Communications in Computer and Information Science 810

Commenced Publication in 2007

More information about this series at http://www.springer.com/series/7899

Serap Kurbanoğlu · Joumana Boustany
Sonja Špiranec · Esther Grassian
Diane Mizrachi · Loriene Roy (Eds.)

Information Literacy in the Workplace

5th European Conference, ECIL 2017
Saint Malo, France, September 18–21, 2017
Revised Selected Papers

Springer

Editors
Serap Kurbanoğlu
Hacettepe University
Beytepe, Ankara
Turkey

Joumana Boustany
University of Paris-Est
Champs-sur-Marne
France

Sonja Špiranec
University of Zagreb
Zagreb
Croatia

Esther Grassian
University of California (UCLA)
Los Angeles, CA
USA

Diane Mizrachi
University of California (UCLA)
Los Angeles, CA
USA

Loriene Roy
University of Texas
Austin, TX
USA

ISSN 1865-0929 ISSN 1865-0937 (electronic)
Communications in Computer and Information Science
ISBN 978-3-319-74333-2 ISBN 978-3-319-74334-9 (eBook)
https://doi.org/10.1007/978-3-319-74334-9

Library of Congress Control Number: 2017964218

Printed on acid-free paper

This Springer imprint is published by Springer Nature
The registered company is Springer International Publishing AG
The registered company address is: Gewerbestrasse 11, 6330 Cham, Switzerland

Preface

The 5th European Conference on Information Literacy (ECIL) was co-organized by the Department of Information Management of Hacettepe University, Turkey, Department of Information and Communication Sciences of Zagreb University, Croatia, and the Information Literacy Association – InLitAs, France. ECIL 2017 aimed to bring together researchers, information professionals, employers, media specialists, educators, policymakers, and all related parties from around the world to exchange knowledge and experience and discuss current issues and recent developments.

The main theme of the fifth conference was "Workplace Information Literacy." In all, 358 proposals were submitted to the conference. Contributions came from 50 different countries (Australia, Austria, Belgium, Botswana, Brazil, Bulgaria, Canada, China, Croatia, Cuba, Cyprus, Czech Republic, Denmark, Estonia, Finland, France, Germany, Hungary, Iceland, Italy, Jamaica, Japan, Kenya, Lebanon, Lithuania, Mexico, Moldova, The Netherlands, Norway, Oman, Pakistan, Poland, Portugal, Qatar, Romania, Russia, Saudi Arabia, Serbia, Singapore, Slovak Republic, Slovenia, South Africa, Spain, Sweden, Switzerland, Turkey, UK, Ukraine, United Arab Emirates, USA).

All submissions were subjected to a double-blind review process. This book consists of a total of 84 selected papers that address many different issues.

Starting with the host organization, the Information Literacy Association, we are grateful to many organizations for their support. We would like to express our deep gratitude to all sponsors for their generous support. Our special thanks go to UNESCO and IFLA, two major organizations that have contributed tremendously to the development of information literacy, for providing their patronage.

We would like to take this opportunity to thank the conference keynote speakers Bonnie Cheuk and Andrew Whitworth; the invited speakers Jean-Philippe Accart and Stéphane Goldstein; the authors and presenters of papers, best practices, PechaKuchas, posters, workshops; and the session chairs. We would like to thank and acknowledge the hard work of the members of the Standing and Program Committees, who invested their time generously to make this event happen.

Our editorial team Sonja Špiranec and Joumana Boustany as well as language editors Esther Grassian, Diane Mizrachi, and Loriene Roy should also be acknowledged here. Special thanks for their hard work and valuable editorial contributions.

Last but not least we would like to thank the local Organizing Committee.

December 2017 Serap Kurbanoğlu

Organization

The European Conference on Information Literacy (ECIL) was co-organized by the Department of Information Management of Hacettepe University, the Department of Information and Communication Sciences of Zagreb University, and the Information Literacy Association – InLitAs.

Standing Committee

Paul G. Zurkowski (Honorary Chair)	USA
Serap Kurbanoğlu (General Co-chair)	Hacettepe University, Turkey
Sonja Špiranec (General Co-chair)	University of Zagreb, Croatia
Joumana Boustany (Co-chair for ECIL 2017)	Université Paris-Est Marne-la-Vallée, France
Szarina Abdullah	MARA Technology University, Malaysia
Buket Akkoyunlu	Hacettepe University, Turkey
Aharon Aviram	Ben-Gurion University, Israel
George Awad	UNESCO Regional Office, Lebanon
Tomaz Bartol	University of Ljubljana, Slovenia
Athina Basha	Albanian Library Association, Albania
David Bawden	City University, UK
Dilara Begum	East West University, Bangladesh
Albert K. Boekhorst	University of Pretoria, South Africa
Alexander Botte	German Institute for International Educational Research, Germany
Christine Bruce	Queensland University of Technology, Australia
Mersini Moreleli-Cacouris	Alexander Technological Educational Institute of Thessaloniki, Greece
Maria Carme Torras Calvo	Bergen University, Norway
Toni Carbo	Drexel University, USA
Paola De Castro	National Institute of Health, Italy
Ralph Catts	University of Stirling, UK
Jerald Cavanagh	Limerick Institute of Technology, Ireland
Kunjilika Chaima	University of Montreal, Canada
Samuel Kai Wah Chu	University of Hong Kong, SAR China
Ioannis Clapsopoulos	University of Thessaly, Greece
John Crawford	Independent Information Professional, UK
Gülçin Cribb	Singapore Management University, Singapore
Lenka Danevska	Central Medical Library, Republic of Macedonia

Lourense H. Das	ENSIL Foundation, The Netherlands
Senada Dizdar	University of Sarajevo, Bosnia and Herzegovina
Noraida Dominguez	University of Puerto Rico, Puerto Rico
Elisabeth Adriana Dudziak	University of Sao Paulo, Brazil
Michael B. Eisenberg	University of Washington, USA
Susana Finquelievich	University of Buenos Aires, Argentina
Almuth Gastinger	University of Science and Technology Trondheim, Norway
Natalia Gendina	Kemerovo State University of Culture and Arts, Russia
Nieves González	University of Seville, Spain
Esther Grassian	University of California, Los Angeles, USA
Eystein Gullbekk	Oslo University, Norway
Thomas Hapke	Hamburg University of Technology, Germany
Päivi Helminen	Helsinki University, Finland
Jos van Helvoort	The Hague University, The Netherlands
Forest Woody Horton	International Library and Information Consultant, USA
Bill Johnston	University of Strathclyde, UK
László Z. Karvalics	University of Szeged, Hungary
Irmgarda Kasinskaite-Buddeberg	Knowledge Societies Division, UNESCO
Anthi Katsirikou	University of Piraeus, Greece
Padraig Kirby	Limerick Institute of Technology, Ireland
Tibor Koltay	Szent István University, Hungary
Rumyana Koycheva	Global Libraries, Bulgaria
Carol C. Kuhlthau	Rutgers University, USA
Claudio Laferlac	University of Malta, Malta
Hana Landová	Association of Libraries of Czech Universities, Czech Republic
Ane Landøy	University of Bergen, Norway
Jesús Lau	Veracruzana University, Mexico
Anne Lehmans	University of Bordeaux, France
Louise Limberg	University of Borås, Sweden
Vincent Liquete	University of Bordeaux, France
Annemaree Lloyd	Charles Sturt University, Australia
Szu-chia Scarlett Lo	National Chung-hsing University, Taiwan
Latifa Mammadova	Ministry of Culture and Tourism, Republic of Azerbaijan
Luisa Marquardt	Roma Tre University, Italy
Vanessa Middleton	Petroleum Institute, United Arab Emirates
Muhammad Sajid Mirza	International Islamic University, Pakistan
Theophilus E. Mlaki	Consultant ICT for Development, Tanzania
María Pinto Molina	Granada University, Spain
Camilla Moring	University of Copenhagen, Denmark
Rajen Munoo	National Library Board NLB Academy, Singapore
Mitsuhiro Oda	Aoyama Gakuin University, Japan
Anna Onkovich	National Academy of Pedagogical Sciences, Ukraine

Chido Onumah	African Centre for Media Literacy, Nigeria
Heike vom Orde	International Central Institute for Youth and Educational TV, Germany
Judith Peacock	Queensland University of Technology, Australia
Zdravka Pejova	Library and Information Consultant, Republic of Macedonia
Manuel Pinto	University of Minho, Portugal
Gloria Ponjuan	University of Havana, Cuba
Maria Próchnicka	Jagiellonian University, Poland
Angela Repanovici	Transilvania University of Brasov, Romania
Laurie Ortiz Rivera	University of Puerto Rico, Puerto Rico
Manuela Rohrmoser	Vienna University, Austria
Jurgita Rudzioniene	Vilnius University, Lithuania
Philip Russell	Institute of Technology Tallaght, Ireland
Ramza Jaber Saad	Lebanese National Commision of UNESCO, Lebanon
Jarmo Saarti	University of Eastern Finland, Finland
Chutima Sacchanand	Sukhothai Thammathirat Open University, Thailand
Armando Malheiro da Silva	University of Porto, Portugal
Diljit Singh	University of Malaya, Malaysia
Jagtar Singh	Punjabi University, India
Kaisa Sinikara	Helsinki University Library, Finland
Eero Sormunen	University of Tampere, Finland
Philipp Stalder	University of Zurich, Switzerland
Jela Steinerova	Comenius University, Slovakia
Gordana Stokić Simončić	Belgrade University, Serbia
Paul Sturges	University of Pretoria, South Africa
Olof Sundin	Lund University, Sweden
Samy Tayie	Cairo University, Egypt
Ellen R. Tise	Stellenbosch University, South Africa
Ross J. Todd	The State University of New Jersey, USA
Ramon R. Tuazon	Asian Institute of Journalism and Communication, Phillippines
Anne Sissel Vedvik Tonning	University of Bergen, Norway
José Manuel Pérez Tornero	University of Barcelona, Spain
Jordi Torrent	United Nations Department of Education, USA
Alejandro Uribe Tirado	University of Antioquia, Colombia
Egbert John Sanchez Vanderkast	National Autonomous University of Mexico, Mexico
Tapio Varis	UNESCO Chair, University of Tampere, Finland
Aurora de la Vega	Catholic University of Peru, Peru
Jose de Jesus Cortes Vera	Autonomous University of Ciudad Juárez, Mexico
Henri A. Verhaaren	Ghent University, Belgium
Sirje Virkus	Tallin University, Estonia
Li Wang	University of Auckland, New Zealand
Sheila Webber	University of Sheffield, UK

Sharon A. Weiner	National Forum of Information Literacy, USA
Barbro Wigell-Ryynanen	Ministry of Education and Culture, Finland
Pradeepa Wijetunge	University of Colombo, Sri Lanka
Carolyn Wilson	University of Toronto, Canada
Tom Wilson	University of Sheffield, UK
Andrew Whitworth	University of Manchester, UK
Michaela Zemanek	Vienna University, Austria
Julia Zhang Xiaojuan	Wuhan University, China

Program Committee

Maryam S. AlOshan	Imam Muhammed bin Saud Univesity, Saudi Arabia
Ines Amaral	Autonomous University of Lisbon, Portugal
Kanwal Ameen	University of the Punjab, Lahore, Pakistan
Tatjana Aparac-Jelusic	University of Zadar, Croatia
Fatima Baji	Ahvaz JundiShapur University of Medical Sciences, Iran
Mihaela Banek Zorica	University of Zagreb, Croatia
Tomaz Bartol	University of Ljubljana, Slovenia
Glória Maria Lourenço Bastos	Universidade Aberta/Portuguese Open University, CEMRI, Portugal
Bojana Boh	University of Ljubljana, Slovenia
Joumana Boustany	Université Paris-Est Marne-la-Vallée, France
Sabina Cisek	Jagiellonian University, Poland
Ioannis Clapsopoulos	University of Thessaly, Greece
John Crawford	Independent Information Professional, UK
Patricia Dawson	Rider University, USA
Mary Jean Tecce DeCarlo	Drexel University, USA
Güleda Doğan	Hacettepe University, Turkey
Orélie Desfriches Doria	Université Jean Moulin – Lyon 3, France
Heidi Enwald	Oulu University, Finland
Helena Francke	University of Borås, Sweden
Fabian Franke	University of Bamberg, Germany
Emmanouel Garoufallou	Alexander Technical Educational Institute of Thessaloniki, Greece
Almuth Gastinger	University of Science and Technology Trondheim, Norway
José Antonio Gómez-Hernández	University of Murcia, Spain
Nieves González	University of Seville, Spain
Allen Grant	Drexel University, USA
Stacey Greenwell	University of Kentucky, USA
Vincas Grigas	Vilnius University, Lithuania
Gaby Haddow	Curtin University, Australia
Lejla Hajdarpasic	University of Sarajevo, Bosnia and Herzegovina
Jos van Helvoort	The Hague University, The Netherlands

Merinda Kaye Hensley	University of Illinois at Urbana-Champaign, USA
Lisa Janicke Hinchliffe	University of Illinois, USA
Baiba Holma	University of Latvia, Latvia
Ma Lei Hsieh	Rider University, USA
Hilary Hughes	Queensland University of Technology, Australia
Maija-Leena Huotari	University of Oulu, Finland
Frank Huysmans	University of Amsterdam, The Netherlands
Martina Dragija Ivanovic	University of Zadar, Croatia
Zhang Jiuzhen	Peking University, China
Nicole Johnston	Edith Cowan University, Australia
Christina Kanaki	Panteion University of Social and Economic Sciences, Greece
László Z. Karvalics	University of Szeged, Hungary
Paulette Kerr	University of West Indies, Jamaica
Tibor Koltay	Szent István University, Hungary
Pavla Kovarova	Masaryk University, Czeck Republic
Liga Krumina	University of Latvia, Latvia
Serap Kurbanoğlu	Hacettepe University, Turkey
Hana Landova	Information Education and IL WG, Czech Republic
Jesús Lau	Veracruzana University, Mexico
Vera J. Lee	Drexel University, USA
Anne Lehmans	University of Bordeaux, France
Louise Limberg	University of Borås, Sweden
Mandy Lupton	Queensland University of Technology, Australia
Juan D. Machin-Mastromatteo	Universidad Autonoma de Chihuahua, Mexico
Afrodite Malliari	DataScouting, Greece
Viviana Fernández Marcial	University of La Coruña, Spain
Konstantina Martzoukou	The Robert Gordon University, UK
Yolande Maury	Artois University, France
Camilla Moring	University of Copenhagen, Denmark
Danuta Nitecki	Drexel University, USA
İnci Önal	Hacettepe University, Turkey
Ágústa Pálsdóttir	University of Iceland, Iceland
Helen Partridge	Queensland University of Technology, Australia
Rosaura Fernández Pascual	University of Granada, Spain
Kornelija Petr Balog	University of Osijek, Croatia
Ola Pilerot	University of Borås, Sweden
Ewa Rozkosz	University of Lower Silesia, Poland
Jurgita Rudzioniene	Vilnius University, Lithuania
Jarmo Saarti	University of Eastern Finland, Finland
Dragana Sabovljev	Zarko Zrenjanin Public Library, Serbia
Chutima Sacchanand	Sukhothai Thammathirat Open University, Thailand
Dora Sales	Jaume University, Spain
Egbert John Sanchez-Vanderkast	National Autonomous University of Mexico, Mexico

Tatiana Sanches	Lisbon University, Portugal
Laura Saunders	Simmons College, USA
Elham Sayyad Abdi	Queensland University of Technology, Australia
Jane Secker	London School of Economics, UK
İpek Şencan	Hacettepe University, Turkey
İrem Soydal	Hacettepe University, Turkey
Eero Sormunen	University of Tampere, Finland
Sonja Špiranec	University of Zagreb, Croatia
Jela Steinerova	Comenius University, Slovakia
Karmen Stopar	University of Ljubljana, Slovenia
Gordana Stokić Simončić	Belgrade University, Serbia
Ivanka Stricevic	University of Zadar, Croatia
Paul Sturges	University of Pretoria, South Africa
Ana Lúcia Terra	Oporto Polytechnic Institute, Portugal
Tania Y. Todorova	SULSIT, Bulgaria
Anne Sissel Vedvik Tonning	University of Bergen, Norway
Yurdagül Ünal	Hacettepe University, Turkey
Zehra Taşkın	Hacettepe University, Turkey
Sirje Virkus	University of Tallinn, Estonia
Zuza Wiorogorska	University of Warsaw, Poland
Andrew Whitworth	University of Manchester, UK
Gunilla Widen	Åbo Akademi University, Finland
Iwan Wopereis	Saskias Research Group, The Netherlands
Mei-Mei Wu	National Taiwan University, Taiwan
Sharon Yang	Rider University, USA
Pan Yantao	Sun Yat-Sen University, China
Sandy Zinn	University of the Western Cape, South Africa

Local Organizing Committee

Joumana Boustany (Chair)	Université Paris-Est Marne-la-Vallée and Information Literacy Association, France
Pierrette Drivet	Retired from IUT Paris Descartes, France

Contents

Data Literacy and Research Data Management

Transliteracy, Reading Literacy, Digital Literacy, Financial Literacy, Search Engine Literacy, Civic Literacy

Science Literacy

Health Information Literacy

Information Behaviour

Information Literacy in Higher Education

Information Literacy in K-12

Information Literacy Instruction

Information Literacy and Libraries

Workplace Information Literacy, Employability and Career Readiness

Workplace Information Literacy: Co-designed Information Experience-Centered Systems and Practices

Mary M. Somerville[1(✉)], Robin Imhof[1], Christine S. Bruce[2], and Elham Sayyad Abdi[2]

[1] University of the Pacific, Stockton, USA
{msomerville, rimhof}@pacific.edu
[2] Queensland University of Technology, Brisbane, Australia
{c.bruce, e.sayyadabdi}@qut.edu.au

Abstract. A collaborative design initiative in a North American academic library was initiated in 2016 to enhance information literacy and enrich learning conditions in the workplace. This paper describes co-workers' information intensive and learning centered design processes, which intend to further collective capacity for 'using information to learn' over a twelve-month period. Throughout, attention focused on aspects of informed learning - being aware of the kinds of information we are using, how we are using information and how different forms of information come together to inform and transform our work. Reflection and dialogue on information experience stories further aimed to inform information experience design - to allow individuals and groups to experience information and the information environment surrounding it in a range of increasingly complex ways which offers them a richer, broader and more effective information engagement experience.

Keywords: Informed learning · Informed systems · Information experience Co-design · Information experience design

1 Introduction

Within University Libraries at the University of the Pacific in Stockton, California, USA, co-workers commenced collaborative design of a workplace communication system and an information exchange initiative in August 2016. The project originated during a campus visit by Dr. Christine Bruce, who founded the concepts of informed learning and information experience. She facilitated three sessions to guide University library participants' exploration of their usage of information to learn in the workplace. Outcomes supported co-design of enabling conditions for learning, through using information, within communication systems and with professional practices. These activities aligned well with the University's strategic plan priorities to: 1. *Foster a vibrant organizational culture by developing a system of shared values and establishing practices that cultivate mutual respect and trust and engaging in effective communication* and 2. *Refine or develop systems and learning opportunities to enhance*

S. Kurbanoğlu et al. (Eds.): ECIL 2017, CCIS 810, pp. 3–10, 2018.
https://doi.org/10.1007/978-3-319-74334-9_1

faculty and staff [1]. In addition, the design activities coincided with University of the Pacific's institutional aspirations to *do more, better.*

With the aspiration to encourage other institutions to consider information experience-centered co-design of organizational systems and practices customized to their local circumstances, this paper situates a workplace information literacy initiative within the scholarly literature, followed by presentation of research methodology and findings. Project phases and concluding reflections summarize progress to date.

2 Background

A relational perspective of information literacy [2], which acknowledges information and learning as core dual components, defines information literacy as having a full repertoire of effective information use experiences. This perspective is the foundation of the more recent concepts of informed learning [3] and information experience [4]. The relational view has also been used to reveal nuanced understanding of information literacy experience in different contexts, such as community [5–7], academic [8–10] and workplace [11–13] settings. Additionally, based on the relational perspective, and to advance information literacy, frameworks such as informed learning design [8], information experience design [11], and informed systems [14, 15], have evolved.

In this organizational effectiveness initiative, informed learning, informed systems, and information experience design are combined to create the theoretical framework of the study. Informed learning, which simultaneously focuses on information use and learning, recognizes the qualitatively different ways of experiencing information and information use, including the relationships between information and its contexts of use [3]. 'Learning' here, adopting the phenomenographic position [16], is a change in how some aspects of the world are experienced or seen. Informed systems advances holistic design thinking to co-create technology-enabled and human-centered systems for workplace communication, decision making, and planning [17], using information to 'learn in action' [17]. Information experience design (IXD) focuses systems and practice design efforts on information experience enrichment [11].

Initial 'proof of concept' evidence linking advancement of workplace information literacy and participatory systems design activities was generated in the academic library at California Polytechnic State University, San Luis Obispo, USA [13]. Soft system design methods [18] that use information to learn guided the organization's three-year exploration, from 2003 to 2006.

A second systems design implementation, conducted from 2008 to 2015 at the University of Colorado Denver, USA, coincided with Bruce's advancement of relational information literacy to informed learning. In response, this research-to-practice initiative focused on "being aware of the kinds of information we are using, how we are using information and how different forms of information come together to inform and transform our work" [19, pp. 8–9]. Soft systems design practices [20], which explicitly advance information and learning, were used to co-create workplace systems and associated practices to further co-workers' engagement with information through what came to be known as informed systems.

In the current customization of informed systems at University of the Pacific, USA, information experience design (IXD) [11] amplifies workplace learning through design activities informed by and focused upon workplace information experience. IXD offers a holistic approach for translating information literacy theory into practice, originating with co-workers' information and learning experience stories. Theoretically grounded in the relational perspective to information literacy [2], this approach ensures inclusive workplace processes that enable use of information in a range of different ways, both during the design process and as a result of the design process.

IXD focuses on a fundamental aspect of relationally viewed information literacy: information experience [4]. Customized to local circumstances, IXD begins with exploration of individuals' information experiences within the situated context. Addressing the centrality of variation in the relational view, information experience design then attends to uncovering variation in revealed experiences. Based on the identified variation, suitable interventions are collaboratively designed and collaboratively implemented to amplify collective experiences of engagement with information to its fullest extent. The enrichment of engaging with information - as well as the capacity for iterative design of learning conditions - expresses workplace information literacy within the relational perspective.

Adopting an information experience design lens in this study, the results of analyzing individuals' stories about how they use information to learn (that is, targeting the building blocks of information literacy mentioned in the IXD framework above) guided systems design and produced organizational practices (as in designing and implementing interventions mentioned in the IXD framework above) that heightened engagement with information in more varied ways, through which collective workplace information literacy capabilities evolved. To advance continuous amplification, reflection and dialogue practices are now integrated into the organizational culture to ensure continuous evaluation and iterative re-design of systems and practices. Collective commitment aims to enable richer experience of and engagement with information to advance workplace information literacy.

3 Stories of Using Information to Learn in the Workplace

Information experience design (IXD) - which places information in the foreground - guided the collective learning catalyzed by analysis of stories about using information to learn and co-design of workplace systems and associated practices. It thereby advanced informed learning, which recognizes that learning is about a shift or change in understanding a phenomenon - in this case, information use. The information stories in this action research initiative were generated over three, 3-h sessions. A facilitator, Dr. Christine Bruce from Queensland University of Technology, in collaboration with other team members, guided participants' thinking and talking about how they used information to learn. Insights, particularly about sharing, saving and using information, subsequently guided choice of technologies and development of practices that produce the conditions for using information to learn within open communication, decision-making and planning systems.

The co-design initiative began with collecting 19 participants' stories of workplace information literacy. In advance of the workshop, participants were asked to reflect on a "best experience of using information to learn at work." The stories were comprised of recollections of job-related information needs and the processes used to obtain information needed. The stories were then shared - through brief spoken summaries - and discussed within the library group. On the second day, department heads convened to identify the 'what, how, and why' aspects of the stories, which has been collected for further reflection and analysis. These questions guided analysis of the stories:

a. What is valued?
b. How does informed learning happen?
c. Where does it happen?

Initial analysis focused on revealing the wide variation in the what, how, and where elements of the information experience stories. Because of their 'thought leadership' responsibilities within the organization, the unit heads both performed analysis on the second day and reported results to the library group on the third day. Concluding discussion explored the next step, coding for analysis of information experience stories. Results would deepen the understanding required to achieve IXD aspirations for informed systems.

4 Informed Learning Story Coding Categories

Stories were next coded according to informed learning categories, which simultaneously focus on information use and learning. More specifically, Academic Support Librarian Robin Imhof led analysis of the qualitatively different ways of experiencing information in the workplace. Coding explored the relationship between information and its contexts of use, including what information is used for, as represented in these categories:

1. Information and communication technologies: harnessing technology for information and knowledge retrieval, communication, and management,
2. Information sources: using information sources (including people) for workplace learning and action taking,
3. Information and knowledge generation processes: developing personal practices or heuristics for finding and using information for novel situations,
4. Information curation and knowledge management: organizing and managing data, information, and knowledge for future professional needs,
5. Knowledge construction and worldview transformation: building knowledge through discovery, evaluation, discernment, and application,
6. Collegial sharing and knowledge extension: exercising and extending professional practices and knowledge bases to workplace insights, and
7. Professional wisdom and workplace learning: contributing to collegial learning through using information to learn to take better action to improve [19].

Coding results revealed that most of the stories recounted individual learning, absent the collective learning activities needed for organizations to be nimble and responsive amidst uncertainty. More specifically, many stories discussed informed learning categories 1–3 that emphasize aspects of information use (technology, sources, processes). Fewer stories described category 4–5 (information curation, knowledge management, knowledge creation, worldview transformation). The workplace informed learning categories of 6–7 (information sharing and workplace learning) were largely absent.

5 Designing New Information Experiences

In response, an Information Curation and Knowledge Management Team (ICKMT) was convened, with representatives from all organizational units and levels. The group's stated purpose was advancement of relational information literacy in both physical and virtual workplace environments. Based on needs identified in information experience stories, team members aimed to co-create conditions for workplace learning. Due to absence in the workplace, informed learning category 6 - collegial sharing and knowledge extension for exercising and extending professional practices and knowledge bases to workplace insights, and category 7 - professional wisdom and workplace learning for using information to learn to take better action to improve - were prioritized. The requisite capabilities necessary to 'bridge' individual and collective learning - categories 4 and 5 - were also determined to be important. So information curation and knowledge management - which provides the foundation for knowledge construction and, ultimately, worldview transformation - were of significance as well. As the co-design team moved from stories to data analysis to informed systems design, participants were guided by information experience design (IXD) perspectives, which places information experience in the foreground. In addition, they knew from organization-wide conversations about the information experience stories that co-workers valued learning from and with each other, and they recognized this as a strength upon which to build. Lastly, they recognized that technology tools and catalytic processes were required to heighten learning within the organization.

6 Informed Systems Co-design: Phase One

Because the organization is engaged in a multi-year, multi-phase facility renovation, ICKMT members decided to focus a co-design pilot on the multi-faceted theme of spaces, services, and resources re-invention. After considering several technology options, which compared and contrasted communication needs and software purposes, the design team unanimously chose the LibGuides blog software for communication, for multiple reasons. First, the Springshare products and platform were used to create research guides and web pages, so software conventions were familiar. Although the LibGuide blog had not been used before, examination revealed that it facilitated easy posting of new information, using similar familiar procedures. Then team members discovered a file size limitation, when they attempted to upload architects' high resolution renderings. So they decided to add a second environment, SharePoint, to which

LibGuide entries could point, if needed. This software had the additional advantage of support by the University's office of information technology.

Very organically, the SharePoint site soon became a repository for other organizational work. For instance, to satisfy the workplace need to curate and preserve committee activities, the SharePoint site became the platform in which to accomplish this work. Coincidently, a mobile computer monitor was built to enable visualization of meeting agendas in library gatherings. This innovation in workplace practices was subsequently furthered when, during unit heads' meetings, the computer-on-wheels (COW) was used to both display meeting agenda and to produce real-time minutes. Through such processes, co-workers learned - with time and practice - to curate, share, and understand workplace information. In addition, they learned to identify information needs and compare needs with available communication channels and possible technology solutions.

7 Informed Systems Co-design: Phase Two

Later this year, Phase Two will look at the breadth and depth of learning achieved through the co-designed systems and associated practices related to comprehensive organizational re-invention and evidenced in the LibGuide and SharePoint environments. Priority will continue to focus on informed learning category 6 - collegial sharing and knowledge extension for exercising and extending professional practices and knowledge bases to workplace insights - and category 7 - professional wisdom and workplace learning for contributing to collegial learning through using information to learn to take better action to improve. In addition, team members will more intentionally look for evidence of categories 4 and 5 - information curation, knowledge management, knowledge construction, and worldview transformation. These elements constitute the 'bridge' capabilities that both enable individuals to contribute their insights to the evolution of collective workplace learning and also enable groups to capture, organize, interpret, and apply information to generate knowledge and, ultimately, wisdom.

Guided by information experience design processes, the ICKMT members will analyze a new set of systems- and practices-enabled stories, which use information to learn. They will expand the original analysis framework - How is informed learning happening? Where is it taking place? What is valued? - and add three more questions: who, why, when. These "6 Ws" constitute the questions used for investigation within the field of journalism. Illustrative of their developing efficacy, team members will also look for these attributes of relational informed learning principles, with the aim of furthering collective workplace information experience:

- Learning is about changes in conception – that is, learning to develop new, more complex ways of conceiving of, or experiencing information.
- Learning always has content as well as process – that is, individuals should be learning about something (disciplinary content) as they engage in learning to be effective information users.

- Learning is about relations between the learner and the subject matter – that is, learning to be an effective information user involves the relations between the learning and the information.
- Improving learning is about understanding the learner's perspective – that is, helping individuals to become better information users requires understanding their ways of conceiving of effective information use [2, p. 174].

This information experience design initiative recognizes that the outcome space represents the relationships between those categories. It depicts the phenomenon as a whole within which learning happens. In other words, learning to fully realize the potential of information experiences requires developing new, more complex ways of conceiving and experiencing the multi-faceted phenomenon. It follows that this manifests as a range of contextualized experiences of varying complexity: a complexity reflecting the purpose for which the information is required, and the subjective knowledge that is developed through the locating and critiquing of the information [2]. The questions then become: "What information … experiences do we want to facilitate or make possible? What information and learning experiences are vital to further our… professional work?" [21, p. 20].

8 Informed Systems Implementation Discussion

Two earlier workplace design studies demonstrated that when professionals become aware of new ways of experiencing the use of information to learn, they can become more effective within new contexts as they learn what is required to make that possible. In other words, professionals' engagement in those knowledge development and learning processes allow them to achieve competence and effective practice. Awareness can be additionally furthered through reflective engagement guided by intentional learning-centered information practices – a process of subjective knowledge development leading to increased understanding [12].

Building upon this strong evidence about the value of explicitly linking information and learning, information experience design is combined in this study with informed systems, to originate organizational capacity building through analyzing informed learning stories. Results in phase 1 informed co-designed systems and practices, which continue to inform redesign efforts in phase 2 that transform collective attention from transactions to transformations [14].

This workplace information literacy approach, grounded in relational information literacy, informed learning, and information experience, anticipates that as understanding of technologies mature, focus shifts naturally from the technology itself and the capabilities needed to use those technologies towards the process of galvanizing information and learning experiences. As results to date at University of the Pacific illustrate, collaborative design of information and learning experiences transforms both learning experience and information experience. This is especially so because IXD has been paired with reflection and dialogue practices that promote iterative design and evaluation processes focused on information use experience. Within this frame, lively conversations quite genuinely catalyze and amplify relational workplace information literacy.

References

1. University of the Pacific: Personal Communication, 6 December 2016
2. Bruce, C.S.: Seven Faces of Information Literacy. Auslib Press, Adelaide (1997)
3. Bruce, C.S.: Informed Learning. Association of College and Research Libraries/American Library Association, Chicago (2008)
4. Bruce, C.S., Partridge, H., Hughes, H., Davis, K., Stoodley, I. (eds.): Information Experience: Approaches to Theory and Practice. Library and Information Science, vol. 9. Bingley, Emerald (2004)
5. Yates, C.: Exploring variation in the ways of experiencing health information literacy: a phenomenographic study. Libr. Inf. Sci. Res. **37**(3), 220–227 (2015)
6. Gunton, L., Bruce, C.S., Stoodley, I.D.: Experiencing religious information literacy: informed learning in church communities. Aust. Libr. J. **61**(2), 119–132 (2012)
7. Demasson, A.E., Partridge, H.L., Bruce, C.S.: Information literacy and the serious leisure participant: variation in the experience of using information to learn. Inf. Res. **21**(2) (2016)
8. Maybee, C., Bruce, C.S., Lupton, M., Rebmann, K.: Designing rich information experiences to shape learning outcomes. Stud. High. Educ. **42**, 1–16 (2016)
9. Hughes, H.E., Bruce, C.S.: International students' experiences of informed learning: a pedagogical case study. Int. J. Pedag. Learn. **8**(2), 106–119 (2013)
10. Lupton, M.: Information Literacy and Learning. Auslib Press, Adelaide (2008)
11. Sayyad Abdi, E.: Information Experience Design in Bruce, C.S., Demasson, A.E., Hughes, H.E., Lupton, M., Maybee, C., Mirijamdotter, A., Sayyad Abdi, E., Somerville, M.M.: Information literacy and informed learning: conceptual innovations for IL research and practice futures. J. Inf. Lit. **11**(1), 8–10 (2017)
12. Forster, M. (ed.): Information Literacy in the Workplace. Facet Publishing, London (2017)
13. Somerville, M.M.: Working Together – Collaborative Information Practices for Organizational Learning. Association of College & Research Libraries/American Library Association, Chicago (2009)
14. Somerville, M.M., Bruce, C.S.: From transaction to transformation: organizational learning and knowledge creation experience within Informed Systems. In: Forster, M. (ed.) Information Literacy in the Workplace, pp. 41–55. Facet Publishing, London (2017)
15. Somerville, M.M., Mirijamdotter, A: Informed Systems in Bruce, C.S., Demasson, A.E., Hughes, H.E., Lupton, M., Maybee, C., Mirijamdotter, A., Sayyad Abdi, E., Somerville, M. M.: Information literacy and informed learning: conceptual innovations for IL research and practice futures. J. Inf. Lit. **11**(1), 16–18 (2017)
16. Marton, F., Booth, S.: Learning and Awareness. Lawrence Erlbaum, Mahwah (1997)
17. Somerville, M.M.: Informed Systems: Organizational Design for Learning in Action. Chandos Publishing, Oxford (2015)
18. Checkland, P., Reynolds, S.: Information, Systems and Information Systems: Making Sense of the Field. Wiley, Chichester (1998)
19. Bruce, C.S., Hughes, H., Somerville, M.M.: Supporting learners in the 21st century. Libr. Trends **60**(3), 522–545 (2012)
20. Checkland, P.B., Poulter, J.: Learning for Action: A Short, Definitive Account of Soft Systems Methodology and Its Use for Practitioners, Teachers and Students. Wiley, Chichester (2006)
21. Bruce, C.S.: Information literacy research and practice: an experiential perspective. In: Kurbanoğlu, S., Grassian, E., Mizrachi, D., Catts, R., Špiranec, S. (eds.) ECIL 2013. CCIS, vol. 397, pp. 11–30. Springer, Cham (2013). https://doi.org/10.1007/978-3-319-03919-0_2

Implementing Library Strategies and Values as a Part of the Workplace Information Literacy

Marja Hjelt[1(✉)] and Jarmo Saarti[2]

[1] University of Tampere, Tampere, Finland
hjelt.marja.a@student.uta.fi
[2] University of Eastern Finland, Kuopio, Finland
jarmo.saarti@uef.fi

Abstract. The paper investigates how the library understanding of the organizational strategy and values affect the adoption of innovations and new services. The paper is based on research and data collected from the adoption of the e-book in Finnish public libraries. The aim is to find out the factors in the libraries' operating culture that support and prevent the introduction of the e-book. It was noted that in the adaptation of new services management needs to market the strategies and motivate the staff in order to encourage the staff to adopt new innovations.

Keywords: E-book · Attitudes · Library staff · Executive board
Public libraries · Finland

1 Introduction

This paper investigates how the library understanding of organizational strategy and values affect the adoption of innovations and new services. It is based on research and data collected from the adoption of the e-book in Finnish public libraries. The aim is to find out the factors in the libraries' operating culture that support or prevent the introduction of the e-book.

Libraries have a two-way impact on introducing innovations. Primarily, the organization must decide on the introduction of innovation and secondly to motivate the staff to accept it [1]. This study identifies the expectations, values and attitudes of the libraries when implementing e-books and related services into the library's collections and services. The research also clarifies what actions are used for the involvement of the staff.

The role of the staff in adopting innovation is to accept it as part of the library service offering and to ensure its delivery to customers. This study focuses on attitudes and social norms that promote or impede the library staff's adoption of e-books and related services as a part of the library's service concept. The study also examines how the library's actions affect the staff's adoption of e-books.

S. Kurbanoğlu et al. (Eds.): ECIL 2017, CCIS 810, pp. 11–20, 2018.
https://doi.org/10.1007/978-3-319-74334-9_2

2 Literature Review

There has been little or no research on information literacy in the adoption of innovations. Instead, learning at the work place as part of the adoption of innovation, attitude building and information literacy has been studied. Research so far has not combined these aspects, but has focused only on one of the topics.

The adoption of innovations has been widely researched. The main theories are the Rogers' *Diffusion of Innovation theory* and the Davis' *Technology Acceptance model (TAM)*. Rogers' [1] theory focuses on an individual's ability to embrace innovation by its perception and suitability according to the individual's experience, values and needs. The key factor for embracing innovation is also the communicability of innovation, that is, how does the community feel about innovation and how is this reflected within the community [1]. Also, Davis's TAM is also approaching the adoption of innovation by its perceived usefulness and ease of use. Experience in the ease of use of the system is characterized by the system usability [2].

The adoption of innovation is dependent on attitudes, and one of the key research studies of attitudes is Erwin's [3]. The knowledge capital, feelings, and behavior of the individual influence the formation of attitudes. The cognitive component is related to the beliefs, assumptions, and attributes that the individual associates with the object of the attitudes. Positive and negative perceptions of the object shape attitudes. Feelings, the Affect component, influence the emergence of positive and negative perceptions. The behavioral component, in turn, refers to previous behavior and experiences [3].

Research on information literacy in the workplace has also focused on learning in the workplace. Lloyd [4] points out that the analysis should focus on understanding the social relationships and activities that enable the development of information literacy but can also limit it. Information literacy comes from practical actions that consist of what is being said and what is being done, and the relationships between these. According to Lloyd [4], information literacy involves understanding the conversations that affect the creation, dissemination, and operational activity of the information. It also involves understanding how information is edited, accepted, or rejected through social activities. Crawford and Irving [5], basing on the Eraut's learning model, argue that formal learning in the workplace is dependent on the workplace's social relations. According to the model, learning is a combination of past knowledge and experiences in the social context [5]. The ways people are learning in the workplace is important and the reliability of the information obtained through the channels was assessed through their own knowledge and experience [5].

3 Methodology

3.1 Framework

The study is framed through Roger's *Diffusion of Innovation*-theory, which is widely used in the innovation research. The starting point is to find out the impact of the operating culture on adopting the innovation. In the operational culture, one includes all the organization's formal and informal rules, practices and behaviors model, values, principles and criteria; and it rises within the framework of the intellectual, material and social practices [6]. According to Rogers [1] a key factor in adoption is the compatibility of lifestyles, social system, and standards.

Rogers' theory is general in nature and provides guidelines for research, but it needs to be complemented by more focused theories to identify areas of innovation adoption. One of the key factors in adopting innovation is the compatibility of innovation with the community values, whose formation is influenced by attitudes. The formation of attitudes can be defined by Davis's *Technology Acceptance Model*, here Aharony [7]. The model has been developed for the adoption of work related information systems into work routines [7] and it is based on the social psychology theory of reasoned action: attitudes and beliefs are related to people's intentions to perform. The key to this model is that attitudes affect our behavior towards innovation. Attitudes are based on the information available to the individual [7].

Work-related information literacy means the ability to find, apply and use information to solve work-related challenges and to employ various suitable data resources at work as Kirton and Barham state [8]. According to Molopyane and Fourie, [8] the American Library Association's Presidential Committee defines the information literate workforce as one that knows how to learn, knows how knowledge is organized, can locate information, and uses information in such a way that others can learn from them.

The adoption of innovation is influenced by the staff's values and attitudes whose background is taught. Information literacy in workplace is also related to learning in the workplace, so Rogers' innovation theory is well suited to the framework of this study.

3.2 Research Questions

The study tries to answer how the libraries' operating culture affects the introduction of e-books. Specifically, we are studying the following:

1. Libraries as innovators:
   1.1. What are the expectations, values, and attitudes of libraries on the adoption of e-books and related services?
   1.2. Regarding e-books and related services what kinds of activities do libraries seek to promote to staff as part of the library service concept?
2. Library staff as innovators:
   2.1. What are the staff's attitudes and social norms that promote or prevent the adoption of e-books and related services (by staff of e-books) as part of a library service concept?
   2.2. What organizational activities and educational features affect the adoption of e-books and related services by the library's staff as a part of the library's service concept?

3.3 Data Collection

The research data is primarily based on interviews. Six libraries were selected for the interviews from different parts of Finland. The libraries are operating as county libraries or are otherwise locally large libraries. The library executive boards were interviewed in a group interview as representative of their organization. Altogether six executive boards interviews were conducted with the average duration of one hour. In addition, five staff members from each library were interviewed, 30 persons in total. The average duration of the interviews was approximately 45 min. The interviews are anonymized in the analysis.

The research data also includes printed material: the library strategies or city's strategies have been used to determine the written values of the library. In addition, the national library strategies in Finland are used. There are references only to the national strategies in the text because the local strategies are also anonymized.

The interview questions of the attitudes and values were drawn up in accordance with the Davis *Technology Acceptance Model*, by studying the interviewees' perception of the usefulness and ease of use of the e-books, as well as exploring information acquisition and use of e-books.

4 Findings and Results

In the following we analyse the strategies and their adoption by the staff from the point-of-view of e-book use and services in the libraries.

4.1 Values and Strategies

In Finland, the operational functions of public libraries are guided by the Library Act and the national library strategy of Ministry of Education and Culture. The strategy of the Council for Public Libraries substantiates national strategy, and the regional and local library and information strategies provide national policies to the local level, considering specific needs of their own operating environment [9].

The core content of the strategies is based on the civic rights of the education and culture [10]. The values of the strategies are passed down from the upper level and complement the libraries' own values when local conditions are observed. In the strategies, values are named with different names, but their meanings are similar in all strategies. In Table 1, the values are combined based on similarities and their meanings are opened in different strategies.

The libraries researched use for executive functions the library's own strategy, city strategy, or city strategy formulated to the library. According to the analyzed strategies, the libraries' mission is very coherent: the library secures and provides culture, information, and learning opportunities to all. It encourages active nationality by strengthening literacy and narrowing the digital divide. The business idea is implemented by providing professional and equitable library and information services, considering customer needs.

Libraries justify the introduction of e-book services by referencing national and local strategies. National strategies guide libraries to follow-up development, but the implementation of services is influenced by local strategies. However, the decision to introduce e-book services has not been made directly under the guidance of the strategy, but the strategies have opened the discussion of implementation.

Table 1. Values and their meanings in different strategies.

Values	Meaning in national strategies	Meaning in local strategies	Meaning in decision making in libraries
Equality	Citizens' equal rights to education despite the place of residence	Library operations must be equal for all customers	Equal opportunities for digital content
Reliability	Reliable and up-to-date content	Professionally selected and trusted collection	
Communality	Library supports the development of civic skills	Encourage active citizenship by strengthening literacy and narrowing the digital divide	Preventing digital exclusion
Open-mindedness	Introduction of new content and services	The development of operations must be creative and bold	Libraries are up to date and offer up-to-date services
Customer orientation	Services and operating culture based on customer needs	Customers involved in the design and development of services	Identify and provide material in the form required by the customer
Availability	Versatile collections	Versatile and multilingual content	Expand the collection in print and in e-book
Accessibility	High quality services and collections	Multi-channel service production for different user groups	24/7 online Services takes disabled into account
Skill/competences	Adequate skills in technology and information management	Expertise must be versatile and fully utilized	
Challenges	New content, self-publishing Local government and economic	Changes in information channels, material formats and people's time usage Economic	From logistics to content

The development of the activities aims to ensure that the library's services are up-to-date. People's habits of searching and using information and literary culture are changing, and at the same time the communication of libraries must change into ways that serve those needs. Libraries should monitor and be involved in development and provide new formats to customers as soon as possible.

The core value of libraries is equality. Equality is aimed at providing equal opportunities for everyone to access digital content and thereby preventing digital exclusion. Equal opportunities for digital content are also aimed at promoting media literacy skills and teaching customers across the digital divide. Digitalization also aims to provide customers different ways to access library collections and to reach new user groups.

Libraries see customer orientations as an important value in introducing e-books. With customer orientation, one aims to provide all material equally to all customers and to identify what kind of material and in what form the customer needs the material at any given time. Ensuring customer orientation requires versatile material, both traditional and digital.

Libraries like that the fact that provision of e-books can promote availability. The availability in sparse-populated areas can be improved by providing e-book collection by remote access to customers' homes, and the use of library material is no longer dependent on library opening hours and distance. E-books can promote the accessibility of content to different customer groups, such as reading and mobility impairments. E-books also expand the collection and individual titles can be found in the collection both in print and in e-book.

The e-book is considered to be content in libraries rather than format. The purpose of the libraries is to provide content, and there is no need to emphasize the forms of content provided. The aim is to provide timely, versatile material and customers should be able to choose in which format they want material to be provided. Libraries should also provide customers access to material that is only provided in digital form. Digitalization also aims to guide the library's operations from the logistics to opening the content.

4.2 The Actions of Libraries Implementing of the E-books to the Staff

The strategies of the libraries raise staff competence and include the requirement that staff should be able to borrow and read e-books so they can teach the library patrons how to use them. It is not enough for the staff to know the technical basics of e-books; they also need to internalize the meaning of e-books in the provision of library services.

After the decision, staff have been informed and introduced to e-book services. Information has focused on informing customers about the service and its implementation. Various channels have been used for information purposes. The staff would want to be informed of the introduction of new services at the earliest possible stage of the change. About e-books, information is primarily sought from the information specialist, who is responsible for them, because their knowledge is more trusted than superiors'.

Staff have been provided with practical guidance in the use of e-books. Guidance has been given orally, in writing and some libraries have produced guidance videos for the use of e-books. The guides have been technical in content, showing how e-book services are used and how to borrow an e-book on different devices. Written instructions and videos are available to the staff on the intranet and to customers on the library's website. The same guidelines are aimed at both staff and customers.

Staff training on e-books and related services has been in-house training in the library. Typically, the information specialist, who is responsible for acquiring e-books is familiar with the services and their use, has prepared and trained the personnel of the library. The training sessions are arranged either centrally at the main library or the information specialist has traveled to the branch libraries to teach their staff. External training experts have not been used to train library personnel. One aim of the internal training has been to show the importance of service in library services.

Libraries have provided for information specialists and librarians responsible for customer guidance external training, as they have a greater need for professional development in digital media. Training for libraries has been outsourced by county libraries in cooperation with national library operators. External training at the regional level has been difficult to organize because not everyone has been able to participate due to long journeys and staff arrangements. Participation in training has been facilitated by streaming and recording training events (Library Chanel). Streaming has provided remote attending, recording and public sharing of recordings familiarizing with the training when it is best suited to work. Recordings have also been used in the library's internal training.

Some of the libraries under investigation operate a so-called "digi-janitor". They are ICT students who are in the library as interns and organize learning sessions as a digital cafe. Their tasks include teaching the use of information technology to the library staff and customers. Typical subjects to be taught are the use of tablets and smartphones, as well as the use of the library's digital services, including e-book services. This has been proven to be a good way to train the staff, but some libraries have also been found it problematic. The staff does not feel the development of their own competence is important if they can transfer the job requiring competence to someone else. Outsourcing is also seen as the library underrating one of its own core services, staff training in the library's own services.

During the deployment phase of the e-book service, staff have been required to take part in training and, as the implementation progresses, to independently access the services and borrow and read e-books. Libraries have also acquired suitable equipment for reading e-books, mainly tablets, so that staff can get acquainted with them. Independent study and peer support has been challenged because the interviewees considered their own knowledge and experience of e-books as weak, making it difficult for them to rely on information from other colleagues.

In the deployment phase of e-book services, e-book services and their use were generally discussed at staff meetings. Subsequently, the topic has only been dealt with if there are changes in the services that customers must be informed of. E-books have been discussed at meetings if there are problems, such as breaks in service, or criticisms have been raised by staff or customers. The staff have found that e-books are not discussed at a general level in meetings, such as issues arising from other duties.

In the informal discussions, e-books are raised as a topic only if there is a need to find solutions to the problems or if there have been changes in the services. Also, discussions with colleagues about e-books are not considered as reliable as discussion about other work issues. Information from a colleague regarding e-books is reviewed by the instructions or by another colleague and attitudes towards colleagues' knowledge of e-books are more critical than other work assignments. Some of the interviewees reported that they trust more information about e-books from their friends than colleagues. Actions are shown in Table 2.

4.3 The Attitudes of Library Staff Towards E-books

Library staff feel that e-books and related services are part of the library's service offering. However, e-book services are considered as complementary and supplementary

Table 2. Actions for implementing e-book service.

Actions	Content	Channel	Realizer	Object
Informing	What is an e-book What is eLibrary Schedule and steps for implementation	Intranet eMail Superior meetings Staff meetings	Information specialist Spokesperson	Staff
Instructions	How to borrow and read e-Book	Person channel Writings instructions Guide videos	Information specialist ICT-librarians	Staff Customers
In-house training	How to use eLibrary	Main library Branch libraries	Information specialist	Staff
External training	E-book in library collections, acquisitions and licensing Technology issues	Seminars	County libraries Libraries.fi Consortium of Public Libraries Regional State Administrative Agency	Information specialist ICT-librarians
Peer support and self-study	Technical know-how Problems	Branch libraries	Staff	Staff
"Digi-janitor"	Technical know-how Problems	Branch libraries	ICT students	Staff Customers

services in the library. They are not seen as the core task of the library. As a supplementary service, e-books are perceived as a very small part of the overall collections and they do not often come up as a topic in customer service situations. Some of the staff have also experienced e-books as threats, as they feel that most customers want to borrow and read a printed book and at the beginning were afraid that e-books would replace printed literature.

Library staff attitudes towards e-book are generated from practical work. The interviewees raise the benefits of the e-book through the e-book's activities. According to staff, customers benefit from e-books because they can be borrowed while traveling and are more convenient to carry with them than a printed book. They also said that the queues for e-books are shorter than the printed book, meaning that the customer gets to borrow an e-book faster than a printed one. E-books are also good for readers with reading disabilities, as it can zoom font size, and e-book services also offer audio books. On the other hand, the issues raised in staff interviews are those commonly used by the e-book marketing in different media. E-book benefits to customers are also viewed as greater for non-fiction and staff feel that students benefit most from e-books. Some staff feel that customers do not read fiction in e-books at all.

5 Discussion and Limitations

The decision of libraries to implement e-book services is based on the strategy of libraries. Library staff are expected to accept e-book services as a part of the library's service palette. However, there is a gap between the expectations of the library management and the staff. The library staff understand and accept e-books as part of the services and collections, but connection with the library's values and strategies seems not to be internalized, and thus their importance in the implementation of strategies is not understood. From this point-of-view, the adoption of an e-book service remains superficial and no real strategic diffusion happens from the management level to the actions of the staff.

Learning in the workplace and information literacy are formed from several external and internal sources and by people who work together [4]. In libraries, the staff are trained in the introduction of e-book services from the point of view of their technical characteristics, but the ideology and strategic goals of e-books in the library's mission have not been clearly discussed with the staff. The gap between the objectives of the library and the staff's adoption of the services arises when the strategic goals are left to the staff's own learning.

Business matters are discussed both in informal discussions and formal meetings. The fewer the staff meetings, the more that informal discussions matter. The importance of team and staff meetings about e-books is emphasized especially when informal discussion about them does not happen. In lobby conversations, the problem arises from the validity of the information received from a colleague. This also emerged in a study by Crawford and Irving [5] where they found that people's resources in the workplace are essential, but the evaluation of colleagues' data's reliability has an effect how it is interpreted. An assessment of the reliability of the data is done on the basis of the colleague's knowledge and experience [5]. Thus, even reliable information can be rejected [11].

There are several factors in creating information needs and affecting what is really happening: the organization's goals and needs are central here [5]. In this study, this did not happen because the strategies were not well-known among the staff. According to Crawford and Irving [5] there may be external drivers, which may generate a need to validate the organization's activities against these objective measures. In this study, external factors pass the poorly understood library strategy, for instance, general discussion about e-books in different media.

Internalizing e-book services for the staff requires formal discussions in the libraries. Information filtering and evaluation through the organization's strategy and values should be seen as part of information literacy in the workplace. The valid implementation of the strategy requires extra effort by the management.

The limitations of this study are that this study addresses only attitudes and values towards e-books and how they affect the adoption of innovation. Nonetheless, the results highlight the same factors as information literacy based on work tasks. Future studies should include how information literacy in the workplace affects adoption and implementation of e-books as an innovation.

References

1. Rogers, E.M.: Diffusion of Innovations, 5th edn. Free Press, New York (2003)
2. Davis, F.D.: Perceived usefulness, perceived ease of use, and user acceptance of information technology. MIS Q. **13**(3), 319–340 (1989)
3. Erwin, P.: Attitudes and Persuasion. Psychology Press, Hove (2001)
4. Lloyd, A.: Trapped between a rock and a hard place: what counts as information literacy in the workplace and how is it conceptualized? Libr. Trends **60**, 277–296 (2011). (fall)
5. Crawford, J., Irving, C.: Information literacy in the workplace: a qualitative exploratory study. J. Librariansh. Inf. Sci. **41**(1), 29–38 (2009)
6. Knuuttila, S.: Kaiken kattava kulttuuri. In: Kupiainen, J., Sevänen, E. (eds.) Kulttuurintutkimus, 3rd edn, pp. 9–31. Suomalaisen Kirjallisuuden Seura, Helsinki (1994)
7. Aharony, N.: Librarians' attitudes towards mobile services. Aslib Proc. **65**(4), 358–375 (2013)
8. Molopyane, J., Fourie, I.: A framework for workplace information literacy in academic contexts Central University of Technology, Free State (South Africa) as case study. Libr. Hi Tech **33**(4), 562–583 (2015)
9. Opetusministeriön kirjastopolitiikka 2015 Yleiset kirjastot: Kansalliset strategiset painoalueet. Opetusministeriön julkaisuja 2009:32. Opetusministeriö, Helsinki (2009)
10. Yleisten kirjastojen neuvoston strategia 2011–2016 (2010). http://www2.kirjastot.fi/File/aca26e87-a1eb-4925-8c56-0491d5751bcf/Ykn-strategia-kirjastoversio-fin.pdf
11. CILIP: Information literacy skills (2012). https://www.cilip.org.uk/cilip/advocacy-campaigns-awards/advocacy-campaigns/information-literacy/information-literacy

Role of Information Culture in Workplace Information Literacy: A Literature Review

Gunilla Widén and Muhaimin Karim(✉)

Information Studies, Åbo Akademi University, Turku, Finland
{gunilla.widen,muhaimin.karim}@abo.fi

Abstract. Information literacy and its related concepts are increasingly important in the digital workplace. How workers use and experience information are dependent on or shaped by the context, such as work tasks, on-the-job experiences, and social aspects. Thus, the role of an organization's information culture would be expected to influence the development of workplace information literacy. This connection however has not been explored previously. The objective of this paper is to focus information literacy on an organizational level. The connection between information culture and information literacy research is explored in an extensive literature review including about 1800 references in these fields of study. The review shows that only few studies address information literacy in connection to information culture (n = 23), which indicates there is a research gap. With the insights from this analysis it is addressed that there is an advantage of combining the two perspectives in future research.

Keywords: Information culture · Information literacy · Information use Information management

1 Introduction

Today's digital workplace is far more information intensive than ever before and the importance of information literacy, what used to be a concept discussed in the context of higher education, has now posed to be relevant and essential in the workplace context. However, despite its increasing importance, the studies conducted on information literacy have predominantly considered it as an individual set of capabilities and often overlooked the contextual influences. There are studies, including Cheuk [1] and Bonner and Lloyd [2] that have examined information literacy in different environments and concluded that how workers use and experience information are dependent on or shaped by the context, such as work tasks, on-the-job experiences, and social aspects. Thus, the role of an organization's information culture influences the development of workplace information literacy. However, previous studies still focus the individual skills in context rather than the other way around, that there are the contextual prerequisites for efficient information use.

The objective of this paper is to focus information literacy on an organizational level, asking how can information literacy be supported by the management? This will be explored from an information culture perspective, which focuses the relationship between individuals and information in their work. There is an understanding that

S. Kurbanoğlu et al. (Eds.): ECIL 2017, CCIS 810, pp. 21–29, 2018.
https://doi.org/10.1007/978-3-319-74334-9_3

values accorded to information, and attitudes towards it are indicators of information culture [3]. The information culture literature underlines the interaction with information within organizations [4]. Combining this line of research with information literacy research could improve a holistic understanding of workplace information literacy and how such purposeful literacies can be nurtured within an organization.

2 Information Literacy

Information literacy has been a concept of library and information science for quite long. Initially the notion of information literacy was used to create awareness in the students to assist them writing their assignments correctly. The objective of developing the level of information literacy within the students was to help them understand the need of information during writing assignments, identify reliable information sources, validate the information and use it appropriately by giving adequate credit to the authors through referencing and citations. It is also about analyzing critically, synthesizing, and solving problems [5–8]. The information literacy concept has also gained interest in other contexts because of the increasing amount of information and the challenges to manage the complex information landscape. In workplace context, information is acknowledged as a resource, but there are still less studies connecting information literacy to work or organizational settings [9–11].

3 Information Culture

Information culture can be defined as "the culture in which the transformation of intellectual resources is maintained alongside the transformation of material resources" [12]. This means, bringing information literacy into workplace context demands a shift in the focus from individual to organizational level. In this study this is operationalized by focusing information culture while it is a perspective underlining the role and value of information for efficient work activities and business performance [12–14]. The values embedded to information and the mindset towards it are the key indicators of information culture in organizational settings [15]. These values and attitudes are influenced by the various layers of organizational culture. Thus, information culture is the elements of organizational culture that influence the management of information [16] and in the same manner information culture is embedded in organizational values, norms and practices that shape the importance and attitude towards information creation and use.

4 Methodology

As part of a larger research project on *The Impact of Information Literacy in the Digital Workplace*, a systematic literature review was administered to gain a comprehensive idea about the role of information culture in workplace information literacy. The query run for this literature review was a part of the project. A total of 1804 scientific papers have been collected focusing on or related to information literacy from major databases such as Science Direct, EBSCO Host, Google Scholar, Library and Information Science and Technology Abstracts (LISTA), Pro-Quest and Web of Science (Table 1). On the second phase of the query, information culture was sought from the pool of these articles.

Table 1. Sources of literature discussing Information Literacy

Databases	Articles extracted
ScienceDirect	1,125
LISTA (EBSCO)	154
Refseek	14
JSTOR	82
Wiley	40
SSRN	31
Google Scholar	13
Emerald Insight	115
ProQuest	70
Sage	160
Total	**1,804**

The goal of this review process was to focus on literature connecting information literacy with management and organizational information culture. The objective of such analysis was to understand whether adequate importance was given to the contextual, social and cultural aspects of workplace information literacy and their extents. The search for literature was initiated in October 2016 and literature were selected from the publication period within 1970 to 2016.

The literature search was conducted in two phases and started with scanning the sources broadly with keywords connected to information activities in the workplace such as information sharing, knowledge creation, information behavior and information handling. In the second phase the keywords were narrowed down to different literacies (Table 2). This means that the pool of papers (n = 1804) represent papers both specifically focusing information literacy and related terms as well as papers that describe information activities in the workplace more broadly.

The search terms used to identify the articles were: information culture, organization culture and organizational culture, a Boolean search string information literacy and information culture and information literacy and culture. With the help of Adobe Acrobat advanced search option, the search terms were sought in the title, abstract and body of the text. Since the objective of this article is to seek previous studies that acknowledge the importance of information culture in the development of information literacy, all articles that mentioned information culture or the cultural aspects were incorporated. Due to the deficiency of studies in organization information literacy, selection criteria were substantially broad. The time frame was from 1970 to 2016; language was English and paper type ranged from peer-review articles to book reviews. From the total set of retrieved articles on information culture and information literacy

Table 2. Final set of keywords used for the systematic literature review

Keywords/databases
Meta literacy
Information literacy
Media literacy
Library instruction
Cultural literacy
Digital literacy
Visual literacy
News literacy
Network literacy
Computer literacy
ICT literacy
Internet literacy

concepts, there were only 23 articles were found, published in peer reviewed academic journals, with some level of information culture perspective. The selection criteria were articles that mentioned information literacy and information culture, articles that discussed information literacy at organizational level and mentioned information culture or organizational culture and articles that connect and discuss information literacy and information culture in the workplace.

The result clearly indicates a potential research gap and deserves more attention. There is considerable debate and criticism on the fact that information literacy has been often studied as an individual set of competencies while information literacy in workplace context involves a complex system of work organization, social relationships and sociotechnical configurations which is a part of the information culture.

5 Results

For the detailed analysis of the literature a clustering method of the studies was executed. The clusters were determined according to the focal area of the study, impact of information literacy and information culture on different parameters and the role of information literacy and culture in workplaces. All the papers analyzed were based on empirical studies. The objective of this sub-grouping is to have a clear understanding of the trend and common aspects of papers discussing both information literacy and information culture. The discussion of the selected articles mostly circumnavigates five major areas of information literacy and information culture. Information culture contributes in these five concerns of an organization:

1. Organizational information and knowledge management
2. Organizational Effectiveness
3. Workplace information literacy
4. Workplace information use
5. Adoption of IT and ICT process and infrastructure.

5.1 Organizational Information and Knowledge Management

Four articles were found discussing the role of information culture in relation to information and knowledge management. Common objectives of the studies were to identify the information behaviors and values that construct information culture in different contexts such as in project teamwork, municipality and knowledge intensive organizations and the role of information culture in knowledge creation, information management and knowledge management practices. The studies found profound effect of information culture in information management. A balanced information culture that promotes effective creation, use and management of information is necessary for seamless organizational information and knowledge management [17–20].

5.2 Organizational Effectiveness

Four articles were extracted that studied the relationship between information culture and organizational effectiveness. The objectives of the studies were to assess information culture in the workplace either by developing typology or by proposing a conceptual model. However, the studies attempted to execute a systematic examination of information culture and its link to concerns such as organizational effectiveness, innovation and employee satisfaction. It is seen that information culture is influenced by leadership style, institutional regulation and information politics. Information culture explains attitudes and values of information and therefore is related to the effectiveness and performance of the organization. Information culture also explains how information is communicated and used and possible measures to assess information culture and performance are addressed. [13, 21–23].

5.3 Workplace Information Literacy

Only two articles discussed information literacy in workplace context in relation to information culture to some extent. The papers underline that the workplace today is increasingly complex and therefore, the capabilities to effectively collect, analyze, assess and synthesize relevant information is imperative. On the other hand, information usage in the workplace is a form of social interaction with people both inside and outside of the organization who are often the prime source of information. Therefore, the critically important competencies must be studied in relation to organizational and information culture, information infrastructure and information technologies. The studies suggested that information literacy should be determined by multiple factors such as: information infrastructure, information sources, human resources, information technologies, management's attitude, policy and information culture. The encouraging information culture helps employees understand the importance of information literacy and value and utility of information in achieving business goal is recognized [9, 31].

The analyzed papers were based on empirical studies applying different methodological approaches such as interviews, case studies and surveys. However, the dominant approach was qualitative studies and case studies. Different kinds of organizations have been studied such as government agency, multinational organizations and national law firms.

Apart from the above mentioned literature, there were five more articles extracted using the search term "information culture". However, these articles concentrated on workplace information literacy and concepts related to that but only occasionally mentioned information culture. Sufficient discussion and linking with the concept of information literacy was not found. Therefore, these articles were kept outside the analysis.

5.4 Workplace Information Use

Four papers focused on the role of information culture in connection to the organizational information use outcomes through systematically identifying information behavior and values that determines organizational information culture. The information culture of an organization is determined by a large number of variables such as its mission, history, leadership, employee behavior and values. Organizations seek and use information to understand the environment they are operating in. Enhancing the information use and its outcomes can be exploited by developing an information culture that fosters conversations and exchange of information. Information culture is put forward to have a profound effect on information management and thus information use outcomes [14, 24–26].

5.5 Adoption of IT and ICT Process and Infrastructure

Four articles discussed the importance of information culture in adopting information and communication technologies. An organization can be influenced by diverse types of information culture in its different operations. The studies suggest that number of specific cultural aspects evolve around the information and communication technology infrastructure. While, the diversity and complexity of information culture creates barrier in the synergy between information and communication technologies and the business itself, a mature and enabling information culture contributes in the easy adoption and use of information and communication technologies. ICT investment and implementation has often failed to produce expected outcomes. The studies pointed out that the key issue is not in the technology rather the social factors such as cultures and individual information capabilities [27–30].

6 Information Literacy and Information Culture

This review shows that previous research has focused information literacy and information culture separately although these two lines of research for sure have a lot in common. We know that information literacy in workplace context is a developing area of research [9–11] and that there is a growing consensus that information literacy is beyond a skill-set when studying it in workplace context.

With the insights from this analysis we would like to address the advantage of combining the perspectives in future research. Information culture research has a lot of aspects to add into information literacy in workplace context. The information culture studies described above highlight the importance of a transparent, open and positive environment towards information and knowledge. Furthermore, information culture affects the information use in organizations, the attitudes towards information, its impact on information infrastructure and how it reduces barriers during implementation of information technologies and systems. The information culture papers also discuss its role in connection to effectiveness, innovation and job satisfaction in organizations. Some papers also focus the perspective of what kinds of skills that are highlighted in connection to efficient information handling as well as the role of information politics in the connection to information culture. Two of the papers have a more specific connection between information culture and information literacy related skills in workplace context highlighting a holistic approach for efficient development of workplace information literacy [9, 31].

The information culture perspective could therefore add to the workplace information literacy discussion on the following insights. Workplace information literacy is not an individual attribute or set of activities, rather a collective attempt in performing the tasks at workplaces. Being a collective approach it includes multiple social and cultural factors that influences the information literacy activities. Apart from the individual skills of information handling, workplace information literacy should be about navigating the organisational level of information awareness. It is important to be able to identify relevant information sources and critically evaluate information needed for problem solving as well as being fluent in navigating the IT landscape of the workplace, but in workplace context the information literacy should also focus aspects like attitudes and values to information, social interaction for knowledge creation, and information use outcomes. From a management point of view this means that individual information handling skills must be supported in interaction with the workplace culture. A successful workplace information literacy programme should take a more holistic approach to information literacy where leadership aspects in connection to information handling is crucial. Acknowledging the cultural aspect in connection to workplace information literacy will also help us design more concrete implementation and assessment frameworks. These should preferably also include quantitative studies considering that most information culture studies so far have used a qualitative approach.

7 Conclusions

The project *Impact of Information Literacy in the Digital Workplace* intends to study information literacy in the workplace and thus addresses the social and contextual influence on workplace information literacy. In order to assess previous studies, the project initiated a literature review on the topic and over 1800 articles were collected. These articles discussed information literacy and concepts relating to and influencing it. From this pool of dataset, papers discussing information culture were separated and later, analyzed. The analysis of these selective papers indicates a substantial research gap in this field. Very few articles were found discussing information culture in direct relation to information literacy. It is therefore suggested that a combination of research on information culture and information literacy would be valuable in the development of the understanding of workplace information literacy as well as in the development of relevant measures to assess information literacy in the workplace.

Acknowledgment. We would like to take this opportunity to thank Academy of Finland for the research grant supporting the project "The Impact of Information Literacy in the workplace" (no. 295743).

References

1. Cheuk, B.: Information literacy in the workplace context: issues, best practices and challenges. In: White Paper prepared for UNESCO, The US National Commission on Libraries and Information Science, and The National Forum on Information Literacy, for Use at the Information Literacy Meeting of Experts, Prague, vol. 12, p. 2004, July 2002. (Retrieved March)
2. Bonner, A., Lloyd, A.: What information counts at the moment of practice? Information practices of renal nurses. J. Adv. Nurs. **67**(6), 1213–1221 (2011). https://doi.org/10.1111/j.1365-2648.2011.05613.x
3. Wright, T.: Information culture in a government workplace: examining records management training and self-perceived competencies in compliance with a records management program. Rec. Manag. J. **23**(1), 14–36 (2013)
4. Oliver, G.: Information culture: exploration of differing values and attitudes to information in organisations. J. Doc. **64**(3), 363–385 (2008)
5. Johnson, A.M.: Library instruction and information literacy. Ref. Serv. Rev. **31**(4), 385–418 (2003)
6. Lupton, M., Glanville, C., McDonald, P., Selzer, D.: Information Literacy Toolkit. Griffith University, Brisbane (2004). http://www.griffith.edu.au/centre/gihe/griffith_graduate. Consulted January 2005
7. Bundy, A. (ed.): Australian and New Zealand Information Literacy Framework: Principles, Standards and Practice, 2nd edn. Australian and New Zealand Institute for Information Literacy, Adelaide (2004). http://www.caul.edu.au/infoliteracy/InfoLiteracyFramework.pdf. Consulted January 2005
8. Wilder, S.: Information literacy makes all the wrong assumptions. Chron. Rev. **51**(18) (2005)
9. Crawford, J., Irving, C.: Information literacy in the workplace: a qualitative exploratory study. J. Librariansh. Inf. Sci. **41**(1), 29–38 (2009)
10. Weiner, S.: Information literacy and the workforce: a review. Educ. Libr. **34**(2), 7–14 (2011)
11. Williams, D., Cooper, K., Wavell, C.: Information literacy in the workplace. In: An Annotated Bibliography. Robert Gordon University (2014). Online Article: Accessed October 2014
12. Ginman, M.: Information culture and business performance. IATUL Q. **2**(2), 93–106 (1988)
13. Curry, A., Moore, C.: Assessing information culture: an exploratory model. Int. J. Inf. Manag. **23**(2), 91–110 (2003)
14. Choo, C.W., Furness, C., Paquette, S., Van Den Berg, H., Detlor, B., Bergeron, P., Heaton, L.: Working with information: information management and culture in a professional services organization. J. Inf. Sci. **32**(6), 491–510 (2006)
15. Oliver, G.: Cultural dimensions of information management. J. Inf. Knowl. Manag. **2**(1), 53–61 (2003)
16. Orna, E.: Making Knowledge Visible. GowerPublishing, Aldershot (2005)

17. Leidner, D.E.: Understanding information culture: integrating knowledge management systems into organizations. INSEAD (1998)
18. Bergeron, P., Heaton, L., Choo, C.W., Detlor, B., Bouchard, D., Paquette, S.: Knowledge and information management practices in knowledge-intensive organizations: a case study of a Québec Public Organization. In: Proceedings of Annual Conference of CAIS/Actes du congrès annuel de l'ACSI, October 2013
19. Svärd, P.: Enterprise content management and the records continuum model as strategies for long-term preservation of digital information. Rec. Manag. J. **23**(3), 159–176 (2013)
20. Vick, T.E., Nagano, M.S., Popadiuk, S.: Information culture and its influences in knowledge creation: evidence from university teams engaged in collaborative innovation projects. Int. J. Inf. Manag. **35**(3), 292–298 (2015)
21. Travica, B.: Information politics and information culture: a case study. Inf. Sci.: Int. J. Emerg. Transdiscipl. **8**, 211–244 (2005)
22. Tien, L.C., Chao, H.S.: Effects of information culture and job satisfaction on the organizational innovation-a study of different leadership styles as a moderatoritle. Adv. Manag. Appl. Econ. **2**(3), 83 (2012)
23. Choo, C.W.: Information culture and organizational effectiveness. Int. J. Inf. Manag. **33**(5), 775–779 (2013)
24. Kirk, J.: Theorising information use: managers and their work. Doctoral dissertation, University of Technology, Sydney (2002)
25. Choo, C.W.: Information seeking in organizations: epistemic contexts and contests. Inf. Res. **12**(2), 12-2 (2007)
26. Choo, C.W., Bergeron, P., Detlor, B., Heaton, L.: Information culture and information use: an exploratory study of three organizations. J. Am. Soc. Inf. Sci. Technol. **59**(5), 792–804 (2008)
27. Menou, M.: Information literacy in national information and communications technology (ICT) policies: the missed dimension, information culture. In: White Paper prepared for UNESCO, Information Literacy Meeting of Experts, Prague (2002)
28. Martin, V.A., Lycett, M., Macredie, R.: Exploring the gap between business and IT: an information culture approach. In: Proceedings of ALOIS 2003, Action in Language, Organisations and Information Systems, pp. 265–280 (2003)
29. Zheng, Y.: Information culture and development: Chinese experience of e-Health. In: Proceedings of 38th Annual Hawaii International Conference on System Sciences, HICSS 2005, p. 153a. IEEE, January 2005
30. Travica, B.: Influence of information culture on adoption of a self-service system. J. Inf. Inf. Technol. Org. **3**(1), 1–15 (2008)
31. Yang, F.: Exploring the information literacy of professionals in safety management. Saf. Sci. **50**(2), 294–299 (2012)

Information Literacy Practices of Researchers in Workplace Information Ecologies

Jela Steinerová(✉)

Comenius University, Bratislava, Slovakia
jela.steinerova@uniba.sk

Abstract. The paper explores information literacy practices of researchers in the context of information ecologies. Selected examples of information behavior studies of researchers and workplace information literacy are reviewed. Information ecologies in workplaces are explained. Findings of a qualitative study of 19 researchers in Slovakia are presented based on methodology of semi-structured interviews and concept mapping. Two concept maps representing issues of barriers and values in information practices are outlined. Findings suggest that multidimensional factors influence workplace information ecologies, mainly disciplinary cultures, values and tasks. Barriers include administrative overload, disintegration of sources and lack of funding. Main values include deep motivation and development of knowledge. Workplace information ecologies can improve research infrastructures and models of information literacy practices.

Keywords: Information literacy practices · Researchers
Workplace information ecologies · Concept mapping

1 Introduction

The purpose of this paper is to explore information literacy practices of researchers in scholarly workplaces in the context of information ecologies. The changing nature of work in digital environment has influenced information behavior of researchers. Digital technologies and social collaborative tools require new, flexible workplace information literacy practices and changing information culture. For example, success factors for distributed work [1] can include an environment of trust and shared ideas and clarity of expectations. Scholarly workplaces include both physical and digital spaces in which workplace information practices change. That is why workplace information literacy [2] in scholarly work needs more attention. In the following sections we will briefly review selected information behavior studies of researchers and concepts of workplace information literacy and information ecologies. We will report on a qualitative study of information behavior of researchers in Slovakia with examples of concept maps of values and barriers. We ask the following research question: Which values and barriers determine workplace information practices of researchers?

S. Kurbanoğlu et al. (Eds.): ECIL 2017, CCIS 810, pp. 30–39, 2018.
https://doi.org/10.1007/978-3-319-74334-9_4

2 Information Behavior Studies and Workplace Information

2.1 Related Studies of Information Behavior of Researchers

Human information behavior studies encompass a variety of models and empirical studies. Many studies pay special attention to professional environment and workplace information behavior [3]. Case [4] has summarized that information behavior models have spread from scientific information to everyday information behavior. First studies were targeted on scientists and engineers, later on researchers in social sciences and humanities. Paisley developed a framework of information use (1968) describing a scientist in an interconnected set of systems, including his personality, work team, formal organization, formal information systems, reference group, membership group, invisible college, political and legal/economic systems [5]. Further studies emphasized the role of scholars as gatekeepers who share information informally. Ellis's studies of scholars lead to his widely recognized model of information behavior [6]. Further highly cited models include especially those by Kuhlthau (ISP), Wilson, and Dervin (sense-making). Fosters' [7] non-linear model of information behavior of scholars identified non-linear processes of opening, orientation, consolidation and cognitive and external factors. Further models considered digital environments and collaboratories. As an example we can mention the theory of remote scientific collaboration by Olson and Olson [8]. Recent trends point to tacit knowledge in information use environments of researchers [9]. The domain analytic approach and disciplinary approaches [10, 11] found differences in information use patterns in disciplines. Research of communication in the sciences identified patterns of online publishing, citation and semantic linking and scientific discovery which are different in disciplines based on weak problem solving (humanities, social sciences) and disciplines with strong problem solving (high level of domain knowledge, sciences) [12]. As opposed to information behavior which is cognitively oriented [13], information practices refer to information use, contexts and social situations. A significant contribution is the use of activity theory by Wilson [14], emphasizing different tools (such as artefacts, mental constructs and norms) used in practices. The model by Byström and Järvelin [3] confirmed relationships between task complexity and information behavior. New models of human information behavior have broadened understanding of the information process towards manifold contextual factors [15, 16], web space searching [17], evolution and social frameworks [18, 19], and holistic ecological approach [20], including workplaces, digital tools and barriers.

2.2 Workplace Information Literacy: Conceptual Background

Workplace digital environments are challenges for development of information literacy practices. Workplaces can be understood as places where people engage in work activities and use information. Recent challenges are raised by electronic and mobile communications. Conceptual analyses of workplace information were presented in the framework of the ENWI project [21, 22]. One of the first frameworks of workplace information of professionals was Taylor's model of information use environments [5]. Although we can find many studies and models of information seeking in contexts, workplace information needs more attention. Contexts of information work were emphasized by Bruce in the concept of informed learning in which she linked information literacy and workplace performance [23]. Both individual and collective factors of experience in communities and disciplines are taken into account, especially social practices of collaboration and information sharing [24]. That is why the concept of workplace information literacy refers to making sense, learning and understanding information environments and power relationships. Workplace information literacy connects workplace information resources with activities and learning. Lloyd [25] enriched the concept of workplace learning by collaborative and socio-cultural practices, environmental contexts, and information landscapes. Sommerville et al. [26] emphasized the cyclical process of cultivating workplace information literacy represented by evidence-based practices, including proficiencies in asking questions, selecting authoritative sources, application of findings and evaluation. Workplace information literacy can be regarded as specific transliteracy based on information resources, information use, learning, teamwork and use of digital tools. Different perspectives on workplace information literacy can be divided into behavioral, relational and socio-cultural approaches in the three contexts of education, workplaces and communities [27]. Abram [2] emphasized that advances in workplace information literacy are based on social networks, collaboration, management of communications, and transfer of skills. As a result information fluency is determined as the ability to find, evaluate and use digital information effectively and ethically in personal and work roles. Abram [2] also points to the fact that educational institutions are regarded as valid targets for workplace information literacy training by impact of professors on students. Another important perspective introduced the concept of professional information literacy based on studies of professions in digital (web) environments [27]. In academic workplaces the concepts of methodological and research information literacies were introduced [28, 29]. Other factors of workplace information literacy cover information use, decision-making, interactions among activities, tasks, tools, technologies, policies and personalities. The question is if the framework of information ecology can contribute to understanding of workplace information literacy practices of researchers.

2.3 Information Ecologies

Information ecologies are defined as dynamic systems of people, practices, values and technologies [30]. They can emerge in different workplaces and contexts (e.g. universities, hospitals, libraries). Holistic views on information environments in contexts are framed by information ecology. A complex model of information environment in organizations was presented by Choo [31], composed by cognitive, affective and situational factors in three dimensions of information use. Information ecology in organizations was determined by Davenport and Prusak [32] as making information meaningful in information management. Environmental sustainability of people, systems and information presented Chowdhury [33]. Sustainable professional information practices were outlined by Liquette [34]. Workplaces can be regarded as information ecologies where information can be shared, and collaboration, interactivity and participation shape communities. Information ecologies cover procedures, goals, values, communities and places of information-related activities. Main characteristics are diversity of components, adaptations between men and networks and co-evolution. In digital workplaces information ecologies open spaces for participation and value-based design of services and products. Critical components are tools for eliminating information overload and risks of information use. For example, Huvila [35] presented social framework of ecology of information work based on studies of archaeologists. In information ecologies links between social and technological contexts and external and internal environments maintain balance in workplace information culture. Collaborative information behavior and information sharing are further concepts which help understand workplace information practices of researchers. In information ecologies cognitive, technological and socio-political dimensions were identified. Principles of knowledge construction include reliance, trust, and culture of critical participation [36]. Workplace information practices of researchers can form information ecologies at micro-level, i.e. individual cognitive, affective and sensorimotor skills, information seeking, relevance assessment and values of information. At macro-level it means management of information resources, systems and services which can inform design of knowledge-based services for individuals and communities of practice of researchers. Information ecologies in scholarly workplaces refer to dynamic places of multiple intertwined factors of digital sources use, social networking, digital publishing, data management, and remote collaborations, integrated by research creativity.

3 A Study of Information Behavior of Researchers

3.1 Research Design and Methodology

A qualitative study of 19 researchers in different disciplines in Slovakia was conducted in 2015–2016. The objectives of the study were to identify information needs and attitudes of researchers to information infrastructures. The design of the study and first results were presented in 2016 [29]. The disciplines included humanities (39%), sciences and medicine (28%), social sciences (22%) and technical sciences (11%). In this paper we report on part of this study with regard to selected information practices, namely barriers and common values. We asked the following questions: What is the influence of workplace information infrastructure on information practices of researchers? Which barriers are most significant in information ecologies? Which values emerge in information ecologies? The methodology of the study was designed using semi-structured interviews, content analyses and concept mapping. Data were coded, categorized and interpreted. Deeper semantic analyses have been applied, including concept mapping. A special concept map of a researcher in information environment was developed, including the components of the research process, the information process, the information infrastructure, and factors of influence [29]. Resulting concept maps represent the collective discourse of researchers.

4 Concept Mapping

Concept mapping was used as a methodology for representation of content analyses of data acquired by interviews. Information landscapes as dynamic representations of information environments cover information literacy practices in disciplines based on discussions [25, 37]. Collective mapping of information practices in workplaces was applied by Whitworth et al. [38]. These maps were used as learning experience. In our approach we used concept mapping to extract key concepts and semantic relations in order to visualize contexts of discourse. In line with similar research [39, 40], we visualized discourse in 25 concept maps. In perceptions of information infrastructures, we found common patterns of expertise, experience and critical analytical information practices manifested in the use of authoritative sources and personal expert networks. Differences stem from problem statements, methodologies, types of data, publishing patterns, participation in social networks and collaboration. As examples, concept maps representing barriers and values are outlined.

4.1 Barriers in Research Information Infrastructures

The concept map Barriers in research information infrastructures identified main barriers as perceived by researchers in their workplaces, namely individual, social, technological, administrative and environmental aspects (Fig. 1).

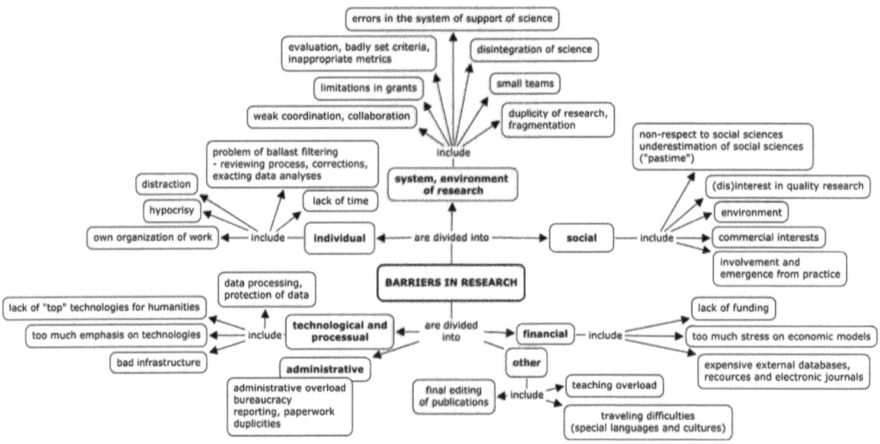

Fig. 1. Concept map barriers in research information infrastructure

Most frequently perceived barriers were administrative overload and lack of funding. Other categories identified technological, personal and social barriers. One researcher put it explicitly: *"We would need financing of that infrastructure. I do not ask for salaries, but for this..." (R19).* These findings point to gaps between information needs of researchers and existing information infrastructures, as found by other studies [41]. Findings confirmed problems of societal interest in the quality research.

Proposals for improvement of information infrastructure were articulated, namely integrated information services, digital systems and repositories, organization of research process, information sharing, interdisciplinary networking and support of young researchers.

4.2 Values of Research Work

Regarding values of research work common attitudes were noted represented by deep motivation of researchers, interest in topics and intellectual pleasure/thrill. (Fig. 2). Researchers identified values involved in social and individual contexts of scholarly activities – from help to people in everyday activities to social significance of basic questions of life. Individual values include freedom of inquiry and characteristics of creative personality based on curiosity and professionality. Values were perceived as dynamic, connected with discovery of new perspectives and creative experience. They are also socially constructed and validated by international community. Values emerge from understanding of a learned scholar and his fascination by knowing. At social level values reflect the social status of science, collaboration and service to society. New discoveries, new practical solutions, new methods and new applications of knowledge were identified as examples of values of research. Generally, values reflect curiosity, knowledge growth and help bridge gaps in knowing. We noted disciplinary differences between sciences (practical solutions, discoveries and quest for understanding life) and social sciences and humanities (broader contexts, interpretations, understanding of people and society in time and space). Values are embodied in personalities of researchers who are main actors of dynamic workplace information ecologies. Similar approach determined value factors of information literacy and information practices of employees (e.g. efficiency, credibility, trust, sustainability) [42].

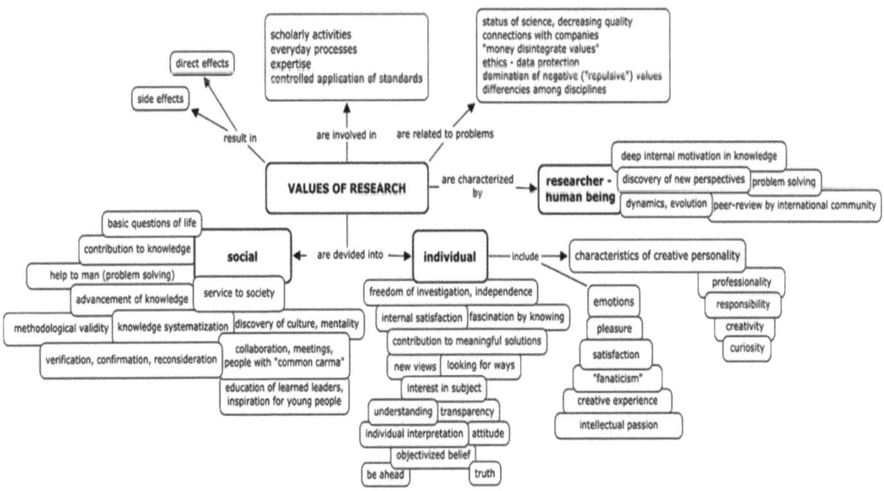

Fig. 2. Concept map values of research

5 Findings: Workplace Information Ecologies

In response to our questions we found that the three most frequently perceived barriers for scholars were lack of funding, administrative overload and understanding of science in society. Workplaces integrate both physical and digital environments. Main perceived problems were bureaucracy and limited access to project funding. Especially in humanities and social sciences researchers perceived insufficient workplace infrastructures, namely access to information sources and expensive technologies. Workplace information infrastructures were perceived as disintegrated. Another frequently mentioned barrier was an inappropriate system of research evaluation. Findings suggest that expertise and methodology are in correlation with workplace information literacy practices of researchers.

Perceived values of research point to deep professional motivation of researchers and the role of their personality. Such values as quest for new perspectives and bridging knowledge gaps are integrated with intellectual pleasure. Values and infrastructures are main components of sustainable workplace information practices of researchers. The position of science in society and promotion of open science were emphasized. Value-based design can support development of more efficient information infrastructures.

Based on the analysed data we can determine workplace information ecologies as dynamic interactions of researchers and hybrid information environments. Diversity of workplace information ecologies was confirmed depending on cultures of disciplines. Differences in disciplines have been manifested in manifold factors, such as problem statement (broad context; narrow context), methodologies, types of data, creativity, procedures, social networking, publishing patterns, collaboration (highly organized or less organized communities). Different information ecologies stem from problem-solving patterns of information use (in sciences, informatics), interpretations and knowledge construction (in humanities), surveys and social interactions (in social sciences). Workplace information ecologies often include digital tools which can add value, but also raise new problems, such as information ethics, security, privacy, copyright. Context-dependent, dialogic and practice-driven workplace information literacy practices have emerged. Digital environments broaden the range of information practices, especially participation in digital communities, networked collaboration, social media, electronic publishing, verification of information and digital literacy.

6 Conclusions

Information practices of researchers can be interpreted from the perspective of workplace information interactions and information infrastructures. Hybrid workplaces include high level of domain and practical expertise of researchers, and make use of methodological literacy, creativity and digital literacy. Findings of our study point to motivation of information practices of researchers embedded in values of research. We also identified main barriers of information practices of researchers, namely disintegrated information infrastructures. Information ecologies were determined as continually evolving dynamic interactions between researchers and information environments. Knowledge of workplace information practices of researchers and factors of workplace information ecologies can help understand information needs of researchers and establish links between theory and value-based design of digital libraries and services. Information literacy practices of researchers differ in disciplines and domains. These differences can form contexts for community-based policies, digital systems, tools and services. Common factors of workplace information ecologies of researchers are research literacy and methodological creativity which should be supported by creative digital tools and practise-based services for researchers. We can also conclude that sustainability of workplace information literacy practices of researchers depends on such values as deep internal motivation and service to societal development. We recommend that information infrastructures should be adapted to information literacy practices of researchers, namely communication, collaboration, interdisciplinary partnerships, data management, academic social networks and new online genres. Workplace information ecologies can support participation in digital communities, cultivation of strategies of digital publishing and digital literacy and develop digital tools for complex worktasks and activities.

Acknowledgements. The paper was developed as part of the research projects VEGA 1/0066/15 Modeling of the information environment of digital scholarship and HIBER, APVV 0508-15.

References

1. Ouye, A.J.: Five Trends that are Dramatically Changing Work and Workplace. Knoll Workplace Research, Knoll Inc. (2011)
2. Abram, S.: Workplace information literacy: it's different. In: Hepworth, M., Walton, G. (eds.) Developing People's Information Capabilities: Fostering Information Literacy in Educational Workplace and Community Contexts, pp. 205–222. Bingley, Emerald (2013)
3. Byström, K.: Information activities in work tasks. In: Fisher, K., Erdelez, S., mcKechnie, L. (eds.) Theories of Information Behavior, pp. 174–178. Information Today, Medford (2005)
4. Case, D.O.: Looking for Information. A Survey of Research on Information Seeking, Needs and Behavior, 3rd edn. 491 p. Emerald, Bingley (2012)
5. Byström, K., Ruthven, I., Heinström, J.: Work and information: which workplace models still work in modern digital workplaces? Inf. Res. **22**(1), CoLIS Paper 1651 (2017). http://InformationR.net/ir/22-1/colis/colis1651.html
6. Ellis, D.: Ellis's model of information-seeking behavior. In: Theories of Information Behavior, pp. 139–142. Information Today, Medford (2005)
7. Foster, A.: A non-linear model of information-seeking behaviour. J. Am. Soc. Inf. Sci. Technol. **55**(3), 228–237 (2004). http://onlinelibrary.wiley.com/doi/10.1002/asi.10359/full
8. Olson, G.M., Olson, J.: Converging on theory from four sides. In: Sonnenwald, D. (ed.) Theory Development in the Information Sciences, pp. 87–100. University of Texas, Austin (2016)
9. Greifeneder, E.: Trends in information behaviour research. Inf. Res. **19**(4) (2014). http://www.informationr.net/ir/19-4/isic/isic13.html
10. Talja, S.: The domain analytic approach to scholars' information practices. In: Fisher, K., Erdelez, S., McKechnie, L. (eds.) Theories of Information Behavior, pp. 123–127. Information Today, Medford (2005)

11. Palmer, C.I., Cragin, M.H.: Scholarship and disciplinary practices. Ann. Rev. Inf. Sci. Technol. **43**(2), 163–212 (2008). https://doi.org/10.1002/aris.2008.1440420112
12. Brown, C.: Communication in the Sciences. Ann. Rev. Inf. Sci. Technol. **44**, 287–316 (2010). (Ed. by, B. Cronin, Information Today, Medford)
13. Ford, N.: Introduction to Information Behaviour, 252 p. Facet, London (2015)
14. Wilson, T.D.: Activity theory and information seeking. Ann. Rev. Inf. Sci. Technol. **42**, 119–161 (2008). https://doi.org/10.1002/aris.2008.1440420111
15. Godbold, N.: Beyond information seeking: towards a general model of information behaviour. Inf. Res. **11**(4), paper 269 (2006). http://InformationR.net/ir/11-4/paper269.html
16. Robson, A., Robinson, L.: Building on models of information behaviour: linking information seeking and communication. J. Doc. **69**(2), 169–193 (2013)
17. Pharo, N.: A new model of information behaviour based on the search situation transition schema. Inf. Res. **10**(1), (2004). http://informationr.net/ir/10-1/paper203.html
18. Spink, A., Cole, Ch. (eds.): New Directions in Human Information Behaviour. Springer, Dordrecht (2005). https://doi.org/10.1007/1-4020-3670-1
19. Spink, A.: Information Behavior. An Evolutionary Instinct. Springer, Heidelberg (2010). https://doi.org/10.1007/978-3-642-11497-7
20. Fidel. R.: Human Information Interaction: An Ecological Approach to Information Behavior, 348 p. MIT Press, Cambridge (2012)
21. Widén, G., Steinerová, J., Voisey, P.: Conceptual modelling of workplace information practices: a literature review. Inf. Res. paper isic08 (2014). (Proceedings of ISIC, Leeds, 2–5 September 2014: Part 1). http://InformationR.net/ir/19-4/isic/isic08.html
22. Byström, K.: Information challenges, challenging information in digital workplaces: report from the European network for workplace information symposium 2015. J. Libr. Inf. Sci. **42** (1), 12–22 (2016)
23. Bruce, Ch.S., Somerville, M.M., Stoodley, I., Patridge, H.: Diversifying information literacy research: an informed learning perspective. In: Hepworth, E.M., Walton, G. (eds.) Developing People's Information Capabilities: Fostering Information Literacy in Educational, Workplace and Community Contexts. Bingley, Emerald (2013)
24. Talja, S., Hansen, P.: Information sharing. In: Spink, A., Cole, Ch. (eds.) New Directions in Human Information Behaviour, pp. 113–134. Springer, Dordrecht (2005). https://doi.org/10.1007/1-4020-3670-1_7
25. Lloyd, A.: Building information resilient workers: the critical ground of workplace information literacy. What have we learnt? In: Kurbanoğlu, S., Grassian, E., Mizrachi, D., Catts, R., Špiranec, S. (eds.) ECIL 2013. CCIS, vol. 397, pp. 219–228. Springer, Cham (2013). https://doi.org/10.1007/978-3-319-03919-0_28
26. Sommerville, M.M., Howard, Z., Mirijamdotter, A.: Workplace information literacy: cultivation strategies for 'working smarter' in 21st century libraries. In: Mueller, D.M. (ed.) Proceedings of 14th National Conference of Association of College and Research Libraries (ACRL), pp. 119–126. Association of College and Research Libraries, Seattle (2009). http://eprints.qut.edu.au/61215/
27. Sayyad Abdi, E., Bruce, C.: From workplace to profession: new focus for the information literacy discourse. In: Kurbanoğlu, S., Boustany, J., Špiranec, S., Grassian, E., Mizrachi, D., Roy, L. (eds.) ECIL 2015. CCIS, vol. 552, pp. 59–69. Springer, Cham (2015). https://doi.org/10.1007/978-3-319-28197-1_7
28. Steinerová, J.: Methodological literacy of doctoral students – an emerging model. In: Kurbanoğlu, S., Grassian, E., Mizrachi, D., Catts, R., Špiranec, S. (eds.) ECIL 2013. CCIS, vol. 397, pp. 148–154. Springer, Cham (2013). https://doi.org/10.1007/978-3-319-03919-0_18

29. Steinerová, J.: Open science and the research information literacy framework. In: Kurbanoğlu, S., Boustany, J., Špiranec, S., Grassian, E., Mizrachi, D., Roy, L., Çakmak, T. (eds.) ECIL 2016. CCIS, vol. 676, pp. 277–285. Springer, Cham (2016). https://doi.org/10.1007/978-3-319-52162-6_27
30. Nardi, B., O'Day, V.: Information Ecologies: Using Technologies with Heart, 232 p. MIT Press, Cambridge (1999)
31. Choo, C.W.: The Knowing Organization. How Organizations Use Information to Construct Meaning, Create Knowledge, and Make Decisions, 354 p. Oxford University Press, New York (2006)
32. Davenport, T.H., Prusak, L.: Information Ecology: Mastering the Information and Knowledge Environment, 255 p. Oxford Univ. Press, New York (1997)
33. Chowdhury, G.G.: Sustainability of Scholarly Information, 231 p. Facet, London (2014)
34. Liquète, V.: Some principles of the durability of the informative professional practices. In: Kurbanoğlu, S., Boustany, J., Špiranec, S., Grassian, E., Mizrachi, D., Roy, L. (eds.) ECIL 2015. CCIS, vol. 552, pp. 99–106. Springer, Cham (2015). https://doi.org/10.1007/978-3-319-28197-1_11
35. Huvila, I.: Social aspects of the ecology of information work. In: Proceedings of International Conference on Information Ecology and Libraries, October 2011, Bratislava, UK, pp. 27–36 (2011)
36. Lehmans, A.: An ecological approach to collaborative knowledge management in small professional communities: sustainable information practices for sustainable work. In: Kurbanoğlu, S., Boustany, J., Špiranec, S., Grassian, E., Mizrachi, D., Roy, L. (eds.) ECIL 2015. CCIS, vol. 552, pp. 107–117. Springer, Cham (2015). https://doi.org/10.1007/978-3-319-28197-1_12
37. Whitworth, A.: Radical Information Literacy. Reclaiming the Political Heart of the IL Movement, 233 p. Chandos, Amsterdam (2014)
38. Whitworth, A., Torras i Calvo, M.-C., Moss, B., Amlesom Kifle, N., Blåsternes, T.: Mapping collective information practices in the workplace. In: Kurbanoğlu, S., Boustany, J., Špiranec, S., Grassian, E., Mizrachi, D., Roy, L. (eds.) ECIL 2015. CCIS, vol. 552, pp. 49–58. Springer, Cham (2015). https://doi.org/10.1007/978-3-319-28197-1_6
39. Novak, J.D., Cañas, A.J.: The theory underlying concept maps and how to construct them. Technical report IHMC CmapsTools, Florida Institute for Human and Machine Cognition, Pensacola (2006)
40. Kinchin, I.M., Streatfield, D., Hay, D.B.: Using concept mapping to enhance the research interview. Int. J. Qual. Methods **9**(1), 52–89 (2010)
41. Vilar, P.: Information behaviour of scholars. Libellarium: J. Res. Writ. Book Cult. Herit. Inst. (2015). Libellarium **VII**(1), 17–39 (2014). http://dx-doi.rg/10.15291/libellarium,v7i1.org
42. Goldstein, S., Whitworth, A.: Determining the value of information literacy for employers. In: Kurbanoğlu, S., Boustany, J., Špiranec, S., Grassian, E., Mizrachi, D., Roy, L. (eds.) ECIL 2015. CCIS, vol. 552, pp. 70–79. Springer, Cham (2015). https://doi.org/10.1007/978-3-319-28197-1_8

Enhancing the Quality of the Library Processes - Benchmarking Workplace Information Literacy and Numeracy Practices and Communication Tools in Two European University Libraries

Núria Balagué[1] and Jarmo Saarti[2(✉)]

[1] Universitat Autònoma de Barcelona, Barcelona, Spain
nuria.balague@uab.cat
[2] University of Eastern Finland Library, Kuopio, Finland
jarmo.saarti@uef.fi

Abstract. The aim of this paper is to investigate how two European university libraries have utilized communication tools to guarantee information literacy and numeracy for academic librarians in order to increase the quality of the services. The paper is based on data about the communication tools implemented and used in the selected institutions. Each communication tool has been defined and their uses compared at each library and its role in their PDCA (Plan-Do-Check-Act) circle considered. The workplace information systems and their valid implementation can help in the organization's strategy work. It also enhances the quality of the library's service processes.

Keywords: Quality management · Communication · Library staff
Academic libraries

1 Introduction

The vision Paul G. Zurkowski had about information literate citizens in the 1970's was one of future citizens and workforce being able to manage the increasing flow of information and what skills they would need daily in the emerging knowledge-based society. The workplace he foresaw is reality at present.

Libraries and their staff need to process a growing amount of information to respond effectively and on time to the needs of their users. It is also important for libraries to show their value to their parent organizations and to society. For instance, at present, academic libraries are not only dealing with documents but becoming increasingly involved in the preservation of a large amount of data gathered by the researchers of their institutions according to open science initiatives.

The ability to evolve with changing needs is a core of the library's culture and its staff members. The need for well-trained staff to select, process and understand a lot of external information, see what implications and circumstances can occur in the library and make rapid and valid decisions is crucial. Therefore, librarians should be not only

S. Kurbanoğlu et al. (Eds.): ECIL 2017, CCIS 810, pp. 40–49, 2018.
https://doi.org/10.1007/978-3-319-74334-9_5

good professionals who create effective processes and provide documented information to researchers, but they also must be prepared to become academics who create the future of the library. They must find, select, and bring together different types of information (e.g., internal and external reports, statistics, and raw data) on a diversity of subjects that when analyzed help the library to find new lines of action.

So, a well-trained staff is needed, not only to be able to deal with professional literature about the library, but also with extensive capabilities of literacy and numeracy skills to facilitate understanding of data and texts within different social contexts (e.g. economic, legal, technological). There is a need for staff prepared to make informed decisions for the appropriate development of libraries.

The aim of this study is to investigate how two European university libraries have used communication and management tools to ensure information literacy and numeracy skills for academic librarians to increase the quality of services.

2 Quality Management is About Information Management

Usually, university libraries have staff with different job profiles (e.g. librarians and supporting staff), and each staff member has knowledge and skills needed to carry out their daily activities. In this sense one can say, that their workplace literacy and numeracy skills are guaranteed. This study is not intended to investigate on individual capacities; instead, the capacity of the workforce is considered as a whole. When working together, the knowledge and skills of each member are merged. We want to reflect here on the needs of high literacy and numeracy skills that must be assumed by the library staff in teamwork.

The term literacy is employed mainly at the present to refer to information literacy, "the ability to access and use a variety of information sources to solve an information need. It includes the development of a complex set of critical skills that allows people to express, explore, question, communicate and understand the flow of ideas among individuals and groups in quickly changing technological environments" [1], and the ability to assess complex contexts.

The term numeracy is employed "to refer to the ability to process, interpret and communicate numerical, quantitative, spatial, statistical and even mathematical information in ways that are appropriate for a variety of contexts" [1].

Technology has helped us to build communication networks and intranets, but the traditional face to face communication is still an important element for the cohesion of teams and the transmission of knowledge. In this study the related literacy, numeracy and communication tools are analysed in a university library setting, with quality management as a background theory which aims to increase customer satisfaction.

3 Libraries Involved in the Study

3.1 University of Eastern Finland Library (UEF)

The University of Eastern Finland was established in 2010 as the result of the merger of the University of Joensuu and the University of Kuopio. With approximately 15,000 students and 2,800 members of staff, the University of Eastern Finland is one of the largest universities in Finland. The university's campuses are located in Joensuu, Kuopio and Savonlinna, about 100 km apart from each other. The library has three campus libraries and a joint library with the university hospital. It has 75 staff members. And it has almost one million printed volumes, about half a million digital book titles and about 20,000 e-journal titles.

One of the main impetuses for introducing quality management system to the library was the fact that the services were to be implemented within a new type of university with the main aim being to provide services in a digital form between campuses [2]. Another goal was to help in the continuing education of the staff [3].

In the implementation of the quality management system the library has utilized modern computer systems. The first phase meant building an extensive intranet as a tool for documentation and service process management. The current phase started in 2015 when new, social media type of tools were implemented for the university. This meant the use of a social media type of intranet and discussion tools, and extensive use of video-conferencing. During this change a special effort has been in staff education and renewal of the management system.

3.2 Universitat Autònoma de Barcelona (UAB)

The UAB Library Service has seven libraries on the Bellaterra campus, one library on Sabadell campus and four libraries located in the University's extension areas. Library holdings include approximately 1,300,000 books, over 80,000 journals, and a well consolidated and ever expanding digital library.

With over 36,000 square meters, the library buildings can accommodate a total of 4,900 readers at a given time. In addition to their physical and digital collections, the libraries offer a full range of on-site and digital services, and the 166 full time equivalent people working in the libraries are ready to serve three million visitors per year and almost the same number of virtual users.

The UAB libraries have been working under a PDCA approach since the early 90's of the last century. Its management is framed by strategic plans and a certified ISO 9001 quality management system.

In addition to the obvious mailings, phone calls and meetings, UAB Library Service has implemented different communication tools to guarantee that its staff is permanently informed on all the issues they need for quality work and is able to provide the best support to users. There is an intranet (run on Liferay), project management software (run on Dotproject), some quality management databases (in-home design on PHP/MySQL) and a quite popular Wiki (run on Redmine). All these tools have as common goals to guarantee the use of upgraded information, to contribute to internal transparency and to encourage all the staff to share information.

4 Methodology and Data Collection

A qualitative research study based on interviews of the library staff was conducted in two academic libraries, Universitat Autònoma de Barcelona Library (UAB) Barcelona, Spain, and University of Eastern Finland Library (UEF), Finland, to compare library service managers' perceptions in each of the institutions. The study utilized the PDCA cycle approach to identify different communication tools and literacy and numeracy practices at different phases of the library activities. The interviews were conducted by the authors who also act as part of the library management, which may have influenced the interviews.

4.1 PDCA Cycle as a Basis for Interviews

The use of the PDCA cycle – known also as the Shewart cycle – was popularized by Deming during the 1950s. Initially it was employed as a tool for product quality control, and later it was recognized as a tool for production process improvement, because of constant interaction among four activities: research, design, production, and sales in conducting a company's business. It was soon considered a well-adapted tool for managing the work carried out by a team. Therefore, the Shewart cycle was redefined, and the four steps renamed as plan, do, check, and act, the PDCA cycle [4, 5].

As the PDCA cycle is a well-known method to conduct activities pursuing improvement, it was considered a good frame to identify different phases of the library activities. The four phases are summarized below:

P: The library plans: The library studies the current situation and gathers data to be used to establish the objectives and processes necessary to deliver results in accordance with the expected output, for instance, in the preparation of the library strategic plan.
D: The library does: Once the plan is ready, it must be implemented. During its daily activities, the library processes are executed and services are provided to library users. Some data is collected to be used later, during the review.
C: The library checks: Data collected during the performance of the activities are analyzed and a review of the actual achievement of the library objectives is prepared. The data are transformed into information used to prepare the next cycle step.
A: The library acts: The findings in the previous phase are the inputs to plan a new cycle. The library should aim towards the future, looking for new targets. Improvement is pursued by setting incremental objectives at every cycle. If the evaluation is showing something that is different from what is expected, it is necessary to put in action necessary adjustments.

4.2 Interviews, Data Collected and Data Analysis

A structured interview was designed with a list of fixed questions that were applied to all the interviewees (see Table 1). The average time to complete it was about 45 min. The interviews took place during April and May 2017.

Table 1. PDCA-cycle and questions based on it.

Cycle phase	Themes
Plan	• What are the main inputs used in the library to plan? [Strategic planning] • What are the main threats to deal with the documentation inputs? • Which communication tools does the library team use to prepare the plan? • Have any problems been detected regarding literacy or numeracy? • Benefits, problems, opportunities
Do	• What are the main inputs used in the library to carry out daily tasks? [Procedures] • What are the main threats in dealing with information in daily work? • Which communication tools does the library team use to do their daily work? • Have problems been detected regarding literacy or numeracy? • Benefits, problems, opportunities
Check	• What are the main inputs used in the library for evaluation and/or audit? [Reports and Data] • What are the main threats to dealing with the internal data collected for charting and analysis? • Which communication tools does the library team use to prepare the annual report and/or evaluation/audit report? • Have any problems been detected regarding literacy or numeracy?
Act	• What are the main inputs used in the library to act? [adjustments to Strategic planning] • What are the main threats to dealing with the results of the evaluation/audit? • Which communication tools does the library team use to prepare its yearly operational plan? • Have any problems been detected regarding literacy or numeracy? • Benefits, problems, opportunities

Both at the UAB and UEF five library middle managers, with working teams consisting of 8 to 22 members, were interviewed. The answers at each university were summarized and then compared and discussed to establish the conclusions based on the findings. In the data analysis, the PDCA-cycle acted as a framework for the comparisons. In addition, the use of communication tools in implementing the PDCA cycle was analyzed.

5 The Libraries' Use of Communication Tools for Quality Work and Challenges in Workplace Information Literacy

5.1 Results of the Survey at UAB Libraries

Plan Phase. At present, UAB Libraries are working under their fifth strategic plan 2015–2018. Main inputs for the plan were internal information: strategic plan 2011–2014 evaluation report, library statistics, user survey, as well as other library reports. University reports on students, research and economic issues were also used to align the new plan with the University's strategic lines. The list of objectives and other reports produced by CSUC, the library consortium to which UAB library is a member, were used as external information inputs, as well as several other reports on university library trends. Finally, a review of best practices was conducted by visiting websites of the first 100 universities in the 2014 edition of Academic Ranking of World Universities.

Different working groups were created and the reports to be processed were distributed to be sure that the staff could combine their daily activities at the library with reading and extracting ideas from the reports. All those interviewed thought that the information was enough and manageable, but some threats to deal with the documentation inputs were referred: dispersion of information to different storage locations, feeling of e-mail overload, information obsolescence, and difficulties in filling the gap between trends and local reality.

The communications tools used by the library to prepare the plan were mainly intranet, e-mail, meetings, and a wiki.

No problems were detected in the comprehension of professional readings in Spanish nor in Catalan and those interviewed indicated that the level of English proficiency of the librarians involved in the planning work was good enough not to affect the comprehension of professional readings. Some contents, not strictly related to libraries as, for instance, information on student demography, statistics on research grants, legal aspects of university financing or future trends on IT, could have presented some difficulties, however all those interviewed agreed that only some occasional difficulties were detected to deal with the complexity of different data.

Do Phase. The UAB libraries emphasize a process approach, the baseline of its ISO 9001 quality management system. Procedures and other documents such as organization charts, process maps, work instructions and any other information required are available for staff on the library intranet. All those interviewed mentioned as input the procedures and other information on the intranet. Other remarks regarded the task plan for objectives and projects for courses, agreements of collaboration with other departments, university services and other user needs.

No threats for the daily work routine were detected. However, e-mail overload was mentioned as a problem. Other comments were, missing personnel due to medical leave or work permit, interruptions, technical failure on the network and being able to know where the information is when you look for something you are not using frequently.

The intranet and e-mail were mentioned as main communication tools and phones, team meetings, the wiki, web, and informal communication.

Those interviewed mentioned that the everyday data are not complex, and that the teams manage well the data related to their specific activities. However, it was pointed out that to survive e-mail overload, some staff just do a very superficial reading, which sometimes leads to a misunderstanding of the information they need to know. Some occasional problems on numeracy have been detected as collecting and preparing statistics is the last priority for some members of the staff.

Check Phase. Main inputs referred to by those interviewed were library statistics, objectives, user demands, user survey, internal reports, and staff feedback.

No threats were detected as those interviewed explained that teams manage well the data related to their specific activities. However, they all agreed on the fact that from time to time mistakes are detected during manual data collection or during changes in methodology.

Regarding communications tools, all those interviewed mentioned the intranet because it contains databases where numerical data are stored and this information is used both to produce the annual report and the reports that will be used during the annual audit. In addition, they all mentioned e-mail, and some referred to team meetings and formal and informal conversations, as well.

No problems of comprehension were reported at a managerial level but there was some mention of sporadic difficulties in some staff with a low level of responsibility.

Act Phase. The main inputs reported were evaluation report, user demands, user survey, and internal reflection on the library operation.

All of the librarians interviewed referred to lack of time and/or staff/ and/or financial resources as main threats. Other threats mentioned were: lack of university's feedback, lack of recognition that discourages the team, and unexpected extra work.

Intranet, e-mail, team meetings and informal communication are the main communication tools in this phase. The review of objectives from the previous year, and decisions on the objectives for the next year require a shared reflection to guarantee good acceptance of the new operational plan, and all interviewed highlighted the importance of face-to-face communication.

No problems of comprehension were detected, but there was one comment about the need for a more accessible and comprehensible evaluation report. No problems were mentioned about numeracy, as the team has already been working with data during its daily activities for a long time.

The use of a PDCA cycle makes management of the libraries and the work teams much easier. However, one of the interviewed mentioned that, in addition, library managers need emotional intelligence to manage a library successfully.

5.2 Results of the Survey at UEF Libraries

Plan Phase. One can divide the data inputs of the planning phase at the UEF in three levels: all the persons interviewed were following university and academic library development at international, national, and home university level. They all followed the main trends in the libraries and in the academic world. The communication channels utilized were journals, internet, and its various tools. Also benchmarking between other libraries was used when planning services.

The library has built a planning cycle based on the PDCA cycle and these tools were utilized by all the persons interviewed. Here the change from static intranet towards interactive social media tools was on-going; also a lot of videoconferencing was used due to the nature of the campus structure of the university. This has enabled the middle managers to involve the staff in the discussion.

The major difference between the middle managers was based on the type of staff. The more they had specialists working in their team, the less they had to act as interpreters of the trends. There also was the notion that the role of the middle managers and especially face-to-face meetings were very important, especially when implementing strategically and fiscally important issues. Also, motivational issues were mentioned: part of the staff thought that planning is not their business but that of the management.

Do Phase. The library's intranet with the documentation it contains was found helpful in conducting the daily tasks. Here also the meetings were very important. Following and analysing feedback and statistics were also important. All the services used the analysis of service anomalies and corrective measures were done automatically and analysed together in meetings.

The main communication tools here were the intranet and ICT communication tools provided by the university. Again, the importance of face-to-face meetings was emphasised.

Check Phase. In the check phase, the annual reporting and yearly management review were mentioned as important tools. The library creates its annual report jointly with the staff and this was found to be a good practice that involves all the staff and increases the understanding of the library's mission and strategy implementation.

At this point, the benchmarking the library does as part of its annual statistics collection was mentioned. This especially helps the middle managers understand how their services succeed compared with other universities. Also, the performance appraisal discussions were found important in checking with the staff on the achievement of library's success.

Act Phase. The persons interviewed all mentioned that the library has been able to build a culture where it is possible to make corrections to the library strategy and service production continuously. Again, especially the specialist staff was mentioned as being able to make these types of corrections more flexibly. They all emphasised the fact that it is also important since the operational environment is changing rapidly.

At the university level, the library has been successful in having members of the staff at all levels, including the governing board. This has helped in affecting the university and its strategy. The most challenging aspect for the staff was the understanding of the university and how it acts. Here the importance of meetings and the role of the middle manager as messenger was again emphasised.

In Table 2 the most important findings from both UEF and UAB libraries are summarised.

Table 2. PDCA-cycle and basic findings.

Cycle phase	Findings
Plan	• A lot of internal and external information has to be processed to produce a good plan • It requires a lot of effort from the middle managers
Do	• Intranet is *one stop shopping* where to find everything that is needed for daily routines • Role of the middle managers as interpreters and messengers is important especially due to the information overflow • Involvement of the staff decreases when library issues are not in focus
Check	• Involvement of all staff on the annual review and reporting helps to strengthen the understanding of the library's mission and strategy
Act	• A culture of improvement facilitate the possibility to make corrections to the library strategy and service production all the time
Complete PDCA-cycle	• Well structured quality management and planning system helps the library in managing the PDCA cycle and its daily tasks • Modern communication tools increase the staff's involvement but it is still very important to hold both formal and informal face-to-face contacts regularly • The pressure of information overload may lead to a superficial scanning that could produce a lack of understanding

6 Conclusions

The library staff has a lot of data available to help them in improving the quality of the library services, but they are not always aware of these resources for decision making in everyday working practices, whether through ignorance or lack of skills to utilize them [6]. Low use of data resources for management could lead the library to not being able to offer quality services, or in the rapidly changing operational environment, their services may even become outdated.

Communication tools play an important role in enabling all the staff to access and use the internal information managed by the academic library [7]. This helps the staff in utilizing it and transforming the knowledge gathered into increasing the quality of the library's services [8, 9]. The study identified several practices where their internal communication network was a facilitator of the library management's strategic goals. These findings also involved some factors related to the communication tools that enabled the use of knowledge for the improvement of the library's services and managing daily routines.

The issues mentioned by librarians in both UAB and UEF libraries are very similar, there were only some differences due to specific organizational structure in each institution. The PDCA cycle approach and a good use of communication tools have fostered a well rooted culture of service improvement.

It seems that the workplace information systems and their valid implementation to active use can help in the organization's strategy work. It also enhances the quality of the library's service processes.

It was also noted that the role of the middle manager is very important. This is because, despite the modern communication tools available, face-to-face contacts and meetings are still the most important managerial tools.

For the staff, it was noted that motivational aspects do affect the ability and the commitment to understand the more abstract issues of library work. It seems that specialized staff is more motivated and self-directing, but mainly within their own professional interests.

References

1. UNESCO: Education for All: A Global Monitoring Report. UNESCO, Paris (2006). http://www.unesco.org/education/GMR2006/full/chapt6_eng.pdf
2. Muhonen, A., Nygrén, U., Saarti, J.: Bringing order out of Chaos: benchmarking tools used in merging university libraries in Finland. In: Woodsworth, A., Penniman, W.D. (eds.) Librarianship in Times of Crisis: Advances in Librarianship, vol. 34, pp. 183–205. Bingley, Emerald (2011)
3. Saarti, J., Juntunen, A.: The benefits of a quality management system: the case of the merger of two universities and their libraries. Libr. Manag. **32**(3), 183–190 (2011)
4. Maruta, R.: Maximizing knowledge work productivity: a time constrained and activity visualized PDCA cycle. Knowl. Process Manag. **19**, 203–214 (2012)
5. Balagué, N., Saarti, J.: Managing Your Library and Its Quality: The ISO 9001 Way. Chandos, Cambridge (2011)
6. Cox, B.: How Libraries Should Manage Data. Chandos, Cambridge (2015)
7. Bats, R.: Internal communication in libraries: are we organizations 2.0? In: Information in e-Motion, Bobcatsss 2012, Amsterdam, pp. 62–66. Bock+Herchen Verlag, Bad Honnef (2012). https://archivesic.ccsd.cnrs.fr/hal-00711162/document. Accessed 22 January 2017
8. Blessinger, K., Hrycaj, P.: Workplace Culture in Academic Libraries: The Early 21st Century. Chandos, Oxford (2013)
9. Atkinson, J.: Quality and the Academic Library: Reviewing, Assessing and Enhancing Service Provision. Chandos, Cambridge (2016)

Information Literacy Across the University and Workplace Reality

Angela Repanovici[1(✉)], Natalia Cheradi[2], Ane Landoy[3], and Silvia Ghinculov[2]

[1] Transilvania University of Brasov, Brasov, Romania
arepanovici@unitbv.ro
[2] Academy of Economic Studies, Chisinau, Moldova
{cheradi, gsilvia}@lib.ase.md
[3] Bergen University Library, Bergen, Norway
Ane.Landoy@uib.no

Abstract. This paper reveals the results of the "Information Literacy across the university and workplace reality" survey. This study revealed which are the most needed information skills for the faculty at the workplace. The questionnaire was addressed to Masters students from two universities in Romania and Moldova, who have a job or have their own business. The results of this study will be taken into account in the improvement of the discipline of Information Literacy and Project Management. The survey targeted a pool of 66 individuals from Transilvania University from Brasov and 53 individuals from the Academy of Economic Studies of Moldova. This study utilized the questionnaire survey method as a research tool, using SurveyMonkey online.

Keywords: Information Literacy · University · Work place · Romania Moldova

1 Introduction

Information Literacy (IL) standards have been defined by many researchers in different ways, covering skills and knowledge that enable individuals to recognize their information needs, and to locate, evaluate and use the needed information, at the same time filtering out the unwanted information. To some extent it also covers the ability to evaluate one's own information seeking process and the consequent final information products. However, an agreement that "IL is important in the workplace has not offered much guidance to universities seeking to prepare their students for professional success" [1]. The initial formulation of IL "was itself a function of a changing workplace where technology was shifting labor from routine manual and cognitive tasks toward more sophisticated behaviors" [2].

The literature shows a lot of programs and courses in IL, but not many instruments to test general IL competence, and what is needed at the workplace [3]. Regarding the complexity of information work, the last decade has seen a shift toward more fine-grained attempts to "identify the discrete information skills needed in business contexts, fleshing out the relationship between traditional library-based definitions of

S. Kurbanoğlu et al. (Eds.): ECIL 2017, CCIS 810, pp. 50–57, 2018.
https://doi.org/10.1007/978-3-319-74334-9_6

IL and the business community's concern for more broadly defined communication and critical thinking attributes" [2].

The capacity to manage information and solve problems in technology-rich environments – that is, to access, evaluate, analyze and communicate information through the use of digital devices and applications – is becoming a necessity, as information and communication technology (ICT) applications permeate the workplace, the classroom and lecture hall, the home, and social interaction more generally [4]. There are many authors who consider the workplace a very important place where IL skills are so important [3, 5–11].

Information Literacy knowledge has become part of professional literacy. Much depends upon this knowledge, particularly, the integration of the population from Romania and Moldova into the new society, as well social cohesion and, inequality exclusion related to access to information.

2 Objectives of These Studies

Currently many acknowledge that we need to implement an IL course in the workplace. One's IL level determines the economic, social and professional status of the specialist of tomorrow. In order to have well-trained and versatile professionals who are able to be part of the European education, it is inevitable that an IL training program be initiated at all levels. The following objectives have been set:

- to ensure the acquisition of accurate IL knowledge and skills of Masters students at Transilvania University, Brasov and Academy of Economic Studies, Chisinau;
- to verify the subjective perception of respondents regarding IL skills, systems and information sources, and other topics of interest related to IL;
- to identify the necessary skills to use information to open one's own business and obtain government funds for financial support, for example STARTUP;
- to research how the university developed critical thinking for their alumni, and provided information on sources of funding for the development of their own businesses;
- to reveal the level of satisfaction of Masters students regarding IL skills;
- to identify issues and initiate proposals on improving users' education via IL programs.

3 Methodology

The operational definition of the variables refers to the alternatives which may characterize these variables (knowledge, preferences, opinions, motivation, informational tools, suggestions, sex, professional category, country). We used the email address list of Masters students (provided by the corresponding departments from the two universities), and emailed them the online version of the survey.

The survey was also distributed via social networks. The information source consists of the 119 participants who replied directly by filling out the online survey. Graduates with a job, or who owned their own businesses, were polled.

Sampling. The survey targeted a pool of 66 individuals from Transilvania University from Brasov and 53 individuals from the Academy of Economic Studies from Chisinau. The sampling method used in the research was the simple random sampling and the applied mechanical step technique, so we chose every third email from the total of 360 emails to which we sent the survey.

Survey Design. A survey is an instrument for collecting data, a logical sequence of 14 questions on the respondents' opinion regarding Information Literacy in general, as well as details such as information tools they used or development of their professional skills. The survey was distributed electronically, and the respondents' opinions and suggestions given during the study were processed automatically in SurveyMonkey. The differences between what employers expect of new employees and what the University perceives those expectations to be, was identified using electronic surveys, in the two universities.

Twenty-five men and 94 women participated in the survey. Of the total number of respondents, 68 people were between 20–25 years of age, 25 people were in the 26–30 years range, and the other 26 were over 30 years old. The Romanian survey was completed by Masters students in medicine, engineering, sociology and communication; the respondents from the Republic of Moldova were Masters students in social sciences and economics.

4 Major Findings

Most of the information necessary to solve various problems in the work-place consists of news from the professional field, professional field information and information about continuing education, as well as. Legal information in the field, and information regarding projects and funding sources. Responses were surprisingly varied regarding the situation when information was needed to make a decision, solve a problem or complete a project. Most were able to solve the problem. Most are happy that the university has helped them develop critical thinking skills and given them available sources of information. Satisfaction levels on IL skills are 3.73 out of 5. Masters students believe that IL skills increase the chances of getting a job and a good salary.

Status of Respondents on the Job Market. The respondents from the Republic of Moldova stating they run their own business account for 11.32% of those surveyed, which is four times higher than the same category in Romania - 3.03%. Conversely, the percentage of inactive respondents from Transilvania University was 16.67% and twice as low from the Academy of Economic Studies (Table 1).

Table 1. What is your status on the job market? N = 119

Options	Romania %	Moldova %
Employee	80.30	81.13
I run my own business	3.03	11.32
Inactive	16.67	7.55

We noticed that the Masters students from the Republic of Moldova are more focused on obtaining knowledge needed for the specific objectives of their own business. In respect of the job and the experience of the research subjects we have not found many essential differences in the research: all of them are at the beginning of their careers and do not have professional experience, regardless of their jobs (Table 2).

Table 2. What is the level of your job? N = 112

Options	Romania %	Moldova %
Management	9.68	18.00
Operational	90.32	82.00

Thus, 9.68% of the Romanian Masters students and 18% of the Moldavian Masters students said they have management jobs. The people specialized at an operational level were present in almost equal ratios: Romania – 90.32%, Republic of Moldova – 82%.

The question *"What type of information do you need at the workplace?"* received the following replies: Romanian and Moldavian groups use different types of information for work activities, but there are some additional differences.

Types of Information Used at the Workplace. The Masters students from the Academy of Economic Studies use more information needed for their professional field and for leisure time; and they search for legal information and professional novelty. The students from Transilvania University prefer information on intellectual property and projects, as well as financing sources. Both categories of respondents actively use different types of information at the workplace in order to achieve results in their activities (Table 3).

Table 3. What type of information do you need at the workplace? N = 116

Options	Romania %	Moldova %
General information	41.27	47.17
Information for leisure time	7.94	11.32
Information necessary in the professional field	76.19	84.91
Information for continuing education	57.14	47.17
Novelty, developments in professional field	69.84	73.58
Legal information in the industry	47.62	62.26
Projects, financing sources	20.63	33.96
Intellectual property rights	11.11	11.32
Information on patents and technological transfer	7.94	7.55

The research subjects were asked to give a short description of the most recent situation when they needed information in order to make a decision, solve a problem or complete a project. Approaching this topic showed a similar situation in the algorithm of information discovery. However, we noticed that the Masters students from the Academy of Economic Studies are more interested in specialized information, the help of colleagues and librarians, while those at Transilvania University are more autonomous in the process of information consumption.

The respondents from Moldova are more supportive of internet resources and library databases. Both categories of respondents perform information searches based on keywords. The relevance of the information is assessed based on the opinions of their peers, of authoritative people, experts and based on the comments of specialists from various media.

University Contribution to the Development of Critical Thinking in Analysing Information. According to the opinion of Romanian and Moldavian respondents, the ideal methods to find information sources are trainings, individual counselling and distance learning. The survey results prove that most respondents believe the university provides a significant contribution in developing critical thinking in analysing information (Table 4).

Table 4. Has the university created the framework for developing critical thinking in analysing information? N = 118

Options	Romania %	Moldova %
Yes	61.54	56.60
No	15.38	13.21
I don't know	12.31	24.53
Comment	10.77	5.66

This supports the importance of IL for both categories, with some differences in the attitude of the Moldavian respondents. They showed a certain degree of uncertainty, accounting for almost 25% when they replied that they did not know the university had the mission to develop such skills.

One respondent from Transilvania University said: "*... I believe that each develops his own logical, critical thinking based on previous daily events and the accumulated knowledge*". Another respondent from the Academy of Economic Studies commented: "*... very little or at all in some cases; student often do not even know how to search an information in the library or even on the internet; they settle with what they find on Google, without filtering the information or analysing its source. Critical thinking is developed in practice, when you face a real situation. At the university you are under the impression that things are evolving 10–15 years later than in the real economy. And we should not blame it on the lack of specialists, but on the university strategies, which turns it into a business and not an institution for educating specialists*". These aspects show there are gaps in the activity aimed at informing specialists within university libraries.

Almost half of the research respondents from both countries gave a positive answer to the question *"Has the university made available information regarding the financing sources for developing your own business or for applying for funding in different projects?"* (Table 5).

Table 5. Has the university made available information regarding the financing sources for developing your own business or for applying for funding in different projects? N = 118

Options	Romania %	Moldova %
Yes	43.75	50.00
No	28.13	30.77
I don't know	17.19	13.46
Not interested	3.13	3.85
Comment	7.81	1.92

There are people in the groups who are indifferent: 3.13% and 3.85% respectively of respondents do not consider this information useful and interesting. This fact confirms the hypothesis regarding the informational load of the master students, given they also have an intensive work program.

Satisfaction with the Information Literacy Skills of Respondents. The matrix response question revealed the opinions and the attitudes of the respondents from both countries about the significance of IL and the degree of satisfaction regarding personal competencies in this field (Table 6).

Table 6. Please reply to the questions below, where 1 = the least, 5 = the most. N = 118

Options	Romania	Moldova
How satisfied are you with your informational competencies?	3.65	3.73
Do you believe that a high level of informational competencies would increase the chances of employment?	4.47	4.42
Do you believe that the wage may be different based on the informational competencies?	4.26	3.85

The weighted average calculated based on the scale questions did not reveal significant differences in assessing personal competencies, but the Moldavian respondents group showed a certain degree of uncertainty in determining the wage according to the informational competencies (score 3.85 vs 4.26 for Romania).

According to the opinions of respondents from both groups under study, the main factor of professional competencies development is personal development, self-education (69.7% Romania and 58.49% Moldova), as well as continuing education (65.15% and 50.94% respectively).

The respondents from the Academy of Economic Studies assign a higher degree of responsibility to the employer (35.85%). However, the role of universities is just as important in the respondents' opinions, for almost half of them (Table 7).

Table 7. In your opinion, who is the main responsible for developing professional competencies? N = 119

Options	Romania %	Moldova %
The university	43.94	50.94
The employer	21.21	35.85
Continuing education	65.15	50.94
Personal development, self-education	69.70	58.49
Others (please specify)	4.55	7.55

There is a difference of opinion between the respondents from the two countries regarding the question *"Do you intend to work in the future in another country?"*. A positive answer was given by 18.18% of Romanian master students and 33.96% from Moldova (Table 8).

Table 8. Do you intend to work in the future in another country? N = 119

Options	Romania %	Moldova %
Yes	18.18	33.96
No	42.42	11.32
I don't know	39.39	54.72

This shows the less stable economic situation in the Republic of Moldova, the increasing migration processes and the uncertain future of youth in their own country. The percentage of people who do not want to leave the country because they already have a satisfying job in Romania is 42.42%.

5 Conclusions

The results of the study demonstrate that the Masters students from Romania are well informed in the information field, since the IL course is included in the curriculum. The respondents from Moldova want more practical information for solving business problems.

The algorithm for searching information, the resources used to solve problems at the workplace, decision making, assessing the relevance and the consistency of the information used by both groups are similar and balanced.

The Masters students from Transilvania University and the Academy of Economic Studies support educational activities at the group level and distance learning at the personal level. Universities, libraries and Masters students should have common responsibilities and coordinated efforts for developing competencies, creating, updating and implementing training programs.

It would be advisable to introduce a mechanism for assessing informational competencies for various specialities (e.g., online tests) that will form the basis of training and information competences development programs.

The current trends in lifelong learning and the continuous improvement of information tools create excellent conditions for university libraries to ensure the development of Information Literacy for people who will leave the university and will be employed, especially throughout a time when employees from the real sector attend professional training courses.

The studies are original, performed for the first time in a university in Romania and Moldova. They may be used by companies, but also universities, to identify the informational needs of graduates in the workplace. The results can be a starting point in the realization of joint employer-university courses building IL skills.

Acknowledgement. CPEA-2015/10014, Modernization of academic library services in Moldova, Eurasia Program.

References

1. Chang, Y.: Assessing students' information literacy skills in two secondary schools in Singapore. J. Inf. Lit. **6**(2), 19–35 (2012)
2. Cyphert, D., Lyle, S.: Employer expectations of information literacy: Identifying the skills GAP. In: Information Literacy: Research and Collaboration Across Disciplines, pp. 53–79. The WAC Clearinghouse, Fort Collins (2017)
3. Caravello, P.S., Herschman, J., Mitchell, E.: Assessing the information literacy of UCLA library's information competencies survey project. In: ACRL Tenth National Conference, pp. 193–202 (2001)
4. OECD: Proficiency in key information-processing skills among working-age adults. In: OECD Skills Outlook 2013: First Results from the Survey of Adult Skills, pp. 55–100. OECD Publishing, Paris (2013)
5. Travis, T.: From the classroom to the boardroom: the impact of information literacy instruction on workplace research skills. Educ. Libr. **34**(2), 19–31 (2011)
6. Kolstad, A.: Flexibility in teaching information literacy by using wikis. In: IFLA Satellite Meeting in Tampere, Finland (2012)
7. Kolstad, A.: Co-teaching in information literacy during work placements: the librarian's role. LIBER Q. **25**(2), 56–86 (2015)
8. Quinn, T., Leligdon, L.: Executive MBA students' information skills and knowledge: discovering the difference between work and academics. J. Bus. Financ. Librariansh. **19**(3), 234–255 (2014)
9. Adamson, C., Dilamarter, D., White, M.: Developing information literacy skills in engineering entrepreneurs: a collaborative approach. In: Interdisciplinary Innovation and Imagination in Engineering Education, pp. 1–5 (2006)
10. Drew, C.: Encouraging use of entrepreneurship information resources: faculty/library collaboration. In: Annual Conference & Exposition, Honolulu, Hawaii (2007). https://peer.asee.org/2072
11. Oehler, A., Höfer, A., Schalkowski, H.: Entrepreneurial Literacy: Empirical Evidence, pp. 1–6 (2012)

Information Literacy of Croatian Subject Indexers

Kristina Feldvari and Kornelija Petr Balog(✉)

Faculty of Humanities and Social Sciences, University of Osijek, Osijek, Croatia
{kfeldvari, kpetr}@ffos.hr

Abstract. The purpose of this paper is to present results of the application of the Cognitive Work Analysis (CWA) framework on the study of the ability of subject indexers in Croatian libraries to find and apply the necessary information in order to perform their work. The research was conducted in April and May 2013 on the sample of 10 subject indexers in five Croatian libraries. During the simulated indexing task, subject indexers were asked to index a few documents in the way they usually perform such tasks at work and to verbally describe their thoughts while performing that task. The analysis of the simulated task data revealed that the biggest problems and obstacles for Croatian subject indexers were related to information searching and retrieval of the final subject access point. Majority of subject indexers in the sample had pronounced difficulties in the search and retrieval phase of the task.

Keywords: Activity analysis · Cognitive Work Analysis (CWA) Information retrieval · Subject indexers · Work-domain analysis

1 Introduction

Information literacy (IL) can be regarded as an umbrella term which encompasses a range of literacies (e.g. information, the Internet, media, digital), each relating to different types of information, such as oral, printed, and digital [1]. The definition also includes a competency list according to which an information literate person is aware of his or her information need, can recognize the information to solve a problem, as well as locate, evaluate, organize, and apply effectively the information needed [2]. On the other hand Goldstein, the director of the CILIP Information Literacy Group (ILG) points out: "it is increasingly recognised that in the workplace, and more so than in academia, information literacy bears a strong relationship to factors driven by context and working environments, and that an approach based on defining a set of generic skills, as taught in educational/academic settings, is not always appropriate for addressing the multi-facetted requirements of employment" [3, p. 6]. The interpretation of IL as a narrow skills-based approach is being questioned as inappropriate for the workplace where a much greater preference is given to the use of people as information sources and relatively little use of libraries [4, 5].

Lloyd also points out that the LIS field used to describe IL only as a basic set of skills without connecting it to the dependency on context [5]. Numerous studies found that workplace IL has a unique discourse and practice and stress out that the IL practice

S. Kurbanoğlu et al. (Eds.): ECIL 2017, CCIS 810, pp. 58–67, 2018.
https://doi.org/10.1007/978-3-319-74334-9_7

manifests itself differently, depending on its context. Those studies also claim that the workplace IL should not rely solely on the study of individual actors taken out of their context, but they should be observed as members of a certain micro professional community – a complex work and practice context [6–8]. In the field of information sciences such an approach, known also under the name of "domain-analysis" was suggested by Hjørland. His approach involves the analysis of knowledge-domains, actors' mental models and their information behavior [9]. One of the most important frameworks used for the study of actors and information environment or context is the Cognitive Work Analysis (CWA) framework. CWA is a work-centered conceptual framework introduced by Vicente [10], Rasmussen et al. [11] and Fidel and Pejtersen [12]. The framework's goal is to perform the cognitive work and context analysis, which is the very thing that Lloyd emphasizes as important in the workplace IL. In CWA, context encompasses a number of constraints and obstacles that mold actors' behaviors while simultaneously requiring a profound understanding of their work and work environment [12].

Numerous research of subject indexing process concludes that the subject indexing in its nature is unpredictable, changeable and interpretative as well as context-dependable [13–15]. The authors emphasize that it is necessary to study not only the process itself as a whole or its individual steps, but also the mental processes of indexers as well as constraints and obstacles subject indexers encounter during their work.

Since our goal was to investigate the ways subject indexers in Croatian academic and public libraries perform their work, which includes the study of actor's information behavior and their work-context (problems and obstacles they encounter while performing work tasks), CWA was seen as the ideal framework. The next section of the paper deals with the description of the framework with a special emphasis on the fourth dimension – activity analysis. This dimension looks, among other things, into the actors' IL skills necessary for performing their work-related tasks.

2 Cognitive Work Analysis Framework (CWA) and Workplace IL

Context in CWA includes a number of constraints and obstacles that mold actors' behaviors. The framework observes human interaction with information in the context of specific goal-driven activities. It is therefore goals that guide activities, regardless of whether they are explicit or implicit, personal or organizational, stable or unstable (situation-dependent). CWA analyses actors' work activities, their organizational relationships, constraints and obstacles they encounter in the work-domain and the actors' personal preferences and priorities. CWA focuses simultaneously on individual actors' (perceptive and cognitive attributes), their work tasks and the contexts in which they operate. Whereas there is an unlimited number of factors that may influence the human-information interaction, CWA offers five dimensions that help the constructor of a controlled vocabulary (e.g. thesaurus) detect various constraints and obstacles that may influence the development of actors' information needs and behavior [16].

Figure 1 illustrates five CWA dimensions [12]. First dimension refers to the work **environment** and encompasses the analysis of elements outside the actors' domain that affect their domain. The analysis of the work environment reveals the context within which the actors operate and provides the understanding for obstacles and constraints under which the actors develop their information needs and behaviour. The second dimension investigates work within the **work domain**. Both the constraints within the work domain and in the work environment limit and affect the actors' information needs, the only difference being that the constraints in the work domain are under control by actors themselves. Constraints found in the work domain are manifold – they are goals, priorities, functions, processes and resources within the work domain.

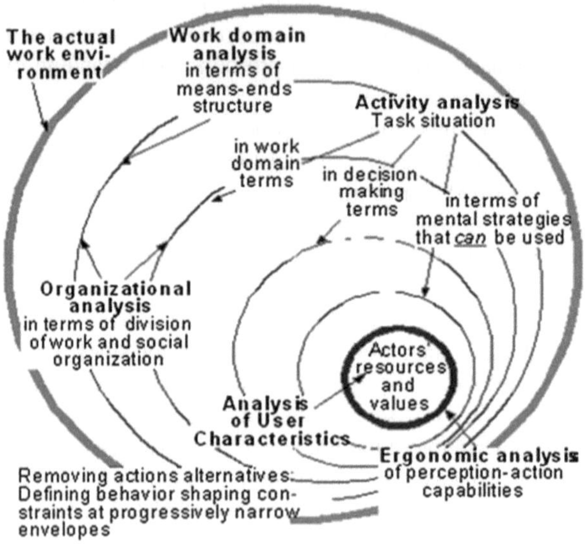

Fig. 1. Cognitive work analysis framework (Source: Fidel and Pejtersen [12])

The third dimension involves **organizational analysis** and deals with the analysis of organizational structure, management style, organizational culture and allocation of roles. Organisational environment, i.e. obstacles encountered in it also affect actors' activities and potential information needs. Fourth dimension, **activity analysis**, examines what actors do to achieve their tasks and this dimension is considered crucial in this framework for investigating actors' information literacy skills. CWA distinguishes between three separate activity analyses: activity analysis in work domain terms, activity analysis in decision-making terms, and activity analysis in terms of strategies that can be used. Activity analysis in work domain terms looks into specific tasks that actors do, explains the goals, constraints, priorities, functions, processes and resources of specific actors' activities and tasks and establishes means-end relationship between them. The analysis also "provides a detailed view of the individual actors' work and framework in which they develop the information needs and information search behaviours" [16, p. 25]. Activity analysis in decision-making terms examines the decisions actors make while performing their activities. This analysis provides an understanding of the actors' work in terms of decision making and focusses in particular on the information they need in order to make decisions and which sources provide useful information. According to Mai, "the purpose of this analysis is to clarify which information people need in order to make certain work-task related decisions, which information is actually available and which information is desirable, but unavailable" [16, p. 25].

The last activity analysis within the fourth dimension relates to search strategies that can be used by actors to find information relevant for specific decision-making activities. The work domain activities shape the decisions the actors make, but the decisions they make shape the search strategies they apply. Search strategies that actors use in a current information system may be good indicators of priorities in their search situations, but they also may be valuable as a foundation for the formulation of search strategies in future information systems. The analysis of strategies should therefore include the questions about possible strategies that actors may employ regardless whether they use those strategies at the moment, or not. To identify possible strategies, the analysis should include strategies individual actors could use to find specific information in an efficient way.

Finally, the fifth, dimension (analysis of actors' resources and values) examines actors experience, education and preferences [16].

It is important to point out that there exists interdependent relationship among all factors in this model. For example, work environment, work domain as well as organisational culture, management and role allocation influence subject department's performance, which in turn influences how individual actors within that department perform their work-related tasks. Work tasks, on the other hand, influence the decisions made by actors, and those decisions, together with actors' attributes, influence actors' information behaviour. It is therefore crucial to analyse all the constraints and obstacles that may shape actors' information behaviour.

3 Research

3.1 Context

Croatian subject indexers operate in a specific work environment – there is no national subject indexing manual or an authoritative and freely available controlled vocabulary list or thesaurus that they could use and apply. Consequently, subject indexing process of Croatian libraries is characterized by various library practices and policies where libraries have differing internal rules and regulations regarding subject indexing process. Finally, at the moment there are several library software programs used by Croatian libraries and the choice of software affects subject indexing practice of a library (through cooperative cataloguing). All this results in inconsistencies of subject indexing process, incompatibilities and system inconsistencies at the national level as well as constraints and obstacles in the work domain of Croatian subject indexers.

3.2 Goal and Research Questions

The goal of our research was to obtain the model of subject indexing process and procedures of Croatian subject indexers using the CWA framework. This goal led to the need to further investigate the applicability of CWA model on the research of subject indexers' IL skills necessary for carrying out their work.

Research questions that guided our investigation were:

1. What are the subject indexing steps of Croatian indexers and what affects them?
2. What sort of information needs and behavior do they demonstrate in their work?
3. What types of sources and information do they use in order to do their work?
4. What type of constraints and obstacles do they encounter in their work?

3.3 Methodology, Instrument, and Sample

Our research sample consisted of ten subject indexers from five Croatian libraries (two indexers per library): there were two libraries with dual function (national and university library and city and university library), one academic and three public libraries. Libraries were chosen according to the following criteria: significance, type and function and library software used (the four most dominant library software used in Croatia are: CROLIST, ZaKi, METELWin and ALEPH). Subject librarians that took part in our research had to be experienced subject indexers (information seeking and searching had to be a component part of their everyday work activities). Sampling was purposeful, based on the researcher's decision.

Since the whole research was conducted from two perspectives: subject indexing department as a whole (which included the analysis and comparison of five subject indexing departments) and the individual subject indexing process, this paper focuses on the latter. The study described in this paper followed qualitative methodology of comparative case study, the controlled comparison method of individual subjecting tasks. The findings were obtained through a simulated subject indexing task as a part of a semi-structured interview. In the simulated indexing task we used two additional research methods: think-aloud method and the analysis of verbal and video recording (all simulated tasks were video recorded). All subject indexers were first asked to describe individual steps of the indexing process on a normal working day and to name all the constraints and obstacles they usually encounter. This gave us insight into the respondents' mental models and strategies. These data were later compared with the data obtained through the simulated indexing task to determine the discrepancies between what indexers do and what they think they do.

Simulated work task concept comes from Ingwersen's cognitive communication model [17] and the practical application of the work-task concept for the solution of information problem during the information seeking process in the work of Byström and Järvelin [18] and Vakkari [19]. The analysis of the verbal report was made according to Someren et al. [20].

During the simulated indexing task, subject indexers were asked to index the document in the way they usually perform such tasks at work and to verbally describe their thoughts while performing the task. All indexers in the sample were asked to index three documents (i.e. articles) that were chosen according to the following criteria: (a) the bibliographic records for the documents must not be included in any Croatian online library catalogue, (b) articles describe contemporary phenomena in a wide area of library and information sciences (LIS) (using new terminology), and (c) articles are of interdisciplinary character (in order to get insight into the information behaviour of indexing specialists in the process of finding and assigning indexing terms from fields other than LIS). All the articles were in the Croatian language. Each indexer was asked to index three (same) articles. Video recordings of simulated indexing tasks of all indexing specialists in the sample were transcribed and segmented into individual indexing steps. Each textual segment was consequently coded and categorized. Coding and categorization followed the model created on the basis of indexing steps described by indexing specialists in the semi-structured interviews that preceded the simulated indexing task. Upon completing the coding and categorization processes we analysed all ten verbal reports and identified the steps shared by all subject indexers in the sample. Those steps served as the foundation for the subject indexing model of Croatian subject specialists. In addition to subject indexing steps, we identified also problems and obstacles that our respondents came across while performing the simulated task. Particular attention was given to the problems and obstacles in browsing and retrieving the appropriate subject indexing term from the available databases (e.g. subject authority file of one's own library, catalogues of other libraries, etc.).

Research was conducted in April and May 2013. First we conducted a semi-structured interview with respondents lasting about 15 min, and then the indexers performed the indexing task. The indexing task itself (indexing three articles) lasted approximately 90 min per indexing specialist.

3.4 Results

Our model has demonstrated that subject indexers get the initial idea of the document topic(s) after the very first reading of the title, author name, abstract and keywords. The idea about the document topic is consequently expressed in the form of the appropriate search terms ('temporary' subject headings) that they then use for further information retrieval. Besides the title, abstract and keywords, subject indexers base those 'temporary' headings also on subtitles or random terms that get repeated in the document, the references or subject headings that are assigned to bibliographic records with the same or similar subjects in their library catalogue database.

Upon the choice of the 'temporary' subject heading, subject indexers search subject headings in their local bibliographic and/or subject authority database. This particular step has great significance because it depends on many factors and is connected with the majority of constraints and obstacles in subject indexing. Combining subject terms into a proper subject heading (string) depends on whether the subject indexer is required to follow library's internal syntactic rules or not. Those subject indexers in our sample (6 out of 10) whose libraries did not have any syntactic rules and did not exercise any control of main- and subheadings did not, as a rule, check the local database for subheadings and combined the subheadings in an arbitrary order.

A subject indexer reaches the final decision on the acceptable subject heading for a certain document after the comparison of 'temporary' subject headings with the existing headings in the subject authority database or the subject headings used in the bibliographic records of their library OPAC.

Constraints and obstacles connected with the process of subject indexing are encountered usually in the third (searching for a suitable subject heading) and sometimes in the fourth step (selection, combining and assigning of final subject headings). The fourth step is also the step which requires subject indexers to demonstrate their IL skills. This step overlaps with ACRL IL standards' indicators and outcomes [21].

The analysis of results identified following constraints and obstacles: constraints of the system, failure to create additional access points (for lead-in terms), no internal syntactic rules, failure to create a scope note field, creating a record for a subject heading that already exists in the system, unauthorized subheadings, no national subject indexing manual and human factors (experience, education, and intelligence). The constraints that are connected to human factors are related to librarians' personal knowledge, education and preferences and are closely connected to IL. An experienced subject indexer is supposed to be well versed and familiar with possibilities and techniques of searching within the library's internal database, other national and international OPACs as well as the Internet. Unfortunately, no subject indexer in our sample used an advanced search option in library OPACs. Another example is the indexer who failed to truncate the search term and was unable to locate the required subject heading although that it existed in the database. Sometimes subject indexers truncate the search terms and consequently increase the recall. The required term appears therefore later on the result list (e.g. fifth page) but indexers only go through the first results page and conclude that the subject heading does not exist in that database. Such a behavior is obviously a result of indexers' impatience and/or their misjudgment of search strategy. Another explanation might be the lack of time for research and searching of the appropriate term.

Apart from searching in reference works (dictionaries, lexicons), the indexers searched also the Internet. While searching the latter no indexer used either phrase-search option or any other Boolean operator (apart from AND). However, there were a couple of indexers in the sample that were extremely familiar with possibilities of other information systems and databases and often applied advanced search techniques.

Four indexers mentioned that one of the constraints in performing their job was the fact that they were unfamiliar with the subject area of the article (i.e. they were in charge of indexing other subject areas in their library). One indexer also mentioned English language as a constraint – this indexer spoke Russian and another language was perceived as an obstacle in finding and researching appropriate terms and subject headings.

Personal knowledge and education, especially when it comes to the knowledge of terminology of the subject area, together with experience in subject indexing are particularly pronounced in the process of "research" of the appropriate term. Namely, those factors determine whether and in what degree a subject indexer is familiar with the proper form of the term accepted by major reference works and which relevant reference works (printed or online) should be consulted in order to verify the (form of the) term –necessary knowledge before the indexer decides on creating a new, authorized, subject heading into the local system.

The last constraint mentioned by the indexer is related to the time necessary for the research of the subject terms and application of various search strategies in order to find the best which would result with finding the right indexing term. This constraint is usually connected with other work tasks indexers are required to do (in addition to subject indexing), amount of material they have to index, and an insufficient number of specialized indexers for certain subject areas (e.g. through formal or some other form of education).

4 Discussion and Conclusions

The foundation of the research of information behavior and IL of subject indexers in this paper is the methodology coming from the multidisciplinary area of human-information interaction (HII). CWA framework used in this paper for examining the IL of subject indexers has five dimensions (work environment, work domain, organization environment, activities and characteristics of actors. The focus of this paper was on the fourth dimension (work activity performed by subject indexers).

The analysis of results obtained through qualitative data collection methods resulted with the subject indexing model of Croatian indexers. According to our findings this model consists of four steps: (1) browsing the document and determining what it is about (aboutness), (2) creation of "temporary" subject headings (key concepts), (3) searching for the final subject heading, and (4) selecting, combining and assigning of the final subject heading(s). It was noticed that all subject indexers prefer using and/or combining subject headings that already exist in their internal database to the creation of new entries or using the entries found in databases of other national or international libraries. This is confirmed by similar research that found that subject indexers heavily rely on existing records and subject heading lists (controlled vocabulary) from their library database [22]. In other words, systems used by subject indexers for their work are utilized not only for the analysis of the document subject but they clearly define and determine the whole process. Constraints and obstacles that are connected with the process of subject indexing are related mostly to the third (searching for appropriate subject heading) and partly to the fourth step (selecting, combining and assigning of final subject headings) of subject indexing.

The findings indicate also that there are present various constraints and problems such as out-of-date and insufficient search capabilities and options of current automated library systems used by Croatian indexers, failure to create additional access points (for lead-in terms), no internal syntactic rules, failure to create a scope note field, creating a record for a subject heading that already exists in the system, unauthorized subheadings, no national subject indexing manual and human factors (experience, education, preferences, lack of time needed for detailed examination and "research" of terms and application of various search strategies in order to find the best which would result with finding the right indexing term. In relation to human factors, our results also show that subject indexers need to be familiar with possibilities and techniques of searching within the library's internal database, other national and international OPACs and databases as well as the Internet.

The majority of indexers in the sample had problems in retrieving the appropriate subject heading which was the reason why they failed to identify the right term in the search phase of the indexing task. Personal knowledge and education, particularly in the sense of being familiar with the subject indexing field and its terminology, is particularly visible and important in the phase of term "research". The last constraint, lack of time, is connected with the other, non-indexing tasks, subject indexers are required to do at their work, the amount of material that needs to be subject indexed and insufficient number of indexers specialized for certain subject areas.

Our findings, although limited by the number of respondents, are consistent with findings of earlier studies [13–15] and confirm that the subject indexing process is unpredictable, changeable and interpretative as well as context-dependable. We can also conclude that CWA framework, especially its fourth dimension is suitable for the research of workplace IL. This is particularly true if we remember the connection between IL and context/discourse [6–8].

Taking into consideration the indexing steps of Croatian indexers together with constraints and problems they face while doing their work, it is foremost necessary to ensure direct guidelines and instructions for the process of subject indexing. We believe that present information systems must be upgraded to include following features: presence and visibility of search capabilities guidelines with a clear description of a single type of search option, *search history (users need to visualize not only their search process but also that of their colleagues and need to be able to see a previously conducted search)*, a keyword search option where all instances of a certain term are found regardless of whether it is as a single word or a phrase, advanced system functions such as an automatic suggestion of possible search terms after a certain number of characters have been entered in the search, advanced system options that would offer corrections in case of misspelled search terms, (e.g. "*Did you mean …?*"), hyperlinks to other records containing relevant indexing terms as well as to semantic tree of associated indexing terms (e.g. preferred, broader, narrower and related term/s).

In addition, present library databases should be made more suitable and user-friendly for searching and retrieving o subject headings. Lastly, subject indexers should be subjected to additional educational training, especially in relation to their IL skills.

References

1. Bawden, D.: Information and digital literacies: a review of concepts. J. Doc. **57**(2), 218–259 (2001)
2. ALA: Presidential Committee on Information Literacy: Final Report. http://www.ala.org/acrl/publications/whitepapers/presidential
3. Goldstein, S.: Information literacy in the workplace. GKIM Matters: Joint J. CILIP's Gov. Inf. Group Netw. Gov. Libr. Inf. Spec. **6**, 6–9 (2016). https://www.cilip.org.uk/sites/default/files/documents/gkim_matters_issue_6.pdf
4. Williams, D., Cooper, K., Wavell, C.: Information Literacy in the Workplace – An Annotated Bibliography, Robert Gordon University, Institute for Management, Governance and Society (IMaGeS), in association with InformAll (2014). http://www.researchinfonet.org/wp-content/uploads/2014/01/Workplace-IL-annotated-bibliography.pdf

5. Lloyd, A.: Information Literacy Lanscapes: Information Literacy in Education, Workplace and Everyday Contexts. Chandos Publishing, Oxford, Cambridge, New Delhi (2010)
6. Mutch, A.: Information literacy: an exploration. Int. J. Inf. Manag. **17**(5), 377–386 (1997)
7. Bruce, C.S.: The relational approach: a new model for information literacy. New Rev. Inf. Libr. Res. **3**, 1–22 (1997)
8. Cheuk, B.W.: Exploring information literacy in the workplace: a process approach. In: Bruce, C.S., Candy, P.C. (eds.) Information Literacy Around the World: Advances in Programs and Research, pp. 177–191. Charles Sturt University, Wagga Wagga (2000)
9. Hjørland, B., Albrechtsen, H.: Toward a new horizon in information science: domain-analysis. J. Am. Soc. Inf. Sci. **46**(6), 400–425 (1995)
10. Vincente, K.J.: Cognitive Work Analysis: Toward Safe, Productive, and Healthy Computer-Based Work. Lawrence Erlbaum Associates, Mahwah (1999)
11. Rasmussen, J., Pejtersen, A.M., Goodstein, L.P.: Cognitive Systems Engineering. Wiley, New York (1994)
12. Fidel, R., Pejtersen, A.M.: From information behaviour research to the design of information systems: the cognitive work analysis framework. Inf. Res. **10**(1) (2004). http://www.informationr.net/ir/10-1/paper210.html
13. Chu, C.M., O'Brien, A.: Subject analysis: the first critical stages in indexing. J. Inf. Sci. **19**, 439–454 (1993)
14. Jones, K.: How do we index? A report of some ASLIB informatics group activities. J. Doc. **39**(1), 1–23 (1983)
15. Mai, J.E.: Deconstructing the indexing process. Adv. Librariansh. **23**, 269–298 (2000)
16. Mai, J.E.: Actors, domains, and constraints in the design and construction of controlled vocabularies. Knowl. Organ. **35**(1), 16–29 (2008)
17. Ingwersen, P.: Cognitive perspectives of information retrieval interaction: elements of a cognitive IR theory. J. Doc. **52**(1), 3–50 (1996)
18. Byström, K., Järvelin, K.: Task complexity affects information seeking and use. Inf. Process. Manag.: Int. J. **31**(2), 191–213 (1995)
19. Vakkari, P.: Task complexity, problem structure and information actions: integrating studies on information seeking and retrieval. Inf. Process. Manag. **35**(6), 819–837 (1999)
20. Someren, M.W., Barnard, Y.F., Sandberg, J.A.C.: The Think Aloud Method: A Practical Guide to Modeling Cognitive Process. Academic Press, London (1994)
21. American Library Association (ALA): Information Literacy Competency Standards for Higher Education (2000). http://www.ala.org/acrl/standards/informationliteracycompetency
22. Šauperl, A.: Subject Determination During the Cataloging Process. Scarecrow Press, Lanham (2002)

Shaping the Future Information Professionals: Searching for the Balance of Job Requirements in Libraries and Education

Radovan Vrana(✉)

Faculty of Humanities and Social Sciences,
University of Zagreb, Zagreb, Croatia
rvrana@ffzg.hr

Abstract. Preparing new information professionals for work is challenging and difficult for organizations like libraries, archives, museums and other public and government institutions as well as for commercial firms seeking highly knowledgeable, skillful and motivated individuals. The paper presents the results from the research study in public libraries in Croatia about their views on knowledge, skills and literacies required for employment in these institutions. The research questions inquire about the understanding of knowledge, skills and literacies of new employees; the adjustment of university study programs to the library practices; and about introduction and frequency of changes of the university study programs. An online questionnaire with nine closed type questions was chosen as the research method. A total of 159 public libraries participated in the research which presents a clear view of public libraries' attitudes about the paper topic, and a need for further and more frequent communication with universities.

Keywords: Employability · Public libraries · Higher education · Croatia

1 Introduction

As the world is changing so are changing the global views on knowledge, skills and literacies of future workforce. Previous experiences in education and employment of students have helped educators and employers construct new paradigms of one's abilities necessary for true inclusion and engagement in the evolving society. One's abilities are commonly defined and described in lists of knowledge and skills forming different types of literacies. It must be noted that the term literacy is now commonly used to describe one's abilities but was previously used in different contexts and with different meanings during the 20th century. Changes in understanding and application of this term in daily use continued to change in the 21st century, especially in different parts of the world based on the level of development of a particular country. Nowadays the term literacy usually has a prefix which explains scope and area of its application. As a result, "the word 'literacy' has begun being used in a much broader, metaphorical sense, referring to other skills and competencies, for example 'information literacy', 'visual literacy', 'media literacy' and 'scientific literacy'" [1, p. 150]. Each skill and

S. Kurbanoğlu et al. (Eds.): ECIL 2017, CCIS 810, pp. 68–77, 2018.
https://doi.org/10.1007/978-3-319-74334-9_8

literacy has its own important function and place in education and society. This is especially true for libraries, archives and museums administrators who evaluate their employee's, knowledge, skills and competencies. To employ the best individuals, the information and cultural institutions must be clear about what to expect of their future employees in terms of work related characteristics. This task is especially difficult if we take into account technology developments, globalization of economy, proliferation of information, evolving new ways of thinking, new emphasis on lifelong education, change of fixed cultural categories into a diversity of perspectives, the emergence of interdisciplinary studies - education has become more student-centered new modes of learning material delivery used by learners [2]. The next part of the paper presents basic facts about the crucial types of literacy as an introduction to the research study which discovered what public libraries in Croatia saw as important knowledge and skills their future employees should possess. Public libraries (269 of them [3]) were chosen as the main research partners as major employers of students studying at the Croatian universities.

2 Literacies and Employability

This part of the paper presents characteristics of several well-known types of literacies and employability. These characteristics are essential for understanding of the research study in the second part of the paper.

2.1 Scientific Literacy

The term scientific literacy refers to the general public's understanding of science [4]. It also describes an approach to science education that assumes a functional level of knowledge of scientific terminology and a familiarity with its writing style [5]. Since its first appearance, scientific literacy has been described extensively, and, as a result, many approaches, views and opinions to understanding of scientific literacy have been created. For instance, in his book on scientific literacies and multi-literacies, Ng [4] offered a view on types of scientific literacy which include nominal scientific literacy; functional scientific literacy and conceptual and procedural scientific literacy. The same author described what a scientifically literate individual should know: to develop a knowledge of the general principles of science; understand the applications of scientific theories, principles and methods to solve problems in society; be able to read and critique media reports; be able to collaborate and communicate with peers and experts; develop an awareness that technology plays a major role in the advancement of science; develop curiosity, persistence and positive attitudes towards lifelong learning of science.

2.2 Digital Literacy

Digital literacy is the ability to use technology, including a computer and mobile devices, to send e-mail, to use common household equipment, to locate and understand information on the web and to use other personal computer based tools [6].

For UNESCO [7], digital literacy is a life skill because it targets all areas of contemporary existence. UNESCO's definition describes best the importance of digital literacy in everyday activities. Libraries are by no means excluded from these activities as their daily operations depend on ICT and ICT related procedures and their users expect even more library services and library material to be accessible by use of ICT [8].

2.3 Media and Information Literacy

Media literacy is a critical thinking skill that enables people to make independent choices with regard to (1) selection of media program and (2) interpretation of the information they receive through the channels of mass communication. It is also understanding of the process of mass communication, an awareness of the impact of the media on the individual and society [9]. Information literacy is a set of abilities requiring individuals to recognize when information is needed and have the ability to locate, evaluate, and use effectively the needed information [10]. Together, media and information literacies embody "essential knowledge about (a) the functions of media, libraries, archives and other information providers in democratic societies, (b) the conditions under which news media and information providers can effectively perform those functions, and (c) how to evaluate the performances of these functions by assessing the content and services they offer. This knowledge should, in turn, allow users to engage with media and information channels in a meaningful manner" [7]. Media and information literacy are important for libraries as "media and other information providers such as libraries, archives and the Internet are widely recognized as essential tools for helping citizens to make informed decisions" [7, p. 16].

2.4 Employability

Finally, educational institutions employ students to support their purposes and goals. "In simple terms, employability is about being capable of getting and keeping fulfilling work. More comprehensively, employability is the capability to move self-sufficiently within the labour market to realise potential through sustainable employment" [11]. Employability could be also described as "the combination of factors and processes which enable people to progress towards or get into employment, to stay in employment, and to move on in the workplace" [12]. To achieve students' employability, higher education institutions constantly adjust their study programs to provide students with new knowledge, skills and competencies in many areas of human endeavor.

3 Research Study

Employability of students is an on-going hot topic which is of interest to higher-education institutions, employers and employees. Levels of their knowledge and skills related to their future jobs and availability of such jobs are of interest to many researchers. For instance, Carroll and Tani [13] analyzed literature about graduate over-education and their job search and concluded that "a substantial proportion of university graduates possess more education than is strictly required for them to perform their jobs, both at labour market entry and later in their careers". Whether or not this is true, remains to be researched in every particular country. This research study puts focus on public libraries in Croatia, a major employer of students of information sciences and other related university studies. The purpose of the research study is finding out what libraries expect from their future employees in terms of knowledge and skills and collecting data about their communication with academic institutions on the topic of study programs. The main hypothesis is that there is a need for more frequent, direct and better communication between libraries and universities about the education of future library employees. The research aimed to find answers to the following questions:

(1) do libraries have a clear understanding of knowledge, skills and competencies based on research of their needs when executing search for new employees?
(2) is there a need for adjustment of the university study programs with the library practice?
(3) who initiates adjustments of the study programs and how frequently do involved parties express their wishes for these adjustments?

An online questionnaire with nine closed type questions was chosen as the research tool. The invitation for participation in the research study was sent to the public libraries in Croatia listed at the Portal of libraries in Croatia at http://www.knjiznica.hr. According to the Statistical yearbook of the Republic of Croatia for 2016 [3], in 2013 (the latest data available) there were 269 public libraries in Croatia. However, a little more than 160 libraries were listed in the Portal of libraries in Croatia and 159 e-mails were delivered without errors on May 12th 2017 with the closing date for participation on May 26th 2017. The total of 105 answer sets collected, is 39% of all public libraries listed in the Statistical yearbook of 2016 and 66% of all invitations sent for participation in the research study.

4 Research Findings

The next part of the paper presents the results of the research study in public libraries in Croatia about the balance of job requirements in libraries and university study programs. The first three questions aimed at discovering what categories of scientific, media and information and digital literacy public libraries want their future employees to possess.

4.1 Categories Related to Scientific Literacy Public Libraries Expect Their Employees to Possess

Scientific literacy is an important aspect of students' education regardless of their future employment. The three most prominent categories (Table 1) chosen by the public libraries in the research study according to their relevance are: evaluation of scientific information resources, possessing an interest in science, and evaluation of scientific information. Public libraries in Croatia are not primarily oriented towards supplying the academic community with information resources but instead they serve as promotors and facilitators of access to popular scientific information. So, these three rather broad categories related to scientific literacy probably fit best to the broad profile of public libraries users in general. Other, more specific research oriented categories were ranked lower.

Table 1. Categories related to scientific literacy public libraries expect their employees should possess (N = 104)

	N	%
Evaluation of scientific information resources	76	73.1
Possessing interest in science	68	65.4
Evaluation of proper and improper use of scientific information	67	64.4
Understanding of research methods	63	60.6
Understanding and interpretation of basic statistics	55	52.9
Reading and interpretation of graphic representation of data	54	51.9
Creation of graphic representation of data	45	43.3
Organization, interpretation and analysis of quantitative data and scientific information	44	42.3
Recognition of a scientific problem	42	40.4
Planning scientific research	41	39.4
Reasoning of conclusions based on quantitative data	27	26.0
Knowledge about scientific concepts	25	24.0
Identification of scientific proof	22	21.2
Understanding of a research plan and its influence on conclusions	22	21.2
Solving quantitative problems by use of probability and statistics	16	15.4
Something else	1	1.0

4.2 Categories Related to Media and Information Public Libraries Expect Their Employees to Possess

The second question (Table 2) aimed at discovering the public libraries' preferences for categories related to media and information literacy as a special group of knowledge and skills. The first three categories are very indicative of the current developments in electronic media in the world. Working with emerging (new) media is a must not only for media companies but also for everyone else getting in touch with the information and communication technology (ICT) influenced media. Social networks have become the mainstream communication media for many and their popularity is constantly growing and attracting new users because "practically everyone's gone mobile, with real-time photo and video sharing becoming the big trend that people are most excited about, especially teenagers" [14]. Following the recent events in media related to so called "alternative facts" [15], Croatian public libraries have recognized that skills for defining true and untrue information and media messages have become essential for their future employees. The need for new skills and knowledge will change and shift as the world changes and as knowledge and skills in these categories become more important for public libraries.

Table 2. Categories related to media and information literacy libraries expect employees to possess (N = 105)

	N	%
Work with new media	87	82.9
Social networks use related skills	81	77.1
Skills for defining true or untrue information and media messages	81	77.1
News evaluation skills	73	69.5
Skills of learning how to work with different media to understand message	71	67.6
Skills for retrieving information from different media to understand a topic	66	62.9
Active location and following of the national, regional and global news	57	54.3
Skills for location of news in different media in order to communicate with people	56	53.3
Global media recognition to better understand messages	43	41.0
Skills for imagining oneself as a part of society by using media	28	26.7
Something else	0	0.0

4.3 Categories Related to Digital Literacy Public Libraries Expect Their Employees to Possess

The third question (Table 3) aimed at finding out what digital literacy related knowledge, skills, and competencies public libraries consider necessary. Again, the three most highly ranked categories were internet searching, writing and editing text and downloading content from the internet. It is worth noting that public libraries have not ranked highly any type of digitization [16] or content (specially video) broadcasting over the internet [17], which are popular categories of knowledge and skills. 58 libraries answered that they wish their employees possess something else (in terms of digital literacy) but didn't give any true explanation about what exactly would they want. Some rude comments were also given, one library questioned the existence of IT support in libraries, one commented about knowing ICT and one suggested learning Wordpress.

4.4 Skills Future Employees Should Possess

Except for the skills enumerated in previous questions, public libraries were asked to choose from the list of personal skills. Librarians' job is to be in contact with library users and the results in this question reflect the need for skills like (Table 4): listening to other people, interpersonal skills, conflict resolution in addition to other skills necessary for normal operation of a library. It is especially positive to observe skills like listening to other people, problem solving and analytical skills and critical thinking highly ranked as these are skills that are highly sought in many professions related to interaction with other people.

Table 3. Categories related to digital literacy public libraries expect employees to possess (N = 105)

	N	%
Internet searching	99	94.3
Writing and editing text	98	93.3
Downloading (content from the internet)	95	90.5
Presentation creation	88	83.8
Digital photo editing	73	69.5
Online questionnaire creation	61	58.1
Use of spreadsheets	60	57.1
Something else	58	55.2
Web page creation by use of HTML	48	45.7
Digitization by use of camera	47	44.8
Video content broadcasting	45	42.9
Sound content broadcasting	41	39.0
Computer illustration creation	32	30.5
Digitization by use of scanner	24	22.9
Online simulation use	22	21.0
Computer animation creation	19	18.1
Web application programming	18	17.1
Mobile application programming	11	10.5

Table 4. Skills important for future library employees (N = 105)

	N	%
Listening to other people	100	95.2
Problem solving	96	91.4
Information retrieval and organization	90	85.7
Analytical skills and critical thinking	81	77.1
Interpersonal skills	71	67.6
Negotiation skills	71	67.6
Decision making	70	66.7
Conflict resolution	62	59.0
Leading and participating in meetings	58	55.2
Leadership	43	41.0
Something else	2	1.9

4.5 Personal Characteristics Library Considers to be Important to Future Employees

When users evaluate their satisfaction with library services – they frequently take into account personal characteristics of librarians. These characteristics are announced in job descriptions in libraries and are part of everyday library operations. The results

(Table 5) indicate that most of personal characteristics offered in this research were important for achieving excellence in work in libraries and were selected by many libraries in this research study. It is interesting to see personal organizational skills and dealing with change uncertainty confrontation ranked low, however, they remain important because personal organization skills are related to work achievements and uncertainty confrontation is needed as we live in the frequently changing world.

Table 5. Personal characteristics important for future library employees (N = 105)

	N	%
Professionalism	102	97.1
Dependability	100	95.2
Creativity	95	90.5
Good oral and written communication skills	92	87.6
Will for learning	92	87.6
Communication and interaction with other teams and networks	80	76.2
Will for taking responsibility	73	69.5
Planning and strategic thinking	65	61.9
Time management	62	59.0
Work under pressure	56	53.3
Personal organization skills	54	51.4
Uncertainty confrontation	47	44.8
Something else	2	1.9

4.6 Frequency of Communication with Academic Institutions About Adjustments of the Study Programs in Accordance with Needs for Knowledge and Skills in the Public Libraries

This question aimed at finding out one of the most important aspects of successful cooperation between libraries and universities. Unfortunately, the frequency of communication between them is very low which does not lead to better understanding of needs for specific knowledge and skills between libraries and universities. 82 public libraries (78.1%) never communicated with academic institutions, 16 libraries (15.2%) did it seldom, 7 libraries (6.7%) communicated occasionally and 0 libraries communicated often or always.

4.7 When Communicating with the Academic Institutions in Croatia on Adjustments of the Study Programs, Who Proposes the Adjustments in Accordance with Needs for Knowledge and Skills in the Public Libraries?

The results of this question revealed that libraries are initiators of communication regarding adjustments of the university study programs more often than academic institutions. Low number of answers indicated a need for more intensive institutional communication as soon as possible. 14 public libraries (50%) proposed the adjustments, 8 public libraries (28.6%) stated that the adjustments are proposed by academic institutions while 6 public libraries (21.4%) stated that both sides propose the adjustments of the university study programs.

4.8 Priorities in Possible Adjustments of the University Study Programs

Libraries have been given an opportunity to prioritize their needs for adjustments of the university study programs in order to hire employees who are better prepared. Their priorities are media and information literacy, followed by digital literacy and scientific literacy. For 65 public libraries (63.1%) in this research media and information literacy was priority, for 25 public libraries (24.3%) digital literacy was priority and for 13 public libraries (12.6%) scientific literacy was priority.

4.9 Frequency of Adjustments of the University Study Programs in Accordance with Needs for Knowledge and Skills in the Public Libraries

Finally, public libraries were asked about the frequency of the adjustments of the university study programs in accordance with their needs for knowledge and skills. The results showed very different views on frequency of the university study programs adjustments. The full study program cycle at the Croatian universities lasts 5 years on average (with exceptions lasting shorter and longer than 5 years) and it is difficult to expect that the study programs will change before the completion of at least one full study cycle followed by the proper analysis of their implementation. However, this question aimed at discovering the position of public libraries on expected frequency of the adjustments and almost all libraries participating in this research declared they would adjust the university study programs in 5 years' time frame or more often and only 2 libraries declared they would wait for more than 5 years (every year N = 11, 10.5%, every 2 years N = 29, 27.6%, every 3 years N = 13, 12.4%, every 4 years N = 23, 21.9%, every 5 years N = 27, 25.7% and less than every 5 years N = 2, 19%). To conclude, public libraries think that their needs for knowledge and skills are changing faster than the university study programs.

5 Conclusion

Finding knowledgeable and skillful workforce is always a dynamic and unpredictable task as there are discrepancies between visions of universities about knowledge and skills needed in libraries and visions of libraries what should their future employees be knowledgeable, skillful and literate in. The abilities of future employees in libraries are already known from the developments in society and can be also recognized and verified from the available lists of knowledge, skills and literacies created by the government and/or originating from research. The research about the Croatian public libraries' views on knowledge, skills and literacies provided answers to all three research questions: (1) libraries have a clear understanding of knowledge, skills and literacies based on research of their needs when executing search for new employees;

(2) there is a need for the adjustments of the university study programs with the library practice; and (3) libraries initiate adjustments of study programs in half cases and want them to happen every 5 years or more often. The main hypothesis was confirmed suggesting the need for more frequent, direct and better communication between libraries and universities. The next step would be intensification of communication between libraries and academic institutions on the adjustments of the study programs.

References

1. Literacy for Life: Education for All. UNESCO, Paris (2005)
2. Lonsdale, M., McCurry, D.: Literacy in the New Millennium. NCVER, Adelaide (2004)
3. Statistical Yearbook of the Republic of Croatia. http://www.dzs.hr/Hrv_Eng/ljetopis/2016/sljh2016.pdf
4. Ng, W.: Empowering Scientific Literacy Through Digital Literacy and Multiliteracies. Nova Science Publishers Inc., New York (2012)
5. Hodson, D.: Towards Scientific Literacy: A Teachers' Guide to the History, Philosophy and Sociology of Science. Sense Publishers, Rotterdam (2008)
6. Leahy, D., Dolan, D.: Digital literacy: a vital competence for 2010? In: Reynolds, N., Turcsányi-Szabó, M. (eds.) KCKS 2010. IAICT, vol. 324, pp. 210–221. Springer, Heidelberg (2010). https://doi.org/10.1007/978-3-642-15378-5_21
7. Digital Literacy in Education. UNESCO, Moscow (2011). http://unesdoc.unesco.org/images/0021/002144/214485e.pdf
8. Pratibha, K., Atram, N.: Digital library services in the digital age. Int. J. Libr. Inf. Sci. **6**, 79–82 (2017)
9. The Praeger Handbook of Media Literacy. Praeger, Santa Barbara, Denver, Oxford (2013)
10. Presidential Committee on Information Literacy: Final Report. http://www.ala.org/acrl/publications/whitepapers/presidential
11. Report Summary: Employability: Developing a Framework for Policy Analysis. http://www.employment-studies.co.uk/report-summaries/report-summary-employability-developing-framework-policy-analysis
12. Workforce Plus – An Employability Framework for Scotland. http://www.gov.scot/Publications/2006/06/12094904/2
13. Carroll, D., Tani, M.: Job search as a determinant of graduate over-education: evidence from Australia. Educ. Econ. **23**, 631–644 (2015)
14. Moreau, E.: Hottest Social App Trends for Teens. https://www.lifewire.com/hottest-social-app-trends-for-teens-3485940
15. d'Ancona, M.: Ten Alternative Facts for the Post Truth World. https://www.theguardian.com/books/2017/may/12/post-truth-worst-of-best-donald-trump-sean-spicer-kellyanne-conway
16. Kendra, M., Proffitt, M.: Advancing the National Digital Platform: The State of Digitization in US Public and State Libraries. OCLC, Dublin (2017)
17. Scardilli, B.: Streaming Video in Public Libraries. http://newsbreaks.infotoday.com/NewsBreaks/Streaming-Video-in-Public-Libraries-97901.asp

Information Literacy of Lawyers in Their Working Environment

Dejana Golenko[1(✉)] and Ljiljana Siber[2]

[1] Faculty of Law, University of Rijeka, Rijeka, Croatia
dejana@pravri.hr
[2] Faculty of Law, University of Osijek, Osijek, Croatia
ljsiber@pravos.hr

Abstract. The research aims at presenting the way legal practitioners in the Republic of Croatia (judges, lawyers, notaries) access relevant sources of information necessary in their profession as well as at defining the problems emerging therefrom. The answers to these questions have been obtained through the study by applying quantitative and qualitative research methods. The analysis results showed that, given the requirements of the labour market, in addition to legal skills, legal practitioners should also develop their information literacy skills. The results will be used to set indicators for creating a learning environment that allows students to continuously and systematically acquire information literacy IL competences required by the global market.

Keywords: Information literacy in the field of law
Information literacy programmes · Legal practitioners · Labour market

1 Introduction

An individual's independence, ability, knowledge, and skills influence their research and all the intellectual and creative activities that they undertake. Their general level of knowledge and their competences are expanded by specific knowledge. Every member of the academic community broadens his/her knowledge specific to their profession by acquiring more detailed specialist knowledge that is subject to frequent and rapid changes.

These changes are brought about by the continuous and rapid development of information and communication technologies as well as changes in higher education. Consequently, some previously acquired information skills may quickly become obsolete and need to be updated with newer ways of searching and finding relevant facts and sources.

The modern working environment requires acquisition of specific competences and information literacy (IL) skills that will enable employees to meet today's expectations of being productive, innovative, and able to transform information to create new knowledge as well as be able to broaden their knowledge of the information landscape in order to compete in globally competitive markets [1]. The main issue in all knowledge-management directed organisations has become the question of competences and their initial activities aimed at motivating the exchange and sharing of

S. Kurbanoğlu et al. (Eds.): ECIL 2017, CCIS 810, pp. 78–86, 2018.
https://doi.org/10.1007/978-3-319-74334-9_9

knowledge. In this context, a number of research studies have been conducted on the topic of information literacy in the working environment [2, 3].

Due to constant developments taking place in new areas and branches of law, further requirements of legal science and the interpretation of law have been laid down not only for Croatian legal scientists but also for legal practitioners (judges, lawyers, notaries). Timely and flawless performance in the field of law can be facilitated only if they demonstrate an extensive knowledge of the specific field, possess the ability to search and use relevant European and international legal sources, and have generic/general IL skills and contextual/specialist IL skills crucial for development of their lifelong competencies not only as members of the academic community but also as jurists.

In the course of their education, law students are taught to search for, retrieve, and quote a number of legal sources (e.g. how to use relevant legal sources, recognize different ways of citing pieces of legislation, and recognize features of legal databases). They also learn to analyse and critically approach a legal issue, establish a legislative framework for legal issues, compare diverse legal systems accessible in various data bases or other sources of information, and evaluate scientific information in different fields of law [4].

2 Previous Research

Numerous authors pointed out that law libraries needed to apply IL programmes and adapt their information services as much as possible to ICT development and changes in the learning environment [5–8]. Thus, Percy Jaysuriya and Kumar suggested that each wave of innovation in legal publishing and development of information technology challenges legal librarians to re-evaluate their information services for students. Students nowadays have higher expectations than the generations before them and hope that rapid technological changes will allow for an easier and simpler research process [9].

On the other hand, a number of authors criticised the research skills of young legal practitioners that enter the labour market [10]. For the most part, this is because IL skills are not the same as 20 years ago due to the rapid development of information and communication technology, the Internet, and new fields of law. Namely, legal practitioners of today are not prepared to do cost-effective research; they are not acquainted with a list of source search tools, they use neither secondary sources nor free sources, and in their research they do not show the ability of conceptual thinking [10].

Employers in the field of law emphasize and even criticize young jurists for their lack of basic information skills and poor practical skills for searching and using online information sources. The foregoing statement has been confirmed by a number of recent research studies. The Westlaw 2006–2007 study compared the research skills of new associates to those of senior associates [11, 12]. The research results showed that the lack of research skills in young associates is an unnecessary cost for law firms and their clients [13].

Authors emphasized that future law practitioners are not educated only at law schools but also on hybrid teaching premises that are built on electronic web sources and new ways of learning, such as eLearning, that makes the Internet the key element in developing students' educational practices [14]. Kaplan and Darvil found it necessary to update teaching methods for new generations of law students [10]. Many authors point out the holistic approach to legal education and demand for discriminating legal skills from the IL skills in the field of law [15].

3 General Presentation of Current Conditions

Despite numerous research studies into the necessary IL skills of legal practitioners in the world, the topic has been underrepresented in the Republic of Croatia. Only a few papers have been written on the importance of formally introducing IL programmes into law schools for students not only during their education but also in lifelong learning programmes [16, 17]. In 2015 and 2016, the project *Iurisprudentia* was carried out at law schools in Croatia with the purpose of improving the status of the legal profession in Croatia through efficient harmonisation of study programmes and labour market requirements. However, this project did not aim to include a detailed analysis of the IL skills of legal practitioners needed for the labour market [18].

4 Research Problem and Research Questions

A deeper understanding of the topic can be acquired only by carrying out extensive research into IL in the working environment of legal practitioners.

In this context, the following research questions arise: To what extent have legal practitioners developed and acquired IL skills and competences necessary for their work during the course of their formal education at law schools? What problems do they have while retrieving and searching for information? Who do they turn to and how do they deal with these problems? What are their employers' expectations? To what extent do their employers facilitate their additional training and education? What part of their formal education should be adapted to the needs of their working environment and their needs of future legal practitioners?

5 Methodology

We looked for the answers to these questions in the study comprising two research stages by applying qualitative and quantitative research methods. From February 2016 until May 2016, the IL programmes were organized for legal practitioners at Judicial Academies in Zagreb, Rijeka, Varaždin, Split, and Osijek, where one of the authors was also the workshop presenter. After carrying out the programmes, the Judicial Academy of the Republic of Croatia administered a workshop evaluation questionnaire.

There were 83 workshop participants. The workshop evaluation data were collected from questionnaires completed by 67 respondents. The workshop participants/respondents were comprised of judges and judicial advisors at district, county, and commercial courts. The workshop was held from February to May 2016 (Table 1).

Table 1. Respondents according to age, gender and length of service

Age	Length of service	Gender
25–35 – 12 respondents	6–10 years – 12 respondents	35 males
35–45 – 20 respondents	11–20 years – 20 respondents	42 females
45–55 – 21 respondents	21–30 years – 21 respondents	
55–65 – 14 respondents	31–40 years – 13 respondents	
	Over 40 years – 1 respondents	

The outcome questionnaire included open-ended and closed-ended questions with a percentage scale and respondents' commentaries. The questions referred to respondents' opinions about the organisation and usefulness of the workshop, as well as the scope of information knowledge and skills that were acquired.

The results of the outcome questionnaire served as a starting point for establishing the framework for the content researched by the authors at the next research stage for applying the qualitative research method of the focus group in order to comprehend the phenomenon context better, in other words the motivation for a particular behaviour of legal practitioners when it comes to information. Namely, recent trends in the field of information behaviour suggest that research should be done on information behaviour and motivation of small groups of users [19]. The focus group consisted of 13 legal practitioners participating in the IL workshop in Osijek in February 2017 with the purpose of researching the participants' information behaviour, their attitudes, and IL comprehension in the context of its application in the workplace (Table 2).

Table 2. Age, gender and length of service in focus group

Age	Length of service	Gender
25–35 – 4 respondents	6–10 years – 4 respondents	3 males
35–45 – 2 respondents	11–20 years – 2 respondents	10 females
45–55 – 5 respondents	21–30 years – 5 respondents	
55–65 – 2 respondents	31–40 years – 2 respondents	
	Over 40 years – 0 respondents	

The questions were divided onto six main topics: information competencies of legal practitioners, sources they used in everyday work, access to and availability of sources, skills and competences of information literacy expected from legal practitioners in carrying out everyday activities, expectations and employers' demands of legal practitioners in the context of Information literacy, and the views of legal practitioners on formal education at law faculties in accordance with the needs of the working environment of future legal practitioners to acquire the necessary skills of information literacy. Within each group of questions subcategories were further elaborated related to specificity of the field of law.

Thirty minutes of conversations and discussions in the focus group of legal practitioners were recorded on a mobile phone voice recorder and the data were processed using VLC media player (free recording software). Since legal practitioners had been acquainted with one another, the atmosphere during the discussion was pleasant and relaxed. One set of questions led to other questions and spontaneously introduced new topics for discussion.

Respondents were labelled as follows: N1, N2, N3, N4, N5, N6, N7, N8, N9, N10, N11, N12, and N13.

Due to the limited scope of operation, we shall point out only the basic categories and the results referring to the research questions.

6 Results

6.1 Information Literacy Skills and Competencies of Legal Practitioners

The results of the evaluation outcome questionnaire, which was administered at the end of the workshop, indicated that legal practitioners rarely used legal databases and relied mostly on printed versions of law commentaries; they obtained relevant information in communication with their colleagues at work.

The foregoing was supported by legal practitioners' responses in the focus group; they obtained necessary information on their own, mostly in their everyday work and they did not use elaborate research techniques or strategies, which additionally slowed down their access to necessary information. Legal practitioners with 10–40 years of service had not attended any form of IL courses [N1, N2, N5, N6, N8, N10, N11, and N13]. They based their research mostly on printed versions of books, articles, and laws. The results showed that legal practitioners with 10 years of service used their information skills more often; they were also more familiar with different online sources, in particular with legal databases that they used in their everyday work. They had received a certain form of IL training at their law schools and had some basic IL skills [N3, N4, N7, N9].

> *We have never been instructed how to draft a judicial decision and we have been required to learn theory by heart; things are different today – there are IL workshops at the faculties and young people have working knowledge of databases and online sources.* [N2]

6.2 IL Skills and Competences that Legal Practitioners Need in Their Everyday Work

The results of the evaluation outcome questionnaire suggested that legal practitioners were expected to develop necessary competences and skills in searching, retrieving, and evaluating information sources and legal databases in new fields of law, for example, the European law.

The responses of legal practitioners in the focus group confirmed this. In their responses, they emphasized the importance of skilful use of relevant information sources, particularly the Croatian legal databases (e.g. Narodne novine/Official Gazette, Ius-Info). Since the Republic of Croatia is a member state of the EU, they were expected to display competence in relevant European databases (e.g. EUR-Lex and CURIA) [N1–N13].

6.3 Problems that Legal Practitioners Face When Accessing and Searching the Required Data in Their Everyday Work

The results of the evaluation outcome questionnaire showed that most legal practitioners expected their circumstances to improve. These improvements referred to allowing more time for research into legal cases and having the possibility to involve services that provide necessary data as well as better access to commercial research tools in the field of law. Access was important since some courts had no access to specialized legal databases (e.g. *Ius-Info*). Moreover, they pointed out the importance of stronger institutional support regarding research in the field of law by means of IT tools.

The responses of legal practitioners in the focus group confirmed these statements. Moreover, the respondents pointed out the problem of restricted financial means of the Croatian courts for the acquisition of legal sources (books, legislation commentaries, and legal databases), that inevitably resulted in accessing mainly free databases [N1–N13].

> *There are a few basic sources of information in our court library – and that is all – we do not have IT experts to support us in search of reliable data.* [N2]

> *We manage to find elsewhere the sources of information that we need – this workshop is a good opportunity, and we mostly manage somehow on our own, the problem is that we do not have access to databases at courts, which inhibits our work – we copy and download the free online sources.* [N1]

6.4 What Do Employers Expect from Legal Practitioners and to What Extent Are Legal Practitioners Granted Further Education and Training in View of Information Literacy?

The results of the evaluation outcome questionnaire suggested that employers recognized the importance of additional education and training in the IL context by including this type of education as a workshop series within the Judicial Academy of the Republic of Croatia. The respondents recommended that they extend this type of education and involve judicial advisors in the education series since judicial advisors will be doing most of the preparatory legal research for judges in the future.

Legal practitioners in the focus group confirmed this and considered that employers expected their employees to improve their computer skills, information skills, and the competences that they needed in their everyday work [N1-13]. Notwithstanding the insufficient funds for supply of necessary sources of information, various training programmes, including the IL programme, had been organized within the Judicial Academy since 2016.

> *We have to learn how to find a piece of legislation in a relevant database.* [N3]

6.5 Should Formal Education at Law Schools Be Changed and Adapted in Accordance with the Working Environment Needs for Acquisition of IL Skills of Future Legal Practitioners?

The results of the evaluation outcome questionnaire showed the respondents' intention to establish a continuous cooperation with law school libraries regarding their participation in IL programmes.

All respondents in the focus group pointed out the necessity of participating in IL programmes at law schools in the Republic of Croatia; from their personal experience, they realised the importance of information sources in solving everyday work problems [N1–N13]. In view of the specificities of a particular branch of law, they assumed that programmes should be created in close consultation with teaching faculty and librarians. They emphasized that librarians would be the most competent in performing these activities because of their experience and knowledge of information sources. They also suggested that these training programmes should be created as courses with ECTS-credit points [N1, N2, N5, N6, N8, N10, N11, and N13]. In this way, all students could improve not only their basic IL skills but also IL skills in the field of law. All participants agreed that information skills and competences of legal practitioners should be updated because new branches of law were emerging due to the rapid development of information and communication technology [N1–N13]. The majority of respondents were not familiar with the fact that law schools provided this form of education and training.

> *It is good to know that law schools provide this form of education.* [N7]

> *Workshops are absolutely necessary and this type of training at law schools is also important – it is crucial to introduce formal IL programmes into law schools.* [N10]

7 Discussion and Conclusion

The analysis of the responses indicated that, given the requirements of the modern labour market, in addition to their professional legal skills, legal practitioners should also improve the IL skills that were important in their everyday work. The reason for this was the rapid development of information and communication technology, and the Internet, numerous legal databases requiring knowledge of different search techniques, and the fact that new fields of law were emerging (particularly in the field of the European law).

The fact is that IL programmes have not been formally introduced in law schools in Croatia. The research results pointed out this deficiency as well as proved the significance of their being introduced. This is supported by the fact that IL is a precondition for lifelong learning and by the need to connect the generic and contextual IL skills of a certain scientific discipline. It is necessary for students – future jurists – to acquire skills and complete IL that will be needed in their everyday life and work. The research itself has motivated the authors to organize periodically IL workshops for legal practitioners at their law schools. Legal practitioners have recognized the importance of IL programmes organized within the Judicial Academy of the Republic of Croatia as well as the importance of lifelong learning in a particular profession.

The research also proved that IL skills were a prerequisite for legal practitioners in Croatia to meet numerous requirements at work. By mastering IL skills, they become competitive on the labour market. In full awareness of the changes that must take place in the value system, the focus of attention should be placed on creating and utilizing intellectual capital by combining knowledge and skills of information literacy. By mastering the skills necessary to work in a certain profession, legal practitioners can increase their individual capacity, which has impact on the efficiency and quality of their organisation as a whole.

The authors of the paper actively promote the introduction of IL into study programmes and the results of this research shall serve as guidelines to adapting the IL to the requirements of the labour market in the field of law.

The results will be used to define the indicators for creation of a learning environment that will allow students to continuously and systematically acquire IL competences in order to become competitive and successful on the global market.

Considering the lack of scientific research papers on this topic, the results of the research contribute to both theoretical and practical reasoning regarding IL in the field of law at the domestic and international level. At a scientific level, the conducted research has opened the path to further research and increased the awareness of the importance of the IL concept in the field of law.

References

1. Lloyd, A.: Building information resilient workers: the critical ground of workplace information literacy. What have we learnt? In: Kurbanoğlu, S., Grassian, E., Mizrachi, D., Catts, R., Špiranec, S. (eds.) ECIL 2013. CCIS, vol. 397, pp. 219–228. Springer, Cham (2013). https://doi.org/10.1007/978-3-319-03919-0_28
2. TFPL Ltd.: Skills for Knowledge Management, TFPL Briefing Paper (1999). http://www.tfpl.com
3. Bruce, C.S.: Workplace experiences of information literacy. Int. J. Inf. Manag. **19**, 33–47 (1999)
4. Ryesky, K.H.: On solid legal ground: bringing information literacy to undergraduate level law courses. J. Effec. Teach. **7**(2), 21–35 (2007)
5. Callister, P.D.: Beyond training: law librarianship's quest for the pedagogy of legal research education. Law Libr. J. **7**(9), 7–46 (2003)
6. Beljaars, B.: Implementing legal information literacy: a challenge for the curriculum. Int. J. Legal Inf. **37**(3), 321–332 (2009)
7. Cuffe, N.: Law student's experiences of information and information technology - implications for legal information literacy curriculum development. http://www.aare.edu.au/data/publications/2002/cuf02169.pdf
8. McLaurin Smith, N., Presser, P.: Embed with the faculty: legal information skills online. J. Acad. Libr. **31**(3), 249–250 (2005)
9. Jayasuriya, P., Kumar H.: Student Services in the 21st Century: Evolution and Innovation in Discovering Student Needs, Teaching Information Literacy, and Designing Library 2.0-Based Services. Georgetown Law Faculty Working Papers. Paper 18. http://scholarship.law.georgetown.edu/fwps_papers/18
10. Kaplan, A.B., Darvil, K.: Think [and practice] like a lawyer: legal research for the new millennials. Legal Commun. Rhetoric: JALWD **8**, 153–190 (2011)
11. Brooks, J.L.K.: Great expectations: new associates research skills from law school to law firm. Legal Ref. Serv. Q. **28**(3/4), 291–300 (2009)
12. A Study of Attorneys' Legal Research Practices and Opinions of New Associates' Reserach Skills (2013). http://www.aallnet.org/sections/all/storage/committees/practicetf/final-report-07102013.pdf

13. Thomson West, White Paper: Research Skills for Lawyers and Law Students 2–3 (2007). http://west.thomson.com/pdf/librarian/Legal_Research_white_paper.pdf
14. Pengelley, N.: Not a box but a window: law libraries and legal education in a virtual world. Aust. Law Libr. **9**(2), 122–127 (2001)
15. Kim-Prieto, D.: The road not yet taken: how law student information literacy standards address identified issues in legal research education and training. Law Libr. J. **103**(4), 605–630 (2011)
16. Golenko, D., Petr Balog, K., Siber, L.: Information literacy programs in the field of law: case study of two law faculties in Croatia. In: Kurbanoğlu, S., Boustany, J., Špiranec, S., Grassian, E., Mizrachi, D., Roy, L., Çakmak, T. (eds.) ECIL 2016. CCIS, vol. 676, pp. 385–393. Springer, Cham (2016). https://doi.org/10.1007/978-3-319-52162-6_38
17. Golenko, D., Vilar, P., Stričević, I.: Academic strategic documents as a framework for good information literacy programs: case study of law faculties in the Republic of Croatia. In: Kurbanoğlu, S., Grassian, E., Mizrachi, D., Catts, R., Špiranec, S. (eds.) ECIL 2013. CCIS, vol. 397, pp. 415–421. Springer, Cham (2013). https://doi.org/10.1007/978-3-319-03919-0_55
18. Iurisprudentia: Improving the Quality of Education at Faculties of Law of the Osijek, Rijeka and Split University. Legčević, J. (ed.) Faculty of Law, Osijek (2016)
19. Bruce, C.: The Seven Faces of Information Literacy. Auslib Press, Adelaide (1997)

From Studio Space and Makerspace to Workplace: Adapting Instruction and Outreach to Fit the Needs of Practitioners from Art to Engineering

Rebecca Kuglitsch(✉) and Alexander Watkins

University Libraries, University of Colorado Boulder, Boulder, USA
{Rebecca.Kuglitsch,Alexander.Watkins}@colorado.edu

Abstract. This paper discusses the specialized instructional needs of creative practitioner communities and consequent tensions students of applied fields face related to their place in the academy. By drawing on the literature of workplace information behavior and exploring the multiple communities of practice that creative practitioners navigate, we suggest information literacy approaches that acknowledge and accommodate their unique needs. If librarians acknowledge an inherent multidisciplinarity, wide ranging use of sources, tacit knowledge, and information use in specialized creation spaces, they can teach information literacy skills that are transferable and meet workplace affordances and needs. This leads to information literacy instruction that resonates with students in these fields and positions them to better succeed in their chosen fields.

Keywords: Professional information literacy · Workplace information literacy Practice-based research · Learning spaces · Practitioner communities

1 Introduction

The specialized instructional needs of creative practitioner communities in academia—the people who apply knowledge to create things, whether art, buildings, or bridges—is frequently neglected in information literacy instruction. Often, library instruction conflates the needs of this group with the needs of traditional scholars. Yet the research necessary for writing an academic paper is markedly different from the research that goes into creating an object or design. Strict adherence to a purely academic approach fails to serve students who will encounter very different norms in their future workplaces, and leads to the impression that information literacy is irrelevant for practitioners' future careers. This can easily demotivate students. A shift to understanding the unique needs and approaches in the applied fields will lead to richer and more effective instruction and outreach to practitioners.

At the same time, the academy tends to silo design and making activities in engineering and in the arts. But phenomenographic evidence suggests that the experience of design is not so different across fields as our academic structures imply [1]. Consequently, we believe that information behaviors across fields can be compared to develop a better understanding of literacy needs across design fields for future success

S. Kurbanoğlu et al. (Eds.): ECIL 2017, CCIS 810, pp. 87–97, 2018.
https://doi.org/10.1007/978-3-319-74334-9_10

in the workplace. In this paper, we take a broader approach to design practitioner's needs and review the literature of information behavior of these groups in order to apply it to student information literacy needs. To do this, we will first review research and information behaviors of practitioner communities, demonstrating similarities across applied fields, and then explore the implications for information literacy instruction.

2 Research for Practitioners

We examine practitioners as a group, ranging from artists to engineers, who nevertheless share research commonalities rooted in the applied nature of their studies. Students in these fields are engaged in a praxis that combines theory with practice. A similar cycle of research-design-build (or create) applies across the group: a studio artist might research a concept, theory or art movement that will inspire their work; architects may do extensive precedent research to inform their design; an engineer might research basic physics concepts to apply to a design. Practitioners in these fields are engaged in reflection about the role of inquiry in design as well, examining the difference between researching for design and design as research. The architecture field is questioning the division that exists between research and practice, and arguing that design practice can also be a way of creating new knowledge [2]. In art practice there is a recurrent debate about whether artists do research: is art a form of inquiry? Critics question whether art is a valid research product or the studio is a valid site for research, yet, "if research is the creation of new knowledge, then the outcome is not merely to help explain things in causal or relational terms, but to fully understand them in a way that helps us act on that knowledge [3]". Because of this move to practice-based research there is an increasing expectation that art students be able to conduct research that is accepted in both the art and academic worlds [3]. Despite the popular conception of engineering as a cut and dried rule-based field, engineers operate in a complex, ambiguous setting, calling for creative synthesis of ideas across fields to develop optimal designs [4]. In engineering, integrating research into design is essential to developing creative solutions to problems.

2.1 Students Work in the Distinct Communities of Academics and Practitioners

Students who are studying to become practitioners, whether they be engineers or artists, exist and work in two distinct but overlapping worlds. They move between a textually oriented academic world, where research leads to carefully constructed arguments, and the practitioner world, where research leads to embodied designs. This requires a shift from thinking about pieces of evidence in developing a rhetorical argument, to thinking about facts, constraints, and specifications as environmentally dependent. An engineer, for example, cannot simply identify a superconductor that meets the most basic needs for a project; they must identify a superconductor that will function within the realistic physical constraints of the project. This need to focus on the embodied output of research requires a different kind of evaluation in practice than it might in academic contexts. Yet as practitioners in the academy, students and faculty move between these two communities of practice, the academic sphere and that of their applied work, each with their own norms, jargon, information sources and requirements.

A central aspect of this is that students must learn to master their field's academic vocabulary and discourse, as well as a practitioner discourse. They are often taught by faculty members who may or may not have participated in the practitioner community and vice-versa; thus they frequently receive mixed messages about requirements. For example, artists need facility with the language of gallery announcements and artist's statements, often rendered in what has been labeled "International Art English" as well as with the theory and jargon laden world of art history research papers [5]. For engineers, architects, or environmental designers a familiarity with technical writing is needed as well as academic language. These students will need to write specifications, technical reports, professional presentations and pitches. Students in these fields will need to write to explain their designs to others who might implement them, to interest potential investors, and to explain how to use a design. Students of practice must be able to fluidly shift between academic and practitioner discourses in the course of a single school day.

Students will also need to move between two different worlds of information behavior. Tenopir and King, for example, note a longstanding difference in use of formal vs. informal communication channels between academic and applied communities in engineering [6]. In their academic work, students learn to privilege formal communication and rely heavily on journal and monographic literature. They are taught to identify academic authority, and to question the credibility of information that has not undergone peer-review. In the world of practice, students need to use informal communications to find the information they need. Grey literature, trade journals, internal documentation, blogs, social media, and personal communication are all key places practitioners find information.

Navigating these multiple communities of practice can be challenging but it is essential for students. By adopting the norms, language, and sources of students' applied as well as academic activities, library instruction can be more effective and relevant to students' future careers. Thus, a recognition of information behavior in practitioner communities underpins effective information literacy for these fields.

2.2 Practitioner Research Relies on Varied Source Types

The key source types in practitioner and academic contexts tend to be drastically different. Though practitioners sometimes use scholarly journals, they tend to find them excessively effortful and frequently out of date [6]. Engineering faculty, for example, rely heavily on journals as one of their top two information sources [7], while practitioners rely on standards and technical reports [8]. Practitioners, especially those in the art and design world rely on trade publications much more than academic publications that highlight new techniques and report on cutting edge art and design practice [9, 10]. For engineers, trade publications are particularly important in the initial scoping and task clarification stage of design [11]. Architects frequently use a wide variety of source types, especially images and video; in one study watching online videos formed a key part of architects information gathering process [12]. For engineers information is accessed in a multiplicity of formats: not only text, but also drawings, photographs, prototypes or mockups, code, or simulations [4]. These varied information sources are particularly rich resources for inspiration and information about current and emerging methods for design. However, often in academic contexts only peer-reviewed journals are taught as acceptable sources, creating a conflict between research students need to perform for their academic work and for their practice. Library instruction is well suited to help practitioner students navigate the complex world of source types and when they would be useful, especially as they may receive mixed messages from their academic and practitioner instructors.

2.3 Practitioner Research Draws from Multiple Disciplines

Practitioner information seeking behavior is inherently interdisciplinary. Across creative and design fields, the ability to identify and assess another field's ideas and apply them in practice is key. Artists seeking information look at "an almost unlimited range" of source types and subjects [13]. Hemming finds that artist's needs are idiosyncratic, they need information with "no epistemic relationship to art [10]". Greer's citation analysis of undergraduate theses found that sources primarily about the fine arts represented just 26% of the citations [14]. Architects frequently use a wide range of online resources for inspiration, site information, and ideas about process [12]. In the authors' experience, architecture students need information from a wide variety of disciplines to successfully complete their designs. These range from architectural precedents to maps and GIS, local history, environmental research, social and psychological information, to health and wellness, and more.

Engineering is similar; to design an engineering solution, information may be drawn from disciplines across the fields of engineering, but also from other areas of design like graphic, architectural and industrial design, as well as the humanities and social sciences [4]. This is necessary because engineers must apply ideas from the sciences to a human context and produce an item for use. A civil engineer, for example, may require information about engineering methods, but also local geology, law, international standards, and construction management. While wide span of disciplines is not absent from academic engineering, it is particularly apparent in industry, where teams tend to work with specialists from a wide range of disciplines, bringing together many areas of expertise, a scenario that is rarely available to students in a classroom context [4].

2.4 Practitioner Research Relies on Tacit Knowledge

In applied fields, experts are often identified by their mastery of a craft and tacit knowledge, rather than solely by academic credentials. Students of practice must be able to recognize others—whether they be professors, project managers, lab managers, or other artists—as information resources, a skill that can be challenging to students trained only in an academic tradition [15]. Practicing artists frequently need to seek out communities of artists for information on materials and techniques and the art market [10]. Mason and Robinson identify an "invisible college" that is an important resource for emerging artists, both for career development (an area artists felt underprepared for by their schooling), as well as for artistic inspiration where they cited conversation and debate as key sources [13]. The architects in Makri and Warick's study frequently sought out their peers' blogs for ideas on their process and what they might do next [12].

Similarly, Allard et al. found that colleagues and team members are a fundamental information source for engineers, although consulting the internet as a first step has increased [16]. Even when using print sources like standards and technical reports, engineering practitioners combine them with tacit knowledge, consulting with colleagues to identify, interpret, and contextualize information [18]. Consulting with colleagues is a way to respond efficiently to active situations when using static technical reports, since colleagues can provide context for decisions and help with how to best apply the information [17]. Colleagues' tacit knowledge was particularly valued for several reasons: first, it was perceived as especially trustworthy; second, it tended to lead efficiently to hard to find documents; and third, colleagues were assumed to be able to validate practices or suggest someone who could [16]. Thus, for engineers even when using textual sources, tacit knowledge is used to enrich the text and make its use more efficient, and this approach is a common thread among practitioner fields.

2.5 Practitioner Research Happens in Unique Spaces

As well as commonalities of practice, these fields share a reliance on designated spaces for building and creation. Their unique spaces—labs, makerspaces and studios—have unique affordances for library outreach, and their own associated information-seeking behaviors that must be acknowledged in information literacy. These spaces of doing correlate with students' future workplaces, allowing information literacy learned in this context to be more easily transferred, consequently promoting critical and creative approaches in the workplace. Studios play a key role in artist's presentation of themselves and in many ways have a performative aspect [19]. They are the site of the all-important studio visits, when curators or dealers come by the artist's studio to evaluate their work for potential shows. Books and other research resources are a hallmark of artist's studios, but how much they are for use or for show is not clear. Labs, somewhat similarly, tend to have a small collection of frequently used works, but again, it is not clear how much they are used. Recent work around makerspaces has extensively discussed how to set them up in the library [20], particularly the public library, but relatively little work has been done about how information use occurs in them. By bringing books and information literacy instruction into these spaces it explicitly ties research to making, important because frequently practitioners class library research as belonging only to the academic side of their work.

3 Understanding the Workplace Information Landscape

As student practitioners move from their academic environment to their new workplace environment, they will find a drastically changed information landscape. In particular, students encounter information scarcity, time constraints, and an increased need to rely on their own personal collections of information.

When artists move from university-provided studio to their own space, the available research resources drastically change. Emerging artists especially do not necessarily have the financial means to purchase all the books or subscriptions they may need to inform their research. Consequently, artists used several places to substitute for a university library including public libraries and bookstores. Artists and designers were just as likely to borrow a friend's copy of a magazine or read it in a bookstore rather than subscribe [13].

Engineers, too, find themselves in a dramatically different resource landscape. First, practicing engineers tend to work under tight time constraints and in a context where much information is proprietary [6]. Additionally, in the workplace it becomes particularly critical to match information needs with level of evaluation: the consequences for selecting the first few resources of a search are minimal in the paper-writing context, but significant in the design process [21]. Moreover, an engineering firm is more likely to provide just in time resources, unlike academic libraries that tend to lean more towards a just in case model, so students need to be comfortable finding information in such situations [8]. Engineers in practice frequently curate and rely on personal collections of information, so a familiarity with methods and tools that support this are key [17]. Understanding how to find information by multiple paths and quickly evaluate whether it is worth sinking their own or their companies resources into obtaining an item is key.

4 Implications for Information Literacy Instruction

Understanding practitioner information literacy needs is especially important for subject specialist librarians who serve practitioners in the arts and engineering, as these librarians mostly come from an academic rather than practitioner educational background. Consequently, they may not be attuned to the unique needs of practitioner students. Indeed 63.2% of art librarians have an undergraduate degree in art history or other humanity, compared to just 20.8% who have a studio art or architecture background. Of the non-LIS advanced degrees held by art librarians 72.8% were in art history or another humanity compared to 12.8% in studio art or architecture [22]. The situation is still more mismatched in STEM. In a 2000 survey of science librarians, 32.2% had some kind of science undergraduate degree at all, only 3.3% had an engineering undergraduate degree, and only 8.9% had an advanced degree in any area of the sciences or engineering [23]. Thus, librarians in such fields may be apt to fall back on academic information literacy models in contexts where a more applied model is appropriate. It is therefore important for librarians to be aware of their own assumptions about user needs, and to actively work to address the needs of practitioners in their library instruction.

4.1 Information Literacy Instruction for Students Moving Between Academic and Practitioner Communities

Librarians need to recognize that students are moving between practitioner and academic worlds, each with different requirements for research. For example, library instruction that focuses on authority codified in peer review and academic credentials can have the effect of minimizing the importance of key practitioner sources such as trade journals, grey literature, blogs, or technical reports. Librarians should teach students about multiple sources of information spanning academic and practitioner communities. By teaching students about the different affordances of various types of sources, we can help them see how these sources work synergistically to inform them about their field. We can show them how practitioner knowledge can be useful for academic writing and how academic knowledge can be useful for their practice. Ideally this will both familiarize them with the important information sources of their future workplaces, as well as demonstrate the continuing usefulness of academic knowledge to their practice.

4.2 Information Literacy Instruction for Multidisciplinary Research

Librarians' academic training may lead them to ignore practitioners' inherently multi-disciplinary and wide-ranging research needs. Academic research typically relies on the information sources and tools of a single discipline. But the needs of practitioners demand library instruction that encompasses a broader range of resources and databases. Librarians should not assume that practitioner students only need to know the primary databases in a specific academic field, but rather should expect that students will want and need to explore the literature of several disciplines. This might include teaching architectural design databases to architectural engineers, teaching social science databases to architects, or showing artists how to navigate philosophy resources. Frequently, instruction to practitioners will also require a willingness to engage with uncommon types of sources. Students from across the spectrum of design and practice may need to be taught to look at materials collections, product catalogs, patents, images, or videos.

4.3 Information Literacy Instruction and Tacit Knowledge

Librarians need to recognize and infuse respect for tacit knowledge into the classroom. By discussing the idea that authority is contextual and that authority and knowledge can come in many flavors, librarians can expose the importance of tacit knowledge. Ideally, librarians would provide examples of tacit knowledge as expert knowledge: master artisans, laboratory technicians, and makerspace machinists. Authority in this context is often validation through social means. Practitioners want knowledge that has proved successful in practice and is validated by others' firsthand experience. Considering the degree to which designers rely on community tacit knowledge, this is an essential skill. As well as explicitly discussing the idea of tacit and practitioner knowledge, librarians can encourage the development of note and record keeping structures that track local experts, as designers and engineers might do in practice. Librarians also might consider encouraging research consultations by framing them as consulting the tacit knowledge of an information professional. By acknowledging and validating the extremely social nature of information seeking in practitioner fields, librarians can develop trust with students in practitioner fields and prepare them to navigate the social aspects of information seeking they will encounter.

4.4 Bringing Information Literacy into Practitioners' Spaces

In the working world, students will frequently encounter research needs, but meeting those needs will relatively rarely take place in a formal library setting. Reaching out to students in their spaces helps set the expectation that research is not only an academic pursuit. Teaching for future workplace environments can encompass teaching outside of the library and in students' spaces. By bringing instruction and outreach into student practitioner spaces such as studios, makerspaces and laboratories, librarians can naturalize the idea of research being integrated in multiple phases of design and production, as well as mimic a workplace context. There has recently been an increasing recognition that information literacy instruction for artists should extend to the studio, especially by attending studio critiques, because the librarian presence in this setting reinforces the connection between the artistic process and the research process [24, 25]. This has the potential to prepare students for a workplace environment where they must talk fluently about their work and how it fits in existing artistic conversations during all important studio visits by curators and gallerists. A similar situation applies in engineering; in the author's experience going out to engineering lab groups, attending poster presentations, and reaching out to engineers in their own spaces normalizes information seeking as part of the design process. Engineers in both the academy and in practice rarely rely on physical library materials, removing one avenue to outreach, but by being present in the spaces engineers use, librarians can demonstrate the importance of information literacy in engineering. Librarians bringing information literacy into practitioner spaces can increase awareness and relevancy of this learning to student's future workplace environments.

4.5 Integrating Information Literacy in the Design Process

Explicitly teaching information literacy and research as threaded throughout the design process is important. When possible, it would be best to teach different skills needed at different points of the design process at the point of need. But for librarians who only have one opportunity to visit a class, it is especially important to model integrating research into multiple design phases. For example, students could map their design process, and the types of information they might need at each stage: identifying a problem, imagining a design, investigating execution, and producing the design. This might adhere to one of the many prescriptive models of design that are explicitly taught in engineering schools, like Radcliffe's Information-Rich Engineering Design, or it might be a more free-flowing process that allows students to define their own model of design [4, 11]. Regardless of how research is integrated throughout the design process, that it happens is necessary for students to learn how to function in the workplace, results in more authentic learning, and in better design outcomes [11].

4.6 Changing Access to Information

It is especially important to acknowledge practitioners' impending loss of access to information after they graduate in teaching transferable information literacy skills. For many students in academic fields, losing access to library resources is unfortunate but does not have a direct bearing on their post-university work. On the other hand, practitioner students will be attempting to directly apply the skills and processes they learned in school to their career. Librarians should specifically teach how to conduct research without academic affiliations and to emphasize tools that practitioners will still have access to. Librarians should also pay particular attention to teaching information management; when intellectual resources represent fiscal and temporal resources, and when students must curate and develop their own personal libraries, as they do in practice, it is especially important to have efficient management systems [17]. By giving practitioners the skills to adapt their research practices to this changed environment we can empower them to continue to use these skills, rather than having them feel that research can no longer be part of their practice in their present situation.

4.7 Intellectual Property

Finally, it is important to address intellectual property. Students in practitioner fields must understand how rights and responsibilities change as a student and as a professional. In the academic context, fair use, copyright, and citation are the most commonly explored aspects of intellectual property, but the world of practice is complicated by patents, trademarks, and trade secrets. Patents and trade secrets are a direct contrast to the academic context where ideas are shared in order to establish primacy; in practice, ideas may be hidden in order to capitalize on them. Consequently, students need to know professional conventions and norms, both for themselves as users of others' intellectual property and to support the creation and safeguarding of their own intellectual property. An engineer, for example, needs to know how to protect their own work with patents–but also to know that perhaps a completed patent is the best source for up to date information [11]. Moreover, a patent is not only potentially the best source of up to date information, resources such as USPTO and Espacenet are freely available sources of detailed technical information.

As well as managing more options for protecting intellectual property, the more permissive standards for fair use in academic contexts may not apply to practitioners in the workplace. So, it is important that instruction equips students not just with how they can use other's work in academic contexts but in future professional situations as well. Yet at the same time as fair use becomes less permissive, there can be more permissive standards for credit-sharing; a student providing a full bibliographic citation of a design inspiration rather than an informal hat tip in a pitch PowerPoint might look out of touch. Consequently, learning to navigate credit-sharing informally is important for professional growth.

5 Conclusion

The ability to transfer information literacy between realms—whether personal, workplace, or academic—is key for students to develop their lives as they want to and to developing an intrinsically motivated understanding of information literacy. In particular in the United States, but increasingly elsewhere, there is a growing tension between university education as vocational preparation and as a purely intellectual endeavor. Especially as students are facing serious financial challenges to attend college and university, a focus on the purely academic can come to seem like a luxury leading to a shift of focus to applied education. But the ability to pursue intellectual questions and lifelong learning should not be reserved for the privileged alone. By linking information literacy to the future careers of practitioners, librarians can give students both the practical skills they need to succeed after graduating while also empowering students in intellectual exploration and the pursuit of knowledge.

References

1. Daly, S.R., Adams, R.S., Bodner, G.M.: What does it mean to design? A qualitative investigation of design professionals' experiences. J. Eng. Educ. **101**, 187–219 (2012)
2. Hensel, M., Nilsson, F. (eds.): The Changing Shape of Practice: Integrating Research Anddesign in Architecture. Routledge, New York (2016)
3. Sullivan, G.: Research acts in art practice. Stud. Art Educ. **48**, 19–35 (2006)
4. Radcliffe, D.F.: Multiple perspectives on engineering design. In: Integrating Information into the Engineering Design Process, pp. 7–19. Purdue University Press (2014)
5. Rule, A., Levine, D.: International Art English. https://www.canopycanopycanopy.com/contents/international_art_english
6. Tenopir, C., King, D.W.: Engineer' information seeking and use. In: Communication Patterns of Engineers. Wiley, Hoboken (2004)
7. Engel, D., Robbins, S., Kulp, C.: The information-seeking habits of engineering faculty. Coll. Res. Libr. **72**, 548–567 (2011)
8. Waters, N., Kasuto, E., McNaughton, F.: Partnership between engineering libraries: identifying information literacy skills for a successful transition from student to professional. Sci. Technol. Libr. **31**, 124–132 (2012)
9. Snow, C.: Architects' wants and needs for information, demonstrated through a university-based information service. In: AP, vol. 27, pp. 112–123 (1975)
10. Hemmig, W.: An empirical study of the information-seeking behavior of practicing visual artists. J. Doc. **65**, 682–703 (2009)
11. Radcliffe, D.F.: Information-rich engineering design. In: Integrating Information into the Engineering Design Process, pp. 46–57. Purdue University Press (2014)
12. Makri, S., Warwick, C.: Information for inspiration: understanding architects' information seeking and use behaviors to inform design. J. Am. Soc. Inform. Sci. Technol. **61**, 1745–1770 (2010)
13. Mason, H., Robinson, L.: The information-related behaviour of emerging artists and designers: inspiration and guidance for new practitioners. J. Doc. **67**, 159–180 (2011)
14. Greer, K.: Undergraduate studio art information use: a multi-school citation analysis. Art Doc.: Bull. Art Libr. Soc. N. Am. **35**, 230–240 (2016)
15. Head, A.J.: Learning curve: how college graduates solve information problems once they join the workplace. Project Information Literacy, Passage Studies Research Report (2012)
16. Allard, S., Levine, K.J., Tenopir, C.: Design engineers and technical professionals at work: observing information usage in the workplace. J. Am. Soc. Inform. Sci. Technol. **60**, 443–454 (2009)
17. Fosmire, M.: Ways that engineers use design information. In: Integrating Information into the Engineering Design Process, pp. 35–43. Purdue University Press (2014)
18. Hertzum, M., Pejtersen, A.M.: The information-seeking practices of engineers: searching for documents as well as for people. Inf. Process. Manag. **36**, 761–778 (2000)

19. Jacob, M.J., Grabner, M. (eds.): The Studio Reader: On the Space of Artists. School of the Art Institute of Chicago: University of Chicago Press, Chicago (2010)
20. Willett, R.: Making, makers, and makerspaces: a discourse analysis of professional journal articles and blog posts about makerspaces in public libraries. Libr. Q. **86**, 313–329 (2016)
21. Fosmire, M.: Information literacy and lifelong learning. In: Integrating Information into the Engineering Design Process, pp. 22–34. Purdue University Press (2014)
22. Brinkman, S.: Census of Art Information Professionals: Preliminary Report of Findings. ARLIS/NA (2017)
23. Winston, M.D.: Academic science and engineering librarians: a research study of demographics, educational backgrounds, and professional activities. Sci. Technol. Libr. **19**, 3–24 (2000)
24. Petraits, E.: Assessing the impact of library instruction on studio-based research: developing a qualitative model. Art Libr. J. **42**, 80–85 (2017)
25. Garcia, L., Peterson, A.: Who invited the librarian? Studio critiques as a site of information literacy education. Art Libr. J. **42**, 73–79 (2017)

Information Literacy Quest. In Search of Graduate Employability

Vjeran Bušelić[1(✉)] and Mihaela Banek Zorica[2]

[1] Zagreb University of Applied Sciences, Zagreb, Croatia
vbuselic@tvz.hr
[2] University of Zagreb, Zagreb, Croatia
mbanek@ffzg.hr

Abstract. Employability of young graduates is one among top goals of the European Union. As today's graduates are expected to work in information-demanding environments, information literacy should play much more important role in linking educational, academic, and economic sectors. Improved communication requires better understanding of the discourse in the employability arena. The results of a bibliometric analysis of scientific discourse of graduate employability domain conducted from the perspective of IL is a valuable starting point for all information professionals interested in appropriate topics on a youth employment agenda.

Keywords: Employability · Graduate employability · Information literacy Bibliometric analysis

1 Introduction

Employability of young graduates is one among top goals of the European Union. EU benchmarks for 2020 for education set the share of employed graduates (aged 20–34 with at least upper secondary education attainment and having left education 1–3 years ago) should be at least 82%[1]. Croatia with little over 60%[2] is par with Greece and Italy in a group of laggers, so this should be a top priority on the Croatian Government Agenda as well. As today's graduates are expected to work in information-demanding environments, information literacy, that originally was promoted during the very earliest identification of information overload as a way to strengthen individual capacities for the use of information tools and thus efficiently address information problems, is certainly an area to look toward for help if not for a complete solution.

Past Croatian research of these issues [1–3] and the latest in this area - [4] clearly points out a lack of dialogue between employers and higher education and suggests mutual understanding as a way to improve. In order to better understand the employers' side, their issues and discourse, a wide bibliometric research of employability domain

---

[1] European Commission, Education & Training Strategic framework 2020 Overview, http://ec.europa.eu/education/policy/strategic-framework_en, retrieved 29/05/2017.

[2] Eurostat, Statistics Explained, http://ec.europa.eu/eurostat/statistics-explained/index.php/File:Employment_rates_of_recent_graduates_(aged_20%E2%80%9334)_not_in_education_and_training,_2005_and_2015_(%C2%B9)_(%25).png, retrieved 29/05/2017.

S. Kurbanoğlu et al. (Eds.): ECIL 2017, CCIS 810, pp. 98–108, 2018.
https://doi.org/10.1007/978-3-319-74334-9_11

is underway in University of Zagreb. Some findings and a road map for information professionals willing to dig into employability domain is presented in this paper.

2 Methodology

For analyzing graduate employability from the perspective of information literacy, publications from Web of Science Core Collection citation database were extracted. Searches were carried out by using the terms "information literacy", "employability", and "graduate". All metadata about authors, journals, and keywords were unified and standardized to enable reliable evaluations. The CiteSpace visualization tool was used for cluster, co-citation, publication portfolio, and keyword analysis [5]. Co-citation and keyword networks were identified and analyzed out of selected employability publications. Most work was done by the end of 2016 and specific details of each analysis are presented in the findings and discussion.

3 Findings and Discussion

Since the goal of this analysis was to investigate correlation between graduate employability and information literacy and identify differences in information science approaches to graduate employability, bibliometric analysis was carried out in two steps. In the first step, the domain of information literacy, as the one information professionals are living in, was compared to one dealing with employability. After that, co-citation and keyword analysis of employability domain was performed with the specific quest to identify the most influential authors and publications dealing with topics of graduate employability.

3.1 Information Literacy and Employability Analysis

Information Literacy and (Graduate) Employability. For this analysis, publications from the WoS Core Collection (WoS CC) citation database were extracted on December 22, 2016 using the terms "information literacy" and "employability". There were 2,975 publications using the term "information literacy" and 2,819 using "employability".

Only 15 publications, which is less than 0.5%, were using both terms – "information literacy" AND "employability".

- It started in 2008 and 2009 with just 1 article, then 0 and then in 2011, there were 2, then 3, 2, 3, 2, 1 in following years. With h-index of 2, only 11 citations in total, avg. of 0.73 citations per item.
- Out of 15 publications, there were 8 conference proceedings, 6 articles and 4 book chapters (all from Chandos Information Professional Series) and 1 editorial.
- Only one of those 15 papers is using exact term "graduate employability". It is a conference proceeding from INTED, Valencia, 2012, with no citation impact.
- The most cited publication (4) is Introduction in the book "Information Literacy Infiltrating the agenda, Challenging minds" by Pope A. and Walton G. from 2011.

- John Crawford is the author with most publications (4) in 2011–13. Two of them are co-authored with Christine Irving. They have only 3 citations (2 + 1 + 0 + 0) in total.

Information literacy is literary not very well connected with employability. There are very few publications connecting information literacy with employability - fewer then 0.5%, and those publications are of very low impact.

Graduates and Information Literacy/Employability. When starting analysis with the term "graduate" and then refining the search with "information literacy" or "employability" many more publications were selected, but with a similar low percentage, still indicating poor interest. However, there are almost five time (4.8) more publications connecting graduate(s) with employability than with information literacy. The search of WoS CC was carried out on January 29, 2017 by using the term "graduate", and then refining the search with "information literacy" and "employability" for the second analysis set. A total of 61,662 publications were found using the term "graduate". Out of those only 156 (0.25%) were found under "information literacy" and 755 (1.22%) dealt with "employability".

The last ten years were very productive. Almost 80% of information literacy publications and almost 95% of those dealing with employability were published in this period (Fig. 1).

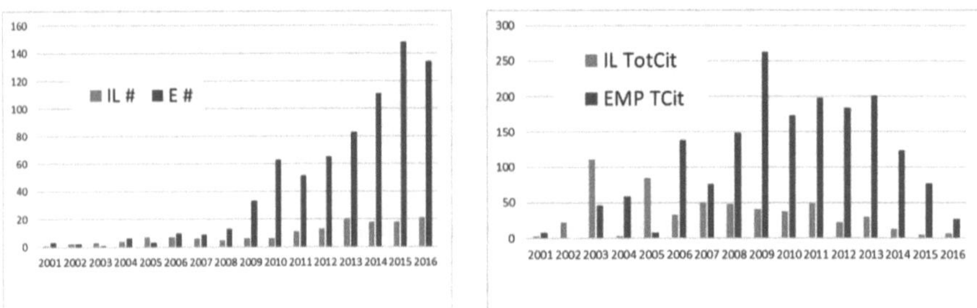

Fig. 1. Comparison of total number and citation count of selected publications in last 15 years

After the economic crisis in 2008, graduate employability publications rose in volume and citation numbers contrary to ones dealing with information literacy. The later did not gaining much scientific attention, even lowering their total citation count.

Information Literacy and Employability Domains. In order to understand differences in domain publishing about information literacy or employability, bibliometric analysis of those two domains were carried out. For this analysis, the previously extracted datasets with 2,975 "information literacy" publications and 2,819 "employability" ones were used.

Information Literacy. The total citation number of selected 2,975 items was 11.211 (a mean of 3.8 citations per item) with an h-index of 40.

- Out of all publications 59.8% were articles, 27.5% were conference proceedings, followed by book reviews (8.4%) and book chapters (7.9%).
- The top cited authors were Lloyd A. (33), Pinto M. (32), Julien H. (27), Irving C. (18), Crawford J. (18), and Bruce C. (18).
- The top 10 cited publications were in the range of 184-80 citations per publication, 9/10 were from ISLS research area.
- Most publications were from Charles Stuart U. (40), Univ. Granada (39), Nanyang Tech. Univ. (39), Queensland Univ. (33), Univ. Illinois (31), and Univ. Sheffield (30).
- 37.5% publications were from USA, 7.2% from England, 6.2 from Australia followed by PR China (5.2%), and Canada (4.6%).
- 63.7% were from the ISLS research area, 21.1% from Education, and 20.7% were from Computer Science.

Employability. The total citation number of selected 2,819 items was 15,668 (a mean 5.6 citations per item) with an h-index of 54.

- Almost two-thirds (63.3%) of all publications were articles, 30.9% were conference proceedings, followed by book chapters (3.2%).
- Top cited authors were De Cuyper N. (29), De Witte H. (23), Lindsay C. (22), Van der Heijden B.I.J.M. (20), and Jackson D. (14).
- Top 10 cited publications were in the range of 330-107 citations per publication, 6/10 were from Health/Nursing (medical) research areas.
- Most publications were from KU Leven (47), Univ. of London (38), Maastricht Univ. (35), Edinburgh Napier Univ. (31), Radboud Univ. Nijmegen (29), and Univ. of Valencia (27).
- 17.1% publications were from England, 15.3% from the USA, 6.8% from Australia followed by Spain (6.2%) and PR China (5.8%).
- 34.3% were from Education, 19.9% from Business Economics and 13.9% from Psychology research areas.

The main difference of these two domains was primarily seen through narrow and compact research area of information literacy publications. Out of total 49 areas, the top three (ISLS, EDU and CS) covering 85% of all publications, versus 68% of top three with almost double the spread – a total of 91 research areas for employability.

The other difference is authors' primary origin. IL authors were primary from the USA (37.5%), where employability is of much brother interest. After England (17.1%), the USA, Australia, Spain, and China were in top10. The Netherlands, Scotland, Germany, Malaysia, and Canada had still respectable percentages of 5.5 down to 3.3%.

Journal Analysis. The breath of the employability domain was mostly visible in publication source analysis. As there were significant differences in the number of journals in LIS space covered by WoS and Scopus [6], for this analysis both were used. From the WoS CC database publications were extracted on December 22, 2016. There were 2,975 publications using the term "information literacy" and 2,819 using "employability". Publications from Scopus database were extracted on December 24, 2016 and there were 5,028 publications using the term "information literacy" and 5,102 using "employability".

Journal analysis confirmed the broad extent of the employability domain as there were 3,163 journals with "employability publications" and only 170 with "information literacy" content. Journals from the domain of employability were ranked according to total number of citations (Tc) from both citation databases, taking in consideration the total number of publications (#) as well (Table 1).

Table 1. Most important journals with employability related content

Tc	Source	S #	S Tc	WoS #	WoS Tc	H-ind	SJR
1	Journal of Vocational Behavior	29	1597	33	1465	101	1,741
2	Education and Training	58	663	14	6	30	0,532
3	Journal of Education and Work	44	384	1	0	18	0,575
4	Urban Studies	12	374	14	291	104	1,567
5	Higher Education Research and Development	17	318	17	213	22	0,936

Analysis of top 20 according to the Journal Subject area and Category shows that most belonged to more than one area (avg. 2.5), and predominantly were from Business, Management and Accounting - Organizational Behavior and Human Resource Management (12), Social Sciences - Education (9), and Psychology - Applied Psychology (6) categories. The narrowness or uniformity of the IL journal domain is confirmed as 17 out top 20 journals were from Social Sciences - Library and Information Sciences domain.

3.2 Employability Domain Analysis

To understand employability, domain co-citation cluster analysis with visualization was performed with a special goal to identify time, most influential authors, and publications, especially ones dealing with graduate employability. All the analysis was carried on with the CiteSpace visualization tool; over 2,703 "employability" publications from WoS CC were extracted on November 28, 2016. Due to the high volume of data for analysis and the large number of publications with citation (1,263) the recommended (default) pruning method was applied. For each time slice (1 year) only the top 50 cited articles were selected.

Period of Active Citation Bursts (1999–2016). When selecting all 36 years, a co-cited network with 1,334 nodes and 3,069 links were formed. It is large and complex data network and, as burst analysis [7] indicated, 84 citation bursts in 36 years, but none before 1999. That was a criteria to shorten the analysis time span without losing confidence from 36 to the last 17 years.

That is why a time period of 1999–2016 was used. By selecting the top 50 references per year, a co-cited network with 662 nodes (cited references) and 1,680 links (co-cited references) was formed. A document co-citation network was built on the methods pioneered by Henry Small [8] that extended from a single-slide equivalent to a multiple-slice network analysis, i.e., a time series of networks in order to detect critical transitions over time more effectively[3].

The top cited employability publications/authors were Fugate [9] with 73 citations, Van der Heijde and Van der Heijden [10] with 70, McQuaid [11] 69 and Rothwell [12] with 68, followed by De Cuyper N., Berntson E., Bridgstock R. and McArdle S. All top 10 cited publications were from the period, 2004–2009.

Table 2. Top bursts (Source: CiteSpace)

Reference	Year	Strength	Begin	End	1999 - 2016
FUGATE M, J VOCAT BEHAV	2004	19,7639	2007	2012	
VAN DER HEIJDE CM, HUM RES MNG	2006	11,7355	2011	2014	
BRIDGSTOCK R, HI EDU RES DEV	2009	10,6264	2014	2016	
MCQUAID RW, URBAN STUD	2005	9,4248	2005	2010	
FORRIER A, INT J HUM RES MNG	2003	7,8477	2006	2011	

As visible from Table 2 most top cited publications were the ones with most intensity in propagation (burst), but it is worth noticing that in most cases it took 3–5 years prior to gain the appropriate attention and acceptance from the scientific community.

Co-citation Cluster Analysis. As a collection of cited documents represent symbols of their scientific ideas, co-citation studies are among the most common used methods in quantitative studies of a field or selected area of interest. In this analysis a multiple-perspective co-citation analysis tool CiteSpace was used with basic scientific principles as explained in [13].

One hundred and ninety one clusters were built. A modularity of 0.8229 and a mean Silouette of 0.3215 confirmed that the homogeneity of these clusters was low. It was because there 179 of them had fewer than 10 nodes/publications (avg. 1.78). They were too small and excluded from any analysis. Out of the remaining 12 clusters with 52% of all nodes, only top 5 (249 nodes, 38%) were discussed (Table 3).

Automated cluster labeling by a tf * idf weighting algorithm [14] extracting terms from publication titles generated a very good interpretation of the topics of the top clusters. The largest cluster #0 with the highest average citation score was the central employability cluster. It contained 8 out of top 10 cited publications. McQuaid [11] and Bridgstock [15] were not included in this cluster as they were leading/forming clusters #1 and #3.

Cluster #1, second largest by number of nodes, was of no interest for this analysis because it dealt with issues of long-term unemployment, a topic that was contrary to our interests. Publications in this cluster were not influential either, with a total citation average of 4.5, the lowest of all analyzed clusters.

[3] Chen C. (2014), The CiteSpace manual v 1.05., pg. 48.

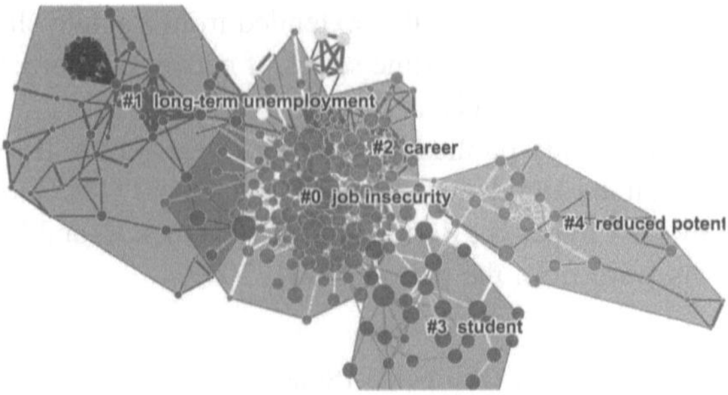

Fig. 2. Top 5 employability clusters (Source: CiteSpace)

Table 3. Top 5 cluster parameters with automated cluster labeling top terms (Source: CiteSpace)

Cluster #	No. of nodes	Avg. TCit	Shilutete	Median Year	Top terms tf * idf weighting algorithm
0	87	16.5	0.786	2007	(26.26) job insecurity; (24.94) temporary employment; (24.94) mediation; (23.77) role; (23.38) employee
1	64	4.5	0.979	2000	(23.14) long-term unemployment; (22.71) buoyant labour market; (22.71) employability gap; (19.96) labour market policy; (19.63) unemployment
2	40	9.6	0.822	2004	(21) career; (16.41) boundaryless career; (15.98) role; (15.89) employability; (14.89) evaluating employability
3	31	16.0	0.935	2010	(17.61) student; (17.44) graduate; (16.44) learning; (15.47) business; (14.77) employability
4	27	6.25	0.924	2003	(17.43) reduced potential; (17.43) innovation; (17.43) examination; (17.43) ict cluster; (16.82) graduate

Graduate Employability Clusters. *Career Cluster (2004).* Cluster #2 was identified as the career cluster, discussing transition from ideas of traditional careers and a "job for life" aspect, concerning the competencies and adaptability of the workforce, towards the "boundaryless career" concept. As seen from Fig. 2, there was a high level of overlapping with the central cluster. Top cited authors were van Dam [16] with 28 citations and a burst parameter of 7,56, Hall [17], 22, 5,90 and Sullivan [18], 21, 3,08.

Discourse used in this cluster was about career approach of employability rather than specific graduate employability. Issues and top terms were "employability" (55), "employees" (30), "career" (24), "relationship" (21), and "job" (17). The terms "study", "research", and "result" were also high on the list but those terms were metadata about publications, not research content. Among 1,092 selected terms, "students" were not mentioned at all, "learning and education" mentioned once, "employment" mentioned twice, "graduates" mentioned three times. Thus, it was a very career oriented discourse and was not specific to graduate employability.

Reduced Potential Cluster (2003). The top term analysis of this cluster with 940 extracted were terms mentioning "graduates" (30), "students" (28), "employability" (26), "university" (18) and "skills" (17) revealed this was a first cluster of our interest. The median year of its publications was 2003. The top cited authors in this cluster were Brown [19] with 23 citations and a burst parameter of 6,17, Knight and Yorke [20] with 17, 4,55, and Barrie with [21], 21, 3,08.

Student Cluster (2010). A second cluster dealing with graduate employability was both up-to date and contained many influential authors and publications lead by the very influential work of Bridgstock [15], 46, 10,63, Rothwell [22], 28, 4,12 and Tomlinson [23], 27, 4,25. In top 10 authors with respectable citations (23–18) were Archer W., Pegg A., Cranmer S., Lowden K., Hinchliffe GW, Boden R. and Mason G. The most active person citing to the cluster was [24].

A term analysis of this cluster with 1527 extracted terms confirmed this was the most important cluster mentioning "students" (62), "graduates" (58), "employability" (46), "skills" (34), and "education" (22) - twice as much as the one from 2003.

Keyword Analysis. Keyword analysis was performed on the entire employability dataset in order to understand importance (by rank, frequency, time of appearance) of graduate employability and related terms and to understand their mutual relationships. Four hundred and nine keywords were identified with 1632 links/relations. After "employability" (#1, 809, 1999) and "employment" (#2, 216, 2000) the most frequent keywords were general ones – "higher education" (#3, 190, 2002) and "education" (#5, 149, 1999), followed by "competence" (#9, 103, 2008), "skill" (#10, 96, 2004), and "student" (#11, 90, 2008). High on a list were also "career" (#15, 67, 2002), "graduate" (#18, 61, 2010), "university" (#19, 60, 2009), and "employability skill" (#25, 49, 2005). At the end, was the explicit term, "graduate employability" (#57, 30, 2008).

Graduate Employability. The term "graduate employability" just started accumulating notice. It was connected to "graduate employment," "human capital," "management," "student," and "skills." Out of 30 publications, the most cited were Boden and Nedeva [25], Wilton [26], and Gedye et al. [27]. Authors with the greatest number of publications on "graduate employability" were Denise Jackson and Samo Pavlin with three articles each (Fig. 3).

Skills and Competences. They terms were traditionally present in employability discourse and better connected with the other terms. Ninety six appearances of the term "skills" were connected with "student," "employability," "experience," "identity," "curriculum," "competence," "university," "perception," "education," "labor market," "satisfaction," "graduate," "training," "boundaryless career," "career," "knowledge," "learning," "higher education," "adult development," "industry," "USA," "geography,"

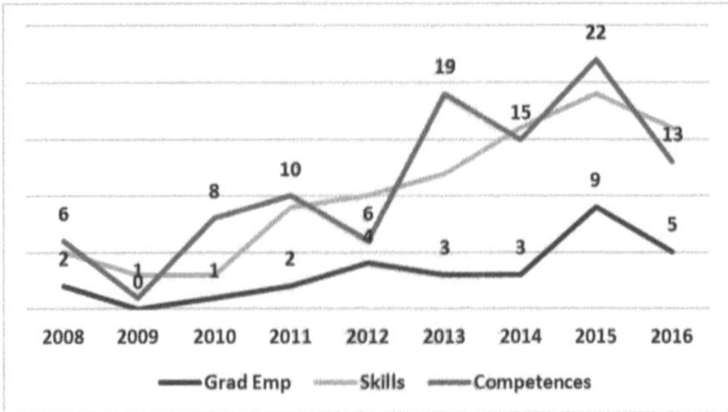

Fig. 3. Graduate employability, skills and competences – history of appearances

"Europe," "learning," "graduate employability," "work", and "employment." "Competence" was found as a keyword 103 times and it was related to "higher education," "validation," "student," "skill," "employability," "system," "opportunity," "performance," "knowledge," "boundaryless career," "graduate," "success," "education", and teamwork (Fig. 4).

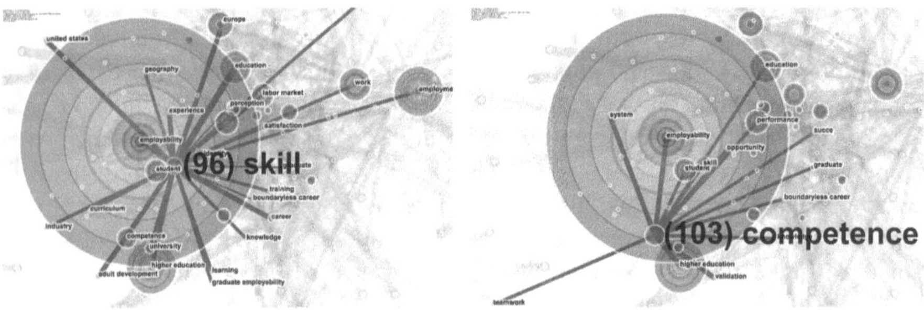

Fig. 4. Skills and competences – relation to other keywords (Source: CiteSpace)

4 Conclusion

Although information literacy is present in the education landscape and successfully includes wider aspects of lifelong learning such as preschool and elementary school education and workplace and health literacy as well, we still lack research in transitional areas such as employability linking education and work.

In research conducted in Croatia [4], the weak nature of the communication between the educational, academic, and economic sectors has been confirmed. Part of the problem lies in terminological mismatches such is the lack of understanding of the role and significance of information literacy on the one side and the terms, skills, and competencies that are required on the other.

The results of a bibliometric analysis of scientific discourse of graduate employability domain conducted from the perspective of IL is a valuable starting point for all information professionals interested in appropriate topics on the youth employment agenda.

References

1. Banek Zorica, M., Spiranec, S.: Assesment of the information competences in the study programs at the University of Zagreb, March 2014
2. Banek Zorica, M., Spiranec, S., Ogrizek Biskupic, I.: What is the employers stand on information literacy – researching employers on expected generic outcomes of their future employees. In: Kurbanoğlu, S., Špiranec, S., Grassian, E., Mizrachi, D., Catts, R. (eds.) ECIL 2014. CCIS, vol. 492, pp. 673–682. Springer, Cham (2014). https://doi.org/10.1007/978-3-319-14136-7_70
3. Bušelić, V., Kovačević, Ž.: High education study program model towards employability. On a way to understand employer's requirements for generic competences. In: Central European Conference on Information and Intelligent Systems (2016)
4. Banek Zorica, M., Špiranec, S., Bušelić, V.: Are we speaking the same language? Croatian employers' IL competency requirements for prospective employees. In: Kurbanoğlu, S., Boustany, J., Špiranec, S., Grassian, E., Mizrachi, D., Roy, L., Çakmak, T. (eds.) ECIL 2016. CCIS, vol. 676, pp. 99–108. Springer, Cham (2016). https://doi.org/10.1007/978-3-319-52162-6_10
5. Chen, C.: Searching for intellectual turning points: progressive knowledge domain visualization. Proc. Natl. Acad. Sci. U.S.A. **101**(Suppl. 1), 5303–5310 (2004)
6. Abrizah, A., Zainab, A.N., Kiran, K., Raj, R.G.: LIS journals scientific impact and subject categorization: a comparison between Web of Science and Scopus. Scientometrics **94**(2), 721–740 (2013)
7. Kleinberg, J.: Bursty and hierarchical structure in streams. In: Proceedings of the 8th ACM SIGKDD International Conference on Knowledge Discovery and Data Mining (2002)
8. Small, H.: Co-citation in the scientific literature: a new measure of the relationship between two documents. J. Am. Soc. Inf. Sci. **24**(4), 265–269 (1973)
9. Fugate, M., Kinicki, A.J., Ashforth, B.E.: Employability: a psycho-social construct, its dimensions, and applications. J. Vocat. Behav. **65**(1), 14–38 (2004)
10. Van der Heijde, C.M., Van der Heijden, B.I.J.M.: A competence-based and multidimensional operationalization of measurement of employability. Hum. Resour. Manag. **45**(3), 449–476 (2006)
11. Lindsay, C., McQuaid, R.W., Lindsay, C.: The concept of employability. Urban Stud. **42** (April), 197–219 (2005)
12. Rothwell, A., Arnold, J.: Self-perceived employability: development and validation of a scale. Pers. Rev. **36**(1), 23–41 (2007)
13. Chen, C., Ibekwe-SanJuan, F., Hou, J.: The structure and dynamics of cocitation clusters: a multiple-perspective cocitation analysis. J. Am. Soc. Inf. Sci. Technol. **61**(7), 1386–1409 (2010)
14. Salton, G., Wong, A., Yang, C.S.: A vector space model for automatic indexing. Commun. ACM **18**(11), 613–620 (1975)
15. Bridgstock, R.: The graduate attributes we've overlooked: enhancing graduate employability through career management skills. High. Educ. Res. Dev. **28**(1), 31–44 (2009)

16. van Dam, K.: Antecedents and consequences of employability orientation. Eur. J. Work Organ. Psychol. **13**(1), 29–51 (2004)
17. Hall, D.T.: The protean career: a quarter-century journey. J. Vocat. Behav. **65**(1), 1–13 (2004)
18. Sullivan, S.E., Arthur, M.B.: The evolution of the boundaryless career concept: examining physical and psychological mobility. J. Vocat. Behav. **69**(1), 19–29 (2006)
19. Brown, P., Hesketh, A., Williams, S.: The Mismanagement of Talent: Employability and Jobs in the Knowledge Economy. Oxford University Press, Oxford (2004)
20. Knight, P.T., Yorke, M.: Learning, curriculum and employability in higher education. In: Learning, Curriculum and Employability in Higher Education, pp. 1–241 (2004)
21. Barrie, S.C.: Understanding what we mean by the generic attributes of graduates. High. Educ. **51**(2), 215–241 (2006)
22. Rothwell, A., Herbert, I., Rothwell, F.: Self-perceived employability: construction and initial validation of a scale for university students. J. Vocat. Behav. **73**(1), 1–12 (2008)
23. Tomlinson, M.: 'The degree is not enough': students' perceptions of the role of higher education credentials for graduate work and employability. Br. J. Sociol. Educ. **29**(1), 49–61 (2008)
24. Jackson, D.: Business graduate employability – where are we going wrong? High. Educ. Res. Dev. **32**(5), 776–790 (2013)
25. Boden, R., Nedeva, M.: Employing discourse: universities and graduate 'employability'. J. Educ. Policy **25**(1), 37–54 (2010)
26. Wilton, N.: Do employability skills really matter in the UK graduate labour market? The case of business and management graduates. Work Employ. Soc. **25**(1), 85–100 (2011)
27. Gedye, S., Fender, E., Chalkley, B.: Students' undergraduate expectations and post-graduation experiences of the value of a degree. J. Geogr. High. Educ. **28**(3), 381–396 (2004)

Information Literacy (IL) in the Academic Context: Is There a Gap Between Employability Competencies and Student Information Literacy Skills?

Jean-Philippe Accart[1,2](✉)

[1] Ecole hôtelière de Lausanne, Lausanne, Switzerland
jean-philippe.accart@ehl.ch
[2] HES-SO, University of Applied Sciences Western Switzerland, Delémont, Switzerland

Abstract. This paper first presents the information literacy competencies in both public universities and institutions of applied learning in Switzerland. Based on the project "Information Literacy at Swiss Universities" launched in 2011, it shows how the Swiss Standards of Information Literacy were designed and applied. These six standards have since been supplemented by related learning objectives. In the second part, the author will answer the question formulated in the title in order to understand if those standards reflect the reality of the job market and the workplace. Two case studies, one at the University of Geneva and the other at Ecole hôtelière de Lausanne in Switzerland (where the author is presently working) are given. In conclusion, he analyses the reasons behind such a gap and proposes several solutions to bridge the gap. Solutions do exist and information professionals hold the key to unlocking information literacy.

Keywords: Information literacy · Standards · Student · University Case studies · University of Geneva · Ecole hoteliere de Lausanne Switzerland

1 Methodology and Overall Approach

This article is a personal reflection, a theoretical approach to the concept of information literacy as applied in Switzerland, and an illustration of the way in which information literacy is applied in both a university setting (at the University of Geneva) and an academic setting (at the Ecole hôtelière de Lausanne) including their strengths and weaknesses.

The methodology consists in comparing and contrasting theory and practice to reach a general conclusion that could be useful for other areas. The result is a set of recommendations regarding what could be done to facilitate students' access to the job market. However, contradictions do exist and it is critical to identify and understand them.

At once a partial study of the literature on a few specific points of interest, the article is also an observation of two distinct academic settings. Observations are very much first person because the author was and is in direct contact with these groups of students and professors, amid a daily environment that sheds light on the value of these six standards

S. Kurbanoğlu et al. (Eds.): ECIL 2017, CCIS 810, pp. 109–118, 2018.
https://doi.org/10.1007/978-3-319-74334-9_12

and how they are actually applied. Alongside relevant stakeholders (usually the faculty), the author lays down a group of criteria and discusses how to go about implementing them. Based on these observations, conclusions are drawn and findings reported.

2 The Creation of the Six Swiss Standards of Information Literacy

A now widely accepted definition of information literacy, formulated by UNESCO, is: "Information Literacy is the capacity of people to recognize their information needs, locate and evaluate the quality of information, store and retrieve information, make effective and ethical use of information and apply information to create and communicate knowledge." [1].

This definition by UNESCO and the standards of the Australian and New Zealand Information Literacy Framework of the Australian and New Zealand Institute for Information Literacy ANZIL [2] and the internationally established Information Literacy Competency Standards for Higher Education of the American Association of College and Research Libraries [3] formed the basis for the development of the Swiss Standards of Information Literacy. A reformulation of the standards was necessary as these had to be adapted to the cultural content of the Swiss target audience. In so doing it was ensured that the contents of all three linguistic cultural regions (German, French, Italian) were fulfilled.

The six Swiss standards in Information Literacy[1] are listed below and each one followed by a short explanation:

1. *The information literate person recognises the* ***need for information*** *and determines the nature and extent of the information needed.*
   The information literate person:
   - defines and articulates the information need referring to a defined purpose;
   - understands the purpose, scope, and appropriateness of a variety of information sources;
   - selects and uses diverse sources of information to inform decisions
2. *The information literate person* ***finds*** *needed information effectively and efficiently.*
   The information literate person:
   - selects efficient methods or tools for finding information
   - constructs and implements effective search strategies
   - obtains information using appropriate methods
3. *The information literate person critically* ***evaluates*** *information and the information seeking process.*
   The information literate person:
   - defines and applies criteria for evaluating information

[1] See: http://www.informationskompetenz.ch/en/about-il/swiss-standards.

- assesses the usefulness of the information obtained
- re-evaluates the nature and extent of the information need
- reflects on the information seeking process and revises search strategies as necessary

4. *The information literate person* ***manages and shares*** *information collected or generated.*
   The information literate person:
   - records information selected and its sources
   - organises, classifies, and stores information using appropriate methods
   - shares information with others
   - keeps up to date with information sources, information technologies, and investigative methods
5. *The information literate person* ***applies*** *prior and new information to accomplish a specific purpose.*
   The information literate person:
   - applies new and prior information to the creation of new knowledge or a particular product
   - communicates the new knowledge or product effectively to others
   - revises the creation and communication process of knowledge or product
6. *The information literate person* ***acts*** *as a responsible member of the information society*
   The information literate person:
   - acknowledges cultural, ethical, and socioeconomic issues related to the use of information
   - conforms with conventions and etiquette related to the use of information
   - legally obtains, stores, and disseminates all kinds of information (Fig. 1).

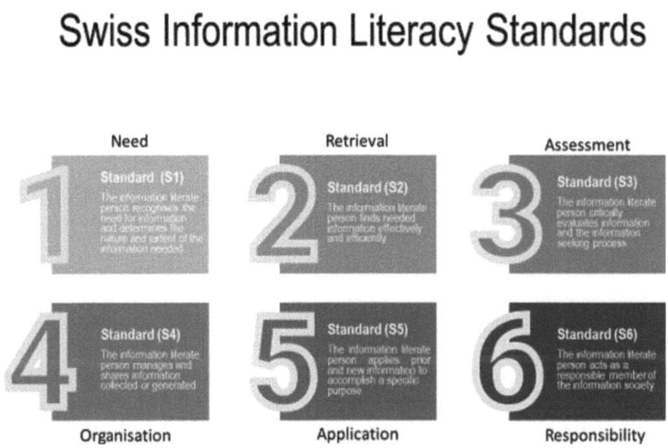

Fig. 1. The 6 Swiss Information Literacy Standards (Source: Christine Walker, Information Specialist at EHL)

These six standards outline the steps required to make sense of information today. The individual plays a central role in our information society. He or she participates concretely in sharing the information that has been gathered and is autonomous in his or her research and decision-making.

These standards can apply to any individual and all stages of his or her personal and professional development. In the two case studies presented today, two student populations – one in a university and scientific setting and the other in an academic and applied sciences setting - will be compared and contrasted as pertains to these six criteria.

3 1st Case Study: Being a Student at the Faculty of Sciences of the University of Geneva

Enrolment at the Faculty of Science of the University of Geneva (UNIGE) was 2,500 students in 2016[2] - including the doctoral programme, and the school recruits professors who are well known in their field, some are even Nobel Prize laureates (maths, physics, for example). UNIGE is ranked 53rd in the Shanghai ranking, which is 5 spots higher than last year. It is second, behind the Ecole polytechnique fédérale de Zürich (EPFZ), among Switzerland's top schools, which are known as Hautes Ecoles Suisses.

UNIGE's library of sciences[3] dates back, in its current configuration, to the 1980s but underwent substantial renovation in 2013 thanks to the generosity of various backers[4]. It covers physics, mathematics, biology and pharmaceutical sciences, among other fields of study, yet some topics are, for historical reasons, housed off-site in and around Geneva (e.g., the life sciences, information technology and astronomy). A few libraries in certain fields have existed since the 18th century. In terms of information literacy, UNIGE's library of sciences is one of the pioneers. Two information officers are in charge of organising classes and regular sessions across all levels of the various academic programmes. Within the library, a specific room is used exclusively for training purposes where demonstrations and classes can be held. Attendance is mandatory, and students must complete a number of exercises online, for which they receive academic credit pursuant to the Bologna Process.

3.1 Applying Information Literacy Criteria at the University of Geneva (UNIGE)

A "training workgroup" was created at the highest ranks of UNIGE in the aim of developing the school's informational culture and:

[2] According to official data from the University of Geneva: https://www.unige.ch/stat/fr/statistiques/chiffresetudiants/.

[3] http://www.unige.ch/biblio/fr/infos/sites/sciences/.

[4] The Schmidheiny Foundation funded these renovations: http://www.fondation-schmidheiny.ch/lafondation.html.

- Creating content for training courses on information skills;
- Leading workshops and courses to improve information literacy;
- Organising training sessions for librarians who are themselves in charge of training students

As part of this workgroup, a cross-discipline "information culture" group at UNIGE's library[5] was created and now manages several projects:

- The autonomous training programme *InfoTrack*[6];
- The organisation of various activities across all campuses;

In 2015, 266 training sessions were held totalling 322 h involving 4,585 participants. The Faculty of Science has the highest participation rates: 103 sessions, 143 h and 1,610 participants. Some 44% of these activities involved the bachelor programme and they were integrated into the university curriculums, 16% at the Master's degree level, 4% doctoral, 5% ongoing education and 31% for other levels.

3.2 Observing UNIGE Students' Information Uptake

For the 4,585 students participating in the information literacy programmes, their knowledge and their understanding of information is substantial, although no studies have been conducted on the Department of Scientific Information, which oversees the university's library[7]. These programmes teach students about plagiarism and how to use software related to bibliographies and referencing. With these skills in hand, UNIGE students are among the Switzerland's best trained in information literacy and with regards to the six previously mentioned criteria.

4 2nd Case Study: Studying at the Ecole hôtelière de Lausanne (EHL)

Enrolment EHL stands at 2,745 students from 114 countries including 58% women[8]. EHL is an international private school specialised in applied education and will be celebrating its 125th anniversary in 2018. It trains, primarily, the future mangers of the hospitality management industry and features a bachelor, master and EMBA programme. It is ranked number one in the world for hospitality management, according to specific criteria[9]. Most of the applicants tend to be in secondary school but sometimes have work experience. In any case, they must express an interest in working in the hospitality field if they want to be accepted. They tend to be so-called Millenials, and

---

[5] "The Library of the UNIGE" is the entity that covers eight specialised libraries under the authority of the Department of Scientific Information (DIS). It contains multiple sites throughout Geneva.

[6] https://infotrack.unige.ch/.

[7] http://www.unige.ch/dis/.

[8] http://www.ehl.edu/fr/a-propos/centre-analyses-institutionnelles.

[9] These criteria are set by the US organisation NEASC (New England Association of Schools Accreditation): https://www.neasc.org/.

the average age of first-year EHL students is 21. Social aspects and networking are strongly encouraged with a plethora of sporting, cultural and musical events being held every year along with parties and other festivities. This component is important at EHL and is very popular – understandably – with students. Classes are taught in English or French, and a wide range of information is only available on the Intranet. Consequently, students are connected all the time to the web and social networks. Projects include market analyses and cross-country comparisons requiring data and statistics. Group work, oral presentations, role playing and quizzes form an integral part of the learning experience and are used successfully to bolster the management theory students learn in classroom settings. This kind of teaching method is specific to schools focused on the applied sciences and is quite different from a university setting where more emphasis is put on theory (Fig. 2).

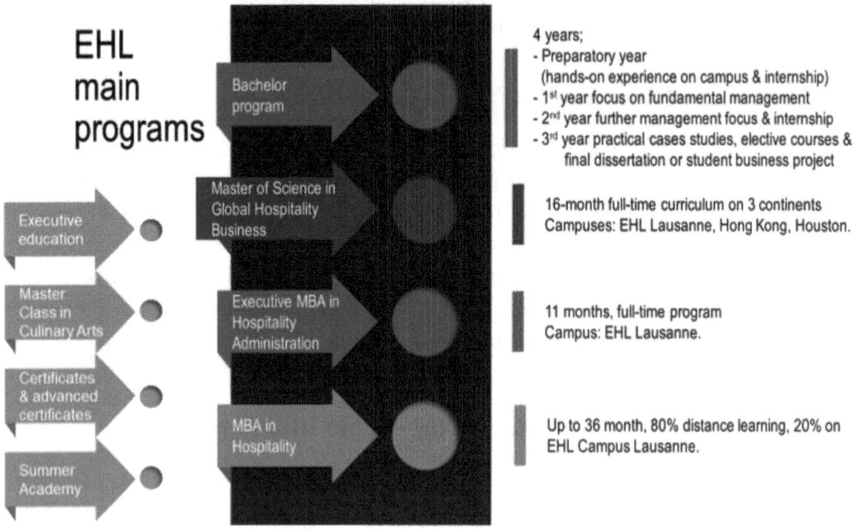

Fig. 2. The main programmes at Ecole hoteliere de Lausanne. (Source: Christine Walker, Information Specialist at EHL)

The EHL library, created 25 years ago, is a traditional academic library, with 35,000 print materials, and a member of the HES network of libraries[10] and NEBIS[11], network of Swiss libraries. Digital resources are no less plentiful with access to over 200 databases and several thousand e-books and online reviews. All resources are available free of charge. Hotel management, finance, business administration, but also gastronomy, tourism and travel, architecture and design or languages are just some of the topics covered. The library easily mee ts information needs (half of EHL students have a library card) but it is not used to the maximum of its capacities for several reasons: insufficient work space, a small support team consisting of five staff members

[10] https://www.hes-so.ch/fr/bibliotheques-hes-so-187.html.

[11] http://www.nebis.ch.

with just one documentation specialist who handles information literacy questions among other tasks, the faculty's sometimes flagging interest in the library. Information culture is not one of the school's strong suits (it has others) and could be improved. For the majority of students, print books or a bricks-and-mortar library are a foreign concept. EHL students are thoroughly digital and sometimes lack general cultural knowledge (although some improve while at EHL). This adds to disparities between the various nationalities represented on-campus in terms of educational and cultural background. The EHL library works to bridge the information culture gap by:

- Welcoming new students during Intro-week or when they return from their internships (the "Welcome Back" period) with a general presentation of the digital resources available to them at the school.
- Organising occasional training sessions on preparing a literature review, parsing sources of information, researching hotel-related data, etc.
- Providing supplemental coaching services for certain classes or projects.
- Holding an annual workshop for new faculty members and academic assistants;
- Providing an 'Introduction to Databases' workshop for BOSC 3 students (3rd year students) and individual marketing projects for MGH students (Master of Science in Global Hospitality Business)
- Publishing demographic and economic data research tips for EMBA students;
- Organising 'Digital Tuesdays', i.e., weekly office hours for all students (Fig. 3).

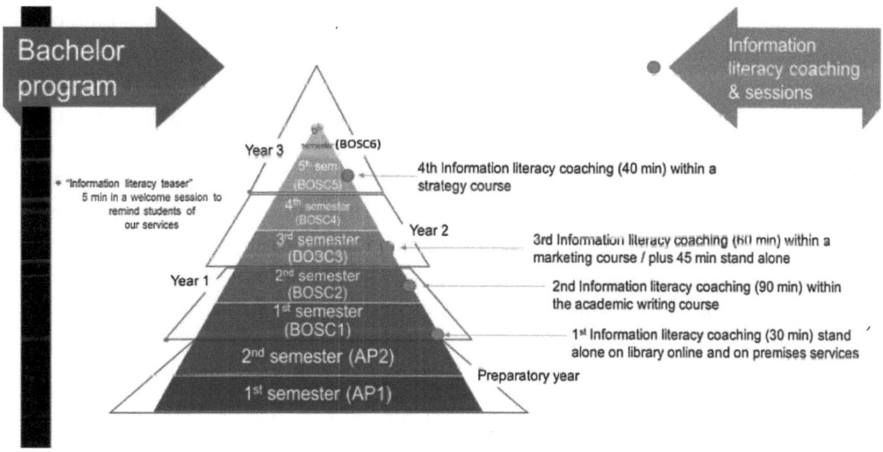

Fig. 3. The bachelor program and information literacy. (Source: Christine Walker, Information Officer at EHL)

4.1 Observing EHL Students' Information Uptake

EHL has an "information training" strategy, which remains largely dormant, geared to students at different stages of their academic experience. Although it is a priority of the dean's office, it is mainly reliant on the prerogative of certain professors who might be willing to clear time for it during their course. The strategy is not implemented school-wide, despite the sizeable financial resources invested in access to databases. One of the knock-on effects is that the six Swiss criteria described above are not applied. Information literacy is therefore uneven across all levels of studies. Many students only become interested in information searches and data research in the final year of their studies. And yet, it does not seem to affect their exam grades, perhaps because more emphasis is put on group versus individual knowledge. Yearlong group work partially compensates for the non-application of the Swiss criteria.

5 What Is to Make of These Observations?

Between these two settings there is a world of difference…and therein lies a certain contradiction. On the Swiss and global job market, EHL graduates are very likely, given EHL's reputation, to find a job in the area of business or hospitality management – despite not really have much in the way of informational literacy skills. EHL alumni generally need these skills at some point in their career and, in response, the library has set up a specific, yet somewhat informal programme whereby they can access the databases. This is a fee-based programme so obviously not all alumni use it. The EHL library thus meets this kind of information need from alumni.

The students of the University of Geneva have real information literacy skills that will serve them well throughout their career. The majority of alumni, however, do not go on to be managers or businessmen, unlike their EHL counterparts. Therefore, the question that arises is the following: are information literacy skills really a prerequisite for professional success? How important are they really? How much value do they have in employers' eyes as the hiring process unfolds?

Let's consider what goes on in a company. An employee's information literacy skills are not recognized in his or her contract and are not mentioned as such in the want ads (we're not talking about job ads for librarians or documentation specialists, obviously). This oversight or misunderstanding on the part of decision-makers leads to an inefficient use of time when it comes to information management. Recent studies show that employees spend over eight hours per week looking for information they need[12]. The waste of time and energy is considerable without the right skills.

[12] Cited in: https://fr.linkedin.com/pulse/combien-de-temps-perdu-%C3%A0-la-recherche-dinformation-c%C3%A9dric-frickert, published 15 May 2017 by Cédric Frickert: "According to a report published by McKinsey, employees spend 1.8 h per day, 9.3 h per week, on average, searching for and gathering information." "Source: Time Searching for Information". Other sources:

• 19.8% of the time of the activity – the equivalent of one day per week of work – is wasted by employees by employees in search of information to do their jobs efficiently; 1/5 of business time is lost looking for information. "Source: Interact".

• A recent webinar provided an interesting statistic by Outsell: the time spent by a manager in search of information has increased 28% since 2002. "Source: IHS Knowledge Collections".

• A new poll revealed that workers needed eight searches to find the right document and information. "Source: SearchYourCloud".

• IDC data shows that "workers spend around 2.5 h every day, or about 30% of the work day, looking for information... 60% of corporate managers estimated that time constraints and incompetence in searching for information prevented their employees from finding the info they need. "Source: Information: The Lifeblood of the Enterprise".

Information literacy skills enable individuals to improve their capacities and general skills and make them more adept at handling related tasks at work, home and socially. This observation is corroborated at the university level where, once the skills have been acquired, they remain an integral part of an individual's skill set, making it easier for them to seek out information, usually without the help of the library (Fig. 4).

Fig. 4. EHL website: EHL key figures: http://www.ehl.edu/fr/a-propos/centre analyses-institutionnelles

EHL students usually acquire these skills but there is room for improvement. For some, the problem is a question of age, education or cultural background while for others the problem is attention deficit disorder (ADHD)[13], a seemingly-ubiquitous affliction nowadays. Students are constantly interrupted by their cell phones or social networks, making it very difficult to concentrate. The idea of reading a book or even a long document is now a feat of almost Herculean proportions.

There are solutions, in both cases, to make up for these shortcomings, including psychological and organisational ones.

6 Conclusion: A Few Recommendations for Both Cases

Multiple causes, multiple solutions: One recommendation is clearly to develop information and digital literacy skills among young students or working adults as early as possible, skills which can be reinforced while at university, regardless of the

[13] http://www.douglas.qc.ca/info/trouble-deficit-attention.

curriculum or type of academic programme. A common information literacy baseline should be established and relevant exams should be required at various stages of students' academic careers.

Being able to search for and critically evaluate all types of information on one's own should be a basic principle of any learning society. The principle of autonomy and access to information in general should be universal across all levels of schooling and in the workplace.

The tools used to seek out information are highly advanced, including search engines that use algorithms and artificial intelligence. These solutions offer good results and are opening up new unexplored areas and allowing us to tap into big data. Data curation and data monitoring are increasingly sophisticated and could help companies, institutions and their employees to access the information they need in less time.

For all the questions aroused briefly mentioned in this article, information professionals have a key role to play in providing support and assistance, and that is the note on which I would like to finish. This role can be played at different levels:

- Using technology and the content creation: we can also leverage technology (creating tutorials and digital services) to create content (either face-to-face or online courses and exercises);
- Supporting and teaching students how to use information: while our pedagogical skills need to improve markedly so we can enable service users to become as independent as possible, and help students search for and understand information.

I firmly believe that informational professionals are capable of rising to this challenge.

Acknowledgments. Translation: Andrew Brenner, Ecole hôtelière de Lausanne (Switzerland). Graphics: Christine Walker, Information Specialist, Ecole hôtelière de Lausanne (Switzerland).

References

1. Catts, R., Lau, J.: Towards Information Literacy Indicators. UNESCO, Paris (2008). http://www.uis.unesco.org/Library/Documents/wp08_InfoLit_en.pdf
2. Bundy, A.: Australian and New Zealand Information Literacy Framework. Australian and New Zealand Institute for Information Literacy (ANZIIL), Adelaide (2004)
3. Association of College and Research Libraries (ACRL): Information Literacy Competency Standards for Higher Education. Association of College and Research Libraries, Chicago (2000)

Professional Practice: Using Case Studies in Information Literacy Instruction Towards Career Readiness

Britt Foster(✉)

California State University, Fresno, USA
brfoster@csufresno.edu

Abstract. The potential of case-based learning, or the use of case studies for information literacy instruction is explored within the context of information literacy for workplace readiness. Taking a constructivist approach, students were asked to use their professional experience to analyze a case study for information needs and resources, and then create a recommendation based on this evaluation. Student learning was assessed through similar reflective prompts applied to their own wine business plan. Using qualitative content analysis, reflections demonstrated students were able to use diverse information sources to apply to complex information needs, mirroring the complex information environment of the modern workplace. Results indicate case-based learning has value for information literacy for career readiness.

Keywords: Information literacy · Career readiness · Constructivism Case study · Reflection

1 Introduction

Case-based learning (CBL), the use of situational scenarios drawn from or inspired by professional or field practice, has been used in multiple disciplines as an instructional design practice, including in library, information, and archival sciences [1–9]. However, there have been only a few studies examining the value of CBL for teaching information literacy skills: for using cases relevant to students' discipline or field of practice to ground information skills within that discipline, and to support the transfer of information skills beyond academic work and into life skills.

This study explores the potential for CBL in information literacy instruction, when one goal of the information literacy instruction is career readiness and supporting the development of information skills for professional practice. Grounded in a constructivist approach to teaching and learning, the instruction session was designed to engage students' professional experience as well as their current knowledge of information resources, and build upon this experience and knowledge to support the development of higher-level information skills. By "practicing" synthesis, evaluation, reflection, and creation of new knowledge in a disciplinary context—all skills identified in the *Framework for Information Literacy for Higher Education* [10]—students model the actions they will perform in the complex information environment of the modern workplace.

S. Kurbanoğlu et al. (Eds.): ECIL 2017, CCIS 810, pp. 119–127, 2018.
https://doi.org/10.1007/978-3-319-74334-9_13

2 Background

2.1 Case-Based Learning

CBL has a connection to libraries in its beginnings. In Garvin's article [11] on the origin and history of CBL at Harvard University, he tells the story of Christopher Columbus Langdell, a student at Harvard Law School who worked in the library and voraciously read and researched court cases. When appointed as a professor and eventually dean of Harvard Law School in the late 1800s, Langdell shifted the instructional approach away from lecture and memorization, and towards close analysis of actual cases, creating opinions based on the application of important central professional ideas [11]. Langdell encouraged students to use the library to find and compare cases to develop their practice, and to master core disciplinary concepts [11].

In this regard, there are parallels to threshold concepts, the theoretical background to the Association of College and Research Libraries' (ACRL) *Framework for Information Literacy* [10], the current document that ACRL uses to inform the way that information literacy is taught in higher education. Threshold concepts require a pedagogical shift away from instruction in library procedures and database "how-tos," and towards the major *concepts* that underpin how we think and talk about information [12]. These can be likened to implicit professional practices—the concepts that practitioners inherently know but cannot necessarily describe to new learners in that discipline [13]. When working across disciplines, as librarians often do through teaching information skills tailored to their students' area of study, CBL may provide the opportunity to support students towards "crossing the threshold" in both information literacy and disciplinary practice [13].

2.2 Constructivism and the Pedagogy of Case-Based Learning

The use of CBL as a constructivist teaching practice centers on its active learning components, learner-centered approach, and integrative instructional design [14, 15]. Constructivist instructors give primacy to the experience of their learner as the foundation of knowledge, and then use instructional experiences, particularly active experiences, to support the creation of new knowledge [16]. Learning experiences are also designed not as discrete units, but connected parts of a larger system: this means that instruction doesn't emphasize skills or applications useful for only a single assignment, but instead, concepts and practices that can be transferred to new situations [15, 17]. CBL serves as a vehicle for constructivist instructional design in providing opportunities for students to bring their experiences into the classroom and apply them to a new scenario through problem-solving, which leads to an expansion of the applicability of these concepts and the creation of new understanding.

Considering the need to apply learning and connect new understanding to existing knowledge structures in order to move beyond memorization and into learning, Nkhoma and Lam [18] hypothesized that using case studies for problem solving would allow students to make those connections that lead to higher-order learning. They found through testing this hypothesis that CBL was an effective method for scaffolding students' existing experience into deeper, more complex knowledge [18]. Scaffolding, in which students are supported through increasingly difficult work with increasing levels of independence, is an important aspect of constructivist and case-based learning [19–21]. In addition, by assigning learners increased responsibility for their learning, students are able to develop greater autonomy in using information either as a group or by themselves, a situation which more closely mirrors the workplace than the traditional librarian-led information literacy lecture/demonstration [22].

Very different from this lecture-based format, CBL is an active learning style which requires students to read, analyze, and problem-solve, potentially in a group learning system. Compared to other active learning styles, Kulak and Newton found that students engaged in CBL performed better on final exams, and demonstrated deeper levels of learning [20]. As with other styles of active learning, CBL is a challenge in that it requires additional preparation on the part of the instructor, and a willingness to be a flexible facilitator in the classroom [21]. For the librarian instructor teaching in a one-shot format, however, this facilitator role may allow the librarian to connect with students on a deeper level, engaging them in conversation and questioning dialog, providing insight and a relationship to learners that can be difficult for a visiting librarian to establish in their brief interactions with students in the classroom [23].

2.3 Case-Based Learning in Information Literacy

While studies examining CBL in information literacy instruction are limited, findings have supported the value of CBL for information instruction. When teaching in the one-shot or single session format, it can be difficult to connect with students and provide a learner-centered experience. Carder [22] states that the prime benefit of case-based, problem-based learning (CBPBL) is providing students with an opportunity to apply information literacy skills in context, making those information skills relevant and engaging to learners, as the instruction session is aligned with their personal and professional interests. Spackman and Camacho [24, 25] found increased attendee satisfaction for case-based instruction sessions compared to IL sessions that did not use cases, and received positive feedback from students and professors about the use of cases in the instruction session.

This connection to professional practice is one of high value to students, and to departments who are concerned with graduates' employability. Using CBL to sync with both the required information skills for a fast-paced business environment and a common instructional design method in MBA programs, Cullen [23] found the use of cases supported students in developing higher-level information skills such as synthesis and evidence-based decision making. Cunningham and Anderson [26] also found that use of case studies encouraged the application of complex information skills, such as "the ability to analyze data, recognize issues, identify and evaluate alternatives, and formulate a conclusion," all in an "unstructured" (p. 5) situation that mirrors real-life, professional work.

What each of these instruction studies demonstrate is the interest of instruction librarians, faculty partners, and students in educational exercises that can be applied to later professional work. By providing situations in which learners can model future practices, information literacy instruction in the CBL model can achieve three things: (1) demonstrate the relevancy of the library to their learners; (2) establish the value of information literacy instruction to students and faculty partners; and (3) support the development of higher-level information skills.

3 Method

The information literacy instruction session using CBL was delivered in ENOL 170: Wine Business, an upper-division undergraduate course for Enology (winemaking) majors, in the Department of Viticulture and Enology at California State University, Fresno. This information literacy module is a segment of the information literacy curriculum for the department: students enrolled in this major receive instruction and are assessed in increasingly complex information literacy concepts as they proceed through their major courses within the department. Each of these instruction sessions and assessment assignments were co-designed by librarians and Enology faculty, and generated by an assessment from the winemaking industry that students needed additional education in oral and written communication, critical thinking, and information literacy skills. The ENOL 170: Wine Business instruction session and assignment are considered a "capstone" experience, or an advanced course in the series that requires students to synthesize existing resources into a new information product, such as a report or presentation, and to reflect on their own information practices and identify areas for improvement.

The ENOL 170 session lasted 50 min. Students were divided into groups of three, four, or five, and told that their group was to roleplay as a consultant group for a wine business. Groups were provided a copy of a wine business case study, as well as questions for a guided group discussion. The case study, *Case Study in Wine Production* [27], describes a wine company who upgrades their water and energy systems in partnership with environmental and energy organizations to reduce resource waste and utility costs. The guided discussion questions asked students to use the case study to identify information needs, resources, and next steps:

1. Where in the case study are there areas of information need?
2. What information resources would you use for these information needs?
3. Based on these findings, what recommendation would you make to the winery for next steps?

Students read and discussed the case study and questions in their individual groups. The class then came together for a whole-group discussion, where students shared their recommendations. Throughout this process, the librarian instructor assumed the role of facilitator, circulating the room, responding to group discussions and recommendations, asking challenging questions, and encouraging students to expand their thoughts and provide reasoning for their decisions.

As their final project for this class, students were assigned a wine business plan. A complex, semester-long assignment, students were required to use many sources, such as a business, marketing, and government resources, in order to complete the plan. To assess information literacy skills, students were given an additional assignment of completing several reflective prompts, to be turned in with the business plan, and then evaluated by the librarian for evidence of information literacy skills. Prompts followed the general flow of the case study discussion questions, asking students to identify information needs, resources used in answering that need, and reflecting on next steps. Prompts provided were:

1. Identify and describe a section of your business plan where you demonstrate application of information in making a decision.
2. What was your information need?
3. What information resources did you use?
4. Say your business has implemented your business plan, and the plan doesn't get the results you hoped for. What would you do next? What information would you need and use?

Responses were collected (n = 13), and analyzed through qualitative content analysis, with close readings used to code for major and minor themes organized into areas of Information Needs, Information Sources, and Actions.

4 Results

4.1 Information Needs

Student reflections focused on information needs appropriate to creating a wine business plan. Major themes identified in Needs were wine consumer demographics and preferences, and information about wine production equipment, specifically types of equipment and equipment costs. Other information needs mentioned frequently were size of production, or how much wine to produce, the cost of buying wine or grapes to make wine, and the cost and determining best location for winery or vineyard land.

4.2 Information Sources

Sources selected to address these information needs were varied, and consisted of relevant and authoritative sources for the stated needs. Major sources of information consulted were government publications, such as the United States Census and United States Department of Agriculture extension documents. Trade publications for the wine industry were a second major source of information. Additional sources consulted with multiple frequencies included experts or peers with relevant experience, and various general internet sources, such as vineyard real estate websites, or winery classifieds pages.

4.3 Actions

Once Needs and Sources were identified, Actions in response to a business challenge were described. Major themes in actions to be taken were to identify the problem within the business plan. Additional actions described included identifying new sources of information, and adjusting practices based on new information gathered.

4.4 Analysis of Results

Throughout their reflections, students demonstrated the ability to identify complex information needs: when describing these needs, phrases such as "multiple factors" and "not straight forward" were used. Consumer demographics and purchasing patterns, a major information need stated in the reflections, required information on age, population, ethnicity, and income, and how these interact with wine purchasing and wine drinking preferences.

Recognizing the complexity of their information needs, students also demonstrated the ability to use a diverse set of information sources that aligned with each facet of their information need. Several reflections described the process of using government sources to define and describe a particular population, such as Millennials or Latinos, and then using wine trade publications to find information on these populations' wine drinking habits. Beyond diverse sources, students also described a variety of methods used to locate information, such as emailing vendors, or interviewing experts in a particular wine grape varietal or winegrowing region. In the ACRL *Framework* [10], the ability to use "various search strategies, depending on the sources, scope, and context of the information need" is defined as an expert behavior—behavior that would be appropriate and effective in the workplace.

It is interesting to consider the prevalence of free or low-cost sources of information used by students for their business plans. Only one student mentioned using journals as a source for their information need. Given the emphasis on scholarly, peer-reviewed articles in earlier courses in this information literacy curriculum, the omission of this source of information is significant. However, the information needs defined by students were generally best addressed by the sources chosen. These sources are also sources that will be easily accessible to students after graduation, once they enter the wine industry and no longer have access to the databases and journal subscriptions provided by the university. Within the context of this assignment, and in line with the learning goals of this instruction session, the use of non-scholarly articles is absolutely appropriate. An area for future research would be an exploration of the motivations and reasoning of students in selecting these sources.

Similarly, peer information, including information from other grape growers or winemakers, was heavily represented in student reflections. In a review of the economic impact of the United States agricultural extension program, Birkhaeuser and Evenson [28] point out that peer-to-peer information is one of the main sources of agricultural information for farmers. As an accessible form of information based in social interaction, students engaging in information seeking from other professionals is a strong indicator that they have begun to adopt the information practices of their field, and suggests that by identifying this information behavior through reflection, CBL can be used to further develop this practice. How students determine which peer to contact, how they obtain that information, and how that information is evaluated would be an additional area of research related to student professional practice and information behavior.

4.5 Limitations

Focused on a single, discipline-specific instruction session with a small sample size at a single university, the results from this study are not generalizable. Without any kind of pre-assessment, it is also difficult to conclude that the evidence of learning in the assessment reflections are a direct result of the case-based design of the information literacy instruction session. Future research and instructional practice may include a pre-instruction reflection to assess student growth, learning, and change as a result of case-based instruction.

5 Discussion and Conclusion

5.1 Discussion

As a result of implementing CBL into information literacy instructional design, the instructor identified several benefits.

Perhaps the most valuable is providing students the opportunity to draw parallels between observed professional information practices, such as that observed during internships, or as described in case studies, and their own professional experience. Observed experiences may be more advanced, and more entrenched in implicit professional practices: what are the motivations behind these practices, and are they efficient? By providing the case study as a static example of these practices, and using guided questions to support student analysis and reflection of professional information practices, students demonstrated that they could then apply this same reflective model to their own "case," as they researched and created a complex business plan. Through further research, it may be determined that students then translate this skill to the workplace for improved information seeking and use practices.

For instructors interested in a constructivist approach to teaching, this CBL exercise also provided the benefit of opening a dialog between students and the instructor during the discussion portion of the class. Students were engaged with the case and eager to compare and share their experiences with the instructor which (1) demonstrated the relevancy of information literacy instruction to the faculty partner, and (2) gave the instructor insight into information scenarios and practices within the discipline, which can be used to improve understanding of information literacy outcomes and future instructional design.

5.2 Conclusion

The results of implementing a CBL-approach to the information literacy instruction session in a wine business class demonstrated the potential of CBL for information literacy instruction. Using a constructivist approach, in which students could apply their previous professional experience and use of disciplinary information resources to a real-life situation, allowed students to complete an advanced analysis of (1) determining information needs; (2) selecting multiple information resources to address these needs; and (3) reflecting upon a change in information-seeking and information-use behaviors in response to new, complex scenarios.

As learners and higher education programs emphasize education not just for academic success, but for life-long learning, instructional design that takes into account professional practice is of great value. By incorporating CBL into their instructional toolkit, librarians and faculty can together support student development of higher-level, real-world information literacy skills.

References

1. Blouin Jr., F.X.: The relevance of the case method to archival education and training. Am. Arch. **41**, 37–44 (1978)
2. Galvin, T.J.: Teaching reference through the case method. J. Ed. Librariansh. **16**, 232–235 (1966)
3. Galvin, T.J.: The Case Method in Library Education and in-Service Training. Scarecrow Press, Metuchen (1973)
4. Harper, J.S., Lamb, S.W., Buffington, J.R.: Effective use of case studies in the MIS capstone course through semi-formal collaborative teaching. J. Inf. Syst. Educ. **19**, 411–418 (2008)
5. Wagner, C.: Teaching information systems management via action memos. J. Inf. Syst. Educ. **15**, 5–7 (2004)
6. Wu, H., et al.: Teaching information security with workflow technology – a case study approach. J. Inf. Syst. Educ. **25**, 201–210 (2014)
7. Wu, H., Xiaohong, Y., Li, Y.: Supporting case-based learning in information security with web-based technology. J. Inf. Syst. Educ. **24**, 31–40 (2013)
8. Moniz, J.R.J.: The use of case studies in library administration courses and work. Libr. Leaders. Manag. **23**, 108–112 (2009)
9. Dow, M.J., et al.: Case-based learning as pedagogy for teaching information ethics based on the dervin sense-making methodology. J. Educ. Inf. Sci. **56**, 141–157 (2015)
10. Association of College and Research Libraries, Framework for Information Literacy for Higher Education (2016). http://www.ala.org/acrl/standards/ilframework
11. Garvin, D.A.: Making the case: professional education for the world of practice. Harvard Mag. (2003). https://harvardmagazine.com/2003/09/making-the-case-html
12. Hofer, A.R., Brunetti, K., Townsend, L.: A threshold concepts approach to the standards revision. Commun. Inf. Lit. **7**, 108–113 (2013)
13. Townsend, L., Brunetti, K., Hofer, A.R.: Threshold concepts and information literacy. Portal Libr. Acad. **11**, 853–869 (2011)
14. Hartfield, P.J.: Reinforcing constructivist teaching in advanced level biochemistry through the introduction of case-based learning activities. J. Learn. Des. **3**, 20–31 (2010)
15. Brooks, J.G., Brooks, M.G.: In Search of Understanding: the Case for Constructivist Classrooms. Merril Education/Prentice Hall, Upper Saddle River, New Jersey (1999)
16. Grassian, E.S., Kaplowitz, J.R.: Information Literacy Instruction: Theory and Practice. Schuman Publishers Inc., New York (2009)
17. Johnson, W.G.: The application of learning theory to information literacy. Coll. Undergrad. Libr. **14**, 103–120 (2007)
18. Nkhoma, M.Z., et al.: Unpacking the revised bloom's taxonomy: developing case-based learning activities. Educ. Train. **59**, 250–264 (2017)
19. Wood, D., Bruner, J.S., Ross, G.: The role of tutoring in problem solving. J. Child Psychol. Psychiatry **17**, 89–100 (1976)
20. Kulak, V., Newton, G.: An investigation of the pedagogical impact of using case-based learning in a undergraduate biochemistry course. Int. J. High. Educ. **4**, 13–24 (2015)

21. McFarlane, D.A.: Guidelines for using case studies in the teaching-learning process. Coll. Q. **18** (2015)
22. Carder, L., Willingham, P., Bibb, D.: Case-based, problem-based learning: information literacy for the real world. Res. Strat. **18**, 181–190 (2001)
23. Cullen, A.: Using the case method to introduce information skill development in the MBA curriculum. J. Bus. Finan. Librar. **18**, 208–232 (2013)
24. Spackman, A., Camacho, L.: Integrated, embedded, and case-based: selling library instruction to the business school. In: Sietz, B. (ed.) Librarian as Architect: Planning, Building, and Renewing: 36th National LOEX Library Instruction Conference Proceedings, pp. 73–78. LOEX Press, Ypsilanti, Michigan (2010)
25. Spackman, A., Camacho, L.: Rendering information literacy relevant: a case-based pedagogy. J. Acad. Librar. **35**, 548–554 (2009)
26. Cunningham, N.A., Anderson, S.C.: A bridge to FARS and information literacy for accounting undergraduates. J. Bus. Finan. Librar. **10**, 3–16 (2005)
27. Garn, J.: Case Study in Wine Production. Wine Bus. Mon. 40–42 (2007)
28. Birkhaeuser, D., Evenson, R.E.: The economic impact of agricultural extension: a review. Econ. Dev. Cult. Change **39**, 607 (1991)

The Role of Sense of Coherence in Knowledge Sharing

Jannica Heinström(✉) and Farhan Ahmad

Information Studies, Åbo Akademi University, Turku, Finland
{jannica.heinstrom, farhan.ahmad}@abo.fi

Abstract. Knowledge sharing is a key competence in a work context. In this study we address knowledge sharing from an individual difference perspective, exploring whether an employee's sense of coherence influences knowledge sharing. Additionally, we investigate whether dedication to diversified learning mediates the relationship between Sense of Coherence (SOC) and knowledge sharing. A survey was conducted in a multinational organization. We received 403 responses. Partial least square structural equation modeling was used to analyze the data. The results show that SOC significantly influences the respondents' self-perceived knowledge sharing activities. However, the relationship is partially mediated by dedication to diversified learning. Results suggest that an employee's knowledge sharing partly arise from personal characteristics. How much is shared in actuality, however, depends on motivation and contextual factors.

Keywords: Sense of coherence · Information mastering · Information literacy Knowledge sharing

1 Introduction

Workplaces are collaborative spaces where success depends on mutual collaboration between employees. Particularly, exchange of task-related information and personal know-how is critical not only for developing new products and services, but also for execution of daily tasks at work. This act of mutual collaboration is known as knowledge sharing. More specifically, it refers to exchange of advice and expertise to help others carry out daily tasks and solve problems [1]. A plethora of research has been done on knowledge sharing, and its importance for organizational as well as individual performance is well established [2–4]. Although an essential activity at the workplace, knowledge sharing is a very complex behavior. An extensive review on knowledge sharing literature by Wang and Noe [5] shows that knowledge sharing is not only influenced by organizational factors such as culture, management support, reward system, diversity and social networks but also by individual characteristics such as self-efficacy, personality, trust and an individual's beliefs about knowledge ownership.

Personal characteristics make individuals predisposed to certain work behaviors and attitudes. Therefore, organizational strategies aimed at enhancing knowledge sharing between employees need to take into account individual characteristics. Previous research has explored the relationship between individuals' personal

S. Kurbanoğlu et al. (Eds.): ECIL 2017, CCIS 810, pp. 128–136, 2018.
https://doi.org/10.1007/978-3-319-74334-9_14

characteristics and knowledge sharing behavior [e.g. 6, 7]. However, sense of coherence, a salutogenic disposition, has not attracted any attention so far, even though research in psychology has clearly established its influence in working life [8].

In our study we, therefore, wanted to investigate the connection between sense of coherence (SOC) and knowledge sharing.

2 Literature Review

SOC describes a resilience to stress, which explains why some people cope well with stressors in situations that others find overwhelming. People with a high SOC find that their environment makes sense, and trust that they have the needed resources to cope with challenging situations [9, 10]. This mindset is also manifested in a work environment [Antonovsky 11, cited from Feldt 12]. Those with a high SOC in general cope better with stress at the workplace and experience less stress symptoms [13, 14]. A strong SOC can moderate feelings of pressure and reactions to work conditions [14].

A person's SOC is also linked to perceptions of the social environment at work. Those with a high SOC generally perceive the organizational climate favorably and believe in their own influence [15, 16]. They feel that they get help from co-workers, can collaborate with them openly and constructively, and perceived the work environment as open with solidarity and free-flowing communication [16, 17]. Those with a low SOC, again, experience more psychological distress and often believe that they lack competence [16]. A study of work-related health resources based on focus-group interviews categorized responses according to the SOC components of comprehensibility, manageability and meaningfulness through deductive content analysis. Comprehensibility was related to reflections with fellow co-workers and participation in discussion with colleagues. Comprehensibility was also linked to open-mindedness such as open discussions, listening and sharing information. Manageability included informal discussions with colleagues which was contrived as important for a positive workplace experience, and responsibility in the form of bringing problems to the attention of others. Meaningfulness at work included the social climate at the workplace and reinforcement from others [18]. Although the study did not focus on knowledge sharing per se, it does highlight the important role of social relations and the sense of influence in work places. Arguably, in workplaces where this is fostered, and for people for whom this comes naturally as part of their SOC, information sharing is more frequent.

A person's SOC is continuously influenced by life experiences and can thereby be influenced by experiences at work [14]. Antonovsky [11 cited from 15] suggested that a sense of influence at work may increase people's general notion of meaningfulness in life. Moreover, he argues that agency at work, such as taking part in collective decision-making, increases the general sense of manageability in life, while the perception of the work environment and one's role within it as making sense increases general comprehensibility. The connection between influence at work and a general sense of meaningfulness in life has, however, not been verified empirically [15]. Despite studies arguing that the work environment influences SOC [15, 19], most studies argue for a relationship the other way around, pointing to studies referring to SOC as a stable concept [17, 20].

A key factor in SOC is the individual's ability to handle stress. Previous research has found that stress and time pressure are significant barriers to knowledge sharing. Time pressure could, in turn, stem from role conflict and role ambiguity. Unclear job expectations cause preoccupation leading in turn to lack of time and resulting in less knowledge sharing [21]. Emotional factors such as burnout have also been found to diminish knowledge sharing [22]. Zhang et al. [22] found that burnout symptoms are stronger predictors of knowledge sharing than personality traits which suggest that interventions aiming at reducing stress and enhancing the workplace climate are more effective in promoting knowledge sharing than focusing only on individual factors. It seems likely that it is not only objective time pressure that influences knowledge sharing behavior but also a person's individual way of experiencing and handling stress. Our aim was to investigate this connection by linking a person's sense of coherence to his/her self-reported knowledge sharing behavior.

3 Methodology

The data for this study was collected from a multinational organization that operates in the energy industry with operation in 70 countries around the world. The survey was distributed through the organization's intranet resulting in 403 responses.

We included three constructs in the study; knowledge sharing, sense of coherence and dedication to diversified learning. All these constructs were measured with multiple items on a seven point Likert scale. Knowledge sharing was measured using a 5-item scale adapted from Yang and Chen [23]. This instrument measures self-reported knowledge sharing, that is, how active in knowledge sharing activities a person experience him/herself to be. Sense of Coherence was measured using a standardized scale developed by Antonovsky [24]. As SOC is a general individual characteristic, manifested in multiple contexts, we also wanted to include a more specific measure of attitude towards work in our study. We, therefore, developed a scale for measuring motivation for workplace learning with a specific focus on openness and dedication to learning in a workplace context. The scale consisted of items that were part of a larger measure of meta-gaming [for conceptual background see [25]].

We named this scale *dedication to diversified learning*. Dedication to diversified learning consisted of four statements: *It is important to critically reflect on what is important for success in my work, and to be open to new approaches, I am learning a lot of things on my free time that are useful for success in my work, I am communicating with different types of people [e.g. with diverse positions, nationalities, characters, education, social class] in my work,* and *It is important for success in my work to be knowledgeable about the people who are not from my own department [e.g. customers, colleagues, competitors].*

3.1 Data Analysis

Partial least square structural equation modeling [PLS-SEM] was used to analyze the data and to explore both direct and indirect influence of SOC on knowledge sharing. Partial least square structural equation modeling is a second-generation statistical technique that allows the measurement of reliability and validity of constructs and estimation of the relationship between them simultaneously [26]. Moreover, this technique is useful for theoretical development, small sample size and non-normally distributed data [27].

3.2 Results

In PLS modeling, the reflective measurement model is assessed before the structural model. Consequently, the measurement model is analyzed for reliability [i.e., the construct measures indicator reliability and internal consistency reliability] and validity [i.e., convergent validity and discriminant validity] [28].

3.3 Measurement Model

Table 1 provides the measurement statistics. According to our analysis, loadings of all reflective indicators is above the threshold value of 0.60 [29]. Moreover, Cronbach alpha and internal consistency values are also above the recommended value of 0.70 [ibid]. Both of these tests show that the measurement model meets the satisfactory reliability.

Table 1. Measurement statistics of construct scales based on reflective indicators

Construct/indicators	Mean	Standard deviation	Indicator loadings	Composite reliability	Cronbach α	AVE
Knowledge sharing	5.71	0.89		0.85	0.79	0.54
KS1			0.72			
KS2			0.81			
KS3			0.70			
KS4			0.81			
Sense of coherence	5.08	0.83		0.82	0.85	0.49
SOC 1			0.67			
SOC 2			0.71			
SOC 3			0.72			
SOC 4			0.79			
SOC 5			0.72			
SOC 6			0.63			
SOC 7			0.66			
SOC 8			0.70			
Dedication to diversified learning	5.60	0.93		0.88	0.71	0.54
DDL 1			0.72			
DDL 2			0.83			
DDL 3			0.68			
DDL 4			0.67			

Table 2. Discriminant validity of the constructs - correlations between constructs

	1	2	3
Knowledge sharing	**0.77**		
Sense of coherence	0.22	**0.70**	
Dedication to diversified learning	0.30	0.38	**0.73**

Bold numbers represent the square roots of the AVEs.

To assess the convergent validity, AVE value of each construct was calculated. As shown in Table 1, AVE value of each construct is above 0.50 [30]. The only exception is SOC that has a very close AVE value of 0.49, and therefore, should not be a matter of concern. Discriminant validity was assessed by using the Fornell and Larcker criterion [31]. According to this criterion, the average variance extracted of each construct should be higher than correlation with other constructs [32]. The results are shown in the Table 2 that confirms the discriminant validity of all constructs.

The measurement model assessment shows that all constructs are reliable and valid, and therefore, we now proceed to the structural model.

3.4 Structural Model

We conducted a step-by-step analysis of the structural model to test the effect of SOC on knowledge sharing, and mediation between them by dedication to diversified learning. First, we focused only on the relationship between SOC and knowledge sharing. Then, we introduced the mediator, dedication to diversified learning, to reassess the relationship between SOC and knowledge sharing. As suggested by Klarner et al. [28], we followed both general guidelines given, for example, by Preacher and Hayes [33] and PLS specific mediation suggestions given, for instance, by Hair et al. [34] and Helm et al. [35] for mediation analysis.

Figure 1 shows the results of step 1. As we can see the direct effect of sense of coherence on knowledge sharing in the absence of the mediator is statistically significant [$\beta = 0.23$]. It shows that SOC positively influences knowledge sharing behaviour. Whether dedication to diversified learning mediates between these two was examined in the second step. As shown in Fig. 2, after introducing the mediator, dedication to diversified learning, we find that SOC has a strong and significant effect on dedication to diversified learning, which in turn has a strong and significant relationship with knowledge sharing. The indirect effect of SOC [i.e. 0.09] via the mediator construct dedication to diversified learning is also significant [$p < 0.01$]. Although the relationship between SOC and knowledge sharing remains significant, the strength of

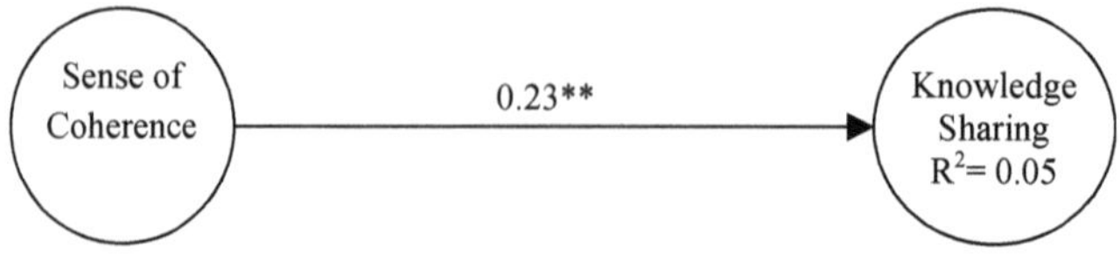

Fig. 1. Structural model without mediator Notes **$p < 0.01$, [two-sided test]

the relationship as well as the level of significance are lower than when dedication to diversified learning was not present. This means that dedication to diversified learning partially mediates the relationship between SOC and knowledge sharing. Overall, we can say that sense of coherence influences knowledge sharing directly and also indirectly through dedication to diversified learning.

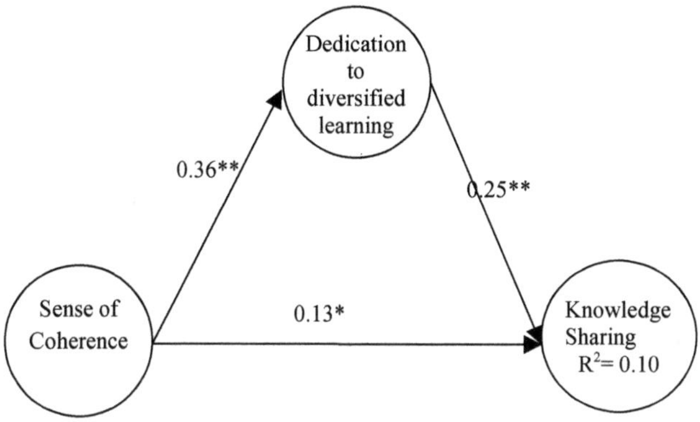

Fig. 2. Structural model with mediator Notes: * $p < 0.05$, ** $p < 0.01$, [two-sided test]

4 Discussion

Our results show that sense of coherence increases knowledge sharing, particularly if mediated by dedication and openness. This confirms that knowledge sharing is influenced by emotional aspects, as well as by cognitive and behavioral aspects [21, 22]. We thereby argue that knowledge sharing can be seen as part of information mastering in a work context.

Information mastering, as coined by Stefan Ek, is a broader concept of information literacy, which manifests in the use of information in managing daily life at work and leisure [36, 37]. Information mastering builds on the concept of sense of coherence. As Ek points out, Antonovsky [10] highlights the role of information in a person's SOC [36, 37]. The stronger your SOC is, the more connected you feel to your environment and the more equipped you are to interpret information you receive. A strong SOC also makes your communication with others flow, so that you not only understand the messages you get, but also feel heard [36, 37]. Here we can see a link to knowledge sharing, which was confirmed in our study.

The relation between dedication to diversified learning and knowledge sharing suggests that the more engaged, open and willing to learn the employee is, the more he/she shares information. Conscientiousness and openness to experience have previously been found to increase knowledge sharing [6, 38]. Sense of coherence creates a sense of being related to your environment, also in the workplace. The stronger you feel this relatedness and the more engaged and invested you are in your work, the more likely you are to share knowledge with your colleagues. This notion underlines the importance of including emotional and attitudinal elements in our understanding of workplace information literacy, as well. This in turn speaks for the relevance of the concept of information mastering [36, 37], also in a work context.

Our study does come with limitations. We used a standardized measure for knowledge sharing as we collected data by a survey. We, however, recognize several challenges in measuring knowledge sharing by self-report. Arguably there is a high risk that respondents would over-estimate their willingness to share as social norms encourage knowledge sharing. Knowledge sharing in itself is also an abstract expression, which lends itself to various interpretations. Nevertheless, the relations we found could be related to previous empirical findings [6, 38] and theoretical concepts [11] and hence appear reliable.

Our results show that a personal characteristic, such as sense of coherence, influences willingness to share information in a work context. This relation is, however, particularly strong if combined with a dedication to work and openness to learning. This motivation, in turn, may be influenced by work tasks and organizational environment. This suggests that a person's knowledge sharing partly arises from personal characteristics, but the degree in which it will be expressed depends on motivation and contextual factors.

References

1. Ahmad, F.: Knowledge sharing in a non-native language context: challenges and strategies. J. Inf. Sci. Online First, 0165551516683607 (2017)
2. Ahmad, F.: Knowledge-sharing networks: language diversity, its causes, and consequences. Knowl. Process Manag. **24**(2), 139–151 (2017)
3. Small, C.T., Sage, A.P.: Knowledge management and knowledge sharing: a review. Inf. Knowl. Syst. Manag. **5**(3), 153–169 (2005)
4. Ipe, M.: Knowledge sharing in organizations: a conceptual framework. Hum. Resour. Dev. Rev. **2**(4), 337–359 (2003)
5. Wang, S., Noe, R.A.: Knowledge sharing: a review and directions for future research. Hum. Resour. Manag. Rev. **20**(2), 115–131 (2010)
6. Cabrera, A., Collins, W.C., Salgado, J.F.: Determinants of individual engagement in knowledge sharing. Int. J. Hum. Resour. Manag. **17**(2), 245–264 (2006)
7. Jarvenpaa, S.L., Staples, D.S.: The use of collaborative electronic media for information sharing: an exploratory study of determinants. J. Strat. Inf. Syst. **9**(3), 129–154 (2000)
8. Levert, T., Lucas, M., Ortlepp, K.: Burnout in psychiatric nurses: contributions of the work environment and a sense of coherence. South Afr. J. Psychol. **30**(2), 36–43 (2000)
9. Antonovsky, A.: Health Stress and Coping. Jossey-Bass, San Francisco (1979)
10. Antonovsky, A.: Unraveling the Mystery of Health. Jossey-Bass, San Francisco (1978)
11. Antonovsky, A.: Health promoting factors at work: the sense of coherence. In: Kalimo, R., Eltatawi, M., Cooper, C. (eds.) Psychosocial Factors at Work and Their Effects on Health, pp. 153–167. World Health Organization, Geneva (1987)
12. Feldt, T.: The role of sense of coherence in well-being at work: analysis of main and moderator effects. Work Stress **11**(2), 134–147 (1997)
13. Albertsen, K., Nielsen, M.L., Borg, V.: The Danish psychosocial work environment and symptoms of stress: the main, mediating and moderating role of sense of coherence. Work Stress **15**(3), 241–253 (2001)

14. Jenny, G.J., Bauer, G.F., Vinje, H.F., Vogt, K., Torp, S.: The application of salutogenesis to work. In: Mittelmark, M.B., Sagy, S., Eriksson, M., Bauer, G.F., Pelikan, J.M., Lindström, B., Espnes, G.A. (eds.) The Handbook of Salutogenesis, pp. 197–210. Springer, Cham (2017). https://doi.org/10.1007/978-3-319-04600-6_20
15. Feldt, T., Kinnunen, U., Mauno, S.: A mediational model of sense of coherence in the work context: a one-year follow-up study. J. Organ. Behav. **21**, 461–476 (2000)
16. Kalimo, R., Vuori, J.: Work factors and health: the predictive role of pre-employment experiences. J. Occup. Psychol. **64**(2), 97–115 (1991)
17. Feldt, T., Kivimäki, M., Rantala, A., Tolvanen, A.: Sense of coherence and work characteristics: a cross-lagged structural equation model among managers. J. Occup. Organ. Psychol. **77**(3), 323–342 (2004)
18. Nilsson, P., Andersson, I.H., Ejlertsson, G., Troein, M.: Workplace health resources based on sense of coherence theory. Int. J. Workplace Health Manag. **5**(3), 156–167 (2012)
19. Togari, T., Yamazaki, Y.: A causal relationship between sense of coherence and psycho-social work environment: from one-year follow-up data among Japanese young adult workers. Global Health Promot. **19**(1), 32–42 (2012)
20. Grevenstein, D., Bluemke, M.: Can the big five explain the criterion validity of sense of coherence for mental health, life satisfaction, and personal distress? Personal. Individ. Differ. **77**, 106–111 (2015)
21. Cleveland, S., Ellis, T.J.: The impact of role conflict, role ambiguity, and locus of control on organizational knowledge sharing practices. In: 2015 48th Hawaii International Conference on System Sciences System Sciences [HICSS], pp. 3801–3810. IEEE (2015)
22. Zhang, J., Zhou, M., Zhang, J.: The interactive effects of personality and burnout on knowledge sharing among teachers. Soc. Behav. Personal.: Int. J. **44**(8), 1267–1280 (2016)
23. Yang, C., Chen, L.: Can organizational knowledge capabilities affect knowledge sharing behavior? J. Inf. Sci. **33**, 95–109 (2007)
24. Antonovsky, A.: The structure and properties of the sense of coherence measurement. Soc. Sci. Med. **36**(6), 725–733 (1993)
25. Huvila, I.: Meta-games in information work. Inf. Res. **18**(3) (2013)
26. Castro, I., Roldán, J.L.: A mediation model between dimensions of social capital. Int. Bus. Rev. **22**(6), 1034–1050 (2013)
27. Vinzi, V.E., Chin, W.W., Henseler, J., Wang, H.: Handbook of Partial Least Squares: Concepts, Methods and Applications, pp. 515–534. Springer Science & Business Media, Heidelberg (2010). https://doi.org/10.1007/978-3-540-32827-8
28. Klarner, P., Sarstedt, M., Hoeck, M., Ringle, C.M.: Disentangling the effects of team competences, team adaptability, and client communication on the performance of management consulting teams. Long Range Plan. **46**(3), 258–286 (2013)
29. Hair, J.F., Black, W.C., Babin, H.J., Anderson, R.E.: Multivariate Data Analysis, 7th edn. Prentice Hall, New Jersey (2010)
30. Amaro, S., Duarte, P.: An integrative model of consumers' intentions to purchase travel online. Tourism Manag. **46**, 64–79 (2015)
31. Fornell, C., Larcker, D.F.: Evaluating structural equation models with unobservable variables and measurement error. J. Market. Res. **18**(1), 39–50 (1981)
32. Wong, K.K.: Partial least squares structural equation modeling [PLS-SEM] techniques using SmartPLS. Market. Bull. **24**(1), 1–32 (2013)
33. Preacher, K.J., Hayes, A.F.: Asymptotic and resampling strategies for assessing and comparing indirect effects in simple and multiple mediator models. Behav. Res. Methods **40** (3), 879–891 (2008)
34. Hair, J.F., Hult, G.T.M., Ringle, C.M., Sarstedt, M.: A Primer on Partial Least Squares Structural Equation Modeling [PLS-SEM]. Sage, Thousand Oaks (2013)

35. Helm, S., Eggert, A., Garnefeld, I.: Modelling the impact of corporate reputation on customer satisfaction and loyalty using PLS. In: Vinzi, V.E., Chin, W.W., Henseler, J., Wang, H. (eds.) Handbook of Partial Least Squares: Concepts, Methods and Applications. Springer Handbooks of Computational Statistics Series, vol. II, pp. 515–534. Springer, Heidelberg (2001). https://doi.org/10.1007/978-3-540-32827-8_23
36. Ek, S.: Om information, Media och Hälsa i en Samhällelig Kontext: en Empirisk och Analytisk Studie [On Information, Media and Health in a Societal Context: an Empirical and Analytic Study]. Åbo Akademis Förlag, Åbo, Finland (2005)
37. Ek, S., Widén-Wulff, G.: Information mastering, perceived health and societal status: an empirical study of the Finnish population. Libri **58**(2), 74–81 (2008)
38. Matzler, K., Renzl, B., Mooradian, T., von Krogh, G., Mueller, J.: Personality traits, affective commitment, documentation of knowledge, and knowledge sharing. Int. J. Hum. Resour. Manag. **22**(2), 296–310 (2011)

Data Literacy and Research Data Management

Training Trainers for Research Data Literacy: A Content- and Method-Oriented Approach

René Schneider(✉)

Geneva School of Business Administration, Carouge, Switzerland
rene.schneider@hesge.ch

Abstract. The paper describes all aspects of a train-the-trainer course that was applied to research data literacy to serve two goals: (a) allowing future trainers to gather and combine content according to the needs of their students and organizational parameters, (b) providing them with essential knowledge concerning didactical approaches to the matter. The course was centered around a series of practical exercises that asked the participants to start with a two dimensional representation of all possible competences and skills to acquire before reducing them to a linear sequence of the concrete course content, and finally the punctual specification of a single lesson.

Keywords: Data management · Research data literacy · Vocational training Train-the-trainer competences

1 Introduction

Based on a theoretical work published in 2013 by the same author [1], the paper will show in detail its transposition to practice by outlining the composition as well as the course of action of a one-day train-the-trainer workshop. This workshop combined domain-specific (i.e., related to research data management) as well as didactical elements that were explained and put into hands-on exercises throughout the whole day, with about one-third of the time being spent for theoretical input and the remaining two-thirds for practice.

The paper will briefly describe the basic and preceding modules and mention all components of the workshop that consisted of

(a) an introductory example course
(b) a methodological approach to create vocational trainings
(c) a specific method to build a two dimensional view on research data management course content representing all aspects of research data literacy
(d) didactical knowledge to structure a course in detail
(e) an overview of already existing courses being available
(f) an exercise to create and visualize a specific course unit.

We will also give diversified references on research data literacy in the introducing part and finally discuss the results of our own study, examining the particular interests and limits of this work.

S. Kurbanoğlu et al. (Eds.): ECIL 2017, CCIS 810, pp. 139–147, 2018.
https://doi.org/10.1007/978-3-319-74334-9_15

2 Theoretical Background

Data, in opposition to information or knowledge, has for a long time been the stepchild of Library and Information Science. They (i.e., data) were generally seen as the mere alphabet or primitive subset for information, which itself (i.e., information) was often defined as "*knowledge* communicated". Thus, by definition and metaphorically speaking, information always oriented its face to the bright sphere of knowledge and showed a rather cold shoulder to the brittle grounds of data. This perspective built the consensus for more than half a century (regardless of the rise of computer technology, i.e. electronic *data* processing) during that time and was not questioned, maybe because the sphere of knowledge bears meaning and allows reasoning about semantics, being itself one of most challenging fields in overall science. But semantics still remains difficult to define and capture exactly, and due to the problem of disambiguation "a camino real" has not been found so far.

Data, on the other hand, are usually quite tangible, with characteristics such as easy to keep, handle, describe, analyze, transform, thus illustrating many pragmatic effects that justify the complete turnover that took place in the last decade. This new scenario is characterized by buzzwords like "big data," "open data," and "linked data." Data is seen as a rather vivid structure that creates information, and allows knowledge extraction via algorithmic processing, which, in turn, leads to the revelation of unknown structures. This shift in perspective has a twofold impact on science:

1. under the form of data science, that is, a scientific paradigm mainly based on a combination of (inferential) statistics and machine learning
2. under the form of research data management including data curation, and thus defined as the "active and on-going management of data through its lifecycle of interest and usefulness to scholarship, science, and education," through activities that "enable data discovery and retrieval, maintain quality, add value, and provide for re-use over time" [2].

In this context, Research Data Management in general, or Data Curation in particular, can be seen as minor concerning quantity (opposed to big, linked, or open data), but major, or at least as important, concerning quality, due to the fact that big data, open data and linked data are scientific movements that need proper data to treat, and well curated data to perform better.

In the eyes of the author this shift in perspective (from knowledge to data) will also lead to major changes in the domain of library and information science and its subdomain of information literacy: the way we understand, treat, compile, and deal with data will, on the one hand, lead to new professional roles (such as data librarians, data archivists and data curators as well as new cooperation between the latter and data managers, data scientists and data journalists) (compare [3]), and, on the other hand, to new training programs in information, or better said, data literacy (see [4] and Sect. 3 of this paper). This means that (a) curricula have to be created, (b) training materials have to be delivered, (c) data-oriented teaching approaches have to be developed, and (d) trainers have to be trained to inform students from all disciplines, and library and information science students in particular, as well as scientists and data professionals as described above.

This article should be considered as a first trial to answer this growing demand and report on an initiative being undertaken in the context of a Swiss project named Train2Dacar (standing for Train the Trainer for Data Curation in Advanced Research). To do so, we will shortly present the modules developed for vocational training in research data management, and describe in more detail a train-the-trainer approach for the creation of flexible and context-adaptive course materials.

3 Research Data Management and Literacy Training

Data literacy [5], as information literacy and data management of any kind, requires training. It is no surprise that training is identified as one of the major services in the realm of research data management [6]. Training – like all forms of education – consists mainly of two components: (1) of knowledge communicated (i.e., information) and (2) the methods used to transfer this knowledge (i.e., formation), in other words, and in its utmost simplicity, the "What" and the "How" of a matter to be taught [7]. A simple training program is usually focused on a certain content to be mediated. In contrast, train-the-trainer programs should cover both aspects. Interestingly, the number of train-the-trainer programs in research data management is not very large, and, if they exist, generally limited to the "What", that is, classical training.

Those classical trainings are already quite numerous [8], with some well known and of high quality (e.g., the ANDS 23 Things on RDM program [9], MANTRA [10], or Essentials for Data Support [11]). As mentioned, train-the-trainer programs are much smaller in number, starting with the Library of Congress Program on Digital Curation [12], where the train-the-trainer aspect is understood as a training program focused on content and given to a limited number of participants whose role is seen as that of multipliers. These multipliers will then train others after having done the initial training. Hence, no real distinction between content and didactical methods and their combination is done.

Since the success of training always depends on the methods used for training, and due to the fact that adult training (or andragogy) differs considerably from classical pedagogy [13], it was decided to add a specific train-the-trainer module for (research) data literacy that combined both aspects with classical modules for research data management. This approach will be presented in the following sections of this paper.

4 Training Trainers for Research Data Management

For a proper understanding of the train-the-trainer workshop described in detail in this chapter, it is important to know that the workshop itself was the last part of a modular vocational training composed of nine modules, with four basic and four intermediate modules (and with a duration of four hours for each module), whereas the latter were specifically dedicated to research data management in digital humanities and thus play a minor role in the context of this paper. The essential thing to understand is the modular composition and division in three types of training modules: basic, immersive, and didactical. The idea behind it was to start with the mediation of factual knowledge and to finish with andragogic (i.e., didactics for adults) skills to further enable the participants to pass on the knowledge acquired and the experiences made to their own clientele, becoming thus multipliers in this new domain. The course was mainly dedicated to librarians and archivists but open to researchers, managers, and computer scientists too.

4.1 Content-Oriented Modules

We will focus on a detailed description of the train-the-trainer module (see Sect. 4.2) and only give a short factual description of the four basic modules. A French and German e-learning module of all modules can be found under www.researchdatamanagement.ch [14].

Module 1: Basics. The training started with some basic definitions and several illustrations explaining what data, scientific data, and research data management mean to all of the sciences as well as their specific disciplines. This introduction was followed by a presentation of the two major theoretical models used in research data management, the data curation cycle and the data continuum model. The second part of the introductory module presented the three basic components that are needed to create the framework in which research data management can take place: policies, data management plans, and guidelines provided by the archive that will ingest the data created during the scientific process. The presentation of the latter document was also seen as a bridge to the subject of long term preservation presented in the second module.

Module 2: Data throughout its Lifecycle. The second module was divided into four sections that addressed different stages of the data lifecycle and their implications for the management of research data with a special focus on long term preservation. Section one was dedicated to the subject of active data management, the handling of data during the research process. The second part aimed to provide an understanding of data storage and discovery infrastructures with a special emphasis on data catalogues, registries and repositories. The subsequent part focused on the description of data (i.e., metadata) and its impact on the findability and (re)usability of research data. The fourth and final section concentrated on basic principles and procedures of long term preservation that ought to ensure long term access and (re)usage of research data. All four sections were accompanied by group work with practical examples that encouraged discussion.

Module 3: Use of Data. The third module demonstrated tools and services to support researchers in discovering, using and reusing data to develop their research further. In the first part of the module, different datasets were uploaded into a visualization tool to show the benefits of data visualization for different research needs. The second part of the module looked into the concepts of Linked Data and the Resource Description Framework (RDF) as a set of techniques that allow integration and combination of heterogeneous data sources, and to address new and challenging research questions.

In a hands-on session, it was illustrated how data can be explored, queried and expanded by means of several external RDF resources already present in the Linked

Open Data cloud using Semantic Web technologies. A RDF dataset was explored to demonstrate the power of linked data and the range of questions that can be asked and answered using the query language SPARQL.

Module 4: Publication and Services. The last module started with a presentation of the major issues concerning the publication and citation of data. To illustrate the added value of data publication, a special focus was set on data papers and data journals. Afterwards, a further focus was set on the problem of dynamic and persistent identifiers for research data, assuring the link between short term and long term repositories.

The module ended with a presentation of the major services that evolve around research data management. After studying the activities related to each service thoroughly, the participants then worked in groups to develop proposals for roadmaps or to describe in more detail the services they are planning to install at their home institutions. The different proposals were then presented and discussed by the participants.

4.2 Method-Oriented Modules

The one day (eight hours) train-the-trainer workshop was designed as an alternation of theoretical inputs and practical exercises, whereas the theoretical parts lasted no longer than 20 min, and emphasis was always placed on the practical parts, including the explanation and discussion of the results obtained during the hands-on sessions.

The workshop started with (1) a short ice-breaking exercise that was immediately followed by (2) a 45-min example course simulating a librarian giving a lunchtime lecture to researchers as an introduction to research data management. This example course included two exercises of minor size (in the middle and towards the end) and followed a didactical model known under the name of e-class reference model [15], a model that was also used for the elaboration of the e-learning modules mentioned earlier [14].

This model was explained in detail in the following part of the training that consisted of (3) a 20-min general introduction to teaching with a special focus on adult learning, a subfield of teaching also known under the term "andragogy."

After a first break, the training continued with (4) another 20 min of theoretical introduction, this time with respect to research data literacy, namely a short lecture based on the paper mentioned earlier, and immediately linked with (5) a one-hour exercise that transformed the theoretical explanations on research data literacy into practical operations similar to those of a non-deterministic algorithm. The exercise was derived from the matrix presented in Table 1 that consists of an attribution of specific skills in the field of research data management to eight major competences in the domain of research data literacy as derived in [1].

The exercise consisted of the elaboration of a metro line based on this attribution, because – metaphorically speaking – the competences in research data literacy (column 1 of Table 1) can firstly be seen as lines of a metro network and secondly the according skills in research data management (column 2 of Table 1) as corresponding stops along these lines. Skills that are difficult to allocate to one single line and that might be stops in another or even more than two lines build intersections between those lines. Thirdly, metro maps are usually divided into zones, generally with respect to their proximity or

Table 1. Competences and skills

Competences in research data literacy	Specific skills in research data management
Identify	Documentation (research environmental, temporal)/ Context/From Information Management to Knowledge Management
Scope	Monitoring Process/Extracting Information from Data Models (and People)
Plan	Data Modeling/Meta Data/Standards Development
Store	Data Analysis and Manipulation/Merging, Mashing, Integration
Protect	Data Preservation/Data Security/Access Authentication/Conditions of Use/Data Legislation
Evaluate	Data Appraisal and Retention/Value of Data/Economic Issues
Manage	Data Appraisal and Retention/Value of Data/Economic Issues
Provide	Facilitation, Communication/Raising Awareness

distance to the center. Hence, the last analogy proposed was the division of the metro map into several zones, such as a central zone which gathered all skills that were to be taught to all participants in a minimal amount of time, and a second zone with those skills that needed more time and a distinct audience.

For the sake of simplicity and according to the distinction made between three lenses in the DigCurV [16] project, namely that of practitioner, manager and executive, special attention was given to the distinction of abilities within these lenses, namely the three capacities "is aware of", "understands", and "is able to". Following these distinctions, it was recommended that participants divide the map into three zones. These zones could be represented by three overlapping zones for practitioners, managers, and executives. Or they could be represented by concentric zones following the distinction within each lens, that is, a central zone for "Awareness Building", an intermediate zone for "Creating deeper understanding" and a peripheral zone "Enabling for Practice" (without necessarily using these labels), or similarly, according to the "23 Things on research data management" distinction between "Getting Started", "Learn More", and "Challenge Me" [8]. Figure 1 shows an idealistic view of the exercise established by the author of this paper. This map was also used during the training for the sake of illustration.

It should be stated in this context that the purpose of this exercise was not to achieve a "first yield" for all aspects of a training program during the one hour given to come to a result, but rather, to bring a group of four to five future trainers with different backgrounds together, and to make them exchange their different points of view via the relay of a two-dimensional map that might be used as a tangible sketch that allows flexible modifications on the one hand, and continuous evolution on the other.

This meant, practically, that several groups of four to five participants were created, and several card sorts [17] were handed out that represented different points of view of the common field-of-interest (in our case research data management and the eight major competences). Further material was given to allow the building of intersections with

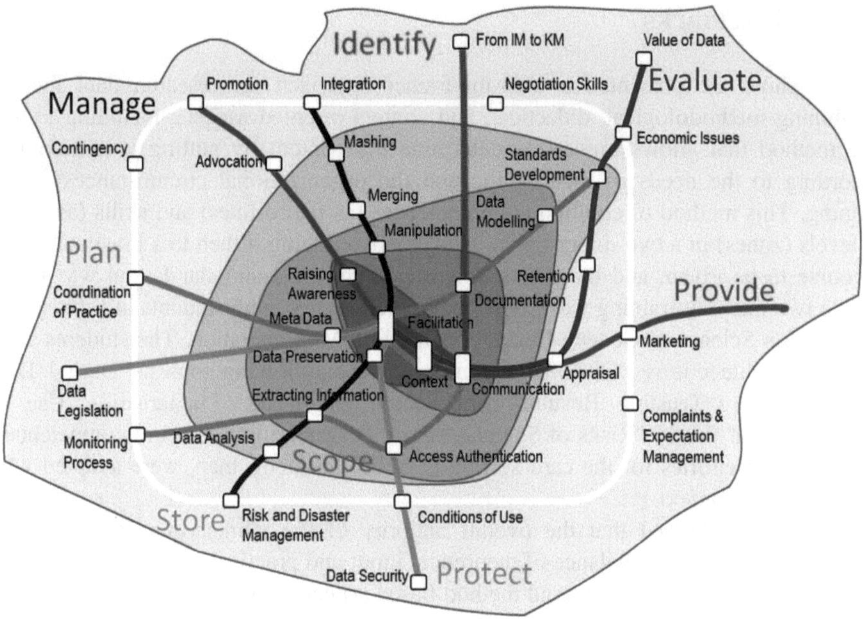

Fig. 1. Metro network derived from Table 1

different colors and the distinction of zones via numbers. After one hour, each group was asked to present the maps briefly, and report on the major outcomes and difficulties that occurred, before switching to the second half of the workshop, which was oriented towards the essential didactical and methodological foundations for the sequential elaboration of a course.

After giving (6) a 20-min general introduction concerning the rough planning of a course, the participants were asked (7) to pick out those contents of the map that they would like to integrate in the course, to create and thus to build a linear subset of the two-dimensional map. To ease the decision, (8) a short overview of existing onsite and online training courses was presented (similar to the one given in Sect. 3 of this paper).

In the final steps of the workshop, the participants (9) selected one peculiar class of the course (one punctual stop in the linear subsection of the two-dimensional map) and worked on the concrete elaboration of a specific lesson. The instructors provided the participants with corresponding sheets that enabled them to plan a course in detail by defining the framework and goals of the course, the theoretical input, practical exercises and didactical methods used including the duration of each of the parts. Each group was then invited to illustrate on a flipchart the content and course of action.

The workshop concluded with short presentations of the results of this last exercise and (10) oral feedback and evaluation given by all participants.

All course materials as well as the results of all groupwork were gathered on a website during the two weeks that followed the course.

5 Final Remarks

In this paper we presented a train-the-trainer approach for research data literacy combining methodological, didactical, and content-oriented aspects, including a flexible method that allows trainers to determine the content by putting it into context according to the needs of their public and the organizational circumstances of the training. This method of combining competences (as metro lines) and skills (as stops) in levels (zones) in a two-dimensional metro map, reducing it then to a linear subset of a course to be given, and the punctual extrapolation of a singular lesson was tested beside two one-day-training workshops in another context with students in Library and Information Science at Geneva Business School of Administration. The students were asked to create courses of different length for the following topics: "Digital Data Management", "Trusting Results from Search Engines", "Plagiarism", "Use of e-readers", and finally "Risks of Social Media". For each topic the core competences, that is, the categories for the card sorting to build the metro map, were adapted with respect to the context.

Experience showed that the overall majority of the workshop participants and students appreciated the balance of theoretical input and practical experience as well as the idea of combining content- and method-based aspects in a setting that allowed them to create mutual training scenarios. However, some participants seemed to have problems with the two-dimensional representation, probably because they prefer an immediate linear or punctual approach to create a limited number of sequential or simply punctual teaching units.

A German and French online-version of this course can be found under www.researchdatamanagement.ch [14].

Acknowledgements. The author would like to thank Eliane Blumer for her contributions during the preparation and execution of the train-the-trainer workshop described in this paper.

References

1. Schneider, R.: Research data literacy. In: Kurbanoğlu, S., Grassian, E., Mizrachi, D., Catts, R., Špiranec, S. (eds.) ECIL 2013. CCIS, vol. 397, pp. 134–140. Springer, Cham (2013). https://doi.org/10.1007/978-3-319-03919-0_16
2. Cragin, M.H., Heidorn, P.B., Palmer, C.L., Smith, L.C.: An educational program on data curation. In: Science and Technology Section of the Annual American Library Association Conference, Washington, DC (2007)
3. Lyon, L., Mattern, E.: Education for real-world data science roles (part 2): a translational approach to curriculum development. Int. J. Digit. Curation **11**(2), 13–26 (2016)
4. Tibbo, H.R.: Digital curation education and training: from digitization to graduate curricula to MOOCs. Int. J. Digit. Curation **10**(1), 144–153 (2015)
5. Koltay, T.: Data literacy: in search of a name and identity. J. Documentation **71**(2), 401–415 (2015). https://doi.org/10.1108/JD-02-2014-0026
6. Jones, S., Pryor, G., Whyte, A.: How to Develop Research Data Management Services - a Guide for HEIs. DCC How-to Guides, Edinburgh: Digital Curation Centre (2013). http://www.dcc.ac.uk/resources/how-guides/how-develop-rdm-services

7. Prongué, N., Schneider, R.: The what and the how of research data management. Towards a unified view of train-the-trainer competencies. In: Proceedings of the 12th International Digital Curation Conference (IDCC), Edinburgh, Scotland, 20–23 February (2017). https://hesso.tind.io/record/1974/files/Poster.pdf
8. Molloy, L.: Research Data Management (RDM) Open Training Materials (2017). https://zenodo.org/communities/dcc-rdm-training-materials
9. Australian National Data Service (ANDS). 23 (Research Data) Things (2016). http://www.ands.org.au/partners-and-communities/23-research-data-things
10. The University of Edinburgh: Mantra – Research Data Management Training (2010–2011)
11. Grootveld, M., Verbakel, E.: Essentials for data support: training the front office. Int. J. Digit. Curation **10**(1), 240–248 (2015)
12. Library of Congress: Digital Preservation Outreach and Communication – Baseline Digital Preservation Curriculum (2017). http://www.digitalpreservation.gov/education/curriculum.html
13. Canadian Literacy and Learning Network: Principles of Adult Learning. Literacy.ca. (2016). http://www.literacy.ca/professionals/professional-development-2/principles-of-adult-learning
14. Mastrandrea, E., Prongué, N., Schneider, R., Stettler, N.: Kursbuch Forschungsdatenmanagement. HTW Chur/HEG Genf. (in press) www.researchdatamanagement.ch
15. Gerson, E.: E-CLASS: Creating a Guide to Online Course Development for Distance Learning Faculty (2000). http://www.westga.edu/~distance/ojdla/winter34/gerson34.html
16. Moles, N.: DigCurV curriculum framework: applications in the development of digital curation vocational training programmes. In: iConference 2014 Proceedings (2014)
17. Hudson, W.: Card sorting. In: Soegaard, M., Dam, R.F. (eds.) The Encyclopedia of Human-Computer Interaction, 2nd edn. The Interaction Design Foundation, Aarhus, Denmark (2013). http://www.interaction-design.org/encyclopedia/card_sorting.html

Data Literacy and Research Data Management: The Croatian State of Affairs

Sonja Špiranec(✉) and Denis Kos

Faculty of Humanities and Social Sciences,
University of Zagreb, Zagreb, Croatia
{sspiran, dkos}@ffzg.hr

Abstract. This report is a part of an international survey on data literacy and research data management and is concerned with the Croatian state of affairs. A key aim of this study is to elicit the practices of Croatian researchers and PhD students regarding the production, dissemination, provision, storage, and description of research data, as well as portraying institutional attitudes towards those issues. By contributing Croatian data this study widens the international perspective on research data management. Findings of this study expose the current levels of awareness and gaps in knowledge and allow creation of structured and well-focused educational activities.

Keywords: Data literacy · Research data management · Academic staff Croatia

1 Introduction

Openness is one of the key premises of contemporary research, which is reflected in many of its facets and processes, like access or diffusion, collaboration, evaluation etc. Although research and scientific knowledge are open by their very nature and intention, just the last decade brought this intrinsic notion to the fore, mainly owing to the availability of new digital technologies and collaborative tools. Conceptually, this premise has elicited a new frame of understandings labelled as "the fourth paradigm in scientific research" [1], which is characterized by new methods and instrumentation enabling scientists to gather huge volumes of data. This development leads to a new type of "data-intensive science" which shifts the attention from the end product of scientific work to documenting the decisions and context from which the research arises [2].

Implications of this data turn, or the "age of data," are described in many documents that reflect the current interest and hype among researchers and funding bodies, and in general at the societal and political level [3–5]. The narrative in these documents focuses on the benefits of open science, data sharing, and the necessity of creating an infrastructure entailing policies, services, tools, repositories, procedures that enable sharing, reusing, collaborating, curation, preservation etc.

However, for the concept of open science to succeed, it certainly takes more than the infrastructure. Willingness of researchers to share their data and use data of others is indispensable, and builds upon an open data culture which is not only anchored in

S. Kurbanoğlu et al. (Eds.): ECIL 2017, CCIS 810, pp. 148–157, 2018.
https://doi.org/10.1007/978-3-319-74334-9_16

attitudes, but also in competencies such as those related to data sharing, filtering, visualizing, linking, using, preserving, retrieving, that is, data literacy (DL). Thus, DL is, next to infrastructure, a key component of doing research in the age of data and data-intensive science.

Nonetheless, despite the impression that we deal with a new "version" of scientific work that brought about profound shifts and genuine new ways of understandings and doing things, as implied by the term "fourth paradigm", it actually represents a continuum in core values and principles in science (e.g., transparency, sharing of knowledge, repeatability, communication) that are accomplished by new approaches and different means. Continuity is also evident when it comes to DL, whose principles and content are standing in close connection to an existing narrative in research and education, namely information literacy (IL). Thus, DL can be perceived as an extension of IL applied within the research process [6]. According to some authors [7] DL has a chance to be more widely accepted by researchers than information literacy, because it is rooted in a research paradigm advanced by researchers, as evidenced by focus group interviews conducted by Colorado State University librarians among faculty members and researchers [8]. Additionally, as research policies and frameworks have nowadays put data-related procedures on their agenda (e.g., the creation of research data management [RDM] plans, the deposit of research data), understanding how to manage, navigate and curate huge amounts of data, that is, DL, has a very good chance to be accepted as a common requirement in research on institutional and system-wide levels.

Despite such potentials, the question of whether or not DL and data practices will be accepted by researchers depends on the existence of an open data culture, which is affected by different factors, as shown in [9]. This study implies that RDM practices and DL are very contextual phenomena, despite the fact that the notion of Open Science is inherently global. As the concrete context is obviously decisive for DL, insights into different contexts and determining contextual forces can shape and strengthen our understandings in DL. This paper is part of a multinational study and contributes to such insights into RDM practices and DL in Croatia.

2 Context of the Study

The effort to provide good support for RDM is a very current issue for Croatia. This is illustrated by projects and initiatives, like OPENAire[1] or SERSCIDA[2], which not only aim to establish a high-quality data infrastructure in Croatian higher education area, but implicitly emphasize the importance of research data management and RDM practices. For instance, OPENAire is focused on establishing the technical infrastructure for reliable digital asset management, while SERSCIDA addresses cooperation and knowledge exchange, but in the field of social science data archiving. Although in both projects infrastructural issues are in the spotlight, research data practices are also of interest as shown by SERSCIDA which elicited insights into research data practices

[1] https://www.openaire.eu/.

[2] http://www.serscida.eu/en/.

among social scientists based on a survey conducted in 2012 [10]. The study revealed that the data social scientists store is often very poorly documented and kept mostly on individual computers with several copies on different computers and media. Access to data is usually allowed only to project team members, but almost half of the respondents believed that their data should be made available either to the general scientific community or publicly available. Social scientists in Croatia consider it important to have access to research data collected by others, but in practice, secondary analysis is rare, and researchers often do not even know whether their data was used. The researchers also stated that data sharing was not part of the research culture.

In addition to projects, policies and statements of governing bodies are additional indicators of the heightened interest in research data. A good example that illustrates support for openness in research, RDM and, implicitly, DL is the recommendation issued by the Croatian Rectors Conference in 2015 [11], which promotes open access to scientific publication and research data and recommends that both open publications and research data should be considered in evaluation procedures and promotion of scientists, scientific projects, and other areas.

3 Objectives and Methodology

A key aim of this study was to elicit the practices of Croatian researchers and PhD students regarding the production, dissemination, provision, storage, and description of research data, as well as portraying institutional attitudes towards those issues.

The study was conducted at the University of Zagreb on a convenience sample of 515 members of academic staff and research students (7.3% of the population) distributed amongst six general subject areas.

The University of Zagreb is the largest university in Croatia employing 7100 researchers, which makes it one of the bigger European universities offering comprehensive access to higher education in almost every field of study. The survey constructed on the Limesurvey service was distributed via e-mail and consists of 24 questions. The data was collected in February, 2017. Data analysis focused on descriptive and frequency analyses.

The achieved sample, constructed based on voluntary participation, consists of two main groups of respondents: academic staff (82.3%) and research students (14.6%). From Fig. 1. it is evident that the respondents were mostly younger and middle-aged researchers, but an important thing to consider is that 83.7% have been involved in research for more than five years. With regard to their gender, 56.3% of respondents were female and 42.7% were male which resembles the distribution in the population. Our attempt to construct a representative sample by inclusion of a minimum of five percent of respondents from every scientific field showed that the interest for the researched topic may vary with regard to subject area.

Figure 2 shows the expected and achieved number (N) of respondents for each of the subject areas. We can see that the survey was very well received in natural sciences, the fields of engineering and technology, medical and health sciences, agricultural sciences and social sciences. However, we have not managed to spark the interest of researchers in the humanities to participate in this survey, even though they have twice

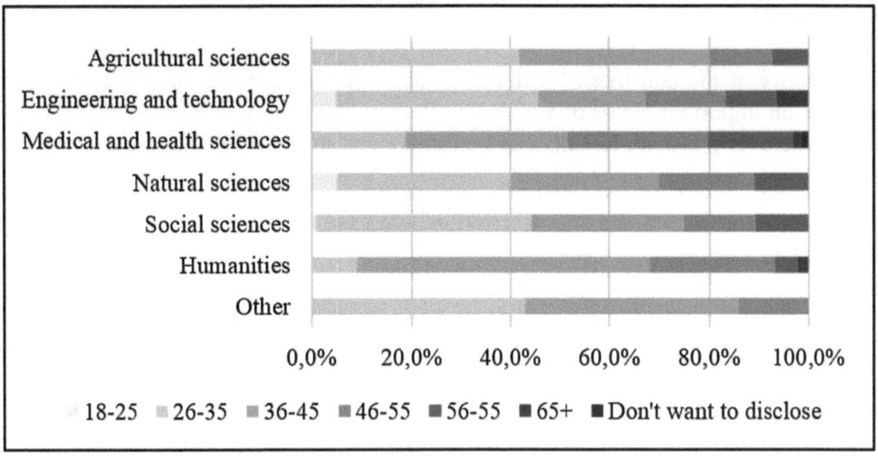

Fig. 1. Age of respondents by discipline affiliation

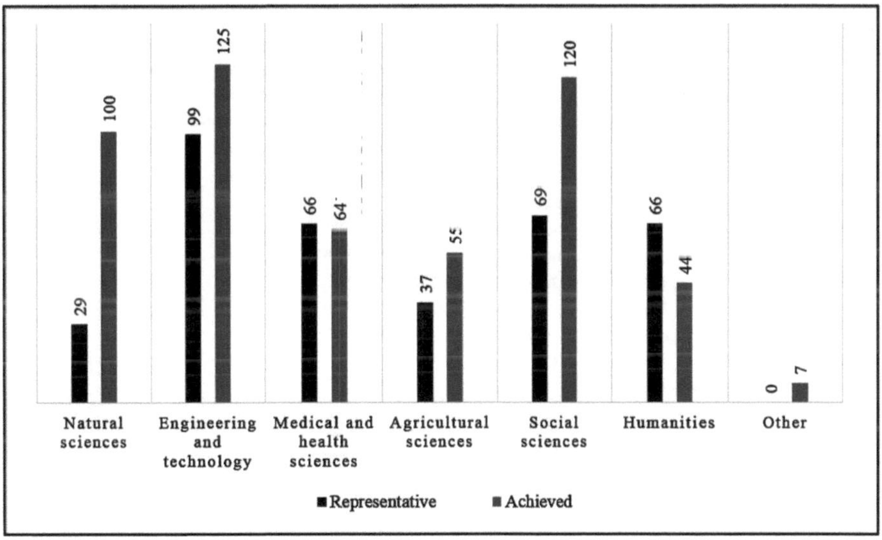

Fig. 2. Comparison of the expected minimum of respondents per field and the achieved number of respondents

as many employed researchers, as the natural sciences. Another important observation is the large number of respondents in the natural and social sciences, which greatly exceeds the expected minimum.

4 Results

The identity of the constructed samples requires that we consider disciplinary differences as an important factor of variability. Presented results will be considered in that sense wherever possible. Results can be categorized in the following way:

1. Type and volume of used and produced data
2. Usage, retrieval, storage and description practices
3. Attitudes towards data sharing
4. Perception of the role of institutions in RDM
5. Educational experience and willingness to participate in education about RDM.

4.1 Type and Volume of Used and Produced Data

In general, the data types most of our respondents use are standard office documents, images and web resources (Fig. 3).

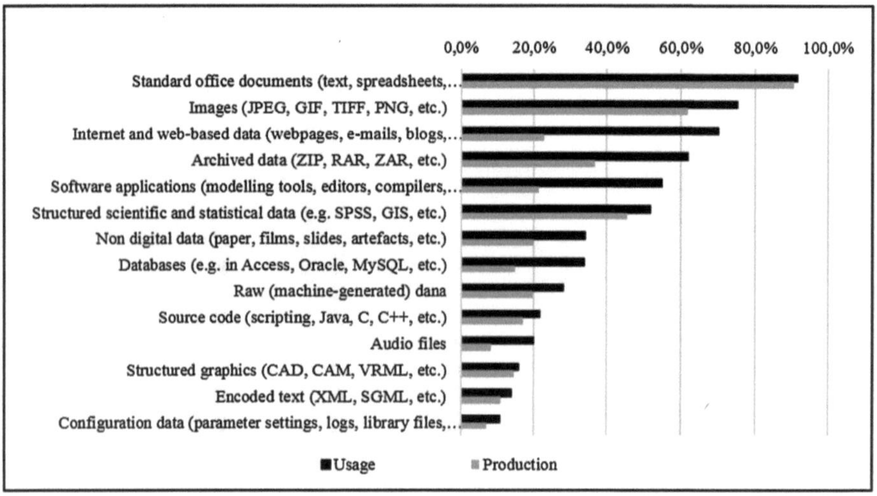

Fig. 3. Comparison of the usage and production of different data types

The production of any data type is, on average, lower then its usage. Differences between subject areas can be seen in higher usage and production of software applications and source code in natural sciences and the field of engineering and technology. Furthermore, differences are seen also in high usage of non-digital data in the humanities (70.5%) while usage of this data type does not exceed 35% in other fields relative to the number of respondents in a given field. Other interesting data types used and produced that were not mentioned by the survey were language corpora and video files.

The volume of the data respondents use (60.2%) and produce (54.37%) can mostly be measured in gigabytes (GB). Only 13.4% use, and 7.8% produce higher volumes of data which exceed one terabyte (TB).

4.2 Usage, Retrieval, Storage and Description Practices

The best insights into researchers' RDM practices come from understanding how they use data, where they retrieve the data they use in their research, and how they store and organize it. Respondents from the University of Zagreb mostly rely on own research skills so the main way they get data for their research are their own research projects (83.9%). On the other hand, 51.3% are prone to rely on their own research network and/or professional and personal connections to get the data they need.

53% use the data they get from outside sources as is, while 55% believe these resources still need a bit of cleaning and some modifications.

The data that 98.1% of respondents create or get from other sources is almost always stored on respondents' own devices. 45.8% also use cloud services, and 18.4% store it on central severs and institutional repositories, while 8.3% use outside repositories. Even though our respondents store the data at least on their own devices, when asked if they would like to store their research datasets beyond the lifetime of their projects, 48.5% said that they strongly disagree with the need for long-term storage, while only 30.1% agreed that it was important. Interestingly, even though only 18.4% store their data in institutional repositories 69.3% do believe that data would be best stored for long-term access at the university.

71.4% of respondents also believe that the university should pay for the storage and public access to the data our respondents created as its employees.

An awareness of the need for long term storage is also shown by description practices and assigning metadata to research datasets. Most of the respondents (55.7%) are familiar with the term "metadata" (uncertain = 15.5%; not familiar = 28.7%), and at least 60% assign some type of metadata to their research datasets. The metadata type added most often is administrative information (Fig. 4). However, when they were

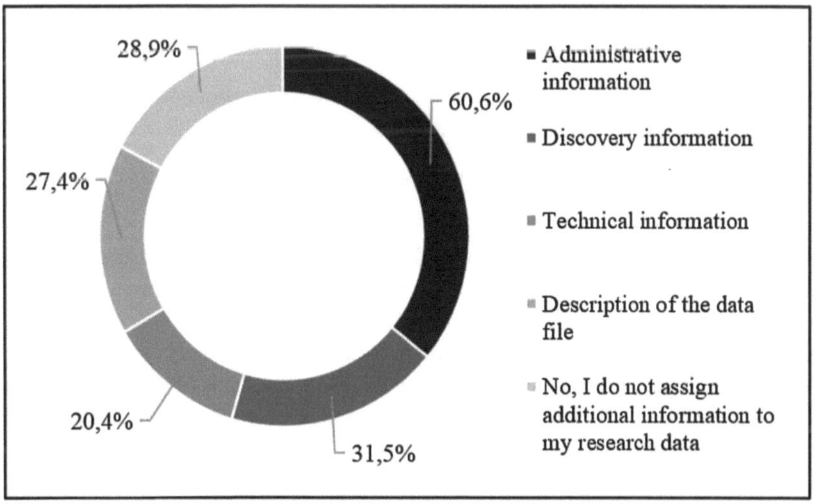

Fig. 4. Additional information respondents assign to their research data

asked how often they use a metadata standard for tagging their data 58.3% answer that they rarely do so. Usage, retrieval, storage and description practices of respondents did not vary across their different subject areas.

4.3 Attitudes Towards Data Sharing

The international survey pays special attention to data sharing practices. Figure 5 shows that respondents from the University of Zagreb usually do share their data and only a small percent say that they do not collaborate with other researchers. However, only 18.1% of that data is truly open to everyone.

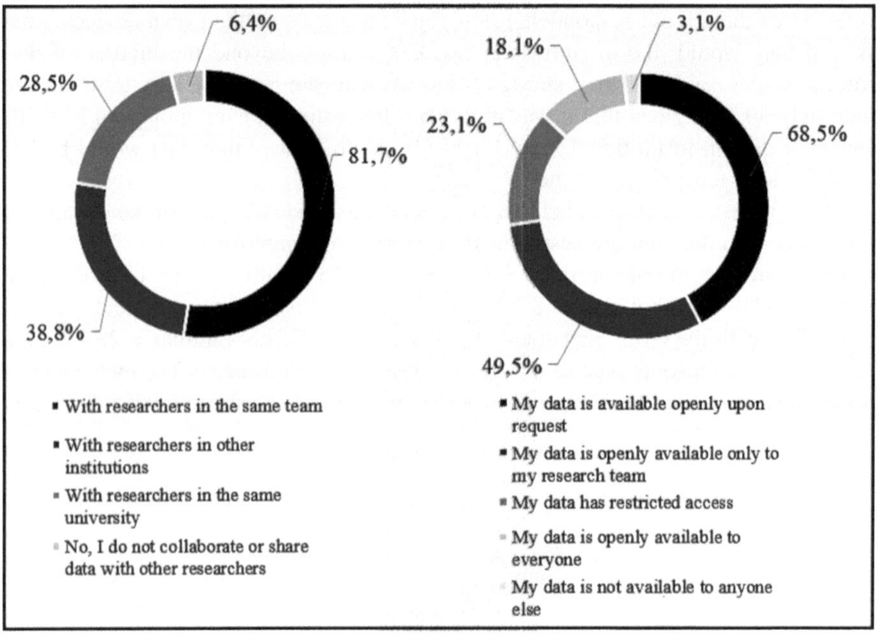

Fig. 5. Data sharing practices

We also asked our respondents about the concerns they have regarding the sharing of their data. With 50.5%, misinterpretation of data is the most common concern, and it is closely followed by misuse of data (48.7%).

However, all types of concerns were present to some extent (fear of losing the scientific edge, legal and ethical issues, lack of resources, lack of appropriate policies and rights protection). Discipline affiliation was not revealed as a contributing factor to the variability in data sharing practices.

4.4 Perception of the Role of Institutions in RDM

When they were asked to consider different institutional practices and how they perceive the role of institutions in RDM, respondents' answers mostly point to the perceived lack of institutional involvement or communication about RDM.

A specific focus in the survey was given to the concept of a Data management plan (DMP). From Fig. 6 we can see that respondents are mostly unsure whether their institution has such a plan, while 34.6% say that such a plan does not exist. Furthermore, other responses revealed that 81% say they have never used a DMP in their research projects and 78.4% say they do not have such a plan in their current research project. However, 35.5% say that they think such a plan would be useful while 59% remain uncertain about its usefulness. Understanding of institutional practices and roles as presented was comparable among different subject areas.

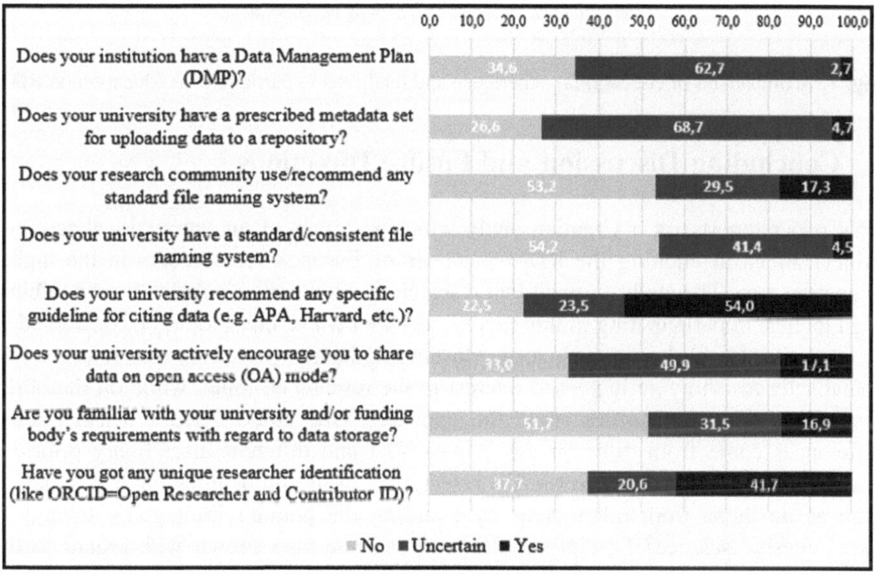

Fig. 6. Perception of the role of institutions and institutional practices

4.5 Educational Experience and Willingness to Participate in Education

One of the key aims of this survey was to establish the need for education and formal training about different RDM topics so that the research team could plan and provide activities to address these educational needs. While our respondents said that they did not have a lot of formal training on RDM, looking at the data (Fig. 7) we could say that their interest in these topics is moderate and similar among the different subject areas.

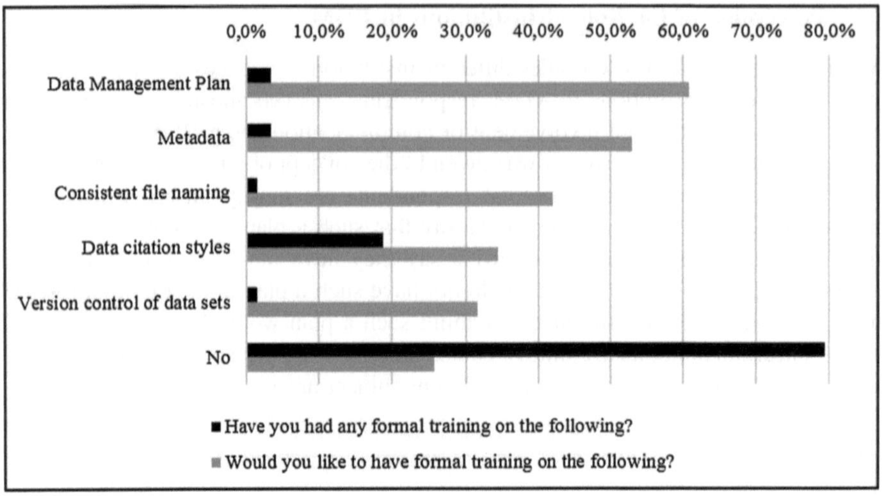

Fig. 7. Comparison of educational experience and readiness to participate in education on RDM

5 Concluding Discussion and Future Directions

This paper reports on a Croatian study which is a part of an international research project aimed at eliciting the RDM practices of European researchers in the higher education area. The study showed that researchers from certain subject areas exhibited high interest in participating in this survey, and we believe this should be considered as an incentive for further investigation. On the one hand, why do natural sciences and social sciences show an increased interest in the researched topic, while on the other, researchers from humanities show the opposite? One could discuss whether these differences come from different disciplinary foci and different disciplinary priorities that distinguish the subject areas. Do researchers in the humanities have as much to gain as do those from other areas by boarding the popular train going towards a data-intensive science? Disciplinary differences were also shown with regard to the data types used in a given field, but RDM and data sharing practices were common among all areas. This leads us to conclude that while the data content naturally differs, the common attitudes among the different subject areas lead to an understanding that there are areas of common interest which could be approached both on the level of institutional policies and educational initiatives focused on broadening the individual researchers' knowledge about RDM. The results given in this report corroborate the findings of previous research projects in Croatia because researchers still store their research data mostly on their own devices with an unsatisfactory level of quality regarding description and preservation. The data has shown that the academic community at the University of Zagreb shows awareness and understands the need to store, describe, share and manage research data but their data-related scientific practices do not reflect that understanding. The data sharing culture has yet to be fully developed because the willingness to share the data rarely takes the form of open public availability of research data. Furthermore, respondents' answers pointed out the perceived lack of institutional involvement or communication about RDM which means that relevant institutions need to do more to encourage knowledge and skills acquisition about RDM. The reported low level of education on researched topics and an already existing moderate interest points to the need to develop DL programs that could shape the will of the academic community that promotes a systematic and sustainable approach to the management of research data. A lot of work for the data librarian!

References

1. Hey, T.: The fourth paradigm – data-intensive scientific discovery. In: Kurbanoğlu, S., Al, U., Erdoğan, P.L., Tonta, Y., Uçak, N. (eds.) IMCW 2012. CCIS, vol. 317, p. 1. Springer, Heidelberg (2012). https://doi.org/10.1007/978-3-642-33299-9_1
2. Gold, A.: Libraries, process, and data. In: Proceedings of the ASIST, vol. 50, no. 1, pp. 1–9 (2013)
3. European Commission: Open Innovation, Open Science, Open to the World. EC, Brussels (2016). http://bookshop.europa.eu/en/open-innovation-open-science-open-to-the-world-pbKI0416263/
4. OECD: Making Open Science a Reality. OECD Publishing, Paris (2015). http://dx.doi.org/10.1787/5jrs2f963zs1-en
5. The Royal Society: Science as an Open Enterprise (2012). https://royalsociety.org/~/media/policy/projects/sape/2012-06-20-saoe.pdf
6. Cox, A.M., Pinfield, S.: Research data management and libraries: current activities and future priorities. J. Librariansh. Inf. Sci. **46**(4), 299–316 (2014)
7. Koltay, T., Špiranec, S.: Libraries meet research 2.0. In: Research 2.0 and the Impact of Digital Technologies on Scholarly Inquiry, pp. 32–52. IGI Global (2017)
8. McLure, M., et al.: Data curation: a study of researcher practices and needs. Libr. Acad. **14** (2), 139–164 (2014)
9. Tenopir, C., et al.: Data sharing by scientists. PLoS One **6**(6), e21101 (2011)
10. SERSCIDA: analysis of existing potentials for the establishment of a social sciences digital data base archive in Croatia (2012). http://www.serscida.eu/images/delivererables/SERSCIDA_D_2_2_Mapping_Report_Croatia.pdf
11. Croatian Rector's Conference: Vrednovanje znanstveno-istraživačkoga rada i promicanje otvorenog pristupa znanstvenim informacijama i istraživačkim podacima (2015). http://www.rektorski-zbor.hr/fileadmin/rektorat/O_Sveucilistu/Tijela_sluzbe/Rektorski_zbor/dokumenti2/Vrednovanje_znanstvenog_rada_i_otvoreni_pristup_znanstvenim_informacijama_Rektorski_zbor.pdf

Data Literacy Education Design Based on Needs of Graduate Students in University of Chinese Academy of Sciences

Wu Ming[1,2(✉)] and Hu Hui[1]

[1] National Science Library, Chinese Academy of Sciences, Beijing, China
{wum,huhui}@mail.las.ac.cn
[2] University of Chinese Academy of Sciences, Beijing, China

Abstract. In the new data-intensive research environment, research data is an important part of scientific findings and every researcher will face sophisticated data management problems during their research life. Solving these data problems requires researchers and students have new skill sets and competencies, which ensure their outputs are accessible, discoverable and reusable. Using the online questionnaire survey method, we conducted a data literacy survey among 59 graduate students of life science in University of Chinese Academy of Sciences (UCAS). The current situation and needs of graduate students' data literacy competences are revealed. On the basis of demand investigation, the data literacy education model of teachers, students and curriculum is constructed, the education content is based on research data lifecycle and includes three levels of learning modes. In addition, the data literacy education implementation scenes for graduate students in UCAS were also designed, and provide evidence for libraries to implement data literacy education services better.

Keywords: Data literacy · Research data management · Data literacy education Graduate students

1 Introduction

In the new data-intensive research environment, research data is an important part of scientific findings, and every researcher will face sophisticated data management problems during their research life, such as data generation and collection, data documentation and processing, data storage and backup, data publishing and sharing. Data literacy has become new skill sets and necessary competencies for researchers and students to solve these data problems [1]. At the same time, many funding agencies, universities and other organizations now have a research data management policy in place, such as the NSF Data Management Plan Requirements which states, "Proposals submitted or due on or after January 18, 2011, must include a supplementary document of no more than two pages labeled 'Data Management Plan'. This supplementary document should describe how the proposal will conform to NSF policy on the dissemination and sharing of research results." And in NIH's view, all data should be considered for data sharing. Data should be made as widely and freely available as possible while

S. Kurbanoğlu et al. (Eds.): ECIL 2017, CCIS 810, pp. 158–168, 2018.
https://doi.org/10.1007/978-3-319-74334-9_17

safeguarding the privacy of participants, and protecting confidential and proprietary data. To facilitate data sharing, investigators submitting a research application requesting $500,000 or more of direct costs in any single year to NIH on or after October 1, 2003 are expected to include a plan for sharing final research data for research purposes, or state why data sharing is not possible. Requirements by different funders to make research data available vary by country, institution, or discipline.

Graduate students are a natural audience for educational programming on data literacy education issues. In the STEM disciplines, graduate students are often expected to carry out most or all of the data management tasks for their own research, and frequently participate in data activities to support team projects [2]. That is to say, this requirement demonstrates that data management skills are needed in a wide range of disciplines and that core skills, as well as discipline-specific training, should be embedded into the graduate curricula [3]. Graduate students are being required to improve and enhance their research data management skills and practices, and data literacy services offer librarians an opportunity to expand their role in the research enterprise within an institution.

In recent years, there has been growing discussion in the literature about how to develop data services and data literacy education in academic libraries. We identified several best practices for teaching data literacy in the literature. The New England Collaborative Data Management Curriculum (NECDMC) is one example of a data management curriculum [4]. Designed collaboratively by librarians from New England academic institutions, it was created for the purpose of using one or more modules to instruct other librarians and researchers about the need for, and use of, good research data management practices. The project, named data information literacy (DIL), consisting of research teams from Purdue University, the University of Minnesota, the University of Oregon, and Cornell University, aims to develop and implement a DIL curriculum in conjunction with university faculty to address these needs [5]. The three central goals for this project are to build infrastructure in the library community for DIL skills, to have students learn DIL skills appropriate to their disciplinary context, and to develop a robust process for librarians to articulate DIL curricula in their research communities. Based on research conducted at Purdue, DIL seeks to incorporate and build upon relevant aspects of information and other literacies to articulate the skill sets needed by graduate students to fulfill their obligations and engage their communities of practice. A central tenant of DIL is the recognition of researchers as producers of data, as well as data consumers. The DataTrain project at the University of Cambridge, aims to build on findings and tools developed in the Incremental project (JISC 07/09 funding strand) by developing disciplinary focused data management training modules for post-graduate courses in Archaeology and Social Anthropology at the University of Cambridge [6]. Another well-known curriculum called MANTRA is an online course from the University of Edinburgh. MANTRA is a free, online non-assessed course with guidelines to help researchers understand and reflect on how to manage the digital data they collect throughout their research. It has been crafted for the use of post-graduate students, early career researchers, and also information professionals [7]. It is freely available on the web for anyone to explore on their own. There are eight online units in this course and one set of offline data handling tutorials. Each unit takes up to one hour, plus time for further reading and carrying out the data handling exercises.

Many libraries have taken on the role of providing instruction in data literacy, but few libraries have addressed the practice aimed at providing data literacy instruction at the life science field. In addition, many libraries have directed their training efforts toward students at the undergraduate and graduate level, rather than focusing on the students' data management behavior and needs in order to design the data literacy instruction. So, this paper chose the graduate students in UCAS as the research objects, designed a questionnaire to investigate their data management behavior and data literacy needs, designs data literacy education implementation scenes and a service model for graduate students in UCAS, and provides recommendations for libraries to improve their implementation of data literacy education services.

2 Methodology

2.1 Questionnaire

We conducted an online survey using Sojump that consists of 30 questions regarding graduate students' own basic information, data management behavior, attitudes, and education related to managing research data. The 12 competencies of Data Information Literacy [2] are used as a guide in designing the survey; further consideration is given to research data lifestyle and the specific situation of graduate students in UCAS. The questionnaire includes two sections and 30 questions. Section one is about personal information of the respondents (Q1–Q3). Section two involves eight parts:

(1) research data basic knowledge (Q6–Q9)
(2) data management plan (Q10–Q13)
(3) data collection and documentation (Q14)
(4) data processing and analysis (Q15–Q18)
(5) data management and preservation (Q19)
(6) data publishing and sharing (Q20–Q21)
(7) research data ethics (Q22–Q23)
(8) needs for data literacy course (Q24–Q30).

In the questionnaire, 28 of the questions are closed-ended in order to facilitate responding and analysis, with options for 'Other' presented where applicable. Two of the questions are open-ended text boxes to obtain additional descriptive information from the participants.

2.2 Participants

We conducted a data literacy survey among 59 graduate students of life science in UCAS. The selection of the respondents mainly takes into account two aspects. The first aspect is different data management behaviors among different disciplines. Life science is one of the main disciplines in Chinese Academy of Sciences and recruits thousands of graduate students including the School of Life Sciences of UCAS, as well as Institute of Botany, Institute of Zoology, Institute of Genetics and Development, Institute of Microbiology and others. Furthermore, in the field of life sciences, the process of research data creation and collection is complex. The analysis and processing of research data is also complicated, and researchers and graduate students face huge amounts of research data and complex data management issues. So this survey chooses life sciences as a starting point, in order to understand their data management behavior and needs. The second consideration is the necessity and feasibility for graduate students in UCAS to receive data literacy instruction. In UCAS, graduate students should finish all of their courses, both compulsory and elective, in their first graduate year, but have not yet started their research work at this stage. Therefore, preparing for future scientific research work, it is necessary and feasible first to cultivate students' research data management ability through credit courses and training lectures.

Our participants come from 22 research institutes in the field of life science of the Chinese Academy of Sciences, such as the Institute of Botany, Institute of Genetics and Developmental Biology, Chengdu Institute of Biology, South China Botanical Garden, Institute of Zoology and others. The research area of participants involves Genetics, Zoology, Biochemistry and Molecular Biology, Botany, Bioengineering, Ecology, Developmental Biology, Cell Biology, Genomics, Marine Biology, and Biochemistry. Overall, the selection of survey samples is in line with the CAS in the field of life science research distribution and has a good representation.

3 Results

3.1 The Status of Graduate Students' Data Literacy

This part intends to offer an overview of the status of graduate students' data literacy, mainly reflecting the data management behavior of graduate students at different stages of the research data lifecycle, including research data basic knowledge, data management plan, data collection and documentation, data processing and analysis, data management and preservation, data publishing and sharing, and research data ethics.

Basic Ideas About Research Data

The Importance of Research Data Management. The question setting and answer option were referenced from the UK Data Archive. Through the investigation of graduate students on the significance of research data management, we can reveal students' awareness and positive attitude on research data management. The survey results indicate that most of the graduate students in the field of life science have a full awareness of the importance of research data management. Among them, the graduate students believe that the main significance of managing their data is promoting innovation and potential (89.83%), reducing the cost of duplicating data collection (86.44%), and encouraging improvement and validation of research methods (83.05%).

Knowledge of Discipline Research Data. This question examines whether students understand and how much they know about research data in their discipline. According to the survey results, most of the graduate students can determine their discipline research data, and statistical and measurement data (88.14%), experimental and simulation results (86.44%) comprise the main data in the life science field.

Policies and Requirements of Research Data Management and Sharing. This question examines whether students understand and how much they know about data management policy and requirements. The survey results indicate that some of the graduate students in the field of life science say they know data management policies and requirements (74.58%), include data policies and requirements in their laboratory (50.85%), and research organization (33.90%). Overall, graduate students lack knowledge about data management policies and requirements, especially regarding journal publishers, data repositories, research funding agencies and other data management policies and requirements.

Research Data Lifecycle. Data often have a longer lifespan than the research project that creates them. Researchers may continue to work on data after funding has ceased. Follow-up projects may analyze or add to the data, and data may be re-used by other researchers. Well organized, well documented, preserved and shared data are invaluable to advance scientific inquiry and to increase opportunities for learning and innovation. So, it is necessary for graduate students to know the concept of the research data lifecycle. According to the UK Data Archive, research data lifecycle includes creating data, processing data, analyzing data, preserving data, giving access to data and re-using data. This question mainly investigates whether the they understand the concept of the research data lifecycle. The survey results indicate that only 20.34% graduate students know something about what the research data lifecycle is, but most of them feel familiar with the research data lifecycle.

Data Management Plan. A data management plan is a formal document that outlines what you will do with your data during and after you complete your research. It describes the data that will be created, the standards used to describe the data (metadata), who owns the data, who can access the data, how long the data will be preserved (and/or made accessible), and what facilities and equipment will be necessary to disseminate, share, and/or preserve the data (NCSU Libraries).

Components of Data Management Plan. The question setting and answer option referenced from NSF, and a data management plan may include:

- the types of data, samples, physical collections, software, curriculum materials, and other materials to be produced in the course of the project
- the standards to be used for data and metadata format and content (where existing standards are absent or deemed inadequate, this should be documented along with any proposed solutions or remedies)
- policies for access and sharing including provisions for appropriate protection of privacy, confidentiality, security, intellectual property, or other rights or requirements
- policies and provisions for re-use, re-distribution, and the production of derivatives

- plans for archiving data, samples, and other research products, and for preservation of access to them.

This question mainly examines whether students understand the concept and specific content of the data management plan. According to the survey results, 90% of the graduate students understand what a data management plan is and can determine the content contained in the data management plan, but there are still 10.17% of students who have no idea about data management plans.

Data Collection and Documentation

The Methods of Recording and Storing Research Data. This topic is mainly to investigate the data collection methods in life science, as well as how the graduate students collect and document their research data during research practice. The results of the survey indicate that, almost all of them have mastered how to collect and record research data. Among them, the most common means of data recording are USB flash disk or mobile hard disk and other portable storage devices (94.92%), personal computer (94.92%), paper or laboratory notebooks (93.22%), and laboratory or office computer (86.44%).

Data Processing and Analysis

Tools and Software of Processing Research Data. The types and formats of life science research data are various and so are the tools and software for processing data. The results of the survey show that data processing and analysis in life science uses basic data processing tools such as Excel, SPSS, and R, and also some special tools for life science such as Primer, Origin Demo, SigmaPlot, STATISTICA, Clustalw, Curve Expert, Click It Graph, Graph Pad, and PRISM. It should be noted that there are still 10.17% of the graduate students who do not know or are uncertain of which tools or software are often used in processing their research data.

The Sources of Research Data. Life science is a complex discipline with large amounts of data and diverse data sources. This topic focuses on investigating graduate students' data sources in their research practice, the results of the survey, Some graduate students have a wide range of research data sources, both their own and team experimental data, but also datasets downloaded from literature, data centers, and data warehouses (59.32%). But we need to pay attention those students who just create their research data personally or rely on their research team (37.29%).

The Standards to Evaluate the Quality of Research Data. Quality control is an important part of research data management. An examination of students' understanding of methods of controlling and evaluating the quality of research data, can reflect their ability level at managing research data. The survey results indicate that the vast majority of graduate students have mastered the methods of data quality control and evaluation, including data authenticity, data integrity, data normative, data reproducibility.

Data Management and Preservation

The Description of Research Data (Metadata). Using metadata to describe research data will keep it understandable and reusable, So, this topic mainly examines attitudes and status of graduate students at understanding and using metadata for description of research data. According to the survey results, most students can describe research data normatively in research practice. They always describe their data following the rules in their research team or laboratory (94.92%), or create data description rules by themselves. However, there are still some students who have never described their research data.

Data Publishing and Sharing

The Way to Publish Research Data. It has become a trend for researchers to submit data in the format the academic journals request when publishing papers. As the survey results indicate, most of the graduate students know how to publish their research data, including submitting it as supporting information for the paper and providing the DOI (76.27%), submitting to the data repository or institutional repository designated (52.54%), and publishing data papers in data journals (50.85%). But on the other hand, there are still some students who say they do not know or are uncertain of how to publish research data.

Research Data Ethics

The Behavior of Data Reference. When we quote research data from others, we should reference the data source in the same manner as citing journal papers. This question mainly investigates graduate students' awareness and behavior when referencing data from someone else. As the survey results indicate, most of them would cite data source normatively (96.61%), and acknowledge the authors of the data sources (52.54%). But there are some students who say they never indicate the data source or do not know how to cite research data normatively.

Research Data Ethics. Many data ethical issues are involved during managing and sharing research data. This topic mainly investigates whether graduate students understand the ethical issues of research data. According to the survey results, many of them know about research data ethics, such as research data ownership (79.66%) and right to informed consent (76.27%), but just a small number of students know about commercial interests, security secrets, and privacy. At the same time, there are 13.56% of students who show that they know nothing about research data ethics.

3.2 The Needs of Graduate Students' Data Literacy

We have investigated graduate students' status of data literacy in life science around the research data life cycle, and now we have several question about what they want to know about research data management, in what way to offer data management courses, and suggestions for data literacy courses.

Attitudes Towards Data Literacy Education. The answer to this question is no doubt yes (essential, 81.36%, important, 18.64%). All graduate students think it necessary to have data literacy education before starting their research and hope to improve their research data management skills.

The Contents Data Literacy Education Needs. We will design course syllabi based on the research data life cycle, so we investigate the specific learning needs through different data management phases. The results of the survey (see Table 1):

Table 1. The contents data literacy education needs

Data management phase	The contents data literacy education needs	%
Data management plan	Elements of data management plan	61.02
	Tools of data management plan	89.83
	Policies and requirements about data management and sharing	81.36
	Research data life cycle	71.19
Data collection and documentation	The type, format and data volume of research data	94.92
	Quality control and evaluation of research data	83.05
	How to document and describe research data in fields	81.36
Data processing and analysis	Tools to process and analyze research data	98.31
	Data visualization	76.27
Data management and preservation	Research data security	91.53
	Research data store and backup	88.14
	Metadata standards for describing research data in fields	81.36
	Research data naming rules	62.71
	Research data version control	47.46
Data sharing and reuse	Retrieval and acquisition external research data	98.31
	ways to publish and share research data	88.14
	Standard for citation of research data	79.66
	Ethics related to research data and protection measures	77.97
	Research data sharing and license agreement	69.49
Teaching approach	Lecture	69.49
	RSS/Alerts	67.80
	Online course	66.10
	Credit course	61.02
	WeChat public, blog and other media	50.85
	Workshop	27.12

4 Discussion

By means of the statistical analysis of the questionnaire survey, the current status and problems of graduate students in life science disciplines about their data literacy are summarized. In addition, the results help us have a better understanding of their needs for data literacy education and provide evidence for libraries to improve data literacy education services. It is shown in Table 2:

Table 2. Suggestions based on the survey results

	Problems description	Suggestions
Basic knowledge about research data	Lack knowledge of discipline data management and sharing policies Lower identification of new scientific data software	Strengthen basic knowledge of research data management in discipline Embedded in the discipline, training in the field of research data management expertise Strengthen the study of data management and sharing policies, such as research funding agencies, Periodical Publishers, etc
Data management plan	Lack ability of understanding data management plan and utilizing of data management planning tools	Strengthen the understanding of research data lifecycle and data management plan. Development the ability of using data management planning tools
Data collection and documentation	Lack ability of discovering and reusing research data in data repository	Enhancement the ability to retrieve data sources such as data platforms, data repositories
Data processing and analysis	Unable to select and use appropriate data processing tools and software; Lack ability of assessing data quality	Strengthen the learning of the appropriate data processing and analysis tools. Introduction of the methods to control the quality of scientific research data
Data management and preservation	Lack ability of specifications metadata, data backup, data security measures	Improvement awareness of protecting data security, learning data backup strategy and measures
Data publishing and sharing research data ethics	Lack awareness of data publication and sharing	Enhancement data sharing awareness and choosing the appropriate way to publish data
Data rights and ethics	Lack awareness of data citing and the rights related to scientific research data	Learning knowledge of data citation and the rights of scientific data management

5 Data Literacy Education Design

Based on survey, the data literacy education model of teachers, students and curriculum is constructe (Fig. 1), the education content is based on the research data lifecycle and includes three levels of learning modes, that is, basic learning, advanced learning and promotion learning. At the same time, we have also designed data literacy education implementation scenes for graduate students in UCAS, and provide evidence for libraries to implement data literacy education services better.

Fig. 1. Data literacy education design

6 Conclusion

In this research, through conducting data literacy investigation among graduate students by means of a questionnaire survey, the current situation of their data literacy and the need to develop them are revealed. Based on the survey results, we developed a tailor-made course to help students improve their data literacy competencies. The results not only provide an implementation program for the improvement of graduate students in UCAS, but also provide a lot of useful information for assisting future librarians in incorporating data literacy skills into their services, especially for academic and research librarians to prepare and develop a data literacy course for their fields' graduate students.

References

1. Association of College and Research Libraries: Working Group on Intersections of Scholarly Communication and Information Literacy. Intersections of Scholarly Communication and Information Literacy: Creating Strategic Collaborations for a Changing Academic Environment. Association of College and Research Libraries (2013)
2. Carlson, J., Fosmire, M., Miller, C.C., Nelson, M.S.: Determining data information literacy needs: a study of students and research faculty. Portal: Libr. Acad. **11**(2), 629–657 (2011)
3. Carlson, J., Johnston, L., Westra, B., Nichols, M.: Developing an approach for data management education: a report from the data information literacy project. Int. J. Digit. Curation **8**(1), 204–217 (2013)
4. NECDMC. http://library.umassmed.edu/necdmc/index
5. Data Information Literacy. http://www.datainfolit.org/
6. DataTrain Project. http://www.lib.cam.ac.uk/preservation/datatrain/
7. MANTRA Research Data Management Training. http://mantra.edina.ac.uk/

Data Literacy Among Charles University PhD Students: Are They Prepared for Their Research Careers?

Barbora Drobikova, Adela Jarolimkova(✉), and Martin Soucek

Faculty of Arts, Institute of Information Studies and Librarianship, Charles University, Prague, Czech Republic
{barbora.drobikova, adela.jarolimkova, martin.soucek}@ff.cuni.cz

Abstract. The goal of our study, based on an extensive survey, is to discover the attitudes toward data sharing and research data management among Charles University doctoral students. The research was carried out as a part of a Data Literacy Multinational Study cooperation project. We have used a Czech version of the data literacy questionnaire presented by Gobinda Chowdhury et al. at the ECIL conference 2016. Results show that doctoral students from all disciplines are willing to share data, but they are not aware of open access principles. Doctoral students have confirmed they share their data at least among their research teams. The results do not show a significant difference in this practice between disciplines. Doctoral students prefer their research data to be preserved for further research.

Keywords: Information literacy · Data literacy · Data sharing · Data sharing practices

1 Introduction

In recent years, the availability and volume of scientific data have grown exponentially. Research funding bodies encourage, or even require, open publication not only of research results, but also publication of involved data as well. Data sharing is an essential component of the direction in which science is moving [1]. This situation creates a need for training in data literacy: a set of competencies that can be defined as the component of information literacy, which enables individuals to access, interpret, critically assess, manage, handle and ethically use data [2].

Before designing any instructional intervention, it is nevertheless necessary to assess the current level of data management awareness, competencies and skills of individual researchers. This is the group, on whom the intervention is focused. The situation in the Czech Republic in the field of scientific data and data literacy has not been assessed so far. Our paper's goal, based on an extensive survey, is therefore to discover the attitudes among doctoral students in the Czech Republic toward data sharing and management. We will use a sample from Charles University in Prague.

Charles University is the largest multidisciplinary, research-oriented institution of higher education in the Czech Republic. It consists of seventeen faculties (individual

S. Kurbanoğlu et al. (Eds.): ECIL 2017, CCIS 810, pp. 169–177, 2018.
https://doi.org/10.1007/978-3-319-74334-9_18

schools) and has more than 50,000 students, 7,500 of whom are doctoral students. The university has approximately 4,600 academics and researchers [3].

The issues of data storage and data access are quite new in the Czech Republic. Charles University does not have its own open research data repository. The university has only collaborated on building a technological infrastructure for data archiving and sharing within research teams in private repositories (ownCloud service) [4].

2 Literature Review

The body of literature on data literacy has been growing steadily for several years. Its core focuses on the definition of data literacy and its main competencies and required skills. As Koltay points out in his reviews of the data literacy field [5, 6], several other labels have been used throughout the literature for the data literacy concept; namely, data information literacy [7], science data literacy [8], data management literacy [9] and research data literacy [10]. There seems to be no definite agreement on the preferred terminology, but data literacy and data information literacy are the most commonly used terms.

The understanding and scope of data literacy has evolved over time; together with its relation to statistical literacy and information literacy. It was used at first only in relation to numerical data; meaning the same thing as statistical literacy or quantitative literacy [11] or even understood as part of statistical literacy [12]. Its meaning was later broadened to cover the collection, processing, manipulation, evaluation and usage of all kinds of scientific data [8]. The foundations of the current scope of data literacy were laid by Carlson et al. with their data information literacy that joined the researcher-as-producer aspect together with the until-then-used aspect of researcher-as-consumer of data. Their concept also changed the view of the data-statistical-information literacy triangle. In Carlson's approach, data information literacy builds on and reintegrates data, statistical and information literacy into an emerging set of skills [7]. The scope of the concept was accepted by other researchers, but the term data information literacy is used only by part of them (for example, see Refs. [13, 14]), while others stick to the term data literacy [2, 6] because of it being more clear and straightforward [6].

So far, the only research in the field of research data in the Czech Republic that has some implications for the data literacy is the dissertation by Pavlaskova [15]. Her work focused primarily on research data from the viewpoint of long-term preservation and archiving, but in the process of her research, she examined different types of data by analysing data appendices from Charles University (Prague) dissertations.

3 Methods

The research was carried out as part of a Data Literacy Multinational Study cooperation project. We used a Czech version of the data literacy questionnaire presented by Chowdhury et al. [16] at the ECIL conference 2016. We distributed it by email to all academics and PhD students affiliated with Charles University.

The structure of the Charles University in Prague is a little different from the institutions the questionnaire has been intended for. Charles University consist of many various faculties, which offer doctoral studies in many disciplines. PhD students were sometimes not able to select his/her discipline listed in the questionnaire. However, the questionnaire is a very suitable starting point for more in-depth research that will follow, and it also offers the possibility of cross-country comparison on a scale till now unparalleled. The questionnaire considers researchers as both producers and consumers of data and focuses on three main topics:

- production and use of data (types of data and volume of data);
- attitudes toward data sharing and data sharing behaviour;
- awareness of various aspects of data sharing (metadata, identifiers and versioning) and data sharing practices.

Data, in the context of this study, is understood very broadly (in line with the definition given by the National Academy of Sciences) as facts, numbers, letters and symbols that describe an object, idea, condition, situation or other factors (National Academy of Sciences, 1999) and independent of its form. It reflects the practices of both natural sciences on one hand and humanities and social sciences on the other.

4 Survey Sample

We decided to use the "census" polling method because of the heterogeneity of the target group. We used the email addresses of academics and doctoral students taken from the Charles University information system.

We collected 1,434 completed questionnaires, 826 of which came from doctoral students and formed the basis for the following analysis (it is approximately 11% of all PhD students at the Charles University).

After we cleaned the data, we always separated the results into for basic scientific areas: humanities (including history and philology), medicine, natural sciences (including mathematics, physics and biology) and social sciences.

5 Research Questions and Hypotheses

As data management is an integral part of science nowadays, we presumed that the willingness and ability to share data and archive them correctly is one of the prerequisites for a successful research career. Hypotheses formulation is therefore guided by a general point of view to consider the current attitudes of doctoral students toward research data sharing and toward descriptions of current practices.

- H1: CU doctoral students are willing to share research data and support open access to data.
- H2: Research teams currently share data, but most probably there exist fundamental differences between subjects.
- H3: Doctoral students view research data archiving as an important prerequisite to further research work.

We used a five-point scale for several questions in the questionnaire. However, for clearer presentation, we merged the answers "I strongly agree" and "I agree" as YES and "I disagree" and "I strongly disagree" as NO.

6 Results Analysis

6.1 CU Doctoral Students are Willing to Share Research Data and Support Open Access to Data (H1)

The research into the attitudes toward research data sharing and the willingness of doctoral students to share data and toward open access produces interesting results. Results show that 64% (n = 826) of doctoral students are not familiar with open access issues. Nevertheless, as further results show, doctoral students do not lack an openness and a willingness to share data (Fig. 1).

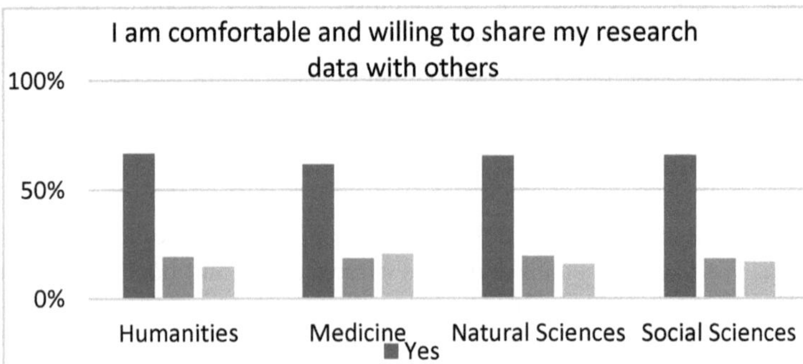

Fig. 1. Willingness to share data

The next attitudinal question on research data sharing concerned doctoral students' opinions on the issue of potential ethical problems that can arise in the process of data sharing, such as whether open data sharing can be contrary to ethical principles (for example, personal data protection). Doctoral students perceive this problem unequivocally as acute, and they mostly expressed that concern (Fig. 2).

As for other potential problems that can arise regarding data sharing, most respondents fear misinterpretation (37%) and misuse of data (33%). On the other hand, lack of policy and lack of resources do not cause concern.

6.2 Research Teams Currently Share Data, But Most Probably There Exist Fundamental Differences Between Disciplines

Outside its research into general attitudes, the questionnaire explored current data sharing practices as well. Here, we see the difference between the humanities and social sciences on one hand, where 36% (n = 179 for humanities, n = 139 for social sciences) of doctoral students do not share data, and medicine and the natural sciences on the other, where only five percent (n = 148) and ten percent (n = 360) report not sharing data. However, the other answers show that most doctoral students from all disciplines share data in some way (Fig. 3).

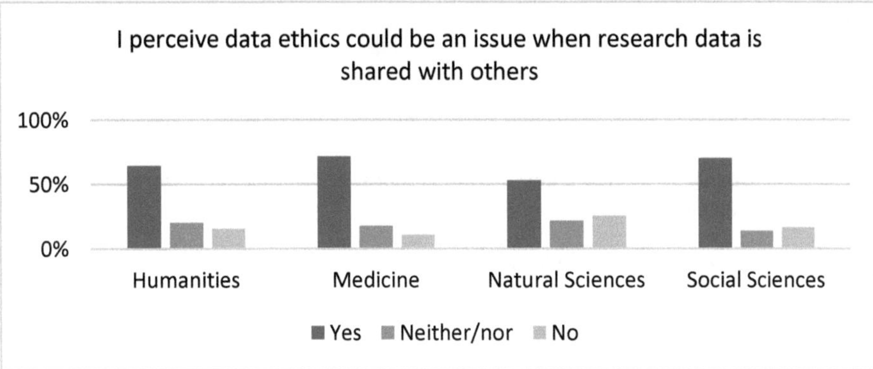

Fig. 2. Data sharing and ethical issues

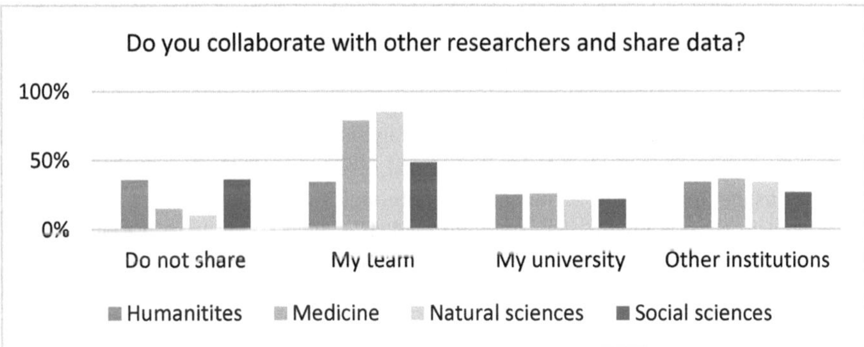

Fig. 3. Data sharing practices

Sharing data does not necessarily mean open access to data, as is shown by answers to the next question on data sharing. The most frequent means of sharing data is upon request. On the contrary, open access is the least frequent method. The smallest share was observed in medicine, with only two percent (n = 148) reporting use of the latter practice. Given the willingness of doctoral students to share data, this situation is more likely caused by a lack of easy solutions for data sharing or ignorance of them (Fig. 4).

6.3 Doctoral Students View Research Data Archiving as an Important Prerequisite to Further Research Work (H3)

On the issue of data archiving, even after a project wherein data was collected or created had concluded, doctoral students expressed themselves relatively unequivocally. The majority of students would welcome the possibility of long-term data

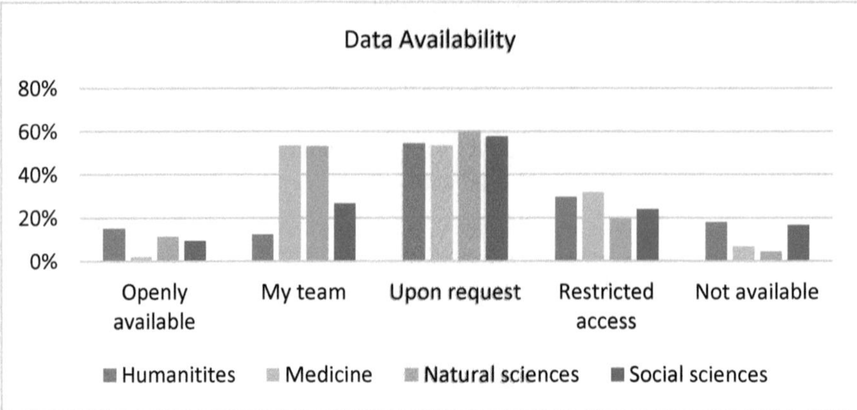

Fig. 4. Data availability

archiving. This question is of the utmost importance to the university. It points to the fact that doctoral students would appreciate the existence of a university data repository. Overall, 90% (n = 826) of all respondents want to archive their data (Fig. 5).

Answers to the question on current data storage practices show that an absolute majority of doctoral students store their data on their own devices (PCs and tablets). The differences between subject areas are negligible. 35–45% of doctoral students use external repositories; usage of cloud-based storage is on the same level. Only in social sciences does use of cloud-based storage exceed 40% (namely 46%, n = 139). Central repository usage appeared in some answers, although the university does not have any central repository as we have already mentioned (Fig. 6). Respondents probably regard subject repositories or repositories of their institutes as central.

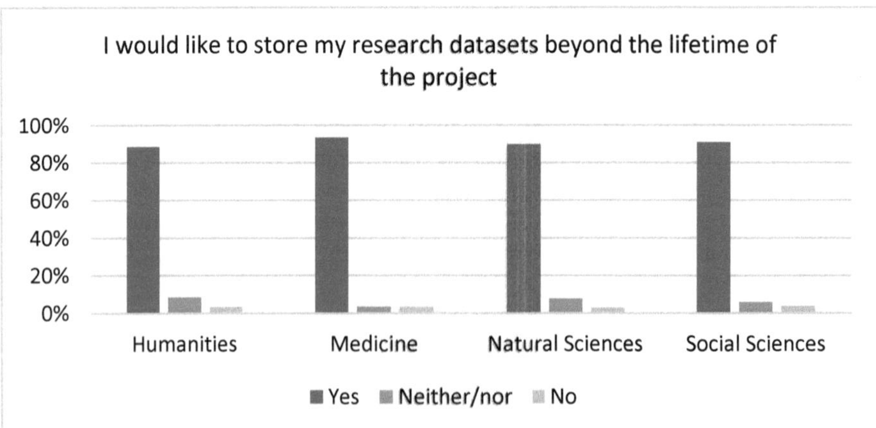

Fig. 5. Research data preservation

Even if they want to store their data, the doctoral students do not in most cases use metadata for data description in their current data archiving practices. Although 60% (n = 826) declare, that they know the term metadata, 39% do not use them at all and 34% (n = 826) rarely.

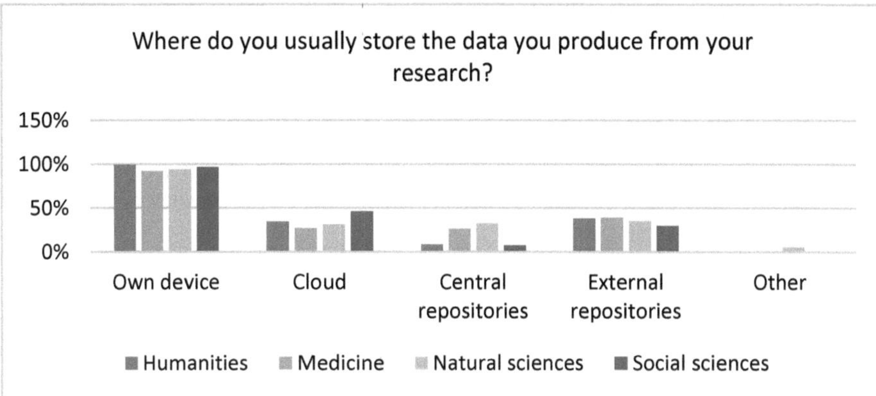

Fig. 6. Data storage

The volume of data that should be stored is substantial for the future building of a central university repository. Currently, most doctoral students use data amounting to numbers in mega or gigabytes. The same volume applies to the data resulting from their research.

7 Limitations of the Study

As the selection may be biased in favour of individuals who already have an interest in data literacy and who may consider data literacy skills more relevant to their work than individuals who do not have such interests, the results cannot be considered a general view in relation to the research population of the Czech Republic.

8 Discussion

We presumed that CU doctoral students are willing to share research data and support open access to data. This hypothesis has been confirmed only partially. The most important finding is, that doctoral students from all disciplines are willing to share data and that they already share them in some way. The concerns expressed in the connection with data sharing, mainly data misuse and misinterpretation and ethical issues, correspond to findings of other studies, for example Tenopir [1]. The difficulty is, that doctoral students in our study are not aware of open access principles and so the requirements for open access to data, that are part of some funding schemes, might cause problems to them.

We also assumed that research teams currently share data, but there likely exist fundamental differences between subjects. Doctoral students have confirmed they share their data at least among their research teams, most frequently upon request. Nevertheless, the results do not show a significant difference in this practice between disciplines. There are probably other factors that influence the willingness to share data, as is shown for example in a study by Kim and Stanton [17].

Our last hypothesis was that doctoral students view research data archiving as an important prerequisite to further research work. This hypothesis has been confirmed. Doctoral students prefer their research data to be preserved for further research. However, they are not skilled in data management, which is probably a consequence of the fragmented approach to data management and data literacy issues at the Charles University.

9 Conclusion

At Charles University, doctoral students are willing to share data. Their attitudes show that they understand this task as an important one in their research careers. They would prefer data preservation for further research to take place in a common university data repository. The results show, on the other hand, that doctoral students are not aware of new trends in data sharing. First of all, they are unfamiliar with open access principles and principles concerning data management. We can say, that they are prepared only partially for their research careers, as they understand the importance of data in their research and they are prepared to share them, but they lack practical data management skills needed to manage their data effectively. For their better preparedness, it will be necessary to introduce data management skills training for doctoral students at the university.

Acknowledgements. The publication was supported by the Charles University programme Progres Q15 "Life course, lifestyle and quality of life from the perspective of individual adaptation and the relationship of the actors and institutions."

References

1. Tenopir, C., Dalton, E.D., Allard, S., Frame, M.: Changes in data sharing and data reuse practices and perceptions among scientists worldwide. Plos One **10** (2015)
2. Calzada Prado, J., Marzal, M.Á.: Incorporating data literacy into information literacy programs: core competencies and contents. Libri **63**, 123–134 (2013)
3. Charles University. Facts and figures. http://www.cuni.cz/UKEN-109.html
4. Cesnet. https://www.cesnet.cz/services/owncloud/?lang=en
5. Koltay, T.: Data literacy: in search of a name and identity. J. Doc. **71**, 401–415 (2015). (Online)
6. Koltay, T.: Data literacy for researchers and data librarians. J. Libr. Inf. Sci. **49**, 3–14 (2017). (Online)

7. Carlson, J., Fosmire, M., Miller, C.C., Sapp Nelson, M.: Determining data information literacy needs: a study of students and research faculty. Libr. Acad. **11**, 629–657 (2011)
8. Qin, J., D'Ignazio, J.: The central role of metadata in a science data literacy course. J. Libr. Metadata **10**, 188–204 (2010)
9. Haendel, M.A., Vasilevsky, N.A., Wurz, J.A.: Dealing with data: a case study on information and data management literacy. Plos Biol. **10** (2012)
10. Schneider, R.: Research data literacy. In: Kurbanoğlu, S., Grassian, E., Mizrachi, D., Catts, R., Špiranec, S. (eds.) ECIL 2013. CCIS, vol. 397, pp. 134–140. Springer, Cham (2013). https://doi.org/10.1007/978-3-319-03919-0_16
11. Hunt, K.: The challenges of integrating data literacy into the curriculum in an undergraduate institution. Iassist Q. (Summer/Fall), 12–16 (2004)
12. Shield, M.: Information literacy, statistical literacy, data literacy. IASSIST Q. Summer/Fall, 6–11 (2004)
13. Frank, E.P., Pharo, N.: Academic librarians in data information literacy instruction: a case study in meteorology. Coll. Res. Libr. **77**, 536–552 (2016)
14. Sapp Nelson, M.R.: A pilot competency matrix for data management skills: a step toward the development of systematic data information literacy programs. J. Escience Libr. **6** (2017)
15. Pavlaskova, E.: Analýza výzkumných dat na základě fondu disertačních prací Univerzity Karlovy v Praze s ohledem na dlouhodobé uložení digitálních objektů (thesis). Praha (2016)
16. Chowdhury, G., Walton, G., Kurbanoglu, S., Unal, Y., Boustany, J.: Information practices for sustainability: information, data and environmental literacy. In: Spiranec, S., Kurbanoglu, S., Landova, H. (eds.) The Fourth European Conference on Information Literacy (ECIL), p. 22. Association of Libraries of Czech Universities, Prague (2016)
17. Kim, Y., Stanton, J.M.: Institutional and individual factors affecting scientists' data-sharing behaviors: a multilevel analysis. JASIST, **97**, 776–799 (2016)

Data Literacy, Collaboration and Sharing of Research Data Among Academics at the University of Iceland

Ágústa Pálsdóttir(✉)

Department of Information Science, University of Iceland,
Gimli v/Sæmundargötu, 101 Reykjavík, Iceland
agustap@hi.is

Abstract. Data literacy and data management have received growing attention in the past years, with open access and data sharing plans as a focus point. The study is part of an international research and the same questionnaire was used by all countries. The focus here is on data practices, collaboration and data sharing among academics at the University of Iceland. Response rate was 15%. Collaborating and sharing data with others was found to be a normal practice in the academics' work. This was done within a rather closed circle of researchers, whom they knew. Thus, their relationship is built on trust that has developed through the collaboration and partnership and it may be assumed that this forms the basis for data sharing. Offering open access to data to everyone was rare. Legal and ethical issues were the main causes of concern for sharing data but other reasons were also identified.

Keywords: Research collaboration · Data literacy · Data sharing Open access

1 Introduction

Research data literacy and data management have received growing attention in the past years. As research funders have started to put emphasis on the valuables of the data and the possibility of reusing it, open access to research data and data sharing plans have become a focus point [1–3]. Data sets are increasingly considered part of the scholarly output and are being distributed as such [4].

This has started to create new demands on researchers, who are faced with complex challenges that they have not previously had to deal with. As a result, there is a growing interest among information specialists in how they can offer support to the research community on how to address these demands. In particular, information specialists who work in academic and research libraries need to be aware of these trends. It is expected that an important function of information service in the coming years will be to offer expertise service at developing data management plans, data description and preservation strategies [5].

Research data literacy has been identified as a sub-discipline of information literacy [6]. In a review article of the importance of data literacy for researchers and the

S. Kurbanoğlu et al. (Eds.): ECIL 2017, CCIS 810, pp. 178–185, 2018.
https://doi.org/10.1007/978-3-319-74334-9_19

possible roles of academic and research libraries in research data management, Koltay [5] defined data literacy as “a specific skill set and knowledge base, which empowers individuals to transform data into information and into actionable knowledge by enabling them to access, interpret, critically assess, manage, and ethically use data” (p. 10). He furthermore pointed out that the definition corresponds strongly with the joint definition by UNESCO and IFLA (International Federation of Library and Information Association) of Media and Information Literacy, which allows individuals to “…access, retrieve, understand, evaluate and use, create, as well as share information and media content in all formats…” [7].

Koltay [5] further noted that data literacy should act as an incentive for researcher to share their data with others. In an examination of the data sharing practices among scientists, Tenopir et al. [8] found that if 85% of participants in their study were interested in using datasets from other researchers if it could be easily accessed. The researcher’s willingness to share their own data, however, was not as great, because 46% do not make their data electronically available to others, while a similar share of them claimed to make at least some of their data available. Other studies have indicated an even lower interest among researchers for making their data openly available to everyone, with the share of those who do so ranging from 25% [9] to 15% [10]. It seems that data is mainly being shared with researchers own network of collaborators [9, 10].

The fact that so many researchers do not share their data openly may be caused by a variety of reasons. Managing research data for sharing is for example a time consuming activity that involves many steps [11], and it may reduce the researchers interest if they feel that they are not being rewarded for the effort that is needed. Tenopir et al. found that the main reasons reported for not sharing data with others were that the researchers did not have sufficient time for it, and a lack of funding. Other barriers reported were not having a place for the data, lack of standards, and that the sponsor does not require data sharing [8]. The fear of researchers regarding legal issues and the misuse of their data has also been described as major barriers for sharing data [9]. Thessen and Patterson have identified the need for both cultural changes and technical advances to encourage and promote data sharing. While the latter is considered easier to solve, cultural differences across disciplines and sub-disciplines call for better understanding [9]. Hatter et al. have added ethical challenges to these, and noted that researchers must also ensure that the ethical standards of academia are being met [12]. It has, furthermore, been pointed out that the data may be a vital asset for the researchers, which they use to promote their career [10].

The aim of the present study is to investigate the data literacy and attitude towards the sharing of research data, among academics at the University of Iceland. To do so, answers to the following research question will be sought: (1) What characterises the data sharing practices of the academics? (2) What challenges are the academics facing regarding data sharing? Recognition of the academics’ attitudes towards the issue of collaboration and data sharing, and the problems and challenges that they are facing, is critical in order to design relevant support for them. The study results may provide important understanding about these issues. The findings can be used by universities to develop data policies and services that assist the research community.

2 Method

This is the Icelandic part of an international online survey that investigates research data literacy and data management, conducted among academic researchers and doctoral students at the University of Iceland. The same questionnaire was used by all participating countries. The online system Lime Survey, which is an open source software, was used for data collection. The survey was sent by email in February and March 2017, to a sample of 225 doctoral students and 567 academic researchers. The response rate for doctoral students was 25% (n = 56) and for academic researchers the response rate was 15% (n = 85). However, the current paper involves only results from the academic researchers. Of those academics who replied to the survey, 51.76% are from the field of social science, 35.30% from science and 12.94% from humanities. A total of 52.94% were men and 47.06 were women.

The questionnaire was translated from English to Icelandic. The measurement instrument consisted of 26 questions in all. A total of 18 questions emphasized data literacy, awareness of data management issues, the extent of collaboration and sharing of research data and the researchers' attitude towards this. In addition, the questionnaire consisted of seven background questions, and one open question.

As previously noted, the content of the survey is data literacy and research data management. It is, however, not possible within the constraints of this paper to investigate all the questions in the survey. Therefore, it was decided to focus on six questions about the following items: the file type of data that the participants normally use for their research, how they usually get the data for their research, how they usually use data that they get from others/outside sources; if they collaborate with other researchers and share data with them, what kind of access to their data they allow others, and finally, if they have any concerns for sharing data with others. All the questions allow multiple answers. The analysis of the data is descriptive.

3 Results

The chapter starts by presenting results about what file type of data the participants use for their research work. This will be followed by results about how they get data for research and what is needed by them to be able to use data from others. After that, results about collaboration with other researchers, data sharing practices, as well as open access and concerns regarding it will be presented.

Figure 1 shows that standard office documents are being used by the overwhelming majority of the participants, or 88.24%. After that come internet and web-based data (64.70%), images (58.82%) and structured scientific and statistical data (52.94%). What is by far the least common to use is configuration data (3.53%) and structured graphics (4.71%). In addition, very few of the participants claim to use software applications (8.24%) and encoded text (9.41%).

Results about how the participants usually get data for their research are presented in Fig. 2. The question contained five statements and the participants were asked to give an answer to all that applied to them.

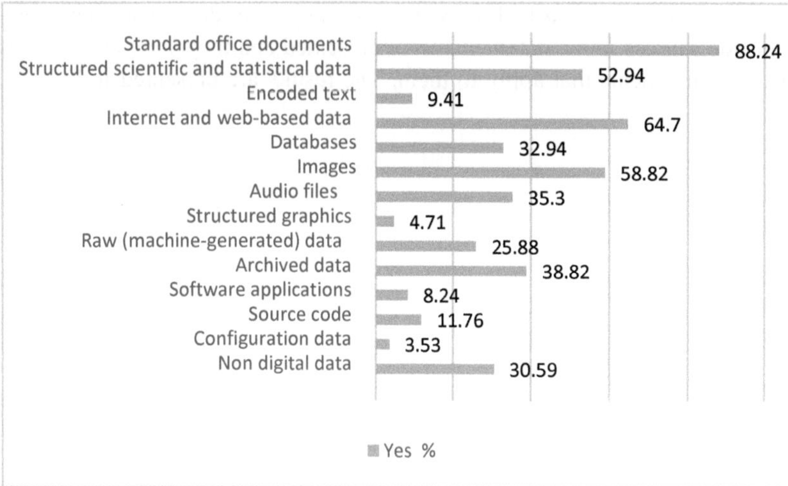

Fig. 1. Please indicate the file type of data that you normally use for your research

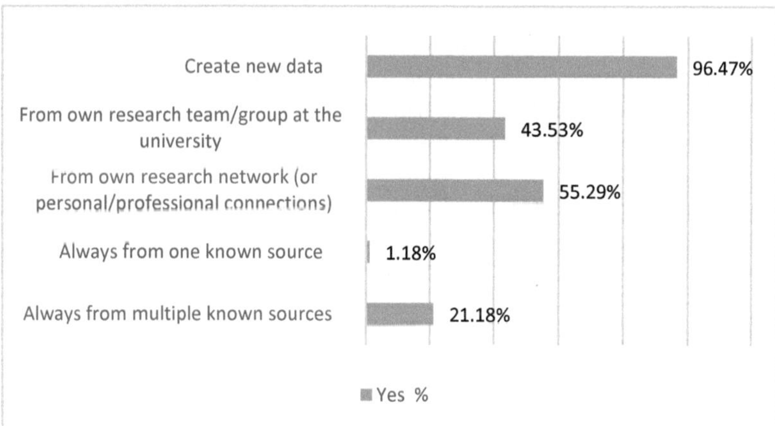

Fig. 2. How do you usually get the data for your research?

Creating new data for research work is what is most common among the participants. As can be seen from Fig. 2, the vast majority of them claim that they usually get data by doing so. Over half of them claim to get data from their research network, while less than half of the participants obtains it from their own research team or group at their university. Getting data always from one known source is almost unheard of among them and the majority of participants do not get data from multiple know sources.

The participants were asked how they usually use data that they get from others/outside sources. Four statements were presented and they were asked to give an answer to all statements that apply to them. The results are presented in Fig. 3.

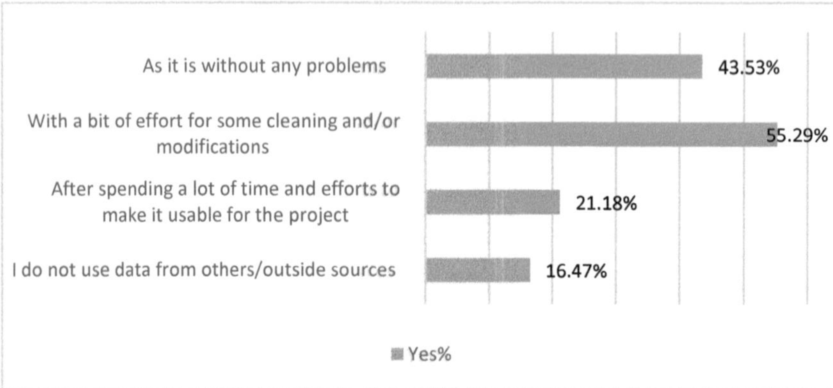

Fig. 3. How do you usually use data that you get from others/outside sources?

From Fig. 3 it can be seen that when data from others/outside sources is being used, over half of the participants needs to put in some effort for cleaning and/or modifying it before the data can be used. Less than half of the participants state that they have no problems using the data as it is. Over twenty percent claim that a lot of time and effort may be needed for making the data usable.

When the participants were asked if they collaborate with other researchers and share their data with them, most of the participants, or 88.24%, claimed that they do so. It is most common (61.18%) to collaborate and share data with researchers that belong to the same research team as they do. In addition, more than half of the participants replied that they collaborate and share data with other researchers in the same university (56.47%) and half of them (50.59%) that they do so with researchers in other institutions.

Figure 4 presents results from two questions. The first one asked what kind of access to their research data the participants provide others with. The second question asked if they have any concerns for sharing their research data with others. At each question, five statements were presented and the participants were asked to give answers to all statements that apply to them.

As can be seen from Fig. 4, the great majority of participants, or 85.88%, do not allow open access to their research data to everyone. Nevertheless, a similar rate of participants (83.53%) do not agree with the statement that their data is not available to anyone else. What is most common is for the participants to have the data openly available to members of their research team (32.94%). A similar share of participants claim to allow access to their data upon request as those who allow access to only some parts of the dataset while other parts have restricted access.

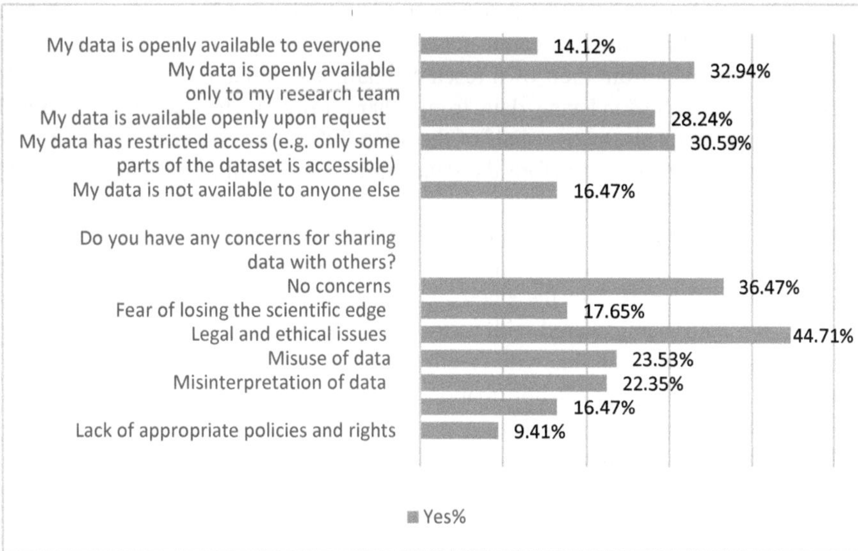

Fig. 4. Open access to research data – Concerns for sharing research data with others

The majority of the participants denied the statement that they had no concerns about sharing their data with others, hence they were worried about it, while over one third of them claimed that they had no concerns. What is most common is concerns about legal and ethical issues. A similar rate, or less than a quarter, of participants claimed that they had concerns about the misuse of shared data as was concerned about the misinterpretation of the data. On the other hand, only less a small rate of participants, or less than 10%, is concerned about the lack of appropriate policies and rights protection in relation to the sharing of data with others (Fig. 4).

4 Discussion

The study sought to contribute to current research into data literacy and the sharing of research data by presenting findings about academic researchers at the University of Iceland. For that purpose the study investigated various aspects related to the data practices, collaboration, open access to data, as well as the challenges and concerns that the academics facing.

The results show that an overwhelming majority of the participants (96.47%) create new data for their research work. When asked what file types they use for their data, the results show that standard office documents is by far the most commonly used (88.24%), which is consistent with the results from the PARSE Insight study (94%). In addition, the results that the majority of participants use web-based data (64.70%) and images (58.82%) is in line with results from the PARSE study [9]. The current study, however, also found that it was common to use structured scientific and statistical data (52.94%).

Besides, creating new data for their research, the majority of participants (55.29%) claim to get data from their research network or through personal/professional connections. Getting data from their own research team or group at their university is also rather common (43.53%). Using data from others however, requires some work on behalf of the participants, as over half of them (55.29%) need to put in some effort for cleaning and/or modifying it before the data can be used, while 43.53% say that they can use it without any problems.

The great majority of the participants claim to collaborate and share data with other researchers (88.24%), which is consistent with the results that a slightly less share of them (83.53%) disagrees with the statement that their data is not available to anyone else. Data is mainly being shared with members of the participants own research teams (61.8%), a finding that is in line with results from the PARSE Insight study (58%) [9], whereas the study by Research Information Network (RIN) found that a lower rate of their participants (37%) did so [10].

The current study, furthermore, shows that more than half of the participants (56.47%) collaborate and share data with other researchers in the same university, and that doing so with researchers in other institutions is only slightly less common (50.59%). This share is quite high compared with the results by Research Information Network (RIN) that 19% of researchers share data openly within their research community [10].

Open access to the research data, on the other hand, is not something that the participants want to offer to everyone, as the great majority of them, or 85.88%, claim that they do not allow it. This is the same result as in the study by Research Information Network (RIN), where 15% of researchers provided open access to their data [10], while the PARSE Insight study found that a higher share of researchers, or 25%, offered open access to data [9]. Results from the study by Tenopir et al. [8], however, show that 46% of those who replied to the question did not make their data electronically available to others.

What is most common is for the participants to have the data openly available to members of their own research team (67.06%). One way to allow others to make use of the research data, although it is not completely open, is to grant restricted access to it. This can be done, for example by granting admission to some parts of the datasets, or by allowing access to the data upon request. However, only about one third of the participants offered these options.

Prior studies have identified various barriers for researchers sharing data with others [8–12]. In this study, the majority of participants (63.53%) claimed to be worried about sharing data with others. Legal and ethical issues were the main cause of concern (44.71%), which is similar to the results found by the PARSE Insight study that 41% of researchers consider legal issues to be a barrier for sharing research data [9]. When other barriers are compared, the results in the current study show that concerns about the misuse of shared data (23.53%) and fear of losing the scientific edge (17%) was much less common and not comparable to the findings of the PARSE Insight study (41% and 27% respectively) [9].

It needs to be kept in mind that the response rate in the study was very low, only 15%. Therefore, the findings cannot be generalized to all academic researchers at the University of Iceland. Nevertheless, the results may provide important understanding about their research data procedures, in particular what characterises their data sharing practices as well as the challenges that they face regarding it.

Taken together, the results indicate that it is usual for the academics in the study to collaborate and share data with others and that it may be considered a normal practice in their work. However, the results also indicate that this is done within a rather closed circle of other researchers whom they already know and have established a relationship of collaboration. It may be assumed that their relationship is built on trust that has developed through the partnership and that this forms the basis for data sharing. The great majority of the participants claims to have concerns for sharing data with others and does not offer open access to their data to everyone. Although legal and ethical issues were reported as the main cause of worry, other reasons were also identified. Thus, it is well possible that it is the combined effect of reasons, rather the individual causes, that has influence on the data sharing practices of the academics.

References

1. Haendel, M.A., Vasilevsky, N.A., Wirz, J.A.: Dealing with data: a case study on information and data management literacy. PLoS Biol. **10**(5), e1001339 (2012). https://doi.org/10.1371/journal.pbio.1001339
2. Koltay, T.: Data literacy: in search of a name and identity. J. Doc. **71**(2), 401–415 (2015)
3. Martin, E.R.: What is data literacy? J. eSci. Librariansh. **3**(1), 1–2 (2014)
4. McMillan, D.: Data sharing and discovery: what librarians need to know. J. Acad. Librariansh. **40**, 541–549 (2014). https://doi.org/10.1016/j.acalib.2014.06.011
5. Koltay, T.: Data literacy for researchers and data librarians. J. Librariansh. Inf. Sci. **49**(1), 3–14 (2017)
6. Schneider, R.: Research data literacy. In: Kurbanoğlu, S., Grassian, E., Mizrachi, D., Catts, R., Špiranec, S. (eds.) ECIL 2013. CCIS, vol. 397, pp. 134–140. Springer, Cham (2013). https://doi.org/10.1007/978-3-319-03919-0_16
7. UNESCO: Media and Information Literacy (2014). http://www.uis.unesco.org/Communication/Pages/information-literacy.aspx
8. Tenopir, C., Allard, S., Douglass, K., Aydinoglu, A.U., Wu, L., et al.: Data sharing by scientists: practices and perceptions. PLoS One **6**(6), e21101 (2011). https://doi.org/10.1371/journal.pone.0021101
9. PARSE.Insight: Insight into Digital Preservation of Research Output in Europe: Survey Report (2009). http://libereurope.eu/wp-content/uploads/2010/01/PARSE.Insight.-Deliverable-D3.4-Survey-Report.-of-research-output-Europe-Title-of-Deliverable-Survey-Report.pdf
10. Research Information Network (RIN): If you build it, will they come? How researchers perceive and use web 2.0. Research Information Network Report (2010). http://www.rin.ac.uk/our-work/communicating-and-disseminating-research/use-and-relevance-web-20-researchers
11. Thessen, A.E., Patterson, D.J.: Data issues in the life sciences. ZooKeys **150**, 15–51 (2011). https://doi.org/10.3897/zookeys.150.1766
12. Hartter, J., Ryan, S.J., MacKenzie, C.A., Parker, J.N., Strasser, C.A.: Spatially explicit data: stewardship and ethical challenges in science. PLoS Biol. **11**(9), e1001634 (2013). https://doi.org/10.1371/journal.pbio.1001634

Date Literacy as Requirement for China's Library and Information Profession: A Preliminary Research on Recruitment Data

Jing Zhang, Qianli Lin, and Peng Xiao(✉)

Sun Yat-sen University, Guangzhou, China
xiaop25@mail.sysu.edu.cn

Abstract. The big data era has arrived. Library and information schools should track the emerging trend among employers demanding skills in working with big data. Educators should be able to respond to the demand for talent in this area by educating graduates and undergraduates to meet social needs. The article provides a preliminary outcome of a long-term research project of the School of Information Management at Sun Yat-sen University using content analysis as a method to study recruitment data, from November 2016 to January 2017. The framework of content analysis comes from earlier research on Data Competence Framework (DCF), which is part of the project, and in this period, 358 positions from 147 libraries and related organizations posted online, 66 of which met at least one competence index of the DCF. The study finds that libraries and information institutions, of different types and across various regions, are becoming more and more interested in data literacy as an ability among their future employees.

Keywords: Data Competence Framework · Data literacy
Chinese library profession · Talent demand

1 Introduction

Data literacy, big data and many other data related concepts have occupied the centre ground of library and information science in China in recent years. The idea of a "Data era" grows in strength and deeply affects our fields by evoking brand-new information needs, changing existing positions, and creating new jobs. More and more Chinese institutions require that their employees demonstrate the capacity to process and manage data. However, LIS schools in China still have not come to an agreement in establishing curriculum related to data science. The Asia-Pacific Congress on Information Discipline Review (CIDR), held in our school last November, was witness this divergence. While some LIS schools are still very conservative in their curricular offerings, some have already tried to replace Information System Management, a traditional program in LIS schools, with a new title: Data Management.

Divergence frequently happens in LIS field, but real questions should be asked: what exactly happens in the job market after the dawn of the data era? What competencies relevant to data are really needed in libraries and information institutions? Have

S. Kurbanoğlu et al. (Eds.): ECIL 2017, CCIS 810, pp. 186–194, 2018.
https://doi.org/10.1007/978-3-319-74334-9_20

any new positions appeared in the field and have any faded out? Answers to these questions would contribute to bridging the gap between conservative ideas and a more "radical" approach that might lead to the building of a solid foundation for the transformation of LIS education.

Collecting and analysing job ads is an established method in answering the questions above. In order to follow the job market over the long haul, the School of Information Management at Sun Yat-sen University launched a project called "Tack the Next Move for LIS" (TNM-LIS) to crawl, preserve, and study job ads data, to arrive at suggestions to cope with current trends.

Though we regard TNM-LIS as an engine for long-term improvement and development, no doubt the rise of "data" is a tipping-point for such a program. Therefore, LIS profession's demands on data literacy became a pilot program for such a project. This paper presents a preliminary outcome of the program, the point of which is showing how we build framework and conduct studies, as well as some analysis of the results of our early data. It should be noted that, the TNM-LIS adjusted its rules of data collecting through such actions as expanding the targeted sources of our crawler. Such adjustment would change the composition of the database and make it not considered rigorous enough to compare data over different given times. But the purpose of TNM-LIS is to follow the practical needs of the LIS profession continuously, not to publish a one-time paper so it is inevitable that the results might be "in flux".

2 Literature Review

Analysis of librarian and information specialists' positions is one of the most common research topics in LIS across various regions and different kind of positions.

Through studying the qualifications and skill requirements of digital librarians in academic libraries, Choi and Rasmussen found that there was an increasing demand for the utilize of digital technologies and resources, management, and communication skills [1, p. 157–167]. Wang et al. sought out contemporary trends of reference librarians and proved reference librarians needed more requirements and higher education background [2, pp. 489–494]. Distance education librarians [3, pp. 500–505], preservation librarianship [4, pp. 646–656], and cataloguing librarians [5, pp. 1–23, 6, pp. 352–363] have been discussed.

Some of the researchers focused on a specific geographical location. Alonso-Regalado and Van Ullen took Latin American and the Caribbean as their scope of study [7, pp. 139–158]. White concentrated on academic libraries in the United States [8, pp. 372–382]. LIS professionals in the UK had been researched by Orme in 2008 [9, pp. 619–633].

Some of the studies focused on requirements of the same position at different levels. Cullen investigated management skills and leadership developments of library and information service workers among senior managers, middle managers, and supervisory managers [10, pp. 138–145]. Entry-level catalogue positions had also been discussed by Hall-Ellis [11, pp. 33–72].

Qualifications and skills also had been taken seriously in academia. Gerolimos and Konsta identified the skills and qualifications librarians needed in modern informational environments [12, pp. 691–699]. Marketing and promotion skills [13, pp. 1–20], information technology [14, pp. 18–21] were taken into consideration in recent years.

3 Methodology

The first step of investigating the library and information profession's requirement on data-related skills is to establish a framework of data literacy to cover all relevant descriptions and positions. In addition, data collecting rules needed to be defined.

This framework of data literacy, named the Data Competence Framework (DCF), was combed through 14 data competence models: UKDA model [15, pp. 11–16], Stephenson and Caravello model [16, pp. 525–540], DataONE model [17, MANTRA model [18], Qin and D' Ignazio Model [19], HKUST model [20, pp. 114–118], MacMillan model [21, p. 4], DataTrain model [22], Carlson model [23, pp. 629–657], Si model [24, pp. 700–724], NECDMC model [25], Prado and Marzal model [26, pp. 123–134], Schneider model [27, pp. 134–140], and ABS model [28]. After extracting these models, the team sorted out five competence dimensions for data literacy: data consciousness, data collection and processing, data analysis, long-term preservation, data reuse, and ethical code. The forms of expression on competence dimensions are understanding data types; drawing up data management plan; collecting data; processing data; analysing statistic by SPSS and Excel; using NVivo to have qualitative analysis; having consciousness to preserve data in a long-term; understanding the method to preserve data; and reusing data consciously and normatively.

By crawling and manual scanning comprehensive recruitment websites, web of university personnel departments, and government agencies' online announcements, a three-month recruitment list was gathered under the guidance of the framework. In accordance with the DCF, the study team examined job responsibilities and job requirements of each position announcements and picked out the ads that conform to at least one of the competence dimensions for data literacy.

4 Four Significant Indicators

To discover the extent of demand for data literacy in China the authors examined the TNM-LIS data from different perspectives. Four significant indicators were chosen to show: regional disparity on data literacy, demand characteristics of talents in different types of libraries, the ratio of education preference, and each position based on location, attribution, and educational limitation of libraries. Due to the restriction on pages, findings can only be discussed briefly.

4.1 About 19 Positions Per Hundred Demand Data Literacy

There were 358 positions from 147 libraries were posted online during November 2016 to January 2017. Under the framework of DCF, the research team obtained 66 positions with data literacy requirements from 29 libraries. About 19% of the positions claim to need for data literacy.

4.2 Regional Distribution of Data Literate Is Centralized

As shown in Table 1, libraries in Beijing had the largest demand (29 positions) for data literacy. And Beijing was followed by Shanghai with15 positions requesting candidates for literacy of data. The percentage of needs for data capacity in Beijing, Shanghai, Zhejiang, Anhui, Yunnan, Chongqing, and Jilin are more than the average. Three-fourths of municipalities in China are on the list, and they are Beijing, Shanghai, and Chongqing. In addition, Beijing and Shanghai have more well-known universities than other regions.

Table 1. Administrative regions' differences in demand on data literacy (Nov. 2016 - Jan. 2017)

No.	Administrative region	Talent demand	Data literacy talent demand	Percentage
1	Beijing municipality	78	29	37%
2	Shanghai municipality	51	15	29%
3	Zhejiang province	26	6	23%
4	Anhui province	9	4	44%
5	Guangdong province	30	2	7%
6	Jiangsu province	23	2	9%
7	Sichuan province	23	2	9%
8	Yunnan province	5	2	40%
9	Chongqing municipality	4	2	50%
10	Jilin province	5	1	20%
11	Jiangxi province	8	1	13%
12	Fujian province	8	0	0%
13	Guangxi Zhuang autonomous region	2	0	0%
14	Hainan province	8	0	0%
15	Henan province	6	0	0%
16	Heilongjiang province	8	0	0%
17	Hubei province	4	0	0%
18	Hunan province	3	0	0%
19	Liaoning province	16	0	0%
20	Ningxia Hui autonomous region	5	0	0%
21	Shandong province	23	0	0%
22	Shaanxi province	11	0	0%
23	Tianjin municipality	2	0	0%
	Total	358	66	18%

4.3 Academic Libraries Require More Data Literacy

The proportion between academic libraries and public libraries is nearly 9–1. Academic libraries attach more importance to the employment of staff with data literacy. It is worth noting that while school libraries were also the target in this survey, none requested data literacy skills in their job vacancy announcements. Since this is a requirement of 8 times as many academic libraries than public libraries, the number of posts were impacted by the academic libraries' data.

4.4 More Than Half Positions Request Master Degree or Above

The chart, Fig. 1, demonstrates that 68.2% (n = 45) of libraries requested that candidates had a master's degree or above. More than half of the institutions set a master's degree as a baseline and one academic library in Guangdong attempted to recruit a Ph.D. as an intelligence analyst.

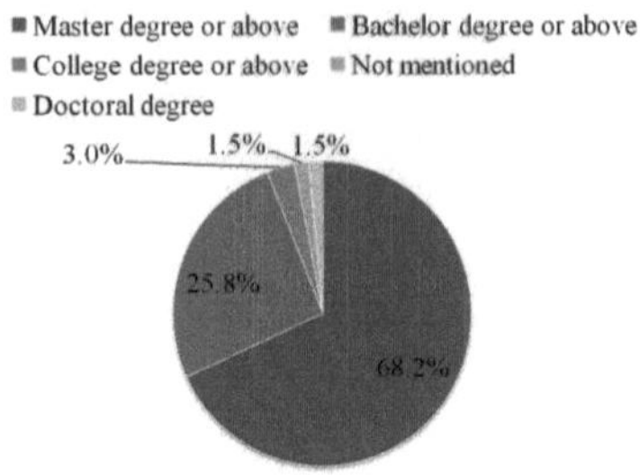

Fig. 1. Percentage of educational requirements (Nov. 2016–Jan. 2017)

5 Tendency Under the Water

5.1 Academic Libraries Have More Consciousness on Data Literacy Than Public Libraries

In the period from November 2016 to January 2017, academic libraries in China advertised a total of 267. And in 22.1% (n = 59) of these positions, employers asked candidates to demonstrate data literacy. The mission, role, responsibility, and function of libraries in different types are distinct; therefore, their demands for data literate also vary to some extent.

Take Peking University Library as an example. The job responsibilities of intellectual property services librarians are collecting and promoting patent data and rendering data services. And they require software development engineers to take charge of data management, data mining, and statistical analysis.

In contrast, the percentage of data literacy job vacancies in public libraries was much lower, at 7.9% (n = 7). This percentage is less than half of that in academic libraries. In 2015, the Ministry of Education of the People's Republic of China updated the Rules and Regulations on Libraries in Institutions of Higher Education [29]. The document indicated that libraries should emphasize statistical works, sort out statistical data, as well as preserving and analysing statistics properly.

5.2 Data-Related Positions in Academic Libraries Show Interest in Higher Educational Background

According to Fig. 2, people with the master's degree may apply for 98.3% (n = 58) of the data-related jobs in academic libraries while only 23.7% (n = 14) of positions required only a bachelor's degree. By comparison, data literacy positions including data literacy librarian and information specialists, need more high educated applicants than the national requirements. The Public Library Law of the People's Republic of China did not mention specific educational requirements for public librarians [31].

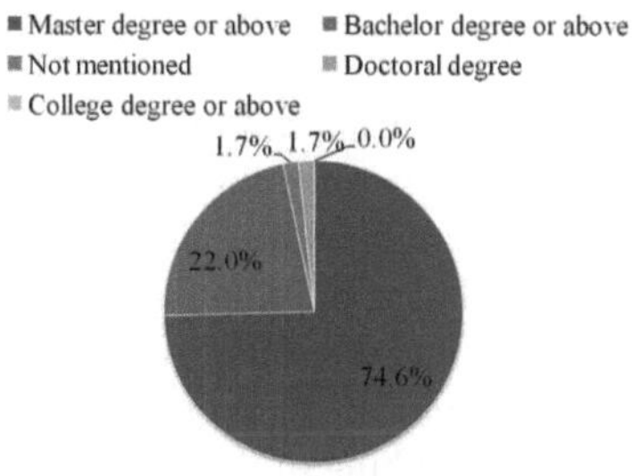

Fig. 2. Educational requirements of positions with demands for data-literacy (Nov. 2016–Jan. 2017)

5.3 Data Literacy Gets More Attention in Some Regions

The demand for data literacy is far greater in Beijing and Shanghai than in other provinces, municipalities, and autonomous regions. Maybe the reason is that these cities have more first-class universities than other areas.

The first-class universities in China usually funded by Project 985 and/or Project 211. One general focus of Project 985 is to construct world-class universities and internationally renowned high-level research-oriented universities [32]. The aim of Project 211 is to build up institutions of higher education to improve the quality of talent cultivation, scientific research levels, and social service abilities. There are 39 Project 985 universities and 116 Project 211 universities in China [33, 34]. According to the lists of Projects 985 and 211, Beijing has the greatest number: 985 or 211 universities among 31 provinces. And the numbers of 211 universities and 985 universities in Shanghai are 10 and 4 respectively, which is the second greatest number in a province.

6 Conclusion

As a pilot program for TNM-LIS, a long-term recruitment data tracking project, the research team conducted research on data literacy. During the period from November 2016 to January 2017, there are 66 positions requesting that applicant candidates possess data literacy. After conducting a content analysis, the authors found a considerable difference in the demand for data literacy among public, academic, and school libraries. And the distribution of geographic location is remarkable.

Through data analysis and content analysis, the team drew several findings. A portion of libraries began to value data literacy and regard data competence as a type of significant manpower capacity, especially in academic libraries. Along with literature studies, the team speculated that there are could be two reasons why academic libraries had more demand for data literacy than public libraries. First, the missions of these two kinds of libraries are different. The role of academic libraries is to cultivate talents and provide services for scholars [31]. The general principles of public libraries are focused on satisfying the needs of citizen's spiritual culture, improving their science and cultural qualities, and promoting social civilization [32]. Second, the policies and regulations for academic libraries and public libraries are different. Rules and regulations for academic libraries in China clearly mentioned data management and preservation, but it was not mentioned in Public Library Law. Meanwhile, policy documents for academic libraries also refer to educational requirements. This policy could affect education background requirements when recruiting new personnel. This might be one of explanations why more libraries affiliated with universities or colleges requested higher academic degrees for candidates applying data literacy position than did public libraries. The team also discovered that the difference of education development might cause varying talent demands of libraries. According to statistics in this study, Beijing and Shanghai are the top two in the ranking of their demand for data literacy. And these two municipalities also possess the majority of 985 or 211 universities. As Project 985, Project 211 is part of a program in the Action Plan for Invigorating Education in China.

These conclusions are based on initial data, so it is still too early to trigger any teaching transformation and education reform based on these findings. But through this research, the potential of TNM-LIS could be explored, and methods of improving the project could be proposed.

References

1. Choi, Y., Rasmussen, E.: What qualifications and skills are important for digital librarian positions in academic libraries? A job advertisement analysis. J. Acad. Librariansh. **35**, 457–467 (2009)
2. Wang, H., Tang, Y., Knight, C.: Contemporary development of academic reference librarianship in the United States: a 44-year content analysis. J. Acad. Librariansh. **36**(6), 489–494 (2010)
3. Tang, Y.: Distance education librarians in the United States: a study of job announcements. J. Acad. Librariansh. **39**, 500–505 (2013)
4. Cloonan, M., Norcott, P.C.: Evolution of preservation librarianship as reflected in job descriptions from 1975 through 1987. Coll. Res. Libr. **50**, 646–656 (1989)
5. Chaudhry, A.S., Komathi, N.C.: Requirements for cataloguing positions in the electronic environment. Tech. Serv. Q. **19**, 1–23 (2002)
6. Kinkus, J.: Project management skills: a literature review and content analysis of librarian position announcements. Coll. Res. Libr. **68**, 352–363 (2007)
7. Alonso-Regalado, J., Van Ullen, M.K.: Librarian for Latin American and Caribbean studies in U.S. academic and research libraries: a content analysis of position announcements, 1970–2007. Libr. Res. Tech. Serv. **53**, 139–158 (2009)

8. White, G.W.: Academic subject specialist positions in the United States: a content analysis of announcements from 1990 through 1998. J. Acad. Librariansh. **25**(5), 372–382 (1999)
9. Orme, V.: You will be …: a study of job advertisements to determine employers' requirements for LIS professionals in the UK in 2007. Libr. Rev. **57**(8), 619–633 (2008)
10. Cullen, J.: LIS labour market research: Implications for management development. Libr. Manag. **25**(3), 138–145 (2004)
11. Hall-Ellis, S.D.: Descriptive impressions of entry-level cataloger positions as reflected in American libraries, AutoCAT, and the Colorado state library jobline, 2000–2003. Cat. Classif. Q. **40**(2), 33–72 (2005)
12. Gerolimos, M., Konsta, R.: Librarians' skills and qualifications in a modern informational environment. Libr. Manag. **29**(8), 691–699 (2008)
13. Okamoto, K., Polger, M.A.: Off to market we go: a content analysis of marketing and promotion skills in academic librarian job ads. Libr. Leadersh. Manag. **26**(2), 1–20 (2012)
14. Khurshid, Z.: The impact of information technology on job requirements and qualifications for catalogers. Inf. Tech. Libr. **22**(1), 18–21 (2003)
15. Meng, X., Li, A.: Scientific data literacy education in overseas academic libraries. J. Acad. Libr. **2014**(03), 11–16 (2014). (in Chinese)
16. Stephenson, E., Caravello, P.S.: Incorporating data literacy into undergraduate information literacy programs in the social sciences: a pilot project. Ref. Serv. Rev. **35**(4), 525–540 (2007)
17. Education Modules. https://www.dataone.org/education-modules
18. Home. http://datalib.edina.ac.uk/mantra/
19. Lessons learned from a two-year experience in science data literacy education. In: Proceeding of the International Association of Scientific and Technological University Libraries. http://docs.lib.purdue.edu/iatul2010/conf/day2/5
20. Wong, G.K.W.: Facilitating students' intellectual growth in information literacy teaching. Ref. User Serv. Q. **50**(2), 114–118 (2010)
21. MacMillan, D.: Sequencing genetics information: integrating data into information literacy for undergraduate biology students. Issues Sci. Tech. Librariansh. **2010**(61), 4 (2010)
22. Data Train Archaeology. http://archaeologydataservice.ac.uk/learning/DataTrain
23. Carlson, J., Fosmire, M., Miller, C.C., Nelson, M.S.: Determining data information literacy needs: a study of students and research faculty. Libr. Acad. **11**(2), 629–657 (2011)
24. Si, L., Zhuang, X., Xing, W., Guo, W.: The cultivation of scientific data specialists: development of LIS education oriented to e-science service requirements. Libr. Hi Tech. **31** (4), 700–724 (2013)
25. New England Collaborative Data Management Curriculum. http://library.umassmed.edu/necdmc/modules
26. Calzada, P.J., Marzal, M.Á.: Incorporating data literacy into information literacy programs:core competencies and contents. Libri. **63**(2), 123–134 (2013)
27. Schneider, R.: Research data literacy. In: Kurbanoğlu, S., Grassian, E., Mizrachi, D., Catts, R., Špiranec, S. (eds.) ECIL 2013. CCIS, vol. 397, pp. 134–140. Springer, Cham (2013). https://doi.org/10.1007/978-3-319-03919-0_16
28. Australian Bureau of Statistics. Draft Statistical Capability Framework. http://www.abs.gov.au/websitedbs/a3121120.nsf/home/ABS+Statistical+Capability+Framework
29. Rules and Regulations on Libraries in Institutions of Higher Education (in Chinese). http://www.scal.edu.cn/sites/default/files/attachment/bzgf/guicheng2015_1.pdf
30. ALA/AASL. Standards for Initial Preparation of School Librarians. http://www2.mcdaniel.edu/slmonline/SLM_550/docs/10_AASL_standard_sch_librarian.pdf
31. Public Library Law of People's Republic of China (Version for Taking Advices) (in Chinese). http://www.chinalaw.gov.cn/article/cazjgg/201512/20151200479628.shtml

32. Action Project of Education (2003–2007) (in Chinese). http://www.szrtvu.com.cn/files/djgz/sdsf/05.htm
33. List of Project 985 (in Chinese). http://www.moe.edu.cn/publicfiles/business/htmlfiles/moe/s238/201112/xxgk_128833.html
34. List of Project 211 (in Chinese). http://www.moe.edu.cn/publicfiles/business/htmlfiles/moe/moe_1680/201002/xxgk_82762.html

Research Data Management in Three Spanish Universities

Alicia Arias-Coello[1(✉)], Clara Simon-Blas[2], Pablo Arranz-Val[3], and Jose Simon-Martin[1]

[1] Instituto Universitario de Evaluación, Universidad Complutense Madrid, Madrid, Spain
{aarias, jsimon}@ucm.es
[2] Universidad Rey Juan Carlos, Madrid, Spain
clara.simon@urjc.es
[3] Universidad de Burgos, Burgos, Spain
parranz@ubu.es

Abstract. Research Data Management (RDM) is an important ability required in the global knowledge environment and essential in the university research context. In this work we will present the results of the application of a web survey of faculties and doctoral students from three Spanish universities, with the aim of knowing their current levels of awareness and gaps in different issues of RDM. This study is part of an international survey on "Base Data Literacy" led by Professor Joumana Boustany from Paris Descartes University. The questionnaire was sent to the research academic staff and student research fellows of the three universities. We received a total of 828 responses, 591 of which were completely filled out. In accordance to the results of this survey we have detected a growing need among research academic staff and research students for RDM skills.

Keywords: Research Data Management · Data management plan Spanish's Universities · Metadata

1 Introduction

Research Data Management (RDM), is defined by Schneider [1] as "a method that enables the integration, curation and interoperability of data created during the scientific process, i.e. the production, access, verification, persistent storage and reuse of this data with the help of adequate and easy-to-use tools in virtual research infrastructures."

In the field of research, within the Horizon 2020 program [2], the European Commission (EC) and the Guidelines for the Regulation on Open Access in Scientific Publications and Research Data [3] define research data as the Information based on actual facts and that can be proved as well as the numerical information that is collected to be analyzed and considered as the basis of a reasoning, a discussion, or a calculation. Statistical results, results of experiments, and observations resulting from field studies, surveys, interviews, and images all constitute examples of research data. Thus, Research Data Management is present in all phases of the research [4] since it includes

S. Kurbanoğlu et al. (Eds.): ECIL 2017, CCIS 810, pp. 195–204, 2018.
https://doi.org/10.1007/978-3-319-74334-9_21

the processes of data creation, planning for reuse, processing, and organization of the same in their structuring and the content analysis, conservation, along with taking into account the security of access, its storage, recovery, public sharing, and reuse. Guidelines on all aspects of the "Participant Portal" were published in 2014 by the European Commission in relation to Horizon 2020 [5].

This reality has led to researchers having to acquire data management capabilities in order to manage huge amounts of data. These capabilities include statistical and computer skills, among others, and the know-how to contextualize the data appropriately in favour of the development of the organization. Leber [6] states that this new task has led to the birth of a new profession that the author calls "data scientist", which is already indispensable in companies as well as in the field of research.

In Spain, today data management in research is a reality that has begun to develop mainly because of the requirements of Horizon 2020, which is beginning to be replicated in national programs.

At the moment, in 2017, Horizon 2020 is a great incentive because all the projects that receive EU funding should develop a data management plan and publish open research data.

As a predecessor of the Spanish situation, we have a report published in 2014 by the Higher Council for Scientific Research (CSIC) [7] on the practices in the management, dissemination, and preservation of data of this institution. In this study, 270 researchers were interviewed and the most relevant conclusions, among others, focused on the insecurity that the interviewees showed regarding control of their own data, the fear of sharing these data, or the idea that the data did not interest others. These results already evidenced the urgency of forming and creating support services for researchers that included the creation, updating, preservation, and dissemination of research data, and for that purpose, university libraries were involved. In this sense, it is important to study Piorun [8], where she argues that these libraries can be very useful since they are experts in the selection of resources, creation of metadata, preservation, organization, and management of data and in providing access to them.

Since 2014, many universities and university libraries have created support services for researchers in relation to data management. One of the most relevant services was created by the Consortium of University Services of Catalonia (CSUC) called "Research Support Working Group", composed of members of all Catalan universities and experts in LIS and technologies of information. This service provides the research groups with a guide for the design of a data management plan (PGD), recommendations for selecting the most appropriate repository for the repository of data, and an open access institutional policy document [9]. Another initiative to support data management, called PaGoDa [10], was developed by the Madroño Consortium of university libraries in the Community of Madrid and the National University of Distance Learning (UNED), that adapted the tool, DMP Online, developed by the Digital Curation Center of the United Kingdom. This consortium also offers support material and advice through each of its member libraries. These initiatives have been very important in Spain, both for the support they provide to researchers and for training in the acquisition of skills in data management.

From the legislative point of view, there are many gaps in our country, one of which refers to data authorship. The law of intellectual property considers authorship in databases as intellectual creations; however, databases containing raw data do not have intellectual property. Licensure that permits data to be published it is usually done through Creative Commons, recommended by the European Commission in 2017.

At the end of 2016, Professor Joumana Boustany, from Paris Descartes University, invited us to participate in the international survey, "Base Data Literacy", for senior and junior researchers at universities. We felt that the timing was very appropriate because 2017 was to be the key date in promoting the management of research data. The results would help us to appreciate a general framework of the Spanish situation. Therefore, the objective of this study is to collect information about RDM of academic staff and doctoral students from Spanish universities. The analysis of the results obtained will allow us to understand the current levels of awareness and gaps in knowledge that will help us develop appropriate data literacy training for the higher education community.

2 Methodology

We used an on-line survey that was designed by Serap Kurbanoğlu (Hacettepe University, Turkey) and Joumana Boustany (Paris Descartes University, France). The survey was translated to Spanish for better comprehension. The questionnaire contains 24 questions, most of which have closed response options and is divided into two sections. The first gathers demographic information including age, gender and educational and professional experience of the respondents. The second explores the opinions of the respondents on different issues of data management: types of data file used in research, volume of data, how you obtain and use the data, where the data is stored, the Data Management Plan, and training in data management.

In accordance with to the objectives of the study, we selected a sample that included research professors and students research fellows from three Spanish public universities representing the three types of Spanish public universities. First, we included the Complutense University of Madrid (UCM) which was created in the century XVI as an example of a traditional university with a large number of professors (more than 5,000) and students (more than 80,000). The second was the Rey Juan Carlos University of Madrid (URJC) as an example of a new university with a medium capacity in number of students (approximately 30,000) and professors (more than 1,400). And, finally, we included the University of Burgos (UBU) an example of a small university in number of students (more than 6,500) and teachers (about 800). The questionnaire was sent only to the research academic staff and student research fellows of the three universities. The number of questionnaires sent were: UCM: 2,740; URJC: 634; and UBU: 425. Of these, 3,301 were addressed to professors and 498 to student research fellows. We received a total of 828 questionnaires, although only 591 were fully completed. The questionnaires received by each University were: 470 of the UCM (response rate 17.1%); 60 of the URJC (response rate 9.5%); 61 of the UBU (response rate 14.3%).

The research was conducted between the months of February and March 2016. Closed-ended questions were analyzed using descriptive statistics including frequency counts and percentages. The data was analyzed statistically with IBM SPSS Statistics.

3 Results

3.1 Respondents Profile

The majority of respondents were research academic staff (84.6%, n = 501) and 15.2% (n = 90) were research students.

As shown in Table 1 the majority of respondents (82.5%) were men older than 36 years of age.

Table 1. Demographic data of the respondents

	Number	Percentage
Gender		
Female	269	45.5
Male	316	53.5
Age		
18–25	17	2.9
26–35	85	14.4
36–45	159	26.9
46–55	198	33.5
56–65	113	19.1
65+	18	3
No reply	1	0.2

As shown in Table 2, 38.2% of the respondents spent more than 20 years dedicated to research.

Table 2. Years involved in research

	Number	Percentage
<5 years	83	14
5–10 years	81	13.7
11–15 years	85	14.4
16–20 years	110	18.6
>20 years	226	38.2
Never involved	6	1

The most frequent work disciplines were the social sciences (35.3%) and natural sciences (24.5%) (Table 3).

The low response rate in the engineering disciplines is due to the fact that in Spain these studies are taught within the polytechnic universities. The low participation in Health Sciences is due to the fact that only teachers of non-clinical subjects have been included in the sample. The percentage of participation in the Humanities is surprising, suggesting that these researchers are using more data-based methodologies.

Table 3. Work discipline

	Number	Percentage
Agricultural science	13	2.2
Engineering	42	7.1
Humanities	71	13.1
Medical and health	66	11.1
Natural science	145	24.5
Social science	209	35.3
Other	45	7.6

3.2 Type of Data Files and Storing Devices

As shown in Fig. 1, the five most widely used file types were:

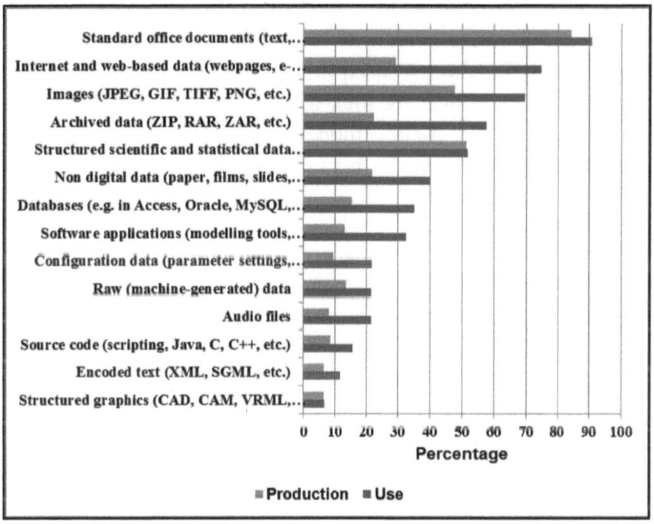

Fig. 1. Type of data files used and produced in research

- Standard office documents (text, spreadsheets, presentations) with 90.7% of respondents.
- Internet and web-based data (webpages, e-mails, blogs, social network data) with 74.8% of respondents.
- Images (JPEG, GIF, TIFF, PNG) with 69.5% of respondents.
- Archived data (ZIP, RAR, ZAR) with 57.5% of respondents.
- Structured scientific and statistical data (such as SPSS, GIS) with 51.9% of respondents.

When asked the type of data they produce in their research, most respondents indicate: standard office documents (84.3%), structured scientific and statistical data (51.3%) and images (47.7%).

With respect to the volume of data they use, the majority of respondents usually used data volumes on the order of GB (44.8%) and MB (45.2%). Only 47 respondents (8%) used data volumes of the order of terabytes. Volumes of data were very similar to those they produced in their research: GB (37.9%) and MB (53.3%).

For most of the respondents (94.3%), the most common way of storing the data generated in the research was to use their own devices (computer, tablet, external drive) or in the cloud (50.3%). Only 17.8% used central servers/repositories of the university or other outside repositories (10%).

3.3 Data Management Plan (DMP)

Figure 2 presents the opinions of academic staff and research students on various aspects related to DMP. A strong majority, 80.4% (n = 591), of the respondents were not aware if their institutions had a DMP and only 10% knew that their institutions had a DMP. Seventy one point nine percent of respondents had never used a DMP in their research, compared to 10% who had used it. This result was consistent with the 8% of respondents who had used a DMP for their current research and 72.6% who said there are not using it. When asked if they thought a DMP actually helps researchers in managing research data, 31.9% of the respondents gave an affirmative answer, compared to 63.8% who did not know.

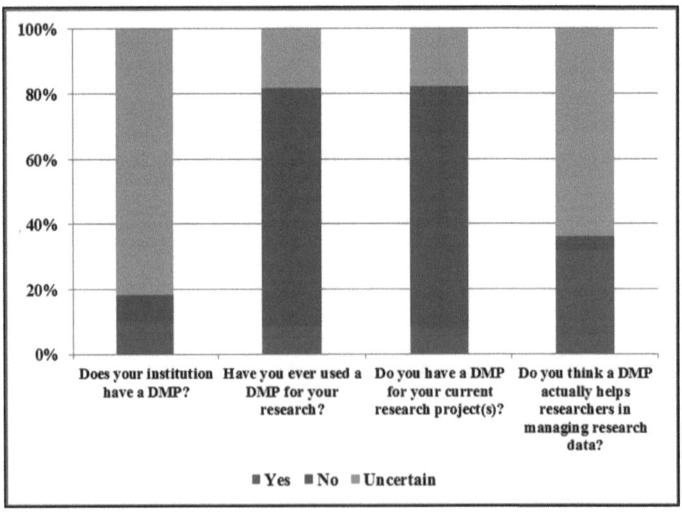

Fig. 2. Opinions about DMP

3.4 Knowledge and Use of Metadata

The survey contains a set of questions about the additional information that researchers include in their research data file from their research.

With respect to additional information, 43.1% of respondents included administrative information (e.g. creator, date of creation, file name, access terms/restrictions,); 41.6% included discovery information (e.g. creator, funding body, project title, project ID, keywords); 23% include technical information (for example, file format, file size, software/hardware needed to use the data,); 24.5% include description of the data file (e.g. file/data structure, field tags/descriptions, application rules,) and 72.6% do not assign additional information to their research data.

Figure 3 summarizes respondents' opinions on metadata. 55.1% of the respondents were familiar with the term "metadata", compared to 39.9% who did not know. Fifty three point five percent of the respondents thought that formal training on metadata would be useful for managing research data and 37.5% did not know. Only 10.9% of the respondents answered that their universities had a prescribed metadata set for uploading data to a repository while 86.1% did not know. Fourteen percent of respondents believed that their research community used/recommended a standard file naming system; where as 52.1% were not aware of it. Only 4.9% of respondents answered that their universities had a standard/consistent file naming system, while 77.7% did not know.

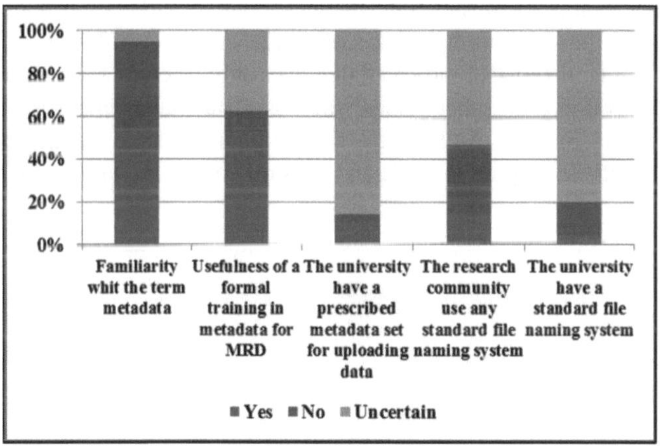

Fig. 3. Opinions about metadata

Figure 4 presents the results on the use of metadata and other ways of identifying data files. Questions have five possible answers: never, rarely, sometimes, often and almost always. Only 10.5% of respondents "often or almost always" used a metadata standard to tag their data. A similar level of response is obtained when asked if they used datasets that are tagged with standard metadata (9.2% indicate often or almost always). Seventeen point eight percent of respondents "often or almost always" used

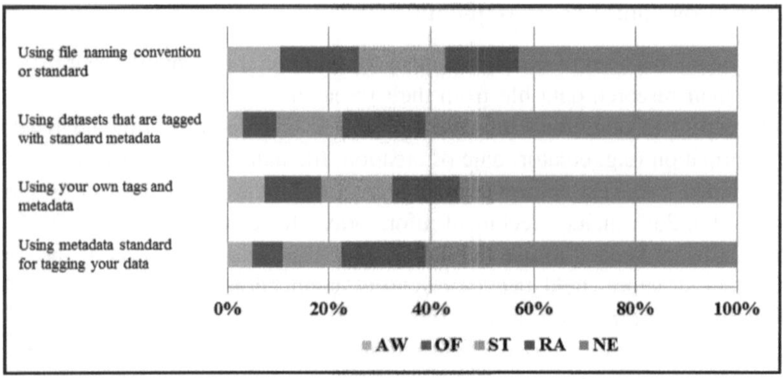

Fig. 4. Use of metadata. AW (Almost Always), OF (Often), ST (Sometimes), RA (Rarely), NE (Never)

their own/in-house (their research team) tags and metadata. Regarding the use of a file naming convention or standard, 25.1% of respondents used it "often or almost always".

3.5 Data Literacy Training

In this section of the questionnaire respondents were asked about their training in some aspects of data management and how they would like to be trained in this matter. Figure 5 presents formal training of the respondents on several issues of data management. Respondents (20.1%) indicated that they only received formal training in data citation styles. Training on other issues, such as Data Management Plan, only wAS provided to 4.6%. Similar results were seen with regards to training on metadata (5.1%), consistent file naming (1.7%), and version control of data sets (2%).

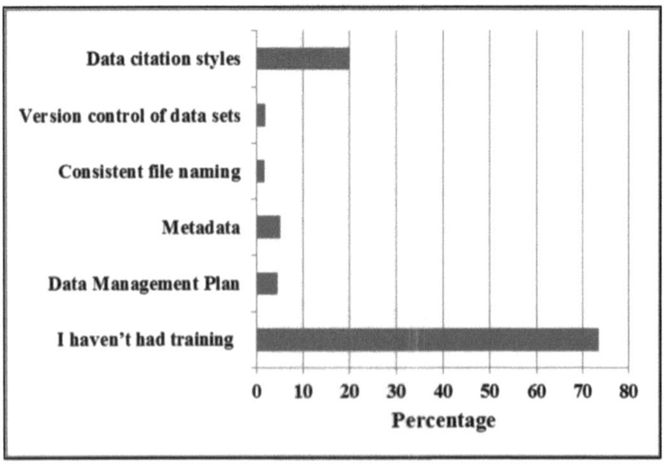

Fig. 5. Formal training received in several issues of data management

Sixty one point four percent of the respondents said they would like to received training on a Data Management Plan, 49.2% on metadata, 42.3% on consistent file naming, 38.9% on version control of data sets, and 37.7% on data citation styles. Only 23.7% of respondents were not interested in receiving training in the above issues.

4 Discussion and Conclusions

This study presents some limitations, among which was the low representation of respondents from University Burgos and the University Rey Juan Carlos. However, the consistency in the results obtained with the different questions may allow us to elaborate on proposals to improve Research Data Management levels at these universities. The results point out the existence of some weak points, such as the current lack of use of DMP in their research activities, such use will need to change in the future when the application of a DMP will become a necessary requirement. Another example was related to the knowledge and use of metadata, where researchers knew the term moderately well, but more than half thought that more training was needed. Similarly this points to the need of a greater involvement of universities in standardization and training activities.

The survey detects the need for strong emphasis on continuing training: more than 60% of respondents agreed to receive training in DMP and more than 40% on metadata and consistent file naming.

In conclusion, according to the results of this survey we have detected a growing need among academic staff and research students for data management literacy skills. In our opinion, the university should offer formal training appropriate to the needs of academic researchers in the different disciplines along with to research students.

References

1. Schneider, R.: Research data literacy. In: Kurbanoğlu, S., Grassian, E., Mizrachi, D., Catts, R., Špiranec, S. (eds.) ECIL 2013. CCIS, vol. 397, pp. 134–140. Springer, Cham (2013). https://doi.org/10.1007/978-3-319-03919-0_16
2. European Commission: Horizon 2020. The EU Framework Programme for Research and Innovation. https://ec.europa.eu/programmes/horizon2020/
3. European Commission: Directorate-General for Research & Innovation (2017). H2020. Programme. Guidelines to the Rules on Open Access to Scientific. Publications and Open Access to Research Data in Horizon 2020. http://ec.europa.eu/research/participants/data/ref/h2020/grants_manual/hi/oa_pilot/h2020-hi-oa-pilot-guide_en.pdf
4. Aydinoglu, A.-U., Dogan, G., Taskin, Z.: Research data management in Turkey: perceptions and practices. Libr. Hi Tech **35**(2), 271–289 (2017). https://doi.org/10.1108/LHT-11-2016-0134
5. European Commission: Research and Innovation. Participant Portal. http://ec.europa.eu/research/participants/portal/desktop/en/home.html
6. Leber, J.: In a Data Deluge, Companies Seek to Fill a New Role. MIT Technology Review: News and Views (2013). https://www.technologyreview.com/s/513866/in-a-data-deluge-companies-seek-to-fill-a-new-role/

7. Román-Molina, J., Bernal, I.: Prácticas en la gestión, difusión y preservación de datos de investigación en el CSIC (2014). https://digital.csic.es/handle/10261/92404
8. Piorun, M.E.: E-science as a catalyst for transformational change in university research libraries: a dissertation. University of Massachusetts Medical School (2013). http://escholarship.umassmed.edu/cgi/viewcontent.cgi?article=1151&context=lib_articles
9. CSUC: Grupo de Trabajo de Apoyo a la Investigación. http://www.csuc.cat/es/investigacion/gestion-de-datos-de-investigacion
10. PaGoDa: Consorcio Madroño. http://www.consorciomadrono.es/primeros-meses-del-portal-pagoda/

Data Literacy and Research Data Management in Two Top Universities in Poland. Raising Awareness

Zuzanna Wiorogórska[1(✉)], Jędrzej Leśniewski[2], and Ewa Rozkosz[3]

[1] University of Warsaw, Warsaw, Poland
z.d.wiorogorska@uw.edu.pl
[2] Wrocław University of Science and Technology, Wrocław, Poland
jedrzej.lesniewski@pwr.edu.pl
[3] University of Lower Silesia, Wrocław, Poland
ewa.rozkosz@dsw.edu.pl

Abstract. We present the results of the Polish part of a study conducted within the framework of the international research project named ReDaM coordinated by the Information Literacy Association (InLitAs). It was a quantitative study based on use of a questionnaire consisted of 25 open-ended and multiple choice questions that was translated from English into Polish. Data were collected from February to the end of April 2017. The target groups were doctoral students and faculty employed at the University of Warsaw and Wrocław University of Science and Technology. The study revealed that a significant number of respondents knew the basic concepts related to Research Data Management (RDM). At the same time, they had not used institutional solutions elaborated in their parent institutions. We did not notice any differences in RDM practices between the fields of study at the two universities. However, we did notice significant differences between academic staff and research students.

Keywords: Data literacy · Data information literacy · Science data literacy Research Data Management · Scholarly information literacy · Poland

1 Introduction

There are several reasons why Research Data Management (RDM) has become an emerging topic of the 21st century discussion among librarians and other information professionals. The common use of ICT tools made research more intensive, technology- and data-driven and led to handling huge volumes of data. However, still most researchers have not been formally trained to manage their own data [1–3]. In this field, RDM has become an area of keen interest in higher education, leading to considerable investment in services, resources, and infrastructure to support researchers' data management needs [4].

S. Kurbanoğlu et al. (Eds.): ECIL 2017, CCIS 810, pp. 205–214, 2018.
https://doi.org/10.1007/978-3-319-74334-9_22

2 Research Data Management–Labelling the Concepts

Terminology confusions happen often while talking about new concepts that have not yet gained global recognition. Here we provide a brief revision of existing terms with an attempt to put them in order to avoid terminology confusion. Also, for the sake of epistemology, it is valuable to investigate the origin and nature of RDM.

Since the education in the field of RDM is strongly connected with educational services offered by libraries, it may be considered as deriving from information literacy (IL), which in turn is linked to the concept of data information literacy. The foregoing term is closely connected to research data services that include RDM, according to Koltay [5] or science data literacy (SDL). In their work, Qin and D'Ignazio [6] stated that, although SDL is somehow similar to information literacy and digital literacy, it focuses less on literature-based attributes and more on functional ability in data collection, processing, evaluation, and use. The concept of digital literacy was described by the American Library Association (ALA) as the ability to use information and communication technology to find, evaluate, create, and communicate information [3].

Research data, as defined by Horizon 2020, the EU Framework Programme for Research and Innovation [7] refers to information, in particular facts or numbers, collected to be examined and considered and as a basis for reasoning, discussion or calculation. The Association of College and Research Libraries (ACRL), for the purpose of its 2014 survey among library professionals, defined RDM as the activities necessary for documenting, maintaining, and making the data collected in the course of research accessible. The data are discipline agnostic and may be in any format [2]. Makani [8] considers RDM in the context of data and information and knowledge discourse; she arguments that effective RDM is one that contributes to innovative and diverse knowledge discoveries, knowledge use, and knowledge reuse.

3 Research Data Management Practices

3.1 Researchers' Awareness

According to literature, there is a little awareness and low levels of comfort and expert self-assessment with the life cycle of research data and RDM topics. This opinion was confirmed by several studies (see e.g. [2, 9, 10]). Moreover, there is a phenomenon that can be named "personalization" or "individual habits"—we can observe individual habits and rules of each organization, research unit, or individual researcher. There is a lack of common practice, the research cultures differ, and a great resistance to changes may be observed [11]. As Burgi et al. [9] remarked, it is difficult to harmonize any of these habits. An OCLC Research Report underlines the importance of education services in raising RDM awareness and it points at two main services: expertise and curation [4]. Libraries have already years of experience in both of these services.

3.2 Identifying and Analyzing the Gaps

Planning initiatives aiming for development of RDM on national level requires an in-depth exploration of existing solutions in this field to avoid duplication and to identify the gaps. The Swiss project may be a good example of such an undertaking [9]. Also, the ACRL Digital Curation Interest Group conducted in 2014 a survey on professional development needs, aimed at librarians involved in the management and curation of research data at their institutions [2].

3.3 Data Management Plan (DMP)

A good DMP helps researchers describe what they are going to do with data during and after their research project, to set up a level of data openness (and thus, possibility of sharing) or confidentiality, and to define the period and conditions of data preservation after the research is completed. DMPs are important part of the research data cycle and they are more and more often required by funding bodies and research institutions [1, 9, 12, 13].

3.4 Existing RDM Education in Different Countries

Not surprisingly, US academic librarians lead in RDM education. Massachusetts Institute of Technology, the University of California, Berkeley, the University of Wisconsin-Madison, Purdue University, Syracuse University, and the University of Minnesota are just few examples [1, 2, 6, 14, 15]. ACRL offers the support of professional development in the field of RDM for librarians. In Europe, under the already mentioned national Swiss project, a group of librarians has been already trained by computer engineers and information specialists and, a website with relevant resources, tools, and guidelines has been created [9]. The University of Tartu, Estonia has offered an RDM course for doctoral students since 2015. The training is integrated into curricula. It is based on personal needs of young researchers and offers individual tutoring [16]. The University of Bristol, UK is developing RDM services; the project focuses on data management assistance, RDM advocacy, and training for researchers representing all disciplines [17].

3.5 Main Conclusions of the RDM Literature Review

RDM depends on institutional strategies and research habits in specific disciplines [9]. RDM education is in the scope of expertise and interest of librarians, however, it should not be provided only by this one group but with close cooperation with other specialists. Pre-assessment tests are crucial before planning and establishing any RDM educational initiatives. One of the ways of such a pre-assessment and a tool to raise awareness of RDM may be a pilot study [6].

4 Polish Study

The study conducted in Poland was a part of international research project, ReDaM, coordinated by the Information Literacy Association (InLitAs) that aimed to collect data about data literacy of academics and research students in higher education institutions. In this paper we present selected results. The purpose of the study was to explore the ways of research data management (RDM) by academic staff and research students and to assess the RDM awareness level of both target groups. Particularly, we wanted to check: (1) what are the Research Data Management practices? (2) are there differences in Research Data Management practices between academic staff and research students? (3) are there differences in Research Data Management practices between two types of higher education institutions, general university vs. university of technology?

4.1 Method

It was a quantitative study. The online survey on the LimeSurvey platform was established to collect data. The questionnaire consisted of 25 open-ended and multiple choice questions, translated from English into Polish. Data were collected from February to the end of April 2017. In this paper, we present only a part of the study, thus, we analyzed responses to selected questions.

4.2 Field

The target groups were doctoral students and faculty employed at the Wrocław University of Science and Technology (WUST) and the University of Warsaw (UW). These two large public universities are highly-ranked, holding second and first positions respectively, in the national rankings of technical universities and universities in Poland, Perspektywy 2016 [18]. These sites were chosen for this research to cover the largest possible number of fields to be represented in the study.

WUST is one of the most dynamically developing technical universities in the country. In 2016 it was granted the logo, "Human Resources Excellence in Research", by the European Commission. This logo is given to institutions that apply the principles of the European Charter for Researchers and the Code of Conduct for the Recruitment of Researchers. There are approximately 34,000 students (including over 800 doctoral students) and over 2,000 research and teaching staff at WUST. WUST has 5,452 registered inventions, over 12,000 publications in journals on the "Clarivate Analytics" Master Journal List, and over 11,000 publications in JCRI indexed journals. What is particularly interesting, and what makes difference between traditional university and the technical one, is that research in WUST focuses on the demands of the industry [19]. Over 74% of participants of the survey conducted during the implementation process of The European Charter for Researchers agreed that WUST provided researcher, including disabled researchers, with flexible working conditions in order to achieve effective research results. And over 60% claimed that WUST supported scientists at all stages of their careers, helping them develop and improve their skills and qualifications and enabling participation in conferences, trainings, and other forms of education [20].

UW is the largest higher education institution in Poland. It is composed of 30 academic and research units and 21 faculties. There are approximately 44,400 students and 6,200 doctoral and postgraduate students (studying, respectively, at 35 and 132 programs). Ten thousand students graduate per year. UW has 3,750 academic teachers, 785 of whom are full professors. It is a research-intensive university: it conducts currently over 1,500 projects financed by national or international research programs, funds, and organizations and produces about 8,700 scientific publications per year. The research potential of UW reflects in the results of the 2016 Nature Index of Rising Stars. The University of Warsaw was ranked 3rd among the institutions of South East Europe. Globally it occupied 96th place [21].

4.3 Data Analysis

We reported descriptive statistics including characteristics of the practices of research data use. The χ^2 test was used to examine differences between two samples. The χ^2 test was used to examine relationships between: (1) some practices and current primary roles, (2) some practices and types of higher education institutions.

Respondents' Characteristics. At WUST, the questionnaire was sent to 5266 respondents and was disseminated via the library webpage. At UW, library authorities denied use of the library mailing list to disseminate the questionnaire; the link to the survey was disseminated through the library webpage and social media platforms. The description and main goals of the study were described precisely in a short memo distributed on every distribution channel. It was filled out by 128 respondents; this low response rate a significant limitation in terms of generalization of results. The low number of respondents may be due to a relatively low number of concerned research students in Poland toward open data issues as well due to little awareness of the life cycle of research data and RDM topics among researchers as proved by several studies mentioned earlier in this paper. That is why the results presented in this paper should be treated as preliminary and refer to the sample only rather than to the whole population. There were more respondents from WUST: 83 (64.8%) than from UW: 45 (35.2%). Among the respondents there were: academic staff (n = 65, 50.8%), and research students (n = 58, 45.3%) and people who indicated other current primary roles (n = 7, 3.9%). The number of academic staff and research students did not differ significantly. The majority of respondents were below the age of 35 years (n = 82, 64.6%), fewer were between 36–45 years (n = 26, 20.5%), and the smallest group above 45 years (n = 19, 14.9%). The gender distribution did not vary significantly; there were 73 (57%) male and 54 (42.2%) female respondents. The largest number of respondents represented engineering and technology (n = 52, 40.6%), natural sciences (n = 28, 21.9%), social sciences (n = 26, 20.3%), and humanities (n = 20, 15.6%) and the smallest, medical and health sciences (n = 2, 1.6%). The low number of medical and health science respondents is explained by the fact that in Poland this is the domain of medical universities and not general or technical higher education institutions. The majority of respondents indicated Poland as their country of origin (n = 126, 98.4%) only two respondents declared another country (The Netherlands, Ukraine).

Practices of Research Data Use. Table 1 presents responses to the questions related to Research Data Management.

Table 1. Distribution of responses to the questions related to Research Data Management

Awareness and application of Research Data Management	Yes		No		Uncertain		χ^2
	n	%	*n*	%	*n*	%	
Familiar with the term 'metadata'	92	71.9	25	19.5	11	8.6	87.86***
Use some standard style for citing research data	76	59.4	43	33.6	9	7	52.61***
Familiar with the concept of Digital Object Identifier (DOI)	82	64.1	40	31.3	6	4.7	67.94***
Have got some unique research identification (for ex. ORCID)	37	28.9	77	60.2	14	10.9	47.64***

Note. *$p < .05$, **$p < .01$, ***$p < .001$.

As Table 1 illustrates, the majority of respondents knew the term 'metadata' (71.9%). A significant number (59.4%) of respondents used a particular standard style for citing research data than did not (33.6%). There were also significant differences in the awareness of what DOI is with 64.1% reporting they were aware of this identifier and 31.3% not aware. A significant difference also was seen in the number of respondents who had (28.9%) a unique research identification (for ex. ORCID) when compared with those who did not have (60.2%) a unique research identification. As indicated by the χ^2 test, there were no statistically significant differences in the answers on the questions related to RDM—presented in Table 1—between the respondents from UW and WUST ($\chi^2 = 3.79$, $df = 2$; $p > .05$, $\chi^2 = 1.75$, $df = 2$; $p > .05$, $\chi^2 = 3.74$, $df = 2$; $p > .05$, respectively).

The χ^2 test also showed that primary role of respondent (academic staff, research student) was not connected with the familiarity with the term 'metadata' ($\chi^2 = .1$, $df = 2$; $p > .05$). We also did not notice any differences between these two groups regarding their familiarity with the concept of Digital Object Identifier ($\chi^2 = 3.74$, $df = 2$; $p > .05$). This result could be explained by the fact that the use of this identifier as a searching tool is gaining popularity in academic environment. Significantly more academic staff (40%) had some unique researcher identification when compared to researcher students (17.2%) ($\chi^2 = 8.68$, $df = 2$; $p < .05$).

Research Data Management Plan. Table 2 illustrates answers to the questions related to RDMP.

As is shown in Table 2, the majority of respondents answered 'No' or 'Uncertain' to various questions related to RDMP. This indicates that respondents have not applied RDMP in their research projects. They also did not know institutional RDMP policies that might be useful in planning individual solutions (only three respondents knew institutional RDMP). However, more respondents recognized (19.5%) rather than did not recognize (13.3%) the importance of RDMP as a supporting tool for researchers in

Table 2. Distribution of responses to the questions related to Research Data Management Plan

Awareness and application of Research Data Management Plan (RDMP)	Yes		No		Uncertain		χ^2
	n	%	*n*	%	*n*	%	
Institution has RDMP	3	2.3	23	18	102	79.7	133.42***
Has ever used RDMP for her/his research	7	5.5	104	81.3	17	13.3	133.42***
Has RDMP for her/his current research project	8	6.3	106	82.8	14	10.9	141.44***
Is of opinion that RDMP helps researchers in managing research data	25	19.5	17	13.3	86	67.2	66.77***
Is of opinion that formal training on metadata would be useful for managing research data	73	57	13	10.2	42	32.8	42.2***

Note. $^*p < .05$, $^{**}p < .01$, $^{***}p < .001$.

their work with raw data. More (57%) noticed the usefulness of formal training for managing research data than did not notice (10.2%).

As the χ^2 test indicated, there were no statistically significant differences in answers to the questions related to RDMP—presented in Table 2—between the respondents from UW and WUST ($\chi^2 = 2.29$, $df = 2$; $p > .05$, $\chi^2 = .14$, $df = 2$; $p > .05$, $\chi^2 = 2.19$, $df = 2$; $p > .05$, $\chi^2 = 2.29$, $df = 2$; $p > .05$, $\chi^2 = 3.79$, $df = 2$; $p > .05$, respectively). Thus, the awareness and application of RDMP did not depend on the type of university.

The χ^2 test also revealed that the primary role of respondent (academic staff, research student) was not connected to the answer whether the institution had RDMP ($\chi^2 = 2.29$, $df = 2$; $p > .05$), whether the respondents had ever applied RDMP ($\chi^2 = 1.5$, $df = 2$; $p > .05$), or whether she or he used RDMP in the current project ($\chi^2 = 3.01$, $df = 2$; $p > .05$). In turn, academic staff and research students differed in their opinion on the role of RDMP as a tool that helps researchers in managing research data ($\chi^2 = 8.34$, $df = 2$; $p < .05$). Academic staff are considerably more often convinced that RDMP supports researchers in use of raw data (24.6%) than research students (12.1%). However, research students (65.5%) were considerably more often convinced—compared to academic staff (46.2%)—about the usefulness of formal training on metadata. The explanation of this results may be correlated in the general, quite specific attitude of Polish researchers towards institutional information literacy.

5 Discussion

The study revealed that a significant number of respondents knew the basic concepts related to Research Data Management. At the same time, they had not used institutional solutions, including the Research Data Management Plan in particular, provided by their parent institutions. Most frequently, the respondents were not aware of existence of such solutions. We did not notice any differences in Research Data Management practices and knowledge of Research Data Management Plan between fields of study at the two universities. However, we did notice significant differences between academic staff and research students in their opinion on the usefulness of RDMP (academic staff more often than research students perceived this tool as useful) and on the usefulness of formal training on metadata (research students more often than academic staff perceived this kind of training as useful). In Research Data Management practice, academic staff differed from research students only in having a unique researcher identification. Academic staff significantly more often than research students had this identifier. This might be linked to their more extensive experience in scholarly publishing since more and more editors require ORCID from the submitting author.

6 Conclusion

Establishing RDMP helps researchers from the beginning of their projects in proper and active thinking about management of research data and its application. It helps avoid later doubts on data authorship and ownership. It is a first step that should be undertaken while planning research. This calls on researchers to consider which type of data will be produced, how much, where it will be stored and for how long preserved, and whether it will be shared or not. Last but not least, RDMP helps save time at the stage of data (or—more generally—research results) publishing. Formal, institutional training on RDMP seems to be the initial phase of data literacy education in Poland. Since June 2015, regular workshops on RDM are organized in Poland approximately twice a year by the Open Science Platform (Pl. *Platforma Otwartej Nauki* http://pon.edu.pl). Still, they are not popular and promoted enough to get to the public awareness of Polish academic community. The workshops, are one-day event for a limited number of participants. Since they are organized on-site in Warsaw they are not easy accessible for many researchers from other cities. That is why some other means of RDM awareness and promotion should be implemented. For example, in the Swiss project mentioned earlier in this paper, one of the expected results are guidelines for researchers and information professionals on RDM to encourage the use of best practices in data management [9].

However, as Carlson et al. [1, p. 635] stated, "any attempt to define a data information program must be aligned with current disciplinary practices and cultures if it is to be relevant to and accepted by its intended audience(s)". We believe that the Polish contribution into the collective intelligence of international ReDaM research project will help fulfill these requirements with regard to recommendations of LIBER working group on E-Science: "when exploring new services, make room for experiments/pilots, keep what works and learn from your mistakes" [22, p. 2].

It should also be mentioned that, according to Polish Law on Higher Education, universities have a statutory obligation to introduce regulations on intellectual property rights management. According to Article 86c of the Law on Higher Education [23], regulations for the management of copyright and related rights, and industrial property rights, as well as rules for the commercialization of research and development findings shall determine, among others: (1) rights and obligations of higher education institutions, academic staff, students and doctoral students with reference to the use and protection of copyright and related rights as well as industrial property rights; (2) rules and procedures to govern the commercialization of research and development findings; (3) rules for the use of assets and facilities of a higher education institution for the purpose of commercialization of research and development findings, and for the provision of scientific and research services. Both WUST [24] and UW [25] have these kind of regulations. Thus, we can risk saying that there is a lack of coherence between introduced—at least at general level—related to regulations on RDM and everyday practice of academic community. We can also with high probability indicate this lack of coherence as an argument for the need of intensification of training on RDM for academic staff.

References

1. Carlson, J., Fosmire, M., Miller, C.C., Sapp Nelson, M.: Determining data information literacy needs: a study of students and research faculty. Libr. Acad. **11**(2), 629–657 (2011)
2. Conrad, S., Shorish, Y., Whitmire, A.L., Hswe, P.: Building professional development opportunities in data services for academic librarians. IFLA J. **43**(1), 65–80 (2017)
3. Johnson, L., Adams Becker, S., Estrada, V., Freeman, A.: NMC Horizon Report: 2014 Higher Education Edition, Austin (2014)
4. Bryant, R., Lavoie, B., Malpas, C.: A Tour of the Research Data Management (RDM) Service Space. Part 1: The Realities of Research Data Management. Dublin (2017)
5. Koltay, T.: Data governance, data literacy and the management of data quality. IFLA J. **42** (4), 303–312 (2016)
6. Qin, J., D'Ignazio, J.: Lessons learned from a two-year experience in science data literacy education. In: Proceedings of the 31st Annual IATUL Conference, 20–24 June 2010, IATUL, West Lafayette (2010)
7. Research & Innovation: Open Science. http://ec.europa.eu/research/openscience/index.cfm
8. Makani, J.: Knowledge management, research data management, and university scholarship: towards an integrated institutional research data management support-system framework. VINE **45**(3), 344–359 (2015)
9. Bürgi, P.-Y., Blumer, E., Makhlouf-Shabou, B.: Research data management in Switzerland: National efforts to guarantee the sustainability of research outputs. IFLA J. **43**(1), 5–21 (2017)
10. Renwick, S., Winter, M., Gill, M.: Managing research data at an academic library in a developing country. IFLA J. **43**(1), 51–64 (2017)
11. Awre, C., Baxter, J., Clifford, B., Colclough, J., Cox, A., Dods, N., Drummond, P., Fox, Y., Gill, M., Gregory, K., Gurney, A., Harland, J., Khokhar, M., Lowe, D., O'Beirne, R., Proudfoot, R., Schwamm, H., Smith, A., Verbaan, E., Waller, L., Williamson, L., Wolf, M., Zawadzki, M.: Research data management as a "wicked problem". Libr. Rev. **64**(4/5), 356–371 (2015)
12. Buddenbohm, S., Cretin, N., Dijk, E., Gaiffe, B., De Jong, M., Le Teiller-Becquart, N., Minel, J.-L.: State of the art report on open access publishing of research data in the humanities (2016). [Other]
13. Higman, R., Pinfield, S.: Research data management and openness: the role of data sharing in developing institutional polices and practices. Program **49**(4), 364–381 (2015)
14. Wittenberg, J., Elings, M.: Building a research data management service at the University of California, Berkeley: a tale of collaboration. IFLA J. **43**(1), 89–97 (2017)

15. Zilinski, L.D., Sapp Nelson, M., Van Epps, A.S.: Developing professional skills in STEM students: data information literacy. ISTL **77** (2014). https://www.learntechlib.org/p/153217/
16. Tarkpea, T., Seiler, V.: Integrating data literacy into information literacy e-course for PhD students. In: Spriranec, S., Kurbanoglu, S., Landova, H., Grassian, E.S., Mizrachi, D., Roy, L., Kos, D. (Eds.) The Fourth European Conference on Information Literacy, (ECIL) 10–13 October 2016, Prague, Czech Republic: abstracts. Association of Libraries of Czech Universities. Prague (2016)
17. Hiom, D., Fripp, D., Gray, S., Snow, K., Steer, D.: Research data management at the University of Bristol: charting a course from project to service. Program **49**(4), 475–793 (2015)
18. Ranking uczelni akademickich 2016. http://www.perspektywy.pl/RSW2016/ranking-uczelni-akademickich
19. Wrocław University of Science and Technology: General Information. http://pwr.edu.pl/en/university/about-us/general-information
20. Politechnika Wrocławska: HR Strategy for Researchers (HRS4R). http://pwr.edu.pl/fcp/xGBUKOQtTKlQhbx08SlkTUhZeUTgtCgg9ACFDC0RDSHRBG1gnBVcoFW8SETZKHg/_users/code_BAlkUKkpKNVI_VBV9XFNBFEZcFiw5Qx0O/europejska_karta_naukowca/hr_strategy_for_researchers_hrs4r.pdf
21. University of Warsaw. http://www.uw.edu.pl/wp-content/uploads/2017/03/prezentacja-2017-en-krotsza-biuro-prasowe-uw-28.03.17.pdf
22. Christensen-Dalsgaard, B.: Ten recommendations for libraries to get started with research data management. LIBER (2012)
23. Ustawa o szkolnictwie wyższym Dz.U.2016.1842 z późn. zm. http://isip.sejm.gov.pl/DetailsServlet?id=WDU20051641365
24. Politechnika Wrocławska. Zarządzenie wewnętrzne 39/2017 z dnia 10 kwietnia 2017r. w sprawie Regulaminu zarządzania własnością intelektualną (2017)
25. Uniwersytet Warszawski. Uchwała nr 68 Senatu Uniwersytetu Warszawskiego z dnia 22 marca 2017 w sprawie uchwalenia Regulaminu zarządzania własnością intelektualną na Uniwersytecie Warszawskim. http://www.monitor.uw.edu.pl/Lists/Uchway/Attachments/4040/M.2017.80.U.68.pdf

Research Data Reshaping Cultural Society: Case of the Lebanese University

Gladys Saade[1] and Dalal Rahme[1,2(✉)]

[1] Faculty of Information Science, Lebanese University, Bauchriyeh, Lebanon
dyssaade@gmail.com, drahmeh@gmail.com
[2] Data Services Librarian, American University of Beirut, Beirut, Lebanon
dalal.rahme@aub.edu.lb

Abstract. Research Data Management (RDM) is a new practice in Lebanese academic institutions. The purpose of this study is to assess technological and organizational needs of one of those institutions, the Lebanese University (LU). A questionnaire was sent to academics from all faculties and branches at LU. The survey measured the demographics of survey respondents, their use of data, the degree of openness and the readiness of researchers to manage, share, and preserve datasets. Results described the concerns, challenges and level of commitment of the researchers to data management and sharing. They revealed a moderate level of awareness of information literacy and RDM practices and gave a preliminary figure of the quantity of data generated at LU allowing participants to express their needs. The paper offers guidance for developing a collection of services to support different activities in this area.

Keywords: Research data management · Institutional repositories
Data sharing · Academic universities in Lebanon · Lebanese University
Open access · Scholarly communication

1 Introduction

The digital revolution has affected all sectors in the society from education, to labor market, to economy, and cultural behavior [1–3]. Technological developments, such as Web 2.0, contributed to consolidating, advancing, and transforming values such as sharing and collaborating. Research Data Management (RDM), a practice that evolved with this technological advancement, is an important way to conduct transparent, ethical, and reproducible research in academia. Since knowledge has long been considered a form of power, detaining information therefore constitutes a step closer to detaining power. RDM best practices equips the research community with this power for it makes data easily accessible to all by centralizing, documenting, and preserving it [4]. In countries that rely on research as a means to develop society, our hypothesis assumes that the application of data management faces logistical challenges including the availability of well-established infrastructures and technical skills. Nevertheless, this issue can be solved by tailoring training and workshops. However, in the context of the Arab world and Lebanon, research rarely contributes to issues related to public life, citizenship, and democracy in a climate dominated by violence, individualism,

S. Kurbanoğlu et al. (Eds.): ECIL 2017, CCIS 810, pp. 215–224, 2018.
https://doi.org/10.1007/978-3-319-74334-9_23

seclusion, and fear of inevitability. The biggest challenge in this context therefore resides in the adoption of new concepts such as collaboration and knowledge sharing. Our research questions are the following: To which extent is the Lebanese University research community in Lebanon willing to apply data management best practices? How does this community perceive of RDM? What is this research community doing to adjust to the new practices in RDM and cooperation?

2 Literature Review

The available literature on research in Lebanon and the Arabic world points to a high degree to the severity of the issues facing the Arab research community. The vast majority of the available published research on this topic focuses on highlighting the problems and shortcomings in this area. This is immediately made apparent through a first look at the titles that show a recurrent use of words such as "obstacles", "desert", "problems", and "information gap" [5–7]. The available studies seem to agree that research in the Arab world suffers from a lack of funding. No Arab country spends more than 0.25 of its Gross National Product on scientific research and most of that funding is spent on salaries [8, 9]. Stephan argues that researchers in Lebanon struggle to reach needed information because the financial, technical and human resources of libraries are limited and channels connecting researchers to each other are weak, hindering collaboration and cooperation efforts [10]. Unlike the trend in the scientific community, researchers in the social sciences tend to avoid collaboration. The literature suggests that social scientists are not likely to collaborate with researchers from other institutions and are even reluctant to collaborate with researchers from their own institution. The research culture seems to be generally based on competitiveness rather than cooperation. In fact, a research study conducted by Fadia Hoteit reaches the same conclusion. She discusses the lack of specialization in research in the Arab world and the lack of cooperation between researchers within one same entity and between different entities [11]. The last factor affecting research production is of historico-sociological nature. Mourtada argues that the development of thought and social structures in Europe has promoted the development of scientific activities. In that context, science therefore came to be recognized as a positive value. This is, however, not always the case in the Arab world [12].

RDM, as a concept, is pushed forward by governments and funding bodies [4, 13] in many countries. Adopting it can contribute to the development of research in Lebanon where there is less collaboration among researchers across Lebanese institutions, slightly better collaboration among researchers from the same institution, and higher collaboration with western institutions [14]. RDM will maximize local collaboration among researchers from different institutions and different fields while minimizing the cost of data collection and reproduction. Considering the weakness and lack of investment in research in the Arab world, the use of RDM and data sharing will strengthen the research production in the region. We believe that the library is well positioned in the academic institution and that specialized data librarians can play a significant role in facilitating data management along with other stakeholders [15]. They need to overcome the previous mentioned barriers as well as the concerns related to legal issues, privacy issues, and consistent procedures in the research life cycle [16].

3 Methodology

Our initial strategy was to target the most prominent academic institutions and research centers in Lebanon. Our attempt was unsuccessful for several reasons mentioned in the literature review. Most of the private institutions were not cooperative. They were also not familiar with the concept we are researching and conveyed a concern about the image of their institutions. This was obvious throughout the discussion we had with their communication offices where some requested to remove the question related to institutional affiliation after we explained what the survey was about. The fact is that all of those institutions work competitively not cooperatively, a common trend in the Arab world since no research policies are available [17]. The results collected were mostly (95%) from the Lebanese University (LU) which led us to consider only LU as our research setting.

LU, established in 1951, is the only public university in Lebanon and the largest in terms of faculties (16), academic staff (8,000), students (79,000) and libraries (62) [18]. It is also the second producer of scholarly works in Lebanon [19].

In order to understand the data management practices and needs across the LU campuses in Lebanon, the study used the survey method to collect the needed data in an anonymous way. Several case studies on data management in academic settings were examined and questions from previous surveys were borrowed and modified to fit the purpose of the study [20, 21]. The survey was administered using an online platform, LimeSurvey, through which each subject received a link allowing only one submission per subject. Questions were made available in three languages: Arabic, English and French. The questions were mostly multiple choice with options to provide free text comments. Analysis of the results such as filtering on aspects of the responses to a particular question and cross tabulations were performed in LimeSurvey as a way to study the relation between the background of the faculty and their interest and engagement in our subject. The questionnaire included 20 questions divided into 5 sections: demographic information, data types and volume, data storage, data literacy, data sharing, and research data management. The survey was conducted between May 1 and May 20, 2017.

Faculty Sample. We were able to obtain 950 email addresses of LU faculty through the university's website. We included faculty members of all academic ranks (professors, associate professors, assistant professors, and instructors) from all faculties and schools. More than 50% of the emails were inactive and undeliverable. The delivered emails informed the participants about the nature of the research, taking their consent before starting the survey.

4 Results

4.1 Demographics

The total number of participants was 161. Fifty two completed the survey; the remaining 109 participants stopped at different stages. Only the complete 52 submissions were taken into consideration for the purpose of this study. People completed the survey in different languages: 11 in Arabic, 20 in English, and 21 in French. As Table 1 shows, respondents in the sample came from different faculties: 8 answers from the engineering school, 7 answers from the humanities, 17 answers from social sciences, 17 answers from natural sciences, 2 answers from agricultural sciences, and only 1 answer from health sciences. The study showed that 38% of those researchers had been involved in research for more than twenty years, 7.69% had sixteen to twenty years of experience in research, 19.23% had between eleven and fifteen years of experience, and 30.77% had five to ten years of experience in research. In terms of gender, female participants constituted 44.23%, male participants constituted 51.92%, and 3.85% of the participants refused to disclose gender information.

Table 1. Number of participants per faculty

Faculty	Number of answers
Engineering	8
Humanities	7
Social sciences	17
Natural sciences	17
Agricultural sciences	2
Health sciences	1
Total	52

4.2 Volume and Type of Data

The volume of data generated by most of the respondents was in gigabytes (57%), a smaller portion of respondents (34%) produced data in megabytes, and fewer participants (3.85%), geoscientists to be more specific, produced data in terabytes. Table 2 shows the type of data used and produced. Researchers worked mostly with standard office documents (78%) and web-based datasets (61%). They rarely used encoded text related formats such as xml (7.6%). Similarly, participants produced largely the same formats: standard office documents (67.31%), structured scientific and statistical data (40.38%), images (38.46%), internet and web-based data (25%), and non-digital data (21.15%).

4.3 Information Literacy

Metadata. As for metadata assignments, 13% added technical information (such as file format, file size, and software/hardware needed to use the data), 25% described the data file structure, 38.5% applied discovery information (e.g. creator, funding body, project title, project ID, keywords, etc.), 40% applied administrative information (e.g. creator, date of creation, file name, access terms/restrictions, etc.) and 34% of the participants did not assign additional information to their research data as per Table 3, below.

Administrative information was applied mostly by natural sciences departments (19.22%), followed by social sciences (28.83%), engineering (13.46%), and humanities

Table 2. Most commonly used and produced data types by LU faculty members

Data type	Used %	Produced %
Standard office documents (text, spreadsheets, presentations, etc.)	78.85	67.31
Internet and web-based data (webpages, e-mails, blogs, social network data, etc.)	61.54	25.00
Structured scientific and statistical data (e.g. SPSS, GIS, etc.)	51.92	40.38
Images (JPEG, GIF, TIFF, PNG, etc.)	51.92	38.46
Archived data (ZIP, RAR, ZAR, etc.)	28.85	9.62
Non digital data (paper, films, slides, artefacts, etc.)	28.85	21.15
Databases (e.g. in Access, Oracle, MySQL, etc.)	25.00	15.38
Software applications (modelling tools, editors, compilers, etc.)	23.08	13.46
Audio files	17.31	5.77
Raw (machine-generated) data	17.31	11.54
Configuration data (parameter settings, logs, library files, etc.)	17.31	11.54
Structured graphics (CAD, CAM, VRML, etc.)	13.46	9.62
Source code (scripting, Java, C, C ++, etc.)	11.54	9.62
Encoded text (XML, SGML, etc.)	7.69	9.62

Table 3. Kind of metadata assigned to research datasets by LU faculty members

Type of metadata	%
Administrative information (e.g. creator, date of creation, file name, access terms/restrictions, etc.)	40.38
Discovery information (e.g. creator, funding body, project title, project ID, keywords, etc.)	38.46
Technical information (e.g. file format, file size, software/hardware needed to use the data, etc.)	13.46
Description of the data file (e.g. file/data structure, field tags/descriptions, application rules, etc.)	25.00
No, I do not assign additional information to my research data	34.62

(13.46%). For discovery information, 17.3% of the answers came from Natural Sciences, 9.61% were from social sciences, 5.76% from humanities, 2% from engineering, and 2% from agricultural sciences. For technical information, 9.61% came from natural sciences, 3.8% from engineering, and 2% from geosciences. When asked about data structure, tags, and application rules, we once again noticed that respondents who applied descriptions of the data files were mostly from natural sciences backgrounds. As for those who did not assign additional information to their research data they mainly came from social sciences backgrounds (15.3%), followed by natural sciences (7.69%), then engineering (3.84%), agriculture (1.92%), and 1.92% was, surprisingly, from the school of information sciences. Almost all (99%) of the participants agreed that the institution should have a predefined metadata set for uploading data into a repository once it exists. More than 52% of the participants expressed interest in receiving formal training on metadata best practices.

Data Citing. Almost half of the researchers (55%) used a standard style for citing their research data; the other half (45%) did not. The LU faculties provide guidelines on citation styles according to 29% of the participants whereas the other 71% of participants were not aware of the existence of such guidelines. As a result, 40% of the participants always cite their data using a standard style, 28% often following a standard style, 29% rarely or never following a standard citation style. Thirty two percent of the academic staff expressed they needed training in this area. Others seemed less interested in the subject.

File Naming. It was found that only 9% of the participants were aware of the importance of the consistency in naming their files while others had rarely (17%) or never (46%) paid attention to being consistent in file naming. The majority (85%) agreed on the role of the university in putting in place a recommendation or a standard for file naming, others (11%) were not aware of its importance and were neither agreeing nor disagreeing to this suggestion and 34% of the participants expressed the need for training.

Version Control of Datasets. When asked if they use a specific tool or technique to easily recognize a specific version of the data set, 8% said they did it always, 20% did it often, 20% did it rarely, and the remaining 52% never did it. Around 5% of the participants had already been trained on version control and 33% wanted to receive training.

4.4 Data Storage

Most faculty surveyed (46.14%) generate their own data sets during research. Also, the same percentage (46.14%) of respondents get data from their research team at the LU. Some researchers (53.85%) have their own research network and connections that provide them with datasets. Despite the finding that most faculty generate and use data sets, almost all of them (88.46%) do not use data repositories to store their data. This lack of awareness is proven given that most faculty (98.08%) say they store their data on their own devices (personal computer, tablet, and external drive). A minority (17.31%) uses the cloud for storage, the remaining participants (11.54%) use either institutional servers or outside repositories and archives to store their data (Table 4). In general, faculty members (77%) understand that data should be preserved for long future access, long after the research is completed. Some (9.6%) did not think about its importance and therefore were neutral (neither agreeing nor disagreeing to storing data for long terms access). Around 13.5% disagreed on the fact that data should be preserved beyond the lifetime of a project.

Table 4. Data storage of most participant

Data storage	%
Own device	98.00
Cloud	17.31
Central servers	5.77
Outside repositories	5.77
Others	3.87

4.5 Data Sharing

More than 53% of the participants would share their data upon request, while 26% have their data openly accessible to everyone, 25% of the participants make their data available only to their research team, 15% refuse to share their data with anyone, and 9.6% allow partial access to their data. Although 44.73% of participants had no concerns related to sharing their data, others had several reasons that made them reluctant to provide data to others: 34.6% were concerned about legal and ethical issues and 26.92% were concerned about the lack of appropriate policies and rights protection (Fig. 1).

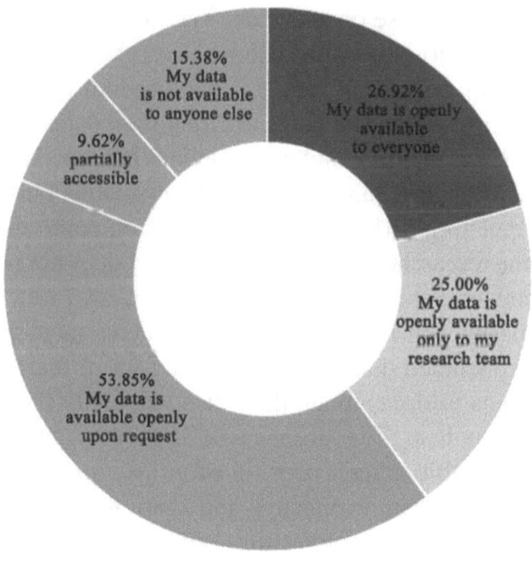

Fig. 1. Researchers sharing their data

4.6 Data Management Plan (DMP)

According to participants (95%), LU does not have a data management plan (DMP) in place. Nevertheless, 5% of the participants were familiar with data management plans and have a DMP in place for their current research. Some of the participants (15%) were not sure what a DMP was. When asked if they had ever used a DMP, 75% of the participants confirmed they have never dealt with it. Putting a DMP in place is essential to 94% of LU researchers, they stated that the institution needs to handle this process.

5 Discussion

The survey revealed the needs and gaps at LU. The fact that 52 participants out of 161 have completed the whole survey may suggest that the majority of the participants did not find the subject relevant to them. On the other hand, we can sense from the complete answers that faculty members at the LU are finding their own ways to apply data management according to the available resources they have in hand. There is certainly a lack of clear policies, infrastructures, and skilled librarians in the institution. The research shows that the LU offered almost no services of any sort to support data management through its campuses. However, participants expressed an interest in the subject of data management and a willingness to be active contributors once an infrastructure is available. Even with a low engagement of the LU libraries in efficiently introducing information literacy practices, researchers are having no major issues in acquiring the data they need from different sources. They are also dealing with almost all the types of data and different volumes. The increase in the volume of data requires good data planning and management. Nevertheless, there is a weakness in other aspects such as data documentation and the use of metadata. The latter is essential for data curation for it allows the researcher to effectively use his dataset in the future without having issues in understanding its content as well as enabling him to share it with others. In addition, respondents expressed weaknesses in citing their datasets especially that there are some guidelines in some faculties and no guidelines in others on how to cite different datatypes, particularly when those are not publically available. Furthermore, organizing information and manipulating it (file naming and version controlling) seems to be the weakest skill among the researchers. Since the university does not provide any means of storage to faculty members, researchers had to find their own way of storing their data through inadequate means. Since none of the respondents mentioned subject specific data repositories, we concluded that they were not aware of their existence. Since LU researchers had no means to disseminate their data efficiently their research data were deemed to ultimately be lost. The absence of data management planning makes researchers of the LU invisible to their peers in other institutions. They do not have the same resources that enables them to manage and share their data in order to advance their research and build significant connections with other scholars in their field.

6 Conclusion

The study results offer a preliminary figure of the management of data at the Lebanese University. It highlighted the strengths, weaknesses and needs of this scholarly community. It also sheds light on the willingness of LU academic staff to work toward enhancements in this area. Most researchers are not reluctant to share data with others. They are willing to cope with new applications of RDM, however they do not have the infrastructure, technical support, or skills to do it. The libraries have a great opportunity to step in and work as a facilitator in this process. Support from the administration is crucial at this level and development of policies and procedures is needed.

7 Recommendations

- Implementation of an institutional repository is crucial at this level to support faculty in managing, sharing, and preserving their research data.
- Development of policies and guidelines is in order to promote a knowledge sharing culture and encourage academics to engage in the activities related to research data management since local funding agencies are requiring data management plans.
- Tailoring of special workshops and training sessions should be done in collaboration with the 62 LU libraries to reinforce information literacy and data management skills.
- Librarians should be empowered through training so they might be able to support faculty members throughout the data life cycle from creation, to documentation, sharing, and preservation of data.

References

1. Bouquillion, P., Matthews, J.: Le Web Collaboratif: Mutations des Industries de la Culture et de la Communication. Presses Universitaires de Grenoble, Grenoble (2010)
2. Dagnaud, M.: Le Modèle Californien: Comment l'Esprit Collaboratif Change le Monde. Odile Jacob, Paris (2016)
3. Rieffel, R.: Revolution Numerique, Revolution Culturelle? Folio actuel. Gallimard, Paris (2014)
4. Surkis, A., Read, K.: Research data management. J. Med. Libr. Assoc. **103**(3), 154–156 (2015)
5. Del Castillo, D.: The Arab World's Scientific Desert. The Chronical of Higher Education, 5 March 2004
6. Allatif, A.L.: Mouawiqat al bahth al ilmi. Al saouddiya (2008)
7. Maadan, S.H.: Waqeh al bahth al ilmi fi al watan al arabi fi dil al fajwa al raqmiyya. Majallat al ouloum al insaniyya, vol. 38 (2012). http://revue.umc.edu.dz/index.php/h/article/view/1337
8. Zahlan, A.: al arab wa tahadiyat al asr. markaz dirassat al wihda al Arabiya, Beirut (1990)
9. Badran, A.: Les Etats Arabes. UNESCO, Paris (2006). http://www.unesco.org/fileadmin/MULTIMEDIA/HQ/SC/pdf/sc_usr05_arab_fr.pdf
10. Stephan, M.: Recherche et Communication. Bahithat, pp. 76–95 (1997)
11. Hotet, F.: al mouwassafat al bahthiya lilrasael al jamiiya fi elm al nafs. Bahithat, pp. 24–40 (1997)
12. Mourtada, A.: The Conditions of Academic Research in the Arab World. Bahithat (1997)
13. Funari, M.: Research data and humanities: a European context. Ital. J. Libr. Inf. Sci. **5**(1), 209–236 (2014)
14. Hakim Rahme, D.: Co-Authorship Patterns at the Medical School of the American University of Beirut between 2004 and 2014. Paper presented at: IFLA WLIC 2016 –

Columbus, OH – Connections. Collaboration. Community in Session 101 - Poster Sessions (2016)
15. Flores, J.R., Brodeur, J.J., Daniels, M.G., Nicholls, N., Turnator, E.L.: Libraries and the research data management landscape. In: Maclachlan, J.C., Waraksa, E.A., Williford, C., (eds.) The Process of Discovery: The CLIR Postdoctoral Fellowship Program and the Future of the Academy, pp. 82–102 (2015). Washington DC: Council on Library and Information Resources. www.clir.org/pubs/reports/pub167/pub167.pdf#page=88
16. Eschenfelder, K.R., Johnson, A.: Managing the Data Commons: Controlled Sharing of Scholarly Data. University Libraries Faculty and Staff Contributions, vol. 15 (2014)
17. Sixth Arabic Report on education and Development (2010). http://fikrconferences.org/sites/default/files/takrir6.pdf. Accessed 28 May 2017
18. Lebanese University Homepage, http://www.ul.edu.lb/. Accessed 28 May 2017
19. Scopus. https://www.scopus.com. Accessed 28 May 2017
20. Questionnaire National Research Data Survey. https://e-infrastructures.at/fileadmin/user_upload/p_e_infrastructures/PDFs/Questionnaire_e-Infra_Research_Data_Survey_Aug15.pdf. Accessed 28 May 2017
21. Tenopir, C., Allard, S., Douglass, K., Aydinoglu, A.U., Wu, L., Read, E., et al.: Data sharing by scientists: practices and perceptions. PLoS ONE **6**(6), e21101 (2011)

Media Literacy

News, Fake News, and Critical Authority

John M. Budd[1] and Kristine N. Stewart[2(✉)]

[1] School of Information Science and Learning Technologies, University of Missouri, Columbia, MO, USA
BuddJ@missouri.edu
[2] Zayed University, Abu Dhabi, United Arab Emirates
Kristine.stewart@zu.ac.ae

Abstract. The purpose of this proposed work is to present a theoretically and methodologically sound grounding for the critical apprehension of what constitutes authoritative news and news sources. The presentation will demonstrate clearly that there are variations in reports of news: intentionally objective news items ("intentionally" in that there is a deliberate attempt at objective reporting), unintentional error in news items ("unintentionally" mistaken), and intentionally false news items ("intentionally" in that there is a deliberate effort to deceive readers). The proposed work will focus on the first and third of the possibilities. Within the functioning of information literacy, it is argued, there is an obligation to recognize the intentionalities for what they are—objective reporting and efforts to deceive. Ultimately, the presentation will suggest ways to realize that obligation.

Keywords: Semiotics · Information literacy · Fake news · Media literacy

1 Introduction

The purpose of this work is to present a theoretically and methodologically sound grounding for the critical apprehension of what constitutes authoritative news "Being dependent on others for what we know makes us vulnerable to those who would exploit this fact in order to spread falsehoods. Making students scientifically literate and more able to distinguish accurate statements from garbage and noise has implications beyond teaching better strategies for writing papers" [1, p. 232]. Steven Sloman and Philip Fernbach are cognitive scientists who study the states of knowledge individuals and communities may have, how to accept degrees of ignorance, and how people may hold illusions of understanding. They examine the limits of rationality when it comes to learning and making decisions, as well as strategies for helping people learn and understand what they need to know. The implications for information literacy, particularly in an era of fake news, are clear and Sloman and Fernbach's lessons will be drawn from again.

The presentation will demonstrate clearly that there are variations in reports of news: intentionally objective news items ("intentionally" in that there is a deliberate attempt at objective reporting), unintentional error in news items ("unintentionally" mistaken), and intentionally false news items ("intentionally" in that there is a deliberate effort to deceive readers). This paper will focus on the first and third of the

S. Kurbanoğlu et al. (Eds.): ECIL 2017, CCIS 810, pp. 227–232, 2018.
https://doi.org/10.1007/978-3-319-74334-9_24

possibilities. Within the functioning of information literacy, it is argued, there is an obligation to recognize the intentionalities for what they are—objective reporting and efforts to deceive. Ultimately, the presentation suggests ways to realize that obligation.

2 Interpretive Challenges of Fake News

Due to changes in the information landscape, students are confronted "with a chaos of information and perspectives and a vast constellation of ever-changing data points that may or may not be true or accurate" [2, p. 311]. Access to high quality journalism has become increasingly more difficult due to the abundance of opinion based information sources disguised as journalism [3]. "Fake news", "alternative facts", and unsubstantiated claims are phenomena which have been largely cultivated in online spaces, such as social media sites, which circumvent traditional methods taught in Information Literacy Instruction (ILI) to interpret information sources.

Social media has elevated the voices of those who otherwise would not have been heard outside of limited circles; this may be seen as both positive and negative. During the "Arab Spring", for example, this "illustrated the collaborative and coercive power of social media" [3, p. 7], amplifying previously silenced voices calling for social justice. Alternatively, it has also given "visibility to deliberate (or ignorant) misinformation, hate speech, incitement to violence and advocacy of terrorism" [3, p. 7]. This has led to the creation of new challenges for students regarding how they base their ideas and decisions on sources of information.

Those unable to or who do not know how unknowing to think critically about what they see or hear online are at risk of falling prey to untruths and ill intended assertions. Unfortunately identifying authoritative sources of information has never been more complicated. Many people seem to take information at face value, believing whatever they read online without question. This issue is exacerbated by the trend of polarized politics. This (and the next) generation of students are watching as adults in their lives have ideas and stances, strictly defined and based on party affiliation or political ideology. Our use of (and reliance on) technologies for access to information compounds confirmation bias, by making it easier. Search engines save information preferences of their users, which means that over time your search engine has become so acquainted with you that it knows your religion, political leanings, and areas of concern [4]. Consequently, even when an individual *actively* searches for information on a topic of interest or concern, the information retrieved by their search engine retrieves siloed information, based on their own information preferences (and pre-existing worldview).

In the 21st century, it seems that people are entitled to both their own opinions, and their own facts. In order to broaden perspectives, individuals must make a concerted and conscious effort to broaden their perspectives; otherwise, they will remain polarized. Knowing the above, however, may present a larger challenge. Whilst working towards the challenges associated with distinguishing accurate statements in the news from both unintentional and intentionally false news items, students risk becoming so cynical about the quality and accuracy of information that they are unable to trust any information.

3 Semiotics

The theoretical grounding for the proposed work is based in Williams' [5] process philosophy of signs. His is a variation on traditional semiotics, where it is presumed that a sign is (primarily) fixed, and that the meaning and interpretants follow necessarily from the sign structure. Instead, in Williams' scheme, "signs are multiplicities and they acquire determinacy through processes of stabilization and destabilization, rather than from externally imposed identities" [5, p. 12–13]. Another way of defining this process structure is to say that a sign does not have an ontological being simply by virtue of its expression. A sign is a product of selection processes that lead to interpretation; the selections are complex and variable, but are products of both linguistic matters *and* intensive elements of attention, discernment, and analysis. It is this last feature of a process theory that applies most pertinently to the proposal's purpose.

Semiotics operates according to a commonly expressed structure, as is indicated by Williams. The diagrammatic representation usually follows a form such as the one below: (Fig. 1)

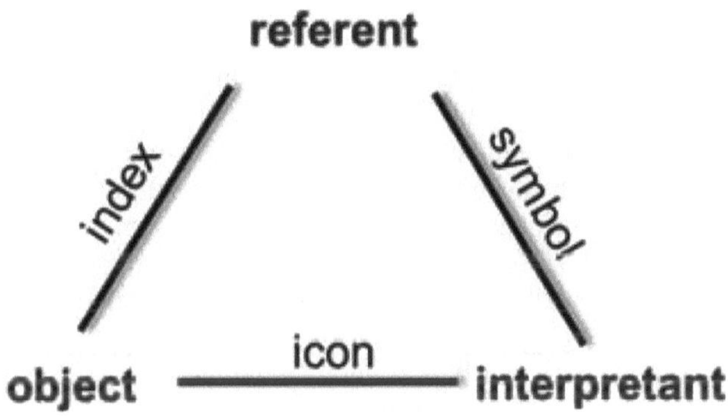

Fig. 1. General structure of Semiotics [6, para. 10]

The structure above has a fairly long history—in one iteration or another—dating back to Charles Sanders Peirce, Charles Morris, and Ferdinand de Saussure (and even to ancient and pre-modern times according to Deely [7]). Peirce articulated some of the earliest principles of signs and the relationships between signs. For example, he [8] writes, "If a sign, *B*, only signifies characters that are elements (or the whole) of the meaning of another sign, *A*, then *B* is said to be a *predicate* (or *essential part*) of *A*" (p. 305, emphasis in original). He elaborates on his particular idea of the interpretant, which is an absolutely essential component of any sign. He [8] says, "There is the *Intentional* Interpretant, which is a determination of the mind of the utterer; the *Effectual* Interpretant, which is a determination of the mind of the interpreter; and the *Communicational* Interpretant, or say the *Cominterpretant*, which is a determination of that mind into which the mind of the utterer and interpreter have to be fused in order that communication should take place" (p. 478, emphasis in original). Peirce elucidates that manifold roles played by the interpretant within any sign structure. This definitional expansion should come as no surprise to those familiar with Peirce; these expansions of the roles of the interpretant are entirely consistent with his Pragmatism, or his insistence that language and its structure by directed *toward* something and should be intended to achieve an end.

Grice [9] explicates what a communicative sign is intended to accomplish:

(i) A communicator C intends *x* to produce some effect E (e.g., a belief, an action) on an interpreter I;
(ii) C intends I to recognize the intention of (i); and
(iii) I's recognition of the intention of (ii) is a reason for the effect E on I (p. 379).

Grice's formulation is quite straightforward, and serves well for most semiotic analysis. The communicative process is, first and foremost, intentional; the intentionality can be taken to mean "deliberate," but it can also have a more phenomenological meaning. That is, the sign, or the communication or utterance, can include the understanding that, for example, the belief is a belief *in* or *of* something. Moreover, the sign's interpretant is a *self*, just as is the communicator. There is not space here to go into detail regarding phenomenology; see Budd [10] for more on the topic.

Barthes [11] elaborates on the definition of a sign in a particularly useful manner, one that illuminates the complexity of communication through signs: "To decipher the world's signs always means to struggle with a certain innocence of objects. We all understand our language so 'naturally' that it never occurs to us that it is an extremely complicated system, one anything but "natural in its signs and rules; in the same way, it requires an incessant shock of observation in order to deal not with the content of messages, but with their making (p. 158)".

As Foucault [12] has warned, a surplus of meaning can intrude upon interpretation (pp. 31–39). Raber and Budd [13] express another element of the sign, this time as it relates to time:

Time has. . . [a] role to play in signification, and this role reveals another essential attribute of the sign and its affinity with the informative object. In order to create and express meaning, signs engage value as well as signification. The meaning of a sign as an instrument of communication depends simultaneously on signification and value, on the relations between signifier and signified within the sign, and on relations between signs. Like signification, value, and therefore meaning, unfolds throughout time (p. 513).

This brief background on semiotics is a bare beginning; it is time to concentrate on Williams [5] and his idea of process semiotics.

4 Process Philosophy of Semiotics

First, the excursus into the work and thought of Peirce, above, has application to Williams process philosophy. One can argue that William's conception follows in the tradition of Peirce's Pragmatic theory of signs. He notes immediately that the meaning of a sign is dynamic; hearken back to Peirce's multiple conception of the interpretant. Williams [5] details his conception of the process philosophy: "The preliminary task of the process philosophy is to define the different processes at work in the sign. It will be argued that they are interdependent and they set conditions for one another. First, the sign is a selection. In order to appear as a sign the threatening message painted on your home had to bring together a set of elements; for instance, the sign is yourself, your door, your thoughts about a message, your feelings, white paint and the shape of a cross. There is a selection of a set, the condition for the appearance of any sign, before there can be meaning (p. 2)".

The form of the sign that is depicted above can therefore be seen as a static representation of one selection, one event that results in the selection of the structure of an iteration of a sign. Williams' depiction of the process is extremely important as a way to conduct information literacy instruction (ILI). In almost every instance in which there is some mode of instruction, there is a semiotic process taking place. It is incumbent upon a teacher to make known the selection, the dynamism which *is* the sign.

One essential point that Williams makes (and it is a point that has great import for information literacy instruction) is that the process philosophy of signs is one of an array of reasoning strategies that any rational person can apply in order to understand communicative action. It is, according to Williams, an extremely important component in the array, and it has unique capacities to foster understanding. He [5] defines his position clearly:

The process philosophy of signs is speculative in so far as it suggests—speculates about—definitions of the sign in order to construct a philosophy aiming neither to base itself on the sciences, nor to offer a complete and consistent alternative to them. Instead, the point is to design a process philosophy of the sign working in critical debate with other ways of thinking about signs, meaning, and the wider systems signs operate in (p. 5).

This qualifier offered by Williams has (at least) a couple of key elements that should be considered in the context of ILI. One is imbedded in the quotation from Williams (above). A sign is imbued with a selection of processes that can be discerned and from which meaning can be inferred. Therefore, the speculation is by no means random or arbitrary; it is grounded in identification of the processes of selection and use that go into rending a sign intelligible. Next, as is evident from what Williams further says, there is something of a dialectical nature of the process philosophy. Williams explicitly acknowledges the dialectic. He [5] writes, "The process is a multiplicity of changing relations and values. . . . The process definition of the sign turns the dialectical account on its head by claiming process as ongoing and ubiquitous alongside secondary processes of relative stabilisation" (pp. 79, 100). Following from the speculative nature of signs within the process conception, Williams notes that there can be internal change in a sign. This leads to the necessity for the recognition of the dialectic, but it is *not* a dialectical exchange between process and structure, since change obfuscates traditional structuralist practices. The tension resides within the sign and the comprehension of the internal changes.

By viewing the process of sign interpretation and the search for meaning as ongoing, there could be constant tensions in interpretation. This is, he says, contrary to structuralism, where form and structure lead to interpretation of meaning. The process philosophy can allow for interpretation of fluid meaning, or of fluid statements about what an utterance means. It is that quality that is most important to ILI and the quest for the meaning of news (and the identification of processes that can be construed as fake or not, despite what may be included in the utterance. Practically speaking, this can lead to a full understanding of the process of discursive practice.

One additional aspect of the process philosophy is pertinent to the practice of ILI, and to the topic of this paper. Williams recognizes that the process sign is political, in that it embraces the event of the political and more generic types of discerning conflict (rather than the narrower definitions of "political"). Williams [5] elaborates by saying, "A process sign determines the political as a problem of description and succession after a novel event which occurs within established frames, where signs shape and give rise to the political as conflict calling for new hypotheses and models" (p. 154).

References

1. Sloman, S., Fernbach, P.: The Knowledge Illusion. Riverhead Books, New York (2017)
2. Allcorn, S., Stein, H.: The post-factual world of the 2016 American presidential election: the good, the bad, and the deplorable. J. Psychohist. **44**, 310–318 (2017)
3. Cerf, V.G.: Can liberty survive the digital age? Commun. ACM **60**, 7 (2017)
4. Loertscher, D.V.: Fake news, a rant, and new standards. Teach. Libr. **44**, 44–45 (2017)
5. Williams, J.: A Process Philosophy of Signs. Edinburgh University Press, Edinburgh (2016)
6. Schneider, F.: A rough guide to the theory of semiotics (2013). http://www.politicseastasia.com/studying/guide-to-the-theory-of-semiotics/
7. Deely, J.: Introducing Semiotic: Its History and Doctrine. Indiana University Press, Bloomington (1982)
8. Peirce, C.S.: The Essential Peirce: Selected Philosophical Writings, Volume 2 (1893–1913). Indiana University Press, Bloomington (1998)
9. Grice, H.P.: Meaning. Philos. Rev. **66**, 377–388 (1957)
10. Budd, J.M.: Phenomenology and information studies. J. Doc. **61**, 44–59 (2005)
11. Barthes, R.: The Semiotic Challenge. University of California Press, Berkeley (1994). Trans. by, R. Howard
12. Foucault, M.: The Archaeology of Knowledge. Pantheon Books, New York (1972). Trans. by A.M.S. Smith
13. Raber, D., Budd, J.M.: Information as sign: semiotics and information science. J. Doc. **59**, 22–507 (2003)
14. Stanford University.: evaluating information: the cornerstone of civic online reasoning (2016). https://sheg.stanford.edu/upload/V3LessonPlans/Executive%20Summary%2011.21.16.pdf

ICT Access and Use by Teachers and Information Professionals: Perspectives and Constraints for the Development of Media and Information Literacy in Brazil

Gilda Olinto[1(✉)], Sonoe Sugahara[2], and Nádia Bernuci[2]

[1] Brazilian Institute of Information on Science and Techology (IBICT), Rio de Janeiro, Brazil
gildaolinto@gmail.com

[2] Brazilian Bureau of Census (IBGE), Rio de Janeiro, Brazil
sonoes@gmail.com, nadiabernuci@yahoo.com.br

Abstract. The Media and Information Literacy Program (MIL) proposed by UNESCO aims at the promotion of a conscious use of information by bringing together academic and public initiatives aware of the relevance of information and communication technology (ICT) in contemporary society. The MIL program elects communication and information professionals and teachers in general as a key professional group. The objective of this work is to collect data on Brazilian MIL professionals: how they are accessing, using, and learning ICT. The data considered in the analyses presented were obtained from the Brazilian Bureau of Census (IBGE). Results suggest that, although they access the Internet for personal use, MIL professionals in Brazil do not have sufficient technological infrastructure at their disposal. Besides, focusing on the sub-category of elementary and high-school teachers, we observed a lack of institutional support for their ICT learning and preparation to act as MIL promoters.

Keywords: Media and information literacy · ICT use · Internet use
Indicators of ICT learning · Information and communication professionals
Brazilian data on ICT

1 Introduction

Although it involves other important dimensions, the concept of MIL (Media and Information Literacy), adopted by UNESCO (United Nations Educational, Scientific and Cultural Organization) [1], places a strong emphasis on generalized access and diversified use of ICT (Information Communication Technologies). Another characteristic of the MIL approach is the specification of professional categories that should be considered in the promotion of MIL. This key professional group includes workers involved in formal and informal education as teachers, librarians and other categories of workers in libraries and museums. We focus here on the Brazilian situation regarding this professional segment, called here the MIL professionals.

S. Kurbanoğlu et al. (Eds.): ECIL 2017, CCIS 810, pp. 233–244, 2018.
https://doi.org/10.1007/978-3-319-74334-9_25

Does Brazil have a favorable perspective for the promotion of MIL and does it have the adequate human resources with the suitable technological infrastructure for this task? To contribute to the answer of these questions, the objective of this paper is to analyze access, availability, and types of use of ICT resources in Brazil by the above-mentioned professional groups. The data used in the analyses of the study were obtained from the national household survey of Brazil's bureau of the census, IBGE (Instituto Brasileiro de Geografia e Estatística) [2]. This survey involved a representative sample of the Brazilian population, involving 356,904 people and 1,100 municipalities. It contained information about general socioeconomic characteristics of respondents. We present here new analyses obtained from microdata available by that institution.

2 The MIL Professionals

The promotion and use of the term MIL can be understood as an effort to bring together two occupational groups—information and communication professionals—to stimulate access to information and knowledge to all types of social groups in all countries. This effort aims at bringing together academic and public policy initiatives that are aware of the omnipresence and relevance of access and effective use of the Internet in contemporary society. The digital era is the amalgam linking all policies and strategies considered by the MIL proposals. "A MIL policy and strategy needs to build upon a concept of media and information literacy that harmonises and encapsulates the large number of related existing literacies that can be identified in the digital age, such as news literacy, television literacy, film literacy, computer literacy, Internet literacy and digital literacy, as well as other emerging concepts like social media literacy" [1, p. 13].

Another related point that seems to motivate the MIL proposal is the appreciation and promotion of the conscious use of information available in the digital world. This consciousness is considered as a guarantee of democracy and citizenship training. Therefore, MIL can be also understood as an effort to build an informational shield that would be able to face the constant menace of manipulation of information as well as the rise of populism and terrorism through social media and other ICT resources. International institutions—such as UNESCO and IFLA (International Federation of Library Associations and Institutions) - are trying to incorporate the term as well as MIL's basic ideas in their proposals towards global democratization of Internet access and effective use. "The goal of MIL is to give people the power to use their rights of free expression, to defend their access to information, to evaluate content, to secure their participation in the process of governing, and to help all voices be heard. At its best, MIL teaches the global public to evaluate available information—including that provided by both formal and informal media—about the world's needs; to make sense of the solutions that are on offer; and to be able to communicate and engage with others proportionately and responsibly, in other words, a bottom up idea" [3, p. 12].

Attention to socially disadvantaged groups is also a characteristic of the MIL proposals. Poor communities, marginalized ethnic minorities, remote groups in rural areas, as well as the promotion of gender equality are considered by this program, notably with the use of ICT resources. About this last subject, also called the gender digital divide, it can be said that a solid academic tradition and several types of evidences already stress the early alienation of women from technology, as well as the lower interest of young girls for hard science and technology as possible career choices [4, 5].

In relation to Internet use, the tendency observed is towards gender parity in access to the Internet, but the persistence of some significant differences when the focus of research is on types of use and appropriation. Women seem to show different interests and abilities when using the Internet, these evidences implying that different information literacy levels can accompany gendered cultures and a gendered education [6, 7]. In other words, ICT gender imbalance can jeopardize women's perspectives in the present knowledge society.

To face these multiple challenges, attention to the educational environment is one of the emphases of the MIL proposals. Specific proposals seem to go in this direction. According to IFLA recommendations [8], governments and institutions should support professional training in MIL and lifelong learning and recognize the importance of these types of competencies and that these should become part of all educational programs and training. Therefore, in addition to information and communication professionals, teachers from all educational levels are to be involved in MIL as a professional group. "… UNESCO model MIL Curriculum and Competency framework for teachers is intended to provide teacher education systems in developed and developing countries with a framework to construct a programme for turning out teachers who are media and information literate. UNESCO also envisions that educators will review the framework and take up the challenge of participating in the collective process of shaping and enriching the curriculum as a living document" [9, p. 19].

Librarians, archivists, and museologists are also valued by the MIL proposals for their pedagogical role as facilitators of information access and use by library and archive users as well as by museum visitors. Museums, archives and libraries constantly face the challenge of competently using TIC resources.

From the discussion above, it can be said that, from the MIL perspective, a group of professional categories can be considered as a key professional group—the MIL professionals—involved in promotion of IT use: these include communication and information professionals as well as teachers in general. These professionals' access and uses of ICT and the Internet, in particular, is therefore an essential starting point for the establishment of public policies on the subject.

3 Data and Methodology

In order to evaluate the perspectives for the promotion of MIL in Brazil, we bring about new information about ICT access and types of Internet use by the above - mentioned MIL professionals. Our analyses focused on the following aspects: Internet access, availability of ITC resources, aspects of Internet use, and forms of ICT training.

We used as our main data source the Brazilian Household Annual Survey of 2015 (known as PNAD survey). This survey collected information about several socioeconomic characteristics of the Brazilian population since 1967. Access and use of the Internet and other ICT devices—microcomputer, cellular phone for personal use, tablet and Internet through television - were included in the 2015 survey, the last survey with microdata available for analysis. A Brazilian classification of occupations (CBO), which follows, as its main reference, the International Classification of Occupations—ISCO-88, is considered in the PNAD. For the statistical analyses presented here, two occupational groups were extracted from the survey microdata. The first group was classified as communication professions and information professionals[1], including librarians, museologists, archivists, and other professionals working as mediators in cultural institutions. The second group involved the category of teacher[2], including pre-school and elementary school teachers, with and without college degree, and college and university teachers.

In 2015 the Brazilian population was 204,860,101 people. But, the total people from whom the survey asked about Internet use were only those 10 years of age and older. Therefore, the total people included in the analyses about Internet access represented 177,656,822 people, excluding more than 27 million children. Other important methodological information is that, in order to count people with access to the Internet, we used a variable with a very general information: "In the last three months did you use the Internet somewhere?". Those who provided a positive answer to this variable represented 103,857,075[3] people.

As complementary data, we also present here information about types of Internet use considered in the annual survey about Internet use for education [10]. From this survey, we obtained information about types of internet use and forms of ICT learning by Brazilian teachers.

4 Internet Access and Types of Internet Access by the Brazilian Population

The first group of information presented here relate to aspects of the contextual and sociocultural characteristics of Internet users in Brazil. This focus tries to detect important dimensions of inequality to take into account in the MIL proposal. Is the Internet reaching people living in rural areas? Is it reaching women and men equally as well as the different racial groups? What is the present impact of age and schooling with regard to Internet access?

Tables 1, 2 and 3, that follow, try to answer these questions about Internet inequalities that might accompany social inequalities.

Although almost 60% of the total population already had Internet access in 2015, including 64% of those living in urban areas, from the tables presented it is possible to conclude that socioeconomic and cultural ambiance show their clear effect on Internet access. The much lower level of access in Brazilian rural areas - half the amount attained in the urban milieu, and affecting 19,767,330 people - suggests the necessity of an urgent attention to this group with respect to ICT.

---

[1] 2611, 2612, 2613, 2616, 3711, 3712, 3713 CBO groups.

[2] 2311, 2312, 2313, 2321, 2330, 2340, 2391, 2392, 2394, 3311, 3312, 3313 CBO groups.

[3] We eliminated from the analyses people who, although informed that they had access, did not answer the questions about type of equipment used for access (393,899 people).

Table 1. Internet access (urban/rural) - Brazilian population 10 years of age and above - 2015

Urban/rural	% with access	N with access	N without access	Total
Urban	64.2	96,953,013	54,032,417	150,985,430
Rural	25.9	6,904,062	19,767,330	26,671,392
Total	58.5	103,857,075	73,799,747	177,656,822

Source: IBGE, Pesquisa Nacional por Amostra de Domicílios, 2015. Microdata.

Table 2. Internet access by race - Brazilian population 10 years of age and above—2015.

Race	% with access	N with access	N without access	Total
White	65.0	52,174,780	28094995	80,269,775
Mulato/black	53.0	50,744,911	45084934	95,829,845
Yellow	71.8	642,736	252194	894,930
Other	44.5	294,648	367624	662,272
Total	58.5	103,857,075	73,799,747	177,656,822

Source: IBGE, Pesquisa Nacional por Amostra de Domicílios, 2015. Microdata.

Table 3. Internet access by gender - Brazilian population 10 years of age and above -2015.

Gender	% with access	N with access	N without access	Total
Women	59.0	54,402,536	37,764,887	92,167,423
Men	57.8	49,454,539	36,034,860	85,489,399
Total	58.5	103,857,075	73,799,747	177,656,822

Source: IBGE, Pesquisa Nacional por Amostra de Domicílios, 2015. Microdata.

Racial groups also show clear differences that accompany expectations based on previous data and theoretical support: black and mixed race groups—a clear majority of the population—had a substantially lower level of Internet access, contrasted with the White and Asian ethnic groups. The good news came from the superior access level among females: women clearly surpassed men in this respect. However, women's Internet access advantage would have to be understood with regard to the purpose of their use, since previous analyses suggest, as mentioned above, that women and men use the Internet for different purposes, which can have a negative impact in this gender group perspective in knowledge society.

The next two graphs (Figs. 1 and 2), analysing the relationship between age and schooling with Internet access, show the strong impact of both variables.

In these two graphs, it is remarkable to observe the negative "slide" effect when age is considered, and the positive "climbing" effect when education is taken into account. A minor observation is that the second age group—between ages 20–29—is in a better position than the previous one, suggesting that Internet access might be still not guaranteed to Brazilian children. In general, however, it seems clear the strong positive

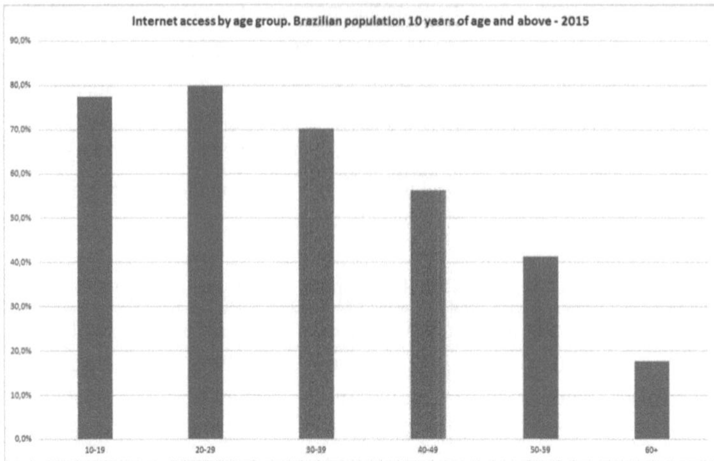

Fig. 1. Internet access by age groups - Brazilian population 10 years of age or more—2015. Source: IBGE, Pesquisa Nacional por Amostra de Domicílios, 2015. Microdata.

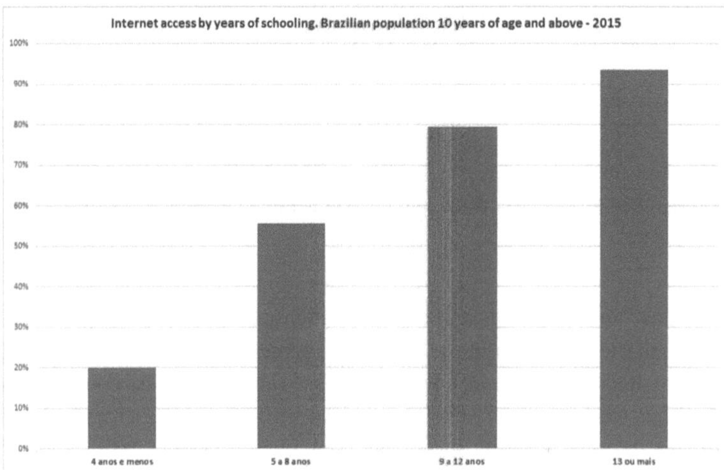

Fig. 2. Internet access by years of schooling - Brazilian population 10 years of age or more—2015. Source: IBGE, Pesquisa Nacional por Amostra de Domicílios, 2015. Microdata.

effect of education and the equally strong negative effect of age in Internet access. These evidences showed the need of attention to both older groups and those with a poor formal education that tend to be alienated from ICT.

We conclude this analysis section of the situation of the general Brazilian population with respect to Internet access by considering the type of ICT device involved in this access. To guide the analysis of the categories presented in Table 4, we consider Internet access by cellular phone, although a rising tendency worldwide, still does not guarantee full access to all types of information available in the net, notably for

Table 4. Internet access by type of access - Brazilian population 10 years of age and above—2015.

Type of access	%	N
Microcomputer only	11.4	11,872,037
Cell phone only	26.8	27,880,200
Micro and cel	44.0	45,748,163
Micro, cel and tablet	10.1	10,525,964
Other types	7.5	7,830,711
Total	100.0	103,857,075

Source: IBGE, Pesquisa Nacional por Amostra de Domicílios, 2015. Microdata.

learning purposes. Besides, access only through the microcomputer can be considered a limitation to several types of use, notably in the use of communication resources, as it is the case of social media.

Data shown in Table 4 indicate that almost 40% of the Brazilian population that had access to the Internet, also attested to using it only by one of these two devices—microcomputer or cell phone-, and not both of them. They had, therefore, a limited possibility of effective use of the net. In a better situation are those that had, at a minimum, microcomputer and cellular phone or more than those types of equipment—just above 60% of users.

As a whole, data presented in this session allow us to conclude that there are still substantial constraints on Internet access in the country from the point of view of socioeconomic and cultural aspects and from the effective availability of basic ICT devices.

5 Internet Access and Types of Internet Access by the MIL Professional Group

Since what we have called the MIL occupational group includes, beside communication and information professionals, Brazilian teachers from all school levels, the initial information sought from the data basis was their total number and the percentage of women involved in these occupations:

Table 5. MIL Occupational group by gender - Brazil 2015.

MIL occupational group	% women	N
Communication and information professionals	49.8	199,005
College and university teachers	51.4	315,391
Elementary teachers with college degree	81.1	3,199,722
Elementary teachers with high school diploma	87.0	291,440
Total	77.6	4,005,558

Source: IBGE, Pesquisa Nacional por Amostra de Domicílios, 2015. Microdata.

It can be emphasized from the above results, that the population of MIL professionals, totals more than 4 million people, the great majority of whom are elementary school teachers. Another highlight was women's participation in these professional categories. It is only among the smaller groups - with low absolute numbers - of communication and information professionals and college and university teachers that we observe gender parity. This professional group's access to the Internet was almost total, ranging from 94 to 99%, for all the above categories with the exception of teachers without college degrees (with high school diploma), only 81.8% of whom indicated that they had some kind of Internet access.

Those who had Internet access—3,795,293 or 94.8% - were asked about their use of the Internet through specific ICT devices. This information is presented in Table 6, below:

Table 6. MIL Occupational group by equipment used for Internet access—Brazil—2015.

ICT equipment	Information professionals (%)	College and university teachers (%)	Elementary teachers with college degree (%)	Elementary teachers with high school diploma (%)
Micro only	7.7	7.4	11.0	16.3
Cel only	2.7	2.0	6.5	18.9
Micro and cel	48.1	42.5	56.7	51.4
Micro, cel and tablet	23.9	26.1	18.3	8.9
Micro, cel, tablet and tv	8.9	14.5	3.5	2.0
Other types	8.8	7.6	4.0	2.5
Total	100.0	100.0	100.0	100.0

Source: IBGE, Pesquisa Nacional por Amostra de Domicílios, 2015. Microdata.

We can consider, as a first approach to the analysis of data in Table 5, that having access to the Internet through only one equipment—as a microcomputer or a cellular phone - would not indicate sufficient basic MIL proficiency. Both from the point of view of their professional training, and from the point of view of their educational activities with students and other Internet users, MIL proficiency would imply access to diversified ITC resources. Although only around 10% of information professionals and college and university teachers did not have at their disposition these two types of equipment, this is the case of more than 32% of elementary teachers with a high school diploma. However, the availability of both ICT devices - micro and cellular - was what better characterized all professional groups: around 50% of the four professional categories considered above. The availability of a tablet, TV or other types of equipment for Internet access, for all of them, was very low.

From the data presented in this section, bout Internet access and types of instrument used for access, we can conclude that basic access is almost guaranteed to all the professional categories selected to represent those involved in MIL training and performance. It can also be stressed the outstanding women's participation in this professional group, information that could be taken into account in efforts to promote MIL: these results illustrate relevance of approaching the gender imbalance in ICT and in career choice in several aspects of MIL programming. Finally, we can point out that diversification of ICT devices for Internet access, as tablet, TV and others, is not yet a reality in Brazil.

6 Purposes of Internet Use and Form of ICT Learning by Brazilian Teachers

To complement the information presented above - about ICT availability by the whole population and by all the country's MIL professionals - we also present here data about the purposes of Internet use and forms of ICT learning by Brazilian teachers, the largest segment of this professional group. These data were obtained from a different data source: the Regional Centre for Studies for the Development of the Information Society (Cetic.br). This non-profit organization promotes annual national surveys about ICT use in the country. The 2015 version of the Survey on the Use of Information and Communication Technologies in Brazilian Schools contains information about a representative sample of teachers from the 8th and 9th elementary school levels and from the 2nd year of high school. A total of 1,631 teachers were included in the sample [10].

Overall, available analyses of this survey show that 98% of teachers already have a college degree, and that 99% also have access to the Internet. Data were also available regarding several types of Internet use by teachers, as shown in Graphic 3, below.

As Graph 3 (Fig. 3) suggests, around 90% of elementary and high school teachers used ICT for communication purposes including sending emails, sending instant messages, and the use of social networks. However, a much smaller percentage of teachers (around 30 to 50%) were involved with activities requiring a more sophisticated use of ICT, such as installing programs, posting videos, and creating blogs. In addition, it was not very common for teachers to have participated in online courses and in forums and discussions, activities that suggest investment in professional improvement: only around 40% seemed to experience these activities. Surprisingly, a much higher proportion of teachers - above 60%- mentioned setting up security devises for computer and Internet use.

Another part of the above-mentioned survey, considers forms of computer and Internet training and continuous education by the teachers in the last 12 months. Graph 4 (Fig. 4), that follows, shows the results to these questions.

In Graph 4, we observe that the great majority of Brazilian elementary and high school teachers seemed to learn about computer and Internet use on their own, through personal contacts, or made use of collaboration networks with teachers outside school. There seemed to be few initiatives made in their own school or by higher educational institutions towards the development of school teachers' ICT literacy.

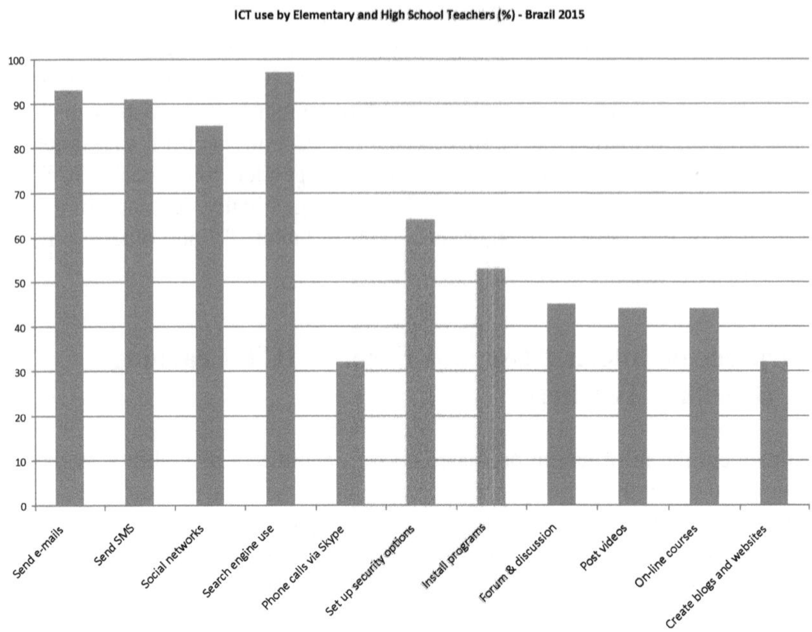

Fig. 3. ICT use by elementary and high school teachers (%) - Brazil—2015. Source: Cetic, ICT in Education 2015.

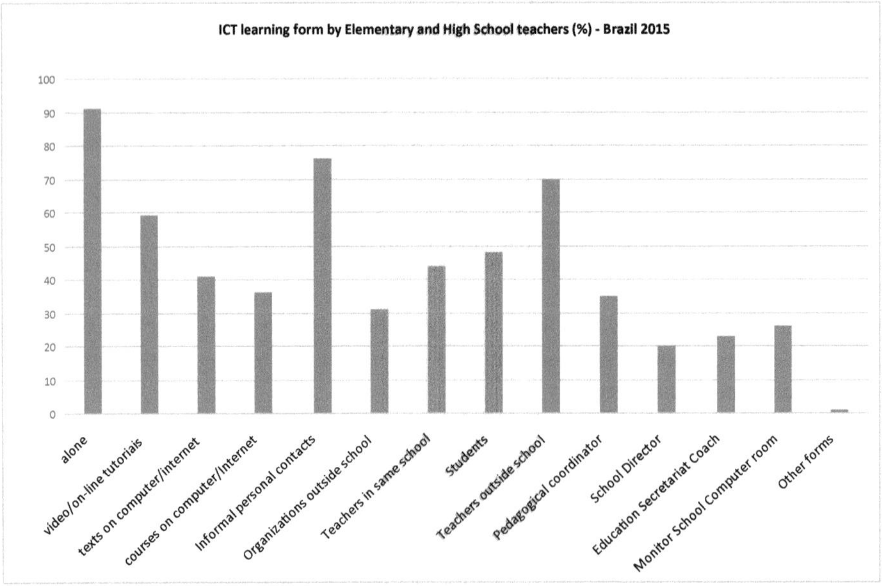

Fig. 4. Forms of ICT learning by elementary and high school teachers (%)—Brazil—2015. Source: Cetic, ICT in Education 2015.

In this section, data presented suggest that some aspects of Internet use are already guaranteed for the Brazilian school teachers for different types of communication purposes. However, uses that require technical training as well uses aimed at learning purposes are still limited for this group. Internet use by teachers do not reflect an institutional or governmental effort towards ICT use in their teaching activities.

7 Concluding Remarks

We discussed here the characteristics and relevance of the MIL proposal by international organizations such as UNESCO and IFLA. The aim of this program is the promotion of information and communication literacy as a means to overcome social inequality, promote empowerment of communities, and guarantee democratic processes throughout the world. The basic professional categories involved in the promotion of MIL are communication and information professionals and teachers—the MIL professionals.

The main purpose of this research was to characterize ICT access, availability, and use by the MIL human resources in Brazil. Data presented were obtained from the annual survey of the Brazilian Bureau of Census of 2015 and from a survey, also carried out in 2015, about ICT use in education from a non-profit organization called Cetic.br.

The first part of the analyses considered the whole Brazilian population revealing some profound inequalities in Internet access: differences in access by the urban-rural dimension, by different ethnic groups, and by age and education are still outstanding in the country.

Subsequent analyses focusing on the MIL professionals suggest that Internet access is guaranteed to them, although large segments of this group do not yet possess the technological apparatus for a more comprehensive action towards MIL in their professional activities. Another characteristic of these professionals, mainly teachers, is the great participation of women, a reality suggesting attention to gender imbalance in the MIL group and to gender issues that should be considered in programs aimed at the training of these professionals.

With regard to types of Internet use by the teachers' subgroup, we observed that there is a generalized use of Internet for personal communication purposes. Also, ICT training appears to be mostly informal, not reflecting institutional efforts in that direction.

As a whole, the discussion and evidences presented here can be considered as an effort to promote the development of MIL indicators, in this case human resources indicators, that could be considered in comparative studies for the identification and promotion of the MIL program in different regions or countries.

References

1. Grizzle, A., Moore, P., Dezuanni, M., Asthana, S., Wilson, C., Banda, F., Onumah, C.: Media and Information Literacy: Policy and Strategy Guidelines. UNESCO, Paris (2013)
2. Instituto Brasileiro de Geografia e Estatística: Pesquisa Nacional por Amostra de Domicílios - PNAD. IBGE, Rio de Janeiro (2015)
3. Moeller, S., Joseph, A., Lau, J., Carbo, T.: Towards Media and Information Literacy Indicators. UNESCO, Paris (2011)
4. Organisation for Economic Co-operation and Development: Gender Equality in Education, Employment and Entrepreneurship: Final Report do the MCM. OECD, Paris (2012)
5. Tomte, C.: Return to Gender: Gender, ICT and Education. OECD, Paris (2008)
6. van Deursen, A.J.A.M., van Dijk, J.A.G.M., Peters, O.: Rethinking internet skills: the contribution of gender, age, education, internet experience, and hours online to medium- and content-related internet skills. Poetics **39**, 125–144 (2011)
7. da Silva, A.G., Olinto, G.: Gender differences in ICT use and information literacy in public libraries: a study in a Rio de Janeiro public library. In: Kurbanoğlu, S., Boustany, J., Špiranec, S., Grassian, E., Mizrachi, D., Roy, L., Çakmak, T. (eds.) ECIL 2016. CCIS, vol. 676, pp. 12–20. Springer, Cham (2016). https://doi.org/10.1007/978-3-319-52162-6_2
8. IFLA Media and Information Literacy Recommendations. Endorsed by the Governing Board of IFLA, at its meeting in Den Haag, The Netherlands (2011)
9. Wilson, C., Grizzle, A., Tuazon, R., Akyempong, K., Cheung, C.-K.: Media and Information Literacy: Curriculum for Teachers. UNESCO, Paris (2011)
10. Regional Center for Studies on the Development of the Information Society: ICT in Education 2015: Survey on the Use of Information and Communication Technologies in Brazilian Schools. CETIC, São Paulo (2016)

A Method Combining Deductive and Inductive Principles to Define Work-Related Digital Media Literacy Competences

Valèria Ligurgo[1(✉)], Thibault Philippette[1], Pierre Fastrez[1], Anne-Sophie Collard[2], and Jerry Jacques[2]

[1] Groupe de Recherche en Médiation des Savoirs, Université catholique de Louvain, Louvain-la-Neuve, Belgium
{valeria.ligurgo, thibault.philippette, pierre.fastrez}@uclouvain.be

[2] Research Center in Information, Law and Society, University of Namur, Namur, Belgium
{anne-sophie.collard, jerry.jacques}@unamur.be

Abstract. How to infer the digital media literacy competences of office workers related to distant teamwork from the observation of collaborative practices? This paper presents a qualitative method that combines deductive and inductive approaches to analyze interviews and observations carried out in ten organizations. From a deductive standpoint, our analysis is anchored in a review of the literature in Computer-Supported Cooperative Work. From an inductive standpoint, our analyses use principles from phenomenography and grounded theory to abstract a theoretical understanding of the studied experiences. The combination of these approaches allows us to examine the way workers experience distant teamwork activities and to consider how their competences reside in their ability to frame the work situations they encounter, and to develop responses accordingly.

Keywords: Digital media literacy · Grounded theory · Phenomenography · Collaborative practices · Distant teamwork

1 Introduction

The ubiquity of information and communication technologies in the workplace has fostered a surge in distant teamwork practices. The LITME@WORK project aims at studying the digital media literacy (DML) competences of office workers related to distant teamwork. Digital media literacy extends the concept of literacy to information and communication technologies by emphasizing not only their informational or digital nature, but also the social dimension and critical understanding of the activity of using technology as a medium of communication [1]. Three complementary angles of analysis are combined by the research teams working on the project:

- The macro-level is focusing on the process of social and discursive construction of DML competences;

S. Kurbanoğlu et al. (Eds.): ECIL 2017, CCIS 810, pp. 245–254, 2018.
https://doi.org/10.1007/978-3-319-74334-9_26

- The meso-level is focusing on the effects of work organization, workplace design and structural conditions (e.g. support, training) on DML competences;
- The micro-level is focusing on understanding digital media uses to define competences in distant collaborative work practices, from the point of view of workers.

The methodological contribution presented in this paper relates to the micro-level analysis conducted to understand how workers use digital media to work collaboratively at a distance and to define the competences they call upon to do so. Instead of defining such competences a priori and attempting to validate their definition, the objective pursued in this project is the very definition of these competences, from the perspective of workers, based on field observation. Hence, our approach to DML competences in distant collaborative work is an interpretive one [2].

The research also veers away from tool-oriented approaches that reduce digital competences to technology-related operational skills [3]. Such approaches define their unit of analysis based on the use of specific software or hardware tools by workers. Rather, we focus on the observed workers' distant collaboration activity, which involves a variety of technologies.

This paper will be dedicated to the description of the qualitative methods we use to pursue these objectives. The question we propose to examine in this article is how to infer competences from the observation of collaborative practices. The first section will detail the type of data that are collected (and how they are collected) as part of this project. Secondly, we will cover the methods for data analysis, which combine deductive and inductive principles. It will be the occasion to discuss the theoretical and methodological consequences of taking an interpretive approach on the definition of competences. Finally, we will use examples from the data we have collected so far to illustrate these principles.

2 Collected Data

We have selected ten cases of Belgian organizations that have introduced changes in their work environment with the intention of enhancing teamwork and distance work with information and communication technologies (ICT) as "flex desks" or teleworking policies for example. The selected cases represent a variety of working contexts in terms of: public/private companies, activity sectors, organization sizes, etc.

For each case, the data collection starts with a global visit of the organization, generally lead by a member of the organization's Human Resources team. Then, six guided-tour interviews are conducted with the team leaders and team members of two teams from two different services. Forty workers and twenty team managers will have been interviewed by the end of the study. A "guided-tour" interview is a camera-recorded interview conducted in the informants' everyday context of work, including their devices and tools [4]. The interview questions (see "selected activities" below) are complemented, whenever relevant, by follow-up questions such as "can you show me how you do that?". These questions invite the informant to show us and comment what is achieved (or not) through collaborative tools to manage a given type of activity (e.g. planning a team meeting). Here, we adopt the principles of connective ethnography [5] to avoid considering the experiences people have online and offline as worlds apart, and examine their online and offline practices as an integrated whole. This leads us to consider the complementarities between the aspects of collaborative work that are achieved by individuals either in the physical presence of their colleagues or in the distance. To do so, the collected data from interviews are complemented by a half-day observation of the team's work environment and practices. Interviews are transcribed and coded using NVivo 11, along with observation notes and field traces (photographs).

3 Data Analysis Principles

3.1 An Interpretive Approach Articulating Deductive and Inductive Coding

We consider competences as not being limited to generic sets of attributes that workers possess and use, defined independently of their context. Indeed, "two workers may be identified as possessing identical attributes but may accomplish work differently, depending upon which attributes they use and how they use them" [2]. Consequently, we aim at defining competences based on the "lived experience of work" [2], i.e. the relationship between the worker and their work environment, taken as inextricably related. In this context, phenomenography [6, 7], which has already yielded abundant discussion in the field of information behavior (see for example [8–11]), comes as an important inspiration for the construction of our method, as it proposes "a research method for mapping the qualitatively different ways in which people experience, conceptualize, perceive, and understand various aspects of, and phenomena in, the world around them" [7].

Adopting an interpretive approach to the workers' perspective on distant teamwork calls for inductive analysis. However, the early stages of our analysis are guided by deductive categories. Our coding process can be seen as a hybrid approach [12] balancing inductive coding from themes emerging in our informants' discourse and deductive coding derived from our theoretical framework. This can be considered as an "abductive matching" in a sense that we create the opportunity to capture and combine the systemic character of the field with the systemic character of our theoretical framework [13]. A first "deductive scan" is applied to the interview transcripts and observation notes, in which we code each part of the material according to the structure of our interview guide. The interview guide covered a series of activities involved in distant collaborative work. These activities were identified by reviewing the literature in the field of Computer-Supported Cooperative Work (CSCW), which provided us with a representative overview of the types of collaborative work activities that are (or could be) supported by existing (and future) technologies (for more details, see [14]). These activities are:

1. Making collective decisions regarding tasks distribution, team governance and roles, and overall team functioning;
2. Managing one's tasks in relation with others;
3. Planning the team's activity;

4. Planning a meeting;
5. Working synchronously in the distance with other team members;
6. Organizing one's workspaces for collaboration;
7. Managing incoming information;
8. Managing outgoing information;
9. Using others to find information;
10. Sharing a collection of documents;
11. Authoring a document collectively.

In our interviews, informants were prompted to describe each activity according to up to eight dimensions: task management, time management, space and distance management, information management, awareness, collective decision making, reflexive tool use, and comprehension of "sociomatics" (for more details, see [14]). The initial coding of our data reflects these deductive categories (activities x dimensions), which were used as a tentative list of activities in which distant collaboration may arise and call for digital media literacy competences. This list allowed us to ensure that a variety of work practices were covered in our data. It also distributed the object of the investigation on several practices and allowed for a fine description of each of them (and possibly for a grouping of some of them based on the data). This represents an alternative to existing phenomenographical inquiries in information science, where researchers have tended to focus on the way people understand a single broad concept, as Bruce [15] did with information literacy, Sandberg [2] with competence in engine optimization, or Smith and McMenemy [16] with political information. In our case, instead of explicitly asking our informants to describe their conception of a general category, such as "distant collaboration" or "digital media literacy for collaboration", we asked them to describe an array of specific collaborative practices they engaged in, and we are using these descriptions to infer what the digital media literacy of distant collaboration is (see below).

Our method shares a combination of inductive and deductive coding and a focus on the description of job expertise with other job analysis methods, such as cognitive task analysis (CTA) [17]. However, CTA seeks to identify strategies and knowledge used by experts to perform one specific complex task, to inform the design of expert systems and instructional material. By comparison, we study the variety of conceptions held by workers (not just experts) regarding a whole range of distant collaboration activities, as they contribute to defining various levels of competence.

The application of the deductive activity categories is followed by the inductive coding of the informants' experiences, with codes describing their actions. From an inductive standpoint, our analyses use principles from the grounded theory method [18, 19] to build a theoretical understanding of the studied experiences. Our informants' discourse and our observations are coded to identify "properties of the subjectivity of actors" [20], which are gradually articulated to define conceptual categories. The categories account for the variation in the different conceptions of distant teamwork practices, in accordance with the principles of phenomenography [6]. This process of deductive and inductive coding is systematically documented in coding memos, which are cross-referenced both with the coded data (interview transcripts and field notes) and with the theoretical memos that articulate conceptual categories into a new conceptual framework. This web of memos guarantees both the grounding of our interpretations into the data [20], and the possibility of internal auditing through dedicated research team meetings, where important coding decisions are explicitly discussed and justified to ensure the visibility, comprehensibility and acceptability of the analysis [21].

3.2 Inferring Competence Definitions

How we infer competences from this coding is not a straightforward process. Two principles of phenomenography define how we initiate this step of our analysis. First, our unit of analysis is the practice, not the individual. A practice is a goal-oriented activity that is potentially distributed across different people, tools and contexts. Distant teamwork practices are coded based both on the informant's discourse on them, and on their traces in the guided tours and in our observations. Second, the coded practices are pooled across our whole sample of informants, so that practices can be compared, contrasted, or grouped both within each informant and between different informants.

Our objective of competence definition imposes at least two requirements on our analysis: we should be able to describe the objects of competence (in terms of situations workers are able to deal with) as well as the nature of a competent response (in terms of situated intentional action).

The issue of the objects of competence is twofold. On the one hand, by describing their practices, our informants provide descriptions of the situations they need to address as part of their work. We use these descriptions as a basis for our analysis to build an inventory of typical problem situations that call for DML competence from the perspective of workers. This inventory may or may not correspond to the eleven activities we surveyed in our interviews. On the other hand, the way they describe these situations depends on their competence. Indeed, a key aspect of professional practice is the ability to properly frame the problem situations that are constitutive of one's work: setting its boundaries, attending to its most relevant features, and imposing a coherence upon it. What Schön [22] calls the "reflective practitioner" is able to frame known situations, and to construct new frames to face novel situations based on their experience.

Our focus on practices (not individuals) as the basic unit for analysis allows us to pool descriptions of practices across all informants, so that we can group together descriptions that refer to the same problem situations, and then, for a given situation, group together descriptions that correspond to qualitatively similar conceptions of that situation. Essentially, our analysis works towards both the identification of the set of distant collaboration situations that call for DML competences, and the identification of the different conceptions of (i.e. different ways of framing) each situation.

As Limberg [8] noted, different conceptions of the same phenomenon can often be hierarchically ordered in terms of their increasing complexity. "More complex ways of experiencing means that the categories comprise more dimensions and a simultaneous awareness of these dimensions." [8]. The analytical process through which we define competences relies on this hierarchical ordering. As one's ability to frame a situation in more or less complex ways is indicative of their competence [2], the ordered conceptions of distant teamwork partly define levels of DML competences.

However, our analysis does not stop at describing how workers understand (i.e. frame) their experience of work in qualitatively different but increasingly complex ways: it must also encompass how they are able to respond to the work situations they encounter. Here, our analysis shifts its focus to the intentional actions performed by our informants based on their understanding of the situation. In this case, competence is not necessarily indicated by the complexity of actions, but rather by their matching with other parameters of the situation. Specifically, we seek to characterize how our informants are able to adjust, in each situation, their actions (what they do) with their tasks (what they are expected to do), their goals (what they want to do), and the actions of the members of their teams (what others do). In this context, although most of the time not all four of these dimensions (actions, tasks, goals, and others' actions) appear together in the description of a given practice, we identify their "successful practices" (when the described dimensions match) and their difficulties (when mismatches occur between them) as markers of greater or lesser competence, respectively.

Of course, framing a problem situation and responding to it are related: "a capability for acting in a certain way reflects a capability of experiencing something in a certain way. The latter does not cause the former, but they are logically intertwined. You cannot act other than in relation to the world as you experience it." [23]. We consider the relationship between these two terms to be a conditional one, with framing being a necessary but insufficient cause to responding.

4 Preliminary Analysis

The following examples illustrate the first steps of the method outlined above, as the analysis is currently underway, which precludes us from presenting its results. The four excerpts presented below feature difficulties expressed by informants about different kinds of distant collaborative practices, representing different types of mismatches between their actions, goals, tasks and others' actions. While the presentation of single excerpts for each problem situation may give the impression of taking the individual (as opposed to the practice) as the unit of analysis, the next steps in the analysis (grouping the pooled practice descriptions by problem situation, and ordering them by complexity) will allow us to contrast different experiences around the same practice. All excerpts are translated from French. Square brackets indicate edits by the research team.

Excerpt 1. In this excerpt, the informant explains how she shares coordination documents by e-mail with her team: "[…] *I've just sent them a brochure and they had to send me their comments back. But it was only comments, not specially working on the brochure. But in that specific case, I found their answers very synthetic. M., the expert, told me, "you should ask them more precise questions if you want more feedback".* […] *So, it's more in the way I manage distant meetings that I must be more precise in the way I communicate.*" (Informant #1, team leader).

From a deductive perspective, this description is coded as: 'authoring a document collectively' and 'space and distance management'. The inductive code we applied to the same excerpt was 'fostering involvement', in reference to the informant's intention to enhance her team members' participation to a project. The informant noted that her former practice did not bring the expected results as it produced answers from the team members that showed too little involvement. Thanks to external support, she then identified how to consider the "distance" parameter of the situation when asking for feedback about future projects by e-mail. This example shows both a mismatch between an ICT-supported action and its initial purpose, and the informant's ability to frame a problematic situation by analyzing the others' actions and finding a solution to improve one's way of working.

Excerpts 2a and 2b. The two following excerpts show how two team members consider the same activity from their own perspective. Informant #2 was asked if he identified any disadvantages to the tools he shares with her teammate: *"As I said earlier, the accounting software for example, it has limitations. The encoding [by multiple users] in the same journal at the same time is not enabled."* (Informant #2, team member).

In a subsequent interview, his colleague was asked to explain the constraint of the tool on parallel encoding: "*No except if... In fact, there are two companies. If somebody's busy with one, you can work on the other. [...] When it concerns certain operations, we organize ourselves. "What are you up to?", "What are you doing?". It's not difficult because we are next to each other. [...] But if you change company [in the accounting software], we can do everything in parallel. [...] Nothing is linked. I can do what I want, he can do what he wants. [...] It's the only time when we can both work on the same tasks at the same time.*" (Informant #3, team member).

Both excerpts are related to our deductive codes 'sharing a collection of documents', 'working synchronously from a distance' and 'reflective tool use'. Informant #2 states that the tool they share prevents them from working at the same time. Informant #3 also considers this limitation, but describes an alternative procedure that enables them to work on the same tasks, but on different companies. Her framing of the situation introduces several additional dimensions, compared to Informant #2's own framing: the possibility of 'managing one's tasks in relation with others' (one of our deductive activity categories) and the way 'being physically present with others' (an inductive code that specifies our deductive 'space and distance management' category) impacts the mutual 'awareness' (another deductive code) of the two colleagues.

Excerpt 3. In this excerpt, Informant #3 explains that she's not able to plan her tasks using a shared calendar, even though she tried: "*I've never been able to plan my workload here. I've tried. I told myself "let's go", I'll take my [Microsoft] Outlook and I'll put the things that I have to do in there. [...] I know that it's my task to encode bank statements for the LLC, everything about the clients, and L. is in charge of the structure. So I would write 'Bank statements'.*" (Informant #3, team member). Asked if she used to visualize her tasks before, she answers: "*Yes, what I had to do, by setting, more or less, the schedule, the number of hours I had to spend for it. For example, I would plan one hour to encode [...] let's say 50 invoices. If I planned one hour, it would never be enough because all the others [tasks and requests] are accumulating during this time so it's impossible to keep a schedule. So, I stopped.*" (Informant #3, team member).

The problematic situation identified by Informant #3 involves the impossibility to plan her tasks using her calendar (which is shared with the whole team). While she is able to 'estimate the workload for each task' (an inductive code that specifies our deductive category of 'managing one's tasks in relation with others'), her difficulty reflects her inability to manage her time, her tasks and the incoming/outgoing information (corresponding to three separate deductive codes) at the same time. Informant #3 attributes this problem to an external cause, namely the work organization in the company. This example points both to the informant's ability to frame the situation in terms of mismatches between her job's requirements, her goals and her actions, and to her inability to find an appropriate alternative to her past practice that would function for her and her teammates.

Excerpt 4. This last excerpt covers the description of the evolution of a practice that results, for the informant, into a more "successful practice" than the previous one. Informant #4 explains how he set up specific tools to better support teamwork and team meetings: "*Whenever we have a team meeting, I've set up tools in Excel where we schematize and categorize actions as open, closed, decisions that are made and so on. [...] This is not the most flexible thing there is but... [...] To sum up, I have the agenda on Excel, and I have everybody's to-do list. When we meet, we look at when we did the list, if a task is open, or I can show everything that we have already done, what is closed, what's in progress, to whom it is assigned, when it needs to be done and a small comment. [...] There are difficulties for those who are less used to that kind of tool, tools that more "project management" oriented. [...] Rather than remembering "what must I do?", the thing is to remember to go check it. It's more about time management for some team members and having the reflex to go in that kind of tool. But it starts slowly. It's been only under way since this year. Before, I would work more on the basis of the meeting minutes... that no one would read. And so I wanted to have something more synthetic.*" (Informant #4, team leader).

Informant #4's goal, as a team leader, is to maintain a high level of 'awareness' (one of our deductive codes) between team members to coordinate the team's different tasks. Consequently, he developed a new project management tool to review and 'plan the team's activity' (another deductive code) during meetings, which he considers as a positive evolution compared to previous practices, like using the meeting minutes as a monitoring tool. He is also able to perceive how this new tool challenges his colleagues' project management habits (which we coded deductively under 'comprehension of sociomatics' and 'reflective tool use').

Informant #4 framed the situation in a way that highlighted its shortcomings (i.e. mismatches between his actions, his goal and the actions of his colleagues: no one read his minutes), and 'experimented new ways of working' (inductive code) to overcome them. This prompted him to 'redefine the terms of collaboration' (inductive code) during team meetings, and to create an instrument that affords collective task reviewing in the future. Besides, he envisioned how the potential pitfalls of the new practice have changed and moved from 'task management' to 'time management' (both deductive codes), and to acquiring the habit of 'remembering the work procedure' (inductive code).

5 Conclusion

Our contribution emphasizes the benefits of combining deductive and inductive approaches to infer the definition of DML competences from the analysis of qualitative data in new or emerging domains of practice. On the one hand, the deductive approach ensures an adequate coverage of the activities and dimensions of the domain of interest, in our case: collaborative ICT-supported work practices. On the other hand, the inductive approach anchors the analysis in the complexity of human practices by examining the individuals' (in our case, the workers') lived experiences without enclosing them in a priori categories defined by experts. The ordering of the informants' conceptions of the problem situations they encounter in terms of their complexity, coupled with the matching of their intentional actions with other parameters of these situations provide the foundation of an interpretive perspective on digital media literacy.

Beyond the specific context of distant work collaboration, we argue that this method affords understanding elements of inter-subjectivity (and not only individual experiences) of an observable phenomenon. It also veers away from monolithic evaluations of competences based on standardized indicators, towards a multidimensional approach of context-based capabilities. However, difficulties may arise when comparisons must be made between different informants and modes of expression, with the risk of either reducing the individual experience of a practice to its simplest form, or to multiply the subjective views without being able to articulate their common ground. This is why this approach requires a time-consuming iterative process between the various cases, thoroughly documented, to obtain a robust analytical model that accounts for the richness of the data, but will potentially be challenged by future societal transformations.

Acknowledgements. The work reported in this article is funded by the Belgian Science Policy Office, under contract BR/143/A5/LITME@WORK. Pierre Fastrez is a Research Associate from the Belgian Fund for Scientific Research - FNRS.

References

1. Buckingham, D.: Digital media literacies: rethinking media education in the age of the internet. Res. Comp. Int. Educ. **2**, 43–55 (2007)
2. Sandberg, J.: Understanding human competence at work: an interpretative approach. Acad. Manag. J. **43**, 9–25 (2000)
3. Buckingham, D.: The future of media literacy in the digital age: some challenges for policy and practice. In: Proceedings of Euromeduc: Media Literacy in Europe: Controversies, Challenges and Perspectives, Bellaria, Italy, pp. 13–24 (2009)
4. Malone, T.W.: How do people organize their desks?: implications for the design of office information systems. ACM Trans. Inf. Syst. **1**, 99–112 (1983)
5. Leander, K.M.: Toward a connective ethnography of online/offline literacy networks. In: Coiro, J., Knobel, M., Lankshear, C., Leu, D.J. (eds.) Handbook of Research on New Literacies, pp. 33–65. Taylor & Francis, New York (2008)

6. Marton, F.: Phenomenography—describing conceptions of the world around us. Instr. Sci. **10**, 177–200 (1981)
7. Marton, F.: Phenomenography—a research approach to investigating different understandings of reality. J. Thought **21**, 28–49 (1986)
8. Limberg, L.: Phenomenography: a relational approach to research on information needs, seeking and use. New Rev. Inf. Behav. Res. **1**, 51–67 (2000)
9. Limberg, L.: Phenomenography. In: Theories of Information Behavior, pp. 280–283. Information Today, Inc. (2005)
10. Yates, C., Partridge, H., Bruce, C.: Exploring information experiences through phenomenography. Libr. Inf. Res. **36**, 96–119 (2012)
11. Bruce, C.: The Seven Faces of Information Literacy. Auslib Press, Adelaide (1997)
12. Fereday, J., Muir-Cochrane, E.: Demonstrating rigor using thematic analysis: a hybrid approach of inductive and deductive coding and theme development. Int. J. Qual. Methods **5**, 80–92 (2006)
13. Dubois, A., Gadde, L.-E.: Systematic combining: an abductive approach to case research. J. Bus. Res. **55**, 553–560 (2002)
14. Collard, A.-S., De Smedt, T., Fastrez, P., Ligurgo, V., Philippette, T.: How is information literacy related to social competences in the workplace? In: Kurbanoğlu, S., Boustany, J., Špiranec, S., Grassian, E., Mizrachi, D., Roy, L., Çakmak, T. (eds.) ECIL 2016. CCIS, vol. 676, pp. 79–88. Springer, Cham (2016). https://doi.org/10.1007/978-3-319-52162-6_8
15. Bruce, C.S.: Workplace experiences of information literacy. Int. J. Inf. Manag. **19**, 33–47 (1999)
16. Smith, L., McMenemy, D.: Enhancing agency through information: a phenomenographic exploration of young people's political information experiences. In: Proceedings of the ASIS&T 2016 Annual Meeting, Copenhagen (2016)
17. Clark, R.E., Feldon, D.F., Van Merriënboer, J.J.G., Yates, K.A., Early, S.: Cognitive task analysis. In: Spector, J., Merrill, M.D., Van Merriënboer, J.J.G., Driscoll, M.P. (eds.) Handbook of Research on Educational Communications and Technology, pp. 577–593. Lawrence Erlbaum Associates, Mahwah (2008)
18. Glaser, B.G., Strauss, A.L.: The Discovery of Grounded Theory: Strategies for Qualitative Research. Aldine, Chicago (1967)
19. Charmaz, K.: Constructing Grounded Theory: A Practical Guide Through Qualitative Analysis. SAGE Publications, London (2006)
20. Lejeune, C.: Manuel d'analyse qualitative. Analyser sans compter ni classer. De Boeck Supérieur, Bruxelles (2014)
21. Akkerman, S., Admiraal, W., Brekelmans, M., Oost, H.: Auditing quality of research in social sciences. Qual. Quant. **42**, 257–274 (2008)
22. Schön, D.A.: The Reflective Practitioner: How Professionals Think in Action. Basic Books, New York (1983)
23. Marton, F., Booth, S.A.: Learning and Awareness. Psychology Press, Abingdon (1997)

Copyright Literacy

Exploring the Need for Intellectual Property Information Literacy for Business and STEM Disciplines

Janis Tyhurst(✉)

King Abdullah University of Science and Technology (KAUST), Thuwal, Saudi Arabia
Janis.tyhurst@kaust.edu.sa

Abstract. A major component of any information literacy training program incorporates training on copyright and fair use. While in the library literature, librarians have provided excellent training on understanding copyright and appropriate use, they have not focused on providing training on other forms of intellectual property (IP), particularly patents. As IP in the form of patents is becoming exponentially more important in the research-to-commercialization process, more work on information literacy training about patents is needed. This paper provides definitions of IP literacy, places the value of IP literacy in a larger context, looks at target audiences, proposes a framework for IP literacy and provides suggestions about the role that librarians can play in developing IP literacies beyond copyright.

Keywords: Information literacy · Information training · Intellectual property Intellectual property literacy

1 Introduction

The emergence of freely available patent databases has opened up new opportunities for librarians to develop new skills and forge new collaborations. Intellectual property (IP) is vital to an innovative and growing economy, with the potential to stimulate employment and job growth as long as people are aware of and able to use IP effectively. Librarians can play an important role in supporting innovation and employment through the integration of IP literacy (IPL) training into their information literacy (IL) programs. Science, technology, engineering and mathematics (STEM) librarians, business librarians and arts librarians can be an important catalyst to spread IPL in their disciplines. Including IPL into academic IL programs enriches understanding that students of the discipline literature have about the role of IP in their studies and future employment. Developing IPL training also encourages collaboration across academic departments and demonstrates the value that librarians bring to the institution. Public Library librarians can use IPL as an opportunity to engage the local community, small-and-medium sized enterprises and entrepreneurs. This paper begins the discussion of IPL by providing definitions of IP literacy, demonstrating the value of IP literacy in a larger context, analyzing target audiences, proposing a framework for IP

S. Kurbanoğlu et al. (Eds.): ECIL 2017, CCIS 810, pp. 257–266, 2018.
https://doi.org/10.1007/978-3-319-74334-9_27

literacy and providing suggestions about the role that librarians can play in developing IP literacies beyond copyright.

2 Definitions of Intellectual Property

The following definitions of intellectual property (IP) are drawn from two major patent offices, the United States Patent and Trademark Office (USPTO) and the World Intellectual Property Office (WIPO).

The USPTO [1] defines IP as, "creations of the mind - creative works or ideas embodied in a form that can be shared or can enable others to recreate, emulate, or manufacture them. There are four ways to protect **intellectual property** - patents, trademarks, copyrights or trade secrets." The WIPO [2, p. 2] defines IP as, "creations of the mind, such as inventions; literary and artistic works; designs; and symbols, names and images used in commerce. Intellectual property is divided into two categories: Industrial Property includes patents for inventions, trademarks, industrial designs and geographical indications. Copyright covers literary works (such as novels, poems and plays), films, music, artistic works (e.g., drawings, paintings, photographs and sculptures) and architectural design. Rights related to copyright include those of performing artists in their performances, producers of phonograms in their recordings, and broadcasters in their radio and television programs."

3 A Working Definition of Intellectual Property Literacy

I propose to use the former American Library Association definition for IL [3] by substituting "intellectual property" for "information" and "intellectual property literacy" for "information literacy": Intellectual property literacy is a set of abilities requiring individuals to recognize when intellectual property is needed and to have the ability to locate, evaluate, and use effectively the needed intellectual property. An intellectual property literate individual is able to: determine the extent of intellectual property needed; access the needed intellectual property effectively and efficiently; evaluate intellectual property and its sources critically; incorporate selected intellectual property into one's knowledge base; use intellectual property effectively to accomplish a specific purpose; understand the economic, legal, and social issues surrounding the use of intellectual property; and access and use intellectual property ethically and legally.

4 Reasons for Developing an IP Literacy Training Component

To understand why developing IPL is important opportunity for librarians, we need to look first at the big picture of the value of IP to the economy. The USPTO report on IP and the U.S. economy [4] states that "IP-intensive industries continue to be a major, integral and growing part of the U.S. economy." This value is demonstrated by the increasing share of IP-intensive industries to the total US gross domestic product (GDP), which increased from 34.8% in 2010 to 38.2% in 2014 or from $5.06 trillion to $6.6 trillion. Figure 1 graphically shows the contributions of IP-related and non-IP-related economic activity to the US GDP in 2010. Figure 2 graphically shows the same contributions in 2014.

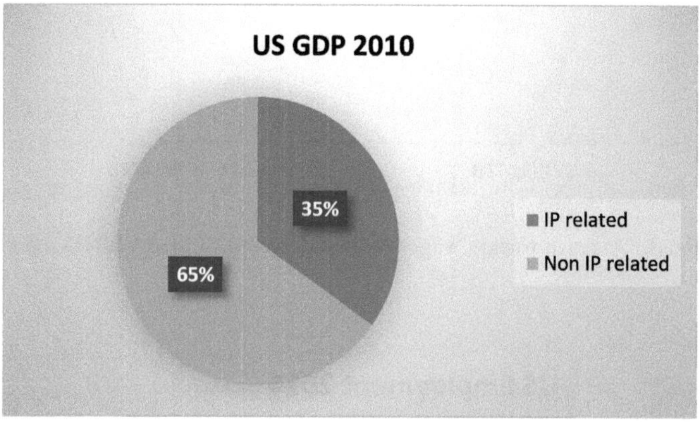

Fig. 1. Contribution of IP to the US GDP in 2010 (2016 USPTO report)

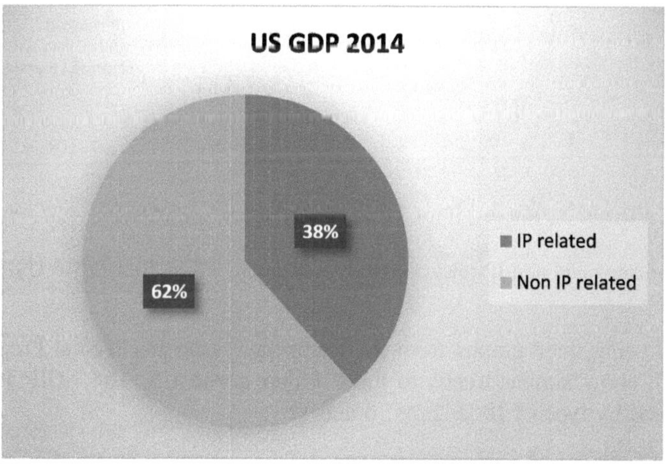

Fig. 2. Contribution of IP to the US GDP in 2014 (2016 USPTO report)

In addition, wages for IP-intensive industries are consistently higher than those for non-IP industries, with IP-related jobs earning a weekly average of 46% more than non-IP-related jobs. IP-intensive industries accounted for 30% of both direct and indirect employment in 2014, or 1 of every 3 jobs. Figure 3 shows the IP-related and non-IP-related average weekly wages in the US in 2014 and Fig. 4 shows the proportions of IP-related and non-IP-related jobs in the US in 2014.

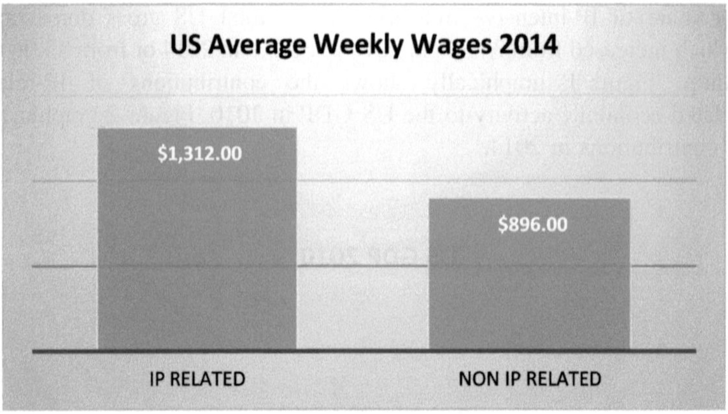

Fig. 3. Average weekly wages in the US in 2014 (2016 USPTO report)

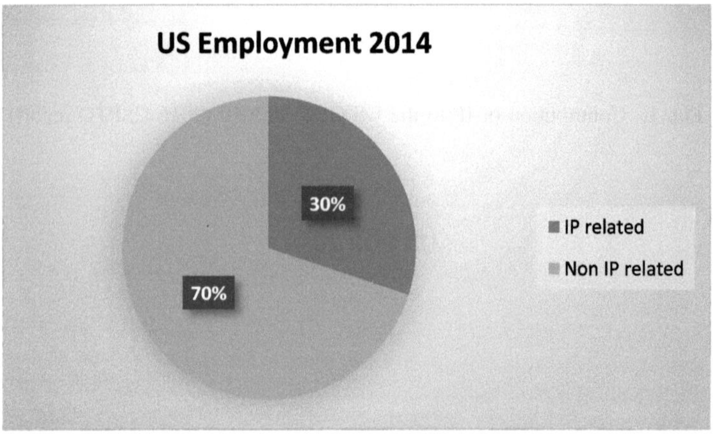

Fig. 4. IP-related and non-IP-related employment in the US in 2014 (2016 USPTO report)

The following three graphs from the European Union Intellectual Property Office (EUIPO) [5] show similar trends to those found in the US. The EUIPO graphs are further refined by type of IP (Figs. 5, 6 and 7).

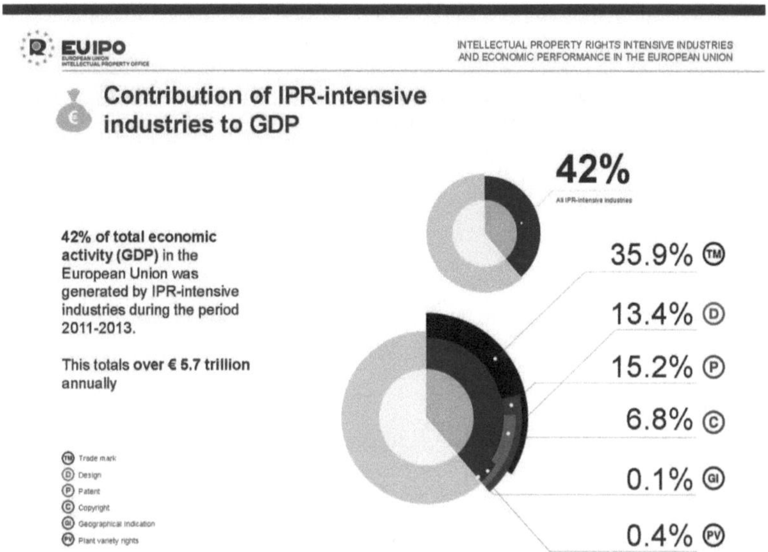

Fig. 5. IP-related employment in the EU in 2015 (EUIPO, Intellectual property rights intensive industries and economic performance in the EU)

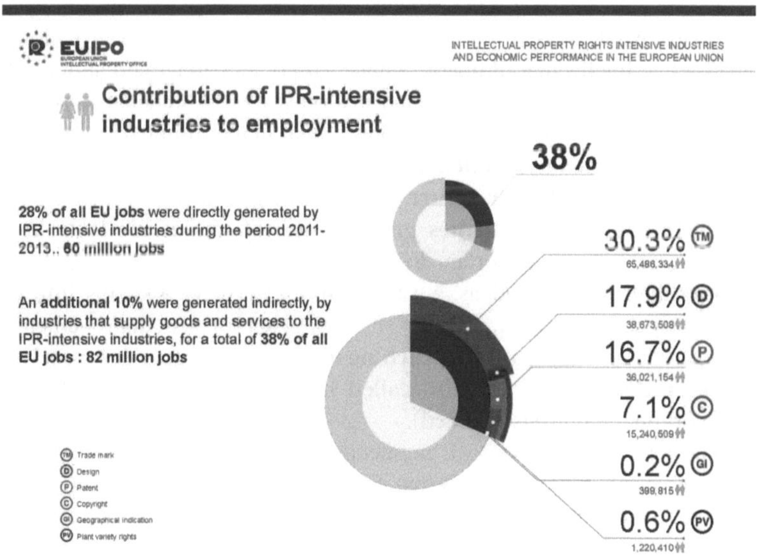

Fig. 6. IP-related employment in the EU in 2015 (EUIPO, Intellectual property rights intensive industries and economic performance in the EU)

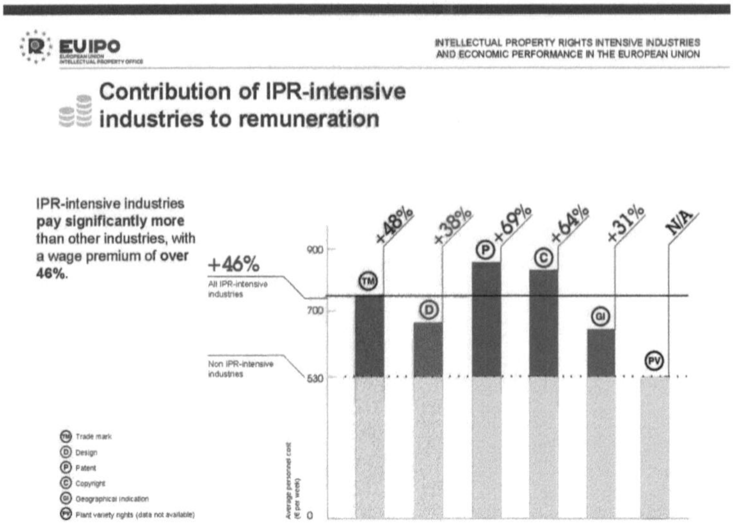

Fig. 7. IP-related employment in the EU in 2015 (EUIPO, Intellectual property rights intensive industries and economic performance in the EU)

5 Who Needs IP Literacy Training?

A recent survey of UK student knowledge jointly run by the National Union of Students (NUS), the Intellectual Property Office (IPO) and the International Property Awareness Network (IPAN) [6, p. 8] found that only 40% of students considered their current awareness of IP to be enough to support them in their future careers. The report also states, "Overwhelmingly, **students felt that a knowledge of IP is important to both their education and their future career**. There is evidence that **IP teaching earlier in their education motivates greater interest among students at FE/HE level…**Students feel it was important to know about IP to ensure everyone receives recognition for their work and ideas, but **they do not perceive a strong link between IP and commercial success….** Many students want to see improvements to IP teaching. In particular, **they want the teaching of IP issues to be more closely-related to their course discipline.** They also called for coverage of IP to extend beyond plagiarism" (original emphasis retained).

Villasenor's [7, p. 1] survey of engineering students at UCLA demonstrated a similar lack of awareness and points out the consequences of this ignorance. In an informal survey of 60 engineering students asking about the different forms of IP, he found that 21% "did not know enough to answer the question 'what is a patent?'" For the other types of IP, he found that 61% could not define a trade secret, 32% could not define copyright and 51% could not define a trademark. He points out that if students are unable to identify IP, how can they be relied upon to "promptly report and fully disclose their patentable inventions" as required by funding agencies funding the research they work on.

Pitkethly [8, p. 163] wrote that the "intellectual property system has several objectives but the most important, especially in the case of the patent system, is providing an incentive for innovation. To provide that potential innovators must be aware of it. The effectiveness of the system thus depends not just on what it provides but on what innovators perceive that it provides. An equally important issue though is whether innovators are sufficiently aware of the system to be able to use it effectively." Librarians are optimally placed to assist in raising awareness of IP.

Intellectual property rights (IPR) exist to encourage and promote the sharing of innovations and new technologies in the public domain while giving the inventor(s) protection for their inventions. To make this a win-win situation, it is critical that IP rights are taught alongside basic IL skills. As Pitkethly [8] wrote, awareness is needed, and not just awareness but a solid understanding of IP and the rights they confer.

6 The Benefits from a Greater Understanding of the Patenting Process and of Patents

Learning how the patent process is structured will help researchers to maximize and streamline their application process and to avoid inadvertently losing their rights to a patent. The following reasons underscore the need for greater awareness and understanding of IP/patents in the STEM and business disciplines.

STEM librarians can introduce IP and patents when introducing resources available for research. Researchers and students need an understanding of how patents fit within the discipline's literature. The technical information contained in patents is often not found elsewhere. **This technical information can be used to prevent research redundancy and direct funding to areas that need more research. It can also be used to strengthen research-funding applications by demonstrating a comprehensive search of all literature, to determine potential areas for further research and to use current and expired patents as building blocks for new technologies. MacMillan [9, p. 157] introduced IPL into his training and concluded that "introducing patent literature to upper-level science students has enhanced their information literacy skills. Students participating in these sessions have a greater understanding of the different types of primary information in their subject areas and the place patents have in their field of study. These students are also more aware of the economic, legal and social issues surrounding the use of information or technologies and the importance of stay abreast of developments in their field".**

Business librarians can incorporate IP when introducing business resources to management and entrepreneurship classes. Just as inventors need to know about IP, future business managers and entrepreneurs need to understand how to identify and protect a company's IP. Understanding the need to do a thorough patent search can prevent inadvertent infringement and potential lawsuits. **Current** patents can be used to identify new, emerging or core technologies. Recent patents can provide indicators of future trends and industries where research and development (R&D) funding should be directed. This in turn helps business managers and entrepreneurs to discover competitors and potential partners or licensing partners. And most basic of all, understanding and awareness of IP allows an inventor or entrepreneur to effectively protect his or her IP by not disclosing it prematurely. Though not within the scope of this paper, it should be noted that Arts librarians can teach about IP for design patents.

For librarians in academic settings, there is an opportunity to work collaboratively with the funding, technology transfer and legal departments at the University as well as with faculty members, researchers and students engaged in innovation. IPL training provides an opportunity for librarians to learn new skills and demonstrate their relevance. Such skills development among librarians benefits the entire university as well as highlights the value libraries and librarians bring to the institution.

7 A Six-Step Framework

Step 1. Begin with an assessment of the target audience's knowledge of IPL. This allows the librarian to understand the current needs of the target audience and it also shows people what they do not know or know well. It is a useful way to attract their attention. There are two parts to a holistic IPL program. The theoretical part covers the patent process, while the applied part focuses on patent searching and analysis.

Step 2. Start the training by defining IP and its place in research and business. Provide a glossary of important terms used in the patent literature. Define what rights are given to a granted patent. Then outline the (general) patent process by asking and answering the following questions: What are the criteria (depending on where the patent will be filed)? What are general timelines and procedures? What is possible to do with the invention while waiting for a patent decision? What are the costs, protections afforded, geographic locations where the patent is enforced? When is it time to consult with legal experts?

Step 3. Discuss some of the common mistakes made by uninformed inventors, including premature disclosure, non-disclosure agreements (NDAs), claims overlaps, trying to patent an invention that is already patented, etc.

Step 4. In the Applied half, start with directions on how to read a patent. Identify the different sections of the patent and explain the purpose and importance of each section.

Step 5. Identify patent search resources. Provide information on the various patent office databases (national and international) and other free patent resources. If there is a subscribed patent database (e.g., Derwent World Patent Index, PatBase, etc.) available, discuss the benefits of using a free vs. a subscribed database.

Step 6. Provide details on how to effectively search for patents using patent record fields and classification schemes. It is useful to create exercises to provide hands-on practice in searching for patents and following patent citations to find additional information. Exercises can be on using keywords, classification systems, how to find the surrounding cited literature, how to determine what stage a patent is in, etc. Discuss what a "State of the Art" (SOTA) search is and when you should be doing a SOTA.

For more detailed and discipline-specific ideas, MacMillan [9], MacMillan and Thuna [10], and Zhang [11] all have written about IPL training in science disciplines or classes, with information on integrating IPL into a class assignment.

8 Librarian Training Options

Librarians can learn about IP via the various training options available from the patent offices (WIPO, EPO, USPTO, national patent offices) and professional associations such as the Patent International User Group (PIUG). Many patent offices are working to increase awareness of IP rights with online training and outreach programs and some even have training materials geared for use in elementary/primary and secondary schools. Understanding the needs of the discipline, business or entrepreneur determines the level of the IPL training needed and allows this training to be adapted and inserted into specialized and general IL training programs. There are many opportunities for librarians to learn more about IP and in turn to translate this new knowledge into IPL training. A list of selected sites with training materials can be found in the Appendix.

9 Conclusion

A lack of awareness and understanding, few examples of how to start a program, and where to get appropriate training are key reasons that IPL is not more widespread and why IPL programs are not offered by librarians. While patents have been around for years, it is only with the advent of online databases that patents have become accessible to anyone with internet access. Online access is creating huge opportunities for librarians in all disciplines to learn new skills and gain new expertise. Prior to online patent databases, patents were seen as the sole responsibility of patent attorneys, IP specialists or technology transfer offices who had access to the patent offices and patent depository libraries. As IP in the form of patents is becoming exponentially more important in the research-to-commercialization process, more work on information literacy training about patents is needed. In providing definitions of IP literacy, placing the value of IP literacy in a larger context, looking at target audiences, proposing a framework for IP literacy and providing suggestions about the role that librarians can play in developing IP literacies beyond copyright, this paper opens the discussion of IPL as part of a librarian's IL training responsibility.

Appendix: Selected Patent Training Resources

Academy of the European Union Intellectual Property Office: https://euipo.europa.eu/ohimportal/en/academy
EUIPO Educational Materials: https://euipo.europa.eu/ohimportal/en/web/observatory/educational-materials
European Patent Office: https://www.epo.org/about-us/office/academy.html
USPTO Webinars and IP E-learning Modules [available in the following languages: English, Spanish, French, Arabic, Russian]: https://www.uspto.gov/learning-and-resources/global-intellectual-property-academy-gipa/uspto-webinars-and-ip-e-learning
WIPO Academy: http://www.wipo.int/academy/en/

References

1. United States Patent and Trademark Office. https://www.uspto.gov/learning-and-resources/general-faqs#1242
2. World Intellectual Property Office. http://www.wipo.int/edocs/pubdocs/en/intproperty/450/wipo_pub_450.pdf
3. American Library Association. http://www.ala.org/acrl/standards/informationliteracycompetency#ildef
4. United States Patent and Trademark Office: Intellectual property and the U.S. economy: 2016 update. https://www.uspto.gov/sites/default/files/documents/IPandtheUSEconomySept2016.pdf
5. European Union Intellectual Property Office: Intellectual property rights intensive industries and economic performance in the EU. https://euipo.europa.eu/ohimportal/en/web/observatory/ip-contribution#ip-contribution_1
6. National Union of Students, the Intellectual Property Office and the International Property Awareness Network: Student attitudes towards intellectual property (2016). http://ipaware.org/wp-content/uploads/2016/10/20121012-IP-report.pdf
7. Villasenor, J.: Intellectual property awareness at universities: why ignorance is not bliss (2012). https://www.forbes.com/sites/johnvillasenor/2012/11/27/intellectual-property-awareness-at-universities-why-ignorance-is-not-bliss/#3851363a13ce
8. Pitkethly, R.H.: Intellectual property awareness. Int. J. Technol. Manag. **59**(3–4), 163 (2012)
9. MacMillan, D.: Patently obvious: the place for patents in information literacy in the sciences. Res. Strat. **20**(3), 149–161 (2006)
10. MacMillan, D., Thuna, M.: Patents under the microscope. Ref. Serv. Rev. **38**(3), 417–430 (2010)
11. Zhang, L.: Developing a systematic patent search training program. J. Acad. Librariansh. **35** (3), 260–266 (2009)

Copyright Literacy Among the Literacies in Hungary

Tibor Koltay[1(✉)], Ferenc Jávorszky[1], and Péter Murányi[2]

[1] Faculty of Pedagogy, Eszterházy Károly University, Rákóczi út 53, 5100 Jászberény, Hungary
{Koltay.Tibor,Javorszky.Ferenc}@uni-eszterhazy.hu
[2] Faculty of Arts, Eötvös Loránd University, Szombathely, Hungary
peterm15@gmail.com

Abstract. This paper paints a picture of the views on copyright literacy in Hungary. The Hungarian Library and Information Science (LIS) community has been introduced to varied literacies, mainly in their native language. The best-known literacy is information literacy, but step-by-step other literacies appear in Hungarian journal and conference papers. Due to the adherence of Hungarian librarians to their native language, there are still abstracting services that deliver abstracts on different LIS subjects that are available in the Hungarian language. Translations of the term *copyright literacy* to Hungarian bears resemblance to information literacy, that is, they are either verbatim translations of the concepts or emphasize literacy's meaning as being educated and having erudition. On this background, the results obtained on a convenience sample of the Hungarian part of an international copyright literacy survey are presented and compared to the findings of two other surveys that used the same questionnaire.

Keywords: IL literature · IL practice · IL survey · Copyright literacy hungary

1 Definitions and Approaches

Although a few papers are expected to approach copyright literacy at this conference, there is still a need to define this concept. Secker and Morrison provided a simple definition of copyright literacy by describing it as "Acquiring and demonstrating the appropriate knowledge, skills and behaviours to enable the ethical creation and use of copyright material" [1].

Harris underlines that we face copyright issues in our daily lives, often without being aware of them. She directs our attention to the fact that, while literacy is defined as competence or knowledge in a specific area, copyright literacy is more specific, because it refers to "identifying copyright-protected materials, navigating fair use and fair dealing, obtaining permissions and licenses where necessary, and recognizing infringement of copyright law". She also points out that knowledge and understanding of copyright regulations can prevent different kinds of infringement, and the lack of knowledge may lead to misunderstandings, as well as preventing the use of readily available materials in new and innovative ways [2].

S. Kurbanoğlu et al. (Eds.): ECIL 2017, CCIS 810, pp. 267–275, 2018.
https://doi.org/10.1007/978-3-319-74334-9_28

The *Information Literacy Competency Standards for Higher Education* stresses the need for copyright literacy, albeit without using the expression itself. Rather, the *Standards* accentuate the awareness of the economic, legal, and social issues related to the ethical and legal use of information [3].

Its successor, the *Framework for Information Literacy for Higher Education Framework* also presents the characteristics of copyright, fair use, open access, and the public domain by directing attention to cultural variability of legal and social construct of intellectual property. The context where it is presented is the value of information that is manifested in various contexts. As it is pointed out, novice learners may struggle with understanding the contradiction between "free" information and the concept of intellectual property as they face rules of citation or warnings about plagiarism and copyright law [4].

The question arises why it is important to study copyright literacy of information professionals. A nationwide survey of 226 academic library staff members in the United States shows that the majority of the respondents have answered copyright-related questions in the workplace. However, only 49% of them regarded themselves prepared to provide copyright information to library users. Charbonneau and Priehs also point out that – besides this perceived lack of competence – various distance education efforts, including the strong presence of Massive Open Online Courses (MOOCs) increase their training needs [5].

2 The Terminology of Literacies and Copyright Literacy in Hungary

While information literacy has been constantly present in the literature in Hungary since the second half of the 1990s, the expression *copyright literacy* appeared only recently [6]. This development fits well into pattern of the emerging terms, more or less closely connected to the concept of information literacy (IL).

The best-known literacy is information literacy, but – in accordance with the above – other literacies appear in Hungarian journal and conference papers, step-by-step. Through these channels, information professionals have become familiarized with the concept of media and information literacy [7], data literacy [8] and green information literacy [9].

The Hungarian Library and Information Science (LIS) community has been introduced to several literacies, mainly in their native language, because informing themselves about developments in LIS-related issues, including literacies in their native language is still the preferred form for Hungarian information professionals. Besides papers, professional journals also offer abstracts on different LIS subjects in Hungarian. These abstracts reflect on diverse professional issues and disclose further concepts, as it was the case of health information literacy.

The term *copyright literacy* is translated into Hungarian differently, but showing similarity to the development of information literacy's translations in the sense that there are literal translations of the expression and translations that express and emphasize literacy's meaning as being educated and having erudition. In the case of copyright literacy, *szerzői jogi műveltség* stresses erudition [10]. If we use the term *szerzői jogi ismeretek*, we emphasise the element of having knowledge about copyright. Using the verbatim translation, raises more complicated issues, because *szerzői jogi írástudás* may raise suspicions that it is related to digital literacy. To be exact, the problem is not in the resemblance, but in the fact that digital literacy in Hungary has been used in a somewhat more restricted meaning compared to its multifaceted and broad understanding conceived by Gilster [11, 12]. Due to the predominance of (ICTs), it is often conceived as nothing else than possessing ICT skills [13]. Although there is still some confusion, in parallel with the appearance of the concept of media and information literacy (MIL) the complexity of digital literacy begins to be better understood and accepted more widely [14].

Competencies related to copyright literacy appear in the National Curriculum for Education (NCE) that regulates the content of public (K12) education. The school subjects that contain elements of copyright literacy are varied, but include computing, literature and media studies. Unfortunately, disproportionately little time is designated for these tasks. If this bottleneck would not exist, there would be, first of all, classes in computing that could inform pupils about the ethical use of information, citing sources used, and plagiarism.

The Hungarian Intellectual Property Office (HIPO) also plays a significant role in the Hungarian intellectual property training system as it offers courses to students of higher education. They give special attention to teacher training, and have organized competitions for teachers to prepare lesson plans on related topics [6].

3 Hungarian Participation in Literacy Surveys

If the appearance of copyright literacy is a novelty, participation in international literacy surveys is not unknown to information professionals in Hungary, though it was only the students of one library school that participated in the first international survey that intended to reveal information about the literacy skills of LIS students [15]. Let us add that this Hungarian contribution brought in a small number of respondents, which nonetheless sufficiently reflected the opinion of the undergraduate students in a small institution, as it had a response rate of 78%.

There is also a survey with Hungarian participation that is still open at the time of writing this text. It is the Hungarian part of the international data literacy survey. This one is different from the preceding surveys, because its potential respondents are not exclusively information professionals, but different researchers from all disciplines. Although this survey is not closed yet, it can be said that – even if its target audience differs from those of earlier ones – the survey in Hungary has been disseminated and publicised with the help of academic and research libraries.

4 The Copyright Literacy Survey in Hungary

4.1 Background

Similarly to the survey on information literacy skills the Hungarian copyright literacy survey was part of an international effort. Surveys were administered with the instrument, developed by Tania Todorova and Tereza Trencheva (Bulgaria), Serap Kurbanoğlu and Güleda Doğan (Turkey), Aleksandra Horvat (Croatia) and Joumana Boustany (France). The findings of the multinational survey in their home countries, based on this methodology were reported in the proceedings of the Second European Conference on Information Literacy [16]. Colleagues from other countries followed suit. Morrison and Secker described the situation in the United Kingdom in 2015. [17] Kortelainen reported on results from Finland [18], while Terra portrayed the copyright literacy competencies of Portuguese LIS professionals [19].

The main goal of this survey was to investigate actual competency levels of Hungarian information professionals, that is, librarians and other library and information science (LIS) professionals in the field of intellectual property rights in general and copyright in particular.

Following the structure of the survey, in this paper we explore:

- The extent of information professionals with copyright related issues;
- The level of awareness of copyright policies and practices within the country and the institutions they work for;
- The opinion of these professionals about the inclusion of copyright-related issues in LIS education and training.

The survey instrument was translated into Hungarian by Tibor Koltay and the translation was reviewed by Eszter Amberg. The Hungarian part of the survey was initiated in October 2014. Information professionals were made aware of the survey and mobilised to respond at KATALIST, the discussion forum of Hungarian LIS professionals.

4.2 Demography

The number of respondents in Hungary was 145, while the survey was consulted by twice as many information professionals, who decided not to respond or who answered only a few questions. In the following, we analyse the data of those who made the effort to respond fully to the survey's questions.

Most of the respondents work in a library and 131 of them indicated the type of library where they are employed, plus two of them did not answer this question, because their library is multifunctional. The majority come from academic and public libraries, and the distribution of their work experience in years of experience was relatively even. The age of the respondents also showed an even distribution: 26 under 30, 36 between 30 and 39, 32 between 40 and 49, 35 between 50 and 60, and 16 over 60.

From the responding information professionals, 52 hold a Bachelor's, 76 a Master's and 10 a PhD degree. There are also 7 librarians with a qualification that is lower than B.A. From those with a PhD, 5 professionals work in academic libraries, 2 in public libraries and 3 in other libraries. With 115 answers, females were in overwhelming majority.

Even though the number of respondents to this survey (145) is relatively low, the Hungarian part of the survey is representative of the state of the profession, even if not in a strictly statistical sense.

4.3 Findings

To interpret the findings as correctly as possible, it seemed sensible to compare the results of the Hungarian survey with two other surveys: the multinational one by Todorova et al. (covering Bulgaria, Croatia, France and Turkey) [16] and the UK survey by Morrison and Secker [17].

General Knowledge and Awareness of Copyright Issues. About 40% of Hungarian information professionals indicated that they are somewhat or moderately familiar with the regulations. However, the level of their awareness about orphan works was below 30%. This demonstrates that, despite the apparent lack of knowledge about orphan works, a substantial extent of copyright awareness is regarded by them to be a pre-requisite for successful digitisation.

International, National and Institutional Regulations and Institutions. To enable comparisons among the answers for this part of the survey, we computed the average of the answers provided for the first four (Likert scale) questions. As we had 145 respondents, it seemed to be conceivable that every question could induce 29 answers, thus producing an average of 3.00. However, this average was not reached in the Hungarian survey. Moreover, in two cases it was lower than 2.00. In the case of national and international regulations, we found that copyright and related law produced an average of 2.63 at the national level, while it was only 1.89 at the international level. Similarly copyright related institutions appeared to be known at the national level with an average of 2.69, while awareness of international regulations performed at the lowest level with 1.81.

All in all – as also partly shown in Table 1 – our findings show consistency with the results of the above surveys about national and international copyright issues and copyleft, because the level of familiarity with these is low among Hungarian information professionals.

The 19% share of the World Intellectual Property Organization (WIPO) and 13% of IFLA confirms that Hungarian information professionals know national regulations

Table 1. The level of awareness on issues related to intellectual property/copyright

	Low	Moderate	Good	Very good	Excellent	Average	UK average
Copyright and related law – national level	35	25	49	30	6	2.63	3.50
Copyright and related law – international level	63	44	30	7	1	1.89	2.27
Copyright related institutions – national level	25	40	44	27	9	2.69	3.24
Copyright related institutions – international level	68	45	24	8	0	1.81	2.09

much better than international ones. Interest in the initiatives of international professional organisation proved to be significantly higher among holders of graduate (Master's) degrees and PhDs.

The number of those who are familiar with Creative Commons Licences is surprisingly low. This is indicated by the fact that 39% chose the option of being not at all familiar, and 18% declared that they are slightly familiar with this concept. That is, the concept was new for more than the half of the respondents.

From among the Hungarian respondents, only 41% know that a national copyright policy exists, and those who are unsure make up an absolute majority with 53%. Whatsoever, we can interpret this fact as a sign of their intent to provide sincere answers.

The discrepancy of opinions about the existence of institutional policies between the proportion of 64% in the UK and 34% in the multinational survey and 49% in the Hungarian one seems to be realistic, because the findings clearly indicate the differences between the copyright policy systems. For the same reason, only 17% of Hungarian information professionals and 15% of the multinational survey indicated that there is a person in their institution in charge of dealing with copyright issues, whereas, in the UK this was the opinion of 64%.

Sources of Information for Copyright Awareness. Among the preferred sources when searching for information on intellectual property and copyright, 65% indicated the web. This result is not surprising. It is even reasonable, as the other two surveys found 71 and 76% ratios. At the same time, we must see that highly preferred sources, such as lawyers (53%), colleagues (54%), the Széchényi National Library and national library organisations (55%) are also reachable through the internet.

On the other hand, choosing lawyers reached surprisingly a high proportion. This becomes even more significant if we compare this result with the findings of the multinational and the UK survey, where this proportion was 26 and 11%, respectively.

As a means of distribution, professional discussion fora are preferred by 40%. This proportion again shows similarity with the other two surveys, while blogs are mentioned by 13%, that is, approximately half of the proportions evidenced in the multinational and the UK survey.

We are speaking about librarians, so it is not by accident that reliance on the professional literature is high with 52%, even if it is lower than in the other two surveys (56% and 70%).

It also of importance that 25% would ask for help and advice from teaching staff and other scholars.

Most of these findings can be seen on Table 2.

Table 2. Preferred sources of information

	Hungary	Four countries	UK
Colleagues	78 (54%)	56%	70%
Lawyers	77 (53%)	26%	10%
Books, articles, etc.	75 (52%)	73%	62%
Websites	94 (65%)	71%	76%
Blogs/wikis	19 (13%)	31%	24%
Professional discussion lists	58 (40%)	40%	47%
WIPO	28 (19%)	17%	13%
IFLA	19 (13%)	24%	9%
National Library and other professional associations	79 (54%)	43%	29% + 59%
Experts from academic and scientific community	36 (25%)	33%	25%

The Importance of Compliance with Copyright Legislations. Compared to the findings of the multinational and the UK survey (81% and 92%) somewhat lower proportion, but still an overwhelming majority (72%) of the Hungarian respondents agree with the statement that services offered by libraries and other cultural heritage institutions require compliance with copyright legislation. Obviously, even this proportion is eminent. Still, 79% of Hungarians show the highest support for the idea that worldwide harmonization of exceptions and limitations to copyright for libraries and archives is necessary. In Bulgaria, Croatia, France and Turkey, the average proportion of the suggestion to WIPO to better define exceptions and limitations to copyright in the digital environment was 74%, while it reached 61% in the UK and 82% in Hungary.

The third suggestion, that is, that the WIPO *Treaty to Facilitate Access to Published Works for Persons who are Blind, Visually Impaired, or otherwise Print Disabled* is an important achievement, attained the highest agreement (90%) among Hungarian respondents (compared to 82% and 87%). However, this result should be treated with caution if we consider that the answers to an earlier question showed awareness of the WIPO below 20%. Most probably, the reason behind the almost unanimous agreement was that Hungarian information professionals support the goals articulated in the treaty, without being familiar with the treaty itself.

The Supposed Level of Self-esteem of the Respondents. There are some peculiar facts that might deserve attention and explanation. The averages produced by female respondents are lower than those of males. A likely reason for this is that females are wary of giving themselves higher scores, although the literature shows conflicting arguments about gender similarities and differences [20–22]. In any case, due to the high proportion of female respondents, the average of answers given by them takes the closest position to the aggregate values. If females gave diverging answers in one direction, the answers by males were almost four times as far in the other direction. All, this is understandable if we take into account that answers given by female respondents were decisive in the Hungarian survey.

It could also be observed that the scores of almost every individual, choosing from the five options of the Likert scale were consequently close to each other. You even might wonder, why did some of the respondents go on with completing the survey, when they gave themselves minimal scores in the first group of questions.

In general, there were only few who gave themselves high scores. It is probably not by accident that one of these was a lawyer.

5 Conclusion

All in all, it can be said that – despite some discrepancies – Hungarian information professionals face similar difficulties as their colleagues in Bulgaria, Croatia, France Turkey and the United Kingdom, when treating copyright-related issues. In other words, there seems to be no significant specificity of the Hungarian context. We can say instead that – despite differences – our findings reinforce what was found in the other three surveys. Unfortunately, this does not mean that the level of knowledge and the awareness of information professionals in these six countries regarding copyright issues would be satisfactory.

The findings of this survey – again similarly to the international survey, mentioned above – also indicate that there is a need for improvement. The survey results themselves underline this, because the overwhelming majority of our respondents support that it is necessary to include intellectual property issues in the curriculum of Library and Information Science education and continuing education.

Accordingly, we can repeat and herewith confirm the words of Todorova et al.: We should increase awareness of information professionals regarding copyright issues. To deepen the level of their knowledge level in this field, LIS curricula and continuing education programs should lay more emphasis on theoretical and practical content on intellectual property issues [16].

Acknowledgments. This paper is one of the outcomes of the research project EFOP-3.6.1-16-2016-00001 "Complex Development of Research Capacities and Services at Eszterházy Károly University".

References

1. Secker, J., Morrison, C.: Copyright and E-learning: a Guide for Practitioners. Facet, London (2015)
2. Harris, L.E.: Copyright literacy and translating copyright to a life skill (2015). http://www.copyrightlaws.com/libraries/copyright-literacy-copyright-life-skill/
3. Association of College and Research Libraries (ACRL): Information literacy competency standards for higher education (2000). http://www.ala.org/acrl/standards/informationliteracy competency
4. Association of College and Research Libraries (ACRL): Framework for information literacy for higher education (2016). http://www.ala.org/acrl/standards/ilframework
5. Charbonneau, D.H., Priehs, M.: Copyright awareness, partnerships, and training issues in academic libraries. J. Acad. Librariansh. **40**, 228–233 (2013)

6. Tószegi, Zs.: A könyvtárosképzés új eleme: a szerzői jogi írástudás [A new element in library and information science education: copyright literacy]. Könyv és Nevelés **18**, 7–21 (2016)
7. Egervári, D.: A digitális írástudás, az információs műveltség és a XXI. századi kompetenciák rendszere [Digital literacy, information literacy and the system of 21st century competences]. In: Networkshop 2017 (2017). http://nws.niif.hu/ncd2014/docs/ehu/028.pdf
8. Koltay, T.: A kutatási adatok és a könyvtár [Research data and the library]. Könyvtári Figyelő **60**, 223–235 (2014)
9. Koltay, T.: A sokarcú információs műveltség néhány új arca [A few new faces of the multifaceted information literacy]. Könyvtári Figyelő **62**, 193–197 (2016)
10. Koltay, T., Varga, K.: Conceptions, ideas, what else? Information literacy in hungary. In: Kurbanoğlu, S., Grassian, E., Mizrachi, D., Catts, R., Špiranec, S. (eds.) ECIL 2013. CCIS, vol. 397, pp. 625–631. Springer, Cham (2013). https://doi.org/10.1007/978-3-319-03919-0_84
11. Gilster, P.: Digital Literacy. Wiley, New York (2016)
12. Bawden, D.: Origins and concepts of digital literacy. In: Lankshear, C., Knobel, M. (eds.) Digital Literacies: Concepts, Policies and Practices, pp. 17–32. Peter Lang, New York (2008)
13. Zsák, J.: A műveltség fogalmának eredete és értelmezésének változásai [The origins of the concept of being educated and the changes of its interpretation]. In: Varga, K. (ed.) A 21. század műveltsége. E-könyv az információs műveltségről. PTE, Pécs (2008). http://www.lib.pte.hu/elektkonyvtar/ekonyvek/elibrary/21szazad/
14. Egervári, D.: A digitális írástudás, az információs műveltség és a XXI. századi kompetenciák rendszere [Digital literacy, information literacy and the system of 21st century competences]. In: Networkshop 2014 (2014). http://nws.niif.hu/ncd2014/docs/phu/028.pdf
15. Saunders, L., Kurbanoglu, S., Boustany, J., Dogan, G., Koltay, T., et al.: Information behaviors and information literacy skills of LIS students: an international perspective. J. Educ. Libr. Inf. Sci. **56**, 80–99 (2015)
16. Todorova, T., Trencheva, T., Kurbanoğlu, S., Doğan, G., Horvat, A., Boustany, J.: A multinational study on copyright literacy competencies of LIS professionals. In: Kurbanoğlu, S., Špiranec, S., Grassian, E., Mizrachi, D., Catts, R. (eds.) ECIL 2014. CCIS, vol. 492, pp. 138–148. Springer, Cham (2014). https://doi.org/10.1007/978-3-319-14136-7_15
17. Morrison, C., Secker, J.: Copyright literacy in the UK: a survey of librarians and other cultural heritage sector professionals. Libr. Inf. Res. **39**, 75–97 (2015)
18. Kortelainen, T.: Copyright literacy in finnish libraries, archives and museums. In: Kurbanoğlu, S., Boustany, J., Špiranec, S., Grassian, E., Mizrachi, D., Roy, L. (eds.) ECIL 2015. CCIS, vol. 552, pp. 202–209. Springer, Cham (2015). https://doi.org/10.1007/978-3-319-28197-1_21
19. Terra, A.L.: Copyright literacy competencies from portuguese LIS professionals. In: Kurbanoğlu, S., Boustany, J., Špiranec, S., Grassian, E., Mizrachi, D., Roy, L., Çakmak, T. (eds.) ECIL 2016. CCIS, vol. 676, pp. 634–643. Springer, Cham (2016). https://doi.org/10.1007/978-3-319-52162-6_62
20. Kling, K.C., Hyde, J.S., Showers, C.J., Buswell, B.N.: Gender differences in self-esteem: a meta-analysis. Psychol. Bull. **125**, 470–500 (1999)
21. Hyde, J.S.: The gender similarities hypothesis. Am. Psychol. **60**, 581–592 (2005)
22. Zell, E., Krizan, Z., Teeter, S.R.: Evaluating gender similarities and differences using metasynthesis. Am. Psychol. **70**, 10–20 (2015)

Copyright Literacy in the Academic Field: Analysis of the Differences Between Faculty, Students and Librarians

Juan-Carlos Fernández-Molina[1(✉)] and Enrique Muriel-Torrado[2]

[1] Universidad de Granada, Granada, Spain
jcfernan@ugr.es
[2] Universidade Federal de Santa Catarina, Florianópolis, Brazil
enrique.muriel@ufsc.br

Abstract. Copyright is involved in many of the educational and informational activities that take place in the environs of higher education, and not only professors but also students and librarians should know its main principles and rules. The aim of this paper is to identify the main differences and similarities in knowledge of the basic matters of copyright literacy among these three sectors of the university community: faculty, students, and librarians. To this end, the results of three different questionnaires in two Spanish universities (Extremadura and Granada) were analyzed. The results reveal that essential mistakes and misunderstandings are shared by all three sectors, although there are some interesting differences as well.

Keywords: Copyright · Information literacy · Academic librarians
University professors · College students

1 Introduction

Copyright is involved in many of the educational and informational activities that take place in the higher education setting. The teaching and research activities of professors, and students′ learning activities, require the use of works whose copyright belongs to third parties. One should therefore be aware of what can and cannot be done with such works without breaking the law. Furthermore, students and professors —and in some cases even librarians— are also creators of intellectual works, so they need to know what rights they hold over the works they have created.

The digital environment has complicated this relationship between the academic community and copyright law, in terms of the new possibilities of use and transmission of digital works, and the legislative reforms of recent years [1]. In the face of this situation, university libraries have attempted to take on the role of advisers and trainers in this area, and are developing numerous information literacy activities focused on copyright law [2]. But, do academic librarians really have the knowledge required to adopt that new role? What is the level of knowledge about copyright on the part of professors and students? Are there common misunderstandings or points of confusion regarding this subject? In order to answer these questions, this paper aims to identify

S. Kurbanoğlu et al. (Eds.): ECIL 2017, CCIS 810, pp. 276–285, 2018.
https://doi.org/10.1007/978-3-319-74334-9_29

and look into the main differences and similarities in knowledge of the basic matters of copyright literacy among the three sectors of the university community: faculty, students, and librarians.

2 Literature Review

Although the past few years have witnessed somewhat more attention to the topic of copyright literacy, publications are still scarce, especially when the focus is on the student population. Deserving mention are two studies in Taiwan [3, 4] that revealed a serious lack of knowledge of the most basic copyright issues. The results of studies by Datig and Russell [5] and by the Joint Information Systems Committee [6] were slightly better, in the latter case probably because only PhD students participated.

Also scanty are studies focusing on faculty members. Smith et al. [7] explored knowledge of copyright among the health science professors of two US universities, making manifest their similarly low degree of familiarity with basic matters of copyright and fair use. Combining interviews and surveys, the study carried out by Sims [8] at the University of Minnesota evaluated the basic copyright knowledge of professors and librarians. The results were better for the librarians, but overall important misconceptions about elementary matters came to light. Particularly interesting is the work by Di Valentino [9] in Canada: a survey showed that many professors do not take full advantage of the information sources available for their teaching activities because they do not feel secure in their knowledge of copyright law and are afraid to infringe it.

Studies focusing on librarians are more numerous, and diverse methodologies have been applied. An early study [10] used a survey directed at librarians, managers of consortia, informed users and corporate rightsholders, with generally poor results. Also poor were the results obtained by Charbonneau and Priehs [11] with a survey aimed to determine copyright awareness and training needs among academic librarians. With their survey carried out in the US, Estell and Saunders [12] looked at the level of familiarity with copyright law among academic librarians; the results were positive in terms of basic knowledge, but insufficient for properly advising users. Even worse are the results reported by Fernández-Molina et al. [13] with a sample of Brazil´s main universities. Under a different focus, the study by Eye [14] exclusively involved library deans and directors, and the results were better, though the questions were very basic. Moreover, their respondents were found to be quite aware of the gaps in knowledge or training of academic librarians, as only 11% thought that LIS schools were providing adequate training in this subject matter. Last but not least, the broad, multinational survey undertaken by the team of J. Todorova (https://copyrightlib.unibit.bg/index_en.php) reveals varying levels of knowledge about copyright in the library profession.

3 Methodology

The three questionnaires that served as the basis for this study were developed in the framework of a research project centered on copyright in the university setting, and two Spanish universities took part (Extremadura and Granada). The survey in Granada was carried out first, exclusively limited for the 94 professors teaching online courses, under the assumption that they would be more aware of copyright matters affecting their teaching activities. A part of the findings appeared in an LIS journal [15]. Afterwards, studies involving 400 undergraduate students and 25 librarians were carried out, in this case at the University of Extremadura, with results also published in part [16, 17].

Given the diverse characteristics of the above respondents, the design of each copyright questionnaire was slightly different, but the three shared common elements surrounding the most basic issues, that is, exceptions and limitations, formal requirements needed, duration, and concept of public domain. In addition, taking into account their increasing relevance in the academic context [18], questions centered on copyleft-type licenses were included. These five basic areas of knowledge regarding copyright and copyleft allowed us to make the comparative analysis presented here.

4 Results and Discussion

In order to achieve an adequate balance between the interests of rightholders and users, copyright is subject to a series of exceptions and limitations. Several of them are useful in the academic environment, for general use (private copying, for the benefit for people with a disability) or specifically addressing the educational realm. Therefore, some basic knowledge of such exceptions and of the conditions and circumstances that allow for their application would be essential for students, faculty and librarians, particularly in the case of matters affecting academics directly—that is, illustration for teaching and quotations for the professors, and library privileges for the librarians.

It should be noted here that the regulation of certain exceptions was modified in recent years, and this development was echoed in the mass media. The most relevant case is that of the private copying exception, sparking intense debate and discussion among specialists and citizens at large, especially due to its controversial 'digital canon' and regulation of the P2P networks. Heated discussion, in this case just by specialists, also surrounded the new regulation of the education exception, owing to the numerous restrictions imposed and to its deficient treatment of online teaching. In turn, the legal modification of library exceptions got no media attention outside the professional sector.

Our question regarding exceptions for teaching was presented in a very general way, simply asking the respondent to say which exceptions and limitations (regarding contents and requisites for application) they were familiar with. They could respond with more than one option; and we supposed that each sector would tend to name the exceptions and limitations that affected their own activity most directly—for example in the case of the professors, illustration for teaching and quotations.

Although it might seem obvious that the private copying exception is the one best known by all three university sectors, given its great impact in the media, what we did not anticipate is that it was more clearly identified than the exceptions closely related to teaching (illustration for teaching, quotations) and library activities (library privileges). Just over half of the professors we queried stated they knew its contents, something hard to justify, especially in the case of the quotations/citations, whose use is essential for research activities. There is also no excuse for the roughly 25% of librarians who admit they do not know the contents of the exception favoring their activity. The results for students were extremely poor except with regard to private copying, and their serious lack of knowledge about the conditions for properly quoting/citing is a worrisome finding (Fig. 1).

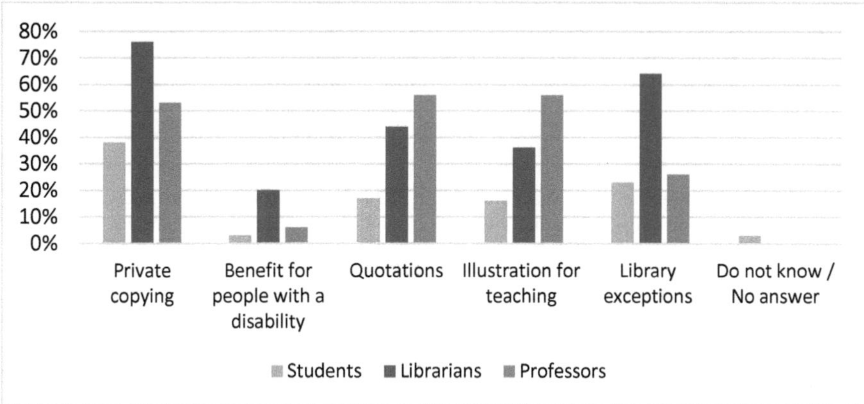

Fig. 1. Copyright exceptions and limitations

One of the most basic questions about copyright is its duration. Because it constitutes a monopoly conceded to the author, its duration is limited. Although each national copyright law has its differences and particularities in this regard, in recent years a process of international harmonization has led to a general rule for its duration, now identical in most countries, 70 years after the author's death. Here we are speaking only of the economic rights, as the moral rights have very different rules in the Latin countries (where the rights of paternity/attribution and integrity are perpetual) and the Anglo-Saxon countries (where they expire at the same time as the economic rights).

The responses to our questionnaire clearly signal the librarians as the only group with a minimally acceptable knowledge of the duration of copyright. It would have been understandable if the error were choosing the option of 60 years, as that was the period established by Spanish law until 1995, when the process of harmonization of the European Union raised it to 70 years; but surprisingly, the majority of both professors and students erroneously chose the option of 50 years. Knowing the duration of copyright implies knowing whether a work we wish to use belongs to the public domain or not, and this is determinant, as we will see shortly, for a series of uses that would not be allowed when dealing with a work whose economic rights remain in effect (Fig. 2).

Closely tied to the previous question, and also essential for any program of copyright literacy, is the concept of and the requirements of the public domain. That is, when and under what conditions a work ceases to have copyright, and can therefore be used freely without requesting permission or making any payment for its use. Although there are different ways of defining public domain, in the case of Spanish legislation — as in the rest of the civil law countries— moral rights play a fundamental role; as mentioned above, the economic rights expire after a period of time, but not the moral rights of paternity/attribution and integrity, which are perpetual. This dual moral/

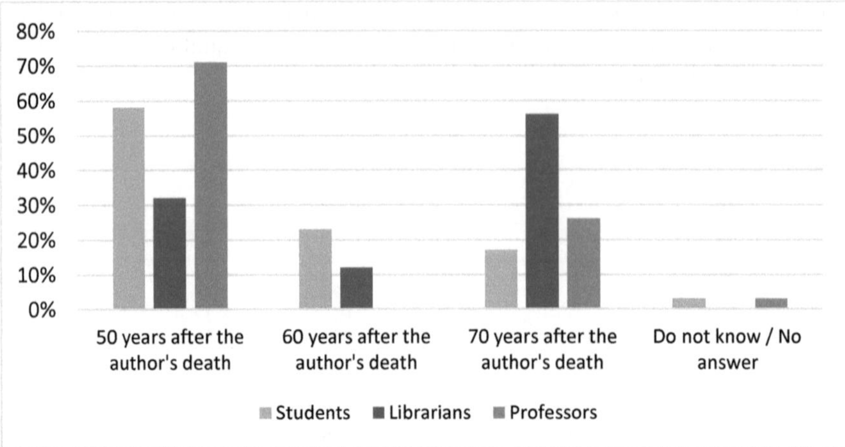

Fig. 2. Duration of copyright

economic nature, and the different durations of the two types of rights, appears to create substantial confusion among the persons surveyed. Although the percentage of correct answers is clearly higher than for the other questions, a good number of individuals, especially in the student body, either believe that the moral rights also expire after some time or, even stranger, think that the work loses its moral rights but not its economic rights. Noteworthy in this case is the high percentage of correct responses from the professors —nearly 80%— surely because they are more aware of their role as authors and the moral component thereof. In contrast, the very negative results from the librarians must be underlined: almost 40% believed that when a work moves to the public domain, the moral rights of the author are also lost (Fig. 3).

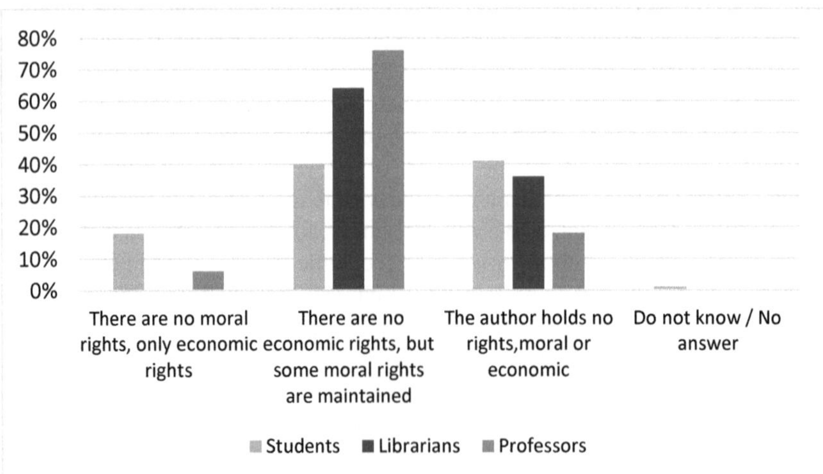

Fig. 3. What does ‘public domain’ mean?

A key element of current copyright law is that no formal procedure is required for a creator to acquire the copyright of an intellectual work. We believe that one question about this point is inevitable for any questionnaire that attempts to gauge basic knowledge about copyright, above all in the academic realm. In this setting most intellectual works generated, whether by professors or students, are not commercial endeavors. Hence almost no one contemplates taking measures (e.g. inscription in the register of intellectual property) to guarantee or enhance legal protection. Yet the fact of the matter is that Spanish law, in agreement with the Berne Convention [19] and all its undersigning countries, establishes that the intellectual ownership of a work corresponds to the author "for the mere deed of its creation" (Article 1 of Spanish Copyright Act). Therefore, while in certain situations inscription in the register of intellectual property may be recommendable, measures such as including a symbol to indicate ownership are not necessary to ensure copyright. For this item on our questionnaire the options were varied, and one or more could be checked: inscription in the registry, copyright symbol, legal deposit… or no requirement at all.

Our expectations of correct responses to this question were low, as we were aware of the generalized misunderstanding [20] that it is not possible to acquire copyright unless something is done to demonstrate authorship. However, the results obtained were even worse than anticipated. Spanish students appear to believe in bureaucracy, as most answered that one needs to register the document, place the copyright symbol on it, and make legal deposit as well. Only 1% responded correctly that no such measure is required. From the professors, in turn, there was a correct response in just 12% of cases. This group tended to insist on the need to register a work.

This surprising finding led us to wonder how students and professors resolve one of the most conflictive situations that can arise between the two groups: the ownership of papers produced as classwork/homework. Evidently, such work is not formally registered or placed in legal deposit, and it is unlikely to carry the copyright symbol. Do students then believe that their work entails no rights at all? And do professors really believe that their students' work has no rights attached and may be used without any sort of restriction? Finally, although the librarians were again the ones with more correct responses to this query (20% answered correctly), their results are only slightly better than the professors, and certainly far from what one would consider the minimal requirements regarding knowledge of copyright law (Fig. 4).

Given the vast development of copyleft-type licenses, especially Creative Commons, and their appropriateness for the university setting, it is also essential to at least be familiar with the underlying philosophy and the basic conditions of this type of license. The corresponding question was plainly stated, not delving into the meaning of the six basic options offered by CC license, but simply limited to the key matter of whether they meant a renouncement of all the rights (moral and/or economic) or instead, if the author decides which rights they maintain and which ones they waive. In this case, the results were very different for the three sectors of respondents, with the librarians attaining better results, roughly two-thirds giving the correct response. Only 21% of the professors answered correctly, their main misconception being that the author renounces all economic rights but not the moral rights. This severe gap in knowledge was totally unexpected, as the professors surveyed divulged their coursework online by means of the OpenCourseWare Consortium, which uses, precisely, Creative Commons licenses.

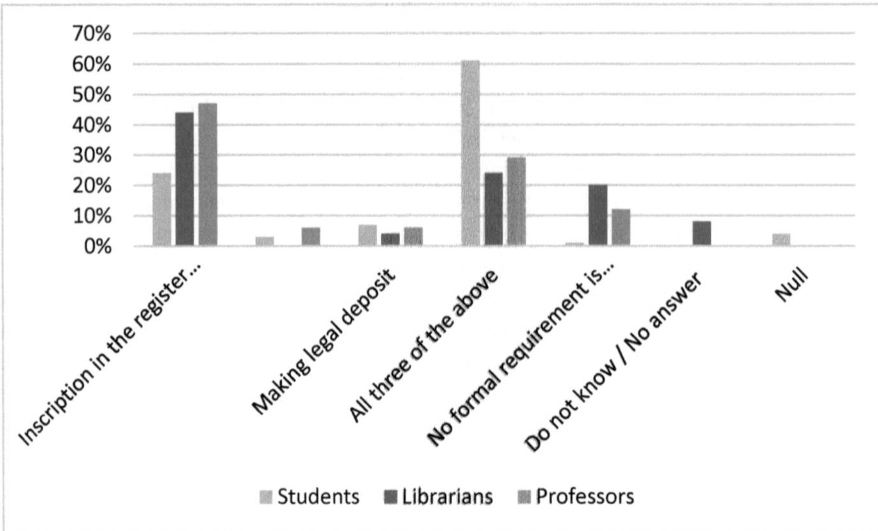

Fig. 4. Formal requirements to acquire copyright

At the same time, it again appears that the professors are acutely aware of moral rights, conceding lesser importance to the rights of an economic nature. This may seem logical in academic arenas. However, they forget that one option under these licenses is that of not allowing derivative works. In other words, they may keep one of their economic rights, the right of transformation. In the end a correct response was given by

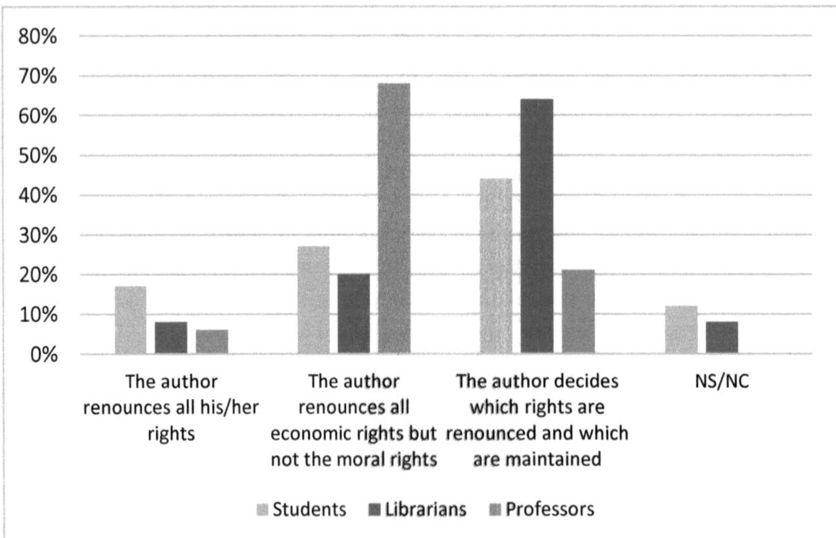

Fig. 5. What are 'copyleft' licenses?

44% of the students, though a noteworthy 12% did not even dare to choose one of the options. These are very disappointing results for an age group held up as "digital natives", supposedly familiar with the new modes of divulging information (Fig. 5).

5 Conclusions

The everyday activities of the three main components of the university population — faculty, students, and librarians— are inevitably connected with copyright legislation, making it essential for all to have adequate training in this area. Because professors and students are both users and creators of intellectual works, they need to know the norms and conditions of use for the copyrighted works of third parties without infringing the law, as well as their own rights and means of protection for their own intellectual creations. Librarians, on the other hand, are in an intermediate position that obliges them to find a balance between respecting the rightholders of informational sources in their library collections and helping users, the faculty and students who wish to make use of the information resources in the broadest manner possible for their activities of learning, teaching and research. Moreover, given the current movement to a more open and free use and distribution of intellectual works, it is crucial for all sectors to at least know the basic principles of this alternative and the different applications for research (open access) and learning (open educational resources) through copyleft-type licenses.

The level of knowledge we detected about the different exceptions and limitations would indicate that none of the sectors has had even minimal training in this area. In all cases the respondents prove to be more familiar with the exception of a general character (private copying), which has had broad repercussion in the media, than with the ones affecting them more directly in their academic/professional activities: illustration for teaching and quotations/citations (faculty and students), and library privileges (librarians). This lack of specific training also comes to light with professors′ and students′ generalized confusion about the duration of copyright, where the librarians achieve clearly better results. The only question where the professors gave acceptable results was regarding the concept of public domain, probably due to their recognition of moral rights in their own role as creators of intellectual works. The results about the formal requirements necessary to acquire copyright of a creation reveal astounding confusion among all three sectors surveyed here, although again the librarians had somewhat better results. Perhaps the most significant finding with this item is that the students are the most demanding sector, widely believing that one must fulfill a number of requisites to obtain copyright. Finally, the degree of knowledge about alternative approaches to copyright, namely CC licenses, is also scanty for all three sectors, but less so among the librarians. The professors paint a truly bleak picture, giving the worst results for this query, yet paradoxically being the main users of such licenses, by means of such items as open access journals, teaching materials distributed as open educational resources, webs, blogs.

The main activities and programs of copyright literacy are designed to provide basic information about these matters to university students, yet the results of our study demonstrate that even university professors lack the minimal knowledge in this field. They need help and specialized counseling not only to deal with the more complex questions related to scholarly communication, but also to resolve the most elementary matters related to copyright and their activity as teachers and researchers. The results also show that the task of training and advising can hardly be taken on by librarians if they do not improve their own knowledge about copyright issues. Fortunately, the positive results obtained in the recent study by Arias-Coello and Simón-Martín (also included in this conference) allow us to be optimistic.

Acknowledgment. This study was supported by the Spanish Ministry of Economy and Competition (Project DER2014-53012-C2-2-R).

References

1. Lipinski, T.A.: Legal issues in the development and use of copyrighted material. In: Moore, M.G. (ed.) Handbook of Distance Education, pp. 451–469. Lawrence Erlbaum, New Jersey (2007)
2. Rodriguez, J.E., Greer, K., Shipman, B.: Copyright and you: copyright instruction for college students in the digital age. J. Acad. Librariansh. **40**(5), 486–491 (2014). https://doi.org/10.1016/j.acalib.2014.06.001
3. Chou, C., Chan, P.S., Wu, H.C.: Using a two-tier test to assess students' understanding and alternative conceptions of cyber copyright laws. Br. J. Educ. Technol. **38**(6), 1072–1084 (2007)
4. Wu, H.C., Chou, C., Ke, H.R., Wang, M.H.: College students' misunderstandings about copyright laws for digital library resources. Electron. Libr. **30**(2), 197–209 (2010)
5. Datig, I., Russell, B.: The fruits of intellectual labor: international student views of intellectual property. Coll. Res. Libr. **76**(6), 811–830 (2015)
6. Joint Information Systems Committee: Researchers of Tomorrow: The Research Behaviour Generation Y Doctoral Students. JISC/British Library, London (2012). http://www.jisc.ac.uk/media/documents/publications/reports/2012/Researchers-of-Tomorrow.pdf
7. Smith, K.H., Tobia, R.C., Plutchak, T.S., Howell, L.M., Pfeiffer, S.J., Fitts, M.S.: Copyright knowledge of faculty at two academic health science campuses: results of a survey. Ser. Rev. **32**(2), 59–67 (2006)
8. Sims, N.: Lies, damned lies, and copyright (mis)information: empowering faculty by addressing key points of confusion. In: ACRL 2011 Conference, Philadelphia, pp. 282–296 (2011)
9. Di Valentino, L.: Laying the Foundation for Copyright Policy and Practice in Canadian Universities. Doctoral thesis, University of Western Ontario (2016). http://ir.lib.uwo.ca/etd/4312
10. Masango, C.A.: Perceptions about copyright of digital content and its effects on scholarship: a South African perspective. Libri **57**(1), 84–91 (2007)
11. Charbonneau, D.H., Priehs, M.: Copyright awareness, partnerships, and training issues in academic libraries. J. Acad. Librariansh. **40**(3–4), 228–233 (2014)
12. Estell, A., Saunders, L.: Librarian copyright literacy: self-reported copyright knowledge among information professionals in the United States. Public Serv. Q. **12**(3), 214–227 (2016)
13. Fernández-Molina, J.C., Moraes, J.B.E., Guimarães, J.A.C.: Academic libraries and copyright: do librarians really have the required knowledge? Coll. Res. Libr. **78**(2), 241–259 (2017). https://doi.org/10.5860/crl.78.2.16584
14. Eye, J.: Knowledge level of library deans and directors in copyright law. J. Librariansh. Sch. Commun. **2**(1), eP1103 (2013). https://doi.org/10.7710/2162-3309.1103

15. Fernández-Molina, J.C., Muriel, E., Vives-Gracia, J., Riera, P., Martín, O.: Copyright and e-learning: professors' level of knowledge about the new Spanish law. In: Aslib Proceedings: New Information Perspectives, vol. 63, no. 4, pp. 340–353 (2011)
16. Muriel-Torrado, E.: Los Derechos de Autor y la Enseñanza en la Universidad: el Papel de la Biblioteca Universitaria. (Doctoral dissertation) University of Granada, Granada (2012)
17. Muriel-Torrado, E., Fernández-Molina, J.C.: Creation and use of intellectual works in the academic environment: students' knowledge about copyright and copyleft. J. Acad. Librariansh. **41**(4), 441–448 (2015)
18. Kapitzke, C., Dezuanni, M., Iyer, R.: Copyrights and creative commons licensing: pedagogical innovation in a higher education media literacy classroom. E-Learn. Digit. Media **8**(3), 271–282 (2011). https://doi.org/10.2304/elea.2011.8.3.271
19. WIPO: Berne Convention for the Protection of Literary and Artistic Works, Paris Act of 24 July 1971, as amended on 28 September 1979. http://www.wipo.int/wipolex/en/treaties/text.jsp?file_id=283698
20. Myers, C.S.: Seven steps to help you become more knowledgeable about U.S. copyright law. Coll. Undergrad. Libr. **23**(3), 343–352 (2016). https://doi.org/10.1080/10691316.2016.1206324

Copyright Literacy in Spanish Libraries, Archives and Museums

Alicia Arias-Coello(✉) and José Simón-Martín

Instituto Universitario de Evaluación,
Universidad Complutense Madrid, Madrid, Spain
{aarias, jsimon}@ucm.es

Abstract. Copyright literacy in Spanish librarians, archivists, documentalists and directors of museums was studied by a web survey as part of multinational research originating from a project funded by the National Science Fund of the Bulgarian Ministry of Education and Science on "Copyright Policy of Libraries and Other Cultural Institutions". The purpose of this study was to examine perceptions, opinions and knowledge of those information professionals with various aspects of copyright and intellectual property, as well as, the need for copyright education. For this study we received a total of 325 responses, 225 of which were completely filled out. This study is the first of its kind in Spain and the results will be compared with those obtained in other countries.

Keywords: Copyright literacy · Spain · LIS · Libraries · Archives

1 Introduction

In Spain, as in France, author rights and copyright do not have the same meaning, although they are closely related. Copyright refers to intellectual property, that is, the rights of a natural or legal person over his work for a certain time. These rights such as the right of recognition of authorship and the right to integrity of the work and also of an economic nature. While individual rights are not transferable, economic rights, which are basically exploitation rights, are transferable and of limited duration over time. On the other hand, the Anglo-Saxon copyright formula is used to designate only the copy right derived from the exploitation rights, and the © symbol is followed by the phrase "all rights reserved". Copyright is also used to reflect the rights of others who have participated in the work, such as translators or the publisher who publishes the book. In this paper we will use the term copyright with the meaning of author rights.

The first rule that regulated author rights in Spain was approved in 1763, which established that the rights to print the work were granted to the author and not to a community or company. From that year were updated these regulations during the eighteenth and nineteenth centuries. The twentieth century was a breakthrough in the recognition of author rights for different types of works and created rights management entities, such as the SGAE, in 1941. In 1942 a standard was published that protected phonograph, in 1966 Cinematographic works and in 1975 legislation in relation to the rights on books. In 1987 the Ministry of Education Culture and Sports published the Law of Intellectual Property that included all kinds of materials generated by an author.

S. Kurbanoğlu et al. (Eds.): ECIL 2017, CCIS 810, pp. 286–293, 2018.
https://doi.org/10.1007/978-3-319-74334-9_30

This legislation has had several reforms over the years to the current law, adopted in 1996, which was modified in part in 2014. This law includes three key issues, such as the protection of making copies of materials, the design of mechanisms for the supervision of management entities and establishes fundamental criteria regarding the rights of authors and works generated in the digital environment.

With regard to training in copyright, in Spain there are several university masters on intellectual property, which include training in copyright and author rights. In these courses are formed the professionals who wish to specialize in this matter. This training has special interest for two reasons, on the one hand because it covers a gap that we have had in Spain for several years referred to this matter and, on the other, because they involve professionals and experts in intellectual property, such as the Instituto Autor (IA), whose mission is to promote and disseminate the study of intellectual property in the European and Latin American fields. It is also important to note, within this training, the Spanish Patent and Trademark Office (OEPM), which is under the Ministry of Industry, Energy and Tourism, where courses and master's degrees on intellectual property are taught.

In 2016, Professor Todorova, from the University Paris of Library Studies and Information Technologies de Sofia and coordinator of the international survey on "Copyright Policies of libraries and other cultural institutions", invited us to participate in this study to learn more about the degree of knowledge that the librarians, archivists, documentalists and directors of museums of our country had on this subject. This survey was generated in Bulgaria in 2013 and by 2014 the results of four countries (Bulgaria, Croatia, France and Turkey [1]) were presented at the 2014 European Conference on Information Literacy. The project has been extended each year to other countries [2–5] and in the third phase of 2016 Spain participated. Therefore, the purpose of this study was to examine perceptions of librarians, archivists, documentalists and directors of museums of their knowledge and opinions with various aspects of copyright and intellectual property. There are no previous studies in Spain on this topic, except those focused on the level of knowledge of basic aspects of copyright between professors, university students and academic librarians [6–8].

The survey was distributed in our country in the months of December 2016 and January 2017 to gather data from librarians, documentalists, archivists and museum managers. At the moment the situation favored us for two reasons, on the one hand the Law of Intellectual Property revised had already been almost two years in force and was widely known and, on the other, this law includes several aspects of relevance as is the protection to the work generated in the digital environment. For these reasons, we considered that it was a very opportune moment to carry out the survey, and in addition, since experiences from other countries had already been presented, we had the opportunity to compare results.

2 Methodology

We used an on-line survey that was created within the framework of the above research project "Copyright Policies of Libraries and Other Cultural Institutions". The survey was translated to Spanish for better comprehension. The questionnaire includes 22 questions, most of which have closed response options and has been divided into four sections, the first includes questions which investigate general knowledge and awareness on copyright issues. The second section explores the opinions of the respondents towards institutional level copyright policy. The third section is about Library and Information Science education. The last section gathers demographic information including age, gender and educational and professional experience of the respondents.

According to the objectives of the study we have selected a sample that includes academic, scientific and institutional libraries, administrative public archives and museums. With the previous criteria we obtained a sample of 960 possible respondents to whom the questionnaire was sent during the month of July of 2016. We received a total of 325 responses, 225 of which were completely filled out, 243 emails were returned. Close-ended questions were analyzed using descriptive statistics including frequency counts and percentages, while open-ended questions were coded using a content analysis. The data was analyzed statistically with IBM SPSS Statistics.

3 Results

3.1 Respondents Profile

We obtained 191 responses in this section. A higher percentage of survey respondents were female (64.9%) compared to male (35.1%). With respect to age, the largest group (55.0%) is in the range between 50 to 60 years, followed by those between 40–49 years (30.9%), while between 30 to 39 years there is only a 7.9%, a point above those over 60 years old. We found that (52.6%) respondents had a connection to the institution where they how had worked for 20 years or more, while 16.8% who worked under 10 years.

The majority of respondents work in libraries (83.5%): academic libraries (57.4%), specialized research libraries (16.5%), and 9.0% in other types of public libraries. Some of the respondents (9.6%) came from professors of LIS, archives (3.7%) and museums (1.6%).

With respect to the highest degree that respondents have, we found that 63.8% have a bachelor's degree, 16.8% possess a master's level diploma and other 16.8% have a PhD. Regarding training areas, most of the sample (45.8%) studied Library Science, 35.8% History Science. Archive science, Cultural Heritage science and Museology are poorly represented, respectively 9.5%, 7.4% and 3.7%.

3.2 Knowledge and Awareness of Copyright

In the first part of the questionnaire, we intended to gather data about general knowledge and opinions of copyright. On a five-point Likert scale ranging from 1 ("not at all familiar") to 5 ("extremely familiar"), the ideal scenario would be that most respondents would reply that they are "very familiar" or "moderately familiar" with the different questions. We represented in Fig. 1 the six aspects of copyright meet this criterion: 55% of participants are familiar with national copyright law; open access, open data, open educational resources (61%); creative commons licenses (56%);

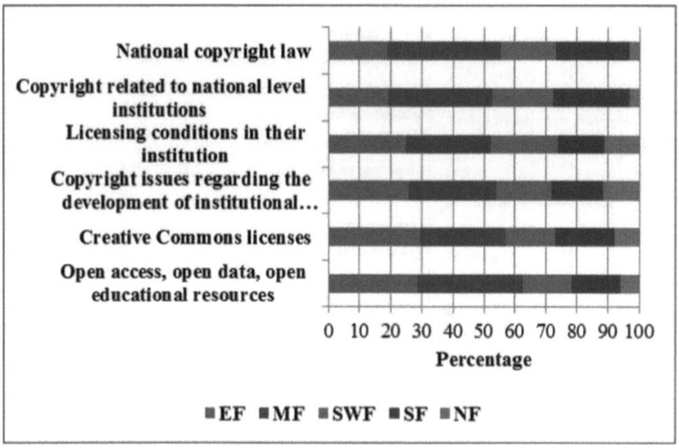

Fig. 1. Level of knowledge and awareness. (NF) = Not Familiar, (LF) = Slightly Familiar, (SWF) = Somewhat Familiar, (MF) = Moderate Familiar, (EF) = Extremely Familiar

copyright issues regarding the development of institutional repositories (54%); copyright related to national level institutions and licensing conditions in their institution (52%). Least familiar topics that include "slightly and no familiarity" responses were: clearing rights (69%); international institutions (53%) and regulation and international institutions (52%). Most respondents (68.2%) described themselves as "extremely or moderately aware" of copyright and intellectual property (IPR) issues. Only 0.9% of respondents were 'not aware at all' of copyright and IPR issues.

The next question of the survey asked respondents where they went to get information about copyright issues. The three top places for information about copyright and its relation to their work are books and articles on the subject (67%), colleagues (60%) and websites (56%). In a smaller proportion there are included, experts from the academic and scientific community (36%), national library and other professional associations (36%), the World Intellectual Property Organization (WIPO) (33%), professional discussion lists (29%) and the International Federation of Library Associations (IFLA) (27.9%). Regarding other resource, Fig. 2 displays the most and least commonly consulted resources.

On the question of the interest in the initiatives of international and national library and other professional associations on issues related to copyright, the respondents can be defined as interested (35.1%), or very much interest (34.6%).

The survey also asked if there was a national strategy for copyright in Spain, and 47.6% of respondents were sure of its existence and 35.6% were uncertain. However, in Spain, there is no formally stablished strategy and it is possible that they confuse strategy with law.

Concerning the national copyright legislation, most respondents (95.7%) knew well the duration of copyright protection, exceptions for private use (82.3%), and exceptions for libraries and educational institutions (84.7%). Only 31.5% of the respondents were

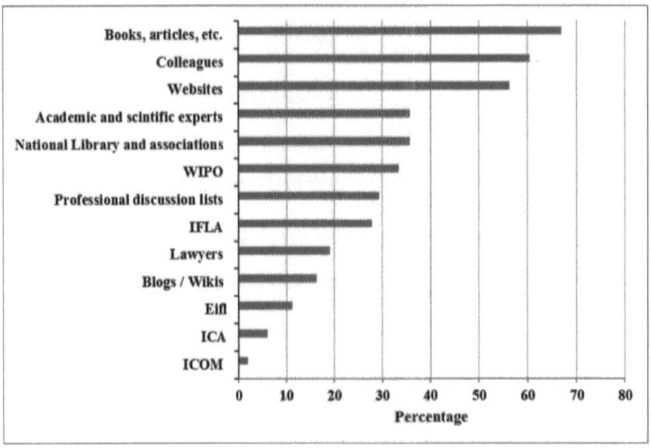

Fig. 2. Copyright information resources consulted by respondents

aware of the existence of the rights for librarians to provide modified copies of works serving the needs of visual impaired patrons. With respect to orphan works (e.g. compulsory license or limitation of liability), only 56.2% of respondents knew its existence (see Fig. 3).

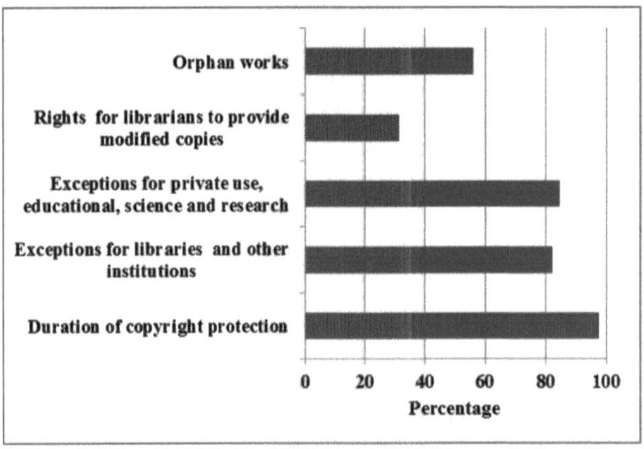

Fig. 3. Issues included in national copyright legislation

Awareness of international copyright initiatives, such as the work of IFLA and eIFL are well known in Spain because 85.9% of respondents were aware of these. Finally, we asked respondents to give their personal opinion with four statements about global copyright policy. 85.9% of respondents agreed with the first statement that library and cultural heritage services should comply with copyright legislation. With respect to the second statement 87.4% of respondents agreed that the World Intellectual Property Organization (WIPO) Treaty to Facilitate Access to Published Works for

Persons who are Blind, Visually Impaired, or otherwise Print Disabled was an important achievement. For the third statement 75.4% of respondents agreed that WIPO should define better exceptions and limitations to copyright in the digital environment. Only 58.8% agreed with the statement that worldwide harmonization of exceptions and limitations to copyright for libraries and archives are necessary.

3.3 Copyright Policy at Institutional Level

In this section the survey explores copyright issues and policies at an institutional level and responses to these are summarized in Fig. 4. Of the respondents 88.3% answered that their organization possesses copyright protected resources and only 5.1% were not sure, and the majority of them (88%) thought institutional copyright policies are necessary for libraries and cultural institutions, only 9.1% never thought about it. Despite the above results, only 33.5% have a copyright policy or internal regulations in their institution, compared to 36% who lack it. Similar percentages are obtained from the question of whether there is a person in charge of questions dealing with copyright issues, 38.6% of respondents said there was a specific person in their institution, compared with 35% that does not have and 26% that are not aware.

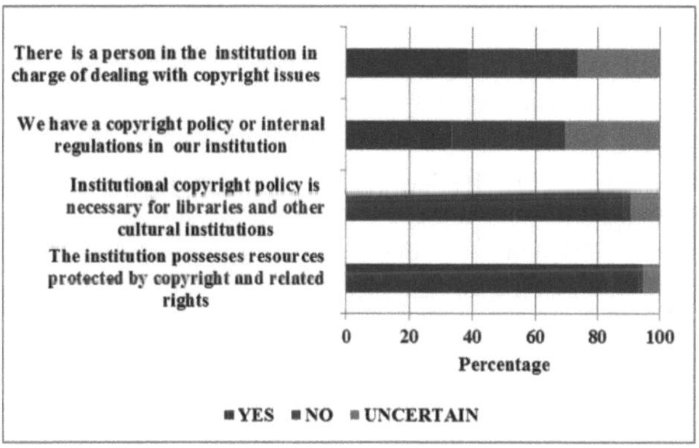

Fig. 4. Copyright policies at institutional level

3.4 Copyright and Education

Almost all of the respondents (96.4%) are in favor of including copyright issues in the curriculum of Library and Information Science Education as well as in continuing professional development (97%). For the question concerning the appropriate level of education to introduce intellectual property, the majority of respondents considered undergraduate level the most appropriated (92.3), followed by master's (50%) and PhD curricula (37.2%).

Figure 5 shows the preferred forms for continuing education on intellectual property and copyright. Training courses is the most popular (cited by 88.5% of respondents), followed by distance learning (65.4%), thematic electronic resources - websites, blogs, wikis, etc. (56%) and thematic workshops (50.8%).

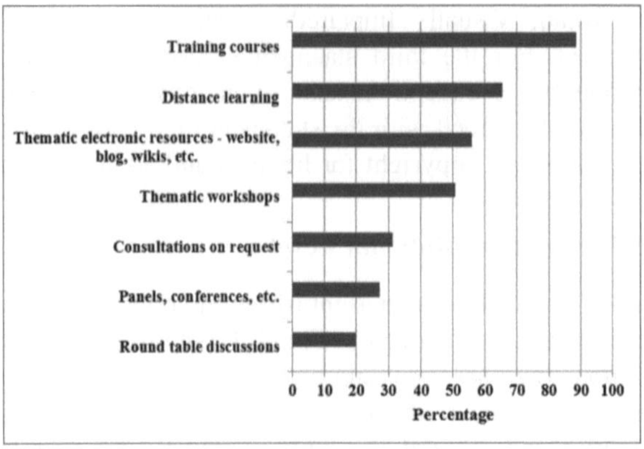

Fig. 5. Preferred forms for continuing education

4 Discussion and Comparisons with Other Countries

In Spain Muriel [8] studies in 2012 the level of copyright knowledge of 25 university librarians, however, it is difficult to make comparisons between both studies due to the difference between objectives, survey questions and answer scales used. Therefore, in this section we will make a comparison between our results and those obtained in countries with similar legislation and library system. These countries are France [4], United Kingdom [2] and Portugal [5]. The main differences between our study and those countries are, in the first place, average age was higher in Spain, most people (55.0%) are between 50 to 60 years old and only 7.9% are below 39 years old. These data appeared to be consistent with the answers to the question about how long the respondents had worked at their current institution. We found that (52.6%) respondents had a connection to the institution where they had worked for 20 years or more. Likewise, in our sample the percentage of people belonging to academic and research libraries is higher than France [4] and Portugal [5] and similar to the UK [2].

In second place, in relation with knowledge and awareness of copyright, levels of copyright literacy appear to be higher in Spain with 68.2% of respondents being either extremely or moderately aware of copyright and IPR issues compared to the other countries. In third place, whit regard to copyright policies within institutions, the two most important differences are, first only 33.5% of Spanish respondent indicate that have a copyright policy or internal regulations in their institution, a similar percentage is obtained in France (34.3%) compared with 63% in UK [2]. Second, 64% of UK respondents had a person responsible for copyright, compared with Spain (38.6%) and France [4] (18.6%)

In fourth place, in relation to copyright education, 92.3% of Spanish respondents thought it should be included in undergraduate curricula for LIS professionals, compared with France [4] (70.2%), Portugal [5] (81.3%) and similar to UK [2] (90%).

5 Conclusions

This study presents the opinion of librarians, archivists, documentalists and directors of museums of their knowledge with various aspects of copyright and intellectual property. The results suggest that the levels of copyright literacy in Spain are, in fact, moderately good in relation to knowledge of Spanish legislation and institutions and awareness of international copyright initiatives. However, many institutions still do not have a copyright policy or adequate resources for their management. Respect to training almost all of the respondents are in favor of including copyright issues in the curriculum of LIS, as well as increase the offer in continuing education.

In conclusion, we think that it is necessary to increase information and knowledge of copyright issues in the sector, since copyright issues are already and will continue to be in the future, even more relevant part of information professional's expertise, and this is emphasized by the need to educate students in this respect

References

1. Todorova, T., Trencheva, T., Kurbanoğlu, S., Doğan, G., Horvat, A., Boustany, J.: A multinational study on copyright literacy competencies of LIS professionals. In: Kurbanoğlu, S., Špiranec, S., Grassian, E., Mizrachi, D., Catts, R. (eds.) ECIL 2014. CCIS, vol. 492, pp. 138–148. Springer, Cham (2014). https://doi.org/10.1007/978-3-319-14136-7_15
2. Secker, J., Morrison, C.: Copyright literacy in the UK: results from a survey of library and information professionals. In: Kurbanoğlu, S., Boustany, J., Špiranec, S., Grassian, E., Mizrachi, D., Roy, L. (eds.) ECIL 2015. CCIS, vol. 552, pp. 191–201. Springer, Cham (2015). https://doi.org/10.1007/978-3-319-28197-1_20
3. Kortelainen, T.: Copyright literacy in finnish libraries, archives and museums. In: Kurbanoğlu, S., Boustany, J., Špiranec, S., Grassian, E., Mizrachi, D., Roy, L. (eds.) ECIL 2015. CCIS, vol. 552, pp. 202–209. Springer, Cham (2015). https://doi.org/10.1007/978-3-319-28197-1_21
4. Boustany, J.: Copyright literacy of librarians in France. In: Kurbanoğlu, S., Špiranec, S., Grassian, E., Mizrachi, D., Catts, R. (eds.) ECIL 2014. CCIS, vol. 492, pp. 91–100. Springer, Cham (2014). https://doi.org/10.1007/978-3-319-14136-7_10
5. Terra, A.L.: Copyright literacy competencies from portuguese LIS professionals. In: Kurbanoğlu, S., Boustany, J., Špiranec, S., Grassian, E., Mizrachi, D., Roy, L., Çakmak, T. (eds.) ECIL 2016. CCIS, vol. 676, pp. 634–643. Springer, Cham (2016). https://doi.org/10.1007/978-3-319-52162-6_62
6. Fernández-Molina, J.C., Muriel, E., Vives-Gracia, J., Riera, P., Martín, O.: Copyright and e-learning: professors' level of knowledge about the new Spanish law. In: Aslib Proceedings: New Information Perspectives, vol. 63, no. 4, pp. 340–353 (2011)
7. Muriel-Torrado, E.: Los Derechos de Autor y la Enseñanza en la Universidad: el Papel de la Biblioteca Universitaria. (Doctoral dissertation) University of Granada, Granada (2012)
8. Muriel-Torrado, E., Fernández-Molina, J.C.: Creation and use of intellectual works in the academic environment: students' knowledge about copyright and copyleft. J. Acad. Librariansh. **41**(4), 441–448 (2015)

Intellectual Property Training of Library and Information Management Bachelor's Students

Tereza Trencheva, Tania Todorova(✉), and Elisaveta Tsvetkova

University of Library Studies and Information Technologies, Sofia, Bulgaria
{t.trencheva, t.todorova, e.cvetkova}@unibit.bg

Abstract. University of Library Studies and Information Technologies (ULSIT) has contributed to the successful dissemination of knowledge in Intellectual Property (IP) field, as there are already 20 years of experience in IP courses for non-lawyers. Although the importance of IP training for the Library and Information Science (LIS) students and professionals is recognized, a study of copyright literacy of specialists from the library and other cultural institutions conducted in Bulgaria in 2013, highlighted serious gaps in the knowledge, awareness and inability of the professionals to deal with copyright issues arising in real work environments. The report presents own *Educational IP model for LIS students at ULSIT*, implemented in the Bachelor's Program "Library and Information Management" from AY 2013/2014 up to now, as an answer on the established knowledge gap.

Keywords: Intellectual property training · LIS higher education Bachelor's degree · Copyright literacy

1 Introduction

In the modern era, called "information society" (already transformed as a knowledge society), we have witnessed the rapid development of human intellectual activity, with the result that produces unique creative goods, products of the personal creativity and innovativeness of the human mind. Specifically this kind of creative goods promote the development of İntellectual Property (IP).

In the theoretical literature there are many IP definitions and interpretations, which are constantly evolving with the technology change. IP by itself, very broadly means the legal rights which result from intellectual activity in the industrial, scientific, literary and artistic fields. Generally speaking, IP Law aims to safeguard creators and other producers of intellectual goods and services by granting them certain time-limited rights to control the use, made of those productions. Those rights do not apply to the physical objects in which the creation may be embodied but instead to the intellectual creation as such.

According to Borisova, Intellectual Property is "property, but not on items of material nature, and upon an intellectual achievements inherently with intangible nature, the so-called intellectual property objects" [1, p. 9]. IP rights must be seen as

S. Kurbanoğlu et al. (Eds.): ECIL 2017, CCIS 810, pp. 294–302, 2018.
https://doi.org/10.1007/978-3-319-74334-9_31

objective and subjective right courses and science. On IP rights, as objectively existing law, in the legal science there is no single opinion. The new information environment imposes new requirements on the competences and adequate knowledge of modern young professionals, who graduated their higher education.

Krasteva summarizes that “this is especially true for the professional fields related to information and social sciences, as currently these sciences are one of the most dynamically developing” [2, p. 108]. The main spheres of realization of the information specialists are: regional and national media, governmental and non-governmental organizations and institutions, and the use of information resources is the basis of their professional activity and condition for their successful realization, they need to be well informed on the IP protection issues. The copyright competence is an essential part of the students’ information literacy in this professional field, especially in terms of Internet usage and digital content.

2 Literature Review

The body of literature on IP/copyright literacy of information professionals and about copyright academic and Continuing Professional Development (CPD) education is substantial and will not be reviewed in depth here. This review will highlight some of the basic documents, initiatives and publications in the field, including: Crews book “Copyright Law for Librarians and Educators” and his updated and revised “Study on copyright limitations and exceptions for libraries and archives”; the guidance of Russell “Complete Copyright: An Everyday Guide for Librarians”; “The Copyright Librarian: A Practical Handbook” by Frederiksen; the eIFL publications “Developing a Library Copyright Policy”, “Treaty Proposal on Limitations and Exceptions for Libraries and Archives” and “Core library exceptions checklist: Does your library law support library activities and services?”; “eIFL-IP Draft law on copyright including model exceptions and limitations for libraries and consumers” as well as “Copyright for Librarians: The essential handbook” by Berkman Center for Internet and Society at Harvard University and eIFL, and “Copyright and E-learning a guide for practitioners” by Secker and Morrison [3–12].

Althought, the copyright-related issues within the LIS and cultural sector are acknowledged in the literature, the themes such as implementations of copyright education into information literacy programs and integration of copyright and licensing issues into the LIS curriculum are actual and require further attention. This was confirmed by Schmidt and English, who investigated in 2013/2014 the copyright/IP instruction in ALA-accredited LIS programs in the USA against practitioner needs of copyright/IP knowledge by comparing LIS course descriptions with survey data from practitioners. They concluded that although recent graduates of LIS programs in the USA are more likely to have had instruction on copyright/IP issues, this instruction is not widespread enough, nor in depth enough to prepare LIS program graduates for the current demands of the workplace [13].

3 Background, Hypotheses and Motivation

University of Library Studies and Information Technologies (ULSIT) has contributed to the successful dissemination of IP knowledge, as there are already 20 years of experience in IP courses for non-laweyers. ULSIT's contribution to the research of IP awareness in information and social sciences is indisputable, considering two projects that are fully focused on the research of future professionals and practitioners. The first one was a survey conducted in 2012 at nine Bulgarian universities (accredited in the professional fields of information and social sciences), which explored the IP awareness among the students as whole. The survey results showed that the students opinion is that IP training is very important and useful for their study and work [17]. Although that importance of training in the IP field for the Library and Information Science (LIS) students and professionals is recognized, the study of copyright literacy of specialists from the library and other cultural institutions, conducted in Bulgaria in 2013, highlighted serious gaps in the knowledge and awareness, and the inability of the professionals to deal with the copyright issues arising in the real working environment [14]. The unsatisfactory level of the copyright literacy of Bulgarian professionals is highlighted in the comparison with the results of a survey among their colleagues from other countries [15].

As an answer on the established knowledge gap, we designed *Educational IP model for LIS students at ULSIT.*

The hypotheses is that: As the main spheres of realization of the LIS future specialists are: libraries, information centers and other cultural institutions, regional and national media, governmental and non-governmental organizations (or with other words – public institutions), and the use of information resources is the basis of their professional activity and condition for their successful realization, they need to be well informed on the issues of the IP protection.

In the process of preparation of the *Educational IP model for LIS students at ULSIT*, we follow some basic conclusions and motivations. *First,* we are convinced that for optimizing the role and quality of library and information education in preparing future professionals in library, information and cultural affairs, according to the new demands of the information and digital reality, and copyright and legal issues - it is important for LIS students to be knowledgeable in the IP field as early as possible during their formal education and to have the sustained development throughout all educational levels [16]. The *second* important factor is that the educational profile of ULSIT is directly related to the dissemination of information and knowledge. Therefore, professional knowledge, skills and experience that students receive during their training are similar to the necessary dissemination of information and knowledge in the IP field. That makes them prepared to work in this area. *Third*, another focus is important, namely, that the object of learning in ULSIT includes a wide range of information products, services, equipment and technologies that are inherently intellectual products and it is logical that students have a good understanding of their IP issues. Therefore, the inclusion of IP matters in the students' curricula in all subjects is natural and necessary, and therefore the efforts are directed towards its realization. *Fourth*, it can be said with conviction that this is the opinion of the students who definitely are interested and willing to acquire more knowledge in IP - an area perceived as modern, relevant and useful. Indicative of this is the fact that each year more students from different disciplines and levels of study write a bachelors' or master's thesis on IP rights, which are successfully defended [17].

4 Educational IP Model for LIS Students at ULSIT

In a knowledge based economy, experts who can interpret IP issues, such as librarians and information specialists are seen as essential. They are responsible for creating a policies of promoting, understanding and resolving legal disputes and conflicts that are unique to this aspect of the Information Society. The way to achieve this is through the educational impact of the IP curriculum. IP can be considered as an information literacy element in university information environment, so to develop successfuly students at the university, and in life, they must learn to use efficiently and effectively the wide variety of information and communication technologies for searching, finding, organizing, analyzing and evaluating the information they need [18].

We developed own *Educational IP model for LIS students at ULSIT* and implemented it in the Bachelor's Program "Library and Information Management" at Library Management Department from AY 2013/2014 up to now. For the needs of this specialty, we have updated the curriculum and prepared the following obligatory courses – "*Intellectual Property*" and "*Digitization and Copyright*" and we also offered elective courses – "*Intellectual Property in Internet*" and "*Law, Media and Advertising*".

4.1 Intellectual Property

The learning outcome of the "*Intellectual Property*" course is for students to obtain the necessary theoretical and practical training for the objects of IP rights and ensure their protection. In the *first module* Legal and Institutional framework at National, European and International level is presented, which will have a particular significance for their implementation in different areas of the modern information society. *The second module* presents the rich variety of IP goods in the fields of literature, art and science, as objects of copyright which are presented from the perspective of holders' rights and their duration, of the moral and material rights of the author, the uses of works and the protection of these rights. The industrial property is represented by inventions, utility models, industrial designs, geographical indications and different types of brands, trademarks, service marks and others. Official publications, institutions, funds and databases, including those on the Internet, through which one can find information about them are presented in *the third module.*

As can be seen from the content of the course, by itself it's basic and aims to introduce the students the wide spectrum of IP objects. IP objects are presented in an attractive way, through a lot of examples which are part of the everyday work of the library specialists. During the seminars students have to be prepared for discussion of different case studies, taken from actual practice. During the semester each student must prepare a presentation according a concrete case study of their choice. Verification of students' knowledge is ongoing throughout the semester and by examination-test. The final score is the average of the monitoring during the semester and evaluation of the exam.

4.2 Digitization and Copyright

In this course topical issues arising over the digitization of cultural heritage, the status of digital resources and observance for copyright, the development of large-scale digitization projects in the U.S. and Europe, the activities of libraries in implementing the digital conversion of cultural materials and on the need of implementation of National Strategy for digitization of cultural and literary heritage – compile the trouble range of the *first module*. The learning content aimed to help the future professionals in the construction of library policies, in accordance with the requirements of the copyright and related rights law in the offering of library services and resources. The current legislative standards and new proposals on exceptions and limitations of copyright for libraries, schools, museums and archives are summarized in the *second module*. It emphasizes the role of libraries as creators of digital content, as gateways for access to digitized information and as a factor in overcoming the digital divide and isolation. The course summarizes the positions of library organizations IFLA, EBLIDA, LIBER, ALA, eIFL etc. and their interaction with the World Intellectual Property Organization (WIPO) and the European Commission in defending the interests of libraries and their users in preparing changes to information legislation, who aimed placing the management of copyright in line with the digital technologies and expand use of Internet. Each module ends with a current assessment, which evaluates the student's involvement in the learning process and class discussions. As final exam task, students are also required to prepare a course work, based on a case study for Bulgarian or foreign cultural institution - examining issues concerning institutional strategies for digitization and institutional copyright policy. The outcomes from the course are that students acquire knowledge and competences to develop successful strategic management in digitization and develop and apply copyright policy in cultural institutions.

4.3 Intellectual Property in Internet

This elective course requires prior knowledge and skills from the previous training course "*Intellectual Property*". The main task of the course is to give students the necessary specialized theoretical and practical training for the management of IP in the digital space. The main task of the *first* module, entitled "*Identification of IP Objects on the Internet*" is: to present İnternet access to IP objects and to clarify copyright powers in the use of works on the Internet. The main task of the second module "*Institutional and Regulatory Framework of IP on the Internet*" is: to reveal the International, European and Bulgarian legislation by relevant documents like WIPO Internet Treaties, EU Directives and Conventions of the Council of Europe and the Bulgarian laws. The institutional framework of the three levels in the areas of IP of information resources on the Internet space are presented, too. The main task of the third module "*Models for the Protection of Intellectual Property on the Internet*" is: to learn how to acquire the right to use works on the Internet - through individual contract or negotiating on a collective basis (through organizations for collective management of copyright). The main methods and structures to build the system for digital copyright management, known as DRM, are shown as equally applicable to individual and collective forms of rights management. This module traces the appearance its applications since 2001 contracts for open access, known as the Creative Commons (CC), and are presented with details and their variations, with the opportunity for adequate implementation by the authors on copyright protection [19]. Teaching is done in an auditorium that includes computers with secure access to the Internet. The teaching is illustrated with concrete examples from practice. Most topics explored are accompanied by demonstration of search capabilities and specific features in generating online contracts. Assessment of students' knowledge is done both throughout the semester and by passing a test.

4.4 Law, Media and Advertising

The course "*Law, Media and Advertising*" provides students with knowledge of the legal framework of the print and electronic media at International, European and National levels. Students acquire specific knowledge regarding the protection of copyright in the creative works and the related rights of the producers and broadcasting organizations, as well as their management and operations.

Emphasis is placed on ethics and responsibilities for working in the media and on forms of IP protection in the presence of disturbances. Sources of advertising in the print and electronic media, such as legal subjects are also covered. They acquire knowledge about the peculiarities of the sources of advertising belonging to the groups of objects of IP for material and moral rights and the duration of ownership. Students get acquainted with the basics of law, and they acquire skills to use legal documents for searching from within the huge flow of information and to comply with their updates. The course is an elective and the assesment of the students' knowledge is by writing a course paper according the course contents in a concrete case study.

5 Other Activities for Informal and Upgrading IP Training

Methodology of teaching the students includes lectures and seminars, interactive and situational methods, application of the approach "learning by doing" and "edutainment", which activates the students' participation. Individual forms of work such as term papers, presentations, individual assignments, communication in e-learning platforms - support the learning process and the current assessment of students' knowledge. Library Management Department features with the active involvement of students in research projects and joint research papers for participation at scientific conferences and symposiums. There are two initiatives in the Library Management Department, which are directed to informal and upgrading IP training of students.

One of them is the work of students in relation to the *Week Dedicated to The International Day of the Book and Copyright Day (23 April)*, where students take part in the organization of this initiative and have the opportunity to publish their first scientific research in the thematic research collection [20].

Also, there is an established tradition in the celebration of the *World Intellectual Property Day (26th April)* as an annually conducted professional forum. The theme of the seminar is determined after the announcement of the slogan from the WIPO. The slogan of the seminar in 2013 was "Creativity: The Next Generation", the slogan for 2014 was "Movies: The Global Passion", the slogan for 2015 was "Intellectual Property – Formula for Success, Creativity and Innovation", the slogan for 2016 was "Internet Liberalization - Formula for Success, Creativity and Innovation", and for 2017 the theme of the seminar was "Intellectual Property, Innovation and Research in a Global Environment". The annual seminar aims to popularize issues directly affecting copyright competence of future library managers, and to become an annual professional forum for the exchange of views, ideas and meetings with prominent experts in the IP field. It is a method to enrich the theoretical knowledge with practical aspects and meeting the academic community with professionals from practice and with leading external experts. The seminars and the published proceedings are always welcomed with great interest by students, professionals, practitioners and those interested in the issues non-specialists lawyers [21].

6 Conclusion

The main aim of the *Educational IP model for LIS students at ULSIT* is for the students to study IP in all educational levels: bachelor, master and doctorate, and in the different forms of education: full time, part time and distance. The teaching methodology combined traditional methods together with informal and upgrading IP training approach. Evaluating our four years of experiences, we need improvement and coordination on the international level. We are interested on the foreign best practices and models for education on copyright, licensing, and other legal issues within the scope of information literacy programs. In this direction, two activities are in realization in 2017.

In May 2017, ULSIT joined the multinational research team for the implementation of the *Copyright Literacy Survey for LIS (Library and Information Science) students (CoLIS)*. The main aim of the survey is to collect data about knowledge, opinions, and experiences of LIS students regarding copyright policies and related issues. Findings will help us to identify better the gaps in the curricula and will allow us to formulate more solid suggestions for improvements.

Also, how to improve the copyright education in LIS field is the on-going discussion, focused on the in-coming professional events in 2017. Our research team will participate in the international symposium on theme "Copyright Literacy and the role of librarians as educators" at ECIL 2017 (European Conference on Information Literacy) and in the Offsite Session "Models for Copyright Education in Information Literacy Programs" for IFLA Congress 2017. This offsite session will be devoted to methodologies for providing a comprehensive knowledge of the legal landscape for copyright, licensing, and related legal and policy issues in libraries and universities [22].

References

1. Borisova, V.: Intellectual Property and Property. University Publishing House Economy, Sofia (2010). (in Bulgarian)
2. Krasteva, R.: Awareness and attitudes of the young people towards the protection of intellectual property on the internet. In: Turnovo, V. (ed.) 10th National Scientific Conference Books-Reading-Comunication, pp. 108–112 (2013). (in Bulgarian)
3. Crews, K.: Copyright Law for Librarians and Educators. ALA, Chicago (2012)
4. Crews, K.: Study on copyright limitations and exceptions for libraries and archives: updated and revised. In: WIPO, Geneva (2015)
5. Russell, C.: Complete Copyright: An Everyday Guide for Librarians. ALA, Chicago (2004)
6. Frederiksen, L.: The Copyright Librarian: A Practical Handbook. Chandos Publishing, Amsterdam (2016)
7. Developing a Library Copyright Policy: An eIFL Guide. eIFL (2012). http://www.eifl.net/english-developing-library-copyright-policy
8. Treaty Proposal on Copyright Limitations and Exceptions for Libraries and Archives: Version 4.3. IFLA (2012). http://www.ifla.org/files/assets/hq/topics/exceptions-limitations/documents/TLIB_v4.3_050712.pdf
9. Core library exceptions checklist: does your library law support library activities and services? eIFL (2016). http://www.eifl.net/system/files/resources/201607/core_library_checklist_online.pdf
10. eIFL-IP Draft Law on Copyright Including Model Exceptions and Limitations for Libraries and Consumers. Based on WIPO Draft Law on Copyright and Related Rights (version 2005): Recommendations by eIFL. EIFL (2016). http://www.eifl.net/sites/default/files/resources/201605/eifl_draft_law_2016_online.pdf
11. Copyright for Librarians: The Esential Handbook. Berkman Center for Internet and Society at Harvard University and eIFL. eIFL (2012). http://www.eifl.net/system/files/resources/201408/cfl_book_download.pdf
12. Secker, J., Morrison, C.: Copyright and E-learning a Guide for Practitioners, 2nd edn. Facet Publishing, London (2016)
13. Schmidt, L., English, M.: Copyright instruction in LIS programs: report of a survey of standards in the U.S.A. J. Acad. Librariansh. **41**, 736–743 (2015)
14. Todorova, T., Trencheva, T.: Copyright literacy in memory institutions: findings from scientific research project in Bulgaria. In: Proceedings of the 3th International Conference on New Perspectives in Science Education, pp. 169–172. PIXEL, Florence (2014)
15. Todorova, T., Trencheva, T., Kurbanoğlu, S., Doğan, G., Horvat, A., Boustany, J.: A multinational study on copyright literacy competencies of LIS professionals. In: Kurbanoğlu, S., Špiranec, S., Grassian, E., Mizrachi, D., Catts, R. (eds.) ECIL 2014. CCIS, vol. 492, pp. 138–148. Springer, Cham (2014). https://doi.org/10.1007/978-3-319-14136-7_15
16. Todorova, T., Peteva, I.: Information literacy competency of LIS students in SULSIT with a special focus on intellectual property. In: Kurbanoğlu, S., Grassian, E., Mizrachi, D., Catts, R., Špiranec, S. (eds.) ECIL 2013. CCIS, vol. 397, pp. 610–616. Springer, Cham (2013). https://doi.org/10.1007/978-3-319-03919-0_82
17. Trencheva, T.: The new reality of intellectual property at the State University of Library Studies and Information Technologies: project initiatives. In: 3rd International Conference "The New Perspectives in Science Education", Florence, Italy, pp. 228–231 (2014)
18. Denchev, S., Trencheva, T.: Intellectual property as a basic part of the University's Information Literacy. In: 2nd International Conference on Education and Management Science (ICEMS 2016), Beijing, China, pp. 74–78 (2016)

19. Trencheva, T.: Intellectual Property in Internet. Za bukvite – Oh pismeneh, Sofia (2014). (in Bulgarian)
20. Parijkova, L. (compl.): The Book – Our More Sensual Present. Za bukvite – Oh pismeneh, Sofia (2014). (in Bulgarian)
21. Trencheva, T. (compl.): Internet Liberalization - Intellectual Property Challenges and Best Practices. Za bukvite – Oh pismeneh, Sofia (2016). (in Bulgarian)
22. Models for Copyright Education in Information Literacy Programs, 23 August 2017, IFLA Offsite Session (2017). https://uwm.edu/informationstudies/research/partnerships/models-for-copyright-education

From Academic Plagiarism to Information Literacy: Mediation in the Ethical Use of Information

Máximo Román Domínguez-López(✉) and Claudia Escobar-Vallarta

Daniel Cosío Villegas Library, The College of Mexico, Mexico City, Mexico
{mrdominguez, cescobar}@colmex.mx

Abstract. This work explores the institutional strategies performed to combat academic plagiarism in Mexican higher education by pursuing two specific aims: 1. To know the role of Mexican university libraries in the processes linked to prevent academic plagiarism; 2. Identify the skills related to copyright and intellectual property pertaining to university librarians. The methodology used is a descriptive and exploratory study of four public universities that offers education in social sciences and humanities located in Mexico City. Information was obtained through a survey of the librarians (data concerning to skills, knowledge and attitudes) and the content revision of information literacy courses or workshops provided by them. Finally, the relation between the librarian's responsibility to restrain this dishonest activity and to promote information literacy, towards achieving the ethical use of information is analyzed.

Keywords: Academic plagiarism · Copyright · Information literacy
Ethical use of information

1 Introduction

In Mexico, academic plagiarism is a matter that has taken greater relevance in recent years due to its incidence at different academic levels; according to Morales [1], plagiarism is a practice that: "has increasingly proliferated, regarding the intellectual creations of scientific, humanistic, technical, pedagogical or educational character, at all levels, [by] teachers and researchers as well as students seeking their doctoral degree". Plagiarism is a phenomenon directly related to the degree of originality of the author and the personality[1] that imprints its creation, however, what strategies or mechanisms are made in Mexican universities to stop or deal with this dishonest practice? Even more, what's the role of the libraries and their librarians facing this important problem affecting the educational sector.

To face this problem, academic and university libraries have had to developed new severe strategies regarding information skills. Actions taken in the library field have

---

[1] Assumed as the characteristic that attach the author with his work, that is, the work has characteristics of the author, either by style or originality, Copyright in Latin America "Personality" is so important that there is a moral right that is inseparable and cannot be waived.

S. Kurbanoğlu et al. (Eds.): ECIL 2017, CCIS 810, pp. 303–312, 2018.
https://doi.org/10.1007/978-3-319-74334-9_32

been reinforced with the development and implementation of various literacy efforts and information skills, particularly directed to new students on how to use information, correct citations, textual quotations, plagiarism in the web environment, among other topics [2]. Through this the students realize many of the economic, legal, and social issues surrounding the use of information, aware of the access and the ethical and legal use of information: "This involves an understanding of risk, an understanding that there are not fixed rules around copyright in many areas, and that it is not their role to sanction and police others' behavior but to work towards mutually satisfactory solutions" [3].

Is also important to analyze the relation between the responsibility of the librarian to stop this dishonest activity and to promote information literacy, to achieve the ethical use of information and their success on its academic trajectory.

2 Academic Plagiarism and its Relationship with Copyright

Among its different meanings, the Dictionary of the Spanish Language, defines plagiarism[2] as the action of stealing, deceiving or copying other people's works[3]. Focusing only on the copy of other works, and leaving aside other elements useful to conceptualize the term, however, in this sense the University of Berkeley, points that academic plagiarism "is defined as the use of intellectual material produced by another person without recognize its source" [4]. Plagiarism is the lack of personal accountability to accredit someone's authorship in a work. Hence the relationship with copyright, because it protects all work fixed in[4] a material medium if it is original[5]. The lack of originality and paternity of a work is then understood as plagiarism, since in theory the plagiarist has no attribution or faculty to recognize authorship over the work. In this context, the following quotation can clarify the act of the plagiary: "Plagiarism is the opposite of absolute originality, but it is born of the same dream. The plagiarist also aspires to the masterpiece. But he is so empty of himself as he believes, that is able to become another, cutting moorings with his 'internal self', rejecting any reference to himself… he also runs the risk of getting lost" [5, p. 371].

In summary, the characteristics of academic plagiarism are related to:

---

[2] From lat., plagium 'action of stealing slaves', 'action to buy or sell free people as slaves', and the gr. Πλάγιος plagiarism 'oblique', 'trickster, misleading'. 1. Action and effect of plagiarizing (copying other people's works). http://dle.rae.es.

[3] A profound revision refers to Marcial the poet (I d.), who helped the confusion by using the word "plagiarism" for the first time in his Epigrama L: "I commend Quinciano, my little books… If they complain of their painful slavery, they come to their aid entirely. And when he proclaims himself to be his master, say that they are mine and that they have been released. If you say it loudly three or four times, you will make the *plagiarist* embarrass." From the Greek "plaguis" (oblique, astute) not from the Latin "plague" (coup) [5].

[4] Fixation, accord to Article 6 of the Mexican Copyright Law is the inclusion of letters, numbers, signs, sounds and images in any medium and which are then allowed to be perceived or reproduced.

[5] The core idea of copyright is the originality that a work must have, however, the Mexican Copyright Law is unclear, opposite to the German case where the matter of originality is akin to philosophical questions and the degrees of originality that a work must have.

1. Lack of originality.
2. No relationship of the personality of the author with the work or creation.
3. Non-existence in the protection of Copyright.

It is necessary to point out that, in the historical evolution of copyright in Mexico, the word plagiarism was related to falsification. The falsification consisted of publishing a work or copying a sculpture, paint, etch or musical work without the express authorization of the author, as evidenced by the Law of 1846 and the Civil Code of 1884. Over time, the copyright ceased to be influenced by the French Civil Code, since Mexico still had many laws from the Iberian Peninsula.

It was in the 19th century that the first provisions on copyright emerged during the Independence and the Reform period. These laws were directed to strengthen the freedom of expression and of the press, rather than with the recognition of an author by the creation of a work. The core of these laws was that the author could leave his work protected over thirty years after his death and the heirs would receive economic remuneration. In this sense, the central idea that encompasses copyright during the 19th century is the originality of a work, nevertheless, Mexican law is imprecise and is open to multiple debates, since it only mentions the following: "The works protected by this Law are those of original creation susceptible to being divulged or reproduced in any form or means" [6, Article 3].

But, what can be considered original? How to determine the originality of a work? What characteristics define a work's originality? Are there degrees of originality when performing a work? These questions have not yet been answered by the Mexican Copyright Law, in the copyright field what for some is considered original for the rest could be a mixture of someone else's ideas. On the contrary, the German Copyright Law (Gesetz über Urheberrecht) accurately indicates the protection of intellectual creations, so the work must reflect the personality of the creator and the level of creativity. That is, creation goes beyond a construction, must do with philosophical issues, where there is a spiritual content, therefore, central to the German law, the individuality is a key factor for the protection or not of a work.

Currently the term plagiarism is not included in the Copyright Law in Mexico, however one article is directly related to the integrity of the work. Article 18 mentions that the author always has the faculty of: "respect for his work, opposing any deformation, mutilation or other modification of it, as well as any action or attempt that causes demerit of it or prejudice the reputation of its author" [6, Article 18]. That's why the term plagiarism does not exist in the Mexican Copyright Law, because most conflicts lay on that article and within the integrity of the work. The development of plagiarism, as we know it today, has varied over time and according technological developments, for example, when the printing press was created, the problem consisted mainly of the abuses committed by editors, printers, booksellers and librarians, who did not give proper recognition of the authorship by stealing someone else's work, for his own economic benefit mainly (*The Statute of Anne*). Now a day, there are a variety of types of academic plagiarism, such as:

1. "Full plagiarism: Total copy of the original content without any change. Generally made by people who do not know the subject.

2. Partial plagiarism: The content is a mixture of two or three different sources, presents a high level of wrong paraphrase and synonyms.
3. Minimalist plagiarism: Plagiarist focuses on the ideas, concepts and opinions of the text. For many it's not considered as plagiarism, hence the confusion. It can be assumed as the theft of ideas or reflections of another.
4. Original source citation: Provides information about the source, but omits data or certain information to retrieve the cited text or even gives false references.
5. Self-plagiarism: Perhaps the most debated, lies in the author intentionally deceiving his readers. Uses his own work (totally or partially), presenting the same idea in a different way" [7].

2.1 Use of Information: From Academic Plagiarism to Information Literacy

Academic plagiarism deals with the use of information, that is, an activity of dishonest appropriation of the ideas or fragments of a work without the proper recognition of the author. Consequently, the ethical use of information has a parallel development to the evolution of the Information Literacy (IL) concept, since Paul Zurkowski defined IL as the use of techniques and skills necessary to use a wide range of information tools and solve a requirement or need for information. According to Zurkowski, "People who have been trained in the application of information resources to their work can be considered literate, competent in information. They have acquired the necessary techniques and skills for the use of the wide range of documentary tools, in addition to primary sources, in proposing informational solutions to their problems" [8].

In this sense, the use of information refers to mental processes, reasoning and principles of ideation[6]. The ethical use of information has been approached from different perspectives and disciplines, such as psychology, sociology, librarianship, administration, among others, as a multidisciplinary area of study. However, there are still terminological inconsistencies. To set up the concept of ethical use, it is necessary refer to Todd [9] who makes a clear assessment of what the use of information is, prior to focusing on the ethical use of information. Use of information, refers to a process of change, approaching on the individual and its cognitions, about "doing something with the information" [9]. A more integral process, that is not framed within the theoretical models of search and retrieval of information, which we are usually familiar with, is a procedure involving the performance of cognitive interaction with information. Here is where the basic principle of copyright begins, in the creation and ideation, to later fix it in a material support.

Wingens [10], mentions the lack of theory regarding the use of information, although there is some research based on generalizations and empirical facts, furthermore in the librarianship developed in Spanish language, exists a controversy on the term "use of information", and the inconsistency of it on its use in the specialized

[6] Ideation is the beginning of any creation of the author and the beginning of the process of designing a work. Ideas in copyright are not protected, however, protection begins when that idea is embodied in a material medium. However, it is important to mention the transcendence of ideation in the process of creating an intellectual work.

literature. When addressing the term of the use of information, it focuses more on the search and retrieval of information bound in libraries and catalogs, rather than the actual "use" of it.

For librarians in Latin America, the law that is framed is the "Right of Author" and not the Copyright, where they substantially change the way of defining the author's moral rights. In short, the use of information is linked with techniques, skills and abilities to use information tools, and with the learning of a person to recognize and identify the correct practices to solve a problem of information. That said, the approach of the librarian teaching activities has developed different strategies ranging from instruction, user training, and development of informational skills to the information literacy.

2.2 Ethical Use of Information; Challenges and Perspectives in Mexican University Libraries

The university library plays an important role on this matter; society expects it to proceed with efficiency and rigor for the recognition of intellectual property, mainly through the sanction of committed cases and the prevention of future omissions: "There is no doubt that every person should have the exercise of their cultural and educational rights guaranteed, both to inform themselves and to express themselves, and with full respect for creative freedom, so that universities and research centers must foresee certain mechanisms which inhibit the presentation, publication or distribution of third-party texts as their own works, since they are harmful acts to others work, lacking any intellectual value and that generate a false reality of its origin, content and authorship, the community and with profound social impact" [1, p. 107].

Relevance of plagiarism in the academic field is not new, it goes back to the first texts of Gilgamesh, considered the oldest literary work the world, and with the first Greek philosophers where the pupils claimed authorship of their masters' works who did not support their ideas. In Mexico, Copyright Law implies that academic plagiarism cannot be understated as a "methodological error". For example, university theses and dissertations have automatic protection since one principle of the referred law, is that the protection of the work exists from the moment they are fixed on a material support, regardless of merit, destiny or mode of expression [6, Article 5]. So, there's an automatic shield for the work since no registration is required at the National Institute of Copyright (INDAUTOR for his Spanish acronym). This lack of formality has put many works and their authorship in question, however, and the institution responsible of resolving such conflicts is the INDAUTOR and its experts. Regarding dissertations and thesis, the failure to cite properly this type of document is considered plagiarism and has also legal repercussions Because the work is being made public from the moment of the degree examination (it's no longer unpublished), the author of the plagiarized work can at any time claim its right to integrity.

Technological advances are ahead on the regulation of this matter, from the printing press until the creation of Internet. For instance, the printing press made it possible for large volumes of works to be spread without the author's' permission, that's why *The Statute of Anne* was established in 1710. At present, the extensive use of the Internet has resulted in a proliferation of new practices that facilitates the access, linking copying and paste, creating a debate in the academic field about the convenience of uploading full theses to institutional repositories or if it is really a good idea. The natural question is, how to avoid academic plagiarism if there is a wide access of information through Internet?

To face this problem, the actions taken in the librarian field have meet two aspects of the information skills:

- Literate: Instructional efforts on information skills, designing specialized courses or classes focused on correct citation practices (how to cite properly, textual quotations, direct and indirect quoting, etc.) and other ways to raise awareness on this subject.
- Knowing our community: User studies help to determine the ethical use of information, before implementing a pedagogical effort, it is necessary to make a diagnosis of the student community.

The study carried out an online survey[7] of librarians working on reference service or related with any informational skills activity. The main purpose of the questionnaire was to explore institutional strategies to face academic plagiarism in higher education, developed in university libraries from the four main public metropolitan universities in Mexico City that offer education in the social sciences and the humanities: The National Autonomous University of Mexico (UNAM), The College of Mexico (Colmex), the Metropolitan Autonomous University (UAM), and the Autonomous University of Mexico City (UACM). The survey was intended to obtain data pertaining to skills, knowledge and attitudes related to copyright and the use of information of the librarians working on these universities; as well as a content review on their information literacy programs and other instructional efforts that address the topic. Questions were mostly of the closed type, although being a small sample, some questions were opened looking to gather more information on the subject. According to this, the responses obtained were grouped into topic categories concerning:

Policies of prevention taken by university libraries:

- 50% do not have any strategy to prevent academic plagiarism at the moment
- 60% does not contemplate the prevention of academic plagiarism on their policies
- Not a single library has a microsite regarding the prevention of academic plagiarism
- 100% considers some sanction regarding the academic plagiarism among its community
- Actions to prevent academic plagiarism driven by the libraries:
- 80% do not offer any course, class or seminar intended to prevent academic plagiarism among their community
- Actions that do exist range from: courses (induction, special classes, general), awareness campaigns among the community and the faculty, and the acquisition of software to detect plagiarism
- Types of sanctions when detecting academic plagiarism:
- Guidance
- Analysis of the cases and the documents

[7] See Appendix A.

- Expulsion, among other administrative sanctions
- Knowledge about the subject (by the librarians):
- 80% do not have basic knowledge about copyright
- 100% claims to know about the ethical use of information
- 50% use the APA bibliographic style standards, the rest vary
- 66% are familiar with software that helps detect academic plagiarism
- 66% participate in some action to raise awareness among their community
- 50% do not participate in the process to evaluate actions of this type in their institution
- 66% of librarians are familiar with the Creative Commons licenses
- 100% claims to be familiar with Open Access
- 100% Support the belief that if a document is available in the Internet, does not imply it can be freely taken
- Information resources addressing plagiarism:
- There are no information resources publicly available, about any literacy initiative to prevent academic plagiarism among these libraries and their communities.

The above data shows that Mexican universities in the metropolitan area need to play a more active role to prevent academic plagiarism among their communities, as the present situation can be assumed as a lack of coordinated efforts and communication between the universities and their libraries, leaving the librarian outside the problem. The librarians recognize the necessity of been prepared about copyright to increase the possibility of effective intervention and strengthen the skills required to avoid the problem, since neither the library staff nor their patrons seem to be aware about the mechanisms of prevention, decisions, consequences and penalties regarding academic plagiarism are effective at their institutions.

In the case of The Colmex (Daniel Cosio Villegas Library), librarians have been concerned and involved in the subject, working on facing the problem from within library science. Some of the actions taken by the library that may work as an example took place in 2016, based on the cooperation of their professional staff: A *Workshop* on copyright and digital plagiarism imparted to the Tepeji Technological Library staff. By first providing the basic elements of copyright, and then by collaboration with the group a working tool called "*Plagiometer*", a graphic and didactic material in the form of a table that consists of visualizing the different manifestations of plagiarism hidden in everyday life and that are often confused or unknown by the academic community. This serves as a metric to measure the level of plagiarism, so that the students could recognize some poor practices in the use of the information, and which was the equivalent to what the National Polytechnic Institute did about the violence in Mexico with the "Violentometer"[8]. A *Survey* was also conducted to determine the behavior from the community of The Colmex when searching for information and how to link it with library activities and services. This helped understand the processes in which library staff were not involved. Finally, the institution's *Ethical guidelines* were revised, to have a wider area of action at the time of detecting academic plagiarism,

[8] More information available at: http://www.genero.ipn.mx/materiales_didacticos/paginas/violentometro.aspx.

generating a posture of faculty towards what they expect from the final works and the dissertations. It was also considered to provide the community with tools (software to detect coincidences) and with more involvement in the information services of the library.

For the Colmex Library, there is a clear position and a working path of the institution about the matter, since plagiarism is included on the institution's Ethical principles. Besides, the library has included on their Information Literacy courses for almost ten years ago, topics concerning the ethical use of information and the necessary practices for assuring it, whose treatment has been considered of great relevance by the faculty and the students. In some cases, promoting the adoption of the IL courses due to the interest of the academic programs or their students to obtain that specific knowledge. In this sense, the library decided to use the digital platform Turnitin, to avoid academic plagiarism, and this has been accepted with enthusiasm by the community.

3 Conclusions

Due to academic plagiarism librarians have the opportunity to create new services and make them available to their community, always guided by the ethical principles emanated from their institution and of associations that promote the ethical use of information. Academic plagiarism is a historical problem, however, currently Information and Communication Technologies, and especially the widespread use of the Internet, have modified certain practices in the use of information. Nowadays disseminating digital content is quicker and more effective, so much that sometimes Mexican Copyright does not respond adequately because of their restrictiveness. An effective strategy is to promote the understanding and recognition of the Open Access movements that works towards the free culture of knowledge, such as adopting Creative Commons licenses or using them to generate educational content. The different software to prevent plagiarism, which have been used so little use in the Latin American academy, can be a good ally when to ensure the quality and truthfulness of the work presented by the students. There is a great diversity of them and some are Open Access sources. Being aware of their existence and disseminating them among their community will increase the value that faculty and students give to our daily work.

Mexican librarians must assume a leading role as the ambassadors of practices and strategies which prevent plagiarism, alerting their community about the different ways in which plagiarism might occur, since these faults range from the most innocent act of neglect to the most elaborate practices of academic piracy. The librarian as a curator and keeper of his collection, must assure the good use of the materials and the quality and authenticity of it. Even though it is not from the library where an effective monitoring of the academic originality should come, in any case library should serve as the main support for university authorities in the strategies they undertake to eradicate these faults within our community, as well as actively participate in the debate or discussion on such strategies. Finally, for today librarians it is fundamental to know the basic elements of copyright to determine that plagiarism contravenes the author's moral rights and deeply harms our community.

Appendix A

Online survey: Strategies against academic plagiarism.

*Required (a: Closed questions; b: Open questions)

1. Position held: *. (b)
2. Does your library have any strategies to prevent academic plagiarism? * (a)
3. Does the library include prevention of academic plagiarism in its community? * (a)
4. Does the library contemplate in its policies some sanction regarding academic plagiarism among its community? (b)
5. What actions does the library do to prevent academic plagiarism in your community? (b)
6. Does the library provide a course, workshop or seminar to prevent academic plagiarism in your community? (b)
7. If so, please provide the URL or other information with public information about the course, workshop or seminar to prevent academic plagiarism in your community? * (b)
8. Do librarians at your institution have basic knowledge of copyright? * (a)
9. Do you know what the ethical use of information is? * (a)
10. What bibliographic style (s) do you use? * (b)
11. Do you know any software that helps to detect academic plagiarism? * (b)
12. Do you participate in any action to raise awareness about these issues in your community? * (b)
13. Does the librarian participate in the process to evaluate such actions in your institution? * (a)
14. Do you use the Creative Commons license for your works? * (a)
15. Are you familiar with Open Access? * (a)
16. If a document is on the network, does it mean that it can be taken freely? * (a)
17. What actions does the institution undertake to detect any situation regarding academic plagiarism? * (b)
18. If your library has a microsite, public information resource, or other support regarding the prevention of academic plagiarism, please provide the URL or other identifying information. * (b)

References

1. Morales Montes, M.A.: Academic plagiarism from the perspective of copyright. Espacio I +D, **5**(2) (2016). http://bit.ly/2raJxMI
2. Domínguez Aroca, M.I.: The fight against plagiarism from university libraries. Prof. Inf. **21** (5), 498–503 (2012)
3. Secker, J., Morrison, C.: From anxiety to empowerment: supporting librarians develop copyright literacy. ALISS Q. **12**(1), 10–13 (2016)
4. College Writing Program: Academic Honesty. University of Berkeley (2017). http://writing.berkeley.edu/students/academic-honesty

5. Maurel-Indart, H., Fólica, L.: Sobre el plagio. Fondo de Cultura Económica, Buenos Aires (2014)
6. Mexican Federal Copyright Law. Chamber of Deputies of the Congress, Mexico (2016). http://www.diputados.gob.mx/LeyesBiblio/pdf/122_130116.pdf
7. Digital Media Rights: How many types of plagiarism are there? (2011). http://www.dmrights.com/en
8. Zurkowski, P.: The information service environment: relationships and priorities. Report ED, vol. 100391. National Commission on Libraries and Information Science, Washington, D.C. (1974)
9. Todd, R.J.: Back to our beginnings: information utilization, Bertram Brookes and the fundamental equation of information science. Inf. Process. Manag. **35**(6), 851–870 (1999)
10. Wingens, M.T.: A general utilization theory: a systems theory reformulation of two-communities metaphor. Knowl.: Creat. Diffus. Util. **12**(1), 27–42 (1990)

Transliteracy, Reading Literacy, Digital Literacy, Financial Literacy, Search Engine Literacy, Civic Literacy

Collaboration and Empowerment in Transliteracy at School

Karine Aillerie[1(✉)], Anne Lehmans[2], and Anne Cordier[3]

[1] Réseau Canopé/Poitiers University, Poitiers, France
karine.aillerie@reseau-canope.fr
[2] Bordeaux University, IMS, Bordeaux, France
anne.lehmans@u-bordeaux.fr
[3] Rouen University, ESO, Mont-Saint-Aignan, France
anne.cordier@univ-rouen.fr

Abstract. Information literacy has long been considered an important aspect in school, as well as in the workplace. Teenagers are the first group affected by requirements based on information skills. Transliteracy occurs as a relevant concept to understand these information practices. Indeed, a holistic approach is needed in order to take into account the multiplicity of contexts of uses and interactions. The research work described here proceeds from a program funded by the French national research agency (ANR Translit 2013–2016) focusing on how high-school students (15–16 years old) manage information with all the available media and tools, individually as well as collectively. Based on ethnographic methodology, the study was carried out between November 2013 and March 2015, in five French high schools during specific learning project based activities. Findings demonstrate that activities and knowledge management on the school workplace must take into consideration complex information skills crossing personal competencies, representations, and self-esteem on one hand, school requirements and context on the other; complex social interactions during information activities; postures and spaces encouraging horizontal learning processes between teachers and students in order to build a community of practice. Our results highlight what is directly visible and what remains implicit. They are likely to be useful for teachers as well decision-makers when designing learning scenarios and guidelines or curricula.

Keywords: Transliteracy · Information literacy · Social interactions Community of practice · High-school

1 Introduction

In the 21st century, the skills required to be successful at school as well as in the workplace involve a high number of proficiencies. These skills include information seeking and problem solving strategies, *a posteriori* validation of information and critical thinking, social skills and collaboration, participation and creativity [1]. Teenagers are the first to be affected by these requirements. “Complex and fascinating” [2] and deeply heterogeneous, their individual information practices beg questions. Far from the “digital natives” myth, their uses are multifaceted, distributed through juvenile

S. Kurbanoğlu et al. (Eds.): ECIL 2017, CCIS 810, pp. 315–321, 2018.
https://doi.org/10.1007/978-3-319-74334-9_33

socialization, daily activities, and educational requirements among others [3]. Transliteracy is found to be relevant in order to understand these information practices. As such this approach joins the theoretical and methodological contributions to a renovated definition of information literacy according to the fast-changing information world and the real practices of users in different settings.

Transliteracy was initially defined by Thomas and colleagues [4] as "the ability to read, write and interact across a range of platforms, tools and media from signing and orality through handwriting, print, TV, radio and film, to digital social networks". In a research project funded by the French National Research Agency, which took place in France from 2012 to 2016, we adopted a more complex definition for this notion of transliteracy. We included "information culture" in context, identifying situations of literacies, media and devices transfers. We analyzed information activity on a transliteracy based approach, while taking into account the social dimension and interactions between individuals. Finally, the researchers involved sought to highlight new forms of "information grammar" [5], transforming fragmented social knowledge into learning potential.

For this contribution, we choose to focus on data collected on the school grounds investigated in this project: five French high schools (15–16 years old students), from four different French areas, during specific learning project-based activities (10th grade, five classes of 30 pupils each). Relying on ethnographic methodology, we studied how students manage information with all the available media and tools, individually as well as collectively.

2 Theoretical and Methodological Framework

Five grounds have been investigated in senior and vocational high schools, over three years and for several weeks (2–18) of observation of dedicated information research activities. During specific educational activities, students (15–16 years old) were required to collectively (by groups of 3–4 members) produce digital outputs such as blogs, videos, travel diaries, slideshows. We aimed to take into account the "social thickness of in progress practices" [6] and then to holistically consider students' information practices and interactions, considering that Transliteracy necessarily grows within communities [7]. According to Liquète [7], the "trans" prefix means in the same time transversal (across different fields of knowledge), and transformation, from uses and practices to knowledge. Thus we have adopted an ecological approach in order to emphasize the role of global context (media and devices available, time and locations where the work took place, collective organizations, teachers' requirements and monitoring) in which one builds its relation to information. On the basis of the "situated" and "distributed" cognition approach [8, 9], we aimed to take into account students and teachers' real uses and their representations. To embed this question of contexts, a multidimensional protocol was set up based on an ethnographic observation involving cross-methodologies: application of an observation grid common to all the fields of investigation, audio recording of the observed situations, pictures, collection of traces (e.g. pupils' productions, drafts and organizational documents, roadmaps provided by teachers, discussions on Facebook, online collaborative documents), students and teachers' interviews. Researchers, alone or in pairs, conducted non-participatory observations, kept a journal of research and carried out flexible exploratory interviews [10] throughout the observed activity, in order to better understand actors' decisions at the moment.

Regarding the elements of observation, each researcher focused mainly on the context of action (dedicated working time, extensions outside the observed situation), the distribution of work within the groups, the individual as well as collective ways to search for information, interactions between pupils, pupils and teachers and between teachers, assessment criteria, the mobilization of various media and tools and moments of transition from one to another. During the observations, we moved regularly from a broad perspective to a narrow one, focusing on a single group, activity or interaction, and then returning to a view of the overall situation [11].

3 Key Results in Analyzing and Processing Information from a Transliteracy-Based Perspective

3.1 Spaces as a Framework for Interactions

Different school contexts were investigated. High-school libraries appeared to be a particularly legitimate and legitimating space for new forms of interactions and interdisciplinarity activities. Teachers and pupils expressed the feeling of being empowered within this specific teaching and learning place, building relationships with each others and working differently than in a regular classroom. A student explained: "When we are in the school library, we work all together, we exchange much more about what we do and how we do it". Other places at school could have been investigated as well (corridors or self-access rooms for instance). We have also observed horizontal relationships between pupils and teachers, who were satisfied to "learn beside and sometimes from their pupils", as witnessed by an English teacher.

It could have been assumed that the computer rooms would have been also favored by the actors, regarding digital projects. *In fact*, the interactions appeared to be impeded there: the inflexible organization arrangement of this kind of places does not favor multi-layouts and group work (space occupied by a computer on a narrow desktop, layout of computers in blocks, for instance), accentuating the division of labor.

In an observation carried out on a school trip abroad, we were especially able to measure the need to take into account the porosities between different contexts in informational situations. The school space extended into the social space when the school librarian precisely invited the students to collect information all over the city, involving the use of personal devices such as mobile phones or tablets. Thus, "intermediate spaces" [12] between school and personal life, face-to-face as well as remote, can support transliteral practices. Moreover, we have been able to observe, even within activities located at school, a strong externalization of interactions among students, especially through the uses of social networking sites and online collaborative tools. Those are pretty much compatible with regulation of group work and the coordination of tasks.

3.2 The Complexity of Collective Organizations

There is a significant difference among teachers depending on their teaching profiles. There are those who assimilate group work with independence and "non-intervention", and those - often school librarians - who view these kinds of projects as an opportunity to promote information literacy activity as a priority. There is, however, a general consensus that there is a need for teacher's attitudes to change. Reduced interventions could be used to encourage interactions among pupils as well as to enhance skills acquired out of school. We have actually observed that teachers mostly allowed groups to organize themselves as they could. This leads to a division of tasks that is carried out according to the media types (e.g. one student searching on the Web, another searching on the library database, another consulting dictionaries, etc.). Transliteracy is therefore not spontaneous, far from it. On the other hand, teachers' monitoring of students' activity is always carried out by the setting up of "boundary objects" [13] such as roadmaps, logbooks or even tutorials, which can be considered as "documents for action" [14].

It is moreover noticeable that an essential factor for activity regulation is the identification by the pupils themselves of their own expertise. For example, a storyboard was spontaneously produced by the group members in order to organize the tasks according to the skills which are individually assigned (bibliography, technical aspects, knowledge organization). A social circulation of the expertise was thus observed among students, who constantly verbalized their actions. As such, social networking sites and online collaborative tools play a great role in collective organizations, especially outside school time as mentioned above. As a result, students tend somehow to confuse the tools used with the organization itself. For instance, "we did a Google doc, Sir!" answered a student when a teacher asked how the group implemented the organization.

3.3 Interactions, Skills and Knowledge

The outputs of interactions (e.g. digital outputs provided by pupils on teachers' requirement) shed light on the identified expertises and tasks which have been distributed within groups. We must point out that the interweaving of different codes (e.g. image, text, sound) was an assessment criteria constantly repeated. We are then not able to assume that the pupils' outputs would have been spontaneously multimedia without this academic demand. In any case, digital outputs highlighted once again skills heterogeneity among pupils and the significant importance of extra-curricular time in the collective organizations. Such an observation leads to question the role of these outputs in the amplification of inequalities among pupils. Indeed, outputs were most often carried out on free time. Then personal devices owned at home as well as technical and informational skills that teenagers already gained, become a major factor of success and distinction. Teachers however must be able to support and train pupils in the classroom or school place in order to formalize and structure knowledge, especially regarding specific requirements such as the diversity of media types employed providing outputs.

Observations demonstrated that skills were largely transformed within the group. Group work allowed for the emergence of a relative complementarity between individuals, either in terms of the distribution of tasks according to the skills and capacities assumed by each member, including leadership effects, or in terms of transfers of expertise from one individual to another or to the whole group. This did not necessarily encourage individual learning, as students may remain confined within or outside their areas of expertise. The distribution of skills and knowledge within the groups was based on three points: collection of information, writing and synthesis, communication. Several and multimedia combinations affected reading and writing tasks: on-screen reading and writing (taking notes) on paper, reading and writing on computer or on paper, reading on paper and writing on computer or even on a phone. In these strategic and cognitive configurations, tools and spaces, personal as well as academic, play indeed an important role.

3.4 The Conditions of a Possible Distributed Literacy

Forms of "distributed cognition" exist when interaction between cognitive technologies linked to a particular environment (a workspace for example) and exchange spaces linked to social arrangements (in a type of task required) create collaborative learning modes [9]. Spaces, media types, devices, finding and processing information methods, can be considered as informational tools. High school students can use a very wide range of tools that are likely to allow them to vary the methods of information access and processing. The choice of tools, and especially ways one uses them, depends initially on what the social environment, firstly at home, offers to each student, even if the statistics show in France a global high rate of digital equipment. School have then to democratize tools and ways to use tools, that students do not usually use, or even know, on a daily basis, especially in three main areas: information seeking (catalogs), information storage and management (indexation), processing and communication (publishing tools). As pupils tend to work a lot outside of school time, special attention must be paid to spaces and settings. They may use public spaces (libraries or school libraries) to continue their work, while they may also have to be satisfied with what they find at home, "information fluent" or not.

4 Conclusions

Our findings highlight that the notion of Transliteracy is built on five key points: the relation to the group (social factor), the relation to semio-technical contexts (spaces, media, devices, procedures for finding and processing information), the relation to legitimacy (cultural factor), the relation to time (temporal factor) and knowledge format (cognitive factor). These elements require particular attention in the context of information literacy strategies.

Activities observed show that the broadest divide is between school culture and individual information practices. On the teachers' side, students' technical abilities are often overestimated. The consequence is a discrepancy between expected and real digital skills [15]. This persistent overestimation tends however to neglect actual learning needs, even basically technical ones. This is a key point, useful for the information literacy field of research as well as for educators. For instance students see their teachers as not technically experts but as information validating experts in relation to educational requirements. They are therefore often requested to help in this validation stage, whereas there is a paradoxical injunction of independence since pupils are summoned to be experts and critics without necessarily having all the cognitive tools to do so. These shifts can slow down group dynamics or creativity. Moreover, whether French high-school pupils still need to improve their proficiency in validation of information and critical thinking, teachers' recommendations are likely to replace pupils' personal reflection. Our findings, and the theoretical angle we choose to implement, highlight the gap between actual cognitive processes and the representation of legitimate knowledge. More precisely, a bridge is to be built between the informational universe of the Web, moving and fuzzy, and the school universe that structures communication, formats and legitimacy.

The ability to manage free time and to work outside schooltime is very unequal [16]. Working outside classroom or schooltime, remotely, requires a pupil's know-how, in the sense of Coulon [17]. It does not only depend on technical skills or mastery of tools, but on a consistent level of self-esteem to take ownership of working methods: e.g. connecting to the school's VLE, consulting documents and taking enough time to learn, in a process of affiliation to the group or class and its activities. As collaborative learning and group work are a major requirement of current education programs, our results point out how much sharing tasks could be time consuming for students leading to reduced cognitive effectiveness. This dilution can be offset by social exchanges between peers, and the emergence of expertise distributed in working groups around certain media such as the blog.

The daily digital tools make it possible to rely on familiar communication formats, common to daily uses as well as academic ones: lists, collections, index, for instance featured on social networking sites or blogs. It is an opportunity for students to create their own spaces-time of socialization and learning, different from the strict time and space frame imposed by school. Our transliteracy based-approach point out that it has to be managed by teachers however. Teenagers are used to listening to music and working at the same time, managing personal and academic purposes at the same moment even with the same tools. The knowledge format remains a benchmark that makes it possible to distinguish what belongs to the content of the knowledge included in a specific and imposed form and that what belongs to the context of learning. The proposal of varied knowledge formats allows the setting up of communication conditions and provides a framework facilitating the emergence of transliteracy skills. The logbook for example, is rather usual in the French educational system and required in activities, but is actually often reduced to a formal and unefficient pedagogical tool. The logbook can however become a real cognitive and didactic tool for training, for storing, sharing and documentarizing collected information. Finally, a specific communication format (for example video) makes it possible for pupils to think about alternative outputs or ways of communication and to reduce the contradictions they perceive between familiar multimedia arrangements and constrained school formats (for example dissertation). The design of information through production of content can also be seen as a mode of grammatization of uses based not only on the procedures but also the critical reflection, not only on problem solving but also on the discovery of questions.

Regarding the keys factors mentioned above, Transliteracy is likely to be facilitated by group work and the multiplication of tools, but rather obstructed by cultural constraints: representations of what is legitimate or not, expressed in traditional knowledge formats. On this matter of cultural construction, representations and construction of meaning, the role of the teacher becomes essential for the emergence of forms of Transliteracy.

References

1. Voogt, J., Roblin, N.: A comparative analysis of international frameworks for 21st century competences: Implications for national curriculum policies. J. Curric. Stud. **44**(3), 299–321 (2012)
2. Boyd, D.: It's Complicated: The Social Lives on Networked Teens. Yale University Press, New Haven/London (2014). https://www.danah.org/books/ItsComplicated.pdf
3. Cordier, A.: Grandir Connectés : les adolescents et la recherche d'information. Caen, C & F Éditions (2015)
4. Thomas, S., Joseph, C., Lacetti, J., Mason, B., Mills, S., Perril, S., Pullinger, K.: Transliteracy: crossing divides. First Monday **12**, 3 (2007). http://firstmonday.org/article/view/2060/1908
5. Chervel, A.: Histoire de la grammaire scolaire. PBP édition (1981)
6. Jeanneret, Y., Souchier, E., Le Marec, J.: Lire, écrire, récrire?. Bibliothèque publique d'information, Paris (2003)
7. Liquète, V.: Can one speak of an "Information Transliteracy"? In: Unesco-Ifap, International Conference Media and Information Literacy for Knowledge Societies, Moscow, Russia, 24–28 June 2012
8. Conein, B., Jacopin, E.: Action située et cognition: le savoir en place. Sociologie du Travail **36**(4), 475–500 (1994)
9. Conein, B.: Cognition distribuée, groupe social et technologie cognitive. Réseaux **2**, 53–79 (2004)
10. Vermersch, P.: L'entretien d'explicitation enformation initiale et continue. ESF, Paris (1994)
11. Grosjean, S.: Étudier la dimension sensible des savoirs produits en contexte de travail. Études de Communication **42**, 47–62 (2014)
12. Cottier, P., Burban, F.: Le lycée à l'ère numérique: usages et recomposition des acteurs. Octares, Toulouse (2016)
13. Star, S.L., Griesemer, J.: Institutionnal ecology, 'translations', and boundary objects: amateurs and professionals on Berkeley's museum of vertrebate zoologie. Soc. Stud. Sci. **19**, 387–420 (1989)
14. Dalbin, S., Guyot, B.: Documents en action dans une organisation: des négociations à plusieurs niveaux. Études de Communication **30**, 55–70 (2007)
15. Dioni, C.: Métier d'élève, métier d'enseignant à l'ère numérique: rapport de recherche pour l'INRP (2008). http://hal.archives-ouvertes.fr/docs/00/25/95/63/PDF/rapportrecherche0208.pdf
16. Le Douarin, L.: Une sociologie des usages des TIC à l'épreuve du temps libre: le cas des lycéens durant l'année du baccalauréat. Recherches en éducation **18**, 11–26 (2014)
17. Coulon, A.: Un instrument d'affiliation intellectuelle. Bull. des Bibliothèques de France **44** (1), 36–42 (1999)

Complex and Multivariable: Methodology of Exploring Digital Literacy and Training Needs Within the Polish SME Sector

Justyna Jasiewicz, Anna Mierzecka, and Małgorzata Kisilowska(✉)

Faculty of Journalism, Information and Book Studies, University of Warsaw, Warsaw, Poland
{justyna.jasiewicz,anna.mierzecka,mdkisilo}@uw.edu.pl

Abstract. A study of information literacy (IL) types, levels, and needs among the Polish small and medium enterprises (SME) was realized in the years 2015–2016, with the Catalogue of Digital Competencies of SMEs (Buchner et al., 2016) as its final product, a diagnosis and education tool, supporting the 'Internet Revolution' education project of Google Poland. Due to multidimensional diversification of the research group, design and implementation of the methodology turned out to be a more complex and challenging task than the catalogue itself. The IL diagnosis phase of the project was realized with different qualitative methods, including desk research, focused group interviews with experts, individual in-depth interviews with entrepreneurs, along with a component of observation, and semantic analysis. Interviews were conducted with the owners and employees of 30 Polish SMEs from various sectors and business branches. The Catalogue of Digital Competences of SMEs was developed with the use of Delphi method, and based on the outcomes of the analysis phase. The methods used during the project enabled identification of key areas of SMEs functioning, and benefits to be achieved as the effect of digitisation of processes, products and/or services. The SMEs sector's information literacy was analysed and described in many aspects, including: size and trade types, location, motivations, types, levels, and shadows of Information and Communication Technologies implementation and information literacy advancement. The project revealed and confirmed the crucial role of methodology and a component of relativity in diagnosing information and digital needs and competencies, in workplace as well.

Keywords: Digital literacy · Information literacy · Methodology design
Small and medium enterprises

1 Introduction and Research Aim

Although the information society has been widely accepted as a common formation of social life in developed countries, the problem of digital divide and information illiteracy still challenges researchers, educators, and politicians. There are many projects and programs concerning development of information and digital skills, addressed to seniors, children, immigrants, unemployed, or people living in distant rural areas,

S. Kurbanoğlu et al. (Eds.): ECIL 2017, CCIS 810, pp. 322–331, 2018.
https://doi.org/10.1007/978-3-319-74334-9_34

aimed in enhancing their competencies as active members of a modern society. Just as the experience and knowledge of people's needs grow, it has become obvious there is no such a thing as universal training for any recipient: their skills, situations, needs or preferences differ significantly.

A study of information literacy (IL) types, levels, and needs among the Polish small and medium enterprises (SMEs) was realized in the years 2015-2016, starting with desk research and interviews with the experts and entrepreneurs (September 2015), through the data collection and analysis phase, up to the design of the Catalogue of Digital Competencies of SMEs [1, 2] as its final product (consulted with the clients in a Delphi study in March 2016), a diagnosis and education tool indicating crucial aspects of IL application, and supporting the "Internet Revolution" education project of Google Poland. The Catalogue was described in detail in [2].

The aim of the project was to develop the Catalogue of Digital Competencies of SMEs as a theoretical framework for diagnosing training activities and education tools in the area of digital literacy in SMEs. Due to multidimensional diversification of the research group, design and implementation of methodology turned out to be a task more complex and challenging than the catalogue itself. The important goal then was to reflect on the complexity of the Polish SME sector and its influence on both information literacy level and education needs.

The following sections present: (a) theoretical background concerning IL and ICT implementation in the SMEs sector, (b) detailed methodology of investigating qualitative and quantitative aspects of ICT application within the Polish SMEs, as well as of developing the Catalogue of Digital Competencies of SMEs, and (c) the product itself, as the outcome of the project.

2 Theoretical Frameworks

ICT adoption in SMEs has been reaching the interest of more and more researchers. The literature review brings an interesting view of several trends in exploring these issues, and refers to different theories and methodologies.

The project on SMEs information literacy being discussed in this paper was mostly based on theoretical backgrounds and methodologies verified in previous projects focused on cataloguing digital competencies, such as the Framework Catalogue of Digital Competencies [3], and the Taxonomy of Digital Competencies of People 50+ [4]. Methodology of cataloguing is based on Bourdieu's [5] theory of class distinction resulting from social inequalities, van Dijk's [6] theory of motivation as a primary factor influencing access and usage of digital media and content, the concepts of information literacy, defined as competencies in finding, evaluating, and effective usage of information [7], and the concept of digital literacy, defined as the skills of using information and communication technologies in different contexts [8]. The foundation of the afore-mentioned Catalogues is the relationality theory of Filiciak et al. [9], defining media literacy as a specific "added value" – a benefit – to any other competencies. Media literacy is not a separate skill, but it enhances people's functioning in all spheres of their lives. Both scope and level of media, digital or information skills depend on one's social, educational, cultural, economic status and needs. There is no ideal competence to be reached, as people all are different and have different needs.

Exploration of information and digital competencies within a workplace is a complex and interdisciplinary action, requiring not only knowledge and expertise of information science, but also of such disciplines as sociology, economy, management or ethnography - and the Catalogue of Digital Competencies in SMEs (being discussed below) was developed by a team of mixed-knowledge project partners.

However, along with the project being described, the compatible concepts and theories have been reviewed in literature. A few of them are discussed briefly by Anna Morgan-Thomas [10], who tried to develop a theoretical conceptualisation of ICT in SMEs to reflect better technology use within this sector and to make it more user-friendly.

The main theories she referred to were: the perspective of technology-in-practice, discussed previously by Orlikowski and Scott [11], the concept of technological affordance, as explored and discussed by the same authors [12, 13], concerning information processes indispensable in economic activities, and the concept of affordances for practice by Fayard and Weeks [14]. The concept of affordances, used mostly in psychology and human-computer interaction, was found to be useful in studying relations between people and technology in organisational contexts. Fayard and Weeks proposed a concept of affordances for practice, joining a technological aspect with Bourdieu's sociological idea of habitus. "Affordance offers a useful way of thinking about how practice is patterned by the social and physical construction of technology, and the material environment and habitus offers a useful way of thinking about how practice is patterned by social and symbolic structures" [14, p. 247].

Just alike the relationality theory, technology-in-practice assumes mutual influence of technology and social context [11]. It considers the effects of ICT implementation in practice. Morgan-Thomas perceives technologies as instruments supporting attainment of skills necessary to realize tasks and to "extract the benefits from use" [11, p. 1126, 15, 16].

There are also researches referring to other theories in surveying ICT adoption in SMEs, like the technology diffusion theory [17] or the complementarity theory [18, 19]. Bocquet, Brossard and Sabatier confirmed that ICT adoption is strongly related to firms' strategies, organizational practices, and competitive environment.

Other research projects focused on specific aspects of ICT in SMEs should also be mentioned here. Ashurst et al. [20] studied relations between ICT implementation and company's development, in particular information literacy and e-business in SMEs. The latter has been proved to be used in two different ways: for innovation and for integrating business processes. They also indicated four IT competencies as particularly important for a company's development: IT leadership, business systems thinking, architecture planning (ability to understand future business needs, with ICT assistance), and making technology work. A link between creative marketing and technology has been found to be crucial in the project.

Higón focused on the role of ICT in innovations of 7505 SMEs from all sectors within the UK [21]. She analyzed the role of different types of ICT applications, referring to variables such as "ownership structure, firm size, market orientation, age and qualifications of managers, and competitive and financial obstacles" [21, p. 685].

Higón found out that the impact of ICT depends on the type of application and innovation activity, as well as the type of firm and management culture.

Factors influencing SMEs' adoption of enterprise applications (like enterprise resource planning, customer relation management - CRM, supply chain management - SCM) were also a subject of research of Ramdani et al. [22]. The study revealed that all three contexts (technological, organisational, and environmental) positively influence the adoption of electronic applications (EA) in SMEs. In other works, the "technology-organization-environment framework" has been proven as influencing the SMEs technological development. "Unlike other types of ICT adoption by SMEs, EA adoption has been found to be influenced by compatibility, complexity, trialability and observability" [22, p. 745].

Durkin et al. [23] tried to discover the scope of social media adoption in SMEs, referring to case studies of eight Irish firms. In the results they offered a theoretical model of customer-oriented social media adoption and utilisation in SMEs. The main point of the model is differentiation (after an assessment of both internal and external operating contexts) of three types of permission marketing: push, pull, and direct. These differentiations support better understanding the ways of social media influence of marketing practices. Finally, they influence reputation, asset management, as well as sales and business development, brand perception, PR, sales and external relationships. The authors found out that the SMEs studies commonly misperceived managing in social media as discrete and operational rather than strategic [23, p. 727]. Actually, the model explains that with social media marketing applied, the clients become seen as "co-producers and influences of the relationship that the company has with them, which has clear managerial implications for the way in which the SME owner-manager does business" [23, p. 729].

The literature review can be concluded with an interesting observation - whatever methodology used in exploring ICT adoption and/or information literacy in a SMEs sector, "a benefit" seems to be a key concept they reach. A benefit perceived either as an incentive and motivation for developing skills and technologies, or as an effect of training and usage of information and digital competencies.

3 Methodology of the Study on ICT Implementation and Information Literacy Levels in the Polish SMEs Sector

Due to the complexity of the research problem and projects' objectives it was necessary to design advanced qualitative methodology. The research project was conducted in four major phases, but in fact it can be described as a multi-level methodological solution. The methodology itself was based on triangulation of qualitative techniques: individual in-depth interviews (as well as dyads and triads), an observation, and a Delphi study. The research project consisted of four main phases: exploratory, field, analytical and cataloguing. Different research methods were selected and applied in each phase.

3.1 The Exploratory Phase

During the exploratory phase review and analysis of existing data and literature as well as interviews with experts and practitioners took place.

The purpose of the analysis was specifically to explore the condition of the Polish SME sector. Sources were selected according to the formal criteria of time (published between 2010 and 2015) and language of publication (Polish for research purposes and English as comparative material). As it comes to the subject criteria, the scope was limited to the characteristics of the Polish SME sector and its current development status. Due to the main purpose of the project, the review focused on investigations of previous initiatives concerning implementation of ICT in SME sector as a whole and in particular types of enterprises.

As a result of the application of the above-mentioned criteria, several types of publications were analysed:

- reports on the condition of the SME sector, including mainly reports on changes in the sector in chronological order, offered mostly by the Polish Agency for Enterprise Development,
- specialist reports on selected aspects of the SMEs functioning (e.g. foreign cooperation, e-commerce, e-banking, innovation, the impact of co-financing);
- research articles on ICT applications in Polish companies - both generic and dedicated to selected technologies (e.g. cloud computing),
- selected English-language publications placing the data about Polish SMEs in a broader context,
- guidelines for SMEs,
- "classical classifications" of business activities (e.g. the Central Statistical Office of Poland - the Polish Classification of Activities).

Second part of the exploratory phase included interviews and consultations with experts and practitioners. The interviews enabled gathering of accumulated practical knowledge and meta-reflection. Among the twenty respondents invited to support the project in the exploratory phase, there were representatives of the third sector, academia and government agencies, specialists in such areas as distribution of the EU funds in SME sector, research and development (R&D) for SMEs, research of Polish entrepreneurship, industry associations. Practitioners were recruited from among the representatives of branches like strategic advice, accounting support, legal advice, finance and banking, telecommunications, Web site positioning, and online communication planning; they were representatives of corporations and SMEs, as well as independent consultants.

3.2 The Field Phase

On the basis of the exploratory phase the set of criteria for a research sample was designed. Selection of the SMEs to be interviewed was executed across seven criteria:

1. size – less than 100 employees, more than five clients;
2. independence – financially and know-how independent (i.e. excluded franchising companies and representatives to the local market), settled in Poland;

3. ICT use – any type of presence on the internet (website, FB fan page, advertisements), use of any ICT solutions in daily work, except fiscal cash register;
4. experience – start-ups, less and more experienced;
5. location – cities, towns, villages, region of Poland;
6. diversity of respondents – age, sex, position in the SME;
7. area of activity – local, international.

Thanks to these advanced criteria of building-up the field research group, it was possible to interview representatives of different SME branches, from various areas of Poland (see Fig. 1).

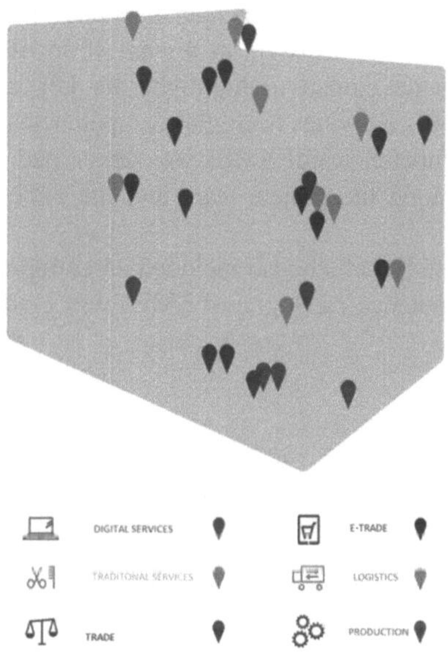

Fig. 1. "Map of branches". Participation of SME branches from various parts of Poland in the field phase of the project.

Field research, consisting of thirty in-depth interviews (including dyads and triads) was conducted in November and the first week of December 2015 at the sites of the companies. Interviews were extended by observation elements that used the natural conditions of the study. Interviews were done by a research team of five.

3.3 The Analytical Phase

Transcripts of interviews and observation cards were prepared after the end of field study.

Then the dedicated tool was applied for the detailed analysis of qualitative data, called "health cards". The "health card" is a form comparable to a patient health record, designed previously by the sociologists Anna Buchner and Katarzyna Zaniewska for research on social network and cultural heritage institutions. It enables detailed registration of data, facilitates navigation through the collected material, and reveals clearly key issues of the study.

The main purpose of this phase was twofold. First, to identify attitudes towards digital technologies in SME. Second, to find out areas most relevant for ICT application, and if they have actually been implemented there. Obtained material made a basis for the last cataloguing phase.

3.4 The Cataloguing Phase

In the results of previous two phases the key areas of SMEs activities were identified, as well as scopes and intensity of digital practices being applied within. These findings were then reviewed by an expert (an SME manager) and revised accordingly. Finally, the proper cataloguing phase could begin as a team effort of researchers and experts. The draft catalogue was developed to highlight the key so-called benefits [2, 3], mapping key areas of SMEs activities to digital competencies. The final version of the Catalogue of Digital Competencies of SMEs was developed in the process of negotiation and verification among the project team and the experts, based on the Delphi method.

Then, in the Delphi study (which also included an entrepreneurial expert), the final shape of the digital competence catalogue of SMEs was gradually developed.

4 Outcomes

The SMEs sector's information literacy was analysed and described in many aspects, including: size and types of trade, location, motivations; types, levels, and tendencies of ICT implementation, and information literacy level. The relational model of digital competences, assuming the scope of the internet use to be shaped by individual needs and interests, allows business owners themselves to manage the process of the company's digitisation by choosing solutions tailored to the company's profile, its offerings and motivation. The methods selected, used and verified during the project, as well as the diagnostic tools developed alongside, enabled identification of key areas of SMEs functioning and its exploration regarding information and digital literacy, and benefits to be achieved as the effect of digitisation of processes, products and/or services. It was found that SME sector operate online within six key areas: Sales, Communication and Promotion, Products or Services, Customers, Market and Competition, and Company Management (see: Fig. 2).

Specific digital competences can yield benefits in each of the areas (see: Fig. 3). Though digital skills may lead to benefits in SME operation, it was also revealed that all of the competences are viewed by the entrepreneurs from the perspective of three main advantages: saving time, saving money, and generating profit.

The Catalogue of Digital Competencies of SMEs was the main research aim and effect of the project [2]. Thanks to the implementation of the relational model it was possible to recognize areas of online activities of SMEs as well as the benefits that can be received in the result of ICT implementation, with the individual scope of the entrepreneurs. As mentioned above, the Catalogue has been and yet is going to be used

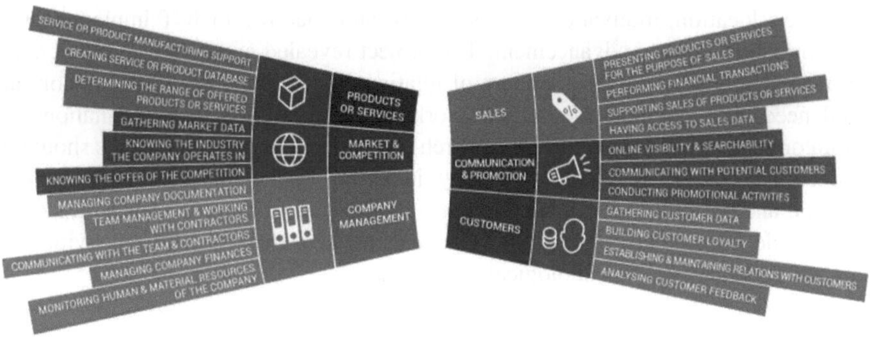

Fig. 2. The Catalogue of Digital Competencies in SMEs: key areas of IL application.

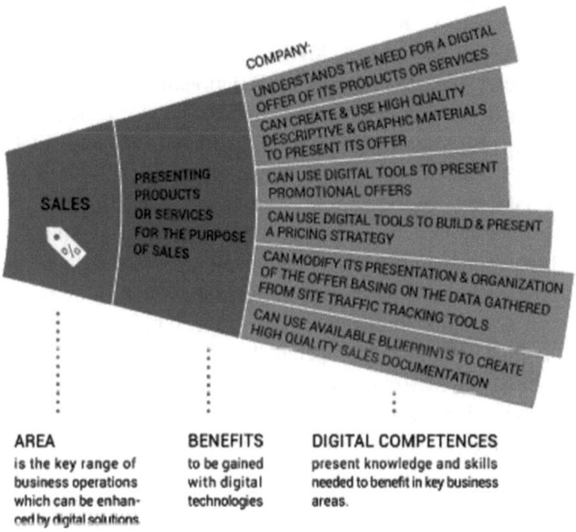

Fig. 3. The structure of the catalogue.

as a foundation and roadmap for strategic implementation of ICT in Polish SMEs, as a framework for designing and realization of profiled education and training services, as well as a tool of diagnosing digital competencies in human resources' management, in particular in recruitment and training processes.

5 Conclusions

The methods selected, used and verified during the project, as well as the diagnostic tools developed alongside, enabled identification of key areas of SMEs functioning and its exploration regarding information and digital literacy, and benefits to be achieved as the effect of digitisation of processes, products and/or services. The SMEs sector's information literacy was analysed and described in many aspects, including: size and trade types, location, motivations, types, levels, and shadows of ICT implementation and information literacy advancement. The project revealed and confirmed the crucial role of methodology and a component of relationality in diagnosing information and digital needs and competencies in the workplace as well. As to its limitations, its exploratory character as a qualitative research has to be mentioned. Its results should be validated in a large-scale quantitative study, including verification in other than Polish economic and cultural contexts. Regarding a dynamic development of ICT, the Catalogue should be regularly revised and updated, as new areas of SMEs activities are being supported by new technological solutions.

References

1. Buchner, A., Zaniewska, K., Filiciak, M., Jasiewicz, J., Kaleta, Ł., Kisiilowska, M., Mierzecka, A., Tarkowski, A.: Katalog kompetencji cyfrowych małych firm (2016). https://centrumcyfrowe.pl/wp-content/uploads/2016/03/IR-katalog-kompetencji.pdf
2. Kisilowska, M., Jasiewicz, J., Mierzecka, A.: Relationality is the key: the family of digital competencies' catalogues and their potential applications. In: Kurbanoğlu, S., Boustany, J., Špiranec, S., Grassian, E., Mizrachi, D., Roy, L., Çakmak, T. (eds.) ECIL 2016. CCIS, vol. 676, pp. 294–303. Springer, Cham (2016). https://doi.org/10.1007/978-3-319-52162-6_29
3. Jasiewicz, J., Filiciak, M., Mierzecka, A., Sliwowski, K., Klimczuk, A., Kisilowska, M., Tarkowski, A., Zadrożny, J.: The framework catalogue of digital competences (2015). https://mc.gov.pl/files/ramowy_katalog_kompetencji_cyfrowych_final_ang_jj_2.pdf
4. Tarkowski, A., Mierzecka, A., Jasiewicz, J., Filiciak, M., Kisilowska, M., Klimczuk, A., Bojanowska, E.: Taksonomia funkcjonalnych kompetencji cyfrowych oraz metodologia pomiaru poziomu funkcjonalnych kompetencji cyfrowych osób z pokolenia 50+ (2015). https://ec.europa.eu/epale/pl/resource-centre/content/taksonomia-funkcjonalnych-kompetencji-cyfrowych-oraz-metodologia-pomiaru
5. Bourdieu, P.: Distinction: A Social Critique of the Judgment of Taste. Routledge, London (2010)
6. van Dijk, J.: The Deepening Divide: Inequality in the Information Society. Sage Publications, Thousand Oaks (2005)
7. American Library Association (2000). http://www.ala.org/acrl/sites/ala.org.acrl/files/content/standards/standards.pdf
8. Eisenberg, M., Berkowitz, B.: Welcome to the Big6 (2012). http://big6.com/
9. Filiciak, M., Mazurek, P., Growiec, K.: Korzystanie z mediów a podziały społeczne. Kompetencje medialne Polaków w ujęciu relacyjnym (2013). https://ngoteka.pl/bitstream/handle/item/215/korzystanie%20z%20mediow%20a%20podzialy%20spoleczne.pdf?sequence=3
10. Morgan-Thomas, A.: Rethinking technology in the SME context: affordances, practices and ICTs. Int. Small Bus. J. **34**, 1122–1136 (2015)
11. Orlikowski, W.J., Scott, S.V.: Challenging the separation of technology, work and organization. Acad. Manag. Ann. **2**, 433–474 (2008)
12. Orlikowski, W.J., Scott, S.V.: What happens when evaluation goes online? Exploring apparatuses of valuation in the travel sector. Organ. Sci. **25**, 868–891 (2014)
13. Scott, S.V., Orlikowski, W.J.: Entanglements in practice: performing anonymity through social media. Mis Q. **38**, 873–893 (2014)
14. Fayard, A.L., Weeks, J.: Affordances for practice. Inf. Organ. **24**, 236–249 (2014)

15. Cragg, P., Mills, A., Suraweera, T.: The influence of IT management sophistication and IT support on IT success in small and medium-sized enterprises. J. Small Bus. Manag. **51**, 617–636 (2013)
16. Wolcott, P., Kamal, M., Qureshi, S.: Meeting the challenges of ICT adoption by micro-enterprises. J. Enterp. Inf. Manag. **21**, 616–632 (2008)
17. Ghobakhloo, M., Tang, S.H.: The role of owner/manager in adoption of electronic commerce in small businesses: the case of developing countries. J. Small Bus. Enterp. Dev. **20**, 754–787 (2013)
18. Milgrom, P., Roberts, J.: Complementarities and fit strategy, structure, and organizational change in manufacturing. J. Account. Econ. **19**, 179–208 (1995)
19. Bocquet, R., Brossard, O., Sabatier, M.: Complementarities in organizational design and the diffusion of information technologies: an empirical analysis. Res. Policy **36**, 367–386 (2007)
20. Ashurst, C., Cragg, P., Herring, P.: The role of IT competences in gaining value from e-business: an SME case study. Int. Small Bus. J. **30**, 640–658 (2012)
21. Higon, D.A.: The impact of ICT on innovation activities: evidence for UK SMEs. Int. Small Bus. J. **30**, 684–699 (2012)
22. Ramdani, B., Chevers, D., Williams, D.A.: SMEs' adoption of enterprise applications. J. Small Bus. Enterp. Dev. **20**, 735–753 (2013)
23. Durkin, M., McGowan, P., McKeown, N., Heller Baird, C., Luo, L., Wang, Y., Han, L., Patino, A., Pitta, D.A., Quinones, R.: Exploring social media adoption in small to medium-sized enterprises in Ireland. J. Small Bus. Enterp. Dev. **20**, 716–734 (2011)

Digital Literacy Practices of Young Children in Informal Learning Spaces

Sirje Virkus[1(✉)], Damiana Koutsomiha[2], and Emmanouel Garoufallou[3]

[1] Tallinn University, Tallinn, Estonia
sirje.virkus@tlu.ee
[2] American Farm School, Thessaloniki, Greece
dkouts@afs.edu.gr
[3] Alexander Technological Educational Institute (ATEI) of Thessaloniki, Thessaloniki, Greece
mgarou@libd.teithe.gr

Abstract. This paper reviews research on digital literacy practices of young children (0–8 years) in out-of-school settings or in informal learning spaces/settings. The purpose of this review is to identify the literature and topics that have arisen from non-school-based or informal space research and to highlight main directions and dimensions. The major research question is: What is the role of informal learning spaces in shaping children's digital literacy practices? This research attempts to bridge the gap that exists between children's uses of digital technology at home and in other informal settings and contributes and highlights the need for studying learning more holistically.

Keywords: Digital literacy · Informal learning · Informal learning spaces Informal learning settings · Out-of-school literacy practices · Learning theory Literacy theory · Young children · Libraries · Museums · Social media Games

1 Introduction

Learning occurs every day in many ways and in a variety of settings. Children do not just learn about their world through formal education, there are the wider influences of home, including parents and siblings, and the community and society in which they live [1]. Learning scientists study learning in a variety of settings and stress that learning develops across multiple timeframes and settings. They emphasize the importance of deep links between formal schooling and the informal learning that takes place at home, libraries, museums, galleries, learning and community centres, clubs, through online activities and among peers [2, p. 1]. A learning environment is becoming increasingly digital, online and informal and children engage in a range of digital meaning making practices in these settings. These practices are under-researched areas in relation to children aged from birth to eight [1, p. 28]. However, an understanding of the connections between digital literacy in formal and informal learning environments is essential to furthering children' digital literacy skills.

S. Kurbanoğlu et al. (Eds.): ECIL 2017, CCIS 810, pp. 332–339, 2018.
https://doi.org/10.1007/978-3-319-74334-9_35

Sefton-Green et al. [1, p. 19] suggest that this offers a broad framework for conceptualising the operational, cultural and critical dimensions of diverse schooled and informal literacy practices, providing a theorised and growing research-evidence base for thinking beyond the focus on "basic skills" that currently prevail in many EU literacy curricula and policy discourses.

2 Methodology

Literature searches were undertaken on computer science, education, library and information science as well as multidisciplinary databases. The search strategy contained three components: terms relating to digital literacy and digital skills, informal learning spaces/settings, informal learning environments and out-of-school settings, and terms relating to young children from birth to eight. Results of various reports were used from relevant educational and library science organizations as well. The review of the literature is framed as a narrative literature review and is organised on emerging themes drawn from the literature.

3 Informal Learning

The literature distinguishes three main forms of learning – formal, non-formal and informal. Literature reviews and theoretical frameworks from various fields provide a variety of definitions of informal learning. Each field provides different ways of defining informal learning and a unique perspective on learning. For example, the informal learning and adult and lifelong learning literature typically examines informal learning from the individual learner's perspective, whereas the workplace learning literature takes an organizational standpoint. Livingstone [3, p. 4] defines informal learning as "any activity involving the pursuit of understanding, knowledge or skill which occurs without the presence of externally imposed curricular criteria". Scheerens [31, p. 2] poses that informal learning is a "truly lifelong process whereby every individual acquires attitudes, values, skills and knowledge from daily experience [...] from family, neighbours, from work and play, from the market place and from the library and the mass media" [as cited in 4].

However, "formal learning is institutionalised (e.g. schools or universities) and follows a mandatory curriculum that defines the learning goals as well as means. Non-formal learning takes place outside the formal education system and is based on voluntary participation in an educational institution (e.g. cooking classes, driving lessons, and language courses). Hence, the learner implicitly controls the learning goals, but the means how these goals are achieved are controlled by the institution, e.g. through a predefined learning agenda or milestones. Informal learning comprises the forms of learning outside both formal and non-formal settings" [5, p. 160]. Bilandzic [5] notes that in practice, the lines between these categories are often blurred.

Thus, learning occurs every day in a multitude of ways and in a range of settings. This learning which is often referred to as "informal learning" has an impact on individuals, organizations, and the economy in many ways [4, p. 1]. For the purposes of this paper the previous classification of informal learning was used. The authors categorized informal learning into several broad categories and stated that organized informal learning can occur in a range of settings including schools, work, the community, and home. Everyday informal learning also takes place at school, work, community, or home, but it does not include an instructor or an organized curriculum, and learners have a range of intentionality in which the learning can be self-directed, incidental, and/or embedded in the process of socialization. In addition, technology has an important role in how learning occurs across all types of learning.

Most of the knowledge and skills that people acquire and adopt throughout their lifetime are based on free-choice-learning activities, as opposed to the formal education system and educational programmes with a dedicated curriculum [5, p. 158].

What are termed "informal learning spaces" are also known more frequently in the literature as 'out-of-school contexts'. The main informal settings, informal spaces or out-of-school contexts explored are libraries, learning centres, museums, galleries, clubs, and community centres.

Additionally, technology has an important role in how learning occurs across all types of learning. Through opportunities such as online learning, massive open online courses (MOOCS), games and simulations, and mobile learning, technology may expand access to learning opportunities [6].

Research on digital literacy practices of young children (0–8 years) in out-of-school settings or in informal learning spaces/settings can be divided into the following topics:

- informal learning in libraries and museums;
- informal learning in mixed settings: learning centers and community centers;
- informal learning via games.

4 Libraries and Museums

Informal learning environments are support systems that are "valuable not as ends, but as means to a greater goal – to helping children grow emotionally, socially, physically, and academically" [7, p. 4]. As far as libraries are concerned they are spaces that foster the evolution of the library role away from being a "gatekeeper" of books, more and more towards being a facilitator for learning and knowledge [5, p. 162]. They form an extensive and pluralistic informal learning setting "that it is equipped to deliver critical early learning resources to young children and families, especially those most in need" [8, p. 5]. Even more, libraries are defined as "informal learning […] non-discipline specific places used frequently by both staff and students for self-directed learning activities and can be within and outside library spaces" [9, p. 59].

By capturing a child's interest and imagination early, librarians intuitively believe that they help children discover that libraries and literacy can be an enjoyable and valued part of their lives. Librarians believe that young children who become regular library users will benefit from the meaningful early literacy experiences available through storytimes. They also believe that this will allow children to develop the early literacy, communication and social skills needed to be ready to learn by the time they enter school [10] and they want children and young people to appreciate intellectual freedom and to actively manage and grow their academic digital footprints [11, p. 151]. In school libraries they "encourage the deconstruction and construction of media messages" and they "help learners develop questions, find, evaluate, analyze, synthesize and synthesized ideas and knowledge with media" [11, p. 150].

Public libraries have traditionally offered early literacy programming to preschool children in the form of storytimes. Through the use of a wide range of high-quality picture books, songs, poetry, fingerplays, puppets and crafts, public libraries have been making literacy fun. They have created inviting spaces for children and their families and caregivers to enjoy literacy-rich, hands-on experiences in an interactive and caring environment [12].

When digital media becomes available to young children early year's library services are devoted into two key areas: providing advice to readers and modeling early literacy activities. And just as librarians are proponents of free access to books and older formal of audiovisual materials, they should provide guidance about access to a range of digital resources from which families and the caregivers of young children can select what best suits their needs [13, pp. 152-155].

Campbell and Kluver [14] pointed out the role of librarians and they proposed the ACE model (Access, Content, and Engagement) as "a framework for thinking about the role of technology and digital media in the library and for responding to the needs of children, parents, and educators in the digital age" [15]. Children's librarians are the ideal media mentors since they are considered to be experienced curators in the evaluation of different types of electronic resources; they are experienced in developing early learning programs; they support lifelong learning, promote reading and equity of access; they have attractive facilities for parents and caregivers who choose them to spend quality time with their children; they maintain close collaborations with community organizations and technology oriented partners to facilitate their projects [14].

Although the majority of the literature is focusing on the informal learning in libraries in many cases libraries and museums are treated as one. They "reach millions of children each year" [8, p. 2] and they "have long held a trusted place in society and a responsibility for preservation, research, education, and access to their diverse holdings" [16, p. 21]. More specifically, "the collections in libraries and museums - books, artwork, scientific specimens, and other cultural artifacts - connect people to the full spectrum of human experience: culture, science, history, and art. By preserving and conserving our material and digital artifacts, libraries and museums link us with humankind's history. These institutions operate as places of social inclusion that promote curiosity, learning by doing, and discovery. In them, we learn about ourselves and others, and enhance the skills that contribute to empathy, tolerance, and understanding" [17, p. 8].

Also, Campbell and Kluver proposed "10 Ways Museums and Libraries Support Community Early Learning Efforts" and they suggested the reasons the most distinct of which are that they "increase high-quality early learning experiences, engage and support families as their child's first teachers, support development of executive function and "deeper learning" skills through literacy and STEM-based experiences, link new digital technologies to learning" [14].

The following distinct cases and research illustrate the aforementioned points and the growing literature on the integration of digital literacies in informal settings.

Calderón (2009) presents an intervention action research that took place in two settings outside school: a computer club and a series of technology-enhanced workshops in a museum in London (UK). The Yew Dell Botanical Gardens in Crestwood, Kentucky, offers nature and garden backpacks as well as "Books and Blankets" baskets that include children's books and blankets for families to read with children in the gardens; and scavenger hunts to develop vocabulary and problem-solving skills. The International Federation of Library Associations issued Guidelines for Library Services to Babies and Toddlers and mentioned best practice examples from the EU and all over the world that were undertaken those past years. Some of these projects are completed but are worth mentioning and some still continue such as Born to read (Nascuts per llegir) in Catalonia, Spain; Boekenpret in the Netherlands; Bookstart in the [19].

Mills et al. [20] designed and implemented a research study in which they used iPads to create digital storytimes for preschoolers. They carefully chose apps and designed hybrid experiences that included both traditional and digital pieces. They then asked participants to fill out a survey describing their reactions to the storytimes and were surprised and pleased to discover the parents and children preferred the digital storytimes.

Jensen et al. [21] elaborated on the early literacy skills in children's libraries and the important role embodied cognition can play in the promotion of early literacy.

The educational program "From the Ancient to the Modern Tablets" aimed to motivate and promote the early literacy and extracurricular reading; establish cognitive links between writing, books and acquiring knowledge with technology; and possess the basic digital skills when using a tablet. A collaboration of the University of Patras, Greece with schools in the framework of the program "Schools go to the University" was established [22].

The Vancouver Public Library ran an eBooks and Apps for Preschoolers program aimed at parents and caregivers of children aged two to six and it included demonstrations on how to use these devices and apps over two 90 min sessions [13].

Another example is the popularity of makerspaces carries a new and fresh perspective in informal learning bringing a do-it-yourself culture [23–25]. With the use of digital technologies, industrial and fine arts anyone can be a co-creator of digital literacy including children.

5 Mixed Settings: Learning Centers and Community Centers

Informal learning initiatives take place in learning and community centers that usually serve under the same umbrella as libraries or museums. For example, Calderón [18] presents an intervention action research that took place in two settings outside school: a computer club and a series of technology-enhanced workshops in a museum in London (UK).

McTavish [26] reexamines traditional notions of literacy by documenting a second grade child's literacy practices in school and out-of-school contexts. Findings show that the focal child recontextualized school literacies in out-of-school spaces and changed them in flexible, playful and technologically contemporary ways. The study offers new knowledge of how school literacy may impact on some children's out-of-school literacies and recognizes that these out-of-school spaces may serve to prepare children more appropriately for the future.

McTavish and Streelasky [27] investigate the ways contemporary childhoods are being shaped by a range of multimodal communicative practices. They discuss two case studies that occurred in two different urban Canadian contexts where they ought to privilege the voices, lives, and meaning-making experiences of two young boys by involving them as active participants in research. Drawing on sociocultural and multimodal theories of learning, the purpose of this research was to investigate the complexity of the everyday communicative practices utilized by young Canadian children in and out-of-school in an attempt to inform the future direction of literacy curricula for children. Although many researchers advocate for children's "voices" to be taken into account in educational research, few report the evidence of engaging children in the research process. In the two cases, the data collection methods provided opportunities for children to express themselves, and revealed the meaning making practices that they valued. The findings also showed how the practices valued and promoted in the focal children's classrooms generally reflected traditional and narrow modes of communication, specifically, print-based, and teacher-directed practices.

6 Informal Learning via Games

Play is a well-documented educational tool, but one that has begun to decline in schools and early childhood education due to the increased pressure for cognitive-based school readiness programs. Video games engage children and help them to develop literacies and competencies outside of the classroom as they open new venues in student's mental exercise, fantasy, creativity, and communication [28].

One of the first studies on multi-touch technology applied to education was "Read-it", a game-based application, designed to support the development of reading skills in children aged 5–7 years old [29]. The results of the pilot experiment showed that children enjoyed playing the game and that the technology was not an obstacle to learning.

In a very recent study Lefteriotis, Giannakos and Jaccheri performed studies to create a framework to include Interactive displays (IDs) in informal learning environments where they were seen as a medium for enhancing students' creativity, and engagement [28].

Cohen and Uhry [30] describe symbolic representation in block play in a culturally diverse suburban preschool classroom. Block play is multimodal and can allow children to experiment with materials to represent the world in many forms of literacy. Combined qualitative and quantitative data from seventy-seven block structures were collected and analyzed. The observed frequency of symbolism used for three levels of symbolism, (1) pre-symbolism, (2) first level symbolism, and (3) second level symbolism was investigated. Results indicated significant differences for first level symbolism or real-world objects. Students reported making homes for Webkinz, indicating an ability to encode multimodally the Webkinz computer game played at home to their school block play. The implications from these findings suggest educators should consider both a sociocultural perspective on playing and children's out of-school experiences on learning. A research agenda that includes multimodality as performance is critical to early childhood education.

7 Conclusions

This review is an attempt to determine behaviors and preferences of children in relation to where, what, when and how they use informal learning spaces; to determine behaviors, attitudes and preferences of children in relation to why they select and use informal learning spaces; to enable evidence based decision making in the development of informal learning spaces; to inform the design of informal learning spaces. The contexts of literacy by Sefton-Green [1] at the micro, meso, and macro level help us put into perspective the issues for informal spaces.

References

1. Sefton-Green, J., Marsh, J., Erstad, O., Flewitt, R.: Establishing a research agenda for the digital literacy practices of young children: a white paper for COST action IS1410 (2016). http://digilitey.eu/ Accessed 19 Jan 2017
2. Sawyer, R.K.: Optimizing Learning: Implications of Learning Sciences Research. OECD/CERI, Paris (2008)
3. Livingstone, D.W.: Adults' Informal Learning: Definitions, Findings, Gaps and Future Research. OISE/UT, Toronto (2001). (NALL Working Paper No. 21)
4. Van Noy, M., James, H., Bedley, C.: Reconceptualizing Learning: A Review of the Literature on Informal Learning. ACT Foundation. Rutgers Education and Employment Research Center (2016)
5. Bilandzic, M.: Connected learning in the library as a product of hacking, making, social diversity and messiness. Interact. Learn. Environ. **24**(1), 158–177 (2016)
6. Kontovourki, S., et al.: Digital literacy in the early years: practices in formal settings, teacher education, and the role of informal learning spaces a review of the literature (2017). http://digilitey.eu/wp-content/uploads/2015/09/WG2-LR-March-2017-v2.pdf
7. Brown, J.S.: 21st century learning environments (2006). http://www.p21.org/storage/documents/le_white_paper-1.pdf
8. Howard, M.L.: Growing young minds: how museums and libraries create lifelong learners (2013). www.imls.gov
9. Harrop, D., Turpin, B.: A study exploring learners' informal learning space behaviors, attitudes, and preferences a study exploring learners' informal learning. New Rev. Acad. Librariansh. **1**(1), 37–41 (2013)
10. MacLean, J.: Library preschool storytimes: developing early literacy skills in children (2008). https://ed.psu.edu/goodling-institute/professional-development/judy-maclean-library-preschool-storytimes
11. Valenza, J., Hobbs, R.: School librarians as stakeholders in the children and media community: a dialogue. J. Child. Media **10**(2), 147–155 (2016)
12. Pratt, M.E., Taylor, M., van Huisstede, L., Gaias, L.M.: A novel take on family involvement: public libraries as early education for the whole family. In: Sutterby, J.A. (ed.) Family Involvement In Early Education and Child Care, pp. 67–90. Emerald Books, Bingley (2016)

13. de Freitas, F., Prendergast, T.: Using digital media in early years library services. In: Rankin, C., Brock, A. (eds.) Library Services from Birth to Five: Delivering the Best Start, pp. 153–167. Facet Publishing, London (2015)
14. Campbell, C., Kluver, C.: Access, content, and engagement: how children's librarians support early learning in the digital age. In: Donohue, C. (ed.) Technology and Digital Media in the Early Years. Routledge, New York (2015)
15. Donohue, C.: Technology and Media in the Early Years. Routledge, New York (2015)
16. Mack, D.L.: Institute of Museum and Library Services (U.S.), & Salzburg Global Seminar. Libraries and museums in an era of participatory culture: a partnership project of the Salzburg GlobalSeminar and the Institute of Museum and Library Services, Session 482 Report, 19–23 October 2011 Institute of Museum and Library Services, Washington, DC (2011)
17. Institute of Museum and Library Services. Museums, Libraries and 21st Century Skills (2009). https://www.imls.gov/assets/1/AssetManager/21stCenturySkills.pdf
18. Calderón, B.: Towards an ecology of learning: children meaning-making with digital technologies in out-of-school settings. Int. J. Learn. **16**(9), 153–167 (2009)
19. IFLA. https://www.ifla.org/
20. Mills, J.E., Romeijn-Stout, E., Campbell, C., Koester, A.: Results from the young children, new media, and libraries survey: what did we learn? Child. Libr. **13**(2), 26–35 (2015)
21. Jensen, C.N., Burleson, W., Sadauskas, J.: Fostering early literacy skills in children's libraries: opportunities for embodied congnition and tangible technologies. In: Proceedings of the 11th International Conference on Interaction Design and Children - IDC 2012, vol. 1, pp. 50–59 (2012)
22. Mystakidis, S., Lambropoulos, N.: Playful blended digital storytelling in 3D immersive elearning environments : a cost effective early literacy motivation method. In: Proceedings of the 2014 Workshop on Interaction Design in Educational Environments. ACM, Albacete (2014)
23. Litts, B.K.: Making learning: makerspaces as learning environments (2015). http://www.informalscience.org/sites/default/files/Litts_2015_Dissertation_Published.pdf
24. Nygren, Å.: The Public Library as a Community Hub for Connected Learning. IFLA 2014, p. 16 (2014). http://library.ifla.org/1014/1/167-nygren-en.pdf
25. Anon: Final recommendations: Europeana Association Network, Task force on public libraries (2015). http://pro.europeana.eu/files/Europeana_Professional/Europeana_Network/europeana-task-force-on-public-libraries-final-report-dec2015.pdf
26. McTavish, M.: "I'll do it my own way!": a young child's appropriation and recontextualization of school literacy practices in out-of-school spaces. J. Early Child. Lit. **14**(3), 319–344 (2014)
27. McTavish, M., Streelasky, J.: Listening to children's voices: children as participants in research. Int. J. Early Child. **44**(3), 249–267 (2012)
28. Leftheriotis, I., Giannakos, M.N., Jaccheri, L.: Gamifying informal learning activities using interactive displays: an empirical investigation of students' learning and engagement. Smart Learn. Env. **4**(2), 1–19 (2017)
29. Sluis, R.J.W., Weevers, I., Schijndel, C.H.G.J.V., Kolos-Mazuryk, L., Fitrianie, S., Martens, J.B.O.S.: Read-it: five-to-seven-year-old children learn to read in a tabletop environment. In: Proceedings of IDC 2004, 1–3 June 2004, Maryland, USA, pp. 73–80 (2004)
30. Cohen, L., Uhry, J.: Naming block structures: a multimodal approach. Early Child. Educ. J. **39**(1), 79–87 (2011)
31. Scheerens, J.: Informal Learning of Active Citizenship at School. Lifelong Learning Book Series, vol. 14. Springer, New York (2009)

Digital Competence of Future Teachers

Jadranka Lasić-Lazić, Krešimir Pavlina, and Ana Pongrac Pavlina(✉)

Faculty of Humanities and Social Sciences, University of Zagreb, I. Lučića 3, 10000 Zagreb, Croatia
{jlazic,kpavlina,apongrac}@ffzg.hr

Abstract. Future teachers are members of the digital generation so the authors are interested to find out what students (future teachers) consider as essential digital competence necessary for their future teaching profession. We are also interested in knowing if they think that competence, which is developed in existing curricula, should be further developed according to modern educational trends. We studied a sample of the students in the humanities and social sciences who are studying at the undergraduate and master's levels for teachers in the Faculty of Humanities and Social Sciences at University of Zagreb, the largest teaching faculty in Republic of Croatia. Research was conducted using a survey with opened and closed questions. Students were asked to rate their attitudes toward the necessary digital competence of future teachers who will educate future generations of digital students using Likert scales.

Keywords: Digital competence · Teachers · Students

1 Introduction

Students who are studying for the teaching profession [1], are members of the digital generation [2], the so-called millennium generation that [3] is classifies as the generation born between the years 1981 and 2000. The synonymous names for the millennium generation are nexters [4], the net generation [5], or generation Y [6]. They are enrolled in modern education. Modern education is defined by changes in educational competencies consisting of eight key competencies [7] that modern educated individuals should exhibit in order to qualify for the future labor market. One of the crucial competencies of modern educated individuals is digital competence. Digital competency relates to the field of information technology. A digitally competent individual possesses the basic knowledge, skills, and attitudes related to the theoretical and practical knowledge of basic applications (tools) for the search, collection, organization, storage, and critical evaluation of information [7, 8]. A great influence on the members of this generation has been made by the technology with which the millennials have grown up [9]. The use of technology is innate to them and they are more geared towards dynamic content than static text. Accordingly, they use different digital technologies at the same time, enabling them to keep in touch with friends. They have a high degree of self-confidence in using technology, that leads to demands for different learning and teaching styles more geared towards group communication [10]. Millennials are surrounded by information and communication technology (ICT) because

S. Kurbanoğlu et al. (Eds.): ECIL 2017, CCIS 810, pp. 340–347, 2018.
https://doi.org/10.1007/978-3-319-74334-9_36

as many as 84% of this generation has at least one digital device for voice or text communication [11]. The research conducted in 2013 [12], involving 60,000 eighth elementary grade students from 21 countries worldwide showed that, by this age, the average student has used computers for six years. Eighty seven percent of students used a computer at home at least once a week by, while this percentage was reduced for use at school (54%) or somewhere else (13%). Off-school computers were used by students for different purposes. At least once a week they created or edited documents (28%), used spreadsheets (11%), created presentations (17%), produced? multimedia presentations (15%), used educational software (18%), used computer programs (10%), and used graphic software (18%). At least once a week outside the school students used the Internet for the purpose of communicating; they sought the information they needed to fulfill their school obligations (52%), used the online encyclopedia or wiki (43%), communicated with others (75%), commented (49%), asked questions (22%) on forums or they answered on questions on forums (24%), wrote blogs (21%), posted pictures or videos (38%), used voice chat (48%), or edited web pages (11%). The computer was used at least once a week for recreational purposes. They searched for activities or places for vacation (28%), read reviews of things they wanted to buy (31%), played games (56%), listened to music (82%), watched videos (68%), or informed themselves (62%).

Since the millennials are constantly surrounded by ICT, the changes that are taking place inevitably affect the educational system. There are eight key competencies that a modern educated individual needs to acquire; "communication in the mother tongue, communication in foreign languages, mathematical competence and fundamental scientific and technological competence, digital competence, learning how to learn, social and civic competence, sense of initiative and entrepreneurship, cultural awareness and expression" [7, p. 3]. Digital competence is highlighted by the fact that the millennials use ICT for private purposes and it is also recognized as one of the core competencies that should be systematically acquired in a formal school environment. A digitally competent individual is a person who possesses basic knowledge, skills, and attitudes pertaining to theoretical and practical knowledge of basic applications for the purpose of searching, collecting, organizing, storing, and critical evaluation of information [7, 8]. An appropriate level of digital competence would enable future teachers to use the educational technology by using computer (software or hardware) in any subject they use to teach their students more knowledge and skills [13].

2 Methodology

The survey was conducted on 94 students of social-humanistic studies for future teachers at the Faculty of Humanities and Social Sciences, University of Zagreb. The questionnaire was divided into five categories of questions and each category consisted of several questions that each student evaluated on Likert scale. Respondents were enrolled in various study programs for future school teachers and it is expected that each of them will need to use knowledge and skills in the domain of digital competence during his or her future teaching work as they will work with students who are members of either the digital or postdigital generation.

3 Results

Table 1 shows that nearly three-quarters of surveyed students were female and only a quarter of surveyed students were male students. These data were backed by the latest report of [14] from the year 2015/2016, according to which a total of 6,278 students at the Faculty of Humanities and Social Sciences studied in the first four years of study, out of which 4,660 were female students.

Table 1. Number (percent) of students per gender

Gender	Number of students
Male	24 (25.5%)
Female	70 (74.5%)
Total	94 (100.0%)

Table 2 shows that the largest number of surveyed students were in their second year of graduate study and the smallest number were in their third year of undergraduate study. During their formal education (primary, secondary, and higher education), students attended various educational subjects aimed at developing the eight core competences of the contemporary educated person [3]. Students were required to estimate how much teaching time was dedicated to the development of individual competence on a scale of 1–5 (with 1 meaning not satisfactory 5 meaning of excellent).

Table 2. Number (percent) of students per year of study

Year of study	Number of students
3rd year of undergraduate study	26 (27.7%)
1st year of graduate study	30 (31.9%)
2nd year of graduate study	38 (40.4%)
Total	94 (100.0%)

Table 3 shows that the highest percent of students estimated that a high amount of teaching time during their education was devoted to the development of communication in the mother tongue (38.30%) and communication in foreign languages (46.81%), whereas a good amount of teaching time was devoted to mathematical competence and basic scientific and technological competence (44.09%) and digital competence (31.91%). As a result, these percentages are followed by an average grade, with the lowest average grade (2.44) of these four competences being allocated to digital competence.

Table 4 shows that the highest percent of students (46.8%) estimated to have a very good level of digital competence. Their attitude can be explained by the fact that the surveyed students were members of the so-called digital generation that is surrounded by ICT and that encourages them to believe in their own digital superiority.

Table 3. Number (percent) of students who expressed their attitudes about development of individual competence during their formal educational process

	Not satisfactory	Enough	Good	Very good	Excellent	Average
Communication in the mother tongue	8	2	14	36	34	3.91
	8.51%	2.13%	14.89%	38.30%	36.17%	
Communication in the foreign languages	4	14	24	44	8	3.40
	4.26%	14.89%	25.53%	46.81%	8.51%	
Mathematical competence and basic competences in science and technology	8	10	41	28	6	3.14
	8.60%	10.75%	44.09%	30.11%	6.45%	
Digital competence	24	24	30	12	4	2.44
	25.53%	25.53%	31.91%	12.77%	4.26%	
Learning to learn	41	21	16	12	2	2.04
	44.57%	22.83%	17.39%	13.04%	2.17%	
Social and civic competences	46	10	20	12	6	2.17
	48.94%	10.64%	21.28%	12.77%	6.38%	
Sense of initiative and entrepreneurship	56	22	12	2	2	1.63
	59.57%	23.40%	12.77%	2.13%	2.13%	
Cultural awareness and expression	24	20	22	22	6	2.63
	25.53%	21.28%	23.40%	23.40%	6.38%	

Table 4. Number (percent) of students who expressed their attitudes about their own digital competence

	Not satisfactory	Enough	Good	Very good	Excellent	Average
Grade your own digital competence	4	4	34	44	8	3.51
	4.3%	4.3%	36.2%	46.8%	8.5%	

Table 5 shows that the highest percentage of students (51.06%) agreed with the claim that only a basic level of digital competence was achieved during formal education and that more levels of digital competence were gained during informal forms of learning (53.19%). The highest percent of students (51.06%) were aware that they will need to be highly digitally competent in their future profession as teachers.

Table 6 shows students' views on their competence to use different categories of information tools. The highest average rating (4.19) was given to the use of presentation tools: almost half (44.68%) of students to knew at least one of these tools very well. This can be explained by the fact that students often use this type of tool during their education. A high average rating was also assigned to video editing tools (3.61), collaboration tools (3.59), audio tools (3.42) and drawing tools (3.38), which most students considered to be very good (34.15%, 42.55%, and 38.30%) or good (34.04%). These results can be explained because these types of tools were used by students to

Table 5. Number (percent) of students who expressed their attitudes on acquired digital competence

	Not agree at all	Disagree	No opinion	Agree	Fully agree	Average
During the formal educational process (elementary school, secondary school, university) I have acquired just the basic level of digital competence	0	18	14	48	14	3.61
	0.0%	19.15%	14.89%	51.06%	14.89%	
Higher levels of digital competence I have acquired during the informal educational process (at various courses, socializing with friends, self-study etc.)	2	4	12	50	26	4.0
	2.13%	4.26%	12.77%	53.19%	27.66%	
I consider that, as a future teacher, I need to be a highly digitally competent	0	4	6	36	48	4.36
	0.0%	4.26%	6.38%	38.30%	51.06%	

Table 6. Number (percent) of students who expressed their attitudes about their skills and knowledge of the use of certain types of information tools

	Not use at all	Have minimum knowledge and skills	Know how to use	Have very good knowledge and skills	Excellent in using	
Audio tools (a tool to work with sound) (for example Skype, Voki, Blabberize, Vocaroo)	8	8	28	36	14	3.42
	8.51%	8.51%	29.79%	38.30%	14.89%	
Drawing tools (for example Paint, Wordle, Queeky, CubeScape, Imaginary City)	2	18	32	26	16	3.38
	2.13%	19.15%	34.04%	27.66%	17.02%	
Collaboration tools (for example Google Disk, Dropbox, Zoho, Class Tools)	4	12	20	40	18	3.59
	4.26%	12.77%	21.28%	42.55%	19.15%	
Graphical tools (for example Photoshop Express, Picnik, Splashup, LunaPic, LoonaPix, Photo Notes)	24	12	22	20	16	2.91
	25.53%	12.77%	23.40%	21.28%	17.02%	
Tools to create a mind map (for example Gliffy, WiseMapping, DropMind, MindMup)	25	20	20	2	2	1.78
	36.23%	28.99%	28.99%	2.90%	2.90%	

(continued)

Table 6. (*continued*)

	Not use at all	Have minimum knowledge and skills	Know how to use	Have very good knowledge and skills	Excellent in using	
Presentation tools (for example Prezi, PhotoPeach, Slideshare, Slidestory, PowerPoint)	0 0.0%	2 2.13%	14 14.89%	42 44.68%	36 38.30%	4.19
Tools to create animations (for example ZooBurst, Pixton, Creaza, ToonDoo, Animatron)	56 59.57%	22 23.40%	8 8.51%	6 6.38%	2 2.13%	1.68
Tools to create video content (for example YouTube, MagToo, Jing, Photobucket)	6 7.32%	10 12.20%	12 14.63%	28 34.15%	26 31.71%	3.61

Note: Respondents use/used at least one of the tools in each group which can also be used for educational process

Table 7. Number (percent) of students who expressed their attitudes about using educational technology in their future teaching work

	Not agree at all	Disagree	No opinion	Agree	Fully agree	Average
In future teaching work I plan to use educational technology for developing educational materials	0 0.00%	2 2.13%	4 4.26%	40 42.55%	48 51.06%	4.42
I believe that by using educational technology, I will facilitate the adoption of knowledge and skills	2 2.13%	0 0.0%	6 6.38%	42 44.68%	44 46.81%	4.34
I believe that by using educational technology in my own future teaching work, I will enable better motivation for my students	2 2.13%	2 2.13%	10 10.64%	46 48.94%	34 36.17%	4.14
I believe that by using educational technology in my own future teaching work, I will establish a positive classroom atmosphere	0 0.0%	2 2.13%	14 14.89%	52 55.32%	26 27.66%	4.08
I believe that by using educational technology in my own future teaching work, I will reduce disciplinary problems	6 6.38%	24 25.53%	34 36.17%	22 23.40%	8 8.51%	3.02
In order to prepare for the use of educational technology in teaching, it will take me more time in comparison with ordinary school lesson preparation	2 2.13%	22 23.40%	34 36.17%	22 23.40%	14 14.89%	3.25

create content intended for free time or to communicate with colleagues. The lowest average scores were achieved by graphical tools (2.91), mind mapping tools (1.78), and animation creation (1.68) which can be explained by the fact that students did not necessarily need to use this skills during their education.

Table 7 shows that most of the students (51.06%) planned to use educational technology in their future teaching work, as they believed that their students will thus be facilitated by acquiring knowledge and developing skills (46.81%). The highest percentage of students agreed with the statement that the technology will motivate students for work (48.94%) and help with the establishment of a positive classroom atmosphere (55.32%). It is interesting to note that the highest percentage of students had no opinion regarding the use of technology to reduce disciplinary problems (36.17%) and that development of teaching materials would be more time-consuming than using classroom teaching (36.17%).

4 Conclusion

The digital generation to which today's students belong has estimated that, on a scale of eight core competences, digital competence is on fifth place according to the amount of time that should be dedicated to its development. While students gave digital competence is in the formal school system this relatively low position, students gave their own digital competence an average rating (3.51). Despite the moderate results at the acquired level of digital competence, it is important for students to become very highly digitally competent as future teachers (4.61). Formal education provided only basic levels of digital competence (3.61) while a higher number of students, on average, rated non-formal learning at a very good level (4.0). Students considered that they are on average very highly competent in digital use of presentation tools (4.19) and have slight competence in using animation tools (1.68) that can be explained by the fact that presentation tools are most used and are, therefore, the most intuitive in their use. It is evident that digital competence is considered by students to be very important from the point of view of their future teaching work to use educational technology (4.42), which is primarily perceived as helping students in acquiring knowledge and skills (4.34) and as a good motivational tool (4.14).

References

1. Chen, W., Lim, C., Tan, A.: Pre-service teachers' ICT experiences and competencies: new generation of teachers in digital age. In: Wong, S.L., et al. (eds.) Proceedings of the 18th International Conference on Computers in Education, Putrajaya, Malaysia. Asia-Pacific Society for Computers in Education (2010)
2. Green, H., Hannon, C.: Their Space: Education for a Digital Generation. Demos, London (2007)
3. Reeves, T.C., Oh, E.: Generational differences. In: Spector, J.M., Merrill, M.D., van Merrienboer, J., Driscoll, M.P. (eds.) Handbook of Research on Educational Communications and Technology, pp. 296–302. Routledge, Abingdon (2008)

4. Zemke, R., Raines, C., Filipczak, B.: Generations at Work: Managing the Class of Veterans, Boomers, X-ers, and Nexter in Your Workplace. Amacon, New York (2010)
5. Tapscott, D.: Grown Up Digital: How the Net Generation is Changing Your World. McGraw-Hill, New York (2008)
6. Oblinger, D., Oblinger, J. (eds.): Educating the Net Gen. EDUCAUSE, Washington, D.C. (2005)
7. European Commission: Key Competences for Lifelong Learning: European Reference Framework. Luxembourg: Office for Official Publications of the European Communities. http://eur-lex.europa.eu/legal-content/EN/ALL/?uri=celex%3A32006H0962 (2007)
8. Tuđman, M.: Teorija Informacijske Znanosti. Hrvatska Sveučilišna Naklada, Nacionalna i Sveučilišna Knjižnica u Zagrebu, Zagreb (2014)
9. Delcampo, R.G., Haggerty, L., Haney, M.J., Knippel, L.S.: Managing the Multi-Generational Workforce: From the GI Generation to the Millennials. Gower Publishing Company, Burlington (2011)
10. Gallardo-Echenique, E., Marques-Molias, L., Bullen, M., Strijbos, J.: Let's talk about digital learners in the digital era. Int. Rev. Res. Open. Distrib. Learn. **16**(3), 156–187 (2015)
11. Pletka, B.: Educating the Net Generation: How to Engage Students in the 21st Century. Santa Monica Press LLC, Santa Monica (2007)
12. Fraillon, J., Ainley, J., Schulz, W., Friedman, T., Gebhardt, E.: Preparing for Life in a Digital Age: The IEA International Computer and Information Literacy Study International Report. Springer International Publishing, Amsterdam (2014). https://doi.org/10.1007/978-3-319-14222-7. International Association for the Evaluation of Educational Achievement (IEA)
13. Computer Science Teachers Association: CSTA K-12 Computer Science Standards: The CSTA Standards Task Force, New York, ACM (2011). https://csta.acm.org/Curriculum/sub/CurrFiles/CSTA_K-12_CSS.pdf
14. Državni Zavod za Statistiku Republike Hrvatske: Studenti u Akademskoj Godini 2015/2016. Državni Zavod za Statistiku Republike Hrvatske, Zagreb (2017). (ISSN 1332-0297)

Financial Literacy Competencies of Women Entrepreneurs in Kenya

Joyce Kinyanjui[1(✉)] and Dennis Ocholla[2]

[1] University of Zululand, Empangeni, South Africa
Joycekinyanjui30@gmail.com
[2] Department of Information Studies, Faculty of Arts, University of Zululand, Empangeni, South Africa
ochollad@unizulu.ac.za

Abstract. Research shows high correlation between financial literacy skills and economic outcomes. This paper summarizes findings of a study on financial literacy competencies of women entrepreneurs in Kenya and how these skills affect their economic empowerment. The study used positivist/post positivist and constructivist approaches associated with Pragmatic paradigm. Data from 400 respondents were collected through questionnaires. Data analysis was through the Statistics and Data (STATA) package. Cross-tabulation analysis and chi-square test of independence were used to analyse relationships between variables. Willingness to invest in risky businesses (49.62%), not shopping around (48.74%), low numeric skills (66.92%), and taking loans without considering the cost (74.05%) are undermining women's economic empowerment demonstrated by the fact that 79.68% of the respondents felt that their financial status was out of control and 83.59% felt uncomfortable about their current debt status. The study was limited to women entrepreneurs in Chuka Constituency who received Uwezo Funds during the 2013/2014 financial year.

Keywords: Sustainable development goals · Financial literacy
Women economic empowerment · Kenya · Chuka constituency

1 Introduction and Theoretical Background

1.1 Information Revolution

Human civilization has been characterized by numerous evolutions, the most notable being hunting and gathering; the domestication of plants and animals; the agrarian revolution; the industrial revolution; and the information revolution. This most recent evolution is the driving force behind development in all spheres of life today [1]. According to [2, p. 14], this is what has led to a fundamental shift in the regime of economic growth towards a new phase called the knowledge economy where knowledge is now regarded as a critical part of the production system.

However, a special kind of literacy beyond functional literacy or the ability to read and write is required for the effective access and utilization of information. This kind of literacy is what is commonly referred to as information literacy (IL). Information literacy is a term that has many related definitions. The majority of the definitions

S. Kurbanoğlu et al. (Eds.): ECIL 2017, CCIS 810, pp. 348–358, 2018.
https://doi.org/10.1007/978-3-319-74334-9_37

include: the ability to know when information is needed; formulation of an effective search strategy using a variety of sources; critical evaluation of the content, accuracy, and source of the information retrieved; and the effective use of that information to meet one's goals, [3].

It is worth noting that different kinds of information and knowledge are required in particular fields. For example, those who would aspire to work in the world of information and communication must be computer literate. Information specialists are therefore now talking about various kinds of literacies. Some of the literacies that have been identified include: functional or basic literacy, cultural literacy, scientific literacy, computer literacy, and business/financial literacy, to name a few [1]. The definition of literacy has therefore been broadened to include multiple literacies or bodies of knowledge, skills, and social practices with which we understand, interpret, and use symbol systems of our culture [4]. Financial literacy (FL) was the focus of this study.

1.2 Financial Literacy

There are many and varied definitions of FL but Hogarth cited in [5] surmised that most definitions of financial literacy include knowledge and the understanding of basic financial concepts and choices in the areas of banking, savings and borrowing, spending wisely, and debt control; good financial planning for the future in case of life events such as retrenchment or for retirement; and the ability to use these to plan and implement financial decisions. Ability to make informed and confident decisions regarding all aspects of one's budgeting, spending and saving, and their use of financial products and services, from everyday banking through to borrowing, investing, and planning for the future is at the core of FL [6]. Similar to IL, for an individual to be considered financially literate, it is assumed that the person has the intellectual ability to understand, find, evaluate, and use information relating to finances, financial products, risks, and any other information relating to his or her financial well-being.

1.3 Women Economic Empowerment

Although there is no set of indicators of women's economic empowerment that cut across all cultures and regions, there is evidence of several characteristics that are relevant and important for economic empowerment across a range of contexts, such as: women's control over income; relative contribution to family support; access to and control of family resources; women's access to employment; ownership of assets and land; access to credit; involvement and/or representation in local trade associations; access to markets; women's representation in high paying jobs; women Chief Executive Officers (CEO); and the representation of women's economic interests in macroeconomic policies, state, and federal budgets [7].

1.4 Barriers to Women Economic Empowerment

Lazo, cited in [8], lists the main obstacles to women's economic empowerment as: illiteracy; lack of awareness; lack of information and knowledge about markets; lack of skills; overall lack of self-esteem and self-confidence; lack of money; lack of job opportunities; and lack of connections. However, illiteracy has been identified as one of the strongest predictors of poverty and is often used to characterize hunger and malnutrition, lack of basic necessities such as safe drinking water and health services, social isolation, exclusion and exploitation, and lack of education that is still experienced in many parts of the world [9]. Low literacy and numeracy levels have therefore become key players in exacerbating social exclusion and alienation for women. [10] describes literacy as the root of society; without literacy there can be no empowerment, much more so for women and girls. Fiedrich and Jellema cited in [11], observe that with increased literacy, women are able to gain access to male-dominated areas of work, learn languages of power that were previously associated with men, and participate in household finances that were previously controlled by men. Therefore, literacy can be the equivalent of powerful tide that lifts all boats [11]. In this paper the broader definition of literacy that includes functional literacy discussed above under Sect. 1.1 is used.

2 Research Problem and Purpose of the Study

Education for women and girls is one of the smartest investments a country can make because it increases economic growth for women and that of a country, improves women's wages and jobs and also empowers them such that they have more say over their lives, are less likely to be subject to domestic violence, participate more in decision making in households, and have an increased sense of their own worth and efficacy [12]. Despite its obvious benefits, gender disparity in education exists in Kenya today, becoming more pronounced in higher education.

According to the Kenya National Bureau of Statistics (KNBS), the net enrolment rates (NER) are the highest ever—74.6% for Early Childhood Development and Education (ECDE), 88.4% for primary schools, and 47.8% for secondary schools [13]. In 2014, 580,921 boys and 711,754 girls (a total of 1,292,675 from 6–13 years) were not enrolled, either because they never attended school or dropped out [14], making this number the eighth highest of any country in the world [15]. According to the Ministry of Education Science and Technology (MoEST), gender parity in access at primary level stood at 97 girls to 100 boys in 2015 but decreased to 89 girls to 100 boys at secondary level and at university, only 30% of students are girls [14].

For those enrolled in school, some do not stay in school long enough to acquire basic literacy and numeracy skills that are critical to acquisition of financial literacy skills. A recent report by [16] indicates that there is high primary school dropout rate at 17.3%; high primary repetition rates between 2% and 7% due to low learning outcomes; low primary retention rate at 82.9%; low transition rate from primary to secondary at 82.3%; and a very low completion of secondary education at 47.8%.

A recent study by the Kenya National Bureau of Statistics determined that 21% of women who were between the ages of 15 and 49 years were illiterate while the percentage for the same age group was lower for men at 8% [17]. The government further puts the percentage of illiterate adults between the ages of 45–49 at 49%. This age bracket is significant for this study as it encompasses adults who are meant to be engaged in wealth creation. The sad irony of illiteracy is that those who need access to knowledge, information, and skills the most, through which they might pull themselves out of poverty, are the ones who are most deprived of this access.

As the government puts every effort to raise the basic literacy levels in the country, the flow of information continues unabated. The amount of information being created everyday is equivalent to that created from dawn of civilization until year 2003. This leads to information overload [18]. Drucker as quoted by [20] once said, "finding, evaluating, and using information efficiently are among the most significant challenges to all professions, particularly in the business world." Large organizations are now hiring information specialists to manage information for them because there is far too much information for any but specialists to find their way around.

For women who are illiterate or just have basic education, acquisition of various functional literacies including FL becomes a great challenge. Lusardi and Mitchell [19] have clearly established that there is a very high correlation between financial literacy and economic outcomes. Women who are not financially literate are excluded from low cost, fair, and safe financial services that are offered by mainstream financial providers such as banks making it impossible for them to achieve sustained economic empowerment. For as long as this form of exclusion remains, the economic empowerment of women will never happen and the term will remain a mere catch phrase and an ever moving target.

Whereas the government has data on literacy, comprehensive data on women entrepreneurs' FL skills is lacking, which makes designing of targeted interventions a near impossibility. The overall aim of the study was therefore to establish the financial literacy competences of women entrepreneurs in Kenya and determine the impact of financial literacy on their economic empowerment.

3 Research Design and Methodology

3.1 Research Design

The study used the mixed method approach that is normally associated with a Pragmatic paradigm. The study combined the Positivist/postpositivist that is associated with quantitative data and Constructivist approaches that emphasizes the socially constructed nature of reality and is therefore associated with qualitative data. The study was carried out using the survey research design because of its ability to capture the complexities of the issues under study using only a small sample of the population. Purposive sampling was used to select 105 women's groups who had obtained loans from the Uwezo Fund in Chuka Constituency in the 2013/2014 financial year.

3.2 Sampling

Both random and stratified sampling technique was applied. The number of respondents from each stratum was proportionate to the size of the different strata of enterprises funded. Possible sampling error was considered. In order to reduce the sampling error, Krejcies's model of sample size determination, as quoted by [21], was used to determine the sample size. The calculation is

$$n = \left(x^2 Npq\right) / \left(d^2 (N - 1) + x^2 pq\right) \quad (1)$$

Where n = desired sample size
N = Target population
P = population proportion (take 0.5)
d = degree of accuracy reflected by the amount of error that can be tolerated in fluctuation of a size about the population and corresponds to the significance level with a standard error of the proportion at the corresponding confidence level
x^2 = the table chi square for one degree of freedom relative to the desired level of confidence ($x^2 = 3.841$ at 95% confidence level).

In the financial years 2013/2014, a total of 105 women's groups obtained loans from the Uwezo Fund in Chuka Constituency. Based on the above calculation, the sample size should be a total of 80 groups. Businesses are categorized into three groups: trade; service; and agriculture. The number of women's groups involved in trade was 38, 17 in the service industry, and 50 in agriculture. In order to calculate the sample proportionate to size, the following formula, as proposed by [22] was used:

Sample size n = 80
Population N = 105
Trade population N1 = 38. To calculate the sample, 80 (38/105) = 29
Service population N2 = 17. To calculate the sample 80 (17/105) = 13
Agriculture population N3 = 50. To calculate the sample 80 (50/105) = 38.

Sample sizes for the different strata were 29 for women groups involved in trade, 13 in service industry, and 38 in agriculture to make a total of 80 women groups. These were selected through random sampling. In order to give the various women groups equal chances of being selected, the names of the women groups in the various business categories were written on a chit and folded. Thereafter, the required numbers of women's groups per categories were picked by one of the research assistants.

The third stage of sampling included the final selection of the women entrepreneurs who were to participate in the research. Each group had an average of 10 women entrepreneurs who met regularly. From each group, a total of 5 women entrepreneurs or 50% of the members participated in the survey. Further sampling at group level was necessitated by the fact that there was a level of homogeneity of the women in the same group as they were involved in running the same business. Collecting data from each member may after some time not yield any new information. It was therefore expected that the total number of women participating in the survey would be 400 women.

3.3 Data Collection

The main instrument for data collection was a questionnaire for the women entrepreneurs. To ensure content validity, information from the literature review was used to construct the questionnaires. The detailed questionnaires had both structured and open-ended questions. The numbers of open-ended questions were minimized to reduce the time taken by respondents to fill in the questionnaire and for the researcher to code, enter, and analyze data. Care was taken to have the open-ended questions follow close-ended related questions. Finally, in order to reduce chances of individual questions being misunderstood, proper question sequencing by making them clear and smooth flowing was followed. In other words, the relation of one question to the next was apparent and questions that were easy to answer came before the more difficult ones [22]. A second interview guide was administered to officers working for the Uwezo Fund.

3.4 Data Analysis

Discrete data was analyzed using the Statistics and Data (STATA) package to generate descriptive statistics such as frequencies (counts) and percentages to describe data on the various variables. Cross-tabulation analysis was conducted to simultaneously analyze the relationship between two or more variables in the study. Causal analysis that is concerned with the study of how one variable affects changes in another variable was used to determine how financial literacy skills affect women economic empowerment which is one of the research questions. A chi-square test of independence was then carried out to assess the degree of association between these variables.

4 Results and Discussion

4.1 Financial Literacy Skills

The following findings of this study were discussed at a conference in Nairobi, Kenya by Kinyanjui and Ocholla [23]. Since financial literacy is a multi-dimensional concept that relates to and overlaps with various other concepts and disciplines [24], the researcher selected some skills especially those that relate to women economic empowerment, identified the percentage of respondents with these skills, and established their correlations. The following Table 1 shows the financial literacy skills that were assessed and the percentage of women entrepreneurs with these skills.

From the list above, 91.93% of respondents had an understanding on the need to diversify business which was demonstrated by the fact that 52.06% of the respondents had other businesses or forms of paid employment. However, this information is not being translated into action as 49.62% of the respondents were willing to invest in a risky business venture.

With regard to financial education, 91.92% of the respondents knew that they had information gaps and yet only 51.26% of the respondents shopped around for financial products and services from different financial products.

Only 33.08% had basic numeric skills required to calculate financial products like loans or even manage basic accounting in businesses like profit and loss. It is no wonder that only 25.95% of the respondents considered the cost of the loan before taking it. With such low skills, it is highly improbable that the women entrepreneurs will become economically empowered.

Table 1. Ranking of financial literacy skills of women entrepreneurs

Rank	Skill	% of women entrepreneurs with skills
1	Understanding of the need to diversify business	91.93
2	Knowing when information is needed	91.92
3	Being the ultimate decision maker	79.55
4	Shopping for Uwezo loan	78.78
5	Checking account transactions/statements	77.02
6	Understanding of business ventures	59.45
7	Shopping for financial products and service from different financial providers	51.26
8	Not investing in a risky business venture	50.38
9	Basic numeric skills	33.08
10	Considering costs before taking a loan	25.95
11	Feeling of being in control of financial status	20.32
12	Feeling of being very comfortable with the current debt status	16.41

A working knowledge of financial institutions, systems and services and a range of analytical skills are critical components of financial literacy. Only 77.02% of the respondents checked their account transaction/statements. Even fewer (6.31%) found it very easy to understand them.

4.2 Women Entrepreneurs' Economic Empowerment

Around half of the respondents (52.14%) indicated that they had an additional business apart from the one funded by loans from Uwezo Fund; 46.35% did not. Sixty four (16.12%) of the total respondents had been in their current business for more than 10 years. This and the fact that 125 (31.49%) of the total respondents were employed and not carrying out their businesses on a full time basis was evidence of their contribution to family support.

Women are accessing finances: an additional 33.08% of the respondents had access to a second loan in addition to the one from Uwezo Fund. Respondents were accessing funds from the bank; 194 (48.99%) of the total respondents used its services, 92 (23.23%) used a *chama*, and 82 (20.71%) used a Sacco. These three provided financial services to more than 92% of the total respondents. Microfinance has been viewed as the panacea for poverty reduction among women but this study contradicted this notion since only 3.79% of the respondents received financial services from Microfinance Bank.

Access to finances does contribute to economic empowerment. From the survey 315 (79.6%) of the total respondents are the ultimate decision makers when it came to their businesses. A smaller percentage, 251 or 63.38% of the respondents, were solely responsible for money management in their households. Lack of control over finances in their businesses and at home was affecting the respondents' capacity to save because only 178 (44.95%) saved on a regular basis. As a whole only 20.32% of the respondents felt in control of their financial status and one of the reasons could be due to over borrowing as only 16.41% felt very comfortable with their current debt status.

The respondents accessed various products with the most common being money from a *chama* (Self Help Revolving Fund). This is not surprising as the women had to be in a *chama* in order to access the Uwezo Fund. The second most common financial service among the respondents was a savings account. Two hundred and thirty two (58.59%) of the total respondents had a savings account either individually or jointly with someone else. It is worth noting that none of the respondents had taken any insurance cover.

Access to credit is one of the measures of economic empowerment. The only challenge is that 21.21% indicated that they did not shop around. Their source of information in most cases was friends and family. This information may not be accurate or objective. Recommendations of a product by the bank may also not have been objective as most likely the officers would have been marketing their products thereby serving their own interests.

Seven (5.34%) respondents took a loan simply because of its availability and only 5 (3.82%) of the respondents considered their financial need at hand. Taking a loan, simply because it is available as opposed to taking a loan to meet a specific financial need points to lack of prudent financial management that is critical for economic empowerment. This is why access to finances only cannot be a measure of women economic empowerment.

Women entrepreneurs were aware of financial concepts like budgeting and saving but appeared to have had some difficulty in implementing this knowledge effectively. Only 30.89% were so disciplined in terms of spending that they had a written record of their expenses.

4.3 Relationship Between Women's Financial Literacy and Women Economic Empowerment?

The study focused on financial literacy skills as a value added product for economic empowerment. In summary, the study investigated whether financial literacy skills were a major factor in women's economic empowerment. The answer is a resounding yes but some financial literacy skills had a greater impact than others. There were some contradictions where women demonstrated certain financial literacy skills but their actions or attitudes did not reflect this. For example, 235 (59.34%) respondents agreed with the statement that a business with a high return is likely to have higher than average risks but 39 (9.85%) of the total respondents still said that they would invest heavily to maximize their return and only 132 (33.33%) of the total respondents said they would consider the investment "too good to be true" and not invest. In addition, there was no statistically significant relationship between recommendations of the above advertised investment and length of time carrying out the current business. The length of time the respondents had been in business did not seem to be a factor in deciding to invest in such a risky venture or not. We can therefore conclude in this case that previous experience was not a basis for making good financial decisions, as advanced by [25].

Women who did not check their financial statements were more likely to feel uncomfortable about their current debt. Out of the 85 respondents who said they did not check their financial statements, 28 (32.94%) were very uncomfortable with their current debt, compared to 10 (11.76%) who were very comfortable with their current debt. Without checking financial statements it becomes difficult to keep track and control one's debt which is one of the indicators of economic empowerment. With excess borrowing women will always be in debt. In such cases, women's economic empowerment will remain a mirage. There was a statistically significant relationship between checking financial statements and thoughts on current debt, at a 5% level of significance meaning that there was a very high correlation between the financial literacy skill of checking financial statements and the economic indicator of feeling very comfortable about ones debt.

Being in control of household finances empowers women economically. For 251 (63.38%) respondents who said that they were mainly responsible for money management in their household, only 17 (6.11%) said they felt that their current financial situation was out of control ALL of the time. The study established that there is a statistically significant relationship between the person mainly responsible for money management in one's household and the feeling about one's current financial situation, at 5% level of significance. As mentioned earlier, positive feelings of one's financial status is one of the indicators of financial literacy skills.

The ability to check financial statements and keeping written records to keep an eye of all expenses are two financial literacy skills that are highly correlated. It is worth noting that keeping written records to keep an eye on all financial records is both a financial literacy skill and an indicator of women's economic empowerment. Out of the 85 respondents who said that they did not check their financial statements, 8 (9.41%) respondents said that they used written records to keep a close eye on expenses. In comparison, out of the 304 respondents who said that they did check their financial statements, 112 (36.84%) respondents said that they used written records to keep a close eye on expenses. By keeping written records to help them keep an eye on expenses, women were more likely to become economically empowered as they would be able to control household expenditure, which in turn would enable them pay their debts and ultimately feel good about their financial situation.

5 Conclusions

Current assumptions by the government that availability of a viable business proposal, previous business records for at least six months, and registration of a business is an indicator of financial literacy skills may not be accurate. The percentage of respondents with various financial literacy skills are outlined in Table 1, above. Willingness to invest in risky business venture (49.62%), lack of basic numeric skills (66.92%), and taking loans without considering the cost (74.05%) was undermining women's economic empowerment which is demonstrated by the fact that 79.68% of the respondents felt that their financial status was out of control and 83.59% felt uncomfortable about their current debt status. Part of the reasons why women felt this way was due to the fact that for some of them they are not the decision makers when it comes to the businesses or household expenditure. Without control, they cannot save. Economic empowerment for most of these women entrepreneurs therefore remained out of reach.

In order to improve women's' financial literacy skills, this paper proposes the following:

1. Establish a functional education system that supports lifelong learning
2. Implement a national literacy and numeracy strategy that ensures learners acquire functional literacy and numeracy
3. Carry out a national survey on financial literacy skills of women entrepreneurs in order to design an evidence based National Financial Literacy Strategy
4. Integrate teaching of financial literacy in the national curriculum from primary level
5. Strengthened legal frameworks that support gender equality including social, political, economic and education equality
6. Create a facilitative environment that allows access to finances from the private sector and other government programmes.

References

1. Bhandary, K.M.: Information Literacy and Librarians Role (2000). http://www.tulc.org
2. Amin, A., Cohendent, P.: Architectures of knowledge: first capabilities and communities. Oxford University Press, New York (2004)
3. Rosenberg, V.: Information literacy and small business. White Paper Prepared for UNESCO, the U.S. National Commission on Libraries and Information Science, and the National Forum on Information Literacy, for use at the Information Literacy Meeting of Experts, Prague, The Czech Republic (2002). http://www.nclis.gov/libinter/infolitconf&meet/papers/rosenberg-fullpaper.pdf
4. Hull, G., Mikulecky, L., St. Ralf, C., Kerka, S.: Multiple literacies: a compilation for adult educators (2003). http://www.cete.org/acve
5. Worthington, A.C.: Predicting Financial Literacy in Australia (2006). http://www.works.bepress.com/acworthington
6. Roy Morgan Research: Australia and New Zealand Survey of Adult Financial Literacy in Australia (2003). http://www.information.net
7. Cheston, S., Kuhn, L.: Empowering Women Through Microfinance (2002). http://www.microcreditsummit.org/papers/empowering_final.doc
8. UNESCO: Women, education and empowerment: pathways towards autonomy. UIE Studies 5 • 1995. Report of the International Seminar held at UIE, Hamburg, 27th January–2 February 1993. http://www.unesco.org
9. Khaldoun, H.: Illiteracy, financial services and social exclusion (2002). http://www.staff.vu.edu.au
10. Dighe, A., Usha, V.R.: Women's literacy and information and communication technologies: lessons that experience has taught. Commonwealth Education Media Centre for Asia (CEMCA) and The Commonwealth of Learning (2006)
11. Gujjar, A.A.: Literacy: a foundation for development of society (2007). http://www.articlesbase.com
12. Sperling, G.B., Winthrop, R., Kwauk, C.: What Works in Girls' Education: Evidence from the World's Best Investment. Brookings Institution Press, Washington, D.C. (2016)

13. Kenya National Bureau of Statistics: Kenya Economic Survey, 2015 (2015a). http://www.knbs.ke
14. Kenya Ministry of Education Science and Technology: 2014 Basic Education Statistics Booklet. Government Printer, Nairobi (2015)
15. UNESCO: Puberty education and menstrual hygiene management (2014). http://unesdoc.unesco.org/images/0022/002267/226792e.pdf
16. Kenya National Bureau of Statistics: Kenya Economic Survey 2016. KNBS, Government Printers, Nairobi (2016)
17. Kenya National Bureau of Statistics: Kenya Demographic and Health Survey 2014. KNBS, Nairobi (2015)
18. Seigler, M.G.: Every two day we create as much information as we did up to 2003 (2003). http://techcrunch.com/2010/08/04/schmidt-data/
19. Lusardi, A. Mitchell, O.S.: Financial literacy and retirement preparedness: evidence and implications for financial education (2007). http://www.EBSCO.com
20. Saulles, M.: New Information Perspective (2007). http://www.emeraldinsight.com/Insight
21. Kenya Institute of Management: Fundamentals of Management Research Methods. Moran Publishers, Nairobi (2009)
22. Kothari, C.R.: Research Methodology: Methods and Techniques. New Age International (P) Ltd., New Delhi (2004)
23. Kinyanjui, J., Ocholla, D.N.: Financial literacy among women entrepreneurs in Kenya: an overview. In: Kwanya, T., Kiplan'gat, J., Wamukoya, J. (eds.) Emerging Trends in Information and Knowledge Management. Eldoret, Moi University Press, pp. 355–366 (2017)
24. Katy, J., Hudson, S., Bush, M.: Tools for survival: an analysis of financial literacy programs for lower income families (2000). http://www.financial-education.org
25. Seghers, A., Manigart, S., Vanacker, T.: The impact of human and social capital on entrepreneurs' knowledge of finance alternatives. J. Small Bus. Manag. **50**(1), 63–86 (2011). https://doi.org/10.1111/j.1540-627x.2011.00344. http://onlinelibrary.wiley.com

Search Engine Literacy

Olivier Le Deuff(✉)

University of Bordeaux Montaigne, MICA, Bordeaux, France
oledeuff@gmail.com

Abstract. The aim of this article is to show that search engine literacy (SEL) can be connected as a transliteracy to digital literacy and information literacy. SEL allows a better understanding of the relationship between information retrieval and technical systems. We show here that teaching Search Engine Optimization (SEO) can be a part of SEL.

Keywords: Literacy · Transliteracy · Search engines · Search engine literacy Google

1 Introduction

If SEO (search engine optimization) is well known, the aim of his article is to show that people's search engine literacy is often very poor. As a professor, I ask my freshmen students every year if they can explain how Google works and how it ranks websites. Not one of my student can answer this question. This is particularly disturbing because my students want to work with information or communication systems. Moreover it demonstrates the failure of their previous education, which should have given them the key to understanding how the main search engines operate.

Many studies have shown that students have great confidence in the results given by Google [1, 2], but they do not develop any critical thinking about its ranking methods.

Moreover, the younger generation is not the only one which does not understand how Google works and how it makes money. In a study of seniors and digital health literacy [3], we have shown that Google was the first tool used to access information on the web (92%). But the design of results is not totally understood by these older users, who very often cannot distinguish between 'natural search results' and ads [4]. At the end of this study, we developed an application to help users evaluate their level of digital health literacy[1]. The results show that the level of health literacy was better than the level of digital literacy because more than 70% of the respondents did not know how Google works.

The aim of this article is to consider search engine literacy (SEL) as an essential part of transliteracy [5]. In fact, search engines like Google are a new kind of media, and major players in information retrieval. Search engine literacy offers the possibility to study the operating mode of Google and to study algorithms from a different perspective from mathematical or computer science approaches.

---

[1] http://www.megatopie.info/testor/enquete.html?e=19.

S. Kurbanoğlu et al. (Eds.): ECIL 2017, CCIS 810, pp. 359–365, 2018.
https://doi.org/10.1007/978-3-319-74334-9_38

This literacy cannot be grounded only on good practices in the use of Google, like the demonstration of advanced research based on simple search literacy [6]. The project of Search engine literacy is more ambitious and calls for a new pedagogy of Google. Later in this article we report on some results of an experiment with our students during a SEO course.

This literacy is a good starting point for explaining the history of the web and the development of a digital and information culture. This is a good method for understanding data literacy and the methods of data treatment. Search engine literacy makes the link between information literacy and data literacy too.

Methodology. This article aims to show the importance of SEL and its relationship with information literacy and culture of information. We want to show here the basis of SEL. This is an exploratory project based on many years of teaching SEO with students in a French i-school. We show here also a project of a French teacher-librarian Florian Reynaud who develops à specific tool to explain search engines.

2 A New Literacy?

2.1 The Search Engine Tradition

SEL is not a totally new literacy. We need to consider older tools for information retrieval before the success of search engines like Google. We think about bibliographic systems, index systems, card systems (like the *Repertoire bibliographique universelle* of Paul Otlet) and other incredible tools like the machine of Emanuel Goldberg [7]. Our ways of searching for information have always been connected with technologies. We always need to imagine sophisticated systems to retrieve information and to satisfy the extent of our information needs. Among these original devices, we think of Jean Hautfuney and the creation of the index of the *Speculum Historiale* written by Jean de Beauvais [8]. That was the beginning of the tradition of indexes and tools for information retrieval (*statim invenire*). After bibliographies and index cards, a new kind of index was created by the Belgian Paul Otlet: the index of all printed documents [9]. It was the 'Google of paper'[2]. We are not in the first age of information, and search engines are not the first generation of 'knowledge machines' [6]. In our age of information, the novelty lies in the computational nature of a search engine's features, which operate on automatic indexing and automated language processing. Nevertheless, it is not impossible to develop historical knowledge of the operating mode of search engines. If learning the information search process requires knowledge of the basic uses of search engines, an ambitious literacy should, rather, involve understanding how they work. That means understanding the context that led to the emergence of Google, in particular the period when leaders like Alta Vista saw a degradation in the quality of their results. Web metadata had been polluted by spam

[2] Louis Wiart, Paul Otlet, L'homme qui inventa le Google de papier. InaGlobal, 01.09.2015. <http://www.inaglobal.fr/histoire/article/paul-otlet-l-homme-qui-inventa-le-google-de-papier-8480>.

keywords. Pornographic keywords and Pamela Anderson's name[3] were used by webmasters to increase their traffic.

The logic is therefore to find a way to grant credit to a resource listed by its URL. The choice made by Sergey Brin and Larry Page was to base their classification algorithm on the importance of references. They chose to build a citation index of the web. This logic was not new, it comes mainly from the work of scientometrics especially that of Garfield, Pritchard and Nalimov. Google belongs to a documentary tradition based on citation logic and on bibliographic methods originally focused on the study of bibliographic references from journals. However the corpus is different since the web is no longer a web of documents for researchers, but a collection of disparate websites. The simplicity and clean interface of Google conceal a complexity that is not understood by users.

2.2 Search Engine Literacy and the Other Literacies

SEL is not a totally new literacy and even less is it disconnected from other literacies that involve information skills on the web. SEL can be considered as a transliteracy that mobilises information skills, digital skills and communication skills.

It is therefore not a separate literacy but rather a literacy that is potentially part of training plans either on the side of information literacy or on the side of digital literacy. It can thus be perfectly described as a transliteracy that makes the link between the two literacies. SEL is also a communication and media literacy. Indeed, we should think of the search engine as a mediation tool that influences content. The evolution of Google makes it a medium in its own right. We find ourselves here aligning with discourses around new media literacies [10]. The challenge is clearly to understand the articulations between content and media.

Search engine literacy allows the link with a citizen conception of information literacy [11], which is precisely a culture of information [12]. This cultural approach implies going beyond good practices to develop a wider and more sustainable knowledge by teaching information and digital concepts. This means better ability to understand the tools used and their foundations. It is also a better cognition and recognition of the technique as part of culture [13, 14]. This implies, therefore, the need to learn the history of the web and the evolution of search engines.

3 SEO as a Strategy of SEL

The challenge is to consider a didactic perspective in teaching search engines, to overcome the "black box" effect, and especially to be able to analyse the results or even criticise them. Indeed, the algorithmic system of search engines relies on computational logic, rather than on logic of analysis. This explains why some research results are disturbed by the high ranking of bad websites with fake news and which are far from the historical truth. For example, a Google search about the historians of the Shoah puts

---

[3] Les meta-tags hors la loi? <http://www.sam-mag.com/archives/metatags.htm>.

forward some negationist websites. This means information literacy must evolve to integrate more and more digital skills. Search engines hide a complexity with a simple interface but the aim is to open the 'black box' following the advice of Johanna Drucker about the necessity to examine the framework:

A frame can extend, intensify, connect, embed, juxtapose, or otherwise modify another frame and perception. The terminology is spatial and dynamic. It describes cognitive processes, not simple actions of an autonomous user, but codependent relations of user and system. In invoking frame analysis as part of the diagrammatic model of interpretation, we have moved from a traditional discussion of graphical formats as elements of a mise en page to a sense that we are involved with a mise en scene or système. This puts us on the threshold of interface and a theory of constructivist processes that constitute the interface as a site of such cognitive relations. Interface is not a thing, but a zone of affordances organized to support and provoke activities and behaviors probabilistically [15, p. 7].

3.1 Learning SEO as a Core Skill for Information Schools

One of the ways to better understand the way search engines work, and especially their ranking methods, is to look at it from an SEO perspective. Students can better understand the key elements used by Google (title markup, domain names, keywords), the page rank and the choices of weighting used in the algorithm.

The observations were made during a course of SEO in a small I-school in France in Bordeaux in DUT Information numérique dans les organisations[4] (digital information in organizations) where we train students for two years. SEO is just a course, which is connected with other courses like metadata history and taxonomies, and markup languages like html and xml. Search engine literacy needs to be connected to many other elements if we want to place it as core content in an I-school curriculum. We can list some essential content:

- The constitution of an index
- History of indexes
- Metadata history, systems and languages
- Human indexing and automatic indexing
- Crawl methods and bots
- Web directories versus Search engines
- Distinction between natural indexing and advertising indexing
- Scientometrics and page rank
- Algorithm and weighting of criteria
- Keyword optimization
- Communication strategies and SEO
- Ethics and search engines
- Personal Data and filter bubbles.

[4] http://www.infonumbordeaux.fr/.

For three years we have experimented with having an SEO contest between groups of students as part of the course. The aim is for them to imagine they are content producers. It is also to apply the SEO methods they have learnt about, to try to place their sites or contents at the top of the hit list on Google. Each year, the choice is based on a request where there are almost no results so that the student productions can best be placed in the first results. The aim of the approach is certainly to be trained in SEO, but the objective is also to pursue the process of training in information retrieval by placing the students on the side of content producers. SEL makes it possible to consider both sides of the information, at the level of the search and also at the level of its production. It makes it easier for students to judge bias in search engines. The principle of motivating students through a logic of challenge or competition also shows that even if search engines avoid too much optimization, search engines' ranking methods differ from human analysis in regard to checking content quality. Therefore, dual training in information retrieval methods and SEO strategies makes it possible to go further in detecting content which is "rubbish". In French, we use 'évaluation de l'information' to describe the analysis of bad contents and the work which allows one to distinguish good contents and relevant websites.

If this type of course seems essential for an I-School education, it is advisable to extend it and offer it earlier on. Without necessarily training in SEO, we could teach how search engines work, especially Google, in an educational perspective.

3.2 Search Engine Pedagogy

Several hypotheses can be envisaged, and are also tested with their students by French colleagues who are teacher-librarians (called in French *professeurs-documentaliste*), to show the students how research results are linked to the constitution of an index[5]. Tools such as Google's custom search can be used to create thematic engines, but you can also rely on specific engines. A *webfinder simulation*[6] is proposed by *professeur-documentaliste* Florian Reynaud in order to be able to use it in class with students. The device makes it possible to understand the steps of classification and how results are ranked. The methods of automatic processing are also explained. It enables understanding of the criteria for ranking information according to the principles of relevance (number of occurrences in connexion to the request), popularity (number of visits), and notoriety (number of links). This also helps learners to understand what an algorithm is with a weighting system.

SEL pedagogy is an important step for information literacy which can show the complexity of the devices and goes beyond the simple satisfaction of an information need (Fig. 1).

---

5 ID Base. Fiches pédagogogiques à l'usage des professeurs documentalistes. <http://idbase.esmeree.fr/>.

6 https://iddocs.fr/webfinder/.

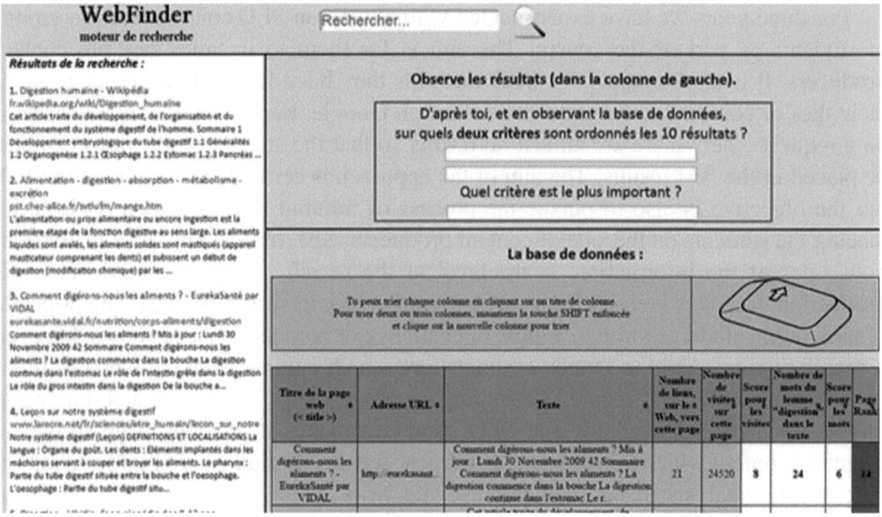

Fig. 1. Webfinder, a tool to understand search engines methods of ranking

4 Conclusion

The description of a culture of information for citizens requires better knowledge of the information retrieval processes and the tools used. SEL cannot be considered a specific literacy. It is a kind of transliteracy and it needs to be connected with information literacy. SEL show the evolution of the methods of teaching information literacy with the will to explain how search engines work, not only the best practices in using them.

Better understanding of search engines, especially through examination of the criteria used for ranking websites, is an important step in the democratization of the search engine and especially Google. It also gives users the means to know when to use Google and when to favour other search methods. Google does not want to publish their algorithm because the firm pretends to protect the truth and to avoid too much SEO optimization. This position shows, too, the will to protect a business model. The democratization of Google appears difficult in this model if users are not well trained and cannot understand the strength and the weakness of such a model. Training students can be the way to imagine that other kind of search engines could be invented in the coming years. Creating an open index [16] of the web could allow alternate models.

Acknowledgment. I want to thank Sheila Webber for reviewing this article. Thanks to Florian Reynaud for the screenshot of his *Webfinder*.

References

1. Hargittai, E., Fullerton, L., Menchen-Trevino, E., Yates-Thomas, K.: Trust online: young adults' evaluation of web content. Int. J. Commun. **4**, 468–494 (2010)
2. Simonnot, B.: De l'usage des moteurs de recherche par les étudiants. In: Simonnot, B., Gallezot, G. (eds.) L'entonnoir. Google sous la loupe des sciences de l'information et de la communication, pp. 31–57. C&F Editions, Caen (2009)
3. Vigouroux-Zugasti, E., Le Deuff, O.: Le senior connecté. In: Saleh, I., et al. (eds.). H2PTM 2015, pp. 174–184. ISTE Editions, London (2015)
4. Le Deuff, O.: La littératie digitale de santé, un domaine en émergence. In: Agostinelli, S., Koulayan, N. (eds.) Les écosystèmes numériques: Intelligence collective, développement durable, interculturalité, transfert de connaissances, pp. 349–369. Presses des Mines, Paris (2016)
5. Thomas, S., et al.: Transliteracy: crossing divides. First Monday **12**(12), 3 December 2007. http://firstmonday.org/htbin/cgiwrap/bin/ojs/index.php/fm/article/viewArticle/2060/1908
6. Wilson, M.L., Ye, C., Twidale, M.B., Grasse, H., Rosenthal, J., McKittrick, M.: Search literacy: learning to search to learn. In: Second International Workshop on Search as Learning (SAL 2016), 21st July, Pisa, Italy (2016)
7. Buckland, M.K.: Emanuel Goldberg and His Knowledge Machine. Greenwood Publishing Group, Westport (2006)
8. Paulmier-Foucart, M.: Ut diligens et intelligens lector requirat: une banque de données du Speculum maius de Vincent de Beauvais. In: De la plume d'oie à l'ordinateur: études de philologie et de linguistique offertes à Hélène Naïs, (Verbum, numéro spécial, Université de Nancy), Nancy, pp. 469–480 (1985)
9. Le Deuff, O.: Utopies documentaires: de l'indexation des connaissances à l'indexation des existences. Commun. Organ. **48**(2), 93–106 (2015)
10. Jenkins, H.: Confronting the Challenges of Participatory Culture: Media Education for the 21st Century. MacArthur Foundation, Chicago (2008)
11. Owens, R.: State government and libraries. Libr. J. **101**(1), 19–28 (1976)
12. Le Deuff, O.: Penser la conception citoyenne de la culture de l'information, Les Cahiers du Numérique. La culture informationnelle **5**(3), 39–49 (2009)
13. Stiegler, B.: La technique et le temps. 1. Galilée: Cité des sciences et de l'industrie, Paris (1994)
14. Simondon, G.: Du mode d'existence des objets techniques. Editions Aubier, Paris (2012)
15. Drucker, J.: Humanities approaches to interface theory. Cult. Mach. **12** (2011). http://svr91.edns1.com/~culturem/index.php/cm/article/download/434/462
16. Lewandowski, D.: Why we need an independent index of the web. arXiv:1405.2212. 9 May 2014

Children's Literacy is Important, but What About Adult Reading Literacy?

Vlasta Zabukovec and Polona Vilar(✉)

Department of LIS&BS, Faculty of Arts,
University of Ljubljana, Ljubljana, Slovenia
{vlasta.zabukovec,polona.vilar}@ff.uni-lj.si

Abstract. We report on a study on adult reading literacy (RL), closely related to information literacy (IL) and very influential in IL development. The level of adult RL, especially its background, is much less investigated than RL of children and young. Existing studies indicate that the level of adult RL in Slovenia is not as high as we would like, which could in the long-term lead to social and economic consequences as well as hinder the principles of democracy and active citizenship. We investigated the factors connected with the adult RL: (1) experiences with past and current promotion of reading (R), attitudes regarding R, family literacy and RL; (2) practices and experiences in lifelong learning and related competences which are influential in the development and maintaining of RL and IL; (3) RL factors investigated in the OECD PIAAC study: content, cognitive strategies, contexts. Our online survey used various types of questions: single/multiple choice, Likert-scale, ranking, open-ended. The sample was purposive (snowball-type) (N = 260) and included adults of all ages, genders, educational and social levels and roles, and various types of housing and residential locations. We gathered information on how the adults perceive and utilize R in its various forms and contexts, what are their attitudes towards the promotion and promotors of R and RL (such as schools, libraries), what practices of lifelong learning and reading culture are present in the society, which contents, contexts of RL are most/least present and how developed are their various cognitive strategies related to RL. Our findings are informative for researchers and teachers in the field of literacies as well as planners of national educational and cultural policies.

Keywords: Reading literacy · Information literacy · Adult reading literacy Lifelong learning · Slovenia

1 Introduction

We are aware of the fact that a lot of has been written to explain the domain in reading literacy (RL) and information literacy (IL). So, it is sometimes very difficult to make coherent conclusions, because several backgrounds, factors and disciplines are included in researching this topic (languages, psychology, pedagogy, library and information science, communication studies and so on). There are many definitions and several operationalisations to reveal RL, which factors are important in developing RL, what kind of impact does RL have in our lives, what is the relationship between RL and IL

S. Kurbanoğlu et al. (Eds.): ECIL 2017, CCIS 810, pp. 366–375, 2018.
https://doi.org/10.1007/978-3-319-74334-9_39

and what kind of applications could be done to improve RL and IL skills. The basic definition of RL, applied in this research, is from PIRLS framework (Progress in International Reading Literacy Study): "*Reading literacy is the ability to understand and use those written language forms required by society and/or valued by the individual. Readers can construct meaning from texts in a variety of forms. They read to learn, to participate in communities of readers in school and everyday life, and for enjoyment.*" [1]. Written language forms, understanding and application were investigated, as it was the case with the PIAAC study (The Programme for the International Assessment of Adult Competencies) [5]. Because the results of PIRLS and PIAAC surveys for Slovenia fourth graders and adults opened several discussions on RL in our society, we were encouraged to start a research on RL among adults.

The last PIRLS in 2011 is the third cycle of study. The fourth-grade students responded to questions designed to measure their reading comprehension in two different situations: reading for literary experience and reading to acquire and use information. In Slovenia, as in ten other participating countries, the level of reading achievement has risen from 2001. In general, it was confirmed that girls had higher scores than boys. The differences were higher for literary than for informational reading. Related to reading comprehension Slovenian fourth-graders got higher scores, so the improvement is evident [3]. Supportive home environment and an early start are crucial in shaping children's RL. For most children, the home provides modelling and direct guidance in effective literacy practices. Young children who see adults and older children reading or using texts in different ways learn to appreciate and use printed materials. It was reported by parents that children with higher reading achievement enjoy reading, are engaged in reading activities more often, have more resources for learning and had attended preschool education [3]. The importance of family and activities to information and reading was first mentioned by D. Taylor in 1983 [2]. D. Taylor at that time explored the social context of home as a key factor in the RL development [2]. She uses this term when she describes different activities in families related to literacy.

PISA 2015 (Programme for International Student Assessment) confirmed that Slovenian 15-year-olds gained better results than OECD average and it was shown that the improvement from year 2006 was really significant [4]. Girls scored much higher than boys. In PISA 2009 the results were elaborated in more details [4] and it was revealed that 15-years old teenagers who read for fun, enjoy reading activities, use self-regulative strategies, and are familiar with strategies of understanding and remembering, had better results in reading than those teenagers who do not possess these skills.

Results on PIAAC [5, 6] survey confirmed that in Slovenia there are 5.6% of adults who attain the two highest levels of proficiency in literacy which is significantly less than the average of 10.6% of adults across OECD countries. In these two levels (4 and 5) adults can integrate, interpret and synthesise information from complex texts that contain conditional and/or contradicting information. 31.2% of adults can understand and respond appropriately to lengthy texts, can identify, interpret or evaluate one or more pieces of information and make appropriate inferences using knowledge text structures and rhetorical devices (Level 3). 24.9% of adults in Slovenia score Level 1 or below in literacy, which means that they can read brief texts on familiar topics and locate a single piece of specific information identical in form to information in the question or instruction.

Our study is inspired also by our recent national project on RL and its contexts, which we found to be primarily linked to educational and cultural policies, of which libraries are an important part [7, 8]. On the basis of our project results some measures were proposed to support a development of RL. Promotion of reading activities should be implemented in all levels of social activities and the support of actual politics is needed. Family reading is one of the most important promotors of reading because it has been confirmed that reading skills develop inter-generationally. It is important to start the literacy process in preschool ages which means that parents and preschool teachers should gain knowledge and skills to adequately support this process [7].

With this research, we aimed to gather information on how the adults perceive and utilize reading in its various forms and contexts. Our findings should be informative for researchers and teachers in the literacy fields as well as planners of national educational and cultural policies.

2 Research

The main focus of this research was:

1. To find out the relationship between past (in childhood) and present reading experiences, especially reading practice, visiting libraries and buying books.
2. To find out what general knowledge do the respondents have about RL and what attitudes and opinions related to RL have been developed, specialy in a context of lifelong learning.
3. To find out what the respondents read, what type of readings they prefer and what kind of cognitive strategies they use in a reading process.

2.1 Sample

Snowball sampling was applied. 260 adults participated in research, 68% were women, 32% were men. 42% of participants were from 21 to 40 years, 28% from 41 to 60 years and 9% above 60 years. 8% of them were students and 62% were employed. Most of them (99%) have finished secondary school or more. 78% of participants were from western part of Slovenia, the minority (22%) comes from eastern part.

2.2 Methods and Procedure

The questionnaire was constructed with three thematic fields: (a) past and actual (present) experiences with reading, (b) reading in a context of lifelong learning and (c) content, cognitive strategies and context of reading. It contained various types of questions: single/multiple choice, Likert-scale and ranking.

Online survey was applied and it took one month to gather data, from April 21 to May 21 2017. Snowball sampling strategy was a convenient way to gather information from respondents of different ages and from different part of Slovenia. Main descriptive statistics and correlational coefficients were computed to explore data.

3 Results and Discussion

Three groups of results will be presented: (1) past and current experiences with reading, (2) reading in the context of lifelong learning and (3) content, cognitive strategies and context of reading.

3.1 Experiences with Reading

The main idea is to explore what kind of memories of their first reading do people have and if these experiences are different compared to present time. Most people confirm pleasant experiences with reading and there are almost no differences between past and present (Fig. 1). The answers were quite homogenous. The correlational coefficient between past and actual experiences is 0.95 ($p = 0.05$).

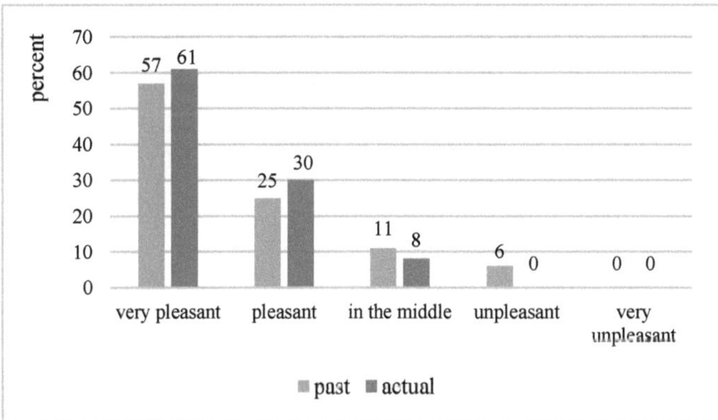

Fig. 1. Past and actual experiences with reading

Figure 2 shows reading practices in the childhood, reading alone or with parents. The correlational coefficient is −0.49 ($p = 0.05$) what means that the majority respondents read alone very often, but reading with parents was not so common in their childhood; a quarter of them sometimes read with their parents.

Further results show that 73% of respondents "very often" or "often" visited the library, their parents bought many books for family members while one fifth bought enormous number of books. 96% of respondents agreed that family literacy is very important. Since the results showed the importance of reading, the correlational coefficients were computed to establish these relations more precisely (Table 1). All coefficients show importance at 5% risk, the highest correlation is between respondents' opinion about family literacy and their visiting libraries in childhood. The relation between buying books and family literacy is quite low.

In the context of reading experiences (Fig. 3), the respondents revealed that teachers promoted reading experiences during lectures the most. But the librarians were not so important in this process as we expected to be. Maybe they did not have so many

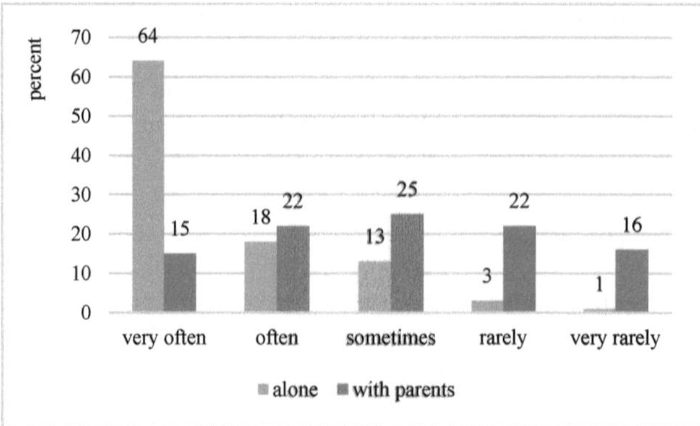

Fig. 2. Reading alone or with parents in a childhood

Table 1. Correlations between buying books, visiting libraries and importance of family literacy

	Visiting libraries	Importance of family literacy
Buying books	r = 0.52 (p = 0.05)	r = 0.20 (p = 0.05)
Visiting libraries		r = 0.90 (p = 0.05)

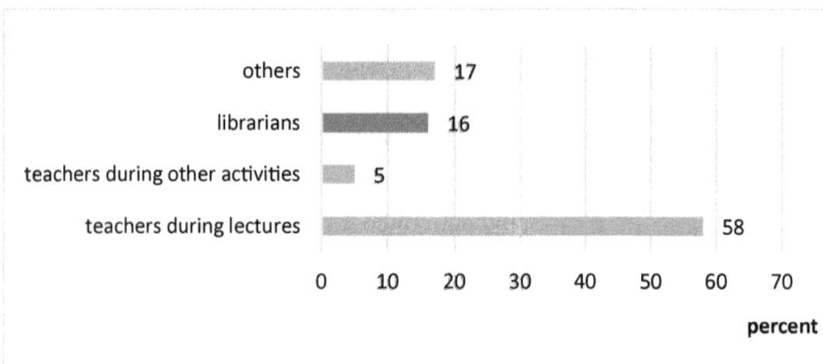

Fig. 3. Promotors of reading in a primary school

opportunities because school libraries had been organized differently in the past and promotion of reading itself was not emphasized. Besides, grandparents were also important partners in reading activities. On the other side, respondents argued that promotors were not important to them because they were really interested in reading itself and they enjoyed it very much.

To get a more complex picture of results, we make some conclusions about past and present experiences on reading. Respondents reported about pleasant memories which are still the same in the present time. In PISA 2009 [4] it was pointed out that enjoying reading activities improves reading skills and brings better results in reading on general. The importance of modelling was not confirmed because we did not ask explicitly about this, but we received information that they did not experience a lot of family reading. Such reading is important not only because of the reading activity, but also because of discussions and interpretations after reading, and especially because for developing understanding and memory skills [4]. Slovenian adults are lacking of these skills [5]. Adults remember that schools were good promotors of reading, especially teachers. But their own interest for reading prevailed; they became their own best promotors of reading. In PIRLS 2011 it was confirmed that interest is one of main factors for RL [4].

3.2 Reading in the Context of Lifelong Learning

Questions in this group are different; some of them related to general knowledge, others ask about opinions or attitudes and some of them ask about experiences.

Respondents explained what RL means for them (Fig. 4). Mostly they explain RL as the ability to read, but other answers are important as well in spite of lower numbers. Besides, their comments on the given explanation are predominantly a combination of all activities, reading, writing, receiving and expressing.

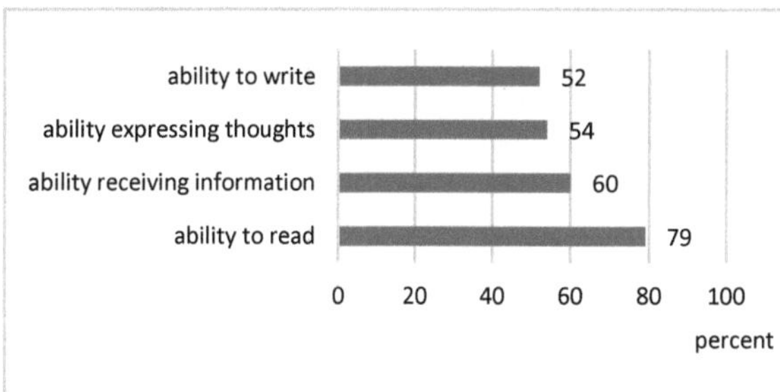

Fig. 4. Explanation of RL

Respondents expressed their opinions on how RL can influence different aspects and areas of life. They were asked to rank options from the most important to the least important (Table 2). General knowledge and life success received the highest position, followed by school and work success. The last three: family, social life and leisure time, have a kind of social notion, and it could be interpreted the RL is in a close relation to social behaviour.

Several activities for developing RL were proposed to the respondents. They had to evaluate which ones will be more suitable for children, teenagers and adults (Table 3). There are some activities which, in their opinion, are suitable for all three groups (voluntary reading activities, reading during family activities and discussions about reading). But on the other side, there are some activities of a more formal nature, like mandatory reading activities, reading activities for school and participation in reading groups. Respondents feel these to be more suitable for children. Others, less formal, are judged to be more appropriate for teenagers: voluntary reading activities, searching information and supporting reading in different situations.

Table 2. Ranking of RL influence

Place	Reading literacy influences...
1	General knowledge
2	Life success
3	School success
4	Work success
5	Family life
6	Social life
7	Leisure time

Table 3. Proposed reading activities for different groups in percentage

Activities	Children	Teenagers	Adults
Voluntary reading activities	64	81	71
Mandatory reading activities	82	49	7
Reading during family activities	61	68	80
Reading activities for school	92	88	12
Searching information	69	91	81
Discussion on readings	90	89	72
Supporting reading in different situations	75	82	76
Participation in reading groups	82	78	65

The next question asked their opinions on which factors influence RL (Table 4). Respondents were asked to rank the options (first rank means the most important position). Content analysis was applied to establish factors which influence RL: personal motivation, social support and technological aspects. Personal motivation is really important and could be realized in developing interest for reading and spending a lot of time reading. Reading and visiting libraries are activities where other people and institutions give an important push for reading. Technological aspects contain use of computer, internet searching and family financial status.

Table 4. Factors which influencing RL

Place	Factors	
1	Interest in reading	Personal motivation
2	Spent time for reading	
3	Support for reading	Social support
4	Visiting libraries	
5	Use of computer	Technological aspects
6	Family financial status	
7	Internet searching	

In this section, it was confirmed that there is a need to practice reading in a lifelong learning context. Adults have gained knowledge on literacy processes and are aware of what RL is. Their understanding is close to the holistic approach on RL; they believe that reading, writing, expressing and receiving are important components of RL. They are aware of RL's impact on learning and also on life in general. This notion was emphasized also in PIRLS, PISA in PIAAC [3–5]. Reading is not only a matter of language, but should be implemented in different learning settings and in different real-life activities. Besides, reading is also an intergenerational activity [7]. On the basis of results about factors which influence RL, it is important to give opportunities to children to develop their interest in reading in different situations. Social support is needed and technical conditions should be offered (computer, internet and financial resources). Experiencing diverse reading activities through lifelong learning is demanding, but it depends on personal development. Children need more structured activities, teenagers are more familiar with and fond of less formal reading activities, especially because of past experiences with formal reading activities which help them upgrade reading activities. For the adults there are activities, especially in families, where certain organization and structure are needed to offer support.

3.3 Content, Cognitive Strategies and Context of Reading

Adults were asked about time spent reading, types of texts, and about internet and printed texts. Besides this, cognitive strategies before, between and after reading were also investigated.

On average, adults read between one and two hours daily. Family reading is not common – they do it less than every 14 days. Adults read newspapers every day. They read printed and internet texts every day (Fig. 5) and they reported that printed texts are easier for reading.

When they have problems with understanding the main idea in the texts they have read they try several strategies such as reading it once again, asking other people or using other reference sources and trying to understand it in context. While practicing

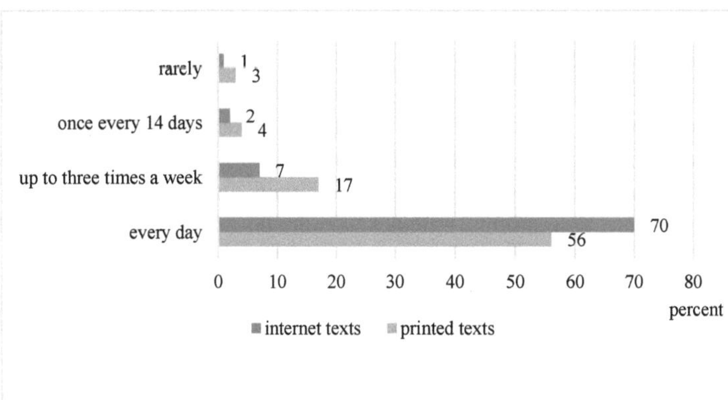

Fig. 5. Reading printed and internet texts

reading activities many adults use reading plans (nearly 90%) and reading summaries (more than 80%), as shown in Fig. 6.

Through reading different texts, literate and informative ones, adults enrich reading practices. Understanding different kinds of information and using them in different contexts provides opportunities to develop RL [4]. Using cognitive strategies for better understanding, pre-reading and after-reading strategies obviously becomes a necessary part of the reading process. PISA 2009 confirmed that teenagers who used different cognitive strategies have better learning and reading results [4].

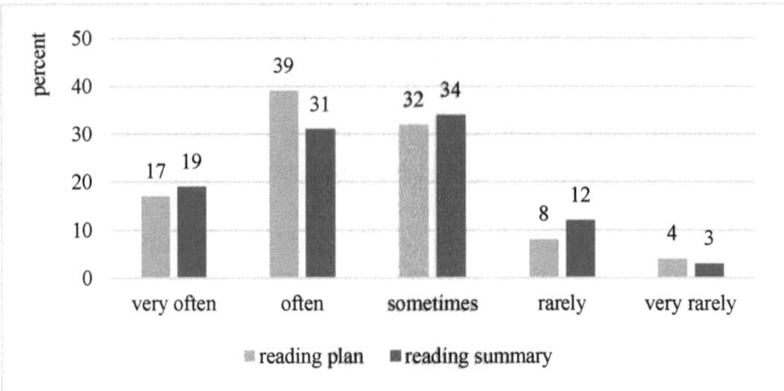

Fig. 6. Frequencies of planning reading and doing summary after reading

4 Conclusions

Our results show different social notions of reading in the past and in the present. It seems that today children need (and often receive) much more encouragement both at home and in school than in the past, but the levels of RL do not progress. Reading policy should be redirected in a way that families, kindergartens and schools promote and support interest and internal motivation for reading. A national strategy is needed for encouraging reading, directed to various stakeholders (teachers in kindergartens and schools, librarians, parents, publishers, policy makers, child doctors, …) – some projects and initiatives are here, but we need to work on a national level to encourage the notion of the life-long nature of reading and increase its reputation, all because of its far-reaching influences. Additionally, different role models and activities for different age groups in various reading settings and situations should be developed and offered, which is a task for professionals such as librarians, teachers, and policy makers. Development of various reading strategies should be encouraged by use of various formats and types of reading materials.

Regarding plans for further research there is a need to invite a more heterogeneous and representative sample. The education level and genders variables will give us more precise information about RL. Some previous studies indicate additional factors to be investigated (such as number of purchased books, and number of books in the home library) to explain RL. And also, elaboration of reading strategies related to different topics and reading materials should be investigated in more details. Then some specific relations between RL in IL should be elaborated.

References

1. About PIRLS 2011 (2013). https://timssandpirls.bc.edu/pirls2011/index.html
2. Knaflič, L.: Kako družinska pismenost vpliva na pismenost otrok [How family literacy influences literacy of children]. Psihološka obzorja [Horiz. psychol.] **11**(2), 37–52 (2002)
3. Mullis, I.V.S., Martin, M.O., Foy, P., Drucker, K.T.: PIRLS 2011 International Results in Reading. TIMSS & PIRLS International Study Centre, Boston College, Chestnut Hill, MA (2012). https://timssandpirls.bc.edu/pirls2011/international-results-pirls.html
4. Puklek Levpušček, M., Podlesek, A., Šterman Ivančič, K.: Dejavniki bralne pismenosti v raziskavi PISA 2009. [Factors of reading literacy in a research PISA 2009], Dissertationes 21. Pedagoški inštitut, Ljubljana (2012). http://www.pei.si/Sifranti/StaticPage.aspx?id=124
5. Skills matter: further results from the survey of adult skills. OECD, Slovenia (2016). http://www.oecd.org/skills/piaac/Skills-Matter-Slovenia.pdf
6. Survey of adult skills. http://www.oecd.org/skills/piaac/
7. Vilar, P., Haramija, D.: Metodologija ciljnega raziskovalnega projekta Kulturni in sistemski dejavniki bralne pismenosti v Sloveniji [Methodology of the target project Cultural and system factors of reading literacy in Slovenia]. In: Prva znanstvena konferenca Raziskovanje v vzgoji in izobraževanju danes? [First national scientific conference Research in education today?], Ljubljana, [in the process of publication; in Slovenian], 27 September 2016
8. Zaključno poročilo ciljnega raziskovalnega projekta V5-1506 – Kulturni in sistemski dejavniki bralne pismenosti v Sloveniji [Final report of the target project V5-1506 – Cultural and system factors of reading literacy in Slovenia] (2016). [unpublished; in Slovenian]

Civil Commitment and the Role of Public Librarians

Hilary Yerbury(✉) and Maureen Henninger

University of Technology Sydney, Sydney, Australia
{hilary.yerbury,maureen.henninger}@uts.edu.au

Abstract. Western culture has developed based on notions that truth, by overcoming falsehood, underpins democracy. Libraries and librarians have played an important part in the provision of information to support democratic processes. This study explored information services offered by the small number of public librarians whose role is to provide information services to employees of local governments, elected representatives and to the general public in Sydney, Australia and their perceptions of their role in supporting the potential for civic literacy to contribute to the quality of public policies and democracy. In the interviews, librarians emphasised the importance of awareness-raising of their role in providing information; some perceived opportunities to highlight existing partnerships or to develop new ones; and community discussions of fake news were seen to give scope for repositioning the services of librarians. The regime of truth relating information access to democratic principles has not yet been replaced.

Keywords: Civic literacy · Information literacy · Local government
Public libraries

1 Introduction

Western culture and democracy have developed based on notions that truth, by overcoming falsehood, underpins democracy, supported by wide dissemination of information. Democracy, as a form of social organisation, is based on notions of truthfulness and rightness, which are used in rational debate to achieve agreement on an issue. Harsin [1] claims that we are currently undergoing a shift from a regime of truth to a regime of post truth (ROPT). "Regime of truth" is a phrase used by Foucault to refer to "a system of ordered procedures for the production, regulation, distribution, circulation and operation of statements" [2, p. 133]. In the late 1970s, when he first began to explore this idea, the responsibility for a statement and the authority of the person making the statement were clear and there were relatively few competing messages, each of which could also be linked to sources of authority and institutions trusted to verify and validate claims. A regime of post truth, according to Harsin, begins to emerge with the fragmenting of sources of information and audiences, including the shifts in expectations that time and space will no longer be barriers to retrieving information; the proliferation of information sources is accompanied by a proliferation of claims and counter-claims about what should be accepted as true, leading people to a

S. Kurbanoğlu et al. (Eds.): ECIL 2017, CCIS 810, pp. 376–385, 2018.
https://doi.org/10.1007/978-3-319-74334-9_40

point where they accept that there is no way to verify truth, and they are prevented from thinking about the bigger issues of social justice and democracy. This study examines the descriptions specialist public librarians give of the work they do, providing services to local government employees and elected representatives at the local level, to explore how they support democratic processes in the community and whether there is any evidence that a regime of post truth is developing in this context.

2 Public Libraries, Local Government Employees, and Democratic Practices

2.1 Public Librarians and Democratic Practices

Libraries and librarians do not exist separate from the rest of society. If Rettig [3] can claim that libraries are a "trusted forum" in contemporary society, it is because they have long been accepted as organisations that are part of a regime of truth, related both to the support of democratic practices and to management of access to scientific literature. Their professional associations usually have a statement similar to that of the Australian Library and Information Association which emphasises this role: "Public libraries have an important role in the development and maintenance of a democratic society by giving individuals access to a wide and varied range of information, ideas, opinions and skills". In the wake of the outcome of the European Union Exit Referendum in the United Kingdom, where some Leave voters subsequently felt they had believed information which was not true [4], and the inauguration of Donald Trump as President of the US where Kellyanne Conway offered alternative facts as an excuse for statements which were patently wrong, there has been an increase in interest in how librarians can provide access to information and support democratic processes. Information literacy in particular has been proposed as a tool which librarians can use to support people not just in their educational processes but also in decisions related to everyday life [5, p. 15].

Public libraries have traditionally been seen to have a significant role in ensuring that people in local communities are well informed, and able to play an active part in the decision-making in their communities. To achieve this, they provide a range of services, from access to a variety of resources, including the World Wide Web as well as local resources, to reference services providing answers to complex questions, to in-house community programs and hosting community forums. They may also be involved in programs intended to develop information literacy [6].

Willingham argues that libraries are "civic agents creating civic agency" [7, p. 97]. The notion of civic literacy emerges from an American view of democracy and engagement in community and society, with its purpose often being stated as increasing participation in the electoral system [e.g. 8]. More broadly, it should be considered in the context of engagement with community and society and its importance in the development of civic agency. Branson [9] suggests that civic literacy can contribute to the quality of public policies and of democratic processes in a community. She notes the importance of public libraries, their collections and their services, in developing civic literacy in members of a community. Information literacy can be seen as fundamental to civic literacy, through its emphasis on understanding and evaluating information presented. Although employees in any level of government, along with elected representatives, are an integral part of civic agency, there appears to be little consideration of the relationship between public librarians and local government employees and the understandings that public librarians might have of it. This study sets out to address this gap.

2.2 Local Government in Sydney and Its Employees

The metropolitan area of Sydney in New South Wales (NSW) currently covers thirty local government areas, generally referred to as councils. Local government is in a state of flux since 2015 when the NSW State Government proposed a series of amalgamations across the state, to reduce the number of councils. This proposal was hotly contested, and although some mergers have gone ahead, others are still before the court. Many councils do not currently have elected representatives (councillors), with their mayors and councillors having been removed in 2016 and the councils put under administration by the State Premier, pending the settlement of the mergers and elections to be held later in 2017. Each local government area previously had its own independent public library service; in councils where amalgamations have taken place, a review of library services is being undertaken. Thus, in almost every council area in metropolitan Sydney, there is uncertainty about the structures and processes of local government, sometimes with an end in sight and sometimes with no indication of when decisions will be finalised.

Each council employs a number of staff with a wide range of responsibilities, which can be divided into four classes of occupation: corporate services and governance, engineering and infrastructure, human and community services and planning and environment [10, p. 8]. Two factors about council workforces are important for this study; the first is that local government employees are generally more highly educated than the general workforce [10, p. 32] and the workforce is older than the general workforce, with 37% of employees aged over 50 (compared to 29%) [10, p. 9]. Across Australia, the number of staff employed by each council varies, as does the number of elected representatives, although the average is around ten.

Some public libraries have established services especially for council employees, although all would provide services on request. These special library services are known as corporate library services. One of the first in Australia was the City of Melbourne's Corporate Library, set up in 1987 to provide services to staff and councillors of the City of Melbourne [11]. In New South Wales, corporate librarians were appointed by a number of councils from the early 2000s, some responsible for collections of materials and others not. The introduction of these services came at a time when public libraries had increasing access to online data bases whereas the council employees did not necessarily have easy access to the internet. Over time, the number of corporate librarians appointed has decreased, for a variety of reasons, including universal access to the internet for council employees with Google seen to remove the need for specialist assistance in searching; changes in organisational structure; shifts in local priorities and the non-replacement of retiring staff.

2.3 Librarians and a Regime of Truth

The professional education of librarians has been positioned within a long-standing regime of truth, incorporating understandings of the authority of information, from reputable publishers and the peer review process, techniques for clearly identifying bibliographic items, the development of search strategies intended to retrieve relevant and appropriate resources, tools for understanding the needs and expectations of groups of information users and of individual enquirers and principles for assuring the quality of information and information resources. At the heart of their practice, or as some would put it at the core of their being [12], has been the provision of resources.

In a context of post-truth and alternative facts, providers of authoritative information across the world have re-asserted the importance of verifying the content of resources before using them. The International Federation of Library Associations has worked with Wikipedia [13] to use the skills of librarians to strengthen the resources posted on Wikipedia, and overcome the criticisms of its user-generated content. Its collaboration with Factcheck.org has led to a poster available in 30 languages, entitled "How to Spot Fake News" [14]. This poster, intended for display in libraries and community centers, provides a set of ideographs which represent an abbreviated form of traditional principles for ensuring the retrieval of quality information.

The emphasis in these concerns with post-truth and alternative facts has largely been on school and academic libraries and their relationship with students and the development of information literacy, and on public libraries and their need to develop an understanding that much that purports to be fact is fictitious. There appears to be no discussion of the information services provided to policy-makers at the local government level, that is, employees of local government and elected representatives.

3 Methodology

Using a practice theory approach [15, 16], in 2017, this study has interviewed the small number of specialist public librarians whose specific role is to provide information services to employees of local governments, elected representatives and to the general public. Six librarians were interviewed, and two more provided written responses; all are women, with at least twenty years professional experience. The purpose of these interviews was to understand the practices of these librarians through their descriptions of their tasks and interactions. Questions elicited responses about the ways these librarians describe their activities, the relationship of the information services provided to broader democratic processes and they also sought to identify possibilities for supporting democratic processes that librarians might wish for. Some questions were framed as an adaptation of Nicolini's interview to the double [17], with participants being asked to describe how they would describe what they do to a public librarian unfamiliar with the concept of the corporate librarian. Each interview lasted between 45 and 60 min, and the audio recordings were transcribed verbatim. The transcriptions were analysed using thematic analysis aimed at identifying key features of the practices of these librarians, in particular those related to elements of civil commitment and information literacy. Approval for the study was given through the Human Research

Ethics Committee of the University of Technology Sydney, with the condition that no participants were to be named and the local government area in which the public library was situated was to be anonymised.

4 Findings

4.1 Practices – a Regime of Truth

The comments of these librarians reveal that their practices are very similar and that these practices are affected by the same external factors. To some extent this is not surprising, because they see themselves as having a group identity, they meet together and have an identity in the wider professional community. On the other hand, the areas in which they work are diverse, affected differently by the current process of mergers.

As a group, they maintain a wiki, whose purpose is describing for other librarians the tasks that make up their work. Here, they identify six tasks: promoting the work of the corporate librarian; involvement in council staff induction sessions; building relationships with staff in council departments; developing a working relationship with individual councillors, developing policy for library services to councillors and council staff and monitoring local government issues. In the interviews, participants provided insight into how they talk about these tasks.

"I provide information and resources to council staff to help them with their work" (L4) is a statement which all participants would acknowledge. Some manage a special collection of material, but most respond to requests for a book or a journal article or a factual answer by using the range of resources available to them through the public library. Most of the requests are "really basic" (L1, L4), although sometimes they fulfil requests for more complex searches (L1). All the librarians mentioned that they provided a current awareness bulletin, usually through using the staff intranet (L4) or as FAQs online (L6), "the modern version" (L5). Much of the work done by these librarians is re-active rather than pro-active (L5, L7), answering expressed needs.

A key part of their practice is verifying information, "sorting quality from dross" (L8) or making sure that council staff have information that can be substantiated. "We can provide "facts" that have been produced by different sources… pointing to different conclusions and can only expect that policy makers will weigh the merits of all the 'facts' and decide appropriately" (L7). In the context of post-truth, "things haven't changed" (L5), "it's not like it's a new thing that libraries are doing" (L2), "we know… to fact check things before we put them on [the staff intranet]" (L1). For L3, it was important to maintain an "emphasis on the local, to know what's happening and have 'the facts right'". Some of the participants expressed concern with how one can understand the notion of 'fact'. Mostly, they reflected that a fact is something that they or council staff "can just look up" (L2), but they make a distinction between the way that they might conduct a search and the way that a member of the council staff might: for a search done by a librarian "they can know that the information is going to be trustworthy" (L5) and by a council staff member on Google, "It's not like quality, is it?" (L4), because the information comes from a source lacking in "authority" (L5). On the other hand, L8 referred to some Google information as being "fit for purpose" although in other cases, she might want staff to recognise that "what they need exceeds what they can find for themselves". For L3, answers to questions which can be substantiated or which come from research-based resources are "actual facts". L4 makes a distinction in the type of question someone might ask in order to explore the idea of fact, when she says: "You know, they might say: we are looking up how this street came to be named… do you have anything in your vertical file? They're kind of solidy [sic] facts aren't they? Do you know what I mean? It's not like: 'we've heard this, is it true?'" Only L2 refers to a broader context reported recently in the Australian media: "a lot of the information has been politicised… it's how you actually [say] that a politician going 'Yeah, I went out in a boat and looked [at bleaching on the Great Barrier Reef]', isn't the same as scientific explanations" (L1).

While all librarians offer information literacy services to council staff, the ways they do it vary. Some are actively involved in induction programs "to new staff" and post information in the relevant intranet page (L4). Whereas L1 notes that it is difficult to get council staff to take part in information literacy programs: "It's not like in the university where staff will come for training … I don't get many people ask" [about information literacy training], L3 reported: "Every now and again, we run information sessions for staff on the corporate library and what's available… So a lot of the time, we can teach them how to access the information themselves or how to use the databases."

4.2 Democratic Processes

All the librarians were able to conceptualise the information services they provide as contributing to the democratic processes in a community, but L7 noted that her manager would have responded "They don't [contribute]". Raising awareness that information exists was seen as fundamental to the democratic processes and to this end, all libraries provided some level of specialist resources for council staff "that's background information for policy" (L4), and this allowed the General Manager in a council dealing with a major issue, to ask: "How did it get to this?" (L3).

L4 and L5 both saw that the public library is involved in the democratic processes of the council itself through its hosting of public exhibitions about changes to council policy, especially planning regulations. L4 had considered hosting a community forum on a contentious issue in the community, but had thought better of it when she realised that "[t]here's 'security guards' at council meetings", presumably to maintain order. Participants also saw the importance of empowering local residents to understand not only local issues but the workings of the decision-making processes, such as "what are the processes for talking at council meetings?" (L2), because "[y]ou're still on your own as a community member to navigate all this stuff" (L1).

Participants identified what they saw as "key trusted partnerships" (L2) in ensuring a well-informed community, and whilst most identified the local newspaper as one of these key partners, other partners listed included local chambers of commerce, key community groups and non-government organisations.

In providing information services to elected representatives, everyone noted that in the past, interactions with elected representatives were easier. The interpretation of the Local Government Act and the introduction of a Code of Conduct (L1) made it "complicated [to be] able directly to interact with councillors" (L2). L3 said she was "not allowed to deal directly with the councillors" and L8 noted that "they don't deal with staff at my level"; L4 described how they used to hand deliver current awareness bulletins to councillors but now have to work "at arms' length" (L1), with the councillors putting in a request to the General Manager or another contact person and L7 noted that "council policy requires councillors to direct their questions through their contact point". The consequence of this is that these specialist librarians no longer have an unmediated relationship with the elected representatives and the best they can do is to provide content for the induction of new councillors after elections or produce a section in the intranet, describing the services they can provide.

4.3 Changes to Practices

"In the past but not so much now", this phrase from L1 was echoed by all participants. There was a common refrain, that in the past, these specialist librarians had had stronger interactions with the council staff and with the elected representatives – councillors. This was clearest in the references to information literacy. "The information literacy part, it has really died off." (L4). Two reasons were given for this, one relating to the skills sets of council staff and the other to easy access to the internet. L8 mentioned that most staff now were tertiary educated and better able to do their own searching. L3 talked about a time when information literacy training was in quite high demand: "it was that change over period where older staff were having to learn" and L4 noted "when we started, people didn't have access to the internet… then people got savvy". She went on to say that when the council arranged access to specialised resources for all staff, it was no longer "the corporate librarian's realm" (L4). On the other hand, L1 reflected: "I think we've sort of almost let that [information literacy] go" and the current situation is one that can prompt these corporate librarians to say: "well hang on one minute, this current news environment is really highlighting basic skills that we can impart to people".

L3 observed a change which for her was a potential threat to the role of the public library as a trusted part of a democratic society. She noted that "we've had to ban a few customers recently. They've done the wrong thing, but this is a place for them…. They can't get help from a lot of [other places in the community]." L4 indicated an anomaly in her council's policy on use of the internet: "[If] you've got your own device, it's free but if you don't…". For L5, "the people who don't [have their own mobile technologies] are probably those who can least afford [to pay for use of the facilities in the public library]".

4.4 And for the Future

Asked to express one wish for something that might enable them to support the democratic processes in their community, a context that L2 described as living "in diverse societies […] where you all don't think the same… [and] there's more than one point of view that's valid," L7 wanted "a way of dispersing the hive mind/mass hysteria and forcing people to think for themselves", and similarly L4 just "want[ed] people to think to ask", to question what they were hearing. L3 and L5 both wanted "access for everybody to information", "for free"; L6 wanted "an injection of funds" to assist in the process of re-focusing public libraries and their staff and L8 wanted "more resources". L2 sought "a better understanding for [librarians] about how [elected representatives] work and how we, as both individual citizens [and] a collective group of citizens, can constructively and ethically influence change". L1, continuing her emphasis on access to evidence-based resources said: "I would just love it if we did a partnership with [the nearby university] and all our staff got a library card… that'd be great".

5 Discussion

These findings suggest at one level that these librarians are working within the long-standing regime of truth. As Byrne [12] suggested, providing resources is at the heart of their practices. They emphasise the significance of appropriate documents and responses from well-founded resources in answering requests and appear to hold a clear sense of what constitutes quality or truth in these circumstances. They are concerned with access to information for council staff and elected representatives and also with ways to ensure that residents in their local community are well-informed about local issues and engaged in local forums. Kemmis [16] however, encourages researchers to look at the context in which practices occur, in particular at policies and conditions at a broader level in the community or society that may impinge on a set of practices.

These librarians are working within a context of trust, where they accept their responsibility for supporting democratic processes leading to empowerment within their community. They show an awareness of their potential to contribute to the quality of public policies, both through provision of information to council staff and through working with staff and community organisations to bring local issues to the attention of residents. However, they are disappointed by their lack of ability to develop what Branson describes as civic literacy [9] to the full, because of the barriers to direct engagement with elected representatives and in some instances because of the contentious nature of local issues which has led to security guards being present at council meetings, a situation out of keeping with the notion of the library as a democratic space.

Another indication of a lack of trust could be perceived in the prohibition of direct contact between these librarians and the elected representatives, spelled out in the codes of conduct for their particular council. Librarians as the providers of information to support decision-making perhaps were seen as having a privileged relationship, protected by the power of the information they provided to support the democratic processes. However, the Councillor Handbook, published by the NSW Department of Premier and Cabinet in cooperation with the Local Government Association of NSW and the Shires Association of NSW in a section on access to information and resources in a chapter entitled Code of Conduct and Acting Ethically, states [18, p. 46] that "Access to council staff expertise must happen through the general manager, or in accordance with a system that is put in place to facilitate and coordinate councillor requests for information or action". Clearly, that privileged professional relationship between information and its use in democratic processes has now been replaced by one where the notion of a personal relationship is more significant and potentially damaging to the democratic process.

Information literacy, seen as fundamental to the development of a well-informed public [6], is both a relatively new practice emerging with the automation of online information services and the popularisation of the Internet and already a skill which these librarians are no longer needed to teach because the skills are well established in the community. Familiarity with the Internet and the search capacities of Google and the appointment of younger university-educated staff has rendered the development in council staff and elected representatives of information literacy by these librarians redundant. Going hand in hand with these developments of increased information literacy among staff and elected representatives and universal access to the internet is the loss to the librarians of their role as gatekeepers over quality information.

Librarians recognised tensions between expectations for current activities and the way they may have performed their tasks in the past. They note the potential conflict between the need for timely responses and in-depth research on a complex issue and the issues arising from the multiplicity of messages in social media and the control over the content of a message from a source deemed authoritative. On the other hand, they also recognise that their professional background has given them a foundation for developing good systems for finding and managing relevant resources, the ability to work across a range of resources and formats and the ability to recognise the information needs of the particular staff member. Further, they are clear that a fundamental ability to evaluate the quality of information resources has not changed, although it may be tested by the often-expressed perception of council staff and councillors that they can identify relevant and appropriate resources themselves.

6 Conclusion

Two factors make it difficult to claim that the established regime of truth is changing significantly, the continued emphasis of these librarians on the provision of well-founded resources related to local issues and their knowledge of how to identify trustworthy resources. However, the blows to the notion of the trustworthiness of the public library and its place as a safe, neutral space for the expression of a variety of ideas may signal a shift towards a new regime of truth. The public library has been one of the institutions upholding the longstanding regime of truth in Australian society. But these factors and the uncertainty surrounding local government area mergers and the position of elected representatives may be threatening this position, especially as they appear to have acted as a deterrent in the uptake of services to support civic literacy.

The emphasis these librarians have given to the importance of awareness-raising of their role in supporting democratic processes and the perceived opportunities to highlight existing partnerships or to develop new ones and to be active in community discussions of issues of local concern were seen to give scope for repositioning the importance of civil commitment and information literacy. The findings of this study imply that all librarians have a role in developing the literacies fundamental to a democratic society. If this means championing a changing regime of truth, this process will include articulating clearly the principles and criteria for judging the trustworthiness of information, including the differences among and between opinion, experience and evidence, and collaborating with others consolidating the new regime.

References

1. Harsin, J.: Regimes of posttruth, postpolitics, and attention economies. Commun. Cult. Crit. **8**(2), 327–333 (2015)
2. Foucault, M.: Power/Knowledge: Selected Interviews and Other Writings, 1972–1977. Pantheon Books, New York (1980)
3. Rettig, J.: New technologies, citizen empowerment, and civic life. In: Qualitative and Quantitative Methods in Libraries: Theory and Applications: Proceedings of the International Conference on QQML2009, Chania, Crete, Greece, 26–29 May 2009, pp. 191-197. World Scientific Publishing, Singapore (2010)
4. Somin, I.: Brexit, "Regrexit," and the impact of political ignorance. Washington Post. Opinion, 26 June 2016
5. Smith, L.N.: Information literacy as a tool to support political participation. Libr. Inf. Sci. Res. **40**(123), 14–23 (2016)
6. Kranich, N.: Civic partnerships: the role of libraries in promoting civic engagement. Resour. Shar. Inf. Netw. **18**(1–2), 89–103 (2005)
7. Willingham, T.L.: Libraries as civic agents. PLQ **27**(2), 97–110 (2008)
8. Milner, H.: Civic Literacy: How Informed Citizens Make Democracy Work. University Press of New England, Hanover (2002)
9. Branson, M.S.: The Role of Civic Education: An Education Policy Task Force Position Paper with Policy Recommendations. Center for Civic Education, Washington, D.C. (1998)
10. Hastings, C., Ryan, R., Gibbs, M., Lawrie, A.: Profile of the local government workforce 2015 report. Sydney Australian Centre of Excellence for Local Government, University of Technology Sydney, February 2015
11. Cameron, R., Bellamy, M.: The City of Melbourne's corporate library. Australas. Public Libr. Inf. Serv. **4**(2), 94 (1991)
12. Byrne, A.: Possibility and imagination: a personal exploration of research and librarianship. Libr. Manag. **38**(2), 11–19 (2017)
13. IFLA: Presenting the IFLA Wikipedia Opportunities Papers. Webpage, 17 January 2017. https://www.ifla.org/node/11131
14. IFLA: How to Spot Fake News, Infographic, 27 January 2017. https://blogs.ifla.org/lpa/files/2017/01/How-to-Spot-Fake-News.pdf
15. Schatzki, T.R.: A primer on practices: theories and research. In: Higgs, J., Barnett, R., Billett, S., Hutchings, M., Trede, F. (eds.) Practice-Based Education: Perspectives and Strategies. Practice, Education, Work and Society, vol. 6, pp. 13–26. Springer, Rotterdam (2012). https://doi.org/10.1007/978-94-6209-128-3_2
16. Kemmis, S., Edwards-Groves, C., Wilkinson, J., Hardy, I.: Ecologies of practices. In: Hager, P., Lee, A., Reich, A. (eds.) Practice-Theory Perspectives on Professional Learning. Professional and Practice-based Learning, vol. 8, pp. 33–49. Springer, Dordrecht (2012). https://doi.org/10.1007/978-94-007-4774-6_3
17. Nicolini, D.: Articulating practice through the interview to the double. Manag. Learn. **40**(2), 195–212 (2009)
18. Local Government and Shires Associations of New South Wales. Department of Premier and Cabinet. Division of Local Government: Councillor Handbook. Division of Local Government, Department of Premier and Cabinet, Nowra, NSW (2012)

Science Literacy

A Study on How to Equip Students with Scientific Communication Skills

Nihal Menzi Çetin[1(✉)] and Buket Akkoyunlu[2]

[1] Hacettepe University, Ankara, Turkey
nmenzi@hacettepe.edu.tr
[2] Çankaya University, Ankara, Turkey
buket@cankaya.edu.tr

Abstract. The purpose of this study was to investigate the effects of scientific communication (SC) curriculum on blog writing skills of sixth-grade students, and opinions of the students and teachers about the curriculum. Through the curriculum, it was aimed to teach students the ability to access and evaluate information, organize information and share it by writing a blog. Students were given three different writing assignments and were asked to share them in their blogs. The first assignment was given for adapting to the writing process. The second and third assignments were assessed to determine the effect of SC curriculum on blog writing skills. At the end of the process, teachers and students were asked about their opinions on SC curriculum and blog writing. Study results revealed that SC curriculum had positive effects on research and writing skills development of the students, and showed that the curriculum was supportive in reaching the course-specific goals.

Keywords: Scientific communication · Digital tools · Blogs · Writing skill Information literacy · Social media

1 Introduction

Scientific communication (SC) is one of the important skills in the 21st century for students, because information and communication technologies change our method of communication [1]. In particular, social media have created new ways for sharing ideas and effective communication. Sharing information on social media has brought about an information explosion on an unprecedented scale. This information explosion has caused the problem of managing information. That is why we need SC skills. SC is a process involving the collection of reliable information and the creation and sharing of scholarly writing. This process requires a set of skills for accessing, evaluating, using, presenting and sharing information in different environments, such as journals and social media. In the literature, SC is defined as sharing research results in oral, written or visual ways [2].

Information and communication technologies present various tools that fulfill information sharing, transferring, and communicating with information, writing and presentation skills. These tools also make it necessary for individuals to obtain new skills [3]. SC curriculum aims to teach students skills like information literacy, and

S. Kurbanoğlu et al. (Eds.): ECIL 2017, CCIS 810, pp. 389–397, 2018.
https://doi.org/10.1007/978-3-319-74334-9_41

presents a frame that enables the students to use these skills with new tools and environments. SC program is aimed at gaining the following basic skills: Access to information, effective listening and note taking, information representation, scientific reading and writing, presenting and sharing information. Social media is an effective tool in teaching information literacy skills because of its ability to interact among individuals, presenting and sharing information and enabling access information [4]. Blogs are online platforms with authentic audiences where students can display their works. [5]. Lacina and Griffith [6] state that blogs' contribution to the development of writing skills makes students research as they write. Blogs combine reading and writing, and students try to write more qualitatively when they know their blogs are read by others. Blogs are considered to be an appropriate environment for students to share information in SC process due to the characteristics mentioned above. Students actively use the Internet to access information, however, when encountering complex research tasks, their current skills were observed to be insufficient [7]. Schedit, et al. [8] indicated that research skill and writing skill of a student are closely associated, and they stated that cognitive and organizational skills displayed in producing new material were more important than the material itself. Research skill required of the student is a complex process that involves not only information gathering, but also evaluation of information sources, critical processing of the information, organizing, and producing new material at the end [9]. All these skills are required to be systematically taught to the students. SC curriculum is designed to meet those needs. In the literature, there are curriculum development studies [10, 11], but authentic environments where students can apply information skills are needed. The SC curriculum developed in this study combines the skills of information literacy and the ability to use social media. The aim of this study is to equip students with SC skills and investigate the effects of the curriculum on students' blog writings. Using the curriculum developed for this purpose, the aim was to teach students the ability to access and evaluate information, organize information, and share it by writing a blog, and students' blogs were assessed as the learning output. The researchers searched the following questions: 1. How have students' blog writing skills changed at the end of the SC curriculum? 2. What are student and teacher opinions of the SC process?

2 Method

2.1 Research Process

Development and implementation of SC curriculum: ASC curriculum was developed by the researchers. Skills were defined from Scherz, Spektor-Levy and Eylon's [12] "Scientific communication: Higher order learning skills" program. In this study, skills were revised and adapted for sixth-graders, and all the components of the curriculum were developed by the researchers. The curriculum has focused mainly on the following skills: Access to information, effective listening and note taking, information representation, scientific reading and writing, presenting and sharing information, all which is called 'SC skills'. Using digital environments is a part of presenting and sharing information and blog usage was taught to students in the curriculum. A website (http://bilimseliletisim.net/) was developed by researchers to deliver the curriculum to students and teachers, and also enables them to reach the content any time and anywhere. The website contains the following components: Lectures with PowerPoint presentations and videos, activities and worksheets for students, lesson plans, and a guide for teachers for implementing the curriculum. The aim was for students to reach both their course and SC curriculum objectives by combining blog writing activity with Turkish Literature (TL) and Information Technology (IT) courses outcomes. Students were given three different writing assignments during the research and they were asked to share them in their blogs. First of all, students were given a presentation about what blogs are and their purposes, and they were guided to start their own blogs. Blog writing activity was conducted under the guidance of course teachers and researchers. Students created their own blog accounts and completed their personal customization. Then, they were tasked with their first blog writing assignment. Their first assignment was to write a column related to a TL course. They wrote their own columns in their blogs by learning column writing in their TL course. The first assignment also had the purpose of preparation of students for the blog writing process. Their second assignment was to research and write about the 'benefits and harms of social media' related to an IT course. The second assignment was also used as a pretest in the experimental study. Later on, students were instructed about SC skills throughout a four-week period. During the instruction, students studied the lectures on the website and completed activities. Students were provided with feedback about their activities. At the same time, a researcher remained available during school hours in order to guide students. Students were given their third blog assignments after the instruction was completed. The third assignment was to research and write about '21st century students' characteristics. The third assignment was used as a posttest in the experimental study. Students' blogs were evaluated through a rubric at the end of the process. In order to support experimental research findings and obtain detailed information about the process, opinions of students and TL and IT teachers on the SC process were obtained and evaluated.

2.2 Research Model

This study used a quasi-experimental research design that compared second assignment scores (pretest) and third assignment scores (posttest) of blog writings of students. One of the existing classes was designated as the experiment, and the other as the control group. According to independent samples t-test results, the experimental and control groups are equal to each other in terms of the pretest scores ($t_{(47)} = 1.07$, $p = .290$). The opinions of the teachers and students about the SC process were obtained and evaluated in the context of the case study. A content analysis method was used to analyze the data obtained from the interviews.

2.3 Study Group

The study was conducted in a private school in the capital in Turkey. Forty-nine sixth-grade students (age 12) and seven teachers participated in the study. The study was implemented in their TL and IT courses and the outcomes are evaluated by the course teachers based on their course-specific criteria. Course evaluations are not included in this study.

2.4 Data Collection

Writing Skills Rubric: The researchers developed a rubric to assess students' blog writing skills. The rubric has seven sub-dimensions that assess four program skills: Organization, language and expression, synthesis, writing bibliography, using different sources, using reliable information sources, and using visuals (see Table 1). The rubric has five criteria from 1 (incompetent) to 5 (exemplary).

Table 1. Sub-dimensions of the rubric and related curriculum skills

Items of the rubric	Curriculum skills
Organization	Presenting and sharing information
Language and expression	Scientific reading and writing
Synthesis	Scientific reading and writing
Using different sources	Access to information
Writing bibliography	Scientific reading and writing
Using reliable sources	Access to information
Using visuals	Information representation

For validity of the rubric, the researchers asked for two expert opinions about relevance with sub-dimensions and curriculum skills. For reliability of the rubric, student blogs were analyzed by a researcher, and 20 randomly selected blogs (40% of the blogs) were analyzed by the course teacher. Raters' training in the use of the rubric is a factor that increases the validity and reliability of the rubric [13]. The course teacher was trained in the rubric criteria before analysis. After the evaluation of blog writings using the rubric, Cohen's Kappa measure for determining agreement between raters was calculated and it is found significantly in harmony at the 0.71 level (p = .000) [14].

Interviews with students and teachers: Interviews were conducted with teachers and students in order to obtain their opinions about SC process. 20 students in the experimental group were interviewed. In these interviews students were asked about their thoughts with regards to blog writing activity and SC instruction. Also four TL teachers and three IT teachers were asked about their opinions regarding the effects of the SC process and blog activity on their courses and students.

3 Findings

Experimental Study Results: Students' posttest scores were calculated and independent t-test was conducted to examine the difference between the experimental and control groups. Results have seen in Table 2:

Table 2. Independent t-test results for the writing skills of students

Group	N	Mean	SD	*t*	*p*
Experimental	25	3.36	0.63	8.78	.000
Control	24	2.14	0.26		

α = .05

As seen in Table 2, there is a significant difference between the experimental and control groups' posttest scores ($t_{(47)} = 8.78$, $p = .000$). After the implementation of SC curriculum, it can be said that the writing skill of the experimental group increased significantly in comparison with the control group. According to the writing skills rubric sub-dimensions, paired samples t-test results of experimental and control groups are shown in Table 3.

Table 3. Paired samples t-test results for the writing skills sub-dimension scores

Group	Writing skill sub-dimension	Pretest		Posttest		*t*	*P*
		M	SD	M	SD		
Experimental	Organization	2.92	0.76	3.68	0.85	−4.321	.000
	Language and expression	2.88	0.78	3.28	0.68	−1.922	.067
	Synthesis	2.52	1.19	2.84	0.99	−1.317	.200
	Using different sources	1.40	0.65	2.76	0.92	−6.107	.000
	Writing bibliography	1.40	0.76	3.64	1.32	−8.615	.000
	Using reliable sources	1.68	1.31	4.28	1.14	−7.612	.000
	Using visuals	2.60	1.38	3.04	1.67	1.066	.297
Control	Organization	2.50	0.78	3.16	0.56	−3.24	.000
	Language and expression	2.96	0.46	3.29	0.62	−2.000	.057
	Synthesis	1.87	1.08	2.04	1.08	−0.659	.517
	Using different sources	1.33	0.92	1.54	0.51	−1.155	.260
	Writing bibliography	1.66	1.13	1.58	0.72	0.303	.765
	Using reliable sources	1.66	1.40	1.83	1.05	−0.517	.610
	Using visuals	2.37	1.21	1.87	1.26	1.252	.223

α = .05

According to the rubric sub-dimensions, the writing skill of the experimental group showed a significant increase in four of seven dimensions (organization, using different sources, writing bibliography, and using reliable sources). In the control group on the other hand, there is significant difference only in the organization sub-dimension. "Organization" refers to putting information in a logical sequence, writing an introduction, discussion and conclusion, ordering and separating the subject into meaningful paragraphs. In this sub-dimension, writing skills of both the experimental ($t_{(24)} = -4.32$, $p = .000$) and the control group ($t_{(23)} = -3.24$, $p = .000$) have significantly increased. "Language and expression" refers to paying attention to spelling rules, and using scientific language. In this sub-dimension, posttest scores of both experimental ($t_{(24)} = -1.92$, $p = .067$) and control groups ($t_{(23)} = -2.00$, $p = .057$)

increased in comparison to pretest scores, however, this increase was not significant. "Synthesis" refers to bringing together gathered information using one's own sentences, and the ability to interpret the information. In this sub-section, posttest scores of both experimental ($t_{(24)} = -1.31$, $p = .200$) and control groups ($t_{(23)} = -0.65$, $p = .517$) increased in comparison to pretest scores, however, this increase was not significant. "Using different sources" refers to using a variety of information sources (different websites, articles, books) when researching. In the study, students used mostly web sources in their research and they benefited from a maximum of four different information sources. In this sub-dimension, postest scores of the experimental group increased significantly compared to their pretest scores ($t_{(24)} = -6.107$; $p = .000$). In the control group, posttest scores were higher than pretest scores at using different sources dimension, but this increase is not significant ($t_{(23)} = -1.15$, $p = .260$). "Writing bibliography" refers to indicating the information sources in accordance with referencing rules. In this sub-dimension, posttest scores of the experimental group increased significantly compared to pretest scores ($t_{(24)} = -8.615$, $p = .000$). In the control group there is a decrease in the posttest scores compared to pretest scores, but this decrease is not significant ($t_{(23)} = 0.303$, $p = .765$). "Using reliable sources" refers to using an information source which is up-to-date, suitable for the purpose of the subject, the source and author of the information is clear, and the content is accurate and objective. The information sources that students use are checked for these criteria and given points. In this sub-dimension, posttest scores of the experimental group increased significantly in comparison to pretest scores ($t_{(24)} = -7.612$, $p = .000$). In the control group, there was no significant difference between pretest and posttest scores ($t_{(23)} = -0.517$, $p = .610$). "Using visuals" refers to use of images, graphics or photos in the presentation of information. It also refers to using relevant visuals in the appropriate place, and making statements about visuals. In this sub-dimension, there is no significant differenve between pretest and posttest scores of the experimental group ($t_{(24)} = -1.066$, $p = .297$). In the control group, posttest scores were lower than pretest scores, but this decrease is not significant ($t_{(23)} = 1.252$, $p = .223$).

Students' opinions about SC process: Students' opinions are grouped into the points they pay attention to as they write blogs, the points they are challenged, positive aspects of writing blog, and what they learned during the SC instruction. Students stated, when writing blogs, they pay attention to writing explicitly and clearly (55%), presentation of information (title, visuals, organization) (60%), spelling and punctuation (55%), writing their own thoughts (30%) and content of the blog (20%). On the other hand 55% of the students stated that they found it difficult to find the relevant information about the topics. According to students, positive aspects of blogging are to learn about the subject (55%), sharing ideas (50%), to inform people (35%), to get comments (20%) and improve their writing skills (20%). Two students stated, by writing blogs, their works have become permanent and they create an archive on the internet. A student said: "*We get a lot of information from blogs. Thanks to blogs, many people can read my thoughts. I can also make my school projects permanent by writing them to my blog*". Students stated, in SC instruction, they have learned well about writing bibliography (90%), search strategies (75%), rules of presenting information

(35%) and finding reliable sources (30%) and transferred these skills to writing blogs. A student stated: "*I used to research my homework from one source and finished it quickly. Now, I look at many sources and try to verify the information. Making research and writing has become more fun. I also learned the reliable web sites*".

Teachers' opinions about SC process: TL course teachers stated that teaching SC skills in combination with courses, engaged technology to the courses, made TL lectures more entertaining, and the curriculum provided alternative activities and methods to the current course. TL course teachers indicated that SC skills positively affected students in reaching their goals. As for blog writing, teachers noted that writing blogs directly affected reading and writing skills, contributed to their ability to express themselves in writing, and reinforced the ability to write columns. A teacher said: "*...blog writing enables students to take part in research process and they had the opportunity to see different opinions and to convey their own views by commenting on other blogs and reading other comments.*" IT course teachers stated that the SC curriculum is in line with their course objectives, and that blog writing, in particular, has improved the students' communication skills on the internet. A teacher said: "*...students learned how to conduct research on Internet with the SC curriculum and they realized that they need to question the accuracy of the source they have found. These skills are in parallel with the information technologies lecture goals.*" IT course teachers stated that blog writing activity has improved the students' ability to express themselves on the Internet and highlighted the fact that students knowing their content being read by others has led them to be more meticulous. They also stated that the fact that students have their own pages in the Internet environment motivated them and developed their sense of responsibility.

4 Conclusion and Discussion

In this study, SC curriculum made a meaningful contribution to the students' development of their writing skills in the sub-dimensions of organization, using different sources, writing bibliography, and using reliable information sources. There was no significant increase in language and expression and synthesis sub-dimensions. It can be said that these skills are acquired in a long period or students transform these skills into performance over time. Different information sources were introduced to the students and scientific article properties were highlighted by having articles in journals and websites reviewed during the SC instruction. Students tried to write blogs in a clear and objective way and to use scientific language as in a scientific article. At the same time, instead of copying and pasting the information they found, they were instructed to reinterpret the information with their own sentences by reading and understanding and they were given small activities during the instruction in order to have them practice their writing skills. It is considered that students need more practice over a course of time in order to make apparent improvement in language and expression and synthesis skills. In the control group, there was no significant increase in writing skill sub-dimensions of language and expression, synthesis, using different and reliable information sources, whereas their organization sub-section increased significantly. This development of writing skills in the organization dimension may be due to the individual efforts of the students or being positively influenced by the articles or other information sources they read while conducting research. Performance of the control group reduced with regards to writing bibliography and using visuals within texts. In general, in both groups, students were observed to have written more carefully in their last assignments.

The writing skill discussed in this study refers to a process that involves students conducting research and presenting their findings in their blogs by interpreting the information they had gathered. The use of blogs in this process has allowed students to share their writings with others and made them pay more attention to what they write. Drexler et al. [15], observed that having their writings read by others increased students' interest for writing. In this study students stated that they were very careful to reach reliable information and to express the information they gathered with their own words, and that they learned the subject they research very well. This suggests that the process of SC has contributed positively to the students' learning. In addition, comments written on their blogs motivated them to correct their works and write more carefully. Similarly, Chong [9] concluded that the feeling of ownership enables students to be more actively involved in research and writing processes. Students learned writing bibliography and search strategies in SC instruction, and used these skills in their research; however they have difficulty finding relevant information. When blog entries were examined, it was observed that students benefited from at most four different sources. They need to research and read more to reach appropriate knowledge. According to the teachers' views, curriculum contributed positively to their course objectives, and provided alternative activities for TL lessons, also offers new environments for the students to demonstrate their writing skills. IT course teachers stated, the curriculum contribute to students establishing communication in a social media and creating their own websites. As mentioned above, the purpose was to enable students to reach their course objectives and SC curriculum objectives simultaneously by combining blog writing activity with TL and IT courses. Teaching information literacy skills in combination with courses is important for students as they develop both these skills and their independent learning and thinking abilities [16]. There are very few studies that combine SC skills including information literacy with primary education curriculum. Kingsawat et al. [17] concluded that learning activities play an important role in the successful integration of information literacy education in the primary education curriculum, and highlighted the necessity to organize activities that allow students individually to conduct research, search for information in different sources, create reports from gathered information, and pay attention to legal and ethical issues in the process. The curriculum implemented in this study is limited to the students of the sixth-grade and TL and IT courses. Integration of SC curriculum with more lessons will provide retention for the acquired skills, and support the lesson objectives. This integration will also eliminate the necessity to allocate separate time to learn related skills. On the other hand the curriculum was implemented a limited period of time. It will be useful to spread the instruction over a wider period of time to assimilate the skills in the curriculum. Lastly, SC curriculum contributed positively to students' writing skills, but the study was conducted in a semi-experimental model and limits the generalization of the results. There is a need for true-experimental studies in the future to reveal the influence of the SC curriculum on writing skills.

References

1. Hurd, J.M.: The transformation of scientific communication: a model for 2020. J. Am. Soc. Inf. Sci. **51**(14), 1279–1283 (2000)
2. White, H.D.: Scientific communication and literature retrieval. In: Cooper, H., Hedges, L.V., Valentine, J.C. (eds.) The Handbook of Research Synthesis and Meta-Analysis, vol. 2, pp. 51–71. Russell Sage Foundation, New York (2009)
3. Kuhlthau, C.C.: Information Skills for an Information Society: A Review of Research. An ERIC Information Analysis Product. Syracuse University Information Resources Publications, Syracuse (1987)
4. Click, A., Petit, J.: Social networking and web 2.0 in information literacy. Int. Inf. Lib. Rev. **42**(2), 137–142 (2010)
5. Lin, M.H., Li, J.J., Hung, P.Y., Huang, H.W.: Blogging a journal changing students' writing skills and perceptions. ELT J. **68**(4), 422–431 (2014)
6. Lacina, J., Griffith, R.: Blogging as a means of crafting writing. Read. Teach. **66**(4), 316–320 (2012)
7. Alamettälä, T.: Information literacy instruction methods for lower secondary education in Finland. In: Kurbanoğlu, S., Boustany, J., Špiranec, S., Grassian, E., Mizrachi, D., Roy, L. (eds.) ECIL 2015. CCIS, vol. 552, pp. 309–313. Springer, Cham (2015). https://doi.org/10.1007/978-3-319-28197-1_32
8. Scheidt, D., Carpenter, W., Fitzgerald, R., Kozma, C., Middleton, H., Shields, K.: Writing information literacy in first-year composition: a collaboration among faculty and librarians. In: Angelo, B.J.D., Jamieson, S., Maid, B., Walker, J.R. (eds.) Information Literacy: Research and Collaboration across disciplines, pp. 219–241. University Press of Colorado, Fort Collins (2016)
9. Chong, E.K.: Using blogging to enhance the initiation of students into academic research. Comput. Educ. **55**(2), 798–807 (2010)
10. Julien, H., Barker, S.: How high-school students find and evaluate scientific information: a basis for information literacy skills development. Lib. Inf. Sci. Res. **31**, 12–17 (2009)
11. Kurbanoğlu, S., Akkoyunlu, B.: Öğrencilere Bilgi Okuryazarlığı Becerilerinin Kazandırılması Üzerine bir Çalışma. HUEF J. **21**, 81–88 (2001)
12. Scherz, Z., Spektor-Levy, O., Eylon, B.S.: Scientific communication: an instructional program for high-order learning skills and its impact on students' performance. In: Boersma, K., Goedhart, M., De Jong, O., Eijkelhof, H. (eds.) Research and the Quality of Science Education, pp. 231–243. Springer, Dordrecht (2005). https://doi.org/10.1007/1-4020-3673-6_19
13. Rezaei, A.R., Lovorn, M.: Reliability and validity of rubrics for assessment through writing. Assessing Writ. **15**(1), 18–39 (2010)
14. Cohen, J.: A coefficient of agreement for nominal scales. Educ. Psychol. Measur. **20**, 37–46 (1960)
15. Drexler, W., Dawson, K., Ferdig, R.E.: Collaborative blogging as a means to develop elementary expository writing skills. Elec. J. Integr. Technol. Educ. **6**, 140–160 (2007)
16. Maitaouthong, T., Tuamsuk, K., Tachamanee, Y.: Development of the instructional model by integrating information literacy in the class learning and teaching processes. Educ. Inf. **28** (2–4), 137–150 (2011)
17. Kingsawat, K., Kwiecien, K., Tuamsuk, K.: Components and factors in integrating information literacy instruction in elementary education using a virtual learning environment. LIBRES Lib. Inf. Sci. Res. Elec. J. **25**(1), 50–77 (2015)

Senior Citizens Science Literacy and Health Self-efficacy Beliefs

Ágústa Pálsdóttir(✉)

Department of Information Science, University of Iceland,
Gimli v/Sæmundargötu, 101 Reykjavík, Iceland
agustap@hi.is

Abstract. The communication of scientific knowledge about health related issues, and the enhancement of science literacy, has been generally recognized as an important factor in relation to lifelong learning about health. The significance of health self-efficacy beliefs has been emphasised in this respect. The study used the Perceived Health Competence Scale (PHCS) to examine the health self-efficacy of senior citizens 60 years and older. A total of 176 participants were divided in two age groups, 87 participants were 60 to 67 years old and 89 participants were 68 years or older. Seniors aged 60 to 67 years with primary education scored significantly lower on four out of eight statements, than those who had higher education, while seniors 68 years and older with primary education scored significantly lower for one statement. Taken together, the results indicate that senior citizens with primary education believe less strongly in their capabilities to effectively managing their health than seniors with higher education.

Keywords: Health self-efficacy · Iceland · Science literacy · Senior citizens

1 Introduction

Inspiring elderly people to take an active part in health promotion and practice a healthy lifestyle in order to stay healthy for as long as possible is essential, both for the individuals and for society. The communication of scientific knowledge about health related issues, and the enhancement of science literacy, is extremely important in this respect and has been generally recognized as an important factor in relation to lifelong learning about health.

Science literacy and health literacy have been described as closely related domains that are somewhat overlapping [1]. Health literacy stands for "the cognitive and social skills which determine the motivation and ability of individuals to gain access to, understand and use information in ways which promote and maintain good health" [2]. In addition, health literacy is closely related to a joint definition by UNESCO and IFLA (International Federation of Library and Information Association) of media and information literacy, which allows individuals to "…access, retrieve, understand, evaluate and use, create, as well as share information and media content in all formats…" [3]. The term media and health information literacy can therefore be used, as it combines the concepts of health literacy and media and information literacy. Many

S. Kurbanoğlu et al. (Eds.): ECIL 2017, CCIS 810, pp. 398–406, 2018.
https://doi.org/10.1007/978-3-319-74334-9_42

definitions exist about science literacy but here a definition is used where science literacy is described as consisting of four interrelated aspects: (1) Context, which refers to a person's ability to identify life situations that involve science; (2) Knowledge, an understanding based on both scientific knowledge and knowledge about science itself; (3) Competencies, being able to identify scientific issues, explain it and use scientific evidence; (4) Attitudes, referring to a person's interest in science, support for scientific enquiry and the motivation to act responsibly [4]. Those who possess science literacy are therefore motivated and able to engage in seeking information, construct new knowledge and use it to control their health related behaviour.

By increasing public understanding in both areas, science literacy and media and health information literacy, it is hoped that people can be helped to make sound choices about their health. This is though not a simple task, nor have efforts at building people's capacity always been effective. Among the factors that have been identified, is people's beliefs and attitudes toward health issues [5].

Social cognitive factors could play a role in this respect. Bandura [6] has pointed out that there is a distinction between obtaining information and acting on the knowledge gained, and has put emphasis on the importance of perceived self-efficacy as a cognitive mediator of action. Self-efficacy beliefs are people's expectations about whether or not they will be able to master a behaviour, and if so, how successful they will be. The emphasis is not on people's skills but on what they believe that they can do with it under different circumstances. Individuals that believe that they have the necessary skills and will be able to perform well at a task are considered likely to be more strongly motivated, to set themselves higher goals and to have the strength to carry out the act than those who are low on self-efficacy beliefs. These factors are crucial in relation to both science literacy and media and health information literacy and explain why self-efficacy beliefs have been identified as important for information solving and lifelong learning [7]. There are some indications that people who are high on self-efficacy beliefs are also more capable of making good decisions about their health, such as seeking advice from health specialists when needed [8] and practice healthier behaviour [9, 10].

The aim of the study is to examine the health self-efficacy of people at the age 60 year and older in Iceland. The paper will seek answers to the following questions: (1) How do senior citizens perceive their health self-efficacy? (2) How does the perceived health self-efficacy relate to the senior citizens age groups, sex and education?

2 Method

The chapter describes the research methods that were used, that is, the collection of data, the measurement instrument, as well as the analysis of the data.

2.1 Data Collection

The data was collected in spring 2012, using an internet and a telephone survey from two random samples of 600 people each, aged 18 years and older from the whole country. The datasets were merged, allowing answers from all individuals belonging to each set of data. The total response rate was 58.4%. The current study involves only participants who are 60 years and older. A comparison of the sample and the population shows that there were more people who are 60 years and older in the sample (27.5%) compared to the population (18.7%).

In Western countries it has been traditional to use the retirement age to define "elderly" [11], and in Iceland elderly is defined by law as people who have reached the age of 67 [12], when it is usual for people to retire. This has, however, been criticised for not taking into consideration the heterogeneity of senior citizens [13]. It has been pointed out that people's chronological age is less important than determinants, like their physical, cognitive and social capabilities [14]. In accordance with the viewpoints, that there is no clearly defined age when people become senior citizens, the associations for senior citizens in Iceland admit those who have reached the age of 60 to become members [15]. However, classifying all seniors together in one age category may obscure differences among them, while comparing sub-groups can generate differences and similarities between them. In view of the above, it was decided that people who have reached the age of 60 should be included in the study, and that those who are at the age 60 to 67 years, a group who is approaching retirement, should be compared with people aged 68 years or older, who have reached the retirement age. Furthermore, it was decided to examine the effects of sex and education on their perceived health self-efficacy [14]. Participants' were 176; 86 women and 90 men. They were divided in two age groups, participants 60 to 67 years were 87 while 89 participants were 68 years or older.

2.2 Measurements and Data Analysis

1. Socio-demographic information included traditional background variables. Based on previous analysis the variables sex and education are used in the current study. Education was measured as the highest level of education completed. Three levels were distinguished: (1) primary education includes those who have finished compulsory education; (2) secondary education includes those who have completed vocational training or secondary school; (3) university education.
2. Age groups. To assess how the experience of health self-efficacy may relate to age, the participants were divided into two groups, those who are aged 60 to 67 years and those who are 68 years and older.
3. Perceived health self-efficacy. The Perceived Health Competence Scale (PHCS) was used to measure the respondents' beliefs in their abilities to control their health. This is an 8-item scale referring to both outcome expectancies and behavioural expectancies. Each statement has a 5-point response scale (1 = Strongly agree – 5 = Strongly disagree). Half of the statements are negatively worded and half of them are positively worded [16].

ANOVA (one-way) was performed to examine difference across the age groups for each statement of the PHCS scale. To examine the effects of sex and education, and how it interacts on the age groups health self-efficacy, factorial analysis of variance (FANOVA) was used.

3 Results

Results about the perceived health self-efficacy beliefs of each age group are presented first. This will be followed by results of how the effects of education interacts on the age groups self-efficacy beliefs, where only results about significant differences will be presented. No significant results were found by the participants' sex.

Results about the age groups perceived health self-efficacy are presented in Fig. 1.

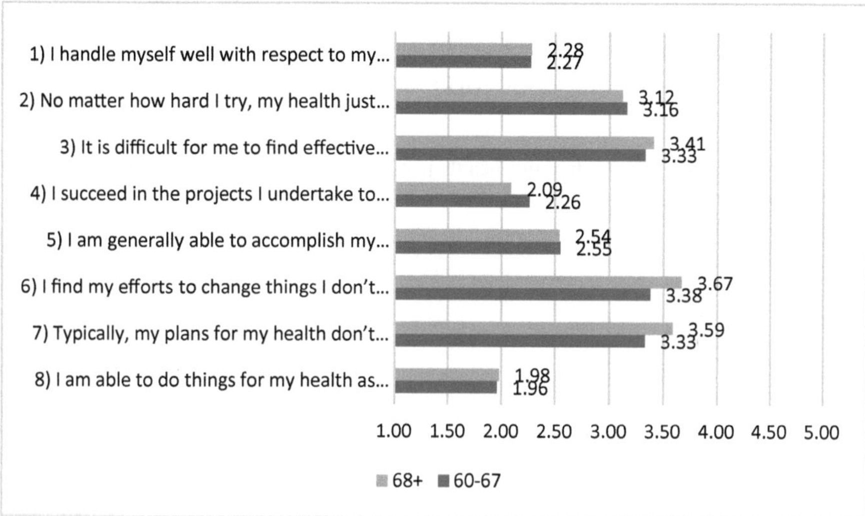

Fig. 1. Perceived health self-efficacy beliefs by age groups

As Fig. 1 shows, for both age groups the mean scores for statements that are positively worded (number 1, 4, 5, 8) are below median (3), which means that the participants were in agreement with them. The mean scores for statements that are negatively worded (2, 3, 6, 7) are above median and therefore the participants disagreed with those statements.

An examination of each statement revealed a significant difference across the age groups for statement 6 "I find my efforts to change things I don't like about my health are ineffective", $F(1,173) = 4.400$, $p = .037$, with the older age group being less in agreement with this than the younger group (Fig. 1).

Factorial analysis of variance (FANOVA) was used to test the statements against education and sex, for each age group. No significant results were found by sex but the analysis revealed significant differences by education for statements 2, 3, 6 and 7. The results are presented in Figs. 2 to 5.

Results about statement 2, "No matter how hard I try, my health just doesn't turn out the way I would like", in Fig. 2, show a significant difference by age and education. Participants in the younger group with primary education did agree with this, as opposed to those who have secondary education ($p < .036$) and university education

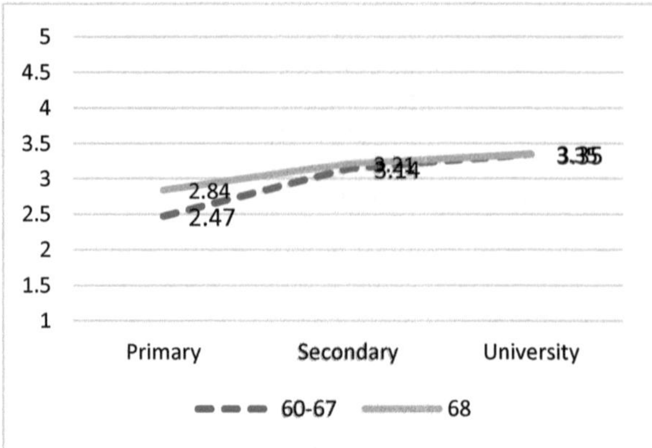

Fig. 2. No matter how hard I try, my health just doesn't turn out the way I would like – differences by age and education

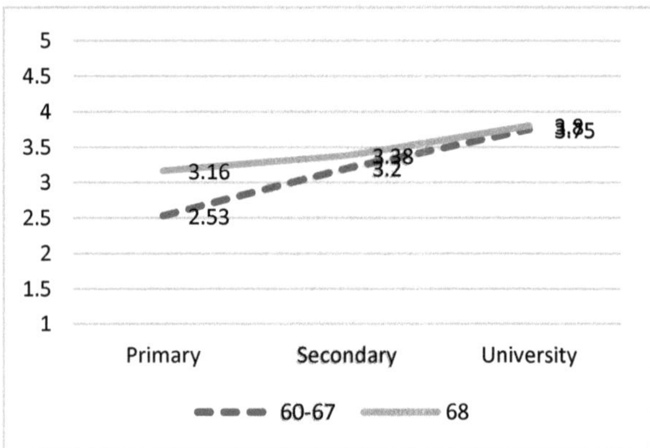

Fig. 3. It is difficult for me to find effective solutions to the health problems that come my way – differences by age and education

($p < .007$). There was not a significant difference across participants with secondary and university education ($p = .407$). Although, no significant difference was found by education for the older age group ($F(2,163) = 1.562$, $p = .213$), the figure shows that participants with primary education agreed with the statement, while those with secondary and university education were in disagreement with it.

Figure 3 shows results for statement 3 "It is difficult for me to find effective solutions to the health problems that come my way". In the younger group, a significant difference was found across participants with primary education, who did agree with the statement, and those with secondary education ($p = .038$) and university education ($p = .000$), who did not agree with it, as well across as participants with secondary and university education ($p = .031$). In the older group, participants in all educational

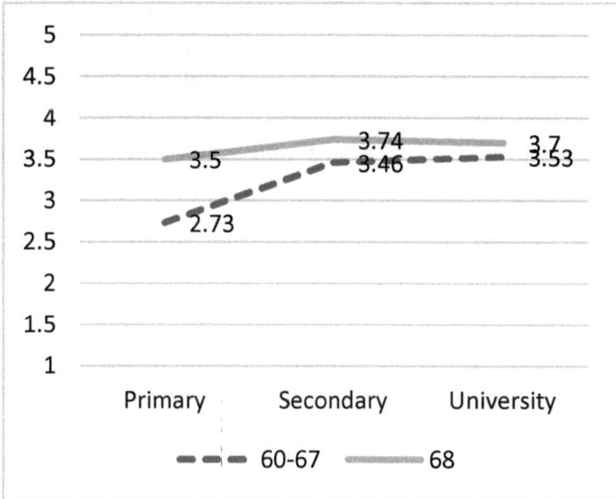

Fig. 4. I find my efforts to change things I don't like about my health are ineffective – differences by age and education

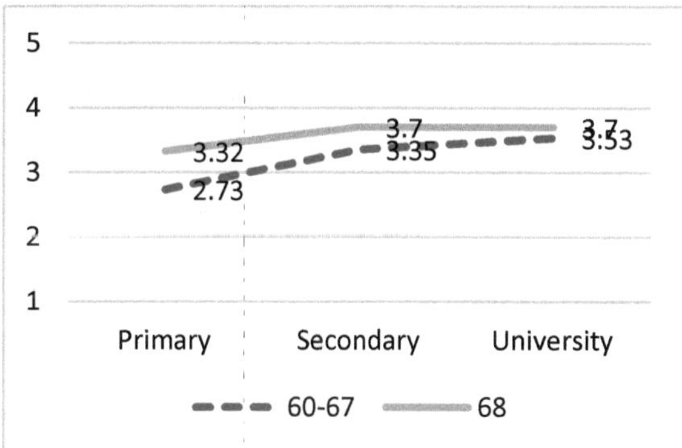

Fig. 5. Typically, my plans for my health don't work out well – differences by age and education

groups disagreed with the statement. Participants with primary education and university education differed significantly (p = .040). A significant difference was not found across participants with primary and secondary education (p = .398) and secondary and university education (p = .137).

Significant difference was found for the younger age group when statement 6, "I find my efforts to change things I don't like about my health are ineffective", was tested against education, see Fig. 4. Participants who have primary education did agree with this as opposed to those with both secondary (p = .009) and university education (p = .005). Significant difference was not found across participants with secondary and university education (p = .733). In the older group, no significant difference was found by education F(2,163) 0,603, p = .548.

Results about statement 7, "Typically, my plans for my health don't work out well", in Fig. 5 show a significant difference by age and education. Participants in the younger group with primary education did agree with this, as opposed to those with secondary ($p = .035$) and university education (=.007). No significant difference was found across participants with secondary and university education ($p = .441$). In addition, no significant difference was found by education in the older age group F (2,163) 1,457, $p = .236$.

4 Discussion

It is crucial to provide senior citizens with opportunities to remain healthy, independent and active members of society for as long as possible. For that, they must be enabled to acquire the scientific knowledge and understanding that is necessary for them to maintain, and preferably to renew, their knowledge of healthy behaviour.

By presenting findings about the perceived health self-efficacy beliefs among people who are 60 years and older, the study sought to contribute to research on science literacy and how it relates to senior citizens possibilities for healthy living, and sustainable health and wellbeing. Instead of classifying all senior citizens in one age category, as quantitative studies often do, the study aimed at investigating similarities and differences among them. This was done by comparing results about two age groups, people who are 60 to 67 years old and those who are 68 years and older. In addition, for each age group, the study explored if the effects of sex and education interacted with age.

The overall results from the current study about the senior citizens perceived health self-efficacy indicate that they have faith in their capabilities to control their own health, and that this does not differ by their age group. However, a closer examination revealed that seniors at the age 60 to 67 years with primary education scored significantly lower on four out of eight statements, than those who had either secondary or university education. The importance of education has been reported in previous studies, with seniors who are more educated being found to score higher on health self-efficacy than those with lower level of education [17–19]. Similar results were, however, not found for seniors who were 68 years and older, as those with primary education were only found to be significantly lower on self-efficacy for one of the statements.

Prior studies have identified health self-efficacy as an important factor at in predicting senior citizens health behaviours. Those who score higher on health self-efficacy have been reported to be more likely to seek advice from health specialists and to be more capable of making decisions about their health [8] and to practice healthier behaviour, than those who are lower on self-efficacy [9, 10].

The skills that are needed for developing science literacy and media and health information literacy are similar. Those who have acquired these skills are motivated and have the abilities to engage in information seeking, constructing new knowledge and to use it to control their health related behaviour [2–4]. Furthermore, the significance of health self-efficacy beliefs has been emphasised in relation to both science literacy and media and health information literacy. Possessing high health self-efficacy beliefs has been identified as important for information solving and lifelong learning [7].

The overall study is limited by a rather low response rate of 58.4%. This is considered satisfactory in a survey but it nevertheless raises the question, whether or not those who answered the survey are giving a biased picture of those who didn't respond. However, the rate of people at the age of 60 years and older in the sample (27.5%) is higher than in the population (18.7%), which strengthens the findings. Thus, the study results may provide valuable information about the perceived health confidence experienced by senior citizens.

5 Conclusion

Taken together, the results from the current study indicate that senior citizens with primary education believe less strongly in their capabilities to effectively manage their health than seniors with higher education, and that they are in need of support that may enhance their self-efficacy beliefs. The communication of scientific knowledge about health related issues has been recognized as an important factor in lifelong learning about healthy behaviour. Likewise, seniors' expectations about their abilities to act on scientific knowledge are of significance. It is essential that they are strongly motivated towards healthy behaviour, as well as having faith in their skills to practice lifelong learning in order to control and improve their health. It is therefore vital that health authorities and health professionals work together to find ways to stimulate this group of senior citizens health competence and motivation towards healthy lifestyles, as well as the enhancing their science literacy.

References

1. National Academies of Sciences, Engineering, and Medicine: Science Literacy: Concepts, Contexts, and Consequences. The National Academic Press, Washington, DC (2016). https://doi.org/10.17226/23595
2. World Health Organization: Health Promotion Glossary. Geneva, World Health Organization (1998)
3. UNESCO: Media and Information Literacy (2014). http://www.uis.unesco.org/Communication/Pages/information-literacy.aspx
4. OECD: PISA 2012 Assessment and Analytical Framework: Mathematics, Reading, Science, Problem Solving and Financial Literacy. OECD Publishing, Paris, France, (2013). http://dx.doi.org/10.1787/9789264190511-en
5. Varner, J.: Scientific outreach: toward effective public engagement with biological science. Bioscience **64**(4), 333–340 (2014)
6. Bandura, A.: Self-Efficacy: The Exercise of Control. W.H. Freeman, New York (1997)
7. Kurbanoglu, S.S.: Self-efficacy: a concept closely linked to information literacy and lifelong learning. J. Doc. **59**(6), 635–646 (2003)
8. Dempster, M., Donnelly, M.: Validity of the perceived health competence scale in a UK primary care setting. Psychol. Health Med. **13**(1), 123–127 (2008)

9. Marks, G.R., Lutgendorf, S.K.: Perceived health competence and personality factors differentially predict health behaviors in older adults. J. Aging Health **11**, 221–239 (1999). https://doi.org/10.1177/089826439901100205
10. Pálsdóttir, Á.: Information behaviour, health self-efficacy beliefs and health behaviour in icelanders' everyday life. Inf. Res. **13**(1), paper 334 (2008). http://InformationR.net/ir/13-1/paper334.html
11. Thane, P.: History and the sociology of ageing. Soc. Hist. Med. **2**(1), 93–96 (1989)
12. Lög um málefni aldraðra nr. 125/1999. (Act on the Affairs of the Elderly)
13. Berger, K.S.: The Developing Person Through the Lifespan, 3rd edn. Worth Publishers, New York (1994)
14. Ries, W., Pöthiga, D.: Chronological and biological age. Exp. Gerontol. **19**(3), 211–216 (1984)
15. Landsamband eldri borgara, http://leb.is/. (Association for senior citizens)
16. Smith, M.S., Wallston, K.A., Smith, C.A.: The development and validation of the perceived health competence scale. Health Educ. Res. **10**(1), 51–64 (1995)
17. Chlebowy, D.O., Myers, J., Mendes, A.N.: Socio-demographic variables and self-efficacy in Caucasian and African American adults with type 2 diabetes. South. Online J. Nurs. Res. **10**(4) (2010). http://www.resourcenter.net/images/snrs/files/sojnr_articles2/Vol10Num04Art11.pdf
18. Clark, D.O.: Age, socioeconomic status, and exercise self-efficacy. Gerontologist **36**(2), 157–164 (1996)
19. Sohng, K.Y., Sohng, S., Yeom, H.A.: Health-promoting behaviors of elderly Korean immigrants in the United States. Public Health Nurs. **19**(4), 294–300 (2002)

Health Information Literacy

Developing Information Literacy in Dependent and Disadvantaged Circumstances: A Transitional Approach in the Digital Health Context

Steven Buchanan(✉), Cara Jardine, and Ian Ruthven

Department of Computer and Information Sciences,
University of Strathclyde, Glasgow, UK
{steven.buchanan, cara.jardine,
ian.ruthven}@strath.ac.uk

Abstract. The purpose of this paper is to advance our understanding of approaches to information literacy skills development in disadvantaged and dependent circumstances, and the role of information behaviour investigations in informing meaningful interventions in context. We report on work with young mothers (<25) from areas of multiple deprivation, seeking to better understand their information needs, and the factors influencing their selective and infrequent engagement with state and voluntary sector information services. We evidence limited progress in addressing digital divide issues, and report young mothers as having multiple and complex information needs, and a dependency upon human information intermediaries due to access and behavioural issues. We discuss design and trial of a tailored digital resource to encourage digital access and use, and in turn literacy development; and report that while found useful by young mothers, usage is likely to be low without human intermediary led intervention. A transitional approach is discussed.

Keywords: Information literacy · Information behaviour · Digital health

1 Introduction

The purpose of this paper is to advance our understanding of approaches to information literacy development in disadvantaged (socio-economic) and dependent (support) circumstances. We report on work with young mothers (age <25) from areas of multiple deprivations (e.g. employment, education, health, crime), seeking to better understand their information behaviours, and the factors influencing their selective and infrequent engagement with state and voluntary sector information services and resources. Identifying a persistent digital divide amongst a high-risk group (health and wellbeing) requiring immediate intervention, we report on the development of a digital resource to provide tailored access to trusted online sources to encourage digital access and use, and in turn, facilitate development of information literacy skills. Our approach to intervention is guided by Eisenberg [1], who reminds us that for information literacy programs to be successful they must be meaningful, and highlights three key

S. Kurbanoğlu et al. (Eds.): ECIL 2017, CCIS 810, pp. 409–418, 2018.
https://doi.org/10.1007/978-3-319-74334-9_43

interwoven components: tasks based on real needs, technology in context, and appropriate information process. In practice, this raised three key research questions:

1. What are the information needs of young disadvantaged mothers?
2. What are the appropriate digital sources to meet these information needs?
3. What would be an appropriate design and approach to digital access and use?

The work responds to calls for "person-based" and "persuasive" approaches to digital health interventions [2], and recognition that "more work is needed to create successful [digital health] engagement strategies" [3, p. 1]. In particular, we illustrate the role of information behaviour investigations in informing meaningful interventions in the problematic context.

Our overarching theoretical framework brought together theories and models of information behaviour and social capital to better understand shared aspects of social integration (understood as access, participation, engagement) in the socio-economic context.

2 Background

The United Kingdom (UK) has one of the highest rates of teenage pregnancy in Western Europe, with associated conception rates correlated to multiple deprivation indexes. At risk groups are disadvantaged and disengaged, with significant health and wellbeing issues reported for both mother and child. In a review of research studies, Trivedi et al. [4] highlights at risk individuals as those: in care; homeless; school underperformers/truants; children of teenage mothers; and from deprived areas. Young mothers are more likely to be single parents, to have experienced family conflict/trauma, not to be in employment, education, or training, and to be at risk of short and long-term mental health issues. Infant mortality rates are higher than those for older women [5], and babies are at greater risk of poor nutrition and childcare [6], and impaired development [7]. Stress and anxiety are heightened amongst young mothers, as are rates of depression [8]. Low literacy levels are also reported [9].

Beyond parenting related information needs, on-going broader support is considered key to long-term success and social mobility [10, 11]; however, a systematic review of the research evidence relating to teenage pregnancy, parenting and social exclusion reports that mainstream services "have often failed to provide the holistic care required to support social inclusion or social re-integration for teenage parents" [12, p. 4], and in particular, to meet diverse needs and preferences. A key recommendation highlighted the need for *tailored* information, advice and support [12]. A UK National Health Service (NHS) review of midwife services [13] highlights similar issues, identifying a lack of age appropriate information, unmet social information needs, and issues of equity of access to information. There have been further follow-on calls for tailored health information [14, 15] and increased digital provision [16], reflecting wider concerns regarding limited online information provision tailored to young people [17]. However, our work examining the information behaviours of first time mothers [18, 19] suggests limited progress in addressing such issues, and reports multiple, complex, and at times competing information needs. Louden et al. [18]

interviewed 22 first-time general population mothers with an average age of 29, and identified information needs relating to: sleeping, milk feeding, weaning, health and infant care, family, activities, and products. Buchanan et al. [19] interviewed 49 professional support workers (family nurses, health visitors, social workers, and voluntary sector support group leaders) working with young mothers (<25) from areas of multiple deprivation, and identified information needs relating to: pregnancy, baby care, finance, family relationships, domestic abuse, education and employment, parent health, and housing. In relation to this, multiple needs could be interrelated, often compounding issues of information overload [19]. For example, financial needs routinely encompassed helping mothers with accessing and understanding state benefits, maternity grants and food and vitamin voucher entitlements; and were often closely linked to housing needs and the fundamental need to provide their child with a habitable home that in situations of sub-standard accommodation or homelessness could present significant health needs for both mother and child.

Low literacy levels (reading and information) are also reported [19], discouraging many mothers from seeking information themselves, and limiting their access to and use of textual information. Issues of misinformation from the use of unreliable sources are reported, as are issues of information comprehension [19]. Practical access barriers are also reported, with many young mothers not possessing a computer and those that do often not able to afford and/or eligible for home internet, and while smartphones are more common, usage can be limited by prepaid credit [19]. Access (and support) is available via public libraries, but few young mothers from areas of multiple deprivations attend library-based groups due to issues of confidence and stigma, which also affects engagement with formal learning programmes more broadly [19]. In such circumstances, many young mothers are dependent upon support workers (e.g. family nurses, health visitors, social workers, voluntary sector support group leaders) as human information intermediaries, particularly when seeking information from external (non-interpersonal and/or digital) sources [19].

In summary, a persistent digital divide is evident amongst a high-risk group with an immediate need for meaningful and persuasive intervention in the problematic context. Reasoning that a formal information literacy program was unlikely to succeed due to complex access and internalised behavioural barriers, our first priority was to develop a tailored digital resource that might encourage digital access and use, and that in turn, might facilitate information literacy development.

3 Methodology

A typology of information needs (research question one (RQ1)) was developed from synthesis of information needs data from previous studies [18, 19] discussed above, with meaningful categories identified via cross-study thematic analysis and iterative pattern coding [20]. Periodic team-based code checking was conducted to check developing categories for coherence, consistence, and distinctiveness [21]. Categorised needs then specified the information services to be provided by the digital resource, and the menu elements of the graphical user interface (GUI).

Appropriate online information sources (RQ2) were identified via service directories and online searches (identified needs providing search parameters), and website content analysis, approached in a systematic and structured manner via selective identification of UK non-commercial state and voluntary sector websites, followed by top-down content analysis of respective webpages. Such an approach has been previously employed [22] to identify digital services and was tailorable to study search parameters. Commercial sites were not included for reasons of trust amongst mothers [18]. Redundant sites (mirrored content and/or link) were also removed. Shortlisted sites were mapped via a matrix to identified information needs, and assigned one or more of the following values: 3. Provides parent tailored information, 2. Is a primary source of information (one or more information needs), 1. Is a secondary source of some information (one or more information needs). The best matches combined 3 & 2 (i.e., a primary source of parent-tailored information for one or more information needs). Selected sites then provided the underlying architecture (information sources) for the digital resource.

To explore design and use of the digital resource (RQ3), individual and small group field trials and discussions were held with young mothers. A purposive approach to sampling defined the key participant inclusion criteria as being a mother aged <25 from an area of multiple deprivation as defined by the Scottish Index of Multiple Deprivation[1], with participants recruited via voluntary sector support groups and the UK National Health Service Family Nurse Partnership (FNP) programme. The resource was described to participants as a resource to provide mothers with tailored access to trusted online information, with the sessions framed as open exploratory discussions to solicit feedback and contribute to further development of the resource.

Ethical approval was obtained via Institutional Ethics Committee, with all experiments run in strict accordance with the guidelines set out by our Institutional Code of Practice on Investigations of Human Beings.

4 Findings

In presenting and discussing our findings we return to our research questions.

4.1 What Are the Information Needs of Young Disadvantaged Mothers?

Synthesis of information needs data from previous studies discussed above [18, 19] identified the following information needs amongst young disadvantaged mothers: pregnancy; labour and birth; child development; child health; parent health; playtime activities; childcare; family relationships; housing; money; legal advice; work, education and training; domestic abuse; stress; and helplines. It is notable that, in comparison to the needs of older (avg. age 29) general population mothers, the needs of young (<25) disadvantaged mothers extend beyond parenting to individual issues of poverty and personal development. A high level of element (information need)

[1] http://www.gov.scot/Topics/Statistics/SIMD.

interactivity is also evident in reports of interrelated needs [19], which is known to be cognitively demanding, requiring systematic and/or simplified learning processes to understand [23], and influencing later design decisions.

4.2 What Are the Appropriate Digital Resources to Meet These Information Needs?

In identifying appropriate online sources to meet identified information needs, an initial list of 98 candidates (websites) was reduced to 36 when redundant sites were removed (a step to simplify design and the user experience, and in particular, reduce cognitive load). Beyond identifying primary sources of information for parents, this step also identified gaps in provision; most notably to meet housing information needs, with the most appropriate source of information being within the voluntary sector rather than the responsible local (state) authority. Once primary online sources were identified for each information need, this formed the initial architecture of the prototype with eight of the fifteen identified websites parent-tailored. During content analysis and mapping, initial child and parent health categories (i.e., pregnancy, labour and birth, child development, child health, parent health) were noted to be logically grouped on existing websites separated by child age (i.e., baby or toddler), and this convention was adopted in our own model, and a general health category also added (for general health needs). In consideration of low literacy and potentially complex and problematic situations, three further categories of additional support were also added: a–z of common terms, helplines, and additional links.

4.3 What Would Be an Appropriate Design and Approach to Digital Access and Use?

The graphical user interface (GUI) was designed to intentionally mirror ubiquitous and widely accepted tablet and smartphone design (see Fig. 1). Cognisant to issues of literacy and cognitive load [19], we considered it beneficial to begin with a GUI design with minimal text, and a simplified architecture that mitigated for issues of information overload common in the initiation and selection stages of information seeking [24] via meaningful (needs based) search processes that expedited access to a single primary source of trusted online information for each category of need. In psychology and cognitive science our categories of need can be considered as schemas, which "can be treated as a single element in working memory and thus heavily decrease cognitive load associated with the performance of later tasks" [25, p.87]. Associated text (category titles) scored 6 in a Flesh-Kincaid readability test indicative of general readability by the adult population. In Big6 terms, we sought to simplify initial steps of task definition, information seeking, location and access.

12 young mothers (aged 15–23) variously attending third sector parent support groups or part of the NHS FNP programme volunteered to provide feedback (via individual and small group sessions). Comments regarding design were mixed. Single direct links to trusted resources were positively commented on by several mothers, and felt to avoid "unnecessary" and "tedious" navigation, and providing "guarantees the information is reliable". However, several mothers also described the design as "plain"

Fig. 1. Prototype GUI design (The launched version of this prototype can be accessed at: http://yoyo.cis.strath.ac.uk/)

and "boring", and suggested that there could be "a more interesting background" and in relation, that it "could be a bit more colourful and not just white". Positive pictures of parenthood were also suggested. Some mothers also suggested having a page beneath each icon providing more links for each topic and additional context and direction such as "general summaries" of the information available beneath.

Some mothers disliked the prototype name ('Mothers Digital Gateway'). It was suggested that "mother" needs to be replaced with a gender neutral term encompassing fathers and carers, and that "gateway" might be replaced with "help book", "helpful info for parents" or "survival guide", although with the latter, when it was mentioned that there already exists a publication titled 'The Young Parents Survival Guide', another participant considered this insulting as she felt it suggests that young people cannot cope with parenthood, and in relation, another commented that, "when you get called a young mum or a young parent, it kind of makes you feel like you're less… because of the way the generations seen as teenagers or whatever… or making you seem less valuable as a parent than older mums". This is an important consideration as stigma is a known issue amongst young mothers [26], with stigma also known to influence information practices [27]. Comments highlight sensitive issues of self-identity, and remind us of the importance of positive constructive communication in progressive situations (i.e., parenthood).

With regard to utility, mothers appeared to intuitively understand the resources' purpose and provided positive feedback regarding categorised information need topics, with none of the topics questioned and three further suggestions made: sexual health, local information and useful phone numbers. Several indicated that they might use the resource with simplified access appearing valued. For example, one mother while browsing linked sites underneath topics commented that without such a resource it can "take forever" to find trusted sites, and another that it was "good to have all the trustworthy sites in one place". Mothers also thought that it should have its own domain with visible links from NHS and public library sites (note: the prototype was located on the parent research project website during these trials).

The trial in itself could also be seen to increase awareness of online resources amongst several participants. For example, one mother while exploring the website link under family relationships commented, "I quite like this one – family lives – I've never seen that one before". However, the majority of participants as part of general discussions also indicated a low use of online sources (favouring interpersonal sources such as family and health visitors instead), and infrequent use of online resources beyond Google. For example, the majority of our participants were unaware of ReadySteadyBaby (NHS Scotland's main online guide to pregnancy and the first 12 months of parenthood), and whilst all knew of Young Scot (Scotland's national information and citizenship resource for young people aged 11–25), none used the website or knew of any peers who did, with the resource described by one as being "not really a thing that young people are actually interested in". In relation, one participant commented more broadly, 'I don't think many people look online for information', a comment supported by another who replied 'I know I don't'.

5 Discussion

Young mothers from areas of multiple deprivations have multiple, complex, interwoven, and at times competing information needs, extending beyond parenting needs shared with general population peers, to individual issues of poverty and personal development. Our findings highlight the importance of situational understanding of information needs, and the potential risks involved in assumptions of homogeneity. Attempting to provide holistic support in such complex circumstances has been a significant and enduring challenge to date with repeated calls for tailored digital support largely unmet. We have demonstrated the role of information behaviour investigations in identifying information needs, and learning needs; to inform meaningful interventions in the problematic context, and in particular, to develop a tailored resource to facilitate and encourage digital access and use. Importantly, given issues of cognitive load, identified categories of information need can also act as schemas to reduce cognitive load during information seeking activity, helping to simplify initial tasks of location and access, and facilitating systematic approaches to information seeking in instances of multiple needs with high element (need) interactivity.

In pilot trials, our young mothers appeared to intuitively understand and interact with the resource, providing positive feedback regarding usability and usefulness, but our findings also suggest that usage is likely to be extremely low by itself. Returning to Eisenberg's [1] three components of effective IL programs, the resource is clearly focused on real information needs, and in meeting those needs helps place technology in purposeful context. It is the third component, process, that requires careful consideration, having to overcome complex access and behavioural issues, the former influenced by digital divide issues, the latter by socio-psychological factors. Given these issues, it is evident that interventions will need to begin in the physical space, and be human intermediary led, which raises further questions of who and how?

We know that young mothers mostly do not use libraries or librarians; but that their support workers (family nurses, health visitors, social workers, voluntary sector support group leaders), beyond being a key source of information in themselves, play a key role in directing and linking young mothers to other information services, groups and resources, and dealing with misinformation [19]. Support workers, as information intermediaries, are therefore ideally placed to utilise the digital resource in their everyday interactions with young mothers, providing access to, and encouraging use of trusted sources of online information, and providing opportunity to discuss and develop information literacy skills in a practical interactive manner. In combination (resource and intermediary), a transitional approach can be applied in the everyday context. However, to be successful, careful consideration has to be given to both the meeting of immediate needs, and longer-term transitions to self-efficacy.

In the learning context, Eisenberg recommends 'continually working with users to help them recognize where they are in the process' [1, p. 43]. This of course requires that there be an agreed upon and understood information process in place that tasks and actions can be related to, and that encourages reflective practice, and develops metacognitive skills. For our purposes such an information process must be adaptable to semi-structured everyday situations, and implementable by non-information professionals, such as nurses, and is reserved for the next stage of this research as part of field trials of the resource involving NHS family nurses providing outreach support to young disadvantaged mothers.

6 Conclusion

A persistent digital divide is evident amongst young mothers from areas of multiple deprivations, who have multiple, complex, interwoven, and at times competing information needs, extending beyond parenting needs to issues of poverty and personal development. There are complex access and behavioural issues to consider, the former influenced by digital divide issues, the latter by socio-psychological factors. Providing support in such circumstances has been a significant and enduring challenge to date.

We have demonstrated the role of information behaviour investigations in identifying information needs, and learning needs, to inform meaningful interventions, and in particular, to develop a tailored digital resource to facilitate and encourage digital access and use in the problematic context. However, while found to provide meaningful and useful access to trusted online information for young mothers, usage is likely to be low without purposeful human intermediary intervention.

The resource can be used by human intermediaries to direct young mothers to tailored and trusted online sources of information, and as a tool to discuss and develop information literacy skills in an interactive and practical manner, developing self-efficacy over time. This requires an information process to be in place that encourages reflective practice and the development of metacognitive skills. It must also be adaptable to semi-structured everyday situations, and implementable by non-information professionals. In combination (resource, intermediary, process), a holistic transitional approach to intervention can then be taken in the problematic context.

References

1. Eisenberg, M.B.: Information literacy: essential skills for the information age. DESIDOC J. Libr. Inf. Technol. **28**(2), 39–47 (2008)
2. Yardley, L., Morrison, L., Bradbury, K., Muller, I.: The person-based approach to intervention development: application to digital health-related behavior change interventions. Med. Internet Res. **17**(1), 30 (2015)
3. O'Connor, S., Hanlon, P., O'Donnell, C.A., Garcia, S., Glanville, J., Mair, F.S.: Understanding factors affecting patient and public engagement and recruitment to digital health interventions: a systematic review of qualitative studies. BMC Med. Inf. Decis. Making **16**(1), 120 (2016)
4. Trivedi, D., et al.: Update on the Review of Reviews on Teenage Pregnancy and Parenthood. Centre for Research in Primary and Community Care (2007). http://www.nice.org.uk/nicemedia/pdf/TeenagePregnancyUpdateReviewFeb08.pdf
5. Torvie, A.J., Callegari, L.S., et al.: Labor and delivery outcomes among young adolescents. Am. J. Obstet. Gynecol. **213**(1), 91–95 (2015)
6. Harron, K., Gilbert, R., Cromwell, D., Oddie, S., van der Meulen, J.: Adversity and Risk of Poor Birth and Infant Outcomes for Young Mothers: a Population-based Data-linkage Cohort Study. The Lancet **388**, 54 (2016)
7. UNICEF: Child Poverty in Perspective: an Overview of Child Well-being in Rich Countries. Innocenti Report Card 7(2) (2007)
8. Raskin, M., Easterbrooks, M.A., Lamoreau, R.S., Kotake, C., Goldberg, J.: Depression trajectories of antenatally depressed and nondepressed young mothers: implications for child socioemotional development. Women's Health Issues **26**(3), 344–350 (2016)
9. Bennett, I.M., Frasso, R., Bellamy, S.L., Wortham, S., Gross, K.S.: Pre-teen literacy and subsequent teenage childbearing in a US population. Contraception **87**(4), 459–464 (2013)
10. Smith, D.M., Roberts, R.: Social inequality and young pregnancy: the causal attributions of young parents in London, UK. Health Place **15**(5), 1054–1060 (2011)
11. Smith, M.L., Gilmer, M.H., Salge, L.E., Dickerson, J.B., Wilson, K.L.: Who enrolls in teen parent education programs? An emphasis on personal and familial characteristics and services received. Child Adolesc. Soc. Work J. 1–16 (2012)
12. Harden, A., Brunton, G., Fletcher, A., Oakley, A., Burchett, H., Backhans, M.: Young People, Pregnancy and Social Exclusion: A Systematic Synthesis of Research Evidence to Identify Effective, Appropriate and Promising Approaches for Prevention and Support. EPPI-Centre, Social Science Research Unit, Institute of Education, University of London (2006)
13. Coltart, L.: Meeting the Needs of Pregnant Teenagers Across NHS Greater Glasgow and Clyde (2007). http://health.cat/ref/pdf.php?search=NHS%20Greater%20Glasgow%20and%20Clyde
14. Berkule-Silberman, S.B., Dreyer, B.P., Huberman, H.S., Klass, P.E., Mendelsohn, A.L.: Sources of parenting information in low SES mothers. Clin. Pediatr. **49**(6), 560–568 (2010)
15. Hagell, A., Coleman, J.: Adolescent Health in the UK Today: Where Next. AYPH (2012). http://www.ayph.org.uk/publications/278_Adol%20health%20in%20the%20UK%20today%2019%20June%202012.pdf

16. Joint Strategic Needs Assessment Under-18 Conceptions in the Lancashire Sub-region 2011/12 (2012). http://www.lancashire.gov.uk/corporate/web/?siteid=6107&pageid=35232&e=e
17. Reading Agency: Libraries and Digital: Research into the Use of Digital Media in Libraries to Develop Audiences for Reading (2011). www.readingagency.org.uk/
18. Louden, L., Buchanan, S., Ruthven, I.: The everyday life information seeking behaviours of first-time mothers. J. Documentation **72**(1), 24–46 (2016)
19. Buchanan, S., Jardine, C., Ruthven, I.: Information Behaviours in Disadvantaged and Dependent Circumstances and the Role of Information Intermediaries (2017), Forthcoming
20. Miles, M., Huberman, A.: Qualitative Data Analysis: An Expanded Sourcebook. Sage (1994)
21. Braun, V., Clarke, V.: Using thematic analysis in psychology. Qual. Res. Psychol. **3**(2), 77–101 (2006)
22. Buchanan, S., McMenemy, D.: Towards a public library digital service taxonomy. In: Lalmas, M., Jose, J., Rauber, A., Sebastiani, F., Frommholz, I. (eds.) ECDL 2010. LNCS, vol. 6273, pp. 425–428. Springer, Heidelberg (2010). https://doi.org/10.1007/978-3-642-15464-5_48
23. Paas, F., Renkl, A., Sweller, J.: Cognitive load theory and instructional design: recent developments. Educ. Psychol. **38**(1), 1–4 (2003)
24. Kuhlthau, C.C.: Seeking Meaning: A Process Approach to Library and Information Services. Libraries Unltd Incorporated (2004)
25. Van Merriënboer, J.J., Sweller, J.: Cognitive load theory in health professional education: design principles and strategies. Med. Educ. **44**(1), 85–93 (2010)
26. Ormiston, R., McConville, S., Gordon, J.: Evaluation of the Family Nurse Partnership Programme in NHS Lothian, Scotland: 2nd Report – Late Pregnancy and Postpartum (2012). http://www.maternal-and-early-years.org.uk/topic/pregnancy/teenage-pregnancy#evidence
27. Lingel, J., Boyd, D.: Keep it secret, keep it safe: information poverty, information norms, and stigma. J. Am. Soc. Inf. Sci. Technol. **64**(5), 981–991 (2013)

Medical Students' Information Literacy Self-efficacy: Longitudinal Study-Protocol Covering a Whole Medical Curriculum

Ann De Meulemeester[1,2](✉), Renaat Peleman[2], and Heidi Buysse[3]

[1] Library and Information Science, University of Antwerp, Antwerp, Belgium
Ann2.Demeulemeester@UGent.be

[2] Knowledge Center for Health Ghent, Ghent University, Ghent, Belgium
Renaat.Peleman@UGent.be

[3] Medical Informatics and Statistics, Ghent University, Ghent, Belgium
Heidi.Buysse@UGent.be

Abstract. Information literacy (IL) and IL self-efficacy (SE) have already been studied in diverse ways by several research groups. However, to our knowledge, no medical curriculum-based studies are available on ILSE. This paper describes the study protocol of the longitudinal study of the evolution in ILSE among individual students as well as cohorts of students throughout (parts of) a complete medical curriculum. A thorough literature study of ILSE within a medical context formed the basis of this research. To evaluate medical-oriented ILSE, a standardized existing ILSE-scale enriched with ten specific medical items was completed, between 2011 and 2016, by all medical students at Ghent University (Belgium), ending with a surplus qualitative study. Data will be analysed statistically. This study will allow to look for cross-sectional as well as longitudinal results. The qualitative study at the end of the research will be performed to clarify some quantitative results.

Keywords: Information literacy self-efficacy · Medical education
Health sciences · Medical curriculum · Higher education

1 Introduction

Medical students are being educated in a more and more digitised world, where a lot of information is freely accessible. Students are continuously confronted with an increase in the amount of information and ambiguity as to the quality of the retrieved information. Technology is continuously changing. To find reliable information in an efficient way, students need good computer and information literacy (IL) skills.

2 Information Literacy

Information literacy is a well-established concept. The definitions of the American Library Association [1], as well as these of the Association of College and Research

S. Kurbanoğlu et al. (Eds.): ECIL 2017, CCIS 810, pp. 419–429, 2018.
https://doi.org/10.1007/978-3-319-74334-9_44

Libraries [2], are widely used in the literature. In 2016 however, ACRL rescinded the "Information Literacy Competency Standards for Higher Education" [2] and adopted an "Information Literacy Framework" proposing a new definition for IL: "Information literacy is the set of integrated abilities encompassing the reflective discovery of information, the understanding of how information is produced and valued, and the use of information in creating new knowledge and participating ethically in communities of learning".

Information literacy is a core component of lifelong learning (LLL) and is no longer limited to traditional education [3]. It can be associated with the development of individual competencies for learning and social responsibility [4] and can be seen as common for all disciplines, learning environments and all levels of education [2].

Information literacy is considered a fundamental ingredient of the academic curriculum and the development of IL competencies is thought to enhance student learning [5, 6]. Research within medical curricula [7] suggests that IL training should be incorporated early in the academic curriculum. However, this should not be limited to the first years but needs to be developed throughout a complete curriculum, to make sure that students improve continuously and retain their acquired IL skills [8]. Hence, teaching IL skills should take place at contextually and appropriate moments of the students' learning process [9]. Recent research by Bazrafkan, Hayat [10], concluded that medical students' IL level should be assessed in different periods. Some researchers [11] suggest that it would be even better to assess IL skills before starting an academic programme.

In the domain of medical and health sciences education, different aspects of IL have been studied; examples within different types of curricula include:

• medical [8–10, 12–18]	• chiropractic [24]
• medical radiation [19–21]	• dentistry [9, 25, 26]
• occupational therapy [22]	• nursing [23, 27–29]
• rehabilitation therapy [23]	• biomedical sciences [7, 30]

3 Self-efficacy

Along with IL, self-efficacy (SE) plays an important role in people becoming lifelong learners [31, 32]. Bandura [33, p. 391] defines perceived SE as "people's judgments of their capabilities to organize and execute courses of action required to attain designated types of performances". Self-efficacy beliefs develop through gradual attainment of skills and experience over time [33]. In his social learning analysis, Bandura [34, p. 191] proposed that "expectations of personal efficacy are based on four major sources of information: performance accomplishments, vicarious experience, verbal persuasion, and physiological states".

The level of SE determines the effort an individual will make and how persistent and resilient this person will be [34, 35]. People with high SE will perceive themselves as capable of successfully completing a task. Self-efficacy beliefs have a positive influence on attaining skills, especially when there are successive performances, by influencing effort, persistence and perseverance [33, 36]. Participation can also have an impact on the level of SE and on higher assessment scores [37]. The more students practice their IL skills and obtain feedback in relation to their efforts, the better their SE beliefs will develop [38]. The specific situation and the domain where SE is evaluated are key elements as they determine the level of SE for a given task within a specific context [33, 39–43].

4 Information Literacy Self-efficacy

It is not sufficient to have the necessary IL skills. An individual also needs to feel confident about these skills and to feel competent about learning and applying them. Today's digital society needs confident, independent, self-regulated learners equipped for LLL. Individuals need to be able to find, evaluate, use, produce and share information and to possess the necessary skills for using information technology in order to do this.

Carson [44] studied the SE beliefs of school library media graduate students. In the measurement, some information specialist skills were integrated. But, it was only 10 years later that "Perceived self-efficacy for information literacy" was introduced as a new research topic within the broader domain of IL [32]. An 89-item SE scale to assess students' perceived IL skills was developed and tested [32].

As Kurbanoglu, Akkoyunlu [45, p. 731] stated, "the attainment of high sense of self-efficacy beliefs is as important as possessing information literacy skills". In other words, if a student feels confident in using his IL skills, he will possibly apply greater effort, persistence and resilience into undertaking problem-solving activities, thinking critically, taking action and trying to take new steps in his learning process. Students with high SE will make sure they have goals and will complete the given task. Those with lower SE, who avoid active learning, are less inclined to develop IL skills that develop LLL [32, 46]. Stokes and Urquhart [28] obtained parallel results in their research and suggest that nursing students who put effort into the learning process and have confidence in their IL skills are more persevering. They found a link between "advanced information literacy self-efficacy", "deep learning style" and the "openness personality". On the other hand, students with a low ILSE belief are more likely to be "surface learners": they will rely more on other students or will stick to their results without making any further effort regarding more literature searching.

Information literacy SE has been associated with higher levels of motivation in students [47] and with academic success [48]. Ross, Perkins [38] concluded in their research that the intrinsic motivation to learn is the most important predictor of higher levels of ILSE. Students need to be proactive and individually pursue the opportunities presented to them within their process of learning. Information literacy courses cannot be limited to teaching IL skills alone. To be effective, learning experiences using these skills should be included in the learning process [6].

Self-efficacy reflects the degree of certainty that a person performs a given task and could therefore be measured by using a self-report scale [40]. The most widely used scale for evaluating SE beliefs relating to IL is the information literacy self-efficacy scale (ILSES) of Kurbanoglu, Akkoyunlu [45] which could lead to reliable and valid results

[49]. There are different studies considering research on ILSE using the ILSES and they are not limited to a specific domain. Here are some examples of research within academic settings using the ILSES 28-item scale within different types of user groups:

• e-leaners [6] • student teachers [45, 50, 51] • student science teachers [48] • post-graduate students [52]	• nursing students [11, 53] • biomedical science students [54] • medical students [55, 56]

Several researchers studied the relationship of the ILSES with an IL assessment [50, 54–56]. Batarelo Kokić and Novosel [50] found a significant correlation between the ILSE beliefs of student teachers and their actual IL competency. Students have the highest SE beliefs in relation to basic IL skills and the lowest for advanced IL skills. Further research is necessary to reveal whether medical students also differ in their SE beliefs regarding basic, intermediate and advanced skills.

Other research demonstrated the relationship between ILSE and computer literacy SE. Erdem [57] concluded that student teachers had either high scores or low/moderate scores on both scales of SE. Results suggest that ILSE and computer literacy SE need to be studied together and that training should be focused on both skills. Usluel [51] investigated the ILSE beliefs of student teachers and reduced the 28-item scale to a reliable 20-item scale. Usluel [51] concluded that the level and duration of ICT usage was a determining factor for students' ILSE beliefs. Kilic-Cakmak [6] used the ILSES to study learning strategies and motivational factors predicting ILSE of e-learners. They concluded that it is necessary to integrate complex tasks where students need to use and improve their critical thinking abilities, because individuals who are able to think critically can deduce, synthesise and integrate information and can therefore evaluate their own thinking process.

Stokes and Urquhart [28] used the 17-item scale of Kurbanoglu, Akkoyunlu [45] and measured the information-seeking behaviour of nursing students according to learning style, personality and ILSE. The researchers concluded that students with advanced ILSE are more extroverted, agreeable, conscientious, emotionally stable, and open [28]. Other researchers developed their own assessment tools. Tepe and Tepe [58] created an ILSE survey and a 25-item IL knowledge test for chiropractic students and found a reliable instrument for measuring self-perceived IL competence, SE and IL knowledge. Mi and Riley-Doucet [59] studied the relationship of nursing and medical students' ILSE beliefs in relation to their orientation towards LLL.

Information Literacy Self-efficacy in the Medical Curriculum. Medical education requires students to practice evidence-based medicine (EBM) and therefore to update their information all the time; caring for patients creates the need for clinically important information about different health-related topics. The practice of EBM is a process of problem-solving, self-directed and LLL. As such, IL is a common element in every aspect of evidence-based education and evidence-based practice [58, 59]. Physicians continuously need to spend time following up developments and advances within their speciality [60]. Medical curricula should therefore pay the necessary attention to IL and LLL.

Information literacy skills and self-regulated learning are not only required for LLL, they are also key factors for success in an increasingly information-based society [45]. "Gaining skills in information literacy multiplies the opportunities for students' self-directed learning, as they become engaged in using a wide variety of information sources to expand their knowledge, ask informed questions, and sharpen their critical thinking for still further self-directed learning." [2, p. 4]. Coaching students in self-regulated learning can help them to improve SE, motivation and performance. In a problem-based medical learning environment, students are required to be engaged in self-regulated learning [61, 62].

The problem-based learning curriculum, however, does not give any guarantees for the development of required self-assessment skills. Self-efficacy is seen as a part of self-assessment because it focuses on a specific task or domain. Research found that students score themselves and their peers depending on their own capabilities. High-achieving students will be stricter in grading themselves, but are accurate about their peers. Low-achieving students are more generous in scoring their peers and themselves [61]. Medical students on the other hand tend to underestimate themselves [63]. The students, however, need to be aware of their own knowledge and performance in order to become self-directed learners [62]. Boud and Falchikov [63] define self-assessment as an act of judging ourselves and making decisions about the next step. An important principle is that students undertake action after the assessment. Langendyk [61] underlined the importance of investigating the impact of early as well as more frequent opportunities for self-assessment. It is clear, within a medical curriculum, where EBM-based practice is established, that IL, SE, self-assessment and self-regulated learning play a key role.

5 Research Protocol

Given the need for large-scale domain-specific longitudinal studies [64], this paper describes the research protocol for ILSE beliefs of medical students feasible in a large-scale longitudinal research. Results of analysed data are no part of this paper and will be published in different research papers.

The study is conducted at Ghent University (Belgium), at the "Faculty of Medicine and Health Sciences," more specifically, within a six-year medical curriculum (mean n/academic year: 1192). Data collection started in 2011 and ended in 2016 with a surplus of qualitative study. Medical students need to pass an entrance examination to be accepted. This represents an important selection criterion within the general competences of the study population. The selection exam consists of two parts: "knowledge and insight in sciences" and "acquiring and processing information". The faculty pays much attention to IL and LLL and for many years has supported the integration and evaluation (examination) of IL training within the first years of the medical curriculum.

In order to collect quantitative longitudinal data for an entire medical curriculum for consecutive years, it was important to get this faculty support. Cooperation with the curriculum manager was crucial for obtaining as high a response as possible. In the first two years of the research, special time was foreseen in the tight lecture schedule to give students detailed study information and the possibility to complete the questionnaire. Afterwards students could, at a chosen free moment, fill in the survey via a digital learning platform, but before a predetermined deadline date.

Instead of creating a new questionnaire the researchers opted to use the validated "Information Literacy Self-Efficacy Scale" (ILSES) from Kurbanoglu, Akkoyunlu [45] like many other researchers [6, 11, 48, 50, 51, 53, 54], and more specifically the seven-factor scale composed of 28 items. The factors are determined by different skills mandatory for a general context of IL education:

- "Defining the need for information"
- "Initiating the search strategy"
- "Locating and accessing the resources"
- "Assessing and comprehending the information"
- "Interpreting, synthesizing, and using the information"
- "Communicating the information"
- "Evaluating the product and process".

Results on this 28-item scale are considered highly reliable and could thus be recommended for measuring IL beliefs among students. Identifying low ILSE beliefs can help to adjust training, motivate students in their ILSE beliefs and stimulate them to participate actively in the learning process. The 28-item scale has been used for various research projects, most of them in the context of student teachers [45, 50, 51] and in relation to computer literacy [51, 57], but to our knowledge never within a complete medical curriculum. However, to evaluate SE, the specific context in which the questions are asked is considered highly important. Therefore, the original scale was enriched with ten specific medical items to evaluate medically-oriented ILSE among students (Table 1) covering basic and advanced medical IL skills. The questions were chosen on an institutional and commercial independent level, usable in a longitudinal study and generalizable to other institutions. Approval for using and extending the 28-item scale was obtained from Serap Kurbanoglu through oral communication.

Table 1. ILSES-M: 10 specific medical questions added to the original ILSES scale

I feel confident to
Use Pico
Search for EBM information
Use a factual database
Use Mesh
Use PubMed
Retrieve an article of an institutional repository
Evaluate bias
Find cited references
Find citing authors
Reference the sources I use in a reference style used in medicine

Students scored their personal degree of confidence on a scale of 0–100. The assessment of the scale was conducted in English; no translation of the original scale was considered as this might generate errors. Flemish students of medicine are familiar with using and reading English resources, as most of their recommended educational manuals are in English. Students were given no time limit for completing the 38-item ILSE in medicine scale (ILSES-M), and all of the questions had to be answered.

To get a better understanding of the cohort of medical students, basic demographic data were collected: date of birth, gender, their college degree and other questions related to their background. Because of the longitudinal nature of the study, only during the two first academic years of the research were all students asked to fill in the background questions; after that, it was limited to first year students.

After the literature survey and outlining of the protocol of the research, approval of the Ethical Committee of the Ghent University was obtained. Students signed the informed consent form stating that the survey was not obligatory and that the results would not affect students' study results. A trusted third party (TTP) made sure that all data was collected and gave every student a unique study number. The TTP made also sure data could be analysed longitudinally.

As pointed out earlier, faculty support was important. All communication to invite students to participate in the research was sent out in the name of the head of the medical curriculum. All students from first-year Bachelor (Y1) to second-year Master's (Y5) were asked to contribute to the survey in the two first weeks of the academic year. Students of the third-year Master's (Y6) were assessed at the end of their academic year, after their final clinical examination.

Collection of the quantitative data started in the academic year 2011–2012 and was collected every year until the academic year 2015–2016. To evaluate the impact of learning and instruction, a post ILSES-M assessment within Y1 was added to the research in 2012. Students of Y1 have an integrated and evaluated course on IL within the context of EBM. Student need to build up a search strategy and to write a paper. Afterwards, they have to peer review two other papers. At the end of their 30-hour course they were asked to fill in the ILSES-M for a second time. Pre- and post-testing is used to evaluate the impact of active learning on students' SE. In addition, Y1 students were also examined on their IL competences. These results will be used to compare their acquired skills with their own ILSE.

At the end of the longitudinal study (March 2016), qualitative research finalised the study. From every study year, a student representative was asked to attend a focus group to discuss the main results of the study. This qualitative study will be of great value since the quantitative results will be discussed and put into context.

All quantitative data will be analysed statistically using SPSS (v24). Data will be described by the mean (Standard deviation [SD]) or median (Inter Quartile Range [IQR]). Principal Axis Factoring and Varimax rotation with Kaiser Normalization will be used for validation of the scale. Cronbach's alpha will be calculated to look for validity of the subscales. ANOVA-tests will be performed to look for differences between multiple groups. Posthoc analyses with correction (Tamhane) will be performed where appropriate. Paired tests will be used to look for within-subject changes over time.

Further analysis of the results will clarify if the ILSES-M is reliable and valid for evaluating students' ILSE beliefs within a complete medical curriculum or within new first-year medical students. Other research questions will look into the development of the ILSE beliefs of students or cohort of students and analyse whether active learning develops higher ILSE beliefs.

6 Conclusion

To the best of our knowledge, no medical curriculum-based studies are available on ILSE. Furthermore, no former longitudinal research on ILSE has been performed. A literature research resulted in the need to assess ILSE within a specific domain, on a larger scale and certainly over a longer period. Setting up a study of this scale would not have been possible without the organisational support of the faculty and moreover without the faculty's own belief that ILSE plays an important role in the development of the medical curriculum objectives of LLL.

This study makes it possible to look for cross-sectional as well as longitudinal results. The qualitative study at the end of the research will help to clarify some quantitative results. All results could be taken into account for further curriculum change at a faculty level, which emphasises the importance of organisational (curriculum) change based on scientific results.

In conclusion, this research is valuable because of the increasing importance of IL in a medical context. Furthermore, the results of this study could lead to guidelines for more adapted ILSE implementation in a medical curriculum.

Acknowledgements. The authors want to thank Nele S. Pauwels (Knowledge Center for Health Ghent, Ghent University, Ghent, Belgium) for critically revising the manuscript. This research did not receive any specific grant from funding agencies in the public, commercial, or not-for-profit sectors.

References

1. ALA: Presidential Committee on Information Literacy: Final Report 1989. http://www.ala.org/acrl/publications/whitepapers/presidential. Accessed 24 July 2006
2. ACRL: Information Literacy Competency Standards for Higher Education 2000. http://www.ala.org/acrl/standards/informationliteracycompetency. Accessed 1 Sept 2006
3. Bruce, C.S.: Information literacy: a framework for higher education. Aust. Libr. J. **44**(3), 158–170 (1995)
4. Boekhorst, A.K.: Becoming information literate in The Netherlands. Libr. Rev. **52**(7), 298–309 (2003)
5. Virkus, S.: Information literacy in Europe: a literature. Inf. Res. **8**(4), 1–56 (2003)
6. Kilic-Cakmak, E.: Learning strategies and motivational factors predicting information literacy self-efficacy of e-learners. Australas. J. Educ. Technol. **26**(2), 192–208 (2010)
7. Kinsley, K., Galbraith, G.M., Herring, M., Stowers, E., Stewart, T., Kingsley, K.V.: Why not just Google it? An assessment of information literacy skills in a biomedical science curriculum. BMC Med. Educ. **11**, 17 (2011)

8. Eskola, E.-L.: Information literacy in medical education: relationships with conceptions of learning and learning methods. Adv. Libr. Adm. Organ. **25**, 203–238 (2007)
9. Dale, S., Campbell, S.: Determining the information literacy needs of a medical and dental faculty. J. Can. Health. Libr. Assoc. **33**(2), 48–59 (2012)
10. Bazrafkan, L., Hayat, A.A., Abbasi, K., Bazrafkan, A., Rohalamini, A., Fardid, M.: Evaluation of information literacy status among medical students at Shiraz University of Medical Sciences. J. Adv. Med. Educ. Prof. **5**(1), 42 (2017)
11. Robertson, D.S., Felicilda-Reynaldo, R.F.: Evaluation of graduate nursing students' information literacy self-efficacy and applied skills. J. Nurs. Educ. **54**(3 Suppl.), S26–S30 (2015)
12. McClurg, C., Powelson, S., Lang, E., Aghajafari, F., Edworthy, S.: Evaluating effectiveness of small group information literacy instruction for undergraduate medical education students using a pre- and post-survey study design. Health Inf. Libr. J. **32**(2), 120–130 (2015)
13. Cullen, R., Clark, M., Esson, R.: Evidence-based information-seeking skills of junior doctors entering the workforce: an evaluation of the impact of information literacy training during pre-clinical years. Health Inf. Libr. J. **28**(2), 119–129 (2011)
14. Carr, S., Iredell, H., Newton-Smith, C., Clark, C.: Evaluation of information literacy skill development in first year medical students. Aust. Acad. Res. Libr. **42**(2), 136–148 (2011)
15. Baro, E.E., Endouware, B.E.C., Ubogu, J.O.: Information literacy among medical students in the College of Health Sciences in Niger Delta University, Nigeria. Prog.-Electr. Libr. **45**(1), 107–120 (2011)
16. Clark, C., Catts, R.: Information skills survey: its application to a medical course. Evid. Based Libr. Inf. Pract. **2**(3), 3–26 (2007)
17. Eskola, E.-L.: Information literacy of medical students studying in the problem-based and traditional curriculum. Inf. Res. **10**(2) (2005). http://InformationR.net/ir/10-2/paper221.html. Accessed 11 Dec 2015
18. Clark, C.: Exploring evidence-based information literacy. In: 3rd International Evidence-Based Librarianship: Evolution of Evidence: Global Perspectives on Linking Research with Practice, Brisbane, Queensland, Australia (2005). https://www.researchgate.net/publication/228414806
19. Thompson, N., Lewis, S., Brennan, P., Robinson, J.: Information literacy skills: medical radiation science students and the internet. Eur. J. Radiol. **1**(2), 43–47 (2009)
20. Baker, S.S., Boruff-Jones, P.D.: Information literacy. Radiol. Technol. **80**(4), 374–376 (2009)
21. Shanahan, M.C.: Information literacy skills of undergraduate medical radiation students. Radiography **13**, 187–196 (2007)
22. Kipnis, D.G., Frisby, A.J.: Information literacy and library attitudes of occupational therapy students. Med. Ref. Serv. Q. **25**(4), 11–20 (2006)
23. Durando, P., Oakley, P.: Developing information literacy skills in nursing and rehabilitation therapy students. J. Can. Health. Libr. Assoc. **26**(1), 7–11 (2005)
24. Weinert, D.J., Palmer, E.M.: Influence of an information literacy course on students' information search behavior. J. Allied Health **36**(1), e1–e12 (2007)
25. Kingsley, K.V., Kingsley, K.: A case study for teaching information literacy skills. BMC Med. Educ. **9**(7), 7 (2009)
26. Ford, P.J., Foxlee, N., Green, W.: Developing information literacy with first year oral health students. Eur. J. Dent. Educ. **13**, 46–51 (2009)
27. Brettle, A., Raynor, M.: Developing information literacy skills in pre-registration nurses: an experimental study of teaching methods. Nurse Educ. Today **33**(2), 103–109 (2013)
28. Stokes, P., Urquhart, C.: Profiling information behaviour of nursing students: part 1: quantitative findings. J. Doc. **67**(6), 908–932 (2011)

29. Andrew, S.: Self-efficacy as a predictor of academic performance in science. J. Adv. Nurs. **27**(3), 596–603 (1998)
30. De Sutter, D.: Librarian teachers on the move: are video tutorials an effective alternative tool for library information literacy instruction? A case study. In: EAHIL 25th Anniversary Conference, vol. 8, issue no. 3, pp. 3–5. European Association for Health Information and Libraries (EAHIL) (2012)
31. Candy, P.C., Crebert, G., O'leary, J.: Developing Lifelong Learners Through Undergraduate Education. AGPS, Canberra (1994)
32. Kurbanoglu, S.S.: Self-efficacy: a concept closely linked to information literacy and lifelong learning. J. Doc. **59**(6), 635–646 (2003)
33. Bandura, A.: Social Foundations of Thought and Action. Prentice Hall, Englewoods Cliffs (1986)
34. Bandura, A.: Self-efficacy: toward a unifying theory of behavioral change. Psychol. Rev. **84**(2), 191 (1977)
35. Pajares, F.: Self-efficacy beliefs in academic settings. Rev. Educ. Res. **66**(4), 543–578 (1996)
36. Lent, R.W., Brown, S.D., Larkin, K.C.: Relation of self-efficacy expectations to academic-achievement and persistence. J. Couns. Psychol. **31**(3), 356–362 (1984)
37. Burgoon, J.M., Meece, J.L., Granger, N.A.: Self-efficacy's influence on student academic achievement in the medical anatomy curriculum. Anat. Sci. Educ. **5**(5), 249–255 (2012)
38. Ross, M., Perkins, H., Bodey, K.: Academic motivation and information literacy self-efficacy: the importance of a simple desire to know. Libr. Inf. Sci. Res. **38**(1), 2–9 (2016)
39. Bong, M., Skaalvik, E.M.: Academic self-concept and self-efficacy: how different are they really? Educ. Psychol. Rev. **15**(1), 1–40 (2003)
40. Cassidy, S., Eachus, P.: The computer self-efficacy website 2003. http://www.psychint.net/selfefficacy/
41. Marsh, H.W., Walker, R., Debus, R.: Subject-specific components of academic self-concept and self-efficacy. Contemp. Educ. Psychol. **16**(4), 331–345 (1991)
42. Pajares, F.: Current directions in self-efficacy research. Adv. Motiv. Achiev. **10**(149), 1–49 (1997)
43. Lin, T.-J., Tan, A.L., Tsai, C.-C.: A cross-cultural comparison of Singaporean and Taiwanese eighth graders' science learning self-efficacy from a multi-dimensional perspective. Int. J. Sci. Educ. **35**(7), 1083–1109 (2013)
44. Carson, C.H.: The development of a scale to measure the self-efficacy of School Library Media Specialists. Sch. Libr. Media Q. **21**(3), 165–170 (1993)
45. Kurbanoglu, S.S., Akkoyunlu, B., Umay, A.: Developing the information literacy self-efficacy scale. J. Doc. **62**(6), 730–743 (2006)
46. Kurbanoglu, S.S.: Self-efficacy: an alternative approach to the evaluation of information literacy. In: Katsirikou, A., Skiadas, C.H. (eds.) Qualitative and Quantitative Methods in Libraries: Theory and Applications. Proceedings of the International Conference on QQML2009, Chania, Crete, Greece, 26–29 May 2009. World Scientific (2010)
47. Pinto, M., Sales, D.: Insights into translation students' information literacy using the IL-HUMASS survey. J. Inf. Sci. **36**(5), 618–630 (2010)
48. Bayral, H., Comek, A.: Examining the relations between science attitudes, logical thinking ability, information literacy and academic achievement through internet assisted chemistry education. Procedia Soc. Behav. Sci. **1**, 1526–1532 (2009)
49. Walsh, A.: Information literacy assessment: where do we start? J. Libr. Inf. Sci. **41**(1), 19–28 (2009)

50. Batarelo Kokić, I., Novosel, V.: The ball is in your court: information literacy self-efficacy and information literacy competence relation. In: Kurbanoğlu, S., Špiranec, S., Grassian, E., Mizrachi, D., Catts, R. (eds.) ECIL 2014. CCIS, vol. 492, pp. 512–520. Springer, Cham (2014). https://doi.org/10.1007/978-3-319-14136-7_54
51. Usluel, Y.K.: Can ICT usage make a difference on student teachers' information literacy self-efficacy. Libr. Inf. Sci. Res. **29**(1), 92–102 (2007)
52. Keshavarz, H., Givi, E., Reza, M., Vafaeian, A., Khademian, M.: Information literacy self-efficacy dimensions of post graduate students: validating a persian version scale. Libri **67**(1), 75–86 (2017)
53. Özbıçakçı, Ş., Gezer, N., Bilik, Ö.: Comparison of effects of training programs for final year nursing students in Turkey: differences in self-efficacy with regard to information literacy. Nurse Educ. Today **35**(2), e73–e77 (2015)
54. De Meulemeester, A., De Sutter, D., Verhaaren, H.: Self-efficacy tests are helpful in the acquisition of information literacy. A case study in first year bachelor students 2012. http://sites-final.uclouvain.be/EAHIL2012/conference/?q=node/564
55. De Meulemeester, A.: The "information literacy self-efficacy scale" and the medical curriculum at Ghent University. In: Kurbanoğlu, S., Grassian, E., Mizrachi, D., Catts, R., Špiranec, S. (eds.) ECIL 2013. CCIS, vol. 397, pp. 465–470. Springer, Cham (2013). https://doi.org/10.1007/978-3-319-03919-0_62
56. De Meulemeester, A., Buysse, H.: Progress testing of information literacy versus information literacy self-efficacy in medical students. In: Kurbanoğlu, S., Špiranec, S., Grassian, E., Mizrachi, D., Catts, R. (eds.) ECIL 2014. CCIS, vol. 492, pp. 361–369. Springer, Cham (2014). https://doi.org/10.1007/978-3-319-14136-7_38
57. Erdem, M.: Self-efficacy levels of teachers in information and computer literacy. World Appl. Sci. J. **2**(4), 399–405 (2007)
58. Tepe, R., Tepe, C.: Development and psychometric evaluation of an information literacy self-efficacy survey and an information literacy knowledge test. J. Chipropr. Educ. **29**(1), 11–15 (2015)
59. Mi, M., Riley-Doucet, C.: Health professions students' lifelong learning orientation: associations with information skills and self-efficacy. Evid. Based Libr. Inf. Pract. **11**(2), 121–135 (2016)
60. Afonso, P., Ramos, M.R., Saraiva, S., Moreira, C.A., Figueira, M.L.: Assessing the relation between career satisfaction in psychiatry with lifelong learning and scientific activity. Psychiatry Res. **217**(3), 210–214 (2014)
61. Langendyk, V.: Not knowing that they do not know: self-assessment accuracy of third-year medical students. Med. Educ. **40**(2), 173–179 (2006)
62. Carr, S.E., Johnson, P.H.: Does self reflection and insight correlate with academic performance in medical students? BMC Med. Educ. **13**(1), 113 (2013)
63. Boud, D., Falchikov, N.: What does research tell us about self assessment. In: Enhancing Learning through Self Assessment, pp. 155–166. Kogan Page, London (1995)
64. Schunk, D.H.: Self-efficacy and academic motivation. Educ. Psychol. **26**(3–4), 207–231 (1991)

Evidence of the Effectiveness of a Digital Tool to Promote Health Service Literacy Among Young University Students

Ilaria Montagni(✉) and Christophe Tzourio

University of Bordeaux, Inserm, Bordeaux Population Health Research Center, Team HEALTHY, UMR 1219, F-33000 Bordeaux, France
{ilaria.montagni, christophe.tzourio}@u-bordeaux.fr

Abstract. University students face for their first time the necessity to find and access health services on their own. Information on health services is easily available online, but young people have difficulties with evaluating its trustworthiness and navigating multiple choices. We produced a digital information tool in the form of an interactive map displaying 88 preselected youth-friendly health services in the Bordeaux area (France). The tool was tested by 319 students who answered a first questionnaire on their knowledge of local youth-friendly health services. Among them, 73 students answered an additional satisfaction questionnaire: 85% declared having obtained clear information through this tool, and 100% felt reassured by the fact that information was advised by experts. Findings suggest that trustworthy institutional digital information tools can contribute to increase students' health service literacy, thus enhancing their access to care.

Keywords: Health information seeking · Health service literacy
Digital information tool

1 Introduction

Most of university students are away from home in a new town and face the challenges of the transition from family dependence to adult autonomy [1]. Despite a well-accepted view that university students are generally in good health [2], routine medical check-ups are recommended at this age (18–24 years), and single health problems, from mild to severe, may raise the need among this specific population to access health care. In an unfamiliar place, finding a health service such as a doctor, a dentist or a gynecologist can be difficult for young people who are breaking from parental guidance. Indeed, burgeoning evidence demonstrates that lack of knowledge about where to get treatment is among the main barriers to receiving appropriate and timely health care [3–5].

In an era of easy access to information provided by new developments in web infrastructures and information and communication technologies [6], this lack of knowledge in a highly connected generation is remarkable. Students have grown comfortable using the Internet to access information even on complex and sensitive

S. Kurbanoğlu et al. (Eds.): ECIL 2017, CCIS 810, pp. 430–439, 2018.
https://doi.org/10.1007/978-3-319-74334-9_45

issues such as health care [7]. However, they seem to feel lost in the online information overload [8], and ask to be guided in the identification of reliable information concerning health services [9]. Results of a survey by the Council of Europe on the information needs of young people show that new generations know how to functionally locate and acquire information from the web [10]. However, they do not have the necessary instruments and abilities to interpret and evaluate such information [11], especially concerning health topics. The next step should be to help students to obtain, use and develop these instruments and abilities in order to become "health literate" as soon as possible. Following the definition provided by Sørensen and colleagues [12], a "health literate" person has the capacity to seek and understand "health information" in order to make appropriate health decisions, including receiving health care. The term "health information" is vague and covers a wide range of information and opinions about health and illnesses, both at the individual and societal levels, including information in relation to a health service [13]. Adapting the definition by Sørensen and colleagues [12], in this paper we use the concept of "health service literacy" described as the capacity to seek and understand information specifically about health services (for instance opening time, staff, service offer, and costs) in order to access them. A "health service literate" person is then expected to be able to obtain, evaluate and finally use information on health services. In other words, "health service literacy" is not the sole knowledge of available health services, but also implies the concrete application of such knowledge to access care.

Previous research showed that young people struggle to navigate autonomously the health care system, and need support with evaluating the reliability of consulted sources [14–16]. As a result, low levels of health service literacy in this population can hamper access to health care contributing to increase morbidity and mortality in young and late adulthood [17].

2 Background to Research

In most of university campuses around the world, students can freely access health services exclusively addressed to them. These health services are on-campus wellness clinics and health promotion centers, whose offer can vary from one country to another. In France, the Ministry of Higher Education and Research established in the year 2007 the creation of campus services of preventive medicine and health promotion called SUMPSS (*Services Universitaires de Médecine Préventive et de Promotion de la Santé*). Each French university is obliged to create a SUMPSS where students can obtain treatment and care for free or with a substantial reimbursement by the French students' health insurance. With a limited staff compared to the large number of students registered at the university, these structures are not able to meet the demand of students who are compelled to seek for health care elsewhere. SUMPSS are additional to all other local health services students can access as any insured French citizen.

Concerning the awareness of both local and campus health services, results from a survey carried out in the USA show that university students do not know where to seek for health care and are not familiar with campus health services [18]. In Australia, data from a similar survey reveal the same alarming findings: students have poor knowledge of available health services and consequently avoid access to health care [19]. In Europe, health service literacy has been less explored. An ongoing cohort study called *i-Share* (internet-based Students Health Research Enterprise) is collecting data on the health status and habits of 30,000 university students across France [20]. Preliminary analyses were conducted in the fourth year of the cohort study (April 2017), on a total of 12,554 students, 9,421 of whom were females (75%). Results showed that 4,622 students (37% of the total sample) declared having refused to consult any general practitioner or specialist in the last 12 months. For 287 of them (6%), the reason was that they did not know where to find a general practitioner or specialist. Similarly, 1,959 students (16%) reported having refused to consult a dentist; for 239 of them (12%), the reason was the same: they did not know where to find a dentist. Finally, among all 9,421 female students, 4,737 (50%) declared not having consulted a gynecologist in the last 12 months. For 973 of them (21%), once again the reason was that they did not know where to find a gynecologist. Drawing on these findings from the *i-Share* survey, we were inspired to look further in the issue of health service literacy in university students.

Health care educators and professionals, as well as parents and professors, face several challenges in ensuring that university students are health service literate. One of the first challenges is to deliver information on health services which is appealing, readable and understandable to a young public. A second challenge is the mean to deliver such information. Today, the Internet and new technologies are the first source of information for young people [7], and digital tools lend themselves to providing, sharing and viewing information in an attractive manner. Digital tools represent then a good way to deliver health information to young adults. However, few are the studies on the effectiveness of these new tools. Finally, a though challenge is increasing students' interest to become health service literate. Face to their academic workload, their worries in their transition to adulthood, and the feeling that information on health services does not concern them because of their young age and good health, students do not express often the need to be informed on their own health or on health issues in general [21].

In an attempt to meet these three challenges, we conducted research with students from the University of Bordeaux, France, by producing an *ad hoc* digital information tool in the form of an interactive map displaying youth-friendly health services in the Bordeaux area.

3 Objective and Research Questions

The primary objective of this research was to examine whether an *ad hoc* digital information tool providing trustworthy information on health services can be effective in increasing students' health service literacy. The following questions were explored:

1. Can an *ad hoc* digital information tool increase students' knowledge of available health services?
2. Are *ad hoc* digital information tools a valid alternative to unguided Internet search of information on health services?

3. Can networks of support like university staff and health care professionals play a pivotal role in helping students in their uptake of online health information seeking?
4. Are the design and usability of *ad hoc* digital information tools determinant in facilitating the acquisition of information on health services?

4 Overview of Methodology

4.1 The servi-Share Study

The present study, called *servi-Share* (services in the *i-Share* project) is nested in the above-mentioned French *i-Share* cohort study [19], whose principal investigators are based at the University of Bordeaux. Four researchers and three public health graduate students from the *i-Share* study, plus seven health care professionals and three industry web-developers constituted the *servi-Share* team for the conception and production of a digital information tool. The tool was an interactive mobile-friendly map displaying 88 preselected youth-friendly health services with detailed information on opening time, staff, service offer, and costs (Fig. 1). We defined as youth-friendly services low-cost or free health care outpatient services addressed, either exclusively or among other population groups, to young people aged 18–24 years. All health domains were taken into consideration, from general health to sexual health, gynecology, and dentistry. The rationale and development of this digital information tool are described elsewhere [20].

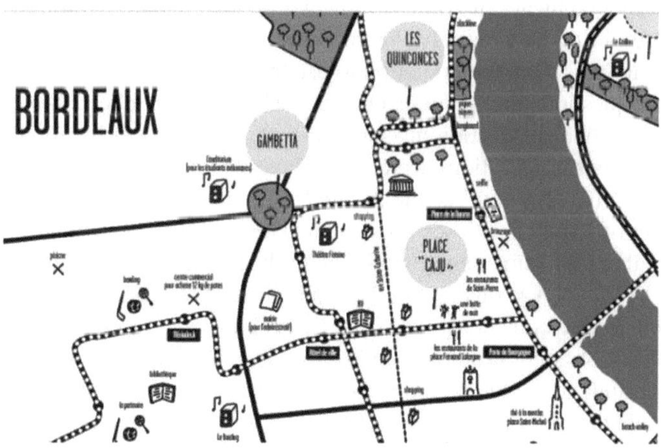

Fig. 1. Screenshot of the *servi-Share* digital information tool (Source: deux degrés)

The *servi-Share* digital information tool was tested and evaluated between September and December 2016 in a sub-sample of students belonging to the *i-Share* cohort study. We chose to contact by e-mail a convenience sub-sample of 1,300 students meeting the following criteria: being a student in one of the universities or post-secondary schools of the Bordeaux area, being aged 18–30 years, and having completed the *i-Share* baseline questionnaire. These 1,300 students were invited in September 2016 by e-mail to click on a link directing them to the *servi-Share* digital information tool. Students were informed that the tool was developed in the larger *i-Share* study, and reassured about the authority behind the information provided. For ethical reasons, participants' usage of the tool could not be registered and health care services that were searched could not be tracked.

The *servi-Share* study was conducted within the regulatory framework of the *i-Share* project by the Commission Nationale de l'Informatique et des Libertés (CNIL; National Commission of Informatics and Liberties; DR-2013-019).

4.2 Questionnaire, Measures and Data Analysis

Prior to the use of the *servi-Share* digital information tool, the sub-sample of 1,300 students was asked to answer an online 7-item questionnaire on knowledge of youth-friendly health services. Questions were embedded in the tool and concerned: (1) place of living (among 119 Bordeaux neighborhoods, 26 municipalities); (2) university location (among 11 different sites of higher education in Bordeaux); (3) how long the participant had been living in the Bordeaux area (from 1 to 24 years); (4) favorite mean of transport (bike, car, public transports, by walk); (5) which types of youth-friendly health services the participant was seeking information for (general health, infections, sexual health, nutrition, mental health, alcohol/tobacco/drugs, health administrative issues, dentist, other specialist, vaccine, radiography and complementary exams, emergencies); (6) the best criterion to choose a youth-friendly health service (low cost, geographical proximity, trustworthiness, short waiting time); and (7) knowledge of youth-friendly health services in Bordeaux.

After two months from the invitation to use the *servi-Share* digital information tool and answer its questionnaire, participants were asked in November 2016 to complete a supplementary online satisfaction questionnaire. A link was sent by e-mail to access a 10-item Google Form. Questions were: (1) "Have you encountered any difficulties in using this tool?"; (2) "Do you like the design?"; (3) "Have you discovered through this tool some youth-friendly health services you had never heard about before?"; (4) "Have you found in this tool some new youth-friendly health services you will access in the future?"; (5) "Will you use this tool in the future instead of other geolocalization search engines if you need to contact a youth-friendly health service?"; (6) "Where would you like to see this tool being promoted and diffused?"; (7) "Through which channels do you think that students should be informed of the existence of this tool?"; (8) "Will you recommend this tool to your friends?"; (9) "What would you like to add to this tool?"; and (10) "How would you rate this tool?". The two questionnaires allowed for comparison of respondents' knowledge of youth-friendly health services in the Bordeaux area before and after the use of the digital tool. The items were created *ad hoc* in order to explore this new research field given that no validated scales to measure health service literacy exist yet.

Additional data on gender, age, field of study (Health Studies, Medicine, Literature and Social Sciences, Scientific Disciplines, Law and Economy, Other, and missing value), health status (very good, good, average, poor, very poor) and services utilization (at least one consultation in the last 12 months with a general practitioner, a dentist, an ophthalmologist, a gynecologist, or another specialist among dermatologist, neurologist, urologist, gastroenterologist, otorhinolaryngologist, psychologist/psychiatrist) were retrieved from the *i-Share* database.

We performed descriptive statistical analyses on data from three databases (*i-Share study* baseline questionnaire, first *servi-Share* questionnaire and second *servi-Share* satisfaction questionnaire) using SAS (V.9.3; SAS Institute Inc., Cary, North Carolina, USA).

5 Results and Discussion

According to the general response rate of *i-Share* participants to other ongoing sub-studies (approximately 20%), we expected at least 300 students to use the *servi-Share* digital information tool and answer the first 7-item questionnaire. Of the 1,300 invited students, a final sample of 319 students (24% response rate) tested the *servi-Share* digital information tool (N = 253 female students, 79%). The invitation to answer the second *servi-Share* satisfaction questionnaire was then sent to all 319 student testers. In total, 73 of 319 students (23% response rate) completed this second questionnaire (N = 58 female students, 79%). Table 1 illustrates the socio-demographic characteristics of the respondents to the first and the second *servi-Share* questionnaires. When comparing these characteristics between the two samples, no differences were found.

We analyzed data in order to provide insight into the four posed research questions.

Concerning the first research question ("Can an *ad hoc* digital information tool increase students' knowledge of available health services?"), results from the first *servi-Share* questionnaire revealed that 187 students (60%) had no knowledge of youth-friendly health services in Bordeaux before using the tool. The majority of them reported avoidance and delay of health care partially due to lack of information on local youth-friendly health services (N = 187, 59%, 4 missing values). Students were mostly interested in obtaining information on the three following types of youth-friendly health services: general practitioner (N = 258, 81%), gynecologist (N = 194, 77% among female students), and dentist (N = 191, 60%). Results from the satisfaction questionnaire indicated that the *servi-Share* digital information tool provided its users with clear information on either new services or services they partially knew (N = 62, 85%). Furthermore, almost the same number of students declared that they would access some displayed youth-friendly health services in the future (N = 61, 84%), suggesting that they were keen to apply received information in order to access health care. When specifically looking at data from students having answered the *servi-Share* satisfaction questionnaire (N = 73), we were able to compare the knowledge of youth-friendly health services before and after the use of the *servi-Share* digital information tool. Before the use of our tool, less than half of the sample (N = 33, 46%, 2 missing values) had declared knowing at least one youth-friendly health service. After the use of our tool, more than two thirds of students (N = 60, 85%, no missing values) declared having acquired new knowledge on youth-friendly health services. Regardless of the knowledge of any youth-friendly health service before the use of the *servi-Share* digital information tool, the proportion of students declaring having obtained new information on youth-friendly health services thanks to our tool was high (84%).

Table 1. The socio-demographic characteristics of the respondents to the first *servi-Share* questionnaire (N = 319) and its satisfaction questionnaire (N = 73).

Socio-demographic variables	First questionnaire *servi-Share*	Satisfaction questionnaire *servi-Share*
Age*	21.7 (2.2)	21.3 (1.7)
Gender		
Female	253 (79.3%)	58 (79.5%)
Male	66 (20.7%)	15 (20.5%)
Field of study		
Health studies	89 (27.9%)	26 (35.6%)
Medicine	56 (17.6%)	11 (15.1%)
Literature and social sciences	86 (27.0%)	18 (24.7%)
Scientific disciplines	28 (8.8%)	5 (6.8%)
Law and economy	29 (9.1%)	6 (8.2%)
Other	21 (6.6%)	4 (5.5%)
Missing	10 (3.1%)	3 (4.1%)
Health status		
Very good	72 (22.6%)	18 (24.7%)
Good	186 (58.3%)	45 (61.6%)
Average	56 (17.6%)	9 (12.3%)
Poor	5 (1.6%)	1 (1.4%)
Very poor	–	–
Consultations with a health professional		
General practitioner	278 (87.1%)	62 (84.9%)
Dentist	136 (42.6%)	34 (46.6%)
Ophthalmologist	120 (37.6%)	29 (39.7%)
Gynecologist	133 (41.7%)	28 (48.3%)
At least 1 other specialist	200 (62.7%)	47 (64.4%)
Total	319 (100.0%)	73 (100.0%)

* Mean age (standard deviation)

Concerning the second research question ("Are *ad hoc* digital information tools a valid alternative to unguided Internet search of information on health services?"), results from the satisfaction questionnaire indicated that the majority of students (N = 50, 68%) would use the *servi-Share* digital information tool instead of other existing search engines. Students considered then this tool as a valid alternative to unguided Internet search of health information.

Concerning the third research question ("Can networks of support like university staff and health care professionals play a pivotal role in helping students in their uptake of online health information seeking?"), almost all students answering the satisfaction questionnaire (N = 70, 96%) reported that promoting the *servi-Share* digital information tool through the official website and social network pages of their university was important to increase its credibility. Students felt reassured by the fact that the information on displayed health services was selected by a pool of public health researchers and health care professionals. This suggests that networks of support like health care experts can help students in navigating online health information.

Finally, concerning the fourth research question ("Are the design and usability of *ad hoc* digital information tools determinant in facilitating the acquisition of information on health services?"), the majority of students from the satisfaction questionnaire did not find any difficulties in using the *servi-Share* digital information tool (N = 67, 92%), and liked its design (N = 55, 75%). Usability and design of *ad hoc* digital information tools may then be determinant in facilitating the acquisition of information on health services. Students appreciated that information was concise and clear, and that plain language was used instead of medical jargon.

6 Limitations and Future Studies

First, the main limitations of this study include the fact that the survey was based on self-evaluation and that only one fifth of the respondents to the first questionnaire completed the second satisfaction questionnaire. As already experienced in other studies within the larger *i-Share* cohort, retaining young university students is an especially difficult task. Young people are involved in a variety of competing activities and bombarded with various marketing messages and appeals for information from a variety of sources. Lack of time and heavy workload are the main reasons why they often refuse to respond to surveys [22]. To achieve success in future longitudinal studies, personalized communications, multimodal contact strategies, thoughtful use of communication technologies, and adherence to customer service principles would be critical [23]. Second, the question of how to assess the effectiveness of digital tools concerning health information is now engendering significant debate in the scientific information, communication and public health community [24]. Future studies are needed to take action in providing evidence of effective methods for monitoring and evaluation of digital tools for health-related information. Third, the small sample of our study and the *servi-Share* tool concerned only university students from the Bordeaux area. However, while generalizability of our findings is limited, the use of short and simple digital information tools to increase health service literacy in students worldwide is recommended and should be consistently studied in future research.

The *servi-Share* tool will be available to all students registered to the *i-Share* website, as it will be displayed on their personal account page in early 2018. For future versions of this tool concerning the Bordeaux area, and for any possible similar tool, the use of a design thinking approach is recommended.

7 Concluding Remarks

In order to increase health service literacy in students, strategies can be adopted to make information appealing, useful and readable to them. Today, new technologies and the Internet are the best means to deliver information on health services to this highly-connected population. However, students feel the need to be reassured on the quality of information found and instructed to evaluate it. Digital information tools can be a valid support to guide young people's online health information-seeking, especially if they are conceived and constructed by experts [25]. The data collected in this study suggest that students' health service literacy is low, but digital information tools have the potential to improve it, provided that the information is trustworthy.

We contributed then to the design of digital information tools with a practical view on how to make it easier for young people to find information about health services in their living area. This specific study on French students provided insights for digital information tools on health services information to be adapted, produced and disseminated in other countries.

Building capacity of any students worldwide to seek information on health services can contribute to their health service literacy, thus promoting their access to care [26] by reducing the risk of making health decisions on the basis of non-credible information [9].

Acknowledgements. The authors would like to thank Tanguy Cariou (University of Bordeaux, Inserm, Bordeaux Population Health Research Center, France) for his contribution to this paper (descriptive analyses). The authors also thank the *servi-Share* and *i-Share* teams for their operational support.

References

1. Kantanis, S.T.: Factors that affect student transition from year 12 to the first year of university: a case study of arts undergraduates at Monash University. In: Conference paper Australian Association for Research in Education, Brisbane (1997)
2. Meier, S., Stock, C., Krämer, A.: The contribution of health discussion groups with students to campus health promotion. Health Promot. Int. **22**(1), 28–36 (2007)
3. Booth, M.L., Bernard, D., Quine, S., Kang, M.S., Usherwood, T., Alperstein, G., Bennett, D. L.: Access to health care among Australian adolescents young people's perspectives and their sociodemographic distribution. J. Adolesc. Health **34**(1), 97–103 (2004)
4. Klein, J.D., McNulty, M., Flatau, C.N.: Adolescents' access to careteenagers' self-reported use of services and perceived access to confidential care. Arch. Pediatr. Adolesc. Med. **152** (7), 676–682 (1998)
5. Tylee, A., Haller, D.M., Graham, T., Churchill, R., Sanci, L.A.: Youth-friendly primary-care services: how are we doing and what more needs to be done? Lancet **369**(9572), 1565–1573 (2007)
6. Garoufallou, E., Chatzopoulou, C., Tzura, E., Maranga, S., Siatri, R., Zafeiriou, G., Antonopoulou, S.: How university students in health care look for information: use and initial appraisal of information resources. In: Kurbanoğlu, S., Boustany, J., Špiranec, S., Grassian, E., Mizrachi, D., Roy, L., Çakmak, T. (eds.) ECIL 2016. CCIS, vol. 676, pp. 412–421. Springer, Cham (2016). https://doi.org/10.1007/978-3-319-52162-6_41
7. Amante, D.J., Hogan, T.P., Pagoto, S.L., English, T.M., Lapane, K.L.: Access to care and use of the internet to search for health information: results from the US national health interview survey. JMIR **17**(4), e106 (2015)
8. Cline, R.J., Haynes, K.M.: Consumer health information seeking on the internet: the state of the art. Health Educ. Res. **16**(6), 671–692 (2001)

9. Ivanitskaya, L., O'Boyle, I., Casey, A.M.: Health information literacy and competencies of information age students: results from the interactive online research readiness self-assessment (RRSA). JMIR **8**(2), e6 (2006)
10. Selwyn, N.: Young people and their information needs in the context of the information society. Technical report from the Directorate of Youth and Sport of the Council of Europe/European Agency for Youth Information and Counseling, Colloquy on youth information, Budapest (2007)
11. Libutti, L.: Young people and information literacy. In: Valente, A. (ed.) Science: Perception and Participation, pp. 69–74. Biblink, Rome (2009)
12. Sørensen, K., Van den Broucke, S., Fullam, J., Doyle, G., Pelikan, J., Slonska, Z., Brand, H.: Health literacy and public health: a systematic review and integration of definitions and models. BMC Public Health **12**(1), 80 (2012)
13. Australian Government: The Privacy Act and Health Information (2008). http://www.alrc.gov.au/publications/62.%20The%20Privacy%20Act%20and%20Health%20Information/definition-%E2%80%98health-information%E2%80%99. Accessed July 2017
14. Paasche-Orlow, M.K., Wolf, M.S.: The causal pathways linking health literacy to health outcomes. Am. J. Health Behav. **31**(1), 19–26 (2007)
15. Niemelä, R., Ek, S., Eriksson-Backa, K., Huotari, M.L.: A screening tool for assessing everyday health information literacy. Int. J. Lib. Inf. Sci. **62**(2), 125–134 (2012)
16. Enwald, H., Hirvonen, N., Huotari, M.L., Korpelainen, R., Pyky, R., Savolainen, M., Salonurmi, T., Keränen, A.M., Jokelainen, T., Niemelä, R.: Everyday health information literacy among young men compared with adults with high risk for metabolic syndrome – a cross-sectional population-based study. J. Inf. Sci. **42**(3), 344–355 (2016)
17. Ickes, M.J., Cottrell, R.: Health literacy in college students. J. Am. Coll. Health **58**(5), 491–498 (2010)
18. Perrault, E.: Students' lack of knowledge regarding healthcare providers' duties, and their preferences for information when selecting new providers. Eur. J. Pers. Cent. Healthc. **3**(1), 113–121 (2015)
19. Schweitzer, R.D.: Problems and awareness of support services among students at an urban Australian university. J. Am. Coll. Health **45**(2), 73–77 (1996)
20. Official website of the i-Share study. http://www.i-share.fr
21. W.H.O.: The Global Strategy for Women's, Children's and Adolescents Health 2016–2030. Every Woman Every Child, New York (2015)
22. Montagni, I., Langlois, E., Wittwer, J., Tzourio, C.: Co-creating and evaluating a web-app mapping real-world health care services for students: the servi-share protocol. JMIR Res. Protoc. **6**(2), e24 (2017)
23. Vincent, K.B., Kasperski, S.J., Caldeira, K.M., Garnier-Dykstra, L.M., Pinchevsky, G.M., O'Grady, K.E., Arria, A.M.: Maintaining superior follow-up rates in a longitudinal study: experiences from the college life study. Int. J. Mult. Res. Approaches **6**(1), 4406 (2012)
24. Baker, D.W.: The meaning and the measure of health literacy. J Gen. Int. Med. **21**(8), 878–883 (2006)
25. W.H.O.: eHealth Tools and Services: Needs of Member States, Geneva (2005)
26. Harper, R.: Development of a health literacy assessment for young adult college students: a pilot study. J. Am. Coll. Health **62**(2), 125–134 (2014)

Demographic Characteristics and Personality Variables as Predictors of Health Information Literacy in Young Adults

Veronika Kuhberg-Lasson(✉) and Anne-Kathrin Mayer

ZPID - Leibniz Institute for Psychology Information, Trier, Germany
{kuhberg,mayer}@zpid.de

Abstract. A quantitative study linking individual differences in health information literacy to personality traits and demographic variables is presented. Vocational students from health-related, commercial, and technical professions ($N = 317$) completed the 30-item version of the NEO Five-Factor Inventory (NEO-FFI-30), a questionnaire measuring the five personality dimensions of neuroticism, extraversion, openness, agreeableness, and conscientiousness, as well as the Health Information Literacy Knowledge Test (HILK). Additionally, each participant indicated his or her gender, age, level of education, and occupation. A multiple regression analysis identified extraversion and education as significant predictors of health information literacy. In addition, a mediating effect of education in the relation between openness and health information literacy was revealed. No significant effects were found for gender, age, and occupation. Possible explanations of the findings as well as implications for promoting health information literacy in young adults are discussed.

Keywords: Health information literacy · Interindividual differences
Personality traits · Demographic factors · Vocational students

1 Introduction

The ability to obtain accurate and intelligible health information is becoming more and more important as the amount of available information and the personal responsibility for health concerns steadily increases. A number of studies has linked health information skills and behavior to positive health behavior as well as informed health decisions and treatment compliance [1–3]. The necessary skills not only include basic information-seeking and processing skills, but also the ability to conduct advanced information searches, to evaluate the quality and trustworthiness of sources, and to understand the potentials and drawbacks of different media [4]. These skills can be summed up in the concept of health information literacy, defined as "the set of abilities needed to: recognize a health information need; identify likely information sources and use them to retrieve relevant information; assess the quality of the information and its applicability to a specific situation; and analyze, understand, and use the information to make good health decisions" [5].

The concept of health literacy information combines the concepts of information literacy and health literacy. Whereas information literacy refers to general abilities to

S. Kurbanoğlu et al. (Eds.): ECIL 2017, CCIS 810, pp. 440–449, 2018.
https://doi.org/10.1007/978-3-319-74334-9_46

"recognize when information is needed and have the ability to locate, evaluate, and use effectively the needed information" [6], health literacy comprises knowledge, motivation and competence to deal with health information in order to make judgments and take health-related decisions in everyday life [7, p. 3], thus including health information literacy and extending to behavior resulting from information acquisition. A third related concept is health information seeking, which is mainly used in the field of information sciences and focuses on information needs, searching behavior (extent of the search and methods used), and evaluation of information, which are all important components of health information literacy. Since all these concepts show close relations to each other, the following remarks not only highlight research in the field of health information literacy, but also transfer relevant findings regarding information seeking and health literacy (as far as they are concerned with the quality of information skills and behavior).

Health information literacy is an essential condition for dealing successfully with health and illness issues at every age, and has thus been studied in different age groups, especially in higher age [8, 9]. Nevertheless, there are some aspects that are specifically relevant for the stage of young adulthood: First, adolescents tend to rely on the advice and support of their parents regarding health matters [10]. Therefore, young adults in the first stages of independence need to develop responsibility for health-related behavior and for designing a social environment beneficial for the health of themselves and possibly of other people. Second, younger age is associated with more information-seeking behavior, especially on the Internet [11], thus requiring abilities in dealing with information overload. Although today's young adults are referred to as the "information age generation", suggesting their familiarity with information media, research reveals problems of this age group in dealing with health-related information. An approach using self-reports [12] identified perceived literacy that was classified as problematic or inadequate in about half the subjects with regard to searching for and evaluating health information and, in about one third, regarding the ability to understand and use health information. The findings correspond with results of a study using an objective knowledge test highlighting deficiencies of American college students in conducting advanced health information searches, judging the trustworthiness of health-related websites and articles, and differentiating between information sources [4].

These shortcomings indicate the necessity to improve health information literacy in young adults. In order to determine a starting point for this endeavor, it is of major importance to identify factors that may influence development and level of sophistication of health information literacy. The present study takes a step in this direction, examining the associations of young adults' health information literacy with sociodemographic factors and basic personality dimensions.

1.1 Significance of Demographic Features

A large body of evidence demonstrates the impact of sociodemographic factors on health information literacy and behavior [11, 13]. One variable identified as a stable factor of influence across the research is education. Several studies revealed correlations between educational attainment and health information literacy, interest in health-related information, and the frequency of information searching [3, 9, 11]. In Germany, people with a lower level of education more frequently stated problematic or inadequate abilities to understand, evaluate, and use health information in comparison to those with a higher educational standard [12]. The same result was found in a European-wide survey: Subjects with a higher level of education reported a higher ability to understand health-related terminology on the Internet and to differentiate between high and low quality of information [14].

Another factor of interest is choice of vocation. So far there is little research exploring the relationship between occupation and health information literacy [16]. As is the case with gender, vocational orientation is expected to be a factor associated with interest in health issues, but not automatically with literacy. But handling of health information as required in health professions should lead to an advanced level of experience and thus have a positive effect on health information literacy. This effect should already be traceable in trainees pursuing a vocation in the medical field compared to those of other vocations.[1]

Based on the empirical findings and considerations outlined above, the following assumptions were tested regarding the effects of demographic variables:

Hypothesis 1. Higher health information literacy is associated with (a) a higher level of education, and (b) working in health-related (compared to non-health-related) vocations.

1.2 Personality Traits

While influences of demographic variations have been well established in research, relationships with personality factors have not yet received much attention. This is surprising, since personality as a stable disposition might well influence attitudes and mechanisms related to the acquisition of health information literacy. While there are some studies analyzing effects of personality on information seeking, [e.g. 17–19], very little research is found in the specific area of health information. Some researchers explored the role of neuroticism mediated by health anxiety in online health information seeking [20], and others have investigated effects of personality on health behaviors, [e.g. 21, 22]. But so far no efforts have been undertaken to examine possible influences of personality traits on objective skills in dealing with health information. Therefore, assumptions about effects of personality traits must be based on the few studies dealing with more general aspects of information behavior. The findings reviewed in the following share the same approach to conceptualizing personality, the broadly accepted five-factor model of personality. This model comprises five basic dimensions [23]: neuroticism, extraversion, openness to experience, agreeableness, and conscientiousness. In a study on the influence of these

[1] Age is considered to be another important factor of influence on health information literacy. However, its effects are not analyzed in the present study because of the homogeneity of the available sample with regard to age. With regard to gender, no clear predictions can be made. Although women tend to report higher need for health information and more interest in health-related issues as well as more information-seeking behavior than men [11], there is no evidence for a higher level of health information literacy among women, [12, 15]. Thus, gender will be included as a control variable only and no predictions about its effects are made.

dimensions on information behavior in students, researchers found patterns of searching behavior that were associated with different personality traits [18]. Whereas both openness to experience and conscientiousness showed a connection to high-quality searching, neuroticism was related to cursory searches. Broad and extensive search behavior was associated with extraversion. In another study, extraverted students were found to be unsystematic in their search, preferring quick solutions and the use of social sources, whereas students high in neuroticism showed difficulties in relevance judgments and insecurity in database searching, and openness to experience was related to broad effortful seeking and critical information judgment [17]. While some studies [17, 18] used self-reports on information behavior, another one examined the role of personality in information behavior tasks related to Web searches [24]. In this study, extraversion was related to problems with executing a task which required information literacy, as well as with a less favorable opinion of the subject's own search skills. Neuroticism was associated with shorter queries and difficulties with relevance judgments, and openness to experience with a broad searching approach (readiness to look at results further down the list of hits in search). Researchers analyzed correlations between different dimensions of self-reported information-seeking behavior and personality traits and found neuroticism to be correlated negatively with almost all dimensions, including those that can be seen as elements of information literacy (such as level of cognitive nature of search, accessibility of source, involvement in resource utilization) [19]. In contrast to neuroticism, positive relations with extraversion, openness, and conscientiousness were found. Summing up these findings, qualitative aspects of information behavior can be shown to be negatively associated with neuroticism and positively with conscientiousness and openness. The results for extraversion are ambiguous, but performance in real tasks points to difficulties related to information literacy. The factor agreeableness does not seem to be of great relevance to information seeking. In view of these insights, the following assumptions are inferred for health information literacy:

Hypothesis 2. Higher health information literacy is linked to a higher degree of conscientiousness and openness to experience as well as to a lower level of neuroticism and extraversion, whereas no correlation with agreeableness is expected.

2 Methods

2.1 Participants

At two vocational schools in Germany, a sample of 352 adolescents and young adults (16 to 34 years, $M = 20.8$ years, $SD = 3.15$; 60.2% female) was gathered. Participants were selected from three types of vocational orientation: Economy and administration (retailers and tax accountant assistants; $n = 112$), technology/mechanics (e.g., industrial mechanics, automotive technicians, electricians; $n = 130$), and health (medical and dental assistants; $n = 110$). In economy/administration, gender was almost balanced (61% female), whereas in health occupations all subjects were female and in technical vocations a predominance of men (73%) was observed. Each vocational orientation encompassed subjects with different levels of education which were grouped according to the German school system: Graduation after nine years (Group 1), after ten years (Group 2), and after twelve or thirteen years of school education (Group 3). Since 35 participants (43% female; 48% in technical, 26% in economic/administrative, and 26% in health vocations) did not fully complete the questionnaire, only 317 datasets were analyzed.

2.2 Measures

Paper-and-pencil measures were used to collect data during regular classroom instruction. Level of health information literacy was measured by the Health Information Literacy Knowledge Test (HILK). A detailed description of the measure is given by Mayer [25]. This questionnaire with 24 fixed-choice items assesses knowledge related to defining information needs, planning information seeking, accessing sources, and scanning information for quality and relevance. The 30-item version of the NEO Five-Factor Inventory (NEO-FFI-30) [26] was used to measure the robust personality dimensions of neuroticism, extraversion, openness, agreeableness, and conscientiousness by five subscales with six items each.

3 Results

Descriptive statistics and psychometric properties of the measures are summarized in Table 1. To test the hypotheses, in a first step, comparisons of means were conducted examining the effects of education and vocational orientation on health information literacy. For education, the assumed relationship to health information literacy could be supported by a significant result ($F(2,316) = 32.00; p < .001, \eta^2 = .20$). A contrast analysis revealed significant differences between low and medium education ($p = .004$) and between medium and high education ($p > .001$), confirming the hypothesis that higher health information literacy is associated with higher education. For vocational orientation, an analysis of variance also resulted in a significant though small effect ($F(2,316) = 3.30; p = .038, \eta^2 = .02$). But a contrast analysis could not confirm the assumed superiority of health vocations, producing nonsignificant results for comparisons with the other vocational orientation.

Table 1. Means (*M*), standard deviations (*SD*), internal consistencies (Cronbach's alpha; in italics on the diagonal), and intercorrelations of the measures used

	M	*SD*	HILK	N	E	C	A	O
HILK	0.42	0.13	*.72*					
Neuroticism N	2.77	0.91	−.07	*.85*				
Extraversion E	3.55	0.62	−.14*	−.25**	*.67*			
Conscientiousness C	4.07	0.58	.03	−.32**	.32**	*.73*		
Agreeableness A	3.79	0.69	.03	−.24*	.07	.22**	*.70*	
Openness O	3.00	0.89	.15**	.12*	−.08	−.20**	−.05	*.76*

*$p < .05$, **$p < .01$

Note. Range of values for HILK: 0–1, for all other scales: 1–5

Second, Pearson *r* correlations were computed examining the relationship of personality traits with health information literacy (see Table 1). As assumed in Hypothesis 2, a negative correlation for extraversion ($r = -.14$, $p < .01$), a positive correlation for openness ($r = .12$, $p < .05$), and no relationship with agreeableness could be confirmed. The expected negative correlations with neuroticism as well as the positive relation to conscientiousness were not found in this sample.

Table 2. Results of regression analysis of health information literacy on demographic and educational variables and personal beliefs (based on 1000 bootstrap samples)

	b	SE (*b*)	β	ΔR^2
Block I				.088, $p < .001$
Constant	0.23	0.05		
Gender (1 = male)	−0.04	0.01	−.15**	
Age	0.01	0.00	.23**	
Block II				.120, $p < .001$
Constant	0.44	0.06		
Gender (1 = male)	−0.02	0.02	−.08	
Age	0.00	0.00	.07	
Education Group 1	−0.13	0.02	−.37**	
Education Group 2	−0.09	0.02	−.34**	
Economic and administrative vocations	−0.02	0.02	−.07	
Technical vocations	−0.03	0.02	−.12	
Block III				.022, $p = .130$
Constant	0.53	0.10		
Gender (1 = male)	−0.03	0.02	−.10	
Age	0.00	0.00	.04	
Education Group 1	−0.12	0.02	−.35**	
Education Group 2	−0.08	0.02	−.33**	
Economic and administrative vocations	−0.02	0.02	−.07	
Technical vocations	−0.03	0.02	−.11	
Neuroticism	−0.01	0.01	−.10	
Extraversion	−0.03	0.01	−.12*	
Conscientiousness	0.01	0.01	.04	
Agreeableness	−.00	0.01	−.02	
Openness	0.01	0.01	.08	
R^2 total				.230, $p < .001$

**p* < *.05*, ***p* < *.01*

Note. *b* = unstandardized regression weight, SE(*b*) = standard error of *b*, β = standardized regression weight; ΔR^2 = increase in variance explained by the predictors.

Third, in order to examine effects of demographic variables in the relationship of health information literacy with personality traits, a multiple regression analysis was conducted. Bootstrapping was chosen to compensate for possible violations of the model conditions regarding the normal distribution of errors and homoscedasticity. Block I contained gender and age as control variables, Block II the level of education and the vocational orientation, and Block III the five scales of the NEO-FFI-30. Since the educational and the vocational variables each comprise three groups, both of them were dummy-coded. In educational attainment, Group 3 (with the highest education) was used as the reference group and compared to both other groups, in vocations, the health-related group was chosen as the reference group.

As represented in Table 2, in Block I the effects of gender and age both reached statistical significance. However, adding education and vocation in Block II led to nonsignificant results for these predictor variables as well as for the newly included vocation variable. In contrast, the effects of both dummy-coded education variables reached significance. These effects remained stable after the addition of the personality variables in Block III. Including demographic variables partly changes the relationship of health information literacy to personality traits identified by correlation analysis: Whereas the correlation coefficient of $r = -.14$ for extraversion almost corresponds to the regression weight of $\beta = -.12$, the significant correlation of $r = .15$ for openness cannot be replicated in regression analysis ($\beta = .08$). This points to an relationship of demographic characteristics with openness, which can be traced down to education by an additional analysis of variance: Openness was slightly higher in the group with the highest education ($F(2,316) = 5.80$; $p < .01$, $\eta^2 = .04$) compared to medium ($p < .05$), and lowest education ($p < .01$) by Bonferroni adjustments.

4 Discussion and Conclusions

This study examined the relationship of personality and demographic characteristics with health information literacy. In Hypothesis 1, positive associations of health information literacy with a higher level of education and a health-oriented vocation were predicted. A strong effect of education was found, confirming the hypothesis and replicating findings from previous research linking health information literacy to general higher education [3]. This result may indicate the importance of school education in the development of the skills that health information literacy is comprised of. Additionally, the effect may be due to an underlying influence of a common third variable such as cognitive ability. Vocational orientation did not show the expected significant effect. This may reflect a training focus in the health vocations analyzed (medical and dental assistants) that emphasizes administration instead of the search for and acquisition of health information. Presumably, training is oriented toward conveying basic knowledge needed for the daily work such as evidence-based practices and standard procedures. Effects of gender and age lost their predictive value after education was entered into the regression equation. This is due to confounding of education with both control variables, as vocational students who have reached a higher level of education are usually older, and a higher percentage of them is female.

In Hypothesis 2, positive associations of openness and conscientiousness as well as negative associations of extraversion and neuroticism with health information literacy were assumed. Using correlation analysis, the assumptions for extraversion and openness could be confirmed. Considering influences of demographic and educational variables in regression analysis led to a nonsignificant result for openness, but left the effect of extraversion almost unchanged, thus confirming negative links between information literacy and extraversion found in other research [24]. Additional analyses revealed the role of education in the relationship between openness and health information literacy: Openness was most pronounced in the group with the highest education which also had the highest level of health information literacy. Extraversion, on the other hand, showed a small but stable negative association with health information literacy in both correlation and regression analysis. This effect is in line with research on the relationship between extraversion and learning [17, 27]: Less successful university students scored higher on extraversion, possibly due to socializing and seeking non-academic outlets. Additionally, extraversion was linked to spontaneous, incidental discovery of useful information [18]. Transferring this finding to health information literacy, lower scores in subjects with higher extraversion could be explained by a broad approach to health information embracing a variety of (social) sources and thus relying more strongly on others in health matters while not placing so much importance on their own competence in dealing with them.

In contrast to previous research [18, 19], no effects of conscientiousness and neuroticism could be detected. This may be due to the fact that the HILK is a measure of objective skills and not of behavior in a given situation. Conscientious people are strong-willed and determined to achieve [23], a personality trait that perhaps only shows effects when a personal interest arises and may therefore be more strongly associated with searching behavior than with underlying literacy skills. The same could be the case with neuroticism: Whereas a neurotic predisposition is related to perceived difficulties with relevance judgements, insecurities, and preferences for confirming information in information-seeking situations [17], it does not necessarily influence the objective health information literacy skills. This view is substantiated by the fact that the one cited study not using self-reports in analyzing information seeking also found only extraversion to be linked to information literacy [24].

Some limitations have to be kept in mind when interpreting the results. Since the study used a cross-sectional design, no conclusions can be drawn regarding the causality of the relationship between personality and health information literacy. Furthermore, the personality dimensions were focused separately, not regarding interrelations and possible typical clusters in relation to health information literacy. Nevertheless, the results of this study bear significance for the practice of information systems and promotion of health information literacy. Though the effects are relatively small, the findings illustrate that personality traits might create impediments to the acquisition of health information literacy. Interventions promoting health information literacy may not in every case have the desired effect due to personality differences. And, while individuals with a lower level of education and less openness to experience might best be served with reliable information from one source that does not require an extended search, such limited information might not be satisfactory to extraverted people needing a variety of sources. In order to adapt health information provided and information-related education, future research should investigate the role of personality in different aspects of health information literacy and behavior such as choice of sources, information retrieval, evaluation processes, and information use.

References

1. Jayanti, R.K., Burns, A.C.: The antecedents of preventive health care behavior: an empirical study. J. Acad. Mark. Sci. **26**(1), 6–15 (1998)
2. Hsu, C.E., Johnson, L., Brooks, A.N.: Promoting health information literacy. Collaborative opportunities for teaching and academic librarian faculty. Acad. Exch. Q. **7**(1), 200–207 (2003)
3. Hirvonen, N.: Health information matters: everyday health information literacy and behaviour in relation to health behaviour and physical health among young men. Acta Univ. Oul. B **133** (2015). http://jultika.oulu.fi/files/isbn9789526210407.pdf
4. Ivanitskaya, L., Boyle, I.O., Casey, A.M.: Health information literacy and competencies of information age students: results from the interactive online Research Readiness Self-Assessment (RRSA). J. Med. Internet Res. **8**(2) (2006). https://doi.org/10.2196/jmir.8.2.e6
5. Medical Library Association Task Force on Health Information: Health Information Literacy Definitions (2003)
6. American Library Association: Presidential Committee on Information Literacy: Final Report (1989)
7. Sørensen, K., Van den Broucke, S., Fullam, J., Doyle, G., Pelikan, J., Slonska, Z., Brand, H.: Health literacy and public health: a systematic review and integration of definitions and models. BMC Public Health **12**(80) (2012). https://doi.org/10.1186/1471-2458-12-80
8. Yates, C., Stoodley, I.D., Partridge, H.L., Bruce, C.S., Cooper, H., Day, G., Edwards, S.L.: Exploring health information use by older australians within everyday life. Libr. Trends **60**(3), 460–478 (2012)
9. Eriksson-Backa, K.: Health information literacy and demographic background in relation to health risks, diabetes and heart disease among older finnish adults. Informaatiotutkimus **33**(3) (2014). Retrieved from Informaatiotutkimuksen paivat 2014, 6. - 7. marraskuuta, Oulun yliopisto, Oulu
10. Gray, N.J., Klein, J.D., Noyce, P.R., Sesselberg, T.S., Cantrill, J.A.: Health information-seeking behaviour in adolescence: the place of the internet. Soc. Sci. Med. **60**(7), 1467–1478 (2005)
11. Wang, M.P., Viswanath, K., Lam, T.H., Wang, X., Chan, S.S.: Social determinants of health information seeking among Chinese adults in Hong Kong. PloS ONE **8**(8) (2013). https://doi.org/10.1371/journal.pone.0073049
12. Schaeffer, D., Vogt, D., Berens, E.M., Hurrelmann, K.: Gesundheitskompetenz der Bevölkerung in Deutschland: Ergebnisbericht. Universität Bielefeld, Bielefeld (2016)
13. Noelke, L., Mensing, M., Kraemer, A., Hornberg, C.: Sociodemographic and health-(care) related characteristics of online health information seekers: a cross-sectional German study. BMC Public Health **15**(31) (2015). https://doi.org/10.1186/s12889-015-1423-0
14. Flash Eurobarometer 404: European Citizens' Digital Health Literacy. A Report to the European Commission (2014)
15. Kutner, M., Greenberg, E., Jin, Y., Paulsen, C.: The Health Literacy of America's Adults: Results from the 2003 National Assessment of Adult Literacy. National Center for Education Statistics, Washington DC (2006)

16. Hirvonen, N., Ek, S., Niemelä, R., Korpelainen, R., Huotari, M.L.: Sociodemographic characteristics associated with the everyday health information literacy of young men. Inf. Res. **20**(1) (2015). https://files.eric.ed.gov/fulltext/EJ1060510.pdf
17. Heinström, J.: Five personality dimensions and their influence on information behaviour. Inf. Res. **9**(1) (2003). https://byupustakawan.wordpress.com/2008/03/15/five-personality-dimensions-and-their-influence-on-information-behaviour/
18. Heinström, J.: Fast surfing, broad scanning and deep diving: the influence of personality and study approach on students' information-seeking behavior. J. Doc. **61**(2), 228–247 (2005)
19. Halder, S., Roy, A., Chakraborty, P.K.: The influence of personality traits on information seeking behaviour of students. Malays. J. Libr. Inf. Sci. **15**(1), 41–53 (2010)
20. Lagoe, C., Atkin, D.: Health anxiety in the digital age: an exploration of psychological determinants of online health information seeking. Comput. Hum. Behav. **52**, 484–491 (2015)
21. Hill, E.M., Gick, M.L.: The big five and cervical screening barriers: evidence for the influence of conscientiousness extraversion openness. Pers. Individ. Differ. **50**(5), 662–667 (2011)
22. Raynor, D.A., Levine, H.: Associations between the five-factor model of personality and health behaviors among college students. J. Am. Coll. Health **58**(1), 73–82 (2009)
23. Costa, P.T., McCrae, R.R.: Revised NEO Personality Inventory (NEO PI-R) and NEO Five-Factor Inventory (NEO-FFI): Professional Manual. Psychol Assess Resour, Odessa (1992)
24. Schmidt, T., Wolff, C.: Personality and information behavior in web search. Proc. Assoc. Inf. Sci. Technol. **53**(1), 1–6 (2016)
25. Mayer, A.-K.: Subjective and objective measures of health information literacy: do they provide complementary or redundant information? In: Kurbanoğlu, S., Boustany, J., Špiranec, S., Grassian, E., Mizrachi, D., Roy, L., Çakmak, T. (eds.) Communications in Computer and Information Science: Workplace Information Literacy, Fifth European Conference, ECIL 2017, Saint-Malo, France, 18–21 September 2017, revised selected papers
26. Körner, A., Geyer, M., Roth, M., Drapeau, M., Schmutzer, G., Albani, C., Schuhmann, S., Braehler, E.: Persönlichkeitsdiagnostik mit dem NEO-Fünf-Faktoren-Inventar: Die 30-Item-Kurzversion (NEO-FFI-30). Psychother. Psychosom. Med. Psychol. **58**(06), 238–245 (2008)
27. De Raad, B., Schouwenburg, H.C.: Personality in learning and education: a review. Eur. J. Pers. **10**(5), 303–336 (1996)

Relationship Between Everyday Health Information Literacy and Attitudes Towards Mobile Technology Among Older People

Heidi Enwald[1,2,3](✉), Noora Hirvonen[1,2,3], Maarit Kangas[4], Niina Keränen[4], Timo Jämsä[3,4], Isto Huvila[2], and Raija Korpelainen[3,5,6]

[1] Information Studies, University of Oulu, Oulu, Finland
{heidi.enwald,noora.hirvonen}@oulu.fi
[2] Information Studies, Åbo Akademi University, Turku, Finland
isto.huvila@abo.fi
[3] Medical Research Center Oulu, University of Oulu and Oulu University Hospital, Oulu, Finland
timo.jamsa@oulu.fi, raija.korpelainen@odl.fi
[4] Medical Imaging, Physics and Technology, University of Oulu, Oulu, Finland
{maarit.kangas,niina.s.keranen}@oulu.fi
[5] Department of Sports and Exercise Medicine, Oulu Deaconess Institute, Oulu, Finland
[6] Centre for Life Course Epidemiology and Systems Medicine, University of Oulu, Oulu, Finland

Abstract. In order to benefit from advanced mobile information technology (AMIT) in e-health services, people need competencies in finding, evaluating, and understanding health-related information in varying everyday life situations, that is, everyday health information literacy (EHIL). This study focused on the relationship between EHIL and AMIT use and attitudes towards it among older adults. A paper questionnaire was posted to a random sample of 1,500 home dwelling subjects aged 65 or more living in Northern Finland. A variety of themes were addressed in the questionnaire including a 4-item version of an EHIL screening tool. The response rate was 61% (n = 918). Older adults with negative attitudes towards or having less experience with mobile information technology were likely to have poor self-estimated EHIL skills. Older people are at risk of marginalization in regard to m-services, and these results should be utilized by decision-makers and software designers in digitalization of services.

Keywords: Health information literacy · Use of technology
Mobile technology · e-Health · Older adults

1 Introduction

At present, technology use is often seen as a necessary prerequisite for older people to be integrated into society and also a factor that relates to active and successful aging. Older people may already be active users of the Internet and computers (seen in this

S. Kurbanoğlu et al. (Eds.): ECIL 2017, CCIS 810, pp. 450–459, 2018.
https://doi.org/10.1007/978-3-319-74334-9_47

paper as "traditional" information technology) but still may be reluctant to use advanced mobile information technology (AMIT) such as smart phones and tablet computers.

Many people between the ages of 60 to 80 are still generally healthy and fit. They want to maintain a high quality of life as long as possible. Their information and service needs differ from those with serious health problems. Individuals are expected to be involved in various aspects of health decision-making [1]. Nowadays, participation also often requires use of advanced information technology. Furthermore, effective participation and use of these kinds of new services require knowledge, skills, and abilities that relate to health information literacy [2].

The aim of this study was to investigate the relationship between everyday health information literacy and the opinions and use of advanced mobile information technology among older people. The research questions were as follows:

How does everyday health information literacy relate to

(1) use of "traditional" information technology,
(2) use of advanced mobile information technology, and
(3) opinions about advanced mobile information technology among older people?

This study is a part of the Gamified Services for Elderly (GASEL) project that examined the requirements for tailored and gamified e-health services in promoting wellbeing and health of older adults [3–5].

2 Background

2.1 Older Adults as Users of Information Technology

Aging populations, age related digital divide, and e-inclusion are fundamental European-wide challenges [6]. In 2016, the Council of European Union [7] published a press release concerning the accessibility of online public services, e.g., the websites and apps of public administrations, hospitals, courts, and other public sector bodies. The findings of Hill, Betts, and Gardner [8] support evidence of a "gray" digital divide that is not only caused by lack of access (first level digital divide) but by lack of use (second level digital divide). At the same time, older adults have been the fastest growing computer and Internet user group [9]. In Finland, elderly people are relatively tech-savvy as 74% of people aged 65 to 74 and 31% of those aged 75 to 89 had used the Internet in the past three months in 2016. Of those aged 65 to 74 years old, 23% and 8% from the older age group had reserved a doctor's appointment online [10].

In recent reports of the GASEL project, it was noted that most of the older people who had used tablets or smart phones had not encountered any major difficulties in their use. Men and those under 70 years old were the most positive in their opinions about mobile information technology [5]. Older adults' frailty and pre-frailty were independently related to the nonuse of AMIT. The frail and pre-frail nonusers also held the most negative opinions on the usefulness or usability of this kind of technology [4].

2.2 The Concept of Health Information Literacy

Health information literacy can be seen as information literacy in the context of health or as a combination of the concepts of health literacy (HL) and information literacy [11, 12]. While the concept of HL, mainly used in health sciences, is usually used to refer to the basic skills people need to be able to function in health care settings, HIL is focused on higher level cognitive abilities to find, evaluate, and understand health information also in everyday life situations. The Medical Library Association (MLA) [12] defines HIL as 'the set of abilities needed to recognize a health information need, identify likely information sources and use them to retrieve relevant information, assess the quality of the information and its applicability to a specific situation, and analyze, understand, and use the information to make good health decisions'.

Based on an operationalization of the MLA's definition of HIL, Niemelä et al. [11] designed a 10-item survey aiming at identifying differences in individuals' everyday HIL (EHIL). Their aim was to develop a simple and practical screening tool that could be used to detect individuals who would benefit from HIL counseling. Hirvonen et al. [13] found that EHIL scores were associated with socio-demographic characteristics as well as health behavior and physical health among young Finnish men. When young men were compared to adults with increased risk for metabolic syndrome, the latter seemed to value health information more but also had more difficulties in knowing who to believe in health issues and in understanding health-related terminology [14].

Niemelä et al. [11] identified three independent factors of EHIL: motivation of finding health information, confidence in one's ability to find, understand and use health information, and evaluation of health information. Furthermore, an item on the ability to understand terminology in health contexts was considered to be 'a fundamental HIL statement' and was analyzed separately. The three-factor structure has been confirmed in subsequent studies [15]. Based on this factor analysis, a shorter version of the tool with one statement representing each factor (motivation, evaluation, confidence, terminology) was proposed [11].

2.3 Older Adults' Health Information Literacy and Information Technology Use

The importance of HL and HIL becomes critical in later age when many health-related decisions are made. Deterioration of HL has been associated with aging (see e.g., a systematic literature review by [16]), poorer health outcomes, and less frequent use of preventive services [17].

Previous studies indicate differences in individuals' HIL based on age, education, economic situation, and health status. HIL has also been positively associated with self-rated health among older people (aged 65–79) [18]. Moreover, seniors may face challenges in understanding the terminology used in health communication. However, research in this area especially among older people is still scarce.

A large study among American adults by Mackert et al. [19] investigated the relationship between HL and health information technology (HIT) adoption. HL was described as the Newest Vital Sign. The use of HIT tools, such as nutrition apps, activity trackers and patient portals as well as the perceived ease of use and usefulness of these applications were under scrutiny. According to the results, patients with low HL were less likely to use HIT tools or perceive them as easy or useful. To our knowledge, this is the first study to examine the relationship between HIL and opinions about and use of AMIT of older adults.

3 Methods and Data Collection

3.1 Data Collection

The study was conducted between November 2014 and January 2015 in Oulu, Finland. Oulu is Finland's fifth largest city with a population of approximately 200,000 of which 14% are 65 years or older [20]. The data were collected with a postal questionnaire sent to a random population-wide sample of 1,500 home dwelling individuals aged 65 or more, speaking Finnish as native language, living in Oulu area. A reminder was sent to the non-respondents four weeks after the first survey. The questionnaire was in Finnish.

The questionnaire, piloted among 11 volunteer seniors, included questions relating to several topics including health status, wellbeing, information behavior, health information literacy, use of technology, and gaming. In this study, responses on questions about EHIL and technology use were utilized. The participants were asked whether they had used a computer, tablet computer, mobile phone, or a touch screen mobile phone in the last 12 months. Moreover, they were asked whether they had Internet access at home, if they had used the Internet, had ever used the Internet with a mobile phone, and if they had ever installed an application to a mobile phone. The response alternatives were: 'Yes, and there were no major difficulties', 'Yes, but it was difficult to do', 'No', and 'I don't know'.

Questions on opinions towards mobile technology were based on the constructs of the Unified Theory of Acceptance and Use of Technology (UTAUT) [21]. The participants were instructed to give their opinion on statements related to their use of mobile information technology devices, such as smartphones or tablets. The statements were as follows: (a) 'I am interested in using mobile information technologies', (b) 'I believe that using mobile information technology is/would be useful in my daily life', (c) 'I believe that using mobile information technology is/would be necessary in my daily life', and (d) 'Using mobile information technology is easy for me'. The response alternatives were: 'Yes', 'No', and 'I don't know'.

Data on EHIL was collected with a shorter 4-item version of the EHIL screening tool [11]. The four statements are: 'I like to get health information from a variety of sources' (motivation), 'It is easy to assess the reliability of health information from the Internet' (evaluation), 'It is difficult to know who to believe in health issues' (confidence), and 'Terms and sentences of health information are often difficult to understand' (terminology).

The study protocol was that of the larger Gamified Services for Elderly (GASEL) project, of which the current study was a part. It was approved by the Ethics Committee of Human Sciences in the University of Oulu (statement 6/2014).

3.2 Data Analysis

The data were analyzed by using the software package SPSS 21 for Windows. The statistical significance of the associations between the categorical explanatory and response variables were analyzed using cross-tabulation with Pearson's chi-squared test.

An exploratory factor analysis with questions relating to use of and opinions about technology was conducted to examine the dimensional structure of the survey. The objective was to investigate whether sum variables could be used for further analysis of the data. The factor analysis showed three dimensions with four questions each. These were labeled: (1) opinions on mobile information technology, (2) mobile information technology use, and (3) "traditional" information technology use. The statements relating to each factor were further analyzed by forming sum variables. First, the statements were rated by giving one point for a 'yes' (indicating use of technology or a positive attitude towards it) response and zero points from other responses. The sum variables reflect the use of traditional technology, use of mobile technology, and opinions towards mobile information technology. The point scale is from 0 to 4 wherein 0 reflects the most negative and 4 the most positive attitude or frequency of use. Further, the sum variables were transformed into binary variables based on point counts:

- 'Traditional' information technology use: accustomed technology users (those with 4 points) and less accustomed technology users (those with 0–3 points).
- AMIT use: people with no experience (0 points) and people with at least some experience (1–4 points).
- Opinions about mobile information technology: people with negative opinions (0 points) and people with at least some positive opinions (1–4 points).

In the analyses, the respondents were categorized into two groups based on whether they perceived problems in the different areas of everyday health information literacy. Agreeing with the statements EHIL1 and EHIL2, and, conversely, disagreeing with the negatively worded statements EHIL3 and EHIL4 were seen as indicators of not perceiving problems in these areas.

4 Results

The response rate was 61.2% (n = 918). The mean age of the final study population was 73.4 (SD 6.8) and 528 (57.5%) of the respondents were females. The responders were approximately 2.5 years younger than non-responders or those who were excluded ($P < .001$), but there was no statistically significant difference in gender distribution ($P = .42$).

4.1 Everyday Health Information Literacy

Of the respondents, 67.4% (n = 590) strongly or moderately agreed with the statement 'I like to get health information from variety of sources' (EHIL1) while 19.8%

(n = 173) were unsure and 12.8% (n = 112) moderately or strongly disagreed. With the statement 'It is easy to assess the reliability of health information from the Internet' (EHIL2), 28.2% (n = 234) agreed, 39.8% were unsure, and 32.0% disagreed. From the respondents, 59.8% (n = 526) agreed, 19.1% (n = 168) were unsure, and 21.0% (n = 185) disagreed that 'It is difficult to know who to believe in health issues' (EHIL3). Terms and sentences of health information were considered difficult to understand (EHIL4) by 58.3% (n = 510) of the respondents; 17.6% (n = 154) were unsure and 24.1% (n = 211) disagreed with this statement.

4.2 Everyday Health Information Literacy and Use of Advanced Mobile Information Technology and Opinions Towards It

Respondents who were confident in their abilities in evaluating online health information, determining whom to believe in health issues, and understanding health related terminology were more likely to use traditional information technologies than those who were unsure of their abilities. In other words, those who perceived problems in these areas of EHIL were more likely to get 4 points in the sum variable ''traditional' information technology use'.

Elderly who were confident in their abilities in evaluating online health information, determining whom to believe in health issues, and understanding health related terminology were more likely to use AMIT than those who were unsure of their abilities. In other words, those who perceived problems in these areas of EHIL were more likely to get more than 0 points for the sum variable 'mobile information technology use' (Tables 1 and 2).

All dimensions of EHIL were linked to opinions towards AMIT. Respondents who did not perceive problems in EHIL were more likely to receive more than 0 points for

Table 1. Cross-tabulations with perceived problems in everyday health information literacy and points in the 'traditional technology' use scale (n = 783).

		Traditional information technology use			
		4 points n = 428 (54.8%)	<4 points n = 354 (45.2%)	Total N = 783 (100%)	Pearson chi-squared
EHIL1 motivation	No problems	296 (57.6)	218 (42.4)	514 (100)	4.73, p = .03
	Problems	133 (49.4)	136 (50.6)	269 (100)	
EHIL2 evaluation	No problems	147 (69.7)	64 (30.3)	211 (100)	**25.81, p < .001**
	Problems	282 (49.3)	290 (50.7)	572 (100)	
EHIL3 Authority	No problems	108 (65.1)	58 (34.9)	166 (100)	**33.84, p < .001**
	Problems	321 (52.0)	296 (48.0)	617 (100)	
EHIL4 terminology	No problems	137 (73.3)	50 (26.7)	187 (100)	**8.97, p = .003**
	Problems	292 (49.0)	304 (51.0)	596 (100)	

Table 2. Cross-tabulations with perceived problems in everyday health information literacy and points in the mobile information technology use scale (n = 728).

		Mobile information technology use			
		>0 points n = 307 (42.2%)	0 points n = 421 (57.8%)	Total N = 728 (100%)	Pearson chi-squared
EHIL1 motivation	No problems	211 (44.2)	266 (55.8)	477 (100)	2.42, p = .12
	Problems	96 (38.2)	155 (61.8)	251 (100)	
EHIL2 evaluation	No problems	94 (50.5)	92 (49.5)	186 (100)	**7.17, p = .007**
	Problems	213 (39.3)	329 (60.7)	542 (100)	
EHIL3 authority	No problems	86 (55.1)	70 (44.9)	156 (100)	**37.12, p < .001**
	Problems	221 (38.6)	351 (61.4)	572 (100)	
EHIL4 terminology	No problems	108 (62.1)	66 (37.9)	174 (100)	**13.67, p < .001**
	Problems	199 (35.9)	355 (64.1)	554 (100)	

the sum variable of 'opinions about mobile information technology'. Therefore, for example, those with the most negative opinions about mobile information technology were more likely to think that it is not easy to assess the reliability of health information obtained from the Internet ($\chi^2(1) = 11.680$, $p = 0.001$) and that health related terminology and statements are often difficult to understand ($\chi^2(1) = 28.095$, $p < 0.001$) (See Table 3).

Table 3. Cross-tabulations with perceived problems in everyday health information literacy and points in opinions about mobile information technology scale.

		Opinions about mobile information technology			
		>0 points n = 376 (49.6%)	0 points n = 382 (50.4%)	Total N = 758 (100%)	Pearson chi-squared
EHIL1 motivation	No problems	269 (54.1)	228 (45.9)	497 (100)	**11.80, p < .001**
	Problems	107 (41.4)	154 (59.0)	261 (100)	
EHIL2 evaluation	No problems	121 (59.9)	81 (40.1)	202 (100)	**11.68, p = .001**
	Problems	255 (45.9)	301 (54.1)	556 (100)	
EHIL3 authority	No problems	96 (60.8)	62 (39.2)	158 (100)	**9.94, p < .002**
	Problems	280 (46.7)	320 (53.3)	600 (100)	
EHIL4 terminology	No problems	122 (66.7)	61 (33.3)	183 (100)	**28.10, p < .001**
	Problems	254 (44.2)	321 (55.8)	575 (100)	

5 Discussion and Conclusions

Older people are rather motivated to seek health information but face difficulties in assessing the reliability of information from online sources and understanding health terminology. Many also find it difficult to know whom to believe on health issues.

More than half of the respondents had used a computer, a mobile phone, had an Internet connection at home, and had used the Internet during the previous year. It should be noted, however, that although Finnish elderly people are relatively tech-savvy, a large proportion of older people still do not use these information technologies. As can be expected, AMIT use is less common among older people: almost 60% of the respondents had not yet used tablet computers or touch screen phones. However, approximately half of the respondents had at least some positive opinions about mobile information technology in that they were interested in it, considered it beneficial, necessary, or easy to use.

Based on our results, the users of both traditional and mobile information technology differ from non-users in that they are more confident in their abilities in evaluating online health information, determining who to believe in health issues, and understanding health related terminology. Also, positive opinions towards mobile information technology were linked to perceiving fewer problems in the areas of EHIL.

Mackert et al. [19] showed that people with low HL were less likely to use HIT tools or perceive them as easy and useful. Our study indicates that perceived problems in HIL are also linked to technology use. Furthermore, the literature on the "gray" digital divide considers lack of use as a key reason for the digital divide for older adults (second level digital divide) [8]. According to our results, those in danger of marginalization from the use of AMIT and mobile e services offered also have difficulties in evaluating and understanding health information.

The strength of this study is the large random population-based sample with a high response rate. Both genders and different age groups of seniors were reached. However, the results reported are based on small number of self-evaluation questions. Even though self-evaluation is a common way to measure HIL and HL, there is an ongoing debate on whether HL represents a skill-based construct or if it more broadly captures personal activation or motivation to manage health [22]. In general, the EHIL screening tool may reflect confidence and motivation rather than actual skills. Furthermore, the analysis did not take into account for confounding factors that may influence both EHIL and AMIT. However, we did not study causal relationships but associations between the variables.

The differences found in this study concerning older adults EHIL skills and use and opinions should be taken into account when designing HIL promotion, targeted and tailored health communication strategies, and intervention studies. Because of this, future EHIL studies should focus on the different aspects of EHIL, for example on skills and abilities to use health information. In addition, older adults with different levels of EHIL and utilization rate of AMIT should be included in designing e-health services targeted for this specific age group. Since older people are at risk of marginalization in regard to m-services, these results should be utilized by decision-makers and software designers in digitalization of services for older people for example through tailoring health contents in these services to better match the users' competencies and preferences.

Acknowledgements. GASEL study has received financial support from the Finnish Funding Agency for Innovation (TEKES). The researchers of Åbo Akademi are part of the HIBA project that is being funded by Academy of Finland.

References

1. Mockford, C., Staniszewska, S., Griffiths, F., Herron-Marx, S.: The impact of patient and public involvement on UK NHS health care: a systematic review. Int. J. Qual. Health Care **24**(1), 28–38 (2012)
2. Suri, V.R., Chang, Y.-K., Majid, S., Foo, S.: Health information literacy of senior citizens – a review. In: Kurbanoğlu, S., Špiranec, S., Grassian, E., Mizrachi, D., Catts, R. (eds.) ECIL 2014. CCIS, vol. 492, pp. 128–137. Springer, Cham (2014). https://doi.org/10.1007/978-3-319-14136-7_14
3. Enwald, H., Kangas, M., Keränen, N., Immonen, M., Similä, H., Jämsä, T., Korpelainen, R.: Health information behaviour, attitudes towards health information and motivating factors for encouraging physical activity among older people: differences by sex and age. In: Proceedings of ISIC, Zadar, Croatia, 20–23 September 2016: Part 2 (2017). http://www.informationr.net/ir/22-1/isic/isic1623.html. Inf. Res. **22**(1), paper isic1623
4. Keränen, N., Kangas, M., Immonen, M., Similä, H., Enwald, H., Korpelainen, R., Jämsä, T.: Use of information and communication technologies among older people with and without frailty: a population-based survey. J. Med. Intern. Res. **19**(2) (2017). http://www.jmir.org/2017/2/e29/
5. Enwald, H., Kangas, M., Keränen, N., Korpelainen, R., Huvila, I., Jämsä, T.: Opinions and use of mobile information technology among older people in Northern Finland – preliminary results of population based study. In: 79th ASIS&T Annual Meeting, Proceedings of the Annual Meeting of the Association for Information Science and Technology, 14–18 Oct 2016, Copenhagen, Denmark, vol. 53 (2016)
6. Niehaves, B., Plattfaut, R.: Internet adoption by the elderly: employing IS technology acceptance theories for understanding the age-related digital divide. Eur. J. Inf. Syst. **23**(6), 708–726 (2014)
7. Council of European Union: More accessible websites across Europe: agreement with European Parliament. Press release (2016). http://www.consilium.europa.eu/en/press/press-releases/2016/05/03-more-accessible-website-across-europa/
8. Hill, R., Betts, L.R., Gardner, S.E.: Older adults experiences and perceptions of digital technology: (dis)empowerment, wellbeing, and inclusion. Comput. Hum. Behav. **48**(C), 415–423 (2015)
9. Heart, T., Kalderon, E.: Older adults: are they ready to adopt health-related ICT? Int. J. Med. Inform. **82**, e209–e231 (2013)
10. Statistics Finland: Finnish residents use the Internet more and more often. Helsinki: Statistics Finland (2016). http://www.stat.fi/til/sutivi/2016/sutivi_2016_2016-12-09_tie_001_en.html
11. Niemelä, R., Ek, S., Eriksson-Backa, K., Huotari, M.-L.: A screening tool for assessing everyday health information literacy. Libri **62**(2), 125–134 (2012)
12. Shipman, J.P., Kurtz-Rossi, S., Funk, C.J.: The health information literacy research project. J. Med. Libr. Assoc. **97**(4), 293–301 (2009)

13. Hirvonen, N., Ek, S., Niemelä, R., Korpelainen, R., Huotari, M.L.: Socio-demographic characteristics associated with the everyday health information literacy of young men. In: Proceedings of ISIC, the Information Behaviour Conference, Leeds, 2–5 September 2014: Part 2 (2015). http://www.informationr.net/ir/20-1/isic2/isic25.html#.VSeH3fmUd1Y. Inf. Res. **20**(1), paper isic25
14. Enwald, H., Hirvonen, N., Huotari, M.L., Korpelainen, R., Pyky, R., Savolainen, M., Salonurmi, T., Keränen, A.M., Jokelainen, T., Niemelä, R.: Everyday health information literacy among young men compared with adults with high risk for metabolic syndrome – a cross-sectional population-based study. J. Inf. Sci. **42**(3), 344–355 (2016). (Special Issue of I3 Conference, at Aberdeen, UK, June 2015)
15. Hirvonen, N., Enwald, H., Nengomasha, C., Abankwah, R., Uutoni W.U., Korpelainen, R., Pyky, R., Huotari, M.-L., Mayer, A.-K.: Validating the factorial structure of the everyday health information literacy screening tool in three different populations. In: Proceedings of ISIC: The Information Behaviour Conference. Extended Abstract for a Poster (2016)
16. Zamora, H., Clingerman, E.M.: Health literacy among older adults: a systematic literature review. J. Gerontol. Nurs. **37**(10), 41–51 (2011)
17. Berkman, N.D., Sheridan, S.L., Donahue, K.E., Halpern, D.J., Crotty, K.: Low health literacy and health outcomes: an updated systematic review. Ann. Intern. Med. **155**(2), 97–107 (2011)
18. Eriksson-Backa, K., Ek, S., Niemelä, R., Huotari, M.L.: Health information literacy in everyday life: a study of Finns aged 65–79 years. Health Inform. J. **18**(2), 83–94 (2012)
19. Mackert, M., Mabry-Flynn, A., Champlin, S., Donovan, E.E., Pounders, K.: Health literacy and health information technology adoption: the potential for a new digital divide. J. Med. Internet Res. **18**(10), e264 (2016). https://www.jmir.org/2016/10/e264
20. Pxnet2.stat: Väestöllisiä tunnuslukuja alueittain (in Finnish). (2013). http://pxnet2.stat.fi/PXWeb/pxweb/fi/StatFin/StatFin__vrm__vaerak/048_vaerak_tau_203.px
21. Venkatesh, V., Morris, M., Gordon, B., Davis, F.D.: User acceptance of information technology: toward a unified view. MIS Q. **27**(3), 425–478 (2003)
22. Smith, S.G., Curtis, L.M., Wardle, J., von Wagner, C., Wolf, M.S.: Skill set or mind set? Associations between health literacy, patient activation and health. Plos One **8**(9), e74373 (2013). http://journals.plos.org/plosone/article?id=10.1371/journal.pone.0074373

Concepts Related to Health Literacy in Online Information Environments: A Systematic Review with an Emphasis on Approach to Information

Anna-Maija Huhta[1(✉)], Noora Hirvonen[1,2], and Maija-Leena Huotari[1]

[1] Information Studies, University of Oulu and Medical Research Center, Oulu, Finland
{anna-maija.huhta,noora.hirvonen, maija-leena.huotari}@oulu.fi

[2] Information Studies, Åbo Akademi University, Turku, Finland

Abstract. This study systematically reviews concepts related to health literacy with an emphasis on the approach to information in their definitions. The focus was set on studies conducted in online information environments. In total, 180 full-text articles were screened and, of these, 71 articles were included in the analysis. Eight different literacy concepts and 17 definitions for them were identified. The most frequently used concepts are health literacy and eHealth literacy. They are used across disciplines. In information science the concept of health information literacy is also used. The approach to information in the definitions varies. Central in health information literacy is the information seeking process. In health literacy definitions the focus is on obtaining information to promote health, usually in a health care setting. eHealth literacy focuses on finding and evaluating online health information.

Keywords: Health literacy · Health information literacy · eHealth literacy Online environments · Systematic review

1 Introduction

The contemporary digital information environment challenges our understanding of what a literate person is. The fast and free flow of information in the web offers us multiple ways to communicate, but it also challenges us with an overload of information and loss of authority and identity [1]. In the context of online health information, competencies related to finding, evaluating, and utilizing information are essential as the amount of health information is rapidly increasing and the possibility to encounter misinformation is apparent.

The term health literacy was introduced in the 1970s following the discussion on health education as a social policy issue [2]. The early health literacy descriptions were built on the understanding of literacy as individuals' reading comprehension, numeracy, and writing skills (e.g. [3]). However, according to Mårtensson and Hensing [4]

S. Kurbanoğlu et al. (Eds.): ECIL 2017, CCIS 810, pp. 460–469, 2018.
https://doi.org/10.1007/978-3-319-74334-9_48

more recent definitions represent health literacy as a multidimensional concept that acknowledges the broadness of skills in interaction with social and cultural contexts. These definitions emphasize the interactive and critical skills needed to use information for making appropriate health decisions [4].

Research on health literacy and related phenomena have been conducted in several disciplines. In the field of library and information science, skills and competencies related to health information have been conceptualized as health information literacy. The concept, introduced by the Medical Library Association [5], combines the concepts of health literacy and information literacy. The concept emphasizes the skills and competencies needed to seek health information and acknowledges the abilities to identify information needs, evaluate the relevance of the found information, and use information to make adequate health choices.

Literacy concepts related to health are diverse and often cross boundaries of disciplines and research areas. However, earlier reviews of health related literacy concepts have usually focused on one particular concept, for example health literacy [4, 6] or eHealth literacy [7–9]. In turn, Lawless et al. [10] conducted a concept comparison of health literacy and information literacy. The results show that these concepts share common attributes, but also unique features [10]. Moreover, the authors suggest that there is a need to explore how different literacy concepts approach information [10]. This review fills in this gap in research.

The aim of this systematic review is to synthesize research on health literacy and related phenomena conducted in different disciplines with a focus on the approach to information in the definitions. As the contemporary health information is increasingly digital, studies conducted in online information environments were chosen for this review. The research questions are: (1) What kinds of health literacy concepts are used in different disciplines when studying health related literacy in an online environment? (2) How do these definitions approach information?

2 Methods

This systematic review follows the Preferred Reporting Items for Systematic Reviews and Meta-Analyses, PRISMA [11], when applicable. This review is interpretive [12] with an emphasis on integrating studies across different disciplines to create a synthesis of the data. Researcher triangulation was utilized as the search strategy was developed in collaboration with the first and second author. The first author conducted all the literature searches and the screening and the second author contributed to the screening process.

2.1 Data Sources and Search Strategy

A search strategy was developed to identify articles that focused on health literacy or a related literacy concept in an online health information environment. The literature search was conducted in six academic databases on April 14, 2016. The databases were Library and Information Science Abstracts (LISA), Applied Social Sciences Index and Abstracts (ASSIA), Education Resources Information Center (ERIC), U.S. National

Library of Medicine premier bibliographic database (Medline), Library and Information Science and Technology Abstracts (LISTA), and The Cumulative Index to Nursing and Allied Health Literature (CINAHL). These databases were seen to best represent the topic and were available through the Oulu University Library. The searches were

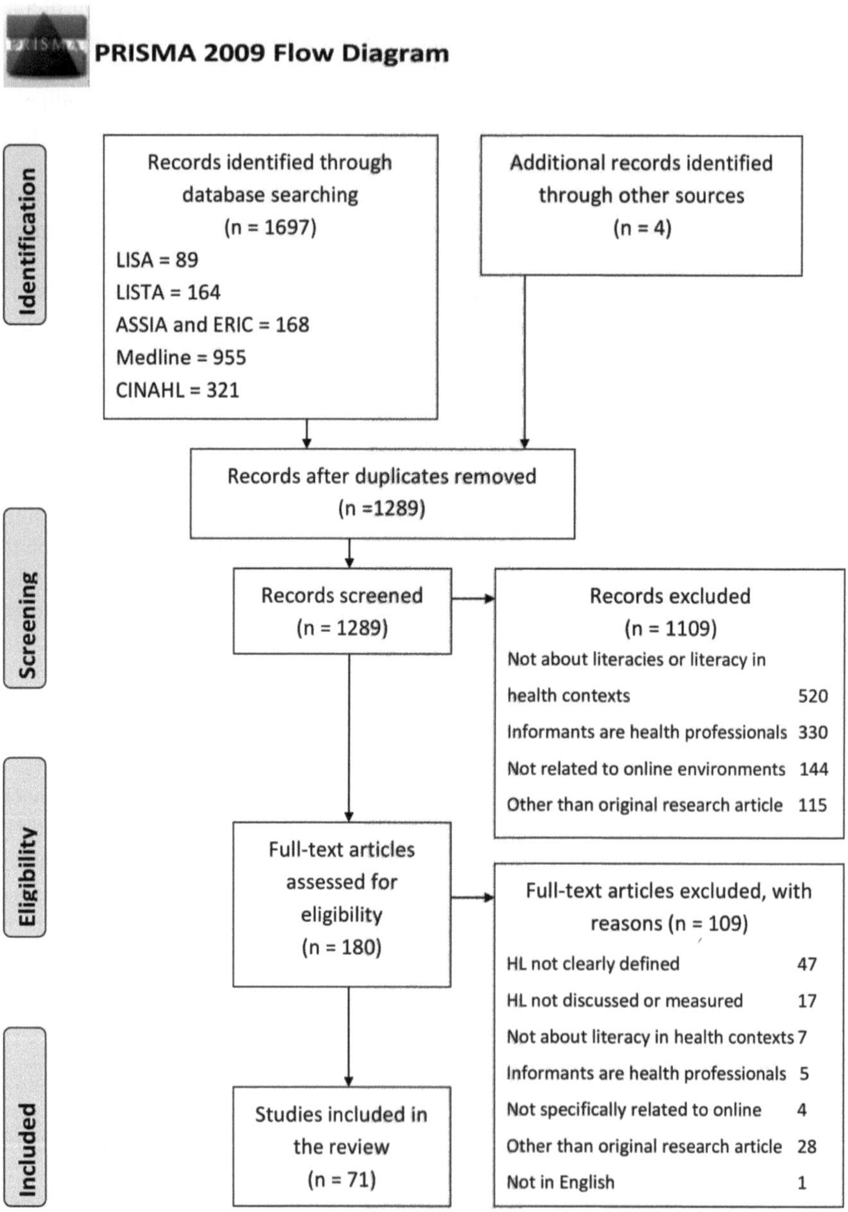

Fig. 1. PRISMA flow diagram [11]

limited to title and abstract and to peer-reviewed articles published in English. A five year time span (from 2011 to 2016) was chosen as the research on online information environments has increased during recent years. The search terms covered three domains, "online", "health" and "literacy", including related terms[1]. Additionally, one academic journal (*Computers in Human Behavior*) was searched manually.

2.2 Study Selection and Analysis of Data

Duplicate references were removed and the titles and abstracts of the articles (n = 1286) screened independently by the first author. The inclusion criteria were discussed and agreed upon by the first and second author. They were set as follows: original research articles written in English, health related literacy as a main topic, lay people as informants, and the context of an online health information environment. A 10% random sample was screened by the second author with an interrater agreement rate of 93%. In total, 180 full-text articles were screened and 109 of them were excluded based on the exclusion criteria presented in the PRISMA flow diagram (Fig. 1). Publication details, discipline of the study (according to the first author's affiliation), and literacy concept with its definition, and other predefined information were extracted from the full-text articles. The analysis focused on the definitions of the concepts that were identified in the eligible articles.

3 Results

3.1 Concepts Related to Health Literacy

In total, 71 eligible articles were included to the review. The articles were from several disciplines but shared a similar focus, namely, to examine health literacy or a related concept in an online information environment. In these articles, eight different literacy concepts were identified with 17 definitions for those concepts (Table 1). The most frequently used concepts were health literacy and eHealth literacy. For the concept of *health literacy,* nine different definitions were identified. Of these the most often referred definition, cited in 26 articles, was the one by Ratzan and Parker [13]. For the concept of *eHealth literacy*, two definitions were identified. Of these, the one initially introduced by Norman and Skinner [14] was referred to in 37 articles.

The majority (n = 41) of the articles represent medical and health sciences, namely, medicine, public health, consumer health, and health education (Table 2). Other fields that were identified are communication and health communication, psychology, library and information science, pharmacy, and sociology or social work.

eHealth literacy as defined by Norman and Skinner [14] (n = 21/41) and health literacy as defined by Ratzan and Parker [13] (n = 12/41) are the most often referred literacy related concepts in medical and health sciences' articles. The concept of eHealth literacy is also most often referred to in the fields of communication and health communication (n = 4/9) and psychology (n = 4/9). In library and information science

[1] Contact the first author for detailed search strategy and full list of reviewed articles.

Table 1. Concepts related to health literacy in the eligible articles (N = 71) and number of articles they are cited in.

The concept	Defined by	Number of articles
Health literacy	World health organization in Nutbeam [15]	4
	World health organization in Nutbeam [16]	1
	Ratzan and Parker [13]	26
	Baker, 2006 [17]	4
	Zarcadoolas et al. [18]	2
	Nutbeam [19]	1
	Berkman et al. [20]	6
	Sørensen et al. [6]	2
	National network of libraries of medicine [21]	1
eHealth literacy	Norman and Skinner [14]	37
	Bodie and Dutta [22]	1
eHealth literacy 2.0	Norman [23]	1
Health information literacy	Medical library association in shipman, Kurtz-Rossi and Funk [5]	1
Everyday health information literacy	Niemelä et al. [24]	1
Mental health literacy	Jorm et al. [25]	3
Oral health literacy	U.S. Department of Health and Human Services [26]	1
"Bad" health literacy	Schulz and Nakamoto [27]	1

Table 2. Represented fields of science (N = 71)

Field of science	Number of articles
Medical and health sciences	41
Communication and health communication	9
Psychology	9
Library and information science	8
Pharmacy	2
Sociology and social work	2

eHealth literacy by Norman and Skinner [14] as well as health literacy by Ratzan and Parker [13] was referred to most often (n = 3/8).

3.2 Definitions of Concepts Related to Health Literacy

Ratzan and Parker [13] define health literacy as "the degree to which individuals have the capacity to obtain, process, and understand basic health information and services needed to make appropriate health decisions". The definition was developed for the U.S. National Library of Medicine and has later been used in several publications promoting public health initiatives (e.g. [28]). The definition focuses on individuals' basic functional health literacy skills, such as reading, writing, and numeracy [4, 29]. Berkman et al. [20] modified the definition by adding to it communication skills, such as listening and speaking.

Health literacy has usually been defined as a set of functional skills [13, 21], although broader perspectives have been introduced. For example, Nutbeam [15, p. 357] defines health literacy as "cognitive and social skills which determine the motivation and ability of individuals to gain access to, understand and use information in ways which promote and maintain good health". Zarcadoolas et al. [18], Sørensen et al. [6], and Nutbeam [16, 19] present health literacy in their definitions as a multidimensional concept that entails a wide range of skills and competencies needed to access, understand, evaluate, and use health information in order to make good judgments and decisions in everyday life to maintain and improve quality of life. Zarcadoolas et al. [18] and Sørensen et al. [6] also suggest that health literacy is a project that can be developed over one's life course.

The concept of eHealth literacy promotes technological skills as part of health literacy. It is originally defined as "the ability to seek, find, understand, and appraise health information from electronic sources and apply the knowledge gained to addressing or solving a health problem" [14]. Bodie and Dutta [22] state that eHealth literacy does not merely refer to searching the Internet for health information, but also entails abilities to understand the found information, evaluate the veracity of this information, discern the quality of different web sites, and use quality information to make informed decisions about health. Norman [23] suggests a concept of *eHealth literacy 2.0* that adds social media related skills to the definition of eHealth literacy. These skills include confidence in expressing oneself clearly in social interactions, ability to synthesize professional and non-professional advice, and comfort and skill in navigating through information found with a mobile device [23].

The concept of *health information literacy* by the Medical Library Association [5] and its re-contextualization *everyday health information literacy* by Niemelä et al. [24] were presented in one article. The concept of health information literacy was developed by combining the concepts of health literacy and information literacy defined by the American Library Association [30] as "a set of abilities requiring individuals to recognize when information is needed and have the ability to locate, evaluate, and use effectively the needed information". Accordingly, health information literacy was defined as "the set of abilities needed to: recognize a health information need; identify likely information sources and use them to retrieve relevant information; assess the quality of the information and its applicability to a specific situation; and analyze, understand, and use the information to make good health decisions." [5, p. 294]. The concept of everyday health information literacy [24, p. 126] sets health information literacy in everyday contexts "as a concept for studying laypersons' general and nonprofessional abilities related to health information."

Other health related literacy concepts that emerged in the articles are mental health literacy, oral health literacy, and "bad" health literacy. The concept of mental health literacy by Jorm et al. [25 p. 182] is defined as "knowledge and beliefs about mental disorders which aid their recognition, management or prevention". The concept of oral health literacy is based on the definition of health literacy by Ratzan and Parker [13].

"Bad" health literacy by Schulz and Nakamoto [27, 31] in turn, refers to "the presence of the ability to understand medical information turned sour by the simultaneous absence of the ability to recognize it as false".

3.3 The Approach to Information in the Definitions of Health Literacy and Related Concepts

The definitions of health literacy and related concepts approach information in different ways. Most of the reviewed definitions presented obtaining information central in gaining an adequate health literacy level. Similar to all of the reviewed definitions is the focus on the ability to understand or comprehend information gained and to utilize the information in a decision-making process. Nutbeam [19] and Sørensen et al. [6] address prior knowledge as an influencing factor when seeking health information. This perspective was absent in other health literacy definitions and in the definitions of eHealth literacy and health information literacy. Critical evaluation of the found information is addressed in four [6, 16, 18, 19] of the nine definitions of health literacy.

The concept of health information literacy emphasizes the information seeking process and, especially, individuals' ability to identify needs for information and potential information sources and to critically assess the relevance of the information gained. The specific attribute of an information need is not addressed in the definitions of health literacy and eHealth literacy. In turn, the critical attribute is addressed in other health literacy concepts such as eHealth literacy by Norman and Skinner [14]. It is especially emphasized in Bodie and Dutta's [22] definition for the same concept.

In the definition of health literacy by Ratzan and Parker [13], health information is understood as basic information that is obtained for decision-making purposes. Other definitions of health literacy, or the definition of health information literacy, do not specify the type of health information that individuals are dealing with. However, the concept of everyday health information literacy specifically addresses health information acquired in everyday life situations. Further, the concept of eHealth literacy was developed to describe the skills needed to engage with online health information [14]. The concepts of mental health literacy and oral health literacy focus on a specific type of health information and the concept of "bad" health information literacy is relevant in the context of false or misleading health information.

4 Discussion

This systematic review shows that several different concepts and definitions are used to examine health literacy or related phenomena in online health information environments. Furthermore, the use of a particular health literacy concept is not restricted to a certain field of science. The most used concepts are health literacy as defined by Ratzan and Parker [13] and eHealth literacy by Norman and Skinner [14]. Surprisingly, these concepts are predominantly used also in the field of library and information science rather than the concept of health information literacy, originally introduced by information science researchers.

The results show that although multidimensional definitions for health literacy have been introduced, the ones used most often in the literature focus on functional skills of an individual. The focus on functional skills in health literacy research and measurement has been criticized because such a perspective does not acknowledge the contextual and societal aspects of literacy (e.g. [4, 29]). It has been suggested that this socio-cultural approach to health literacy research should be focused on as it helps to create wider understanding on the socially derived information practices that facilitate people to become health literate [32]. The wide use of the concept of eHealth literacy since its initiation implies that there is a need to conceptualize the skills and competencies needed to act in online environments.

The approach to information in the examined definitions varies. Common to the definitions is to present information as a tool that helps individuals to make better health decisions or to promote their health. Lawless et al. [10] note that the concepts of health literacy and information literacy have many common characteristics such as the perspective on literacy with multiple dimensions. Unique for the concept of information literacy is the emphasis on search skills, search strategies, and finding information [10]. This perspective can be seen highlighted also in the concept of health information literacy.

In health literacy research the emphasis is on the communication that takes place in health care settings [10] and health information is often seen as medical information obtained through health services (see e.g. [29]). In turn, the concept of eHealth literacy focuses on health information obtained online. Health information literacy research highlights that people seek and use different types of health information from a variety of sources. Critical evaluation of information is included in the definitions of eHealth literacy and health information literacy but in only few of the health literacy definitions. On the other hand, some of the health literacy definitions recognize information seekers' prior knowledge as an influencing factor when obtaining information. In the concept of health information literacy individuals' prior knowledge is seen as the basis for identifying information needs.

As the results show, the different definitions for concepts of health literacy and related concepts overlap, and many similar attributes can be identified in them. Yet, the lack of consistency in defining a certain concept may lead to poor theoretical constructs and difficulties in their operationalization for measurement purposes.

This systematic review is among the first to investigate health literacy concepts across disciplines and as such has its limitations. As the focus of the review was on studies conducted in online information environments, the results do not fully describe the changing phenomena. Other limitations include the search strategy and databases that were used to search literature. These choices had an effect on the type of studies that could be found.

Future studies should critically examine the definitions of health related literacy concepts. The focus of the investigation should be placed on gaining deeper understanding of the different perspectives and science philosophical background assumptions of health literacy and related research. Also, it should examine how the transforming online information environment and practices embedded in it are taken into consideration in the development of health literacy and related concepts.

References

1. Bawden, D., Robinson, L.: The dark side of information: overload, anxiety and other paradoxes and pathologies. J. Inf. Sci. **35**(2), 180–191 (2009)
2. Simonds, S.K.: Health education as social policy. Health Educ. Monogr. **2**, 1–25 (1974)
3. American Medical Association: Council on scientific affairs, ad hoc committee on health literacy. Health literacy: report of the council on scientific affairs. JAMA **281**(6), 552–557 (1999)
4. Mårtensson, L., Hensing, G.: Health literacy – a heterogeneous phenomenon: a literature review. Scand. J. Caring Sci. **26**, 151–160 (2012)
5. Shipman, J.P., Kurtz-Rossi, S., Funk, C.J.: The health information literacy research project. J. Med. Libr. Assoc. **97**(4), 293–301 (2009)
6. Sørensen, K., Van den Brouck, S., Fullam, J., Doyle, G., Pelikan, J., Slonska, Z., Brand, H.: (HLS-EU) consortium health literacy project European: health literacy and public health: a systematic review and integration of definitions and models. BMC Public Health **12**, 80 (2012)
7. Bautista, J.R.: From solving a health problem to achieving quality of life: redefining eHealth literacy. J. Literacy Technol. **16**(2), 33–54 (2015)
8. Gilstad, H.: Toward a comprehensive model of eHealth literacy. In: Jaatun, E.A.A., Brooks, E., Berntsen, K.E., Gilstad, H., Jaatun, M.G. (eds.) Proceedings of the 2nd European Workshop on Practical Aspects of Health Informatics (PAHI 2014), Trondheim Norway, pp. 63–72 (2014)
9. Griebel, L., Enwald, H., Gilstad, H., Pohl, A.-L., Moreland, J., Sedlmayr, M.: eHealth literacy research – Quo vadis? Inf. Health Soc. Care (2017, Epub ahead of print)
10. Lawless, J., Toronto, C.E., Grammatica, G.L.: Health literacy and information literacy: a concept comparison. Ref. Serv. Rev. **44**(2), 144–162 (2016)
11. Moher, D., Liberati, A., Tetzlaff, J., Altman, D.G.: The PRISMA group: preferred reporting items for systematic reviews and meta-analyses: the PRISMA statement. PLoS Med. **6**(7), e1000097 (2009)
12. Harden, A., Thomas, J.: Mixed methods and systematic reviews: examples and emerging issues. In: Tashakkori, A., Teddlie, C. (eds.) SAGE Handbook of Mixed Methods in Social and Behavioral Research, pp. 749–774. SAGE, Thousand Oaks (2010)
13. Ratzan, S.C., Parker, R.M.: Introduction. In: Selden, C.R., Zorn, M., Ratzan, S.C., Parker, R. M. (eds.) National Library of Medicine Current Bibliographies in Medicine: Health Literacy. NLM Pub. No. CBM 2000-1. Bethesda, MD: National Institutes of Health, U.S. Department of Health and Human Services (2000)
14. Norman, C.D., Skinner, H.A.: eHealth literacy: essential skills for consumer health in a networked world. J. Med. Internet Res. **8**, e9 (2006)
15. Nutbeam, D.: Health promotion glossary. Health Promot. Int. **13**(4), 349–364 (1998)
16. Nutbeam, D.: Health literacy as a public health goal: a challenge for contemporary health education and communication strategies into the 21st century. Health Promot. Int. **15**(3), 259–267 (2000)
17. Baker, D.W.: The meaning and the measure of health literacy. J. Gen. Intern. Med. **21**(8), 878–883 (2006)
18. Zarcadoolas, C., Pleasant, A., Greer, D.: Advancing Health Literacy: A Framework for Understanding and Action. Jossey-Bass, San Francisco (2006)
19. Nutbeam, D.: The evolving concept of health literacy. Soc. Sci. Med. **67**, 2072–2078 (2008)
20. Berkman, N.D., Davis, T.C., McCormack, L.: Health literacy: what is it? J. Health Comm. **15**, 9–19 (2010)

21. National Network of Libraries of Medicine: Health literacy. Definition (2013). https://nnlm.gov/professional-development/topics/health-literacy
22. Bodie, G.D., Dutta, M.J.: Understanding health literacy for strategic health marketing: eHealth literacy, health disparities, and the digital divide. Health Mark. Q. **25**(1–2), 175–203 (2008)
23. Norman, C.D.: eHealth literacy 2.0: problems and opportunities with an evolving concept. J. Med. Internet Res. **13**(4), e125 (2011)
24. Niemelä, R., Ek, S., Eriksson-Backa, K., Huotari, M.-L.: A screening tool for assessing everyday health information literacy. Libri. **62**(2), 125–134 (2012)
25. Jorm, A.F., Korten, A.E., Jacomb, P.A., Christensen, H., Rodgers, B., Pollitt, P.: Mental health literacy: a survey of the public's ability to recognise mental disorders and their beliefs about the effectiveness of treatment. Med. J. Aust. **166**(4), 182–186 (1997)
26. U.S. Department of Health and Human Services: Oral health. In: U.S. Department of Health and Human Services (ed.) Healthy People 2010, Washington, DC. U.S. Government Printing Office (2000b)
27. Schulz, P.J., Nakamoto, K.: "Bad" literacy, the internet, and the limits of patient empowerment. In: AAAI Spring Symposium Series: Artificial Intelligence and Health Communication. 2011 March Presented at: AAAI Spring Symposium Series: Artificial Intelligence and Health Communication, Palo Alto, CA, 21–23 March, pp. 65–69 (2011)
28. Nielsen-Bohlman, L., Panzer, A.M., Kindig, D.A.: Health Literacy: A Prescription to End Confusion. National. Academies Press, Washington (2004)
29. Guzys, D., Kenny, A., Dickson-Swift, V., Threlkeld, G.: A critical review of population health literacy assessment. BMC Public Health **15**, 215 (2015)
30. American Library Association. Presidental Committee on Information Literacy. Final report. American Library Association, Chigago (1989). http://www.ala.org/acrl/publications/whitepapers/presidential
31. Allam, A., Schulz, P.J., Nakamoto, K.: The impact of search engine selection and sorting criteria on vaccination beliefs and attitudes: two experiments manipulating Google output. J. Med. Internet Res. **16**(4), e100 (2014)
32. Lloyd, A., Bonner, A., Dawson-Rose, C.: The health information practices of people living with chronic health conditions: implications for health literacy. J. Librariansh. Inf. Sci. **46**(3), 207–216 (2014)

Examining Energy Information Literacy with an Adaptation of the Everyday Health Information Literacy Screening Tool

Teija Keränen[1(✉)], Noora Hirvonen[1,2], and Maija-Leena Huotari[1]

[1] Information Studies, Medical Research Center, University of Oulu, Oulu, Finland
{teija.keranen,noora.hirvonen, maija-leena.huotari}@oulu.fi
[2] Information Studies, Åbo Akademi University, Turku, Finland

Abstract. This study explores energy information literacy by applying an adapted version of an everyday health information literacy (EHIL) screening tool. For this study, the original EHIL tool was modified by adjusting its ten statements to an energy context. Data were collected with an online survey from students present for the academic year in 2016–2017 (n = 11,381) at the University of Oulu. Statistical analyses include an exploratory factor analysis and comparison of mean factor scores. Survey items on respondents' background were also included in the analyses. The response rate was 12.2% (n = 1,390). The screening tool's factorial structure was found to be multifaceted and to resemble that of the original EHIL tool with three factors: motivation ('motivation'), confidence in finding energy information ('confidence'), and perceived ability to evaluate it ('evaluation'). Mean factor scores varied by gender and field of study. The study is among the first to examine energy information literacy.

Keywords: Energy information literacy · Screening tool · Everyday life Health information literacy · Online survey

1 Introduction and Objectives

1.1 The Concept of Energy Information Literacy

Transitions in energy production and consumption are currently taking place on many levels of society. At the same time, global energy demand is increasing and there is a need to mitigate climate change by reducing greenhouse gas emissions. Cleaner, more energy efficient technologies have been developed in recent years and governments have made efforts towards more sustainable paths in energy production [1]. Energy related decisions are made not only on a energy market or policy levels but also on an individual level through choices people make in their everyday lives when acting as energy consumers and, increasingly, producers. The understanding that people develop on energy issues guides these decisions [2]. In this study, we focus on people's abilities to seek, evaluate, and use energy related information in everyday situations and

S. Kurbanoğlu et al. (Eds.): ECIL 2017, CCIS 810, pp. 470–480, 2018.
https://doi.org/10.1007/978-3-319-74334-9_49

introduce the concept of energy information literacy (EIL). Furthermore, we explore the applicability of an everyday health information literacy (EHIL) screening tool adapted to an energy context.

The concept of EIL is connected to energy literacy (EL) which refers to people's skills to make informed energy-related choices. A broadly used definition of EL by DeWaters and Powers [3] consists of cognitive (knowledge), affective (attitudes and values), and behavioural aspects. DeWaters and Powers state that an energy literate individual "has a sound conceptual knowledge base as well as a thorough understanding of how energy is used in everyday life, understands the impact that energy production and consumption have on all spheres of our environment and society, is sympathetic to the need for energy conservation and the need to develop alternatives to fossil fuel-based energy resources, is cognizant of the impact that personal energy-related decisions and actions have on the global community, and – most importantly – strives to make choices and exhibit behaviors that reflect these attitudes with respect to energy resource development and energy consumption" [3, p. 45]. Another related concept is green information literacy which refers to conventional information literacy skills expanded to include sustainable thinking, that is, considering how information behavior, information choices, and information actions influence the environment [4].

Our examination of the concept of energy information literacy is based on an application of the concept of health information literacy that was introduced in the early the 2000's. It was defined as "the set of abilities to recognize a health information need, identify likely information sources and use them to retrieve relevant information, assess the quality of the information and its applicability to a specific situation, and analyze, understand, and use the information to make good health decisions" [5, p. 294]. The definition was framed within two related concepts: health literacy and information literacy. In a similar manner, we propose that the concept of energy information literacy may be used to refer to information literacy in an energy context: to abilities needed to recognize an energy-related information need; identify likely information sources and use them to retrieve relevant information; assess the quality of the information and its applicability to a specific situation; and analyze, understand, and use the information to make good decisions in terms of energy.

While energy literacy refers to energy-raleted knowledge, attitudes, and intentions or behavior [3], energy information literacy emphasizes the meta-cognitive abilities that form the basis for lifelong learning such as being able to locate relevant information and to evaluate and use it effectively (see [6]). These abilities can be considered especially important in the contemporary, constantly changing information environment. For a long time, the concept of information literacy was mainly applied in educational settings. More recently, the focus of information literacy research has expanded to everyday life context as well. Yet, there is still a significant gap in this area of research [7].

1.2 Assessment of Energy Information Literacy

Energy literacy has been assessed based on self-reported behaviour and energy literacy tests, namely, what people say, do, and know [8]. Mainly it has been evaluated quantitatively and from the perspective of rational decision-making in energy related issues [9] or as the ability to evaluate energy use of household appliances [10]. Target groups have been, for example, middle school and high school students [3] or households [9].

In the context of health, Niemelä et al. [11] designed an everyday health information literacy (EHIL) screening tool based on the Medical Library Association's definition of health information literacy. The screening tool was meant to detect individuals or groups with problems related to their interest and motivation, finding, understanding, evaluating, or using health information, but being literate at the average level (being able to read). The tool consist of ten statements (EHIL1–EHIL10) to which participants are asked to respond in a scale from 1 (strongly disagree) to 5 (strongly agree). The tool was found to have a multifaceted structure with three factors: motivation to seek information ('motivation', EHIL1, EHIL3, EHIL2, EHIL9), confidence in finding information ('confidence', EHIL10, EHIL8, EHIL5, EHIL4), and perceived abilities to evaluate information ('evaluation', EHIL7, EHIL6) [11, 12].

1.3 Objectives

To our knowledge, this study is among the first to examine energy information literacy. It aims at exploring energy information literacy by applying an adapted version of the EHIL screening tool. The research questions are set as follows:

Q1: What is the factorial structure of the everyday energy information literacy (EEIL) screening tool?
Q2: Do mean factor scores vary across respondents' background variables?

2 Method

2.1 Data Collection

The data were collected with an online survey sent to all students present for the academic year 2016–2017 at the University of Oulu, Finland, in January 2017 (n = 11,381). The response rate was 12.2% (n = 1,390). The original EHIL screening tool was modified to an everyday energy information literacy (EEIL) screening tool by adjusting its ten statements to an energy context:

EEIL1. It is important to be informed about energy issues.
EEIL2. I know where to seek energy information.
EEIL3. I like to get energy information from a variety of sources.
EEIL4. It is difficult to find energy information from printed sources (magazines and books).
EEIL5. It is difficult to find energy information from the Internet.
EEIL6. It is easy to assess the reliability of energy information in printed sources (magazines and books).
EEIL7. It is easy to assess the reliability of energy information on the Internet.
EEIL8. Energy related terminology and statements are often difficult to understand.

EEIL9. I apply energy related information to my own life and/or that of people close to me.

EEIL10. It is difficult to know who to believe in energy issues.

The respondents were provided with a short definition of energy by explaining that, in this context, energy refers to energy used by households mainly for lighting and warming as well as energy used by traffic and industry.

Also, questions gathered demographic items on the respondents' backgrounds. The respondents were asked about their year of birth, gender, highest education, work situation, income, major field of study, and whether their studies relate to the energy industry or electricity market. Further, they were asked about their place of residence, the type of house or appartment they lived in, home ownership, and living arrangements.

2.2 Data Analysis

The internal consistency of the 10-item everyday energy information literacy screening tool was analysed using unstandardised Cronbach's alpha. The principal component analysis was chosen as the extraction method in the exploratory factor analyses because the aim was to describe the factorial structure of the screening tool. According to the Kaiser-Guttman-criterion, all factors with an eigenvalue of >1 were extracted. To improve the interpretability of the extracted factors, an orthogonal rotation (Varimax criterion) technique was applied, yielding statistically independent factors.

Mean factor scores were calculated with the regression method, and one-way analyses of variance (ANOVA), and independent samples t-tests were performed to examine whether the mean factor scores varied across demographic variables and respondents' field of study. The relationship between factor scores and respondents' background variables were analysed with analysis of variance (ANOVA) using standardized factor scores where the mean is set to 0 and standard deviation to 1. Thus, a negative value refers to below the mean and a positive value to above the mean factor score. Standardized mean factor scores are presented in homogenous subsets: each subset comprises a set of means that do not differ from each other significantly (Tables 3 and 4 in the Results section). Statistical analyses were performed using the IBM Statistical Package for the Social Sciences (SPSS) version 22.0.

3 Results

3.1 Respondents' Characteristics

The respondents' mean age was 28.1 years and 57.0% (n = 785) were female. The majority of the repondents were full-time students (n = 923, 66.5%), lived in a city with a population over 50,000 (n = 1212, 87.3%), lived in a rental apartment (n = 1078, 77.6% and had less than a 2,000 euro monthly household income (n = 866, 62.6). Nearly half (n = 594, 42.8%) lived alone and 39.6% (n = 550) in a household of two people. The respondents had majors in the Faculty of Natural Sciences (n = 249, 17.9%), Humanities (n = 229, 16.5%), Educational Sciences (n = 214, 15.4%),

Medicine (n = 206, 14.8%), Engineering (n = 179, 12.9%), Information Technology and Electrical Engineering (n = 122, 8.8%), Business (n = 98, 7.0%) and other faculties (Architecture n = 36, 2.6%; Biochemistry and Molecular Medicine n = 20, 1.4%; Mining School n = 27, and 1.9%, other n = 8, 0.6%). Of the respondents 13.2% (n = 183) reported to have studies related to energy industry or electricity market, and 44.7% (n = 621) already had an academic degree.

3.2 The Factorial Strucure of the EEIL Screening Tool

The internal consistency of the 10-item everyday energy information literacy (EEIL) screening tool was evaluated with Cronbach's alpha and it was .701. The Kaiser-Meyer-Olkin measure of sampling adequacy value was .735, indicating that the samples were adequate to consider the data as normally distributed. Barlett's test of sphericity was significant ($p < .001$). The screening tool's factorial structure was found to be multifaceted (see Table 1). Three factors were indentified and labeled as follows (labels in parenthesis): confidence in finding and understanding information ('confidence'), motivation to do so ('motivation'), and perceived ability to evaluate information ('evaluation').

Table 1. Results of exploratory factor analyses (rotated component matrix) of data collected from Finnish university school students (n = 1,390). For the purpose of clarity, only factor loadings >.50 are printed in the table.

Component		1	2	3
Confidence	EEIL2 I know where to seek energy information	−.656		
	EEIL4. It is difficult to find energy information from printed sources (magazines and books)	.633		
	EEIL5. It is difficult to find energy information from the Internet	.730		
	EEIL8. Energy related terminology and statements are often difficult to understand	.637		
Motivation	EEIL1. It is important to be informed about energy issue		.774	
	EEIL3. I like to get energy information from a variety of sources		.761	
	EEIL9. I apply energy related information to my own life and/or that of people close to me		.687	
Evaluation	EEIL6. It is easy to assess the reliability of energy information in printed sources (magazines and books)			.797
	EEIL7. It is easy to assess the reliability of energy information on the Internet			.785
	EEIL10. It is difficult to know who to believe in energy issues			−.597
	Total variance explained	55.7%		

Table 2. Descriptive statistics for the three everyday energy information literacy factors.

	No. of items	M (SD)	Skewness	Kurtosis	Alpha
Confidence	4	3.47 (.53)	−.124	−.233	.641
Motivation	3	3.73 (.71)	−.408	−.050	.599
Evaluation	3	2.92 (.70)	−.024	−.3027	.618

As can be seen in Table 2, mean factor scores were the lowest for 'evaluation' and the highest for 'motivation' in the whole sample. In further analysis, standardized mean factor scores are used (regression method).

3.3 Differences by Respondents' Background

Significant age differences were found in mean factor scores for 'motivation' and 'evaluation'. Older students (>25 years) had higher scores in 'motivation' but lower scores in 'evaluation' when compared to younger students (<25 years) (see Table 3).

Table 3. Standardized mean factor scores (regression method) by age in homogenous subsets.

Age	N	Subset for alpha = 0.05			F, p*
		Factor 1: confidence			1.68, .169
25–30	324	.092			
23–25	279	.015			
>30	333	−.008			
<23	433	−.072			
		Factor 2: motivation			8.95, <.001
23–25	279	−.162			
<23	433	−.093	−.093		
25–30	324		.049	.049	
>30	333			.209	
		Factor 3: evaluation			4.67, .003
>30	333	−.160			
25–30	324	−.004	−.004		
23–25	279	.025	.025		
<23	433			.110	

*ANOVA; Tukey HSD. Uses Harmonic Mean Sample Size = 333,803; the group sizes are unequal; the harmonic mean of the group size is used; type I error levels are not guaranteed.

Male students' mean factor scores were higher in 'confidence' (M = 0.413 vs. M = −0.300, t(1290) = 13.653, p < 0.001) and lower in 'motivation' (M = −0.060 vs. M = 0.060, t(1290) = 2.193, p = 0.028) when compared to female students. The difference was not significant in 'evaluation' (M = 0.055 vs. M = −0.049, t (1290) = −1.906, p = 0.066).

The humanities' and educational sciences' students had the lowest and engineering students the highest mean factor scores for 'confidence' (Table 4). Natural sciences' and engineering students, and students in other fields (architecture, biochemistry and

Table 4. Mean factor scores by students' (n = 1,390) field of study.

Faculty	N	Subset for alpha = 0.05*				F, p**
		Factor 1: Confidence				18.2, <.001
Education	214	−.376				
Humanities	225	−.289	−.289			
Other	90	−.155	−.155			
Natural Sci.	247		.003	.003		
Medicine	202		.030	.030		
Business	97			.211		
Info. Techn. & Electrical Engineering	115			.348		
Engineering	177				.516	
		Factor 2: Motivation				3.32; .002
Info. Techn. & Electrical Engineering	115	−.315				
Business	97	−.198				
Humanities	225	−.030	−.030			
Education	214	−.012	−.012			
Medicine	202	.019	.019			
Engineering	177	.113	.113			
Natural Sci.	247		.122			
Other	90		.130			
		Factor 3: Evaluation				
Business	97	−.179				2.37, .021
Medicine	202	−.107	−.107			
Education	214	−.072	−.072			
Humanities	225	−.040	−.040			
Info. Techn. & Electrical Engineering	115	−.020	−.020			
Other	90	.049	.049			
Natural Sci.	247	.108	.108			
Engineering	177		.192			

*Mean factor scores (regression method) **ANOVA; Tukey HSD, means for groups in homogenous subsets are displayed. Uses Harmonic Mean Sample Size = 333,803; the group sizes are unequal; the harmonic mean of the group size is used; type I error levels are not guaranteed.

molecular medicine, mining school, and non-specified) had the highest mean factor scores both in 'evaluation' and 'motivation'. Business school and information technology and electrical engineering students, in turn, received the lowest scores in 'motivation'. Students in business school and medicine received the lowest scores in 'evaluation'.

Further, there were significant differences in mean scores for each factor based on whether a respondent's studies related to energy industry or electricity market or not. Those whose studies were related to these issues ($n = 181$) received higher mean factor scores in 'motivation' ($M = 0.245$ vs. $M = -0.053$, $t(1290) = 3.728$, $p < 0.001$), 'evaluation' ($M = 0.198$ vs. $M = -0.023$, $t(1290) = 2.767$, $p = 0.007$), as well as 'confidence' ($M = 0.312$ vs. $M = -0.055$, $t(1290) = 4.630$, $p < 0.001$).

4 Discussion

The everyday energy information literacy (EEIL) screening tool's factorial structure was found to be multifaceted. It resembled that of the original everyday health information literacy (EHIL) screening tool and its three factors: motivation and confidence in finding information ('motivation', 'confidence'), and perceived ability to evaluate it ('evaluation') [12]. Also some differences were found. In the original EHIL tool, EHIL2, 'I know where to seek health information', was included in 'motivation'. In the present study, in turn, a similar statement in an energy context, EEIL2, was included in the factor labeled 'confidence'. EHIL10, 'It is difficult to know who to believe in health issues', was included in 'confidence' in earlier studies in health context, whereas in the context of energy EEIL10, 'It is difficult to know who to believe in energy issues', was part of 'evaluation'.

The factor scores were found to vary by gender, age, and field of study. Older students had higher mean scores in 'motivation' and lower mean scores in 'evaluation' when compared to younger students. Similarly, in a study on everyday health information literacy, older adults were found to be more motivated to seek health information but less confident in their abilities to determine who to believe in health issues and understanding terminology when compared to younger people [13]. In a study on energy literacy by DeWaters and Powers [3], high-school students had more positive attitudes and values toward energy issues than middle-school students. However, in behavioral items the result was the opposite: middle-school students were more likely to attend to energy saving [3].

Educational level has been found to be connected to energy literacy [3] as well as to health information literacy [15] in earlier studies. In the present study, the study population was homogeneous in terms of its educational level, namely, they were all university students. However, their EEIL scores were examined based on their field of study and some differences were found. The engineering students had high mean factor scores for all three factors. Also natural sciences' students had high mean factor scores for 'evaluation' and 'motivation' as well as students categorized in the 'other' category. The humanities' and educational sciences' students, in turn, had the lowest scores for 'confidence'. The business school students had relatively low scores in both 'motivation' and 'evaluation'. Also students in information technology and electrical engineering received low scores in 'motivation', and medical students, in turn, in 'evaluation'.

Further, significant differences were found in mean scores for each factor based on whether a respondent's studies related to energy industry or electricity market or not. These findings indicate that students whose studies involve energy related issues are more likely to be motivated to seek for energy information, and confident in their abilities to find and evaluate the information. In a study by Cotton and colleagues [14], a large proportion of students in Architecture, Design, and Environment, Geography, Earth, and Environmental Science as well as Marine Science and Engineering considered themselves as experts or quite knowledgeable in energy issues. In turn, students in Nursing and Midwifery, Social Science and Social Work, and Psychology were less confident in their energy knowledge [14].

In this study, male students' scores were higher in 'confidence' and lower in 'motivation' when compared to female students. In a similar vein, men scored higher in energy literacy tests based on knowledge [14] and women, in turn, had better scores in energy related values, attitudes, and self-efficacy [3]. Interestingly, in a study by Cotton and colleagues [14], male respondents were more likely to cite the Internet as important in contributing their understanding of energy issues, while female respondents found TV, friends, and family as important energy information sources. Also in studies on everyday health information literacy, men, and especially young men, have been found to have lower motivation than women to seek information [13]. Gender differences could be expected to explain some of the educational differences since in some fields the gender distribution tends to be rather uneven. In this study, the Educational Sciences' and Humanities' students were predominantly women and the students in Engineering and Information Technology and Electrical Engineering predominantly men. This reflects the student body at the University of Oulu. However, although male students in general were less motivated to seek for energy information than female students, engineering students received high mean factor scores in 'motivation'.

The results are indicative and should be replicated in other populations. Further, everyday energy information literacy should be studied in connection to energy consumption and production actions as well as attitudes. Information literacy is not important only in education but these competencies also guide everyday decisions. Therefore, everyday information literacy in diffent settings deserves to be examined further.

5 Conclusions

To our knowledge, this study is among the first to propose and examine the concept of energy information literacy (EIL). Moreover, the study contributes to further modification of the everyday health information literacy (EHIL) screening tool to other contexts, in this case, the context of energy. The factorial structure of the everyday energy information litracy screening tool is similar to that of the everyday health information literacy screening tool with three factors: motivation and confidence in finding information ('motivation', 'confidence'), and perceived ability to evaluate it ('evaluation'). Moreover, significant differences in factor scores were found based on respondents' background, namely, gender and field of study. These findings indicate that this screening tool has potential to be applied in the context of energy and to be further transfered to other contexts as well. The tool can be used to detect individuals or groups who lack motivation or have difficulties in finding or evaluating information on a topic. Information and guidance may be tailored to better match people's needs based on the responses to the tool's statements.

Acknowledgements. The study is funded by the Strategic Research Council, Finland, Project n:o 292854.

References

1. International Energy Agency: Energy and Climate Change. World Energy Outlook Special Report 1 (2015). https://www.iea.org/publications/freepublications/publication/WEO2015SpecialReportonEnergyandClimateChange.pdf
2. Stern, P.C.: Individual and household interactions with energy systems: toward integrated understanding. Energy Res. Soc. Sci. **1**, 41–48 (2014)
3. DeWaters, J.E., Powers, S.E.: Energy literacy of secondary students in New York State (USA): a measure of knowledge, affect, and behavior. Energy Policy **39**(3), 1699–1710 (2011)
4. Kurbanoğlu, S., Boustany, J.: From green libraries to green information literacy. In: Kurbanoğlu, S., Špiranec, S., Grassian, E., Mizrachi, D., Catts, R. (eds.) ECIL 2014. CCIS, vol. 492, pp. 47–58. Springer, Cham (2014). https://doi.org/10.1007/978-3-319-14136-7_6
5. Shipman, J.P., Kurtz-Rossi, S., Funk, C.J.: The health information literacy research project. J. Med. Libr. Assoc. **97**(4), 293–301 (2009)
6. American Library Association: Presidential Committee on Information Literacy: Final Report (1989). http://www.ala.org/acrl/publications/whitepapers/presidential
7. Martzoukou, K., Sayyad, A.E.: Towards an everyday life information literacy mind-set: a review of literature. J. Doc. (in press)
8. Sovacool, B.K., Blyth, P.L.: Energy and environmental attitudes in green state of denmark: implications for energy democracy, low carbon transitions, and energy literacy. Environ. Sci. Policy **54**, 304–315 (2015)
9. Brounen, D., Kok, N., Quigley, J.M.: Energy literacy, awareness, and conservation behavior of residential households. Energy Econ. **38**, 42–50 (2013)
10. Attari, S.Z., DeKay, M.L., Davidson, C.I., Bruine de Bruin, W.: Public perceptions of energy consumption and savings. Proc. Natl. Acad. Sci. U.S.A. **107**(37), 16054–16059 (2010)
11. Niemelä, R., Ek, S., Eriksson-Backa, K., Huotari, M.-L.: A screening tool for assesing everyday health information literacy. Libri **62**(2), 125–134 (2012)
12. Hirvonen, N., Enwald, H., Nengomasha, C., Abankwah, R., Uutoni, W.U., Korpelainen, R., Pyky, R., Huotari, M.-L., Mayer, A.-K.: Validating the factorial structure of the everyday health information literacy screening tool in three different populations. In: ISIC: The Information Behvaiour Conference, University of Zadar, Croatia, 20–23 September. Extended Abstract for a Poster (2016)
13. Enwald, H., Hirvonen, N., Huotari, M.-L., Korpelainen, R., Pyky, R., Savolainen, M., Salonurmi, T., Keränen, A.-M., Jokelainen, T., Niemelä, R.: Everyday heath information literacy among young men compared to adults with high risk for metabolic syndrome – a cross-sectional population-based study. J. Inf. Sci. **42**(3), 344–355 (2016)

14. Cotton, D.R.E., Miller, W., Winter, J., Bailey, I., Sterling, S.: Developing students' energy literacy in higher education. Int. J. Sustain. High. Educ. **16**(4), 456–473 (2015)
15. Hirvonen, N., Niemelä, R., Ek, S., Korpelainen, R., Huotari, M.-L.: Socio-demographic characteristics associated with the everyday health information literacy of young men. Inf. Res. **20**(1) (2015). paper: isic25

Subjective and Objective Measures of Health Information Literacy: Do They Provide Complementary or Redundant Information?

Anne-Kathrin Mayer(✉)

ZPID - Leibniz Institute for Psychology Information, Trier, Germany
mayer@zpid.de

Abstract. The present study examines the psychometric properties and the usefulness of the Health Information Literacy Knowledge Test (HILK), a 24 item multiple-choice test which aims at assessing knowledge related to determining a health information need, searching and accessing information, and evaluating its relevance and quality. 144 German university students completed the HILK together with established subjective measures of health (information) literacy and health status. Correlations of the HILK with subjective measures were at least marginally significant, supporting the assumption that both types of measures assess related constructs. In multiple regression analyses, HILK scores predicted mental and physical health status while there were no associations between subjective health (information) literacy with both health measures. It is concluded that the HILK is a research tool which complements subjective assessments of health literacy and might even be more useful when it comes to predicting health outcomes.

Keywords: Health information literacy · Health literacy · Assessment Health status · Questionnaires · Knowledge tests

1 Introduction

Participating actively in health decisions requires individuals to obtain information from multiple sources, to evaluate it and to relate it to their life situation. The concept "health information literacy" has been introduced to denote the comprehensive set of abilities that enables individuals to specify their health information needs and to seek, retrieve, evaluate, and use health information to make adequate health decisions [1]. As explained by Niemelä and collegues [2], health information literacy combines two concepts from different research traditions, namely "health literacy" [3] and "information literacy" [4]. Thus, research may draw on theorizing from both fields. While numerous studies in medical sciences, public health, information sciences, and psychology have provided evidence for associations of the broader concept "health literacy" with health outcomes, the use of health care services, and health cost [5], research on "health *information* literacy" is still in its infancy although interest in this set of knowledge and skills has considerably increased during the last two decades. A search in the PUBMED database

S. Kurbanoğlu et al. (Eds.): ECIL 2017, CCIS 810, pp. 481–490, 2018.
https://doi.org/10.1007/978-3-319-74334-9_50

with "health AND information AND literacy" as a combined search term yielded 364 documents published in 2000–2005, 865 documents published in 2005–2010, and 340 documents published in 2011 and the first four months of 2012 [6].

Still, there is a lack of empirical findings regarding the concept and its relations to health outcomes which may partly be attributed to problems with measurement, particularly to the lack of assessment tools [7]. To measure an individuals' amount of health literacy, an almost unmanageable number of instruments has been used [8, 9], many of them including relevant facets of health information literacy. Particularly for the assessment of "everyday health information literacy", a screening tool was developed which includes questions about individuals' competence and motivation to deal with health information [2]. However, all these tools only capture self-reports about the general or illness-specific ability to deal with health information. While such subjective measures are usually characterized by high reliability, their validity has often been questioned. Generally, subjective or "perception-based" assessments of abilities often do not correlate with "objective" or "performance-based" indicators of the respective abilities, i.e. with the results of achievement or knowledge tests [7, 10, 11].[1] Especially individuals with low competences and – at the same time – little experience with their use tend to overestimate their abilities [12]. Therefore, questionnaires are only of limited suitability for the valid assessment of competences.

On the other hand, commonly used objective health literacy measures like the Test of Functional Health Literacy in Adults [13] the Rapid Estimate of Adult Literacy in Medicine [14] or the Newest Vital Sign [15] have also been criticized because they only reflect the basic verbal and numerical skills needed to read and understand health information ("functional health literacy"; [16]) but fail to reveal individual differences in more advanced knowledge and skills making up health information literacy. Only a few objective tests have been developed to assess more advanced competences which are necessary for processing information in research contexts but are irrelevant or overly demanding for individuals without medical and statistical education [17, 18].

Therefore, the Health Information Literacy Knowledge Test (HILK) was developed to fill in the gap between measures assessing basic functional skills and advanced research-related information-seeking and evaluation skills. The HILK is a standardized multiple choice-test which aims at assessing self-reports of knowledge about health information seeking and evaluations of everyday health information from sources like newspapers, brochures, books or websites which are (also) designed for people without academic background. It is assumed that this knowledge is needed to systematically plan and conduct information searches and to evaluate the results of these searches, thus forming the basis of development of the respective skills. The present paper reports on the construction of the test and presents findings on its reliability and usefulness in a sample of university students from non-medical domains.

---

[1] In this paper, I will use the terms "subjective" versus "objective" measures as synonyms to "perception-based" versus "performance-based" measures [7].

1.1 Construction of the Health Information Literacy Knowledge Test (HILK)

The construction of the HILK is based on the premise that it is possible to decompose the process of seeking and evaluating health information into a sequence of steps which has to be passed through (sometimes repeatedly) until individuals either feel that their information need is basically satisfied or decide to abort the process for other reasons. Thus, descriptive process models from general information literacy research were screened for their applicability and relevance in the health context. Finally, the decision was made to derive the skill decomposition underlying the test from the well-established Big6 skills approach [19] which is sufficiently validated and precise to derive assumptions about the subskills which should be included in the HILK. Two of the Big6 skills ("Synthesis" and "Evaluation") were not included as they refer to skills which are predominantly needed in the academic context and are difficult to tap by means of a standardized knowledge test.

In addition, the Information Problem-Solving Model (IPS; [20]) appeared fruitful for our analysis of subskills because it includes a distinction between getting a "rough" overview of quality and relevance of an information source ("scanning") and analyzing information in more detail and depth (evaluating). While the latter step is doubtlessly central to understanding health information, the former is important to quickly decide whether a source is worth to be considered in detail or should be abandoned because of irrelevance or insufficient quality. Thus, knowledge and skills related to the step of "scanning" are essential to manage the huge amount of information available (particularly on the internet), and, thus, will help to prevent individuals from experiencing "health information overload" [21]. Based on these considerations, we ended up with a skill decomposition which comprises four skills with two subskills each:

(1) **Specification of information need** (Define information problem; Identify information needed),
(2) **Planning the search** (Know available resources; Determine search strategy),
(3) **Locating and accessing information** (Identify type of source; Access source),
(4) **Scanning information** (Assess relevance and quality; Orient within source).

A pool of 57 initial multiple choice-items was constructed covering each subskill with at least four items. Each item consists of a question, and –for some items– supplementary materials. Items require participants, for example, to recognize adequate sources to satisfy an information need, or to evaluate health materials (e.g., snapshots of websites or extracts from books) with regard to their relevance or quality. For each item, three answer options are provided. In most items, participants have to evaluate each option separately (see Fig. 1 for a sample item). The number of "true" options ranges from none to three. In the remaining items, participants are required to select one of the three options as the "best" or "correct" answer or mark the item with "don't know". Item scores are calculated as the proportion of options marked correctly, and the total score is computed as the arithmetic mean of all item scores, ranging from 0 to 1.

Which of the following aspects point(s) to the appraisal that a specific internet board/forum on health is a reliable discussion platform?			
	Does apply	**Does not apply**	**Don´t know**
(a) The board is provided by an approved organization (e.g., a university or a patient organization).	□	□	□
(b) Medical experts (e.g., physicians) take care of board.	□	□	□
(c) The board explicitly points to the fact that internet information cannot replace seeing a physician.	□	□	□

Fig. 1. Sample item of the HILK test (options a, b, and c should be marked as "does apply")

To test the quality of the scoring key and to clarify item wording if necessary, an "expert study" was conducted. 11 psychologists with experience in information literacy research worked on the preliminary item pool. Four items were dropped from the item pool because experts did not reach acceptable consensus (>80%) about the correct options, and minor changes to item wording were made. The resulting 53-item pilot version of the HILK was applied in two studies (Study 1: 138 psychology students; Study 2: 99 students of law and economics) to shorten the test. Based on results of exploratory factor analyses, item analyses and semantic considerations related to content validity, the instrument was reduced to a 24-item version. In this version, each of the subskills listed above is represented by at least one item.

1.2 Hypotheses and Research Questions

The present study seeks to provide empirical evidence for the reliability and validity as well as the usefulness of the HILK in sample of university students from non-medical domains. Thus, three research questions and four hypotheses are pursued.

Adequate reliability or precision of measurement is a prerequisite for the use of a test. A common presumption among researchers is that a research tool should show an internal consistency (Cronbachs alpha) of at least alpha = .70. Therefore, the first research question is:

Research Question 1. Does the HILK show adequate reliability?

The second research question refers to the validity of the HILK, and, thus, to the question whether the test measures what it intends to measure:

Research Question 2. Does the HILK show adequate validity?

To answer this question, the HILK scores would preferably be related to other validated *objective* measures of health information literacy, like other knowledge or achievement tests. However, as mentioned in Sect. 1.1, no such measures exist, and the available health literacy test are inappropriate for this purpose because they are unable to uncover individual differences in well-educated samples or because they were developed for individuals with medical and statistical education [17, 18]. Thus, in the present sample, only associations of the HILK with established *subjective* measures of health information literacy and the related construct of health literacy were examined. As discussed above, associations between questionnaires and achievement tests related to the same competences are usually weak [10, 11]. Still, we assumed that:

Hypothesis 1. Higher health information literacy knowledge is associated with higher levels of subjective health information literacy **(Hypothesis 1a)**, and subjective health literacy **(Hypothesis 1b)**.
A third research question refers to the usefulness of the HILK:

Research Question 3. Is the HILK a useful test in the sense that it provides information about the level of health information literacy which is not already provided by questionnaire measures?

To give an answer to this question, the predictive value of objective and subjective health (information) literacy measures for participants' current physical and mental health status was analyzed. If the HILK is a nonredundant measure of health information literacy, it should possess incremental validity, which means that

Hypothesis 2. HILK scores explain additional variance in measures of (a) mental as well as (b) physical health when the subjective level of health information literacy is controlled for.

2 Methods

2.1 Participants and Procedure

Participants were 144 German university students (80.5% humanities or languages, 19.5% mathematics or computer sciences) aged between 18 and 33 years ($M = 23.40$, $SD = 2.96$); 69% of them were female. Data collection took place in supervised group sessions in the university's computer labs. Participation in the studies was voluntary; participants were financially compensated.

2.2 Measures

The 24-item final version of the HILK was used as an objective assessment of health information literacy. For the subjective assessment of health (information) literacy, three self-report questionnaires were used: The Everyday Health Information Literacy Screening Tool (EHIL; [2]) comprises 10 statements referring to an individual's ability and motivation to search, evaluate, understand, and use health information from different sources. Participants indicate their agreement with the items on a 5-point Likert scale.[2] The eHealth Literacy Scale (eHEALS; [22, 23]) aims at assessing health literacy related to the use of electronic sources. The scale comprises eight items which are answered on

[2] The tool was translated into German independently by two researchers (the author and a PhD student), and discrepancies were resolved by discussion. An English native speaker then back-translated the test which lead to minor refinements of wording.

a 5-point Likert scale. In addition, the European Health Literacy Survey (HLS-EU-Q47; [24]) was administered. 47 statements describing health-related behaviors are rated with reference to their perceived difficulty on a 4 point scale. From the answers, a health literacy index comprising all 47 items is computed.

Finally, as a measure of subjective health status, the German Health Survey – Short Form (SF-12; [25]) was used. The SF-12 is a self-report questionnaire which comprises 12 questions referring to various aspects of health-related quality of life (e.g., subjective evaluations of overall health status or the ability to perform specific social and physical activities). By aggregating weighted item scores based on the scoring algorithm provided by Bullinger and Kirchberger [25], two measures are derived, representing self-assessments of physical health (PH) and mental health (MH).

3 Results

HILK total scores varied between .36 and .86. Together with the arithmetic mean of $M = 0.63$ (standard deviation $SD = 0.11$), this indicates that the test has medium difficulty and is able to differentiate between levels of health information literacy in well-educated samples. To answer Research Question 1, reliability estimates were computed by the statistical software R using the "psych" and "userfriendlyscience" packages. For Cronbach's Alpha, a value of 0.78 (95% confidence interval: 0.73 – 0.83) emerged which may be interpreted as adequate for a research tool. However, as is generally known, Cronbach's Alpha has many drawbacks [26]: The coefficient is only a consistent estimator of the population internal consistency when certain rigid assumptions are met. Particularly the assumption of unidimensionality may not be taken for granted as the test covers a heterogenous domain of knowledge and, thus, may include several subdimensions. Revelle's Omega which does not rely on the assumption of unidimensionality, yielded a value of .80 which is also in the adequate range.

With reference to Research Questions 2 and 3, first intercorrelations of all measures were computed with SPSS (Version 23). The correlation coefficients as well as descriptive statistics of all measures are reported in Table 1. While the self-report questionnaires were highly intercorrelated, their correlations with the HILK were smaller but at least marginally significant, confirming Hypothesis 1a and b.

Table 1. Descriptive statistics, reliabilities, and intercorrelations of the health (information) literacy measures.

	M(SD)	HILK	EHIL	e-HEALS	HLS-EU-Q47
HILK	0.63 (0.11)	–	$.22^{**}$	$.13^{+}$	$.13^{+}$
EHIL	3.41 (0.44)	–	–	.52***	$.57^{***}$
eHEALS	3.33 (0.59)	–	–	–	$.44^{***}$
HLS-EU-Q47	33.39 (6.22)	–	–	–	–
SF-12 (MH)	42.07 (10.90)	$.20^{**}$	.06	−.04	$.11^{+}$
SF-12 (PH)	53.62 (6.16)	$.15^{*}$	−.04	.00	.00

$^{***}p < .001$; $^{**}p < .01$; $^{+}p < .10$ (one-tailed)

The multivariate associations between subjective and objective health (information) literacy, and health (see Hypothesis 2a and b) were examined in two multiple blockwise regression analyses with mental health and physical health as dependent variables. In the first block of the regression, the three subjective measures were entered as predictors into the regression equation.[3] In the second block, the HILK score was added. Mental health could not be predicted by the subjective health literacy measures in the first block of the analysis. Including the HILK in Block 2 lead to an increase of explained variance by 3.5% ($F = 4.96$, df 1/135, $p < .05$), resulting in an overall marginal significance of the regression (see Table 2, upper panel).

Table 2. Results of blockwise multiple regression analyses predicting mental and physical health from health ınformation literacy and health literacy measures.

Predictor	*b*	SE(*b*)	β	*t*
Dependent variable: SF-12 mental health ($R^2 = 0.060$, $F[4, 135] = 2.14$, $p < .10$)				
Constant	28.97	8.30		3.49^{**}
EHIL	.39	2.74	.02	.14
eHEALS	−2.61	1.86	−.14	−1.40
HLS-EU-Q47	.23	.19	.13	1.25
HILK	20.06	9.01	.19	2.23^{*}
Dependent variable: SF-12 physical health ($R^2 = 0.028$, $F[4, 135] = 0.961$, $p = .341$)				
Constant	50.97	4.77		10.69^{***}
EHIL	−1.45	1.57	−.10	−.92
eHEALS	.21	1.07	.02	.20
HLS-EU-Q47	.03	.11	.03	.25
HILK	9.50	5.17	.16	1.84^{+}

$^{***}p < .001$; $^{**}p < .01$; $^{*}p < .05$; $^{+}p < .10$
Note. b = unstandardized regression weight, SE(b) = standard error of b, β = standardized regression weight; t = t-value of regression weight; R^2 = variance of the dependent variable explained by the predictors.

For physical health, a similar pattern emerged. There were no significant associations with and, consequently, no prediction of physical health by the measures in the first block of the analysis. Including the HILK in Block 2 did not lead to a significant prediction of physical health overall (see Table 2, lower panel). However, the regression coefficient for the HILK proved to be marginally significant, and the increase of explained variance amounted to 2.4% (F = 3.37, df 1/135, p < .10).

[3] Because all predictors were intercorrelated, the results were checked for evidence of multicollinearity which might bias the coefficients. All variance inflation factors were < 1.77 and all tolerances were > 0.56. These values are well below the values of VIF = 10 and tolerance < 0.2 which are usually assumed to indicate that collinearity might constitute a problem [27].

4 Discussion and Conclusions

The present paper introduces a new standardized multiple-choice test for the assessment of health information literacy, the knowledge and skills needed to seek and basically evaluate everyday health information. The 24-item version of the HILK was applied in a sample of university students with a non-medical background to evaluate its psychometric properties and usefulness. Estimates of internal consistency indicate that, in spite of some heterogeneity, the HILK is sufficiently reliable for research purposes (see Research Question 1). However, the dimensionality of the test should be further examined by means of exploratory as well as confirmatory factor analyses in larger samples which are more heterogenous with regard to age and education.

Regarding validity (Research Question 2), correlational analyses support the assumption that the HILK is associated with the EHIL as subjective measure of health information literacy. Associations with two health literacy measures were less close and only marginally significant but pointed into the expected positive direction. Generally, correlations between the HILK and the questionnaire measures are only in a low to moderate range. On the one hand, this finding may be attributed to the limited conceptual overlap of the HILK and the subjective measures. While the HILK covers knowledge about seeking and evaluating everyday health information from printed, digital or personal sources, the questionnaires are either restricted to dealing with information from digital sources [23] or are conceptualized broader and also refer to the motivation to deal with health information [2] or the application of information [24]. On the other hand, the low correspondence of objective and subjective measures has been demonstrated in numerous studies on cognitive abilities [11] and has been corroborated for scholarly information literacy [28]. Thus, future studies should take a closer look at discrepancies between subjective and objective health information literacy measures to examine the causes of these discrepancies and their consequences for health information behavior and decision making. In addition, efforts should be undertaken to validate the HILK by relating scores to behavioral indicators of health information literacy, such as performance in standardized information search or evaluation tasks.

The usefulness of the test (Research Question 3) is demonstrated by the finding that the HILK predicted mental and (marginally) physical health status while there were no associations of the questionnaire measures with both health indicators. Thus, knowledge related to seeking, accessing, and evaluating everyday health information goes along with higher levels of mental well-being as well as physical health. Because the results are based on a homogeneous sample of university students, these findings may not be ascribed to individual differences in level of education which has been identified as an important predictor of health literacy as well as health status [29]. Still, additional studies should demonstrate the generalizability of findings by including samples from different educational backgrounds. As the correlational design of the study prevents causal interpretations, longitudinal research is needed to identify the mechanisms linking knowledge about health information seeking with health status. Nevertheless, it can be concluded that the HILK is a reliable and valid research tool which complements self-report questionnaires of health information literacy. The HILK might even be more useful than these more established tools when it comes to predicting health outcomes.

References

1. Medical Library Association Task Force on Health Information: Health Information Literacy Definitions (2003)
2. Niemelä, R., Ek, S., Eriksson-Backa, K., Huotari, M.-L.: A screening tool for assessing everyday health information literacy. Libri **62**(2), 125–134 (2012)
3. Sørensen, K., Van den Broucke, S., Fullam, J., Doyle, G., Pelikan, J., Slonska, Z., Brand, H.: Health literacy and public health: a systematic review and integration of definitions and models. BMC Public Health **12**(1), 80 (2012)
4. American Library Association: Presidential Committee on Information Literacy: Final Report (1989)
5. Berkman, N.D., Sheridan, S.L., Donahue, K.E., Halpern, D.J., Crotty, K.: Low health literacy and health outcomes: an updated systematic review. Ann. Intern. Med. **155**(2), 97–107 (2011)
6. Ivanitskaya, L.V., Hanisko, K.A., Garrison, J.A., Janson, S.J., Vibbert, D.: Developing health information literacy: a needs analysis from the perspective of preprofessional health students. J. Med. Libr. Assoc. **100**(4), 277–283 (2012)
7. Schulz, P.J., Hartung, U.: The future of health literacy. In: Schaeffer, D., Pelikan, J.M. (eds.) Health Literacy. Forschungsstand und Perspektiven [Health Literacy. State of Research and Perspectives], pp. 79–92. Hogrefe, Goettingen (2017)
8. Altin, S.V., Finke, I., Kautz-Freimuth, S., Stock, S.: The evolution of health literacy assessment tools: a systematic review. BMC Public Health **14**, 1207 (2014)
9. Haun, J.N., Valerio, M.A., McCormack, L.A., Sørensen, K., Paasche-Orlow, M.K.: Health literacy measurement: an inventory and descriptive summary of 51 instruments. J. Health Commun. **19**(Suppl. 2), 302–333 (2014)
10. Brackett, M.A., Mayer, J.D.: Convergent, discriminant, and incremental validity of competing measures of emotional intelligence. Pers. Soc. Psychol. Bull. **29**(9), 1147–1158 (2003)
11. Freund, P.A., Kasten, N.: How smart do you think you are? A meta-analysis on the validity of self-estimates of cognitive ability. Psychol. Bull. **138**(2), 296–321 (2012)
12. Kruger, J., Dunning, D.: Unskilled and unaware of it: how difficulties in recognizing one's own incompetence lead to inflated self-assessments. J. Pers. Soc. Psychol. **77**(6), 1121–1134 (1999)
13. Parker, R.M., Baker, D.W., Williams, M.V., Nurss, J.R.: The test of functional health literacy in adults: a new instrument for measuring patients' literacy skills. J. Gen. Intern.Med. **10**(10), 537–541 (1995)
14. Davis, T.C., Long, S.W., Jackson, R.H., Mayeaux, E.J., George, R.B., Murphy, P.W., Crouch, M.A.: Rapid estimate of adult literacy in medicine: a shortened screening instrument. Fam. Med. **25**(6), 391–395 (1993)
15. Weiss, B.D., Mays, M.Z., Martz, W., Castro, K.M., DeWalt, D.A., Pignone, M.P., Hale, F.A.: Quick assessment of literacy in primary care: the newest vital sign. Ann. Fam. Med. **3**(6), 514–522 (2005)
16. Nutbeam, D.: Health literacy as a public health goal: a challenge for contemporary health education and communication strategies into the 21st century. Health Promot. Int. **15**(3), 259–267 (2000)
17. Ivanitskaya, L., Boyle, I.O., Casey, A.M.: Health information literacy and competencies of information age students: results from the interactive online research readiness self-assessment (RRSA). J. Med. Internet Res. **8**(2), e6 (2006)
18. Steckelberg, A., Huelfenhaus, C., Kasper, J., Rost, J., Mühlhauser, I.: How to measure critical health competences: development and validation of the critical health competence test (CHC test). Adv. Health Sci. Educ.: Theory Pract. **14**(1), 11–22 (2009)

19. Eisenberg, M.B., Berkowitz, R.E.: Information Problem Solving: the Big Six Skills Approach to Library, Information Skills Instruction. Ablex Publishing Corporation, Norwood (1990)
20. Brand-Gruwel, S., Wopereis, I., Walraven, A.: A descriptive model of information problem solving while using internet. Comput. Educ. **53**(4), 1207–1217 (2009)
21. Chan, Y.M.: Predictors of health information overload within internet users. Int. J. Inf. Commun. Technol. Res. **2**(12), 881–887 (2012)
22. Norman, C.D., Skinner, H.A.: eHEALS: the ehealth literacy scale. J. Med. Internet Res. **8**(4), e27 (2006)
23. Soellner, R., Huber, S., Reder, M.: The concept of ehealth literacy and its measurement. J. Media Psychol. **26**, 29–38 (2014)
24. Sørensen, K., Van den Broucke, S., Pelikan, J.M., Fullam, J., Doyle, G., Slonska, Z., Brand, H.: Measuring health literacy in populations: illuminating the design and development process of the european health literacy survey questionnaire (HLS-EU-Q). BMC Public Health **13**(1), 948 (2013)
25. Bullinger, M., Kirchberger, I.: Fragebogen zum Gesundheitszustand – Manual [Health Survey – Manual]. Hogrefe, Goettingen (1998)
26. McNeish, D.: Thanks Coefficient Alpha, We'll Take it From Here. Psychological Methods (accepted for publication) (2017)
27. Field, A.: Discovering Statistics Using IBM SPSS statistics, 4th edn. Sage, London (2013)
28. Rosman, T., Mayer, A.-K., Krampen, G.: Combining self-assessments and achievement tests in information literacy assessment: empirical results and recommendations for practice. Assess. Eval. High. Educ. **39**, 1–15 (2015)
29. Van der Heide, I., Uiters, E., Boshuizen, H., Rademakers, J.: Health literacy in Europe: the development and validation of health literacy prediction models. Eur. J. Public Health 25 (suppl_3) (2015)

Information Behaviour

Information Horizons of Croatian Physicians

Kornelija Petr Balog[1(✉)] and Ivana Turk[2]

[1] Faculty of Humanities and Social Sciences,
University of Osijek, Osijek, Croatia
kpetr@ffos.hr

[2] City and University Library of Osijek, Osijek, Croatia
turk.ivana@gmail.com

Abstract. This paper looks into the information horizons of Croatian family medicine physicians and clinicians with the aim of determining whether they differ from the findings of previous studies. In this pilot-study we used a map drawing technique and follow-up interviews. The sample consisted of ten physicians: (five family medicine physicians and five clinicians) from Osijek, Croatia. Clinicians were interviewed in 2015 and family medicine physicians in 2017. Respondents were asked to place the information sources on mental maps according to their importance and frequency of usage. The results show that clinicians use more information sources than family medicine physicians, which is particularly true for online peer-reviewed sources. Younger physicians use a higher number of information sources than older physicians (they rely heavily on professional literature and peer advice). Viber group messaging was identified as a new channel of communication for family medicine physicians.

Keywords: Information behavior · Information horizons · Information sources Mental maps · Physicians · Work environment

1 Introduction

Information literacy (IL) today should no longer be considered to be a process consisting of only mastering a set of skills in order to access, disseminate or present information because it is a much more complex phenomenon. According to Lloyd [1] it requires developing an understanding of what constitutes information in a specific setting and is therefore manifested as the product of implicit and explicit social activities that are situated and collective.

In today's workplace, regardless of whether it is a primary school classroom, a government agency or a hospital (workplace), IL is considered today to be the most important factor for successful job performance now and in the future [2]. The majority of us usually encounter IL in an educational setting where the interaction with information is structured, organized and enshrined in authorized bodies of knowledge [3]. In this setting, the primacy is given to canonical, objective and explicit knowledge, and the focus is on the performance of an individual [1]. On the other hand, the workplace is a social setting where the information landscape can be often described as messy and complex. It usually consists of a range of practices that entwine to contribute to the collective work performance. Workplace knowledge is characterized and shaped by the

S. Kurbanoğlu et al. (Eds.): ECIL 2017, CCIS 810, pp. 493–502, 2018.
https://doi.org/10.1007/978-3-319-74334-9_51

use of canonical as well as non-canonical sources (e.g. experience, tacit knowledge, etc.). Workplace learning is sometimes formal and has the form of training, but more often it is informal and happens at the moment of practice [4]. It seems that the current educational understanding of information literacy has just started to take into account social practices fundamental for information literacy in context-dependent settings.

In our research we used the methodology of information horizons (IH) which deals with mental maps where individuals position various sources according to their preferences and significance [16]. IH is an evolving theoretical framework proposed by Diane Sonnenwald back in 1999 with a purpose of closer exploration of human information behavior [17]. IH framework is closely related to the concept of IL because it involves the investigation of, among other things, one's ability to find and access the necessary information.

This paper presents the findings of the pilot-study that looked into the information horizons of Croatian family medicine (FM) physicians and clinicians in the context of their work practice. The FM physician is defined as a doctor working in the first line of patient care as general practitioner (GP) or a family doctor. A clinician is a doctor working in the hospital and/or a doctor with a specialization.

2 Information Needs, Sources and Information-Seeking Behavior of Physicians: Literature Review

The profession of a physician is one that constantly requires searching for information. Consequently, there are a number of studies available on information behavior of physicians.

Clark and colleagues' review of 47 papers published from 1996 to 2011 on the information behavior of physicians and nurses revealed that the information needs of physicians are usually related to information on diagnosis, medications, treatment, epidemiology, prognosis and aetiology [5].

An issue that can negatively affect the information needs of physicians is information overload. Considering that in the medical field information from research doubles every 20 years, this is a pronounced problem [6]. Haynes determined, for instance, that an internal medicine doctor should read 19 medical articles daily in order to keep updated [7]. In such a setting it would be impossible for physicians to retain all the knowledge required to treat patients over the course of their careers. Therefore, they need to be able to search for and retrieve necessary information that would refresh and update their knowledge efficiently and effectively.

A review by Dawes and Sampson that looked into 19 studies ranging from 1978 to 2001 (where the majority of the studies included family medicine physicians, and only two included specialists) found that the majority (13 studies) reported text sources as the primary source of information, four studies reported colleagues, and one found electronic sources to be the primary source [8]. In the more recent review conducted by Clark and colleagues, it is evident that electronic resources have become more and more significant – the most popular resource among physicians was the Internet, followed by textbooks, colleagues, journals, professional websites, drug compendiums and medical libraries as the least utilized source [5]. More recent studies report of the prevalent use of online (both authoritative and non-authoritative) sources by physicians [9–11]. Those sources are mostly used near the physicians' point-of-care, and very rarely at home or in a library [9]. The research also shows that general practitioners use a limited number of websites, have problems with assessing the quality of the found information, and often feel inadequate to formulate a correct query [11].

In Croatia, only one study from 2009 into the information behavior of Croatian clinicians was detected. It was conducted for the purposes of a doctoral dissertation [12]. The study found that when clinicians needed new medical information, the majority of respondents (56.1%) used books and journals, 19.5% sought an opinion from a colleague, and only 6.7% used an online medical database. In addition, as many as 62.4% of respondents did not use online medical databases at all, and only 33.9% used Medline. The study also showed that clinicians had a low level of awareness and usage of EBM resources (only 3.3% used the Cochrane Library). According to this, the information behavior of Croatian physicians was much closer to the behavior of physicians in the Dawes and Sampson study (covering the period 1978–2001) where the respondents follow the traditional pattern of information-seeking behavior.

3 Research

3.1 Context

The World Health Organization's (WHO) Report from 2016 gives evidence about the shortage of physicians in some areas of the world. Among those are countries of the Eastern Mediterranean Region, which is the geographical location of Croatia [13]. In addition, the Euro Health Consumer Index (EHCI) for 2016 states that Croatia holds the 19th place (out of 35 countries) in the ranking of healthcare systems in Europe [14]. Finally, ever since Croatia became a member of the EU it started recording a chronic shortage of physicians. Physicians, especially younger ones, are emigrating to other EU countries in pursuit of better working conditions. In 2016, the average age of a health-care professional in Croatia was 49.5. The highest number of physicians were in the age group 55–59, and the lowest in the age group 35–39. Physicians of the latter age group are those who most frequently leave the country and find jobs outside Croatia [15]. Therefore, the physicians who stay in Croatia are coping with an increasing number of patients and a health system burdened by many problems.

3.2 Goal and Research Questions

The goal of this research was to investigate the information horizons of Croatian physicians, more precisely, FM physicians and clinicians, with the aim of determining whether there are differences in the information sources they use considering the differences in their medical practice.

The research questions that guided our research were: Is there a difference in the number of information sources used for the purposes of performing work tasks by our two respondent groups? Is there a difference between the two groups in positioning information sources (i.e. printed and online) and interpersonal sources (e.g. colleagues) on their information horizon (IH) maps? Which sources are more preferred by FM physicians and which by clinicians? Is there a difference in the use of information sources between physicians investigated in 2015 and those investigated in 2017?

3.3 Methodology, Instrument and Sample

The framework of the information horizons used in this research focuses on source preferences of individuals and emphasizes the importance of investigating how contexts, situations and social networks shape an individuals' information behavior. We chose this methodology because it gives a good insight into the mental processes and mental maps of human information behavior.

In our study we used a map drawing technique proposed by Savolainen and Kari [16], accompanied by a short follow-up interview in which the respondents clarified why they put certain sources and channels on their mental maps. Due to space constrictions, this paper focuses on data collected through mental maps and a follow-up interview. In addition to the explanation of maps, the interview also asked whether there were sources that respondents wanted to use in the past, but could not for any reason.

All physicians were asked to fill in the mental maps with the information sources they use for their work (Fig. 1). They were instructed to place information sources used most frequently in Zone 1 (Z1) (innermost circle), sources used slightly less frequently in Zone 2 (Z2), and sources least frequently used in Zone 3 (Z3). After the respondents completed the maps they were asked to explain them. Additional questions that guided the participants' explanations of the mental maps were modelled according to Tsai [18]. They were asked what sources and in which situations they give preference, which sources they tend to avoid and why, which sources are consulted when they have difficulties in solving problems at work, and whether there was a source they wanted but were unable to use and was therefore not in their map.

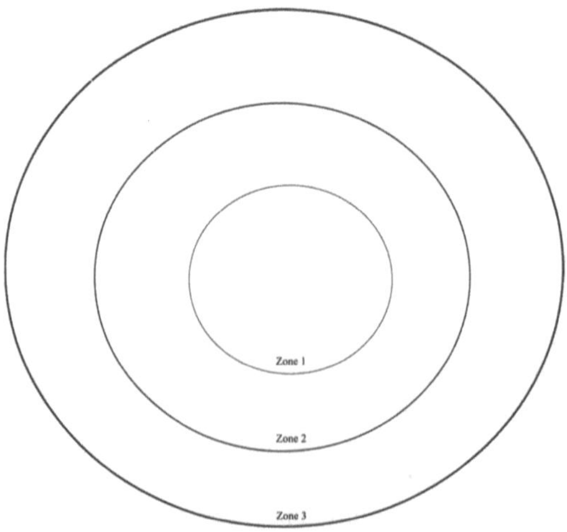

Fig. 1. Mental map used in our research

The sample of our pilot-study consisted of 10 physicians – five FM physicians and five clinicians – all from the town of Osijek, Eastern Croatia. Five physicians (4 clinicians and 1 FM physician) were part of an earlier study from 2015 [19] and the other five were investigated in April 2017. Half of the sample were younger physicians, under 40 years of age (2 FM physicians and 3 clinicians) and the other half were older, over 40 years of age (3 FM physicians and 2 clinicians). Table 1 gives additional demographic data of the sample.

Table 1. Demographic data of the sample

Code	Age	Gender	Specialization	Graduation	Years of experience
C1	45	F	Clinical and anatomic pathology	1996	15
C2	50	M	Neuroradiology	1989	23
C3	36	F	Radiology	2003	12
C4	36	F	Gynecology and obstetrics	2003	12
C5	34	M	Nuclear medicine	2007	10
FM1	59	F	Family medicine	1982	31
FM2	34	F	Family medicine	2008	9
FM3	32	F	Family medicine	2008	7
FM4	51	F	Family medicine	1991	25
FM5	54	F	Family medicine	1982	25

Data collected from the maps was analyzed by descriptive statistics adopted by Savolainen and Kari [16]. In Savolainen and Kari's study, they calculated the number of sources/channels in each zone. They also weighted sources and channels by multiplying a source/channel by 3 in Zone 1, 2 in Zone 2, 1 in Zone 3, to see the weighted scores of each of the sources or channels.

3.4 Results

According to the results of this study, ten participants included 59 unique information sources or channels on their information horizon maps (sources or channels mentioned several times were counted only once). Among which, 27 sources are in Zone 1 (with a total weight of 81), 16 in Zone 2 (total weight 32), and 16 in Zone 3 (total weight 16). FM physicians listed 27 sources whereas clinicians listed slightly more (32). The highest number of sources for both groups were found in Zone 1 (FM-13, clinicians – 14), while the other two zones had fewer sources, equally distributed (FM – 7; clinicians – 9).

We categorized the information sources and channels mentioned by the physicians into six categories: interpersonal sources, library, reviewed online sources, non-reviewed online sources, professional literature and pharmaceutical sources. The complete list of sources per category can be seen in Table 2.

Some sources were mentioned more than once. The most frequently mentioned information sources in Zone 1 are: PubMed (6x), the Internet (6x), colleagues (5x), books/professional literature (2x), HALMED (Agency of Medicinal Product and

Table 2. Distribution of sources per category

Categories of information sources in actors' mental maps	
Group	Sources
Interpersonal sources	Yahoo (colleagues); colleagues – peers; subject specialists; colleagues not connected to work; congresses and meetings; e-mail communication with patients; Viber (communication with colleagues)
Library	Librarians
Reviewed online sources	PubMed; Pathology Outlines; Medscape; Medline/PubMed; radiopaedia.org; Royal College of Obstetricians and Gynaecologists; UpToDate; journal Gynaecologia et Perinatologia; Portal of the Croatian Society for Gynecology and Obstetrics; ATA [American Thyriod Association] guidelines; EMedicine (Medscape); Internet – professional online sources and peer-reviewed journals; Internet – education; HALMED [Agency of Medicinal Product and Medical Devices of Croatia]; Cochrane; Collegium Antropologicum; Medicus (Croatian medical journal)
Non-reviewed online sources	Google; Internet – other sources; Internet – popular sources; Croatian Health Insurance Fund (CHIF)
Professional literature	Books (other publications); scientific articles; older professional literature; medical textbooks (especially MSD manual); medical journals
Pharmaceutical sources	Leaflets, pharmaceutical companies and brochures, pharmaceutical representatives

Medical Devices of Croatia) (2x), and the Croatian Health Insurance Fund (CHIF). In Zone 2 three sources were mentioned more than once: books/professional literature (3x), Medscape (2x), and UpToDate database (2x). In Zone 3, three sources were used more than once: colleagues (4x), pharmaceutical materials (3x), and books/professional literature (2x).

Table 3 presents weighted sources per respondent groups. Our findings show that clinicians use more online-reviewed sources (weight 37) than FM physicians (weight 23) and when they do, they tend to place them in either Zone 1 or 2. The second next preferred sources for clinicians are interpersonal sources (weight 17) and they use them slightly more often than FM physicians (weight 13). FM physicians on the other hand use slightly more non-reviewed online sources (weight 9) and pharmaceutical sources (weight 4). Libraries and librarians are barely a part of information horizons of physicians in our sample – only one clinician (radiologist, age 36) put librarian in Zone 3. Our results also showed that younger doctors (under the age of 40) use far more information sources (35 sources; weight 76) than their older colleagues (24 sources; weight 53). Also, they tend to rely quite a lot on professional literature (e.g. textbooks) and interpersonal sources. For example, they put professional sources in all three zones (Z1-2, Z2-2, Z3-2; weight 14), whereas their older colleagues place those sources only in zones 2 and 3 (Z2-1; Z3-1, weight 3). Similarly, interpersonal sources seem to be quite important to young doctors – Z1-5, Z2-1, Z3-3 (weight 20). In contrast, their

Table 3. Summary table of weighted sources per respondent group

Category	Clinicians				FM physicians				No	Total weight
	Z1	Z2	Z3	Weight	Z1	Z2	Z3	Weight		
Professional literature	1	3		**9**	1	1	3	**8**	9	17
Reviewed online sources	8	6	1	**37**	5	3	2	**23**	25	60
Interpersonal sources	4		5	**17**	3	2		**13**	14	30
Non-reviewed online sources	2		1	**7**	3			**9**	6	16
Library			1	**1**					1	1
Pharmaceutical sources			1	**1**		1	2	**4**	4	5
Total	15	9	9	**72**	12	6	7	**57**	59	129

older colleagues value the importance of peer advice, but not to the extent as their younger counterparts (Z1-2, Z2-1, Z3-2; weight 10). Older doctors, on the other hand, look for information on the Internet (non-reviewed sources) putting it in zones 1 and 3 (Z1-4, Z3-1; weight 13) more often than their younger colleagues (Z1-1; weight 3).

Follow-up interviews gave better insight into reasons why certain information sources were placed in a certain zone. FM physicians placed in Z1 sources that meet their most frequent needs: communication with patients (they need to adjust their vocabulary so that the patient understands them and therefore read popular medical articles online), checking on drugs (HALMED), checking on administrative regulations (CHIF), doing online tests that are required for relicensing. Clinicians put in Z1 the sources mostly required for diagnosing and solving a particular medical problem. Those sources mostly refer to reviewed online medical sources and colleagues. Clinicians also take extreme care to confirm the validity of results and medical solutions found in information sources and recheck the information in other sources for clues (S1).

Among other interesting findings was the fact that FM physicians seemed to use Viber group messaging as a new communication channel. Namely, in 2017 we noticed a higher utilization of mobile devices for the purposes of consultations with peers among FM physicians. Although communication through Viber groups did not come up that often in the mental maps of our respondents (only one FM physician placed it in Z2), follow-up interviews revealed that all four FM physicians interviewed in 2017 frequently use Viber group consultations. FM physicians interviewed in 2015 did not use that channel for communication with colleagues. Clinicians, on the other hand, do not seem to use Viber and did not mention it.

Follow-up interviews also revealed that several of our respondents (FM2, C3, C5) wanted to use some online data-bases in the past, but did not have access to them (there was no institutional and/or national subscription).

4 Discussion and Conclusions

This paper presents findings of the pilot-study about the information horizons of family medicine physicians and clinicians. Altogether ten doctors were investigated – five in 2015 (one FM physician and four clinicians) and five in 2017 (one clinician and four

FM physicians). Clinicians in our sample were of various specializations: clinical and anatomic pathology, neuroradiology, radiology, gynecology and obstetrics and nuclear medicine. Five doctors in the sample were under 40 years of age, and five were over 40. Two respondent groups were chosen because although they belong to the same discipline (medicine), their information needs and information behavior tend to differ in some degree. It is our belief that findings of this pilot-study might give more information about the sources of information of Croatian physicians, and would help academic and clinical libraries in Croatia develop a better information support system for FM physicians and clinicians, who tend to differ slightly in their information needs and sources used.

Altogether 59 unique information sources and communication channels were placed on information maps. In order to manage those sources more efficiently, we grouped them in six categories: interpersonal sources, library, reviewed online sources, non-reviewed online sources, professional literature, and pharmaceutical sources.

Judging from the type of sources found in Zone 1, particularly sources that were mentioned by more than one respondent, we might conclude that doctors in our sample tend to be more inclined to use electronic resources (both reviewed and non-reviewed) which could be considered to be primary sources for them. In the second place of preference are colleagues, followed by professional literature (mainly textbooks). Similar results were obtained in a study by Clark and colleagues [5]. On the other hand, this deviates slightly from the findings of an earlier Croatian study which found that clinicians relied primarily on textbooks, then on colleagues and lastly on online databases [12]. Such a discrepancy is, however, expected since the earlier Croatian research was conducted in 2009. Unfortunately, medical libraries were not part of the information horizons of our respondents. Although clinicians work in a hospital with a medical library, only one placed the library in Z3. One of the possible reasons for this might be the fact that going to the library takes up too much time and is too slow for them, and their follow-up interviews emphasized the timeliness and speed of access to information.

Our results show that clinicians use information sources slightly more than the FM physicians. However, both respondent groups place the highest number of sources in Zone 1, which indicates that those are the sources with which they are the most familiar and most frequently use. Also, those are obviously the sources they trust the most. Both groups placed fewer sources in the other two zones (equal number of sources per zone).

The usage of information sources is closely related to the nature of the doctors' work – FM physicians interact with patients and must be able to communicate the information about the illness to the patient in an appropriate way making sure the patient understands the message. Also, since they cover all areas of medicine they need to constantly check the information about drugs and possible changes that have occurred. Lastly, they have a lot of administrative duties and must keep up with all the changes and regulations regarding patients' rights about medical equipment and treatment. Clinicians, on the other hand, do not get as frequently in touch with patients and are much more concentrated on the specific illness or medical problem for which they are specialized. For them, validity and trustworthiness of the source and medical advice as well as the speed of access to the information source, is of great importance. In that regard, clinicians (especially younger ones – C3, C4) value greatly peer advice, but only if the colleagues are close by and they can get their feedback immediately. Otherwise, if there are no colleagues at the workplace that can be asked, older clinicians conclude that that option is too slow for them (C2) and look for answers online and on their own. According to information needs of physicians identified by our research (such as diagnosing, medicating, treatment) our findings are similar to those identified by Clark and colleagues [5].

We also noticed that, in comparison with the older doctors in the sample, the younger doctors use far more information sources and consultation (with older and more experienced colleagues), which may be attributed to their inexperience and insecurity.

Another new channel of information that was observed, especially among FM physicians investigated in 2017, is a Viber group texting for advice and support. The Viber group consists of other peers and they regularly exchange experiences and give each other advice on any topic related to their everyday work problems.

The findings from our pilot-study clearly show that workplace information gathering and workplace knowledge of Croatian physicians working in Osijek, Eastern Croatia, is sometimes characterized by the use of canonical (e.g. text-books), but more often by the use of non-canonical sources (e.g. experience, colleagues) which is consistent with earlier studies [4]. Information seeking is mostly done in the work setting, rarely at home, and almost never in the library, which is consistent with the earlier research [9].

The findings presented in this paper are results of a qualitative study. Due to the small sample, results are only indicative and cannot be considered as final conclusions about the information horizons of Croatian physicians. However, we believe that these findings may serve as a starting point for more detailed investigation of the information horizons of physicians, particularly bearing in mind the lack of research studies on this topic in Croatia.

References

1. Lloyd, A.: Trapped between a rock and a hard place: what counts as information literacy in the workplace and how is it conceptualized? Libr. Trends **60**(2), 277–296 (2011)
2. National Forum on Information Literacy. http://infolit.org/workplace-information-literacy/
3. Gherardi, S.: Community of practice or practices of a community? In: Armstrong, S., Fukami, C. (eds.) Sage Handbook of Management Learning, Education and Development, pp. 514–530. Sage, Thousand Oaks (2009)
4. Sawchuck, P.: Adult Learning and Technology in Working-Class Life. Cambridge University Press, Cambridge (2003)
5. Clarke, M.A., Belden, J.L., Koopman, R.J., Steege, L.M., Moore, J.L., Canfield, S.M., Kim, M.S.: Information needs and informatio-seeking behaviour analysis of family medicine physicians and nurses: a literature review. Health Inf. Libr. J. **30**, 178–190 (2013)
6. Wyatt, J.C., Sullivan, F.: ABC of health informatics-keeping up: learning in the workplace. Br. Med. J. **331**, 1129–1132 (2005)
7. Haynes, R.B.: Where's the meat in clinical journals? ACP J. Club **119**, A22–A23 (1993)
8. Dawes, M., Sampson, U.: Knowledge management in clinical practice: a systematic review of information seeking behavior of physicians. Int. J. Med. Inform. **71**, 9–15 (2003)

9. Lialiou, P., Mantas, J.: Online information seeking behaviour by nurses and physicians: a cross-sectional study. In: Sermeus, W., Procter, P.M., Weber, P. (eds.) Nursing Informatics 2016, pp. 33–37. IOS Press, Amsterdam (2016)
10. Mikalef, P., Kourouthanassis, P.E., Pateli, A.G.: Online information behaviour of physicians. Health Inf. Libr. J. **34**(1), 58–73 (2017)
11. Schuers, M., Griffon, N., Kerdelhue, G., Foubert, Q., Mercier, A., Darmoni, S.J.: Behavior and attitudes of residents and general practitioners in searching for health information: from intention to practice. Int. J. Med. Inform. **80**, 9–14 (2016)
12. Markulin, H.: Analiza informacijskih potreba i načina uporabe informacijskih izvora na uzorku liječnika hrvatske kliničke bolnice [Information Seeking Behaviour and Use of Information Resources among Physicians in a Croatian Clinical Hospital]. Liječn Vjesn **136**, 256–260 (2014)
13. WHO. World Health Statistics 2016: Monitoring Health for the SDGs (2016). http://www.who.int/gho/publications/world_health_statistics/2016/en/
14. Health Consumer Powerhouse. Euro Health Consumer Index (EHCI) 2016: Report (2017). http://www.healthpowerhouse.com/files/EHCI_2016/EHCI_2016_report.pdf
15. Glas Slavonije: Prosječna dob liječnika je 46 godina, a 1189 ih odlazi raditi u EU, 10 October 2016. http://www.glas-slavonije.hr/314087/1/Prosjecna-dob-lijecnika-je-46-godina-a-1189-ih-odlazi-raditi-u-EU
16. Savolainen, R., Kari, J.: Placing the Internet in the information source horizons: a study of information seeking by Internet users in the context of self-development. Libr. Inf. Sci. Res. **26**(4), 415–433 (2004)
17. Sonnenwald, D.: Evolving perspectives on human information behavior: contexts, situations, social networks and information horizons. In: Wilson, T., Allen, D. (eds.) Exploring the Contexts of Information Behaviour, pp. 176–190. Taylor Graham, London (1999)
18. Tsai, T.: Information horizons of Taiwanese graduate students. In: Reilly, M. (ed.) iConference Proceedings, pp. 233–246 (2010). https://www.ideals.illinois.edu/bitstream/handle/2142/14911/InformationHorizons_iConference_Tsai0106.pdf?sequence=2
19. Turk, I., Petr Balog, K.: Informacijski horizonti hrvatskih stručnjaka različitih profesija [Information horizons of Croatian experts in different professions]. Libellarium **9**(2), 321–354 (2016). https://doi.org/10.15291/libellarium.v9i2.267

Seeking Serendipity: The Art of Finding the Unsought in Professional Music

Iwan Wopereis[1(✉)] and Michiel Braam[2]

[1] Open University of the Netherlands, Heerlen, The Netherlands
iwan.wopereis@ou.nl

[2] ArtEZ University of the Arts, Arnhem, The Netherlands
m.braam@artez.nl

Abstract. Serendipity is a valuable constituent of professional work. In order to 'control' the phenomenon it is important to gain insight in its processes and influencing factors. This study examined two cases of serendipitous information behavior in professional improvised music, a domain often associated with unpredictability. The aim of the study was to validate McCay-Peet and Toms' latest model on work-related serendipitous experiences. The study followed a semi-structured interview procedure that consisted of three one-hour interview sessions to select cases and collect data. Results show that our data fit the model. Process elements like 'trigger', 'connection', 'valuable outcome', 'unexpected thread', and 'perception of serendipity' were identified, as well as factors such as 'trigger-rich', 'openness', and 'prepared mind'. We also identified other factors (i.e., 'curiosity', 'interest', and 'initiative') that might influence serendipitious discovery. Additional (multi) case studies are necessary to generalize findings.

Keywords: Information behaviour · Information seeking
Serendipity · Music

1 Introduction

Serendipity is a relatively young concept that is increasingly used in formal and informal communication [1, 2]. From its inception until now, different meanings have been assigned to it, making it a somewhat *fuzzy concept* [3–5]. Originally, serendipity refers to the act of "… making discoveries, by accidents and sagacity, of things [someone is] not in quest of …" [1, p. 2]. This description emphasizes chance and unpredictability, as well as perceptiveness and knowledge as important constituents of the discovery made. Recent definitions have added certain 'qualities' to conditions, processes, and products of serendipitous discovery. 'Pleasant surprise' [6], 'fortunate happenstance' [6], or 'happy discovery' [7] for instance stress positivity in serendipitous outcomes. Further, additives like 'prepared mind' [2] and 'gift' [3] underline the importance of ability as prerequisite to notice serendipity. Well-known examples of highly significant serendipitous discoveries by 'gifted' professionals are Post-it, X-rays, aspartame, and penicillin. In general terms these examples can be categorized as "finding B, when looking for A." This 'quality-free', simplified rule of serendipitous behavior applies for many situations in daily and professional life. Most of us will

S. Kurbanoğlu et al. (Eds.): ECIL 2017, CCIS 810, pp. 503–512, 2018.
https://doi.org/10.1007/978-3-319-74334-9_52

probably recognize this rule when the Internet is purposefully searched for information. For instance, it is not unusual that during a work-related, goal-directed search in Google the search engine results page (SERP) presents to you one or more references to sources not relevant to the search at hand but valuable for solving other (latent) professional problems.

Serendipitous discovery seems to have a positive effect on individual, group, communal, and societal well-being and functioning [4, 5]. It also has a strong link to innovation and creativity, two highly valued features of contemporary work [4, 8]. Consequently, it probably goes without saying that it is important to understand serendipitous processes and products as well as the factors that influence them. Initial research on serendipity mainly focused on identifying and categorizing examples of serendipity and distinguish so-called serendipity patterns (see [1, 2]). The emphasis in current research is much more on revealing conditions for serendipity and disentangling serendipitous processes. Results of this line of research are often models that go beyond insight into processes; these models aim to help control serendipity too, a seemingly paradoxical situation [3].

A promising contemporary 'serendipity model' has been constructed by McCay-Peet and Toms [4]. Their model consolidates previous models of serendipity and explains serendipity broadly, in a professional, work-related context. Interestingly, their definition of serendipity resembles the original 'neutral' definition, saying that it is "[a]n unexpected experience prompted by an individual's valuable interaction with ideas, information, objects, or phenomena." (p. 1474). McCay-Peet and Toms analyzed 15 examples of serendipity in depth to construct the model. However, in order to become robust, it is important to validate the model in various contexts [9]. Our study contributes to 'model robustness' and examines work-related examples of serendipty in the domain of professional improvised music making. We chose this domain as it is often associated with unpredictable outcomes and processes prone to risk, (happy) accident, and surprise [3, 11, 12]. The study specifically aimed to find examples of serendipity in music information (seeking) behavior (see [13]). Before we expand on the study's research questions, we first briefly summarize McCay-Peet and Toms' serendipity model. Table 1 provides summary definitions of the model's constituents; Fig. 1 shows how these constituents relate to each other.

McCay-Peet and Toms' model consist of seven elements (see Table 1, E1–E7). According to their model a serendipitous experience starts with a trigger (E1), connects–after a possible delay (E2)–trigger and the individual's knowledge base (E3), leads to a follow-up action (E4) that, in turn, results into a valuable outcome (E5). Within one or more of these 'steps' the individual experiences unexpectedness (E6). Finally, the individual perceives the situation as serendipitous (E7). Since valuable outcome and perception of serendipity can occur before the follow-up has been ended, the latter is 'faded' in the figure. The model of McCay-Peet and Toms also identifies factors that may facilitate the process of serendipity. These factors can refer to interactions the individual has with the environment, labeled in Table 1 as 'external' (F-Ex) or describe features of the individual only, labeled in the same table as 'internal' (F-In).

Figure 1 shows how the seven elements (E1–E7) of an serendipitous experience are intertwined in time. It furthers emphasizes that several external (F1-Ex to F4-Ex) and internal factors (F5-In to F7-In) influence these elements.

Table 1. Constituents of the McCay-Peet and Toms serendipity model (see [4])

Elements and factors	Definition
Trigger (E1)	A verbal, textual, or visual cue that initiates or sparks an individual's experience of serendipity
Delay (E2)	The interval that may occur when an individual perceives a *trigger* but does not immediately recognize a *connection* between the *trigger* and the individual's knowledge and experience
Connection (E3)	The recognition of a relationship between the *trigger* and the individual's knowledge and experience
Follow-up (E4)	Action taken to make the most of a *trigger* or *connection* and obtain a *valuable outcome*
Valuable outcome (E5)	The positive effect of the serendipitous experience both realized and projected
Unexpected thread (E6)	The unexpected chance, accident, or surprising element that is evident in one or more of the *trigger*, *connection*, *follow-up*, or *valuable outcome* elements of the serendipitous experience
Perception of serendipity (E7)	An experience is understood or regarded to be serendipitous based on awareness of its *trigger*, *connection*, *valuable outcome*, and *unexpected thread*
Trigger-rich (F1-Ex)	An environment that contains sensory cues that have the potential to spark serendipity
Highlights triggers (F2-Ex)	Something or someone who highlights, points to, or otherwise alerts an individual to *triggers*
Enables connection (F3-Ex)	Something or someone who encourages explorations, critical thinking, and the sharing of knowledge and ideas that make it possible to see relationships between information and ideas
Enables capturing (F4-Ex)	Something or someone who helps an individual record or copy a *trigger* for later use
Openness (F5-In)	To be curious or open or receptive to experience. Openness may describe a personality trait, conscious strategy, or a temporary state
Ability to make connections (F6-In)	To be able to think critically or creatively about relationships between encountered ideas, information, and phenomena and the individual's own knowledge and experience
Prepared mind (F7-In)	The individual's knowledge and experience

Note: E = element in model; F = factor that may facilitate serendipity; Ex = external; In = internal

The aim of our study was to validate McCay and Toms model of serendipity in the domain of professional improvised music. However, we were also curious about the relationship between serendipity and creativity, and more specifically between serendipity and improvisation, a salient instance of musical creativity [11, 12]. Therefore, we started the research discussing contemporary definitions of serendipity [1, 2, 4] and relating it to improvisation. After this discussion, examples of serendipity were collected and analyzed using McCay-Peet's research procedure [5].

We formulated three research questions:

- RQ1: How can we best define work-related serendipity in a creative domain like music and how does it relate to concepts like creativity and improvisation?
- RQ2: Does the model of McCay-Peet and Toms explain how work-related serendipitous (information) behavior unfolds in professional improvised music?
- RQ3: Does the model explain conditions that may influence the process of serendipity within the aforementioned context?

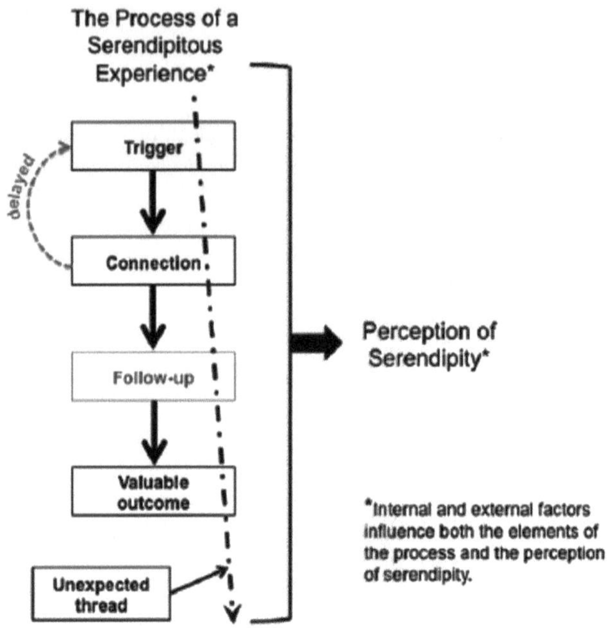

Fig. 1. The process of a serendipitous experience (Source: JASIST, 66, p. 1468)

2 Method

2.1 Subject

This study explored serendipitous information behavior of the second author, a professional musician with over 30 years of experience in jazz and improvised music; we will use the abbreviation MB to refer to him. MB's prior knowledge on the concept of serendipity is substantial, which made him an ideal 'reflection partner' throughout the study. MB acquired knowledge on serendipity when he initiated and conducted a musical project entitled 'Serendipities'. This project included the composition and performance of 17 pieces of music, each referring to existing serendipities, like *Post-it*, *Penicillin*, and *Aspartame* (see also [14]). The 13-piece big band 'Bik Bent Braam' performed 'Serendipities' several times in 2010. MB's knowledge on serendiptiy was helpful to define and delimit the concept and to discuss its relationship with concepts like *creativity* and *improvisation* (RQ1, see also [3]). Further, his knowledge on serendipity helped to select the serendipitous cases for validating the McCay and Toms model (RQ2 and RQ3).

2.2 Procedure

Data Collection. The first author took the interview that followed the semi-structured method of McCay-Peet [5] to collect data. This quadripartite interview protocol includes questions about (a) the work of the participant, (b) the definition of serendipity, (c) specific examples of serendipity, and (d) serendipity in general. The study's focus was on the third part, namely the collection and analysis of work-related examples of serendipitous experiences. The interview consisted of three separated one-hour parts. The first sub interview registered the first three consituents of the interview protocol (a, b, c), the second interview focused on the last two parts (c, d), and the last interview was used as 'member check' in order to improve reliability, accuracy, and validity (see also [9]). Before the interview, the participant received an email that included contemporary definitions of serendipity [1, 2, 4] and the question to think of one or more examples of work-related serendipity. The three (sub) interviews were recorded with an Olympus-VN Digital Voice Recorder and transcribed.

Data Analysis. McCay-Peet and Toms' model on serendiptiy [4] functioned as the initial framework for the analysis of the interview. The first author used the same thematic analysis method [10] to identify additional relevant themes.

3 Results

This study validated McCay-Peet and Toms' serendipity model by analyzing two cases of serendipity in the domain of professional improvisational music. To select proper cases, we first discussed the concept of serendipity, which resulted in a delineation of the concept. We start the results section with this conceptual analysis (RQ1) and subsequently describe and explain the cases in light of the model (RQ2 and RQ3).

3.1 Definition

RQ1. MB's first response to the three definitions of serendipity [1, 2, 4] that were presented to him was: "This [MB points to the definitions on a piece of paper] is actually very useful for everything I do. … What's here is all about improvisation." However, he then boldly states that the three definitions "have nothing to do with serendipity" as they do not explicitly mention that someone should be "in search of something else" when being exposed to the unsought. As such, his view on serendipity equals the rule mentioned in the Introduction saying that serendipity is "finding B, when looking for A." MB stresses that serendipity without preconceived search component resembles 'coincidence', an important ingredient of his music though.

With regard to improvisation, MB tries "… to have as few expectations as possible in advance" when he starts to play. This position towards the improvisational act has developed over the years: "The more I improvise and the longer I do it, I think that I should really sit 'completely empty' there [in other words, on stage], and then I'll see what will happen. That means, it can never be a serendipity, because I'm not looking for something." However, primed by this study, the issue how his improvisational music making relates to serendipitous experience kept him busy. During the member check in the third interview MB nuanced his initial view on improvisation and search. "I think it is difficult not to be in search of something during an entire concert." "During a concert, you actually start completely empty. … And at some point something [musically] happens and you start investigating it, which is a search for a concrete solution. During this search new things can be discovered." MB illustrates this by mentioning an example to investigate a certain chord, because it sounds so awful (in this case, a C Majeur 7 or c-e-g-b): "And then [while performing] you discover that a reversal of notes can result in an interesting rhythmic pattern in which the original notes of the chord actually sound much nicer. … It [i.e., the unsought finding] becomes part of your 'backpack' [MB's metaphor for his musical knowledge base]". MB stresses that during an improvisation he wants to discover new things and that he is not very eager to make intense use of his 'backpack'. However, he also admits that "… it's not for nothing it's there…" and that such instants of musical knowledge (e.g., patterns) often sound good, because of training.

Serendipity and improvisation, thus, seem to have a relationship. Although MB mentions some examples (e.g., finding an interesting rhythmic pattern when solving the problem of an awful sounding tetrad), these examples of serendipity where not included in the analyses. Instead, we focused on serendipitous experiences on a higher level of professional music making, namely the planning, execution, and evaluation of musical products, like a concert.

3.2 Cases

MB mentioned several examples of work-related serendipity during the three interview parts. We selected two striking cases to study in depth, of which one was an instance of 'serendipity in information science' or SIS (see [3]).

Case 1: Toxic. The first case, Toxic, can be categorized as SIS. During a search for musical information on YouTube, this system recommended MB to watch the music video 'Toxic' of pop musician Britney Spears. This recommendation surprised MB: "[This kind of music] takes place completely out of my comfort zone. Let's say that Britney Spears does not have my direct interest. Excellent singer, nothing wrong with that, but it's not the kind of music I would normally listen to." Despite this, MB remembered the song 'Toxic' and that it included unusual (synthesizer) strings. At that time he was working on a programme for a 20-piece conservatory student band, called ArtEZ Big Collective [15], that also included six stringed instruments. The latent need for songs with strings for the ArtEZ Big Collective became manifest when MB saw the recommendation to watch 'Toxic'. Watching the video incited MB to write an arrangement for the conservatory band. It was performed at the 34th Music Meeting, a renowned world music festival in Nijmegen, the Netherlands. This case is a typical example of 'finding B (i.e., an unexpected, but potentially interesting song for a big band), when looking for A (musical information for another purpose)'.

Case 2: Globe. The second case, Globe, refers to a musical project named 'Globe Orchestra.' The organization of the 15th edition of the Music Meeting, assigned this project to MB as musical leader. The rationale of the project was to form a group of musicians from different corners of the world (i.e., The Tuva Ensemble from Tuva, The Bisserov Sisters from Bulgaria, The Ndere Troupe from Uganda, and improvisers Fred van Duynhoven and MB from the Netherlands) and perform a series of concerts at the Music Meeting and other musical sites in the Netherlands. MB's initial idea was to let the band members "create a fusion of world music." For that reason he prepared some rough drafts for possible pieces of music. However, after the first rehearsals it became clear that this plan would not work. Tuvan, Bulgarian, Ugandan, and Dutch musical traditions were too distinct to start a kind of 'fusion band' right from the beginning. Further, it was difficult to communicate on preconceived musical plans, because not all musicians could speak English. "We have rehearsed for one week. I think during the second day of the rehearsal, I threw away all my initial musical plans and ideas for the project. And my thoughts were: This does not make any sense." This feeling was omnipresent in the group. The musicians then decided to interact musically with their instruments (or voices) using their own musical idiom as starting point. MB continues: "[Y]ou have to stick much closer to the traditions of the musicians and learn from them." At that time he realized that he was about to learn things he had never learned before, due to the remarkable composition of the group musicians. As from that moment (that is: day two of the rehearsal) the musicians decided to look much closer to each others musical traditions and tried to connect them in musical pieces that emerged during the rehearsals. Time pressure probably geared up the process. In the end, the new 'democratic' approach to music making proved to be succesfull. The musicians created an interesting musical programme that was performed several times in the two weeks after the rehearsal period. Thus, in search for a musical repertoire, the musicians 'found' a new approach to create music for heterogenous groups of musicians in an effective and enjoyable way. This valuable outcome became one of the 'cornerstones' of MB's professional work: starting projects without preconceived plan, 'empty', with a professional attitude that includes curiosity, interest in fellow musicians, and initiative.

3.3 Validation

RQ2. McCay-Peet and Toms' model consists of seven elements (see E1–E7 in Table 1 and Fig. 1). The first element 'trigger' (E1) was present in both cases. In the case 'Toxic' the trigger was a recommendation by YouTube. MB explained this trigger (E1) and elaborated on the technology behind recommendations: "There's also a negative side to it. When someone is searching the [YouTube] system and gets something in the right column, he/she is inclined to select the first videos in the list. … There is a danger that you don't think anymore …What kind of society we'll get when Google or YouTube search for you? Then we'll get an *algorithmic society*." MB is aware of the fact that search algorithms influence the selection of sources and that a critical stance towards music information search is necessary (see also [16]). "Although I don't believe in conspiracy theories, I think these companies try to create mainstream. You can control mainstream, not chaos." As such, it is not strange that MB experienced 'surprise' (i.e., 'unexpected thread', E6) when the video Toxic (i.e., mainstream music) was recommended to him by the YouTube system. In the second case the trigger included the observation that in a project that consists of a heterogeneous group of musicians preconceived musical ideas do not work [E1]. MB connected this experience to his knowledge that musical improvisers should enter their professional musical projects 'open-minded', and start them 'as empty as possible' (E3, see also Sect. 3.1). In these projects it is important the individual musician "… should be curious and take initiative." To MB's surprise [E6] all musicians had such an attitude. It contributed to the success of the new 'democratic' approach to music making [E5] where deliberation between musicians was strictly musical. This approach to music making developed further over the years and became MB's standard approach to professional musical projects. As such, this serendipitous experience can be understood as major event in MB's professional career. He classified it as "a wonderful experience, that was very influential… and very positive. I can remember that I enjoyed every moment immensely." The serendipitous experience in the first case didn't have such impact on MB's professional work. However, it's outcome proved to be valuable [E5] as the arrangement of the musical song Toxic became part of the repertoire of the ArtEZ Big Collective.

RQ3. McCay-Peet and Toms' model distinguish seven factors that may influence serendipity (see F1–F7 in Table 1). In the case, Toxic, MB perceived the YouTube system as 'tigger-rich' (F1) that highlights triggers (F2) well. However, MB also pointed to the inadequacies of recommender systems (i.e., "it makes worlds small, mainstream", cf. [16]). According to MB, internal (personal) factors like 'openness' [F5], 'ability to make connections' [F6], and 'prepared mind' [F7] were also clearly present in this case. For instance, a firm 'prepared' musical knowledge base makes it possible to recognize an interesting musical video, value it's content, and relate it to a musical need. Further, a critical and open mind, results in a better use of recommender systems in musical databases, making the 'algorithmic space' a bit larger. MB also mentioned the 'prepared mind' in the second case, Globe. "Of course, you need to know something about music, otherwise it [trigger and/or connection] will just pass by." MB mentioned other personal characteristics that might influence a serendipitous experience. The first was curiosity. This characteristic relates to openness, but includes also a kind of action. By mentioning 'initiative' as a second feature, MB emphasized the importance of 'action'. According to MB, someone should be 'in search of something' in order to 'find the unsought'. The last personality feature MB mentioned was 'interest in fellow musicians'. Interest relates to curiosity and increases the chance to witness serendipity. During the first part of the interview, when discussing the Globe Orchestra case, MB stated that the musical environment has hardly any influence on serendipity. "Both open projects and delineated projects can result in serendipitous experiences. It is hard to say when it [serendipity] happens.… You will get different outcomes, I think. But, the situation doesn't matter: creative or boring." Despite this remark, the second case proved to be exceptional fertile ground for serendipity. Such a musical environment that consists of a wide variety of curious, interested musicians seems to facilitate more professional growth than less musically varied environments.

4 Discussion

This study validated McCay-Peet and Toms' model on work-related serendipity in the domain of professional music. Two cases on professional music information behavior were analysed. Before selecting cases, we discussed and analysed the concept of serendipity and its relation with improvisation (RQ1). We concluded that 'being in search of something else' is a prerequisite for 'finding the unsought' [2]. The two selected cases met this criterion. Further, we found that serendipity can be a consituent of improvisation. MB recognized this possibility (see also [3]). However, this study did not analyse serendipity on a 'microlevel' in depth, as it is difficult to recall concrete instances by means of a semi-structured interview. Future research should address the issue of serendipity in improvisation on a microlevel. We think that (video) observation and cued retrospective reporting (see [17]) is a promising research method to capture serendipity on a micro-level. In this study, we analysed work-related serendipitous experiences on a meso-level (the planning, creation, performance, and evaluation of a concert). The McCay and Toms' model proved to be useful to distinguish serendipitous processes (RQ2) and conditions for serendipitous discovery in these cases (RQ3). We identified important consituents of the process of serendipitous experience (e.g., E1, E3, E5, E6, and E7) and factors that influence serendipitous discovery (e.g., F1, F2, F5, and F7). Interestingly, we found other (personality) factors that might promote serendipitous discovery in creative domains. In professional music, personality characteristics like 'curiosity', 'initiative', and 'interest in others' (i.e., fellow musicians) seem to enhance serendipitous discovery. Of course, additional research is needed to generalize these findings.

5 Conclusion

Seeking serendipity may sound as a paradox, just like controlling it [3, 18]. However, results of this study and other research provides increasing evidence that we can influence and stimulate it. We think that future research should differentiate levels of analysis (e.g., micro-, meso-, and macro-level), domains (e.g., leisure, education and training, and work) and contexts (e.g., SIS) in order to scrutinize the phenomenon. Collecting cases and analyzing them in multi-case studies might be an interesting next step to further validate promising models like that of McCay-Peet and Toms.

References

1. Merton, R.K., Barber, E.: The Travels and Adventures of Serendipity. Princeton University Press, Princeton (2004)
2. Van Andel, P.: Anatomy of the unsought finding. serendipity: origin, history, domains, traditions, appearances, patterns and programmability. Br. J. Philos. Sci. **45**, 631–648 (1994)
3. McBirnie, A.: Seeking serendipity: the paradox of control. Aslib Proc. **60**, 600–618 (2008)
4. McCay-Peet, L., Toms, E.G.: Investigating serendipity: how it unfolds and what may influence it. J. Assoc. Inf. Sci. Technol. **66**, 1463–1476 (2015)

5. McCay-Peet, L.: Investigating work-related serendipity, what influences it, and how it may be facilitated in digital environments. Ph.D. thesis. Dalhousie University, Halifax (2013)
6. Wikipedia (2017). Serendipity. https://en.wikipedia.org
7. Oxford dictionaries (2017). Serendipity. https://en.oxforddictionaries.com
8. Díaz de Chumaceiro, C.L.: Serendipity and its analogues in Runco's problem finding, problem solving, and creativity. Creativity Res. J. **10**, 87–89 (1997)
9. Yin, R.K.: Case Study Research: Design and Methods, 5th edn. Sage, Thousand Oaks (2014)
10. Braun, V., Clarke, V.: Using thematic analysis in psychology. Qualitative Res. Psychol. **3**, 77–101 (2006)
11. Wopereis, I.G.J.H., Stoyanov, S., Kirschner, P.A., Van Merriënboer, J.J.G.: What makes a good musical improviser? an expert view on improvisational expertise. Psychomusicol. Music Mind Brain **23**, 222–235 (2013)
12. Wopereis, I., Derix, E.: Seeking creativity: a case study on information problem solving in professional music. In: Kurbanoğlu, S., Boustany, J., Špiranec, S., Grassian, E., Mizrachi, D., Roy, L., Çakmak, T. (eds.) ECIL 2016. CCIS, vol. 676, pp. 428–436. Springer, Cham (2016). https://doi.org/10.1007/978-3-319-52162-6_43
13. Lavranos, C., Kostagiolas, P.A., Martzoukou, K., Papadatos, J.: Music information seeking behaviour as motivator for musical creativity: conceptual analysis and literature review. J. Doc. **71**, 1070–1093 (2015)
14. Dekker, J.: Gestures: a film for Bik Bent Braam's musical program 'Serendipities'. Motion picture. https://vimeo.com/13074765
15. ArtEZ Conservatorium: ArtEZ big collective, motion picture. https://www.youtube.com/watch?v=PgI73SasntU
16. Wolf, C.T.: DIY videos on YouTube: identity and possibility in the age of algorithms. First Monday, **21**(6). http://dx.doi.org/10.5210/fm.v21i6.6787
17. Van Gog, T., Paas, F., Van Merriënboer, J.J.G., Witte, P.: Uncovering the problem-solving process: cued retrospective reporting versus concurrent and retrospective reporting. J. Exp. Psychol. Appl. **11**, 237–244 (2005)
18. Corneli, J., Jordanous, A., Guckelsberger, C., Pease, A., Colton, S.: Modelling serendipity in a computational context. arXiv:1411.0440v5 [cs.AI] (2017)

Measure of Healthcare Professionals' Behavioral Outcomes Using a Social Learning Theory

Rubina Bhatti and Salman Bin Naeem(✉)

Department of Library and Information Science,
The Islamia University of Bahawalpur, Bahawalpur, Pakistan
dr.rubytariq@gmail.com, salmanbaluch@gmail.com

Abstract. To measure the healthcare professionals' (HCPs) behavioral outcomes (knowledge, attitude, intentions, and behaviors) about specific health information resources available online in order to determine the stage of behavioral change using social learning theory. A cross-sectional survey was conducted in 36 District Headquarter Hospitals (DHQs), 89 Tehsil Headquarter Hospitals (THQs), 293 Rural Health Centers (RHCs), and 2455 Basic Health Units (BHUs) in Punjab, Pakistan. The survey population comprised of rural HCPs (e.g., physicians, surgeons, and gynecologist) working in primary and secondary healthcare facilities of Punjab province, Pakistan. The results of the study concluded that majority of the HCPs' knowledge of online healthcare information resources is limited. However, their attitude and intention towards using the online healthcare information resources for day-to-day clinical practice is positive. The study recommends a need to launch promotional and educational activities through which HCPs' interest and awareness about online healthcare information resources and services should be persuaded.

Keywords: Healthcare professional · Behavioral capability
Social learning theory · Information resources

1 Introduction

Healthcare professionals (HCPs) need a wide range of patient-specific information to make clinical decisions about the patients [1, 2]. Seeking information in a timely way is essential for improved patient care decisions [3]. Healthcare professionals seek information from different information resources that include personal collection, colleagues, seniors, and online databases. The continued availability of information provides self-reliance and better approach to patient care outcomes. However, the unavailability of information during the clinical decision making process is likely to increase the chances of uninformed or delayed patient care decisions. It also increases the chance of medical errors such as wrong diagnosis or error in administering treatment [4, 5] which ultimately reduce the quality of patient care outcomes.

The identification of information needs, information accessibility and its availability are among the factors that stimulate HCPs to seek healthcare information for patient care decisions; this is an area which has been explored and reported by many

S. Kurbanoğlu et al. (Eds.): ECIL 2017, CCIS 810, pp. 513–525, 2018.
https://doi.org/10.1007/978-3-319-74334-9_53

LIS professionals and researchers around the world [6–8]. Few studies have been conducted in Pakistan to explore the Primary Care Physician's (PCP) clinical information needs, information access, information seeking patterns and barriers in seeking clinical Information [9–12]. Several studies conducted to investigate the attitude of HCPs toward using information sources [13, 14], using specific electronic information resources such as Internet and online resources for seeking healthcare information [15–17], ascertaining the HCPs' information needs [10, 11, 18], exploring HCPs' information seeking patterns, determining the attitude of HCPs toward using library [9, 19]. The majority of these studies on information behaviors focus on primary care physicians or general practitioners (GPs) [6, 14].

Many studies have explored various aspects of physicians' information behavior [20, 21]. The results of these studies showed wide variations in physicians' attitude while seeking healthcare information. Primary care physicians mostly preferred to seek healthcare information from 'human sources' that included colleagues, senior doctors, and pharmaceutical representative [9, 10, 12]. The second most preferred source type was print sources in which PCPs like to seek information from books and journals [22, 23]. The use of digital libraries and electronic resources available on the Internet was also found to becoming an increasingly preferred information sources among HCPs [20, 23]. The growing number of HCPs consider the Internet as a significant, useful and speedy source for seeking healthcare information for patient care decisions [24, 25]. According to them, most of the information they need related to patient care decisions is available on the Internet [25, 26]. Several studies have investigated the use of the Internet for seeking healthcare information for patient care decisions [13, 14]. The literature indicated that physicians' attitudes played a significant role not only in its acceptance but also in the efficient use of Internet and online information resources during clinical practice [27, 28].

Naeem et al., reported that the majority of the PCPs frequently need healthcare information for patient management, staying current, continuing medical education and evidence for policies. However, they occasionally need information related to teaching and research. They frequently need information sources related to protocols and guidelines for treatment, latest research, clinical trials, evidence-based medicine and health status indicators [10]. In another study, librarians who recorded the clinical questions, raised by PCPs, indicated that MEDLINE or similar databases were the best source to answer the 43% of the clinical questions raised by PCPs during clinical practice. The study also drew a comparison to the preferred sources of answering the clinical questions between librarians and PCPs. Forty-three percent of librarians as compared to 1% of PCPs that reported MEDLINE searches as their first choice of information source to answer the clinical questions. Databases were used by only 3% of PCPs [29].

Previously a very little is known and reported in the literature about HCPs' behavioral outcomes on online healthcare information resources and services here in Pakistan. Therefore, this study was conducted with an aim to measure the behavioral outcomes of the HCPs working in primary and secondary healthcare facilities of Punjab, Pakistan.

2 Methodology

A cross-sectional survey was conducted in 36 District Headquarter Hospitals (DHQs), 89 Tehsil Headquarter Hospitals (THQs), 293 Rural Health Centers (RHCs), and 2455 Basic Health Units (BHUs) in Punjab, Pakistan. The survey population comprised rural HCPs (i.e., physicians, surgeons, and gynecologist) working in primary and secondary healthcare facilities of Punjab province, Pakistan. A total population of the study comprised (N = 4033). Of the 4033 HCPs, 2273 (56.36%) was working in primary healthcare and 1760 (43.64%) secondary healthcare. The minimum sample size of the study calculated was (n = 357) with confidence level = 95%, and margin of error = 5% using Krejcie and Morgan sample size table [30]. Using quota sampling the researchers divided population into four strata: HCPs of BHUs (stratum A), RHCs (stratum B), THQs (stratum C), DHQs (stratum D). The proportions of these strata in the population identified in order to select the minimum number of participants from the each stratum while taking into consideration the proportions of each stratum in the population. In order to meet the minimum number of required sample size (n = 357), 9% sampling proportion from each stratum found adequate to reach the minimum sample size of the study. The reason for using a quota sampling was to assemble the representative proportion from different groups of the entire population with respect to their healthcare facilities (e.g., BHUs, RHCs, THQs and DHQs).

A social learning theory identified from the literature of health behavior to be used in the present study. The important variables (knowledge, attitude, intentions, behavior, expectations, and self-efficacy) and relating questions to this theory were identified and incorporated in the questionnaire in order to collect the data from respondents on these variables: to log onto PubMed, I need special software; PubMed is only for HCPs (behavioral capability); compared to other Internet sources for healthcare information PubMed is? PubMed is essential tool for my work; if I need an answer to a clinical problem I intend to consult PubMed (Expectations); how confident are you in your ability to find information on the Internet? How confident are you that the Internet has information you need? (Self-efficacy).

To prevent respondents from answering non-relevant questions a skip logic, also known as branch logic, was used in the survey. It created a custom path through the survey that varied based on the respondent's answers. Five-point Likert type scale from 'strongly disagree' to 'strongly agree' was used to measure the HCPs' attitude, intentions, and behavior. A questionnaire was first pre-tested with five experts and then pilot tested on a sample of 15 HCPs from a target population. Cronbach's alpha coefficients used to assess the content reliability and internal consistency of the questionnaire. A Cronbach's alpha score (0.83) for 27 items related to social learning theory indicated a very high reliability of the scale.

The collected data analyzed using Statistical Package for Social Sciences (version-20). The data related to social learning theory (e.g., attitude, intentions, behaviors, expectations, self-efficacy) were measured on interval scale and presented in mean and standard deviation. Analysis of Variance (ANOVA) statistics were used to assess any significant difference in the attitude, intentions, and behaviors of HCPs of five different healthcare facilities (e.g., BHUs, RHCs, THQs, DHQs, Others). The non-parametric statistics Kruskal-Wallis were applied to find any differences in the perceived threat and perceived self-efficacy among HCPs of five different healthcare facilities. Similarly, Mann-Whitney U statistic was used to determine any differences between HCPs' enrollment in post-graduation and perceived level of threat and efficacy.

2.1 Response Rate

Over 2000 phone calls were made to almost 2000 HCPs in order to seek their participation in the survey, of which 1204 HCPs agreed to participate in the study. A copy of questionnaire was posted to HCPs who agreed to participate. Of the 1204 HCPs, 396 returned the completed questionnaire with a response rate (32.89%), after three follow-up with a gap of two weeks. On the other hand, an online link to the questionnaire was sent to 660 HCPs through WhatsApp, out of which 118 responded with a response rate (17.87%). Overall, the response obtained from HCPs against targeted response from different healthcare facilities was (100%). Since there is an inverse relationship between sample size and the margin of error, larger sample size is likely to yield smaller margins of errors. Therefore, the researcher continued obtaining responses even after reaching the minimum sample size of (n = 357). Overall, the data was collected from 517 HCPs through the questionnaire on variables important to the social learning theory (e.g., behavioral capability, expectations, and self-efficacy).

2.2 Ethical Approval

The study was begun after the approval of the Departmental Research Committee of the Department of Library and Information Science, and Advanced Studies and Research Board of The Islamia University of the Bahawalpur. Pakistan.

3 Results

3.1 Measure of Behavioral Outcomes

Of the 517 respondents, the overwhelming majority of 351 (67.9%) were male. Most of the respondents 199 (38.5%) worked in BHUs. The difference in gender of healthcare professionals (HCPs) was much higher in secondary than primary healthcare facilities. Using post hoc chi-square analysis, a statistically significant difference with a small effect size was found in the gender distribution of HCPs in different healthcare facilities such as BHUs, RHCs, THQs, DHQs, and others (χ^2 (4) = 11.141, p = .025, Cramer's V = .147) (Table 1).

The largest group of HCPs were in the health facilities of BHUs and the smallest were in RHCs. Majority of the HCPs in primary and secondary healthcare facilities were young and less experienced. The age group with the highest number of HCPs was 21–30 years. The majority of them 103 (38%) worked in BHUs. Only 15 (2.9%) were in the age group of 51–60 years (Table 1).

Table 1. Demographic information (gender, age group, and clinical experience)

	Primary healthcare		Secondary healthcare		Others (N = 36)	Total (N = 517)	χ^2 value	*p*-value	Cramer's V
	BHUs (N = 199)	RHCs (N = 63)	THQs (N = 118)	DHQs (N = 101)					
Gender									
Male	144 (41%)	33 (9.4%)	76 (21.7%)	70 (19.9%)	28 (8%)	351 (67.9%)	11.141	.025*	.147
Female	55 (33.1%)	30 (18.1%)	42 (25.3%)	31 (18.7%)	8 (4.8%)	166 (32.1%)			
Total	199 (38.5%)	63 (12.2%)	118 (22.8%)	101 (19.5%)	36 (7%)	517 (100%)			
[a]*Age Group*									
21–30	103 (38.0%)	32 (11.8%)	69 (25.5%)	53 (19.6%)	14 (5.2%)	271 (52.4%)	24.210[a]	.216	.019
31–40	65 (34.6%)	23 (12.2%)	41 (21.8%)	43 (22.9%)	16 (8.5%)	188 (36.4%)			
41–50	23 (53.5%)	6 (14.0%)	8 (18.6%)	4 (9.3%)	2 (4.7%)	43 (8.3%)			
51–60	8 (53.3%)	2 (13.3%)	0 (0.0%)	1 (6.7%)	4 (26.7%)	15 (2.9%)			
Total	199 (38.5%)	63 (12.2%)	118 (22.8%)	101 (19.5%)	36 (7%)	517 (100%)			
[b]*Clinical Experience*									
<5	107 (39.3%)	31 (11.4%)	68 (25.0%)	53 (19.5%)	13 (4.8%)	272 (52.6%)	16.767	.180	.401
6–10	52 (33.1%)	19 (12.1%)	33 (21%)	39 (24.8%)	14 (8.9%)	157 (30.4%)			
11–15	14 (38.9%)	6 (16.7%)	8 (22.2%)	4 (11.1%)	4 (11.1%)	36 (7%)			
15>	26 (49.1%)	7 (13.7%)	9 (17.6%)	5 (9.8%)	5 (9.8%)	52 (10%)			
Total	199 (38.5%)	63 (12.2%)	118 (22.8%)	101 (19.5%)	36 (7%)	517 (100%)			

*The difference is significant at the 0.05 level.
Cramer's V effect size: 0.1 small, 0.3 medium, 0.5 large [38].
[a]5 cells (25.0%) in age group have expected count less than 5. The minimum expected count is 1.04.
[b]8 cells (32.0%) in working experience have expected count less than 5. The minimum expected count is .07.

Two hundred and seventy two (52.6%) respondents had less than 5-years of clinical experience, while another 47.4% had a working experience between 6 to 15> years (Table 1).

The interpretation of the *p*-value of the age group and clinical experience is not reported due to the violation of chi-square assumption as reported by Yates, Moore & McCabe in 1999 that "no more than 20% of the expected counts are less than 5" [39].

The behavioral outcomes (e.g., knowledge, attitude, intentions, and behaviors) were measured on important variables related to social learning theory. The knowledge of the respondents about online resources and services were measured on 6 statements (Table 2). They were asked "do you know about PubMed"? Of the 415, only 105 (25.3%) responded "yes" but majority 310 (74.7%) responded "no" (Table 2).

Table 2. Measure of behavioral outcomes (knowledge)

Statements	N		BHUs (N = 199)	RHCs (N = 63)	THQs (N = 118)	DHQs (N = 101)	Others (N = 36)	Total (N = 517)
I know about PubMed	415	Yes	30 (7.2%)	10 (2.4%)	31 (7.5%)	29 (7%)	5 (1.2%)	105 (25.3%)
		No	131 (31.6%)	41 (9.9%)	61 (14.7%)	58 (14%)	19 (4.6%)	310 (74.7%)
I know about HEC digital library	412	Yes	7 (1.7%)	2 (.5%)	4 (1%)	2 (.5%)	1 (.2%)	16 (3.9%)
		No	152 (36.9%)	48 (11.7%)	88 (21.4%)	85 (20.6%)	23 (5.6%)	396 (96.1%)
To log onto PubMed, I need special Software	92	Yes	6 (6.5%)	1 (1.1%)	3 (3.3%)	4 (4.3%)	1 (1.1%)	15 (16.3%)
		No	21 (22.8%)	5 (5.4%)	23 (25%)	25 (27.2%)	3 (3.3%)	77 (83.7%)
To use HEC digital library, I must have Static IP address from Internet service providers (ISPs)	30	Yes	3 (10%)	1 (3.3%)	3 (10%)	2 (6.7%)	2 (6.7%)	11 (36.7%)
		No	8 (72.7%)	3 (75%)	6 (66.7%)	2 (50%)	0 (0%)	19 (63.3%)
PubMed is only for health care professionals	92	Yes	21 (22.8%)	6 (6.5%)	23 (25%)	23 (25%)	2 (2.2%)	75 (81.5%)
		No	7 (7.6%)	3 (3.3%)	4 (4.3%)	1 (1.1%)	2 (2.2%)	17 (18.5%)
I have enough knowledge of specific information resources available online	132	Yes	10 (7.6%)	3 (2.3%)	9 (6.8%)	10 (7.6%)	0 (0%)	32 (24.2%)
		No	35 (26.5%)	9 (6.8%)	29 (22%)	20 (5.3%)	7 (5.3%)	100 (75.8%)

A statistically significant difference with a small effect size was existed among the HCPs of different healthcare facilities in their knowledge about PubMed "χ^2 (4) = 11.315, P = .165, Cramer's $V = .023$)". HCPs from DHQs and THQs were more aware with the PubMed as compared to HCPs of other types of healthcare facilities. Only 16 (3.9%) HCPs indicated that they know about HEC digital library, whereas, majority 396 (96.1%) mentioned that they did not know about it (Table 2).

The respondents who knew about PubMed and HEC digital library were asked the follow-up questions (e.g., to log onto PubMed, they need special software; to use HEC digital library, they must have IP address). Of the 92 respondents, 15 (16.3%) responded "yes" and 77 (83.7%) responded "no" that they need a special software to log onto PubMed (Table 2).

Surprisingly, only 30 respondents responded to a statement "to use HEC digital library, I must have a static IP address from ISPs" (Static IP address is required to access the HEC digital library). Of the 30, 11 (36.7%) responded "yes" and 19 (63.3%) responded "no". Those who responded to a statement "to log onto PubMed, I need special software" were asked a follow-up question of whether "PubMed is only for healthcare professionals", Of the 92 respondents, 75 (81.5%) responded "yes" and 17 (18.5%) responded "no" (Table 2).

3.2 Measure of Behavioral Outcomes (Attitude)

The respondents who indicated that they know about PubMed and HEC digital library were asked a set of six follow-up questions in order to assess their attitude toward Internet and online healthcare information sources. All the six statements relating to attitude received mean scores between 2.95 to 4.21 indicating that the majority of the respondents were either 'agreed' or 'neutral' with the statements, for example: "PubMed is an essential tool for my work" (M = 4.21, SD = .632), and "the Internet is an essential tool for my clinical practice" (M = 4.19, SD = .693). However, they were 'neutral' with the statements such as: "compare to other Internet sources for health information, HEC digital library is beneficial" (M = 3.36, SD = .929). Analysis of variance (ANOVA) showed no significant difference in the attitude of HCPs of different healthcare facilities $F(4, 272) = 2.617$, $p = .127$ (Table 3).

Table 3. Behavioral outcomes of the healthcare professionals (HCPs)

	Mean	Std. deviation	*F*	*p*-*value*
**Respondents' attitude*				
PubMed is an essential tool for my work	4.21	.632	2.617	.127
The Internet is an essential tool for my clinical practice	4.19	.693		
Compare to other Internet sources for health information, PubMed is beneficial	4.12	.602		
The information available on Internet is largely reliable	3.67	.837		
Compared to other Internet sources for health information, HEC digital library is beneficial	3.36	.929		
HEC Digital library is an essential tool for my work	2.95	.524		
**Respondents' intentions*				
I intend to use PubMed weekly	3.95	.784	.496	.739
If I need an answer to a clinical problem, I intend to consult PubMed.	3.94	.793		
I intend to use HEC digital library weekly	3.70	.811		
If I need an answer to a clinical problem, I intend to consult HEC digital library	3.65	.852		
**Respondents' behavior*				
If I need an answer to a clinical problem, I consult PubMed	2.01	1.212	3.963	.004
I use PubMed weekly	2.00	1.122		
If I need an answer to a clinical problem, I consult HEC digital library	1.61	.623		
I use HEC digital library weekly	1.60	.623		
***Respondents' confidence*				
How confident are you in your own ability to find information on the Internet? (Self-efficacy)	2.57	.913	6.515	.000
How confident are you that the Internet has information you need? (Expectations)	3.41	1.148	5.960	.000

Level of significance <.05.
*Scale: 1 = Strongly Disagree, 2 = Disagree, 3 = Neutral, 4 = Agree, 5 = Strongly Agree.
**Scale: 1 = Totally Unconfident, 2 = Slightly Confident, 3 = Reasonably Confident, 4 = Very Confident, 5 = Totally Confident.

3.3 Measures of Behavioral Outcomes (Intentions)

A set of four statements asked in order to assess HCPs' intention to use healthcare information resources (e.g., PubMed and HEC digital library). The mean values of the HCPs responses to all these four statements ranged from 3.65 to 3.95 indicating their intention to use PubMed and HEC digital library on a 'weekly' basis. They also agreed to consult PubMed and HEC digital library for finding answers to clinical problems. Analysis of variance (ANOVA) found no significant difference in the intentions of HCPs of different healthcare facilities in using PubMed and HEC digital library $F(4, 272) = .496$, $p = .739$ (Table 3).

3.4 Measures of Behavioral Outcomes (Behaviors)

All four statements relating to behavior received a mean scores ranged from 1.60 to 2.01 indicating that majority of the HCPs disagreed with these statements (e.g., if I need an answer to a clinical problem, I consult PubMed; I use PubMed weekly; If I need an answer to a clinical problem).

Using Analysis of Variance (ANOVA) we found a statistically significant difference among the behaviors of HCPs of different healthcare facilities $F(4, 274) = .3.963$, $p = .004$. Using a post hoc Tukey statistics, a statistically significant difference was found in the statement "I use PubMed weekly" among the responses of HCPs of DHQs and BHUs (MD = .483, p = .041) and also HCPs of DHQs and RHCs (MD = .745, p = .012). The difference was also significant between the responses of BHUs and RHCs in the statement of "I use HEC digital library weekly (MD = .339, p = .036), and between the HCPs of DHQs and RHCs (MD. 512, p = .001) in a same statement. A statistical difference was also found in the statement of "if I need an answer to a clinical problem, I consult HEC digital library". This difference was significant among the HCPs of BHUs and RHCs (MD = .348, p = .041), and DHQs and RHCs (MD = .743, p = .004) (Table 3).

3.5 HCPs' Confidence on Their Own Abilities to Find Information from the Internet (Social Learning Theory)

Respondents were asked a question related to "self-efficacy" or the degree of perception of one's ability to find the useful information. This statement received a mean score 2.57 indicating that majority of the respondents were "reasonably confident" in their own ability to find information on the internet. A post hoc Analysis of Variance (ANOVA) statistics indicated a significant difference in the self-efficacy of HCPs of different healthcare facilities (e.g., BHUs, RHCs, THQs, etc.,) $F(4, 380) = 6.515$, $p = .000$ (Table 3).

A post hoc Tukey HSD statistics indicated that this difference was significant between the HCPs of DHQs with BHUs (MD = .470, p = .001), RHCs (MD = .454, p = .046), and any other (MD = .802, p = .001). A difference was also significant between HCPs of THQs with BHUs (MD = .328, p = .051), and any other (MD = .660, p = .014). The HCPs of DHQs had a higher self-efficacy as compared to HCPs of

BHUs. However, no significant difference in self-efficacy was found between the HCPs of RHCs and THQs (Table 3).

The majority of the respondents were "reasonably confident" that the Internet has the information they need. A statistically significant difference was found in the expectations of HCPs of different healthcare facilities $F(4, 379) = 5.960$, $p = .000$ (Table 3). A post hoc Tukey HSD analysis indicated that this difference was significant between the HCPs of DHQs and BHUs (MD = .478, p = .019), or any other (MD = 1.157, p = .000). A difference was also significant between HCPs of THQs and any other (MD = .959, p = .003). However, no significant difference was found between the HCPs of BHUs and RHCs, and BHUs and THQs. However, HCPs working at DHQs were more confident that the relevant information is available (expectations) as compared to HCPs of BHUs and Any other.

4 Discussion

The results of the study showed that HCPs' knowledge about online healthcare information resources such as PubMed and HEC digital library was quite low. The majority 74.7% of the HCPs were unaware of PubMed, and 96.1% of the HEC digital library. Of the 105 (25.3%) HCPs (who were aware bout the PubMed), 15 (16.3%) were not aware about how to use PubMed. The percentage of awareness about PubMed and HEC digital library in our population was quite low as compared to other studies in which they reported the use of PubMed among HCPs in variety of clinical settings that ranged from 23% to 71%, showing a strong level of awareness [29–33]. PubMed, which is one of the most useable and accessible research databases in medicine, allows free searches and access to abstracts and in some cases to full-text articles of resources indexed in Medline [34]. A research study reported that the use of PubMed and other online resources led to a 10% increase in accurate diagnoses [35]. Similarly, the results of our study showed that majority of the HCPs reported that "Internet is an essential tool for their clinical practices". They were of the opinion that the information available on the Internet is largely reliable. However, only 15% of the HCPs in our population indicated that "PubMed is an essential tool for their work". Whereas, Only 18.18% indicated that "PubMed is beneficial as compared to other Internet sources for health information".

Ward et al, reported that attitudes of physicians is a significant factor as to doctors' acceptance and use of online information from their clinical settings [28]. The majority of the HCPs' intention was positive, they agreed to use and consult healthcare information sources (e.g., PubMed and HEC digital library) in order to find the answers of clinical problems. However, their behavior was not active. They were not using and consulting PubMed/HEC digital library to find the answers of clinical questions. The application to change behavioral capability includes provision of awareness and trainings about PubMed and HEC digital library to HCPs. In the literature, three factors that shape behavioral action were reported when a health communications theory is adapted to information seeking behaviors. These factors were classified as: (i) predisposing factors; providing a reason behind the behavior or motivate a person for change. Predisposing factors included knowledge, beliefs, attitude, and readiness to change;

(ii) enabling factors that enable a person to seek new information and realize his motivation, it includes infrastructure, available resources, skills, and information technology; and (iii) reinforcing factors that come into play to reward a behavior. The sustainability of behavioral actions depend a lot on reinforcing factors; if a behavior get rewarded, it is likely to increase the chances that a behavior will continue. Conversely, if a person failed to get the desired results, it is likely to decrease the chances that behavior will continue. Librarian or institutional support, seniors or expert influence, are among the factors that predispose and reinforce behavior change [36, 37]. The responses measured on variables such as 'expectations' and 'self-efficacy' indicated that majority of the HCPs were reasonably confident that the Internet has all the information they need (expectations).

There is a need for HCPs to be taught how to search on the Internet to find relevant information in order to increase their level of confidence. There is a need to conduct information literacy programs aimed at changing the information behaviors of HCPs. Different promotional and educational strategies such as to increase interest and awareness among HCPs through seminars, exhibits and brochures, training the HCPs by conducting workshops, hands-on training or demonstrating on computers, are required to increase awareness, knowledge, influence attitude, beliefs, facilitate information technological access, develop skills, reinforce behaviors and build health science librarians or institutional support in order to increase the use of PubMed and other online resources such as HEC digital library that will ultimately increase the patient care outcomes.

Due to population dispersion, data collected for this study through a survey method has its own limitations. The results could be subject to personal biases as well as HCPs' ability to understand the questions. Every effort was made to minimize the bias by maintaining the internal consistency of the questions. The questionnaire was reviewed for content validity by five experts.

5 Conclusion

The results of the study concluded that the majority of the HCPs' knowledge of online healthcare information resources is limited. However, their attitude and intention towards using the online healthcare information resources for day-to-day clinical practice is positive. The study recommends launching promotional and educational activities through which HCPs' interest and awareness of online healthcare information resources and services are increased. The results of this study carry some important practical implications for health sciences librarians, policy makers, and professional associations such as Pakistan Library Association (PLA) and Health Department to introduce the strategies that could help improve the behavioral outcomes of HCPs so they could be able to utilize the healthcare information from HEC digital library, PubMed and other online resources effectively, which could ultimately increase the quality of patient care decisions.

References

1. Cimino, J.J., Li, J., Graham, M., Currie, L.M., Allen, M., Bakken, S., Patel, V.L.: Use of online resources while using a clinical information system. In: AMIA Annual Symposium Proceedings 2003, vol. 2003, p. 175. American Medical Informatics Association (2003)
2. Bates, D.W., Cohen, M., Leape, L.L., Overhage, J.M., Shabot, M.M., Sheridan, T.: Reducing the frequency of errors in medicine using information technology. J. Am. Med. Inform. Assoc. **8**(4), 299–308 (2001)
3. Friedman, C., Gatti, G., Elstein, A., Franz, T., Murphy, G., Wolf, F.: Are clinicians correct when they believe they are correct? Implications for medical decision support. Stud. Health Technol. Inform. **84**(1), 454–458 (2001)
4. Allen, M., Currie, L.M., Graham, M.J., Bakken, S., Patel, V.L., Cimino, J.J.: The classification of clinicians' information needs while using a clinical information system. In: AMIA 2003 (2003)
5. Donaldson, M.S., Corrigan, J.M., Kohn, L.T. (eds.): To Err is Human: Building a Safer Health System. National Academies Press, Washington, D.C. (2000)
6. Coumou, H.C., Meijman, F.J.: How do primary care physicians seek answers to clinical questions? A literature review IRP. J. Med. Libr. Assoc. **94**(1), 55 (2006)
7. Davies, K.: The information-seeking behaviour of doctors: a review of the evidence. Health Inf. Libr. J. **24**(2), 78–94 (2007)
8. Norbert, G.L., Lwoga, E.T.: Information seeking behaviour of physicians in Tanzania. Inf. Dev. **29**(2), 172–182 (2013)
9. Naeem, S.B., Ahmed, S., Rabbani, M.W.: The impact of hospital libraries on patient care and clinical decision-making: a survey of teaching hospitals. J. Hosp. Librariansh. **13**(2), 120–130 (2013)
10. Naeem, S.B., Ahmed, S., Ishfaq, K.: Information needs and sources of doctors working at remote government health facilities in Pakistan. J. Health Inform. Dev. Ctries. **7**(2), 141–152 (2013)
11. Naeem, S.B., Bhatti, R.: Clinical information needs and access in primary health care: a comparative cross-sectional study of rural and non-rural primary care physicians. Health Inf. Libr. J. **32**(4), 287–299 (2015)
12. Bhatti, R., Naeem, S.B., Jamil, R.M., Shah, S.T.: Internet-based information usage pattern of paediatricians: a survey of Southern Punjab, Pakistan. Libr. Philos. Pract. (2014)
13. Bennett, N.L., Casebeer, L.L., Kristofco, R.E., Strasser, S.M.: Physicians' Internet information-seeking behaviors. J. Contin. Educ. Health Prof. **24**(1), 31–38 (2004)
14. Dorsey, M.J., Detlefsen, E.: Investigating information-seeking behaviors of primary care physicians who care for older depressed patients and their family caregivers: a pilot study. J. Can. Health Libr. Assoc./Journal de l'Association des bibliothèques de la santé du Canada **26**(4), 111–116 (2005)
15. Torre, D.M., Wright, S.M., Wilson, R.F., Diener-West, M., Bass, E.B.: Family physicians' interests in special features of electronic publication. J. Med. Libr. Assoc. **91**(3), 337 (2003)
16. Boissin, F.G.: Information-seeking behaviour and use of the internet by French general practitioners: a qualitative study. Health Inf. Libr. J. **22**(3), 173–181 (2005)
17. Meats, E., Brassey, J., Heneghan, C., Glasziou, P.: Using the Turning Research Into Practice (TRIP) database: how do clinicians really search? J. Med. Libr. Assoc. **95**(2), 156 (2007)
18. Lappa, E.: Undertaking an information-needs analysis of the emergency-care physician to inform the role of the clinical librarian: a Greek perspective. Health Inf. Libr. J. **22**(2), 124–132 (2005)

19. Nail-Chiwetalu, B., Ratner, N.B.: An assessment of the information-seeking abilities and needs of practicing speech-language pathologists. J. Med. Libr. Assoc. **95**(2), 182 (2007)
20. Gavino, A.I., Ho, B.L., Wee, P.A., Marcelo, A.B., Fontelo, P.: Information-seeking trends of medical professionals and students from middle-income countries: a focus on the Philippines. Health Inf. Libr. J. **30**(4), 303–317 (2013)
21. Prakasan, P.M.: Information needs and use of healthcare professionals: international perspective. DESIDOC J. Libr. Inf. Technol. **33**(6), 465–471 (2013)
22. McGettigan, P., Golden, J., Fryer, J., Chan, R., Feely, J.: Prescribers prefer people: the sources of information used by doctors for prescribing suggest that the medium is more important than the message. Br. J. Clin. Pharmacol. **51**(2), 184–189 (2001)
23. Urquhart, C., Turner, J., Durbin, J., Ryan, J.: Changes in information behavior in clinical teams after introduction of a clinical librarian service. J. Med. Libr. Assoc. **95**(1), 14 (2007)
24. Maharana, R.K., Dha, A.P., Pati, S.: Exploring the information seeking behavior of medical science professionals: a case study of Veer Surendra Sai Medical College, Burla, Odisha. Int. J. Inf. Dissem. Technol. **3**(1), 62 (2013)
25. Garcia-Cosavalente, H.P., Wood, L.E., Obregon, R.: Health information seeking behavior among rural and urban Peruvians: variations in information resource access and preferences. Inf. Dev. **26**(1), 37–45 (2010)
26. Oweghoro, B.M., Adeleke, I.T., Mshelia, P.P., Ogundiran, L.M., Yusuf, A.M., Adeoti, D.I.: Knowledge, access and use of internet-based health information for personal healthcare among employees of the foremost Nigerian University. Am. J. Health Res. **3**(1–1), 25–31 (2015). Special Issue: Health Information Technology in Developing Nations: Challenges and Prospects Health Information Technology
27. Adeleke, I.T., Asiru, M.A., Oweghoro, B.M., Jimoh, A.B., Ndana, A.M.: Computer and internet use among tertiary healthcare providers and trainees in a Nigerian public hospital. Am. J. Health Res. **3**(1–1), 1–10 (2015). Special Issue: Health Information Technology in Developing Nations: Challenges and Prospects Health Information Technology
28. Ward, R., Stevens, C., Brentnall, P., Briddon, J.: The attitudes of health care staff to information technology: a comprehensive review of the research literature. Health Inf. Libr. J. **25**(2), 81–97 (2008)
29. González-González, A.I., Dawes, M., Sánchez-Mateos, J., Riesgo-Fuertes, R., Escortell-Mayor, E., Sanz-Cuesta, T., Hernández-Fernández, T.: Information needs and information-seeking behavior of primary care physicians. Ann. Fam. Med. **5**(4), 345–352 (2007)
30. Krejcie, R.V., Morgan, D.W.: Determining sample size for research activities. Educ. Psychol. Measur. **30**(3), 607–610 (1970)
31. Lindberg, D.A., Siegel, E.R., Rapp, B.A., Wallingford, K.T., Wilson, S.R.: Use of MEDLINE by physicians for clinical problem solving. JAMA **269**(24), 3124–3129 (1993)
32. Bowden, V.M., Kromer, M.E., Tobia, R.C.: Assessment of physicians' information needs in five Texas counties. Bull. Med. Libr. Assoc. **82**(2), 189 (1994)
33. Richwine, M.P., McGowan, J.J.: A rural virtual health sciences library project: research findings with implications for next generation library services. Bull. Med. Libr. Assoc. **89**(1), 37 (2001)
34. Lokker, C., Haynes, R.B., Wilczynski, N.L., McKibbon, K.A., Walter, S.D.: Retrieval of diagnostic and treatment studies for clinical use through PubMed and PubMed's Clinical Queries filters. J. Am. Med. Inform. Assoc. **18**(5), 652–659 (2011)
35. US National Library of Medicine: Fact Sheet MEDLINE (2016). https://www.nlm.nih.gov/pubs/factsheets/medline.html

36. Falagas, M.E., Ntziora, F., Makris, G.C., Malietzis, G.A., Rafailidis, P.I.: Do PubMed and Google searches help medical students and young doctors reach the correct diagnosis? A pilot study. Eur. J. Intern. Med. **20**(8), 788–790 (2009)
37. Burroughs, C.M., Wood, F.B.: Measuring the Difference: Guide to Planning and Evaluating Health Information Outreach. National Network of Libraries of Medicine, Pacific Northwest Region (2000)
38. Cohen, J.: Statistical Power Analysis for the Behavioral Sciences. Lawrence Erlbaum Associates, Inc., Mahwah (1988)
39. Yates, M.: The Practice of Statistics. Macmillan, Basingstoke (1999)

Academic Reading Format Preferences and Behaviors in Mainland China

Peng Xiao[1], Yantao Pan[1](✉), and Jiuzhen Zhang[2]

[1] Sun Yat-sen University, Guangzhou, China
{xiaop25,puspyt}@mail.sysu.edu.cn
[2] Peking University, Beijing, China

Abstract. This study has investigated format preferences for academic reading and reading behaviors of Chinese undergraduates, postgraduate students, Ph.D students and post doctorates, to see whether they like reading academic materials in print or electronically. This study adopted the Academic Reading Questionnaire (ARQ) originally designed by Mizrachi, and 1,165 valid on-line questionnaires were collected in mainland China. The ARQ survey in China shows students' strong preference for paper or printed materials compared to electronic versions. This result is not surprising, compared to results from other countries. However, it is interesting to find the rise of smartphones to be an important course reading device among Chinese students.

Keywords: Reading format preference · Reading behavior · Print reading Electronic reading · Academic reading

1 Introduction

In the year 1999, the Chinese Press and Publishing Institute started the National Reading Survey, which takes a close look at citizens' reading behaviors in mainland China. The survey contains a question on citizens' preference on reading format. In 2012, more than 70% of respondents tended to "read by holding a printed book in their hands", [1]; in 2013, 66.0% of respondents still wanted to hold a book [2]; in 2014 and 2015, the number dropped to 57.2% (2014) and 57.5% (2015) [3, 4]; in the latest report from 2016, the number hit its lowest mark at 51.6%, in the meantime, the ratio for digital reading has continuously risen eight years in a row [5].

However, a series of recent research studies suggests that scholars and college students are still loyal to printed academic materials [6, p. 301]. But it is impossible for the academic circle to wall itself off from the reading format revolution. The real problem is when will they accept reading courses and academic materials electronically? Not being prophets, the most we can do is to keep paying attention to the changes in learning and academic groups' relevant behaviors and preferences. This paper presents a new study of this kind in China. The study reported by this paper was performed in 2015, and follow-up research is still on-going. This is an independent study, as well as part of a bigger program called Academic Reading Format International Study (ARFIS).

S. Kurbanoğlu et al. (Eds.): ECIL 2017, CCIS 810, pp. 526–534, 2018.
https://doi.org/10.1007/978-3-319-74334-9_54

2 Literature Review

From 2015, many scholars from different countries have published their results of ARFIS research, including Estonia [7], Croatia [8] and Qatar [9]. ARFIS has built a model for these research projects, including this paper, based on the foundation of Mizrachi's studies performed at the University of California, Los Angeles [6, 10]. Most of these studies presume students still prefer the print format to electronic, but with variations in different countries.

Since ARFIS and relevant research studies have become widely known, the authors see no necessity to make more passing references. It is more important for this study to review some significant research conducted in mainland China.

In 2008, Xiaobin Huang and his students performed a study on how undergraduates' reading behaviors are influenced by digital media, which gathered data from 100 undergraduates and 103 graduate students at Sun Yat-sen University [11, p. 53]. Time spent in reading digital course materials is rising and the convenience of the electronic format received wide acclaim among students. Another study conducted by Zha et al. aimed to explore users' perception of the ease of use and usefulness of print and electronic resources in Chinese university libraries [12]. Though the research team emphasized that users are undergoing a transfer of usage behavior from print to electronic resources, from 273 respondents of their study, only 12.09% would make electronic resources their first choice. Other than quantitative research on university students and library users, Yuan et al. provided another approach of reading format preference research in China. They performed a controlled experiment on 20 students. The reading test was divided into two groups, one for a paper book and another for an e-book, to see the difference between the two formats. They believe this research shows that "*paper reading favors systematic thinking, deep understanding and long-term memory, and digital reading boosts the ability of information access*" [13, p. 36].

3 Methodology

This study adopted the Academic Reading Questionnaire (ARQ). Based on the premise of keeping ARQ's original meanings and research purposes, the questionnaire was translated into Chinese with slight modification on expression for better understanding among local groups. The version used in China's study consists of 16 five-point Likert-style questions, along with some other questions gleaning respondents' background details. Respondents were asked to rank from "Strongly disagree" to "Strongly agree" in each Likert-style statement.

In order to provide a panoramic scope for the format preference issue, from March to July 2015, with the help of scholar network, we posted the ARQ online and randomly invited students from 33 universities and colleges from 17 cities to fill out the questionnaire. 1,165 valid on-line questionnaires were collected in mainland China. Though the survey was accomplished, additional research, including in-depth interviews on Chinese students and scholar groups are still carried out to gain explanation of the qualitative results. While the interview section is still in process, this paper only provides preliminary results of China's situation.

3.1 Demographic Information of Respondents

Response rates by gender are 37% male and 63% female. 56.91% (n = 663) of respondents are between 20 and 24 years old, and the mean of respondents' age is 24.31. The distribution of ages may relate to the sample's enrolment status, shown in Fig. 1.

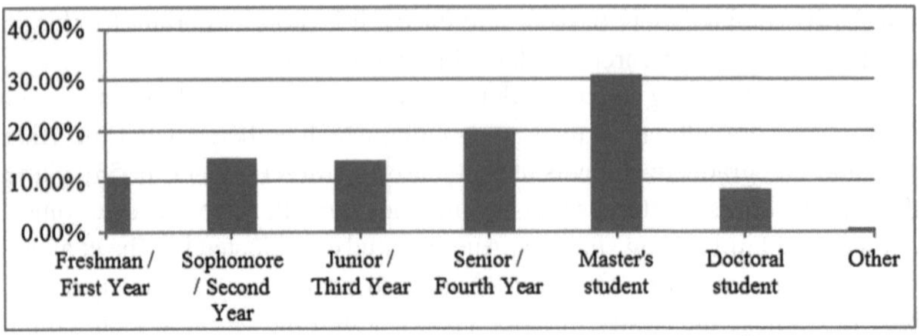

Fig. 1. Respondents' current status

28.5% (n = 332) of the total study are in social science; 12.70% (n = 148) are in engineering. The distribution is slight in liberal arts, science and medicine (10.04%, 10.9% and 10.73% respectively). A large number of responses (27.12%) choose "other" (n = 316). According to our interview research so far, there is a great possibility that management students tend to choose this answer ("other"), since in recent years, management has become regarded as an interdisciplinary subject.

4 Result

4.1 Reading Devices for Electronic Courses

Eight options are offered as answers for respondents in the question "I read my electronic course readings on a: __ (multiple-choice questions)". It's normal to see 72.02% (n = 839) of laptop computer use, which usually ranks first in similar research around the world, but surprisingly, the most popular answer in China is "Phones" (73.91%, n = 861) as Fig. 2 illustrates.

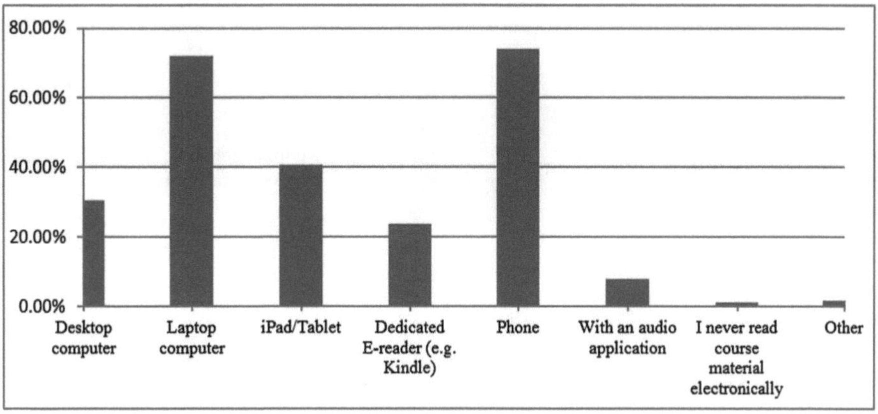

Fig. 2. Popular reading devices for electronic courses

4.2 General Preference on Academic Reading Format

Questions inquired about respondents' general preference, from the ARFIS questionnaire, including:

- I prefer to print out my course readings rather than read them electronically
- I prefer to read my course readings electronically
- I prefer to have all my course materials in print format (e.g. book, course reader, hand-outs)
- I like to make digital copies of my printed course materials
- I prefer electronic textbooks over print textbooks.

Together, in Figs. 3 and 4, the answers to these questions denote respondents' strong preference for print format while reading and using academic materials.

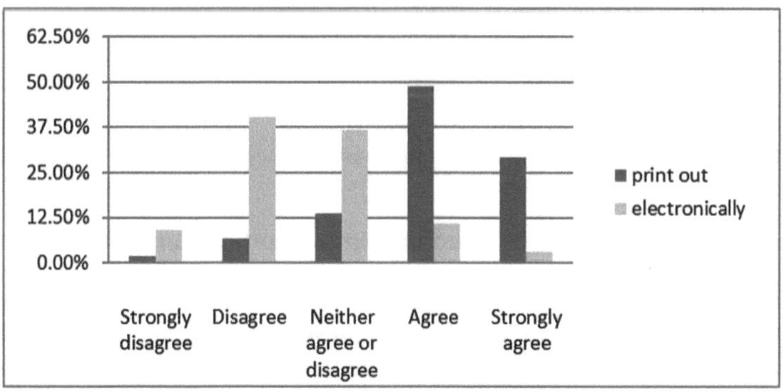

Fig. 3. Preference of reading in print or reading electronically

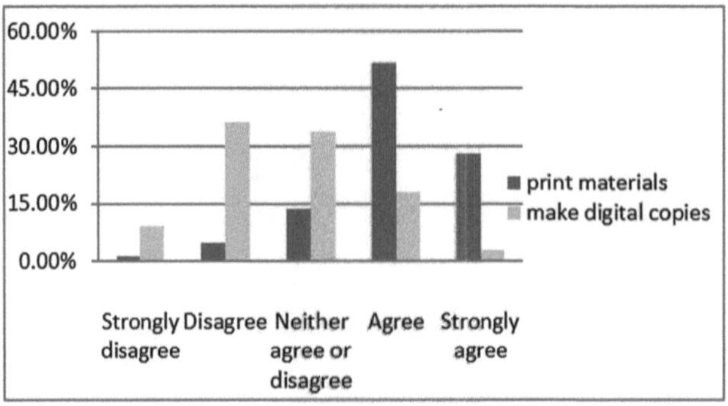

Fig. 4. Preference of printing materials or making digital copies

4.3 Recognition on Printed Learning Environment

The investigation of students' recognition when using printed materials includes inquiry on remembering and focusing. Figure 5 below states that nearly 60% (n = 692) of the students agree or strongly agree that they remember best when reading in print. This result demonstrates printed materials' advantage, but the percentage is much lower than that in Mizrachi's research [6, p. 305]. At the same time, over 80% (n = 937) agree or strongly agree with paper materials' positive effect on focusing, roughly even with Mizrachi's result.

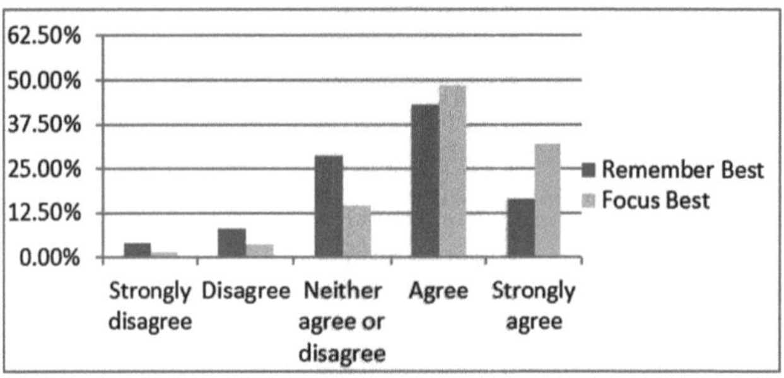

Fig. 5. Engagement when reading in print: remember (Question 1) and focus (Question 12)

4.4 Learning Behavior and Its Relationship to Reading Format

The ARQ asks three questions about learning behavior and its relationship to academic reading format. Figure 6 shows a preference that respondents are more likely to highlight and annotate when they are engaging printed materials. Figure 7 illustrates that 74.85% (n = 872) express tendency to review course readings if they are in print. However, in the meanwhile, it is not too hard to notice that electronic reading also accounts for a certain percentage of "Agree" and "Strongly Agree" in Fig. 6.

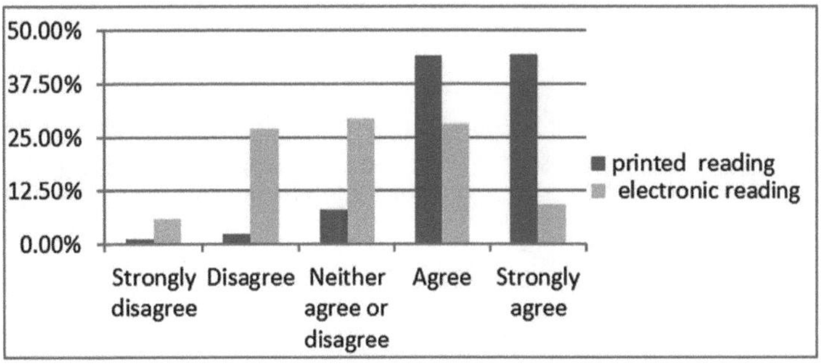

Fig. 6. Highlighting/annotating printed reading (Question 7) and electronic reading (Question 11)

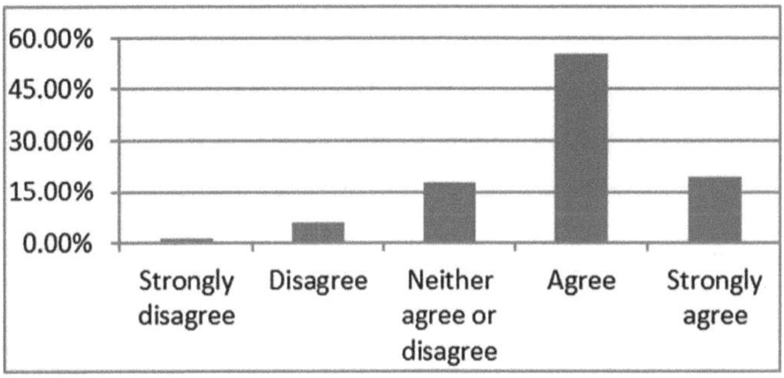

Fig. 7. Agreement for reviewing if reading materials are printed

4.5 Factors that Influenced Format Preference: Language, Length and Convenience

Length of the reading could be an important variable in choosing a different format. The designer of ARQ, adopted in this study, tends to use seven pages as a watershed for choosing to read in print or electronically. Figure 8 shows 78.28% (n = 912) of respondents want to (agree/strongly agree with) read paper materials when their reading tasks are over seven pages. When materials are less than seven pages, only 28.58% (n = 333) will read in electronic format.

So far this research demonstrates an overwhelming preference for printed materials in an academic context. Convenience could be one of the reasons that students are accustomed to using printed materials, and also the cause for electronic readings failing to catch up. Only about 30% (29.27%, n = 341) of respondents agree or strongly agree that reading electronically is more convenient than reading in print.

Language was often regarded as another factor in selecting reading format. But in our survey, only 25.49% (n = 297) of students confirmed (agree/strongly agree with) that their preferred format depends on the language of the reading.

However, our questionnaire offers another interesting angle to examine language's effect. As shown in Fig. 9, the respondents disagree or strongly disagree that they will tend to read electronically when materials are in their native language. And in Fig. 10,

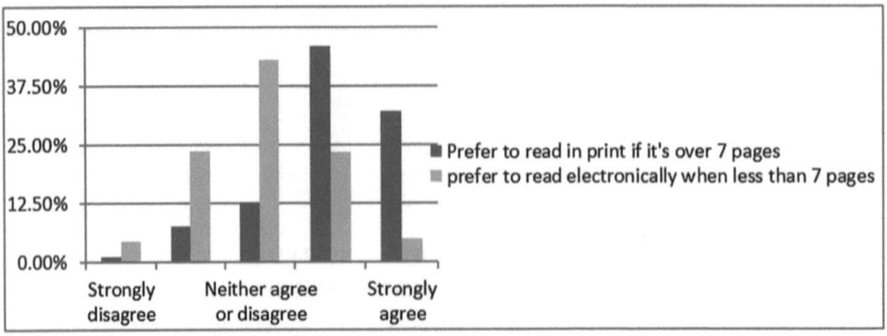

Fig. 8. 7 pages as the watershed for reading in print or electronically (Question 4, 8)

nearly 60% (59.91%, n = 698) of participants claim that they prefer to read foreign language materials in print. It is worth mentioning that the most popular foreign language in China's colleges and universities is English, because English has been a compulsory subject in the National College Entrance Examination (known as "Gao Kao") for a long time.

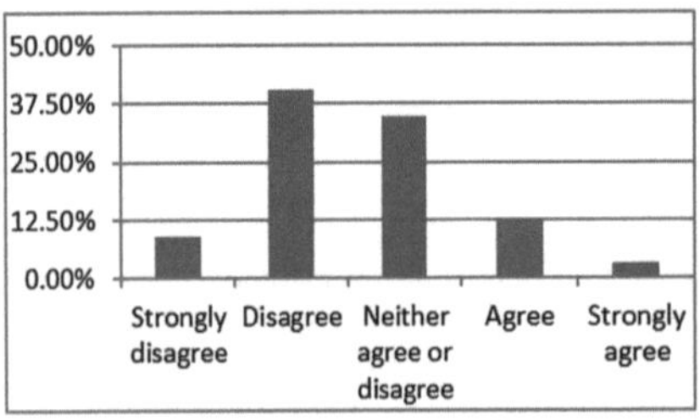

Fig. 9. Preferring to read course readings electronically rather than in print when they are in my native language

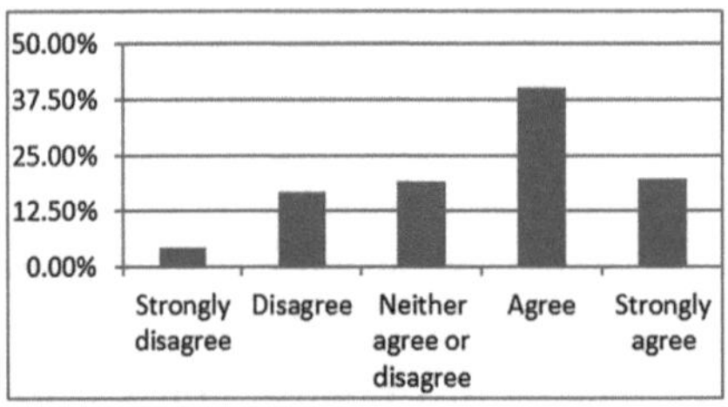

Fig. 10. Preferring to read foreign language material in print rather than electronic

The last possible factor is visual or other limitations. The distribution of answers to this question is actually pretty even: 48.41% (n = 564) of participants point out that these kinds of limitations have influenced their preference for electronic or print format.

5 Discussion and Conclusion

The ARQ survey in China no doubt shows students' strong preference for paper or printed materials compared to electronic versions. Though further research to find out possible reasons are still being conducted, possible options include: the natural advantages of printed materials in course and academic reading, such as "convenience" mentioned above, limited resources of electronic textbooks, and Chinese families and universities' stress on eye-protection.

The survey result is not surprising. Stressing that scholars and students still prefer print materials but not electronic ones has become more and more common in the field of LIS and the discipline of education. However, we need to notice that we are now only in the dawn of the digital age. Electronic/digital reading environments are evolving, strengthening devices' usability, adopting fresh surfaces and breeding new software. And more importantly, the meaning of "in print" has remained the same for a long period, but the content of "electronic" could be changing day by day. Only a few years ago, iPads and tablets popped up and became one of the dominating digital reading devices. That is why, in this study, we are strongly appealing to scholars, librarians and information specialists' attention to Fig. 2, which indicates the rise of smartphones as an important course reading device. In common sense, phones are not for course and academic reading, but nearly 74% of students choose phones as a choice when engaging electronic courses. This may relate to Chinese customers' tendency to buy cell phones with bigger screens, as an IDC report in May 2017 indicates: "*The share of less than 5 Inch screen size smartphone reduced to 21.2% in Q1 2017 from 40.3% in Q1 2016. The focus of China-based vendors remains on bigger screens, 9 out of 10 smartphones shipped by China-based vendors were 5 inch and above in Q1 2017.*" [14]. It could be a unique case which cannot be repeated again in other countries at the moment, but could also be a signal of a new era.

References

1. More than 70% of Chinese are Still Fond of the Reading in Print. http://media.people.com.cn/n/2013/0419/c40606-21194650.html
2. 11th National Reading Survey issued. http://hen.chinadaily.com.cn/n/2014-04-22/NEWS19051.html
3. Interpretation of 12th National Reading Survey. http://book.ifeng.com/a/20150504/14604_0.shtml
4. 13th National Reading Survey. http://book.sohu.com/20160421/n445248790.shtml
5. 14th National Reading Survey. http://book.sina.com.cn/news/whxw/2017-04-18/doc-ifyeimqy2574493-p2.shtml
6. Mizrachi, D.: Undergraduates' academic reading format preferences and behaviors. J. Acad. Librarianship **41**(3), 301–311 (2015)
7. Põldaas, M.: Print or electronic? Estonian students' preferences in their academic readings. In: Kurbanoğlu, S., Boustany, J., Špiranec, S., Grassian, E., Mizrachi, D., Roy, L., Çakmak, T. (eds.) ECIL 2016. CCIS, vol. 676, pp. 238–246. Springer, Cham (2016). https://doi.org/10.1007/978-3-319-52162-6_23
8. Pešut, D., Živković, D.: Students' academic reading format preferences in Croatia. New Libr. World **117**(5/6), 392–406 (2016)
9. Johnston, N., Salaz, A., Alsabbagh, L.: Print and digital reading preferences and behaviors of university students in Qatar. In: Kurbanoğlu, S., Boustany, J., Špiranec, S., Grassian, E., Mizrachi, D., Roy, L., Çakmak, T. (eds.) ECIL 2016. CCIS, vol. 676, pp. 247–255. Springer, Cham (2016). https://doi.org/10.1007/978-3-319-52162-6_24
10. Mizrachi, D.: Undergraduates' academic information and library behaviors: preliminary results. Ref. Serv. Rev. **38**(4), 571–580 (2010)
11. Xiaobin, H., Xiaoyan, L., Ziming, L.: Investigations and analyses of the influences of digital media on university student reading behaviors. Libr. Inf. Serv. **52**(2), 53–56 (2008)

12. Zha, X., Li, J., Yan, Y.: Understanding usage transfer from print resources to electronic resources: a survey of users of Chinese university libraries. Serials Rev. **38**(2), 93–98 (2012)
13. Yuan, X., Wang, J., Liu, L.: Experimental study on reading comprehension effects of paper reading and digital reading. J. Libr. Sci. Chin. **41**(9), 35–46 (2015)
14. China-based Vendors Now Contribute More Than Half of Indian Smartphone Market in CY Q1 2017: IDC India. https://www.idc.com/getdoc.jsp?containerId=prAP42557317

Information Grounds in the Eyes of the First-Year Information Management Students

Sabina Cisek(✉), Paloma Korycińska, and Monika Krakowska

Faculty of Management and Communication, Institute of Information and Library Science, Jagiellonian University, Cracow, Poland
{sabina.cisek,paloma.korycinska,monika.krakowska}@uj.edu.pl

Abstract. The main purpose of this paper has been to discover how novice information management students perceive "their" information grounds, that is places/social settings in which people seek and share information while being involved in a focal activity. The ability to comprehend one's own information behavior, including the identification and interpretation of "encountered" or "visited" information grounds, serves as a basis for, inter alia, the development of one's information culture and literacy, which is particularly important for future information professionals/scientists. The reported research is empirical and exploratory in nature, based on a text analysis method. The sample included 67 first-year information management students of the Jagiellonian University in Cracow. The following outcomes have been confirmed: (1) students are generally able to identify different information grounds following Fisher's trichotomy of places, people, and information-related phenomena; (2) the concept of information grounds seems to be a good starting point for teaching information behavior theories.

Keywords: First-year students · Information behavior · Information grounds Information professionals · Students of information management University teaching

1 Introduction

Exploration of information behavior, knowledge of various information tasks undertaken by users as well as awareness of their own, individual activities in this respect are elements of human information culture in its broad sense, in particular – for information professionals/scientists.

The inspirational aspect of the content presented, in line with introducing various methods of information flow diagnosing (including observation, self-realization, interpretation, and analysis) are important in the didactic process in the field of information behavior. The ability to perform one's own specific activities in response to information as a **conscious** reaction to it has an impact on the modification of individual information behavior and development of information competencies. At the same time, being aware of information processes in one's own professional and private life as well as managing information in the context of information activities related to the entire external

S. Kurbanoğlu et al. (Eds.): ECIL 2017, CCIS 810, pp. 535–544, 2018.
https://doi.org/10.1007/978-3-319-74334-9_55

environment of the user, who functions in it both individually and in groups, makes it possible to recognise information needs and behavior of other people. All these elements are essential in order to improve information culture, and in the context of life-long education.

Information behavior, just like information competencies, is a complex umbrella concept referring to a variety of features supporting the user in the constantly evolving information society. Cognitive skills, dynamic information seeking, critical and independent thinking, problem solving, understanding the ways of information and knowledge organisation are indispensable to be able to function in both professional and everyday-life information environments. Such competencies are fundamental in the education process of information management students who acquire information on human abilities, activities, and ways of feeling one's needs, seeking, managing, sharing, and using information in a variety of contexts and circumstances [1, 2].

The ability to professionally identify and understand information needs and behavior, both one's own and someone else's, is not innate; quite the opposite – one has to learn it. The education of students in this field is not simple, at least at the beginning of the information science program. Thus, education should include social and emotional approach in the presented models of information behavior as well as observation and understanding of everyday information activities and their context in the social environment, both the one familiar to and personal for the student and the one newly encountered by her/him. All that may be helpful in interpreting information behavior and encouraging students to explore this extremely important research area.

One of the models presented to the first-year students in the undergraduate program of information management at the Jagiellonian University in Cracow, Poland (JU) – particularly useful in this context – is Karen Fisher's information grounds (IG) idea, within the social and affective paradigm. To find out whether the components listed are truly important for the entire process of realizing and understanding observed (one's own and someone else's) information behavior, an analysis of the way of interpreting information grounds and the ability to identify them by the first-year students was carried out.

Thus, the main purpose of the reported research was to check whether the students are aware of their participation in information grounds at all, which is related to the evaluation of their knowledge of information behavior and information processes. Secondly, an attempt was made to find out whether the students can recognise the IG in which they participate as well as identify the most typical information grounds and the components that shape these communities. Thirdly, another goal was to capture the affective elements indicating involvement in information grounds and the linguistic, lexical, and semantic categories defining these synergistic environments. Here, the aim was, among others, to diagnose whether and what kind of an affective load or emotions determined the assignment of meaning to and understanding of the concept of IG.

This paper consists of six parts: introduction; theoretical framing – the concept of information grounds; material, methods, and participants; findings and discussion; conclusions; limitations and recommendations for future research.

2 Theoretical Framing – the Concept of Information Grounds

The idea of information grounds (IG) has been developed and empirically investigated by Fischer and her colleagues since the 1990s [3]. Now it constitutes one of the most influential concepts in information behavior research, contributing to deeper understanding of everyday contexts in which information seeking, sharing and transfer occur [4]. The investigation of information grounds involves comprehensive qualitative and quantitative studies of various groups of users, the role of social factors, standards and roles undertaken by people, the locations and affective approach to information processes occurring in these places [5]. The emergence of information grounds was observed – inter alia – in the following communities and groups of people: immigrant communities [3], public library users [6], school students [7], university students [5], virtual groups [8], mobile network users [9], stay-at-home women [10], participants of the Second Life virtual world [11], social media [12] as well as coffee shop clients in the context of military conflicts [13].

The interdisciplinary model of information environments has been developed on the basis of several theories. The key concepts on which the information ground scheme is founded include: (a) social constructionism, an epistemological approach according to which the perception and understanding of reality is subjective because of its permanent interpretation and interactions with other users [14], (b) Dervin's Sense Making metatheory, focusing, among others, on seeking/making the order and sense of reality [3], (c) Granovetter's concept of the Strength of Weak Ties, according to which weak bonds between people are the most valuable in the process of information acquisition and flow; they also determine integration of diverse groups of users and development of extended social networks, which enables interaction and information exchange with people of similar convictions [15], (d) the theory of Small Worlds by Elfreda Chatman, which makes it possible to diagnose various normative information activities in the groups in which participants have little contact with the persons who do not belong to the sociocultural environment of the little worlds created around themselves [16], (e) Oldenburg's approach which emphasizes the role of the place and space in which the user functions. Location, both in the real world and in cyberspace, may have an exceptional importance and create space for social relations, be characterized by a special climate (atmosphere) and interior design which increases emotional welfare supporting or activating information processes, in particular – information acquisition, sharing, transfer and response to it. It should be emphasized that the initial concept of the third place by Oldenburg, which served as a basis for the development of the idea of information grounds, may also refer to the location of professional activity (place of work) and formal processes of education (schools, universities), where mutual social relations are strengthened [3].

The concept of information grounds was formulated in reference to the aspects of the trichotomic relationship – involving people, places, and information-related phenomena. These attributes, having affective and social dimensions, include, among others, the size and type of membership, familiarity, actor roles, social roles, emotions and motivations of the participants of information grounds, focal activities undertaken in each space, conviviality, creature comforts, location and permanence, privacy, and noise level [5]. The characteristic qualities of information grounds include: incidentality, neutrality, social interactiveness in the process of information flow and diversity of the participants who influence one another. It is also significant that participants are involved in formal and informal ways of information sharing, which makes information transfer multi-directional while the information obtained is used in a non-conventional way. Users benefit in a physical, affective, cognitive, and social sense. The information ground which makes the basis for a variety of social, cognitive, and informational processes is referred to as the grand context, including several sub-contexts, which are created by individual participants, their perspective, subjective understanding of reality, phenomena, and objects. The sub-context may also be defined by the physical surroundings, the architecture of the interior and the place [17]. The affective elements characterizing information grounds condition the evaluation of events, the place, and people. In this way, they determine the importance and level of adjustment to the context of the situation or information circumstances. They may also serve as grounds for an increased emotional arousal with positive qualities, which activates certain kinds of information behavior [18].

The theory of information grounds makes it possible to diagnose various information activities of their participants. Exposing the element of emotional involvement in information transfer and sharing in specific, small, socio-cultural communities motivates the students to reflect upon and study information behavior, both in the academic community and in the context of everyday life.

3 Material, Methods, and Participants

The reported mixed-method research was empirical and exploratory in nature, based on a document/text analysis technique and content analysis (of written accounts) [19]. The goals of our study are stated in the Introduction section of this paper.

The research was carried out in a group of 95 first-year full-time undergraduate students of information management at the Institute of Information and Library Science of the Jagiellonian University between November 2016 and January 2017. The study was executed in four groups in different periods of time because of different class schedules of the groups. In class, the students were taught the theory of information grounds. The most important components and assumptions of this concept were listed and characterized and the examples from the relevant literature were presented. At the same time, the students were required to carry out – as a compulsory assignment – a few days observation of information grounds, those familiar to and frequented by them as well as the new ones, and then prepare their characteristics in writing. Selected essays were verified during oral presentations. The descriptions were sent directly to the university e-learning platform Pegaz, which is used to offer online courses. Eventually, 67 essays were collected. They were characteristics of information grounds by students who actively participated in the Information Behavior course offered in the first semester of the undergraduate program.

Table 1. Types and aspects of information grounds named by the students

Type and aspect	Number of characteristics	Percentage (N = 146)
People-related	Total: 1	0.7
"A man on a tram"	1	
Places-related	Total: 144	98.6
Means of transport	34	23.3
Catering facilities	30	20.5
Social meetings	18	12.3
Waiting rooms in clinics	13	8.9
School/university	13	8.9
Mass events	12	8.2
Shop	10	6.8
Home/family meeting	6	4.1
Internet communicators	2	1.3
Library	2	1.3
Other	4	2.7
Information-related	Total: 1	0.7
Information meetings	1	

Table 2. Attributes of information grounds named by the students

Attributes	Number of characteristics which included a given attribute (quality)	Percentage (N = 146)
Location and permanence	139	95.2
Conversation topic	137	93.8
- Non-specified (chit-chat/ small talk)	72	49.3
- Specified	65	44.5
Type of information behavior observed	78	53.4
Membership type	46	31.5
Focal activities	42	28.7
Familiarity	33	22.6
Noise level	27	18.5
Emotions and motivations of participants	18	12.3
Conviviality	12	8.2
Actors' roles	8	5.4
Membership size	8	5.4
Social roles	7	4.8

The entire contents of 67 students' essays sent to the university e-learning platform Pegaz was manually transferred to a Word file and processed using QDA Miner licensed software. In the corpus thus created, 146 (N = 146) characteristics of information grounds were distinguished. Students could label them freely as, for example, "A waiting room in a clinic" or "A train journey". The following tasks were carried out: (1) thematic categorisation of the material in terms of the type of the information ground described using the trichotomy of people – places – information-related phenomena (Table 1), (2) thematic categorisation using the list of pre-defined criteria corresponding to IG properties (cf. Table 2) in order to define the completeness and thoroughness of the characteristics prepared by students, (3) inductive tagging of expressive acts of speech, that is utterances expressing the cognitive and emotional attitude of the message sender to what he or she is saying; the same part of the analysis focused on looking for the signs of emotions in students' utterances, (4) tagging the fragments that fulfilled the genre requirements of a narrative (micro-stories), (5) mechanical frequency analyses and calculations illustrating the difference in the capacity of characteristics.

4 Findings and Discussion

The collected characteristics of the students' information grounds differed in terms of capacity: the shortest one included two words, the longest – 192 words, while the average was 83 words. Table 1 presents the results of the analysis of the material with the focus on the type and aspects of the IG described, using Fischer's trichotomy – people, places, and information-related phenomena [5].

In the examined sample of the first-year information management students, the information grounds having specific frameworks in public space turned out to be the easiest to capture and understand by the students, and link with their own experience. In general, identification is correct, but the indication of home is surprising. It should be mentioned that in Polish scholarly literature and teaching practice, information grounds are translated literally as "temporary information places". The adjective "temporary" strongly emphasizes the transient, elusive and short-term nature of the communication exchange and, above all, the instability and unpredictability of the communication settings. In this context, qualifying one's own home and, in two cases, even traditional Christmas family meetings (Christmas Eve dinner) as information grounds may be seen in two ways: as an erroneous identification or as a possible confirmation of the attitude of the respondent to the bonds in his or her family. This doubt cannot be resolved using the method of obtaining empirical material applied in the study, thus, *ex abundanti cautela*, these indications should be considered erroneous or at least debatable from the point of view of compatibility with the definition of information grounds presented to the students beforehand.

The indications revealed in the empirical material are, by and large, quite general, and usually repetitive, most often with a concise explanation only, including the examples provided by the teacher. One should not forget, however, that the characteristics examined were created either during classes, that is in limited time, or as homework, both as a result of the teacher's instruction, which, because of the inherent factor of coercion, may encourage students to adopt conservative attitudes. What stands out against this background is less obvious identifications revealing a greater degree of reflection and true intention to translate one's own experiences into the language of information grounds. They include, in the category of "Places": a meeting of Anonymous Alcoholics, a casting announced by a television station, regular meetings of people who participate, free-of-charge, as audience members in the Polish TVN talk-show, "a charity event" (as labelled by a student) – work for Caritas, a charity, and the following description that was identified in Table 1 as "A man on a tram": "One day, when I was on a tram going back from university (…), half-way through my journey a man got on the tram and took a seat opposite the door. When the tram left the tram stop the man communicated the following message: 'I'd like to invite you to visit my Facebook page 'GAY. The fundamental rights of the European Union'. He repeated this message two, maybe three, more times and then got off. I was very much surprised by the form of communicating this information. Although passengers were talking, when they heard this man, they all went silent and focused their attention on him. In my case, because of my major, it was an extraordinary experience. Of course, I was too flustered to go to the website immediately while on the tram, but I checked it out when I got home. The type of information: incidental discovery of information".

The measure of cognitive attractiveness of the concept of information grounds is, in our opinion, the number of attributes that the students could assign to the IGs identified by them. Table 2 presents the quantitative distribution of qualities included in the examined characteristics (students' essays).

The majority of students' opinions reveal information grounds as places where people create ad hoc, incidental communities because of a joint operational aim, but the exchange of information occurs in them as a side effect. As for such IGs as means of transport, shops, cafés or mass events, the respondents emphasized the trivial and random nature of the conversations made. This is of great importance, because it means that they independently identified the communication situations in which the phatic function of the language was realized, the one used to maintain interpersonal relations without any informational value and/or direct practical application of the messages.

The degree of the completeness of the characteristics of information grounds provided in Table 2 shows that they were usually shallow and quite general, probably because they were written hastily to meet the requirements of the course. This is also confirmed by the sloppiness of preparation as some of the essays were sent using smart phones, they included spelling mistakes and lacked diacritical marks. Given these circumstances, the relevance of essay contents deserves to be praised.

The descriptions analysed, despite their perfunctory nature, may serve as a source of valuable didactic information on how first-year students, 19–20-year-old in Poland, who belong to the generation of digital natives perceive the rules of social co-existence and communication barriers. Here, the interesting observations are the following: "[on the train] people have more information to convey because they do not know each other", "[at a friend's party] despite the difference in age and interests, we were at the same place and occasion, which made interaction possible between people who normally do not talk to one another". In the first comment, the respondent is aware of the phenomenon of communication disinhibition related to the sense of anonymity in a public place, while in the second, the respondent reveals the awareness of the existence of social separatisms, based on her own observations, which are abolished in IG.

The characteristics were developed as class assignments, which is probably why they are impersonal and, as such, deprived of an emotional focus. They are dominated by a reporting tone, noun phrases and enumerations in the syntactic layer, for example a list of issues discussed in the conversations of the participants of a given IG. Just in ten percent of them IG is described in the first person, from the perspective of a participant/witness/observer of a communication event, with semantic qualities related to emotions. In four descriptions, there were some stylistic figures, in particular self-irony employed by a student to evaluate his own attempt to use a conversation with a shop assistant as a pretext to flirt ("and then I told her a weak joke").

In the research reported here, it was assumed that the narrative character of an utterance was an important indicator of the communicative nature of information grounds understood as the ease with which first-year students of information management may learn it, that is include it in their personal repertoire of possible scripts used in the perception of social reality. Putting one's individual experience in the form of a story/fiction is the fundamental human sense-making strategy, as noted by, for example, Dervin [20]. Therefore, it was assumed that the more micro-stories in the material studied, the greater the probability that the students did try to use the IG concept as a filter facilitating the interpretation of various communication events, including their own and someone else's emotions that lay the foundation for or were the consequence of these events. The impact of the conditions in which the students performed the task, however, was underestimated, as a result of which the material included only four comments developed using a narrative scheme or even revealing the qualities of a micro-feature. They focused on the information behavior of the people observed at a playground, a bank, in a means of transport ("A man on a tram") and a village shop.

5 Conclusions

Our research intended to find out whether the novice information management students are aware of their participation in information grounds at all, as well as recognise the IG in which they take part, and are capable of naming attributes/components of the observed information grounds. As a theoretical basis, we used Fischer's approach and concepts [3, 5]. Generally speaking, no flagrant mistakes in the identification of information grounds were discovered in the collection of the students' IG descriptions. But there were some ambivalent indications, six in total (4%), in which the IG pointed out were home/family and university classes. As it was impractical to determine the motivation behind these indications, they were treated as probable mistakes and, at the same time, signals of possible instability/fluidity of the respondents' idea of the differences between information environments that Oldenburg [21] included in the category of the first, second and third places, which is definitely worth a separate study. Also, it was interesting to observe that the attributes of IGs named by the JU students (see Table 2) are noticeably similar to those identified by Fischer et al. in their investigation of college students' information grounds [5].

Most often (77%), the respondents identified IGs as places where the phatic function of the language could be fulfilled. From the perspective of the organisation of the didactic process at the first year of study at the Institute of Information and Library Science of the Jagiellonian University, this confirms the rationale of offering such courses as "Social Communication and the Media" and "Introduction to Linguistic Pragmatics" along with the class "Information Behavior". In this way, the communication events experienced by students may be explored in a multifaceted and interdisciplinary way. In addition, the didactic methods applied in teaching the theory of information behavior should be extended to include the component of the organisation of experiences and knowledge by means of a story.

In the light of the results obtained, the IG concept is a good starting point in the introduction to the theory of information behavior in the first year of the information management program because, first of all, it refers to the information situations and behavior that the students are familiar with in everyday life and, secondly, it considers the emotional element which is noticed and felt by the students.

6 Limitations and Recommendations for Future Research

The present findings and conclusions ought to be seen as partial and tentative, because of two reasons. *Primo*, the technique of obtaining empirical material adopted in our study was not optimal for evaluating the cognitive (and emotional) receptiveness of students with regard to information grounds. The IG characteristics developed in class or as homework frequently appeared to be generic (basic), perfunctory, and lacking deeper personal insights or stories. Therefore, at the next stage of exploration, the techniques applied should not be subject to the distorting effect of coercion/duty.

Secundo, only a convenience sample of information management students from one university was used. To acquire a more comprehensive picture of the perception of IG by future information professionals as well as the didactic value of the theory of information grounds, further research – involving different universities in various countries – is needed.

References

1. Fisher, K.E., Erdelez, S., McKechnie, L.E.F. (eds.): Theories of Information Behavior. Information Today, Medford (2005)
2. Savolainen, R.: Information behavior and information practice: reviewing the "umbrella concepts" of information-seeking studies. Libr. Quart. Inf. Community Policy **77**(2), 109–132 (2007)
3. Fisher, K.E., Naumer, C.M.: Information grounds: theoretical basis and empirical findings on information flow in social settings. In: Spink, A., Cole, C. (eds.) New Directions in Human Information Behavior, pp. 93–111. Springer, Dordrecht (2006). https://doi.org/10.1007/1-4020-3670-1_6
4. Fisher, K.E., Julien, H.: Information behavior. Ann. Rev. Inf. Sci. Technol. **43**(1), 1–73 (2009)
5. Fisher, K.E., Landry C.F., Naumer, C.: Social spaces, casual interactions, meaningful exchanges: 'information ground' characteristics based on the college student experience. Inf. Res. **12** (2) (2007). http://www.informationr.net/ir/12-2/paper291.html

6. McKechnie, L.E.F., McKenzie, P.: The young child/adult caregiver story time program as information ground. In: Library Research Seminar III, Kansas City, MO, 14–16 October 2004 (2004)
7. Spencer, C.L.: The social information grounds of Māori secondary school students. In: Bilal, D., Beheshti, J. (eds.) New Directions in Children's and Adolescents' Information Behavior Research, pp. 191–213. Emerald Group Publishing Limited, Bingley (2014)
8. Talip, B.A., Narayan, B., Edwards, S.L., Watson, J.: Digital ethnography as a way to explore information grounds on Twitter. Qual. Quant. Methods Libr. **5**(1), 89–105 (2016)
9. Counts, S., Fisher, K.E.: Mobile social networking as information ground: a case study. Libr. Inf. Sci. Res. **32**(2), 98–115 (2010)
10. Fisher, K.E., Landry, C.F.: Information and everyday life: the role of affect in the information behavior of stay-at-home mothers. In: Nahl, D., Bilal, D. (eds.) Emotional Design: The Emergent Affective Paradigm in Information Seeking and Use Research, pp. 211–234. Information Today, Medford (2007)
11. Lin, P., Eisenberg, M.B., Marino, J.: Second life as an information ground: implications for collaborative information behavior (2010). http://www.academia.edu/492941/Second_Life_as_an_Information_Ground_Implications_for_Collaborative_Information_Behavior
12. Narayan, B., Talip, B.A., Watson, J., Edwards, S.: Social media as online ınformation grounds: a preliminary conceptual framework. In: Urs, S.R., Na, J.-C., Buchanan, G. (eds.) ICADL 2013. LNCS, vol. 8279, pp. 127–131. Springer, Cham (2013). https://doi.org/10.1007/978-3-319-03599-4_15
13. Rohman, A., Pang, N.: Seeking common ground: coffee shops as information grounds in the context of conflict (2015). https://www.asist.org/files/meetings/am15/proceedings/submissions/papers/48paper.pdf
14. Tuominen, K., Savolainen, R.: A social constructionist approach to the study of information use as discursive action. In: Vakkari, P., Savolainen, R., Dervin, B. (eds.) Information Seeking in Context. Proceedings of an International Conference on Research in Information Needs, Seeking and Use in Different Contexts, 14–16 August 1996, Tampere, Finland, pp. 81–96. Taylor Graham, London (1997)
15. Granovetter, M.S.: The strength of weak ties. Am. J. Sociol. **78**(6), 1360–1380 (1973)
16. Burnett, G., Jaeger, P.T.: Small worlds, life worlds, and information: the ramifications of the information behavior of social groups in public policy and the public sphere. Inf. Res. **13** (2) (2008). http://InformationR.net/ir/13-2/paper346.html
17. Williams, R.D., Smith, C.A.: Constructing the information ground of the campus disability center. Libr. Inf. Sci. Res. **38**, 285–291 (2016)
18. Krakowska, M.: Koncepcja tymczasowych miejsc informacyjnych ("information grounds") i rola emocji w badaniach zachowań informacyjnych użytkowników. In: Kocójowa, M. (ed.) Biblioteki, Informacja, Książka: Interdyscyplinarne Badania i Praktyka w 21 Wieku (w Dziesięciolecie Śmierci prof. dra hab. Wiesława Bieńkowskiego). ePublikacje Instytutu INiB UJ, vol. 7. INIB UJ, Kraków (2010). http://skryba.inib.uj.edu.pl/wydawnictwa/e07/n-krakowska.pdf
19. Flick, U. (ed.): The Sage Handbook of Qualitative Data Analysis. Sage Publications Ltd., London (2013)
20. Dervin, B.: On studying information seeking methodologically: the implications of connecting metatheory to method. Inf. Process. Manag. **35**, 727–750 (1999)
21. Oldenburg, R.: The Great Good Place: Cafes, Coffee Shops, Bookstores, Bars, Hair Salons, and Other Hangouts at the Heart of a Community (improved reprint). Da Capo Press, Boston (1999)

Information Literacy of Elderly People: Bridging the Digital Gap

Iva Zadražilová(✉)

Charles University, Prague, Czech Republic
iva.zadrazilova@gmail.com

Abstract. The aim of this paper is to present the methods and results of qualitative research focused on the use of the Internet by senior citizens in the Czech Republic. These results offer a unique insight into the situation which is terminologically described as a secondary digital divide. The purpose of the qualitative research was to recognize and describe what topics seniors are interested in, what their motivation to use the Internet is and how and why they search for information. The outcomes define the senior citizens' fields of interest, information behaviour and the level of their searching skills. The research is part of a doctoral thesis oriented to elderly people, their information literacy skills and secondary digital gap.

Keywords: Information literacy · Senior citizens · Digital divide · Internet Information and communication technologies

1 Introduction

The digital divide is a term discussed in various professional communities. This phenomenon emerged at the turn of the 21st century with the rapid development of technologies that control all spheres of human life. The possibility to access information technology and the ability to use it has begun to strongly influence the social, economic, cultural and political integration of individuals into society. The development of today's information society brings with it many new possibilities, but also new barriers for those who cannot or do not want to adapt to a fast pace [1, 2]. Hence, significant differences arise between different groups of citizens, which are mainly determined by the use of information and communication technologies and the degree of their adaptation to everyday life [3].

The original definitions of the digital divide emphasized in particular the physical access to the Internet and the ownership of modern technologies – this is what we today call the primary digital divide [3]. With the development of the Internet and information and communication technologies however, we can observe that in economically stabilized and developed societies it is no longer the physical access and ownership that is the core issue; inequalities are most evident in capabilities or competencies of individuals to use these technologies effectively. Physical access as the original digital divide indicator is slowly losing importance. Another stage, called the secondary digital divide, has been identified [2]. Secondary digital divide emerges between groups of people who

S. Kurbanoğlu et al. (Eds.): ECIL 2017, CCIS 810, pp. 545–554, 2018.
https://doi.org/10.1007/978-3-319-74334-9_56

have access to and own technology, but their use skills are diametrically different. The digital divide makes it impossible for an individual or group to access information and options that are commonly available to the population on the opposite side of the divide. In this context, it is becoming increasingly important to explore the use of the Internet by a selected group, and to implement this knowledge in particular into the structure of lifelong learning.

According to data of the Czech Statistical Office [4], the overwhelming dominance of the youngest age groups in the use of the Internet has been steadily weakening in the recent years. In 2011, one fifth of all Internet users in the Czech Republic were older than 55 years and the number of these users is growing dynamically [4]. Based on demographic forecasts, we can see that this trend will continue along with the aging of the population. According to the latest data, the percentage of people aged 55 to 74 who used a computer or the Internet in the past three months is approximately 52% [4]. In the future, we can expect the number of senior Internet users to grow more and more rapidly. At present, retirement age is already reached by people who are accustomed to using Internet technology automatically both in work and in personal life.

Hence, the decision to focus empirical research on seniors was motivated by this fact, but also followed from the focus of my dissertation on information literacy in relation to the digital divide. My aim was to explore this phenomenon in respect of a specific target group. I was interested in identifying the needs that arise for this group in working with the Internet as well as in how these needs are satisfied.

1.1 Review of Recent Literature

Why do we want to explore how this target group uses the Internet, how deep the digital divide is and what can be done to mitigate it, in the first place? Old age as a stage of life is as important as any other stage and deserves the same emphasis on development. The period of old age stretches over 20–30 years and is in terms of its length similar to the age of youth and early adulthood. If older people are to be able to cater to their own needs and continue to live independently in their homes, they need to be able to get information and work with it. People of this age today commonly use the Internet and have their goals and needs that reflect their personal motivation, skill level and level of information literacy. At the same time, this group is described as one of the most vulnerable to digital exclusion, as many studies suggest [5–7]. The authors in principle agree that the more information and communication technologies (the Internet) will become the exclusive infrastructure of communication and information access, the more those who do not use the Internet at all or use it less effectively will be disadvantaged. This may be called the paradox of information literacy [1].

Research on the target group of senior citizens and their use of the Internet suggests that older people feel the need to learn some specific skills [8], that they commonly use the Internet and have some degree of information literacy. Among the aspects that influence their motivation to use the Internet are their capabilities and the amount of time and effort invested in learning [7].

Other research [9] identifies a number of differences in the use of the Internet by different target groups. This includes studies that have demonstrated that people of different sex, age, education, and Internet experience spend their time online differently. The general conclusion is that the Internet will increasingly reflect the social, economic and cultural relationships existing in the offline world, including inequalities [10].

In the Czech Republic, however, no qualitative research has yet been carried out to investigate the real needs of seniors in working with the Internet and how they are met.

2 Research Methods

2.1 Research Strategy

The aim of the research was to obtain detailed and complete information on the work of seniors with the Internet. Since I did not have sufficient data about the issue examined, I chose qualitative type of research. I attempted to get as much information as possible and to find regularity in the obtained data to determine new hypotheses or theories. In view of the type of research, the grounded theory design appeared as the most appropriate research strategy. Its main objective is to create a theory that will show what is important in the area under examination. Although the data from qualitative research cannot be generalized to describe the entire population, it has helped to get a better idea of how and why seniors use the Internet, what their information needs are, how they satisfy them, and what influences their information behaviour.

2.2 Definition of Research Topic and the Main Research Question

The main research question was defined as follows: How are the seniors' interests concerning information on the Internet satisfied? Given the emphasis on the experience of respondents in relation to everyday use of the Internet and work with information, the research was primarily concerned with the information behaviour of seniors and their information and media literacy. The main goal was to determine how seniors satisfy their needs and how they use the Internet.

In order to achieve maximum unity in what can be understood as satisfaction of interests, two specific topics were selected, which were discussed in interviews with respondents. These were the areas where seniors' interests are satisfied and areas where seniors consider their needs unsatisfied and encounter barriers. These topics were reflected in individual research questions:

1. In what areas do seniors feel that their interests are being met?
2. What practices do seniors use to satisfy their interests?
3. In what areas do seniors feel that their interests are not being met?
4. Where do they feel barriers to satisfying their interests?

These questions were subsequently elaborated into more detailed sub-questions that were asked in the interviews. To determine how seniors approach working with information, I applied the structure of the interview the Global Media and Information Literacy Assessment Framework: Country Readiness and Competencies (MIL), which is used to describe levels of individual competencies with respect to MIL. The MIL Assessment Framework proposes 12 major competencies [11]. These competencies were reflected in individual questions; as an illustration I provide three primary aspects of the standard:

- MIL component 1: Recognizing the demand for, being able to search for, being able to access and retrieve information and media content.
- MIL component 2: Understanding, assessment and evaluation of information and media.
- MIL component 3: Creation, utilization, and monitoring of information and media content.

Further questions concerned the frequency of technology use, the barriers, and help. Identification of the areas in which seniors would like to learn more and improve their skills was part of the focus.

2.3 Selection of Respondents

To select the research sample, the non-probability method of purposive sampling, combined with self-selection sampling was chosen. Since the objective of the research was not to observe representativeness as it is for instance understood in quantitative research, it was possible to choose non-probability sampling, which is commonly used in qualitative research. An essential characteristic of this type of selection is that the method of choosing a research sample is usually not fixed in advance and could change during the research. Purposive sampling is based solely on the researcher's judgment as to what should be observed and what can be observed. His or her conclusions can hardly be generalized. The researcher must clearly, accurately and openly define the population that his or her sample actually represents.

Therefore, the respondents were selected to meet the criteria I set at the beginning of the research. I addressed some of the respondents as a follow-up to previous contact with them. I was casually familiar with these potential participants and approached them in person. These were students of the University of the Third Age (three individuals) or participants of seminars I hold for seniors (two individuals). The rest of the respondents recruited from my contacts (parents or grandparents of my acquaintances, colleagues, etc.). It turned out in one case that the respondent had previous experience with qualitative research, albeit in another field.

2.4 Sample Characteristics

The originally expected number of respondents ranged between seven and ten respondents. The final number was not predetermined and was based on sample saturation. The interviews took place between March and April 2017. All the respondents I had pre-selected agreed with the interview and the final sample included nine respondents. I also had other respondents who wanted to become part of the research, but once the sample was saturated, there was no need for interviews with them. I contacted six respondents by e-mail and three respondents by phone. Two respondents are partners and live in a common household. A personal semi-structured interview was conducted with all respondents. Respondents were selected on the basis of the following criteria:

1. Respondent falls into the 65+ age group. This age category was set with respect to the age definition of a senior, as I understand it for the purposes of the dissertation. No upper age limit was set.
2. The respondent has experience with handling modern information and communication technologies and commonly uses these technologies (the respondent is computer-literate). Fulfilment of this condition was verified when the respondent was addressed by asking the following self-assessment questions prior to arranging an appointment: Can you turn on the PC? Are you able to launch the Internet? Do you know how to open a browser? Are you able to enter a simple search query?
3. The respondent has access to the Internet (not only at home, also from a library).

Full anonymity was ensured for the respondents; they are referred to by fictional surnames in the research. Similarly, all the other names mentioned by the respondents in the interviews were also deliberately changed.

Seven women and two men participated in the research. Coincidentally, without taking this criterion into account in advance, six respondents have a university degree; one respondent even holds an associate professor degree. The difference between the youngest and the oldest respondent is 25 years, i.e., a whole generation.

2.5 Data Collection Methods

Through the interview, it is possible to penetrate more deeply, get a great deal of data, while giving the respondents the time and space to accurately express themselves and communicate their own stories. Due to certain mobility constraints faced by this target group, each interview was conducted at one time, during one meeting. Interview time ranged from 25 to 39 min. Two interviews took place in a café chosen by the respondents. Two interviews took place in the flats of the seniors situated in a home for the elderly. Three interviews took place in the flats or homes of the respondents. One interview took place in the respondent's office, and one conversation was conducted over Skype with a respondent who was at home. These were environments that the seniors know well and feel positive about. Therefore, the assumption that in an atmosphere of familiar and safe environment, respondents will be more willing to answer thoroughly and openly the questions asked was confirmed. During the data collection process, I slightly modified some of the questions, also on the basis of working with the data already collected. This can be illustrated by the question of whether seniors can imagine their lives without the Internet, which was not included in the original script.

Questions and sub-questions were therefore predetermined, but during the interview, according to the semi-structured interview method, the respondents were asked additional questions based on the dynamics of the interview and the information provided by the respondents. These questions were to lead to a deeper understanding of the phenomenon under examination and to the clarification of information obtained from the respondents. The questions were formulated so as to allow the respondent to reconstruct and describe his or her experience in relation to the use of the Internet and information and communication technologies as accurately as possible. Taking into account the specifics of the target group of seniors, I encouraged respondents to tell me their story or describe specific examples and situations. Respondents also gave oral and written informed consent stating that they are familiar with and agree to the course of the research. Since the identity of the respondents was known to me, anonymity was ensured at least in the sense that the true identity of the research participants would not be known to anyone else.

All interviews were recorded using voice recording software. I then transcribed all the recordings literally. Transcripts are not edited stylistically and are left in the natural language as uttered. The next phase of working with the data was open coding. In this stage, I divided the text into units to which I assigned names and continued to work with the newly-tagged fragments.

I organized the categories that emerged from open coding into the structure of subcategories and main categories. In the open coding stage, six key categories were analysed; the description and detailed analysis of their meaning was produced by the so-called "showing of cards" technique.

3 Findings

The categories that will be presented below were created with regard to the goal of the research, which is in particular an effort to find an answer to the question of how are the seniors' interests concerning information on the Internet satisfied? For the sake of clarity, I include the subcategories that I used in determining the final main categories (Table 1).

Table 1. Main categories and subcategories

Main category	Subcategory
Personality aspects in working with technology	Barriers and problems in using technology, level of trust in the virtual environment, motivation, attitude to working with the Internet, personification of the Internet, experience with and self-confidence in working with ICT
Influence of the environment	Milestones in working with technology, helpers and teachers, media influence
Internet of daily life	Current use of the Internet, everyday use, technology used
Information literacy indicators	Information skills, area without skills, proven procedures
Satisfied and unsatisfied needs	Recognized and unrecognized needs, areas of interest satisfaction, procedures for satisfying needs, need for communication
Education	Interest in education

3.1 Personality Aspects in Working with Technology

The research has shown that the individual and his or her personality are an integral part of technology use. The barriers and problems that accompany the work with technologies and the Internet have been identified as significant issues. The origin of a barrier was often associated with previous negative experience, the respondent's concern that something would go wrong in the process or simply with uncertainty. Personality aspects were also reflected in respondents' level of confidence in interacting with the online environment, whether it was an a priori feeling of mistrust of the Internet as such or, on the contrary, uncritical confidence in the accuracy of the information found. The question of respondents' motivation to start using the Internet was mostly linked to the need for communication, whether within the family or at work. Another motivation category was curiosity or leisure. The respondents' attitude to working with the Internet depended on their time and space to try something new, as well as on whether they identified themselves as active or passive users and whether they perceived the computer as a close person or friend. The analysis revealed that self-confidence of respondents, their knowledge and skills, and relying on their own judgment and the ability to find what they need are also important factors.

3.2 Influence of the Environment

The influence of the environment on the individual working with the technology has proved a crucial category. The support of family or friends plays an enormous role for the target group of seniors, and this category was strongly emphasized by all respondents. Family members (mostly younger age groups) or friends act not only as teachers, who initiated the respondents into working with technology, but in particular as advisers who can provide immediate help when a current need or a technical problem arises. All respondents, without exception, would not be able to cope without help from outside.

3.3 Internet of Daily Life

This category emerged in connection with questions asking the respondents to describe their current way of using the Internet. More or less identical frequencies of Internet usage with respondents turning it on every day have been identified. The Internet of daily life can be used to refer to a set of activities, such as following news, searching for specific information, using Internet banking, playing games, e-mailing, shopping, working activities, and map and timetable orientation. This category also involved identification of the software or hardware owned or used by the respondents.

3.4 Information Literacy Indicators

Effective use of information and communication technologies implies a degree of information literacy. Respondents described the skills they have as well as areas without the required skills. It was interesting to find that MIL Standard competencies appear in this case both in the areas where seniors are confident and also where they feel they lack orientation. A typical area where respondents mostly feel secure is the forwarding and passing of information and the ability to find the information they need. It is important to note that they are for the most part satisfied with the first results they receive and do not search further. Nevertheless, there was an effort to verify certain types of information from multiple sources. The area that was mentioned as a big unknown is working with files and photos in general. Respondents also frequently mentioned that they are returning to proven procedures that they had recorded in writing without computer.

3.5 Satisfied and Unsatisfied Needs

The analysis of codes in this category identified the satisfied and unsatisfied needs, and perhaps surprisingly, also the unrecognized needs that the respondents could not correctly identify. The need for communication, whether by e-mail, Skype or social networking, has proved an essential need, which is principally satisfied. Respondents also described their procedures for satisfying their information needs and searching for a certain type of information. They agree that they can find what they need and do so through search engines, such as Google, where they enter a query into the search box. Some are also able to refine the query in order to get as precise information as possible. However, few respondents used advanced search techniques. Instead, they often referred to the trial and error method. Respondents also explained that they do not feel the need to search for certain information or to learn to engage in a specific activity (typically online shopping). Or, alternatively, they would be interested in some activity, but they do not know that it exists and do not encounter it.

3.6 Education

The last category of education broadly followed from the previous category. It was identified as a tool for addressing unsatisfied needs. Some respondents have a negative view of the offer of educational events that is rather limited and often fails to meet their needs. They declare their interest in education provided, for example, by libraries as institutions that they perceive as geographically and socially close. It turned out that many of them had already participated in a certain type of educational events and were satisfied. Most of the time, however, they are not very active in searching for them and prefer to wait for events that appear in their neighbourhood or on recommendation of others.

4 Discussion and Conclusion

The research provided some insight into the situation of Internet use by people over 65 in the Czech Republic.

The seniors' interest in information on the Internet does not substantially differ from common needs of working age users. Elderly people approach the Internet and work with information and communication technologies on the basis of their personality aspects and their past experience. However, the perception of virtual environment as trustworthy and the motivation for starting to use the Internet play a crucial role in this target group. They also perceive the problems and barriers that naturally occur on the way, but solve them with relatively high self-confidence or with the help of close family members or friends. The influence of the environment is therefore a crucial factor that has shaped their current level of skills. Everyday use of the Internet is taken for granted as a regular habit that is part of their activities. If they do not focus on searching for specific information, it is exactly the Internet of daily life that forms the framework of their interests and represents a key feature of the current use of the Internet by this target group. Their work with information includes all indicators of information literacy, albeit naturally at different levels. They can identify the need, search for the information in different ways and in different sources, evaluate it, pass it on and use it. They rely on their established and proven practices that they have adopted. They also openly admit which skills they do not possess or do not wish to acquire. They are aware of a great deal of their needs and know how to satisfy them; they identify other needs as unsatisfied due to lack of knowledge or ignorance of the process. Research has also shown a relatively large area of needs that are unrecognized. This is why seniors welcome new knowledge to help them meet their interests as regards information on the Internet and the opportunity to participate in education in this area.

Seniors have no problem adapting to new technologies and using them as they need. As indicated by other publications [6, 12], once they accept these technologies into their lives, they will see them as invaluable help and, despite the barriers they encounter, will be motivated to use them. However, in accordance with the findings of other authors [13], the results of the research also point to the fact that older people may experience certain limitations to effective use of the Internet due to the lack of intermediate skills and that the area where they lack any skills may be more extensive than it would seem from a superficial look. This is where the secondary digital divide, as understood by Dijk [2, 10, 13] emerges. As confirmed by other authors [6, 14], education is a vital tool for alleviating the secondary digital divide and strengthening the skills of this target group. This is a need that elderly people perceive and declare and they have so far been trying to fulfil it mainly through the people around them. We may ask the question whether it would not be useful to focus also on this target group and to offer education on such topics as how to teach a senior to work with the Internet in a meaningful way [9]. Education in this field, for instance through special lessons and programmes provided for seniors in libraries, will help them stay active and integrate into society.

References

1. Lupač, P.: Za hranice digitální propasti. Slon, Praha (2016)
2. Van Dijk, J.: The Deepening Divide: Inequality in the Information Society. Thousand Oaks, California (2005)
3. Attewell, P.: The first and second digital divide. Sociol. Educ. **70**, 252–259 (2001)
4. Český statistický úřad. https://www.czso.cz
5. Castells, M.: The Internet Galaxy: Reflections on the Internet, Business, and Society. Oxford University Press, Oxford (2003)

6. González-Oñate, C., Fanjul-Peyró, C., Cabezuelo-Lorenzo, F.: Use, consumption and knowledge of new technologies by elderly people in France, United Kingdom and Spain. Comunicar **45**, 19–28 (2015)
7. Larsson, E., Larsson-Lund, M., Nilsson, I.: Internet based activities (IBAs): seniors' experiences of the conditions required for the performance of and the influence of these conditions on their own participation in society. Educ. Gerontol. **39**(3), 155–167 (2013)
8. St. Jean, B., Rieh, S.Y., Kim, Y.M., Yang, J.Y.: An analysis of the information behaviors, goals, and intentions of frequent Internet users: findings from online activity diaries. First Monday **17**(2), 2 (2012)
9. Choi, J.H., Moon, J.Y., Kang, J., Kim, S., Lee, I.: Seek or provide: comparative effects of online information sharing on seniors' quality of life. Commun. Assoc. Inf. Syst. **34**, 513–531 (2014)
10. Van Dijk, J., Van Deursen, A.: The digital divide shifts to differences in usage. New Media Society. 7 (2013)
11. Global Media and Information Literacy Assessment Framework: Country Readiness and Competencies. http://unesdoc.unesco.org/images/0022/002246/224655c.pdf
12. Nägle, S., Schmidt, L.: Computer acceptance of older adults. **41**, 3541–3548 (2012)
13. Van Dijk, J.: The evolution of the digital divide - the digital divide turns to inequality of skills and usage. In: Bus, J., Crompton, M., Hildebrandt, M., Metakides, G. (eds.) Digital Enlightenment Yearbook, pp. 57–78 (2012)
14. Hargittai, E., Hsieh, Y.P.: Digital inequality. In: The Oxford Handbook of Internet Studies (2013)

Information Literacy in Higher Education

Prediction of Academic Performance of the University Students Through Their Use of Library Electronic Resources and Their Self-efficacy

Tariq Mahmood Chohan[1], Rubina Bhatti[2], and Salman Bin Naeem[2(✉)]

[1] The Islamia University of Bahawalpur, Bahawalpur, Pakistan
tmchohan@iub.edu.pk
[2] Department of Library and Information Science, The Islamia University of Bahawalpur, Bahawalpur, Pakistan
dr.rubytariq@gmail.com, salmanbaluch@gmail.com

Abstract. The objective of the study was to assess the influence of students' self-efficacy and their use of electronic resources on their academic performance. A survey was conducted in The Islamia University of Bahawalpur, Pakistan in which 307 students participated from five different faculties. A questionnaire was developed to gather the data for this study on variables related to demographic information of the respondents, their use of 'library's electronic resources', 'self-efficacy', and 'academic performance'. The results of the study concluded that the use of library's e-resources has a significant influence on the academic performance of the students. However, it has a negative influence on students' self-efficacy due to availability of wide ranging e-resources. The results of the study also concluded that self-efficacy is not correlated with academic performance of the students, however, it is negatively correlated with the use of university library's e-resources.

Keywords: Self-efficacy · Electronic resources · Academic performance University library · Pakistan

1 Introduction

University libraries develop their information resources and services in order to assist the students in their academics. University library's collection is largely based on the recommended and additional books prescribed in the syllabi of different programs offered by the University. It provides an opportunity to students, who are unable to buy the recommended books because of various reasons (e.g., cost, non-availability of books in local market), to find, read and borrow the books from a library. In addition to that, libraries subscribe e-resources, which are mostly supportive to the recommended textbooks, in order to provide additional and the latest information to students on a topic. Moreover, university libraries design services to enable students to be information literate in order to access, use and exchange the information in need. Such

S. Kurbanoğlu et al. (Eds.): ECIL 2017, CCIS 810, pp. 557–567, 2018.
https://doi.org/10.1007/978-3-319-74334-9_57

services are provided in the shape of trainings and workshops. The aim of many of these services are to ultimately influence the capacity of students in order to make them able to be more confident in their abilities.

The self-efficacy has been defined by Bandura as "beliefs in one's capability to organize and execute the courses of action required to manage prospective situations". It is also described as "a person's belief in his ability to attain desired outcomes" [1]. Many psychologists and academicians have realized the fact that an individual's self-efficacy, or person's belief in his ability or capability, is largely correlated with how he learns and behaves. Many students find it difficult to study, learn and get good marks not as a result of physical impairment or low intelligence, but due to their perception of being unable to do academic work [2]. Thus perceived, self-efficacy is a substantial element of performance which works somewhat independently of underlying skills [3]. "Self-efficacy beliefs contribute to effective performance". It increases motivation, and helps to keep focus on tasks and efforts, and also decreases "self-defeating negative thinking" and anxiety [1]. Students are not motivated to learn if they perceive low self-efficacy [4, 5].

Availability of electronic information resources through the library (e.g., online databases) and wide acceptability and usage of these resources by students are likely to influence their academic performance. Previously many studies reported a positive impact of "electronic information resources" on students' academic performance [6, 7].

Bandura concluded that a person with higher self-efficacy is likely to choose difficult and challenging tasks, remain persistent and perform them successfully [1]. Similarly, academic achievement is also largely dependent on a person's belief of being in-charge of their own fate [8]. The persons who are successful and high achievers do not attribute their fate to fortunate or vagaries of chances but they attribute their success to their power of decision, determination, persistency and hard work [9]. In a same way, students who find themselves unsuccessful in the classroom/academics and perceive themselves poor in studies are more likely to develop a syndrome that includes many types of self-defeating motives such as low motivation and low self-efficacy [10]. According to Tella and Tella, ability and previous performance achievements are the determinants to perceive strong self-efficacy. Both are also taken as strong predictors of subsequent performance [9].

Self-efficacy beliefs in academic differ from discipline to discipline. For example, students might have higher self-efficacy in one discipline but low in another [11, 12]. Whereas, Ren concluded that people like to perform the activities in which they perceived to have a higher self-efficacy [13]. Wang et al., reported that people with high self-efficacy are at advantaged to use e-resources more frequently and get maximum out of these resources in terms of learning as compared to people with low self-efficacy. Generally, low self-efficacy leads toward unfamiliarity and feelings of uncomfortable with e-resources and services [14].

Many studies conducted previously in order to determine the relationship between self-efficacy and the use of e-resources have concluded a positive relationship between these two variables. Similarly, self-efficacy and use of e-resources have also a positive impact on academic performance [6, 7, 15–17]. A study ascertained that male students have higher self-efficacy as compared to female students [15]. Self-efficacy is positively correlated with academic achievement, and it is a strong predictor of academic performance [9].

The computer self-efficacy explained as "an individual's perceptions of his or her ability to use computer in the accomplishment of task rather than reflecting simple component skills" [18]. Self-efficacy has significant influence on the adoption and use of e-resources, library and Internet and on academic performance [18]. Previously, few studies explored the impact of self-efficacy on information technology use [18, 19]. Igbaria and Livari conducted a research study to assess the relationship between computer self-efficacy and computer use. The results showed that computer self-efficacy is correlated with "perceived ease of use". It showed that an increase in the level of computer self-efficacy will likely to increase the level of "perceived ease of use". However, an indirect correlation found between the "perceived usefulness" and "perceived ease of use" [19]. Together, Self-efficacy and task performance positively influence "perceived ease of use". However, if a person is given prior training, it weaker the influence of "self-efficacy" and "task performance" on "perceived ease of use" [20]. General training courses on computer or information communication technology (ICT) are not likely to influence employee's self-efficacy level. However, specific need-oriented hands on trainings have a significant influence on "self-efficacy" and "perceived ease of use". Decker reported that the level of "self-efficacy" remain the same for two and half year after the training [21]. Zhan, Li, Duan and Wu conducted a research study to assess the influence of self-efficacy on learner's attainment. The findings revealed a positive relationship between self-efficacy and learner's attainment. If a learner has a positive self-efficacy towards learning, his attainment level will also be high as well [22]. Waldman conducted a survey research study at "Baruch College" to assess the role of students' self-efficacy on their library's e-resources search and use. The results showed a positive relationship between the use of library and its e resources. Moreover, the students who showed their interest to learn about searching and using e-resources were likely to have higher self-efficacy [11].

Previously, many research studies indicated that self-efficacy influence academic performance and the use of e-resources [17, 23–26]. But, these variables and their correlations are not tested in public sector universities of South Punjab. Therefore, this study was conducted with an objective to assess the relationship among "self-efficacy", "the use of e-resource" and "academic performance" of the students at the Islamia University of Bahawalpur, Punjab, Pakistan.

The findings of the study will be significant to the librarians of the participating university in order to understand the strength or weakness of the relationship among "self-efficacy", "use of electronic information sources" and "academic performance" of the students. Previously, not much of the work on students' self-efficacy has been done by the community of library and information scientists in Pakistan. Therefore, this study will help draw their attention towards this important variable and its relation with "the use of library's e-resources" and "academic performance" of the students.

The results of this study will also be very helpful for university librarians, administrations and policy makers to understand the level of self-efficacy among students, its role in the "use of library's e-resources" and "influence on academic performance". Understanding with these three variables "self-efficacy", "use of electronic resources", and "academic performance" will help them to tailor their services accordingly for the betterment of the students. The results will also provide an opportunity to organize trainings sessions for students according to their exact stage of self-efficacy (low, medium, high) in order to make them self-efficient. These training programs will not only help them to eradicate the problems arise while using e-resources but will also help them to use these resources frequently and effectively that will ultimately improve their academic performance.

2 Methodology

A survey was conducted in The Islamia University of Bahawalpur, Pakistan. All the regular enrolled BS, Master, M. Phil students in the faculty of arts, science, Islamic learning, and management science were the population of this study. A questionnaire was developed to gather the data on variables related to demographic information of the respondents, their use of the library's e-resources, self-efficacy, and academic performance. Self-efficacy was measured using a set of 13 statements; these statements were related to "I can manage to solve difficult problems related to ICT use", "I am confident (or feel strongly) that I can figure out the solutions of any problem", and "I always stick to my aims to accomplish my goals". However, academic performance was measured using Grade Point Average (GPA) in each semester. A pre-tested questionnaire administered among the population through convenience sampling. The data analyzed using "Statistical Package for Social Sciences". "Pearson Correlation Coefficient" statistics was used to assess the correlation between the self-efficacy and academic performance. Linear Regression model was used to determine the influence of "self-efficacy" and "the use of electronic resources" on "university student's academic performance". A four-point Likert type scale from "not at all true" to "exactly true" was used to collect the data for this study. Alpha value for this study was set at .05.

2.1 Response Rate

A total of 500 copies of questionnaire were distributed among the respondents in a university library, class rooms of different departments, and male and female hostels of the university. Of the 500 copies, 307 filled copies were retuned with a 61.4% response rate. Of the 307 copies of questionnaire, six questionnaires were filled carelessly and not valid for data analysis. They were discarded. One questionnaire was discarded randomly to keep the 300 questionnaire for data analysis.

3 Results

3.1 Respondents' Demographic Information

The majority (n = 157; 52.3%) of the respondents were male and 143 (47.7%) were female. The gap in gender distribution was not wider. The mean age of the respondents was 20.75 years with SD = 2.97, minimum age of the respondents was 17 years and a maximum age 38 years with a range of 21 years. The median age of the respondents was 20 years. The mode (most repeated) age of the respondents was 19 years. A majority of the respondents (n = 168; 56.9%) were enrolled in BS program, 95 (32.2%)

were at master level, 12 (4.1%) were enrolled in M. Phil programs, 9 (3.1%) were in PhD programs, and 11 (3.7%) were enrolled in other programs. Respondents from the faculty of science comprised the largest group (n = 145; 48.3%); 84 (28%) were from faculty of arts; 28 (9.3%) were from faculty of Islamic learning; 31 (10.3%) were from faculty of pharmacy; and 12 (4%) respondents were from the faculty of management science.

3.2 Respondents' Grade Point Average

The mean GPA of the respondents was 3.34 with standard deviation .367, with a minimum GPA 2.10 and maximum GPA 4.00. The GPA was ranged between 1.90 points. The median GPA was 3.30, and mode was 3.20 GPA.

3.3 Use of Library's Electronic Information Resources

Most respondents (n = 241; 80.3%) have used the library's e-resources. However, 59 (19.7%) respondents have not used the library's e-resources.

3.4 Frequency of Library's Electronic Information Resources Use

A majority (n = 112; 37.3%) of the respondents reported their frequency of library's e-resources as at least once a week; 53 (17.7%) reported their use of library's e-resource as daily, 49 (16.3%) use at least once a month, and 22 (7.3%) use less than once a month. However, 42 (14%) respondents have never used library's e-resources.

3.5 Measure of Self-efficacy

Respondents were asked a set of 13 statements in order to measure their level of self-efficacy. All of these statements received a mean score ranging from 3.01 to 3.79 indicating a good level of self-efficacy. The majority of the respondents considered two statements "exactly true": "I am confident (or feel strongly) that I can figure out the solutions of any problem" (Mean 3.79, SD 5.565), and "I can manage the problems in my life so, I can focus on my studies" (Mean 3.50, SD 3.231). However, majority of the respondents ranked all other nine statements as "moderately true". These statements were; "to achieve better grades I have to look after my health" (Mean 3.39, SD 2.634), "If I am in trouble, I can usually think of a solution" (Mean 3.34, SD 1.831), "I know I will get a good position in my career if I do well in my studies" (Mean 3.32, SD 1.099), and "I have fair support from my family to excel in my studies" (Mean 3.28, SD 2.057), etc. (Table 1).

3.6 Relationship Between Use of University's Library E-Resources and Self-efficacy

Spearman's rho statistics were used to assess the influence of library's e-resources use on respondents' self-efficacy. The results showed a statistically negative relationship between the two variables (Spearman's rho (140) = −.279, p = .001) (Table 2).

Table 1. Measure of self-efficacy

	Statements	Valid	Mean	Std. deviation
	I am confident (or feel strongly) that I can figure out the solutions of any problem	284	3.79	5.565
	I can manage the problems in my life so, I can focus on my studies	278	3.50	3.231
	To achieve better grades I have to look after my health	278	3.39	2.634
	"If I am in trouble, I can usually think of a solution"	280	3.34	1.831
	I know I will get good position in my career if I do well in my studies	278	3.32	1.099
	I have a fair support from my family to excel in my studies	281	3.28	2.057
	"I always stick to my aims to accomplish my goals"	287	3.27	2.099
	"Thanks to my resourcefulness, I know how to handle unforeseen situations"	274	3.24	4.398
	"I can manage to solve difficult problems"	258	3.17	.904
0	I attend my classes no matter how busy I am	275	3.17	1.043
1	I am certain I can manage the time to do all my class assignments	277	3.15	2.670
2	"I am confident that I could deal with unexpected events"	279	3.03	.990
3	I can remain calm in difficulties	283	3.01	2.615

"Scale: 1 = Not at all True, 2 = Hardly True, 3 = Moderately True, 4 = Exactly True"

3.7 Relationship Between Frequency of Electronic Resource's Use and Self-efficacy

Table 2 shows a relationship between the frequency of electronic resource's use and self-efficacy. The results showed a significant negative relationship existed between the frequency of library's e-resources use and respondents' self-efficacy. It means the increase in frequency of electronic information resources cause a decrease in the level of self-efficacy Spearman's rho (130) = −.191, p = .030.

3.8 Relationship Between Library's Electronic Information Resources Use and Academic Performance

In order to assess the relationship between the frequency of library's electronic information use and academic performance, the researcher used a Spearman's rho statistics. The results of the Spearman's rho showed a statistically positive correlation between the frequency of library's e-resources use and respondents' academic performance. It means the respondents who use library's e-resources regularly also get higher GPA as compared to those who use library irregularly, Spearman's rho (278) = .174, p = .004 (Table 2).

Table 2. (a) Relationship between use of university's library e-resources and self-efficacy. (b) Relationship between frequency of e-resource's use and self-efficacy. (c) Relationship between library's e-resources use and academic performance

(a)

			Use of library's e-resources	Efficacy
Spearman's rho	Use of library's electronic resources	r_s	1.000	−.279**
		p-value	.	.001
		N	300	140
	Efficacy	r_s	−279**	1.000
		p-value	.001	.
		N	140	140

(b)

			Efficacy	Library's e-resources use
Spearman's rho	Efficacy	r_s	1.000	−.191*
		p-value	.	.030
		N	140	130
	Library electronic resource's use	r_s	−.191*	1.000
		p-value	.030	.
		N	130	278

(c)

			GPA	Use of library's e-resources
Spearman's rho	GPA	r_s	1.000	.174**
		P-value	.	.004
		N	300	278
	Use of library's electronic resources	r_s	.174**	1.000
		P-value	.004	.
		N	278	278

**. < P = 0.05

3.9 Correlation Between Respondents' Self-efficacy and Academic Performance. Respondents' Academic Performance Were Measured Using Their Grade Point Average (GPA)

However, a set of 13 statements were asked to measure the self-efficacy of the respondents. "Pearson Correlation Coefficient" statistics was used to determine the correlation between self-efficacy and academic performance of the students. No statistically significant relationship found between the two variables Pearson *r* (140) = .078, *p* = .361 (Table 3).

Table 3. Correlation between respondents' self-efficacy and academic performance

		GPA	Efficacy
GPA	*R*	1	.078
	P-value		.361
	N	300	140
Efficacy	*r*	.078	1
	P-value	.361	
	N	140	140

3.10 Influence of Self-efficacy and Electronic Resource's Use on Academic Performance

Linear Regression model was used to determine the influence of self-efficacy and e-resource's use on university student's academic performance. No statistically significant influence was found of self-efficacy and electronic information resource's use on the academic performance of the students (Table 4).

Table 4. Influence of self-efficacy and electronic resource's use on academic performance

Model	R	R square	Sum of squares	Mean square	F	Sig.
1	.157[a]	.025	.463	.231	1.605	.205[b]
			18.303	.144		
			18.766			

a. Predictors: (Constant), Efficacy, How often do you use the library's electronic resources?

4 Discussion

The results of our study showed that majority (80.3%) of the students have used the library's subscribed e-resources, and the percentage of e-resources use is quite high as compared to other studies conducted previously in South Punjab, Pakistan in which the students' use of library's e-resources reported between 40% to 68.6% [27, 28].

Our study showed a negative relationship between the frequency of library's e-resources use and students' self-efficacy. Whereas, studies conducted previously in order to determine the relationship between self-efficacy and the use of e-resources have highlighted a positive relationships between the two variables [6, 7, 15–17]. The one reason for this negative relationship could be the size of the e-resources. The more the students explore the library's e-resources, the more they feel overwhelmed and abandon the skills they gained to retrieve the required information out of the flood of information. Therefore, the exposure to more information resources may cause a decrease in the level of students' self-efficacy. Similarly, no significant relationship between the students' self-efficacy and their academic performance was found. However, the literature indicated that the self-efficacy is correlated with academic achievement [8]. Self-efficacy is a strong predictor for academic performance [9]. Previously, many research studies indicated that self-efficacy influence academic performance and the use of e-resources [17, 23–26].

The results of our study showed a positive correlation between the frequency of e-resources use and academic performance. It means that the students who use library's e-resources regularly also get higher GPA as compared to those who use library's e-resources irregularly. These finding are consistent with the findings of studies conducted previously, in which they reported that the availability of e-resources through library (e.g., online databases) and wide acceptability and usage of these resources by students are likely to influence their academic performance. Previously many studies reported a positive impact of "electronic information resources" on students' academic performance [6, 7].

Overall, the results of our study found no significant influence of self-efficacy and e-resource's use on the academic performance of the students. However, the studies conducted previous reported that self-efficacy and the use of e-resources have a positive impact on academic performance of the students [6, 7, 15–17].

The limitations of the study include; a survey method was adopted to collect the data for this study which has its own limitation and survey statements are always subject to respondents' understanding. However, in pre and pilot testing phase of the questionnaire revisions were made to make it easy and understandable to the students. The data collected for this study was based on respondents' perceptions about their level of self-efficacy as well as the data they reported (e.g., about their GPA, the use of e-resources) is not verified by any other mean, that is likely to lead towards the findings which are not consistent with the findings reported in the literature. The other limitation may be the use of general self-efficacy scale, (students' general self-efficacy) which may not have any direct impact on their academic performance and use of e-resources. Therefore it is desirable that in future researches the use of e-resources, their academic performance, and level of self-efficacy may be verified by other resources as well. Instead of using general self-efficacy scale to determine the correlation with the use of e-resources, it is ideal that computer/Internet self-efficacy scale may be used.

5 Conclusions

The results of the study concluded that the use of library's electronic information resources has a significant influence on the academic performance of the students. However, it has a negative influence on self-efficacy of the students. The results of the study concluded that self-efficacy is not correlated with academic performance of the students, however, it is negatively correlated with the use of university library's electronic information resources.

6 Recommendations

On the basis of the conclusion following recommendations are made;

- There is a need for information literacy and instruction programs to be organized in order to increase awareness among students about different subscriptions and other electronic resources by a library. These sessions will also be helpful in developing a capacity and self-efficacy among students and it will make them able to access and use and electronic resources effectively.
- A separate computer lab in each department should be developed in order to facilitate effective access and use of library's electronic resources.
- The use of scholarly search engines such as Google Scholar and HEC Summon search for all database should be promoted among students instead of general search engine.
- Various library's services and sources need to be promoted among students in order to increase the use of these resources and services (e.g., library's orientation registration facility, HEC digital library resources, IUB VPN services, online public access catalogue, friend of library program, HEC summon search for all database, availability of M. Phil and PhD theses, and scholar's room).

References

1. Bandura, A.: Self efficacy, vol. 4, pp. 71–81. Academic Press, New York. http://www.des.emory.edu/mfp/BanEncy.html
2. Estrom, T.J.: Self-concept and its implications for counselors. Niger. J. Clin. Counselling Psychol. **2**(1), 125–135 (1996)
3. Bandura, A.: Social Foundations of Thought and Action. Prentice Hall, Englewood Cliffs (1986)
4. Schulte, S.J.: High self-efficacy and high use of electronic information may predict improved academic performance. Evid. Based Lib. Inf. Pract. **3**(2), 35–37 (2008)
5. Akram, B., Ghazanfar, L.: Self efficacy and academic performance of the students of Gujrat University, Pakistan. Acad. Res. Int. **5**(1), 283 (2014)
6. Ramayah, T., Aafaqi, B., Ignatius, J.: Role of self-efficacy in e-library usage among students of a public university in Malaysia. Malaysian J. Lib. Inf. Sci. **9**, 39–58 (2004)
7. Ukachi, N.B., Onuoha, U.D., Nwachukwu, V.N.: Students' attitudes as a determining factor to electronic information resources use in university libraries in South-West, Nigeria. DESIDOC J. Lib. Inf. Technol. **34**(4), 333–341 (2014)
8. Komarraju, M., Nadler, D.: Self-efficacy and academic achievement: why do implicit beliefs, goals, and effort regulation matter? Learn. Individ. Differ. **30**(25), 67–72 (2013)
9. Tella, A., Tella, A., Ayeni, C.O., Omoba, R.O.: Self-efficacy and use of electronic information as predictors of academic performance. Electron. J. Acad. Spec. Librariansh. **8** (2), 12 (2007)
10. Richardson, C.S., Norman, A.S., Shawn, N.O.: Educational Psychology, 7th edn. McGraw-Hill, Boston (1998)
11. Waldman, M.: Freshmen's use of library electronic resources and self-efficacy. Inf. Res. **8** (2), 150 (2003). http://informationr.net/ir/8–2/paper150.htm

12. Ozer, E.A., Akgun, O.E.: The effects of irrational beliefs on academic motivation and academic self-efficacy of candidate teachers of computer and instructional technologies education department. Proc.-Soci. Behav. Sci. **25**(197), 1287–1292 (2015)
13. Ren, W.H.: Library instruction and college student self-efficacy in electronic information searching. J. Acad. Librariansh. **26**(5), 323–328 (2000)
14. Wang, C.H., Shannon, D.M., Ross, M.E.: Students' characteristics, self-regulated learning, technology self-efficacy, and course outcomes in online learning. Dis. Educ. **34**(3), 302–323 (2013)
15. Lent, R.W., Lopez, F.G., Bieschke, K.J.: Mathematics self-efficacy: sources and relation to science-based career choice. J. Counseling Psychol. **38**(4), 424 (1991)
16. Pajares, F.: Self-efficacy beliefs in academic contexts: an outline. Emory University, Division of Educational Studies Website: http://www.des.emory.edu/mfp/efftalk.html. Accessed 8 Aug 2016
17. Kuo, Y.C., Walker, A.E., Schroder, K.E., Belland, B.R.: Interaction, Internet self-efficacy, and self-regulated learning as predictors of student satisfaction in online education courses. Int. High. Educ. **31**(20), 35–50 (2014)
18. Compeau, D.R., Higgins, C.A.: Computer self-efficacy: development of a measure and initial test. MIS Q. **1**, 189–211 (1995)
19. Igbaria, M., Iivari, J.: The effects of self-efficacy on computer usage. Omega **23**(6), 587–605 (1995)
20. Liu, L., Grandon, E.E.: How performance and self-efficacy influence the ease of use of object-orientation: the moderating effect of prior training. In: Proceedings of the 36th Annual Hawaii International Conference on System Sciences, 6 Jan 2003, pp. 10-pp. IEEE (2003)
21. Decker, C.A.: Training transfer: perceptions of computer use self-efficacy among university employees. J. Career Tech. Educ. **14**(2) (1998)
22. Zhang, J., Li, F., Duan, C., Wu, G.: Research on self-efficacy of distance learning and its influence to learners' attainments. In: Proceedings of the International Conference on Computers in Education (ICCE)/SchoolNet, pp. 1510–1517 (2001)
23. Laguna, K., Babcock, R.L.: Computer anxiety in young and older adults: implications for human-computer interactions in older populations. Comput. Hum. Behav. **13**(3), 317–326 (1997)
24. Lærum, H., Ellingsen, G., Faxvaag, A.: Doctors' use of electronic medical records systems in hospitals: cross sectional survey. BMJ **323**(7325), 1344–1348 (2001)
25. Ford, N., Miller, D., Moss, N.: The role of individual differences in internet searching: an empirical study. J. Am. Soc. Inf. Sci. Technol. **52**(12), 1049–1066 (2001)
26. Murero, M., Rice, R.E.: The Internet and Health Care: Theory, Research, and Practice. Routledge, Abingdon (2013)
27. Khan, S.A., Khan, A.A., Bhatti, R.: Internet access, use and gratification among university students: a case study of the Islamia University of Bahawalpur, Pakistan. Chin. Librariansh. Int. Electron. J. **1**(32), 1–4 (2011)
28. Khan, A., Ahmed, S.: The impact of digital library resources on scholarly communication: challenges and opportunities for university libraries in Pakistan. Lib. Hi Tech News. **30**(8), 12–29 (2013)

Outcomes and Challenges of Offering an Information Literacy Compulsory Undergraduate Credit Course: A Mexican Case

Jesus Lau[1,2](✉), José Luis Bonilla[3], and Alberto Gárate[3]

[1] Instituto de Ingeniería/DSAE, Universidad Veracruzana, Juan Pablo II y Ruiz Cortines, 94294 Boca del Río, Veracruz, Mexico
jlau@uv.mx

[2] PIMSA-Catedra Distinguida, CETYS Universidad, Mexicali, Mexico

[3] CETYS Universidad, Calz. CETYS s/n. Col. Rivera, 21259 Mexicali, Baja California, Mexico
{joseluis.bonilla,albertogarate}@cetys.mx

Abstract. The aim in this paper is to report the learning experience evaluation of an information literacy (IL) undergraduate compulsory credit course in a country where information and research skilled lecturers are scarce. Students should begin to develop information competencies during their K-12 education; however, this is seldom the case in the Mexican educational system where students enroll at universities with limited IL training. CETYS University, whose IL evolution has been previously reported in the ECIL Conference Series, made the decision to offer a compulsory eight-credit course for all first-year students. The implementation of the course had the challenge of hiring faculty who did not have, in most cases, IL facilitation experience. The outcome of the first cohort of 17 groups that included 361 students was that the students did have a positive learning outcome, according to the two technique-assessment study but did identify important opportunities to improve the course and the facilitation process.

Keywords: Information literacy credit courses · Information competencies credit courses · Information literacy credit course assessment · Information skills teaching · Information competencies lecturer assessment · Undergraduate information literacy courses

1 Introduction

As stated in the abstract, the aim of this paper is to report the evaluation of an information literacy (IL) undergraduate compulsory credit course in a country where information-skilled lecturers are generally scarce [1]. The subject is discussed addressing the information competencies (info-competencies) challenges at the high school level, followed by a description of the CETYS University case, and the strategies taken to enhance info-competencies of newly-registered students, among them the adoption of an eight-credit face-to-face IL course titled "Management of Information (MI)" for all new university entrants. The adoption of the course had the aim of helping students develop basic information skills as they start their undergraduate programs. Students who enroll in

S. Kurbanoğlu et al. (Eds.): ECIL 2017, CCIS 810, pp. 568–575, 2018.
https://doi.org/10.1007/978-3-319-74334-9_58

higher education tend to have limited information skills [2], apparently, an international trend [3]. According to PISA (Program for International Student Assessment) evaluation results, Mexican students rank among those from nations with the lowest reading scores, a basic skill for information competency attainment. Mexican students received 423 points compared to the OECD average of 493 points. However, the outcome is more or less similar to other developing economies such as those of Brazil and Colombia [4]. CETYS requires high school candidates to take the admission College Board Examination, but only two factors: verbal and mathematics, a fact that makes it difficult to identify student info-competencies qualifications as they enter the institution that is the largest private university in Baja California, the Northernmost Mexican state that borders California, USA. As reported in previous ECIL Series Publications [5], the university has over 7,500 students and holds the Western Association of School and Colleges accreditation (WASC), a major achievement, as one of only six institutions with American accreditation in Mexico. Since 2007, CETYS has identified and adopted a set of desirable qualities that students ought to achieve before they graduate. These profile characteristics are understood as special education elements that make CETYS different from of other institutions of higher education [6]. One element is Information Culture, understood as a set of information, technology and communication related competencies. The ultimate goal of this element is to graduate students with abilities to access, evaluate, and use information with support of both traditional and technological resources to respond and solve their personal and professional needs within their discipline and level of education [6]. The strategy to deploy the Information Culture "element" has several actions, among them IL studies to assess information competencies and faculty information demands, development of an IL rubric for undergraduate syllabus, and the use of iSkills, Sails and an in-house instrument to monitor IL competencies of students; outcomes that have also mostly been reported in previous ECIL Series Publications [5]. A follow up to these strategies is the creation of the cited management of information (MI) course in 2016 that all new students take during their first two semesters.

2 How the Course Content Evolved

In 2014, when the curriculum of all programs of the University underwent evaluation to update them according to changes in the job market and the disciplines they covered, a criterion was agreed upon by college committee participants that 20% of the courses of all degree-granting programs should contribute to the development of core skill characteristics of the generic graduate profile, among them, information culture, i.e., information competencies [6]. The set criteria pivoted on the resolution to offer an IL course to all students. The decision meant the creation of an eight-credit course (4 h per week) that was called, as stated, Management of Information (MI). The course is compulsory and has to be taken during the first year at university. The syllabus was developed by a team of three humanities faculty members who submitted the proposal for discussion and input to the heads of the three campus libraries that make up the University Library System. It must be mentioned that other Mexican universities who offer IL credit course do not seem to have documented their experiences. A quick social network media question to IL colleagues reported a handful of universities offering credit courses as optional or compulsory.

The syllabus was organized into five thematic units. The first focused on the discussion of information society and culture, the second covered information literacy standards in Mexico, the third was on how to conduct information research, and finally, the fourth and fifth were devoted to bibliographic resources management. The learning goal of the course was the development of the eight core competencies stated in the Mexican Information Literacy Standards [7] through the selection of a research topic by students, according to their discipline. Students selected a topic and identified all possible information resources in preparing an end-of-term paper, applying research methodology and following the APA citation style (American Psychological Association).

3 Implementation of the Course

The implementation period was brief because the plan was approved shortly before the beginning of the following academic year. The biggest challenge was the administrative recruitment of several lecturers. Faculty members were invited by academic coordinators from each campus. Prospective instructors needed to have had at least a Master's Degree and the subject qualifications, a hurdle that was difficult to overcome because there were 17 subject area groups to teach at the three university campuses. CETYS had only four professional librarians at the time. They were invited to teach the IL course at all the campuses, along with lecturers from other disciplines. Some of project faculty agreed to teach more than one group.

All lecturers hired at the Tijuana Campus had a Master's Degree, except two who had Ph.Ds., among them two were librarians, the campus library director and a reference librarian. Three of the faculty had some publication experience and none of them were members of the National System of Researchers, a Mexican (SNI) government body that certifies and awards recognition to those who publish their research output. According to this body, Mexico had 18,500 SNI members in 2012, among 369,000 faculty, although only 89,000 (24%) were full-time and assumed to have research skills, because they devoted all their working time to universities [1]. However, academic coordinators who carried out the lecturer recruitment did not require the SNI designation for the MI facilitation.

Recruited lecturers were invited to attend a two-hour teaching introduction to the course, where, in addition to a talk, they received a copy of all teaching materials (an e-Booklet of nearly 200 pages) for the IL course taught at Universidad Veracruzana: "Information Competencies for Learning" by Jesus Lau that included 40 learning exercises [8]. They also received a copy of the institutional APA style manual, and the booklet on how to prepare of academic papers, both publications edited by CETYS [9, 10]. The facilitation of the course kicked off, as stated, with 17 groups with an enrollment of 361 students. After the course began, lecturers had occasional meetings at each campus during the semester to share and improve their MI experiences. Unfortunately, there was no library leadership to provide faculty IL training one of the campuses.

4 Course Overall Evaluation

The exploratory overall evaluation was conducted after the first semester concluded. For convenience, the assessment was conducted at the Tijuana campus, where one of the researchers teaches and where more professors were hired, a total of nine. The selected campus is similar in size to the one at Mexicali but with twice the number of students as Ensenada. The process included three research techniques, the first one a questionnaire with 27 closed questions to identify the knowledge and skills gained by students during the IL course. The survey also included three open-ended questions designed to (1) help understand what students had done to learn; (2) identify the learning activities the lecturer used to promote learning; and (3) to identify the main student learning experiences in the different MI lessons. There were 315 out of a potential of 361 answers from students who had attended one of the 17 MI courses. The results of the survey are not part of this report but they will be used as part of a planned longitudinal assessment. The second technique was the organization of a discussion group held with seven of the nine lecturers who facilitated one or more courses at the Tijuana campus. The objective of the MI faculty focus group was to analyze their teaching experience, what they had achieved, what was missing in the course, and what should be done in subsequent learning experiences. Finally, the third technique was an exploratory analysis of IL skills developed by students. They were asked to share, on a voluntarily basis, two papers they wrote: the end-of-term MI paper and one completed near the end of their previous high school year.

5 The Voice of Lecturers – Faculty Focus Group

IL lecturers, as the key actors of this new course, were invited to have a meeting at the library during the final week of the semester. The meeting was attended by seven out of nine faculty who were part of the initial team. The goals of having this focus group were to learn and record the teaching experience, and to gather data to document and publish the results for the sake of improving future developments in the course. The session was video recorded with the permission of the participants. Four sets of basic questions comprised the assessment dynamic: (1) How did you feel during the facilitation of the course? What did you feel went right and what did not? (2) How did you feel about training for MI teaching? What would you suggest for other new lecturers? (3) What are the skills required to facilitate the MI course?, and (4) What syllabus improvements did you identify? The discussion lasted an hour and a half, as programed. The video was transcribed for qualitative inductive analysis to identify content categories. The main qualitative results are summarized as follows:

(1) **Course – Right Decision.** Lecturers agreed that the institutional decision to offer this course as a compulsory requirement was the proper decision and was beneficial to students. They enjoyed this new teaching experience.
(2) **Achievement.** They were quite certain that students achieved good learning levels, even in some subjects that may sound "simple and familiar," such as how to evaluate information and go beyond simple Google searches.

(3) **Benefits.** Most students benefited from the MI course, especially those with a certificate from the so-called National High School (standard program in Spanish) and the Bilingual High School (half of the standard program in English), who had fewer information competencies. However, students who were accepted in the International High School certification (standard program in English with extra courses taught by teachers from other parts of the world) were more information-qualified.
(4) **Concern.** Lecturers stressed that the information skills learned in MI are likely to be lost if they are not practiced in other undergraduate program courses.
(5) **Syllabus Complexity.** Lecturers made it clear that it took more effort than expected to understand the structure and logic of the syllabus. They found it complicated to devote a unit to the subject of the knowledge society and then work separately on the many (eight) information competencies. They recognized that they did not cover all the info-competencies because of time limitations and their own limited lecturer IL skills.
(6) **Training – Team Work.** A common statement from participants was that there was not enough training to grasp the scope of the course. One of them stated that any MI facilitator should master research methods, IL, and information and communication technologies (ICT). Participants stated that the facilitator should approach this course as a workshop where they ought to play a coaching role. They recognized that their strengths, some were strong in IL (librarians) or others were strong in research methods (lecturers with doctoral degrees). Their suggestion was to employ team teaching where these strengths could be pulled together for the benefit of students.
(7) **Discipline Focus.** A challenge that they expressed was the difficulty and, in some cases, the impossibility of focusing on the discipline-specific needs of the different undergraduate programs, such as use of style manuals that differed from APA and the mastering of databases in fields unknown to lecturers.
(8) **Opportunity to Seize.** The MI course should capitalize on the wide and rich variety of information resources across the border with California, USA, such as universities and research centers located in nearby San Diego. Thus, librarians ought to build cooperative library bridges to benefit the MI course.
(9) **Limited Knowledge Construction.** Lecturers assumed that the students read digital formats, including note-taking using pictures, was a limiting factor for knowledge construction because students spent a rather short time reasoning and doing metacognition, thus limiting memory retention. Elaboration of posters, note-taking exercises, and plain bibliographic notes were used to induce students to devote more time to MI understanding and learning.

6 Student Information Competencies Evaluation

A request was sent to all Tijuana Campus MI students to voluntarily participate in the evaluation process by sending a copy of their MI end-of-term paper along with a paper they completed during their last semester of high school. An electronic repository was established so that they could upload the papers. Of the 122 students who responded to the request only 52 sent both papers. An alphabetic list was compiled (104 papers in total, half from high school and the rest MI essays). The 52 students represented all groups. The papers were reviewed in terms of ten variables where each variable had an arbitrary value of 10 points so that the highest positive outcome would yield 100 points. The variables had therefore no weight related to the required effort, difficulty, or time spent by students.

The comparison of both papers showed positive results but with room to improve. The variable, "Table of contents", had limited growth because it went from 37% to 40%; "Structure of the Paper" increased from 69% to a significant 96%; "Writing Composition (Argument)" and "Citations" had dramatic jumps, the first from 54% to 81% and the second from 46% to 98%; "Paraphrasing" also had increase from 69% to 100%; "Academic Information Sources", and "Information Sources in other Languages" (mainly English) went up, the first from 35% to a high of 81%, and 29% to 67% doubling the high school score compared to the first year MI university course. "References" had, on the other hand, from 69% to 100%; "Advanced Use of Word Processing" had early 100% progress, but it was still low, reaching the bottom figure of 21%. "Use of Graphics and Tables" had limited growth from 17% to 21% (See Table 1).

Table 1. High school versus undergraduate papers

Paper indicators fulfillment Value 10% each	High School 52 papers = 100%	Undergraduate 52 papers = 100%
1. Table of contents	37%	40%
2. Structure: introduction, discussion and conclusion	69%	96%
3. Writing composition (argument)	54%	81%
4. Citations	46%	98%
5. Paraphrasing	69%	100%
6. Academic information sources	35%	81%
7. Information sources in other languages	29%	67%
8. References – style	63%	100%
9. Use of advanced word processing	12%	21%
10. Use of graphics and tables	16%	28%
Total	**43% papers**	**71% papers**

Additional information about the paper comparison yielded that high school papers 11.4 pages in length compared to 24.2 pages for the undergraduate MI course. In other words, students showed excellent improvement in this quantitative indicator. "Information Sources in Other Languages", mostly in English jumped from 4.5 to 13.9. The overall results show information competencies for the 52 high school papers was 43% for the ten indicators with a value score for each, while the first year undergraduate MI increased to 71%. The qualitative evaluation of the MI 52 student papers gave an indication that the MI course and the lecturer facilitation were successful. However, there was room for improvement, mainly for the elements "Table of Contents", "Use of Advanced Word Processing", and "Use of Graphics and Tables".

7 Conclusion

The decision to create and offer a compulsory IL course to all undergraduate students regardless of the program they attended was a positive step in the curricular development of CETYS University, certainly promising in terms of the information culture qualification of future graduates. The requirement of this IL eight-credit course enabled the institution to pave the way to accomplish its strategic information culture goal as a graduate profile element. The aim of the course syllabus was to foster eight information competencies [7]. The implementation of the course, however, had the challenge of recruiting professors with solid information competencies, that is, faculty with experience in accessing, retrieving, evaluating, and using information for research beyond their use in teaching. This CETYS MI course is one of the few ventures in Mexico that required the course for all students. Unfortunately, no literature was found that documented previous cases with such courses. Although this study was only valid for the studied cases, the sample evaluation of the first deployment of the MI course in Tijuana yielded important results that will potentially help the university to improve the MI syllabus and the recruiting and selection of lecturers, the outcome of the evaluation of the Tijuana Campus MI courses, using a lecturer focus group, and the comparison of high school and MI final papers provided indicators to conclude that:

(1) The overall outcome of the course was highly positive for several paper assessment variables or elements. Students made progress in the qualitative comparison of the papers written in the last high school semester compared to those completed during the MI undergraduate course, especially in the core IL indicators. The weaker skills were mostly noted for those indicators related to ICT (See Table 1).
(2) The course program may need to be adjusted to focus more on information competencies and less on the theoretical knowledge society unit, according to lecturer focus group feedback.
(3) The lecturer profile needs to be more specifically defined. Because it is too general for recruitment ideally SNI qualifications should be required. Even though the student-learning outcome was the hiring of better information and research-skill qualified professors may still improve the course learning performance.
(4) The teaching MI team of nine lecturers had uneven qualifications –only two had a doctoral degree and the rest had no publication experience –and had information skills than library lecturers, who in turn also lacked publication experience crucial for information communication. These factors need to be further evaluated. Team-embedded IL is an option to be considered to complement and benefit from the individual strengths of lecturers.
(5) The focus group results showed that lecturers were unaware of their own IL skills limitations and were generally satisfied with their IL facilitation performance.
(6) Training of lecturers is needed especially training in use of databases, search strategies, and the drafting of student learning exercises.

(7) Although students did improve their information skills, further study is needed to assess additional factors in regard to the library role and lecturers' IL skills impact, mainly among those whose lecturers whose information competencies were higher because they held a Ph.D.
(8) The study results will be forwarded to the university authorities for potential IL course implementation improvement.

The CETYS experience requiring every incoming student to take the MI eight-credit course was a welcome decision by faculty. It will potentially be useful for future graduates who may have a solid information culture and be able to benefit from and contribute to the wealth of information available within reach of most computers and ICT tools.

References

1. Tuiran, R.: La Educación Superior en México 2006–2012: Un Balance Inicial. http://red-academica.net/observatorio-academico/2012/10/03/la-educacion-superior-en-mexico-2006-2012-un-balance-inicial/. Accessed 25 May 2017
2. Cortés-Vera, J.J.: El Desarrollo de Competencias Informativas en Estudiantes Universitarios. Una Visión sobre Avances y Perspectivas desde la Universidad Autónoma de Ciudad Juárez. In: Hernández, P. (ed.) Tendencias de la Alfabetización Informativa en Iberoamérica, pp. 233–262. Centro Universitario de Investigaciones Bibliotecológicas UNAM, México (2012)
3. Julien, H., Gross, M., Latham, D.: Survey of Information Literacy Instructional Practices in U.S. Academic Libraries. College and Research Libraries (pre-print). http://crl.acrl.org/content/early/2017/01/30/crl17-1024.full.pdf+html. Accessed 14 Feb 2017
4. OECD: Nota país: Programa para la Evaluación Internacional de Alumnos (PISA), PISA 2015 – Resultados (2015). https://www.oecd.org/pisa/PISA-2015-Mexico-ESP.pdf. Accessed 25 May 2017
5. European Conference on Information Literacy: ECIL Conference Series (n/d). ilconf.org. Accessed 17 Feb 2017
6. Gárate, A., Rocha, J.: Plan de Desarrollo CETYS 2020. CETYS Universidad, Mexicali, B.C., México (2011)
7. Cortés, J., González, D., Lau, J., Moya, A.L., Quijano, A., Rovalo, L., Souto, S.: Declaratoria: Normas sobre Alfabetización Informativa en Educación Superior (2002). http://bivir.uacj.mx/dhi/documentosbasicos/Docs/Declaratorias/DeclaratoriaTercerDHI.pdf
8. Lau, J.: Curso Gestión de la Información: Competencias Informativas para el Aprendizaje. Universidad Veracruzana, Boca del Río, Veracruz, México (2015, unpublished manuscript)
9. Bonilla, J.L., Montes, M.E.: Guía para Elaborar Trabajos Académicos: desde Nociones de Redacción hasta los Pasos para hacer Distintos Trabajos. Instituto Educativo del Noroeste, A.C., Mexicali (2015)
10. Bonilla, J.L., Montes, M.E.: Manual de Presentación de Trabajos Escritos. Instituto Educativo del Noroeste, A.C., Mexicali (2015)

Where to Now? New E-learning Concepts and Co-creation at the Technical University of Denmark

Andrew Cranfield(✉) and Thomas Jensen

DTU Library, Kongens Lyngby, Denmark
{ancra, tsko}@dtu.dk

Abstract. From 2014 to 2016 DTU Library was involved in a large multi-institutional publicly funded DEFF (The Danish Electronic Research Library) project entitled "E-learning, information literacy and library services" that focused on enhancing links between education and employability, including information competencies. As a part of this project, DTU Library and The Royal Library, Copenhagen, developed and implemented a MOOC (Massive Open Online Course) on academic information seeking. This paper will analyze and discuss how we have used the results and experiences from the DEFF project to develop and further qualify our e-didactic and e-learning endeavors. The second part of the paper will look to the future and how a new DEFF funded project running will seek to establish new solutions taking their inspiration from the concept of co-creation. We will discuss underlying theory of the two DEFF projects, target groups, and how experiences and conclusions from the first DEFF project influenced and charted the direction of the second DEFF project.

Keywords: MOOC · E-learning · Co-creation · Information seeking
Information retrieval · Information literacy

1 The World's First MOOC About Academic Information Seeking

In the fall of 2013, a large group of university libraries in Denmark decided to engage in a joint project entitled "E-learning, Information Literacy, and Library Services". The project was funded by Denmark's Electronic Library (DEFF) and ran from 2014-2016. One of the primary focus points of this work was to discover how the Danish university libraries would best be able to become a relevant partner for our respective educational institutions [1].

First and foremost those involved wanted to investigate how libraries could enhance their position as an important part of university education by embedding librarians and library services in the Learning Management Systems used by our various institutions. However, it was also suggested that a smaller part of the effort should explore the potential and possibilities for libraries in the relatively new area of the Massive Open Online Course (MOOC).

S. Kurbanoğlu et al. (Eds.): ECIL 2017, CCIS 810, pp. 576–584, 2018.
https://doi.org/10.1007/978-3-319-74334-9_59

At this point since both The Technical University of Denmark (DTU) and University of Copenhagen (DTU) were using the Coursera platform (one of the leading global platforms for delivering MOOCs), DTU Library and Copenhagen University Library saw this as an opportunity to achieve the goal of developing a MOOC centred on academic information seeking.

1.1 Creating the MOOC

In the beginning of 2014 a project group was formed consisting of four information specialists from each library. During the spring of that year the group began discussions about the proposed content of the MOOC. The fact that the group's members came from two different institutions quickly made us realise, that we needed to begin by having an exhaustive debate about what we wanted to incorporate in the MOOC. Both parties wanted to develop a MOOC that would be relevant to the users at our respective institutions while appealing to a global user audience within academia. In the end we decided to create a MOOC primarily focused on undergraduate students but in such a way that it would still be suitable the wider audience of individuals who would like to become more proficient information seekers.

Consultations with representatives from both universities pedagogical units led the project group to begin the development of the content by first creating the MOOC's learning objectives and then secondly creating the quizzes that should test the participants at the end of each module. This helped to pinpoint the different aspects on which the course would focus. The learning objectives of the MOOC state, that after passing the course, one would be able to:

- Identify your information needs
- Evaluate databases and other information resources
- Set up search strategies and use various search techniques
- Formulate search strings based on your own research assignment
- Identify relevant material types
- Undertake critical evaluation of your sources
- Search more efficiently on the internet
- Avoid plagiarism
- Cite correctly
- Work with reference management tools
- Document your search process

The content tries to mirror the scenario that the student goes through in the process of seeking information for a research assignment at an academic level. The basic elements of information seeking are introduced and arranged into three individual modules that should be taken in the proposed order.

1. Preparing your search process
2. Performing your searches
3. Evaluating your search results

The backbone of the three modules are 21 videos. Quizzes and small assignments supplement and test the learning process, informing the participants along the way on whether or not they have achieved the necessary level of knowledge. The quizzes must be taken for the participant to pass the course. For participants who are writing an actual academic paper or project, the assignments contribute directly to their own search process. One assignment asks the participant to "Identify the learning targets in your curriculum or study program. What are the formal requirements in relation to the use and documentation of literature?". In this way the participant is encouraged to take on the process of searching for academic literature within their local context.

1.2 Results and Experiences

The "Academic Information Seeking" MOOC was launched on the Coursera platform in early December 2015. The team behind the MOOC was uncertain about the response and about whether or not a course with such a relatively narrow subject would be of interest to more than maybe just a few fellow librarians within the academic world. Fortunately this uncertainty proved to be unnecessary (Table 1).

Table 1. Statistics from December 2015 to May 2017 "Academic Information Seeking" [2]

Total visitors	15,021
Total enrolled learners	6,794
Active learners	3,736
Course completers	389
Payments	62

These numbers may not be all that impressive compared to the most popular courses on the largest MOOC platforms providing access to e-learning content from a long list of the world's most prestigious universities. However, from an academic library perspective, the numbers represent an interest that far exceeds even our most optimistic expectations.

Apart from generating a large number of users following and active in the course, "Academic Information Seeking" attracted users from all over the world. The course had participants from 155 countries, as indicated in red, below [2] (Fig. 1).

Fig. 1. Participants from around the world (Color figure online)

When it comes to the participant's student status the numbers show that this MOOC has a slightly higher portion (38%) of its participants who are currently full-time students or part-time students compared to the average Coursera course (32%). [2]

The course is very well reviewed by the participants. Ninety two reviews rated the course 4.5 on a 5 point scale. The content have received 929 (98%) likes and 22 (2%) dislikes [2]. Thirty two learner stories and 25 written reviews are almost entirely filled with positive and encouraging feedback and statements like these:

> "I've really enjoyed the course and I'm sure it will help me in the future research. I'm currently pursuing a PhD and at one point I've realized I'm not being systematic about collecting literature" [2].
> "…I will apply it on my own work and share it with my students" [2].
> "I'm a medical student and I took this course to write a review article" [2].

1.3 Integrating the Lessons Learned

In the process of developing and releasing "Academic Information Seeking", we have learned a lot about the potential strengths and weaknesses of delivering e-learning in a MOOC format.

Some of the videos have successfully been integrated into our regular on-campus courses, using the flipped classroom concept, where students watch a set of videos before going to face-to-face sessions.

However, choosing the right selection of videos to watch before an on-campus course can sometimes be a bit challenging. To make sure that the students feel obligated to watch the videos before class, it should be clear to them, not only how they would benefit from seeing them, but they should also be informed about how their performance in class and the topics covered there depend heavily on them watching the videos beforehand.

Therefore, the didactical set-up should incorporate elements that secure the interconnectedness between the videos and the classroom activities. One of our courses at DTU Library gives students the chance to earn 2.5 ECTS points and in this particular course we now use a set of videos from the MOOC in connection with a live quiz session in the online tool, Socrative. The students are informed about this quiz and they are told that the classroom instruction is structured in a way that requires them to watch the videos. They use their mobile phones to test if they have picked up on the key learning points from the videos and the library instructors are given an overview of the student's level of knowledge. In this way the combination of videos and quizzes helps the instructors to adapt the classroom activities to a level that is suitable for the group as a whole as well as for the individual student.

In some cases students are supposed to watch only one or two videos before an on campus course. A prime example of this is in connection with the library's course in reference management that specifically deals with the reference management tool, Mendeley. Using the video about how to create a Mendeley account before the face-to-face instruction saves time and enables the instructor to address more in-depth issues during the 90 min that the course lasts.

In her report, "Flexible concepts for integrating the virtual library into educational learning environments", Schreiber highlights a set of challenges relevant to the project in general that are also recognisable within the MOOC project [3]. First of all it demonstrates that there is a substantial discrepancy between the e-didactical theory and the reality in the academic world - for instance the challenge of involving and engaging students in the construction of learning objects and learning content. The team behind the MOOC project took some small steps in order to try and incorporate input from DTU students about the learning content but it proved difficult to engage the students in this process. They have a hard time trying to describe, the learning content that they would like to see in the MOOC about searching for academic information. The most common reaction to the suggestions put to them would be something like "well, that sounds ok, I guess".

Schreiber also points out the challenge of making the embedded learning content in an LMS or in this case a MOOC, sufficiently relevant and interesting to different students [3]. The MOOC format requires that the content is relatively generic and that somewhat limits the relevance of the videos in a local context and in connection to specific courses. That often demands tailor-made content and subject specific examples if the course is to really make a difference. The MOOC also lacks a focus on local services and search interfaces. Consequently we have decided to reopen the learning content and produce new videos. The new versions will be based on the original scripts but the new videos will be shorter, lasting approximately 2–4 min instead of 4 to 8 min. They will be more suitable for a local audience due to an enhanced focus on specific topics of relevance to DTU students.

An evaluation of the project showed that the students thought that the original videos were informative and supportive [4]. However, the students also indicated that the videos generally could have been more personal, inspiring, and innovative. It was also suggested in the evaluation that the videos needed to do a better job in motivating and engaging the participants.

As mentioned before it is very difficult to get qualified input from students by just asking them what they would like to have if they have no special qualifications or prior knowledge about the subject. One way of overcoming this challenge is by including the students in a co-creation process.

2 Co-creation – Concept and Framework

The concept of co-creation is not easily defined, as it means different things to different people – a quick GOOGLE search turns up over 23 million results. Prahalad and Ramaswamy define co-creation:

"**Co-creation** is a management initiative, or form of economic strategy, that brings different parties together (for instance, a company and a group of customers), in order to jointly produce a mutually valued outcome. Co-creation brings the unique blend of ideas from direct customers or viewers (who are not the direct users of the product) which in turn gives a plethora of new ideas to the organisation" [5].

This leaves us with some idea, but perhaps a rather vague one. In the framework of a university library the above definition can be contextualised to mean delivering services to our stakeholders, i.e. students, teachers and researchers, generating new ideas and encouraging joint responsibility, not just for the learning outcomes, but also for the processes and methodologies themselves.

We also note that co-creation is a term that is intrinsically positive. This is illustrated in this statement by Voorberg et al. when they reviewed a segment of the available literature: "We conclude that co-creation and co-production has primarily symbolic value and seems to be considered as values in themselves" [6]. If we accept or partly accept this conclusion, then it is imperative for our project here at DTU Library to construct a working definition of co-creation that will focus on process, methodology, and outcomes.

In order to do this we have adapted the model as proposed by Jens Ulrich in his working paper for VIA University College as we believe that this provides a framework from which to work [7].

The model below is based on co-creation with citizens in a local government setting (and is not unrelated to concepts of civil engagement and community empowerment), but the main points are, we believe, transferable to student engagement and student learning within a university/university library perspective (Fig. 2).

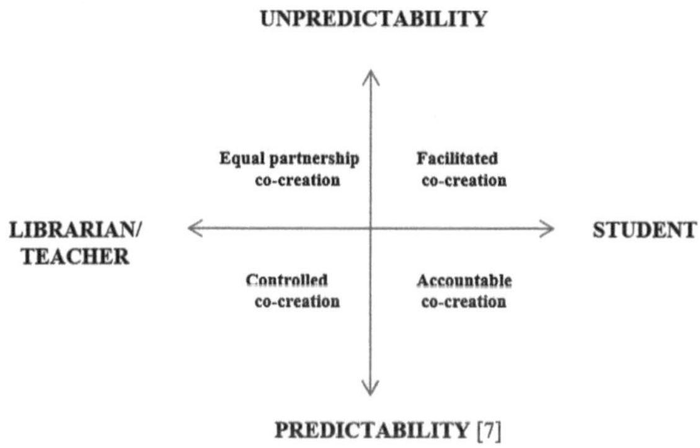

Fig. 2. Co-creation model

The model shows different ways of "sharing" co-creation with, in this case, students at DTU. The y-axis shows the level of predictability/unpredictability, that the organization is willing or capable of accepting, while the x-axis shows us the influence of the partners in relation to each other. In the following we will delve into more explicit descriptions of the four types of co-creation.

2.1 Controlled Co-creation

In this scenario the library staff would seek to control the process with a high level of structure, a high level of predictability, high accountability, and a focus on well-defined professional outcomes. In this model library staff are the senders and the students the receivers in a classic communication model and the power relations are traditional and well understood. In all actuality most teaching/learning activities at the library are planned and implemented with some level of controlled co-creation – examples of this could be input to course work or the opportunity to evaluate a relevant course.

2.2 Accountable Co-creation

In this scenario the emphasis is on students taking responsibility for their own learning in an environment where the results of the process are relatively predictable. Here the teacher/librarian takes on the role of facilitator and the student or students take on a greater degree of independence and accountability. It is the role of the teacher/librarian to ensure that the learners are given the appropriate tools and knowledge to move the process forward themselves due to ideas of self- motivation and empowerment. Classic group work or workshops could be examples of accountable co-creation.

2.3 Equal Partnership Co-creation

Equal partnership co-creation can be defined by the fact that the end result is not pre-defined and there is a high level of unpredictability. The teacher/librarian is a partner in the process rather than an authority or facilitator. The ambition is not to steer the creative endeavors. Since the librarian/teacher identifies the problem or challenge to be addressed, the solution, therefore, is in the hands of the students themselves. An example of this could be that the librarian/teacher defines the learning outcomes, but it is the students themselves who define or in part define the methodologies and didactic form.

2.4 Facilitated Co-creation

In the case of facilitated co-creation the outcomes are not defined beforehand and the responsibility for these is primarily with the students. It is the students themselves who have identified the learning needs and the librarian/teacher acts as a "coach" on the sidelines of the learning process. The learning environment is no longer necessarily the classroom or library but could be off-campus or even in the student's home. An example of this could be that the students "book-a-librarian" who visits a study group at home to help answer questions that turn up during the time the students complete a written report.

2.5 Reflections on the Model

The model introduced by Jens Ulrich – though it takes its starting point from co-creation thinking with a local government and municipality setting – has proved useful in our thinking about co-creation with students when focusing on information competencies and information learning. Obviously many learning forms and co-creation processes may blend different aspects from the four examples and in our setting and context of the library will seldom exist as "clean" versions.

Another important aspect to consider is that of motivation. As already stated the whole concept of co-creation has positive connotations and in the local government setting much of the motivation for involvement will be linked to ideas of civic society, civic engagement, and empowerment. In a university setting these motivational factors do apply but whether they are enough to ensure engagement is unclear and, therefore, other motivational aspects for students must be and will be considered before the start of our project. Students at the Technical University of Denmark are, as students all over the world, presented with a plethora of different activities and the motivation to get involved in a co-creation project may not be top of the agenda. So, some sort of reward system should be considered, such as awarding extra ECTS points, arranging for short-term employment, supporting conference participation, or providing letters of recommendation.

For those librarians who will be involved in the project it will mean putting aside the hierarchical role of "the teacher" and participate in creating a space for collaborative learning and creativity.

2.6 Co-creation – Where to Now?

Our experience at the library tells us that the students are highly motivated for learning about information retrieval and academic searching when it is closely linked to a specific course where these information competences come into play and are most relevant. Therefore, we have joined forces with a specific teacher – with whom we have worked closely over a number of years – with the intention of building on this existing cooperation to include fifth semester students in a co-creation process to investigate, design, and implement working strategies for good information praxis. A small number of students will be invited to join the co-creation project that will run in conjunction with the academic course itself – the students will also follow the previously mentioned generic course that the library offers (academic information retrieval) and will be rewarded with 5 ECTS points – 2½ points for the co-creation participation and 2½ points for the library course. All of the participating students will also receive a letter of recommendation outlining the details and outcomes of the co-creation project.

In their review of the literature Voorberg et al. point out that many of the co-creation projects and initiatives that they describe have little, or in some instances no, focus on the outcomes of these endeavors [6]. The focus is on the process and the methodology – and as stated before the positive value in co-creation itself. We are well aware of this challenge.

3 Conclusion

Reflecting on the four different ways of working with co creation (controlled co-creation, accountable co-creation, equal partnership and facilitated) it is clear to us from our experiences in the first DEFF project that elements from all four scenarios were beneficial. Our intention is to work from the perspective of an equal partnership. This will pose challenges to us as library professionals as we attempt to leave our (or part of) our professional identity at the door as we enter a space for new learning, new roles, and new outcomes. This will, of course, also pose challenges to our students who are not necessarily comfortable or familiar with their new role where they take a larger responsibility for the teaching/learning process than is the norm in a traditional university setting.

References

1. Harbo, K., Jensen, T.S.: How can the digital library contribute to employability? Nord. J. Inf. Lit. High. Educ. **8**, 20–29 (2016). https://noril.uib.no/index.php/noril/article/view/257. Accessed 18 May 2017
2. Coursera Analytics
3. Schreiber, T.: Fleksible koncepter for integration af det virtuelle bibliotek i uddannelsernes læringsmiljøer (2015). http://www.deff.dk/nyheder/ni-fleksible-koncepter-til-integrationen-af-e-biblioteket-i-laeringsmiljoeerne/
4. Lykke, M., Svarre, T., Skov M.: Evalueringsrapport: evaluering af digitale læringsprodukter til udvikling af studerendes informationskompetencer (2016). http://www.deff.dk/fileadmin/user_upload/DEFF/publikationer/Oevrige/DEFF_Evalueringsrapport_Elearning.pdf
5. Prahalad, C.K., Ramaswamy, V.: Co-creation experiences: the next practice in value creation. J. Interact. Mark. **8**, 5–14 (2004)
6. Voorberg, W., Bekkers, V., Tummers, L.: Co-creation and co-production in social innovation: a systematic review and future research agenda. In: EGPA Conference (2013). http://www.lipse.org/upload/publications/Co-creation%20and%20Co-production%20in%20Social%20Innovation%20A%20Systematic%20Review%20and%20Future%20Research%20Agenda.pdf
7. Ulrich, J.: Samskabelse – en typologi, p. 15 (2016). http://docplayer.dk/18053900-Samskabelse-en-typologi.html

Some Predictors of University Students' Information Literacy

Danica Dolničar(✉) and Bojana Boh Podgornik

Faculty of Natural Sciences and Engineering,
University of Ljubljana, Ljubljana, Slovenia
{danica.dolnicar,bojana.boh}@ntf.uni-lj.si

Abstract. The study investigated the predictive power of scientific literacy (SL), ICT use, self-concept, self-efficacy and motivation of 139 undergraduate university students on their information literacy (IL) before taking a compulsory credit-bearing IL course. Knowledge tests were administered for IL and SL, and questionnaires for ICT use and psychological factors. All predictors together accounted for 33.3% of the variance in the pre-test IL level. Significant positive predictors included SL and self-concept about learning, while external controlled motivation correlated negatively with IL. ICT tools and Internet confidence were poor predictors of IL. Internal motivation played a suppressor role in the model. The IL study course significantly improved the IL of students, with a mean difference of 16.38%; the students who scored poorly on the pre-test, benefited more than others.

Keywords: Information literacy · Higher education · Multiple regression
Scientific literacy · ICT use · Self-concept · Motivation

1 Introduction

Information literacy (IL) is often mentioned in connection with other literacies such as scientific literacy (SL) or ICT literacy. Indeed, there are elements of IL in the latter two. While IL is defined as an intellectual framework for understanding, finding, evaluating, and using information [1], SL denotes knowledge and understanding of scientific concepts and processes. The description of scientific competencies from the PISA science survey includes multiple IL-related elements, such as 'Identifying scientific issues by identifying the keywords to search for scientific information' [2]. In terms of ICT literacy, a European framework for digital competences, DigComp [3], identifies five essential areas: information, communication, content-creation, safety, and problem-solving. Several of those can be associated with the IL domain in the area of information especially 'identifying, locating, retrieving, storing, organizing and analysing digital information, judging its relevance and purpose'. The focus in ICT literacy is on the mastery of tools as opposed on the mastery of information. Our focus was on the richness of the ICT experience (frequency of use) and confidence, two attributes

S. Kurbanoğlu et al. (Eds.): ECIL 2017, CCIS 810, pp. 585–594, 2018.
https://doi.org/10.1007/978-3-319-74334-9_60

possessed by the so-called generation of "digital natives". Surprisingly, studies [4, 5] have found that digital nativeness *per se* has not been sufficient for using information in a creative and critical way, neither in the light of digital nor IL competencies.

There are other personal factors, besides knowledge and skills, that could potentially have an effect on the students' IL level, their academic self-concept (knowledge of one's academic ability), general self-efficacy (belief in one's capabilities [6]), motivation (both internal and external), and learning strategy. High academic self-concept and domain-specific self-efficacy were reported to have had positive effects on the information seeking knowledge only when paired with high intelligence [7, 8], pointing to the importance of ability-tailored IL training. According to Serap Kurbanoglu [9], students with low self-efficacy were less inclined to develop the IL competencies for lifelong learning. Broad academic motivation was found important in the development of IL competencies [10, 11]. However, the research often investigated the role of motivation on the IL self-efficacy rather than measuring IL knowledge. Both intrinsic (internal) and extrinsic (external) academic motivation, but especially the intrinsic motivation to know, were positively related to IL self-efficacy [12]. The effect of learning strategies and motivation on the IL self-efficacy was studied by Kiliç-Çakmak [13]. Metacognitive strategies and the control belief of learning were both found to affect multiple IL dimensions. Due to an important role of the motivation, components of motivational design were incorporated in both the AASL IL standards [14] and in the ACRL IL framework [15].

Based on the above findings, the aims of our study were:

- To investigate the influence of several predictors of the information literacy (IL) of university students, measured by the Information Literacy Test (ILT):
  - Scientific literacy (SL), measured by the Scientific Literacy Test (SLT);
  - Use of information and communication technologies (ICT use), measured by four subscales: frequency of using software (ICT-S), frequency of using hardware (ICT-H), number of study courses that involved ICT (ICT-C), confidence when using the Internet (ICT-I);
  - Psychological parameters, measured by a questionnaire with seven subscales: self-concept about learning (SC-L), self-concept about problem-solving (SC-P), general self-efficacy (SE), internal motivation (IM), autonomous external motivation (EM-A), controlled external motivation (EM-C), use of metacognitive learning strategies (LS).
- To evaluate the ability of university students for IL improvement within a dedicated credit-evaluated study course (ILSC), designed according to the ACRL IL standards.

In the research hypotheses we predicted that

- Students' SL, ICT use, academic self-concept, general self-efficacy, academic motivation and learning strategy all have positive effects on IL;
- The IL study course would significantly improve the IL of all students.

2 Materials and Methods

2.1 Measuring Instruments

Information Literacy Test (ILT). A 40-item multiple-choice knowledge test [16] was applied. For each item, only one of the four given options was correct, yielding one point. The content covered all 5 ACRL IL standards for higher education [1].

Scientific Literacy Test (SLT). A knowledge test, comprising 6 problem-based tasks with 23 items in total, was used. The problems, covering popular science topics, were selected from the 2006 PISA science items [17]. Although most items were of a multiple-choice type, some were open ended and had to be evaluated and scored individually (one point per item).

ICT Use Survey. A 35-item scale, with four subscales, was applied from a previous study [5]. The frequency of using software (ICT-S, 16 items) and hardware (ICT-H, 4 items) was measured on a 5-point Likert scale with the following categories: never, less than once a week, multiple times a week, almost every day, and multiple times a day. The third subscale (ICT-C, 5 items) concerned the number of study courses that involved the ICT use. Lastly, the subscale confidence when using the Internet (ICT-I, 10 items) was tested with a series of statements on a 5-point Likert scale, with options ranging from strongly agree to strongly disagree.

Self-concept/Self-efficacy/Motivation/Learning Strategy Questionnaire. A 70-item 5-point Likert type questionnaire [18] was applied that was composed previously as a synthesis of the Self-description questionnaire III (SDQ, [19]), Generalized self-efficacy scale (GSE, [20]), and the Academic motivation questionnaire [21]. The scale was subdivided into 7 subscales: self-concept about learning (SC-L, 10 items), self-concept about problem-solving (SC-P, 10 items), self-efficacy (SE, 10 items), internal motivation (IM, 13 items), autonomous external motivation (EM-A, 6 items), controlled external motivation (EM-C, 6 items), and the use of metacognitive learning strategies (LS, 15 items).

2.2 Information Literacy Study Course (ILSC)

A compulsory 45-h, 3 credit IL course was aligned with the 5 ACRL standards. Lectures, seminar work and practical exercises were delivered/lead by the authors of this contribution using the same methodology and teaching style. Traditional teaching methods were combined with project- and problem-based active learning methods with examples selected from the fields of study. In addition to information sources available in the library or freely on the web, all students had access to professional scientific and patents databases, according to the university licenses.

2.3 Test Group and Testing

One hundred and thirty nine undergraduate students enrolled in three different faculties at the University of Ljubljana participated in the study. The structure of the sample is presented in Table 1.

Table 1. Sample structure by gender, study year and study programme.

Grouping by	Group	Frequency	%
Gender	Male	19	13.7
	Female	120	86.3
Study year	1st	6	4.3
	2nd	103	74.1
	3rd	30	21.0
Study programme	Health sciences	61	43.9
	Biology education	38	26.3
	Graphics technology	29	20.9
	Geotechnology/mining	11	7.9

Prior to taking the course, the students' IL levels were assessed with the ILT (pre-test), which was administered again after the course (post-test). Other tests and surveys used in this study (SLT, ICT use and motivation-related subscales) were taken before the IL course.

The testing was implemented via the online survey system 1ka (1ka.si) or in a printed form, in classrooms supervised by the teacher. An introductory protocol was applied before testing, providing instructions, and explaining the purpose of the study, voluntary participation, and anonymity. Testing was undertaken in years 2014 and 2015.

2.4 Data Analysis

Reliability of the tests/surveys was measured via the Cronbach's alpha. Correlations among variables (scales and subscales) were examined with the Pearson's correlation coefficient. Effectiveness of the ILSC was measured with the paired-samples t-test, comparing ILT results on the pre-test and post-test. Groups were compared using the ANOVA. The predictive power of SL, ICT use, and psychological subscales on IL was calculated with multiple linear regression (MLR). ILT pre-test score was used as a dependent variable. The IBM SPSS statistics package (version 24) was used for the data analysis.

3 Results and Discussion

3.1 Basic Descriptive Statistics and Cronbach Alpha

Basic descriptive statistics (mean and standard deviation) for all variables (dependent and independent) are given in Table 2. In the case of ILT and SLT knowledge tests, the percentage of correct answers is shown; in others, with the exception of the ICT-C subscale (number of ICT-rich courses), an average score on 5-point Likert scale is displayed. Also shown are the reliability of each subscale as Cronbach's α and the corresponding number of subscale items. The reliability of the ICT-H (hardware use) subscale could not be determined.

Table 2. Mean, standard deviation, reliability and number of items for all variables.

Topic	Scale/subscale	M	SD	α	Items
Information literacy	ILT (pre-test)	67.97	12.62	0.738	40
	ILT (post-test)	84.35	6.85		
	ILT (difference)	16.38	10.04		
Scientific literacy	SLT	67.91	13.54	0.607	23
ICT use	ICT-S (software)	2.68	0.35	0.710	16
	ICT-H (hardware)	3.22	0.59	N/A	4
	ICT-C (courses)	4.95	2.05	0.666	5
	ICT-I (Internet confidence)	3.50	0.54	0.783	10
Self-concept	SC-L (learning)	3.84	0.46	0.757	10
	SC-P (problem solving)	3.45	0.50	0.747	10
Self-efficacy	SE	3.73	0.46	0.812	10
Motivation	IM (internal)	3.57	0.50	0.830	13
	EM-A (autonomous external)	3.93	0.50	0.670	6
	EM-C (controlled external)	3.38	0.60	0.655	6
Learning strategy	LS	3.61	0.40	0.629	15

3.2 Information Literacy Study Course Effectiveness

Comparison of the ILT pre-test (M = 67.97, SD = 12.62) and post-test scores in percentages (M = 84.35, SD = 6.85) showed an improvement on the post-test. The paired sample t-test confirmed that the mean difference of 16.38% was statistically significant with a large effect size ($p < 0.001$, $d = 1.61$). The effectiveness of the ILSC on the test group was thus proved; students significantly improved their IL.

3.3 Influence of the Study Year

While no significant differences in IL (pre- and post-test) based on gender were found with a t-test, comparison of the study years, investigated with the ANOVA and Tukey's post-hoc test showed a significantly higher score on the pre-test for third year students, while the first and second year students did not differ significantly. On the post-test, the difference diminished, and was not statistically significant. The results are in line with our previous findings [16], implying that a gradual increase of the IL occurs with study years, even without a specific ILSC. An increase in the IL and a smaller post-test difference proved the benefit of the ILSC, especially in the lower study years. There were also some differences evident when the first and second year students' results were grouped together, and compared to the third year students, in other variables (Fig. 1).

Namely, both groups exhibited a similar level of SL (Fig. 1, left), but the third year students used software more often and were also more confident on the Internet (Fig. 1, right).

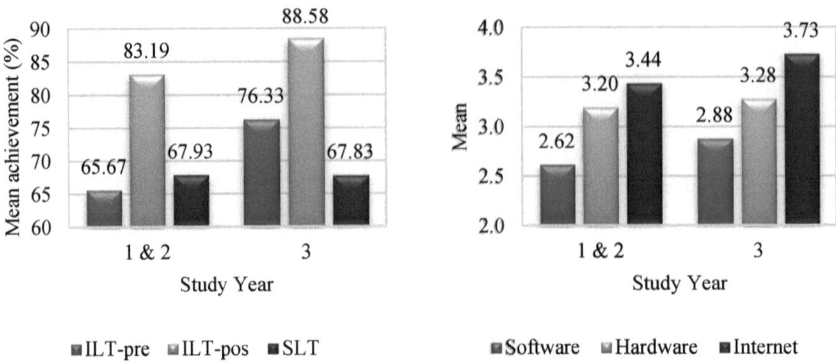

Fig. 1. Differences in IL (pre- and post-test), SL and ICT use by study years

3.4 Correlations Between Variables

Zero-order correlations (Pearson's r) between the independent (predictor) variables as well as with the ILT pre-test, post-test and pre-test/post-test difference scores are displayed in Table 3. Statistically significant correlations are shaded. The significance level p is <0.05 when r < 0.22, and <0.01 otherwise.

Table 3. Zero-order correlations between model variables.

	ILT-pre	ILT-pos	ILT-dif	SLT	ICT-S	ICT-H	ICT-C	ICT-I	SC-L	SC-P	SE	IM	EM-A	EM-C
ILT-pos	0.61													
ILT-dif	-0.84	-0.08												
SLT	0.41	0.25	-0.34											
ICT-S	0.10	0.00	-0.12	-0.02										
ICT-H	-0.10	-0.11	0.06	-0.14	0.38									
ICT-C	-0.01	0.04	0.04	0.04	0.16	0.03								
ICT-I	0.10	0.07	-0.08	-0.06	0.23	0.10	0.03							
SC-L	0.18	0.03	-0.21	0.07	0.12	0.03	0.15	0.10						
SC-P	0.16	0.09	-0.14	0.07	0.35	0.14	0.16	0.25	0.28					
SE	0.14	-0.01	-0.18	0.00	0.24	0.15	0.08	0.32	0.41	0.64				
IM	-0.03	0.00	0.05	-0.14	0.30	0.12	0.12	0.25	0.61	0.36	0.52			
EM-A	0.13	0.08	-0.10	0.03	0.16	-0.09	0.13	0.05	0.42	0.15	0.26	0.54		
EM-C	-0.23	-0.16	0.18	-0.07	0.02	0.09	-0.04	0.01	-0.03	-0.31	-0.21	0.01	0.27	
LS	-0.10	-0.13	0.03	-0.02	0.18	0.02	0.11	0.02	0.46	0.16	0.30	0.57	0.53	0.14

Only three variables correlate significantly with the ILT pre-test score, the correlations ranging from moderate positive (r = 0.41) for scientific literacy, small positive (r = 0.18) for self-concept about learning, and small negative (r = −0.23) for controlled external motivation. The first result confirms that the scientific and information literacy are relatively closely connected. The negative correlation with the controlled component of the external motivation (where students are motivated by grades, teachers and other people) implies that students who do not rely on external motivation have acquired more IL knowledge than those who do.

While the ICT use was not significantly correlated with IL on the pre-test (r = 0.10), there was a moderate correlation found between hardware and software use (r = 0.38), and a weak link between the software use and confidence on the Internet (r = 0.23). Software use was also moderately correlated with the internal motivation (r = 0.30) and self-concept about problem solving (r = 0.35) while confidence using the Internet was moderately correlated with the self-efficacy (r = 0.32) and weakly to the problem solving self-concept (r = 0.25).

Six strong correlations were observed among psychological subscales. Internal motivation was strongly linked to the autonomous external motivation (r = 0.54), but also to the self-concept about learning (r = 0.61), self-efficacy (r = 0.52), and learning strategies (r = 0.57). Self-efficacy was strongly correlated with the self-concept about problem solving (r = 0.64). Learning strategies and autonomous external motivation also had a strong connection (r = 0.53).

Table 3 reveals a high correlation (r = 0.60) between the ILT scores on the pre-test and post-test and a very strong negative correlation (r = −0.84) between the pre-test and the pre-test/post-test difference, indicating that the students with the lower starting level of IL have improved on the post-test more than students with a better pre-knowledge on IL.

Table 4. Predicting the students' IL level before taking the course (bolded are the statistically significant predictors)

	Unstand. Coeff.		Stand. Coeff.			95.0% Confid. Inter. for B		Correlations		
Predictor	B	Std. Err.	β	t	Sig.	Lower	Upper	Zero-order	Partial	Part
(Constant)	13.890	5.756		2.413	0.017	2.499	25.281			
SLT	**0.545**	**0.124**	**0.336**	**4.382**	**0.000**	**0.299**	**0.791**	**0.409**	**0.364**	**0.319**
ICT-S	1.989	1.249	0.139	1.593	0.114	−0.482	4.460	0.095	0.140	0.116
ICT-H	−0.449	0.705	−0.053	−0.637	0.525	−1.844	0.945	−0.104	−0.057	−0.046
ICT-C	−0.176	0.184	−0.072	−0.955	0.342	−0.541	0.189	−0.007	−0.085	−0.069
ICT-I	1.054	0.743	0.114	1.419	0.158	−0.416	2.524	0.104	0.125	0.103
SC-L	**2.589**	**1.053**	**0.238**	**2.458**	**0.015**	**0.505**	**4.674**	**0.179**	**0.214**	**0.179**
SC-P	−0.253	1.035	−0.025	−0.245	0.807	−2.302	1.795	0.158	−0.022	−0.018
SE	0.708	1.187	0.064	0.596	0.552	−1.642	3.057	0.135	0.053	0.043
IM	**−2.411**	**1.206**	**−0.237**	**−2.000**	**0.048**	**−4.797**	**−0.025**	**−0.035**	**−0.175**	**−0.145**
EM-A	**2.874**	**1.002**	**0.283**	**2.868**	**0.005**	**0.891**	**4.857**	**0.126**	**0.248**	**0.209**
EM-C	**−1.918**	**0.706**	**−0.229**	**−2.715**	**0.008**	**−3.315**	**−0.520**	**−0.226**	**−0.235**	**−0.197**
LS	**−2.722**	**1.193**	**−0.218**	**−2.283**	**0.024**	**−5.082**	**−0.362**	**−0.100**	**−0.199**	**−0.166**

3.5 Predicting the IL Level of Students

A multiple linear regression analysis was used to develop a model for predicting the student IL level before taking the course from twelve independent variables (SLT, four ICT and seven psychological subscales). The model was able to account for 33% of the variance in the IL level; $F(12, 126) = 5.25$, $p < 0.001$, $R^2 = 0.333$. The statistically significant predictors are bolded in Table 4. All three predictor variables with a significant zero-order correlation with the IL level (scientific literacy SLT, self-concept about learning SC-L and controlled external motivation EM-C), had a significant partial effect in the full model. Their contributions to IL variance, calculated by partitioning R^2 by multiplying β values with zero-order correlations from Table 4, were 13.7% (SLT), 5.2% (EM-C) and 4.3% (SC-L). Internal motivation IM had a significant negative effect in the model, but since its zero-order correlation with ILT was 0, it played a suppressor role, strengthening the effect of the self-concept about learning. The autonomous external motivation EM-A had a positive effect in the model; although it was only weakly correlated with the ILT, it influenced other variables in the model (removing EM-A also dropped IM, EM-C and LS from the model). The learning strategy (LS) had a negative influence in the model, which was in line with its small (albeit non-significant) correlation with the ILT. The reason may be that some of the items in this subscale could be perceived by students as negative or socially inadequate (e.g. asking the teacher/other students for help, or rearranging one's notes after the lecture). General self-efficacy and self-concept about problem solving had no influence on the level of IL.

4 Conclusions

The study confirmed that the information literacy of students can be influenced by their competencies in related disciplines, by their psychological traits/preferences, and by the IL specific study course. Constructing a multiple linear model from a sample of 139 students we found out that:

- The best predictor of IL was scientific literacy (accounting for 16.71% of the variability).
- Overall richness of ICT use and confidence on the Internet had no significant influence on the IL level in our study. This ties in with earlier research that found that digital natives were not necessarily information literate [4].
- Motivation and related factors were not very well correlated with the IL. Only the self-concept about learning was found to be a positive predictor of IL and the controlled external motivation was a negative predictor. In other words, students with a good grasp of their academic ability had a better chance of utilizing it when acquiring IL knowledge. This could be connected with findings that low-performers often overestimate their IL skills [22]. On the other hand, students relying primarily on the outside motivation also attained a lower IL level. Therefore, close attention should be paid to the motivational aspects of the IL education, as was suggested by [23], to include both intrinsic and extrinsic motivation. Internal motivation,

although not directly correlated with IL in our case, enhanced the effect of self-concept about learning in the model.

- The effectiveness of the IL study course was proven. The comparison of the ILT pre-test and post-test scores showed a mean difference of 16.38%, and the improvement of students' IL was statistically significant. The students that scored poorly on the pre-test, improved more than others. Therefore, the introduction of an IL course seems to be most beneficial for students with initially low levels of IL.

Acknowledgements. The study was financially supported by the Slovenian Research Agency, project J5-5535. The following researches participated in the preparation of tests and questionnaires used in the project: Tomaž Bartol and Andrej Šorgo (IL test, ICT use survey), Saša A. Glažar (SL test), Mojca Juriševič and Margareta Vrtačnik (Self-concept/Self-efficacy/Motivation/Learning Strategy Questionnaire), Blaž Rodič (setting e-versions on the online survey system 1ka.si).

References

1. ACRL: Information Literacy Competency Standards for Higher Education. American Library Association (2000). http://www.ala.org/acrl/standards/informationliteracycompetency
2. Catts, R., Lau, J.: Towards information literacy indicators. In: Conceptual Frame-Work Paper. UNESCO, Paris (2008). http://www.ifla.org/publications/towards-information-literacy-indicators
3. Ferrari, A.: DIGCOMP: a framework for developing and understanding digital competence in Europe. In: Punie, Y., Brečko, B.N. (eds.) Joint Research Centre of the European Commission (2013). http://publications.jrc.ec.europa.eu/repository/bitstream/JRC83167/lb-na-26035-enn.pdf
4. Fraillon, J., Schulz, W., Ainley, J.: International Computer and Information Literacy Study: Assessment Framework (2013). http://research.acer.edu.au/ict_literacy/9
5. Šorgo, A., Bartol, T., Dolničar, D., Boh Podgornik, B.: Attributes of digital natives as predictors of information literacy in higher education. Br. J. Educ. Technol. **48**(3), 749–767 (2017)
6. Bandura, A.: The explanatory and predictive scope of self-efficacy theory. J. Soc. Clin. Psychol. **4**(3), 359–373 (1986)
7. Rosman, T., Mayer, A.-K., Krampen, G.: Intelligence, academic self-concept, and information literacy: the role of adequate perceptions of academic ability in the acquisition of knowledge about information searching. Inf. Res. Int. Electron. J. **20**(1), 1–20 (2015)
8. Rosman, T., Mayer, A.K.: Moderating effects of domain-specific self-efficacy on the relationship between intelligence and information-seeking skills. In: 16th Biennial EARLI Conference for Research on Learning and Instruction, Limassol, Cyprus (2015). https://www.zpid.de/pub/research/2015_rosman_EARLI-paper_limassol.pdf
9. Serap Kurbanoglu, S.: Self-efficacy: a concept closely linked to information literacy and lifelong learning. J. Doc. **59**(6), 635–646 (2003)
10. Crow, S.R.: Information literacy: what's motivation got to do with it? Knowl. Quest. Chic. **35**(4), 48–52 (2007)

11. Mortimore, J.M., Wall, A.: Motivating African-American students through information literacy instruction: exploring the link between encouragement and academic self-concept. Ref. Libr. **50**(1), 29–42 (2009)
12. Ross, M., Perkins, H., Bodey, K.: Academic motivation and information literacy self-efficacy: the importance of a simple desire to know. Libr. Inf. Sci. Res. **38**(1), 2–9 (2016)
13. Kiliç-Çakmak, E.: Learning strategies and motivational factors predicting information literacy self-efficacy of e-learners. Australas. J. Educ. Technol. **26**(2), 192–208 (2010)
14. Standards for the 21st-Century Learner. American Association of School Librarians (AASL) (2006). http://www.ala.org/aasl/standards/learning
15. ACRL: Framework for Information Literacy for Higher Education. American Library Association (2016). http://www.ala.org/acrl/standards/ilframework
16. Boh Podgornik, B., Dolničar, D., Šorgo, A., Bartol, T.: Development, testing, and validation of an information literacy test (ILT) for higher education. J. Assoc. Inf. Sci. Technol. **67**(10), 2420–2436 (2016)
17. OECD: PISA released science items (2006). http://www.oecd.org/pisa/38709385.pdf
18. Juriševič, M., Baggia, A., Bartol, T., Dolničar, D., Glažar, S.A., Kljajić Borštnar, M., et al.: Motivational aspects of information literacy in higher education. In: International Conference on Excellence Innovation Creativity Basic-Higher Education Psychology (2016). http://www.icieconference.net/images/Conference_Program_Detailed_Book.pdf
19. Marsh, H.W., O'Neill, R.: Self description questionnaire III: the construct validity of multidimensional self-concept ratings by late adolescents. J. Educ. Meas. **21**(2), 153–174 (1984)
20. Schwarzer, R., Jerusalem, M.: The general self self-efficacy scale (GSE). In: Weinman, J., Wright, S., Johnston, M., (eds.) Measures in Health Psychology: A User's Portfolio Causal and Control Beliefs, Windsdor, UK, pp. 35–37 (1995). https://userpage.fu-berlin.de/health/engscal.htm
21. Vrtačnik, M., Juriševič, M., Ferk Savec, V.: Motivational profiles of Slovenian high school students and their academic performance outcomes. Acta Chim. Slov. **57**(3), 733–740 (2010)
22. Mahmood, K.: Do people overestimate their information literacy skills? A systematic review of empirical evidence on the Dunning-Kruger effect. Commun. Inf. Lit. **10**(2), 199–213 (2016)
23. Hess, N., Kathryn, A.: Motivational design in information literacy instruction. Commun. Inf. Lit. **9**(1), 44–59 (2015)

The "Real World" Relevance of Information Literacy

Karen F. Kaufmann[1,2](✉)

[1] Information Systems School, Queensland University of Technology (QUT), Brisbane, QLD, Australia
Karen.f.kaufmann@gmail.com
[2] San Jose State University Gateway PhD, San Jose, CA, USA

Abstract. This doctoral study aims to learn undergraduate student perceptions of the relevance of information literacy competencies applied to academic work. The study also intends to learn what students identify as factors that make information literacy relevant. This paper presents preliminary findings providing new insights for improving pedagogical work, supporting academia goals such as retention and completion, and improving how to communicate the value of information literacy competencies as transferable competencies to the "Real World". Using a pragmatic epistemological and methodological approach, the research design includes a cross-sectional mixed-methods two-stage sequential study.

Keywords: Information literacy · Framework · Socio-cognitive relevance
User relevance · Higher education · Academic work · Threshold concepts
Real world

1 Introduction

Research has documented that "the most prominent and consistent determinant of information literacy is student perception" [1 p. 132]. Using Relevance Theory as the theoretical underpinning for this study, Socio-Cognitive Relevance (SCR) is being investigated using the cognitive and communicative principles of Relevance Theory [2]. The cognitive principle of Relevance Theory is utilized in this study examining the "cognitive" principle of relevance of Information Literacy Competencies (ILC) identified to be measured as "meaningful" [3–6]. The communicative principle of Relevance Theory examines the "socio (social)" principle of relevance of ILC identified to be measured as "usefulness" [3, 7–10]. For this study, information literacy competencies specific to higher education will be as described by the newly adopted 2016 Association of College and Research Libraries (ACRL) Framework and Threshold Concepts in combination with the 2000 ACRL Standards [14].

The primary research question for this mixed methods sequential study asks:

- How is information literacy relevant to undergraduate student academic work, from a socio-cognitive user view?
- The secondary research questions ask:

S. Kurbanoğlu et al. (Eds.): ECIL 2017, CCIS 810, pp. 595–604, 2018.
https://doi.org/10.1007/978-3-319-74334-9_61

- What are undergraduate student perceptions of the socio-cognitive relevance of IL competencies to their academic work?
- What are factors impacting the socio-cognitive relevance of IL competencies to academic work?

2 Literature Review

The information literacy competencies in this study are mapped to the Association of College and Research Libraries Information Literacy Framework [9] and Standards [10]. When considering the user-view, relevance is identified when information has meaning or is meaningful in relation to context - such as academic work [4, 6, 9, 10]. Socio-cognitive relevance is the perception of something being useful and meaningful [11]. Using the theory of relevance as a framework, this study aims to contribute to the growing literature in information literacy and the nascent space in information science literature on socio-cognitive relevance [2, 12, 13].

The information literacy (IL) Framework is intended, as per the ACRL [14] filing and adoption, to broaden the scope of learning, research, scholarship and pedagogy, as well as embrace the notion of threshold concepts, metacognition and self-directed learning that our technology and information climate now encourages and even demands. Edwards [15] found that a student's ability to discern a change in their awareness of new knowledge (threshold concept) may cause changes in learning outcomes. IL education and research has been shifting to recognize the rich information ecology of the 21st century. The notions of threshold concepts and meta-literacy are core concepts of the revised Framework for Information Literacy for Higher Education recognizing behavioral, affective, cognitive, and metacognitive engagement [14].

Threshold Concepts are discipline specific spaces that provide for new understanding for thinking, practicing, and building associations within that discipline. The new Framework for Information Literacy for Higher Education is informed by threshold concepts including the work of Wiggins and McTighe [16] based on the seminal research of Meyer and Land [17]. The Framework adopts six frames that anchor information literacy concepts with a set of knowledge practices and dispositions components identified for each.

The concept of IL as the core meta-literacy for users in academia, business and as lifelong learners is a topical thread that fills current literature [18]. Meta-literacy is part of the rich paradigm of relevance inquiry and information ecology of interdependent factors where people, information, and technology interact. The literature that supports further inquiry of student perceptions of ILC and learning indicate the complex interplay of ILC, learning, and their relevance to academic work [18–22]. This speaks to the information ecology influences that may be contextual, situational, social, topical, relational, inferential, cognitive, behavioral, or motivational. These influences may affect how students may perceive ILC as relevant as they employ ILC in their academic work.

Van der Henst et al. suggest that "Everything else being equal, the greater the cognitive effects achieved by processing an input, the greater its relevance" [23, p. 4].

This concept continues in their work of reasoning experiments, and they suggest that this comparative linguistic approach can be considered as to what is relevant to the user: the relevance in the context of other premises, such as prior knowledge. "The relevance of a piece of information is relevance to its user" [23, p. 4]. Inherent in this thinking, is the implicitness of relevance, which several authors have noted and called for continued empirical evidence - evidence to consider and possibly discover implicit attributes of relevance [24]. Implicit attributes of relevance might include attitude [25], intuitive understanding [26], emotions [24], and multi-dimensionality or meaning that relevance can be judged by different users having different perceptions [3]. Researching student perceptions of the relevance of ILC to academic work may inform the information science and academic communities of ways to enhance ILC relevance to improve academic success. If the usefulness (socio) and meaningfulness (cognitive) of ILC are identified, and mapped to the Frames and Standards, gaps in relevance that impact student understanding and therefore application to their academic work can be addressed in teaching and integration in curricula development. Identifying factors of relevance identified by students will assist understanding of what makes these competencies useful and meaningful to them as they use information. The possible transferability of these factors to non-academic contexts - the "Real World" - such as workplace, health related information use, employment seeking information use, and everyday information use may be applied.

Information literacy viewed through a theoretical lens of socio-cognitive relevance is an area of study that is open to exploration and is a topic that has emerged in more current literature in the field of information science [4, 6, 7, 13, 19, 27–31].

3 Research Method

The pragmatic approach to this study aligns mixed methods to the research inquiry including the abductive connection of theory and data. The inter-subjective relationship to the research process aligns transferability of inference from data [28].

This is a two stage cross sectional explanatory mixed methods study. The methodology and results from the first quantitative stage informs the methodology used for the second qualitative stage [29]. The mixed methods approach is used with the intent of producing a "superior product" [30, p. 17].

Data collection for stage one of the study uses an online survey divided into four sections. Section one of the survey has an introduction, instructions, and consent to participate. Section two has four questions asking about the student experience and specific tasks associated with completing an academic paper with required sources. Section three defines "usefulness" and "meaningfulness" and has ten ILC identified for students to rank the relevance of the competency. The ILC questions use a four point Likert-type scale for ranking how useful and meaningful the ILC were when used to complete their academic task. The final question in this section asks for students to indicate their perception of improvement of ILC using a sliding scale ranking. Section four of the survey is a Thank You & Follow-Up with five demographic questions and the opportunity for participants to indicate interest in participating in the second stage focus groups.

Data collection for stage two used focus groups. Four focus groups were conducted after the stage one online survey had been completed and data reviewed. A discussion guide was used to conduct each focus group session. The survey data was used to inform the development of the focus group discussion guide. Participants were provided a participant packet that included an instruction page, consent to participate, and a student version of the discussion guide to refer to during the focus group session.

The stage one quantitative data analysis was conducted using SPSS v24 and Excel software. The stage two qualitative data analysis was conducted using thematic analysis. Thematic analysis was used to review, interpret, and identify key themes and then factors from the focus group data. Thematic analysis is described as "a method for identifying, analyzing and reporting patterns (themes) within data" [31, p. 79]. Using thematic analysis provides for coding for specific research questions, providing for a theoretical [31] abductive approach, that supports the methodology of this study.

Using the pragmatic mixed methods sequential approach, the quantitative and qualitative data are integrated and analyzed to provide context and connections of the mixed methods data and to ultimately attempt to answer the sequential and primary research questions.

3.1 Sample Design

The sample for the survey was a non-random purposive participant pool; 392 undergraduate students were given the opportunity to volunteer to participate in the online survey. The online survey had 140 responses resulting in a 35.7% response rate. From this pool of 140 responses, 134 valid student participants emerged. The cross section of the survey participants include representation from fourteen different classes situated across ten academic programs. Age, gender, academic status, and student status were well represented and distributed.

Stage two used purposive non-probability sampling. The stage two qualitative sequence of this study included four focus groups with a total of ten student participants. The first two focus groups had taken the stage one online survey and indicated their interest in participating in the focus groups in the final section of the survey. The second two focus groups had received on-campus information literacy instruction for a class that required a writing assignment. Participants were invited during the on-campus instruction to indicate interest in participating in a focus group for this study.

4 Findings

Preliminary findings and data analysis of the mixed methods study provides information about undergraduate student perceptions of the relevance of information literacy competencies when applied to an academic task. The second stage of the sequential study provides qualitative data indicating what students say are factors that make information literacy competencies relevant to their academic work. Together, these two stages of the study when integrated, intended to answer the primary research question:

How is information literacy relevant to undergraduate student academic work, from a socio-cognitive user view?

4.1 Quantitative - Stage One

Using a Likert-type scale participants ranked the SCR of the ILC as being useful and meaningful for successful completion of their academic paper assignment [3, 4, 6, 8, 12, 25–27, 31, 32]. Responses showed 88.6% of participants did use information literacy competencies to complete their writing assignment. The average ranking of each of the ILC on a four point Likert-type scale was the highest rank possible in the survey described as "very relevant". Participant choices for ranking the SCR of ILC were: (1) not relevant, (2) somewhat relevant, (3) relevant, or (4) very relevant.

Section 3 of the survey asked five demographic questions and included an additional space for participants to indicate if they would like to participate in a focus group.

The demographic data includes age range, gender, academic status, student status, and current program of study of the participant pool. Using SPSS v24, the bivariate analysis indicates there was neither an association of strength to the ordinal variables (Spearman's Rho) nor to the nominal variables (Lambda) and the SCR of ILC. These findings importantly assist in understanding that participant perceptions of ILC were not bound by age, gender, academic status, student status, or academic program. This data complemented Franklin's [32] study findings that demographics were not predictors of or highly correlated to the perception of the importance of information literacy competencies.

4.2 Qualitative - Stage Two

Preliminary thematic analysis of the four focus group transcripts unveil one overarching or "uber" factor and six key factors of SCR to ILC. Related to these key factors of SCR, fourteen dimensional factors of SCR to ILC were identified. The key factors and dimensional factors and the interplay of meanings of these factors, are related, and intertwined. They may be described as nuanced with shades of emphasis implicated by the language, context, and meanings that students shared. These associations or the integration of the SCR to the ILC may indicate the application of these factors of SCR to ILC as possible threshold concepts. The "implicitness" and multi-dimensionality of meaning of relevance as perceived by users was empirically identified in this study [24].

This paper will focus on the key factor of SCR to ILC, described as "Real World Application". These are two-dimensional factors; personal relevance and professional relevance, are associated with this key factor. "Real World Application" was coded when participants expressed their perceptions of the application of ILC as it relates to the real world.

Here are a few examples of how focus group participants expressed their perceptions of how ILC are SCR or useful and or meaningful to a "Real World Application".

> *"I think understanding that past- you know post college- you're still going to use these [ILC] - that's important to understand."*

"I think it's kind of half-and-half for me. [...] I'm probably not plagiarizing anyone, but just, it's for right now in college that you need to know you're not plagiarizing - and in the real world you need that."

"Maybe, ahm, if you're going to be telling the students... you could tell them how it's [ILC] not just relevant for here at the college, but later on in life you'll probably need to be able to use IL being able to get good sources."

"Um, in terms of usefulness I found, any of the texts that included case studies that showed how the information that you were reading or learning could be applied to the field, I found that I guess if we're gauging these in terms of usefulness and meaningfulness, I found that useful; and it showed how you can use the information. In terms of meaningfulness the - having high level technical data um- good descriptions of the technology being studied at least in the program that I'm in that was helpful to have the breakdown of how it should work from a technological standpoint and then the case studies that show here's how you apply the technology you're learning to a real world example."

Here are a few examples of how focus group participants expressed their perceptions of how the dimensional factor of "Personal Relevance" related to the "Real World Application" of ILC as a factor of SCR.

"For my sources, when somebody would go on to talk about a real life example to tell how this could affect people- real life examples was a factor."

"I agree, it did add to writing in the paper and our knowledge. Cause that's where looking up these things to write about the paper, we kind of learned them [ILC] as we're going through that."

Lastly here are a few examples of how focus group participants expressed their perceptions of how the dimensional factor of "Professional Relevance" related to the "Real World Application" of ILC was a factor of SCR.

"Yes, useful, added to my knowledge; meaningful [ILC] will help in my actual career."

"Yes, and you don't have to be in the field of technology to use that [ILC]. You're going to use these[ILC] again in any professional field, and at some point in your life. Understanding that maybe will make it more relevant to someone who is just now learning them."

"Learning about copyright, licensing, and plagiarism stuff like that it's useful for me because the profession I want to go into I don't want to code a game and then have somebody steal that code for the game if I make it open source and use it to make money off of the code that I wrote. And it's meaningful because at the same time you don't want other people to have to go through that where you're stealing their work and profiting off of it."

Participants indicated that "Real World Application" of ILC increased the relevance of ILC to their academic work. Personal and professional relevance were impactful dimensions of relevance that mattered to the application of ILC to their academic work, connecting new possible information spaces to their current information ecology. A shade of emphasis related to this factor mentioned by students was the importance of clearly identifying and articulating the Real World Application of ILC. This is important to avoid a possible barrier to this factor of relevance and increase the understanding and perception of the value of ILC to their Real World.

As noted in the introduction, student perceptions of information literacy is a strong determinant to information literacy [1]. Therefore, providing the knowledge base of how ILC are relevant beyond their academic tasks provides opportunity for perception to be impacted.

5 Implications and Conclusion

Relevance… "The perception that something is interesting and worth knowing" [33, p. 1]. Exploring the socio-cognitive relevance of ILC through expressly including both the newly adopted 2016 ACRL Framework and the 2000 ACRL Standards as competencies has not yet been studied. This "niche" study of socio-cognitive relevance and the newly identified enmeshed ILC within the "community" of IS, provides for new data and understandings of the impact of these related and intertwined constructs in the information ecology of college students. The "niche" markets for this study include: academia, education, communication, psychology, social science, information science information professionals, lifelong learning partners, and foundations. The study may provide insights into how students perceive the value of ILC for the "Real World"-recognizing ILC as transferable skills for workplace environments, social, and everyday information needs. The more meaningful ILC are to the student academic experience, the greater the opportunity for student success, lifelong learning and career success [34].

Identifying the factors of SCR that students have identified will assist understanding what makes these competencies useful and meaningful to them as they use information. The implementation of these factors to non-academic contexts, such as the workplace – "The Real World" - has potential to increase the relevance of ILC to users. Revising the survey tool used in this study to accommodate a workplace task ethos may be a possible instrument for workplace task ILC relevance assessment.

The "Real World" application of ILC expressed by focus group students as a factor of SCR - the crossing of a threshold of understanding if you will - expressed as a perception in either personal or professional dimensions, unveiled some new data. A possibly new understanding was that students were connecting the "Real World" application of ILC to information uses beyond their current academic work and, in fact when they did, ILC became more SCR - useful and meaningful - to the students. Goldstein and Whitworth [35] in their work with information literacy in work environments, drew an association of workplace IL competence to efficiency, competitive advantage, and employee satisfaction. They also acknowledged this related to the often questioned impact of IL instruction in academia. This study provides empirical data reflecting and connecting ILC impact and possible implicitness of relevance from the academic information ecology to the "Real World".

In the book titled *Managing the Millennials* [36], Espinoza and Ukleja identified that a key to motivating the millennial workforce is helping them find meaning in what they do. They are kept motivated by seeing how what they do matters. In contrast, de-motivation occurs when millennials are not allowed to bring their creativity and passion to their work. Millennial learners and workers are looking for the useful and meaningful (SCR) information spaces to apply ILC. This may add credibility to the integrated, dimensional factors of the "Real World" socio-cognitive relevance of information literacy competencies as millennials cross these thresholds of new understandings.

In a recent case study, Conley and Gill [37] developed a survey to learn business professionals' views and gain insight as to the relevance of IL in the workplace and student IL competencies as potential hires in their businesses. They sought to validate the relevancy of IL for business professionals. Given the research they cited and lack of agreement on terminology, they found it paramount to define and explain IL for the business professionals taking the survey. Their findings resonated with the findings of this study that affirmed the need to specifically articulate what IL is and how it connects to the "Real World" and to students' immediate academic task.

This study's preliminary findings showed the majority of undergraduate students found ILC to be "very" useful and meaningful (SCR) to their academic work. The study also indicated that the "Real World" application of ILC - beyond academic work - in personal and professional dimensions including the workplace, increased the socio-cognitive relevance of ILC when articulated to students.

Acknowledgments. Exceptional gratitude to my supervisors, who have guided this work by their expertise, insight, and care. Each of these researchers bring academic rigor and insights for which I am so very grateful. Thank you - Dr. Elham Sayyad Abdi (QUT Principal Supervisor), Professor Sylvia E. Edwards (QUT Associate Supervisor) and Dr. Lili Luo (SJSU, External Supervisor).

Much gratitude to Beta Phi Mu for selecting this study for the 2017 Eugene Garfield Doctoral Dissertation Fellowship.

The Queensland University of Technology (QUT) granted permission for this research: Ethics Clearance #1500000893. Seminole State College of Florida (SSC) Institutional Research Board approval June 23, 2016.

References

1. Poll, R., Payne, P.: Impact measures for libraries and information services. Libr. Hi Tech **24** (4), 547–562 (2006)
2. Wilson, D., Sperber, D.: Relevance theory. In: Horn, L.R., Ward, G. (eds.) The Handbook of Pragmatics, pp. 607–632. Oxford, Blackwell (2004)
3. Borlund, P.: The concept of relevance in IR. J. Am. Soc. Inform. Sci. Technol. **54**(10), 913–925 (2003)
4. Cosijn, E., Ingwersen, P.: Dimensions of relevance. Inf. Process. Manag. **36**, 533–550 (2000)
5. Hjørland, B.: Epistemology and the socio-cognitive perspective in information science. J. Am. Soc. Inf. Sci. Technol. **53**(4), 257–270 (2002)
6. Saracevic, T.: Relevance: a review of the literature and a framework for thinking on the notion in information science. Part II: behavior and effects of relevance. J. Am. Soc. Inform. Sci. Technol. **58**(13), 1915–1933 (2007)
7. Hjorland, B.: Domain analysis: a socio-cognitive orientation for information science research. Bull. Am. Soc. Inf. Sci. Technol. **30**(3), 17–21 (2004)
8. Saracevic, T.: Relevance: a review of and a framework for the thinking on the notion in information science. J. Am. Soc. Inf. Sci. **26**(6), 321–343 (1975)
9. Framework for Information Literacy for Higher Education [Internet]: American Library Association (2016). http://www.ala.org/acrl/sites/ala.org.acrl/files/content/issues/infolit/Framework_ILHE.pdf. Updated 11 January. Accessed 28 Jan 2016

10. Information Literacy Competency Standards for Higher Education [Internet] (2000). http://www.ala.org/acrl/standards/informationliteracycompetency. Updated 1 September. Accessed 26 Sept 2014
11. Borlund, P.: The concept of relevance in IR. J. Am. Soc. Inform. Sci. Technol. **54**(10), 913–925 (2003)
12. Hjorland, B.: The foundation of the concept of relevance. J. Am. Soc. Inform. Sci. Technol. **61**(2), 217–237 (2010)
13. Hjørland, B.: Epistemology and the socio-cognitive perspective in information science. J. Am. Soc. Inform. Sci. Technol. **53**(4), 257–270 (2002)
14. ACRL Standards Committee: ACRL Board of Directors Action. http://acrl.ala.org/ilstandards/wp-content/uploads/2015/01/Framework-MW15-Board-Docs.pdf. Accessed 16 Jan 2015
15. Edwards, S.: Panning for Gold: Information Literacy and the Net Lenses Model. Auslib Press, Adelaide (2006)
16. Wiggins, G., McTighe, J.: Understanding by Design. Association for Supervision and Development, Alexandria (2004)
17. Meyer, J., Land, R.: Threshold Concepts and Troublesome Knowledge: Linkages to Ways of Thinking and Practising within the Disciplines. University of Edinburgh Edinburgh, Economic and Social Research Council, London (2003)
18. Marcum, J.W.: Rethinking information literacy. Libr. Q. **72**(1), 1–26 (2002)
19. Steinerova, J.: Ecological dimensions of information literacy. Inf. Res. **15**(4), 27 (2010)
20. Maybee, C.: Undergraduate perceptions of information use: the basis for creating user-centered student information literacy instruction. J. Acad. Librariansh. **32**(1), 79–85 (2006)
21. Kwon, N., Onwuegbuzie, A., Alexander, L.: Critical thinking disposition and library anxiety: affective domains on the space of information seeking and use in academic libraries. Coll. Res. Libr. **68**(3), 268–278 (2007)
22. Bruce, C.: Information literacy as a catalyst for educational change. A background paper (2004)
23. Van der Henst, J.B., Sperber, D., Politzer, G.: When is a conclusion worth deriving? A relevance-based analysis of indeterminate relational problems. Think. Reason. **8**(1), 1–20 (2002)
24. Steinerova, J.: Seeking relevance in academic information use. Inf. Res. **13**(4) (2008)
25. Cuadra, C., Katter, R.: Opening the black box of "Relevance". J. Doc. **23**(4), 291–303 (1967)
26. Saracevic, T.: Relevance reconsidered. In: Proceedings of the Second Conference on Conceptions of Library and Information Science (CoLIS 2). ACM Press (1996)
27. Cosijn, E.: Relevance judgements within the context of work tasks. In: 1st International Conference on Information Interaction in Context. ACM, New York (2006)
28. Morgan, D.: Paradigms lost and pragmatism regained: methodological implications of comgining qualitatvie and quantitative methods. J. Mix. Methods Res. **1**(1), 48–76 (2007)
29. Teddlie, C., Yu, F.: Mixed methods sampling a typology with examples. J. Mix. Methods Res. **1**(1), 77–100 (2007)
30. Johnson, R., Onwuegbuzie, A.: Mixed methods research: a research paradigm whose time has come. Educ. Res. **33**(7), 14–26 (2004)
31. Braun, V., Clarke, V.: Using thematic analysis in psychology. Qual. Res. Psychol. **3**(2), 77–101 (2006)
32. Franklin, K.: The importance of information literacy: insights from the next generation of scholars. In: ACRL Twelfth National Conference, Minneapolis, Minnesota, 7–10 April 2005

33. Helping students find relevance [Internet] (2013). http://www.apa.org/ed/precollege/ptn/2013/09/students-relevance.aspx. Updated September. Accessed 1 Dec 2015
34. Li, H.: Information literacy and librarian-faculty collaboration: a model. Chin. Librariansh.: Int. Electron. J. (24) (2007). http://doi.org/10.7282/T3TQ61PF
35. Goldstein, S., Whitworth, A.: Determining the value of Information Literacy for employers. In: Forster, M. (ed.) Information Literacy in the Workplace, pp. 67–84. Facet Publishing, London (2017)
36. Espinoza, C., Ukleja, M.: Managing the Millennials, 2nd edn. Wiley, Hoboken (2016)
37. Conley, T., Gil, E.: Information literacy for undergraduate business students: examining value, relevancy, and implications for the new century. J. Bus. Financ. Librariansh. **16**(3), 213–228 (2011)

Information Culture of Students in the Academic Environment – Finding One's Way Through Studies

Krista Lepik(✉) and Katrin Kannukene

University of Tartu, Tartu, Estonia
{krista.lepik,katrin.kannukene}@ut.ee

Abstract. This study focuses on information related values, norms, and practices of information management students at the Institute of Social Studies, University of Tartu, Estonia. 100 interviews, conducted by students during qualitative research methods classes in 2015 and 2016, were analyzed by applying concepts of constructivist grounded theory. The preliminary results indicate the need to focus on students' information culture related issues already in the beginning of studies by introducing context-dependent values, norms, and practices to the newcomers. Shared values and understandable norms related to student-faculty communication, information about support in urgent situations or earlier communication practices with faculty members are but a few examples of means that can aid students in the academic environment.

Keywords: Information culture · Information literacy · Students Student-faculty communication · Estonia

1 Introduction

Today, the university presents an information-rich environment with challenges for both faculty members and students. This paper discusses initial results of a recent qualitative study that aims to understand students' values, norms and practices – that is, their information culture [1] when they attempt to retrieve course-related information from their teachers and fellow students. The students we studied (N = 100) were expected to enroll in several courses (at least for 24 European Credit Transfer and Accumulation System points) each semester. Therefore, they had many questions concerning enrollment and home assignment deadlines, home assignment descriptions, and many other practical issues related to academic life. Many students in our sample were Open University students. In addition to their studies, they worked and had parental duties. Academic issues played a small yet important role of their lives and their need to obtain correct, timely information about their studies was critical. Thus, in our paper, we dealt with information culture related to their organizational context not information culture regarding the contents of studies such as homework, information seeking, and avoiding plagiarism.

S. Kurbanoğlu et al. (Eds.): ECIL 2017, CCIS 810, pp. 605–614, 2018.
https://doi.org/10.1007/978-3-319-74334-9_62

The aim of our study is to propose information culture related practical recommendations to our colleagues teaching courses about learning skills in higher education and also to other parties who may be interested in supporting the social well-being and information culture of students.

2 Theoretical Framework

Information literacy (IL) in higher education has been one of the most popular topics of our field [2, 3]. Very often it has been regarded as a set of skills that can be taught in schools, universities, libraries, and other settings [4, 5], embraced by standards by SCONUL, ACRL, and other associations. In these kind of approaches, IL means "the adoption of appropriate information behavior to obtain, through whatever channel or medium, information well fitted to information needs, together with critical awareness of the importance of wise and ethical use of information in society" [6, p. 336]. Yet, in [7], the authors stress the importance of contextualizing IL in the notion of information culture, that is, in information-related values, norms and practices [1]). Information culture should thus be treated as reaching beyond socially enacted practices [8] "purely in organizational context" [7, p. 24] towards civic citizenry asking critical questions about information production, ownership, and distribution [7]. Indeed, the notion of information culture has previously been tackled in the context of organizations: predominantly in companies and firms [9, 10], universities [11], or the health sector [12], and always the information culture of employees of organizations has been the object of interest.

Besides explaining the theoretical framework of our object of inquiry, some remarks also need to be added about previous studies on information practices of students. As IL skills have been considered "a core competency … through all levels of formal learning" [13, p. 25], a vast number of publications has been dedicated to IL skills of students: from developing new models to help students obtain these skills [5] to assessing these skills [14]. Most publications stressing IL skills tap on the students' need to find appropriate information for home assignments (see for a classical example in [15]) or develop academic skills [16], while some also pay attention to life outside academia [17, 18]. However, these works, with few exceptions [19, 20], miss the importance of information culture among students within their groups of fellow-students and the students' need for studies related information that remains outside the scope of information sought for home assignments and students' everyday life.

Considering the example of students, we seek balance between the aforementioned approaches to information culture. Students as course mates form relatively coherent groups where group dynamics and sense of community start shaping relationships in and practices of these groups during years of study – thus enabling researchers to study information culture within this kind of groups. At the same time, the agency of students entails a possibility to play an active role in the formation of information culture within their group and also negotiate studies related information culture at their department. This also adds a civic dimension to the information culture [7, 21]. Although dimensions of information culture offer multiple ways to tackle this notion, we also need to pay more attention to particular analytical aspects in the study of information culture of students.

Therefore, we follow the definition of information culture as "manifested in the organization's values, norms, and practices that have an impact on how information is perceived, created and used" [9, p. 793]. Information culture in the context of students' academic life may have different manifestations than in organizations but the core components of information culture are still the same. While values can be seen as "the deeply held beliefs about the role and contribution of information to the organization, as well as the principles that define how information ought to be created and used" [9, p. 793], we need to consider beliefs about ways of creating, transferring, contributing or using of information, depending on academic context. Norms – "rules or socially accepted standards that define what information behaviors are normal or to be expected in the organization" [9, p. 793] may also have different manifestation in students' information culture. As we can see in the next chapter, the main set of (explicit) norms in the case of students is embedded in the Study Regulations. So, in our analysis, the focus will be on definitions about information behaviors are considered normal or expectable among students. This way, a turn from rather abstract values can be made towards expectations about information practices. Eventually, there are practices, "repeated patterns of behavior that involve organizational roles, structures, and forms of interaction" [9, p. 793], embedded in experiences of students, regarding their interaction with fellow students, faculty members, academic affairs specialists, and other related parties in academic life.

The notions of 'values', 'norms', and 'practices' inform the main research question of our study: through which values, norms, and practices can we conceptualize information culture of students based on the example of information work students at the University of Tartu? By having some understanding of students' information culture, we can move on by discussing what practical steps can be taken by faculty members, tutors, librarians or academic affairs specialists in order to support different dimensions of information culture of students. Yet before presenting results and discussing on information culture of students, we introduce the context of our study.

3 Studies Related to the Information Infrastructure at University of Tartu, the Institute of Social Studies

We conducted our study in the Institute of Social Studies, at the University of Tartu. The University of Tartu is the largest and oldest university in Estonia, the number of students in the Institute of Social Sciences is one of the largest enrollments compared to other institutes at our university: as of May 1, 2017, there are 670 students [22]. In addition to over 70 faculty members, there are five academic affairs specialists who support students. The Library of Social Studies is at the disposal of students during workdays. Not very far from the institute, students can prepare their home assignments at the University of Tartu Library main building. In addition, there are few tutors, students who volunteer to support newcomers.

At the University of Tartu, the most important document regulating studies is the Study Regulations that pays attention to different learning related activities from enrollment to courses to graduation issues. It also regulates the few deadlines for making information available for students in the Studies Information System (SIS).

The SIS enables students to enroll in courses, see timetables, their course plans, and the results of their exams. The SIS is complemented by Moodle where faculty members can post course related materials, send notifications, organize forums, and where students participate in courses. For group communication, the information work students of the Institute of Social Studies use private Facebook groups that support both their information needs and sense of community [23].

4 Methodology of the Research

Our study involves 100 University of Tartu students who studied in the information work related curriculums of Information Management, Information and Records Management, Librarianship, and Information Environments. The interviews were conducted from 2015 to 2016 in the framework of qualitative research methods courses; both interviewers and interviewees were students at this course. In total, 123 interviews were conducted during the courses, 23 of which were omitted from this study where interviewees did not clearly granted permission to use their interviews for further research. Our sample consisted mostly of second and third year students, both those taking courses through regular face-to-face courses along with open university learners. As the information work students at our university are predominantly female, we did not use information about gender in the process of labeling the interviews as it may reveal the identity of male interviewees. Interviews are quoted in the following text by referencing them according to the time of conducting the interview (for example 2015 S), form of study (RS as regular study, or OU as open university), year of study (2nd or 3rd), and the corresponding number for the order within particular course group. The composition of our sample is depicted in Table 1.

Table 1. Composition of the sample.

Year (Semester)	Form of study	Year of study	Number of students in our sample
2015 (Spring)	Regular study (RS)	2nd	12
2015 (Spring)	Open university (OU)	2nd	26
2015 (Spring)	Open university	3rd	14
2015 (Fall)	Open university	3rd	14
2016 (Spring)	Regular study	2nd	7
2016 (Spring)	Open university	2nd	27

In order to conduct interviews, the students used a list of interview questions compiled by one of the authors of this paper. In accordance with the principles of conducting semi-structured interviews, the students as interviewers were fully free to ask additional questions or change the order of questions if needed. However, as the interviews were conducted as home assignments and for most of the students it was the first time to conduct a semi-structured interview, the quality of the interviews varied. In some interviews, the aforementioned principles of semi-structured interviewing were applied flawlessly while in others, the interviewers had too strictly followed the list of questions – thus, these interviews may lack the depth of an assisted conversation.

We have analyzed the semi-structured interviews by applying principles of constructivist grounded theory [24]. In the beginning of the analysis, we used open coding to make sense of the interviews, and then, by applying axial coding, we were able to group the codes in coherent code families that formed the structure of analysis. We examined each code-text relationship carefully, often used memos and discussed both codes and memos to ensure consistent usage of codes. These measures contributed to both intra-coder and inter-coder reliability. In addition, the relatively large number of interviews coupled by careful reflection of our work hopefully enabled us to gain a complete and reliable understanding of the phenomenon at hand.

5 Results

Presenting the initial results of our study, we have focused on information culture among students in the framework of their academic life. The analysis of values, norms, and practices has indicated that most clearly it is possible to tackle information culture of students through different kinds of interactions, both pleasant and problematic, both in and outside a classroom. The accounts of these interactions can be treated as litmus papers revealing the aforementioned values, norms, and practices, but also tensions between them. In general, students' information culture is embedded in their interactions to faculty members and other staff at the university on one hand and in their relationships with fellow students, on the other.

Values in students' information culture are related to their interactions with faculty members both during and between classes or learning sessions; the latter is particularly important for Open University students. Many expectations towards faculty members are bound to their interpersonal skills. As the expert position of faculty members is mostly taken for granted, students value a positive attitude, open-mindedness (including openness to questions), friendliness and treating students as equals. These traits help students feel welcomed at the university and find more easily some courage to ask questions during or between classes. The tonality of faculty-members' messages (both oral or written) serves the same purpose: while elementary politeness is important, positive attitude also encourages students even if the contents of the message are actually negative (about low grade of the home assignment, for example). In case e-mail or Moodle feedback is the main channel to keep in touch with faculty members, students mentioned feeling highly sensitive about the contents of received message especially when they sensed the feedback they receive is not about the contents of their work, but about themselves: "*like when she is criticizing my home assignments I can understand that the critique is about my work not about letting me know how stupid I am*" (2015S_OU_3rd_2). Sometimes, interviewees also recognized the subjective nature of tonality by admitting their own negative prejudice toward some faculty member.

In addition, students' values and expectations about information culture were strongly shaped by ways they perceived the position of teachers as somewhat superior compared to students. An important manifestation of this position was revealed when we considered ways students turned towards faculty members in their everyday speech or e-mails. Students considered calling teachers 'Teie'/'You' (compared to the formal pronoun of 'Sie' in German instead of using informal 'du') very important. Unless the teacher had permitted otherwise, interviewees expected to come the initiative to use 'Sina' or informal 'You' from the teacher. Besides stressing the position of faculty members through means of language, students valued taking time to think through their messages to faculty members. Students tried to formulate messages so that it would take faculty as little time as possible to reply these messages, and thus, students hoped to receive the replies as soon as possible. 'As soon as possible' can, according to interviews we analyzed, be a very 'fluid' notion: while students were not expecting in most circumstances any reply from the faculty member during weekends, the expectations to receive a reply during weekdays varied greatly from receiving it during the same day when an e-mail was posted to an entire week. There can be exceptions, too, in cases where the supervisor had agreed to respond quickly.

Concerning fellow students, a certain degree of collectivity illustrated the relationships. From the interviews, a rather careful choice of the addressee in a problematic situation was revealed. Some interviewees justified writing to a faculty member first by stressing the importance to get first-hand information especially when they felt their questions were personal or embarrassing. Meanwhile, some interviewees stressed consulting faculty member "only [when] in dire trouble" (2016S_OU_2rd_11) as they felt it impolite to disturb a faculty member or leave 'silly' impression of themselves. It was very common for students to ask their course mates first and then turn to the faculty member by writing a collective letter with fellow students to specify some issue that might be in students' opinion relevant to everyone. In the latter case, both Facebook and Moodle served the needs of students. First, they used Facebook as a site to quickly consult other students and check whether they had similar understandings of the problem. Thus, there was a chance that some diligent course mate already knew the answer. Secondly, the forums in Moodle enabled students to receive formal answers to questions by all course mates.

The line between students' values and norms towards obtaining needed information can be very thin. In addition to the Study Regulations document, students' information culture also involves some shared understandings about how things are supposed to be done. The usage of formal 'you' can be seen as politeness towards faculty members but it is social as well and related to certain kind of normativity. This relates to whether fellow students would accept some kind of behavior as "*many course mates do not probably like it when a student stresses her friendship with a faculty member and says [familiar] 'you' to the faculty member*" (2015S_ OU_3rd_6), or whether students in a study group have agreed with the faculty member to use familiar 'you'. Likewise, uncontested was the norm of writing polite e-mails to ask something of faculty members: writing e-mails correctly is not just part of respecting them, but also part of feeling like a professional information worker. The same is expected of faculty members although, supporting tonality in faculty members' messages was if not equally, then considered even more important.

The norms span from formal learning environments and e-mail correspondence to social media. When students talked about faculty-students' relationships on Facebook, this environment was oft-mentioned as a place where to see real friends not 'friends' as mere contacts. Thus, being a 'friend' with a faculty member was considered to be exceptional and only in cases of "*being involved in a strong collaboration*"

(2015S_ RS_2nd_2) such as writing a graduation thesis, familiarity with the faculty member prior to enrollment in the university, or creating some professional contact after graduation. To keep in touch with faculty members, there are other, more official channels such as e-mail or Moodle "*where the borders between official and familiar interactions are not to become blurred so easily*" (2015S_ OU_2nd_26). In addition, transferring school-related communication into other environments was mentioned tiresome both for students and faculty members.

The practices as part of information culture were outlined through previous repeated behavior of students. The most common practice students mentioned in our interviews was writing e-mails to faculty members. Relying on certain values and norms, e-mails were usually written because of some homework assignments (to ask whether the assignment was understood correctly, or to post it), cases of being absent from a seminar, sending a draft during supervision, but also when students needed some information about an internship. All these cases are formal, thus nurturing the formal relationship between the student and a faculty member. Especially in case of Open University students who are present only during study sessions and communicate with faculty members mostly through e-mail, the strong formality in their academic experiences can explain their reluctance to use social media for communicating with faculty members: the contrast between perceptions of the university and social media as such was overwhelming.

Another distinguished set of practices was related to 'crisis situations' in classroom or e-mail communication. By 'crisis situations' we mean unexpected, usually urgent and unpleasant situations that do not occur on regular basis, but are still significant. Examples included cases when the home assignment or its deadline was changed, there was some misunderstanding about the tonality of message, the faculty member did not reply e-mails) Keeping in mind this kind of cases, students mentioned the need to have as clear 'rules of game' as possible. Despite a certain amount of confusion, the particular situation usually needed to be solved quite quickly. The respectable position of faculty members thus came with a responsibility to show the initiative in solving crises, but also to follow each case as an example of desirable work related behavior to students who are future information professionals.

6 Discussion

Previously, there has been some focus on information culture among academic staff in higher education [11]. In our paper, we analyzed the information culture among university students as part of the very same information environment. Recognizing information culture in a group of fellow students regardless of previous practical knowledge about one's field or earlier experience in the university shifts our focus from IL centered approaches [4, 5, 14, 15] towards information culture related aspects: how do newcomers' find their way through studies in their peer group with certain emerging values, norms, and practices? Each year, new students find themselves struggling to find out about the 'unwritten rules' concerning the ways information is being treated or mediated at their university. In the face of classes related to 'academic self-management' or 'learning to learn', or when students have the available help of student tutors, or are engaged in stand-alone IL courses, some of this struggle has been relieved, yet we propose an additional dimension that concerns students as members of their new group or community of practice.

By drawing on the results of our study we suggest that the emerging information culture in a group of students is rather independent and self-organizing, possibly containing values and norms that new students take along from their previous contexts. The values are related to professionalism and societal position of faculty members as representatives of the university, but also to their fellow students as companions and 'supportive shoulders' for next three years. The norms, linked to politeness in academia, 'appropriate' behavior in different communication sites (both formal and informal), and perceived professional behavior, form an invisible foundation of information culture between course mates. And then, there is the matter of practices, shaped by both values and norms, but also newly emerging experiences about diverse situations. These situations are not always as peaceful as we all hope, in fact, some of these can be urgent, stressful and distracting. Thus some guidelines for possibly re-emerging 'crisis situations' would be useful. The practices, in turn, nourish future values and norms, stories, and even 'urban legends' circulating in the academic environment. There is a threat, however, that information culture of students may drift too far away from the previously existing information culture in the university, causing a potential clash of cultures and thus hinder academic progress of both students and faculty members.

Recognizing context and group dependency of information culture even within the same institution, it is nearly impossible to suggest fixed set of rules to enhance information culture among students. We stress the importance of dealing with aspects mentioned in the previous section in the framework of already existing 'academic self-management' classes. Even more, by considering the civic dimension of information culture [8], we suggest that shaping information culture of students can only take place in mutual collaboration and negotiation. Also, a subject of discussion would be formulation of information culture with its' implicit and explicit manifestations or, in other words, besides all kinds of guides and instructions, do the students really need another set of rules? If yes, then how can we make sure the students really rely on this set of rules? If no, then how to provide support for students who feel themselves as if on a slippery ice when it comes to communicating with faculty members or making agreements with fellow students? It may be a problem that students' tutors or classes related to 'academic self-management' or 'learning how to learn' can discuss, yet firstly, it needs to be publicly acknowledged that the information culture is equally important issue next to topics like 'how to use your library's databases' or 'who to turn to when you need…'. There are few clichés like 'student's best friend is another student' that are repeatedly reminded to newcomers, but these clichés are merely a tip of the iceberg of the information culture in its entire richness.

Our paper presented initial results about inquiry into the information culture of students. There is also some insight into students' information culture in social media [23]. In our paper, the main focus was on students' information culture related predominantly to the need to obtain correct information about their studies on time; we do recognize the need to elaborate this topic in our future research. Furthermore, different aspects of information culture of students still need discovering such as forms of collaboration between students, course-work related information culture (including writing homework, avoiding plagiarism, and information seeking) to name but a few. There is the need to move on from our current state of fragmented view of the information culture of students towards a multifaceted model that takes into account the nature of the academic context. In addition, we are keenly interested in scrutinizing the topic of information culture not only in Estonia, but also in international contexts to pay attention to the context-specificity of students' information culture.

7 Conclusion

To conclude, we emphasize the importance of tackling students' information culture when it comes to the organizational context of studies. As newcomers to a particular academic environment, students are 'flooded' with new information, yet there are still implicit norms which get introduced during studies by coincidence. Our suggestion is to present such unwritten norms and conventions during the first semester of studies in order to avoid misunderstandings and confusion. The university as an information-rich environment contains not only subject-related information. It also contains the invisible net of values connected to faculty members and fellow students, norms bound to academia and professionalism, and already-established practices possibly nurturing new values and norms. In turn, these norms have nodes consisting of 'whys and hows' of creating, transferring, contributing, and using information. Having a conscious viewpoint to information culture of one's group or community of practice is handy all through the university life, but also later, when the student has graduated, and the fresh alumna or alumnus finds her- or himself on the labor market, facing, in fact, similar kind of problems.

Acknowledgements. The authors are grateful for the support of Archimedes Foundation and the Institute of Social Studies at the University of Tartu, supporting participation on ECIL 2017 conference. We also thank students who agreed to have excerpts from their interviews included in this paper. Last but not least we thank the referees of this article for their helpful criticisms and suggestions.

References

1. Choo, C.W.: Information Management for the Intelligent Organization: The Art of Scanning the Environment, 3rd edn. Information Today, Medford (2002)
2. Rader, H.B.: Information literacy 1973–2002: a selected literature review. Libr. Trends **51** (2), 242–259 (2002)
3. Virkus, S.: Information literacy in Europe: a literature review. Inf. Res. **8**(4), paper no. 159 (2003). http://informationr.net/ir/8-4/paper159.html
4. Doyle, C.S.: Information Literacy in an Information Society: A Concept for the Information Age. ERIC Clearinghouse, Syracuse (1994)
5. Seiler, V., Miil, K., Lepik, K.: How to fit teaching of information literacy in with students' needs: an on-line credit course model from the University of Tartu library. Liber Q. **22**(1), 42–63 (2012)

6. Johnston, B., Webber, S.: Information literacy in higher education: a review and case study. Stud. High. Educ. **28**(3), 335–352 (2003)
7. Webber, S., Johnston, B.: Transforming information literacy for higher education in the 21st century: a lifelong learning approach. In: Hepworth, M., Walton, G. (eds.) Developing People's Information Capabilities: Fostering Information Literacy in Educational, Workplace and Community Contexts, pp. 15–30. Bingley, Emerald (2013)
8. Lloyd, A.: Information literacy as a socially enacted practice: sensitising themes for an emerging perspective of people-in-practice. J. Doc. **68**(6), 772–783 (2012)
9. Choo, C.W., Bergeron, P., Detlor, B., Heaton, L.: Information culture and information use: an exploratory study of three organizations. J. Am. Soc. Inform. Sci. Technol. **59**(5), 792–804 (2008)
10. Widén-Wulff, G.: Business information culture: a qualitative study of the information culture in the finnish insurance business. Inf. Res. **5**(3), paper no. 77 (2000). http://informationr.net/ir/5-3/paper77.html
11. Lauri, L., Heidmets, M., Virkus, S.: Information literacy and information culture in higher education institutions in Estonia. In: Kurbanoğlu, S., Boustany, J., Špiranec, S., Grassian, E., Mizrachi, D., Roy, L. (eds.) ECIL 2015. CCIS, vol. 552, pp. 509–516. Springer, Cham (2015). https://doi.org/10.1007/978-3-319-28197-1_51
12. Zheng, Y.: Information culture and development: Chinese experience of e-health. In: Proceedings of the 38th Annual Hawaii International Conference on System Sciences, HICSS 2005, p. 153a. IEEE (2005)
13. Breivik, P.S.: 21st century learning and information literacy. Change: Mag. High. Learn. **37** (2), 21–27 (2005)
14. American Library Association: Information Literacy Competency Standards for Higher Education (2000). http://www.ala.org/acrl/ilstandardlo.html
15. Kuhlthau, C.C.: Inside the search process: information seeking from the user's perspective. J. Am. Soc. Inf. Sci. **42**(5), 361–371 (1991)
16. Marcum, J.W.: Rethinking information literacy. Libr. Q. **72**(1), 1–26 (2002)
17. Horgan, A., Sweeney, J.F.: Young students' use of the internet for mental health information and support. J. Psychiatr. Ment. Health Nurs. **17**(2), 117–123 (2010)
18. Špiranec, S., Kos, D.: Information literacy practices and student protests: mapping community information landscapes. Inf. Res. **18**(3), paper C39 (2013). http://informationr.net/ir/18-3/colis/paperC39.html
19. Bøyum, I., Aabø, S.: The information practices of business PhD students. New Libr. World **116**(3/4), 187–200 (2015)
20. Pilerot, O.: A practice-based exploration of the enactment of information literacy among PhD students in an interdisciplinary research field. J. Doc. **72**(3), 414–434 (2016)
21. Le Deuff, O.: Library 2.0 and the culture of information: new paradigms? Cadernos de Biblioteconomia, Arquivistica e Documentao **1/2**, 20–28 (2011)
22. Õppijate arv. http://www.ut.ee/oppijate-arv/
23. Peeduli, K.: Facebooki peidetud rühm ja kogukonnatunne [Secret group in Facebook and the sense of community]. Graduation Paper. University of Tartu, Tartu (2016)
24. Charmaz, K.: Constructing Grounded Theory, 2nd edn. SAGE, Los Angeles (2014)

Information Overload in a Disciplinary Context

Sirje Virkus, Sigrid Mandre(✉), and Elise Pals

Tallinn University, Tallinn, Estonia
sirje.virkus@tlu.ee, sigrid.mandre@tlulib.ee,
pals.elise@gmail.com

Abstract. The purpose of this paper is to present the results of a study that explored how students from four different disciplines perceive information overload and cope with this phenomenon. We have formulated three research questions: How do students perceive information overload? How do students cope with information overload? What are the disciplinary differences in coping with information overload? The research involved a mixed methods research strategy, using both quantitative and qualitative methodologies, built into a two-stage research design. The first stage was a small-scale questionnaire survey among students from four disciplines: psychology, mathematics, informatics, and information science. The second stage involved the collection of qualitative data. In-depth interviews with students were conducted from four disciplines (psychology, mathematics, informatics, and information science). In this paper the authors will present the results of this study.

Keywords: Information overload · Information literacy · Students Higher education · Questionnaire survey · Interviews

1 Introduction

Information overload is not a new phenomenon and has been around for much longer than the phrase itself. However, in the past decade the importance of information overload has increased substantially because of the rapid growth of digital information through social networks, mobile devices, and various sensors (i.e. the Internet of things). New types of data, often unstructured and volatile, are being generated at an accelerating rate. The rate of data creation is faster in the early 21st century than at any time in the past [1]. Meadow and Yuan [2] have even suggested that instead of information overload we have data overload.

Eppler [3, p. xvii] believes that information overload is one of the key challenges of the digital age. Although information overload is not an entirely new phenomenon, we need to approach it differently today. Marques and Batista [4] indicate that current trends and evolving technologies such as the internet of things, transmedia, and the combined use of various devices and communication channels encourage a new thinking on the problem of information overload and a new layer on the information overload problem has emerged, which is the issue of communication overload.

S. Kurbanoğlu et al. (Eds.): ECIL 2017, CCIS 810, pp. 615–624, 2018.
https://doi.org/10.1007/978-3-319-74334-9_63

The aim of this paper is to present the results of a study that explored how students from four different disciplines perceive information overload and cope with this phenomenon. The paper is structured as follows. The first section presents a literature review providing a definition of information overload, related terms, and discusses some relevant research related to information overload. Research methodology will be explained in Sect. 3. Section 4 provides the empirical research findings focusing on the ways in which bachelor's students perceive and cope with information overload. The last section presents conclusions drawn from the empirical study.

2 Literature Review

According to the bibliometric analysis, the number of publications on information overload has increased and the phenomenon has been the subject of numerous studies from a variety of disciplines. In the Web of Science database, 2,469 publications were received under the topic area "information overload" in the period from 1990 to 2017 in January 2017. In the beginning of 1990s there were only few information overload research publications but the number of publications has been growing steadily; for example, 222 publications were published in 2014, 237 publications in 2015, and 240 in 2016. The highest contribution to information overload research comes from the computer science research community. Fifty-six percent (1382) of publications come from the subject area of computer science, followed by engineering 20.5% (507), business economics 11.4% (281), information science and library science 10.2% (251), and telecommunications 5.4% (134).

2.1 The Term and the Definition of Information Overload

According to Grimshaw [1] the term "information overload" can be traced back to 2,300 years ago. Levy [5, p. 501] believes that complaints about an overabundance of books date back at least as far as the sixteenth century. An entire issue of the Journal of the History of Ideas in 2003 was devoted to exploring the early modern information overload demonstrating that during the years 1550–1750, the production, circulation, and dissemination of scientific and scholarly texts accelerated tremendously and Europe experienced a kind of "information explosion" [6, p. 2]. However, one of the first social scientists to notice the negative effects of information overload was the sociologist Georg Simmel who hypothesized in the beginning of the last century that the overload of sensations in the modern urban world caused city dwellers to become jaded and interfered with their ability to react to new situations [7, p. 662].

Several authors believe that the term "information overload" was mentioned the first time in 1964 by an American social scientist Bertram M. Gross in his book "The Managing of Organizations: the Administrative Struggle" [8, 9]. However, Levy [5] indicates that in a scholarly monograph of Richard L. Meier "A Communications Theory of Urban Growth" (1962) there was a section entitled "The Threat of Information Overload". In an article "Operation Basic: the retrieval of wasted knowledge" (1962) Gross [10] argued that the accelerating rate of publication was threatening science and society with an "information crisis" and leads citizens to an information overload. Some years later, several other authors, for example, Boulding [11] and Ackoff [12] used the term "information overload" in their publications. The American writer and futurologist Alvin Toffler further popularized the term "information overload" in his seminal book "Future Shock" in 1970. [as cited in 5]

Several authors have stated that there is no single generally accepted definition of information overload [13–18]. Jones [7, p. 660] notes that information overload can be defined as the state of an individual or system in which excessive communication inputs cannot be processed and utilized, leading to breakdown. One of the most used has been referred to as inverted u-curve [19, 20], that essentially establishes a cause-effect relationship between the amount of information available and the capacity of individuals to make decisions [4, p. 4]. Jones [7, p. 660] notes that information overload occurs because the degree to which we can effectively process information is limited by the finite capacity of human cognition. However, some authors have introduced the notion of "perceived information overload" as a concept that is measurable [1].

However, Grimshaw [1] believes that in the early 21st century there is a consensus that information overload refers to a state where the flow of information exceeds the cognitive capacity to process it. Several authors highlight the need to connect information overload with the available time of managing or processing information [4, 16, 21].

2.2 Related Terms

Within the research community several other terms have been also used by different authors in addition to "information overload". For example, "information overflow" [17, 22], "infobesity" or "information obesity", "intoxication" [23], "information anxiety" [24], "information avoidance" [1], "information pollution", "cognitive overload" [25], "sensory overload" [26], "communication overload" [27], and "knowledge overload" [28]. A term, "information fatigue syndrome" was even coined to name a related psychological malady [6, p. 1]. In addition, the term "information overload" has evolved into phrases such as "information glut", "data glut" and "data smog" [29, 30].

A synonym for information overload in the research publications is frequently information overflow – these terms are used equally and without any distinction [17, 22]. Information anxiety originates from the ever-widening gap between what we understand and what we think we should understand. Wurman [24] describes frustrating situations giving rise to information anxiety, for example situations in which the individual does not understand information or feels overwhelmed by the amount of information to be understood [as cited in 17, p. 614].

Batista and Marques [4] suggest extending the concept of "information overload" with a wider idea that also includes "communication overload", and in that way integrating the challenges posed by today's communication technologies. They believe that these two concepts are closely interrelated. Communication overload means that the exchange of information and the communication messages that people deal with exceed their capacity to manage them. This is what regards analyzing information and messages content, filtering out what seems more relevant or that should be given attention to so that contents can be digested. They note that many of the issues published under the information overload topic are, in fact, communication overload problems and challenges [4, p. 6]. However, the interest in communication overload is apparently still very low [4, p. 14].

2.3 Research on Information Overload

Information overload has been explored in several disciplines: for example, in computer science, engineering, business economics, library and information science, telecommunications, management science, educational sciences, psychology, health care sciences, communication studies, mathematics, public administration, neurosciences, and sociology.

According to Savolainen [17] the first study specifically focusing on the phenomena of information overload was presented by Miller in 1962. In his 1956 study he showed that short-term memory has a limited capacity and it could hold on average seven items (plus or minus two items). Given the limitations of the memory span, individuals processing information try to cope with the eventual overload by drawing on adjustment strategies such as queueing or filtering [17, p. 612].

Early information overload research had a focus on cognition, and this still continues to be an important topic [31]. In later works the focus is also on the causes of overload; for example, information and communication technologies like electronic mail, social networking tools, or mobile technologies [14–17, 31–33]. Other areas that are explored in the literature include organizational change and personal adaptation strategies, and human-computer interaction design for enabling interruptions to be a positive source of information [1]. However, technology is both a principal cause and main solution to information overload in today's society [34].

The psychological and physical consequences of information overload can have an impact on the individual, organisational, and societal levels. For example, the Basex Report "shows that Information Overload costs the U.S. economy ca. $900 billion per year" [35, p. 1]. Several studies have found that information overload leads to information anxiety, depression, work stress, loss of job satisfaction, boredom, bad redundancy, distraction, loss of workers' efficiency, decrease of productivity, high blood pressure, insulin resistance, heart disease, and information fatigue syndrome [9, 16, 17, 36, 37]. Information overload also influences negatively job performance, decision making, and personal relationships [15, 38], causing constraints on the ability of the individuals to solve problems [4, p. 6] and reducing the quality of decisions.

In the engineering field, recommender systems are the most explored area. It is believed that they can reduce the negative impact of information overload. In mathematics, the algorithms that allow the improvement of recommender systems efficiency continue to be a major research area. In social sciences, research on recommender systems and information filtering techniques and on email overload is in focus. In business, management and accounting themes, the reduction of information overload to improve consumer choices and decisions in the online environment are explored. In the organizational context technostress has also been in focus [4, p. 11]. According to Eppler and Mengis [16] early management research focussed mainly on accounting, management information systems, organization science, and marketing and explored how the performance and decision making of an individual varies with the amount of information he or she is exposed to. Brey [36] notes that modern management and organization studies explores "how information overload negatively affects productivity and worker well-being and how information overload may be managed more effectively". In the fields of information technology, library and information studies, and management information systems the main focus is on "how information systems may be developed and set up so as to help reduce information overload" [36, p. 2].

Batista and Marques [4, p. 16] note that although the majority of the literature found places attention on the fields of individuals and organizations, they see that the issues of information and communication overload are also problems that affect and are affected by societies themselves, which is a perspective that deserves to be further researched. According to Savolainen [17, p. 613] sociologists have explored information overload at a general level and found it as a major factor affecting the quality of life in the information society.

It is also Savolainen [17] who notes that issues of information overload have predominantly been explored in work-related contexts, particularly management and decision-making, while studies focusing on these phenomena in non-work contexts are fairly rare. However, there are also several studies that focus on information overload in the educational context [39–48]. It is believed that students can learn effectively when requirements of cognitive processes in the learning activities do not overload the limited capacity of working memory; when the requirements of the cognitive activities make heavy demands on the working memory, learning can be ineffective [49].

Information overload has changed also our information behaviour. According to Rowlands et al. [50] this new form of information seeking behaviour can be often characterised as being horizontal, bouncing, checking, and viewing in nature. Thus, the "wide availability of information that we are currently witnessing brings additional importance to the problem, making it urgent that individuals and organizations continually develop techniques and strategies to filter, select, and process the most appropriate information to solve their problems" [4, p. 6].

3 Methodology

The literature review informed the design of our research project. The purpose of this research was to investigate the ways how students experience and cope information overload in four disciplinary contexts – in psychology, mathematics, informatics, and information science. Three research questions were formulated: (1) How do students perceive information overload? (2) How do students cope with information overload? (3) What are the disciplinary differences in coping with information overload?

The research involved a mixed methods research strategy, using both quantitative and qualitative methodologies, built into a two-stage research design. The first stage was a small-scale questionnaire survey among bachelor's students from four disciplines at Tallinn University: psychology, mathematics, informatics, and information science. The results of the survey provided a broad picture of a phenomenon and helped to identify relevant interview questions. The second stage involved the collection of qualitative data. In-depth interviews with eight students were conducted in four disciplines (psychology, mathematics, informatics, and information science). Descriptive analysis was applied to the questionnaire survey data while the qualitative data were analyzed using a constant comparative method of data analysis.

The empirical data were gathered through structured questionnaires from 82 bachelor's students and through in-depth semi-structured interviews with eight bachelor's students. The participants were mainly recruited through the study counsellor and specialists of the academic units. The data were gathered in spring 2017.

Of the survey participants 57 (69.5%) were females and 25 (30.5%) males. Twenty four respondents were from informatics, 22 from information science, 19 from psychology, and 17 from mathematics. The ages of the respondents ranged from 19 to 46.

Semi-structured interviews were conducted with eight bachelor's students from psychology, mathematics, informatics, and information science. Four students were females and four males. The ages of the interviewees ranged from 20 to 42. The interviews took place over about one hour.

The participants were asked about their experience with information overload (questionnaire study and interviews) and their copying strategies with information overload (interviews). The results of the study are presented in the following section.

4 Results

All students in the study were familiar with the concept of information overload.

According to the results of the questionnaire survey among 82 students almost half (46.3%) of the respondents did not consider information overload as a real problem. They believed that they are able to find relevant information and they had knowledge and skills to cope with information overload. Several respondents also pointed out that they liked to be in the information environment and surrounded by information and they did not feel that there was too much information. However, to the question if they had experienced information overload, 81% of the respondents answered "yes". The main complaint was that it was sometimes difficult to distinguish the relevant information from the large amount of unnecessary information.

A majority of the respondents stated that the abundance of information is most often related to studies. It occured also in relation to social media; Facebook was used by 81 (98.8%) respondents, YouTube by 67 (81.7%), Instagram by 60 (73.2%) respondents.

Sixty one percent of the respondents felt that they checked their e-mails or mobile phone messages too often. Thirty three respondents felt the need to check e-mails and messages a few times a day, 27 respondents few times per hour, and 12 respondents every few minutes.

The majority of respondents (51) found that they had rather good information seeking skills, 16 respondents felt that they can handle infomation more or less, and 14 respondents felt that their information skills are very good. Only one student found that his information skills were rather bad.

Problems occured if computers or mobile phones were used for a long time; for example, 90.2% of the respondents felt the lack of time for other activities while 78% experienced concentration problems, 57.3% had sleeping problems, 56.1% felt stress,

48.8% felt that they were nervous, 46.3% felt agitation, and 23.2% mentioned depression. Thirty seven point eight percent of the respondents felt anxious when they were away from the Internet.

All eight interviewed students confirmed that they had experienced information overload. However, six students found that information overload was a serious problem and two students regarded it as a marginal problem. Most of the interviewed students very seldom watched television or read printed books and their main communication tools were mobile phones or laptops. However, informatics students reported that, because of their study field, they used various technological tools for testing purposes. They all found that their information skills were rather good. They acknowledged that they had used multitasking but no one confirmed that they were very good in it. The main problems caused by information overload were concentration problems, fatigue, sleeping, and headached. Two students reported stress and one mentioned that he had even thought that he should go to the doctor and ask for antidepressants.

The strategies for coping with information overload were explored through the interviews. The major strategies mentioned by students for coping with information overload were prioritizing, filtering, withdrawal, eliminating, ignoring, queuing, blocking, and information handling skills development. For example, several students believed that prioritizing strategy lead to greater focus on tasks and helped to get things done. The filtering strategy was favoured especially in online environments in helping weed out useless and irrelevant material. The withdrawal strategy was used to keep the number of information channels, social media tools, and sources to a minimum. Three interviewees also used eliminating, ignoring, and blocking strategies. nformation science students highlighted the importance of developing information handling skills.

There were not clear differences in results between different disciplines. However, it seemed that students from information science and psychology perceived information overload to be a problem more often than students from informatics and mathematics. For example, nine students from informatics found that information overload was a problem and 15 thought that it was not a problem. Seven students from mathematics found that information overload was a problem and 10 thought that it was not a problem. At the same time 17 information science and 11 psychology students found that information overload was a problem and five information science and eight psychology students thought that it was not a problem.

However, although many questionnaire respondents did not consider information overload as a problem, many of them recognized that they have experienced it. For example, 20 informatics, 18 psychology, 16 information science, and 13 mathematics student experienced information overload. Only six information science, four mathematics, and four informatics and one psychology student never experienced information overload.

Students from all disciplines reported various consequences of information overload and copying strategies. There were not clear disciplinary differences. Importance of the development of information skills or information literacy was highlighted by information science students and one psychology student who had a work-related relationship with the library. They believed that knowledge of databases and information resources as well as information finding, evaluating, and using skills helped to avoid information overload. Informatics students used various information and communication technology more often than students from other disciplines as it was part of their learning process.

5 Conclusions

The study is based on experiences of bachelor's students' information overload. The study aimed to get an overview of students' perception of information overload and the strategies students employed to cope with the overload problems.

As a result of the questionnaire findings we can conclude that, although many respondents did not consider information overload as a problem, a majority experienced it. Information overload was mainly related to studies and social media. The majority of study participants found that they had rather good information seeking skills. Long-term use of computers and mobile devices caused distraction from other activities, concentration and sleeping problems, stress, nervousness, agitation, tiredness, headache, and even depression. Most of the interviewed students very seldom watched television or read printed books and their main communication tools were mobile phones or laptops. The strategies for coping with information overload were explored through interviews. The major strategies mentioned by students for coping with information overload were prioritizing, queuing, filtering, withdrawal, eliminating, ignoring, blocking, and developing of information handling skills.

There were not clear differences in results between different disciplines. However, it seemed that students from information science and psychology perceived information overload to be a problem more often than students from informatics and mathematics.

References

1. Grimshaw, D.J.: Information Overload. Oxford Bibliographies Online (2016). http://www.oxfordbibliographies.com/view/document/obo-9780199756841/obo-9780199756841-0133.xml
2. Meadow, C.T., Yuan, W.: Measuring the impact of information: defining the concepts. Inf. Process. Manag. **33**(6), 697–715 (1997)
3. Eppler, M.J.: Foreword. In: Marques, R.P.F., Batista, J.C. (eds.) Information and Communication Overload in the Digital Age, p. xvii. IGI Global, Hershey (2017)
4. Batista, J.C., Marques, R.P.F.: An overview on information and communication overload. In: Marques, R.P.F., Batista, J.C. (eds.) Information and Communication Overload in the Digital Age, pp. 1–20. IGI Global, Hershey (2017)
5. Levy, D.M.: Information overload. In: Himma, K.E., Tavani, H.T. (eds.) The Handbook of Information and Computer Ethics, pp. 497–517. Wiley, Hoboken (2008)
6. Rosenberg, D.: Early modern information overload. J. Hist. Ideas **64**(1), 1–9 (2003)
7. Jones, G.: Information overload. In: Christensen, K., Levinson, D. (eds.) Encyclopedia of Community: From the Village to the Virtual World, vol. 2, pp. 660–663. Sage, London (2003)
8. Yan, L.: The value of social media for patients: social supports, networking, and learning in online healthcare communities. Doctoral Dissertation. University of Washington (2012)

9. Terra, A.L.: Email overload. Framing the concept and solving the problem – a literature review. In: Marques, R.P.F., Batista, J.C. (eds.) Information and Communication Overload in the Digital Age, pp. 22–44. IGI Global, Hershey (2017)
10. Gross, B.M.: Operation basic: the retrieval of wasted knowledge. J. Commun. **12**(2), 67–83 (1962)
11. Boulding, K.E.: The ethics of rational decision. Manag. Sci. **12**(6), B161–B169 (1966)
12. Ackoff, R.L.: Management misinformation systems. Manag. Sci. **14**(4), B147–B156 (1967)
13. Butcher, H.: Meeting Manager's Information Needs. Aslib, London (1998)
14. Bawden, D., Holtham, C., Courtney, N.: Perspectives on information overload. Aslib Proc. **51**(8), 249–255 (1999)
15. Edmunds, A., Morris, A.: The problem of information overload in business organisations: a review of the literature. Int. J. Inf. Manag. **20**(1), 17–28 (2000)
16. Eppler, M.J., Mengis, J.: The concept of information overload: a review of literature from organization science, accounting, marketing, MIS, and related disciplines. Inf. Soc. **20**(5), 325–344 (2004)
17. Savolainen, R.: Filtering and withdrawing: strategies for coping with information overload in everyday contexts. J. Inf. Sci. **33**(5), 611–621 (2007)
18. Jackson, T.W., Farzaneh, P.: Theory-based model of factors affecting information overload. Int. J. Inf. Manag. **32**(6), 523–532 (2012)
19. Eppler, M.J.: Information overload and information quality. In: Cantoni, L., Danowski, J.A. (eds.) Communication and Technology, 5th Volume of the Handbook on Communication Sciences, pp. 215–232. De Gruyter Mouton, Berlin (2015)
20. Schroder, H.M., Driver, M.J., Streufert, S.: Human Information Processing: Individuals and Group Functioning in Complex Social Situations. Holt, Rinehart and Winston, New York (1967)
21. Schick, A.G., Gordon, L.A., Haka, S.: Information overload: a temporal approach. Acc. Organ. Soc. **15**(3), 199–220 (1990)
22. Lee, D.H., Brusilovsky, P.: Fighting information overflow with personalized comprehensive information access: a proactive job recommender. In: Third International Conference on Autonomic and Autonomous Systems, ICAS 2007, p. 21. IEEE (2007)
23. Yang, C.C., Chenb, H., Honga, K.: Visualization of large category map for internet browsing. Decis. Support Syst. **35**(1), 89–102 (2003)
24. Wurman, R.S.: Information Anxiety. Doubleday, New York (1989)
25. Vollmann, T.E.: Cutting the Gordian knot of misguided performance measurement. Ind. Manag. Data Syst. **91**(1), 24–26 (1991)
26. Libowski, Z.J.: Sensory and information inputs overload; behavioural effects. Compr. Psychiatry **16**(3), 199–221 (1975)
27. Meier, R.L.: Communication overload: proposals from the study of a university library. Adm. Sci. Q. **7**, 521–544 (1963)
28. Hunt, R.E., Newman, R.G.: Medical knowledge overload: a disturbing trend for physicians. Health Care Manag. Rev. **22**(1), 70–75 (1997)
29. Jones, S.G.: Understanding community in the information age. In: Jones, S.G. (ed.) Cybersociety: Computer-Mediated Communication and Community, pp. 10–35. Sage, Thousand Oaks (1995)
30. Shenk, D.: Data Smog: Surviving the Information Glut. Harper Edge, San Francisco (1997)
31. Sobotta, N.: A systematic literature review on the relation of information technology and information overload. In: 2016 49th Hawaii International Conference on System Sciences (2016). https://www.computer.org/csdl/proceedings/hicss/2016/5670/00/5670a858.pdf

32. Allen, D.K., Shoard, M.: Spreading the load: mobile information and communications technologies and their effect on information overload. Inf. Res. **10**(2), paper 227 (2005). http://InformationR.net/ir/10-2/paper227.html
33. Szóstek, A.M.: Dealing with my emails: latent user needs in email management. Comput. Hum. Behav. **27**(2), 723–729 (2011)
34. Elwert, S.: Information overload making your head explode? (2013). http://www.wnd.com/2013/01/information-overload-making-your-head-explode/
35. Spira, J.B., Burke, C.: Intel's war on information overload (2009). http://iorgforum.org/wp-content/uploads/2011/06/IntelWarIO.BasexReport1.pdf
36. Brey, P.: Preface. In: Strother, J., Ulijn, J., Fazal, Z. (eds.) Information Overload: An International Challenge to Professor Engineers and Technical Communicators. Wiley-IEEE Press (2012)
37. Benselin, J.C., Ragsdell, G.: Information overload: the differences that age makes. J. Librariansh. Inf. Sci. **48**(3), 284–297 (2015)
38. Bawden, D., Robinson, L.: The dark side of information: overload, anxiety and other paradoxes and pathologies. J. Inf. Sci. **35**, 180–191 (2009)
39. Paulo, H.F.: Information overload in computer-mediated communication and education: is there really too much information? Implications for distance education. Master's thesis, University of Toronto (1999)
40. Battle, J.C.: The effect of information literacy instruction on library anxiety among international students. Doctoral Dissertation. University of North Texas (2004)
41. Bradford, G.R.: A relationship study of student satisfaction with learning online and cognitive load: initial results. Internet High. Educ. **14**(4), 217–226 (2011)
42. Chen, C.-Y., Pedersen, S., Murphy, K.L.: Learners' perceived information overload in online learning via computer-mediated communication. Res. Learn. Technol. **19**(2), 101–116 (2011)
43. Chen, C.-Y., Pedersen, S., Murphy, K.L.: The influence of perceived information overload on student participation and knowledge construction in computer-mediated communication. Instr. Sci.: Int. J. Learn. Sci. **40**(2), 325–349 (2012)
44. Shrivastav, H., Hiltz, S.R.: Information overload in technology-based education: a meta-analysis. In: Proceedings of the Nineteenth Americas Conference on Information Systems, 15–17 August 2013, Chicago, Illinois (2013). https://pdfs.semanticscholar.org/ff94/d26c6b4711216b6e034072b0cbbc2fae10fd.pdf
45. Blundell, S., Lambert, F.: Information anxiety from the undergraduate student perspective: a pilot study of second-semester freshmen. J. Educ. Libr. Inf. Sci. **55**(4), 261–273 (2014)
46. Pant, M.K., Negi, U.: Redeeming the information overload: a case study on Doon University, Dehradun. Library Philosophy and Practice (e-journal), paper 1304 (2015). http://digitalcommons.unl.edu/libphilprac/1304
47. Kurelovic, E.K., Tomljanovic, J., Davidovic, V.: Information overload, information literacy and use of technology by students. Int. Sch. Sci. Res. Innov. **10**(3), 908–912 (2016)
48. Ojo, O.J.: Information Anxiety and Information Overload of Undergraduates in Two Universities in South-West Nigeria. Library Philosophy and Practice (2016). http://digitalcommons.unl.edu/cgi/viewcontent.cgi?article=3760&context=libphilprac
49. Beetham, H.: An approach to learning activity design. In: Beetham, H., Sharpe, R. (eds.) Rethinking Pedagogy for a Digital Age: Designing and Delivering E-Learning, pp. 26–40. Routledge, Oxford (2007)
50. Rowlands, I., Nicholas, D., Williams, P., et al.: The Google generation: the information behaviour of the researcher of the future. Aslib Proc.: New Inf. Perspect. **60**(4), 290–310 (2008)

Information Literacy and Learning in Higher Education: A Thought Experiment

Michael Flierl(✉)

Libraries, Purdue University, West Lafayette, IN, USA
mflierl@purdue.edu

Abstract. The nature of the relationship between information literacy (IL) and learning is important for academic librarianship and higher education. This paper will use a philosophical tool to investigate this relationship – a thought experiment. This is a type of creative narrative meant to advocate for or against a certain idea. The thought experiment will provide evidence for a strong connection between IL and learning. This suggests that one's theoretical IL position implies certain commitments with regard to what learning is and how it should be fostered in higher education. Therefore, one method to progress IL theory is to look to learning theory. Explicit considerations on the nature of learning can yield more nuanced understandings of IL.

Keywords: Thought experiment · Information literacy theory
Learning theory

1 Introduction

In a higher education context, learning and information literacy (IL) have a close relationship. But what is the nature of this relationship? What are the implications for one's perspective on this topic? This paper will investigate these questions through a thought experiment – a method employed primarily in philosophy but also in other fields like physics. Thought experiments can "help explicate a concept and its area of application more precisely" [1, p. 92]. For example, by imagining himself chasing a beam of light, Einstein was better able to understand the properties of light which aided developing the Special Theory of Relativity. We will imagine the ideal of IL abilities and knowledge, and from there explore the relationship between IL and student learning from a new perspective. This paper will argue that if one takes the position that IL is more than generic skills, this logically entails that IL in a higher education context involves learning disciplinary content. Therefore, academic librarians concerned with IL and IL theory ought also to be concerned explicitly with theories of learning. To take a theoretical stance concerning IL is to simultaneously take a position about how students learn. Accordingly, more deliberate considerations of what student learning is, and how it occurs, can lead to more nuanced understandings of IL.

S. Kurbanoğlu et al. (Eds.): ECIL 2017, CCIS 810, pp. 625–633, 2018.
https://doi.org/10.1007/978-3-319-74334-9_64

2 IL and Learning in Higher Education: Theoretical Context

There is excellent theoretical literature about the relationship between IL and learning. We will discuss three perspectives. While this will not cover the entirety of scholarship on the relationship we want to investigate, it shows that serious intellectual energy has been brought to bear on the relationship between IL and learning. This underscores the importance of the relationship between IL and learning. First is Lloyd's socio-cultural approach that argues against a decontextualized, skills-based conception of IL in favor of one that takes into account the "complex contextualized practice, processes and interactions that enable access to social, physical and textual sites of knowledge" [2, p. 570]. An expert in IL is one who can navigate an information landscape that includes social and historical elements, among others. Context is key.

Bruce's seminal work, *Informed Learning*, draws strong theoretical ties between information use and learning, based in phenomenography and variation theory. She states that "content is learned through effective interaction with information" [3, p. 2]. While using information more creatively and intentionally is not a necessary precondition for learning, using information is "one dimension of the complex phenomenon we know as learning" [3, p. 15]. By crafting learning environments where students are more intentionally and creatively using information, students can learn disciplinary content and use information in more sophisticated ways.

Whitworth takes a radical or critical approach to IL, utilizing such philosophers as Habermas and Bakhtin in his work, *Radical Information Literacy: Reclaiming the Political Heart of the IL Movement* [4]. Whitworth uses a dialectic of the philosopher Bakhtin to analyze the relationship between IL and learning. Historically, Whitworth argues that IL has been viewed as *monologic*, think monologue from one point of view. This is problematic because the nature of learning is *dialogic*, where multiple perspectives and speakers are present. As a result of this conflict, authority about information becomes too concentrated and institutionalized. This results in an insidious form of inequality where those with less power and ability do not even recognize their own position.

Lloyd, Bruce, and Whitworth are not all in direct dialogue with one another. For instance, Whitworth's work is more concerned with the nature of IL – defining his own analysis as philosophical while defining Bruce's approach as relational [4, p. 80]. Additionally, Bruce is more directly concerned with pedagogy than Whitworth. However, what is most important to note is that all three theories explicitly deal with IL in the context of education and learning. This context, whether it be socio-cultural, political, or phenomenographic, affects how each theoretician defines what IL is, and what IL is capable of. The theoretical relationship between IL and learning exists and it is important.

3 Thought Experiments

There is no single definitive definition for the concept of 'thought experiments.' For the sake of expediency, we will provide a brief working definition to ground our discussion. The Stanford Encyclopedia of Philosophy states "Thought experiments are devices of the imagination used to investigate the nature of things… Most often thought experiments are communicated in narrative form…" [5]. So thought experiments are typically a story with the aim to investigate something without new empirical data. Another way to put this would be – 'what can we learn by using our imagination?'.

Thought experiments have contributed positively to the fields of philosophy, mathematics, physics, history, social sciences, and Christian theology, among others [5]. In philosophy and the physical sciences many thought experiments are created to argue for or against a theory or position. Another purpose of thought experiments is to clarify a concept to make a theory easier to understand [5]. Thought experiments can be a tool, aiming, like empirical experiments, to help us better understand the world. Also like empirical experiments, thought experiments are concerned with issues of reliability [6] and internal and external validity [7].

Let us now discuss an actual thought experiment – the trolley problem [8]. Imagine you see a speeding trolley in the distance and you are by a lever that can change the trolley from one track to another. Ahead of the trolley are five people unable to move. On an adjoining track is one person unable to move. You have two choices. You can do nothing and let the five people die or you can activate the lever ensuring the trolley kills one person. Rather than have a dry discussion about whether weighing the number of lives at stake in a decision should enter into an ethical calculus – the trolley problem provides a narrative through which to have that kind of conversation. We can now ask some interesting questions that have serious repercussions: Is activating the lever the right thing to do? What if there were only two people on the original track, or a hundred – would that change one's position?

This thought experiment goes beyond creating an interesting hypothetical situation. It can help reveal our ethical positions and intuitions. Let us say that we argue that pulling the lever is the right thing to do. This is a classic consequentialist position – where what is right depends on the consequences of one's actions. The result of one person dying is better than five people dying, so pulling the lever is the right thing to do. But let us explore this position further. What if instead of pushing a lever, one could push a very corpulent individual (for you are too thin) in front of the tracks to slow down the Trolley and save the five people [9]. Would that change one's decision? The consequences of the decision are the same, five people alive with one person dead. It passes the consequentialist test. Yet shoving someone onto trolley tracks hardly ever seems like an ethically acceptable thing to do. Perhaps we might need to clarify further what kind of consequences we take into account, or develop some boundaries of ethical action. For instance, never being forced to do something that would cause one extreme psychic harm, like murdering someone would [10].

In analyzing what has traditionally been considered to be successful philosophical thought experiments, like Quine's 'Gavagai' or Searle's 'Chinese Room,' Gomila states the following, "their contribution consists of the explicit formulation of our intuitions by means of a resort to boundary situations…The extraordinary situations depicted surprise us, mobilize our intuitions, obliging us to clarify them…" [11, pp. 87–88]. The trolley problem, like most thought experiments, pushes our thinking to creative extremes with the end goal of furthering the field of ethics and clarifying our ethical positions and intuitions. This is the general approach to thought experiments this paper will take. We will creatively push our thinking concerning IL and learning to an extreme so as to more effectively analyze and clarify the relationship between the two.

4 A Thought Experiment About IL and Student Learning

4.1 Kiki

Our thought experiment is the following: Kiki is a graduating student at State University who possesses extraordinarily sophisticated knowledge, abilities, perceptions, and/or experiences of IL. In fact, for whatever IL theory one subscribes to, Kiki is as close to the ideal as humanly possible, though she is not "perfect" in any sense. Her abilities could be defined by the skills of finding and evaluating information or something more complex such as having passed through all of the Association of College & Research Libraries (ACRL) threshold concepts for IL [12]. She is a sophisticated consumer and creator of information, engaging with information from any source with a critical eye. Kiki is knowledgeable about the socio-political and ethical aspects of information processes and structures too. She is aware of issues about contemporary journalism, peer-review, and open access in academia, or news algorithms on social media like Facebook. As one can imagine Michael Jordan's seemingly inhuman feats of athleticism, or Einstein's brilliant intellect applied to physics, one can imagine a woman named Kiki with superior IL abilities.

This paper will consider two fundamental questions: 1. Is it *possible* for Kiki to have become this sophisticated (for Kiki surely was not born this way) without using her IL knowledge, abilities, or experiences to learn disciplinary content at State University?; and 2. Is it *plausible* for Kiki to have become so advanced without learning disciplinary content? We will then discuss implications for academic librarianship as a result of how one answers these questions.

4.2 On the Possibility of the Thought Experiment

Arguing that it is possible for Kiki to have become so advanced in IL without learning subject content strongly implies a "generic" approach to IL given that Kiki developed her IL abilities in complete isolation from learning disciplinary subject content [13, p. 5]. IL instruction in this sense means IL is the subject content to be taught, distinct from disciplinary content. IL becomes equated to the skills or processes of using library databases, employing checklists about authority and relevance for academic articles, etc. Additionally, it is not necessarily the case that to develop such skills (especially if they are considered generic) they need to be applied to learn disciplinary content. One can learn how to search more effectively for psychology journals without learning about psychology – or learn about important features of datasets without learning about the discipline the datasets originates from. While knowing about psychology can help one limit their search terms or create more specific, and therefore better, search strings, one's abilities could also improve by learning about search engine optimization, and Boolean operators. At least some of these factors are discipline agnostic.

It is important to note here that one could argue that this is a straw man argument. It is not too difficult to paint a generic approach to IL in unflattering colors – reducing academic librarianship to walking students through tedious checklists and boring bibliographic instruction. Additionally – we have an issue with motivation. Why would anyone want to learn to use information simply for its own sake and not for the sake of something else? I submit the strongest argument for answering affirmatively would take the position that IL has (at least some) intrinsic value: it is valuable, at least in part, for its own sake and not for the sake of something else.

One analogy could be in jogging. One could jog for the numerous health benefits and so treat it as instrumentally valuable. On the other hand, one could simply enjoy jogging intrinsically and do it for its own sake – for no other reason. Lastly, a person could want to jog for its health benefits, but also because they simply enjoy jogging. It is possible that Kiki enjoys learning about how to find, evaluate, and use information for its own sake, at least partially. She could find learning how to use information inherently worthwhile and interesting, and so could be a brilliant IL autodidact. This addresses our motivation issue. Kiki's motivation to become so proficient in IL does not have to be based in academic success. She could be a proto-LIS researcher who finds information issues inherently worthwhile.

There still can be a relationship between IL and learning – it is simply not strong. It is what we can call a 'thin' relationship, where IL skills or abilities can be applied *later* to disciplinary content. For instance, a day after a student learns about a rubric to assess the authority of an information resource, that student applies the test to a few journal articles he finds. In Kiki's case – we can imagine her simply being lazy. She does not want to spend the time thoroughly evaluating and synthesizing information for a research paper. Rather, she exclusively uses basic search strings in Google to adequate academic results. Given a thin relationship between IL and learning, it is possible for Kiki to be so advanced without having applied her superior IL abilities to learn subject content.

4.3 On the Plausibility of the Thought Experiment

If one does not think it is plausible for Kiki to become so advanced without having used her abilities to learn disciplinary content, this implies one takes a position that the generic perspective does not accurately represent the entirety of what IL is or does. In other words, if one does not think our thought experiment is plausible, the generic IL perspective is intuitively or theoretically inadequate. While IL can include generic skills, IL as a whole is more than a set of generic skills, and there is more than a thin relationship between IL and learning disciplinary content. I submit that the majority of academic librarians are in this camp – and the purpose of this paper is to draw out implications for our intuitions concerning what we will call a 'thick' relationship between IL and learning in higher education.

One way to argue for this approach would be to draw from parallels to learning subject content. To learn to play the piano – one does not play scales exclusively. Rather, one learns things like scales so that one can play a song or piece. Generic skills and knowledge is ultimately applied in a disciplinary context. Playing scales helps one play pieces better or helps one gain the dexterity necessary to play a piece. In the same way, one should learn to use information in a disciplinary context so that one can learn disciplinary content. While the information environment in one discipline may be different than another, one cannot plausibly learn how to use information without learning how to use information in a specific context. If a piano player cannot apply a technique they are trying to refine (by practicing scales) to play a piece, then what is the point of practicing the technique? Similarly, if one does not use generic IL skills in the classroom to cultivate learning, then why would academic librarians teach generic skills? This is not to say that IL is a necessary pre-condition for the ability to learn, or that IL has a causal relationship with student learning. Rather, this is the view that IL *can* facilitate, enable, or augment disciplinary learning.

Further justification for our thought experiment to be implausible are examples found in the library and information science (LIS) literature. For example, IL is perceived as "essential to 'evidence-based practice'" in nursing and can contribute to justifying changing an existing practice or help determine ethically appropriate care [14, p. 1237]. Incorporating IL into a business school curriculum produced benefits for librarians, by providing insight on course design, as well as faculty, "increasing interest in defining course objectives more clearly and engaging students in development of information literacy competence" [15, p. 316]. Another study using thematic analysis found that IL can have an important role to play in active learning environments, enabling learning subject content or helping students engage "in disciplinary ways of knowing" [16, p. 709]. An ACRL report titled *Academic Library Impact on Student Learning and Success: Findings from Assessment in Action Team Projects* detailed the results of ACRL Assessment in Action projects from over 50 institutions of higher education [17]. While the ACRL report is not necessarily generalizable to all of academia, it still evidences how IL can contribute to student learning. It notes that "Students benefit from library instruction in their initial coursework," "Library use increases student success," "Collaborative academic programs and services involving the library enhance student learning," and "Information literacy instruction strengthens general education outcomes." [17, pp. 1–2]. IL can can contribute to student learning in various ways.

Lastly, acquiring such advanced abilities without learning disciplinary content could simply be considered *prima facie* absurd. To think of someone like Kiki who would not bring her IL talents to bear to learn in the classroom defies common sense. This is a legitimate position to hold because the aim of our thought experiment is more exploratory than argumentative. The goal is to highlight where we stand on this important topic and to draw out some important repercussions as a result of where we stand.

5 Discussion

Similar to the trolley problem, our thought experiment can help make some assumptions and implications of taking a specific position more explicit so as to more properly analyze them. Let us first discuss the implications for the thin position. First, there are serious pragmatic issues. If academic librarians take this stance towards the relationship between IL and learning, then they will have a difficult time justifying the resources and time for embedding IL into curricula, and rightfully so. Few people will be as intrinsically motivated to learn about IL as Kiki.

Additionally, academic librarianship could become marginalized if it cannot clearly argue for a strong, direct link between our expertise and a valuable mission of any college or university, viz. student learning. College and university libraries continue to compete for resources as institutions demand more accountability and evidence for how libraries help their institution meet their teaching and learning mission [18, p. 6]. Arguing that IL has a thin theoretical link to learning, even in this best-base scenario with Kiki, would be problematic for academic librarianship at large. It unnecessarily limits what IL is capable of, as evidenced by current literature and theory. What use are such IL abilities, no matter one's theoretical IL stance, if Kiki does not use them to learn? To say that Kiki's situation is possible is a Pyrrhic victory at best.

Let us now discuss the implications of the thick position – that Kiki's situation is not plausible. This implies some kind of *direct* relationship between IL and learning. This statement is not a revelation. As we have shown earlier, major IL theorists and LIS literature have already determined this in various ways. Our thought experiment can help bring to light an important implication of this view. If IL has a direct and thick relationship with learning and it is more than generic skills, then our theoretical approach to IL has implications for how we, as academic librarians and IL theorists, conceive of learning. Perhaps more importantly, the inverse is also true. How we conceive of learning can have implications for how we conceive of IL.Therefore, IL theory can advance from discussions not directly considering information use. Somewhat paradoxically, explicit considerations of the nature of learning completely separate from considerations of information can help refine our understanding of IL.

For example, perhaps one subscribes strongly to the ACRL threshold concepts. One finds threshold concepts appealing and intuitive theoretically. Here, it makes sense that learning about how authority is constructed can fundamentally transform the way one views scholarly information. Yet, given what we have discussed, this position also implies a strong position for threshold concepts as a legitimate theory that, at least partially, explains what learning is and how it happens. There are important consequences for taking this position. For example, Meyer and Land themselves broach some difficulties of threshold concepts relating to issues of "hierarchy and relations of power within learning environments and academic communities more widely" [19, p. 374]. Who decides the thresholds of a discipline? Does this create an unfair power dynamic between teachers and students, or administrators and teachers? This discussion could make one more cautious about threshold concepts as a whole, which in turn may have consequences for how one views threshold concepts in relation to IL. Embracing debates within learning theories can allow more sophisticated analyses of IL theories.

Another example: do students learn what 'good' writing is by reading multiple examples of what is considered to be 'good' writing? Or, would students learn better by reading varying levels of writing [20, p. 1065]? A constructivist might argue for the former position, while a variation theorist would certainly argue for the latter. Bruce, for instance, takes variation theory as a basis for her Informed Learning approach to IL [3]. Her IL theory is intertwined with her position on what learning is. It is plausible that once an academic librarian concerns herself with issues pertaining to learning and participating in scholarly dialogue about the nature of learning that she takes a new theoretical position on IL, or amends her previous stance. Perhaps one is skeptical of the variation theory perspective because of its common research methods, e.g. learning studies and phenomenographic interviews.

Again, something seemingly far removed from IL theory could have serious implications for IL theory. Seeing learning through the lens of threshold concepts is qualitatively different than seeing learning through the lens of variation theory. In a similar way, the ACRL New Framework takes a qualitatively different approach to IL than Informed Learning. Explicitly discussing the merits of learning theories like behaviorism, cognitivism, constructivism, social constructivism, variation theory, and others, would be useful to the LIS field and for IL research. Such dialogue would enable new and interesting perspectives on what IL's role is, and how it can be best employed, in higher education. Such discourse takes place in other fields, like medical education [21].

Accordingly, it is important that academic librarians make dialogue and debate about learning theories more explicit. The more sophisticated reasons and arguments an academic librarian can make with regard to taking a specific theoretical stance on learning, the more sophisticated reasons and arguments an academic librarian can make to take a specific theoretical stance on IL. Arguing for the benefits of one IL approach should include discussion about what learning theory underpins one's IL approach, why such a learning theory is attractive and appropriate, etc.

If academic librarians conceive of IL as being more than mere discrete skills, this entails a thick relationship between IL and learning. Given this strong relationship, librarians working in higher education then would benefit from more open and intentional dialogue about learning theory. To advance IL theory, LIS researchers and practitioners should draw from learning theory.

6 Conclusion

This paper used a thought experiment to analyze the relationship between IL and learning. We have demonstrated that there are theoretical and pragmatic reasons to perceive a strong link between IL and learning. Accordingly, to advance IL theory academic librarianship must turn its attention towards theories of learning – and discuss explicitly what learning is and how it should take place. Commitments to certain theories of IL are also making certain commitments to what learning is and how it is best achieved. This may or may not align with what we already believe what learning is. Moreover, one's theoretical approach to learning (whether made explicit or not) could affect one's theoretical approach to IL. The relationship we examined is not one-way. What is important is to be unequivocal about the role learning plays in IL. If there is a strong and direct relationship between IL and learning, then academic librarianship should turn to and debate learning theory to advance IL theory.

References

1. Brendel, E.: Intuition pumps and the proper use of thought experiments. Dialectica **58**, 89–108 (2004)

2. Lloyd, A.: Information literacy landscapes: an emerging picture. J. Doc. **62**(5), 570–583 (2006)
3. Bruce, C.S.: Informed Learning. American Library Association, Chicago (2008)
4. Whitworth, A.: Radical Information Literacy Reclaiming the Political Heart of the IL Movement. Chandos Information Professional Series. Elsevier Science, Burlington (2014)
5. Brown, J.R., Fehige, Y.: Thought experiments. In: Zalta, E. (ed.) The Stanford Encyclopedia of Philosophy (2017, forthcoming). https://plato.stanford.edu/archives/sum2017/entries/thought-experiment/
6. Klee, R.: Physical space effects and philosophical thought experiments. Metaphilosophy **39** (1), 89–104 (2008)
7. Wilson, J.: VII—internal and external validity in thought experiments. In: Proceedings of the Aristotelian Society, vol. 116, no. 2, pp. 127–152 (2016). https://doi.org/10.1093/arisoc/aow008
8. Foot, P.: The problem of abortion and the doctrine of the double effect. In: Foot, P. (ed.) Virtues and Vices and Other Essays in Moral Philosophy. Basil Blackwell, Oxford (1978)
9. Thomson, J.J.: Killing, letting die, and the trolley problem. Monist **59**, 204–2017 (1976)
10. Smart, J.J.C., Williams, B.: Utilitarianism: For and Against. Cambridge University Press, Cambridge (1973)
11. Gomila, A.: What is a thought experiment? Metaphilosophy **22**(1 and 2), 84–92 (1991)
12. Association of College and Research Libraries: Framework for Information Literacy in Higher Education. Association of College and Research Libraries (2015)
13. Lupton, M., Bruce, C.S.: Windows on information literacy worlds: generic, situated and transformative perspectives. In: Practising Information Literacy: Bringing Theories of Learning, Practice and Information Literacy Together. Centre for Information Studies, Charles Sturt University, Wagga Wagga, N.S.W., pp. 4–27 (2010)
14. Forster, M.: A phenomenographic investigation into Information literacy in nursing practice — preliminary findings and methodological issues. Nurse Educ. Today **33**(10), 1237–1241 (2013)
15. Fiegen, A.M., Cherry, B., Watson, K.: Reflections on collaboration: learning outcomes and information literacy assessment in the business curriculum. Ref. Serv. Rev. **30**(4), 307–318 (2002)
16. Maybee, C., Doan, T., Flierl, M.: Information literacy in the active learning classroom. J. Acad. Librariansh. **42**(6), 705–711 (2016)
17. Association of College and Research Libraries: Academic Library Impact on Student Learning and Success: Findings from Assessment in Action Team Projects. Prepared by Karen Brown with contributions by Kara J. Malenfant. Association of College and Research Libraries, Chicago (2017)
18. Association of College and Research Libraries: Value of Academic Libraries: A Comprehensive Research Review and Report. Researched by Megan Oakleaf. Association of College and Research Libraries, Chicago (2010)
19. Meyer, J.H.F., Land, R.: Threshold concepts and troublesome knowledge (2): epistemological considerations and a conceptual framework for teaching and learning. High. Educ.: Int. J. High. Educ. Educ. Plan. **49**(3), 373–388 (2005)
20. Pang, M., Marton, F.: Interaction between the learners' initial grasp of the object of learning and the learning resource afforded. Instr. Sci. **41**(6), 1065–1082 (2013)
21. Torre, D., Daley, B., Sebastian, J., Elnicki, M.: Overview of current learning theories for medical educators. Am. J. Med. **119**(10), 903–907 (2006)

Required Skills for Teachers: Information Literacy at the Top

Tatiana Sanches(✉)

Institute of Education, Lisbon University, Lisbon, Portugal
tsanches@fpie.ulisboa.pt

Abstract. This study seeks to contribute to a reflection on teachers' training and professional development in the field of information literacy, in Portugal. Aspects regarding teacher training and their role as spreaders of knowledge and multipliers of good practices are problematized. UNESCO's curriculum for teachers and ACRL guidelines are used methodologically as the central thread of this interpretation. From here we seek to explain how a higher education institution – an Institute of Education, which is devoted to the professional development of educators, including teachers, has engaged in information flit-eracy actions through training interventions, in recent years. The study concludes that through sharing and dialogue within the librarian profession, but also within the sphere of education professionals - teachers and trainers - the best training practices in university libraries can be consolidated. Finally, certain points for reflection and debate concerning this theme are proposed.

Keywords: Information literacy · Teacher education
Librarian teacher cooperation · Higher education · Portugal

1 Introduction

The increase of compulsory education has created optimal conditions for more students to reach higher education, mobilising a great mass of teaching professionals all over the world and posing countless challenges for the teaching profession, especially in the transition of the 20th to the 21st century, including:

- teaching has become student-centered
- there is greater access to information
- more choice and diversity of training courses
- there is an interception of the digital era in teaching tools
- training interventions for online environments have been created and adapted.

The explosion of information, in a multimedia and digital context, has become a fertile area for exploring, communicating and spreading information, thus enabling new knowledge to be learned, created and taught. This scenario poses questions regarding the skills future and in-service teachers must acquire and develop. These skills will give them more intervention capacity, because not only will they benefit their role as spreaders of information, but they will allow them to develop the ways in which they

S. Kurbanoğlu et al. (Eds.): ECIL 2017, CCIS 810, pp. 634–644, 2018.
https://doi.org/10.1007/978-3-319-74334-9_65

learn and are updated. Thus pre-service and in-service teachers are agents and subjects of new learning.

The study now presented intends to explore these characteristics and the way teachers can prepare specifically for dealing with information, developing their information literacy. On one hand, this includes knowing how to search, choose, organise, evaluate and present information in an ethical and legal manner, and giving them better conditions to communicate it. On other hand, it will benefit teachers because information skills will allow them to deal with teaching and learning environments that are constantly developing, and it will support them in their professional development and in their lifelong learning. In the first part of this article, a reflection is conducted on the impact of information literacy in the educational and learning context, analysing processes and trajectories teachers may explore while developing their skills, particularly information literacy. In the second part, a case of specific information literacy training course in Portugal, directed towards teachers and conducted by a university library, is presented. Both sections aim to show how Information Literacy proves to be a set of vital required skills for teachers.

2 Information Literacy as a Fundamental Skill for Teachers

In 2006 the European Parliament [1] recommended a set of key skills for lifelong learning, an important milestone in the definition of a comprehensive strategy in the field of education, where skills are defined as a blend of knowledge, abilities and attitudes that are suitable for each performance context. Key skills are said to be those that support personal fulfillment, social inclusion, active citizenship and employment. The debate became very interesting as some authors spoke of the importance of preparing teachers for the challenges of the 21st century, namely in Europe, so as to act in a changing society. Persson [2, p. 13] stated that "If professionals in education are to prepare an even more diverse group of learners for much more challenging work they will need substantially more/new knowledge and radically different lifelong skills than most now have". Some years later, a study [3] concluded that learning objectives will focus more on skills than on knowledge, that learning will be more adapted to the needs of real life and that individuals will be more active and connected to their environment, and therefore teachers themselves will become lifelong learners. Flores and Coutinho [4, p. 7] also mentioned that teachers' work implies new ways of regarding teaching, knowledge and the role of schools and teachers. Perrenoud [5] had already looked into what are the essential skills for teachers, having highlighted innovative practices and also emerging skills, that is, those that should guide pre-service and in-service training, contribute to the fight against school underachievement and, on the other hand, develop citizenship, resort to research and emphasise reflective practice. In fact, teachers must pay attention to their professional training and development, as has also been demonstrated by the research on the theme [6]. The scope and responsibility of functions is clear, as well as perception of the social impact of this profession.

This initial approach shows that teachers are key actors in a changing social context, particularly in an information society. These changes have greater impact on learning and are precisely based on the exchange of information and on the way knowledge is generated, but also how the information is searched, chosen and used. That is why the expertise to deal with information in a vital skill for any citizen in the 21st century, especially for professionals whose primary material is information and knowledge.

New teaching and learning practices are also important for this reflection. Student-centred teaching requires the use of digital and multimedia-based learning resources. Digital libraries and repositories facilitate the reuse of digital content, allowing access to a variety of sources and boosting the formation of critical thinking and the creation of more complex ideas, while encouraging students to use the resources and reinterpret them [7]. To develop all these skills Information Literacy is crucial. The American Library Association, through its Association of College and Research Libraries Division [8], defines this concept, explaining that an individual qualified with information skills should be

- capable of determining the need for information and its extent
- accessing information efficiently and effectively
- critically evaluating information and its sources
- incorporating the information chosen in his knowledge base
- using the information effectively to fulfill a specific objective
- understanding the economic, legal and social implications of the use of information
- knowing how to access and use it ethically and legally.

The same document adds that the development of skills within information literacy makes individuals more capable of dealing with information in the several spheres of activity throughout life [8]. As Esteves states [9, p. 37], the huge amount of information made available to everyone today can be considered to be very positive, as well as an increasingly easier access to the extensive knowledge stored there. On the other hand, the excessive abundance of information makes it indigestible for a single individual and the quality (rigour, validity) of available information is very unequal. So new needs emerge, associated with information processing and organisation and with the adoption of a critical point of view about its quality. The teacher's role also includes promoting the learning of information literacy, seeking to incite in students the attitude needed for the development and practice of skills to be better learners. This is the reason why libraries all over the world are organizing and providing specific training to promote information skills.

Through their official position, two entities – UNESCO and ALA/ACRL – have been legitimizing the importance of information literacy skills in teaching training. Both marked their positions regarding information literacy and its concept, its social influence and the way the educational and technological context affect learning and have impact on this profession, stressing the importance of mastering information for effective lifelong teaching and learning. The guiding document *Information Literacy Standards for Teacher Education* [10, p. 1], states that "Teachers play a key role in providing students with diverse opportunities to learn how to use information wisely." This vital document provides tools for teachers so that librarians can prepare specific training for them and, on the other hand, the evaluation of this kind of training can be carried out, with comparable results and benchmarking. Librarians working in higher education, especially in teacher and education professionals' training schools, can plan and implement their training with this specific target audience in mind. The structure followed in this document is exactly the same as the one found in the *Information Literacy Competency Standards for Higher Education* [8], presenting the information literacy learning standards, which turn into performance indicators and are accompanied by practical examples regarding goals to attain. In turn, UNESCO issued official guidelines that frame and describe the composed concept of Media and Information Literacy (MIL), recently publishing a set of documents which relate the capacity to deal with information and with media in a critical, informed manner: the guiding document *Media and Information Literacy: Policy and Strategy Guidelines* [11], and the document *Global Media and Information Literacy Assessment Framework: Country Readiness and Competencies* [12] fit these purposes. Both include the concept of information literacy combined with that of media literacy. The reason for this is the need to provide citizens with the necessary skills to search, experience and benefit from the freedom of expression and of access to information, whatever the support may be. These documents seek to correspond to current convergence trends of radio, television, internet, newspapers, books, archives and physical and digital libraries into one single platform, thus regarded as means to access information, irrespective of the channel. Therefore, information literacy is introduced considering the diverse contexts for its use and with the purpose of fully integrating and developing these skills in personal, educational and social spheres. UNESCO's commitment to promote MIL is visible not only in the above mentioned documents, but also in the document *Media and Information Literacy Curriculum for Teachers* [13]. This document took into account the importance of integrating MIL in the formal training of teachers, thus enabling a process which aims to reach and develop the capacities of million of young people through their teachers, working as a catalyst of this specific knowledge. Media and information literacy expand the movement for civic education which incorporates teachers as the main agents of change.

3 Teaching Information Literacy to Teachers Around the World

The study of information literacy as a fundamental skill for teachers is not new. For instance, Huang and Yang [14] address the technological changes that have had an impact on the field of education, stressing the need to develop knowledge in teachers, given the challenges, changes and skills that must be developed in an educational digital ecosystem. Although focused on the impact of technologies in schools, Schrum et al. [15] also mention the importance of preparing school leaders, teachers and educators for the future, given their decisive role with students in the 21st century. The increasing prominence of information literacy in teacher training is underlined by Kovalik et al. [16], who stress the teacher's role and responsibility in teaching information literacy, sustaining the idea of becoming proficient in the mastery of this matter and teaching it. Their study presents the results of an inquiry (covering 46 USA higher education establishments), which relates data about teachers' knowledge, inclusion and information literacy evaluation in teacher training programmes, as well as collaboration between teachers and librarians to teach these skills. The conclusions reiterate the importance of including information literacy education in pre-service teacher training curricula. This has been studied in different parts of the globe, with glaringly different implementation speeds in different countries.

In the United States, in Ohio, a cross-sectional study had already been carried out in 2009 at a higher education establishment with teacher training [17]. It reports several implementation phases of the teacher training programme on information literacy, highlighting the close collaboration between librarians and teachers and the success achieved, though there is no standard manner of incorporating information literacy in terms of curricula. In Croatia, a study by Kokic [18] shows how difficult it is to evaluate learning in information literacy in this context. Although there are learning objectives connected to the expected results of information literacy (based on international standards), these are limited. On the other hand, as the syllabi are not yet aligned with the guiding documents, recommendations favour a more consistent integration of these learnings in terms of curricula. In Greece [19], the Department of Primary Education of the School of Education (Aristotle University of Thessaloniki) defined a program to integrate information literacy education in the first years of teacher training courses. After three years of implementation, since 2010–11, the outcome was very positive, one of the students' conclusions being that "the IL course is not an end in itself but an introductory stage in which they learn to utilize IL tools in a context to build on their IL confidence." [19, p. 24]. In Brazil a report describes an experiment [20] consisting of a training workshop for in-service teachers. The idea was to develop information skills in public basic education teachers, considering the absence of programmes integrated in the curriculum and also, according to the authors, considering that information is an enhancer of knowledge. So, if it is developed based on public inclusion policies, it will have positive consequences on education and on a large scale, as an ally in the development of skills, especially for content mediators, as teachers are [20, p. 61]. From Russia and Uzbekistan [21] there are also reports already seeking to reflect further on the inclusion of UNESCO's guiding documents, adapting them to the local reality and implementing models that may be integrated in these countries in terms of pre-service teacher training. In light of the same documents, Alves and Varela [22] analyse the trainers' training needs, in this case in Portuguese-speaking African countries. Based on this analysis, they consider UNESCO's [13] model to be the best for media and information literacy training, because it ensures a broader, more adequate learning of the subjects related to information.

Some authors have mentioned the importance of addressing information literacy as a skill to be taught in pre-service teacher training as well as in the professional development teachers should seek to carry out over their career. Shipman et al. [23] refer to this exactly, relating in-service teachers' information search and use habits to training previously carried out during their initial training, thus stating that the results of information literacy training are long-lasting, accompanying teachers throughout their professional performance. The importance of information literacy is already recognised as a skill to be integrated in teachers', trainers' and educators' training. This awareness is not only manifest in the experiments reported, as those described above, but also in the prospective questioning of intervenors, and in the theoretical reflections this topic has triggered. For instance, Perzycka's [24] theoretical reflection substantiates the important of studying and applying information literacy more consistently, from the in-depth analysis of the conditions it is made of, as well as from dialogue with theory from which practices may benefit.

4 A Case of Specific Training in the Portuguese Context

Numerous studies have analysed and reflected upon pre-service teacher training, and Portugal is no exception. Most authors agree that there are training processes that complement each other in pre-service training: the curricular part, based on learning subjects, and training in the context of a professional internship, which seeks to ensure preparedness for professional reality [25]. Silva [26, p. 26] states that teacher training is a continuous, systematic, wholistic, transversal and organised process, present in every moment of the teaching career. The Portuguese law (D.L. no. 240/2001, of 30 August) actually establishes the professional performance profiles of professions related to teaching (including kindergarten teachers and basic and secondary education teachers). Cannas and Moreira [27, p. 46] declare that, as the main agents of the educational process, teachers may be the authors of innovative, reflexive action when they participate as protagonists in implementing good pedagogical practices.

The University of Lisbon is the biggest university in Portugal, with 18 Schools (Faculties and Institutes) and around 50,000 students, 3,500 teachers and 2,500 staff. There are 22 academic libraries, organised by themes according to the areas of education and research of each autonomous unit. The Institute of Education, currently with about 900 students, is one of these schools, devoted to research, training in education and training in Portugal. It is important to mention that since 2010, the library of the Institute of Education, which previously depended on a single institution – the Faculty of Psychology and Educational Sciences – has been supporting the research and education of the two institutions created that year – the Faculty of Psychology and the Institute of Education, of the University of Lisbon.

The library has sought to align with international standards, providing two modalities of information literacy training: in the classroom and occasionally via elearning (requested by teachers), and in open enrolment workshops, based on a training programme developed by its librarians. The analysis that follows concerns this last contribution. The experiment carried out by the library of the Faculty of Psychology and Institute of Education has a ten-year record of user training, but this study focuses only on the most recent year. The construction of the current training plan was based on previous experience and on international guiding documents. Considering the ALA and UNESCO documents [10, 13], we sought to address all the skills that are part of the requirements for teacher training, relating them to the established standards and to the learning goals of each module offered, always bearing in mind their contextual application. The information-literate teacher education student:

(1) defines and articulates the need for information and selects strategies and tools to find it.
(2) locates and selects information based on its appropriateness to the specific information need and the developmental needs of the students.

(3) organizes and analyzes the information in the context of specific information needs and the developmental appropriateness for the audience.
(4) synthesizes, processes, and presents the information in a way that is appropriate for the purpose for which information is needed.
(5) evaluates discrete pieces of information as well as the entire information seeking process.
(6) knows how to ethically use and disseminate information.

The MIL curriculum for teachers is framed based on three content areas:

1. Knowledge and understanding of media and information for democratic discourses and social participation.
2. Evaluation of media texts and information sources.
3. Production and use of media and information.

This training offer seeks to remedy the failings of several students in information literacy and contribute to the development of skills in searching, evaluating and transmitting information, trying to combine both guideline documents, but also considering the ACRL Framework [28].

The preparation of this intervention took into account the needs indicated by several users and was formulated in an appealing way, seeking to match the level of education and the level of complexity inherent to each training proposal. Work started on the training plan in order to change the organisation established the previous year as regards its curricular plan, length, schedule, evaluation and promotion. The didactic materials were also reconsidered. The presentation text available in the institutional sites to publicise these sessions was composed as follows:

The library continues to promote workshops aimed at developing skills in the good **use of information resources**, especially designed to support academic goals. The volume of information currently available requires students have the necessary skills to search, evaluate, select, use and present information in an ethical and effective manner. That is why we have designed a programme for the continuous development of these skills:

1 - Searching and selecting in electronic resources
2 - Quoting and referencing with the APA 6th norm
3 - Managing bibliographic references with Endnote web
4 - Organising information for theses and dissertations
5 - Oral and Power Point presentations.

The main feature is related to the idea that information literacy responds to several requests which, in the case of these students, may be divided into two assumptions. One regards academic goals: completing work for different subjects; obtaining an academic degree, by presenting a dissertation or thesis at the end of the course; conducting research, for which bibliography must be managed in depth (showing information has value [28]). The other regards the need for future teachers to incorporate what they learn into their scope of knowledge, then to retransmit it and adjust it in different contexts for their own future pupils (showing scholarship as conversation [28]).

Alongside the information skills practiced in a training context (the rooms where the training takes place are equipped with computers so students can carry out exercises), we also considered it important to complement training with different examples, in view of future adjustment needs of information literacy to different contexts.

Based on a systematic evaluation performed at the end of the sessions, the outcome of the training sessions carried out in 2016/2017 was very positive. This evaluation used a Lickert scale, with scores between 1 (dissatisfied) and 4 (very satisfied), comprising the following ten issues:

- General quality of the trainer's exposition
- Content organisation
- Relevance of the topics covered
- Clarity of the exposition
- Adequacy of training to student needs
- Trust in the information provided by the trainer
- Supporting documentation
- Quality of the tutorials presented
- Adequacy of training to students' level of knowledge
- Comfort of the room.

The results of the questionnaires given to users in every session are proof of the positive feedback regarding this programme. In 2017 a group of five programmes were carried out, each one containing five two-hour workshops. During the first semester of 2017, 25 sessions were thus carried out, taught by three librarians who trained a total of 207 students, having had a 95% global average rating in terms of satisfaction (Table 1).

Table 1. Information literacy programme, taught during the 1st semester of 2017.

Workshops taught	Students involved	Satisfaction
1. Searching and selecting in electronic resources	35	92%
2. Quoting and referencing with the APA 6th norm	50	95%
3. Managing bibliographic references with Endnote web	47	95%
4. Organising information for theses and dissertations	48	95%
5. Oral and Power Point presentations	27	97%

Besides information retrieval or organisation strategies, another aspect introduced concerns strategies for presenting information, providing some practical ideas to deal with communicating and presenting ideas (showing authority is constructed and contextual, and information creation as a process [28]). This evaluation indicated the consolidation of our training practices and certainly the trainers' commitment to helping users in a personalised manner to develop their information literacy skills.

5 Final Remarks

All formal learning requires the use of resources based on information. Following librarians' steps, teachers seek to facilitate the reuse of content, allowing access to a variety of sources and enhancing the development of critical thinking and the creation of more complex ideas, as they encourage students to use and reinterpret resources [29]. Students and teachers use information resources to carry out much of their activity, which implies the capacity to understand, access, evaluate, use and manage a vast range of documents. Hence teachers need to devote some time to learning new information organization, management tools and ways to present academic work. In turn, librarians must have thorough knowledge of these topics and allow them to be taught so they can be reproduced, particularly when being taught to teachers.

We sought to show how important it is to recognise the teacher's role as a multiplier of information literacy. The paper focused on the importance of teachers' information literacy and discussed a training intervention developed by a higher education institution in Portugal to engage information literacy skills and competencies in the professional development of educators. The literature review and observation of practices converge towards the same conclusions: the key importance of information literacy in teacher education and how teachers themselves are aware of it. Therefore, librarians must make their contribution, providing information resources and the training needed to use them to the full.

Everyone involved should understand to what extent they need to develop greater expertise, particularly if they are leading similar processes, seeking to correspond to these specific needs. Such sharing should be based above all on dialogue between these two professionals – librarians and teachers – so that both can converge towards common goals. As this alignment of interests and efforts is essential, in the future it will be important that international documents are converted into national guidelines in Portugal, consolidating and standardising the training offer for teachers, which would increase the scope and impact of information literacy. The actions librarians can develop at this level are fundamental, for they are the basis for the creation and development of transversal skills in lifelong learning, for which teachers are indispensable actors and partners.

References

1. European Parliament and the Council: Recommendation of the European Parliament and the Council of 18 December 2006 on key competences for lifelong learning. In: Official Journal of the European Union, L394 (2006)
2. Persson, M.: A vision of European teaching and learning: perspectives on the new role of the teacher. The Learning Teacher Network, Karlstad (2006)
3. Ala-Mutka, K., Redecker, C., Punie, Y., Ferrari, A., Cachia, R., Centeno, C.: The future of learning: European teachers' visions. In: Report on a Foresight Consultation at the 2010 eTwinning Conference, Seville, February 2010
4. Flores, M.A., Coutinho, C.: Formação e trabalho docente: tendências e desafios atuais. De Facto, Sto. Tirso (2014)

5. Perrenoud, P.: Dix nouvelles compétences pour enseigner: invitation au voyage. ESF, Paris (1999)
6. Conceição, C., Sousa, O.: Ser professor hoje: o que pensam os professores das suas competências. Revista Lusófona de Educação **20**, 81–89 (2012)
7. McGill, L.: Transforming curriculum delivery through technology: JISC Programme Synthesis Report (2011). http://www.jisc.ac.uk/media/documents/programmes/curriculumdelivery/curriculumdeliveryfinalreport.pdf. Accessed 24 Apr 2017
8. ALA: Information Literacy Competency Standards for Higher Education. Association of College and Research Libraries, American Library Association, Chicago (2000). http://www.ala.org/acrl/sites/ala.org.acrl/files/content/standards/standards.pdf
9. Esteves, M.: Construção e desenvolvimento de competências profissionais dos professores em contexto de aprendizagem em rede. In: Pryjma, M.F., Oliveira, O.S. (eds.) O desenvolvimento profissional docente em discussão, pp. 23–46. UTFPR, Curitiba (2016)
10. ALA: Information Literacy Standards for Teacher Education. Association of College and Research Libraries, American Library Association, Chicago (2011). http://www.ala.org/acrl/sites/ala.org.acrl/files/content/standards/ilstandards_te.pdf
11. UNESCO: Media and Information Literacy: Policy and Strategy Guidelines. UNESCO, Paris (2013). http://unesdoc.unesco.org/images/0022/002256/225606e.pdf
12. UNESCO: Global Media and Information Literacy Assessment Framework: Country Readiness and Competencies. UNESCO, Paris (2013). http://www.uis.unesco.org/Communication/Documents/media-and-information-literacy-assessment-framework.pdf
13. Wilson, C. et al.: Media and Information Literacy Curriculum for Teachers. UNESCO, Paris (2011). http://www.unesco.org/new/fileadmin/MULTIMEDIA/HQ/CI/CI/pdf/media_and_information_literacy_curriculum_for_teachers_en.pdf
14. Huang, R., Yang, J.: Digital learners and digital teachers: challenges, changes, and competencies. In: Spector, J.M., Ifenthaler, D., Sampson, D.G., Isaías, P. (eds.) Competencies in Teaching, Learning and Educational Leadership in the Digital Age, pp. 47–56. Springer, Cham (2016). https://doi.org/10.1007/978-3-319-30295-9_4
15. Schrum, L., Niederhauser, D.S., Strudler, N.: Competencies, challenges, and changes: a US perspective on preparing twenty-first century teachers and leaders. In: Spector, J.M., Ifenthaler, D., Sampson, D.G., Isaías, P. (eds.) Competencies in Teaching, Learning and Educational Leadership in the Digital Age, pp. 17–32. Springer, Cham (2016). https://doi.org/10.1007/978-3-319-30295-9_2
16. Kovalik, C.L., Jensen, M.L., Schloman, B., Tipton, M.: Information literacy, collaboration, and teacher education. Commun. Inf. Literacy **4**(2), 145–169 (2010)
17. Earp, V.: Integrating information literacy into teacher education: a successful grant project. Behav. Soc. Sci. Librarian **28**(4), 166–178 (2009)
18. Kokic, I.B.: Information literacy for future teachers. World J. Educ. **2**(1), 45–54 (2012)
19. Bougatzeli, E., Togia, A., Papadimitriou, E.: Developing an information literacy course for teacher education students in Greece. Int. J. Lit. **21**, 17–26 (2015)
20. Silva Neto, C.E., Freire, G.H.A.: Competência em informação: relato de experiência. RACIn **2**(2), 44–63 (2014)
21. Gendina, N.: Integrating the personal information culture concept and the idea of media and information literacy offered in the UNESCO curriculum for teachers: experiences of Russia and Uzbekistan. In: Kurbanoğlu, S., Boustany, J., Špiranec, S., Grassian, E., Mizrachi, D., Roy, L., Çakmak, T. (eds.) ECIL 2016. CCIS, vol. 676, pp. 543–554. Springer, Cham (2016). https://doi.org/10.1007/978-3-319-52162-6_54
22. Alves, F.M.M., Varela, A.V.: Formação de formadores em Media and Information Literacy (MIL) para países lusófonos africanos. Revista Brasileira de Biblioteconomia e Documentação. **13**(n. especial), pp. 254–271 (2017)

23. Shipman, T., Bannon, S.H., Nunes-Bufford, K.: The information-seeking habits of in-service educators. Coll. Res. Libr. **76**(2), 120–135 (2015)
24. Perzycka, E.: Teacher's learning processes of information competences in the network society – proposed theoretical model and methodological solutions. New Educ. Rev. **40**(2), 180–188 (2015)
25. Loss, A.S., Caetano, A.P.V., Ponte, J.P.: Formação de Professores no Brasil e em Portugal: pesquisas, debates e práticas. Annris, Curitiba (2015)
26. Silva, C.: Tornar-se professor ou o itinerário formativo: entre formação inicial, indução profissional e formação contínua. In: Flores, M.A., Carvalho, M.L., Silva, C. (eds.) Formação e aprendizagem profissional de professores: contextos e experiências, pp. 17–40. De Facto, St. Tirso (2016)
27. Cannas, A.C., Moreira, J.A.: O perfil profissional docente em contextos educativos diferenciados. Whitebooks, St. Tirso (2015)
28. Association of College and Research Libraries [ACRL]: Framework for information literacy for higher education (2015). http://www.ala.org/acrl/standards/ilframework
29. McGill, L.: Transforming curriculum delivery through technology: JISC Programme Synthesis Report (2011). http://www.jisc.ac.uk/media/documents/programmes/curriculumdelivery/curriculumdeliveryfinalreport.pdf

Recognizing the Influence of Disciplinarity on Student Inquiry

Jean-Pierre V. M. Hérubel and Clarence Maybee(✉)

Purdue University, Libraries, West Lafayette, IN, USA
{jpvmh, cmaybee}@purdue.edu

Abstract. Upper-level undergraduate students need to recognize the role that disciplinary cultures play in the creation and dissemination of scholarship. This will empower students to navigate scholarly literature with a deeper understanding of how disciplinarity shapes their inquiry. When asking students to engage with scholarship, teachers often direct them to specific journals, without making the selection process explicit. Information literacy may be situated within disciplinary or communal contexts, often highlighting the need for recognizing authority. However, these descriptions may fall short of explaining the nuanced forces shaping such authority, and how disciplines, sub-disciplines, or multi-disciplines package information. Using Hérubel's definitional model describing characteristics of disciplinary cultures, this paper offers a lens for working with undergraduate students to enable them to understand how it shapes the information they encounter and its potential influence on their own scholarly efforts.

Keywords: Disciplinary literacy · Higher education · Interdisciplinary Information literacy · Multidisciplinary · Undergraduates

1 Introduction

Knowledge is undifferentiated until disciplined [1, 2]. Even when disciplined, coherence of historical knowledge is situated within the contextualized disciplinary formations of historical practice and disciplinary research protocols [1]. In higher education, undergraduate students are enculturated into academic disciplines, requiring them to understand disciplinary information practices. Information literacy efforts may play an important role in the enculturation process. Simmons [3] highlights the potential for librarians to adopt a mediating role in which they assist students in understanding and applying disciplinary information practices. Adopting such a role requires information literacy learning opportunities to be grounded in an "understanding of what disciplines are and how information practices are a part of them" [4, p. 323].

Higher education teachers, including librarians, tend to focus on explaining specialized and disciplinary knowledge, rather than having the students engage in the inquiry, discovery and debate that continually shapes knowledge [4]. Educators need to focus on enculturating students by providing them with guided opportunities to practice. In so doing, teachers must enable students to become aware of the information practices cultivated and used within the discipline. One such information practice that

S. Kurbanoğlu et al. (Eds.): ECIL 2017, CCIS 810, pp. 645–653, 2018.
https://doi.org/10.1007/978-3-319-74334-9_66

is critical for student learning is recognizing that academic journals reflect and serve different specializations of research.

Successfully finding appropriate information requires discernment of how scholarship is executed and disseminated. Information literacy efforts in higher education do not typically aim to make students aware of the nuances of disciplinary cultures and how disciplines, sub-disciplines, or multi-disciplines package information. A teacher or librarian in a higher education history course (the example used throughout the paper) may direct students to resources and journals specific to topics the students are pursuing. However, historical scholarship is found in many journal venues that privilege different theories, perspectives, and approaches. The easiest approach is to find journals identified with one's topic—but, any constellation of academic history journals may offer a rich spectrum of journals relevant to the student's inquiry. This paper broaches this concern by introducing disciplinary cultures and their respective characteristics as a lens through which undergraduate history students may understand disciplinary characteristics of the information they encounter and its potential influence on their own scholarly efforts within the class.

2 Approach and Methodology

Disciplinary literacy is grounded in and emerges from Hérubel's definitional model of disciplinary cultures to frame examples of history journals. Ulrichsweb.com was used to ascertain disciplinarity of target journals as well as individual journal publishers' websites for scope and purpose of journals selected as illustration. We also examined *America: History & Life* and *Historical Abstracts* by keyword for discussions of how disciplinary cultures affect or inform findings.

2.1 Information Literacy in the Disciplines

In higher education, information literacy is typically viewed as a general set of information skills that are applicable across contexts. However, it may also be understood in other ways, such as socio-technical [5, 6] or socio-cultural practice [7, 8], in which information literacy focuses on enabling learners to adopt information practices that are a sub-set of the practices within a social context, such as an academic discipline. Drawing different approaches together, the GeST Windows framework suggests that various conceptualizations of information literacy can be seen across a range that includes generic and situated models [9]. A situated approach would encompass generic information skills while also focusing specifically on how information is used within an academic discipline. When understood as situated, information literacy efforts tend to involve engaging students in authentic information practices of a given discipline.

The Framework for Information Literacy for Higher Education [10] produced by the Association of College and Research Libraries (ACRL) is concerned with how information is used within contexts, highlighting information use and production, and how it is enmeshed with ideas such as authority and value. *The Framework* also emphasizes the role of communities in negotiating meaning within a context. However, the *Framework* stops short of closely examining information literacy in relationship to disciplinarity. Contrasting with Simmons [3], who argues for greater librarian involvement, *The Framework* [10] suggests a division of labor in which disciplinary faculty take primary responsibly for teaching higher education students disciplinary information practices. Regardless of who does the teaching, it is important that students understand and engage in the information practices used by the discipline in which they are studying. Farrell and Badke [4] caution that teachers tend to focus on content, and therefore, may not spend course time shedding light on disciplinary information practices. Disciplinary literacy, including an understanding of disciplinary information practices, can guide information literacy efforts to enable students to learn and make inquiries within their disciplines.

3 Information Literacy and History Students

Drawing from disciplinary literacy, a hypothetical course will be used to exemplify how awareness of some aspects of disciplinary information practices can advance the work of undergraduate students studying history. Extending the evaluative aspect of information literacy, applying a nuanced disciplinary lens deepens students' ability to navigate and communicate their scholarly ideas. Undergraduates seeking a degree in history must successfully complete an upper-level undergraduate course in historiography and historical methods. This course covers the history of historical research and scholarship, as well as historical theory, its achievements, controversies, and schools of thought, etc. Additionally, students are introduced to a suite of technical methodologies, as well as theoretical approaches used in past and current historical practice. Primary and secondary resources and scholarship are introduced within the context of the research process. Figure 1 outlines a historical research process students may be introduced to in the course.

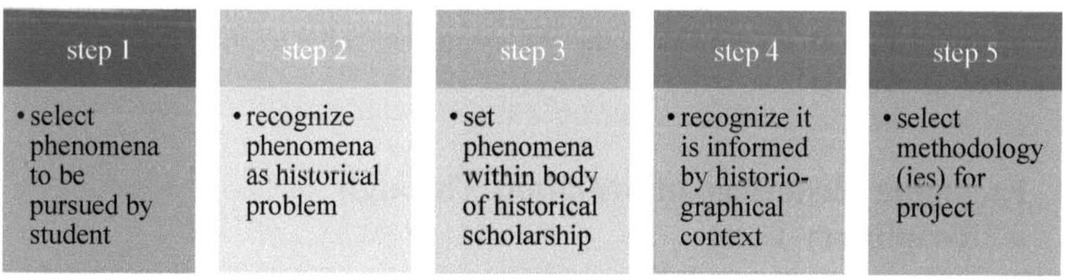

Fig. 1. Historical research process

Instructors typically cover the use of monographs (book-length studies) as well as scholarly journals devoted to history scholarship; however, the larger landscape of history journals, including specializations and methodological and theoretical perspectives, are not typically broached. Consequently, discussion of history journals, and their respective foci and intellectual protocols, must include disciplinary cultures and how different journals influence students' engagement with historical information.

Examining history journals may sensitize students to the richly layered and far-ranging intellectual concerns of historical research.

For methodological purposes, history students need to be both cognizant and capable of discerning these characteristics to practice historical inquiry successfully. Teachers need to introduce students to the plethora of journal scholarship, which invites them to experience historical research within a larger intellectual context. Teachers may introduce a suite of history journals with various specializations and characteristics of different approaches, methodologies, and so forth. Students are then asked to identify and articulate different disciplinary orientations represented by these journals. When disciplinary cultures are introduced, questions of finding appropriate information and analytical comprehension become a central concern in student learning. Students must understand that the proliferation of history journals indicates the presence of rich epistemologies, approaches, and historiographical concerns driving historical research. Journals are a reflection of specialization, emphasizing methodological, theoretical, or period and subject foci (see Fig. 2).

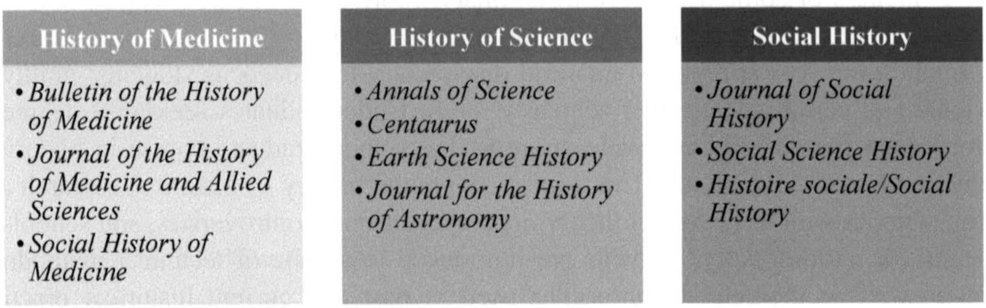

Fig. 2. Examples of specialization of history journals

A proliferation of journals exists alongside general academic history journals purporting to display representative scholarship for the entire history profession. Given this landscape of journals, how does the history student come to grasp the enormity of historical scholarship?

4 Engaging Historical Information Through a Disciplinary Lens

All academic knowledge depends upon academic disciplines, which are responsible for the vetting of pedagogy, research, and legitimization of subjects pursued. Disciplines guide approaches taken, theoretical perspectives and methodologies as well as dissemination of scholarship. Students are exposed to disciplinary cultures through instructors, who filter their teaching and vetting of learning via the spectrum of disciplinary alignments (see Fig. 3).

Recognizing these kinds of disciplinary approaches will influence the information students gather and inform their research activities. Introducing students to the ideas in the model outlined in Fig. 3 allows them to acknowledge disciplinary, and especially

Disciplinary	Subdisciplinary	Interdisciplinary	Multidisciplinary
• A highly defined approach with specific methodological and technical characteristics. Specialized nomenclature and consensus-driven protocols and procedures. • ***Examples-- History, Philosophy*** • ***Journal Examples-- American Historical Review; Revue Historique***	• A highly specialized approach within a disciplinary framework with specific objectives, utilizing unique methodologies and techniques. • ***Examples-- History of Science, History of Education*** • ***Journal Examples-- History of Science; History of Education Quarterly***	• Two or more disciplines come together to examine a topic or set of topics and meld into a permanent relationship. • ***Examples-- Historical Sociology, Historical Anthropology*** • **Journal Examples--** ***Journal of Interdisciplinary History; Cultural & Social History***	• Two or more disciplines providing unique perspectives to explore phenomena, while retaining their singular characteristics. • **Examples—Latin American Studies, American Studies** • **Journal Examples--** ***Journal of Canadian Studies; Middle Eastern Studies***

Fig. 3. Typology of disciplinary formations [11]

epistemological, orientations addressing what it means to find and interpret history journal articles, analyze those articles, and determine how historians privilege various perspectives. Once a topic is chosen, the student is exposed to an in-depth approach to journals and their respective disciplinary orientations—specifically, how each journal privileges its unique/particular position within an ecology of disciplinary orientations. As outlined in Fig. 4, each journal presents the student with a set of characteristics that address that journal's emphases, distinguishing it from other journals.

American Historical Revew	Social Science History	Journal of Modern History
• general, all periodizations • not highly specialized • not geographically-based • larger focused studies • no modeling • narative-based • low usage of data & statistical visualizations	• informed by social sciences • modeling • data & statistically oriented • social scientific theories imployed • high usage of data & statistical vizualizations	• European focused • from Renaissance to 20th century • all fields & specializations • no model or social science theory • low usage of data & statistical visualizations

Fig. 4. Characteristics of history journals

The challenge for students is to develop an appreciation for history journals other than what is easily accessible. This is particularly true for social history, history of science and technology, and cultural history, among other interest concentrations. The more complex the historical phenomena, the more a student will encounter journals incorporating various disciplinary approaches. Reflective of the intellectual fermentation occurring in historical studies, students may be asked to examine journal statements which typically outline the disciplinary approaches emphasized by a specific journal:

> ...the official peer-reviewed journal of the Social History Society (SHS), aims to address disciplinary shifts, and create a dialogue between social and cultural historians. The journal emphasizes the ways the 'social' and 'culture' are mutually constitutive and that study of one enables a deeper understanding of the other. The *and* in our title is important: all submissions to the journal should aim to contribute to the understanding of both cultural and social history.—***Cultural and Social History***

> ...founded to employ the methods and insights of other disciplines in the study of past times and to bring a historical perspective to those other disciplines. JIH still publishes methodologically innovative articles and reviews in the "new history" style that it pioneered and has now developed for twenty-five years–successfully integrating a variety of topics without limit to a particular geographical area or chronological period. In the past few decades, historians have begun to see how disciplines asking similar questions can influence and borrow from one another. History is not merely the sum of "facts"–famous names, dates, inventions, and battles–presented in chronological order. The understanding of people's belief systems, the practices and institutions that supported those beliefs, the way human beings nourished and protected their lives, the economic activities that sustained them, the conflicts that arose from such activities, the processes of resolving those conflicts–these are what motivate particular historical questions.—***The Journal of Interdisciplinary History***

> ...advances the study of the past, publishing peer-reviewed original articles that combine empirical research with theoretical work, undertake comparisons across time and distance, or contribute to the development of quantitative or qualitative methods of analysis. The interdisciplinary research community of social scientists – historians, sociologists, economists, political scientists, anthropologists, and geographers – that form the membership of the Social Science History Association and its research networks benefit from the high-quality articles provided by the journal.—***Social Science History***

Academic history privileges the analytical over the narrative, often assuming knowledge grounded in epistemologies informed by social science disciplines, (e.g. economics, political science, anthropology or sociology), as well as humanities, (e.g. literary studies, philosophy, art history). For example, if students were seeking social history or history of science they would encounter history journals utilizing various insights, approaches, and theoretical perspectives that challenge their preconceived notions of history as narrative—story telling. Various configurations appear—

- subdisciplines, such as:
  - economic history
  - history of education
  - history of science & technology
  - visual anthropology
- interdisciplines, such as:
  - visual studies
  - historical sociology

- multidisciplines, such as:
  - American studies
  - medieval studies.

As exemplified for social history in Fig. 5, disciplinary cultures are even more articulated when examined further.

Fig. 5. Approaches and perspectives related to social history

Successful historical research and comprehension of disciplinary cultures demand an ability to find and articulate the findings within a spectrum of disciplinary approaches found in history journals. The above examples of disciplinary cultures illustrate both nuances and approaches, as well as possible methodologies, and techniques borrowed from other non-history disciplines. To express this more granularly, Fig. 6 demonstrates synergies that may influence what the student interprets from his or her reading of a journal article.

A student researching medieval Burgundian agriculture may find studies replete with nomenclature, sociological theory based modeling, as well as cartographic and data display, which is as important as the article's narrative analysis and conclusions. Various articles will privilege certain key emphases, while focusing on particular insights. Medieval agricultural economies present the student with many epistemological problems and can be approached via different disciplines and methodologies. Consequently, the student will need to read and analyze articles that may influence their

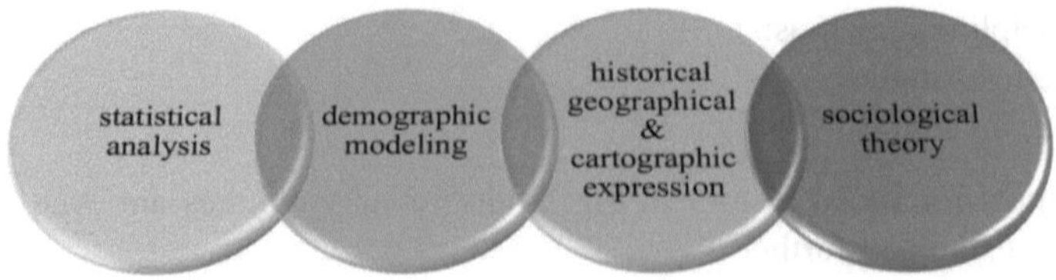

Fig. 6. Elements found in an article on medieval agricultural production in Burgundy

information gathering. Depending upon the student's comprehension of disciplinary borrowings, consultation with disciplinary and/or information literacy instructors is paramount.

What are the consequences of using various history journals and respective emphases? Retrieving and selecting relevant journals and utilization of articles as references for papers and presentations is firmly grounded in historiography and historical methodologies: historiography framing the student's argumentation within the formal context of previous historical scholarship, and utilization of theories, methodologies, and techniques. Without a sound understanding of how disciplinary influences affect their research project, students may not be able to find and evaluate appropriate materials. Improper or misappropriation of ideas contained in articles may actually distort and deform a student's argument, and referencing articles with minimal intellectual relevance can only delegitimize a student's efforts. Therefore, teachers should introduce disciplinary literacy as an essential animating approach to information usage in historical scholarship.

An important caveat beyond the retrieval of articles is the need to examine the journal's purpose and focus; each issue contains the general statement and protocols identified with the journal's *raison d'etre*. Appropriation of various terminology associated with disciplinary specializations may influence a student's findings and argument. If students are unaware of its meaning, the inappropriate use of terminology may undermine the intent or argument of a paper. Making students aware of the disciplinary aspects of how information is created and disseminated advances learning in the historiography and historical methods course, and sensitizes students to the world of academic journals in all disciplinary areas.

5 Concluding Observations

This paper frames the necessity to understand disciplinary cultures and their unique protocols of theories, methodologies, and techniques. Enculturation to disciplinary cultures, including an understanding of the influence of disciplinarity on the dissemination of scholarship, offers students a rich ground for engaging with information to accomplish successful research in the field of history. Expanding the concept of authority put forth in information literacy models (e.g., ACRL 2015), recognizing how history journals reflect varying historical specialization further frames the diversity of possible approaches to any given subject or historical problem. How the student interprets the problem, and the array of possible methodologies, theories, and techniques open to them, influences their argumentation, and results.

This paper establishes the necessity of sensitizing students to disciplinary literacy when learning to use information to recognize and utilize journal literature effectively. Student discernment of disciplinary characteristics allows them to achieve a more nuanced understanding of historical knowledge and its dissemination in the journal literature. Future work includes developing an articulated and nuanced approach to enabling students to understand journal literature using concrete examples. This will include a project focused on the history of education that will showcase disciplinary literacy as a intermediary lens within the larger context of information literacy. History is only one example of using disciplinary literacy, as this approach can be used to foster elements of information literacy in other disciplinary venues.

References

1. Hérubel, J.-P.V.M.: Being undisciplined; or traversing disciplinary configurations in social science and humanities databases: conceptual considerations for interdisciplinarity and multidisciplinarity. In: Witt, S.W., Rudasill, L.M. (eds.) Social Science Libraries: Interdisciplinary Collections, Services, Networks, pp. 25–39. De Gruyter (IFLA Pub.), Berlin (2010)
2. Hérubel, J.-P.V.M.: Disciplinary morphologies, interdisciplinarities: conceptualizations and implications for academic libraries. In: Mack, D.C., Gibson, C. (eds.) Interdisciplinarity and Academic Libraries: ACRL Publications in Librarianship, No. 66, pp. 17–53. ACRL, Chicago (2012)
3. Simmons, M.H.: Librarians as disciplinary discourse mediators: using genre theory to move toward critical information literacy. Port. Libr. Acad. **5**, 297–311 (2005)
4. Farrell, R., Badke, W.: Situating information literacy in the disciplines: a practical and systematic approach for academic librarians. Ref. Serv. Rev. **43**, 319–340 (2015)
5. Marcum, J.W.: Rethinking information literacy. Libr. Q. **72**, 1–26 (2002)
6. Talja, S., Tuominen, K., Savolainen, R.: "Isms" in information science: constructivism, collectivism and constructionism. J. Doc. **61**, 79–101 (2005)
7. Lloyd, A.: Framing information literacy as information practice: site ontology and practice theory. J. Doc. **66**, 245–258 (2009)
8. Lloyd, A.: Information Literacy Landscapes: Information Literacy in Education, Workplace and Everyday Contexts. Chandos, Oxford (2010)
9. Lupton, M., Bruce, C.S.: Windows on information literacy worlds: generic, situated and transformative perspectives. In: Lloyd, A., Talja, S. (eds.) Practicing Information Literacy: Bringing Theories of Learning, Practice and Information Literacy Together, pp. 4–27. Charles Sturt University, Wagga (2010)
10. Association of College and Research Libraries (ACRL).: Framework for Information Literacy for Higher Education. ACRL, Chicago (2015). http://www.ala.org/acrl/standards/ilframework
11. Hérubel, J.-P.V.M.: Subject specialization and subject dispersion in historical scholarship: qualitative preliminary explorations in disciplinary cultures. COLLNET J. Scientometr. Inf. Manag. **6**, 131–144 (2012)

A Model of Collaboration Building Between Teaching Faculty and Librarians at Earlham College: Viewed from Educational Development and Relationship Marketing

Tayo Nagasawa(✉)

DHIER/Research Development Office of University Library, Mie University, Tsu, Japan
nagasawa.tayo@mie-u.ac.jp

Abstract. Regarding collaboration building between teaching faculty and librarians in university education, there were a large number of practical reports on information literacy instruction projects in collaboration with teaching faculty. However, most studies did not focus on analyses of teaching faculty-librarian relationships in themselves, and few explained those relationships in terms of conceptual or theoretical frameworks. The purpose of this paper is to explain collaboration building between teaching faculty and librarians from the viewpoints of conceptual and theoretical frameworks. A grounded theory regarding collaboration building, which was constructed based on a case study of Earlham College in the United States, was interpreted in terms of educational development. As a result, librarians' strategic approaches were located not only in instructional development which was concerned with enhancing course design, but also in relationship marketing which focused on building long-term relationships with customers in order to facilitate mutual value creation.

Keywords: Faculty-librarian relationship · Collaboration
Information literacy instruction · Grounded theory · Educational development
Relationship marketing · Earlham College

1 Introduction

In order that undergraduates build a foundation of workplace information literacy for their future, colleges and universities have considered information literacy (IL) as part of graduate attributes. Librarians had opportunities to join a discussion group about IL initiatives, and approached teaching faculty and curriculum committees so that information literacy instruction (ILI) could be integrated into their instructional and curriculum design. In the context of these educational reforms, a constructive relationship between teaching faculty and librarians should be recognised [1, 2].

Parallelled with collaboration between teaching faculty and librarians in various IL settings on campus, collaboration building with teaching faculty has been studied in Library and Information Science. There were a large number of "how-we-done-it-good" reports and essays with IL settings done in collaboration with teaching faculty [3]. Most studies did not focus on teaching faculty-librarian relationships in themselves, however,

S. Kurbanoğlu et al. (Eds.): ECIL 2017, CCIS 810, pp. 654–664, 2018.
https://doi.org/10.1007/978-3-319-74334-9_67

and few explained those relationships in terms of conceptual or theoretical frameworks. The purpose of this paper is to explain collaboration building between teaching faculty and librarians in university education from the viewpoints of conceptual and theoretical frameworks.

2 Literature Review

Based on a literature review on collaboration building between teaching faculty and librarians in university education, the following points were clarified: (1) the number of research papers on this topic was considerably fewer than the number of practical reports; (2) there were a limited number of researchers who continued studying this topic; and (3) only a few papers applied conceptual or theoretical frameworks [4]. This literature review implied that a more theoretical research should be conducted on this topic, and teaching faculty-librarian collaboration building should be analysed with theoretical frameworks.

Only a few papers have applied conceptual or theoretical frameworks to this topic. Black et al. [5], Machin et al. [6] and Amante et al. [7] analysed their findings in terms of conceptual frameworks, which were constructed by themselves based on literature reviews and their own experiences. Knapp [8], Julien and Given [9], Julien and Pecoskie [1], Phelps and Campbell [3] and Nagasawa [4] analysed their findings in terms of conceptual or theoretical frameworks: Knapp applied social structure in institutional sociology, Julien and Given and Julien and Pecoskie applied social positioning in information behaviour, Phelps et al. applied relationship marketing, and Nagasawa applied educational development in higher education research.

Since a limited number of previous studies applied conceptual or theoretical frameworks, no specific framework was identified as a core framework for this topic. Among conceptual or theoretical frameworks applied in the previous studies, educational development would be a useful framework to interpret collaboration building. Although most previous studies did not necessarily mention it clearly, various approaches and components regarding educational development were confirmed to be embedded in the contexts [4].

3 Conceptual Framework: Educational Development

Educational development is a comprehensive concept which contains instructional development, curriculum development, organisational development and professional development. Instructional development is mainly concerned with enhancing course design to support student learning, and emphasises more technical aspects of developing teaching and pedagogical planning skills. Curriculum development focuses on developing programmes of study such as selecting and designing the courses or learning modules that fit the curriculum and enable achievement of the learning objectives. Organisational development is about maximising an institution's resources to meet organisational objectives and to achieve broad institutional missions by supporting policymakers and decision makers in their strategic planning and implementation regarding learning and teaching. Professional development is concerned with the teaching faculty's development as scholars [10].

Previous studies on building collaboration between teaching faculty and librarians in university education have applied approaches and components concerning educational development directly or indirectly. Black et al. contained instructional development as one of the main strategies to build collaboration with teaching faculty [5]. Machin et al. analysed collaboration building in the process of curriculum development [6]. Based on a literature review, Bruce proposed five dimensions of teaching faculty-librarian partnerships similar to the above educational development approaches [11]. Moreover, based on a systematic literature review, Nagasawa constructed a conceptual framework for collaboration building between teaching faculty and librarians in university education. One of librarians' main strategic approaches was educational development including instructional development, curriculum development and organisational development [4]. These previous studies indicated that educational development could give conceptual lenses to interpret librarians' collaboration building with teaching faculty in university education.

4 Methodology

There is a grounded theory on collaboration building between teaching faculty and librarians in college education. This grounded theory was constructed based on a qualitative case study of Earlham College in the United States, and answered the following research questions: "what are the librarians' main approaches to teaching faculty which librarians could promote to build collaboration between teaching faculty and librarians" and "what are the causal conditions inside/outside libraries which promote collaboration between teaching faculty and librarians" [12]. As a benchmark, Earlham College was selected in terms of purposeful sampling, in particular, maximum variation sampling. Earlham College is a private liberal arts college located in Richmond, Indiana. Since the 1960s, its diverse practices on collaboration building between teaching faculty and librarians have resulted in better student outcomes [13], and have influenced many college and university libraries [14].

The data such as books, articles, interview data, archival records, administrative documents, reports, dissertations, data on physical artifacts, and observation data were collected between March 2004 and September 2014, and analysed by open-, axial- and selective-coding using an inductive method, in particular, a grounded theory approach [15]. As a result of the analysis, a grounded theory was constructed. This Earlham model consisted of categories including librarians' strategic approaches and intervening conditions. As categories of librarians' strategic approaches, "customised ILI", "instructional support for teaching faculty" and "interpersonal communications" were discovered. As intervening conditions, "leadership of library directors", "librarians as instructors", "librarians' faculty status", "small community", "flat hierarchy" and "teaching faculty as educators" were discovered [12] (Fig. 1). In order to complete a grounded theory, the Earlham model was analysed in terms of conceptual and theoretical frameworks including educational development.

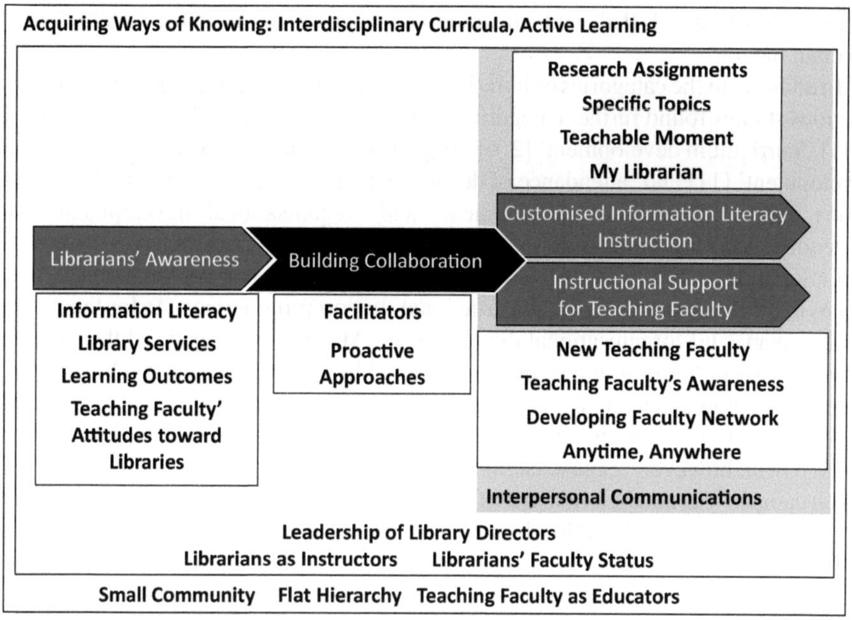

Fig. 1. The Earlham model

5 Results and Discussion

5.1 Librarians' Strategic Approaches

Concerning categories of librarians' strategic approaches, the Earlham model consisted of "customised ILI", "instructional support for teaching faculty" and "interpersonal communications". Based on a literature review and their own experiences, Black et al. constructed a 'Librarian-faculty collaboration model' in order to integrate customised ILI into courses. Librarians took opportunities to 'build relationships' with teaching faculty such as sending library newsletters and visiting their offices. In addition, librarians provided 'faculty development' workshops with teaching faculty in collaboration with educational development units on campus [5]. These approaches were entirely the same as "customised ILI", "instructional support for teaching faculty" and "interpersonal communications" in the Earlham model. Regarding "instructional support for teaching faculty", Bruce also proposed 'academic development partnerships', where librarians engaged in learning initiatives or faculty development programmes mostly in collaboration with institutional academic department units [11]. As for "interpersonal communications", based on a literature review, their own experiences and focus group interviews with teaching faculty, Amante et al. proposed 'the Librarian-library/faculty relationship model'. One of the components was 'communication', which played a key role in personalised contact and in establishing channels to facilitate interaction, and influenced on '[teaching faculty's] trust in librarians and library services' [7]. This was similar to "interpersonal communications" which was located in an infrastructure to promote "customised ILI" and "instructional support for teaching faculty" in the Earlham model.

In addition to the categories of librarians' strategic approaches in the Earlham model, previous studies found further categories such as 'working with other campus units' [5, 6, 11], 'curriculum development' [2, 6], 'organisational development' [6, 11], 'research development' [11] and 'attendance of departmental meetings' [16]. Most of these categories except 'curriculum development' and 'organisational development' were embedded in the Earlham model even though they were not extracted as categories: for example, librarians collaborated with other campus units such as departmental secretary offices in the process of designing instructional support programmes. As for 'curriculum development' and 'organisational development', Machin et al. analysed their collaboration process in 'curriculum development', and Shane explained 'curriculum development' and 'organisational development' processes on campus [2, 6]. At Earlham College, librarians were not involved in curriculum development nor organisational development, however, because taking numerous efforts at managing conflicts and politics on campus was not their first priority. Instead, librarians have focused on their efforts in building interpersonal relationships with teaching faculty both in formal and informal settings.

5.2 Intervening Conditions in Libraries, Institutions and Societies

Concerning categories of intervening conditions in libraries, the Earlham model consisted of "leadership of library directors", "librarians as instructors" and "librarians' faculty status". Based on a literature review and her own experiences, Shane proposed 'factors affecting the creating and implementation of a campus-wide IL programme', which meant intervening conditions in order to build collaborations between teaching faculty and librarians in institutional IL settings. Shane's model included similar categories to the Earlham model, such as 'librarian faculty status', 'library directors' commitment level' and 'librarians' leadership and marketing skills' [2]. Based on comparative case studies of three liberal arts colleges, Taylor extracted factors which resulted in successful ILI. These factors were intervening conditions in libraries and institutions. 'Leadership of librarian', which was extracted as the most important factor, was similar to "librarians as instructors" in the Earlham model [17].

As for categories of intervening conditions in institutions, the Earlham model consisted of "small community", "flat hierarchy" and "teaching faculty as educators". Taylor indicated 'size of colleges', which was similar to "small community" in the Earlham model. 'Faculty attitudes, acceptance and utilization of programs' was relative to "teaching faculty as educators" who were interested in teaching and educational development in the Earlham model [17]. Julien and Pecoskie revealed 'unequal power relationships' which was opposite to "flat hierarchy" in the Earlham model, and analysed traditional campus hierarchies and cultures had influenced on this power imbalance [1]. Since Earlham College considers equality and consensus important based on Quakerism, 'unbalanced power relationships' between teaching faculty and librarians, like Julien and Pecoskie indicated, was not recognised. Based on a literature review, Hardesty explained the culture of teaching faculty: teaching faculty favoured facts in subjects and research over process and teaching. Thus, teaching faculty were not interested in working with librarians [18]. These faculty cultures, which Julien and Pecoskie and Hardesty indicated, differed from the campus culture including "flat hierarchy" and "teachers as educators" at Earlham College.

In addition to the categories of intervening conditions in the Earlham model, previous studies found further categories such as 'librarians' attitudes toward teaching faculty', 'teaching faculty attitudes toward libraries/librarians', 'accrediting bodies' and 'IL competency standard'. As for 'librarians' attitudes toward teaching faculty', Julien and Given analysed that such librarians' attitude prevented librarians from building good collaborations with teaching faculty [9]. At Earlham College, librarians' rivalry attitudes toward teaching faculty were not recognised because librarians regarded themselves as playing a different role to the teaching faculty. As for 'teaching faculty attitudes toward libraries/librarians', librarians have struggled to understand such teaching faculty attitudes so that librarians could build good relationships with teaching faculty. Therefore, many librarians have studied 'teaching faculty attitudes toward libraries/librarians' [19]. In the Earlham model, this component was embedded in categories even though it was not extracted as a category. As for 'accrediting bodies' and 'IL competency standard', Shane proposed these factors as external factors which affected campus-wide IL programmes [2]. Since librarians at Earlham College started to collaborate with the teaching faculty in order to contribute to their own institutional purposes, these external factors were not extracted.

5.3 Collaboration Building as Educational Development

In addition to comparison to previous studies, the Earlham model should be interpreted in terms of educational development. The Earlham model showed how, in order to integrate "customised ILI" into courses, librarians built good relationships with teaching faculty based on "instructional support for teaching faculty" and "interpersonal communications". Since the main strategic approaches focused on individual teaching faculty and their courses, the Earlham model was located in instructional development which was concerned with enhancing course design to support student learning [10].

Context and Mission	national, political/institutional/disciplinary
Principles, Values and Ethics of Practice	practice in context/ evidence-based practice/ focus on learning/ collegiality/ values & ethics
Educational Development Units	Institutional mandate/ organisational structure/ role of educational developers/ target audience/ strategies for educational development
Educational Development Expertise	understanding teaching & learning/ understanding academic culture/ leadership/ project management/ development of expertise/ networking at local, national & international levels
Evaluating Practice	Impact of educational development on practices/ effectiveness of educational development strategies/ measurement of educational quality/ scholarship of educational development

Fig. 2. Conceptual framework of educational development

Regarding educational development, Taylor and Colet proposed a conceptual framework. Resulting from case studies of educational development practices in Canada, Switzerland, Denmark, Belgium and France, previous studies on learning and teaching development, and the experiences of educational developers, Taylor and Colet framed this framework which conceptualised the major dimensions of development that crossed cultures, institutions and disciplines. The framework was composed of context and mission; principles, values and ethics of practice; educational development units; educational development expertise; and evaluating practice [10] (Fig. 2). This framework would be useful to interpret components of educational development.

Context. In the Earlham model, "acquiring ways of knowing" as a causal condition was in an institutional context, not in national or disciplinary contexts. Recently, national initiatives to improve the quality and cost-effectiveness of higher education have been influencing educational development practices. Earlham College was not motivated by national initiatives, however. In order to contribute to the institutional mission, which was "acquiring ways of knowing" as the educational objective, librarians at Earlham College started to collaborate with teaching faculty in the 1960s.

Principles, Values and Ethics of Practices. Appreciating and working in the local context was important for educational development: a comprehensive knowledge of the community, a commitment to the priorities, and needs of individuals and groups in the community [10]. Librarians at Earlham College appreciated the potential needs of teaching faculty before approaching them. After seeing the priorities and needs of individual teaching faculty or the College, librarians committed to target teaching faculty with high priority to IL component or ILI. Taylor and Colet indicated knowing one's context required more than passive observation [10]. Librarians at Earlham College shared issues, challenges and resources with teaching faculty and the College based on active participation in the community such as "interpersonal communications" with teaching faculty in various settings. "Librarians' faculty status" helped librarians with participating in all-campus faculty meetings and committees, and, consequently, with knowing the current priorities and needs on campus.

Evidence-Based Practice. As well as systematic use of sound research, best practices raised the credibility and impact of educational development practices [10]. Librarians at Earlham College coordinated with teaching faculty who had successfully collaborated with librarians in their courses, as presenters of instructional support programmes. This meant librarians used best practices in explaining libraries to teaching faculty. It helped other teaching faculty not only with better understanding how librarians could help their courses but also by raising their credibility.

Collegiality. Taylor and Colet indicated educational development was optimised when collegiality characterised individual initiatives and the general relationships among educational developers, teaching faculty, students, administrative and technical staff and academic administrators [10]. Under the context of "flat hierarchy", librarians at

Earlham College have facilitated collegiality as an infrastructure of instructional development based on "instructional support for teaching faculty" and "interpersonal communications". It helped with optimising "customised ILI".

Expertise. As well as being expected to understand teaching and learning, and academic culture, educational developers should identify change agents and their own leadership roles in promoting and sustaining the development of learning and teaching in their academic communities [10]. At Earlham College, librarians approached target teaching faculty whenever signs of changes were recognised. When the curriculum committee had started to discuss revision of the curricula, librarians proposed to the curriculum committee integrating "customised ILI" into new courses in the process. Taylor and Colet indicated regular contacts helped educational developers building visions for learning and teaching on campus [10]. Librarians at Earlham College built these visions based on participating in formal and informal settings such as all-campus faculty meetings and committees, and faculty buffets. "Librarians' faculty status" promoted librarians to participate in the campus community, and "small community" brought opportunities for librarians to communicate the teaching faculty on campus.

5.4 Collaboration Building as Relationship Marketing

The Earlham model indicated that librarians' main strategic approaches were to build good relationships with teaching faculty. These relationships played an important role as an infrastructure to integrate "customised ILI" into their courses. Thus, librarians' strategic approaches at Earlham College were located in relationship marketing as well as in instructional development. Grönroos defined relationship marketing as follows: "Relationship marketing has emerged, or rather re-emerged, as a marketing paradigm. Marketing and management based on customer relationships is seen as an alternative to focusing on transactions or exchanges of goods and services for money. Firms choosing a service perspective as their strategic approach almost inevitably have to focus on relationships with their customers and other stakeholders…" [20, p. 23].

There are many articles which apply relationship marketing in Library and Information Science, such as collaboration building between libraries and library users. There were no articles except Phelps and Campbell, which focused on collaboration building between teaching faculty and librarians in university education, however [3]. Phelps and Campbell have verified relationship building between teaching faculty and librarians in terms of the Trust and Commitment Theory, which was proposed by Morgan and Hunt, and have identified what contributes to and deters from teaching faculty-librarian relationships [3]. In addition, Amante et al. indicated "relationship marketing should be researched and applied to university libraries and, more specifically, to the study of faculty-librarian relations" [7, p. 100]. Besant also pointed out a tenet of relationship marketing became the engines for achieving the library's main values or contributions to the parent institution's purpose [21]. As previous studies mentioned, relationship marketing could also give conceptual lenses to interpret the Earlham model.

Key Aspects of Relationship Approaches. Viewed from service management and marketing, Grönroos proposed key aspects of relationship approaches to customers: (1) service was support for customers' individual processes that facilitated their value creation, and this support was enabled when knowledge and skills were used on resources; (2) the ultimate goal was to facilitate value creation for the customer, which in return enabled the service provider to capture value from the relationship, with service as a mediator; (3) service was a process, where the service provider's resources and the customer often interacted to some extent; (4) as a service provider, the resources of the firm's offering could be of any kind including physical goods, service activities and information [20, pp. 2–3]. In the Earlham model, librarians have supported teaching faculty's individual course design process by means of "customised ILI" so that the course design could be optimised. In the process, librarians coordinated library services such as various kinds of information resources and ILI with assignments and courses. "Customised ILI" resulted in facilitating value creation, which enhanced learning outcomes. In order to design "customised ILI" in their courses, librarians shared goals and means of courses and assignments based on interactions with teaching faculty.

Key Relationship-Based Characteristics. Grönroos also proposed key relationship-based characteristics: (1) the service provider and customer engaged in long-term business contact; (2) the relationship required that the service provider gained insight into the customer's everyday process; and (3) the goal of the relationship was mutual value creation [20, p. 3]. In the Earlham model, librarians engaged in long-term contact with teaching faculty. From the beginning when teaching faculty were hired, "My librarians" have been building relationships and collaborations with the teaching faculty in various settings. Because of the long-term relationships, "My librarians" gained insights not only into the teaching faculty's courses and assignments but also into their personal interests. It resulted in designing "customised ILI" more effectively, which created value for their courses. In order to gain these insights, "My librarians" communicated teaching faculty during their everyday processes such as designing "customised ILI", "instructional support for teaching faculty" and "interpersonal communications". Consequently, building collaboration between teaching faculty and librarians turned out mutual value creation. Since students became information literated, teaching faculty gained to optimise their course design and to enhance learning outcomes. The Library was actively integrated into the education process in the College.

6 Conclusion

The purpose of this paper was to explain collaboration building between teaching faculty and librarians in university education from the viewpoints of conceptual and theoretical frameworks. Based on an interpretive case study, a grounded theory based on Earlham College was analysed in terms of educational development. As a result, librarians' strategic approaches and the intervening conditions of the Earlham model were located in instructional development. In addition, these approaches, which built long-term relationships with teaching faculty for mutual value creation, were also located in relationship marketing. Future research is needed to compare the Earlham model with more grounded theories which were constructed based on other case studies.

Acknowledgements. The author would like to acknowledge people who supported this research: Dr. Ronald R. Powell, emeritus professor, School of Library and Information Science, Wayne State University, USA, for the first direction of this research; the librarians and teaching faculty at Earlham College for their assistance in the field research; the archivists at Earlham College, and the librarians at Wayne State University, Mie University and Nagasaki University for their assistance in collecting documents; Professor Hiroshi Itsumura, Graduate School of Library, Information and Media Studies, University of Tsukuba, Japan for giving advice on this paper.

This research was supported by the Grant-in-Aid for Scientific Research in 2004 and 2005, offered by the Japanese Society for the Promotion of Science (Research Project Number 16700239: Grant-in Aid for Young Scientists B).

References

1. Julien, H., Pecoskie, J.: Librarians' experiences of the teaching role: grounded in campus relationship. Libr. Inf. Sci. Res. **31**(3), 149–154 (2009)
2. Shane, J.M.Y.: Formal and informal structures for collaboration on a campus-wide information literacy program. Resour. Sharing Inf. Netw. **17**(1/2), 85–110 (2004)
3. Phelps, S.F., Campbell, N.: Commitment and trust in librarian-faculty relationships: a systematic review of the literature. J. Acad. Librariansh. **38**(1), 13–19 (2012)
4. Nagasawa, T.: A systematic review on building collaboration between teaching faculty and librarians in university education **77** (2017, in press). (in Japanese)
5. Black, C., Crest, S., Volland, M.: Building a successful information literacy infrastructure on the foundation of librarian-faculty collaboration. Res. Strat. **18**, 215–225 (2001)
6. Machin, A.I., Harding, A., Derbyshire, J.: Enhancing the student experience through effective collaboration. New Rev. Acad. Librariansh. **15**, 145–159 (2009)
7. Amante, M.J., Extremeno, A., da Costa, A.F.: Modelling variables that contribute to faculty willingness to collaborate with librarians. J. Librariansh. Inf. Sci. **45**(2), 91–102 (2012)
8. Knapp, P.B.: The Monteith College Library Experiment. Scarecrow Press, New York (1966)
9. Julien, H., Given, L.: Faculty-librarian relationships in the information literacy context. Can. J. Inf. Libr. Sci. **27**(3), 65–87 (2003)
10. Taylor, K.L., Colet, N.R.: Making the shift from faculty development to educational development. In: Saroyan, A., Frenay, M. (eds.) Building Teaching Capacities in Higher Education, pp. 139–167. Stylus, Sterling (2010)
11. Bruce, C.: Faculty-librarian partnerships in Australian higher education: critical dimensions. Ref. Serv. Rev. **29**(2), 106–115 (2001)
12. Nagasawa, T.: Intervening conditions inside and outside libraries in order to build collaboration between teaching faculty and librarians in education: based on a case study of Earlham College. In: Kurbanoğlu, S., Boustany, J., Špiranec, S., Grassian, E., Mizrachi, D., Roy, L., Çakmak, T. (eds.) ECIL 2016. CCIS, vol. 676, pp. 587–597. Springer, Cham (2016). https://doi.org/10.1007/978-3-319-52162-6_58
13. Hardesty, L., Hastreiter, J., Henderson, D. (eds.): Bibliographic Instruction in Practice: A Tribute to the Legacy of Evan Ira Farber. Pierian Press, Ann Arbor (1993)

14. Grassian, E.S., Kaplowitz, J.R.: Information literacy instruction. In: Bates, M.J., Maack, M.N. (eds.) Encyclopedia of Library and Information Sciences, 3rd edn., pp. 2429–2444. CRC Press, Boca Raton (2010)
15. Strauss, A., Corbin, J.: Basics of Qualitative Research. Sage, London (1998)
16. Henry, J.: Academic library liaison programs. Libr. Rev. **61**(7), 485–496 (2012)
17. Taylor, S.K.: An Examination of Course-Related Library Instruction Programs at Three Small Private Liberal Arts Colleges. Kansas State University, Manhattan (1991)
18. Hardesty, L.: Faculty culture and bibliographic instruction: an exploratory analysis. Libr. Trends **44**(2), 339–367 (1995)
19. Ducas, A.M., Michaud-Oystryk, N.: Toward a new enterprise: capitalizing on the faculty-librarian partnership. Coll. Res. Libr. **64**(1), 55–74 (2003)
20. Grönroos, C.: Service Management and Marketing. Wiley, Hoboken (2015)
21. Besant, L.X., Sharp, D.: Upside this! libraries need relationship marketing. Inf. Outlook **4**(3), 17–22 (2000)

Developing Information Literacy in Interdisciplinary Classrooms: Engaging with Diverse Literacies

Kristen M. Schuster[1] and Kristine N. Stewart[2](✉)

[1] Department of Digital Humanities, King's College London, London, UK
kristen.schuster@kcl.ac.uk
[2] Zayed University, Abu Dhabi, United Arab Emirates
kristine.stewart@zu.ac.ae

Abstract. Preparing students for their masters' dissertations requires understanding their abilities, needs and academic goals. This means faculty should provide multiple opportunities for students to develop and demonstrate information seeking skills and have opportunities to apply these skills to research practices. To contextualize challenges advisors face, this paper will describe methods lecturers can use to support masters level dissertation research in an interdisciplinary department. The challenges of teaching information literacy in a diverse academic environment will also be discussed. Evidence and descriptions will be empirical, but will shed light on the obstacles teaching staff may face when supporting student acquisition of information literacy skills at the post graduate level.

Keywords: Graduate students · Information literacy · Interdisciplinary studies

1 Introduction

Frameworks for information literacy provide a set of guidelines for assessing and improving students' research skills. Namely, they support reflective practices that advisors and students can engage with over the course of a dissertation project. Preparing students for their masters' dissertations requires understanding their abilities, needs and academic goals. This means advisors should provide multiple opportunities for students to develop and demonstrate their understanding of a research topic – either through information seeking or information use. Granted, this is easier said than done, particularly in post-graduate interdisciplinary courses where students will have a wide range of research and writing skills.

Research indicates that students may reach the level of postgraduate studies where they are expected to perform research, but lack basic information literacy abilities [1]. One component of this research focuses on lecturers not regularly reflecting on when and how students gain the ability to meet these standards. During the dissertation process this may be particularly problematic because it could result in students misinterpreting existing research, their research framework, or the methods for interpreting

S. Kurbanoğlu et al. (Eds.): ECIL 2017, CCIS 810, pp. 665–670, 2018.
https://doi.org/10.1007/978-3-319-74334-9_68

their research data. In this light, it is important to provide students with multiple opportunities to demonstrate their understanding of the research process.

Informal and continuous reflective assessment is one way to pro-actively address these potential shortcomings. This requires advisors engage with their students and provide support so that students develop information seeking, evaluation and selection skills that support critical and effective research practices. While it is likely that students have received library instruction at some point in their undergraduate coursework, or even participated in library instruction sessions at the recommendation of their advisor, it is important to augment these experiences with discipline specific knowledge. This is to say, advisors may not be responsible for teaching their students information seeking skills, but they are responsible for supporting the application and continued development of these skills in discipline specific contexts. Engaging with students in informal and ongoing conversations about their practices, opinions and efforts to use information gathered during research encourages them to proactively reflect on the relevance of their research question, and to begin crafting effective research methodologies. Simultaneously, it is an opportunity for advisors to evaluate their methods for providing feedback and support. In the remaining portions of this paper we will describe the dissertation advising process in the Department of Digital Humanities at King's College London. This description will frame a discussion of the ways reflective teaching supports the application of effective information literacy skills.

2 Dissertations in the Department of Digital Humanities at King's College London

The Department of Digital Humanities offers five master's degrees: MA Digital Asset and Media Management (MA DAMM), MA Digital Curation (MA DC), MA Digital Humanities (MA DH) MA in Digital Culture and Society (MA DCS) and an MA in Big Data, Culture and Society (MA BDCS). Four of the MA programmes (MA DAMM, MD DH and MA BDCS) are taught solely at King's College. The MA DC programme is taught at both King's College and at the iSchool at Humboldt University. Each degree program uses different methodological approaches to help students engage with theories of information and manifestations of information in digital environments. For example, the MA DAMM program focuses on identifying and describing the value of asset management in media environments like newspapers, magazines and television. The MA DC programme focuses evaluating and developing frameworks for digitizing and preserving cultural heritage, while the MA DH programme focuses on methods for engaging in computational humanities research and work. Lastly, the MA DCS and MA BDCS use digital methodologies to investigate trends in social networks and information systems. Each program requires students complete a dissertation.

The Department of Digital Humanities student handbook describes the dissertation in broad terms: "The individual project and dissertation is a compulsory part of the MA… Each student will undertake a research project in an area related to one or more of the modules they are taking. Each student will be assigned a member of staff as dissertation Supervisor" [2, para 7]. Although the guidelines indicate that students should draw on topics they have explored in their coursework, they are encouraged to look beyond these topics and develop original research. Thus, it is important that students articulate how their topic relates to their course of study. This academic year, dissertation topics range from studies of media convergence in Chinese news industries, case studies of metadata and knowledge organization systems in digital palaeography projects and critical assessments of social media platform end-user agreements.

There is a standard timeframe dissertation advisors use to collect and evaluate student progress. First, students submit a dissertation prospectus, which includes a short abstract that summarizes the student's research interests and a tentative bibliography of 15–20 scholarly sources. Advisors review these abstracts and either volunteer to supervise a student, or are assigned to supervise students. In theory abstracts provide a framework for assessing whether students are able to articulate a research theme and understand the function of a research question. Additionally, it is an opportunity to evaluate whether students are familiar with literature relating to their chosen topic. The dissertation prospectus is an opportunity to assess students' existing abilities and is an opportunity to discuss potential research strategies. These strategies typically focus on information seeking and evaluation processes that support developing an annotated bibliography. Providing support when students begin their research is essential, and one way to do this is through supporting information seeking for the literature review.

Completing a literature review and research methodology requires discussing broad topics or themes identified in a dissertation prospectus and refining them. Encouraging students to experiment with different search strategies is important. Instead of simply showing them how to use different library tools in a format similar to one-shot library instruction, it is more effective to discuss search strategies and the use of keywords the student came up on their own, or took note of while reading. Preparing students to describe and analyse the articles, websites and books they will use during their literature review requires discussing these sources and helping students design an outline and writing strategy. Although not required, students are encouraged to write an annotated bibliography. The annotated bibliography is more than an opportunity for students to practice referencing scholarly materials, it is a way for them to practice identifying and describing arguments they believe will support their evaluations of a research topic or theme. Additionally, it is a way for them to practice summarizing (but not necessarily paraphrasing) scholarship in relation to their own interests. Students who complete their annotated bibliography are in a position to reflect on and revise the research question proposed in their dissertation prospectus. This process of reflection is an opportunity for students to flesh out their annotations for their literature review. Additionally, their description of scholarly research presents an opportunity for them to identify different research methods, and to select a methodology that will support sampling and data analysis.

Given the diversity of topics and varying levels of research experience, dissertation supervisors need to ensure students are capable of conducting data collection and analysis. Supporting students during the early stages of their dissertation project by providing disciplinary expertise while they write their annotated bibliographies and literature reviews is one way to do this. This level of supervision allows advisors to engage in reflective teaching practices. As a pedagogical method, reflective teaching supports ongoing and informal assessment of student work. During an MA dissertation, this level of support is important because students are novice researchers, often with limited information seeking and evaluation skills. The following section will discuss how reflective teaching supports a dynamic implementation of information literacy instruction.

3 Advising and Informal Assessment

Thus, we argue that engaging in reflective teaching allows students to practice a variety of information literacy skills. Information literacy is "firmly connected to instruction around research strategies" [3, p. 45] and as such, is integral to questions and methods for investigating a topic. As the Association of College & Research Libraries [4] notes, the environment of higher education and information ecosystem are rapidly changing, thereby changing the roles of both students and teaching faculty. Students now assist in the creation of new knowledge, which bears great responsibilities regarding understanding and using information and scholarship ethically. The role of teaching faculty has changed in regards to the creation and assessment of curricula and assignments that "foster enhanced engagement with the core ideas about information and scholarship within their disciplines" [4, p. 2].

Although graduate students are a common topic in LIS literature, their role as researchers is not frequently discussed [5]. There is a consensus in information literacy research that identifying a research need is an important first step in the research process, and as Graduate students with thesis requirements will be expected to delve deeper into the literature to identify research questions and fulfil their information needs [6]. This requires greater assistance and training than graduate students not required to perform original research. Given the diverse perspectives on the structure and function of information in these degree programs, dissertation advising requires advisors support students in developing clear research questions and developing appropriate methodologies. Providing support when students begin their research is essential, and one way to do this is through supporting information seeking for the literature review.

Dissertation advising is a process of supporting the development of a research question students can answer. This means it is essential advisors support students' exploration of literature on their topic. While discussing research interests and supporting the development of research questions, dissertation advisors have the opportunity to engage in reflective teaching practices. In the book, *Reflective Teaching in Higher Education*, Ashwin [7] poses some key questions to help guide reflective teaching:

- When did we become aware of particular problems?
- How can we learn from what didn't (or hasn't been) going well?
- What tools and practices have we been using?

This means that advising is (in theory) an ongoing conversation about students' understanding of a topic and their conception of how to investigate it. As such, information seeking and evaluation supports the development of a research methodology. By asking students to reflect on problems and milestones (i.e. achievements) and to describe their information seeking practices, advisors can in turn go through the same steps and reflect on whether they are providing appropriate support.

Encouraging students to produce knowledge, as opposed to simply summarize existing knowledge, encourages them to take risks and challenge the contents and format of different information sources. Dissertation advisors can play a role in ensuring students effectively engage in critical analyses – that is to say, feedback supports a process of refining research questions. This requires regular and informal input from supervisors so that students are receiving discipline specific advice on methods for identifying and negotiating challenges in the research process. Informal and regular feedback still requires planning on the advisor's part.

Assessment is a process of providing students with constructive feedback on their understanding of research materials. Adding to this basic understanding Nicol and Macfarlane-Dick describe feedback as "information about how the student's present state (of learning and performance) relates to [research] goals and standards" [8, p. 2]. In this light, assessment encourages students to connect individual concepts discussed in their dissertation prospectus with broader concepts discovered while writing their annotated bibliography. Biggs describes a similar process, constructive alignment, where "…students construct meaning through relevant learning activities" [9, p. 2]. In the aligned system, teaching methods and assessment tasks align "with the learning activities assumed in the intended outcomes" [9, p. 2]. It is not always possible or necessary to provide rigorous or official continuous feedback. Informal feedback, however, can be just as meaningful and successful in achieving desired outcomes. For example, asking students to share drafts of their annotated bibliography is a way to monitor their information seeking and evaluation skills. It is also an opportunity to reflect on whether they are addressing their research topic appropriately. In this light, informal and continuous assessment encourages students to actively participate in learning processes, and makes the expertise and advise of supervisors' points for conversation and critical engagement with information. Overall, reflective teaching encourages the development of meta-disciplinarity, which in turn will support their understanding and use of research methodologies [10].

4 Conclusion

During the dissertation process, reflective teaching offers an opportunity to identify and frame information seeking and evaluation and use it as a process that empowers students to engage in research. Shifting learning processes from lectures to student participation in no way minimizes the teacher's role in the learning process. Instead, it changes the research dynamic and can encourage students to engage in self-motivated and ongoing assessment and feedback processes. The aforementioned responsibilities of both students and advisors become more complex in an interdisciplinary environment due to variations in concepts, commonly accepted vocabulary and research orientations. This requires students negotiate a wide range of standards for information seeking and use, and advisors engage in reflective teaching practices and meaningful assessments to identify challenges encountered by students regarding internal contexts (e.g. extent of student knowledge and level of experience) and external contexts (e.g. information seeking behaviours and abilities) [11].

References

1. Conway, K.: How prepared are students for postgraduate study? A comparison of the information literacy skills of commencing undergraduate and postgraduate information studies students at Curtin University. Aust. Acad. Res. Libr. **42**, 121–135 (2011)
2. King's College London, Department of Digital Humanities.: Student Handbook (2017). https://www.kcl.ac.uk/artshums/depts/ddh/study/handbook/assessment/taught/dissertation.aspx
3. Lloyd, A.: Information Literacy Landscapes. Chandos Publishing, Oxford (2010)
4. Association of College and Research Libraries. http://www.ala.org/acrl/standards/ilframework
5. Exner, N.: Research information literacy: addressing original researchers' needs. J. Acad. Res. **40**, 460–466 (2014)
6. Rempel, H.G.: A longitudinal assessment of graduate student research behavior and the impact of attending a library literature review workshop. Coll. Res. Libr. **71**, 532–547 (2010)
7. Ashwin, P. (ed.): Reflective Teaching in Higher Education. Bloomsbury, London (2015)
8. Nicol, D.J., Macfarlane-Dick, D.: Formative assessment and self-regulated learning: a model and seven principles of good feedback practices. Stud. High. Educ. **31**, 199–218 (2006)
9. Biggs, J.: Aligning teaching for constructing learning. The Higher Education Academy (2003). https://www.heacademy.ac.uk/knowledge-hub/aligning-teaching-constructing-learning
10. Winberg, C., Barnes, V., Ncube, K., Tshinu, S.: Postgraduate students' experiences in interdisciplinary research studies. S. Afr. J. High. Educ. **25**, 1003–1020 (2011)
11. Newby, J.: Entering unfamiliar territory: building an information literacy course for graduate students in interdisciplinary areas. Ref. User Serv. Q. **50**, 224–229 (2011)

Information Literacy in K-12

A Performance-Based Test for Assessing Students' Online Inquiry Competences in Schools

Eero Sormunen[1(✉)], Roberto González-Ibáñez[2], Carita Kiili[3], Paavo H. T. Leppänen[4], Mirjamaija Mikkilä-Erdmann[5], Norbert Erdmann[5], and María Escobar-Macaya[2]

[1] Faculty of Communication Sciences, University of Tampere, Tampere, Finland
eero.sormunen@uta.fi
[2] Departamento de Ingeniería Informática, Universidad de Santiago de Chile, Santiago, Chile
{roberto.gonzalez.i,maria.escobarm}@usach.cl
[3] Department of Education, University of Oslo, Oslo, Norway
c.p.s.kiili@iped.uio.no
[4] Department of Psychology, University of Jyväskylä, Jyväskylä, Finland
paavo.ht.leppanen@jyu.fi
[5] Department of Teacher Education, University of Turku, Turku, Finland
{mirmik,nwmerd}@utu.fi

Abstract. In this paper, we introduce a performance-based test for measuring adolescents' competences in online inquiry. The test covers four competence dimensions: (1) searching and selecting relevant sources, (2) identifying the main ideas presented in the sources, (3) evaluating the credibility of the sources, and (4) synthesizing information across the sources. We implement a technological solution called NEURONE to carry out this routine. The scoring of the test data is demonstrated by presenting preliminary results of a case study. Finally, we discuss the strengths and limitations of the test.

Keywords: Online inquiry competences · Information literacies
Performance-based tests · Schools · Pupils

1 Introduction

The breakthrough of the Web in the late 1990s gave a boost for research on information literacy (IL). The enormous and ever expanding information resources of the Internet gave new potential to develop online research as an integrated element of learning [1]. The heterogeneity and complexity of Web information resources directed the interests of various research communities on the issues of efficient searching and critical evaluation of information [2]. Skills related to online research and learning became a genuine multidisciplinary research field.

This paper aims to contribute to IL research by introducing a performance-based online test designed to measure online inquiry competences. Performance assessments are characterized by the use of open-ended tasks and complex problems that require

S. Kurbanoğlu et al. (Eds.): ECIL 2017, CCIS 810, pp. 673–682, 2018.
https://doi.org/10.1007/978-3-319-74334-9_69

students to display their skills in several types of performance that usually focuses on higher-order skills [3]. Our assessment, targeted for adolescents, measures skills needed when solving a problem with online information. We will introduce the main elements of the assessment and a case study that helps to understand how students' skills are evaluated. The assessment aims at providing timely information of students' skills for improving instructions both in classrooms and in school libraries.

2 Approaches to Assess Online Inquiry Competences

Assessment approaches for IL are divided into three main categories [4]: (1) Fixed-choice tests are good for measuring students' acquisition of declarative knowledge. McCulley [5] calls fixed-choice instruments knowledge tests. The strength of this approach is that data collection is easy to administer in large volumes and scoring can be automated. (2) Performance assessments (or performance tests) require students to apply their knowledge and skills with tasks simulating the real world tasks. (3) Rubrics are scoring tools for qualitative rating of authentic, often complex student work. Rubrics and performance tests are not exclusive categories since rubrics can also be applied in scoring performance tests.

2.1 Information Literacy Tests

Library institutions in higher education have actively developed fixed-choice tests, such as SAILS [6] applying the IL competency standards. However, there have been only a few attempts to develop instruments to measure younger students' skills. Some fixed-choice tests of IL skills have been developed for primary or secondary students [7, 8]. We did not find any examples of performance tests in the LIS literature.

Fixed-choice tests, such as SAILS, have been systematically validated and are widely used but suffer from three basic limitations: (1) They measure what the student knows rather than what she/he can do; (2) They are strongly contextualized into the library environment neglecting the Web as an information and learning environment; (3) Only limited attention is given to the information use [9].

2.2 Online Research and Comprehension

In educational sciences, research on literacies has increasingly begun to explore online research and comprehension [10, 11]. Online research and comprehension refers to the Web-based activities of locating, critically evaluating, synthesizing, and communicating information when students solve an open-ended problem with the help of online information [10]. Thus, this approach overlaps with IL but research focuses only on skills needed on the Internet environment. This line of research has designed, implemented and applied performance-based assessment for increasing our knowledge on students' online inquiry skills [12].

2.3 Evaluation of Information Interactions

Research on task-based information interaction [see 13] offers a solid theoretical ground to develop tests for IL with authentic or simulated tasks. Further, experimental studies on interactive information retrieval process provide us with models and tools to capture and analyze search logs. Systems, such as Coagmento, collect users' actions during search tasks. The system can collect actions and their outcomes, such as mouse clicks, queries, visited pages, saved pages, and highlighted text extracts [14].

3 A Novel Performance Test for Online Inquiry Competences

Our literature review indicates that the LIS community has neglected the development of assessment methods beyond fixed-choice knowledge tests. This is unfortunate since present instruments do not help us to understand how students apply their conceptual, declarative, and procedural knowledge in authentic online inquiry tasks. The gap in measuring higher-level learning outcomes obviously limits the possibilities to develop IL instruction. Novel performance-based assessment methods are needed also for evaluating the effectiveness of instruction.

Performance-based assessment designs try to build a balance between natural research design, realism, and control. Various dimensions of online inquiry competences require authentic tasks in which testees can demonstrate their mastery of competences. Tasks completed in the actual Internet would be authentic but lack control of the changes in Internet resources and other confounding factors. To control these it is necessary to build closed test environments simulating the Internet [10].

3.1 Tasks

Though simulated online inquiry tasks are complex, they can be divided into stages or phases which appear quite consistently across tasks [13, 15]. Structuring tasks into stages simplifies assessment since each competence dimension can be assessed within one stage where specific scoring methods can be applied. The test instances can be varied by changing the topic, the sources, or the answer required.

In the assessment, students perform a scenario-based task that measures the interrelated online inquiry skills of searching and selecting relevant sources, identifying important information in the selected sources, evaluating credibility of sources, and synthesizing information across multiple sources. After students have been introduced to a simulated task-scenario, students conduct the task in four phases matching the above listed competence dimensions.

3.2 Developing a Task on a Controversial Issue

To demonstrate our approach, we designed a task on a controversial issue. In the beginning of the assessment, students receive an email from a student representing another school. In the e-mail, he gives a tip to students on how to earn some money for a field trip by making a magazine that can be sold to parents and acquaintances. He also suggests that students compose an article titled "Computer-gaming has both advantages and disadvantages" for the magazine. In the article, students should also give a recommendation on how adolescents should use computer-games. Finally, he asks students to search for three Web sources and write an article on the basis of them.

In the first phase (Search and Selection), the student is required to use a search engine to locate three relevant sources. In the closed test environment (see Sect. 3.3 for more details), the document collection contains only three relevant and 17 non-relevant sources. The content and layout of the relevant sources were designed by the research team to simulate authentic Web pages. The non-relevant pages were directly downloaded from the Web but internal links were deactivated. The non-relevant sources also dealt with computer gaming and related themes but did not discuss potential advantages and disadvantages of gaming to players. If the student fails to find all relevant sources in the first phase, the missing ones are given when he/she moves to the second phase. This ensures that all students have equal chances to succeed in the later phases independently of their success in searching.

In the second phase (Identifying and Collection), the student is asked to identify two text extracts per page which include relevant information for the task. The aim is that the student reads the relevant sources and tries to make sense of their content. The relevant sources were designed to approach the topic from different perspectives: health, learning, and aggressive behaviour. The sources varied in their argumentation so that one source presents supportive reasons, one counter-reasons, and one both. The student highlights the fragments of text considered as the most important.

In the third phase (Critical Evaluation), the student is asked to evaluate the credibility of each source by rating them with stars (ranging 1–5) and to justify the ratings. The relevant pages included three different types of sources: a short newspaper article, a press release of a university, and a blog posting of a medical expert. This was supposed to reflect the wide variation of texts that the Internet offers.

In the final phase (Synthesis), the student is required to compose the short article to the school magazine. The fragments of texts identified in the second phase (Identifying and Collection) were available for the student, and she/he could also visit the pages. Students were expected to compose their synthesis by utilizing all sources, and give a balanced review on the advantages and disadvantages of computer gaming.

3.3 Development of the Test System

To implement the above test, we developed an online environment called NEURONE (oNlinE inqUiRy experimentatiON systEm) as part of the Finnish-Chilean iFuCo project (2016–2018). NEURONE comprises four major modules that assess the following online inquiry skills: search, identify main ideas, evaluate information critically, and synthesize information. These modules are materialized through a set of components, resources, and tools deployed in a controlled environment. The first module consists of a search engine and a navigational system that operate on a closed collection of Web pages. Within this component a user can search for information in a system that mimics the appearance of well-known search engines (Fig. 1). Moreover, Web pages can be explored and bookmarked for later usage. The second module provides access to the bookmarked Web pages and a tool for collecting fragments of text called snippets from the pages. The third module allows users to revisit Web pages bookmarked so that they can evaluate them. Finally, the fourth module provides access to bookmarked pages, the main snippets collected from them, and a form to compose the text that synthesize information found from the sources.

Fig. 1. Snapshot of NEURONE's search module user interface in the Finnish language (Legend: *Tehtävä* = Task; *Mitä piti tehdä?* = What is the current task?; *Tutoriaali* = Tutorial; *Valittuja sivuja n* = *n* Bookmarked pages; *Hae* = Search.) displaying search results. Other snapshots and additional information of NEURONE can be found at http://www.neurone.info.

To better scaffold students in NEURONE, the modules were connected with contextualized instructions and automated tutorials before each stage. Moreover, to increase the engagement within the system, both the tasks and the tutorials were guided by fictitious characters that were represented as avatars.

NEURONE was developed through an iterative process that let us improve its usability, test structure, and content. Specifically, we conducted three pilots with elementary school students. Overall, 38 students from three schools participated in these pilots completing the test in pairs or individually. The analysis of system logs, on-site researcher observations, and users' comments revealed several software bugs and unclear instructions, tutorials, and task guidelines. All these issues were fixed.

4 A Case Study

In this paper, we report the results of a case study conducted in two classes of sixth graders from one primary school in Finland. There were 36 students, 19 girls and 17 boys aged 12 to 13 years. The goal of the case study is to demonstrate the administration of the test and scoring of students' online inquiry competences. Note that the small dataset allows us to make decriptive statistical analysis only.

4.1 Test Arrangements

The test session was arranged at school during a regular 45-min lesson. Before the students arrived to the class, computers were started and logged into the NEURONE system. A researcher read aloud short written guidelines to students before they started the test. Students were advised to work at their own pace but be aware that the system will alarm when the maximum time in each phase is close to the end. Students were encouraged to ask for help if they faced problems with the system. Spare laptop computers were available to avoid potential problems with the school's equipment.

4.2 Scoring

In scoring students' online inquiry competencies, various approaches need to be applied because the assessed data vary from dimension to dimension. In two first dimensions, we applied automatic procedures in the search log data. In two latter dimensions, scoring was based on a rubric.

Searching and Selecting Relevant Sources. In order to demonstrate the utility of our test approach, we score students' performance at this stage through two specific measures. Given the nature of the task (search three relevant Web pages) a recall-based measure is a natural choice. We applied an adapted version of recall as defined in [16]. Recall(s) corresponds to the ratio between the total number of relevant pages bookmarked by student *s* (relevant coverage) and the total number of relevant documents (here three) in the collection (Eq. 1). However, recall alone turned out to be a vulnerable measure because some students learned to select relevant pages by randomly bookmarking pages and letting NEURONE inform when they got a hit. SearchScore(s) is a process-based measure that takes into account students' selection behaviors. It corresponds to the ratio of the total number of relevant documents bookmarked and the total number of pages bookmarked (Eq. 2). The denominator penalizes for the high number of bookmarked pages. We weigh the ratio by five to scale the score between the range 0–5.

$$\mathrm{Recall}(s) = \mathrm{RelevantCoverage}(s)/\text{Total no of rel pages} \tag{1}$$

$$\mathrm{SearchScore}(s) = 5 * \mathrm{RelevantCoverage}(s)/\mathrm{ActiveBookmarks}(s) \tag{2}$$

Identifying the Main Ideas from a Source. To evaluate whether students were able to identify two text extracts that contained main ideas from each Web page, an automatic procedure was launched to compare students' snippets and the actual main ideas. The list of main ideas from each document was identified and compared to the text fragments selected by the student. If students' selections match (partial or exact) with the main ideas of the page, he/she received one point. Additional matches of other snippets with the same idea did not give points. As a result, a student could receive two points from each page and altogether up to six points in this stage.

Justifications for Credibility Evaluations. Evaluation of credibility was scored in terms of the justifications presented by students for their credibility evaluations for each three sources (see e.g., [17]). Students scored two points by presenting at least two relevant justifications, one point for one relevant justification, and zero points if students were not able to present any relevant justifications. The maximum score was six points.

Synthesizing Information Across Sources. This dimension was scored in terms of quality of source-based argumentation. The scoring rubric took into account the following four aspects in students' articles: (1) how well argumentation relied on multiple sources; (2) whether students' source-based argumentation considered both sides (advantages and disadvantages), (3) quality of source-based arguments, that is, whether arguments were complete (playing violent computer games increases aggressive behaviour) or incomplete (playing computer games increases aggressive behaviour), and (4) richness of argumentation. The maximum score was four points.

4.3 Results

Search and Selection. Results show that 11 students (31%) found all relevant pages (Recall = 1), 16 students (44%) found two (Recall = 0.67), and nine students (25%) found only one of the relevant pages (Recall = 0.33) within the given time limit of eight minutes. Recall does not take into account if the student had bookmarked pages randomly. To address this limitation, we applied our second measure Search Score. The average search score was 2.46 (SD = 1.1). Only three students (8.3%) had bookmarked all three relevant pages straight without miss selections (Search Score = 5).

In the group of 11 students, who demonstrated maximum recall (Recall = 1), four students bookmarked eight or nine pages. This indicates that they had not really tried or been able to assess the relevance of pages they had retrieved and opened. Their search scores fell below the average (<2.46). In the group of 9 students, who succeed to find only one relevant page, two measures give equal scores (recall = 0.33; Search Score = 1.67) since none of the students practiced with random bookmarkings.

Identifying and Collecting Important Ideas. The students scored on average, 4.36 (SD = 0.96) out of six points in the main idea identification task. All students were able to identify at least two extracts that included main ideas, however only 6% of them (3 students) were able to score the maximum 6 points. The majority of the students identified four or five relevant extracts. One interesting aspect to note was that the student who achieved the highest score in this stage was among the low achievers in the previous phase according to our search score with only 1.66 points. Students with the highest search score obtained four or five points in the collection stage.

Justification of Critical Evaluations. The results show students' limited abilities to evaluate the credibility of online sources. The total mean score for credibility evaluation was 2.00 (SD = 1.79) out of six points and the mean scores for single sources varied from 0.53 to 0.75 (max. 2 points). One fourth of the students were unable to present any relevant justification to any of the three evaluated sources. Furthermore, only few students were able to present multiple justifications for their evaluations. The proportion of students that presented multiple justifications for their evaluation at least in one of the evaluated sources was 27.8%. Only one student presented multiple justifications in all of his source evaluations. Almost all justifications (n = 75) were confirming the credibility. Only 7% of justifications indicated some skepticism.

Synthesis. Although students performed quite well in the main idea identification task, they had difficulties in source-based argumentation. The mean score on quality of source-based argumentation was 2.06 (SD = 1.07) out of four points. From all students 11% were unable to include any complete source-based arguments into their article. Additionally, 11% of students showed either one-sided argumentation or they relied only on one source in their argumentation. Students may have faced difficulties in deep level of processing of texts that was shown in quite big proportion of incomplete arguments. In total, 22% of arguments were incomplete lowering the quality of students' argumentation. Four points was achieved by 8% of students showing rich and precise argumentation throughout their composed article.

5 Discussion and Conclusions

We argue that the assessment of online inquiry competences is a multidisciplinary research issue, and tackling the challenges of performance-based testing calls for interdisciplinary research efforts. We responded to the call by introducing a test approach that provides new features informed by previous research both in LIS and educational sciences. The notion of inquiry task is bridging researchers in task-based information interaction [13] and online research and comprehension [10]. They provide a solid theoretical ground to the design of test assignments.

Our specific contribution was to apply search log analysis methods developed in interactive information retrieval research [18] to score students' searching performance. To the best of our knowledge, the automatic analysis of search logs has not been used earlier in similar tests. The closed test environment (controlled task and document collection) offers an enormous potential for the search log analysis beyond what can be done in the open Web environment. The analysis may focus both on output variables (e.g. recall and precision) and process variables (e.g. search behaviours such as click-through behavior). For a longer list of measures, see [16, 18].

Expanding the analysis of searching beyond the overall performance scores is important from the view point of developing pedagogical practices. Performance measures tell us the level of searching skills in the tested group of students. However, if we want to develop teaching of online inquiry competences, and especially searching skills, it is more important to know what patterns of searching behaviour make the difference between high and low performers. This is a way to identify unproductive searching practices in particular contexts, design teaching interventions to tackle them, and tools for scaffolding students' learning, for example, see [19].

The NEURONE-Assessment was able to capture a comprehensive set of complex skills with the task that was reasonable in length for younger learners. In the design, we varied different task types. For example, when students were able to select important ideas with the snippet tool instead of the note-taking tool, they were probably not overwhelmed before the last, the most demanding open-ended task. Varying the task types probably also increases students' engagement in the task.

Our case study demonstrated how the novel test approach, as implemented in NEURONE, can be applied at the level of primary education and how the scoring of students' performance in four dimensions of online inquiry competences can be operationalized. We demonstrated what kinds of scoring can be applied in the obtained dataset. We also demonstrated how a rich search log (and overall system log) can be used in quality and validity control.

The study has several limitations. The paper introduces new ideas based on previous multidisciplinary research and one implementation of those ideas. We demonstrated one set of scoring methods without validating them at this point. In the limited dataset, we could demonstrate how the test works in practice. However, the case study does not allow us to generalize empirical results to a wider population.

In conclusion, we have contributed to the development of performance assessments in online inquiry competences. Based on an interdisciplinary approach, we designed, planned, and implemented a novel test for online inquiry competences. Moreover, we demonstrated that our approach can be applied in the field and that it opens promising avenues to develop performance tests which exploit search logs at full capacity and evaluates performance across the entire online inquiry task.

Our work on the performance test continues. About 340 6th-graders in ten Finnish schools performed the test in four topics during the Spring term 2017. In addition, hundreds of Chilean students will take the test during the first half of 2018.

Acknowledgements. The study was part of the iFuCo project funded by the Academy of Finland (grant's no. 294186) and the National Commission for Scientific and Technological Research (CONICYT) in Chile (grant's AKA/EDU-03). The authors thank the schools participating in the study. We are especially grateful to Daniel Gacitúa Vásquez who made an enormous job in building the NEURONE system. We also thank Andras Varga for the layout desings, and Elina Hämäläinen, Nina Kullberg, Mirka Junikka, Teemu Mikkonen and Tuulikki Alamettälä for organizing the tests.

References

1. Kingsley, T., Tancock, S.: Internet inquiry: fundamental competencies for online comprehension. Read. Teach. **67**, 389–399 (2014)
2. Stordy, P.H.: Taxonomy of literacies. J. Doc. **71**, 456–476 (2015)
3. Baker, E.L., O'Neil, H.F., Linn, R.L.: Policy and validity prospects for performance-based assessment. Am. Psychol. **48**, 1210–1218 (1993)
4. Oakleaf, M.: Using rubrics to assess information literacy: an examination of methodology and interrater reliability. J. Am. Soc. Inf. Sci. Technol. **60**, 969–983 (2009)
5. McCulley, C.: Mixing and matching: assessing information literacy. Commun. Inf. Lit. **3**, 171–180 (2009)
6. Lym, B., Grossman, H., Yannotta, L., Talih, M.: Assessing the assessment: how institutions administered, interpreted, and used SAILS. Ref. Serv. Rev. **38**, 168–186 (2010)

7. Majid, S., Chang, Y.-K., Foo, S.: Auditing information literacy skills of secondary school students in Singapore. J. Inf. Lit. **10**, 44–66 (2016)
8. Foo, S., Majid, S., Chang, Y.K.: Assessing information literacy skills among young information age students in Singapore. Aslib J. Inf. Manag. **69** (2017, pre-print)
9. Sparks, J.R., Katz, I.R., Beile, P.M.: Assessing digital information literacy in higher education: a review of existing frameworks and assessments with recommendations for next-generation assessment. Am. Educ. Res. J., 1–34 (2017)
10. Leu, D.J., Forzani, E., Rhoads, C., Maykel, C., Kennedy, C., Timbrell, N.: the new literacies of online research and comprehension: rethinking the reading achievement gap. Read. Res. Q. **50**, 37–59 (2015)
11. Cho, B.-Y., Woodward, L., Li, D., Barlow, W.: Examining adolescents' strategic processing during online reading with a question-generating task. Research Report No. RR-16-32. Educational Testing Service, Princeton (2016)
12. Kennedy, C., Rhoads, C., Leu, D.J.: Online research and learning in science: a one-to-one laptop comparison in two states using performance based assessments. Comput. Educ. **100**, 141–161 (2016)
13. Järvelin, K., Vakkari, P., Arvola, P., Baskaya, F., Järvelin, A., Kekäläinen, J., Keskustalo, H., Kumpulainen, S., Saastamoinen, M., Savolainen, R., Sormunen, E.: Task-based information interaction evaluation: the viewpoint of program theory. ACM Trans. Inf. Syst. **33** (2015). Article no. 3
14. González-Ibáñez, R., Shah, C.: Coagmento: a system for supporting collaborative information seeking. Proc. Am. Soc. Inf. Sci. Technol. **48**, 1–4 (2011)
15. Kuhlthau, C.C.: Seeking Meaning: A Process Approach to Library and Information Services. Libraries Unlimited, Westport (2004)
16. Shah, C., González-Ibáñez, R.: Evaluating the synergic effect of collaboration in information seeking. In: Proceedings of the 34th International ACM SIGIR Conference on Research and Development in Information Retrieval, SIGIR 2011, pp. 913–922. ACM, New York (2011)
17. Kiili, C., Laurinen, L., Marttunen, M.: Students evaluating internet sources: from versatile evaluators to uncritical readers. J. Educ. Comput. Res. **39**, 75–95 (2008)
18. Shah, C., Hendahewa, C., González-Ibáñez, R.: Rain or shine? Forecasting search process performance in exploratory search tasks. J. Assoc. Inf. Sci. Technol. **67**, 1607–1623 (2016)
19. Kiili, C., Coiro, J.L., Hämäläinen, J.: An online inquiry tool to support the exploration of controversial issues on the internet. J. Lit. Technol. **17**, 31–52 (2016)

Lower Secondary School Teachers' Experiences of Developing Inquiry-Based Approaches in Information Literacy Instruction

Tuulikki Alamettälä(✉) and Eero Sormunen

Faculty of Communication Sciences, University of Tampere, Tampere, Finland
{tuulikki.alamettala, eero.sormunen}@uta.fi

Abstract. Inquiry-based assignments are commonly used in information literacy (IL) instruction. However, guiding pupils through the inquiry process is challenging as the school's traditional instruction practices are teacher-centered. Yet, there are teachers who continuously develop their personal pedagogies in IL instruction, but we have very little research insight into that. This paper reports on a two-year longitudinal case study based in the classrooms of a lower secondary school teacher. The teacher and her two colleagues were engaged in enhancing their pedagogical practices in IL instruction. The findings based on interviews and classroom observations indicate that the teachers use various types of assignments and instructional activities for IL instruction.

Keywords: Information literacy instruction · Teachers
Lower secondary schools

1 Introduction

Previous research into information literacy pedagogies indicates that IL receives minimal specific attention in teacher education [1]. Studies among practicing teachers suggest that IL instruction is often weakly designed, concentrates mainly on technical aspects and leaves the crucial stages of the learning process without adequate attention [2]. Although the overall picture of the current situation in schools is overshadowed, there are teachers who continuously develop their instructional practice in IL [3].

Pedagogical models for IL instruction have been developed within library and information science. Guided Inquiry might be one of the most established, research-based frameworks [4]. There is also a body of literature introducing related instructional designs from the viewpoint of teachers' professional development [5]. The problem is that these models have not been integrated into national development projects and are not widely applied in schools.

In this paper, we focus on the micro level: what happens in classrooms where a lower secondary school teacher develops her professional practice in IL instruction. We adopted a longitudinal approach enabling us to study IL instruction in various curricular situations during a two-year period. The aim of the study is to create a better

S. Kurbanoğlu et al. (Eds.): ECIL 2017, CCIS 810, pp. 683–692, 2018.
https://doi.org/10.1007/978-3-319-74334-9_70

understanding of teachers' IL instruction practices and their ways of developing their methods in IL instruction.

2 The Framework of the Study

Most scholars in education acknowledge that teacher-directed instruction as well as the sole use of textbooks and workbooks are no longer meaningful pedagogical practices [6]. Inquiry-based learning is a well-known learner-centered pedagogical approach that actively involves students in their own learning. Inquiry-based learning requires the learner to observe, ask questions, discover gaps in their own knowledge base and study resources to bridge these gaps [7, 8].

The need to improve students' information literacy is closely connected to the progress towards learner-centered pedagogies. Inquiry-based assignments, such as essays, are commonly used in IL instruction since they require independent acquisition and use of information sources. However, adoption of new pedagogical practices is still a challenge for teachers as they have to guide students to work independently in information environments that teachers cannot fully control [4].

2.1 Guided Inquiry

Guided Inquiry (GI) [4] is grounded in Kuhlthau's extensive studies of the Information Search Process (ISP) model [9]. GI is built around the ISP with specific direction for guiding students in each phase of the inquiry process. It is based on the idea that information literacies are best learned by training appropriate information practices in a genuine collaborative process of inquiry.

GI divides the inquiry process into eight phases: (1) open, (2) immerse, (3) explore, (4) identify, (5) gather, (6) create, (7) share, and (8) evaluate. The teacher steers the process with instructive interventions, offering targeted support for the specific phases of the process. GI emphasizes the phases before collecting information (i.e., phase 5). Students are prepared for information gathering by arousing their curiosity, sharing what is already known, building up background knowledge, and exploring ideas [4].

Students are guided to enhance their learning by using three inquiry tools. *Inquiry journals* help reflect on personal learning. *Inquiry logs* help keep track of important information sources. *Inquiry charts* help visualize ideas about the topic being studied. GI applies two types of collaborative forum. The whole class (*inquiry community*) is used to introduce and motivate the assignment and share results. Small groups (*inquiry circles*) are the main forum for learning activities.

GI recommends that teachers and librarians with varied expertise are organized to create flexible teams. Teams plan and supervise the inquiry. The school librarian is a specialist on information resources. Teachers work as curriculum content experts [4].

2.2 Pedagogical Practices in Finnish Schools

It has been argued that teachers in Finland have good opportunities for professional development. Teacher education is research-based and offers teachers knowledge and methods to develop teaching and to solve pedagogical problems [10]. It has been argued that the curricular framework supports the change of practices. However, the mainstream form of instruction has appeared to be quite conservative using traditional instructional methods with textbooks [11].

The Finnish national core curriculum presents the objectives and core contents of all school subjects, and describes the mission, values, and structure of education. Municipalities, schools and teachers themselves draw up their own local curricula within the national framework [12]. This approach provides teachers with an opportunity to take their own classroom context into account.

The national core curriculum for basic education emphasizes the learning goals in *multiliteracies*. Multiliteracies are defined as being competences associated with acquiring, interpreting, producing and evaluating a variety of texts. By definition, multiliteracies strongly overlap with information literacy. Multiliteracies should be developed in all teaching and learning, integrated into all school subjects [12].

3 Research Setting

This paper reports on a two-year case study in the classrooms of a lower secondary school teacher and her two colleagues who were engaged in enhancing their pedagogical practices in IL instruction. Guided Inquiry was introduced to the teachers but they were free to apply it as they saw fit. The aim was to create a better understanding of the pedagogical challenges that teachers face when they apply inquiry-based approaches as an everyday school practice. The research questions of the study were:

1. What kind of pedagogical designs do teachers develop for inquiry-based information literacy instruction?
2. To what extent were the observed pedagogical designs similar to the designs of Guided Inquiry?
3. How do teachers experience their possibilities and success in developing inquiry-based information literacy instruction in their everyday school context?

3.1 School Context

Compulsory education in Finland consists of a nine-year comprehensive school system, from the age of 7 to 16. The first 6 years are spent at primary school under the leadership of a classroom teacher. For the last 3 years, pupils move to lower secondary school where classes are taught by a variety of subject teachers.

This study followed the work of a Finnish language and literature teacher for two years from the 7th to the 8th grade. The lower secondary school studied also serves as a teacher training school in Southern Finland and has approximately 300 students. The school is a part of, and works in close collaboration with, the local university. It functions as an environment for development, experimentation and research for its own employees and university researchers. It can be argued that the school represents the current state of the art in research-based pedagogies.

3.2 Participants and Modules Studied

Data were collected during the 2015–2016 and 2016–2017 school years. The Finnish language and literature teacher (the Teacher for short) taught three parallel classes (19–20 pupils per class). She had six courses with them during the study period. We collected data during the first, third and fourth courses. The courses were chosen as it was easy to see that their learning goals were explicitly associated with IL themes. Two history teachers were also involved since the Teacher organized the third course in close collaboration with a history course. One of the history teachers taught two of the classes, and the other took one class.

The Teacher has a Master's degree and subject teacher education in Finnish language and literature. She has 11 years of work experience in teaching. She has supervised student trainees for five years. The history teachers were experienced teachers with similar work roles.

The Teacher planned and implemented three modules for information literacy instruction. Modules 1 and 3 were part of Finnish language and literature courses (Finnish language for short). Module 2 was integrated into a joint project of Finnish language and history. In module 1 (Sep 2015), pupils made a brochure about social media. In module 2 with history (Apr–May 2016) pupils gave a presentation and wrote a fictive text about the Finnish Civil War. In module 3 (Sep–Nov 2016), each pupil prepared and presented an argumentative speech.

3.3 Data Collection and Analysis

Data were collected through thematic interviews, which are designed to provide insight into what participants know and think about the research question [see e.g. 13]. The first author interviewed the Teacher for the first time at the beginning of her first course in August 2015 and for the final time after the fourth course in April 2017. The themes of the pre-interview were built on the Teacher's earlier experiences regarding IL instruction: what kind of problems she had faced, what kind of development needs had arisen and which Guided Inquiry activities she found useful. In the last interview, the Teacher was asked about her experiences of the whole two-year period: what new things she had experienced, how implementation had succeeded and how she felt that the pupils or the Teacher had benefitted from the projects. The pre-interview lasted 30 min and the post-interview 15 min.

Additionally, the Teacher was interviewed before and after each module. The pre-interviews dealt with the learning goals and the practicalities of the courses. Experiences of the modules were surveyed with post-interviews. The history teachers were interviewed regarding the second module too. The interviews lasted from 15 to 35 min. The Teacher was interviewed separately, the history teachers together.

In order to get an overall picture of what was happening in the classrooms, the first author observed all the relevant project lessons (3–4 lessons per class during the first module, 8–10 lessons per class during the second module, 3–5 lessons per class during the third module) and wrote memos. Lessons lasted 45–75 min. The memos and all the material that was handed out during the lessons were used as a support material for analysing the interview data.

Data were exposed to content analysis. The analysis was divided into two parts; descriptive and analytical. In the descriptive part, data were analyzed based on the research questions and taking the research setting into account. In the analytical part, data were exposed to deductive, theory-guided, content analysis. In the deductive content analysis, the themes are drawn from existing theoretical ideas that the researcher brings to the data [14] - in this case from Guided Inquiry [4].

The transcribed interviews were hand-coded directly into the text documents. The interviews were reviewed with attention paid to the research questions for themes. The observation memos and the handouts were used to support the analysis. Lastly, the themes were interpreted using Guided Inquiry as an analytical framework.

4 Results

The results of data analyses are presented one module at time. Firstly, the themes and goals of the module are introduced. Next, the applied design patterns are presented (1st descriptive part), and compared with the designs of the Guided Inquiry (analytical part). Finally, teachers' experiences are described (2nd descriptive part).

4.1 Module 1

The first module was carried out with the 7th graders during the Fall term of their first year at lower secondary school. The pupils created a brochure about social media for 5th graders emphasizing how to use it appropriately. The Teacher said that the main learning goal was for the pupils to learn to seek information and to apply it in writing for a target audience. Netiquette was the learning goal in the subject content.

Design. The Teacher defined the target audience so that the pupils had to think about how to transform the text from the sources into their own text in order to write clearly enough for younger children. The work was done in pairs so that the pupils would learn to cooperate and to share their knowledge. Group discussions at the beginning of the project aimed to activate interaction and collaboration between pupils. The pupils were guided to use inquiry logs for keeping track of information sources.

Guided Inquiry. The Teacher borrowed the idea of inquiry logs from GI. As recommended in GI, she chose a project theme that she felt was familiar to the pupils and she let the pupils choose their subtopics. The thinking here was to engage pupils in their work. GI also emphasizes that pupils should be prepared to seek information by stimulating their curiosity and interests, and sharing what is already known. The Teacher aimed to achieve this by letting pupils discuss the theme, firstly in inquiry circles and then working together in an inquiry community.

Experiences. The Teacher reported that most pupils seemed to enjoy the project. She thought that the pupils had learned about seeking and using information, as well as about working in pairs. However, the Teacher saw huge differences in how well pupils sought and then used information. The Teacher reported that a common problem was that many inquiry logs were not filled in completely and some others were lost. Most of the pupils finished the project in a hurry. Incomplete bibliographies were one indicator of this hurry. The use of information sources was somewhat problematic. The Teacher saw copying and pasting from Wikipedia. Some pupils used low quality websites as their sources.

All things considered, the Teacher thought that the assignment was probably too complicated. Several things were calling for the pupils' attention at the same time. The Teacher concluded that simpler assignments would be more useful. She suggested that a more concrete example of the end product should have been shown to the pupils. The observations confirmed that the pupils seemed to wait for specific instructions on what and how they should do. The Teacher was not satisfied with the inactive use of inquiry logs (on paper). She argued that an electronic log might have been more effective.

4.2 Module 2

The Teacher cooperated with two history teachers for the second module. It was carried out during the Spring term. In the history course, pupils gave a presentation about the Finnish Civil War. In the Finnish course, the pupils wrote a fictive text which they based on facts learned during the history lessons. The teacher team hoped that pupils would learn to seek and use diverse information sources and to present justified opinions. The Teacher wanted the pupils to learn that seeking information contributes to fictive writing and is a part of it. Learning criticism of sources was set as an important goal by the history teachers. From the pedagogical point of view, the Teacher expected joint teaching units to give more time to the first phases of inquiry and the pupils could then concentrate more thoroughly on the theme.

Design. Pupils' orientation to the theme was emphasized in the design of the unit. The pupils paid a visit to a museum to see an exhibition of the Finnish Civil War before the project started. The visit was expected to perform as a cognitive and emotional trigger encouraging the pupils to think about the theme and inspire them in their work.

The teacher team wanted pupils to learn to manage their sources more systematically and continued to guide them in the use of inquiry logs. The logs were in electronic format. In order to offer diverse information sources to the pupils, the history teachers brought books from their own collections and also gave the pupils tips about useful internet sites. The assignments were done individually for both subjects, but some activities were also done in inquiry circles. In history, the pupils had group discussions about their themes and about how to outline the topics. In Finnish, the pupils gave written feedback to their classmates in the middle of the writing process as well as afterwards. In history, the pupils got feedback from the others at the end.

Guided Inquiry. Some pedagogical designs used in the module were similar to GI. The pupils' curiosity was stimulated by a museum visit, the pupils were free to choose their topics within the main theme, and inquiry logs were used. The pupils wrote their own texts individually but worked at some point in inquiry circles. More time and attention was devoted to the first phases of the inquiry process: open, immerse, explore. The three teachers formed a learning team – as emphasized in GI. GI also encourages the team to offer the pupils a variety of sources as the history teachers did.

Experiences. The Teacher noted that the work done in history influenced the pupils' activities in her class. The pupils chose topics that they knew about and got ideas from the history class. The Teacher felt that the pupils made progress in process writing. The fictional writing process did not require much information seeking as the pupils used information that they had already found for their history work. However, the Teacher saw that some learned about acquiring information for writing fiction.

According to the history teachers, the pupils were positive about the assignment and seemed to find and choose topics of their own interest. The museum visit motivated pupils for the learning task. The history teachers felt that even those who were not initially interested in history showed some signs of engagement. They also argued that pupils paid more attention to the language of their presentations than they usually do. The history teachers reported that pupils learned about subject content, information seeking and evaluation. The pupils who had used the inquiry log managed to synthesize information across sources better than those who had not used it. The history teachers experienced that most pupils' problems dealt with finding and analyzing information. They did not use eagerly the sources offered by the teachers.

The teacher team also noticed that some pupils had difficulties getting started and choosing the topic and some changed their topic if they did not find information at once. Copying and pasting caused a minor problem. Although the inquiry logs were in electronic format this time, they were not actively used.

All of the teachers were quite satisfied with the second assignment apart from the fact that there was too little time for shared activities between subjects at the end. They suggested that a shared launch of the module would have been useful, too. The Teacher expressed that organizing the project in one class at a time instead of in parallel in three classes would be one way to enhance collaboration.

4.3 Module 3

The third module was again a one-subject course in Finnish language and it was carried out in the Fall term of the second school year with pupils who were now 8th graders. Each pupil gave a five-minute speech about a theme of their choice. The aim was to convince the audience of one's message, and to learn to justify one's opinions. The Teacher's aim was that the pupils recognize what they already know about the subject matter and to analyze what kind of further information they need. The Teacher emphasized that seeking information was not the main issue but that it would help to complete the task. The pupils needed information to justify their opinions.

Design. Before handing out the assignment, the Teacher asked pupils to think about what could be improved at their own school, in their hometown and in Finland. She wrote some of the pupils' answers on the blackboard and then explained the assignment. She emphasized that pupils need to seek information in order to justify their message. She prepared worksheets for the pupils to write down what they know about the subject in advance. In addition, pupils were asked to plan what kind of further information they would need and where to find it. Inquiry logs were again used in printed form.

Guided Inquiry. Pupils' own choice, inquiry logs and emphasis of the first phases of inquiry associated the designs with GI. The Teacher wanted pupils to concentrate especially on what they already know and thus emphasized the immerse phase of GI.

Experiences. According to the Teacher, the third module went as planned. Most pupils managed to perform at their own level. They learned about giving a speech but only a few had searched for information for their speeches. The observations revealed that some pupils pondered their topic selection for a very long time. Some thought that they did not need any information or could not search for it. Not all filled in the worksheet. Again, the inquiry logs were incomplete. The Teacher reported that pupils had problems when choosing a topic for their speech, when seeking information and when justifying their opinions. Some pupils had not prepared their speeches at all.

The Teacher felt that she should have emphasized more the importance of seeking information and provided more personal guidance for pupils. She argued that the pupils failed to see seeking information as a learning goal. She suspected that there were too much content in the worksheets. She thought that it might have been better to seek information separately, before pupils began planning the speech. On the other hand, she hesitated to make seeking information a separate part of the process.

5 Discussion and Conclusions

The current study explored how inquiry-oriented teachers develop information literacy instruction as part of their everyday school practices. The practices of information literacy instruction are typically studied in the context of a single teaching unit. We adopted a wider perspective by monitoring how the Teacher taught her three classes during two school years. Data were collected by taking a sample of three assignments, each from a different course. The advantage of this approach is that we could study pedagogical practices in varying curricular contexts. However, all three assignments were part of the same curricular track both for the Teacher and for pupils. We may think that this increases the validity of our data since varying modules and courses shed light on the Teacher's pedagogical ideas and practices from varying angles.

Findings. The results show that the teachers are ready to apply diverse assignments in IL instruction. The teachers implemented four assignments. None of them was a traditional essay. The formats were a brochure, a presentation, a fictive text and a speech. Diverse assignments lead to diverse inquiry processes, activities and guidance.

Guided Inquiry emphasizes similar issues as the Finnish curriculum. Thus, the teachers were partly familiar with them. They devoted attention to the first phases of the inquiry process (open, immerse, explore, identify) and introduced various designs for how to do this. They also gave more space for pupils to choose topics that interested them. Inquiry logs were introduced to the pupils. The pupils worked in different groups and the teachers also worked partly as a team. But, apart from Guided Inquiry, the librarian was not involved. In Finland, different professions tend to be quite territorial and cooperation is not always self-evident.

The teachers experienced that investment of their time in the first phases of inquiry paid off: the pupils seemed to find topics that interested them. They also seemed to gain from cooperation between the two subjects. The teachers saw that pupils who used inquiry logs managed to synthesize information across sources more effectively than those who did not use them. Choosing the topic, finding and analyzing information was difficult for some pupils. Sometimes it was difficult to strike a balance between phases. For example, emphasizing the pupils' own knowledge (immerse) could lead to passivity when seeking information (explore, identify, gather). Technical problems and a lack of IT-skills occasionally steered pupils' attention towards technical issues instead of working on information and writing.

It seemed that not all pupils are attuned to working in a learner-centered way and are waiting for clear instructions. This may affect motivation and cause indifference to the assignments which was evident with some pupils. But, all in all, the teachers felt that inquiry-based learning is a fruitful approach and that the meaning of information seeking is something that should be emphasized to the pupils.

Future Research. The work reported here is part of a broader study. We also collected survey data in the classroom of pupils' online inquiry attitudes, self-efficacy and practices. In addition, the pupils completed online tests which measured their skills in searching the web and evaluation of sources. The surveys and competence tests were carried out at the beginning, in the middle and at the end of the research period both in the three classes taught by the Teacher and in two control classes at the same school. Thus, we can analyse the long-term changes in various variables among the pupil population and compare them with the Teacher's experiences.

Limitations of the Study. The case study focused on one teacher and her two colleagues at a teacher training school. Subsequently, the results cannot be generalized to Finnish lower secondary schools or other schools. However, we may expect that the ecological validity is good since the teachers were planning and implementing their pedagogical ideas as part of their regular work in the framework of the national and local curriculum.

Conclusions. Our concluding remarks are the following: We have introduced a novel approach for case studies on the practices of IL instruction in schools. Our longitudinal approach enables teachers to concentrate on development of the instruction across a long period of time. For the researcher, it helps to dig deeper into teachers' pedagogical practices by exploring IL instruction in varying curricular contexts. The empirical findings suggest that teachers use various types of assignments and instructional activities for IL instruction.

Acknowledgements. The study was funded by the Faculty of Communication Sciences at the University of Tampere, Finland. The authors thank the teachers participating in the study. We also thank our colleagues at the TRIM research center for their constructive comments on the early version of the manuscript.

References

1. Tanni, M.: Teacher Trainees' Information Seeking Behaviour and Their Conceptions of Information Literacy Instruction. University of Tampere, Tampere (2013)
2. Limberg, L., Alexandersson, M., Lantz-Andersson, A., Folkesson, L.: What matters? Shaping meaningful learning through teaching information literacy. Libri **58**(2), 82–91 (2008)
3. Sormunen, E., Alamettälä, T.: Guiding students in collaborative writing of Wikipedia articles – how to get beyond the black box practice in information literacy instruction. In: Viteli, J., Leikomaa, M. (eds.) Proceedings of EdMedia 2014 – World Conference on Educational Multimedia, Hypermedia and Telecommunications, vol. 2014, no. 1, pp. 2122–2130 (2014)
4. Kuhlthau, C.C., Maniotes, L.K., Caspari, A.K.: Guided Inquiry: Learning in the 21st Century, 2nd edn. Libraries Unlimited, Santa Barbara (2015)
5. Kiili, C., Mäkinen, M., Coiro, J.L.: Rethinking academic literacies; designing multifaceted literacy experiences for pre-service teachers. J. Adolesc. Adult Lit. **57**(3), 223–232 (2013)
6. Selander, S., Kress, G.: Design för Lärande – Ett Multimodalt Perspektiv. Norstedt, Stockholm (2010)
7. Hmelo-Silver, C.E., Chinn, C.A., Chan, C.K., O'Donnell, A.M.: International Handbook of Collaborative Learning. Routledge, New York (2013)
8. Chu, S.K.W., Tse, S.K., Chow, K.: Using collaborative teaching and inquiry project-based learning to help primary school students develop information literacy and information skills. Libr. Inf. Sci. Res. **33**(2), 132–143 (2011)
9. Kuhlthau, C.C.: Seeking Meaning: A Process Approach to Library and Information Services, 2nd edn. Libraries Unlimited, Westport (2004)
10. Jyrhämä, R., Maaranen, K.: Research orientation in a teacher's work. In: Niemi, H., Toom, A., Kallioniemi, A. (eds.) Miracle of Education: The Principles and Practices of Teaching and Learning in Finnish Schools, pp. 97–111. Sense Publishers, Rotterdam (2012)
11. Korkeamäki, R.-L., Dreher, M.J.: Early literacy practices and the Finnish national core curriculum. J. Curric. Stud. **43**(1), 109–137 (2011)
12. Finnish National Board of Education. Perusopetuksen opetussuunnitelman perusteet. (National Core Curriculum of Basic Education.) (2014). http://www.oph.fi/download/163777_perusopetuksen_opetussuunnitelman_perusteet_2014.pdf
13. Cohen, L., Manion, L., Morrison, K.: Research Methods in Education. Routledge, New York (2000)
14. Mayring, P.: Qualitative content analysis. Forum Qual. Sozialforschung/Forum Qual. Soc. Res. **1**(2), Article no. 20 (2000)

Information Safety Education of Primary School Children in Libraries

Pavla Kovářová(✉)

Masaryk University, Brno, Czech Republic
kovarova@phil.muni.cz

Abstract. This paper presents the results of evaluation research of a loosely connected series of information safety lessons designed for all nine primary school grades and organized by libraries. All lessons took place in two libraries and in three other schools in the Czech Republic from 2013 to 2017. The author used evaluation questionnaire and participatory observation to evaluate lessons at the first two levels of Kirkpatrick's model. Librarians can use the results as arguments for lesson effectiveness, for transfer of the lessons to other libraries and for planning other information safety lessons according to children's needs. Results have shown that children evaluated the lessons positively. Children actively participated in activities. They liked to share their experience and opinions, but also showed some incorrect preconceptions. The analysis focused on the content of the lessons, the influence of the institution where they took place, the form of lessons, the school teacher and the ways of engaging students.

Keywords: Information literacy education · Information safety Libraries · Primary schools · Research

1 Introduction

Information safety is a part of Media and Information Literacy [1]. The importance of this topic is evident not only from its inclusion in information literacy standards [2] and primary school curriculum [3], but mostly from risky information behaviour of children. A question is, which topics and to what extent are they discussed with children in practice. Information safety is not sufficiently anchored in the Czech primary school curriculum [2]. Only technical basics are covered in the first five grades; more topics (including the first mention of information evaluation) are assigned to the higher grades, but a great number of information safety topics are still explicitly missing (schools can teach them but it is not necessary). Time allocation for the whole information and communication technology education is only one hour per week for lower level (grades 1 to 5 together, not each year) and the same for higher grades (grades 6 to 9).

In the case of children in primary schools (children aged 6 to 15 years) we can identify risk behaviours in the area of obtaining, evaluating and creating information. When obtaining information, students infringe copyright [4]. Another problem may be access to inappropriate information [5]. In evaluating information, the speed of access to information is often crucial, whereas they consider the quality of information only to a limited extent [6]. Information generation mainly concerns communication that is

S. Kurbanoğlu et al. (Eds.): ECIL 2017, CCIS 810, pp. 693–702, 2018.
https://doi.org/10.1007/978-3-319-74334-9_71

often carried out in the Internet environment. Therefore, it is important to include all three components of Media and Information Literacy in primary school education.

Hence, a conception of education for primary school students was developed, which guarantees that students of each grade go through a lesson, utilizable not only in the library, as a way of gradually building up their knowledge, skills and attitudes to limit their risk behaviours. If preventive measures are not sufficient, students should be aware of possible procedures for addressing information safety incidents. All lessons were evaluated according to Kirkpatrick's model [7]. The subject of this paper is a presentation of part of the results covering the first two levels of this model (reaction and learning), based on an evaluation questionnaire and participatory observation.

2 Literature Review

Copyright infringement is considered undesirable but commonplace. Finnish research has found a relationship between the intensity of this behaviour and its perception as acceptable; 71% of adolescents (15–16 years) illegally downloaded a file in the past year; 14% do it on a daily basis, although 60% considered it morally wrong [4]. The reasons for illegal software downloading by children (8-18 years) were mostly financial, but also included the argument that a lot of people do it (33%) [7]. Only a third of the children were convinced that uploading software to the Internet without paying is illegal. Children's access to inappropriate information, such as pornography, extremism, aggression, hate messages, self-harm or drugs, can negatively affect their psychological development [9]. The Czech Republic ranks first among the countries in terms of the number of children who have seen in the past 12 months some of the monitored types of content (43% of children), while it ranks fifth in pornography with 28% of children [5]. In evaluating information, children face the problem of lack of critical thinking in favour of fast Internet access [6]. According to Czech research [10], 33.2% of children on the Internet always tell the truth and, on the other hand, 2.49% absolutely believe what others say about themselves on the Internet. Both figures point to a problem of information evaluation.

The risk behaviour of children when communicating over the Internet lies above all in sharing information that may be misused. Adolescents (10–19 years old) were willing to make public 13 of the 18 items of monitored personal information and less often used privacy settings compared to adults [11]. One-third of social network users do not know how to change privacy settings [12]. One-third of adolescents share their password with friends, and one-quarter do not know that uploaded content cannot be permanently deleted [13]. Even in this respect, Czech children have used the Internet to a greater extent and have more experience with risk factors than children from other European countries. In 2011, 72% of Czech children had a social network profile, with 33% a public profile, and 14% had experienced misuse of personal data in the past 12 months [5]. More than 20% of Czech children (11–17 years old) share personal information, starting from the most common items: name and surname, facial photographs, e-mail, school address, and phone number [14]. Their own "sexy" photographs or videos were posted by 7.41% and sent on request by 12.14% of Czech children [14], despite the fact that 77.50% considered such behaviour risky.

Communication with Internet friends is a practice admitted by 54.30% of children; 26.92% of children said their Internet friend asked them to keep their Internet communication secret, and 40.22% of children would agree to a personal meeting [14]. Children often mistakenly believe that they would know that they are communicating with an adult [15]. The sharing of personal information and the risky behaviour of Czech children is increasing every year [14].

Nevertheless, children may not be just victims; education also plays an important role in preventing them from becoming offenders. In the United Kingdom, 25% of adolescents have tried to break into their friend's Facebook account, even though they were aware that it was wrong [16]. Perpetrators of cyberbullying are often not aware that their behaviour harms others; they consider their behaviour an innocent game [15]. Czech children perpetrators most often use hacking into an account (24.93%), verbal attacks (12.22%), identity theft (8.97%), humiliation through a photograph (6.75%) and threats and intimidation (5.73%) [14].

As far as preventing cyber-attacks is concerned, the most common method according to parents is active mediation (93%). In terms of monitoring (45%) and technical mediation (17%), the situation in the Czech Republic corresponds to the average of the countries monitored. Restrictive strategy, on the other hand, is frequent (72%), but not as much as in other countries [5]. Active mediation including education led to the reduction of risk behaviours and harm to children on the Internet, while technical mediation does not influence risk behaviours [17]. Application of all mediation strategies decreases as children grow older, especially between 14 and 15 years of age [5]. Parents' approaches also vary according to their age, education, and place of residence [18], which may indicate more vulnerable groups. The influence of peers in mediation is also considerable, especially in the Czech Republic [5], which contributes to cooperative learning.

Despite the key role of parents, Czech children in comparison with other countries most often ignore what their parents say about Internet behaviour (54% of children) [5]. This supports active mediation by other entities, including libraries [19–21]. Already in 2011, 6% of children used libraries as a source of information about information safety [5]. Czech libraries offer individual lessons in information safety, however, compared to information search topics, their numbers are much lower [22]. They also actively participate in the international Safer Internet Day [23]. Publications describing experience with library information safety lessons are no longer exceptional (for example see [24–29]). Even though one-off lessons have their value, conceptual solutions were recommended to increase knowledge of responsibility and safety in the digital environment in each grade (K1 to K12) [30]. Previous research has confirmed that libraries, as well as schools, students and their parents welcome the possibilities of conceptual information safety education in libraries [31].

3 Conception of Education in Information Safety

Primary school students often use the Internet intensively [5]. Even when they do not, it is advisable to prepare them in time for the use of the Internet for various purposes, whether obtaining or creating information is involved. As described above, it is necessary to gradually develop the knowledge, skills and attitudes in all three components of media and information literacy, depending on needs and abilities.

The methodology is primarily intended for use in libraries and corresponds to a constructivist paradigm. To increase students' motivation and achieve better knowledge transfer, all lessons use active and cooperative learning; the instructor is essentially a facilitator of knowledge [32–34]. Activities usually presented as a game are based on common situations imaginable in real Internet use by students of a given age. The methods of Reading and Writing for Critical Thinking and the learning framework formed by evocation (reminders of what is already known about the topic), realization of meaning (passing on new information) and reflection (verification of understanding and links between previous and new pieces of knowledge) are often utilized.

Each lesson lasts 90 min (two school units) and is intended for one class. They are designed to require minimal technical equipment. Students leave the lesson with material from the reflection stage for a follow-up with the teacher and with five questions the students should discuss with their parents. The conception consists of nine loosely connected lessons, each of which is intended for one primary school grade:

1. Pros and Cons of Computers: Students should become aware of the positives and negatives of using a desktop, notebook, tablet, smartphone and e-book.
2. Ten Rules of Safe Internet: Children should be aware of basic safety measures when using the Internet and the reasons for their use.
3. Digital Footprints in a Network: The lesson highlights the threats related to communication and inadequate evaluation of information on the Internet.
4. Who is behind the Monitor: Students should categorize information according to the degree to which it can be misused and suitable personal answers.
5. Work with Information Resources: The lesson teaches how to work with printed and electronic resources, including the basics of assessing their credibility.
6. Polyjuice Potion: By introducing social engineering techniques, the lesson leads to a healthy mistrust and recommendations for work with a password.
7. Up and Download: Based on real-world situations and media reports, the lesson presents means of dealing with copyright works in an electronic environment.
8. Detective Stories on Facebook: Using real-life stories, students are informed of Internet threats and possible protective and defensive measures.
9. The Life of a Media Report: The lesson shows the procedures for evaluating media messages (argumentation and possible manipulation).

4 Methods

This paper presents part of the results of the evaluation of lesson effectiveness according to Kirkpatrick's model [7]. It focuses on reaction and learning. All lessons were realized in two different libraries (one in a small town, one in a big one, each cooperating with one school) and in three other schools in the period from 2013 to 2017. The libraries and schools were selected by purposive sampling. Libraries have been cooperating with schools for several years and are active in information literacy education. Two of the other schools collaborate with libraries on lessons held on their premises. But both libraries and schools did not cover the topics of information safety prior to the research. For the third school it was the first experience with a lesson by a librarian. Lessons were given by the author or by a librarian in the presence of the author as a third-party observer. Most of the lessons were attended by teachers of the class, in some cases (higher grades) they actively participated in the lesson.

There were 59 observations in total (numbers for each lessons are shown in Table 1). Observation was documented in the form of field notes. An analysis of these notes resulted in five thematic areas being defined: location of the lessons, the primary school teacher, the form of lessons, work of individual students and the choice of the subject. Given the objective of this paper, partial findings revealed through individual activities are not specified; instead the paper presents general findings about students' attitudes regarding the issue of information safety as such and whether their response corresponded to the reasons behind their use (e.g., connection to real Internet experiences).

Table 1. Number of observations and students for each lesson

Lesson	Observations	Students	Lesson	Observations	Students
1	7	124	6	8	190
2	9	238	7	2	48
3	8	193	8	4	115
4	15	366	9	2	42
5	4	82	Total	59	1398

Smile sheets as a form of evaluation questionnaire were used in lessons provided between 2015 and 2017. We used a simple questionnaire where each student wrote a comma under one of three smilies (smiling, neutral, frowning). Smile sheets with a greater number of commas than the total number of students were discarded.

5 Results

Basic lesson evaluation at the level of reaction according to Kirkpatrick's model [7] was revealed by smile sheets. The overall assessment of lessons is shown in Table 2.

Students generally evaluated the lessons positively; however, according to the teachers, the worse ratings by students in higher grades were due to a more critical view that older students have of any form of administered education. The results show that continuous changes in the settings of lessons led to improved student ratings, according to the smile sheets and observations.

The lessons that took place at schools received more negative ratings. This influence was confirmed through observation in all lessons tested in both environments. At school, students were more focused on the teaching routines; they required a break regardless of the activities, although they were able to concentrate on activities for the entire duration when the same lesson was given in a library. In the library, students

Table 2. Final assessment of lessons based on smile sheets

Grade	Lesson title	Number of lessons	Positive	Neutral	Negative
1	Pros and cons of computers	6	94	15	5
2	Ten rules of safe Internet	8	149	28	23
3	Digital footprints in a network	4	82	14	4
4	Who is behind the monitor	5	97	24	2
5	Work with information resources	3	34	25	3
6	Polyjuice potion	6	112	12	2
7	Up and download	2	0	23	25
8	Detective stories on Facebook	1	13	19	11
9	Life of a media report	2	7	24	9

were more cooperative, more active, and less afraid to express their opinion, especially when they were not sure if it is correct.

Whether the lesson takes place in a school or a library, it is always crucial how the teacher accepts it, because he or she should follow up. Teachers responded positively to the obtained material created by students during the lesson and had support for their own lessons. Similarly, the teacher's reaction had an impact on other classes in the school, in particular on their expectations about the lessons in general. Teachers appreciated the form of the lessons, accentuated co-operation and learning games. They perceived positively the content of lessons associated with the educational programme (see [3]), and often commented that they had learned new information themselves. The teachers mainly wanted the children to realize the negatives of the Internet and to use other information sources as well as to find other ways of spending their leisure time. The presence of the teacher had a positive influence on the management of the lesson. It was particularly helpful in calming the students when they were asked to evaluate the activity, but at the same time it did not hinder their active participation.

Like teachers, students also perceived the form of the lesson positively, especially when non-traditional learning methods were selected and a clear goal was pursued. Worksheets played an important role in this effort. When students were to discuss a topic without more specific information, they felt frustrated and focused on elements that did not help them achieve the set goal. Movement activities were instrumental in directing attention in all grades, but particularly in lower grades. For example, in a teaching game involving throwing a dice, the dice was not passed around but students had to come one by one to the instructor to throw it and then returned to their place. Most students actively completed the lessons (sometimes after modification), but it was always important to have an alternative solution for some students (e.g., those with mild autism). The activities were chosen and managed in such a way that the students were guided by means of practical tasks to find appropriate solutions that were generalized in the reflection and put into the context of everyday life.

In the lower grades, students were motivated as soon as they learned about the connection of the lesson with the Internet; starting from grade five (second level of primary school), it was crucial to convince the students that the content would be useful in practical life. This was a problem especially with the Copyright Act because the students believe that no one can detect their violations and thus sanctions are irrelevant to them. However, after some modifications, even the older students were convinced, which was evident from their questions on how to deal with their specific issues (such as how to quote, how to block a person who sends aggressive messages on Facebook). Across the grades, students were actively participating no later than in the second part of the lesson, particularly by sharing their own experiences and opinions. A similar breaking point between the first and second level of the primary school was evident in the spontaneity of students, when almost all of the younger students wanted to share the results of their work, whereas the interest of the older students was exactly the opposite. It was therefore necessary to have techniques to make sure that the objective criteria for the presenter's selection are clear.

Differences among students were obvious not only between individual grades, but also within them. Starting from the lesson for grade one there were big differences in computer literacy among students, but not so much in information literacy. In each class in grades one-three there were several students without any Internet experience. On the other hand, already in lessons for grade one there were students who were knowledgeable, not about terminology, but about possible uses of a computer, tablet and the Internet (mostly stereotypical and narrowly focused). When information literacy was more accentuated, such as in an orientation regarding information sources or information evaluation, the differences between students were smaller.

The choice of the topic for a grade played a key role in ensuring a connection with practice and preparing the students for activities that will soon occur and for which the students have so far no specialized knowledge. The choice was usually commented on by teachers several months after the lesson, when they contacted the instructor and shared that the situation had changed and the theme of the lesson had proven necessary.

The first lesson varied depending on the students' experience, for instance in the choice of practical examples (for example, the use of mobile applications). It was these practical examples that the students remembered most often. Similarly, the second lesson led students to learn certain safety measures, explained through specific situations with a simple solution (for example, it is not acceptable to write the school's address to an Internet friend). Students in the third grade were still often inclined to simple solutions, even though that would more closely reflect real practice. Students in the fourth grade not only remember what information they should not share, but are also able to apply the rules to questions that were not previously discussed. Students who worked in the fifth lesson with electronic resources (Wikipedia and a website) were at the start more enthusiastic than the other groups, but when they evaluated the information found and the quality of resources, they observed that those who worked with a book achieved the best results. Grade six students were well aware of their Internet experience and it was therefore necessary to confront the students with their limited knowledge through definitions of Internet threats and legal sanctions already in the first activity. In contrast, in Lesson seven, students were aware of their limited knowledge of the Copyright Act, but did not consider it a problem. It was necessary to make the first activity entertaining and also to show a connection with their lives (role play, especially on the subject of plagiarism when creating a paper). Grade eight students were mostly aware of the positive aspects of the Internet. They had some information about the negatives, but considered them to be too distant. They shared a lot of experience of people they have known (only exceptionally their own experience). The last lesson accentuating manipulation in the media proved to be the most problematic one in terms of connection with students' lives. They were aware of the existence of the media, but their reception was mostly limited to social networks and YouTube. Students' attention was only captured when practical examples of manipulation they may encounter in the environments they use were presented.

6 Discussion

The results of smile sheets and observations have confirmed the importance of factors influencing the effectiveness of active and cooperative learning [32–34], especially the role of the teacher, the learning environment and the choice of teaching methods. With appropriately set activities, the students were guided through the subject matter to find solutions to problematic situations themselves. Students' motivation was higher, the more the problem was close to their lives and the less traditional forms of teaching were used (using, for example, movement or game components).

Links to students' real lives were well suited to the problems and activities in the Internet environment that have been identified by research [4–6, 8–16]. Although students often knew the safety measures, their behaviour did not match that knowledge. For example, they knew how to create and use a password, but they were surprised to learn that there have been cases when an offended friend had misused it for bullying or that it is common procedure to use a pet's name or the year of birth when trying to break into an account. They did not say this was the way they work with passwords, but their reactions were obvious. It has therefore proven useful to present the issue in the context of the results of research on student Internet behaviour. Despite the links to the Internet, the lessons have shown that it is appropriate to focus not so much on computer literacy but rather on information literacy, which at present does not correspond to primary school educational programmes [3]. On the other hand, it encourages cooperation between libraries and schools in addressing information safety issues.

Similarly to the findings of the EU Kids Online [5], students often said they ignored their parents' efforts to create a setting for safer behaviour on the Internet; they wanted to decide for themselves on the basis of what they considered to be a problem. In terms of technical mediation, they knew some of the measures, but they were usually seeking them only after they encountered a problem (for example, blocking communication). Students were surprised by the privacy options offered for instance by Facebook and showed interest in their use, such as limiting their parents' access to some information. They were often not familiar with monitoring methods that parents can use, which may be due to the fact that they are not so widespread [5].

7 Conclusion

The results showed evaluation at the first two levels of Kirkpatrick's model. These results can be used as arguments for lessons' effectiveness, for transfer of lessons to other libraries and for planning other information safety lessons according to children's needs. Lessons based on a constructivist pedagogical paradigm were evaluated by children positively in smile sheets. That was indicated also by observation. Children were active in all activities and they shared their own experience and opinions concerning work with information and information technologies. However, they also showed some incorrect preconceptions, such as which kind of behaviour is not classified as cyberbullying, or the belief that their reaction should be stronger aggression. The results clearly indicate that even though primary school students are sometimes labelled as "digital natives", information safety lessons are relevant, in particular when they are placed within a conceptual framework and connected with students' lives, the subjects taught at school, and discussions in families.

References

1. Global Media and Information Literacy Assessment Framework: Country Readiness and Competencies. UNESCO, Paris (2013)
2. Kovářová, P.: Role bezpečnosti v rámci informační gramotnosti. ProInflow **2**, 106–130 (2010)
3. Příloha, č. 1 k Opatření ministryně školství, mládeže a tělovýchovy, kterým se mění Rámcový vzdělávací program pro základní vzdělávání. http://www.nuv.cz/uploads/RVP_ZV_2016.pdf
4. Aaltonen, M., Salmi, V.: Versatile delinquents or specialized pirates? A comparison of correlates of illegal downloading and traditional Juvenile crime. J. Scand. Stud. Criminol. Crime Prev. **2**, 188–195 (2013)
5. Livingstone, S., Haddon, L., Görzig, A., Ólafsson, K.: Risks and Safety on the Internet: The Perspective of European Children. Full Findings. LSE, London (2011)
6. Hunter, I.: Information literacy and the Google generation: teaching research skills to sixth-formers. Leg. Inf. Manag. **13**, 107–111 (2013)
7. Kirkpatrick, D.: Revisiting Kirkpatrick's four-level model. Train. Dev. **1**, 54–59 (1996)
8. Majority of youth understand copyright but continue to download illegally. Read. Teach. (1), 120 (2004)
9. Sheridan, L.P., Grant, T.: Is cyberstalking different? Psychol. Crime Law **6**, 627–640 (2007)
10. Szotkowski, R., Kopecký, K., Krejčí, V.: Nebezpečí internetové komunikace IV. Univerzita Palackého v Olomouci, Olomouc (2013)
11. Walrave, M., Vanwesenbeeck, I., Heirman W.: Connecting and protecting? Comparing predictors of self-disclosure and privacy settings use between adolescents and adults. Cyberpsychol.: J. Psychosoc. Res. Cyberspace **6** (2012)
12. O'Neill, B.: Trust in the information society. Comput. Law Secur. Rev. **5**, 551–559 (2012)
13. Joiner, R., Gavin, J., Duffield, J., Brosnan, M., Crook, C., Durndell, A., Maras, P., Miller, J., Scott, A.J., Lovatt, P.: Gender, internet identification, and internet anxiety: correlates of internet use. CyberPsychology **4**, 371–378 (2005)
14. Kopecký, K.: Rizikové formy chování českých a slovenských dětí v prostředí internetu. Univerzita Palackého v Olomouci, Olomouc (2015)
15. Safer Internet for Children: Qualitative Study in 29 European Countries - Summary Report. http://ec.europa.eu/public_opinion/archives/quali/ql_safer_internet_summary.pdf
16. Weaver, A.: Facebook and other Pandora's boxes. Access **4**, 24–32 (2010)

17. How Can Parents Support Children's Internet Safety? http://eprints.lse.ac.uk/42872/1/Howpercent20canpercent20parentspercent20supportpercent20childrenpercentE2percent80percent99spercent20internetpercent20safetypercent28lseropercent29.pdf
18. Álvarez, M., Torres, A., Rodriguez, E., Padilla, S., Rodrigo, M.J.: Attitudes and parenting dimensions in parents' regulation of internet use by primary and secondary school children. Computers **67**, 69–78 (2013)
19. Ranguelov, S.: Summary report education on online safety in schools in Europe. New Horiz. Educ. **3**, 149–163 (2010)
20. Martin, N., Rice, J.: Children's cyber-safety and protection in Australia: an analysis of community stakeholder views. Crime Prev. Commun. Saf. **3**, 165–181 (2012)
21. Moreno, M.A., Egan, K.G., Bare, K., Young, H.N., Cox, E.D.: Internet safety education for youth: stakeholder perspectives. BMC Public Health **1**, 543–548 (2013)
22. Kovářová, P.: Information literacy education and the educational needs of teaching librarians: the Czech Republic in comparison with the other visegrad four countries. In: Kurbanoğlu, S., Boustany, J., Špiranec, S., Grassian, E., Mizrachi, D., Roy, L., Çakmak, T. (eds.) ECIL 2016. CCIS, vol. 676, pp. 644–654. Springer, Cham (2016). https://doi.org/10.1007/978-3-319-52162-6_63
23. Zapojené organizace. http://www.saferinternet.cz/sid-2017/730-zapojene-organizace.html
24. Thinking about Digital Footprints. http://bellbulldogreaders.edublogs.org/2013/10/06/thinking-about-digital-footprints/
25. In the Fishbowl. http://www.coetail.com/bqdressler/tag/digital-footprint-2/
26. Teaching Children About Digital Footprints. http://primarytech.global2.vic.edu.au/2013/02/22/teaching-childre-about-digital-footprints/
27. Digital Citizenship, Digital Footprint & Digital Literacy. http://lswetnam.blogspot.cz/2013/08/digital-citizenship-digital-footprint.html
28. Digital Citizenship at CMS. http://www.mightylittlelibrarian.com/?p=1081
29. Lesson plan: Who Am I? http://eprints.bbk.ac.uk/8667/3/8667.pdf
30. Citizenship in the Digital Age: Sample Lesson Plans for Grades 1–12. http://schools.nyc.gov/NR/rdonlyres/3CA0188D-66A2-490C-9E90-1EFCADA92F8C/0/Citizenshipinthedigitalage.pdf
31. Kovářová, P.: Six views on information safety education in libraries. In: Kurbanoğlu, S., Špiranec, S., Grassian, E., Mizrachi, D., Catts, R. (eds.) ECIL 2014. CCIS, vol. 492, pp. 703–712. Springer, Cham (2014). https://doi.org/10.1007/978-3-319-14136-7_73
32. Grecmanová, H., Urbanovská, E., Novotný, P.: Podporujeme aktivní myšlení a samostatné učení žáků. Hanex, Olomouc (2000)
33. Kasíková, H.: Kooperativní učení, kooperativní škola. Portál, Praha (1997)
34. Poling, D.A., Hupp, J.: Active learning through role playing: virtual babies in a child development course. Coll. Teach. **4**, 221–228 (2009)

School Librarians' Attitudes Towards Teaching Information Literacy

Vincas Grigas[1(✉)], Anna Mierzecka[2], and Roma Fedosejevaitė[3]

[1] Vilnius University, Vilnius, Lithuania
vincas.grigas@mb.vu.lt
[2] University of Warsaw, Warsaw, Poland
anna.mierzecka@uw.edu.pl
[3] Vilnius, Lithuania
roma.fedosejevaite@gmail.com

Abstract. The objective of the research is to outline school librarians' attitudes towards teaching information literacy by analysing teaching experience, the scope of courses taught, and attitudes towards motivation of teaching. Respondents to the survey were librarians from secondary schools in Lithuania and Poland. Respondents for the research were selected from the top 250 best secondary schools in Lithuania and Poland accordingly. Data for this study was gathered using Computer-assisted web Interviewing (CAWI) technique. The results of the survey showed that school librarians had more positive emotions about their teaching motivation than negative ones. We saw that school librarians concentrate more on finding information, but are less actively involved in developing skills on the use of the information found. Also, school librarians are more prone to speak about information sources and specific tools to find it rather than organising their teaching activities as a platform for building up learning experiences. For better insight, the analysis was carried out comparing results from Lithuania and Poland as well as linking emotions with job meaningfulness.

Keywords: School librarian · The Big6 · Information literacy
Motivation for teaching

1 Introduction

The American Association of School Librarians (AASL) describes the school librarians' duties as "working with members of the school community to develop the policies, practices, and curricula to guide student learning" [1, p. 17]. School librarians could potentially play a major role in infusing IL concepts and skills into secondary school curricula as well as enhancing implementation of IL knowledge practices and dispositions into the secondary school education system. Evidence suggests that emotions experienced by librarians during their educational duties may be included among the most important factors for improving their teaching proficiency [2]. It suggests a need

R. Fedosejevaitė—Independant Researcher (MPsy), Vilnius, Lithuania.

S. Kurbanoğlu et al. (Eds.): ECIL 2017, CCIS 810, pp. 703–712, 2018.
https://doi.org/10.1007/978-3-319-74334-9_72

to evaluate school librarians' attitudes towards teaching, their experience in implementing IL, their potential to be ambassadors of IL at schools, as well as the ability to prepare secondary school students to be consumers and creators of information who can participate successfully in collaborative spaces.

Although there are studies which concern librarians' emotions related to professional tasks [2, 3], the affective dimensions of instructional work of school librarians need more detailed investigations. Emotions influence the efficiency and efficacy of teaching significantly, so we decided to conduct research among school librarians in Lithuania and Poland to gain knowledge of their feelings related to performing teaching, as well as job meaningfulness evaluation. Due to the lack above of IL teaching standards which are officially recognised (neither country has an official recommendation regarding which IL standard to use), the diversity of the courses is considerable. That is why we also examined the school librarians' teaching activities, using the Big6 model as a universal framework to assess content taught. The goal of this research was to recognise the IL situation from the school librarians' perspective and to understand better school librarians' attitudes towards developing IL skills in schools. Poland and Lithuania were chosen as countries that started implementing IL activities almost at the same time and under similar conditions (shortly after the collapse of communists' regimes and the Soviet Union at the end of the nineties). The cultural and social as well as the economic context are similar as well.

2 Theoretical Background

2.1 School Librarians as Teachers

A considerable amount of literature has been published on analysing the role of school librarians [4–8]. Today, school librarians are not only managers of school libraries but, according to AASL, are also playing different roles, such as information specialist, teacher, instructional partner, and program administrator [1]. The research conducted by Wine allowed her to discuss the radical change in the role of school librarians and to conclude that their skills and competencies predispose them to fulfil leadership roles in technology integration into classroom instruction [4]. Asselin made similar conclusions [9].

We would like to focus on the role of the school librarians as teachers throughout this paper. The responsibility and importance of this task are clear when we refer to the AASL guidelines, where the duties of school librarians are described as empowering students to be: "critical thinkers, enthusiastic readers, skilful researchers, and ethical users of information" [1, p. 8]. Although the previous studies reveal the significance of this job, it does not correlate with the level of support they receive at school. As Ash-Argyle and Shoham stated: "Despite their potential role as lead educators of IL skills in the school community, school librarians tend to be invisible to students, teachers and headteacher" [8, p. 119]. According to the literature reviewed by Lo and Chiu [5] the problems school librarians are faced with are similar in many countries: a lack of resources, time, certified programs and training opportunities, recognition of school librarians' qualifications, as well as the fact that many teachers and administrators still do not understand the concept of IL and are not aware of the role which school librarians can play in this process. Another important issue is the school librarians' perception of their own readiness to implement IL education. Several researchers have found that school librarians perceive themselves as having a low level of IL skills [6, 10, 11], there are also studies which prove the necessity to improve the degree of those skills [11–13].

2.2 Teaching Librarians Emotions

In many cases, the level of the school librarians' job satisfaction is low [5, 8, 14–16]. The studies above provide grounds for a statement about potential difficulty with the affective dimension of teaching activity. Thus, in this paper, we will pay particular attention to emotions as factors for school librarians' professional identity. According to Garganté et al. emotion related to teaching should be understood as a "specific set of teachers' knowledge on the affective dimension of their teaching" [17, p. 163]. The significance of emotions as a factor influencing the process of instruction was highlighted by a study of Beauchamp and Thomas who indicated how strongly the emotions might affect teachers' attitude, culture and discipline [18]. There are also studies which focus particularly on the emotions of librarians during instructional work [2, 7, 19–21]. The researchers have noticed that teacher-librarians' emotions differ depending on their approaches to teaching [7], but also on organisational factors, self-conception, interpersonal factors and teaching agenda [2, 21]. The investigation conducted by Julien and Genuis show that considering emotions of librarians as educators may influence significantly their job performance, as well as that of a library as an organisation [2, 21]. Grigas et al. examined emotions related to different aspects of academic librarians' teaching. They found that the most positive evaluations were given to consistency and positive attitude toward teaching, while the most pessimistic evaluations were given to effort that teaching requires and feeling of tenseness during the teaching process [22]. Another important issue connected with the emotions is a feeling of performed job meaningfulness. The feeling of meaningfulness is crucial to work engagement and motivation [23]. Lo and Chiu's study confirms that school librarians' dedication and belief in the positive results of their work influence essentially an overall learning procedure [5, p. 8].

2.3 Information Literacy Programs at Schools

Considering the nature of school librarians' work we should notice that unlike other teachers there is no widely accepted syllabus or standards that school librarians on which they may base their teaching. This causes huge diversity in IL instructional programs. Throughout this paper, we would like to examine the affective dimension of different aspects of the teaching process; this is the reason we also need a framework to compare the differences between instructional work done by our respondents, as this may influence the emotions as well. There are a few models which may be used by school librarians to support their teaching efforts, that is, the Big6, REACTs, Pathway to Knowledge, FLIP IT, and I-Search [24, 25, pp. 33–76, 91–126]. We have decided that the Big6 model will be the most useful for our purposes. The Big6, developed by Eisenberg and Berkowitz [26] defines information problem-solving regarding a research process and is a teaching approach widely used all over the world, from kindergarten through higher education [27–29]. The unique character of this model results from its construction: it comprises a unified set of information skills, which taken together, form a process useful whenever people are faced with an information problem or with making a decision that is based on the information. The Big6 involves the following six stages [30], which are outlined in Table 1, Sect. 4.2.

Table 1. Percent sometimes (3) and often (4) evaluation criteria were chosen in Lithuania and Poland sample and differences between countries

Information literacy skills	Percent of 3 and 4		Difference between countries (p)
	LT	PL	
1. Define the information problem	81%	83%	0.198
2. Identify their information needed (to solve the information problem)	71%	92%	**0.000****
3. Determine all possible sources relevant to problem	69%	90%	**0.000****
4. Select the best sources	85%	96%	**0.001****
5. Locate sources	90%	97%	**0.000****
6. Find information within sources	87%	96%	**0.003****
7. Engage (e.g., read, hear, view, acquaint themselves with information)	65%	86%	**0.000****
8. Extract relevant information	81%	91%	0.013
9. Organize from multiple sources	52%	79%	**0.000****
10. Present the information	54%	64%	**0.001****
11. Judge all above-mentioned actions' effectiveness (does it solve a problem)	53%	62%	**0.002****
12. Judge all above-mentioned actions efficiency (whether it was possibly better)	47%	57%	**0.002****
Average overall	**70**	**83**	
Average by Big6 steps:			
1. Task definition (1st and 2nd skills)	76%	88%	
2. Information seeking strategies (3rd and 4th)	77%	93%	
3. Location and access (5th and 6th)	89%	97%	
4. Use of information (7th and 8th)	73%	89%	
5. Synthesis (9th and 10th)	53%	72%	
6. Evaluation (11 and 12)	50%	60%	

**$p < 0.005$

The study by Wolf et al. metacognition research on task performance by eighth-grade students, proves the usefulness of the Big6 as a framework for scientific research [27]. In our study, it offers a clear framework to find out about the content of the teaching programs performed by librarians in different schools.

3 Method

3.1 Data Collection and Participants

The study was conducted in the form of a survey using Computer-assisted web Interviewing (CAWI), with data being gathered via an online survey tool 1KA.SI, open source software that allows a use of the semantic differential technique, a type of a rating scale designed to measure the connotative meaning of attitudes towards teaching.

Data collection started on 6th of March 2017 and came to an end on 31st of March 2017. Respondents to the survey were librarians from secondary schools in Lithuania and Poland. Respondents for the research were selected from the top 250 best secondary schools in Lithuania and Poland accordingly (we used official school ranking lists in Lithuania and Poland). Invitations to take part in the survey were sent to 500 schools. By the end of the survey period, data was gathered from 230 librarians (143 from Lithuania (LT) and 87 from Poland (PL)) – response rate was 46%. Data was collected following confidentiality procedures.

Teaching experience of the participants: less than 5 years (LT – 19%; PL – 8%); between 5 and 10 years (LT – 33%; PL – 12%); between 11 and 15 years (LT – 19%; PL – 17%); between 16 and 20 years (LT – 14%; PL – 8%); more than 20 years (LT – 15%; PL – 55%).

Type of lectures librarians implement in Lithuania and Poland: Several hours long mandatory Information Literacy courses integrated into curricula (LT – 4.4%; PL – 20.7%); Several hours long optional Information Literacy courses are not included in curricula and students can choose the course freely (LT – 16.2%; PL – 8.6%); Individual consultations to individual students or to group when is a need to solve particular information seeking issues (LT – 47.1%; PL – 32.8%).

3.2 Measures

The questionnaire has four parts. In the first part there are two questions: what type of information literacy lectures do they implement and for how long have they implemented information literacy teaching activities.

In the second part there are 12 items on which information literacy skills they develop during teaching activities at a school library in the first part. Each item was evaluated through the four-point Likert scale: 1 – never; 2 – seldom; 3 – sometimes; 4 – often. The design of this part was based on the Big6 six-stage model.

In the third part there are five pairs of adjectives dedicated to evaluating motivation for teaching. Teaching librarians' emotions were evaluated through a seven-point Likert rating scale. Semantic differential scores were transformed to fit in a scale ranging from −3 to +3 and a middle or neutral point of a zero (0). The design of this part was built on research conducted by counterparts in Spain who analysed affective dimensions of university professors about their teaching by exploring it through the semantic differential technique [22].

In the fourth part respondents were asked to respond regarding work meaningfulness [31]. Each item was evaluated through the seven-point Likert scale: 1 – Strongly disagree, 2 – Disagree, 3 – Slightly disagree, 4 – Neutral, 5 – Slightly agree, 6 – Agree, 7 – Strongly agree.

This research seeks to address the following questions: 1. What are school librarians' attitudes towards teaching information literacy? 2. How have the attitudes been affected by country, experience, and type of lectures? 3. How does work meaningfulness evaluation correlate with teaching emotions and developing IL skills?

3.3 Analytical Approach

We compared the average scores–averages and standard deviation (STD.)–of IL skills development and adjectives to find the most positively valued pairs of adjectives and the most often developed skills. We explored the Pearson correlation between the school librarians' activities on developing IL skills and motivation for teaching. We analysed the differences in the means of each of the Big6 model stages, motivation for teaching and job meaningfulness scale by applying independent samples T-test. We used multiple regression analysis to link motivation for teaching with job meaningfulness. Internal reliability was evaluated by Cronbach's alpha and criterion validity.

4 Findings

The high reliability of the questionnaire (Cronbach's alpha 0.849) and excellent reliability for the second, third and fourth parts of the questionnaire (Cronbach's alpha ranging from 0.914 to 0.933) let us analyse findings of this study with confidence.

4.1 General Results

First, let us look at the general evaluation of how often librarians develop IL skills during teaching activities at a school library.

The difference between the highest and the lowest mean was 0.98 (LT) (Std. 0.82) and 1.06 (PL) (Std. 0.74). Highest results are seen in locating and accessing information (5th and 6th skill), information seeking strategies (3rd and 4th skill) and task definition (1st and 2nd skill). Almost all, except the first and eighth items, were statistically significantly different ($p < 0.005$). Lithuania showed a lower mean in almost all items in comparison with Poland.

The single most noticeable observation to emerge from the data comparison was that school librarians from Lithuania in contrast to their counterparts from Poland are less likely to develop skills required to work with information sources. Also, it should be noted, that the standard deviation between the results in all items is quite high (around 0.8).

School librarians in both countries have a very positive motivation for teaching (average):

- Feelings regarding your attitude towards teaching (Positive - negative) (LT – 5.22; PL – 6.09);
- Significance of teaching to you personally (Irrelevant - relevant) (LT – 5.4; PL – 6.18);
- Your attitude to your future improvement as a teacher (Pessimistic - optimistic) (LT – 5.32; PL – 6.12);
- While teaching you feel (Tense - calm) (LT – 4.6; PL – 5.71);
- Feelings that you have about teaching (Intrusive - pleasant) (LT – 4.94; PL – 5.69).

The highest difference between Poland and Lithuania is in assessing feeling while teaching (mean difference 1.11). Lithuanian school librarians seemed to be more tense while teaching than colleagues from Poland and evaluated it lowest (mean 4.6) of all five items. All the elements are statistically significantly different ($p < 0.005$).

No insights can be made from the correlation analysis (no strong correlation) of information skills and motivation for teaching.

We made a multiple regression analysis to link teaching of IL skills with job meaningfulness. Our analysis showed no statistically significant relation.

School librarians think that their work is important and they have a meaningful job (average):

- The work that I do is important (LT – 6; PL – 6.2);
- I have a meaningful job (LT – 6; PL – 6.1);
- The work that I do makes the world a better place (LT – 5.7; PL – 5.8);
- What I do at work makes a difference in the world (LT – 5.3; PL – 5.5);
- The work that I do is meaningful (LT – 5.9; PL – 5.8).

By contrast school librarians reflected a bit less positively on their personal contribution in embracing or making the world a better place, and they are less likely to be confident in their ability to make a difference in the world.

4.2 Analysis of Information Literacy Skills Development

For a better understanding of the results, a deeper look into every item is needed. To see the differences between Lithuania and Poland and compare them all, we converted the results to a percentage equivalent. We decided to measure what percent of the highest evaluation criteria (sometimes and often) were chosen. We think it helped us to clarify which of the information skills are developed most often.

School librarians from Poland showed a deeper involvement in teaching IL skills on an average of 13%. The signalling items are 3, 4, 8, and 9, which differ more than 20% each. All of them are related to the requirement of higher order skills with which to deal.

No items in the case of Lithuania reached more than 90% while in the case of Poland we even have six highly evaluated cases such as number 2, 3, 4, 5, 6, and 8. It shows that school librarians in Poland give much attention to information seeking strategies, information location and access, and use of information.

Synthesis and Evaluation steps were evaluated least – on average 62% and 55%. It shows that far too little attention is being paid to the results of the whole process – organisation of information sources, presentation of the information, judgement of whether a problem was solved and whether it was possible to do better. Two discrete reasons emerged from this. One is that type of IL lectures implemented has a direct impact on how often Synthesis and Evaluation steps were evaluated more positively. Those who implement several hours long mandatory IL courses integrated into the curricula more often develop skills outlined in the Synthesis and Evaluation steps. Second, those, who work in the field for a longer time (between 16 and 20 years), evaluated their involvement in the development of skills outlined in the Synthesis and Evaluation steps more often.

However, in other items, there was no such consistency that those who have longer experience in the field more often than others develop IL skills numbered from 1 to 8. We found out that more experienced librarians develop a much wider range of information literacy skills in the case of Lithuania, in contrast to the case of Poland – we cannot find a clear difference in the elaboration of IL skills analysis by librarians' experience in the field.

5 Discussion

The results of the study showed school librarians' eagerness to implement stages of IL on a different level. School librarians are more prone to develop IL skills which are related to process (second and third stages), and less likely to develop skills related to using the results (content) reached after implementing the process (fourth and fifth stage). These results provide further support for the hypothesis that school librarians concentrate on finding information, but are less actively involved in developing skills in the use of the information found. Also, this leads us to an insight that school librarians are more prone to speak about information sources and specific tools to find it rather than organising their teaching activities as a platform for building up learning experiences.

Poland and Lithuania results differ in statistical significance, and we can see a tendency that Polish results are higher than Lithuanian ones. Many factors may cause these differences. We paid attention to the two possible explanations: (1) school librarians in Poland are more mature and experienced than the ones in Lithuania; (2) Polish participants more often teach several hours' long mandatory IL course integrated into the curricula. The official status of educational duties may cause more positive emotions arising from the perception of the importance of the job and the ability to develop a wider range of IL skills.

The current research was not specifically designed to evaluate factors related to the impact of outside factors. This research will serve as a base for future studies on what scope of IL is implemented at schools and what is the school librarian's motivation for teaching. A further study with more focus on school librarians' knowledge of IL and teaching methods are therefore suggested.

6 Conclusions

The empirical findings in this study provide an understanding about the way IL is developed at schools. This study showed that librarians from both countries taught students to locate sources, to select the best sources, and to find information within sources mostly, but gave little attention to the evaluation of information seeking and the efficiency of actions implemented during the process. Implementation of the fifth and sixth stages of the Big6 depended on the type of IL courses and experience in the field. Those more experienced and those who implement mandatory courses are the school librarians who develop higher order IL stages. Standard deviation between the results in all items is quite high (around 0.8) and proved that school librarians in their engagement in IL activities are not a homogenous group.

According to theoretical background – school librarians do not feel confident about teaching. This study has shown that librarians are not confident in their role of being teachers, but are proud of being named as teachers. Although the results of this research does support the idea that emotions experienced by teaching librarians depend on their teaching experience or type of lectures they are instructing. The results show that teaching activities have great importance for librarians and their attitude is quite positive about them.

References

1. American Association of School Librarians. Empowering Learners: Guidelines for School Library Media Programs. American Association of School Librarians, a Division of the American Library Association, Chicago (2009)
2. Julien, H., Genuis, S.K.: Librarians' experiences of the teaching role: a national survey of librarians. Libr. Inf. Sci. Res. **33**, 103–111 (2011)
3. Heidi, J., Shelagh, K.G.: Emotional labour in librarians' instructional work. J. Doc. **65**, 926–937 (2009)
4. Wine, L.D.: School librarians as technology leaders: an evolution in practice. J. Educ. Libr. Inf. Sci. **57**, 207–220 (2016)
5. Lo, P., Chiu, D.K.W.: Enhanced and changing roles of school librarians under the digital age. New Libr. World **116**, 696–710 (2015)
6. Shyh-Mee, T., Kiran, K., Diljit, S.: Examining school librarians' readiness for information literacy education implementation. Malaysian J. Libr. Inf. Sci. **20**, 79–97 (2015)
7. Wheeler, E., McKinney, P.: Are librarians teachers? Investigating academic librarians' perceptions of their own teaching skills. J. Inf. Literacy **9**, 111–128 (2015)
8. Ash-Argyle, R., Shoham, S.: Professional self-efficacy and role perception of school librarians and their impact on the development of students' information literacy: an evidence-based study. J. Inf. Literacy **8**, 118–140 (2014)
9. Asselin, M.: Teaching information skills in information age: an examination of trends in the middle grades. School Libr. Worldwide **11**, 17–36 (2005)
10. Smith, J.K.: Secondary teachers and information literacy (IL): teacher understanding and perceptions of IL in the classroom. Libr. Inf. Sci. Res. **35**, 216–222 (2013)
11. Kamal, M.A., Othman, N.: Training and development for library and media teachers in selected Malaysian school resource centres. J. Educ. Practice **3**, 77–86 (2012)

12. Streatfield, D., Shaper, S., Markless, S., Rae-Scott, S.: Information literacy in United Kingdom schools. J. Inf. Literacy **5**, 5–25 (2011)
13. Ismail, S., Dorner, D., Oliver, G.: Local studies teachers' perspectives of information literacy education in primary schools. IPEDR **47**, 76–80 (2012)
14. Cheng, P.-Y.: Perceiving usefulness: the perception of users on school libraries and librarians in Hong Kong. Doctoral dissertation, Charles Sturt University, Wagga (2012). http://researchoutput.csu.edu.au/R/?func?dbin-jump-full&object_id?35229&local_base?GEN01-CSU01
15. Zhan, W., Zhou, Y., Liu, Z.: Burnout analysis of influencing factors for school librarians. Libr. Inf. Serv. **56**, 69–73 (2012)
16. Oberg, D.: Libraries in schools: essential contexts for studying organizational change and culture. Libr. Trends **58**, 9–25 (2009)
17. Garganté, B., Meneses, J., Monereo, C.: Affective dimension of university professors about their teaching: an exploration through the semantic differential technique. Univ. Psychol. **13**, 161–173 (2014)
18. Beauchamp, C., Thomas, L.: Understanding teacher identity: an overview of issues in the literature and implications for teacher education. Cambridge J. Educ. **39**, 175–189 (2009)
19. Walter, S.: Librarians as teachers: a qualitative inquiry into professional identity. Coll. Res. Libr. **69**, 51–71 (2008)
20. Langmead, A., Otis, J.M., Warren, C.N., Weingart, S.B., Zilinksi, L.D.: Towards interoperable network ontologies for the digital humanities. Int. J. Humanit. Arts Comput. **10**, 22–35 (2016)
21. Julien, H., Pecoskie, J., Reed, K.: Trends in information behavior research, 1999–2008: a content analysis. Libr. Inf. Sci. Res. **33**, 19–24 (2011)
22. Grigas, V., Fedosejevaitė, R., Mierzecka, A.: Librarians as educators: affective dimensions experienced in teaching. In: Kurbanoğlu, S., Boustany, J., Špiranec, S., Grassian, E., Mizrachi, D., Roy, L., Çakmak, T. (eds.) ECIL 2016. CCIS, vol. 676, pp. 619–633. Springer, Cham (2016). https://doi.org/10.1007/978-3-319-52162-6_61
23. Spreitzer, G.M., Kizilos, M.A., Nason, S.W.: A dimensional analysis of the relationship between psychological empowerment and effectiveness, satisfaction, and strain. J. Manag. **23**, 679–704 (1997)
24. Eisenberg, M.B.: Information literacy: essential skills for the information age. DESIDOC J. Libr. Inf. Technol. **28**, 39 (2008)
25. Thomas, N., Crow, S., Franklin, L.: Information Literacy and Information Skills Instruction: Applying Research to Practice in the 21st Century School Library Libraries Unlimited. Santa Barbara, CA (2011)
26. Eisenberg, M.B., Berkowitz, R.E.: Information Problem-Solving: The Big Six Skills Approach to Library and Information Skills Instruction. Norwood/Ablex, Jamaica/NJ (1990)
27. Wolf, S., Brush, T., Saye, J.: The Big Six information skills as a metacognitive scaffold: a case study. Sch. Libr. Media Res. **6** (2003). http://news.ala.org/ala/mgrps/divs/a
28. Heath, R.A.: Toward learner-centred high school curriculum-based research: a case study. J. Libr. Inf. Sci. **47**, 368–379 (2014)
29. Eisenberg, M.B.: Information literacy: essential skills for the information age. DESIDOC J. Libr. Inf. Technol. **28**, 39–47 (2008)
30. Eisenberg, M., Berkowitz, B.: Welcome to the Big6 (2012). http://big6.com/
31. Bunderson, J.S., Thompson, J.A.: The call of the wild: zookeepers, callings, and the double-edged sword of deeply meaningful work. Adm. Sci. Q. **54**, 32–57 (2009)

Information Literacy Instruction

Identifying Good Practices in Information Literacy Education; Creating a Multi-lingual, Multi-cultural MOOC

Lyn Robinson(✉) and David Bawden

Centre for Information Science, City, University of London, London, UK
{l.robinson, d.bawden}@city.ac.uk

Abstract. This presentation reports an analysis of good practices in information literacy (IL) education, with particular reference to practices which may be incorporated in the design on a Massive Open Online Course (MOOC). Based on an analysis of published literature and reports, analysis of existing IL MOOCs, and expert opinion, it presents good practice eleven area: IL definition and models; IL content and contexts; pedagogical frameworks; teaching and learning methods; interaction and collaboration by learners; structuring of learning materials; assessment methods; multi-lingual and multi-cultural aspects; IL outside higher education; MOOC management; and MOOCs in LIS and IL.

Keywords: Information literacy · MOOCs · Good practice · Multilingual Multicultural · Self-assessment

1 Introduction

This paper reports an analysis of good practices in information literacy (IL) education, with particular reference to practices which may be incorporated in the design on a Massive Open Online Course (MOOC). It is the first stage of an Erasmus+ project, Information Literacy Online (ILO), to create a MOOC for IL, with an emphasis on multi-lingual and multi-cultural aspects, and on continual participant self-assessment.

The project partners are: Barcelona, Graz, Frankfurt (DIPF), Hildesheim, London (City), Ljubljana, and Zadar. The MOOC will focus on students in higher education, while being accessible to high-school students and to adults in lifelong-learning. It will be multi-lingual (English, German, Spanish, Catalan, Slovenian and Croatian), and reflecting both culturally distinct and language-specific issues in IL, and will have a focus on technology-supported participant self-assessment.

This presentation reports the first stage of the project, carried out between January and May 2017. This is an analysis of current good practices in teaching and training for IL, to guide the structure, content, nature of interaction, and pedagogical practices of the MOOC. No attempt was made to identify 'best' practice; rather to identify good practice relevant to the context of the ILO MOOC. The aim was to identify approaches which had been reported to have successful application in several relevant contexts, without ignoring recent, and hence less widely-reported, promising examples. Because

S. Kurbanoğlu et al. (Eds.): ECIL 2017, CCIS 810, pp. 715–727, 2018.
https://doi.org/10.1007/978-3-319-74334-9_73

of the diversity of the approaches and issues, and the need to focus on perceived relevance to the ILO MOOC, the approach is necessarily less formal than that of a systematic review.

This is a work in progress, and will be kept updated to guide development of the ILO MOOC through the duration of the project.

Only a summary of this extensive review is given here, with limited indicative references, and with emphasis on the aspects of particular interest to ILO: multi-lingual and multicultural content, and participant self-assessment. The full report, with 17,000 words, 280 references, and numerous examples, will be deposited in the Humanities Commons repository.

2 Methods

Since the literature (published and unpublished) is extensive, and practice rapidly developing, the focus was on materials created in the last five years, with a date of 2012 or later, although particularly significant older material was also included where appropriate. The aim was not to produce a comprehensive bibliography, but rather a selective list of resources providing evidence of good practice: for MOOCs generally, with emphasis on multi-lingual and multicultural aspects; for IL learning, where it is relevant to the MOOC context; and for technology-supported self-assessment.

Sources used were: Internet search engines; Internet sources (specialist blogs, associations, curricula); bibliographic databases (Library and Information Science Abstracts (LISA), Library and Information Science and Technology Abstracts (LISTA), Web of Science, Educational Abstracts, British Education Index, Educational Resources Information Centre (ERIC), Applied Social Sciences Index and Abstracts (ASSIA); citation indexes to follow up relevant sources; library catalogues (City University of London, University College London, London University Senate House Library, British Library; contents lists of relevant journals (Journal of Information Literacy, Communications in Information Literacy, Nordic Journal of Information Literacy in Higher Education, British Journal of Educational Technology); contents of books series (European Conference on Information Literacy Proceedings) and multi-authored monographs.

A detailed analysis of the features of 21 existing IL MOOCs was also carried out, both to assess general good practice and to identify any which might be, in some respects, exemplars for the ILO MOOC.

Comments on aspects of the draft report were obtained from a small number of IL experts in the UK, Germany, Slovenia and Croatia, to assess the validity of the conclusions.

3 Summaries of Good Practice

Eleven aspects of good practice were examined; these emerged from the analysis as being the issues discussed in the literature, rather than being pre-defined, with the exception of topics in Sects. 3.7 and 3.8, which were included as being of importance for the design of the IL MOOC. The findings for each are summarised here.

3.1 IL Definition and Models

Not all reported IL educational initiatives state the definition or model of IL being used. However, it is good practice to state these explicitly, as they help in making rational and explicable decisions about the way the initiative is designed. An initial division can be made into the older style of linear, skills-based models, and the more recent, and more holistic models; though an over-simplification, this is in accord with the way the models are typically regarded, Walsh [1] describing them as 'competence' and 'relational' models respectively. While most IL provision is designed around one model, it is possible to 'pick and mix'. For example, an IL programme at the University of Maynooth combined elements from the ANCIL model and the ACRL Framework [2], while it appears feasible to combine the older ACRL Standards with their newer Framework [3, 4]. Nor are the models necessarily very different in practice; for example, one IL programme was mapped to ANCIL, but the originators noted that it could equally be mapped to the SCONUL 'Pillars' model [5].

For the ILO project, given the general trend towards broader conceptual definitions of IL rather than the older skills-based definitions, and the desirability of having an internationally recognised basis for a multi-cultural MOOC, the UNESCO definition of media and information literacy is the most suitable [6]. Models of this kind have criticised for offering little specific guidance for designing IL training; this may be countered by using a more specific model of IL within the general definition. The UK Open University model, which specifies detailed competencies at several levels in five areas, is a good example [7].

Therefore the definition of IL for ILO would be "a set of competencies that empowers citizens to access, retrieve, understand, evaluate and use, create, as well as share information and media content in all formats, using various tools, in a critical, ethical and effective way, in order to participate and engage in personal, professional and societal activities", with competencies specified in five areas: understand and engage in digital practices; find information; critically evaluate information, online interactions and online tools; manage and communicate information; collaborate and share digital content.

3.2 IL Content and Contexts

A very wide variety of individual topics have been included in IL educational programmes, including those described as digital literacy, media literacy, metaliteracy, etc. In order to try to define realistic, broad core, those topics appearing in two or more of the main IL models were identified. This leads to the following set of 16 core concepts, with the proviso that there is overlap between them, and that terminology is not used consistently in all models:

- understand the information environment (in the widest sense)
- use digital tools effectively
- recognise information needs, and how to address them
- know relevant information resources
- find and access information
- critically evaluate information and information sources

- critically evaluate online interactions and online tools
- manage information
- collaborate in information handling
- share digital content ethically
- become an independent and self-directed learner; and a lifelong learner
- learn to learn; develop metacognition
- understand ethical issues of information
- present and communicate information
- create information products
- synthesize information and create new knowledge

This set of topics is recommended as the basis for the development of the ILO MOOC, though not all will be included from the start.

A perennial issue has been the appropriate balance between generic and subject- or context- specific IL material [8]. In general, good practice has moved in the direction of greater specificity, with a recognition that IL provision is more meaningful to students the more it can be made contextual to their situation [9]. On the other hand, creation of generic teaching materials has been recommended, for economy and to encourage re-use. We conclude that good practice for ILO will be to create an initial set of generic models and materials in such a way that they can be readily modified, customised or extended for use in specific contexts.

3.3 Pedagogical Frameworks

Only a minority of reports of IL training programmes mention any explicit pedagogical framework, and there is no single pedagogical framework which has been widely used in the creation of IL learning materials. Rather, a variety of frameworks have been used, seemingly *ad hoc*, for both the creation and the application of IL materials, among them Biggs' constructive alignment pedagogy, Bloom's taxonomy of educational objectives, Honey Mumford learning styles, and Kolb's experiential learning style theory. Despite criticism of the uncritical use of learning styles, it seems that this kind of framework has value for IL instructional design, not least in reminding designers not to rely a limited repertoire of activities. Knowles' andragogy, the principles of learning by autonomous adults [10], has seemingly not been explicitly applied in IL education, though it seems apposite for use in the largely self-regulated learning environment of a MOOC, as does Schön's reflective practice, which has had some limited use in IL education [11].

3.4 Teaching and Learning Methods

A wide variety of methods have been used in the teaching of IL, and much has been written about them, though mainly in the context of face-to-face classes [12]. Even considering only online provision, "The variety of methods employed illustrates that there is no magic bullet approach to IL" [3]. Such studies as have been done find little demonstrable difference in effectiveness between particular instructional methods, on between face-to-face and online delivery, and between online instruction with different degrees of interaction.

In general, good practice for IL education has sought to combine learning approaches, including:

- didactic explanation (via text, video, animation, audio), with videos increasingly acceptable as an alternative to face-to-face presentation and text-based online instruction
- active learning exercises, individual or collaborative, short "one off" or longer duration
- resource evaluation, by checklist or by longer qualitative assessment
- information creation, reflective writing, creation of resource lists

These have been delivered face-to-face, by online instruction, or by self-directed independent learning.

The online tutorial has been a staple tool for teaching IL since the late 1990s, a general move away from static text-based tutorials to those with more interaction and audio/visual content; the latter is typically more appealing to students, but does not necessarily result in better assessed learning outcomes. A very common structure is a two-part tutorial, with an instructional component followed by an active learning component: quiz, exercises, etc.

IL tutorials have typically been followed by an individual student in isolation, but are increasingly including online communication and collaboration (synchronous and asynchronous) with instructor, or collaboration with fellow students. Self-paced learning units may be valuable for self-directed learning, and for the development of a habit of lifelong learning [13].

There is no standardisation, or agreed best practice, in what software to use in producing IL learning materials, although the increasing use of open source software is notable. Increasing provision of IL learning online has led to the creation and use of small, discrete 'bite sized' learning objects. These have the obvious advantages of being relatively quickly produced, modified and shared, and are convenient for learners to access and use. On the other hand, it is recognised that to be realistic, activities in distance education should take days, weeks or months rather than short discrete minutes of time, and allow for critical reflection and perhaps collaboration. 'Bite size' materials must therefore be carefully integrated into longer duration programmes to be effective.

Gamification, using games in learning situations and introducing game-like elements into instruction generally, has been found to be a good way of involving and enthusing students, and improving student engagement and learning, not least in MOOCs [14, 15]. It has been found to be useful for information literacy learning, initially in the form of physical in-class games, and more recently as digital games [1, 16]. There are few fully developed IL games, and these are very demanding of time and expertise to build, monitor and support. There has been considerable criticism of many IL instructional games, as having game elements artificially added on; a form of dressed-up assignment. Whatever form they take, IL games must be fully integrated into the rest of the course, and contribute in a useful way to the other things participants are doing; not a thing on their own, not a game for the sake of it. Further, as not all participants will like the game approach, it should be optional; there should be ways of using the instructional materials without the game elements.

3.5 Interaction and Collaboration by Learners

Good practice is now to include as much interaction, with the system, and collaboration, with other students, in online IL instruction, reflecting general pedagogical opinion on the value of active and social, collaborative, learning. Since online IL instruction was introduced in the late 1990s, the trend has been to provide more interaction for active learning, to supplement or replace passive didactic instruction [17, 18], although the definition of what counts as interaction varies considerably between writers [19]. Interactive exercises with real resources, rather than pre-set simulations, are much more realistic, and hence better for learning, but they need to be updated each time the course runs, because the digital resources used will change. In any event, provision of effective interaction is generally more time-consuming than providing simpler forms of tutorial.

The newer instantiations of IL instruction generally support collaboration between learners whenever possible. For example, the ANCIL model emphasises the value of collaborative learning, based on real needs, wherever possible [20]. There must, however, be some similarity of subject or context between learners, for collaboration to be meaningful.

3.6 Structuring of Learning Materials

Relatively little attention has been given to categorising and structuring learning materials for IL instruction, with the exception of the creation of IL learning objects to be as reusable as possible.

Designing materials for IL instruction, online tutorials in particular, in such a way that that that they can easily be re-used by others, and modified by their originators, has been seen as desirable ever since such materials were first created [21]. Initially these were intended for local re-use, and kept in an institutional repository, while the current trend is to treat them as Open Educational Resources (OERs) for general re-use, kept in an open access repository, such as GitHub and SoftChalk Cloud. To be effectively reusable, reusable learning objects (RLOs) for IL instruction should observe certain general conditions, some of the most significant being that they should:

- have clearly stated learning objectives and outcomes
- be generic, and focus on broad IL goals, rather than being course- or subject-specific; this increases shelf-life and applicability, but at the cost of losing the losing the benefits of contextualisation
- cover the smallest feasible amount of material, as this makes it more flexible and easier for other to reuse in different contexts
- address multiple learning styles and preferences, through inclusion of different activities in each object
- always include some check of knowledge, as this will be needed by some potential users
- be flexible, by, for example, providing multiple points of access, and giving the choice to take a concluding assessment
- be consistent in design with similar RLOs, so students do not have to learn a new process each time

- be intuitive to use; technical solutions should not get in the way of learning
- have appropriate licensing conditions, allowing wide re-use
- use generally accepted standards wherever applicable, including accessibility standards
- use only widely available, ideally open-access, software and resources, allowing wide re-use

Other than this concern for creating IL materials as RLOs, there has been some interest in using constructivist and/or connectionist principles in the design of IL instruction, but this is not universally accepted. Various instructional design frameworks have been applied, of which the most popular have been ADDIE and IDEA [22].

3.7 Assessment Methods

Assessment has always played a part in IL instruction, with a limited variety of methods used: as an initial pre-instruction assessment, to check student's prior knowledge; as a check of understanding after each session; and as a post-course assessment, which may also be a summative examination for credit, while frequent formative assessment fits with currently popular models of 'bite sized' instructional activities [23, 24]. There is, however little agreement on good practice for self-evaluation by participants, so this aspect of the ILO project will be genuinely innovative.

The well-tried multiple-choice quiz remains the predominant form of assessment, but this has limitations. There is a problem if static assessment questions are tied to online information sources that changes often, while questions of principle, which will be unchanging, run the risk of being either trivial, when the answer is self-evident or lacking context, or debatable, when there is no right answer. Alternatives to quizzes are reflection and portfolios, 'selfie' photographs illustrating understanding, search task completion, and critical incident questionnaires.

Assessment by an instructor remains the popular method, although peer assessment by other participants, though rarely used so far in IL instruction, can be effective. Self-assessment remains little tried, beyond a simple, and sometimes unrealistic self-assessment of overall capability before and after a course of instruction. Some IL tutorials and MOOCs offer brief self-assessment quizzes, though they may have the problem of not recording completion or performance [25].

3.8 Multi-lingual and Multi-cultural Aspects

Although there are many descriptions of IL training in particular countries or regions, they generally do not analyse national cultural variations. There have been very few examples of multi-lingual provision for IL education, nor of explicit and detailed consideration of such education might be adapted to students from different cultural backgrounds. There is, as Simon [26] puts it "a dearth of literature exploring how library instruction and information literacy instruction is conducted in colleges and universities in non-English speaking countries".

This is despite the fact that in an early paper addressing this topic, Johnson and Webber [27] wrote that "in terms of local and national culture, the information literature person is a self- and socially-conscious being, rather than a simple repository of skills and knowledge. This is underlined by cross-cultural difference, where issues of behaviour and acceptability of kinds of information become sensitive". Setting aside language issues, there are questions of different academic linguistic styles, unfamiliar cultural references and religious, historical and political allusions, different learning styles, and different patterns of engagement with various types of media. There may be particular problems in the expression of IL concepts, typically formulated in English, in other languages. Simon [26] notes the difficulties faced by Israeli students in converting Hebrew concepts into the kind of formalised keyword approach necessary for database searching, while Boolean searching itself may be problematic for non-English speakers [28].

There are relatively few examples of multi-lingual IL provision. Three typical examples of those which do exist include: the INFLOW IL model, developed within the EC 7th Framework Programme between 2010–2014, and mainly intended for younger students though with some applicability to university students, developed in English and translated into French and Spanish [11]; digital IL instructional games with a multilingual interface (English, Bulgarian, Italian and Swedish) being produced in the Erasmus+ project 'Transforming information literacy instruction in the university environment through the serious games approach (tiLIT)' [29]; and the UNESCO IL MOOC, to be instantiated in English, Arabic, Greek, Spanish, and Hindi, as well as in English [30].

Although there have been many descriptions of IL education in various countries and regions, there have been few accounts of what differences local culture may make. a number of writers, as noted below, have alluded to this, but few have given specific detailed recommendations. It may be difficult to distinguish issues due to culture from those due to language or previous educational curricula. Similarly, relatively few writers have used any recognised framework in analysing cultural differences. Where a formal framework has been used, it is invariably Hofstede's 'Five Dimensions of Culture' [31].

It has been argued that the older forms of IL models are poorly suited to deal with cultural aspects of IL, and that critical information literacy approaches, because of their support for multiple perspectives and support for societal as well as personal development, are superior, particularly in transitional and post-conflict societies [32, 33].

The most extensive set of studies of IL education in different cultural settings have been those of Dorner and Gorman, drawing on analyses of the contexts of Asia and Oceania, and summarised by Dorner [34]. They argue that IL education for this extensive region must be contextual and sensitive to local needs, and in favour of explicit consideration of cultural factors, using Hofstede's dimensions, in planning IL education in developing countries. Models using a critical form of IL are favoured over those based on the older skills-based frameworks, especially approaches based on Bloom's taxonomy, as these may not be suitable for all cultures. Applying these ideas to IL education in Laos, they suggest that student-centred learning may not appropriate, that collaborative group-working will be better accepted than individual work, and that learning activities should be particularly clearly defined and structured.

Given that there is very little agreement on good practice here, the LO project should be genuinely innovative.

3.9 IL Outside Higher Education

IL education has generally been developed for students in higher education, taking Bachelors and Masters degrees in universities and colleges. There has been some limited consideration of IL in three other contexts: younger students, typically in schools; in workplaces and professions; and for the general public [35–37]. There are a few examples of cross-sectoral applications, with IL materials developed for a university being used in a public library, or those developed for school pupils being offered to parents and alumni, but these are unusual.

To allow for materials developed for university students being applicable in other contexts, the key factors seem to be they be sufficiently broad in coverage, generic in subject, and in discrete bite-sized units; this will maximise the chance of their reuse in this way.

3.10 MOOC Issues: General and Management

MOOCs (massive open online courses), generally understood as online courses in any subject area with unlimited enrolment, first appeared in 2008. Increased usage, and many new providers, led to 2012 being described as the 'year of the MOOC'. Then disenchantment, due to very poor completion rates (usually well below 10%), concerns about quality, and problems of sustainability, with providers potentially putting in a lot of effort for little financial return. Subsequently, there has been a revision of ideas, and progress on a more realistic basis, as well as consideration of the wider place of MOOCS in lifelong learning; for overviews of MOOCs and their development, see [38–41]. This therefore an appropriate time for reconsidering the value of MOOCs for IL instruction.

From the beginning, a distinction was made between two main types of MOOC: cMOOCs, or connectivist MOOCs, based on a constructivist approach, with learning happening mainly through social interaction, and xMOOCs, or extended MOOCs [in the sense that they generally extend other forms of education or professional development for most learners], have a traditional course structure, with a linear syllabus, largely controlled by instructors, with limited interaction between learners. A variety of other categories of MOOCs have been suggested, for example LOOCs (little open online courses), SOOCs, (small open online courses), SPOCs (small private online courses), and SMOCs (synchronous massive open online courses), and the the 'mini-MOOC', a course with a narrow subject focus, based explicitly on pedagogical principles, using automated online assessment, created with the aim of helping large numbers of participants learn specific skills within the topic. There is no longer any sharp distinction between the forms of MOOCs, and it seems that IL MOOCs in the future, including the ILO MOOC, will share the characteristics of more than one kind.

Many factors have been identified as affecting student recruitment and retention in MOOCs, including student background and motivation, pedagogical design, the extent to which the MOOC can be tailored to the need of its users, ways of encouraging student access, and the extent to which it is integrated into other learning [40, 42, 43]. Of course, many participants in a MOOC are not concerned about completion. They are auditing the material for interest, or as a 'taster' for the subject, and do not necessarily want to follow to the end. It seems therefore desirable for IL instruction MOOCs to be designed in such a way as to allow incorporation their materials into 'blended learning' within a university, while allowing independent learners to follow the whole MOOC course, and also encouraging auditing and 'drop ins'.

It may be noted, with respect to the multilingual intention of the ILO MOOC, that the English language predominates in MOOCs generally. A study carried out in early 2016, examining the 4950 MOOCs listed in the Class Central database, showed that, although MOOCs in 17 languages could be identified, English language courses accounted for 76%, and five languages (English, Spanish, French, Chinese and Arabic) accounted for 95% [44]. As a comparison, the MOOC-list website offered MOOCs in 30 different languages in March 2017, but with English still predominant.

3.11 MOOCs in LIS and IL

Although it seems that there is a natural synergy between the open and individual learning offered by MOOCs and the the ethos of library/information services, there have been very few examples of LIS involvement with MOOC development [39, 45].

A number of MOOCs have developed for the teaching of IL. 21 were identified in the preparation of this report, described in sufficient detail for their features to be analysed; this analysis appears in the full report. In summary, it has to be said that their natures are so varied, all having been developed for a particular context, need, or available expertise, that it is difficult to draw general lessons of good practice. They vary from a course aimed at teaching the basics of IL to new university students, to a course for young people on UNESCO's MIL ideas, to one of the concept of metaliteracy, to a short 'any time' course on plagiarism issues.

It may be said, however, that these examples suggest that offering the MOOC for an initial defined period with active instructor support, followed by availability for self-paced use at any time (perhaps within a defined time period after the instructor-led phase, to avoid the materials becoming obsolescent), is attractive in maximising use.

4 Conclusions

The analysis of good practice in IL education reported here will form the basis for the design and development of the ILO MOOC. The most salient factors are: balancing a broad and inclusive understanding of IL, with a more detailed and specific model; using a pedagogical framework to ensure a variety of appropriate interactions and activities; creating small RLOs to aid flexible reuse; and adopting innovative approaches to the multilingual and multicultural aspects, and to self-assessment.

References

1. Walsh, A.: Playful information literacy: play and information literacy in higher education. Nordic J. Inf. Literacy Higher Educ. **7**(1), 80–94 (2015)
2. Dodd, L.: Embedding information literacy through critical skills, collaboration and a new curriculum. SCONUL Focus **68**, 37–41 (2017). https://www.sconul.ac.uk/page/focus-68. Accessed 23 Feb 2017
3. Reichart, B., Elvidge, C.: Information literacy in the changing landscape of distance learning. Pennsylvania Libr.: Res. Practice **3**(2), 144–155 (2015)
4. Stewart, K.N., Broussard, D.M.: Promoting empowerment through metaliteracy. In: Jacobson, T.E., Mackey, T.P. (eds.) Metaliteracy in Practice, pp. 135–158. Facet, London (2016)
5. Gleeson, C., Verlander, P., Hardisty, J.: Developing a new co-ordinated approach to information literacy at the University of Chester. SCONUL Focus **68**, 42–46 (2017). https://www.sconul.ac.uk/page/focus-68. Accessed 23 Feb 2017
6. UNESCO: Global media and information literacy assessment framework (2013). http://unesdoc.unesco.org/images/0022/002246/224655e.pdf#page=22. Accessed 30 May 2017
7. Open University: Digital and Information Literacy Framework (2017). http://www.open.ac.uk/libraryservices/pages/dilframework. Accessed 22 Feb 2017
8. Peters, J., Hathaway, H., Bragan-Turner, D.: Does discipline matter? In: Martin, A., Rader, H. (eds.) Information and IT Literacy: Enabling Learning in the 21st Century, pp. 77–87. Facet, London (2003)
9. Wang, L.: Chapter M. In: Global Perspectives on Information Literacy: Fostering a Dialogue for International Understanding. ACRL Student Learning and Information Committee, pp. 130–144 (2017). http://www.ala.org/acrl/sites/ala.org.acrl/files/content/publications/whitepapers/GlobalPerspectives_InfoLit.pdf. Accessed 6 Apr 2017
10. Knowles, M.: The Adult Learner, 7th edn. Butterworth-Heinemann, London (2011)
11. McNicol, S., Shields, E.: Developing a new approach to information literacy learning design. J. Inf. Literacy **8**(2), 23–35 (2014)
12. Burkhardt, J.M.: Teaching Information Literacy Reframed: 50+ Framework-Based Exercises for Creating Information-Literate Learners. Facet, London (2016)
13. Mi, M.: Application of instructional design principles in developing an online information literacy curriculum. Med. Ref. Serv. Q. **35**(1), 112–121 (2016)
14. Lameras, P., et al.: Essential features of serious game design in higher education: linking learning attributes to game mechanics. Br. J. Educ. Technol. (2016). https://doi.org/10.1111/bjet.12467
15. Borras-Gene, O., Martinez-Nuñez, M., Fidalgo-Blanco, A.: New challenges for the motivation and learning in engineering education using gamification in MOOC. Int. J. Eng. Educ. **32**(2B), 501–512 (2016)
16. Wintermeyer, A., Knautz, K.: Meaningful implementation of gamification in information literacy instruction. In: Kurbanoğlu, S., Boustany, J., Špiranec, S., Grassian, E., Mizrachi, D., Roy, L. (eds.) ECIL 2015. CCIS, vol. 552, pp. 350–359. Springer, Cham (2015). https://doi.org/10.1007/978-3-319-28197-1_36
17. Mery, Y., Newby, J.: Online by Design: the Essentials of Creating Information Literacy Courses. Rowman and Littlefield, Lanham (2014)
18. Mery, Y., DeFrain, E., Kline, E., Sult, L.: Evaluating the effectiveness of tools for online database instruction. Commun. Inf. Literacy **8**(1), 70–81 (2014)
19. Stiwinter, K.: Using an interactive online tutorial to expand library instruction. Internet Ref. Serv. Q. **18**(1), 15–41 (2013)

20. Secker, J., Coonan, E. (eds.): Rethinking Information Literacy: a Practical Framework for Supporting Learning. Facet, London (2013)
21. Courtney, M., Wilhoite-Mathews, S.: From distance education to online learning: practical approaches to information literacy instruction and collaborative learning in online environments. J. Libr. Adm. **55**(4), 261–277 (2015)
22. Mullins, K.: IDEA model from theory to practice: integrating information literacy in academic courses. J. Acad. Libr. **42**(1), 55–64 (2016)
23. Oakleaf, M.: Dangers and opportunities: a conceptual map of information literacy assessment approaches. Portal: Libr. Acad. **8**(3), 233–253 (2008)
24. Turnbow, D., Zeidman-Karpinski, A.: Don't use a hammer when you need a screwdriver: how to use the right tools to create assessment that matters. Commun. Inf. Literacy **10**(2), 143–162 (2016)
25. Lowe, M.S., Booth, C., Tagge, N., Stone, S.: Integrating an information literacy quiz into the learning management system. Commun. Inf. Literacy **8**(1), 115–130 (2014)
26. Simon, C.R.: Library and information literacy instruction in Israeli colleges and universities: a preliminary survey. Int. Inf. Libr. Rev. **45**(3/4), 108–113 (2014)
27. Johnson, B., Webber, S.: As we may think: information literacy as a discipline for the information age. Res. Strat. **20**(3), 108–121 (2003)
28. Zhao, J.C., Mawhinney, T.: Comparison of native Chinese-speaking and native English-speaking engineering students' information literacy challenges. J. Acad. Libr. **41** (6), 712–724 (2015)
29. Encheva, M.: Teaching information literacy courses in the context of library and information science education in Bulgaria: challenges and innovative approaches. J. Libr. Adm. **56**(5), 595–602 (2016)
30. UNESCO: Register for online media and information literacy course for youth (2016). http://www.unesco.org/new/en/communication-and-information/crosscutting-priorities/gender-and-media/women-make-the-news-2016/register-for-online-mil-course. Accessed 29 May 2017
31. Gill, C.: Hofstede's cultural dimensions and differences across cultures. Oxford University Press blog (2017). https://blog.oup.com/2017/03/hofstede-cultural-dimensions. Accessed 23 Mar 2017
32. Hicks, A.: Cultural shifts: putting critical information literacy into practice. Commun. Inf. Literacy **7**(1), 50–65 (2013)
33. Špiranec, S.: Chapter K. In: Global Perspectives on Information Literacy: Fostering a Dialogue for International Understanding, ACRL Student Learning and Information Committee, pp. 110–120 (2017). http://www.ala.org/acrl/sites/ala.org.acrl/files/content/publications/whitepapers/GlobalPerspectives_InfoLit.pdf. Accessed 6 Apr 2017
34. Dorner, D.G.: Chapter E. In: Global Perspectives on Information Literacy: Fostering a Dialogue for International Understanding, ACRL Student Learning and Information Committee, pp. 47–59 (2017). http://www.ala.org/acrl/sites/ala.org.acrl/files/content/publications/whitepapers/GlobalPerspectives_InfoLit.pdf. Accessed 6 Apr 2017
35. Laubersheimer, J., Ryan, D., Champaign, J.: InfoSkills2Go: using badges and gamification to teach information literacy skills and concepts to college-bound high school students. J. Libr. Adm. **56**(8), 924–938 (2016)
36. Forster, M. (ed.): Information Literacy in the Workplace. Facet, London (2017)
37. Kingori, G., Njiraine, D., Maina, S.: Implementation of information literacy in public libraries. Libr. Hi Tech News **33**(2), 17–22 (2016)
38. Haber, J.: MOOCs. MIT Press, Cambridge (2014)
39. Alman, S., Jumba, J. (eds.): MOOCs Now: Everything You Need to Know to Design, Set Up, and Run a Massive Open Online Course. Libraries Unlimited, Santa Barbara (2017)

40. Rieber, L.P.: Participation patterns in a massive open online course (MOOC) about statistics. Br. J. Educ. Technol. (2016). https://doi.org/10.1111/bjet.12504. Online Early View
41. Pope, J.: What are MOOCs good for? MIT Technol. Rev. (2017). http://www.technologyreview.com/533406/what-are-moocs-good-for. Accessed 9 Mar 2017
42. Hew, K.F.: Promoting engagement in online courses: what strategies can we learn from three highly rated MOOCs. Br. J. Educ. Technol. **47**(2), 320–341 (2016)
43. Salmon, G., et al.: Designing massive open online courses to take account of participant motivations and expectations. Br. J. Educ. Technol. (2016). https://doi.org/10.1111/bjet.12497. Online Early View
44. Stratton, C., Grace, R.: Exploring linguistic diversity of MOOCs: implications for international development. In: Proceedings of the Association for Information Science and Technology, vol. 53, no. 1 (2016). http://onlinelibrary.wiley.com/doi/10.1002/pra2.2016.14505301071/epdf. Accessed 12 Mar 2017
45. Pujar, S.M., Tadasad, P.G.: MOOCs - an opportunity for international collaboration in LIS education. A developing country's perspective. New Libr. World **117**(5/6), 360–373 (2016)

International Students' Expectations of Information Literacy Instruction

Nicole Johnston[1(✉)], Meggan Houlihan[2], and Jodi Neindorf[1]

[1] Edith Cowan University, Perth, Australia
{n.johnston,j.neindorf}@ecu.edu.au
[2] New York University Abu Dhabi, Abu Dhabi, UAE
meggan.houlihan@nyu.edu

Abstract. This paper presents the findings of a case study that investigated international university students' expectations and experiences of information literacy across two countries. The results from this case study provide insights that can be utilized by librarians working with international students, to plan and develop their information literacy instruction classes and programs. Armed with an awareness of what international students' expectations and experiences with information literacy programs are, librarians can develop more meaningful instruction that better meets the information needs of international students. Moving beyond the pilot survey, the researchers aim to improve the survey instrument and collaborate with librarians in several countries to collect data from institutions and universities around the world. Exploring and comparing results from a truly global population will only enhance library services to international students and help librarians better understand the specific information needs of international students.

Keywords: International students · Information literacy · Case study · Survey

1 Introduction

As the internationalization of higher education continues to flourish, which recently expanded from 1.3 million students studying outside of their home country in 1990 to 5.0 million studying away in 2014 [1], colleges and universities are increasingly concerned about how to best serve this student population. Academic libraries are no different. There has been a plethora of literature, both scholarly and non-scholarly, published on international students and various aspects of the academic library, in hopes of providing better services and programs to this population. A recent systematic review of library and information science (LIS) literature on international students and academic libraries found that while there are numerous publications on it, there is a lack of original research conducted on the topic. Most published pieces focused on "what we did" scenarios [2], where authors typically described a successful lesson, activity, or outreach event targeting international students. The authors called for LIS researchers and practitioners to incorporate evidenced-based research, results, and recommendations into their practice to improve services to international students.

S. Kurbanoğlu et al. (Eds.): ECIL 2017, CCIS 810, pp. 728–737, 2018.
https://doi.org/10.1007/978-3-319-74334-9_74

Working to address this gap in the literature, this paper presents the findings of a case study that investigated international university students' expectations and experiences of information literacy across two countries. A case study was selected as the best possible research method in order to gain both quantitative and qualitative feedback from respondents. The pilot study included the creation and distribution of an online survey that measured international university students' experiences and expectations of information literacy instruction, key questions and topics addressed include:

- what is information literacy
- expectations of the benefits of research skills to academic success and their future career
- expectations of research assistance
- expected content in library instruction sessions
- previous experience of information literacy.

The pilot study was conducted at two different academic institutions located in two separate continents, Edith Cowan University located in Western Australia and New York University Abu Dhabi (NYUAD) located in Abu Dhabi, United Arab Emirates (UAE). Edith Cowan University serves over 27,000 undergraduate and graduate students, and 4,000 international students from over 100 different countries attend the university annually [3]. NYUAD is composed of 1,050 undergraduate students representing 110 different nationalities [4]. Both institutions have culturally diverse campuses with unique student populations. The results from this case study provide insights that can be used by librarians working with international students, to better plan and develop their information literacy instruction classes and programs. Armed with an awareness of what international students' expectations and experience of information literacy programs are, librarians can develop more meaningful instruction that meets the information needs of international students.

2 Literature Review

There is a growing body of literature related to international students and academic libraries, and this literature review intends to provide a brief overview of the topic. According to a systematic review of LIS literature on information literacy and international students by Houlihan et al. [5], there were only 23 scholarly articles published between 1990 and 2014 that utilized authentic research methods to investigate information literacy and international students. This study also revealed that library instruction, library experience, and information seeking were the most popular research topics addressed within the data set. The authors also identified key recommendations on how to best serve international students from the data set which included, campus collaboration, staff training, assessment, cultural awareness, and library instruction [5].

Much research has been conducted on enhancing library instruction efforts to increase student participation, satisfaction levels, and learning within library instruction sessions and outreach programs targeted to international students. Language-based recommendations are numerous. In order to enhance library instruction sessions for international students, Amsberry [6] made several recommendations related to language including the notion that library instructors should clearly pronounce all words, use simple grammar and vocabulary, eliminate jargon, and utilize student feedback, in order to better communicate with international students. Conteh-Morgan [7] presented a series of suggestions for the incorporation of language acquisition theories into library instruction sessions in order to improve student learning. Martin et al. [8], collaborated with English as a Second Language (ESL) instructors to embedded information literacy skills and instruction into ESL composition classes. The program was very successful, and allowed international students to feel more comfortable around librarians. There is also some literature that looks at international students' knowledge of academic integrity and conventions. Han [9] found in his study on the information literacy development of higher research ESL students that the scholarly reference style and academic requirements for quality of sources in Australia differed from the students' home country of China. Hughes [10] also found that international students were unused to the academic conventions that were required of them, such as referencing and plagiarism.

Orientating international students to the academic library is another instruction area ripe with literature. Hoffman and Popa [11], wrote about the need to provide personalized library instruction for international students, and encourage staff training so staff are better able to help identify when international students were struggling with library resources and services. Liestman and Wu [12] experimented with offering library orientations for international students in their native language, and suggested further research on library instruction and orientations in students' native tongues. Lunger and Kubo created a tiered orientation program that consisted of "a campus orientation presentation, library orientation and tours, information literacy workshops, and international peer-advisor training" [13, p. 605]. Assessment data concluded that international students who used the library were more likely to ask for help [13, p. 616].

3 Method

This case study presents the findings of an exploratory study that was conducted in Australia and the UAE, which investigated international students' expectations and experiences of information literacy. The overarching aim of the pilot study was to distribute a survey at two global universities, collect feedback and data, improve the survey instrument, and expand the survey to include other universities around the globe, while also increasing the number of survey participants. The online survey, conducted via Qualtrics, consisted of five demographic questions and thirteen questions related to information literacy instruction, including previous, current, and future expectations and experiences of information literacy. In Australia, convenience sampling was used to disseminate the survey, and it was disseminated through the library at Edith Cowan University. The survey was added to the library news webpage and promoted in information literacy classes, as well as emailed to lecturers to disseminate. There was a low rate of return. In the UAE, the survey was disseminated on behalf of the NYUAD Library through emails from select faculty members to students enrolled in their classes. There was an intermediate return rate.

4 Findings

This section provides detailed information about the survey data related to demographics, prior library experience, understanding information literacy, and expectations of information literacy.

4.1 Demographics

A total of 49 international students partially or fully completed the pilot survey, and demographic data from both institutions varied. Students were allowed to abstain from any question, thus making results of respondents vary by question. Twenty-five international students completed the survey in the UAE and 24 international students completed the survey in Australia. The authors defined an international student as one who studied outside his/her home country. Data showed that participants from the UAE pilot survey were from 24 different countries including, Bulgaria, Ethiopia, Ukraine, and India. Thirteen (52%) of participants were male, and 21 (84%) of students were between the ages of 18–21. The respondents were studying a wide array of academic disciplines, most heavily in science and economics. All students were enrolled in undergraduate programs, and it should be noted that NYUAD is primarily an undergraduate campus. In the Australian survey, students who completed the survey hailed from the Middle East, including Iran, Saudi Arabia and Kuwait, Asia, including India, China, and Vietnam, and Europe. 15 (63%) of the respondents were female with 13 (54%) of the respondents being over 30. The respondents were studying in a range of majors and degrees including undergraduate, Masters and Ph.D. degrees in education, nursing, marketing, and computer science.

4.2 Prior Library Experience

Understanding international students' prior information literacy experiences is crucial to understanding how to best serve this population. As seen in Fig. 1, there were mixed responses to how often international students visited a library prior to arriving at university. 11 (48%) of the students studying in Australia had visited a library more than once a week prior to coming to university, with only one student (4%) having no access to a school library and three (13%) never having visited a library. Of the 24 students in the UAE who responded, 12 (50%) students stated they only occasionally used the library prior to arriving at university. Six (25%) students used a library more than once a week and only one (4%) respondent did not have access to a library.

Many students had mixed responses about being previously taught research skills by a librarian prior to arriving at university. 12 (52%) students in Australia and 13 (54%) students in the UAE had never participated in a library instruction session. Four (17%) students in Australia reported having been taught a library research skill through a one-on-one consultation with a librarian, while seven (29%) students in the UAE attended one - four library workshops with a librarian in high school.

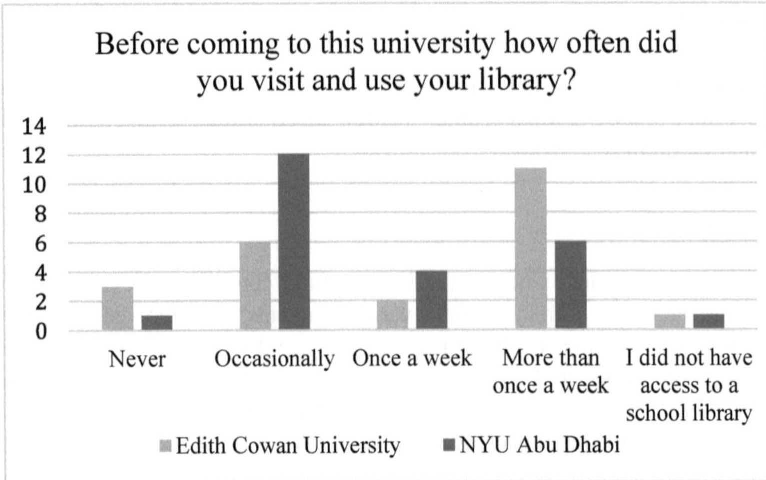

Fig. 1. Before coming to this university how often did you visit and use your library?

4.3 Understanding Information Literacy

There were 24 responses in the Australian survey and 25 responses in the UAE survey to the question: what is your understanding of information literacy? Respondents were able to select more than one definition. As you can see in Fig. 2, 16 students in Australia (67%) and 20 students in the UAE (83%) understood information literacy as: recognize when information is needed and have the ability to locate, evaluate, and use information effectively. In the Australian survey, 11 students (46%) reported that information literacy is: being able to use information to learn something; and only four (17%) respondents stated that they had no understanding of information literacy. While in the UAE survey, 12 respondents (50%) stated that information literacy is: being able to use information for class; and only three respondents had no knowledge of information literacy.

When it came to answering the question: how important do you think having research skills is for completing your degree? 22 (95%) of the respondents in Australia felt it was important or very important, and 21 (67%) respondents in the UAE felt it was important or very important. Overall, only one (4%) of the respondents in the Australian survey thought research skills were unimportant for passing his/her degree. 18 (78%) of the respondents in Australia and 22 (70%) respondents in the UAE felt that library services were extremely important or important to the success of their studies.

The students were asked, as international students, what barriers they encountered when they began studying at their respective universities. Respondents could select more than one answer. As seen in Table 1, the biggest barrier for both countries was academic writing. For Australian students the next biggest barriers were referencing and finding resources in the library. For the UAE students, the next biggest barrier was referencing followed by conducting research.

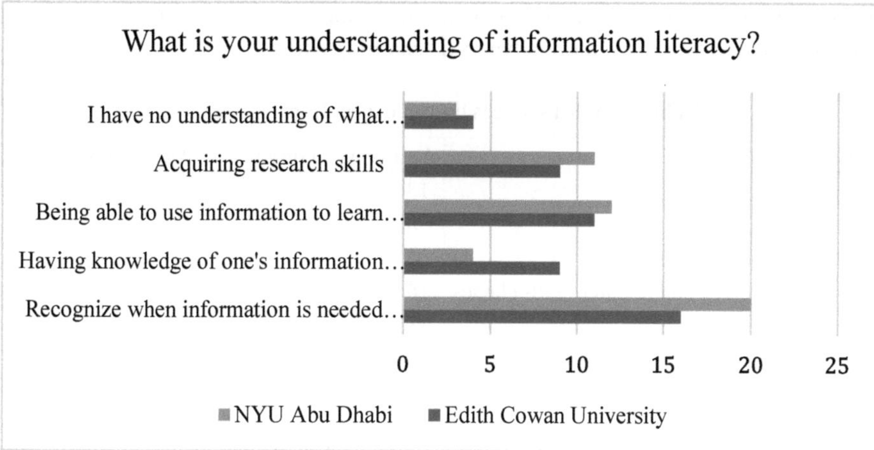

Fig. 2. What is your understanding of information literacy?

Table 1. What barriers did you encounter when you started studying at this university?

Barriers	Australia responses	UAE responses
Reading in English	4	2
Finding resources in the library	12	7
Academic writing	17	13
Understanding academic integrity rules at the university	9	5
Conducting research	6	9
Referencing and citations	13	10
I encountered no barriers	0	3
Other (please specify)	4	2
Total	**65**	**51**

4.4 Expectations of Information Literacy

Students were also asked what services they expected from the library, as well as what library services they could expect from a one-on-one interaction with a librarian. Respondents could select more than one response. As seen in Table 2, students in both countries felt that providing access to books and databases was the most important library service followed by access to computers and study space. Students also specified that they wanted more quiet study space and longer borrowing times. When it came to one to one interactions, the majority of Australian students felt that librarians should give them assistance finding resources for assignments followed closely by teaching them how to use the library's resources. With the students studying in the UAE, it was the reverse with the majority of students expecting librarians to assist them with finding resources for assignments closely followed by teaching them how to use the library's resources. Students also specified they would like more subject specific advice related to research and to be shown more advanced searching skills.

Table 2. What services do you expect from a library?

Library services	Australia responses	UAE responses
Computers and internet	18	24
Orientation tours	8	5
Providing books and databases	23	24
Information literacy and research skills classes	16	12
Study space	18	23
Other (please specify)	4	0
Total	**87**	**88**

Respondents were asked about which library workshops they thought would help them with their studies, as well as if they thought there should be specific library workshops for international students. Many of the students in Australia thought that using library databases, finding resources, and writing skills would help them most on their studies. The respondents in the UAE also felt that using library databases, writing skills, and using citation management software would be useful workshops for them. The other responses stated that workshops on resources for systematic reviews would be helpful.

In response to the question on whether there should be specific library workshops for international students, 13 (57%) of the students located in Australia and 12 (50%) of students located in the UAE felt that there should be specific library classes for international students. Students participating in both surveys suggested the most important workshop to be offered should be how to use online library databases. The UAE survey responses also highlighted the importance of academic writing and citations. Finally, respondents were asked how important they think information literacy/research skills are to their future careers. Both surveys yielded similar results. Twenty-one (92%) of the respondents in Australia and 20 (80%) respondents in the UAE felt information literacy and research skills were important or very important to their future career. No respondents thought information literacy and research skills were not at all important.

5 Discussion

This section provides further insight into information literacy expectations, prior library experience, and collaboration.

5.1 Information Literacy Expectations

In general, students in both Australia and the UAE had similar expectations of both the academic library and librarians. International students, included in this pilot study, expected libraries to provide access books and databases, computers, and study spaces. The respondents' main expectations of one-on-one interactions with librarians were how to use the library's resources and assistance finding resources for assignment. In both countries barriers international students faced included academic writing, referencing, finding resources, and conducting research. These barriers also translated into the suggested library workshops for international students. Students suggested workshops in finding resources and using library databases, writing skills, and using citation management software. The finding that referencing is a barrier correlates with other authors' findings that international students often lack knowledge of referencing and citation rules and need instruction in finding resources for their research [9].

5.2 Library Experience

In the Australian survey, although most international students had visited a library before coming to university, most of the students had never attended a library research class before coming to the university. On the other hand, a majority of respondents located in the UAE stated they occasionally visited a library prior to arrival at university (50%) and never attended a library workshop (46%). This is useful data for librarians to be aware of as the knowledge that international students have limited and varied previous experience with libraries. Instructional experiences can influence how topics for information literacy programs and one-on-one sessions are developed. The international students in this study, with limited previous research skills training, stated they would like information literacy workshops on topics, such as finding library resources and citations. Most international students also feel there should be specific library classes for international students. This fits with Hoffman and Popa [11], who advocate for the need to provide personalized library instruction for international students. Creating active and engaging library workshops will better serve this population.

5.3 Collaboration

Since international students, included in this case study, ranked academic writing skills as one of their main barriers to their academic success, along with finding resources and referencing. This data provides unique opportunities for librarians to collaborate with academic writing staff, in order to provide instruction programs that meet both the writing and information literacy needs of international students. The NYUAD Library reiterates the importance of critical research and critical writing by collaborating on outreach programs, such as capstone boot camps, research breakfasts, and orientation efforts, with the Writing Center. The relationship is so strong that the Writing Center moved into Research Services, located in the library, in 2015. Zhang [14] suggested that libraries should offer writing workshops, in addition to traditional library workshops. There are endless possibilities for on-campus and off-campus partners to create innovative programming and instruction to better prepare international students for academic success.

6 Conclusion

This pilot study on international students' expectations and experiences of information literacy seeks to fill a gap in LIS literature by using an evidenced-based research method to better understand this student population. Study findings show that international students have varied past and present expectations and experiences with information literacy, but a majority of respondents agreed that information literacy and research skills are helpful to their future careers. The findings also suggest that the international students who participated in the survey, came to university with little prior information literacy instruction and face barriers to academic success, including academic writing, finding resources, and referencing. LIS researchers interested in investigating their international student population and information literacy may want to recreate this pilot survey at their home institutions. The authors also advocate for the use of mixed methods when researching this population. Interviews, focus groups, and research diaries would add an interesting dimension to this topic and contribute to a growing body of work on this topic. The pilot study results, as well as future survey results, will be of great use to the library community as librarians can use the results to prepare information literacy instruction that meets the needs of international students as well as establish collaborative programs with academic writing departments.

References

1. The State of International Student Mobility (2015). http://monitor.icef.com/2015/11/the-state-of-international-student-mobility-in-2015/
2. Click, A.B., Wiley, C., Houlihan, M.: The internationalization of the academic library: a systematic review of 25 years of literature on international students. Coll. Res. Libr. **78**(3), 328–358 (2017)
3. About ECU. http://www.ecu.edu.au/about-ecu/welcome-to-ecu/about-ecu
4. By the Numbers - NYU Abu Dhabi. http://nyuad.nyu.edu/en/admissions/student-profiles/by-the-numbers.html
5. Houlihan, M., Wiley, C., Click, A.B.: International students and information literacy: a systematic review. Ref. Rev. Serv. **45**(2) (2017, pre-print)
6. Amsberry, D.: Talking the talk: library classroom communication and international students. J. Acad. Libr. **34**(4), 354–357 (2008)
7. Conteh-Morgan, M.: Connecting the dots: limited English proficiency, second language learning theories, and information literacy instruction. J. Acad. Libr. **28**(4), 191–196 (2002)
8. Martin, J.A., Reaume, K.M., Reeves, E.A., Wright, R.D.: Relationship building with students and instructors of ESL: bridging the gap for library instruction and services. Ref. Serv. Rev. **40**(3), 352–367 (2012)
9. Han, J.: The experiences of Chinese PhD students in Australia: encountering information literacy challenges. J. Inf. Literacy **6**(1), 3–17 (2012)
10. Hughes, H.: International students using online information resources to learn: complex experience and learning needs. J. Further Higher Educ. **3**(1), 126–146 (2013)
11. Hoffman, I., Popa, O.: Library orientation and instruction for international students: the University of California-Davis experience. RQ **25**(3), 356–360 (1986)
12. Liestman, D.: Reference services and the international adult learner. Ref. Libr. **33**(69–70), 363–378 (2000)

13. Langer, C., Kubo, H.: From the ground up: creating a sustainable library outreach program for international students. J. Libr. Adm. **55**(8), 605–621 (2015)
14. Zhang, L.: Communication in academic libraries: an East Asian perspective. Ref. Serv. Rev. **34**(1), 164 (2006)

The Impact of Creativity on Information Literacy Instruction

Zachary Newell(✉)

Simmons College, Boston, MA, USA
zlnewell@gmail.com

Abstract. The author has been researching and reflecting on the importance of creativity in enhancing the information literacy classroom, particularly in the context of an academic library. The author approaches research with an increasing interest in exploring creativity as part of the ACRL Framework and the way the creative information literacy component fits into the holistic approach of a changing, more engaging curriculum on college campuses. Recently, the author conducted a research study that explored the role of creativity in information literacy. By examining the impact of library instruction on various formats of student learning, this paper will reflect on the definition of creativity, how it is implemented in the library classroom, and the results of a recent research study that outline next steps and opportunities.

Keywords: Information literacy · Reflective pedagogy · Creativity Arts · ACRL Framework

1 Introduction

The author has been researching and reflecting on the importance creativity plays in enhancing the information literacy classroom, particularly in the context of an academic library. The author's preliminary belief in approaching information literacy is that the library should not be so focused on the user as a consumer of a service, but instead on the student as both a growing organism and as a reflective learner. The research is rooted in larger theories on pedagogy—critical and reflective pedagogy, but also within the intersection of phenomenology, liminality and third space theory. Central to this research is the idea of pushing the academic library to be a greater participant in engaged learning. The basis for engaged learning stems from an interest in being more intentional in teaching and constructing learning in the classroom, and also in embracing creative approaches to learning through creative pedagogy—that the learning process is never entirely predictable. The challenge for the researcher comes from defining creativity. In asking for a more creative approach to library instruction, does the research ask for librarians to be more artistic or to physically create something?

The researcher has employed the use of a survey as a first step in garnering feedback in defining and implementing creativity in the library classroom. The survey is comprised of closed questions as well as some open-ended questions. The qualitative

S. Kurbanoğlu et al. (Eds.): ECIL 2017, CCIS 810, pp. 738–748, 2018.
https://doi.org/10.1007/978-3-319-74334-9_75

component provides the framework for the researcher to examine the motivations across academia in general, the library specifically, in dissecting opinions about creativity—how it is defined, what it means, and how it is attached to other theories of learning; but it also allows the researcher to study the impact of creative approaches to teaching information literacy on student learning. While there are a series of questions that are facilitated by the introduction of the framework, and how those questions frame a larger question about creativity and the theory/pedagogy it informs, the driving question for the research is: How do librarians characterize the role of creativity in their teaching/learning process?

2 Review of Literature (Brief)

Creativity is loosely defined, with little formal research for its application in library instruction. In *Fostering Creativity—a holistic framework for teaching creativity,* a framework for creativity is presented that calls for cultivating a psychological disposition that frees students from "self-constructed obstacles." Students, the authors argue, are endowed with the creative problem solving strategies and the capacity to apply creative techniques [1]. This involves readjusted thinking in order to reframe a problem and to search efficiently, and to plan time for repetition and reflective thinking. The goal of academia, according to Alison James and Stephen Brookfield in their recent book, *Engaging Imagination*, is to create lively classrooms and help students become critically reflective [2].

Before we send students to books, periodicals, and websites, we need to teach them *about* information. The new Information Literacy Frames provide an opportunity for both instructors and librarians working together to draw on critical literacy theory, or critical pedagogy, where the instructor introduces topics and directs learning but does so with student input and by valuing student experiences. In *Information Literacy and Reflective Pedagogical Praxis*, Jacobs explains that critical pedagogy invites creative, reflective dialog. Jacobs explains that "To teach students about personally meaningful information and non-analytic information processes means first and foremost to create a space where inner life can be nurtured, where creativity can emerge, where students can love the questions" [3]. Play facilitates five cognitive processes involved with creativity: problem framing, divergent thinking, mental transformations, practice with alternative solutions, and evaluative ability [4].

In a recent talk entitled *The Liminal Library*, Fister cites the new ACRL Frames as moving away from competencies that placed too much emphasis on observing the rules of finding and evaluating information. The shift from linear-based competencies to threshold concepts represents a place in an intellectual journey that is between understanding—what Fister refers to as liminality. Liminality represents a journey in navigating uncertainty through a "transferrable learning experience . . . by increasing self-knowledge and confidence," by participating in the making of meaning [4]. This making of meaning comes through a state of questioning and probing, where students can rethink assumptions and participate in the making of knowledge (creation) as a continuous, successive dialog for the way information fits into a personal context of understanding. Students are no longer receivers of a standard of information, but participators in a new reality of exploration and discovery that contributes to establishing a new voice based on independent experiences and a self-created authority. The environment is no longer dominated by process (standards) but integrated into a conversation about the place of information in one's own life.

In an academic setting, the researcher seeks to explore the connection between the new ACRL Framework, the way it is used and implemented, conceptually, and its effectiveness in precipitating the way creativity is manifested in the classroom, practically. The researcher suspects that little study has been done assessing the impact and/or effectiveness of creativity as a manifest extended from the new ACRL Framework. Paired with metaliteracy, technologies that facilitate creative learning through the academic library, and other pedagogies explored as part of student engagement across campuses, the researcher suspects that there is a growing interest in exploring creativity as part of the Framework, and the way the creative information literacy component fits into the holistic approach of a changing, albeit, more engaging, curriculum on college campuses.

3 Definition of Creativity

The researcher defines creativity in information literacy as "the ability to engage learners through a critically reflective process in order to foster divergent thinking, and where conversation and questioning is encouraged to challenge and reshape identities" [5]. The definition is extrapolated from the review of literature. So that a holistic definition is presented, creativity in the library classroom is also defined as a process where learners are encouraged to play, explore and transform in a context that allows for managed failure—failure framed by reflection and iteration and less by penalty and closure. Providing a definition invited a foundation of assumptions in which respondents could work, but also a point of departure to reflect more concretely on differing interpretations of creativity.

4 Sources of Research Material

Information literacy, defined as the ability to locate, access, evaluate, and use information efficiently, effectively and within legal and ethical guidelines (ACRL, 2000) has evolved in the past two years to include a Framework for Information Literacy in Higher Education (ACRL, 2015) that grows out of a belief that information literacy as an educational reform movement will realize its potential only through a richer, more complex set of core ideas. The Framework is based on conceptual understandings that organize many other concepts and ideas about information, research, and scholarship into a coherent whole—a cluster of interconnected core concepts, with flexible options for implementation, rather than one set of standards or learning outcomes. The *Framework* depends on these core ideas of "metaliteracy", with a special focus on metacognition, or critical self-reflection, as crucial to becoming "more self-directed in a rapidly changing ecosystem."[1]

The researcher's project sought to examine creativity in the library classroom, and how the ACRL Framework might influence or facilitate these creative approaches. The researcher contends that creativity is infiltrating learning in higher education. A survey represents the quickest way to garner feedback while providing insight into further in-depth qualitative research.

The survey is comprised of 28 questions, utilizing scaled, multiple choice and open-ended questions. In the survey, librarians are asked to reflect briefly on their teaching and their students' learning in their instruction/information literacy sessions. The researcher used an information literacy listserv established by the American Library Association (ALA) to target librarians and faculty who teach information literacy classes, and who are actively involved in interpreting the Framework and applying the concepts into their teaching. The survey was sent out in two (2) different phases. The questionnaire contains three (3) parts:

(1) questions about the approaches to information literacy;
(2) the way the Framework advocates for changes to that approach, or facilitates creative practice;
(3) how a creative approach to information literacy contributes to transformative learning (impact on student learning, or success).

5 Data Collection, Analysis, Results

When reporting the results of the study the researcher used a questionnaire whose face validity was established by experts (practitioners in the field of information literacy instruction). The survey was pilot tested on a subset of participants and edited/tailored before final implementation.

The researcher compiled data via survey questions that were then transcribed. The researcher created a series of "a priori" codes that were derived from the conceptual framework, the list of potential research questions, the actual research questions, the list of survey questions, and problem areas. The researcher used "a priori" codes to help decide which concepts and themes to communicate in the evaluation as well as how the data should be organized and coded.

The researcher worked to categorize the data by themes. They were then matched to what the researcher determined were "emergent codes", those that were drawn out from the data. The emergent codes were paired with the pre-set codes to see which overlapped. The major codes/themes, as recorded by the researcher and confirmed by two additional researchers, include "creative teaching", "creativity in learning", "connection to the information literacy framework", "challenges/barriers", and the "role of library in providing creativity."

[1] The Framework allows for flexibility, outlining six different concepts: Authority Is Constructed and Contextual; Information Creation as a Process; Information Has Value; Research as Inquiry; Scholarship as Conversation; Searching as Strategic Exploration.

The responses to the survey can be broken down into five broad themes:

(1) creativity in teaching
(2) creativity in learning
(3) the role of the library in providing creativity
(4) barriers to being creative in the classroom
(5) connection to the Information Literacy Framework.

The total number of people who entered the survey was 227, and 121 of those respondents completed the survey in its entirety (n = 121). Of the full responses, 64 (53.8%) are considered faculty; 48 (40.3%) do not have faculty status. Of the 121, 50.4% (n = 60) have been in the profession ten (10) or more years. Respondents overwhelmingly—79.3% (n = 96), stated that they teach standalone information literacy classes, also known as one-shot style instruction classes (non-credit bearing), which equated to less control over the implementation of class instruction. The five categories below represent the most important questions under the broad themes. Some of the questions were not directly as important to the current study, but insightful for further a study on creativity in information literacy. A few of the important ancillary questions not reviewed as broad themes will be reviewed in the discussion section below.

5.1 Creative Teaching

The primary question in the broad theme of creative teaching asks: Would you consider your approach to information literacy instruction to be "Creative"? 101 respondents, or 83.5%, answered that their approach can be considered creative. The researcher believes that the answer corresponds to the definition outlined at the beginning of the survey (for consistency and clarity), and with respondents' notions of creativity as defined in their responses. The largest themes in affirming creative practice in the library classroom, ten respondents explicitly stated an interest in creating "out-of-the box" assignments with a variation stating an interest in experimenting with techniques and approaches in the classroom, or more overtly, "shaking things up." Seven respondents stated a direct relationship to "fun" activities, with three specifically relating fun to a variation of gamification, video animation or storytelling. Of the three respondents, two cited active learning exercises as part of gaming. Another five respondents cited activities or narratives explicitly as directly relating to students and as responsible for personalizing the connection to students, which takes learning a new and unanticipated direction. Five respondents stated that they employ hands-on activities, understanding concepts and resources on their own time.

One of the later, follow-up questions asked if there is an opportunity for any of the instructors to offer any of the following as part of their class:

- Problem framing
- Divergent thinking
- Mental transformations
- Practice with alternative solutions
- Evaluative ability.

The survey also asked if information literacy classes include dialog for the way information fits into a personal context of understanding. Both of the questions were further expanding the survey definition of creativity while getting respondents to think about relating information to everyday experiences, how students can use the information to solve problems and decipher authority, and evaluate different pathways for appropriating and utilizing the information.

5.2 Creativity in Learning

In order to avoid putting the onus on instructors in the classroom, it is imperative to perceive shifts in learning from students. How does a desire on the part of students necessitate a change to the way classes are taught? How does creativity in the classroom change the kind of learning the library provides? Many of the answers explained that creativity is linked to engaging students in an iterative process, challenging preconceived notions about information, and creating a learning environment in which students want to participate. Many of the responses indicated a variation on a theme that the more emotional and reflective, the more engaging and meaningful the learning is for the students. Twenty respondents cited creativity as more fun, or that it creates more buy-in for the students, and that the engagement improves the learning experience. Eight responses cited creativity as facilitating a change to the approach in teaching, and therefore a more substantial shift for students (qualified by saying in one response that teaching is cross-disciplinary and beyond the confines of the library). Other responses touched on reaching students with different learning styles, enabling learners in their own way, and using creativity to change the purpose of library instruction.

The question was asked: In your opinion, does creativity in the classroom transform the library experience, and does it engage students in the research and learning process? Ninety-five, or 78.51%, responded in the affirmative, and almost unanimously cited engaging the learner in the classroom as part of the transformative experience, and furthermore, that creativity is empowering to students. Creativity offers real learning and personalizes the learning experience. One response was that creativity extends the reach of metacognition and makes it part of [their] learning experience. Another respondent offered that creativity as transformative experience is basic educational theory (Dewey, Vygotsky) on how and why we learn best–application, investment, approval, engagement.

5.3 Connection to the Information Literacy Framework

The study on creativity looked into the ways the ACRL Framework might influence thinking about creative approaches to teaching information literacy, and toward creative approaches to information on behalf of students/learners. The first question on the Framework was: In your opinion, does the ACRL Framework support creativity for students? The question asks respondents to explain their answer. The ACRL Framework is new and veiled in general concepts that can be interpreted in various ways, without an overt reference to creativity. The questions allow respondents to reflect on what is stated in the Framework. Twenty-seven of the 121 respondents indicated that the Framework supports engagement. Tailored to engagement, nine respondents indicated that the Framework made learning more "fun"—more dynamic for meeting student needs. Similar to engagement, five respondents answered that the Framework supported creativity in a variation of higher thinking, and made learning more personal and inspirational for students. Respondents suggested a connection to pedagogical influences of Bloom's taxonomy and influences of contextualism.

The researcher must also ask: does a departure from the standards provide more flexibility, more of an opportunity to be creative? In your opinion, is the ACRL Framework more flexible than the standards? Please explain. The question was intended to garner some reflection from respondents—for those who have given the Framework some thought and for those who have not. The vast majority of respondents agreed that, yes, the Framework is more flexible. One hundred and ten respondents, or 90.1% said yes, but there were some variations in qualifying the "yes" attached to an agreement for the flexibility. Many agree that flexibility is not always a good thing. Many respondents agree that the standards were too prescriptive, but the clear guidelines were helpful in providing outcomes for teachers and students. The flexibility of the Framework, while viewed as generally positive, comes with what the researcher might describe as a general anxiety for how to implement something that is so flexible. The Framework is seen by a few respondents as less flexible if used as a measuring tool —for outcomes and assessment. As a guide toward understanding, it is more flexible, and with this means using what works for the librarian while potentially ignoring other parts. This also means the potential for the Framework to work in isolated parts rather than holistically.

The question was also asked: How, if at all, does creativity fit into the ACRL Framework? A majority of respondents indicated that creativity does fit into the ACRL Framework. The responses that affirmed the connection did so by citing a relationship between the concepts and the flexibility they offered. There is a clear connection for some between the concepts—a shift from the outlined, "mechanical" process of the standards—and the flexibility, or freedom, offered by the Framework. This would allow librarians the ability to offer fresh and inventive ways for teaching information literacy, especially outside of the traditional classroom perspective. The nature of information and scholarship is evolving, and simple bound theses and five-paragraph essays are no longer the norm. Being able to have the flexibility in the framework for video and other media projects is useful (even if not addressed directly)." Even if the Framework does not directly address the idea of creativity, it allows flexibility and freedom in interpreting and applying the concepts, in this case, "Information Creation as a Process," for allowing the construction of knowledge. "Ideas in the Framework guide how instructors think about accessing, evaluating and utilizing information. I think it is a more holistic way of thinking about information. This can affect the activities instructors plan by encouraging creativity in teaching students the practical as well as the philosophical ideas about information in general and in a library setting."

5.4 Barriers

If the ACRL Framework provides flexibility, or the "permission" to engage students in more meaningful ways, what are the barriers to implementing creative practice in the classroom? The question was asked: In your opinion, does creativity in the classroom transform the library experience, and does it engage students in the research and learning process? Please Explain. The researcher felt this was one of the more important questions in terms of understanding a pivotal change in the approach toward information literacy instruction. Of the 121 responses, 26 said either "no" or that they were not sure if creativity could transform the library experience. Many of the "no" responses cited a one-shot (one-time, fifty-minute instruction class) as a hurdle to implement creativity in the classroom, and therefore were unable to "assess" its impact. A few of the "no" responses also stated that it depends on the learners. Others were hesitant to embrace the correlation between creativity and a transformative class, citing hesitation in embracing a definition of creativity as effective. One response said that the idea of creativity is too broad. If tied to learning objectives, creativity could be transformative.

The researcher noticed that many of the respondents had a hard time grappling with the definition of creativity. It was hard for some to separate the definition from ideas associated with artistic practice, even with a brief definition outlined at the beginning of the survey. Those who responded in the affirmative almost unanimously cited engaging the learner in the classroom as part of the transformative experience and that creativity is empowering to students. Creativity offers real learning and personalizes the learning experience. One response offered that creativity extends the reach of metacognition and makes it part of [their] learning experience.

From the outset of the survey, respondents overwhelmingly—79.3% (n = 96), stated that they teach standalone information literacy classes, also known as "one-shot" style instruction classes (non-credit bearing), which equated to less control over the implementation of class instruction. Yet, when an ancillary question near the end of the survey was asked about collaborating and coordinating with other faculty classes, 103 respondents, or 85%, acknowledged that they do collaborate in some form (Table 1). It is unclear if the role of collaboration as it is currently practiced provides a meaningful correlation between information literacy class collaborations and creative classroom practice.

Table 1. Collaboration between the instruction class and other faculty taught classes

Do the activities offered in the instruction class coordinate (collaborate) with other faculty taught classes, or are they offered independent of other classes?		
Answer options	%	n
Yes, collaboratively	38.0	46
No, independently	8.3	10
Both, collaboratively and independently	47.1	57
Other (please specify)	6.6	8

5.5 Role of Library in Providing Creativity

Gauging the role of the library is to discern perceptions about the place of the library on a College campus. More specifically, there is an opportunity to gauge how learning is perceived in the context of information literacy and within the space of the library. What do you think is the role of the library in employing creative practice in support of learning? Most of the responses to this question did not go into too much depth. The majority of the responses did reaffirm the need for creativity in the library, and the best way to get there is by employing collaborations with faculty and other groups, such as the First Year Experience office or the Writing Center. A large number of respondents also cited engagement, a recurring theme in relating creativity to teaching students. Respondents also viewed creativity as an opportunity to act as leaders in the field, and as an opportunity to sell what librarians do with the premise that the library is the largest classroom. Finally, respondents noted an obligation to support and promote creativity in conjunction with other pedagogical practices and as an opportunity to take more risks in taking a leadership role in the classroom and among peer faculty outside of the library. Those respondents who had a tenuous view of the role of creative practice in support of learning and felt that sound pedagogical practice was more important than being creative. Another respondent said that the library is not an actor, while yet another said the library should stop trying to be everything to everybody. The respondents see a role/need for creativity but also see barriers in implementing a creative classroom.

What are the implications of a creative classroom on teaching and learning? How do you think the ACRL Framework would foster "transformative learning" as it relates to creative practice? A few respondents felt that the Framework would construct a personal relationship to information for students, and in that context could act as a guide for "transformative learning." It encourages a wider range of information literacy concepts, a more critical approach to knowledge creation and academic practice and encourages a more student centered (student engaged) approach to information literacy. It has the potential to offer librarians and students greater flexibility and a chance to be more reflective. The Framework, one respondent noted, provides reflection about what librarians are doing and why. It directly addresses transformative learning and incorporates creative practice into the knowledge practices and dispositions of many of the frames. The Framework also provides the impetus to try different things and to better assess student learning.

6 Discussion

The idea of creativity has its foundations in library and information science. The library is a place that historically has promoted convergent thinking. Even with changes in the way higher education views information literacy, there are opportunities for librarians to help students develop capacities for divergent thinking. Creativity and what this means for librarians as educators creates opportunities for re-thinking the library as a catalyst for transformation across higher education. This is revealed in the survey.

The survey represented a rather lengthy attempt at garnering feedback on a topic that, while not new, is difficult to define and pinpoint. The survey might have received more feedback had the number of questions been reduced to between eight and 12 of the most basic questions. As it stands, 28 questions represented a survey that was probably too long. The nature of the research, which involves delving into definitions of creativity and theory on teaching, including transformative theory, requires interactions with teaching librarians and with students.

It is also worth exploring more of the barriers and opportunities to implementing the creative classroom and what this means for both instructors/librarians and students. It is also worth exploring assessment initiatives of information literacy instructors, and how instructors assess the creative classroom—specifically identifying the correlation between those who say they are creative in teaching and the perception of student and/or faculty satisfaction. Areas for further research that were touched on in the survey include the relationship, or correlation, between the creative classroom and student grades, and the way in which collaborations across campus are used to bolster the creative classroom, as well as how best to leverage those collaborations/partnerships for student success. Additionally, it is worth exploring the way the ACRL Framework pairs with other standards and rubrics in facilitating a campus-wide conversation about the role of creativity, especially as it might garner feedback on the way collaborations are formed and/or solidified in implementing creative ways for teaching information literacy. This is especially important given recent discussion about framing a personalized meaning to information while addressing information that exists in "fake" or "alternative" spheres.

In the survey, the researcher should have provided an opportunity for respondents to define creativity in their own terms. It remains difficult to characterize creativity after delving into a literature review that outlines components of reflective and critical pedagogy/information literacy. In surveying practitioners, they do not have access to the same line of thinking about the ways creativity are molded and shaped from the pedagogical mold (literature review) seen by the researcher.

There is an interpretive and descriptive approach to the research that explores different ways in which librarians and students experience and respond to creativity and to various phenomena and situations in the world around them. The researcher would need to delve further into the research to obtain a view into both students and librarians' life-worlds (inner world of immediate experience) and to understand their personal meanings—the way they respond to creative stimuli in different contexts in the library, but with a focus on the library classroom. It is especially important to hear from students, those who are receivers of information literacy instruction. While the study focused primarily on practitioners within the library (librarians), it would also be fruitful to expand research to a wider sphere of LIS professionals—those outside the immediate realm of the library. In that case, a qualitative study would be appropriate for follow-up. A qualitative study has already been started, specifically involving interviews and classroom observation, in order to gain direct interaction in defining terms and gathering opinions about approaches to teaching.

References

1. Berg, H., Taatila, V., Volkmann, C.: Fostering creativity - a holistic framework for teaching creativity. Dev. Learn. Organ. **26**(6), 5–8 (2012)
2. James, A., Brookfield, S.: Engaging Imagination: Helping Students Become Creative and Reflective Thinkers. Jossey-Bass, San Francisco (2014)
3. Jacobs, H.: Information literacy and reflective pedagogical praxis. J. Acad. Librariansh. **34**(3), 256–262 (2008)
4. Fister, B.: The liminal library. LILAC (2015). http://barbarafister.com/LiminalLibrary.pdf
5. Elmborg, J.K.: Libraries as the spaces between us: recognizing and valuing the third space. Ref. User Serv. Q. **50**(4), 338–350 (2011)

Threshold Concepts and Information Experience in IL Professional Education: Curriculum Design for Online Learning

Virginia M. Tucker(✉)

School of Information, San José State University, San José, CA, USA
virginia.tucker@sjsu.edu

Abstract. Information literacy (IL) professionals are engaged in teaching, mentoring, and collaboration, roles that call for deep understanding of strategies for navigating the information environment. The relatively new construct of *information experience* provides insights into these integrative roles and is considered together with the theoretical construct of *threshold concepts*. Threshold concepts in the library and information science (LIS) domain have been explored for professional search expertise and for information literacy. The discussion extends from the IL professional's roles to the experiential realm of threshold knowledge in online learning. Practical illustrations of designing online curriculum for information professionals based on threshold concept research findings are provided.

Keywords: Information experience · MLIS education
Information professional education · Online education · Online learning
Threshold concepts

1 Introduction

Information literacy professionals are engaged in teaching, mentoring, and collaboration, roles that call for deep understanding of information structures, learning design, and tactics for navigating the information environment. These roles extend to facilitating and furthering the understandings of others in significant ways as well. The relatively new construct of *information experience* [1] provides insights into these integrative roles, and *threshold concept* theory [2] provides a framework for exploring the knowledge necessary to advancing as an information literacy (IL) information professional. Developing as an information professional for these roles involves learning in formal degree programs as well as continuing career development. This paper focuses on higher education programs for new IL professionals. Much of this learning is taking place in a diverse and responsive online landscape. It discusses the information experience and threshold concepts research literature, exploring the intersection of these two constructs for how they can guide instructional design and deeper understanding of essential knowledge for this learner group. Illustrations are provided for online learning activities for IL professionals including ways to engage students in discussions and how to sequence assignments to support threshold learning.

S. Kurbanoğlu et al. (Eds.): ECIL 2017, CCIS 810, pp. 749–758, 2018.
https://doi.org/10.1007/978-3-319-74334-9_76

2 Learning Environment

Educational programs for IL information professionals cover preparation in discipline knowledge, research methods, and a range of library and information science (LIS) literacies as well as strategies for putting these new learnings into practice in different information work venues and when taking on different roles. Given accelerating growth in online learning programs for MLIS (and similar degree) students, this paper focuses on instructional activities that are effective in the online environment. Lifelong learning is part of the continuing development of skills for information professionals. There is likewise increasing growth of MOOCs and online certificate programs [3, p. 149–150], typically for augmenting one's skills in a specific area (e.g., digital curation or data visualisation). The discussion that follows is primarily centred on professional degree programs, such as the MLIS, that prepare students with core knowledge and competencies.

An information professional is called upon to teach, design curriculum, mentor, collaborate, and facilitate, in addition to being able to organise, manage, and retrieve information in a wide range of formats. Competencies that support these roles are delineated for graduates of MLIS programs and for members of LIS professional organisations. These competences are often divided between enabling or 'soft' skills (critical thinking, initiative, flexibility, communication) and concepts, such as knowledge structures, information ethics, and collection management [4, 5]. Professional responsibilities extend to furthering the skills of others, whether formally or in informal tutoring roles, particularly in the realm of information literacy and search methods. Broadly speaking, we help others move forward in how they experience information in their communities, workplaces, and professions, and we influence what they find, what they determine to be of value, and even how they contribute to online content and metadata. Indeed, a key element in distinguishing one's identity as an information professional is that, entwined with our own information experience, we play a facilitative role in the information experience of others [6]. Yet another defining characteristic is that these multiple roles are integrative in that we perform them holistically, fluidly adapting to circumstances.

Knowledge demands of the IL professional may include subject domain expertise, depending on the workplace and position. Medical and legal information knowledge are primary examples where understanding of terminology, ethics, and research methods is essential for information professionals [7, 8]. Domain knowledge can begin with familiarity with vocabulary but it extends beyond terminology. As an example, a law librarian needs to have a deep understanding of the legal profession's ethics, standards, reasoning, and what might be considered the culture of the justice system in which he/she practices and supports information needs, whether for attorneys or self-represented litigants. Finally, the online learning environment is inseparable from the online information culture: "digital information is a key learning, employment, cultural, and everyday life resource" [3, p. 5].

3 Research Constructs

In order to build a path to better understanding of the integrative roles of IL information professionals and the environment in which they acquire their knowledgebase, the research literature of two constructs is explored: information experience [1] and threshold concept theory [2]. Threshold concepts in the LIS domain have been explored for professional expertise in the search environment [9] and for information literacy [10, 11]; this sets the stage for rich discussion of the IL educator's roles and the experiential realm of threshold concepts specific to ontological shift for the educator-as-learner. The information experience construct and the theoretical lens of threshold concepts are considered together initially because they both address elements of integration and identity that are critical to understanding evolving roles. It is also important within this discussion to hold in mind that the primary purpose of threshold concepts is to guide curriculum design. Complementing this purpose is the synergistic construct of information experience, serving as an aid to conceptualising our information worlds that are "subjective and individual, imprecise, uncertain and fluid, and at times richly disruptive" [12, p. xxi].

3.1 Information Experience

Information experience has emerged in recent years as a research construct focused on a holistic approach to studying how people experience and engage with information. The construct considers people and the ways they relate to their information worlds as inseparable [13]. Still in a nascent stage, information experience has been studied using a range of methodologies, including phenomenography, grounded theory, and ethnomethodology [1]. It is important to note that studying information experience is different from studying information behaviour, a research domain going back to the 1970s. As an example, information behaviour research considers skills, techniques, and the attributes of study participants. Exploring information experience looks at the broader experience of the participants, studying concepts involved and taking a holistic approach to understanding their engagement and interrelationships with information.

In a recent study, the information experiences of highly experienced information professionals (30-plus years of experience) were found to be distinct in several ways: (i) they involve deep and profound engagement with the information environment due to a depth of understanding about the processes and players in that environment; (ii) they extend to taking a role in facilitating the information experiences of others; (iii) their knowledge of critical concepts transforms their experience [6]. This third attribute, knowledge of critical concepts, has been shown to include some concepts that are threshold concepts, evidencing how the two constructs can cross-inform in a study specific to information professionals.

3.2 Threshold Concepts

Threshold concepts have been studied across a wide range of academic disciplines and, within LIS, for search expertise and information literacy, with considerable attention gained in 2016 when the Association of College and Research Libraries (ACRL) adopted the new Framework for Information Literacy for Higher Education [10]. The threshold concepts framework supports understanding of transformative learning that "opens up new territory once it has been traversed. Because these new ways of thinking cannot be accessed until the student has moved through the portal, the threshold concept is an obstacle for the learner who is unable to pass through it" [9, p. 152]. Mastering a threshold concept "involves learning to see some aspect of the world in a totally new, transformative, and often counter-intuitive manner. Following such transformed understanding, continued and profound learning associated with the concept becomes possible" [9, p. 150]. A threshold concept has five main characteristics:

- Transformative: causing a shift in perception and identity. Once a threshold concept is understood, the learner experiences a major shift in perception, simultaneously with identity shift. "New understandings are assimilated into our biography, becoming part of who we are, how we see, and how we feel" [14, p. 2].
- Troublesome: initially counter-intuitive or uncomfortable. A learner may have to wrestle with a threshold concept in order to fully understand it. Troublesomeness is "an instigative or provocative feature which unsettles prior understanding, rendering it fluid and provoking a state of liminality" [15, p. xi].
- Irreversible: unlikely to be forgotten or unlearned. Once a threshold concept is understood, it is unlikely to be unlearned; the experience is rather like the adage about learning to ride a bicycle. Meyer and Land also pointed to the "difficulty [learners] experienced looking back across thresholds…and attempting to understand (from their own transformed perspective) the difficulties faced from (untransformed) student perspectives" [2, p. 5].
- Integrative: exposing something where the connectedness was not previously understood. The integrative characteristic involves learning to accommodate new information and grasping previously hidden interrelatedness of phenomenon [16].
- Bounded: having "terminal frontiers" that border other thresholds into new conceptual areas. The "bounded" characteristic is considered to be present less often than the other four characteristics of threshold concepts [2, p. 6].

In addition to having these five characteristics, a threshold concept also affects a learner's discourse about the new knowledge, ways of reconstituting the knowledge, and sense of identity. These attributes have been studied in more recent years as threshold concept theory has continued to develop. In understanding a threshold concept, "an integration of new knowledge occurs which requires a reconfiguring of the learner's prior conceptual schema and a letting go or discarding of any earlier conceptual stance. This reconfiguration occasions an ontological and an epistemic shift" [15, p. xi]. Ontological shift is closely coupled with the transformative nature that is at the core of a threshold learning experience.

Another aspect of threshold concepts is that they are defined both by the new pathways made available to a learner and by the barriers they pose. A threshold concept will indeed open up a new and previously inaccessible way of thinking—but it also "represents a way of understanding or interpreting or viewing something without which the learner cannot progress" [2, p. 412]. It is a portal but it also represents a barrier to the learner who is unable to pass through.

Threshold Learning and Course Design. Threshold concepts grew out of the goal to improve curriculum design, and there are three broad considerations when applying the theory to this purpose: "(a) sequence of content; (b) processes through which learners are made ready for, approach, recognise, and internalise threshold concepts; (c) ways in which learners and teacher recognise when threshold concepts have been internalised" [17, p. 199]. Threshold concepts are "jewels in the curriculum" [17, p. 198] and focusing on them when making decisions about course content can help educators with the tendency to stuff in too much "knowledge bulk" [16, p. 4]. Creating opportunities for students to wrestle with threshold knowledge means the instructor needs patience as well as tolerance for some uncertainty to be experienced by students. Ensuring that students have venues for sharing their confusion (finding out they are not alone) and working through it, rather than getting stuck, is critical. This approach challenges the instructor to listen closely for signs of both misunderstanding and understanding, developing a "third ear…[to] understand what students do not understand…[and to] foster appreciation of the tough conceptual and emotional journeys they have to make" [17, p. 200].

The troublesome nature of new knowledge can in fact be immensely beneficial to the learner. Meyer and Land referred to "stuck places" and "conceptual difficulties" as allowing for the possibility of transforming the learner's perspective, and noted that such instances can hold sway for educators as well [18]. They suggest ways to support these experiences in the curriculum: "The task for course developers and designers here is to identify, through constructive feedback, the source of these epistemological obstacles, and subsequently free up the blocked spaces. This might be achieved, for example, by redesigning activities and sequences, through scaffolding, recursiveness, provision of support materials and technologies or new conceptual tools, through mentoring or peer collaboration" [18, p. 377].

As this discussion is focused on online course design, it is useful to note that the nature of the online learning environment shares two important attributes with threshold learning experiences: both embody ambiguity and liminality. As described by Macleod and Ross, the digital space of online learning leads to "social engagement and hierarchy becoming less clearly defined" [19, p. 15] which means the instructor's role is altered in significant ways. They propose that the opportunities for similarly altered learning pathways are likewise significant, arguing that the instructor's role becomes "to participate and provoke in creative and playful ways that open up passages or possibilities" [19, p. 15].

Threshold Concepts and Information Literacy. The development of a theoretical framework involves stages of maturation, and information literacy and threshold concepts have intersected in their evolutions in recent years. One of the earliest studies of threshold concepts in information literacy was conducted by Blackmore [20] who focused on their troublesome aspects. Two of her findings are of particular note. First, that *contextual awareness* was a threshold concept. Second, that the teaching of specific skills should be de-emphasised in favor of "increasing student understanding of how they are already engaging with information and how they need to build on that to succeed in an academic context" [20, p. 9]. Carrying this forward into course design, Blackmore advocated shifting the "focus from 'teaching the use of' to 'promoting understanding of' information products [that] may at first seem very subtle, but can potentially lead to a major shift in developmental direction" [20, p. 9]. This early finding pointed the way towards concepts-based instead of skills- and tools-based curriculum in information literacy. Since then, threshold concepts within the LIS domain have been studied for search expertise [9] and more extensively for information literacy [10, 11], as noted above.

4 Learning Activities

To animate this discussion of theoretical constructs and to build upon it for understanding IL professional education, examples of implementation are provided, drawn from two courses in an online MLIS program [21]. One course is a core class required of all students that covers database design, vocabulary design, and essential principles of information organisation and retrieval. During the semester, students work in small groups to design and build databases for non-traditional objects and to develop small controlled vocabularies. The second course is an elective on advanced search methods for which the previous course is pre-requisite; it covers techniques and concepts for searching online, including strategies, database content, search options, and understanding the information environment. The course includes extensive hands-on experience with subscription search engines, such as ProQuest Dialog™, Web of Science™, and LexisNexis™. Class sizes are typically 35 students who live in all timezones across the U.S. and Canada with two to three students in each class in other countries.

Instructional activities are described below in the context of each course, along with the threshold concepts or principles they support. This covers: (1) ways to sequence assignments and other learning activities to maximise opportunities for students to discover critical understandings on their own, the result being more wrestling with new content but also more 'stickiness' (irreversibility) of concepts learned; and (2) peer interactive learning and online discussions integrated with task-based assignments.

4.1 Sequencing

The first element for the course design is the sequencing of concepts in the content as covered in assignments and in course readings and other media formats, such as videos, audio recordings, and narrated lectures. In order to create opportunities for students to discover critical knowledge and experience threshold learning, the sequencing is guided by constructivist principles and scaffolding [18]. As an example, students typically arrive knowing about bibliographies but see them as no more than a list of publications an article's author was diligent to include to credit works cited. When they discover through an assigned search task that at first seems impossible (e.g., to go forward in time and find what articles have cited a seminal work in the last five years), they have eye-opening experiences that go beyond learning how to use a citation indexing tool and on into grasping how research literature and scholars have impact within the information environment. Once this happens, they never look at bibliographies, the research process, or content creation the same way. They have learned that subject searching is possible in ways other than through keywords or controlled vocabulary terms.

Throughout the classes, students begin with instruction and assignments that create opportunities to wrestle with and discover concepts for themselves in active and participatory assignments. Many learners in the U.S. have had educational experiences of being taught-to-the-test, and creating opportunities for discovery minimises a parallel of being taught-to-the-threshold, being told what the threshold concept is and then working to learn it. Only near the end of the term do we discuss some of the research literature about threshold concepts. This sequencing means that students are given range for discovery experiences and have greater potential for ah-ha learning moments. It also means their learning experiences may be characterised by being rather uncomfortable initially with a sense that the new knowledge is counter-intuitive and troublesome, yet this leads to more lasting and irreversible learning.

4.2 Discussions Three Ways

Discussions in the online learning environment are laden with both positive and negative aspects that differentiate them from in-class discussion activities. Because online discussions are most typically asynchronous, students experience lag time in the engagement and miss the quick back and forth of conversational discourse, but they can benefit from having time to formulate and articulate their ideas before posting. Students who might hesitate to engage in a real-time and/or face-to-face discussion may be more forthcoming and more apt to post responses to classmates. In addition, depending on how discussions are set up and the learning management system (LMS) being used, students can subscribe to discussion threads, enabling them to respond more quickly and engage more fully in threads of interest. Three ways of using discussion forums are described, each with illustrations from one of the two MLIS courses described above.

Discussion Linked to Task-Based Assignment. In the information retrieval course students evaluate a website using information architecture heuristics and then design an improved sitemap. In preparation for this assignment, they engage in a two-stage discussion, starting with questions about their own experience with the site, then a second round of questions that exposes them to threshold knowledge related to information environment and information seeking behaviour. Questions include: Is the site designed to support or encourage browsing behaviours? What might site architects take into account when their target users come from a wide range of cultural and social backgrounds? Using this multi-staged approach helps move students through critical thinking and reflection before they wrestle with the analytical and designing elements of the larger assignment. This is where the ah-ha moments then tend to take place.

Discussion with Peer Engagement and Problem Solving. Another activity in the information retrieval course is learning to use database design software. Students first design the database structure, then implement it in the software, so that database records can be entered and search form pages built. For many students who have a humanities or social sciences background, the structural concepts underlying the assignment are particularly challenging, and the online environment can exacerbate the sense of loneliness when confusion arises. To prepare for the larger assignment, each student builds a mini-database and posts the link to its search page where others test it and comment. If there is a problem, a solution is worked out quickly within the discussion forum. The discussion forum keeps this potential troublespot from being a dead-end. Students are able to learn the essential concepts about information structures by designing and building them hands-on, collaboratively, and with immediate feedback.

Discussion and Reflective Writing. Reflective writing is used in both courses, primarily as individual assignments, yet it is also effective for students to share some of their commentaries in discussion forums in order to gain from seeing the range of ideas and reactions from their classmates. This broadens their learning experiences in ways that might happen in hallways in place-based classes but not so easily in online learning environments. Issues of authenticity arise, as in most online forums: self-preservation may be present in any reflective writing, although this is well balanced by the online 'masks' that allow us to speak what we otherwise would not [22].

5 Discussion

In considering the online learning environment for information professionals, it is worthwhile to underscore that it is inseparable from the broader context of the online digital environment in which we work, communicate, and tend to daily tasks. The illustrations for ways to structure online learning activities so that students engage with each other as members in an online community have parallels in the virtual workplace where they want to thrive and continue with their lifelong learning. This paper contributes to the growing literature of "pedagogic engagement within the threshold concept framework perspective" [23, p. 470] and to how educators can effectively integrate threshold knowledge into the classroom [24]. Questions for further discussion include: What learning activities described in the case illustrations might be adapted for use in IL courses for non-information professionals? What activities might be guided in a similar way for MLIS courses in other core areas, such as reference services, collection management, or information ethics and intellectual freedom? What other activities in the online learning environment are especially effective for supporting and/or provoking threshold learning experiences? And, how are IL educators, themselves lifelong learners, affected by curriculum that is guided by threshold concepts?

6 Conclusion

This paper presents a research context for the varied roles that information professionals take on in the online environment using the two constructs of threshold concepts [2] and information experience [1]. It discusses how these roles are integrative in nature and how they demand deep understanding of information structures and ways to navigate the information environment. Ultimately they result in enabling students to join in fully as a member of the information professional community. Online education for IL professionals, such as MLIS degree programs, are used as the learning venue, and learning activities are described for courses in information retrieval system design and advanced search that illustrate ways to support information professionals in developing understanding of critical knowledge. Design of the courses is guided by threshold concepts, and the sequencing of activities, such as task-based discussions, support opportunities for threshold learning experiences. This paper has positioned the literature from the two research areas of threshold concepts and information experience as a foundation to the illustrations of learning activities, in order to engage with the "research-practice nexus" [25]. This framing is intended to generate debate, scholarly conversation, and further creativity among IL educators.

References

1. Bruce, C.S., Davis, K., Hughes, H., Partridge, H., Stoodley, I. (eds.): Information Experience: Approaches to Theory and Practice. Emerald Group, Bingley (2014)
2. Meyer, J.H.F., Land, R.: Threshold concepts and troublesome knowledge (1): linkages to ways of thinking and practising within the disciplines. In: Rust, C. (ed.) Ten Years on Improving Student Learning, pp. 1–16. Oxford Centre for Staff and Learning Development, Oxford, UK (2003)
3. Anderson, A., Johnston, B.: From Information Literacy to Social Epistemology. Elsevier, Amsterdam (2016)
4. International Federation of Library Associations (IFLA): guidelines for professional library/information educational programs (2012). https://www.ifla.org/publications/guidelines-for-professional-libraryinformation-educational-programs-2012
5. American Library Association (ALA): knowledge and competencies statements developed by relevant professional organizations (n.d.). http://www.ala.org/educationcareers/careers/corecomp/corecompspecial/knowledgecompetencies
6. Tucker, V.M.: The expert searcher's experience of information. In: Bruce, C.S., Davis, K., Hughes, H., Partridge, H., Stoodley, I. (eds.) Information Experience: Approaches to Theory and Practice, pp. 239–255. Emerald Group, Bingley (2014)
7. American Association of Law Librarians (AALL): competencies of law librarianship (2010). http://www.aallnet.org/mm/Leadership-Governance/policies/PublicPolicies/competencies.html
8. Medical Library Association (MLA): MLA's competencies for lifelong learning and professional success (2016). http://www.mlanet.org/p/cm/ld/fid=39
9. Tucker, V.M., Weedman, J., Bruce, C.S., Edwards, S.L.: Learning portals: analyzing threshold concept theory for LIS education. J. Educ. Libr. Inf. Sci. **55**(2), 150–165 (2014)
10. Association of College and Research Libraries (ACRL): framework for information literacy for higher education (2016). http://www.ala.org/acrl/standards/ilframework
11. Townsend, L., Hofer, A.R., Hanick, S.L., Brunetti, K.: Identifying threshold concepts for information literacy: a Delphi study. Commun. Inf. Lit. **10**(1), 23–49 (2016)
12. Todd, R.J.: Preface. In: Bruce, C.S., Davis, K., Hughes, H., Partridge, H., Stoodley, I. (eds.) Information Experience: Approaches to Theory and Practice, pp. xxi–xxiii. Emerald Group, Bingley (2014)
13. Yates, C., Partridge, H., Bruce, C.: Exploring information experiences through phenomenography. Libr. Inf. Res. **36**(112), 96–119 (2012)
14. Cousin, G.: Neither teacher-centred nor student-centred: threshold concepts and research partnerships. J. Learn. Dev. High. Educ. **2**, 1–9 (2010)
15. Land, R., Meyer, J.H.F., Baillie, C.: Preface: threshold concepts and transformational learning. In: Meyer, J.H.F., Land, R., Baillie, C. (eds.) Threshold Concepts and Transformational Learning, pp. ix–xlii. Sense Publishers, Rotterdam (2010)

16. Cousin, G.: An introduction to threshold concepts. Planet **17**, 4–5 (2006)
17. Land, R., Cousin, G., Meyer, J.H.F., Davies, P.: Implications for course design and evaluation. In: Meyer, J.H.F., Land, R. (eds.) Overcoming Barriers to Student Understanding: Threshold Concepts and Troublesome Knowledge, pp. 195–206. Routledge, New York (2006)
18. Meyer, J.H.F., Land, R.: Threshold concepts and troublesome knowledge (2): epistemological considerations and a conceptual framework for teaching and learning. High. Educ. **49**, 373–388 (2005). https://doi.org/10.1007/s10734-004-6779-5
19. Macleod, H., Ross, J.: Structure, authority, and other noncepts. In: Land, R., Bayne, S. (eds.) Digital Difference: Perspectives on Online Learning, pp. 15–27. Sense Publishers, Rotterdam (2011)
20. Blackmore, M.: Student engagement with information: applying a threshold concept approach to information literacy development. In: Proceedings Third Biennial Threshold Concepts Symposium, Sydney, Australia (2010)
21. San José State University, School of Information: Masters of Library and Information Science program. http://ischool.sjsu.edu/programs/master-library-and-information-science-mlis
22. Todd, R.: The thing itself: on the search for authenticity. Penguin Group, New York (2008)
23. Meyer, J.H.F.: Threshold concepts and pedagogic representation. Educ.+ Train. **58**(5), 463–475 (2016)
24. Meyer, J.H.F., Timmermans, J.: Integrated threshold concept knowledge. In: Land, R., Meyer, H.F., Flanagan, M.T. (eds.) Threshold Concepts in Practice, pp. 25–38. Sense Publishers, Rotterdam (2016)
25. Bruce, C.S.: Information literacy research: dimensions of the emerging collective consciousness, a reflection. Aust. Acad. Res. Libr. **47**(4), 220–238 (2016)

Information Literacy and Libraries

Libraries as a Support of Informed Citizens – The Balancing Act Between Library's Good Quality and Austerity Measures

Petra Düren[1], Ane Landoy[2(✉)], and Jarmo Saarti[3]

[1] Department Information,
Hamburg University of Applied Sciences, Hamburg, Germany
petra.dueren@haw-hamburg.de
[2] University of Bergen Library, Bergen, Norway
ane.landoy@uib.no
[3] University of Eastern Finland Library, Kuopio, Finland
jarmo.saarti@uef.fi

Abstract. In a time of rapidly expanding information possibilities, including "fake news", libraries as guardians of the quality of information have become even more important. In our era, however, it is the guardians of confirmed information themselves and information literate citizens that must be enabled to decide what facts to rely on. At the same time, new public management (NPM) is changing the way libraries, both public and academic, are allowed to act in their local communities. The effect of the "age of austerity" with libraries being closed due to an ongoing economic crisis must also be taken into account. The changing circumstances call for new leadership, new competences and new tasks in libraries. In this paper the authors will present results of European studies on changes in libraries as a result of implementing NPM. While it is evident that the environment and the libraries are changing, it is, however, not clear that the changes are going in only one direction, or how they actually will be impacting the need for more information literate citizens.

Keywords: Finland · Germany · Information literacy · Leadership style Management style · New public management · Norway

1 Introduction

Librarians and libraries as guardians of quality information are more important than ever before. Librarians also play an important role in the support of citizens becoming information literate and thus able to decide what facts to rely on, within a society where the amount of information available is exploding: "Data is growing faster than ever before and by the year 2020, about 1.7 MB of new information will be created every second for every human being on the planet" [1]. At the same time the libraries are under pressure by many forces including the impact of new public management (NPM) on public organisations. In this paper the impact of new public management on how the libraries can act within their local communities, especially with regards to their role as a support for information literate citizens, will be analysed. After an overview of

S. Kurbanoğlu et al. (Eds.): ECIL 2017, CCIS 810, pp. 761–768, 2018.
https://doi.org/10.1007/978-3-319-74334-9_77

some earlier research on NPM and libraries, a pilot study in three countries will be presented. In this study, academic and public library leaders have been interviewed to find their thoughts on libraries supporting the informed citizens while under the pressure from NPM, and the austerity measures following from the ongoing economic crisis.

2 NPM and Libraries – Some Earlier Research

New public management emerged as a part of a broader neoliberal focus on policy and public administration taking place all over the world, and NPM-inspired reforms have become widespread from the 1990's onward. Despite national variations in the scope and depth of changes, NPM reforms originate from similar economic theories and normative values, placing economic efficiency and budgetary control as priorities for government.

The often-stated aims of these reforms are to enhance the responsiveness of government to citizens, to stretch the effectiveness of scarce public resources and to move decision-making closer to the constituents of the public sector. Devolution of responsibility and decision power to lower levels of government is a core feature in NPM programs. By transferring power to managers, NPM reforms aim to streamline functions and reduce redundancy and waste [2].

For activities considered to be best implemented directly by the private sector, outsourcing has emerged as a core policy goal: specific services and functions (such as maintenance, control, and advice) are contracted out to private companies in the belief that specialisation and competition encourage cost cutting and economic efficiency, and thus enhances the use of public resources [2]. Achieving greater efficiency in public-service provision and administration has brought into attention some unintended and unanticipated consequences, many now well-documented in the literature.

True political decentralisation to democratically elected lower level representatives or civic society stakeholders has seldom been a priority when weighed against the contrary goal of increased decision-making efficiency. As one critic of NPM has stated, “Market-driven managerialism can run counter to self-governance, as it is structured around the idea of happy consumers rather than involved citizens” [3, p. 35, 4].

It is important to acknowledge that similarities in the direction and characteristics of administrative reforms adopted during the 1980s and 1990s define NPM better than any well-defined doctrine or suite of adoption administrative tools. While generalizations about the policy reforms associated with NPM are possible, their adoption always reflects local institutional histories, cultures and policy goals. While NPM is well documented within the overall public sector, not a lot research has been done on implementing the NPM practices in libraries.

In the library environment NPM includes the need to develop strategies, plan budgets based on the strategies, and ensure that the goals are met. Customer satisfaction is seen as the most important goal. Libraries also have had to implement accounting of cost and activities, and performance-measurement with an emphasis on output and outcome instead of input, as well as benchmarking to compare the library's processes, cost and activities with those of other libraries [5, p. 163]. Summarized by Pors and

Johannsen [6, p. 52]: "NPM is a movement that tries to transfer principles from private sector into the public sphere" and with this into libraries. In libraries NPM manifested itself as supporting a transition towards product-orientation, improving the quality of library service delivery, develop output-orientation and to ensure market and consumer-oriented behaviors. There has also been an attempt to change from bureaucratic and hierarchical organizations to more modern flexible and leaner forms of management [6, p. 52].

NPM can therefore be said to make libraries want to transform their organizational identity from a public service organization into a more business-like identity [7, p. 251], and NPM at times may also lead to an overemphasis on the financial aspects instead of the societal added value, leaving less possibilities for potentially financial risky creative or innovative activities. Also, there may be less opportunities for a participative management style, as negotiations and agreements may lead to additional costs [8, p. 9].

Library leaders need to improve their strategic management competences, as Vallet [8, p. 12] has shown from the Flemish library world. Düren [5, p. 163] agrees: "the management has to develop a strategy with vision, mission and strategic goals. It has to plan annual programme budgets based on cost and activity accounting to show how-efficient and effective their work is."[..] "Consequently, public [as well as academic] libraries have to leave their professional comfort-zone behind, or as a public library-director said '…we have to leave familiar grounds'" [8, p. 14].

However, the introduction of NPM in libraries is not necessarily in conflict with library core values but can be interpreted as tools for library management. A Danish study shows that librarian "identity" can both be in conflict and in harmony with NPM logics. Kann-Christensen shows that both at field level and organizational level the librarian logic, regarding user contact and promotion of information, and culture are crucial issues. Furthermore it is shown that the librarian as profession in principle is not opposed to either pressure for efficiency nor continuous change of the library. However one can identify a resistance towards changes in the library that take away the possibility for the librarians to influence their organization and work [9, p. 217].

Düren [5] has demonstrated how a German academic library can use the Balanced Scorecard to develop and implement a strategy, as a result of growing pressure from NPM-inspired reforms in the German public sector, and Saarti and Juntunen [10] showed the benefits of a quality management system in merging university libraries in Finland. Kann-Christensen and Andersen investigated a Danish county library and found that libraries are caught between the demands of being cost-effective and accountable to the needs and whishes of the patrons. This means that user satisfaction is seen as very important for legitimizing the library's existence [11].

Apart from these international studies from Denmark, Belgium, Germany and Finland one will see that within the field of library research, NPM has not been thoroughly investigated. The authors believe that a comparative perspective will provide library leaders and researchers with new insights.

The main research questions of this study are:

1. To what extent are library leaders equipped to provide the library sector with a new leadership and management style?

2. How can the libraries, in a squeeze between the demands for better service and less money, find a way to train citizens in information literacy?

3 Methodological Issues

To answer the two research questions the authors conducted a pilot study in Germany, Finland and Norway, interviewing academic and public library leaders to find out how NPM and the resulting austerity measures impact the citizens' training in information literacy and what can be done to ensure sufficient support of informed citizens.

For the qualitative expert interviews the library directors, one from a public library and one from an academic library in each country, were contacted and asked the following:

1. Libraries should nowadays be guardians of confirmed information and of information literacy as a tool for citizens to be able to decide for themselves what facts to rely on. At the same time, New Public Management is changing the way libraries, both public and academic, are allowed to act in their local communities. These changing circumstances call for new leadership and new leader roles in the libraries. To what extent are you as a library leader equipped to do this? (e.g. management skills, leadership skills, budget for skill enhancement/education, cooperation).
2. How does your library in a squeeze between the demands for better service and less money find a way to train citizens in information literacy?

Especially interesting is to see what is expected from libraries in different European countries and how they are supported through resources for this new task.

The content analysis of the interviews were conducted based on the questions and compared in order to find similarities and dissimilarities between the library sectors and countries.

4 Research Results

Table 1 shows some details about the library leaders interviewed for this pilot study and their library.

Table 1. l Libraries that participated in this pilot study

Type of libary/country	Full time equivalent (FTE) 2017	Leader of this library since
Public library/Germany	5.25	1997
Academic library/Germany	20.5	2006
Public library/Finland	197.5	2014
Academic library/Finland	50	2015
Public library/Norway	106	2011
Academic library/Norway	110	2015

Germany. The director of the public library in Germany mentioned that some of the aspects of the NPM, such as quarterly reports and a specific report about public and academic libraries in Germany (the BIX – Bibliotheksindex) have ceased to exist. Those were relevant methods to show the activities of this library, even if the relatively extensive tasks relating to providing information literacy competences only have been depicted on the brink. Since 2000 the then reduced amount of staff has been the same, which means that this library only has 80% of its needed personnel capacity. Through the implementation of the RFID-technology at least the opening hours could be kept. Due to lack of resources known deficits that need attention in information and digital literacy cannot be resolved, and programs to support this cannot be implemented. Also some support programs like "Lesen macht stark: Lesen und digitale Medien" ("Reading makes strong: reading and digital media") are extensively bureaucratic and the library cannot participate. At least there is a well-thought-of municipal professional training program, in which the library's staff can participate and keep their professional competences up to date. Also helpful is that this library has a good reputation and with this can choose its spheres of activity as well as its cooperation partners relatively freely.

At the moment this library tries to modernise its guaranteed offers for schools through the relatively easy application for state funds to buy a carrying case for iPads. With this the classic guided tour for school classes shall be replaced through an action bound rally. The library's digital services and resources will thus be communicated in a transparent and modern way. On the other hand some programs needed to be stopped (at least temporarily) because they are too time-consuming and need too many of the limited resources, such as the "Kinder- und Jugendbuchwochen Schleswig-Holstein", an annual event in November in which over 500 school classes and groups from nurseries are invited into libraries and schools as a project for the promotion of literacy.

To have the chance to at least once in a while be able to plan and execute activities such as gaming actions or information about topics such as child-proof locks of smartphones and child protection in the internet, the library needs cooperation partners. Often the library is not the protagonist of these activities, but only offers the environment in which it can take place. The library director wishes the library could be more active in offering its own activities. This cooperations help create more ties to the community and raise recognition. To be able to be more active in this field of activity they try to unleash more personnel hours through more digitalization, including the methods of payment in the library, through constant reviewing the library's processes, through outsourcing tasks and through optimizing the library's catalog to reduce questions of users. Nevertheless, for the older pupils as well as adults information literacy programs can only be executed on request and if the resources are free at that moment and not as part of a regular program.

The director of the German academic library who was interviewed for this pilot study makes clear that nobody asked his library formally or informally to be a guardian of confirmed information literacy as a tool for citizens. He thinks that libraries can contribute to this, but that maybe the university's decision makers are not aware of this possibility. For most people libraries are still only places to store books. And therefore this library is not equipped for this task.

Nevertheless, this library tries to fulfill its role as guardian of confirmed information and of information literacy for its students, and for this they have established a part-time position that helps professors in all of the university's departments through teaching "Information competence", which some of the departments demand regularly.

As this library has no resources for this task nor a mandate to act as guardians of confirmed information and of information literacy as a tool for citizens, they only fulfil this for their students in the above mentioned extend.

Finland. The public library director mentioned that these new evolving services are a very important part of the new tasks the libraries must include in their services. The director is also very active in improving theses services, attends courses and includes the staff in strategic discussions. The director had a long working and management history, that seemed to definitely help in focus on the new and emerging service changes.

Also in this library there have been some budgetary cuts, but according to the director not as drastic as in some other public libraries in Finland. This has meant resource allocation to the strategically important tasks and the teaching and empowerment of users in information literacy issues is one of these strategic choices in their library. In addition they have been able to use automation in removing routines from the library staff to the computers.

The director of the Finnish academic library had not received any formal training from his own university. Instead the director had a lot of previous managerial and financial education and experience from previous tasks, including entrepreneurship. Also the active updating of one's knowledge from the professional field (internet discussion and professional papers) was important.

The information literacy teaching was seen as one of the main function in the library: "Although the staff has been reduced radically we have not cut back the teaching in the same proportion; we have been reorganizing so that the level of the teaching could be maintained and even enhanced/developed." Some minor adjustments have been done, including increasing the group sizes and diminishing contact teaching. But the director mentioned that if more staff cutbacks are going to happen this will also effect the teaching provided by the library.

Norway. How are changing circumstances related to NPM influencing library leadership in Norway? The library directors that were interviewed in Norway are uncertain of what the effects of NPM are in the Norwegian library world. They both see the call for plans and controls as supportive of development. Both find that there is a certain amount of freedom in "framework budgeting". However, if they want to develop, funding has to be found through external project funding. At the same time, changes in the skillset of the library employees are possible, but require more time and a lot of patience. Both felt that they have the necessary skills for leading their libraries, skills that have been acquired through further education and practices. The public library leader has worked in other library leadership positions before, and in central library organisations for decades. The academic library leader worked in other mid-level management positions in the library for several years.

The library in a squeeze between demands for better service and less money needs to prioritize, and to be active in applying for funding for development projects. The public library prioritizes to train refugees and immigrants, children and seniors in computer skills and languages. The upper secondary schools in the municipality have quite good libraries themselves now, so the pupils from there are no longer a primary target group. Information literacy is not yet well developed in the public library, however the librarians are up-skilling themselves for this task.

The university library director sees her staff being more actively involved in trying to embed themselves in the academic departments, anticipating needs and being proactive. They wish to offer information literacy as student services, and also to help the departments fulfill their obligation to deliver transferable skills to the students as part of the learning goals.

The Norwegian library leaders see collaboration between different groups of libraries as a necessary way forward.

The library leaders that participated in this pilot study are generally equipped to provide the library sector with a new leadership and management style (research question number 1). They know about the importance of strategic planning and (re) allocation of resources, the need of process optimisation, to find cooperation partners and to constantly educate oneself and their members of staff to hold their professional competences up to date.

This leads to research question number 2, as leaders have to prioritize what they can do – considering the few resources they have - to fulfill their library's task as guardians of quality information, as can be seen in the public library in Germany, in which only children from nurseries and young pupils are in the focus of the programs for information literacy, or in Norway, where the public library is specialized in programs for refugees and immigrants, children and seniors. They find ways to train citizens in information literacy through reorganising their libraries, outsourcing as well as cooperations. And they are aware that they need to find ways to avoid further cutbacks.

5 Conclusions and Further Research

As this pilot study only shows the opinions and experience of six library leaders one must be careful when drawing conclusions. The aim was to generate a broad point-of-view which will lead to further research. Following this pilot study more qualitative interviews must be conducted, to be able to develop concrete hypotheses which then can be tested through a representative quantitative research.

But one can state based on findings here that the NPM has definitely had an effect on the management of the libraries. The directors are more aware of the policies and economic pressures that are affecting the public sector, including the libraries. It also seems that if the library director is active in strategic work and can influence the decision makers, the library can also gain when being able to present its value for the community. It also seems that the NPM policies are effecting the strategic work of the libraries pointing it to the direction discussed earlier in Sect. 2, especially towards economic efficiency. There also seems to be a limit from budget cutbacks after which the service production is not anymore possible at an agreeable level.

In Finland information literacy is seen as a strategic and important task for both academic and public libraries and it seems that it is also seen as one of the tasks that the libraries want to prioritize. This can be interpreted that the library can also make strategic decisions on the issues that are important for the libraries, but it seems that the experience and education of the director has an effect especially on the strategic work and how one succeeds in it.

In Germany the academic library is not seen as an institution that has the competences and should see as one of its tasks to be guardians of confirmed information and of information literacy as a tool for citizens. And even to support students in this, the library has only minimum resources, not nearly enough in the public library information literacy is seen as an important task, but resources are only made available for children and young pupils, and even those are not adequate. Older pupils and adults are not in the focus of implementing programs for information literacy.

In Norway the public library prioritizes to train refugees and immigrants, children and seniors in computer skills and languages. The adults "in between" are left out. The university library has the skills and the mandate to aid the academic departments in supplying transferable skills to the students, and information literacy is considered one of these skills.

References

1. Marr, B.: Big Data: 20 Mind-Boggling Facts Everyone Must Read. Forbes 30.09.2015. https://www.forbes.com/sites/bernardmarr/2015/09/30/big-data-20-mind-boggling-facts-everyone-must-read/#35c775c617b1. Accessed 04 May 2017
2. Eakin, H., Eriksen, S., Eikeland, P., Øyen, C.: Public sector reform and governance for adaptation: implications of new public management for adaptive capacity in Mexico and Norway. Environ. Manag. **47**(3), 338–351 (2011)
3. Box, R.: Running government like a business: implications for public administration theory and practice. Am. Rev. Publ. Adm. **29**, 19–43 (1999)
4. Olssen, M., Peters, M.A.: Neoliberalism, higher education and the knowledge economy: from the free market to knowledge capitalism. J. Educ. Policy **20**(3), 313–345 (2005). https://doi.org/10.1080/02680930500108718. Accessed 04 May 2017
5. Düren, P.: Public management means strategic management. Libr. Manag. **31**(3), 162–168 (2009)
6. Pors, N.O., Johannsen, C.G.: Library directors under cross-pressure between new public management and value-based management. Libr. Manag. **24**(1/2), 51–60 (2003)
7. Skålén, P.: New public management reform and the construction of organizational identities. Int. J. Publ. Sect. Manag. **17**(3), 251–263 (2004)
8. Vallet, N.: The odyssey of Flemish public libraries facing opportunities and threats when becoming strategic partners in urban development. Libr. Manag. **36**(8/9), 1–18 (2015)
9. Kann-Christensen, N.: Forestillinger om forandringer: Organisatoriske forandringer i to danske folkebiblioteker. Ph.D. dissertation, Royal School of Library and Information Science, Copenhagen (2009)
10. Saarti, J., Juntunen, A.: The benefits of a quality management system: the case of the merger of two universities and their libraries. Libr. Manag. **32**(3), 183–190 (2011)
11. Kann-Christensen, N., Andersen, J.: Developing the library: between efficiency, accountability and forms of recognition. J. Doc. **65**(2), 208–222 (2009)

Assessing a Library's Support for Overlooked Components of a University's Learning Culture

Jon R. Hufford(✉)

Texas Tech University, Lubbock, TX, USA
Jon.hufford@ttu.edu

Abstract. The three-year inquiry focuses on assessing the size of a university library's support for engaged-learning courses and for student populations. In doing this, it models an effective way to obtain data from campus information systems. The inquiry's research questions are, how can libraries identify courses where the library supports engaged-learning courses, and how can libraries target their efforts for maximum impact on student learning in overlooked components of the campus' learning culture. Focused questions serving as data-gathering goals to answer the research questions are, how many students enrolled in these courses, and how many students in each class year passed a course each semester with a library assignment. Analysis of data collected can result in additional studies providing comprehensive assessments of the library's effect on student-learning outcomes. Among other things, the inquiry found 22% of students enrolled during the study took part in engaged learning involving a library assignment.

Keywords: Assessment · Library services · Information literacy
Higher education · Learning culture

1 Introduction

Institutions of higher education conduct assessments to show that they are committed to student learning. Libraries participate in their institutions' assessment programs by measuring the quality of the services offered to their campus clientele, including the services that support student-learning outcomes. Numerous publications have recorded library contributions to the parent institution's assessment goals.

These kinds of assessments are regular events on many campuses, and they measure important elements of a campus learning culture. However, some elements of the culture are hardly ever assessed. Apart from classroom and online teaching and the availability of services like those offered by a library, successful student learning is also dependent on such sometimes difficult to measure factors as:

- the impact of programs incorporating engaged-learning activities
- student mentoring by faculty and librarians
- student, faculty, and administrator behavior and attitudes
- individual motivation, expectations, capacities, and readiness to learn.

These elements of the culture are often not part of the classroom or online experience and therefore usually are not measured by typical assessment tools. The result of this is that measuring an entire campus learning culture in a comprehensive and detailed

S. Kurbanoğlu et al. (Eds.): ECIL 2017, CCIS 810, pp. 769–780, 2018.
https://doi.org/10.1007/978-3-319-74334-9_78

manner seldom occurs. This is unfortunate because all elements of a campus culture encourage and support learning.[1]

Libraries and their parent institutions need to assess how and to what extent they are affecting student learning through their contributions to these elusive elements of the campus culture. They also need to assess their level or size of support for and effect on learning of a wide range of student populations over extended periods. The results of these kinds of assessments will lead to a more thorough and detailed understanding of a library's quantitative and qualitative contributions to the mission and goals of its institution [1, p. 350].

The main purpose in doing this assessment at one institution is to model an effective way other libraries can obtain data using campus information systems [1, p. 351]. The focus on assessing the size of Texas Tech University Library's support for courses with engaged-learning activities and for particular student populations over three years is a demonstration of how the model can be applied. Follow-up studies of the courses and student populations targeted by this inquiry will assess the library's impact on student learning. The research questions of the inquiry relate directly to the inquiry's main purpose of modeling an effective way to obtain data using campus information systems. They are:

1. How can libraries identify courses where library resources and services support engaged-learning courses?
2. How can libraries target their efforts for the maximum impact on student learning in overlooked and/or discrete components of the campus' learning culture?

Focused questions serving as data-gathering tools to both accomplish the local assessment and, in doing so, to answer the inquiry's research questions are:

1. How many courses with engaged-learning activities require the use of library resources and services? How many students enrolled in these courses?
2. How many students in each class year (freshman, sophomore, junior, and senior) passed a course each semester with a library assignment that required the use of library resources and services?[2]

---

1 In an article published in May 2013, the author proposed a plan for assessing a library's contribution to these neglected elements of the campus learning culture. See "Can the Library Contribute Value to the Campus Culture for Learning?" *Journal of Academic Librarianship* 39(3) (May 2013): 288–296. The present article reports on implementation of a portion of the plan at Texas Tech University Library. Implementation of these and additional elements of the plan are reported in "The Academic Library and the Culture for Learning," *Portal: Libraries and the Academy* 16(2) (April 2016): 349–372.

2 Engaged learning occurs when students participate in determining the direction their learning takes. They "may be involved in the decision-making that determines the class's activities and experiences. They perform research, discuss issues, create their own projects, and use technology to make discoveries based on their choices. The professor serves as a coach or facilitator who guides the students to the course's goals. Service learning, community-based learning, learning communities, undergraduate research, internships, writing-intensive courses, and collaborative assignments and projects are different teaching and learning programs or methods that incorporate engaged learning experiences in one way or another" [1, p. 351].

2 Justification for Study and Research Questions

Though the inquiry occurred at one institution, other universities can use its unique method. The method can result in more comprehensive assessments than otherwise of a library's impact on the parent institution's mission and goals, and, through follow-up studies, on student learning outcomes. This can be especially helpful for large universities offering hundreds or thousands of credit courses each year. An inquiry using this method need not end with measuring levels of support, though size is an important way to assess a library's contributions to its institution's goals. Analysis of the results can help identify components that need more study. For example, the data collected in this inquiry for focused question one can lead to a follow-up inquiry in which the courses identified as having engaged-learning activities, and library support for the activities, can result in more effectively assessing the library's impact on student learning in these courses.

In addition, the data collected for focused question two can lead to another inquiry that compares students taking the targeted courses who had a library assignment requiring use of library resources and services, and passed the course, to students who took the same courses but who did not have the library assignment. Did fewer students taking these courses without a library assignment get a passing grade? Another follow-up inquiry could track and assess the learning outcomes of the students who took the courses targeted by focused question two to determine whether having library assignments during their tenure in college had any effect on their learning from one semester or year to the next. The present inquiry identified student populations that are now available for further study to determine whether information literacy classes, library assignments, and/or use of library resources and services have any effect on their learning outcomes.

The data collected for the two research questions of this study enrich a library's analyzing and planning processes in assessment. The result is more informed decision-making. Engaged learning plays an important role in the curricula of higher education. Many educators believe students learn better through engaged learning. Colleges and universities must assess the learning outcomes of engaged learning activities just as they assess other teaching and learning methods to find out how successful the activities are in promoting learning and how well institutions support them. Quantitative and qualitative evidence of what the library contributes to support the engaged-learning activities of courses provide a more in-depth understanding of how well the library supports its institution's mission and those goals that focus on support for student learning.

Research question two, concerned with the discovery over a three-year period of the percent of students in each class year (freshman, sophomore, junior, and senior) who passed a course with an assignment that required that they find and use library resources and services, is associated with traditional classroom and online teaching and learning. However, many libraries do not normally collect this kind of statistical data, and therefore it often goes unreported in the profession's published literature or a library's annual reports. This unique information matters because it can provide an understanding of the progressive impact a library has on designated groups of students over extended periods.

3 Literature Review

The author used several keywords associated with "engaged learning," along with several keywords associated with "library support," to search in databases for published sources relating to focused question one. In addition, he searched using keywords associated with "longitudinal studies," along with keywords associated with "library assignment," for sources associated with focused question two. The author examined only sources published between 2000 and 2014, and that discussed the topic from an institutional perspective. He searched in Web of Knowledge, Scopus, and several EBSCO and FirstSearch databases. Portions of this literature review derive from previous research published by the author [1, p. 352].

Sources providing an overall administrative perspective discuss the library's role in supporting the entire campus learning culture only cursorily or implicitly. Often, they argue for an alignment of the library's mission, goals, and assessment program with those of the parent institution and with the institution's accreditation processes. Library support for the elements of a campus learning culture that this study targets is not addressed in the content of these sources.

In one such source, Bowlby discusses organizational performance assessment and reviews several organizational performance assessment programs available online, including the Association of College and Research Libraries' ACRLMetrics and the Association of Research Libraries' StatsQUAL™ [2]. She maintains that libraries using these programs to assess their organizational performance have subsequently integrated their library's planning and performance with the parent institution's mission and goals, which usually includes a general statement supporting engagement. In another source, Franklin reports that the University of Connecticut (Storrs) Libraries set-aside goals focused on collections and traditional library services and instead developed a strategic plan that focused on the goals its parent institution identified as essential components of its plan [3]. The university identified undergraduate education, graduate and professional education, research, scholarship, creative activity, diversity, and public engagement as the areas it wanted to emphasize. The library not only used these areas as a framework for its strategic plan but also reorganized its staff to align the Library's organizational structure to better support the university's academic goals.

In a rather unusual approach to aligning the library's mission, goals, and assessment program to those of its parent institution, Trinity University's (San Antonio, Texas) Coates Library used an opportunity made available to the university during its accreditation review as a means of integrating its information literacy goals with the university's goals. Zald and Millet recount how the library, motivated by a competition initiated by the Southern Association of Colleges and Schools, developed a Quality Enhancement Plan to improve student learning across the curriculum [4]. The plan called for librarians to work with teaching faculty to develop, implement, and assess student-learning goals for courses taught in the academic departments. Following the university's acceptance of the plan, librarians and faculty began integrating the library's information literacy program with the goals of the academic departments and the mission and goals of the university.

The Value of Academic Libraries: A Comprehensive Research Review and Report [5], researched by Megan Oakleaf and published online in September 2010 by the Association of College and Research Libraries, advocates, among other things, the kind of research undertaken by this study. However, it does not mention any completed research concerned with the elements of the learning culture targeted by this study's questions. The report's purpose was to review in a comprehensive manner the quantitative and qualitative research literature on library assessment, gaps in the research, appropriate research methodologies for academic libraries, and best practices for demonstrating the value of libraries in an institutional context. Also, several assessment "perspectives" are discussed, including student learning outcomes assessment. The research agenda found in the report focuses on areas where an academic library affects its institution's mission and goals [5, pp. 101–128].

Faculty members in academic departments have written about the campus learning culture that includes the elements this study is concerned with more extensively than librarians have, yet they do not mention the library's role. A representative group of these faculty members, concerned about the future of higher education, call for a complete change of campus cultures "in a manner that deepens and broadens learning" in *Transforming Undergraduate Education: Theory that Compels and Practices that Succeed,* a monograph published in 2012 [6]. The book's authors believe student-centered learning is important. However, they believe teachers often neglect this kind of learning.

In the book's first chapter titled "The Theoretical Arguments and Themes," Harward summarizes the ideas discussed more thoroughly in the following chapters [7]. He provides an explanation of what a supportive campus learning culture is like, advice on how to improve it, and a strategy for assessing it. Other chapters in the book discuss such issues as the need to focus on engaged learning, the failure of institutions of higher education to graduate students who know how to learn, the long-neglected aims of liberal education, and returning civics to liberal education. Chapters especially relevant to the research reported in this article are "The Theories, Contexts, and Multiple Pedagogies of Engaged Learning" by Lynn Swaner [8], "Reuniting the Often Neglected Aims of Liberal Education: Student Well-Being and Psychosocial Development" by Bergen-Cico and Bylander [9], and "Liberal Education and the Policy Landscape" by Schneider and Humphreys [10]. Swaner examines engaged learning and its dimensions [8, pp. 80–86]. She concentrates on service learning, learning communities, and undergraduate research. Swaner believes that a culture of engagement can act as a catalyst to bring about improvements in student learning. Bergen-Cico and Bylander maintain that liberal education in the United States is in a deplorable state and that one reason for this is that college students experience high levels of psychological distress [9, p. 97]. Schneider and Humphreys identify and discuss successful high-impact educational practices like first-year seminars and experiences, common intellectual experiences, learning communities, and writing-intensive courses [10, p. 292].

In a chapter of another book titled "Leading Higher Education Teaching, Learning, and Innovation," Debowski discusses the roles leaders in higher education can play in constructing and promoting an exceptional learning environment. The author, another member of higher education's teaching profession, asserts that there is now a "greater understanding of the need to develop an educational environment that is constructive, supportive, and innovative for both teachers and students" [11, p. 252]. As she sees it, one of the conditions for the success of this kind of environment is a focus on the student. She explains that, "although teachers are a major determinant of student satisfaction, … [students'] assessments of their experience will also be based around the administrators, facilities, service groups, other teachers, and infrastructure that they have encountered" [11, p. 261].

Various articles describe a systems approach or strategic planning project that focused on support for student-centered learning. Collins, Friday-Stroud, and Ashley describe a systems approach to creating and sustaining a campus culture centered on student learning [12]. They discuss how administrators and faculty members can support the culture and use a systems model to identify inputs, "throughput" processes, and outputs associated with a campus system. The authors also offer suggestions for successfully applying their approach. Nowhere in their article are libraries mentioned.

Blumberg writes about a strategic planning project done at the University of the Sciences in Philadelphia in 2001/2002 that identified strategic imperatives to direct the university's planning through 2010 [13]. One of the imperatives was to establish a culture of student-centered learning and living. The university's administration appointed a planning team to lead the effort to create objectives, action steps, and outcome indicators for student-centered learning and living. In addition, it tasked the University Teaching and Learning Center with educating faculty and supporting their efforts to implement learning-centered teaching in their classes. The project may have been more successful if librarians had been involved.

Hendricks et al. report on a project done at the College of Saint Catherine (Saint Paul, Minnesota) in 1991 whose initial goal was to find ways to improve recruitment and retention of students at the College [14]. However, the project quickly evolved into one of building a new campus culture for learning. In addition to problems with recruitment and retention, college administrators had become aware that the campus was also suffering from fragmentation. Faculty, staff, and students felt isolated. The complete separation of the teaching and research responsibilities of faculty from the supporting activities of the student affairs staff was especially noticeable. This growing awareness led to action, and the college decided to establish a team of faculty and staff to address the problem. The team developed a plan that built on the institution's newly revised core curriculum. The plan linked faculty efforts in the area of academic learning to student affairs staff efforts in the area of student development. Neither this source nor the previous one authored by Blumberg mention the campus library's contribution to the projects described.

Several published sources report the results of longitudinal assessments of student populations. None of these studies evaluated the neglected components this study targets. In addition, they did not include the library in their research projects. An important research project of this kind is the National Center for Education Statistics' National Education Longitudinal Study (ELS) conducted in 2002 and 2004 [15]. The study provided data on trends in transitions experienced by students proceeding through high school and into postsecondary education or careers.

The sources discussed above describe contributions to research in one or more of the areas of library assessment, engaged learning, college learning cultures, or longitudinal studies of students. However, they do not report on the kind of inquiry done in this present study. Nor do they discuss any studies that used the same model and questions for gathering data.

4 Research Design

The state of Texas requires all faculty teaching in Texas higher education institutions to submit syllabi of all courses they teach for inclusion in a publicly searchable online database [16]. Texas Tech University uses DigitalMeasures [17], a leading web-based faculty activity reporting system, to meet this obligation. Syllabi of courses taught at Texas Tech since the spring of 2011 are available to the public in the institution's DigitalMeasures database. The author searched in all the syllabi of courses taught between the spring of 2011 and the summer of 2013 for the keywords "service learning," "civic learning," "engaged learning," "learning communities," "undergraduate research," "collaborative assignments," "collaborative projects," "community-based learning," "internships," or "writing intensive courses" and for several keywords associated with "library support." The online searching disclosed that syllabi for 99 courses included at least one of the terms in the group of terms associated with "library support" and at least one of the terms in the group of terms associated with "engaged learning." The author carefully examined printed copies of the syllabi of these courses in order to answer focused question one, which is concerned with library support for engaged learning.

Staff at Texas Tech University's Office of Institutional Research provided the author with the statistical data needed to answer focused question two, which is concerned with finding the percent and number of students in each class year who passed a course with an assignment requiring the use of library resources and services. They provided the enrollment, class year, and passing grade data of those courses found in DigitalMeasures with syllabi that included keywords associated with "library assignment," and that thus met the requirements of focused question two.

5 Findings for Focused Questions

The author searched in the syllabi of courses stored in DigitalMeasures and taught from the spring semester of 2011 to the summer semester of 2013[3] and found 99 unique courses that included at least one of the terms in the text of their syllabi associated with "engaged learning" and one of the terms associated with "library support" (see Table 1). After carefully examining the printouts of these syllabi, the author determined that all of them required students enrolled in the courses to participate in an engaged learning activity or activities where they were required to find and use library resources and services (see footnote 2 for all activities included in engaged learning). Texas Tech University's Office of Institutional Research provided enrollment numbers for these courses.

[3] Data for the fall semester of 2013 was not available during the implementation of this study.

Table 1. Number of courses from spring 2011 to summer 2013 meeting requirements of focused question one

	Spring 2011	Summer 2011	Fall 2011	Spring 2012	Summer 2012	Fall 2012	Spring 2013	Summer 2013	Totals for the study period
Courses taught	14	7	17	14	4	17	18	8	99
Students enrolled	3,419	636	5,695	3,201	638	4,306	2,670	682	21,247

The syllabi of the 99 courses state, using various wording, that research using the library's resources and services for writing a term paper or for a presentation is required. Often the research is for a term paper requiring the use of a particular citation style manual with the number of works to cite. Assignment descriptions frequently point out that the paper requires analysis and/or critical thinking on the part of the student. A number of the assignments require a particular element in the paper's structure, such as inclusion of a literature review, description of the study's methodology, or hypothesis statements. Several of the undergraduate courses are writing intensive, internships, or undergraduate research courses, and some of the graduate courses prepare graduate students for thesis or dissertation projects. Seven of the undergraduate courses require service-learning activities. These activities are usually associated with reflection papers or journals, class presentations based on the experience gained and including an annotated bibliography, supervised service work, agency evaluations, or content papers based on the experience. Sometimes a syllabus identifies the library's website with particular resources on it that it recommends for use to complete the research project. Occasionally an assignment identified the liaison librarian for the academic department offering the course as a resource person or as a presenter for one of the class meetings [1, p. 360].

Continuing to use DigitalMeasures, the author identified syllabi of undergraduate courses taught between the spring semester of 2011 and the summer semester of 2013 that included in their text at least one of the terms associated with "library assignment."[4] Any kind of library assignment, not just those including engaged-learning activities, were counted. The author examined these syllabi to verify that they in fact contained an assignment that met the requirements of focused question two. Subsequently, the Office of Institutional Research provided the student enrollment by class year and passing-grade data of these courses. The number of students enrolled in the courses who received passing grades was broken down by class year and within each class by semester of the period covered by the study. The author compared the resulting numbers with total class enrollments for each semester. The percentages of students in the sophomore, junior, and senior classes who passed a course with a library

[4] The terms associated with "library assignment" include "research assignment," "library project," "research project," "writing assignment," "paper assignment," and "term paper assignment."

assignment requiring use of library resources and services ranged from 5.3 to 15.5% per semester and 17.2% to 36.4% per year. The percentages of students in the freshman classes who passed a course with this kind of assignment ranged from 8.7 to 30.6% per semester and 40.2% to 62.6% per year.

6 Discussion and Conclusions Pertaining to the Research Questions

This inquiry's method, using an online system to provide a researcher with data for all the courses taught at a university, is new and has not been previously discussed in the published literature, as it is reported in the literature review above. The inquiry succeeded in modeling an efficient and effective way, using an online resource, to assess a library's level or size of support for courses with engaged-learning activities and for particular student populations over an extended period. In doing this, it answered its two research questions. Libraries can identify courses where their resources and services, including information literacy instruction, support engaged-learning courses, and they can target their efforts for the maximum impact on student learning using their parent institution's online systems. Numerous institutions of higher education located in many countries store data such as class enrollments, grades, and even course syllabi in online databases. Many of them permit researchers, including librarians, to access aggregated data from their databases to conduct research projects. Therefore, librarians at numerous institutions should be able to do studies like this one.

The method assures that the population assessed is complete. This is especially important for large universities that offer hundreds or thousands of courses. Without the comprehensive searching available through an institution's online system, a library's assessments of its effect on courses can only reach segments of the course offerings and student populations. A comprehensive reach is especially important when determining the level or size of library support for the parent institution's mission and goals. The size of a library's reach in supporting courses says much in assessments at the institutional level.

However, the most important outcome of this inquiry is that it has targeted courses with engaged-learning activities and student populations for further study, and it speaks to research question two. Texas Tech University Library, and other libraries using the same method, can do follow-up studies that can focus on the library's efforts for the maximum impact on student learning in courses and student populations. Monitoring the stored online data of the courses targeted by this inquiry's focused questions over time will facilitate comparisons of the grades of students taking courses with library assignments and those taking the same courses but without such assignments.

7 Conclusions Pertaining to the Local Assessment

Analysis of this inquiry's collected data elicits definite conclusions when using it for local assessment. Considering Texas Tech University's declared emphasis on engaged learning in its several manifestations and its desire to promote engaged learning throughout its curricula of around 4,500 courses offered each year [18], one can conclude that the Library's contribution to only 99 of those courses with engaged-learning activities during the three-year period of the study is unimpressive. A total of 21,247 students were enrolled in these 99 courses during the period of the study, while a total of 96,444 students were enrolled at Texas Tech University during the period of this study. This means that 22.0% of all the students enrolled from the fall of 2010 to the summer of 2013 took part in engaged learning activities involving an assignment requiring use of library resources and services [19, pp. 367–368].

One may conclude after studying the data above that Texas Tech librarians need to persuade more faculty members to add library assignments to their courses with engaged-learning activities. To begin with, the author distributed copies of the 99 syllabi with engaged-learning activities and assignments requiring use of library resources and services to the liaison librarians who are responsible for the academic departments that sponsor these courses for follow-up. Some of the assignments need to be improved, and the librarians are the best advocates for this improvement. In addition, the librarians who provide information literacy classes will begin brainstorming for strategies to increase the library's support for courses with engaged-learning activities.

The data collected and analyzed to find the percent of undergraduate students in each class year who passed a course meeting focused question two's criteria revealed that the freshman classes had the highest percentages with a range of from 8.7% (summer 2012) to 30.6% (fall 2011). The sophomore classes had a percentage range of 6.4% (summer 2012) to 15.5% (spring 2012), the junior classes 5.3% (summer 2011) to 12.5% (spring 2012), and the senior classes 6.8% (summer 2013) to 12.8% (spring 2011). Required core courses with library research assignments have large numbers of freshmen and this is the reason for the higher percentages for the freshman classes. The significance of the numbers and percentages for all the classes may be arguable. However, one could conclude after reviewing the data that the liaison librarians need to do a better job of persuading their faculty that it is important for their students to acquire library research skills.

8 Further Research Needed

Additional questions can lead to the measurement of other hitherto neglected elements of the learning culture. Some of these questions are:

- How has the college or university documented the connection between student well-being measures and learning? Does the library play a role in this connection?
- When using flourishing and resiliency scales [20] or when tracking behavioral patterns, attitudes, and dispositions from survey data, what changes are revealed when collections of students are compared throughout their undergraduate careers? What has brought about these changes? Has the library played a role in any changes?

Academic and research libraries need to recognize the importance of collecting and analyzing data pertaining to these neglected components of assessment—components such as the library's contributions to increasing student engagement in a successful learning culture. Assuming student learning-outcomes assessment continues to play an important role in higher education and complete, accurate, and continuous analysis of the success of student learning continues to be the goal, then a variety of different methods of assessment must be implemented regularly to obtain a more complete picture of what is taking place.

References

1. Hufford, J.R.: The academic library and the culture for learning. portal: Libr. Acad. **16**(2), 349–372 (2016)
2. Bowlby, R.: Living the future: organizational performance assessment. J. Libr. Adm. **52** (6/7), 626–652 (2012)
3. Franklin, B.: Surviving to thriving: advancing the institutional mission. J. Libr. Adm. **52**(1), 94–107 (2012)
4. Zald, A.E., Millet, M.: Hitching your wagon to institutional goals. In: Wilkinson, C.W., Bruch, C. (eds.) Transforming Information Literacy Programs: Intersecting Frontiers of Self, Library Culture, and Campus Community, pp. 119–130. Association of College and Research Libraries, Chicago (2012)
5. Oakleaf, M.: The Value of Academic Libraries: A Comprehensive Research Review and Report. Association of College and Research Libraries, Chicago (2010)
6. Harward, D.W., Finley, A.P. (eds.): Transforming Undergraduate Education: Theory that Compels and Practices that Succeed. Rowman and Littlefield, Lanham (2012)
7. Harward, D.W.: The theoretical arguments and themes. In: Harward, D.W., Finley, A.P. (eds.) Transforming Undergraduate Education: Theory that Compels and Practices that Succeed, pp. 3–33. Rowman and Littlefield, Lanham (2012)
8. Swaner, L.E.: The Theories, Contexts, and Multiple Pedagogies of Engaged Learning: What Succeeds and Why? In: Harward, D.W., Finley, A.P. (eds.) Transforming Undergraduate Education: Theory that Compels and Practices that Succeed, pp. 73–89. Rowman and Littlefield, Lanham (2012)
9. Bergen-Cico, D., Bylander, J.A.: Reuniting the often neglected aims of liberal education: student well-being and psychosocial development. In: Harward, D.W., Finley, A.P. (eds.) Transforming Undergraduate Education: Theory that Compels and Practices that Succeed, pp. 91–108. Rowman and Littlefield, Lanham (2012)
10. Schneider, C.G., Humphreys, D.: Liberal education and the policy landscape. In: Harward, D.W., Finley, A.P. (eds.) Transforming Undergraduate Education: Theory that Compels and Practices that Succeed, pp. 281–299. Rowman and Littlefield, Lanham (2012)
11. Debowski, S.: Leading higher education teaching, learning, and innovation. In: Roccio, J.E., Al-Dairy, M.A., Buskins, W. (eds.) Handbook of College and University Teaching: A Global Perspective, pp. 251–266. Sage, Thousand Oaks (2012)
12. Collins, J., Friday-Stroud, S., Ashley, C.: A systems approach to creating and sustaining an assessment culture. Int. J. Educ. Res. **5**(2), 152–167 (2010)
13. Blumberg, P.: Beginning journey toward a culture of learning-centered teaching. J. Stud. Cent. Learn. **2**(1), 69–83 (2004)
14. Hendricks, S.H., Kari, N.N., Richter-Norgel, E.: The Catherine connection: building a learning culture. About Campus, pp. 25–28, May/June 2000

15. U.S. Department of Education, National Center for Education Statistics: Educational Longitudinal Study of 2002 (ELS: 2002): Base-Year to Second Follow-Up Data File Documentation. In: NCES 2008-347. Department of Education, Washington DC (2007)
16. Texas Legislature: Public Access to Course Information. Texas House Bill 2504, 81st Texas Legislature, 8 May 2009
17. DigitalMeasures. http://www.digitalmeasures.com
18. Texas Tech University: Making It Possible: Strategic Plan 2010–2020. Texas Tech University, Lubbock (2010)
19. Texas Tech University: Online Fact Book. http://www.irim.ttu.edu/Factbook/
20. The Resilience Center: The Resilience Scale. http://www.resiliencescale.com/index.html

Dare to Share the Silence: Tools and Practices of Contemplative Pedagogy in a Library Brain Booth

Marissa M. Mourer[1] and Katia G. Karadjova[2(✉)]

[1] Eastern Washington University, Cheney, WA, USA
mmourer@ewu.edu
[2] Humboldt State University (HSU), Arcata, CA, USA
katia.karadjova@humboldt.edu

Abstract. A research study at a rural, public university revealed interest among college students in engaging in mindfulness and contemplative practices within their university library. This study also identified a gap between interest in contemplative pedagogy among faculty and their engagement in contemplative practices within this newly-created library space, The Library Brain Booth. This study shares the results of visits to the Library Brain Booth by both first-time and returning participants. It also provides mean usage time at each of the following stations that were created to support mindfulness and contemplation: biofeedback, color-relax, game-relax, light-relax, read-relax, silent-relax, sound-relax, audio-meditate, prompt-meditate, video-meditate, gratitude-express, and virtual reality-immerse. The results of the study are intended to support the explicit promotion of metacognition and mindfulness in the academic process, both through mindfulness activities within the library for students, and through contemplative pedagogy in information literacy instruction.

Keywords: Contemplative pedagogy · Contemplative studies
Academic libraries · Information literacy · Mindfulness
Undergraduate students

1 Introduction

In this research study, we aimed to identify willingness to engage in mindfulness and contemplation practices among college students in their university library. This study also aimed to identify interest in contemplative pedagogy in the workplace for educators, including librarians. Mindfulness as an academic activity was promoted to the campus community through an innovative and newly-created physical space within the university library, entitled Library Brain Booth, providing participants with activities and tools that could support exploration of mindfulness and contemplation. These activities and tools were chosen for both their accessibility to a diverse and novice audience as well as for potential popularity or novel interest. The stations created were biofeedback, color-relax, game-relax, light-relax, read-relax, silent-relax, sound-relax, audio-meditate, prompt-meditate, video-meditate, gratitude-express, and virtual reality-immerse.

S. Kurbanoğlu et al. (Eds.): ECIL 2017, CCIS 810, pp. 781–790, 2018.
https://doi.org/10.1007/978-3-319-74334-9_79

We created the innovative Library Brain Booth space to address an important gap in our educational and workplace environments: the known benefits of practicing mindfulness as a metacognitive activity toward academic and workplace success. With willingness to engage in mindful practices as an academic activity established, further research could be supported that would explore the ability of specific tools and activities to impact academic success and cultivate mindfulness among students. It could also support efforts for librarians to partner with departmental faculty to embed contemplative pedagogy into information literacy instruction and measure its impact on both students and faculty.

2 Literature Review

College students must navigate between two major factors affecting their performance and wellbeing, namely, copying with stress [1–3] and dealing with distractions to sustain productive cognitive activities [4]. Contemplative pedagogy offers methods that support the development of student attention and emotional balance as well as techniques that support creativity and course content learning [5].

Mindfulness is a mental state of focused attention in the present moment without judgmental perspectives. Scholars and practitioners have discussed mindfulness theories and practices at-length [6–10] and its positive effects on the human wellbeing [11, 12].

The literature suggested that mindful practices could have a positive impact on student learning [6, 13, 14], on reducing emotional exhaustion and improving workplace satisfaction and effectiveness [15, 16], and on supporting mental health [11, 17].

Engagement with mindfulness and contemplative pedagogy supports such proven activities as intentional brain breaks, emotional self-regulation, and singular focus.

Intentional brain breaks: taking as little as a few minutes to give the brain a break from thinking, can lead to better focus and better academic study outcomes [6, 18].

Emotional self-regulation practice [11]: educators ask students to engage in courageous conversations both in- and outside of the classroom. Teaching contemplation and mindfulness is a way to prepare students to more successfully engage in those conversations while also teaching the cultivation of patience and compassion for diverse viewpoints [19].

Singular focus: many students struggle with attempting to multitask as well as foster strong, singular focus when it is needed for short or sustained periods of time. Mindfulness training has quite immediate impacts on attention and focus [19, 20].

Some scholars and practitioners have gone even further by designing and conducting ongoing mindfulness training in the classroom across curriculum to support an attentive, present-centered, and non-reactive mental mode [13, 21] as well as by development and standardization of mindfulness qualities scale for college students [22].

Lately, librarians have started to pay attention to mindfulness and to engage with mindful practices [20, 23, 24]. Just a few university libraries have started to dedicate time and spaces to mindfulness activities. Most of these libraries focus primarily on meditation. Our project is the first one to involve a broader spectrum of mindfulness activities, that offer intentional brain breaks to students, faculty and staff.

3 Methodology

3.1 Research Question

The study's overall research questions are as follows: Among the campus community is there interest and willingness to engage in mindful practices within the library's academic setting? Will participants return? If there is interest, what is the mean duration of use for each station?

3.2 Quantitative Approach

We designed a LibGuide for the Library Brain Booth to provide overall information for all participants, and a contemplative pedagogy section for campus educators. Drawing data from the LibGuides statistics section, the viewing rate of the LibGuide was 1,191 views from August 29 through December 31, 2016, with most views occurring in September.

Shortened Google url's linking to the LibGuide were created to track views via clicks. The shortened url's were used in targeted promotions to three campus groups: college students, staff, and faculty, including librarians. Email communications were sent via the opt-out campus system. 32 students, 16 staff, and 51 faculty viewed these emails.

Additionally, small printed flyers were created with a unique url to share with students via tabling events during freshmen orientation, multicultural welcome events, and on library whiteboards. The viewing rate of this unique url was 128 students.

We also provided a voluntary student sign-up form at those tabling events who wished to be added to an email group for direct communications. A total of 120 students signed up.

3.3 Qualitative Approach

We designed a moderate participant observation study [26], influenced by focused ethnography [25], where the primary data collection format was video recordings of each session. The video camera was visibly perched above eye-level at the front of the room. Researchers were stationed outside of the classroom, serving as identifiable, limited participants [26]. Researchers obtained informed consent and answered questions outside of the classroom. Participants could invite us into the space for support at any time.

We did not have any interested parties who declined to participate in the study. Due to the continuous video recording in the Library Brain Booth classrooms, those who wished to use the Library Brain Booth stations were required to provide their informed consent to enter the classroom and be video recorded for the study. Although we did not have any participants decline to participate in the study, there were printed opt-out flyers with links to freely-available online mindfulness resources to support those who declined.

We designed the study so that the total number of visits to the Library Brain Booth would be tracked via the required signed consent forms collected. One-time or returning participants were confirmed using these forms, which included printed name and date.

It was determined that video data analysis would be centered on recording aggregated station visit lows, highs, and means as well as observations of participant interactions.

The Library Brain Booth was hosted twice weekly for two-hour sessions. We hypothesized that classroom set-up might impact Library Brain Booth station usage, so two different classroom locations were chosen and in both only natural outside light was used. One classroom hosts individual mobile desks. Two to four desks would be grouped together for each station. The second classroom has long tables in rows not easily moved. Seats were arranged on both sides of a row with one to two stations available in any given row.

3.4 Limitations

Participants did consent to being audio recorded, yet most informing dialogue between participants and researchers took place outside of the designated classroom space at the point of getting informed consent. Since this study, audio recordings have been collected.

Based on early observations of the video data, it was determined that a follow-up study would be required to introduce one tool at a time or to discuss multiple-station usage with participants through interviews or focus group settings. All station visits of any length were initially recorded, yet required time to engage with activities and tools was diverse. A visit of any length could not be decidedly determinant of either preference or ability to support mindfulness practice for everyone. Absence of a visit to a station could also not concretely be concluded to be due to a lack of interest, and could be attributed to lack of time or lack of awareness. Defining what constituted activity or tool engagement without asking participants directly was also not deemed appropriate. Additional study using interview or focus group techniques is necessary.

4 Results

Overall, the results showed significant interest in mindfulness tools and activities within an academic library setting among college student participants in the Library Brain Booth. Interest in mindfulness tools and activities in the workplace among college staff and college faculty could only be demonstrated through engagement with digital promotional material.

4.1 Participation

One-Time and Returning Visits Recorded. In the fall of 2016, from the first day of operation on August 31 through the week of finals on December 14, we tracked attendance by completed informed consent forms.

The total number of visits to the Library Brain Booth in fall 2016 was 240. Of the visitors, students made up the largest percentage at 95% (n = 228), along with 3% (n = 8) staff and 2% (n = 4) faculty. We did not have any community member participants.

We were also seeking to understand if interest transcended the initial novelty of the space. Of the total participants, 12% (n = 28) returned on at least one more occasion.

4.2 Station Usage and Duration

We prompted participants to stay for any length of time during the operating hours. Thus, no participant could participate more than 120 min. We also informed them that they could come outside of the classroom to ask us questions or to seek station support. It was intentional to be outside of the space and to not provide direct instruction. We also encouraged them to move station furniture or tools as they desired, including to combine station offerings.

We note that given the lengthy visits of many participants, especially among returning participants, the overall limited operating hours of the Library Brain Booth may have been a significant factor on returning participants. Efforts to offer both purposefully shorter sessions and an open, dedicated space with circulating materials are underway because of this study (Table 1).

4.3 Participant Observations

An anonymous comment card was available for participants to voluntarily provide written comments while in the Library Brain Booth. A total of 74 comments were received. In comparing the written comments with the video data by date, we could not associate individual station usage to participant preference or benefit with any degree of certainty.

> *"It was cool although I didn't stay long, felt more relax [sic] & at peace."*

> *"I feel a lot lighter, not as tight, I don't feel that tension, however slight, in my head or body. It's great to get my mind off of everything, even just for a few mins. Biofeedback was my favorite!:)"*

Interactions Among Participants. The Library Brain Booth was not a dedicated silent space, and this was communicated to participants. Unless participants arrived together, interactions were extremely limited. Even those who arrived together were seen to separate and participate silently. Interactions tended to be of a necessary nature in that a participant either wanted to share the same station or needed another participant to move to access a station.

The biofeedback and virtual reality-immerse stations were observed to have more interactions, and participants were seen assisting each other, sharing phones and VR videos.

While activity around a station by more than one person was found to pique interest among other participants, it was more common to see participants actively disengaging from others in the space. Disengagement was observed as turning one's body or averting gaze, not acknowledging the arrival of others, and closing eyes where activities permitted.

Table 1. Library brain booth station tools and duration of time spent by low, high, and mean.

Station Description. Combined use of station tools together is also noted	Low	High	Mean
Biofeedback. This station featured four mobile heart-rate variability biofeedback units and with operating instructions **Combined with:** Color-relax, read-relax, gratitude-express, game-relax, and prompt-meditate	1	21	5
Color-relax. This station featured coloring pages, both those freely available online and in commercial coloring books. Colored pencils and colored felt, odorless markers were provided **Combined with:** Biofeedback, light-relax, sound-relax, and video-meditate	1	39	9
Game-relax. This station provided a wooden labyrinth puzzle, several decks of cards, and a rotating selection of commercial board games and puzzle games. Traditional puzzles were not included **Combined with:** Biofeedback, noise-relax, and virtual reality-immerse	1	29	7
Light-relax. Two light lamps were set-up along with instructions and manufacturer's cautions **Combined with:** Color-relax, read-relax, gratitude-express, game-relax, and prompt-meditate	1	19	6
Read-relax. A rotating selection of the 30 curated books was offered each session. Signage notified participants that all were circulating and specially cataloged for easy searching **Combined with:** Color-relax, read-relax, gratitude-express, game-relax, and prompt-meditate	1	29	7
Silent-relax. Silent participation was not required. For participants who wished to use the space in silence, sound-isolation headphones were provided. Because silent-relax was always done in combination with other activities, the data represent station combination of these **Combined with:** Prompt-meditate, game-relax, light-relax, and read-relax	4	12	7
Sound-relax. Featured two plug-in sound machines with headphones **Combined with:** Color-relax, light-relax, and participants' own projects	1	60	9
Audio-meditate. A CD player and headphones were provided with four guided meditation CD's **Combined with:** Was not used in combination	2	12	7
Prompt-meditate. Printed mindfulness prompts, including mindfulness activity cards, were provided for an electronic-free option **Combined with:** Biofeedback and light-relax	1	17	3

(*continued*)

Table 1. (*continued*)

Station Description. Combined use of station tools together is also noted	Low	High	Mean
Video-meditate. Two laptops, with headphones, were provided along with signage listing several free online guided meditations. Five guided meditation DVD's were also purchased for the library's collection and noted on the signage **Combined with:** Color-relax	2	16	5
Gratitude-express. Large sheets of paper and markers were laid out on tables with some of the sheets blank and some containing a "Gratitude Log" **Combined with:** Biofeedback	1	20	6
Virtual reality-immerse. Four goggles were purchased for device compatibility. A list of VR-friendly immersive experience video links and manufacturer's instructions were provided. Participants had to bring their own or borrow a participant's smartphone **Combined with:** Biofeedback	1	35	8

Tools purchased based on affordability and recommendations. Products are noted, but are not endorsements. Biofeedback: emWave™; Light: Lightphoria Lamps™; Sound: SONEic™; Prompt: Growing Mindful™; Virtual Reality: Tepoinn™, Samsung™, and Freefly™.

Classroom Design. No discernible difference was observed in station usage, participant interactions, or time at stations across the two classroom configurations. Layout did impact station discovery.

In the classroom with individual seating, participants were observed walking haphazardly for longer periods of time before pausing to view or engage with stations. In the classroom with table rows, participants were generally observed to access the stations in a left-right, front-back order, except for returners who directly headed to stations of interest. Rows required more interaction to access a tool being blocked by another participant.

The researchers have received verbal requests for meditation benches and yoga mats. We acknowledge the potential interest in design elements or equipment that would delineate it from a traditional library space. Written comments included: "*Nice idea-better layout might be chairs facing individual stations/desks w/barriers; Cool idea-maybe add something to the room so it's not just desks; Pillows, blankets of color!*"

5 Conclusions/Discussions

The overall goal of providing mindfulness activities within the university library setting is to introduce metacognition more explicitly, particularly to college students as part of the academic process and to faculty and staff in the workplace. It is hoped that situating metacognition via mindfulness will normalize the practice and lead to greater exploration of its positive impacts on academic and workplace success for students, staff, and faculty.

Looking at the literature on library programing [27, 28], and given the voluntary, incentive-free, no-credit nature of the Library Brain Booth, we established that the number of participants (n = 240) demonstrated significant interest among college students. Exploring the potential time burden placed on students to learn outside of the classroom through a broader, critical examination of library offerings is warranted. Toward that end, we have just concluded a spring 2017 study offering direct, microlearning opportunities.

A shorter visit duration at the Library Brain Booth or at a station was not deemed to be less beneficial to participants, especially as we reviewed comments such as these: *"Perfect little break from school; Wonderful experience. Nice little break!; Great for a break!; Just scoped everything out. Next time I'll choose one."*

We cannot conclude that the space must be silent. For example, participants were rarely observed to speak in the Library Brain Booth, but the sound of voices may be viewed negatively or differently than nature sounds or white noise. We believe that preference for sound is important to explore and may have impacted initial or returning participation.

Overall, some tools and activities were observed to be easy to learn, but may not support our aims to promote mindfulness and contemplation. An illustrative example of this is coloring pages. While we recorded lengthy coloring sessions and devoted attention among some participants, others were observed to frequently scan the room or their phones. Explicit connection to mindfulness practice and the role of metacognition in academic efforts was found to be crucial in situating the tools and the Library Brain Booth mission.

One way in which we believe we can accomplish making metacognition more explicit is to capitalize on the observations made about participants' choices for station combinations, and support shorter visits. We observed some activities and tools to be complementary. We plan to present those combinations more explicitly and intentionally. For instance, given the ease of use of color-relax, game-relax, light-relax, read-relax, and sound-relax, we plan to promote pairing these with biofeedback, audio-meditate, prompt-meditate, and video-meditate with stronger messaging around intentional brain breaks.

Finally, our study also showed an existing gap between engagement with digital tools centered on contemplative pedagogy and in-person faculty participation. A follow-up study focused solely on engagement with contemplative pedagogy, aside from faculty's own mindful practice, would better identify this gap. We encourage librarians to conduct follow-up studies in this area. We believe that librarians are well-positioned to adopt contemplative pedagogy in their information literacy instruction and to serve as resources for departmental faculty, who may be willing to explore its use in their courses. As a workplace effort, we argue that further study is warranted to support professional development and support our holistic selves at work to support caring, patient, and inclusive work with students.

Acknowledgements. We would like to thank the HSU Sponsored Programs Foundation for two grant awards to make the purchasing of all the tools possible.

References

1. Coiro, M., Bettis, A., Compas, B.: College students coping with interpersonal stress: examining a control-based model of coping. J. Am. Coll. Health **65**(3), 177–186 (2017)
2. Denovan, A., Macaskill, A.: An interpretative phenomenological analysis of stress and coping in first year undergraduates. Br. Educ. Res. J. **39**(6), 1002–1024 (2013)
3. Li, M., Yang, Y.: A cross-cultural study on a resilience-stress path model for college students. J. Couns. Dev. **94**(3), 319–332 (2016)
4. Cheong, P., Shuter, R., Suwinyattichaiporn, T.: Managing student digital distractions and hyperconnectivity: communication strategies and challenges for professorial authority. Commun. Educ. **65**(3), 272–289 (2016)
5. Zajonc, A.: Contemplative pedagogy: a quiet revolution in higher education. New Dir. Teach. Learn. **2013**(134), 83–94 (2013)
6. Hassed, C.: Mindful Learning: Reduce Stress and Improve Brain Performance for Effective Learning. Shambhala Publications, Boston (2015)
7. Khazan, I.: The Clinical Handbook of Biofeedback: A Step by Step Guide for Training and Practice with Mindfulness. Wiley, Chichester (2013)
8. Langdon, S., Jones, F.W., Hutton, J., Holttum, S.: A grounded-theory study of mindfulness practice following mindfulness-based cognitive therapy. Mindfulness **2**(4), 270–281 (2011)
9. Paulson, S., Davidson, R., Jha, A., Kabat-Zinn, J.: Becoming conscious: the science of mindfulness. Ann. N. Y. Acad. Sci. **1303**(1), 87–104 (2013)
10. Vago, D.R., Silbersweig, D.A.: Self-awareness, self-regulation, and self-transcendence (S-ART): a framework for understanding the neurobiological mechanisms of mindfulness. Front. Human Neurosci. **6** (2012)
11. Cayoun, B.: Mindfulness-Integrated CBT for Well-being and Personal Growth: Four Steps to Enhance Inner Calm, Self-confidence and Relationships. Wiley, Chichester (2015)
12. Rogers, H.: Mindfulness for the Next Generation: Helping Emerging Adults Manage Stress and Lead Healthier Lives. Oxford University Press, New York (2012)
13. Hartel, J., Nguyen, A., Guzik, E.: Mindfulness Meditation in the Classroom. J. Educ. Libr. Inf. Sci. **58**(2), 112–115 (2017)
14. Rechtschaffen, D.: The Mindful Education Workbook: Lessons for Teaching Mindfulness to Students. W.W. Norton & Company, New York (2016)
15. Hülsheger, U.R., Alberts, H.J.E.M., Feinholdt, A., Lang, J.W.B.: Benefits of mindfulness at work: the role of mindfulness in emotion regulation, emotional exhaustion, and job satisfaction. J. Appl. Psychol. **98**(2), 310–325 (2013)
16. Leroy, H., Anseel, F., Dimitrova, N.G., Sels, L.: Mindfulness, authentic functioning, and work engagement: A growth modeling approach. J. Vocat. Behav. **82**(3), 238–247 (2013)
17. Bettis, A.H.: Comparison of two approaches to prevention of mental health problems in college students: enhancing coping and executive function skills. J. Am. Coll. Health, 1–10 (2017)
18. Bamber, M.D., Schneider, J.K.: Mindfulness-based meditation to decrease stress and anxiety in college students: a narrative synthesis of the research. Educ. Res. Rev. **18**, 1–32 (2016)
19. Shapiro, S.L., Brown, K.W., Astin, J.A.: Toward the integration of meditation into higher education: a review of research. Center Contempl. Mind Soc. (2008). http://www.contemplativemind.org/admin/wp-content/uploads/2012/09/MedandHigherEd.pdf
20. Moniz, R., Eshleman, J., Henry, J., Slutzky, H., Moniz, L.: The Mindful Librarian: Connecting the Practice of Mindfulness to Librarianship. Chandos Publishing, Oxford (2015)

21. Morrison, A.B., Goolsarran, M., Rogers, S.L. Jha, A.P.: Taming a wandering attention: short-form mindfulness training in student cohorts. Front. Human Neurosci. **7** (2014)
22. Arunya, B., Thamilselvan, P.: Development and standardization of mindfulness qualities scale for college students. Indian J. Posit. Psychol. **8**(1), 64–67 (2017)
23. Mastel, K., Innes, G.: Insights and practical tips on practicing mindful librarianship to manage stress. LIBRES: Libr. Inf. Sci. Res. Electron. J. **23**(1), 1–8 (2013)
24. Ruhlmann, E.: Mindful librarianship. Am. Libr. **48**(6), 44–47
25. Knoblauch, H.: Focused ethnography. In: Forum Qualitative Sozialforschung/Forum: Qualitative Social Research, vol. 6, no. 3 (2005)
26. Wolcott, H.F.: The Art of Fieldwork. Altamira Press, Walnut Creek (2005)
27. Loos, A.T.: The role of librarians in promoting digital wellness: a case study. Public Serv. Q. **13**(1), 32–40 (2017)
28. Turner, L.: Word of mouth and library workshops: let's get people talking. Coll. Res. Libr. News **78**(3), 142–143 (2017)

Information Culture and CETYS University WASC Accreditation: the Library as Stakeholder

Rubén F. Martínez-Rocha[1(✉)], Jesús Lau[2], and Eduardo R. Díaz[1]

[1] CETYS Universidad, Tijuana, Mexico
{ruben.martinez,eduardo.diaz}@cetys.mx
[2] Universidad Veracruzana, Veracruz, Mexico
jlau@uv.mx

Abstract. This paper analyzes CETYS (Center for Technical and Higher Education) University's information culture experiences from the empirical perspective of the librarians. The goal is to analyze the development of information culture (IC) as well as the actions that have been undertaken and the proposals that are yet to be considered to consolidate IC. CETYS is immersed in an educational evolution and has succeeded in meeting the high standards of the Western Association of Schools and Colleges (WASC, USA). The institution viewed IC as an element that ought to distinguish and characterize graduates of any academic program that the university offers. IC is considered a seminal element to train professionals to understand their information needs, how to search, evaluate, and use information. The study of the IC outcome is assessed here, relying on the institutional plans and reports for five of the eight objectives where the librarians were involved. These achievements have enabled faculty, students, and librarians to prepare themselves for a cultural change around information.

Keywords: Information culture · Information literacy · Higher education CETYS University

1 Introduction

As part of the action plan to achieve Western Association of Schools and Colleges (WASC) international accreditation, obtained in 2012, the *2020 Development Plan* of CETYS University [1] remarks that information culture is a Differentiating Element of the CETYS Graduate: and thus, it has been linked to the very mission of the institution since its inception, proposing to highlight this particular subject as a distinctive characteristic of its graduates. Also, IC is counted among the academic goals that are supported by the library and one of the six elements that characterize graduates from all educational levels, taught, and developed through innovative concepts and state-of-the-art teaching methods during their learning process. These initiatives will help graduates succeed in their professional lives and to achieve notability for counting with other distinctive EDEC's [1], besides IC, such as the following:

S. Kurbanoğlu et al. (Eds.): ECIL 2017, CCIS 810, pp. 791–799, 2018.
https://doi.org/10.1007/978-3-319-74334-9_80

- Liaison
- Sustainability
- Internationalization
- Social responsibility
- Entrepreneurship and innovation

The role of librarians has been vital for the implementation of IC in the institution's academic and pedagogical process, to achieve the aforementioned goals, and to execute the corresponding actions; librarians' roles have also been as crucial participants, and have been submitted to change, analysis, and organized and systematic professional and labor processes. Given that it is more than half-way between 2010 and 2020, it is now time to assess and, from the perspective of the librarians, empirically study the actions undertaken through this IC initiative through assessing their impact and identifying unfinished actions with the goal of identifying pending objectives.

2 IC and Conductive Actions

According to Menou [2], IC is the ability of individuals or groups to use information in the best way. CETYS takes this concept and implements it through its' 2020 plan [1]. One of the first actions undertaken in 2009, directed to achieve international accreditation and the implementation of IC, was the creation of an Information Literacy Development course with the participation of librarians and faculty that achieved good progress and some results [3, 4]. As Lau [3] reports, the follow-up actions, involving librarians, outlined to WASC, for the development and implementation of EDEC's with IC, are:

1. *Standardization of personnel service capacity and competences:* The opportunity of participating with professional librarians able to supply the library services that the community demands with the same quality in every library in the system.
2. *Standardization of service capacity, based on the expected demand of the student population at each campus.* - Every library shall have the same standardized facility and service infrastructure that corresponds to the capacity and dimensions of each campus.
3. *Completion of the service catalog that shall be offered in the libraries at each campus.* - Increase the service catalog, currently limited by restrictions of space, personnel, and technology.
4. *A new personnel recruitment plan for the libraries in the CETYS system.* - Offer new services, requiring professional librarians, and increase the current workforce.
5. *A professional development plan for the personnel of all libraries in the CETYS system.* - Current library personnel shall be updated and professionalized.
6. *Formulate learning results, and the corresponding assessment mechanisms to evaluate the extent of knowledge of the services offered by the system libraries among the students, and the degree to which they are being used.* - Development, application, and assessment of bibliometric elements capable of measuring the impact of the actions undertaken, to aid in decision-making processes.

The institution's library system is one of the support elements provided for faculty members, supplying the necessary information resources for cultural development, research, and diffusion. Thus, the library works in tandem with the institution and as a participant in action plans (initiatives) that indicate the path and objectives to follow. These initiatives are budget allocations that permit the achievement of the goals set in the *2020 Development Plan*, a vital document for the CETYS evolution process. The four initiatives that libraries have to develop and execute for the implementation of IC are:

A. *Infrastructure consolidation.* - Build optimal and versatile spaces that satisfy the demands of the community; improve and extend existing ones.
B. *Improvement of the archives.* - Increase the quantity and quality of the library archives, stressing the format diversity and time relevance that the community requires. This includes print, digital, and remote resources.
C. *Recruitment of professional human resources.* - Increase the current workforce with the recruitment of library specialists, or specialists in other areas related to the institution's academic offerings.
D. *Personnel professionalization and training.* - Promote the intellectual and professional development of librarians through support grants for graduate studies, library science training, or through updating courses.

It shall be noted that the actions reported by Lau [3] directly coincide with the initiatives of the libraries; thus, action 1 is linked to initiative A, actions 2 and 3 are linked to initiative B, and so forth. This shows that the work, actions, and initiatives are coordinated towards the achievement of one sole common objective.

3 Achievements

The achievements of EDEC, in relation to its objectives, were reported by Lau [5], who included the diagnosis and consultation processes for the entire CETYS community. Two main diagnostic actions can be highlighted: a population-based study of information literacy, and a bibliometric analysis to the research and dissemination of publications with a bibliography of all current academic plans.

"A study called "Demanda y competencias informativas de académicos (DECIA)" (Faculty information demand and competence) was carried out, comprising the entire part-time and full-time teaching staff, during the first semester of 2012. The results revealed that the faculty requires greater informational and technological demand and competence, and that the impact of information literacy promotion in the classroom is low" [3].

The bibliometric analysis reported that: "analysis of faculty papers, and academic programs, to evaluate their use of information, shows that a major part of the teaching staff, that have published papers, requires more updated information, and better scientific content. The results also revealed that faculty members required more consultation of information, and more paper publication" [3].

The results of all these studies guided the determination of action measures. One of these was to create a list of strategies for faculty members to follow. To that end, a list of 50 actions was compiled, and a committee was created for the design and implementation of an Information Literacy Development category.

Another of the undertaken actions was the development and implementation of a six-credit course, called *Information Management*, mandatory for all first-semester students. This course was jointly developed with the librarians and it has been taught by them since the second semester of 2015.

As part of the evaluation of the student's literacy, the institution, through its' Center for Academical Development and Improvement (CDMA), devised and applied a pilot instrument in 2012 [6] for 469 students, obtaining results that were later contrasted with subsequent tests. In particular, this test, conducted at the institution with the help of the librarians, was designed to follow up on these evaluations in subsequent years. There was also the application of two tests that looked for evidence of the students' degree of information literacy skills at a given moment during their period at CETYS. One of these tests was the *SAILS* test, applied in 2013 to students who had a certain degree of English language knowledge, from a sample of 300 students from different semesters. The second test, applied in 2015, used the *iSkills* assessment system, and also measured student information literacy. It was applied to 554 students with some degree of knowledge of the English language. The results of both tests will be discussed later [6].

Finally, within the taken actions, the elaboration and publication of a writing and style manual stand out. Similarly, seven articles have been published derived from the research, diagnosis, and implementation processes that have produced good results. These publications demonstrate the progress achieved in CETYS on the topic of IC. Said articles are cited in this paper and have been exhibited in fora of such standing as ECIL.

4 Objective of This Research

The goals set with the international accreditation indicate that, by 2020 [1], qualitative and quantitative progress made in each one of the determined initiatives and objectives shall be shown. This compels the institution to set strategies to assess the efficiency and efficacy of the undertaken actions. This raises the following three questions that involve the three main beneficiaries of these goals and that will be answered by the results:

1. How is the faculty of CETYS University reacting to the challenge of improving their information literacy?
2. How are CETYS University students reacting to the challenge of improving their information literacy?
3. How are librarians performing with regard to strategies to consolidate the development of information literacy?

5 Methodology

CETYS University developed a critical mass of reports and studies concerning the topic of this paper [3, 6, 7]. To benefit from these resources, this paper was developed with a qualitative research approach where institutional and public documents were used and organized to answer questions posed by researchers and scholars [5, 8]. Additionally, an ethnographical approach was used [5, 8] to contextualize the impact of the actions undertaken on the subject of libraries in the current general learning environment of the institution. Given that one of the authors of this paper is currently occupying a strategical position in the library and is part of the team in charge of the development of the corresponding EDEC, that experience was essential for information compilation and contextualization.

Information compilation was done between September 2016 and March 2017 and the analysis of the reports and documents cited in this paper has allowed the determination of some conclusions that will be reported later. Additionally, the authors of this paper have access to non-published internal reports of the institution such as results of DECIA, the local assessment instrument, the *SAILS* test, and *iSkills* hard data and recommendations found in these documents helped in the generation of the conclusions. Once information compilation was finished, it was analyzed in terms of IC, in accordance with the guidelines set by the accreditation agencies, and the current education model of CETYS University. This comparison made the determination of the degree of information literacy of library users possible.

6 Results

Regarding DECIA results, data found in this study show that faculty training is needed to make better use of the library. Additionally, they need to develop their information literacy further and use information technologies more [9] to be promoters of IC in the classroom themselves. The bibliometric analysis evidenced the obsolescence of the resources used to elaborate the analyzed publications and the basic and complementary bibliography of some academic programs. The high academic importance placed on textbooks for certain subjects is evidenced here as well [4].

The list of capabilities to be developed in teachers is completed and the assigned categories are determined, allowing for a more systematic and organized development [10]. Also, the Information Management course is already being taught with 485 passing the course to date.

The results obtained in the tests that measure the students' information literacy also showed interesting data. As in the case of the *SAILS* test, that showed [6] that the students had low information research abilities. The *iSkills* method demonstrated that some topics, such as information research and evaluation, are below average and similar results were found with the local assessment instrument [3, 6].

Both finished manuals have imposed a systematic and standardized order in the constant elaboration of written papers in class (reports, essays, research papers), and they have contributed to the fulfillment of the compromise of educating students with the competences that modern society demands [11, 12]. The same has happened with the publications and congress participations. This resulted in documented progress made in the subject [4, 6, 7, 9, 10, 13] with respondents starting to implement the good habit of documenting and reporting all research.

Regarding the results obtained from library initiatives, and based solely in unpublished internal reports of the institution, it can be seen that once WASC accreditation was achieved in 2012, facility and service renovations were carried out in the Tijuana library and a community library was built in Ensenada. The only pending subject is the renovation and expansion of the Mexicali library, that has been delayed due to natural disaster (earthquakes).

The acquisition, updating, and extension of print, digital, and remote information resources have been steadily achieved without any setbacks and constant advancement has continued. Only once, in 2015, were the 2020 goals revised downwards because they were estimated well above the current perspective. Today, they are adjusted to more realistic figures and goals.

There are two reference cases already (Mexicali and Tijuana), and the percentage of library science specialists present at the beginning of the WASC accreditation process (5%) increased, reaching 33% to date. There are currently eight library science professionals in the institution: three at the postgraduate level, and five at the undergraduate level. Thus, the librarian team at CETYS University as the most professional in the state of Baja California.

We have the permanent support of the administrators of the institution to attend training courses and the necessary economical resources to fund the professional education of four future librarians who are currently pursuing graduate library science studies.

7 What is Left to be Done? (Recommendations)

Regarding library improvements, the construction and existing facility remodeling agenda must continue because the ever-increasing demand for services and space, at times, render the existing facilities insufficient. On the other hand, communication with faculty members has to be consolidated in order to promote the use of the library and its services. Consequently, it is also necessary to make progress in the improvement of the library collection, searching for better resources. The library service catalog will be completed by the second semester of 2017, involving a wider, permanent and programmed variety of courses, workshops, and seminars. As part of this course catalog, courses on information literacy development, use of information and quotation management systems, the ethical use of information, and plagiarism prevention will be permanent offerings. It is suggested to reactivate the information literacy program for newcoming faculty members, to help them achieve an optimal performance of their teaching duties, and to be up to par with the implemented IC.

The completion and consolidation of new library positions, such as a collection system developer and a library service coordinator in Ensenada, shall be continued with the recruitment of professionals, Regarding professional training, advances are satisfactory, even though they are made in line with educational processes. Currently, graduate-level education is being supported and these processes will last for a few more years.

The use of scientific publications, such as monographs, has to be promoted against the use of obsolete textbooks. Faculty research and publications have to be encouraged. As has been previously suggested [9], teaching has to be more efficiently linked to the use of information technologies and electronic resources through the use of the library portal. Research and article publishing have to be promoted, with libraries contributing horizontally. The holistic IC model has to be consolidated [1]. The drive shall not wane with time, it must keep going.

Finally, the institution shall develop its own assessment instrument, in Spanish, that allows it to permanently assess the advancement that each graduate shows in the subject of IC. Based on results, the processes shall be adjusted, and goal corrections shall be suggested. Table 1 summarizes all this:

Table 1. Past, ongoing and pending actions and initiatives.

Actions - initiatives	Facts	Ongoing	Pending
1. *Personnel competence standardization.* **A.** *Infrastructure consolidation*	• Building construction, extension demodulation • 50 strategies	• Category creation • Creation institutional assessment tools	• Reactivation of information literacy development courses for faculty members
2. *Standardization of service capabilities* ***B.*** *Improvement of the archives*	• Information management course • Style manual • Information literacy development courses • Article elaboration	• Info. management course • Promotion of the use of style manuals • Future article publication	• Implement collection development • Foster research
3. *Service catalog* ***B.*** *Improvement of the archives*	• DECIA diagnosis • Bibliometrics • Constant archive improvement	• New construction plans • Increase electronic collections	• Add new services • Foster the use of the library among faculty members • Goal achievement
4. *Recruitment of new personnel* **C.** *Recruitment of professional human resources*	• Three new professional librarians	• A coordinator	• Consolidate staff
5. *Professional development* **D.** *Human resource professionalization and training*	• Constant training and support to graduate programs	• Graduate studies	• Finish and continue
6. *Assessment instruments*	• Applied: SAILS, iSkills, institutional	• In development: proprietary instrument	• Finish and apply

8 Conclusions

To date, halfway between the 2010 and the 2020 goals, CETYS University constantly makes efforts to comply with and uphold the objectives. Once the necessary and pertinent adjustments have been done, the work has to keep advancing. The institution is immersed in a change process and librarians are part of this process. The results obtained from the application of *SAILS*, *iSkills*, and the institutional instrument show data that reveal deficiencies that can be corrected through work and pertinent actions. These deficiencies include the low efficiency in information research evidenced by the *SAILS* test and the institutional assessment instrument where students showed acceptable information research skills, but showed deficiencies in information evaluation. These aspects showed improvement upon application of the *iSkills* system, and in comparison with the institutional instrument.

Regarding the information management course, still in existence, 485 students trained in information literacy have been enrolled in two semesters. Thus, the proposal of a strategy, and the design of a (quantitative) instrument to assess their learning, and the degree that information literacy has favorably influenced (qualitative) it, are in order. The degree of IC will be measured at the moment of graduation.

Regarding infrastructure, advancements in space demand, and adaptation of existing spaces to the needs of new technologies and services offered in the libraries have been minimal. In addition to this, there is an increasing demand for space, due to an increase in the student population mainly at the senior secondary and undergraduate levels that has caused the oversaturation of the existing spaces and insufficiency in some moments of the day.

The institutional instrument for assessment of information literacy, and thus the success of IC in the institution, has to be reevaluated and restructured. It will be elaborated in Spanish, in order to avoid the uncertainty that arises from not knowing whether results obtained with the *SAILS* test and the *iSkills* method are partly due to imperfect knowledge of the English language or if they truly show a lack of information literacy [6].

The role of the library and the professional librarian is essential throughout this process of IC achievement. Consequently, to achieve the goals for 2020, and implement them, librarians have to remain motivated as do the academic and student communities so that they demand better services and the support for their professionalization and training can continue.

References

1. CETYS University: Development Plan 2020. IENAC, Mexicali, Mexico (2011)
2. Menou, M.: Cultura, Informação e Educação de Profissionais de Informação nos Países em Desenvolvimento. Ciência da Informação **25**(3) (1996)
3. Lau, J.: Information Culture – EDEC: 2012–2016 Report. Internal report, CETYS University (2017)

4. Lau, J., Gárate, A., Osuna, C.: Walking from concepts to facts: a holistic information literacy approach experience at the university level. In: Kurbanoğlu, S., Grassian, E., Mizrachi, D., Catts, R., Špiranec, S. (eds.) ECIL 2013. CCIS, vol. 397, pp. 302–308. Springer, Cham (2013). https://doi.org/10.1007/978-3-319-03919-0_39
5. Creswell, J.W.: Research Design: Qualitative, Quantitative, and Mixed Methods Approaches. Sage, Thousand Oakes (2014)
6. Lau, J., Machin-Mastromatteo, J.D., Gárate, A., Tagliapietra-Ovies, A.C.: Assessing Spanish-speaking university students' info-competencies with iSkills, SAILS, and an In-House instrument: challenges and benefits. In: Kurbanoğlu, S., Boustany, J., Špiranec, S., Grassian, E., Mizrachi, D., Roy, L., Çakmak, T. (eds.) ECIL 2016. CCIS, vol. 676, pp. 327–336. Springer, Cham (2016). https://doi.org/10.1007/978-3-319-52162-6_32
7. Machin-Mastromatteo, J.D., Beltrán, O., Lau, J.: Piloting a holistic information culture program: the experience of CETYS Universidad system of libraries. In: Kurbanoğlu, S., Špiranec, S., Grassian, E., Mizrachi, D., Catts, R. (eds.) ECIL 2014. CCIS, vol. 492, pp. 350–360. Springer, Cham (2014). https://doi.org/10.1007/978-3-319-14136-7_37
8. Brown, A.: The place of ethnographic methods in information systems research. Int. J. Mult. Res. Approaches **8**(2), 166–178 (2014)
9. Machin-Mastromatteo, J.D., Virkus, S.: Doing online relearning through information skills (DORIS): a mutual shaping perspective for information literacy research and practice. In: Kurbanoğlu, S., Grassian, E., Mizrachi, D., Catts, R., Špiranec, S. (eds.) ECIL 2013. CCIS, vol. 397, pp. 380–385. Springer, Cham (2013). https://doi.org/10.1007/978-3-319-03919-0_50
10. Lau, J., Bonilla, J.L., Gárate, A.: Diving into deep water: development of an information literacy rubric for undergraduate course syllabi. In: Kurbanoğlu, S., Špiranec, S., Grassian, E., Mizrachi, D., Catts, R. (eds.) ECIL 2014. CCIS, vol. 492, pp. 570–579. Springer, Cham (2014). https://doi.org/10.1007/978-3-319-14136-7_60
11. Bonilla, J.L., Montes, M.E.: Guide to Write Academic Papers. CETYS University, Tijuana (2012)
12. Bonilla, J.L., Montes, M.E.: Manual for Submission of Written Works. CETYS University, Tijuana (2013)
13. Machin-Mastromatteo, J.D.: Two years of information culture development for supporting higher education: initiatives, teacher's perceptions and future actions. In: Kurbanoğlu, S., Boustany, J., Špiranec, S., Grassian, E., Mizrachi, D., Roy, L. (eds.) ECIL 2015. CCIS, vol. 552, pp. 517–526. Springer, Cham (2015). https://doi.org/10.1007/978-3-319-28197-1_52

Theoretical Framework

Exploring Information Literacy Through the Lens of Activity Theory

Hazel Hall, Peter Cruickshank(✉), and Bruce Ryan

Centre for Social Informatics, Edinburgh Napier University, Edinburgh, Scotland
{h.hall,p.cruickshank,b.ryan}@napier.ac.uk

Abstract. Activity Theory (AT) is presented as a framework for explaining Information Literacy (IL) as a technologically mediated social practice. This is achieved in the context of a study conducted in 2016 on the information gathering and sharing activities of Scottish community-level elected representatives. This work demonstrates the value of AT as (i) a tool for IL research that seeks to present information practices in their social contexts, and (ii) as a means of highlighting underlying issues within the social environment under review through the identification of contradictions within the activity system.

Keywords: Activity Theory · Information Literacy · Hyperlocal democracy Libraries · Lifelong learning

1 Introduction and Background

The theme of this paper is Activity Theory (AT) as a framework for exploring Information Literacy (IL) as a technologically mediated social practice. The value of AT is discussed with reference to a research project entitled Information Literacy for Democratic Engagement (IL-DEM). IL-DEM was funded by the Information Literacy Group of the Chartered Institute of Library and Information Professionals in 2016 to investigate the ways in which community-level elected representatives (community councillors) in Scotland undertake two related information activities: (i) seeking and sharing the opinions of the citizens that they represent with higher tiers of government, and (ii) finding and sharing information from higher tiers of government with the citizens that they represent.

The main finding of the analysis presented below is that AT is an appropriate tool for IL research of this nature. Its main strengths are found in the processes of preparing data collection tools and the extraction of 'meaning' from interview data. In addition, AT is especially powerful at identifying contradictions between the activities under scrutiny in research projects. In this case, since IL was viewed through the lens of AT, barriers to information sharing, and the stimulation of change in information practice, came to the fore as strong themes in the findings of the empirical work.

1.1 Activity Theory

AT is a framework that relates human activities to their social contexts. It provides a language for making sense of complex, real-world activities in cultural and historical

S. Kurbanoğlu et al. (Eds.): ECIL 2017, CCIS 810, pp. 803–812, 2018.
https://doi.org/10.1007/978-3-319-74334-9_81

contexts. As such, AT is not a predictive theory, but rather a tool that can be deployed with empirical data to develop understanding of the activities of actors [1].

AT developed from the work of Soviet psychologists such as Vygotsky [2], Mironenko [3]. They wished to understand human activities as systemic and socially-situated phenomena. A general account of AT's early history can be found in the work of Mironenko [3]. In Library and Information Science (LIS) research the application of AT in has been discussed more fully by Wilson [4].

One of the most frequently cited models of AT, and the one deployed in the study reported here, is that advocated by Engeström [5–7]. This version brings technology and context together into a unit of analysis called an 'activity system'. In Engeström's model *subjects* (people) use *tools* (which may be physical, e.g. technology, or cognitive, e.g. skills [7]) to attempt to achieve *objects* (or objectives). *Subjects*' activities spring from one or more *motivations*, that is, the reasons for attempting to achieve the objective(s) or goal(s) of the activity. Activities are constrained by social and/or workplace contexts [1, 4]. Contexts comprise *tools*, the *community* (in AT terms, this may be may be the *subject*'s immediate work group or team, or the wider organisational community, or society at large [4], that is, stakeholders in activities), the *rules and norms* of the community [8], and the *division of labour* around the activities [7]. The *outcome*(s) are distinct from the *object*(s) because they are the consequences of activity, and include unexpected results. It is also important to note that *objects* can change over time. For this reason Wilson introduced the concept of process within activity systems into his work on AT [4].

Issues within an activity system are explained through tensions and *contradictions*. These may be found: (i) within elements (e.g. *tools*, *subjects*); (ii) between elements (e.g. between a *subject* and a *rule*); (iii) between a central activity at one point in time and a central activity later on; and (iv) between activities [5]. AT also suggests that collaborative activities can be *co-ordinated* (participants work independently towards goals and using methods which they have not set), *co-operative* (participants set the common goals), or *co-constructive* (participants set the goals and methods) [9].

The language of activities, AT constructs, and contradictions hence provides a ready-built analytical framework for understanding underlying issues around any social activity. As such, AT has been used in studies of a number of workplace contexts, for example, use of mobile data by police [10], and in a variety of subject domains including LIS in general (as noted above), [7]. There are also examples of its prior use in IL research, [11]. However, to date, AT has not been deployed in research that considers IL in the context of 'hyperlocal' democracy – democracy 'pertaining to a town, village, single postcode or other small, geographically defined community' [12]. Hyperlocal is interesting in this IL context because it implies that physical/face-to-face information interactions and channel-shifting are inherent, as will be seen below.

1.2 Community Councils

Prior to discussing the means by which IL can be explored through the lens of AT, it is worth providing some background information on the local context of the research study that served as the test site here.

Scotland's local government was subject to major reorganisation in 1975 [13]. Community councils were established as part of this process. Their creation was meant to address fears that citizens might feel remote from the democratic process due to the reduction in the number of local authorities in the new local government structure.

The regulation and support of community councils is currently delegated to Scotland's 32 local authorities. Local authorities are responsible for the 'definitions' of their community councils' areas and numbers of members, for running community council elections, and for providing much of their (somewhat meagre) funding. The 'definitions' are found in documents known as 'Schemes'. Most Schemes also state how community councils are run, and they provide examples of activities that they may undertake with reference to relevant legislation. Membership of any community council comprises voting members (elected and co-opted), and non-voting, ex-officio members (local authority councillors, members of the Scottish Parliament, and members of the UK Parliament whose wards and constituencies overlap the community council's area).

Unlike the vast majority of Europe's democratic systems, community councils are *not* bodies of government [13, 14]. Although they are conceived in the legislation as representative bodies for particular geographic localities, they have no duties to deliver services, nor can they raise taxes. Each community council is set up to 'ascertain, co-ordinate and express to the local authorities for its area, and to public authorities, the views of the community which it represents, in relation to matters for which those authorities are responsible, and to take such action in the interests of that community as appears to it to be expedient and practicable' [15], so their role is explicitly centred on information. They also have a limited role in planning: they may comment on planning applications, such as from the change of use of a garage to an office in a conservation area, to large housing or industrial developments.

The community council system in Scotland faces a number of challenges. The main problem is that it relies almost entirely on the voluntary efforts of community councillors, and they have no funding for the hire of additional professional assistance [16]. As a result, many community councils struggle to fill their vacancies. Indeed in some parts of the country community councils do not exist at all [13, 17–20]. The demographic profile of the volunteer community councillor population is also an issue, particularly in terms of information literacy. Typically community councillors are older citizens who have not benefited from any formal information skills training over the course of their lifetime, whether at school or in the workplace. This means that few have developed adequate skills to deal with the tasks of gathering, processing and presenting information on their communities' views. This is reflected in the low numbers of community councils known to use the Internet to engage with, and/or obtain information from, their citizens [18–20].

Whereas the information practices in local government have previously been the subject of academic research [e.g. 21, 22], this study is significant as the first to have considered the information literacy of *volunteers* active in *hyperlocal* government.

1.3 The IL-DEM Project: Motivation and Methods

The main purpose of IL-DEM was to understand reasons for, and seek solutions to, some of the manifest problems outlined above. Community councils' low use of the Internet was one stimulus. It was also deemed important to examine other channels for information sharing such as face-to-face, letters, and telephone. This is because of the hyperlocal nature of the work of community councils. Contact can shift rapidly from one channel to another when information is shared within community councils. For example, a conversation might begin at a formal meeting or in a chance encounter, then may be continued via social media, and again at the next community council meeting.

Data were collected for IL-DEM through hour-long semi-structured interviews with community councillors (n = 19) between 21 November and 9 December 2016. The councillors were based in a various localities across Scotland. These ranged from areas with low to high deprivation, and remote rural to highly urban environments. The interviewees were asked to specify their age by decade. The breakdown was one interviewee in his/her 30s, three in their 40s, nine in their 50s, four in their 60s, and two in their 70s. The interviewees served on community councils in eight local authority areas: Aberdeen, Argyll and Bute, Edinburgh, Fife, Glasgow, Perth and Kinross, Renfrewshire, and Shetland.

The interviewees responded to a call for participation in the project that was posted to an online discussion board for community councillors, and the national community council web site. Community council liaison officers, i.e. the local authority staff charged with supporting community councils, were also made aware of the project by email and through discussion board postings.

The interview questions were generated with reference to project research questions and dominant themes from a review of the literature. As well as prompting the interviewees to speak about information literacy in general, as well as their own information practices, the questions were designed to address other related topics such as lifelong learning, social capital and citizenship. The interview schedule was piloted with staff from the Improvement Service (the national improvement service for local government in Scotland) prior to implementation.

The AT constructs described in [1] and elements of the SCONUL 7-pillar model of information literacy were used both (i) to inform the development of the interview schedule, and (ii) to manually code the data following transcription of the interviews. The latter was achieved by listing the research questions and the AT constructs in the top row of a spreadsheet, with the interview questions in the left-hand column. Then relevant data from each interview were copied into the spreadsheet cells according to (i) interview question and (ii) research question or construct. Text-concatenation allowed for the assembly of all data thematically for analysis.

It should be emphasised that the focus of the discussion below is not the findings of IL-DEM *per se*, nor their articulation with the SCONUL pillars, but the deployment of AT in a research project concerned with IL. This is achieved with reference to two information activities undertaken by the community councillors interviewed: (i) their sharing information about citizens' opinions to higher authorities; and (ii) their sharing of information from higher authorities to citizens.

The main findings of the empirical work completed for IL-DEM on the practices of community representatives in exploiting information channels for citizen engagement, and their relationship with the SCONUL pillars, are found in the IL-DEM project report, and a paper presented at *Information: interactions and impact (i3)* 2017 [23, 24]. These relate that, despite the high level of education and self-efficacy of community councillors, their democratic activities are not fully underpinned by information practices in line with the SCONUL 7 pillars.

2 Alignment of Data from the IL-DEM Project to AT Constructs

Since the purpose of this paper is to explore the value of AT in IL research, the constructs of AT introduced above are reframed below with reference to data gathered for a project concerned with IL (IL-DEM). Some examples are also given of project findings that emerged from this process of deliberately considering the IL-DEM data through the lens of AT and its constructs. It should be noted, however, that these examples are for illustration only: the full project findings are found in other outputs that report the empirical study from the perspective of a contribution to the body of extant work in IL [23, 24].

2.1 Subjects

In some cases, the application of AT constructs to IL can be challenging. For example, an initial problem may be the definition of *subjects* following practice in AT. The particular challenge faced in the IL-DEM project was whether to treat individual community councillors as the *subjects* (on the basis that they are the people who are involved in the activity), or for this label to be assigned to the community councils as 'inanimate' groups of actors. Such a decision is important in studies of information behaviour and use, given that there may be a need for findings to be presented at the level of the individual, the group, or from both perspectives.

In partial resolution of this question, a decision was taken to treat individuals as 'interviewees', and community councils as collective *subjects*, in this work. This follows practice in other studies that have used AT in library and information science research. For example, in their study Detlor, Hupfer and Smith class libraries as *subjects*, having collected their data by interview with individuals [7].

2.2 Motivations

At the outset it was anticipated that community councillors would find it easy to report the reasons why they were motivated to undertake information activities in response to the requirements of the legislation for community councils, and the content of local authority Schemes. This proved to be the case: the majority of interviewees (14) provided data on their reasons for engaging in information activities that fitted with the *motivation* construct of AT. In addition, the interviewees explained the more general *motivations* to volunteer as a hyperlocal representative.

2.3 Objects and Outcomes

Interview questions about the information roles of community councils, and the extent to which they are successful in meeting the requirements of these, allowed for the activity system under review to be considered with reference to the AT constructs of *objects* (the goals that the *subjects* wish to achieve through their activities) and *outcomes* (the actual results of activities).

In line with the legislation, it was anticipated that the main *object* of community councillors' information activities would be to gather, process and convey information about their citizens' opinions. The analysis of the interview data using AT constructs confirmed this. For example, 15 interviewees recognised the importance of information sharing *objects*: one said 'We don't transact actions, we don't have any financial power. Our currency is information.'

The consideration of *outcomes* surfaced evidence of poor information practices within community councils. For example, two interviewees from the same community council admitted that its 'mailing list [includes] 60-odd people, which is nothing given that that there are 25,000 people in the area'. Another interviewee joined her community council specifically to make it share information with its community but, at the time of interview, she was considering resignation due to a lack of support from her colleagues.

2.4 Tools

In AT, *tools* are the physical or mental devices used by *subjects* in their activities. Interviewees were therefore asked about information sources and channels used to (i) gather information about local issues, and (ii) to share information with their citizens. This allowed for the identification of a range of *tools* including bodies (e.g. local authorities) and individuals (e.g. citizens by word of mouth) as information sources, as well as traditional media (e.g. local press) and Internet sources (e.g. Facebook). Commentary on the perceived usefulness of such *tools*, and the level of comfort that community councillors experience when using them, provided further data for interpretation when the full project findings were applied to the SCONUL model.

2.5 Rules and Norms

Taking into account the AT construct of *rules and norms*, the regulations and conventions that mediate activities and relationships within the activity system under review were identified as part of the IL-DEM project. This brought to the fore the *rules and norms* imposed on community councils (the legislation and Schemes), as well as a number devised by community councillors themselves to improve information practices within their community councils. These included, for example, processes decided at local level to minimise information overload, such as only reviewing planning matters that impinge directly on the area covered by the community council. The consideration of the AT constructs of *rules and norms* in respect of information activities amongst this group was also useful in revealing the factors that influence the ways in which information tasks are undertaken by community councils, including whether or not they are undertaken at all.

2.6 Community

Prior to entering the field, of the types of *communities* (the AT terminology for stakeholder groups) that develop around the information activities of community councillors were already known: fellow community councillors; the citizens that they represent (especially those who engage with their community councils); and functionaries such as the local authority officials and councillors who interact with community councils. These were confirmed in the data collected and analysed, with additional commentary provided on levels of engagement across the *communities*.

2.7 Division of Labour

Division of labour in AT refers to the manner(s) in which work is allocated among various actors in the activity [7]. For this reason interviewees were asked about task-allocation for information-related activities within their community councils. The data gathered provided detail on a range of approaches to task allocation e.g. according to individual skills, or designated community council roles, such as online communication. Thus AT was found to be useful in establishing an overview of the means by which information-related tasks are allocated in community councils.

A challenge of considering the IL-DEM data with reference to the construct of *division of labour*, however, was to take into account the extent to which it is mediated by *rules and norms*. In short, it proved difficult to find clear-cut distinctions between these two constructs.

3 Discussion and Conclusions: The Value of Deploying Activity Theory in the IL-DEM Project

Following the analysis of the full data set, with reference to AT constructs as described above, it was possible to portray the information activities and relationships of the *subjects* in the IL-DEM project in an activity diagram. This is shown below in Fig. 1.

The use of AT in this project was valuable first because it allowed for the completion of the data collection and analysis processes in a systematic way. When preparing the main tool of data collection, for example, reference to the main AT constructs (as outlined above) ensured that relevant and useful interview data were collected: the simple process of checking that each of the constructs was 'covered' in the interview schedule ensured that it was comprehensive enough to extract the data required to answer the IL-DEM project research questions from the output of the interviews. Equally, AT furnished a ready-made framework for coding the project data to then generate an analysis of activities reported by the interviewees in the social context under review. In addition, having prepared the data in this way, it was possible to see alignments between the data categorised under the AT constructs and the

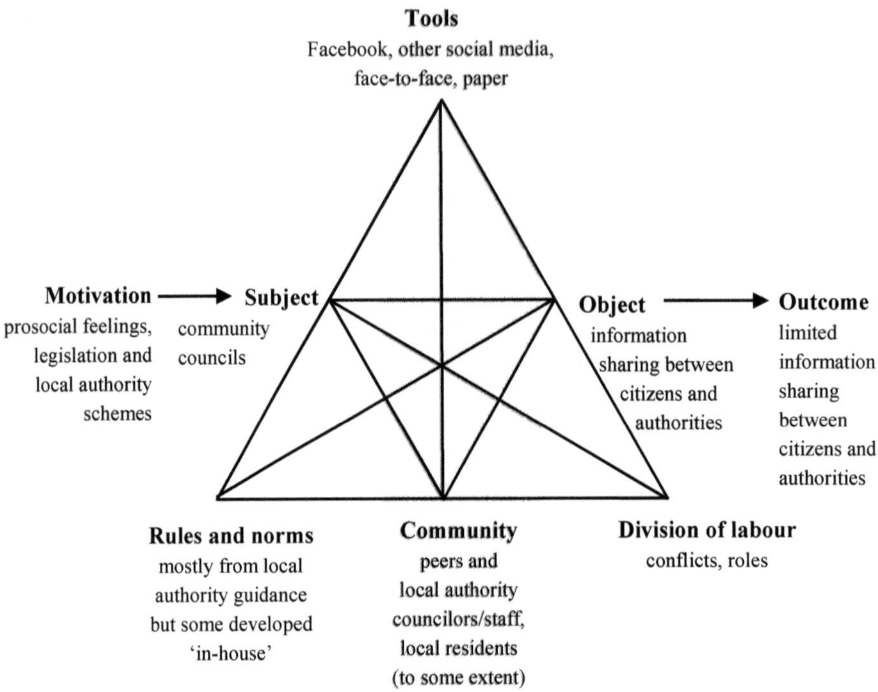

Fig. 1. Activity system for community councillor information activities

SCONUL IL pillars. For example it was found that data relevant to both *tools* and *community* in AT fit with the *gather* and *present* pillars.

The second main benefit of deploying AT in this work was that it brought to the fore a number of important findings on the level of information literacy amongst community councillors in Scotland, and the factors that influence this – it was key to answering the core research questions of the IL-DEM project. Of particular interest here are the contradictions identified from the data set, not least because these can serve as the foundations of the future practical benefits of completing this work, by 'exposing opportunities for change' [7]. For example contradictions uncovered in the data set pointed to the status of community councillors as part-time volunteers who do not have time to undertake all possible information sharing activities. This helps explain community councils' low use of the Internet to engage with citizens.

A further benefit of using AT in this work was that it led to the generation of the project's three main recommendations: (i) community councillors should lobby for suitable training, and take part in an audit of their information skills and practices, with leadership and support from the Improvement Service; (ii) community council liaison officers should do more to emphasise the value of information skills in supporting community councils' statutory role of representing citizen opinions; and (iii) public library services should extend their roles to support community councils.

The deployment of AT in a project such as this, however, is not without its challenges. Some decisions on constructs are difficult to make, as illustrated above with reference to the question of *subjects* in the IL-DEM project. Similarly, here the distinctions between the constructs of the *rules and norms* and *division of labour* were not always clear. The definition of the activity system itself can also raise questions. In the case of Scottish community councils and information sharing for example, it could be argued that there are actually two activity systems in operation: one for information that is disseminated in one direction, and a second for the other.

Despite these challenges, this work has shown that AT is valuable to research design in projects concerned with group information practices. In addition, AT can contribute to the generation of findings that contribute to the development of existing models (in this case the SCONUL 7 pillars). Since activity diagrams provide a snapshot of the system under review at a certain time, a further benefit of deploying AT is in longitudinal studies where the impact of earlier interventions can be observed. This would be particularly interesting in the case of the Scottish community councils, should the recommendations summarised in the project report be implemented [23, 24].

Acknowledgements. The authors are grateful to CILIP's Information Literacy Group for project funding, and to the community councillors who took part in the research.

References

1. Wilson, T.: A re-examination of information seeking behaviour in the context of activity theory. Inf. Res. **11** (2006)
2. Vygotsky, L.S.: Mind and Society. Harvard University Press, Cambridge (1978)
3. Mironenko, I.A.: Concerning interpretations of activity theory. Integr. Psychol. Behav. Sci. **47**, 376–393 (2013)
4. Wilson, T.: Activity theory and information seeking. Annu. Rev. Inf. Sci. Technol. **42**, 119–161 (2008)
5. Engeström, Y.: Learning by Expanding: An Activity-Theoretical Approach to Developmental Research. Orienta-Konsultit, Helsinki (1987)
6. Allen, D., Karanasios, S., Slavova, M.: Working with activity theory: context, technology, and information behavior. J. Am. Soc. Inf. Sci. Technol. **62**, 776–788 (2011)
7. Detlor, B., Hupfer, M.E., Smith, D.H.: Digital storytelling and memory institutions: a case study using activity theory. In: ASIST 2016 (2016)
8. Allen, D., Karanasios, S., Norman, A.: Information sharing and interoperability: the case of major incident management. Eur. J. Inf. Syst. **23**, 418–432 (2014)
9. Bardram, J.E.: Collaboration, Coordination and Computer Support: An Activity Theoretical Approach to the Design of Computer Supported Cooperative Work. Aarhus University, Aarhus (1998)
10. Karanasios, S., Vardaxoglou, G., Allen, D.: Innovation in UK law enforcement: the emergence of mobile data. In: 15th Americas Conference on Information Systems (AMCIS 2009), pp 1–10 (2009)
11. Abdallah, N.B.: Activity theory as a framework for understanding information literacy. In: Kurbanoğlu, S., Grassian, E., Mizrachi, D., Catts, R., Špiranec, S. (eds.) ECIL 2013. CCIS, vol. 397, pp. 93–99. Springer, Cham (2013). https://doi.org/10.1007/978-3-319-03919-0_11
12. Radcliffe, D.: Here and Now: UK Hyperlocal Media Today (2012). http://www.nesta.org.uk/publications/here-and-now-uk-hyperlocal-media-today

13. Goodlad, R., Flint, J., Kearns, A., Keoghan, M., Paddison, R., Raco, M.: The Role and Effectiveness of Community Councils with Regard to Community Consultation. Scottish Office Central Research Unit, Edinburgh (1999)
14. Glasgow City Council: The Scheme for the Establishment of Community Councils (2013)
15. UK Government: Local Government (Scotland) Act 1973 (1973)
16. Bort, E., Mcalpine, R., Morgan, G.: The Silent Crisis: Failure and Revival in Local Democracy in Scotland. Jimmy Reid Foundation, Glasgow (2012)
17. McIntosh, N., Alexander, A., Cubie, A., Leicester, G., Mackay, E., Millar, M., Smith, M., Watt, M.: The Report of the Commission on Local Government and the Scottish Parliament. Scottish Office, Edinburgh (1999)
18. Ryan, B.M., Cruickshank, P.: Community Councils Online. Edinburgh Napier University, Edinburgh (2012)
19. Ryan, B.M., Cruickshank, P.: Community Councils Online. Edinburgh Napier University, Edinburgh (2014)
20. Cruickshank, P., Ryan, B.M., Smith, C.F.: Disconnected democracy? a survey of Scottish community councils' online presences. Scott. Aff. **23**(4), 486–507 (2014)
21. Wilson, T.D., Streatfield, D.R., Mullings, C.: Information needs in local authority social services departments: a second report on Project INISS. J. Doc. **35**(2), 120–136 (1979)
22. Wilson, T.D., Streatfield, D.R.: You can observe a lot: A study of information use in local authority social services departments conducted by Project INISS, Postgraduate School of Librarianship and Information Science, University of Sheffield, Sheffield, (occasional publication no. 12) (1980). http://informationr.net/tdw/publ/INISS/
23. Hall, H., Cruickshank, P., Ryan, B.M.: Information Literacy for Democratic Engagement. Edinburgh Napier University, Edinburgh (2017). https://communityknectdotnet.files.wordpress.com/2017/02/il-dem-stakeholder-report-january-2017.pdf
24. Cruickshank, P., Hall, H., Ryan, B.M.: Practices of Community Representatives in Exploiting Information Channels for Citizen Engagement. Paper presented at information: interactions and impact 2017, Aberdeen, 27–30 June 2017 (2017). http://www.napier.ac.uk/research-and-innovation/research-search/outputs/practices-of-community-representatives-in-exploiting-information-channels-for-citizen

Alternatives to Being Information Literate

Isto Huvila(✉)

Department of ALM, Uppsala University, Uppsala, Sweden
isto.huvila@abm.uu.se

Abstract. In contrast to the relative abundance of conceptualisations of "information literacy", the earlier research has placed considerably less attention on its alternatives. The findings show that there are shades of being less and non-literate beyond a mere lack of necessary skills or engagement in inappropriate practices. Information illiteracy can be experienced as a problem but it can also represent a conscious choice for delimiting and organising information practices. From a theoretical and practical perspective, this study suggests that both information literacies and information illiteracies should be taken into account in information literacy research and education, and when developing and deploying information systems and services to compensate for the lack of literacies.

Keywords: Information literacy · Information illiteracy · Information anxiety Satisficing

1 Introduction

There are several competing views of what information literacy is. The approaches range from treating information literacy as one skill, or a set of skills or competences to conceptualising it as a socially enacted practice and as a capability enacted through situationally and contextually conditioned practices [1–4]. Even if there are specific areas and aspects of information literacy that are considered under researched [5, 6], there is a serious dearth of systematic work on the lack of information literacy, or in broader terms, alternatives to being information literate.

The aim of this article is to focus on that particular gap and to extend the understanding of the alternatives to being information literate by explicating nuances and dimensions of 'information illiteracy' beyond simple binaries. Unlike the earlier literature seems to suggest both explicitly and implicitly, it is suggested that there are many more shades of being less and non-literate than a mere lack of necessary skills or engagement in inappropriate practices.

2 Literature Review

Information literacy has been conceptualised in the literature from several competing metatheoretical perspectives [4, 7]. In contrast to the earlier conceptualisation of information literacy as a generic acontextual skill, the more recent research has tended

S. Kurbanoğlu et al. (Eds.): ECIL 2017, CCIS 810, pp. 813–821, 2018.
https://doi.org/10.1007/978-3-319-74334-9_82

to emphasise it as a social and situated (or sociotechnical, [3]) phenomenon rather than an individual trait, and stressed the plurality of information literacies and information literacy practices [8]. Limberg, Sundin and Talja, who define information literacy as "purposeful information practices in a society" [7, p. 95], note that within the newer research in the area, it is possible to identify at least three different meta-theoretical approaches, which all in a broad sense, belong to the "alternative approaches" [8] that contest the idea of information literacy as one generic skill. However, instead of having led to paradigmatic changes in the field, it seems that the new perspectives have increased the diffusion of views and created fault lines between different professional and scholarly schools in the information literacy community [4, 7]. Whereas the competence-oriented perspectives tend to be based on the assumption that information literacy can be graded (e.g., Wallis [9]) and it is possible to create instruments for measuring the level of information literacy [10, 11], the practice-based approaches have focused on explicating the contextual and situational fit, appropriateness and purposefulness of information literacy practices [7, 8].

In contrast to the abundance of literature and perspectives as to what information literacy is, there has been significantly less attention to the alternatives of being information literate, or to counter-paraphrase Lloyd [12], practices within which information literacies are not enacted. This is conspicuous, especially because the idea of the lack or inadequacy of information literacy in general, or particular information literacies, permeates the literature independent of its underlying metatheoretical assumptions. In some cases, authors have referred to different levels of information literacy ranging, for instance, from low to high (e.g., Wallis [9]) and in quantitative levels, it is not uncommon to use scales to measure levels of information literacy [13]. Socioculturally and, for instance, phenomenographically oriented research use different vocabulary and are less inclined to measure the 'level' of information literacy but also these types of studies embrace the idea of grading in their pursuit of improving information literacies or to make them more purposeful [7, 14].

The literature contains also somewhat sporadic references to information illiteracy. It is typically portrayed in the context of skills-based approaches as a state of lacking information literacy (skill or skills) [15–18]. Both Green [15] and Lin [16] criticise the dichotomy literacy/illiteracy. Lin [16] notes that the term information literacy itself is problematic in that it may lead to assuming information illiteracy in people. A common trait of the conceptions of information illiteracy is that they fall within the much-criticised derogatory discourse of the information poverty of 'needy users' [19–21]. In contrast to the assumptions embedded in this discourse, unorthodox information practices [22], or as Green [15] emphasises, non-participation in information literacy education, does not (automatically) make anyone an incapable information illiterate.

3 Methods and Materials

The empirical material consists of sixteen qualitative interviews of archaeology professionals from a Nordic country with special interest in issues pertaining to the archiving and preservation of archaeology. The groups of informants represent a convenience sample. Following the convention of information literacy research in a workplace context where the term is not used by the informants themselves, the interviews and analysis of transcribed interview records focused on the analysis of the "application of information literacy" [23], and particularly, in the context of this study, on the application of information illiteracies. All interviews were conducted by the author, taped and transcribed by a professional transcriber. The interviews lasted, on average, 60 min. The interviews focused on the interviewees' professional work, and their views on the current state and future prospects of archaeological information management. For reporting purposes, the interviewees were assigned false names (Table 1). The analysis of the interview transcripts was based on close reading [24] of the interview transcripts. A detailed description of the empirical approach and its limitations has been presented in two earlier texts [25, 26].

Table 1. Interviewees

Interviewee	Description
Mohamed	Finds information administrator at a national institution (responsible for the management of archaeological finds)
Travis	Administrative director of a contract financed archaeological department at a regional museum
Eunice	Archivist, information manager at a national institution
Faunia	Administrative director of a contract financed archaeological department at a regional museum
Liesel	Finds administrator at a national institution
Bentley	Coordinator at a private archaeology consultancy
Precious	Researcher in archaeology at a Swedish university
Zero	Field archaeologist at a private archaeology consultancy
Hamish	Archivist at a national institution
Delia	Coordinator at a contract archaeology department at a regional museum
Jeremiah	Archivist at a national institution
Hanna	Data archivist working at a data archive
Sam	Administrator at a county administrative board
Nombeko	Researcher in archaeology at a Swedish university
Park	Information manager at a national institution
Baines	Researcher in archaeology at a Swedish university, data archivist working at a data archive

4 Analysis

An analysis of the interview record exposed examples of practices or competences that can be classified as different alternatives to being information literate. The breakdown is not suggested to be exhaustive of all possible practices, but rather a first step towards developing a broader understanding of how to conceptualise and explicate the phenomenon of not being information literate, and its implications for the information literacy field.

4.1 Barrier to Purposeful Information Practices

The analysed interview record contained several references to classical 'information illiteracy' cited in the literature, a lack of abilities and capabilities to engage in purposeful information practices in a particular situation. The interviewees made remarks both of their own lack of information literacy and that of others, and how their and others' information literacy has positive and negative implications on the information work of the both parties Interviewee Nombeko discussed in detail the inadequacy of the information literacy practices of her colleagues (i.e., others) by noting that archaeological documentation, which is produced in field as a part of excavations and surveys is not adequately standardised to be easily reused at a later stage by researchers such as herself, and, for instance, by landowners with an interest in knowing the limits of archaeological sites on their property. In contrast, for instance, Bentley expressed his frustration that he, himself, did not know how to manage and what to do with the large number of digital photographs taken at an excavation, how many of them should be archived and included in the excavation report, and what should be done with the "remaining 90%, what do we do with them for example?". Instead of being an example of an individual inability of the particular interviewee, comments made by others, including Mohamed, Travis, and Hanna, it was apparent that the practices of archaeological information management in the studied country as a whole were not information literate enough to deal with digital photographs. Different interviewees described various types of *ad hoc* strategies that themselves could be described as innovative information literacies but that in the end, especially in the societal context (cf. [7]), clearly lacked purposefulness.

4.2 Opportunity to Avoid Information Interactions

Simultaneously to causing anxiety, the lack of abilities and capabilities provided interviewees opportunities to legitimise their avoidance of engaging in specific information interactions and in a broader sense, in particular information practices. Bentley describes that the inability to produce perfect documentation of archaeological sites gives archaeologists a relative freedom to do as they feel best: "the priority is that something gets done". Another example, that recurred in several interviews (e.g. Mohamed, Eunice, Faunia, Liesel, Sam), were comments that 'we' cannot undertake a particular (information) task like appraising or deaccessioning a particular document or a set of data, because 'we' were not there when the document was created or data was collected, and implicitly, in practice, because we lack (or can be argued to lack) an adequate competence to do so. Eunice gave a more explicit example of this when she described how, according to her, archivists have a tendency to come and "point to the laws and regulations saying that we have to do it like this, because it is the directive", ending the discussion of different alternative approaches to managing information and archival records.

4.3 Opportunity for Alternative Information (Literacy) Practices

In contrast to being a barrier, the analysed data also contains examples of how the lack of particular information literacy could become an opportunity to engage in alternative information practices. Liesel describes that the difficulty in finding and obtaining documents from the archive located at her own institution means that she often searches for and retrieves them online whenever they can be found on the webpages of the organisations that originally produced them. On a more general level, Zero noted that the lack of routines opens up possibilities to engage in information practices that are relevant for the situation.

Travis described a relatively extreme situation with close to a complete dearth of information literacy with a specific type of information. According to him, his organisation was more or less lacking any functional practices to work with the management of any type of digital information. Instead of seeing this a mere problem, he commented that in the end, it gives him close to complete freedom to start to develop purposeful information practices (i.e., information literacy) as he and his organisation considers best without the need to take into account legacy practices and literacies that could hinder the process.

5 Discussion

5.1 Beyond the Literacy/Illiteracy Dichotomy

The analysis revealed several noteworthy aspects of the lack of information literacy that warrant further consideration. Firstly, it is apparent that like information literacy, the lack or inappropriateness of information literacy is not a binary phenomenon. There are degrees and nuances of how purposeful certain information practices are in a specific situation. Similarly, there is individual variation in whether or how something is experienced as sub-optimal and how it affects different individuals and groups that are engaged in particular information literacy practices. For some, ambiguous information practices may appear as a form of information illiteracy whereas others might see the flexibility as a clever strategy. Therefore, also the outcomes of the alternatives of being information literate can be either positive or negative. Deficient information literacy can hinder purposeful information practices like reusing archaeological documentation but it can also help field archaeologists to produce documentation that is particularly relevant to the situation when the documentation is being created. In the analysis, it became especially apparent that information illiteracy in producing, organising and managing information is tightly intertwined with the problems of using information and vice versa. This observation highlights the significance of extending the inquiry of information (il)literacies enacted in the situation of seeking and using a particular piece of information to those playing out in the situation when it was created, organised and managed not only as important skills as Huvila [6] suggests, but also as two intimately related sides of the same constellation of practices.

The paradox of the contextual and situated nature of the lack of 'adequate' information literacy is similar to that of information literacy itself. However, an explicit consideration of the perplexity of their being and not-being as a double paradox can be helpful in bringing clarity both to the problematic dichotomisation of information literacy and illiteracy, and the similarly problematic assumptions of the complete situatedness and contextuality of all information literacy practices that effectively negate the possibilities for any generalisations even on an analytical level.

Instead of considering information literacy alone, it could be useful to extend the perspective to the deficiencies of information literacies as well. The lack of particular information literacies and the presence of alternative information (il)literacies can be conceptualised as comparable scales that are similarly bound to situation and context as information literacies. It is further conceivable that in addition to multiple information literacies, individuals also have several information illiteracies intertwined with their information literacies. Elaborating the perspective makes it possible to extend analysis to understand the implications of the combination of these practices in relation to different implicit and outspoken purposes in a situation and context. Explicit consideration of illiteracies also makes it easier to appreciate why a person can be (from an information literacy educators' perspective) simultaneously information illiterate and competent (cf. [15]). Instead of being absolutely information illiterate, an individual can be engaged in information illiteracy practices that make an educator perceive them as information illiterates, whereas in practice, they are simultaneously enacting information literacies that make them capable of pursuing purposeful information work. From this perspective, it is apparent that information illiteracy is not necessarily a negative phenomenon.

A better understanding of how information literacies and illiteracies relate to and interact with each other could be suggested as helpful in developing information literacy education, understanding of information practices and situational purposefulness, to develop information systems that better take both the competences and incompetences of their users into consideration, and instead of necessarily eliminating all information illiteracies, compensate part of them with relevant information services. This would be another legitimate strategy to help individuals in their information work, as Huvila [22] has suggested.

5.2 Literacy and Illiteracy, or Beyond

After criticising the literacy-illiteracy dichotomy and simultaneously using the two terms throughout this text, it is necessary to ask whether the terms are appropriate to use. It is possible to argue that the notions of information literacies and information literacy practices also incorporate illiteracies, even if they would not have been discussed in explicit terms, or that the absence of information literacy in information practices is an indication of information illiteracy. For instance, the sociocultural perspective [7], which posits that information literacy is enacted as a part of certain practices [27, 28], indirectly suggests that there are other practices within which information literacy is not enacted. To an extent these are, or incorporate information practices (or, as according to some researchers, all work and practices have an informational element [29, 30]), and they do not incorporate information literacy, they can be conceived to enact information illiteracy.

In the present study, references to the notion of information illiteracy and information illiteracies served a dual function. The use of an explicit term to refer to the lack or deficiency of purposeful information practices offers the possibility of explicating them in an analytical sense and contrasting practices with each other. At the same time, it opens an opportunity to discuss and nuance the earlier conceptualisations of information illiteracy. After having said that, a final question remains as to whether literacy-illiteracy is enough. A complementary notion missing from the spectrum and that makes at least some theoretical sense could be perhaps termed *information unliteracy* (ability to engage in counter-purposeful information practices). The question is, however, whether making such a further distinction is empirically useful. It could be enough to acknowledge that particular practices can be purposeful or unpurposeful in different contexts and appear as information literacies or illiteracies depending on the specific situations and purposes considered.

6 Conclusions

This study has shown that there are nuances in being information illiterate beyond a mere state of lacking. Information illiteracy can be related to avoidance of work and various strategies of evading the need to master work-related information and information work practices. Some of these practices can be negative from an individual and organisational workplace perspective, whereas some have positive implications in one or both of the contexts. The present study posits that information illiteracy can have different nuances that partly come close to alternative forms and types of information literacies and partly to strategies of coping without self mastering necessary information and information work practices. The findings suggest that the lack of information literacy in general and specific types of information literacies in particular, can be experienced as a problem, but they can also represent a conscious choice for individuals and groups to delimit and organise their information practices in order to better manage their everyday lives. From a theoretical and practical perspective, this study suggests that both information literacies and information illiteracies should be taken into account in information literacy research and education, and when developing and deploying information systems and services to compensate for the lack of literacies.

Acknowledgements. This study has been conducted under the auspices of the Archaeological information in the digital society project, funded by the Swedish Research Council Grant (VR) grant 340-2012-5751. The work is also affiliated with the The Impact of Information Literacy in the Digital Workplace (DiWIL) project at Åbo Akademi University, Finland funded by the Academy of Finland.

References

1. Stordy, P.: Taxonomy of literacies. J. Doc. **71**(3), 456–476 (2015)
2. Lloyd, A.: Framing information literacy as information practice: site ontology and practice theory. J. Doc. **66**(2), 245–258 (2010)
3. Tuominen, K., Savolainen, R., Talja, S.: Information literacy as a sociotechnical practice. Libr. Q. **75**(3), 329–345 (2005)
4. Bawden, D.: Information and digital literacies: a review of concepts. J. Doc. **57**(2), 218–259 (2001)

5. Crawford, J., Irving, C.: Information literacy in the workplace: a qualitative exploratory study. J. Librariansh. Inf. Sci. **41**(1), 29–38 (2009)
6. Huvila, I.: The complete information literacy? Unforgetting creation and organisation of information. J. Librariansh. Inf. Sci. **43**(4), 237–245 (2011)
7. Limberg, L., Sundin, O., Talja, S.: Three theoretical perspectives on information literacy. Hum. IT **11**(2), 93–130 (2012)
8. Eckerdal, J.R.: To jointly negotiate a personal decision: a qualitative study on information literacy practices in midwifery counselling about contraceptives at youth centres in Southern Sweden. Inf. Res. **16**(1) (2011)
9. Wallis, J.: Information-saturated yet ignorant: information mediation as social empowerment in the knowledge economy. Libr. Rev. **52**(8), 369–372 (2003)
10. Hernon, P., Schwartz, C.: Information literacy: time to move beyond more of the same? Libr. Inf. Sci. Res. **36**(3/4), 133–134 (2014)
11. Stewart, C.: Measuring information literacy: beyond the case study. J. Acad. Librariansh. **37** (3), 270–272 (2011)
12. Lloyd, A.: Information literacy as a socially enacted practice: sensitising themes for an emerging perspective of people-in-practice. J. Doc. **68**(6), 772–783 (2012)
13. Walsh, A.: Information literacy assessment: where do we start? J. Librariansh. Inf. Sci. **41** (1), 19–28 (2009)
14. Hicks, A., Lloyd, A.: It takes a community to build a framework: information literacy within intercultural settings. J. Inf. Sci. **42**(3), 334–343 (2016)
15. Green, R.: Information illiteracy: examining our assumptions. J. Acad. Librariansh. **36**(4), 313–319 (2010)
16. Lin, P.: Information literacy barriers: language use and social structure. Libr. Hi Tech **28**, 548–568 (2010)
17. Perelman, L.: Information illiteracy and mass market writing assessments. Coll. Compos. Commun. **60**(1), 128–141 (2008)
18. Mensching, G.E., Mensching, T.B. (eds.): Coping with Information Illiteracy: bibliographic instruction for the information age. Papers Presented at the Seventeenth National LOEX Library Instruction Conference Held in Ann Arbor, Michigan, 4–5 May 1989. Pierian, Ann Arbor (1989)
19. Hedemark, A., Hedman, J., Sundin, O.: Speaking of users: on user discourses in the field of public libraries. Inf. Res. **10**(2) (2005)
20. Haider, J., Bawden, D.: Conceptions of "information poverty" in LIS: a discourse analysis. J. Doc. **63**(4), 534–557 (2007)
21. Olsson, M.R.: Re-thinking our concept of users. Aust. Acad. Res. Libr. **40**(1), 22–35 (2009)
22. Huvila, I.: Information Services and Digital Literacy: in Search of the Boundaries of Knowing. Chandos, Oxford (2012)
23. Sundin, O., Francke, H.: In search of credibility: pupils' information practices in learning environments. Inf. Res. **14**(4) (2009)
24. DuBois, A.: Close reading: an introduction. In: Lentricchia, F., DuBois, A. (eds.) Close Reading: A Reader, pp. 1–40. Duke University Press, Durham (2003)
25. Huvila, I.: Awkwardness of becoming a boundary object: mangle and materialities of reports, documentation data and the archaeological work. Inf. Soc. **32**(4), 280–297 (2016)
26. Huvila, I.: 'If we just knew who should do it', or the social organization of the archiving of archaeology in Sweden. Inf. Res. **21**(2) (2016)
27. Sundin, O., Francke, H., Limberg, L.: Practicing information literacy in the classroom: policies, instructions, and grading. Dan. bibl. **7**(2/3), 7–17 (2011)

28. Lundh, A.: Studying information needs as question-negotiations in an educational context: a methodological comment. In: Information Research, vol. 15, no. 4. Special Supplement: Proceedings of the Seventh International Conference on Conceptions of Library and Information Science – Unity in Diversity – Part 2 (2010)
29. Hill, M.W.: The Impact of Information on Society. Bowker-Saur, London (1999)
30. Huvila, I.: How a museum knows? Structures, work roles, and infrastructures of information work. JASIST **64**(7), 1375–1387 (2013)

Librarians' Understanding of Information Literacy in Academic Libraries in Bulgaria: A Case Study

Katia G. Karadjova[1,2(✉)]

[1] Queensland University of Technology (QUT), Brisbane, Australia
[2] Humboldt State University (HSU), Arcata, CA, USA
katia.karadjova@humboldt.edu

Abstract. This study aims at illuminating a culturally situated understanding of Information literacy (IL) contextualized by a particular landscape in terms of a specific geographic region with related socio-cultural characteristics. The understanding of IL defines the frameworks for teaching IL in academic settings and impacts pedagogy. The study embraces the *constructivist* worldview through the lens of a socio-cultural theoretical framework and employs *instrumental* (with *exploratory* and *ethnographic* elements) case study approach. The research design includes: field observations and analysis, unobtrusive data set(s) collection and examination, artifact analysis such as websites, and in-depth interviews with Bulgarian academic librarians. This study addresses the need to apply culturally grounded approaches to IL to better serve specific groups. It will add to the international pool of knowledge in the field and will benefit Bulgarian academic librarians by providing a view of their understanding of IL and possibly facilitate further inquiry into suitable framework and practices.

Keywords: Information literacy · Academic library · Bulgaria

1 Introduction

Information literacy (IL) has signified a practical and strategic concept to information professionals since its emergence in the 1970s. IL encompasses the ways we discover, value and use information. The understanding of IL defines the frameworks for teaching IL in academic settings and impacts pedagogy. From a (social) constructivist point of view understanding is an activity of the individual mind and these interpretations of reality are culturally derived and historically situated. The body of literature suggests that IL understanding may vary in different parts of the world depending on factors such as historical perspective and socio-cultural characteristics [1–3, etc.].

South-East Europe (SEE) has been identified as one of the geographic regions in the world which is lagging behind global IL developments. Many countries there have been experiencing challenges since "IL is a highly contextual phenomenon, circumscribed by different socio-technical, political or historical factors" [2]. Hence, existing frameworks and best practice models from abroad cannot be copied or nested into IL policies.

S. Kurbanoğlu et al. (Eds.): ECIL 2017, CCIS 810, pp. 822–832, 2018.
https://doi.org/10.1007/978-3-319-74334-9_83

Bulgaria is an old country in SEE with rich history and long-standing cultural traditions. The Bulgarian state was founded in 681 CE and thus dates from the time of the Eastern Roman Empire (Byzantium). Bulgarians have their own language, Bulgarian, and have given the Cyrillic alphabet to the world [4, 5]. Bulgaria became a part of the European Union in 2007, which triggered significant legislative transformations after 45 years (1944–1989) of communist regime and consecutive economical hardship. Bulgarian librarianship has been going through significant changes since 1989, concurrently with the democratic reforms in that country after the end of the communist era, by transforming the librarian's role as a curator and gatekeeper to a new user-oriented paradigm of librarianship. The ongoing makeover of Bulgarian libraries has been amplified not only by the changing political and social milieu, but also by the cycles of economic turmoil and recovery in Bulgaria, as well as by the increasing implementation of new technologies.

The concept of 'information literacy', also called in Europe 'information competence' [6], is relatively new to the Bulgarian library field and practices. IL scholars in the Central - and East-European regions have started to address the significance of specific socio-cultural contexts [2, 7]. This study aims at illuminating a culturally grounded understanding of IL contextualized by a particular landscape in terms of a specific geographic location, Bulgaria, with related socio-cultural characteristics.

2 Literature Review

The literature review focuses on overviews of IL as a concept, IL in academic libraries including in particular Southeastern European countries, and the emerging need for culturally grounded approaches to IL.

2.1 Information Literacy as a Concept

IL has signified a practical and strategic concept to information professionals since its emergence in the 1970s [8, 9]. The first definition of the term "information literacy" was linked to work-related skills, namely, as stated by Zurkowski [10], "people trained in the application of information resources to their work can be called information literates." Most definitions of IL include the following elements: critical thinking, resource-based learning, and life-long learning [8].

Table 1 below represents the two main groups of approaches to IL identified for the purpose of this study: **generic-skills approach** and **contextualizing approaches**. Many of the contextualizing approaches have derived from studies on IL in **different 'cultures'**

With all of these taken into account, 'the context' represents a much more complicated milieu, which would explain why homogenous approaches to IL tend to create contradictions across contexts. For example, suggestions about exploring IL experiences of higher educators in other cultures in terms of other parts of the world [1] or at the workplace in different countries [22] support the notion that a focus on not-yet-studied various contexts results in a need for new agenda in IL research [24]. In the same way that there are different faces of information literacy [1, 13], there are

Table 1. Approaches to IL

Generic-skills approach	Beyond the generic-skills approach	IL in different 'cultures'
ALA [11] Delphi study, Doyle [12] ACRL IL Standards Due to ALA's definition this was the primary approach to IL in North America but not necessarily in other countries.	• ***Relational*** **approach** [1, 13–15] • ***Social context*** approach [14, 16, 17] • ***Sociotechnical practice*** [18] • ***Information landscapes*** [19, 20] • ***Radical information literacy*** [3]	Educational arena, workplace, etc. [1, 16, 21–24] Suggestions to study 'cultures' in terms of other parts of the world (education, Bruce [1]; the workplace in different countries, Jinadu and Kaur [22], etc.)

many ways of understanding, experiencing and conceptualizing the phenomenon [1, 16, 20, 21, 23]. It is important to consider the contradictions across contexts and the importance of the context to understanding the complexity of IL [24]. Taking the view that an information literate person engages with information in a particular *landscape* [19, 20] and acknowledging the inequality in access to information [3] based on political, socio-cultural and other differences in specific landscapes, both advance further the notion that IL understanding should be investigated in particular settings in different parts of the world instead of just imposing outside understandings and frameworks.

As a researcher, my intention is to use a socio-cultural approach to investigate IL understanding among Bulgarian academic librarians. This will account for the significant roles that social relations, culture and community play in learning and specifically in higher education [25].

2.2 IL and Academic Libraries

Literature reviews have revealed that IL as practiced in higher education and academic libraries outlines a landscape that has a particular user population and is influenced by perceptions and trends in relation to learning and teaching in academic settings. The activities of academic librarians in the higher education settings [20] encompassed: *information sharing and two-dimensional advocacy for IL.* One dimension focused on improving information practice in the interest of students. The second focused on the librarian's status in relation to roles outside of the academic library; *identifying ways to measure and prove the worth of IL education* to the academic community and then sharing these accomplishments with the IL instruction community; *librarians' reflection on their own pedagogical knowledge* and ways to develop it further; and *reflexivity about teaching skills* as well as ways to improve their own experiences and the learning experiences of students [20].

Table 2 below represents the two identified approaches in academic libraries. It also shows IL publications about Southeast-European Countries where Bulgaria is located.

Table 2. IL in academic libraries

Generic-skills approach in academic libraries	Beyond the generic-skills approach	Southeastern Euro-countries
• Boff and Johnson [26]; Cunningham and Lanning [27]; Doyle [12]; Hollister [28]; Johnson and Webber [29]; **Korobili et al.** [30]; Sharkey [31]; O'Hanlon [32]; Stanger [33]; etc. • Standards and frameworks based on decontextualized understanding of IL regarded as *generic skills*.	Complex phenomenon, which serves as a catalyst for learning [1, 13, 14, 16, 34, 35] Education *landscape* [19, 20]	• **Korobili et al.** [30] • Špiranec and Pejova [2] • Yankova [36] • Todorova and Stoikova [37]

Overall, in the higher education landscape the practice of IL was "situated, shaped, interpreted and constituted through a Western educational discourse that emphasizes and values individual achievement" [20, p. 64]. There are two major views of IL in this landscape. The first one regards information as objective and external in relation to the user and focuses on the development and application of skills, thus defining IL as a measurable set of abilities. The other view highlights the subjective and transformational aspects of the information experience [1, 14, 34], and the emphasis is not on developing skills but on empowering students to recognize "the variations in experiencing information in a reflective and critical way" [20, p. 64].

Southeastern European Countries. Scholars have conducted studies on investigating attitudes, perceptions and practices of IL among academic librarians in relation to specific countries and Southeastern Europe is represented by Greece [30].

The term 'information literacy' was mentioned in a few professional Library and Information Science publications in Bulgaria in relation to the ALA's (1989) definition [36, 37]. An overview of IL in Southeastern Europe [2] outlined the variables that influence the IL paradigm in many countries of the region as follows: *traditions in education*; *traditions in librarianship*; *demands of the labor market*; and *the wider political & socio-technical context*.

Summary. Overall, the body of literature suggests that IL understanding may vary in different parts of the world depending on factors such as historical perspective and socio-cultural characteristics [1–3, 7]. These factors provide different contexts for the IL phenomenon. Hence, existing frameworks and best practice models from abroad cannot be copied, imported and nested into IL policies. This leads to the conclusion that that there is an existing need of applying culturally grounded approaches to IL to better serve specific groups. Bulgaria is only just now adopting a user paradigm. Going from generic-skills approach to beyond generic-skills approach seems to be a critical shift that might need to happen. The potential beyond generic-skills approach needs to be well contextualized in terms of the Bulgarian context. The understanding of IL in Bulgarian academic libraries has not been researched so far. This study will address the existing gap by investigating how Bulgarian academic librarians understand IL and possibly facilitate further inquiry into suitable framework and practices.

3 Methodology

3.1 Research Question

The central qualitative question is *How do Bulgarian academic librarians understand IL?*

3.2 Qualitative Case Study

This study embraces the *interpretivism (social constructivism)* worldview through the lens of a socio-cultural theoretical framework. It follows Vygotsky's notion that *understanding* is social in origin and the development of knowledge structures and knowledge formation in general take place within socio-cultural contexts. Qualitative case study research empowers the researcher to explore a real-life, contemporary bounded system, namely, a case, through in-depth data collection involving multiple sources of information and reports, which provide a case description and case themes [38]. The intent is to explore and generate insights into Bulgarian librarians' understanding of IL by employing *instrumental (*with *exploratory* and *ethnographic* elements) case study [39].

Defining and Bounding the Case. Defining the case for this study led to selecting the setting of Bulgaria taking into account that Bulgarian academic libraries are spaces in which the country's culture and traditions in education are reflected. The older libraries could be considered keepers of culture and they might have strong influences on other libraries. In terms of bounding the case, the artifacts to be analyzed and the academic librarians to be interviewed will be selected from different academic libraries representing the types identified below.

The participant profile in this study defines 'Bulgarian academic librarian' as follows: Bulgarian professional librarian employed in Bulgarian academic library. Three types of universities and respectively their libraries has been identified for the purpose of this study as follows:

Type 1: Library Studies related, that is Bulgarian University of Library Studies and Information Technologies, Sofia;
Type 2: General, broad scope universities in terms of disciplines, older and newer, for example, the libraries of Sofia University (SU) and New Bulgarian University (NBU).
Type 3: Specialized Universities, for example, the libraries of Sofia Medical University, University of Architecture, Civil Engineering and Geodesy at Sofia.

The identification of the different types was essential in relation to the need to assure fair representation of different Bulgarian academic libraries.

The Research Design includes: field observations and analysis, unobtrusive data set(s) & artifacts collection and examination and at the end in-depth interviews with approximately 15 Bulgarian academic librarians.

Field Observations. The researcher plans to observe the environment and activities in three different academic libraries (each representing one of the three types), and to take field notes in regards to analyze and identify any relations to IL understanding and application. The daily activities of the academic librarians as well as their behavior while interacting with library patrons might be a rich source of information to draw on in terms of exploring their understanding of IL. The same could be said about the library environment, including signage, dedication and use of library space, available resources and services. The field observations and field notes might, also, help with identifying possible locations and options for unobtrusive data set(s) collection & artifacts to examine and analyze.

The Unobtrusive data set(s), documents & artifacts to be collected and examined in relation to any possible mentioning of or affiliation with the explored phenomenon, namely, information literacy, are: (1) publications, presentations, and posters by academic librarians in Bulgarian; (2) handouts, flyers, and such; (3) publications from professional organizations such as newsletters, conferences (if any), organization's mission, vision, policy documents and materials, and such; (4) grants & corresponding findings or developments. Some other unobtrusive data set(s) might be identified, collected and examined as well. All other available information related to the cultural differences in how Bulgarian librarians understand IL will be explored. These could include any relevant historical and political interpretations, university- and institutional-wide policies, evidence supporting culturally specific views of academia on a national scale, etc. A possible challenge could be gaining access past possible gatekeepers of the information, but this will be investigated.

Identified artifacts will be examined and analyzed, such as websites and tutorials. For example, the researcher plans to examine Bulgarian academic libraries' websites in relation to IL understanding and activities.

Interviews. The researcher plans to conduct qualitative, in-depth interviews (digital and/or face-to-face) with approximately 15 academic librarians from different academic libraries in Bulgaria representing the three types of academic libraries. The goal is one interview per participant and having 1–2 participants from different academic libraries representing the three types of universities. The interview script is semi-structured and contains open ended indicative questions. The interviews will be conducted, recorded by voice recorder and transcribed in the Bulgarian language. Specific parts will be translated into English as necessary.

In this study the intention is to align with interviewing for "conceptual analysis of the person's understanding of a topic" [40], namely, *understanding of IL*. Investigating perceptions through open-ended questions will allow exploring information through the views of Bulgarian academic librarians. The context of their work places, social interactions and cultural views shaped by historical predispositions of the particular geographic region, the Balkans, are expected to shape their understanding of IL.

The goal will be to achieve thick description of the case and its context, then use categorical aggregation to establish themes or patterns [41]. The researcher will create and organize files for data, read through texts, make notes and formulate some initial codes. The next step will be to identify common themes through cross-data analysis. The researcher will follow a specific coding manual [42]. The method of analysis will be a process that involves constant comparison in regards to data collection to allow the exploration of unexpected information.

3.3 Challenges and Strategies for Validating Findings

Since an *instrumental* (Bulgaria) with *exploratory-ethnographic* elements *case study* has been selected, as an approach of inquiry the validation of findings will be done by *triangulation*, which includes field observations, unobtrusive data set(s) & artifacts analysis and qualitative in-depth semi-structured interviews. The data collection plans, procedures and analysis have been refined through pilot testing [39, 41]. Also, the quality of the design of the case study will be examined in relation to four tests commonly used in the social sciences: construct validity, internal validity, external validity, and reliability [41].

4 Pilot Study

The pilot study could be helpful not only with refining the data collection and analysis plans but also with clarifying the conceptual framework of the study [39, 41, 43].

Following the research design the researcher conducted **observations in two academic libraries** and completed initial analyses of **one unobtrusive data set**. Then the researcher conducted **three interviews** with librarians representing library types two and three.

4.1 Results

Observations. The researcher took detailed notes about space use, collections and access, offered services, and visible activities and interactions at the libraries. The analysis of the notes revealed many similarities in terms of services and at the same time significant differences in terms of access between the two libraries.

Unobtrusive data set. The only major publication in Bulgarian related directly to IL identified so far is the conference proceedings of a symposium with international attendance, *Information Literacy – Training Models and Best Practices*, held in Varna, Bulgaria in 2012. This was the first and only event so far held in the country, which directly addresses IL.
The initial review of these conference proceedings revealed that:

- The terms used interchangeably as an equivalent or closely related to the term IL were three: (1) *Информационна Грамотност* – Information Literacy; (2) *Информационна компетентност* – Information Competency; and (3) *Информационна Култура* – Information Culture.
- A lot of the publications referred directly to the ALA (1989) definition of IL and the generic-skills approach. These publications were using the term (1) *Информационна Грамотност* – Information Literacy. Other definitions mentioned were a definition declared at a 2012 International Conference on *Media- and Information Literacy* in Moscow and an IFLA definition from 2006. No other approaches to IL were mentioned.
- Most of the authors in the collection are professors at the Bulgarian University of Library Studies and Information Technologies, Sofia.

- It seems that sometimes the meaning of information literacy has been considered equivalent to subject content knowledge in terms of subject expertise and subject publications expertise.

Further examination and analyses of the texts are expected to reveal more details and particularities.

Interviews. Initially identified cross themes from the interviews:

- Pressure to catch up with developments and best practices in the outside IL paradigm;
- Some familiarity with ALA's (1989) definition of IL and imported examples of best practices affiliated with the generic-skills approach;
- Expressed emphasis on subscription to online databases with content in English and on how to search in them.
- At the same time, acknowledgment that students do not use these databases because of two reasons: (1) Students do not need to use them since all they need is a textbook in relation to most of the courses' curricula. Apparently lecturing is still the highly predominant pedagogy. Professors require attending lectures and studying from lecture notes and/or the content of the required textbook. (2) The content of the databases is in English or Russian and most of the students are not well versed in any of these languages.
- Faculty members and doctoral students use the databases but not directly. A typical practice is to request from a librarian to find and deliver the full text of specific articles or to prepare a bibliography on a specific topic. Then the faculty member reviews the bibliography and requests the full text of all or some articles to be retrieved and delivered by the librarian.
- Pressure to develop IL education practice, for example, IL courses and workshops. Library orientation, introduction to library collections and library services, when available, are considered IL instruction.
- Bulgarians in general do not like to seek help.

4.2 Initial Findings

As expected, the pilot study has informed the research design. Linear design was not optimal. The data of each one of the methods informed the other two.

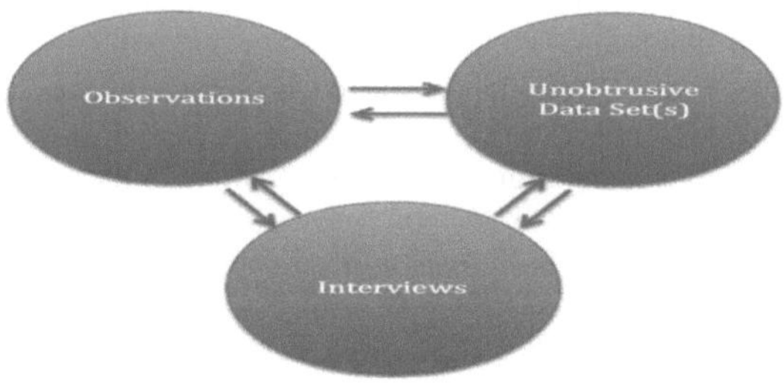

An early finding that has significance is that IL is being related to subject area competency. This finding has been underpinned by the data from each one of the methods (observations, unobtrusive data set analysis, and interviews).

Also, the preliminary findings on the context suggested how Bulgarian academic librarians were setting the boundaries of IL, for example, instruction seemed to be limited to how to use the library. The substantial difference in access between the two visited libraries is expected to have significant impact on it.

All of the three interviewed librarians mentioned pressure to catch up with developments and best practices in the outside IL paradigm mostly in relation to grants coming from the European Union. One of them was expected to design and develop a pilot IL program/course and seemed to feel quite unsure how exactly to approach this. This suggests that the findings of this study could be helpful in facilitating further inquiry into suitable framework and practices.

5 Discussion

The intrinsic quality of the IL agenda is embodied in understanding and utilizing "the power of effective information use in all social and cultural contexts" (Bruce, as cited in Whitworth, 2014, p.b.c.). The full study of information literacy understanding among Bulgarian academic librarians will add to the international pool of knowledge in the field and address the need to apply culturally grounded approaches to IL to better serve specific groups. Also, the study will benefit Bulgarian academic librarians by providing a view of their understanding of IL and possibly facilitate further inquiry into suitable framework and practices.

Acknowledgements. I would like to thank my supervisory team, Dr. Christine Bruce, Dr. Mary Ann Harlan and Dr. Elham Abdi for their continuous support.

References

1. Bruce, C.: The Seven Faces of Information Literacy. Auslib Press, Adelaide (1997)
2. Špiranec, S., Pejova, Z.: Information literacy in South-East Europe: formulating strategic initiatives, making reforms and introducing best practices. Int. Inf. Libr. Rev. **42**(2), 75–83 (2010)
3. Whitworth, A.: Radical Information Literacy: Reclaiming the Political Heart of the IL Movement. Chandos Publishing, Oxford (2014)
4. Rusev, P.: Origine, nature et developpement de la culture Bulgare durant treize siecles. Etudes Balk. **17**(3), 3–15 (1981)
5. Katsikas, S. (ed.): Bulgaria and Europe: Shifting Identities. Anthem Press, London (2010). http://www.ebrary.com
6. Virkus, S.: Information literacy in Europe: a literature review. Inf. Res.: Int. Electron. J. **8**, 159 (2003)
7. Koltay, T., Špiranec, S., Karvalics, L.Z.: Research 2.0 and the Future of Information Literacy. Chandos Publishing, Amsterdam (2016)
8. Pawley, C.: Information literacy: a contradictory coupling. Libr. Q. **73**(4), 422–452 (2003)

9. Limberg, L., Alexandersson, M., Lantz-Andersson, A.: What matters? Shaping meaningful learning through teaching information literacy. Libri: Int. J. Libr. Inf. Serv. **58**(2), 82–91 (2008)
10. Zurkowski, P.: The Information Service Environment: Relationships and Priorities. National Commission on Libraries and Information Science, Washington, DC (1974)
11. American Library Association (ALA): Final Report from the Presidential Committee on Information Literacy, January 1989. http://www.ala.org/ala/professionalresources/infolit/index.cfm. Accessed 26 Jan 2010
12. Doyle, C.: Outcomes Measures for Information Literacy Within the National Education Goals of 1990. Final Report to National Forum on Information Literacy. Summary of Findings, ED351 033. ERIC Clearinghouse on Information and Technology, Syracuse (1992)
13. Bruce, C.S.: Information literacy programs and research: an international review. Aust. Libr. J. (ALJ) **49**(3), 209–218 (2011)
14. Bruce, C.S., Edwards, S.L., Lupton, M.: Six frames for information literacy education. Italics **5**(1), 1–18 (2006)
15. Gunton, L., Bruce, C., Davis, K.: Information literacy research: the evolution of the relational approach, pp. 1943–1963. IGI Global (2015)
16. Bruce, C.: Information literacy research: dimensions of an emerging collective consciousness. Aust. Acad. Res. Libr. **31**(2), 91–101 (2000)
17. Marcum, J.W.: Rethinking information literacy. Libr. Q. **72**(1), 1–26 (2002)
18. Tuominen, K., Savolainen, R., Talja, S.: Information literacy as a sociotechnical practice. Libr. Q. **75**(3), 329–345 (2005)
19. Lloyd, A.: Information literacy landscapes: an emerging picture. J. Doc. **62**(5), 570–583 (2006)
20. Lloyd, A.: Information Literacy Landscapes: Information Literacy in Education, Workplace and Everyday Context. Chandos Publishing, Oxford (2010)
21. Bruce, C.S.: Information literacy research and practice: an experiential perspective. In: Kurbanoğlu, S., Grassian, E., Mizrachi, D., Catts, R., Špiranec, S. (eds.) ECIL 2013. CCIS, vol. 397, pp. 11–30. Springer, Cham (2013). https://doi.org/10.1007/978-3-319-03919-0_2
22. Jinadu, I., Kaur, K.: Information literacy at the workplace: a suggested model for a developing country. Libri **64**(1), 61–74 (2014)
23. Lloyd, A.: Information literacy: different contexts, different concepts, different truths? J. Librariansh. Inf. Sci. **37**(2), 82–88 (2005)
24. Lloyd, A., Williamson, K.: Towards an understanding of information literacy in context: implications for research. J. Librariansh. Inf. Sci. **40**(1), 3–12 (2008)
25. Wang, L., Bruce, C., Hughes, H.: Sociocultural theories and their application in information literacy research and education. Aust. Acad. Res. Libr. **42**(4), 296–308 (2011)
26. Boff, C., Johnson, K.: The library and first-year experience courses: a nationwide study. Ref. Serv. Rev. **30**(4), 277–287 (2002)
27. Cunningham, T.H., Lanning, S.: New frontier trail guides: faculty-librarian collaboration on information literacy. Ref. Serv. Rev. **30**(4), 343–348 (2002)
28. Hollister, C.: Bringing information literacy to career services. Ref. Serv. Rev. **33**(1), 104–111 (2005)
29. Johnson, B., Webber, S.: Information literacy in higher education: a review and case study. Stud. High. Educ. **28**(3), 335–351 (2003)
30. Korobili, S., Malliari, A., Christodoulou, G.: Information literacy paradigm in academic libraries in Greece and Cyprus. Ref. Serv. Rev. **36**(2), 180–193 (2008)
31. Sharkey, J.: Towards information fluency: applying a different model to an information literacy credit course. Ref. Serv. Rev. **34**(1), 71–85 (2006)

32. O'Hanlon, N.: Information literacy in the university curriculum: challenges for outcomes assessment. Libr. Acad. **7**(2), 169–189 (2007)
33. Stanger, K.: Implementing information literacy in higher education: a perspective on the roles of librarians and disciplinary faculty. LIBRES: Libr. Inf. Sci. Res. Electron. J. **19**(1), 1–6 (2009)
34. Bruce, C.S.: Informed Learning. Association of College and Research Libraries, American Library Association, Chicago (2008)
35. Hughes, H.E., Bruce, C.S., Edwards, S.L.: Models for reflection and learning: a culturally inclusive response to the information literacy imbalance. In: Andretta, S. (ed.) Change and Challenge: Information Literacy for the 21st Century, pp. 59–84. Auslib Press, Blackwood (2007)
36. Yankova, I.: The Modern Library: The University Library in Contemporary Education. St. Kliment Ohridski University Press, Sofia (2004)
37. Todorova, T., Stoikova, D. (Ed): Information Literacy – Training Models and Best Practices. Conference Proceedings. Sofia: Za bukvite-O pismeneha Press (2012)
38. Creswell, J.W.: Qualitative Inquiry and Research Design: Choosing Among Five Approaches, 3rd edn. Sage, Thousand Oaks (2013)
39. Simons, H.: Case Study Research in Practice. SAGE Publications Ltd., London (2009)
40. Brinkmann, S., Kvale, S.: InterViews: Learning the Craft of Qualitative Research Interviews. Sage, Thousand Oaks (2015)
41. Yin, R.K.: Case Study Research: Design and Method, 5th edn. Sage, Thousand Oaks (2014)
42. Saldaña, J.: The Coding Manual for Qualitative Researchers. SAGE, Los Angeles (2016)
43. Maxwell, J.A.: Qualitative Research Design: An Interpretive Approach. Sage, Thousand Oaks (2013)

Information Literacy Vis-a-Vis Epidemic of Distrust

Helena Lipková(✉), Hana Landová, and Adéla Jarolímková

Faculty of Arts, Institute of Information Studies and Librarianship, Charles University, Prague, Czech Republic
{helena.lipkova, hana.landova, adela.jarolimkova}@ff.cuni.cz

Abstract. Information literacy has long been understood in a broad context as the ability to evaluate information and select it based on the quality and trustworthiness thereof. However, trust still seems to be an underestimated phenomenon that urgently requires more attention. Recent developments have made us realize that users may not consider information to be credible, unless it meets a theoretical set of criteria anchored in the definition of quality information. The decisive factor that leads either to the acceptance, or the rejection, of information is "trust". If information professionals are to execute their fundamental role as information mediators successfully, they must thoroughly understand this phenomenon in order to become trusted members of the "social bubbles" of those that come from different social groups and classes. This literature review examines the extent to which trust has been researched from the perspective of information science. The prime resources were the LISA, LISTA and LISS databases used during the time period: 2007–2016.

Keywords: Trust · Trustworthiness · Information literacy · Literature review LISA · LISTA · LISS

1 Introduction

Trust makes social action possible [1]. Trust represents one of the fundamental social bonds. It is a crucial sociological phenomenon that influences in a fundamental way the deepest pillars on which a society functions. Recent theoretical views have been developed not only in the field of psychology but also in a number of other social science disciplines. In highly-complex societies, the essential nature of trust is expressed in broader ties and contexts than just on the personal level of relationships between individuals. With the development of an information society, the topic of trust is discussed more often, especially in relation to technology, information and information sources and virtual communities. Meanwhile, these issues have a direct impact on the field of LIS. Their topicality and urgency are also apparent in our everyday lives, as well as in the increased number of published papers on the topic [2]. In order to fulfill the role of librarian and information specialist jobs during the era of information explosion and the development of an information society, a thorough understanding of the phenomena of trust and trustworthiness in their varied forms and expressions and

S. Kurbanoğlu et al. (Eds.): ECIL 2017, CCIS 810, pp. 833–843, 2018.
https://doi.org/10.1007/978-3-319-74334-9_84

throughout their entire life-cycle is essential. The results of our research in this area can help us understand the basic principles that create suitable conditions for creation of trust and its further development. They help us to analyze impulses that lead to loss of trust and conditions for its restoration. This theoretical skill has potentially significant influence on the practical work of information specialists. Based on it, we can more easily identify the possible reasons why some segments of the population show greater tendencies to trust certain forms or certain types of information, information sources, experts, and so on. The findings of this research can help us provide recommendations on how to approach trust construction among recipients of information, mediators and information sources as such, that is, in what way do we disseminate and share information literacy with individual segments of the population. The research data can also provide tips on better design of information services, information systems and their UX interfaces so that trust features are emphasized as well as the trustworthiness of all elements and actors. In recent years, a lot of research articles have dealt with many of the above-mentioned topics. They have grown significantly in number, in the LIS field as well. Together with the quantity of papers, the fragmentation of areas researched has also expanded. This literature review has the objective of clarifying the current state of research in the field, and of mapping current research focus and suggestions for future research.

2 Methodology

To identify relevant articles in the LIS domain, we used the following databases: LISA, LISTA and LISS. We used descriptors to search for articles, that is, "Trust (Sociology)" (LISA) and "Trust" (LISTA, LISS), along with keywords such as trust, trustworthiness, credibility and reliability. We chose the keywords based on preliminary research of the most relevant articles; in some cases, the interchange of the terms – trust, confidence and credibility – occurred. This corresponds, however, to the way that the authors themselves codify the content in their articles based on the keyword "trust". We limited our searches back to 2007. This particular time period - beginning with the financial crisis in 2007–2008 and continuing until the more recent era of fake news and alternative facts - seemed to be the most relevant.

The removal of duplicate and irrelevant records resulted in 555 entries that we reviewed for content analysis. Given that the subject descriptors in the databases do not provide deeper information on the context of the topic of trust and its relationship to other topics, we decided to use our own coding system for the analysis. The basic hierarchical structure, including various aspects of the topic "trust", was created based on theoretical work on this topic from other fields and based on a preliminary analysis of records searched. During an open coding process, the original codes were combined with other related terms that capture the context of the topic "trust" in each particular article. The coding, using the Atlas.TI[1], was conducted in two phases. In the first phase,

[1] Atlas.ti is a tool for qualitative analysis of large bodies of textual, graphical, audio and video data. It allows systematic coding and conducts an in depth analysis. See details of the tool at atlasti.com.

we focused primarily on the main topics of the articles in the search and on tagging important documents. We have used the terms and keywords identified in the following parts of the database record: title, keywords, descriptors and abstract. Several key documents were studied thoroughly in order to select the most valuable terminology and get a detailed insight into the particular topic. We always assigned them a code at the lowest level possible, complemented with a more general code in cases where the article discussed broader aspects of a topic. In the second phase, we worked on making the codes more specific and on the general filling-in of others. Based on the frequency of incidence of individual codes and the joint (common) incidence of certain codes, we then created an overview of topics that works from the field of information science and library sciences currently addressed, together with trust. On the other hand, we identified topics that are currently lacking in contemporary LIS literature. We have listed examples of work that addresses individual topics; the selection thereof is based on the individual assessments of the authors.

3 Results

3.1 Trust in Relation to an Object

The first, most distinctive, aspect of this literature review is the form of relationships that have been most often monitored in research done so far. In this part, we distinguished mainly between the following relationship groups:

(a) between individuals;
(b) between the individual and a group;
(c) between the individual and an institution;
(d) between the individual and technology;
(e) between the individual and information

Point (e) was considered so important – from the LIS perspective – that it was extracted and later categorized as part of a separate section (*see* Sect. 3.3).

Relationship Between Individuals. Most articles written from this perspective address the trustworthiness of professionals of various types (for example, physiotherapists, doctors, and archivists). In relation to informational professions, the trustworthiness of information professionals is mentioned only generally [3]. The published studies analyze successful techniques for trust construction [4]. The significance of trustworthy information mediators and curators is also described [5, 6], as well as the importance of disseminating critical information literacy (that is, in academic/university libraries – [7]). Only exceptionally do the articles mention the issue of trust in relation to emerging information professionals as they build their professional identity [8].

Relationship to a Group. The most frequent topic in this area is trust in relation to virtual communities, namely in social media of various types. Key points of interest are the topics of creating and maintaining trust in communities [9, 10], knowledge sharing [11–13], creating user-generated content [14] and the benefits of these communities in building social capital [15]. The authors also focus on specifics of sharing health information and/or data [16, 17] and information related to customer evaluations and recommendations [18–21]. Trust and commonality of interests are perceived as a condition for the success of automated recommendation systems [22].

Relationships in the Workplace. Articles on building and developing relationships in the workplace came in second place, mainly those with emphasis on the influence of corporate culture on creating trust among employees [23, 24], efficiency in achieving common goals [25–27], and trust as a condition for efficient set-up of knowledge management in an organization [28, 29]. Another aspect being monitored is the relationships with business partners [30].

Relation to Institutions. In relation to institutions like libraries, the most discussed topic was the significance of libraries, namely public libraries, in the process of building social capital [31]. Libraries are important elements in determining social reputation, identification, culture, social relation and interaction zones belonging to members of the public. The main factors influencing a library's potential to contribute to the creation of social capital are analyzed (e.g. [32, 33]). Research studies compare selected institutions (see Miller 2014), or investigate the importance of the activities of public libraries in the integration of marginalized or disadvantaged groups [34].

Trust in the Technology. The research on individual trust in technology most often related to the issue of technological environments enabling the development of online business relationships (e-commerce, m-commerce and e-marketplaces in general) [20, 35, 36]. We devoted a separate chapter to the often-recurring topic of online banking [37]. From a perspective of statistical incidence, technologies in relation to the development of e-government represent the third most represented topic [38]. The most often observed perspective is the approach to adoption of technologies and options for boosting trust in newly-introduced technologies.

3.2 Trust Construction

Another crucial topic we researched in the context of the issue of trust vs. distrust as a societal phenomenon was the question of trust construction. This is a relatively broad concept, and thus it was necessary to define more detailed topics. We identified several specific areas; among them are trust construction principles, personal conduct and communication, and their impact on trust construction.

Trust Construction Principles. The basic principles for trust construction are most often researched in relation to the question of trust when sharing information within a specific community [26]. A correlation to trust in institutions or businesses or in online trade (e-commerce) or in social networks also often occurs [39]. Questions on the role of communications and communication strategy (including marketing and various campaigns) also appear significantly as one of the basic principles for trust construction in the field of business; including the implementation of new technologies (online shopping, online banking) [40]. Several studies have been devoted to the principles and axioms based on which people develop trust in individual information sources [41, 42].

Personal Conduct. The topic of personal behavior – the behavior of the individual as an important factor in trust construction - receives noticeably less attention in the literature. The only areas with more significant representation in completed studies involves the issue of personal behavior in social networks and online communities [17], or possibly its role in trust construction within a community in general [28]. There is a frequent intersection with the topic of leadership here [43].

Communication – Impact on Trust Construction. The topics of communication and communication strategy in the context of trust construction are very often tied to building trust in institutions, companies and brands [44], the same as with the field of image building in general. This is a direct intersection with the fields of marketing and promotion. Communications play a very important role in the area of pushing the implementation of new technologies and building trust in new tools. This fact presents itself particularly strongly in relation to issues of online shopping (e-commerce) and social networks. In the field of technology, there is a very strong bond between the quality design of a technology or an online platform and the marketing or communications strategy. Most studies in this area consider good communications as one of the key principles for trust construction.

Brand. Avery similar pattern for mutual bonds can be seen in publications devoted to the question of trust in a specific brand. Building trust in a brand and building a trustworthy image are very closely tied to building trust in a company or institution. At the same time, we also discovered many studies devoted specifically to building trust in a brand in e-commerce environments. We repeatedly identified elements such as communications, including marketing strategies and campaigns, as topics related to trust construction in the areas of trade and business.

Design and Information Processing. Because a large part of the research in the field of trust construction is focused on questions related to trust in technologies, it was important to devote time to questions on the influence of information system design and information processing on boosting trust among users. A typical example is the question of building trust of the patients in systems for e-health cards/records [45] and, depending thereon, in choice of physician. Several studies also reflect on the importance of design for e-commerce systems on the success and credibility of a given company [36]. The connection to perceived risks related to use of information systems, i.e. in the field of online banking [46] show up significantly. Issues such as threats to privacy and misuse of personal data are generally critical to building trust in technologies and information systems.

Trust, the construction thereof and development thereof are to a large degree questions of intuition, emotions and the personal experiences of each individual. There is already research available devoted to the psychological aspects of trust construction as part of business relations, including the role prejudice plays: both interpersonal and cultural [47]. There has been only one small piece of research done in the field of differences in building trust between institutions and people. The completed research focuses mainly on the topic of social trust and trust construction between the government and citizens [48]. Another very interesting topic is the situation in international organizations and companies where employees work in virtual teams, only meet together exceptionally in online environments, and the issue of building trust in employers and in colleagues has a different dynamic than in a typical work environment [49, 50].

3.3 Trust in Information Resources

Trust in information sources is already one of the main areas addressed by LIS; this is a matter of principle. However, not all topics in this area are covered to an equal degree. We identified four main areas:

- those that concern information sources in general
- attributes of trustworthy sources of information
- trust in social networks
- the role of trust in searching for health-related information.

Trust in Information Sources in General. The literature primarily addresses new technologies and their influence on trust in information sources. Here, we can find a number of topics that are given greater attention. Issues such as information literacy and critical assessment of sources primarily belong here [7], as do trust in electronic sources, namely webpages [51], and the relationship between information sources and assessing relevance [52] and reliability. Digital archives and repositories, researched also in relation to scientific communications [53–55] are an independent group of information sources for which trust plays a big role in their usage.

Attributes of Trustworthy Information Sources. Research on attributes of trustworthy information sources once again focuses primarily on webpages, social networks and the aforementioned digital archives and repositories. A relatively large portion of literature is devoted to the trustworthiness of health-related sources (see below). Attributes are also assessed in relation to online shopping and e-commerce in general. It appears that design, usability and easy navigation can have great importance in creating trust; more so than quality of content [56]. Several models have been formed, that is, an Integrated Layer Model of Trust. Trust in information taken from sources is influenced by trust in the source on which trust in the medium has an impact. This relates to a tendency to trust as such [42]. Part of the article guides (the reader) to educating users, mainly students, in the area of assessing the trustworthiness of information sources.

Trust in Social Networks. The most represented topic in the field of information sources is trust in social networks. Social networks serve rather for seeking information and sharing it. Here, they research the role of trust in sharing information and knowledge. Trust is viewed, for example, as one of the dimensions of social capital that contributes to shared knowledge creation [16]. Combining the concepts of social capital, social networks and trust appears in several other works [13, 39, 57]. The topic of trust in social networks is also very often connected to various aspects of online shopping, that is, online reviews of goods, and intentional building of virtual communities on the part of the seller. Social networks are also tied to searching for sources of health-related information, because online patient communities are an important source of information as well as a support tool [58]. Trust is discussed on various levels: interpersonal trust and systems of trust or a community level of trust and trust in connections made [57]. The authors focused specifically on Facebook, Twitter and Wikipedia, which are characterized as social media [15, 59, 60].

Searching for Healthcare-related Information. Special attention is given to the role of trust in searching for information related to health and health status. This topic ranks among the most frequently searched information on the internet overall. This undoubtedly relates also to greater emphasis on the health literacy of citizens, mainly in Western nations, responsibility for one's own health, and a greater role in decisions thereon. The main research focus includes evaluation of the trustworthiness of webpages devoted to healthcare issues and also the assessment of the role of social networks and communications on health-related information and trust therein [17, 61]. As concerns the criteria, a systematic overview of criteria for evaluating the quality of webpages has been elaborated [62].

3.4 Other Aspects of Trust Research

Trust Theory. As a part of the review, we were also interested in the degree of representation of theoretically-oriented articles on the topic of trust. The statistical incidence of such articles, compared to other categories, ranked at a relatively low level. From the LIS perspective, we consider the following articles most interesting; some of them are of a more general nature and others have a narrower focus: [63, 64].

Violation of Trust and Trust Reconciliation. Violation of trust does not rank among the most emphasized topics. The most often researched is the risk of violation of trust; and this as actual or anticipated, mainly in relation to personal data, online shopping and online banking and payments [65]. This topic is also presented as trust in institutions, primarily governmental ones [38]. Publications devoted to questions of reconciliation of trust appeared only sporadically in our research sample – whether it involved general aspects or descriptions of specific processes/procedures. A typical example is a case study from the field of e-commerce and reconciliation of trust in the company-client relationship after an episode of trust violation (leak of personal data) [30]. Generally, that is, not just in relation to trust reconciliation, one can state that publications focused on best practices appear only rarely.

The detail codes networks for the above mentioned topics as a result of qualitative data analysis in Atlas.ti are visualized in the ECIL presentation on the ECIL conference website.

4 Conclusions

A literature review has shown that, as part of LIS journals, the issue of trust is discussed mainly in the following areas: trust in a person, an institution or an object; trust construction; and – as is to be expected – trust in information sources. However, even among these strongly-represented topics, there are areas that have not yet been processed in detail. One example could be the bond of trust in a professional (a librarian) and professional growth. Generally, for example as part of the topic of trust construction, a study is lacking that focuses on the role of the individual (user, librarian, information specialist, other professional, leader) and his/her behavior. In the fields of information sources and social networks/media, attributes of trustworthy information sources and trust in health-related information online and on social networks are most often discussed. Traditional information sources are represented by archives, but in digital form. Very striking is the almost complete absence of the question of trust in traditional media. This is very interesting, for traditional print media still make up a significant part of library collections and the sources that individuals work with in general. Essentially, publications devoted to best practices for enhancing trust among communities and users, including policies to boost contributions to social capital, are almost completely missing. Very little attention has been paid, according to our review, to research on trust in librarians and information professionals in general, be it from the point-of-view of the public or among library users. Publications that already have excerpts in expert databases have yet, to a large degree, to capture the topic of fake news in general, or in relation to information literacy. Most often this topic is researched in connection with social media, but this research does not offer a comprehensive view on the topic. However, one can expect rapid growth in the number of publications capturing various aspects of this topical issue. By no means does this paper provide a detailed description of publications on the topic of trust in the LIS literature. We suggest it be considered a starting point for deeper research in particular thematic areas. Also, we aimed to point out the relevance of the topic to the area of media and information literacy – at least in two very important ways:

(1) Trust in various information resources (including individuals and institutions) and search tools affects very much the way people seek information and the attention they pay to evaluation of information found. This should be taken into consideration during IL programs.
(2) Also, trust in the library and librarians becomes a very important issue and needs to be cultivated and nourished, should libraries and librarians still play one of the crucial roles in the IL development.

Acknowledgements. The research was supported by the Charles University programs Progres Q15 "Life course, lifestyle and quality of life from the perspective of individual adaptation and the relationship of the actors and institutions".

References

1. Weber, L.R., Carter, A.I.: The Social Construction of Trust. Kluwer Academic/Plenum Publishers, New York (2003)
2. Harper, R., et al.: Trust, Computing and Society. Cambridge University Press, Cambridge (2014)
3. Flinn, A., Shepherd, E.: Questions of trust (and distrust). Arch. Sci. **11**, 169–174 (2011)
4. Franks, T.: Trusted librarian: service model offers best practices for new subject librarians. Pract. Acad. Librariansh.: Int. J. SLA **6**, 1–16 (2016)

5. Duranti, L., Rogers, C.: Educating for trust. Arch. Sci. **11**, 373–390 (2011)
6. Deschamps, C., Serres, A.: Les outils de curation nous obligent à réinventer des mécanismes de confiance Documentaliste. Sciences de l'Information **49**, 35 (2012)
7. Tewell, E.: Toward the resistant reading of information: Google, resistant spectatorship, and critical information literacy. Libr. Acad. **16**, 289–310 (2016)
8. Hoy, M.: Relationships, trust and learning: experiences of emerging professionals working in collecting institutions. Arch. Sci. **11**, 391–408 (2011)
9. Carey, M., Meyer, H.: The influences of participation and moderation on the development of a sense of virtual community. Int. J. Web Based Communities **12**, 326–341 (2016)
10. Zolfaghar, K., Aghaie, A.: A syntactical approach for interpersonal trust prediction in social web applications: combining contextual and structural data. Knowl.-Based Syst. **26**, 93–102 (2012)
11. Jalonen, H.: A framework for dealing with fundamental knowledge problems through social media. VINE: J. Inf. Knowl. Manag. Syst. **44**, 558–578 (2014)
12. Rahman, M., Hussain, B.: The impact of trust, motivation and rewards on knowledge sharing attitudes among the secondary and higher secondary level students'. Libr. Rev. **63**, 637–652 (2014)
13. De Meo, P., Nocera, A., Rosaci, D., Ursino, D.: Recommendation of reliable users, social networks and high-quality resources in a social internetworking system. AI Commun. **24**, 31–50 (2011)
14. Chung, N., Han, H., Koo, C.: Adoption of travel information in user-generated content on social media: the moderating effect of social presence. Behav. Inf. Technol. **34**, 902–919 (2015)
15. Warren, A.M., Sulaiman, A., Jaafar, N.I.: Understanding civic engagement behaviour on Facebook from a social capital theory perspective. Behav. Inf. Technol. **34**, 163–175 (2015)
16. Zhao, J., Ha, S., Widdows, R.: The influence of social capital on knowledge creation in online health communities. Inf. Technol. Manag. **17**, 311–321 (2016)
17. Sillence, E.: Seeking out very like-minded others: exploring trust and advice issues in an online health support group. Int. J. Web Based Communities **6**, 376–394 (2010)
18. Park, J., Lee, H., Lee, J.: Applying social exchange theory in IT service relationships: exploring roles of exchange characteristics in knowledge sharing. Inf. Technol. Manag. **16**, 193–206 (2015)
19. Olapiriyakul, K., Kangsirikul, S.: The role of web-forum in knowledge sharing and its impacts on consumer's purchase intention in e-marketplaces. Int. J. Innov. Learn. **12**, 283–293 (2012)
20. Shin, D.: User experience in social commerce: in friends we trust. Behav. Inf. Technol. **32**, 52–67 (2013)
21. Kuo-Lun, H., Judy, C., Xiang-Ying, W., Hsi-Peng, L., Hueiju, Y.: Antecedents and consequences of trust in online product recommendations: an empirical study in social shopping. Online Inf. Rev. **34**, 935–953 (2010)
22. Bhuiyan, T.: A survey on the relationship between trust and interest similarity in online social networks. J. Emerg. Technol. Web Intell. **2**, 291–299 (2010)
23. Al Hawari, M.A.: Comparative study of trust as a knowledge sharing enabler and its influence on organisational culture. J. Inf. Knowl. Manag. **11**, 1250014 (2012)
24. Mackenzie, M.: Manager communication and workplace trust: understanding manager and employee perceptions in the e-world. Int. J. Inf. Manag. **30**, 529–541 (2010)
25. Savolainen, T., Lopez-Fresno, P., Ikonen, M.: Trust-communication dyad in inter-personal workplace relationships – dynamics of trust deterioration and breach. Electron. J. Knowl. Manag. **12**, 232–240 (2014)

26. Savolainen, T., Lopez-Fresno, P.: Trust as intangible asset - enabling intellectual capital development by leadership for vitality and innovativeness. Electron. J. Knowl. Manag. **11**, 244–255 (2013)
27. Tsai, M., Cheng, N.: Understanding knowledge sharing between IT professionals – an integration of social cognitive and social exchange theory. Behav. Inf. Technol. **31**, 1069–1080 (2012)
28. Marouf, L.N., Agarwal, N.K.: Are faculty members ready? Individual factors affecting knowledge management readiness in universities. J. Inf. Knowl. Manag. **15**, 1650024 (2016)
29. Khvatova, T., Block, M., Zhukov, D., Lesko, S.: How to measure trust: the percolation model applied to intra-organisational knowledge sharing networks. J. Knowl. Manag. **20**, 918–935 (2016)
30. Choi, J., Nazareth, D.: Repairing trust in an e-commerce and security context: an agent-based modeling approach. Inf. Manag. Comput. Secur. **22**, 490–512 (2014)
31. Vårheim, A.: Public libraries: places creating social capital? Libr. Hi Tech **27**, 372–381 (2009)
32. Karadeniz, Ş., Yilmaz, B.: The library in the context of the social capital. Inf. World **16**, 180–203 (2015)
33. Schlak, T.: Social capital as operative in liaison librarianship: librarian participants' experiences of faculty engagement as academic library liaisons. J. Acad. Librariansh. **42**, 411–422 (2016)
34. Vårheim, A.: Gracious space: library programming strategies towards immigrants as tools in the creation of social capital. Libr. Inf. Sci. Res. **33**, 12–18 (2011)
35. Lin, J., Wang, B., Wang, N., Lu, Y.: Understanding the evolution of consumer trust in mobile commerce: a longitudinal study. Inf. Technol. Manag. **15**, 37–49 (2014)
36. Guzzo, T., Ferri, F., Grifoni, P.: A model of e-commerce adoption (MOCA): consumer's perceptions and behaviours. Behav. Inf. Technol. **35**, 196–209 (2016)
37. Cockrill, A., Goode, M., Beetles, A.: The critical role of perceived risk and trust in determining customer satisfaction with automated banking channels. Serv. Mark. Q. **30**, 174–193 (2009)
38. Gjermundrød, H., Dionysiou, I.: A conceptual framework for configurable privacy-awareness in a citizen-centric eGovernment. Electron. Gov.: Int. J. **11**, 258–282 (2015)
39. Sánchez-Franco, M., Buitrago-Esquinas, E.M., Yñiguez-Ovando, R.: What drives social integration in the domain of social network sites? Online Inf. Rev. **39**, 5–25 (2015)
40. Lee, J., Park, D., Han, I.: The different effects of online consumer reviews on consumers' purchase intentions depending on trust in online shopping malls: an advertising perspective. Internet Res. **21**, 187–206 (2011)
41. Marton, C.: Quality of health information on the Web: user perceptions of relevance and reliability. New Rev. Inf. Behav. Res. **4**, 195–206 (2003)
42. Lucassen, T., Schraagen, J.M.: Propensity to trust and the influence of source and medium cues in credibility evaluation. J. Inf. Sci. **38**, 566–577 (2012)
43. Jameson, J.: Leadership of shared spaces in online learning communities. Int. J. Web Based Communities **7**, 463–477 (2011)
44. Young, S.K.: Application of the cognitive dissonance theory to the service industry. Serv. Mark. Q. **32**, 96–112 (2011)
45. Walker, D.M., et al.: Trust me, I'm a Doctor: examining changes in how privacy concerns affect patient withholding behavior. J. Med. Internet Res. **19**, 52–67 (2017)
46. Hussain, C., Irani, Z., Abbasi, M.S., Nizamani, H.A.: Acceptance of online banking information systems: an empirical case in a developing economy. Behav. Inf. Technol. **32**, 668–680 (2013)

47. Séamas, K., Noonan, C.: Anxiety and psychological security in offshoring relationships: the role and development of trust as emotional commitment. J. Inf. Technol. **23**, 232–248 (2013)
48. Tamilina, L.: The impact of welfare state development on social trust formation: an empirical investigation. Electron. J. Knowl. Manag. **7**, 501–508 (2009)
49. Pangil, F., Chan, J.M.: The mediating effect of knowledge sharing on the relationship between trust and virtual team effectiveness. J. Knowl. Manag. **18**, 92–106 (2014)
50. Zhang, Y., Fang, Y., Wei, K., Chen, H.: Exploring the role of psychological safety in promoting the intention to continue sharing knowledge in virtual communities. Int. J. Inf. Manag. **30**, 425–436 (2010)
51. Tashtoush, Y.M., Zaudan, A., Alsmadi, I.M.: Implications for website trust and credibility assessment. Int. J. E-Entrepreneurship Innov. **3**, 17–33 (2012)
52. Xu, Y.: Relevance judgment in epistemic and hedonic information searches. JASIST **58**, 179–189 (2007)
53. Yeo, G.: Trust and context in cyberspace. Arch. Rec. **34**, 214–234 (2013)
54. Faniel, I., Kriesberg, A., Yakel, E.: Social scientists' satisfaction with data reuse. JASIST **67**, 1404–1416 (2016)
55. Tenopir, C., Levine, K., Allard, S., Christian, L., Volentine, R., Boehm, R., Nichols, F., Nicholas, D., Jamali, H., Herman, E., Watkinson, A.: Trustworthiness and authority of scholarly information in a digital age: results of an international questionnaire. JASIST **67**, 2344–2361 (2016)
56. Pengnate, S., Antonenko, P.: A multimethod evaluation of online trust and its interaction with metacognitive awareness: an emotional design perspective. Int. J. Hum.-Comput. Interact. **29**, 582–593 (2013)
57. French, A.: An empirical analysis evaluating trust in social networking. Int. J. Web Based Communities **11**, 4–24 (2015)
58. Rowley, J., Johnson, F., Sbaffi, L.: Trust judgements in online health information seeking. Health Inform. J. **21**, 316–327 (2015)
59. Kourouthanassis, P., Lekakos, G., Gerakis, V.: Should I stay or should I go? The moderating effect of self-image congruity and trust on social networking continued use. Behav. Inf. Technol. **34**, 190–203 (2015)
60. Rowley, J., Johnson, F.: Understanding trust formation in digital information sources: the case of Wikipedia. J. Inf. Sci. **39**, 494–508 (2013)
61. Kusumi, T., Ogura, K., Miura, A.: Development of a support group using a virtual space for cancer patients. Int. J. Web Based Communities **10**, 445–465 (2014)
62. Zhang, Y., Sun, Y., Xie, B.: Quality of health information for consumers on the web: a systematic review of indicators, criteria, tools, and evaluation results. JASIST **66**, 2071–2084 (2015)
63. Khosrowjerdi, M.: Trust in people, organizations, and government: a generic model. Int. J. Electron. Gov. Res. **12**, 55–70 (2016)
64. Mai, J.E.: Classification in a social world: bias and trust. J. Doc. **66**, 627–642 (2010)
65. Hong, I., Cha, H.: The mediating role of consumer trust in an online merchant in predicting purchase intention. Int. J. Inf. Manag. **33**, 927–939 (2013)

Author Index

MIX
Papier aus verantwortungsvollen Quellen
Paper from responsible sources
FSC® C105338

If you have any concerns about our products,
you can contact us on
ProductSafety@springernature.com

In case Publisher is established outside the EU,
the EU authorized representative is:
Springer Nature Customer Service Center GmbH
Europaplatz 3, 69115 Heidelberg, Germany

Printed by Libri Plureos GmbH
in Hamburg, Germany